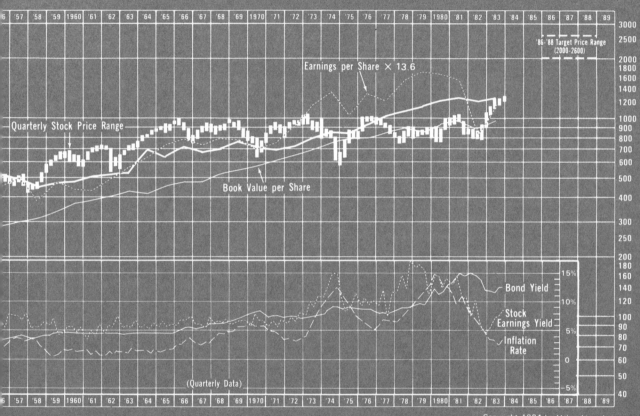

Earnings per Share × 13.6

Quarterly Stock Price Range

Book Value per Share

'86-'88 Target Price Range
(2000-2600)

Bond Yield

Stock Earnings Yield

Inflation Rate

(Quarterly Data)

Fundamentals of
Investment Management

FUNDAMENTALS OF INVESTMENT MANAGEMENT

SECOND EDITION

Geoffrey A. Hirt

Associate Professor of Finance
DePaul University

Stanley B. Block

Texas American Bank/Fort Worth Chair of Finance
Texas Christian University

1986

Homewood, Illinois   60430

The first edition of this book was published under the title
Fundamentals of Investment Management and Strategy.

© RICHARD D. IRWIN, INC., 1983 and 1986

ISBN 0-256-03355-2

Library of Congress Catalog Card No. 85–80013

Printed in the United States of America

4 5 6 7 8 9 0 D 3 2 1 0 9 8 7

PREFACE

In developing this book, we have attempted to employ a style that falls somewhere between the descriptive texts of the 1960s and the highly mathematical books designed primarily for graduate students.

While we accept many of the tenets and assumptions of an efficient market environment, we nevertheless carefully explain the importance of fundamental and technical analysis. Three chapters are devoted to the process of fundamental stock selection. Furthermore, we devote a chapter to special situations: in the chapter we examine investment strategies for which the efficient market hypothesis may not be fully operative in that there may be superior returns even on a risk-adjusted basis.

As is true of most investment texts, the primary emphasis is on equity investments. The individual security as well as a potential portfolio of investments are considered. There is a strong emphasis on evaluating appropriate risk-return trade-offs and the implications of modern portfolio theory.

Even though stocks are given the major attention throughout the text, a key strategy is to recognize all investment outlets as part of the feasible set. Some investments work best during inflation or other forms of economic upheaval, while others prosper in more stable times or even periods of disinflation. While we do not purport to be able to tell how to forecast the future with any high degree of certainty, the well-trained student should be aware of all options open for investment. For this reason, we take a hard look at the bond market and investment strategies that are appropriate for the type of volatile interest rates that we have had in the last decade.

We also examine such investment alternatives as real estate, commodities and financial futures, previous metals and gems, and collectibles (coins, stamps, art). We take a more systematic approach to these investments than do most other texts—by carefully evaluating risk-return trade-offs, trading costs, problems of illiquidity, and timing considerations. Whether the student chooses to engage in these investments or not, he or she is almost certain to be eventually approached with suggestions or proposals, and should be aware of the advantages and disadvantages of each.

A number of major changes have been included in this revised edition. There are three new chapters: Duration and Reinvestment Concepts, Stock Index Futures and Options, and International Securities Markets. The material on duration is highly innovative for an undergraduate textbook, yet the student should have no major difficulty in following the concepts. The chapter on

stock index futures and options reflects a desire on the part of the authors to be as up-to-date as possible in the coverage of new financial instruments. Finally, the chapter on international investment stresses the international dimension of investments.

There is also new material related to such diverse topics as the emerging financial service industry, Reagan economic policies, zero-coupon bonds, the personal computer as related to investments, arbitrage pricing theory, the "small-firm" effect, the Black-Scholes Option Pricing Model, and so on.

In the revised edition a greater effort was made to introduce concepts of risk and return in a very systematic fashion early in the text. Chapter 1 has been substantially revised toward this end. The later material on valuation directly relates back to this first chapter.

Also there are substantially more discussion questions and problems in the revised edition (approximately one third more than in the first edition). The instructor's manual has been expanded to include over 1,000 objective questions as well as transparency masters.

At the back of the book, the reader may observe over 30 pages of historical tables on stock prices, interest rates, and other economic or financial data. Both the student and the instructor can readily compare current values with past trends. Such topics as election-year performance, interest rate peaks, etc. can be easily viewed in these tables.

We wish to thank those who contributed directly to the preparation of the first edition and the second edition, particularly Roger Potter for his valuable help in the development of the material on estate planning and his supportive efforts in working with us on the questions and problems. Special thanks go to Carl Luft for his contribution of the Black-Scholes Option Pricing Model material. We also wish to recognize Becky Hurtz for her help in developing test material and Vincent Clemente for his aid in the instructor's manual.

For their valuable reviews and helpful comments on the first and revised edition, we are grateful to Keith E. Boles (University of Colorado, Colorado Springs), Jerry D. Boswell (College of Financial Planning), Paul Grier (SUNY-Binghamton), John D. Markese (DePaul University), John W. Peavy III (Southern Methodist University), Tom S. Sale (Louisiana Tech University), Ira Smolowitz (Siena College), Frank N. Tiernan (Drake University), Bismarck Williams (Roosevelt University), Sheri Kole (Copeland Companies), Art Schwartz (University of South Florida), Jane H. Finley (University of South Alabama), Don Taylor (University of Wisconsin, Platteville), Carol J. Billingham (Central Michigan University), and Gerald A. Blum (University of Nevada, Reno).

We also wish to express our thanks to Dave Ritzwoller for his help in proofreading the manuscript and Alexandra Ladias for her assistance in indexing the manuscript. We further wish to thank our respective institutions for their administrative help.

Finally, we are especially grateful to our families for their patience and tolerance throughout the project.

Geoffrey A. Hirt
Stanley B. Block

CONTENTS

Part Three
Fixed Income and Leveraged Securities   266

FUNDAMENTALS OF
INVESTMENT MANAGEMENT

Part One

INTRODUCTION TO INVESTMENTS

In Part One of the text, we establish the groundwork that is essential to the development of investment strategy and the management of financial resources.

The place to begin is with the setting of investment objectives. Not only is this the first step in any well-managed investment program, but it is often the most important ingredient. Among the factors the investor considers are willingness to take risks, desire for current income, need for liquidity, and tax considerations. The reader also considers the concepts of risk and return and examines historical rates of return on different types of investments. Career opportunities in the areas of investments and security analysis are also described in Appendix 1–B to Chapter 1.

A discussion of security markets follows in Chapter 2. An important distinction is made between primary markets (for new issues) and secondary markets (for existing issues). We discuss the major organized exchanges, such as the New York Stock Exchange, the American Stock Exchange, and the Chicago Board Options Exchange, as well as the over-the-counter market. We also take a look at future developments in the securities industry relating to computerized security trading.

In Chapter 3 the actual steps necessary to participate in the market are considered, with a description of the types of accounts that can be opened, the forms of orders that can be executed, and the commission costs involved. Tax considerations are also covered, with an emphasis on the proper timing of investment decisions to minimize taxes. The issue of individually managed accounts versus mutual funds is the final item of consideration in Chapter 3.

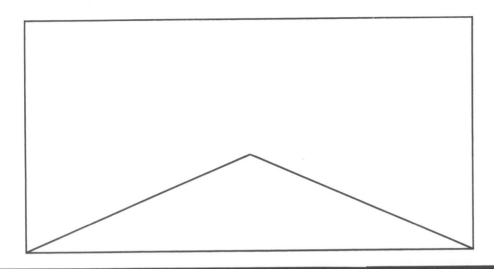

As part of the goal of establishing the groundwork for investment management in Part One, sources of investment information are covered in Chapter 4. The reader is presented with an overview of aggregate economic data sources generated by the government and industry/company data developed by investment advisory services, such as Value Line and Standard & Poor's. The uses of periodical indexes, journals, and computer data bases are also highlighted.

Chapter 1

THE INVESTMENT SETTING

In the last decade, we saw an unusual series of economic events. Oil went from $2 to over $30 a barrel. Gold went from $35 an ounce to $875 and then fell by over 60 percent. Silver increased from $4 an ounce to over $50 an ounce and then declined by 80 percent. Interest rates moved between 8 percent and 20+ percent, and inflation was at double-digit levels, moderating only at later points in time. This was in sharp contrast to the stable economic environment of the 1950s and 1960s.

How does one develop an investment strategy in such an environment? Suggestions come to the investor from all directions. He or she is told how to benefit from the coming monetary disaster as well as how to grow rich in a new era of prosperity. The intent of this text is to help the investor sort out the various investments that are available and to develop analytical skills that suggest what alternates might be most appropriate for a given portfolio.

We shall define an investment as the commitment of current funds in anticipation of receiving a larger future flow of funds. The investor hopes to be compensated by forgoing immediate consumption, for inflation, and for taking a risk.

The process of investing may be both exciting and challenging. The first-time investor who pours over the financial statements of a firm and then makes a dollar commitment to purchase a few shares of stock often has a feeling of euphoria as he or she charges out in the morning to secure the daily newspaper and read the market quotes. Even the professional analyst may take pleasure in leaving his Wall Street office to evaluate an emerging high technology firm in Austin or Palo Alto. Likewise, the buyer of a rare painting or late 18th-century U.S. coin may find a sense of excitement in attempting to outsmart the market. Even the purchaser of a bond or money market instrument must do proper analysis to assure that anticipated objectives are being met.

However, the seasoned investor often learns that there are failures that go with successes. The professional money manager is under tremendous pressure to outperform the popular market averages, and failure to do so may mean loss of a valuable account or perhaps a job. The individual investor may also feel a sense of frustration as he or she observes a "sure thing" go sour. The primary task is to establish your investment objectives so that both successes and temporary setbacks can be reasonably anticipated and accepted as part of the process.

FORMS OF INVESTMENT

In the text, we break down investment alternatives between financial and real assets. A financial asset represents a financial claim on an asset that is usually documented by some form of legal representation. An example would be a share of stock or a bond. A real asset represents an actual tangible asset that may be seen, felt, held, or collected. An example would be real estate or gold.

In Table 1–1, we list the various forms of financial and real assets.

As indicated in part A of Table 1–1, financial assets may be broken down into five categories. *Direct equity claims* represent ownership interests and

TABLE 1–1   Overview of Investment Alternatives

A. Financial assets
    1. Equity claims—direct:
        Common stock.
        Warrants.
        Options.
    2. Equity claims—indirect:
        Investment company shares.
    3. Creditor claims:
        Savings accounts.
        Money market funds.
        Commercial paper.
        Treasury bills.
        Bonds (straight and convertible to common stock).
    4. Preferred stock (straight and convertible to common stock).
    5. Commodity futures.
B. Real assets
    1. Real estate—office buildings, apartments, shopping centers, personal residences.
    2. Precious metals—gold, silver.
    3. Precious gems—diamonds, rubies, sapphires.
    4. Collectibles:
        Art.
        Antiques.
        Stamps.
        Coins.
        Rare books.
    5. Other:
        Cattle.
        Oil.
        Common metals.

include common stock as well as other instruments that can be used to purchase common stock, such as warrants and options. Warrants and options allow the holder to buy a stipulated number of shares in the future at a given price. Warrants usually convert to one share and are long-term in nature, whereas options are generally based on 100 share units and are short-term in nature.

Indirect equity can be acquired through placing funds in investment companies (such as a mutual fund). The investment company pools the resources of many investors and reinvests them in common stock (or other investments). The individual enjoys the advantages of diversification and professional management (though not necessarily higher returns).

Financial assets may also take the form of *creditor claims* as represented by debt instruments offered by financial institutions, industrial corporations, or the government. The rate of return is often initially fixed, though the effective yield may vary with changing market conditions. Other forms of financial assets are *preferred stock,* which is a hybrid form of security combining some

of the elements of equity ownership and creditor claims, and *commodity futures,* which represent a contract to buy or sell a commodity in the future at a given price. Commodities may include wheat, corn, copper, or even such financial instruments as Treasury bonds or foreign exchange.

As shown in part B of Table 1–1, there are also numerous categories of real assets. The most widely recognized investment in this category is *real estate,* either commercial property or one's own residence. For greater risk, *precious metals* or *precious gems* can be considered, and for those seeking psychic pleasure as well as monetary gain, *collectibles* are an investment outlet. Finally, the *other (all-inclusive)* category includes cattle, oil, and other items that stretch as far as the imagination will go.

Throughout the text, each form of financial and real asset is considered. What assets the investor ultimately selects will depend on his or her investment objectives as well as the economic outlook for the future. For example, if the investor believes that inflation will be relatively strong in the future, there may be a preference for real assets that have a replacement value reflecting increasing prices. In a more moderate inflationary environment, stocks and bonds may be preferred.

THE SETTING OF INVESTMENT OBJECTIVES

The setting of investment objectives may be as important as the selection of the investment. In actuality, they tend to go together. A number of key areas should be considered.

Risk and Safety of Principal

The first factor that the investor must consider is the amount of risk that he or she is prepared to assume. In a relatively efficient and informed capital market environment, risk tends to be closely correlated with return. Most of the literature of finance would suggest that those who consistently demonstrate high returns of perhaps 20 percent or more are greater-than-normal risk takers. While there may be some clever investors who are able to prosper on their wits alone, most high returns may be perceived as compensation for risk.

And there is not only the risk of losing invested capital directly (a dry hole perhaps), but also the danger of a loss in purchasing power. At 8 percent inflation (compounded annually) a stock that is held for four years without a gain in value would represent a 36 percent loss in purchasing power.

The investor who wishes to assume low risks will probably confine a large portion of his or her portfolio to short-term debt instruments in which the party responsible for payment is the government or a major bank or corporation. Some conservative investors may choose to invest in a money market fund, in which the funds of numerous investors are pooled together and reinvested in high-yielding, short-term instruments. More aggressive investors may look toward longer-term debt instruments and common stock. Real assets, such as gold, silver, or valued art, might also be included in an aggressive portfolio.

It is not only the inherent risk in an asset that must be considered, but also the extent to which that risk is being diversified away in a portfolio. Though an investment in gold might be considered risky, such might not be fully the case if it is combined into a portfolio of common stocks. Gold thrives on bad news, while common stocks generally do well in a positive economic environment. An oil embargo or foreign war may drive down the value of stocks while gold is advancing, and vice versa.

The age and economic circumstances of an investor are important variables in determining an appropriate level of risk. Young, upwardly mobile people are generally in a better position to absorb risk than are elderly couples on a fixed income. Nevertheless, each of us, regardless of our plight in life, has different risk-taking desires. A surgeon earning $200,000 a year may be more averse to accepting a $2 per share loss on a stock than an aging taxicab driver.

One cruel lesson of the last decade is that those who thought they were buying conservative investments often found quite the opposite to be true. For example, an 8 percent U.S. government bond maturing in 1998 was trading at 75 percent of its stated value in the mid-1980s.

Current Income versus Capital Appreciation

A second consideration in the setting of investment objectives is a decision on the desire for current income versus capital appreciation. Though this decision is closely tied to an evaluation of risk, it is a separate matter.

In purchasing stocks, the investor with a need for current income may opt for high-yielding, mature firms in such industries as public utilities, machine tools, or apparel. Those searching for capital gains may look toward smaller, emerging firms in high technology, energy, or electronics. The latter firms may pay no cash dividend at all, but the investor hopes for an increase in value to provide the desired return.

Liquidity Considerations

Liquidity is measured by the ability of the investor to convert an investment into cash within a relatively short period of time with a minimum capital loss on the transaction. Most financial assets provide a high degree of liquidity. Stocks and bonds can generally be sold within a matter of minutes at a price reasonably close to the last traded value. Such may not be the case for real estate. Almost everyone has seen a house or piece of commercial real estate sit on the market for weeks or months.

Liquidity can also be measured indirectly by the transaction costs or commissions involved in the transfer of ownership. Financial assets generally trade on a relatively low commission basis (perhaps 1 or 2 percent), whereas many real assets have transaction costs that run from 5 percent to 25 percent or more.

In many cases the lack of immediate liquidity can be justified if there are unusual opportunities for gain. An investment in real estate or precious gems

may provide sufficient return to more than compensate for the added transaction costs. Of course, a bad investment will be all the more difficult to unload.

The investor must carefully assess his or her own situation to determine the need for liquidity. If you are investing funds to be used for the next house payment or the coming semester's tuition, then immediate liquidity will be essential, and financial assets will be preferred. If funds can be tied up for long periods of time, bargain-buying opportunities of an unusual nature can also be evaluated.

Short-Term versus Long-Term Orientation

In setting investment objectives, you must decide whether you will assume a short-term or long-term orientation in managing the funds and evaluating performance. You do not always have a choice. Those who manage funds for others may be put under tremendous pressure to show a given level of performance in the short run. The appliers of pressure may be a concerned relative or a large pension fund that has placed funds with a bank trust department. Even though you are convinced your latest stock purchase will double in the next three years, the fact that it is currently down by 15 percent may provide some discomfort to those around you.

Market strategies may also be short-term or long-term in scope. Those who attempt to engage in short-term market tactics are termed *traders*. They may buy a stock at 15 and hope to liquidate if it goes to 20. To help reach decisions, short-term traders often make use of technical analysis, which is based on evaluating market indicator series and charting. Those who take a longer-term perspective try to identify fundamentally sound companies for a buy-and-hold approach. A long-term investor does not necessarily anticipate being able to buy right at the bottom or sell at the exact peak.

Tax Factors

Investors in high tax brackets will have different investment objectives than those in lower brackets, or tax-exempt charities, foundations, or similar organizations. An investor in a high tax bracket may prefer municipal bonds (interest is not taxable), real estate (with its depreciation and interest write-off), or investments that provide tax credits or tax shelters, such as those in oil and gas or railroad cars.

In recent times many investment advisers have cautioned investors not to be blinded by the beneficial tax aspects of an investment but to look at the economic factors as well.

Ease of Management

A final item of consideration in setting up an investment program is ease of management. The investor must determine the amount of time and effort that can be devoted to an investment portfolio and act accordingly. In the stock

market, this may determine whether you want to be a daily trader or to assume a longer-term perspective. In real estate, it may mean the difference between personally owning and managing a handful of rental houses or going in with 10 other investors to form a limited partnership in which a general partner takes full management responsibility and the limited partners merely put up the capital.

Of course, there is a minimum amount of time that must be committed to any investment program. Even when investment advisers or general partners are in charge, their activities must be monitored and evaluated.

PROFILE ANALYSIS

The editors of *Consumer Guide* have developed an interesting survey to see what types of investments are appropriate for investors, based on their age and economic circumstances. The questionnaire is presented in Appendix 1–A. After you have read this chapter you may want to try it. You can apply the questions to your own or your family's economic conditions.

MEASURES OF RISK AND RETURN

Now that you have some basic familiarity with the different forms of investments and the setting of investment goals, we are ready to look at concepts of measuring the return from an investment and the associated risk. The return that you receive from any investment (stocks, bonds, real estate) has two primary components: capital gains (or increase in value) and current income. The rate of return from an investment can be measured as:

$$\frac{\text{Rate of}}{\text{return}} = \frac{(\text{Ending value} - \text{Beginning value}) + \text{Income}}{\text{Beginning value}} \qquad (1\text{--}1)$$

Thus if a share of stock goes from \$20 to \$22 during 1986 and also pays a dollar in dividends during the year the total return is 15 percent. Using Formula (1–1):

$$\frac{(\$22 - \$20) + \$1}{\$20} = \frac{\$2 + \$1}{\$20} = \frac{\$3}{\$20} = 15\%$$

Where the formula is being specifically applied to stocks, it is written as:

$$\frac{\text{Rate of}}{\text{return}} = \frac{(P_1 - P_0) + D_1}{P_0} \qquad (1\text{--}2)$$

Where:

P_1 = Price at the end of the period.
P_0 = Price at the beginning of the period.
D_1 = Dividend income.

Risk

The risk for an investment is related to the uncertainty associated with the outcomes from the investment. For example, an investment that has an absolutely certain return of 10 percent is said to be riskless. Whereas, another investment that has a likely or expected return of 12 percent, but also the possibility of minus 10 percent in hard economic times and plus 30 percent under optimum circumstances, is said to be risky. An example of three investments with progressively greater risk is presented in Figure 1–1. Based on our definition of risk, investment C is clearly the riskiest because of the large uncertainty (wide dispersion) of possible outcomes.

In the study of investments, you will soon observe that the desired or required rate of return for a given investment is generally related to the risk associated with that investment. Because most investors do not like risk, they will require a higher rate of return for a more risky investment. That is not to

FIGURE 1–1   Examples of Risk

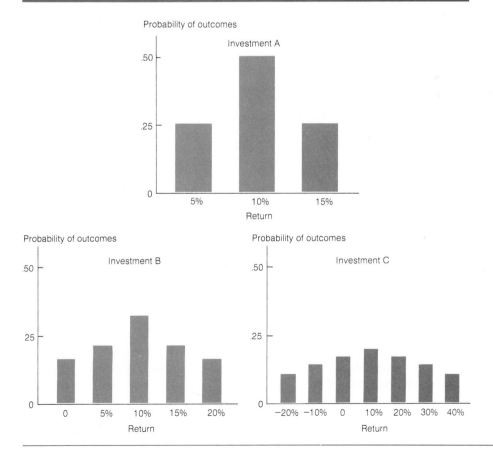

say that investors are unwilling to take risks—they simply wish to be compensated for taking the risk. For this reason, an investment in common stocks (which inevitably carries some amount of risk) may require an anticipated return 4 or 5 percent higher than a certificate of deposit in a commercial bank. This 4 or 5 percent represents a risk premium. You never know for sure whether you will get the returns you anticipate, but at least your initial requirements will be higher to justify the risk you are taking.

ACTUAL CONSIDERATION OF REQUIRED RETURNS

Let's consider how return requirements are determined in the financial markets. Although the following discussion starts out on a theoretical "what if" basis, you will eventually see empirical evidence that different types of investments do provide different types of returns.

There are basically three components that make up the required return from an investment:

A.   The real rate of return.
B.   The anticipated inflation factor.
C.   The risk premium.

Real Rate of Return

The real rate of return is the return that investors require for allowing others to use their money for a given time period. This is the return that investors demand for passing up immediate consumption and allowing others to use their savings until the funds are returned. Because the term *real* is employed, this means it is a value determined before inflation is included in the calculation. The real rate of return is also determined before considering any specific risk for the investment.

Historically, the real rate of return in the U.S. economy has been of the magnitude of 2 to 3 percent. However, in the 1980s it has been somewhat higher (4 to 6 percent). It is possible that the greater volatility in the financial markets (in terms of interest rates and stock prices) has led to this higher real-rate-of-return requirement. Over the long-term, perhaps 3 percent may still be the most reasonable estimate.

Anticipated Inflation Factor

The anticipated inflation factor must be added to the real rate of return. For example, if there is a 3 percent real-rate-of-return requirement and the anticipated rate of inflation is 5 percent, we combine the two to arrive at an approximate 8 percent required return factor.[1] Combining the real rate of return and inflationary considerations gives us the required return on an investment be-

---

[1] We use the word *approximate* to denote that mathematical procedures actually produce an answer slightly over 8 percent.

fore explicitly considering risk. For this reason, it is called the risk-free required rate of return or, simply, *risk-free rate (R_F)*.

We can define the risk-free rate as:

$$\text{Risk-free rate} = (1 + \text{Real rate})(1 + \text{Expected rate of inflation}) - 1 \qquad (1\text{-}3)$$

Plugging in numerical values, we would show:

$$(1.03)(1.05) - 1 = 1.0815 - 1 = .0815, \text{ or } 8.15\%$$

The answer is approximately 8 percent. You can simply add the real rate of return (3 percent) to the anticipated inflation rate (5 percent) to get an 8 percent answer or go through the more theoretically correct process of Formula 1–3 to arrive at 8.15 percent. Either approach is frequently used.

The risk-free rate (R_F) of approximately 8 percent applies to any investment as the minimum required rate of return to provide a 3 percent *real return* after inflation. Of course, if the investor actually receives a lower return, his real rate of return may be quite low or negative. If the investor receives a 4 percent return in a 5 percent inflationary environment, there is a negative real return of 1 percent. The investor will have 1 percent less purchasing power than before he started. He would have been better off to spend the money *now* rather than save at a 4 percent rate in a 5 percent inflationary economy. In effect, he is *paying* the borrower to use his money. Of course, real rates of return and inflationary expectations change from time to time, so the risk-free required rate (R_F) also changes.

We have now examined the two components that make up the minimum risk-free rate of return that apply to any investment (stock, bonds, real estate, etc.). We now consider the third component, the risk premium. The relationship is depicted in Figure 1–2.

FIGURE 1–2   The Components of Required Rate of Return

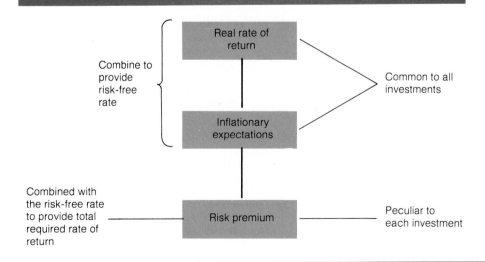

Risk Premium

The risk premium will be different for each investment. For example, for a federally insured certificate of deposit at a bank or for a U.S. government Treasury bill, the risk premium approaches zero. All the return to the investor will be at the risk-free rate of return (the real rate of return plus inflationary expectations). For common stock, the investor's required return may carry a 4 or 5 percent risk premium in addition to the risk-free rate of return. If the risk-free rate were 8 percent, the investor might have an overall required return of 12 to 13 percent on common stock.

+ Real rate	3%
+ Anticipated inflation	5%
= Risk-free rate	8%
+ Risk premium	4% to 5%
= Required rate of return	12% to 13%

Corporate bonds fall somewhere between short-term government obligations (virtually no risk) and common stock in terms of risk. Thus, the risk premium may be 2 to 4 percent. Like the real rate of return and the inflation rate, the risk premium is not a constant, but may change from time to time. If investors are very fearful about the economic outlook, the risk premium may be 8 to 10 percent for a high-risk investment.

The normal relationship between selected investments and their rates of return is depicted in Figure 1–3.

There have been a number of empirical studies that tend to support the risk–return relationships shown in Figure 1–3 over a long period of time. Perhaps the most widely cited is the Ibbotson and Sinquefield study presented in Table 1–2, which covers data from 1926–83. Note the high-to-low return scale is in line with expectations based on risk.[2] Of particular interest is the first column, labeled geometric mean. Nonstatisticians will be pleased to know that this is simply the compound annual rate of return. The arithmetic mean in column 2 is an average of yearly rates of return and has less meaning. We will study the concept of standard deviation (column 3) later in the text.

Because the study covered over half a century (including a decade of depression), the rates of return are somewhat lower than those currently available in the economy. This is particularly true for the bonds and Treasury bills shown in the table.

In Table 1–3, you see a study by Salomon Brothers, an investment banking firm, that covers 14 different investment categories and the CPI (consumer price index).

---

[2] Similar long-term studies of financial assets by Fisher and Lorie produced the same type of risk–return relations. Examples include Lawrence Fisher and James H. Lorie, *A Half Century of Returns on Stocks and Bonds* (Chicago: University of Chicago Graduate School of Business, 1977); James H. Lorie and Lawrence Fisher, "Rates of Return on Investment in Common Stock," *Journal of Business,* January 1964, pp. 1–17; and Lawrence Fisher and James H. Lorie, "Rates of Return on Investment in Common Stock: The Year-by-Year Record 1926–1965," *Journal of Business,* July 1968, pp. 219–316.

FIGURE 1–3   Risk-Return Characteristics

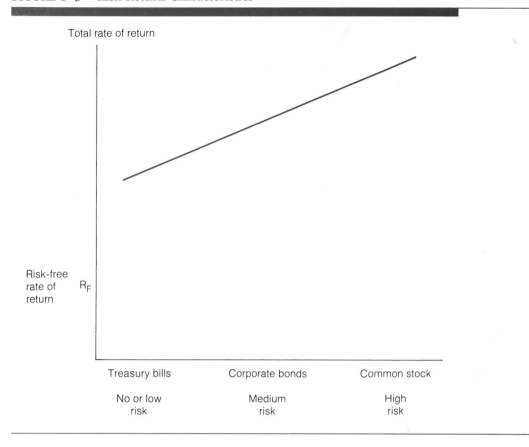

TABLE 1–2   Annual Returns of Financial Assets (1926–1983)

Series	(1) Geometric mean	(2) Arithmetic mean	(3) Standard deviation
Common stocks	9.6%	11.8%	21.4%
Small stocks	12.8	18.7	36.5
Long-term corporate bonds	4.2	4.4	7.6
Long-term government bonds	3.5	3.7	7.4
U.S. Treasury bills	3.1	3.2	3.2
Inflation	3.0	3.1	5.0

Source: *Stocks, Bonds, Bills and Inflation, 1984 Yearbook* (Chicago: R. G. Ibbotson and Associates, Inc., 1984), p. 5.

TABLE 1–3   Compounded Annual Rates of Return*

	15 years (ranking)		10 years (ranking)		5 years (ranking)		1 year (ranking)	
Oil	20.4%	(1)	10.1%	(4)	14.8%	(2)	0.0%	(8)
Coins	17.3	(2)	21.4	(1)	11.3	(5)	7.4	(3)
Gold.	16.3	(3)	9.5	(6)	7.4	(8)	−4.0	(12)
U.S. stamps.	16.1	(4)	17.1	(2)	9.8	(6)	−4.0	(13)
Chinese ceramics.	13.7	(5)	5.9	(14)	15.7	(1)	3.0	(6)
Silver	11.7	(6)	7.2	(12)	2.4	(13)	−25.2	(15)
Diamonds.	10.4	(7)	9.8	(5)	6.1	(9)	0.0	(7)
Farmland	9.6	(8)	9.4	(7)	3.3	(12)	−0.7	(9)
Treasury bills.	9.0	(9)	10.1	(3)	12.7	(4)	9.4	(2)
Old masters	8.5	(10)	9.1	(8)	1.5	(14)	14.3	(1)
Housing	8.5	(11)	8.6	(10)	5.8	(10)	5.5	(4)
Consumer price index . .	7.2	(12)	7.9	(11)	7.9	(7)	4.6	(5)
Bonds.	5.7	(13)	6.3	(13)	4.6	(11)	−7.2	(14)
Stocks.	5.3	(14)	9.0	(9)	13.5	(3)	−1.2	(10)
Foreign exchange.	3.0	(15)	0.9	(15)	−4.9	(15)	−3.0	(11)

* Values computed through June 1, 1984.
Source: Salomon Brothers Inc.

The study is different from Table 1–2 in that it covers real assets as well as financial assets. The information runs through June 1, 1984.

For the 15-year and 10-year periods, real assets tend to dominate the return rankings. This is primarily due to the high rate of inflation that was present during the 1970s and early 1980s. Real assets, because of increasing replacement value and scarity, tend to perform best during periods of high inflation. However, in the 5-year column, you will observe that many real assets, such as silver, diamonds, farmland, and gold performed poorly as inflationary expectations diminished in the 1983–84 time frame. Stocks, which were poor performers over the 15- and 10-year periods, showed a strong performance during the five-year time frame. The one-year rankings are almost meaningless because of short-term influences.

Because much of the material in the Salomon Brothers study was gathered during one of the most inflationary time periods in U.S. history (aided by major oil price increases), you should not overly generalize from the results. Over longer periods of time, common stock tends to perform at approximately the same level as such real assets as real estate, coins, stamps, etc.,[3] with each

---

[3] Examples of longer-term studies on comparative returns between real and financial assets are: Roger G. Ibbotson and Carol F. Fall, "The United States Wealth Portfolio," *The Journal of Portfolio Management,* Fall 1982, pp. 82–92. Roger G. Ibbotson and Lawrence B. Siegel, "The World Market Wealth Portfolio," *The Journal of Portfolio Management,* Winter 1983, pp. 5–17. (While Ibbotson and Siegel showed superior returns for metals between 1960 and 1980, metals have greatly underperformed other assets in the 1980s). Alexander A. Robichek, Richard A. Cohn, and John J. Pringle, "Returns on Alternative Media and Implications for Portfolio Construction," *Journal of Business,* July 1972, pp. 427–43.

tending to show a different type of performance in a differing economic environment. More will be said about the impact of inflation and disinflation on investments in later parts of the text.

Determining the Risk Premium

We have attempted to demonstrate the importance of risk in determining the required rate of return for an investment. As previously discussed, it is the third key component that is added to the risk-free rate (composed of the real rate of return and the inflation premium) to determine the total required rate of return. How does one *actually* go about determining the risk that is to be rewarded from a given instrument?

Systematic and Unsystematic Risk

You will recall that earlier we defined risk as related to the uncertainty of outcomes for a given investment. But it is not just the risk for an individual security that must be considered. Financial theory also requires that we consider the relationship between two or more investments to determine the combined risk level. Part of the risk of one investment may be diversified away with a second investment. For example, an investment in an oil company may be somewhat risky in nature because oil prices may drop, but if you have a second investment in a petrochemical company that will benefit from lower oil prices, then you have diversified away part of the risk. Similarly, investments in foreign stocks often move in the opposite direction of investments in U.S. stocks. If you combine stocks from two or more countries, part of the risk is diversified away. Because diversification can *eliminate* part of the risk in an investment, not all risk is thought to be compensated for by proportionally higher returns.

   Financial theory can be used to break down risk which is systematic and unsystematic in nature. We'll talk about the latter item first. Unsystematic risk is risk that can be diversified away in a well-constructed portfolio and thus is not assumed to be rewarded with higher returns in the financial markets. It represents the type of risk described in the preceding paragraph. Systematic risk, on the other hand, is inherent in the investment and cannot be diversified away, and is assumed to be rewarded in the marketplace. The relationship is indicated below.

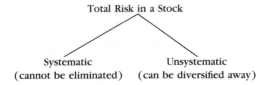

Total Risk in a Stock

Systematic   Unsystematic
(cannot be eliminated)   (can be diversified away)

   Systematic risk is measured by the related movement of a stock to the market. Even in a totally diversified portfolio, each stock will be vulnerable to changes in the *overall* market even if individual characteristics of the stocks

have been largely diversified away. Based on systematic risk, if the market goes up or down by 10 percent, our stock may go up or down by 10 percent. The joint movement between a security and the market in general is defined as the beta coefficient. If a stock has equal volatility to the market (if the market changes by 10 percent, the stock changes by 10 percent) the beta coefficient is 1. If the stock is 50 percent more volatile than the market, the beta coefficient is 1.5 and so on. Systematic risk, as measured by the beta coefficient, is assumed to be compensated for by higher potential returns. That is, stocks that have high systematic risk or betas are assumed to provide higher returns to compensate for the additional risk. This same type of risk analysis can be applied to other types of investments as well.

In Chapter 19, we will give a more thorough mathematical definition of how you separate out systematic and unsystematic risk. It is enough for now that you understand that the differences exist, and that the two forms of risk are not equally compensated. In the prior discussion of unsystematic risk, we mentioned the importance of diversifying away nonmarket-related risks. We discussed oil versus petrochemicals as representing potential for diversifying oil price risks. Also foreign stocks versus U.S. stocks were given as an example. Undoubtedly you can think of others. The auto part replacement market may move in the opposite direction of new auto sales; the same can be said for the market for defense systems and public works projects. In order to establish an efficiently diversified portfolio, the investor must consider how projects correlate with each other. Generally, highly correlated projects provide little diversification benefits, while projects that have low correlations or are negatively correlated provide maximum diversification benefits.

Summary of Return Considerations

Based on our analysis to this point, we can say that each investment requires a total return that comprises a real rate of return, compensation for inflationary expectations, and a risk premium. The risk premium should be related to systematic risk (as opposed to unsystematic risk).[4]

When you get to Chapter 6, "Valuation of the Individual Firm," you will see how the required rate of return influences the valuation of an investment. You should also be aware that just because an investor has a required return expectation does not mean that the expectation will be met. For example, an investor may purchase a bond with an expected return of 10 percent. But if the inflation expectations go up, the new required return on such a bond may now be 13 percent. The only way for the old bond to offer the going market rate, based on its low 10 percent interest payments, will be for the bond to go down in value. This lower value will offer the *new* bondholders the return they desire but will mean *old* bondholders are suffering market value losses in the

---

[4] Some analysts prefer to view risk in terms of internal corporate considerations such as business or financial risk. Our emphasis for now is on systematic risk.

meantime. They started out hoping to receive 10 percent, but now their annual rate of return will be less because of the drop in the bond value.[5] The same thing can happen to common stock investors.

WHAT YOU WILL LEARN

The first part of the book covers the general framework for investing. You will look at an overview of the security markets (New York Stock Exchange, Chicago Board Options Exchange, etc.). Then you will examine the basics for participating in the market, such as opening an account, executing an order, investing individually or through a mutual fund, and so forth. Also in the first section of the book, you will become familiar with sources of important investment information so that you can begin to make your university or public library a valuable asset.

You will then go through the classic process of analyzing and valuing a security. You will start with examining the economy, then move to the industry level, and finally to the actual company. The authors go through the process of actually putting a value on a stock. There is also heavy emphasis on financial analysis. One chapter provides an in-depth analysis of The Coca-Cola Company to demonstrate the procedures that should be utilized in identifying the strengths and weaknesses of a company. For enthusiasts of charting and other forms of technical analysis, we examine the advantages and disadvantages of such approaches.

You will then move from stocks to bonds. Your level of interest should not diminish because bonds also offer an opportunity for income, and, surprisingly, for large gains or losses. Because an emphasis of the book is to give the student a wide investment horizon from which to choose, we then consider a variety of other investment alternatives. These include convertible securities and warrants, put and call options, commodities and financial futures, stock index futures and options, and real assets such as real estate and precious metals. We realize some of these terms may have little meaning to you now, but they soon will.

In the latter part of the book, we also consider the concepts of portfolio theory and how to put together the most desirable package of investments in terms of risk and return. We also consider the consequences of investing in a reasonably efficient stock market environment, one in which information is acted upon very quickly. Can superior return be achieved in such a setting?

The final chapter is devoted to estate planning. You can see the consequences of decisions made now and later on your ultimate wealth.

Many students taking an investments course are not sure of their ultimate career goals. We hope this course can be equally valuable to a future banker, CPA, insurance executive, marketing manager, or anyone else. However, for

---

[5] Of course, if inflation expectations go down, the required return would be less and the bond price would go up. Now investors would receive a return higher than the 10 percent they initially expected.

those specifically considering a career in investments, the authors present a brief summary of career opportunities in the second appendix at the back of this chapter, Appendix 1–B.

IMPORTANT WORDS AND CONCEPTS

Investment	**Real rate of return**
Financial assets	**Inflationary expectations**
Real assets	**Risk-free rate**
Direct and indirect equity	**Risk premium**
claims	**Systematic risk**
Creditor claims	**Unsystematic risk**
Portfolio	**Diversification**
Capital appreciation	**Beta**
Liquidity	

DISCUSSION QUESTIONS

1. How is an investment defined?
2. What are the differences between financial and real assets?
3. List some of the key areas relating to investment objectives.
4. Explain the concepts of direct equity and indirect equity.
5. How are equity and creditor claims different?
6. Do those wishing to assume low risks tend to invest long-term or short-term? Why?
7. How might investing in something generally considered to be risky actually decrease an investor's risk?
8. What are some types of appropriate investments for investors in high tax brackets who wish to diminish their tax obligation?
9. How is "liquidity" measured?
10. Explain why conservative investors who tend to buy short-term assets differ from short-term traders.
11. Why is there a minimum amount of time that must be committed to any investment program?
12. In a highly inflationary environment, would an investor tend to favor real or financial assets? Why?
13. What are the two primary components that are used to measure the rate of return achieved from an investment?
14. Many people think of risk as the danger of losing money. Is this the same way that risk is defined in finance?
15. What are the three elements that determine how much an investor should require in return from an investment?
16. What is the normal historical level for real rate of return in the United States? Why has it been higher than this in the 1980s?

17. Explain how an investor receiving a 4 or 5 percent quoted return in an inflationary environment may actually experience a negative real rate of return.

18. Rank order the following items in terms of the risk premium they should receive; go from the lowest to the highest.
   Certificates of deposit at a bank.
   Unexplored gold mine in Africa.
   Common stock for large companies.
   U.S. government Treasury bills (short-term).
   U.S. government bonds (long-term).
   Corporate long-term bonds.
   Common stock of small companies.

19. What is the difference in meaning between the arithmetic and geometric mean as shown in the study in Table 1–2?

20. In the Salomon Brothers study in Table 1–3, observe the relative performance of stocks versus silver over 15 years and over 5 years. Explain why the reversal took place.

21. Why is *all* risk not thought to be compensated by proportionally higher return?

22. If stocks are combined into a portfolio, is it their systematic or unsystematic risk that is being reduced?

23. Explain the concept of a beta coefficient. Should large beta stocks have higher or lower required rates of return?

24. If required returns in the market turn out to be larger than initially anticipated, what is likely to happen to the market value of a previously purchased asset?

25. In considering Question 24, suggest some factors that might have caused the required rate of return to go up.

PROBLEMS

1. The stock of Dynamo Corporation went from $25 to $28 last year. The firm also paid 50 cents in dividends. Compute the rate of return.

2. In the following year, the dividend was raised to 70 cents. However, a bear market developed toward the end of the year, and the stock price declined from $28 to $22. Compute the rate of return (or loss) to stockholders.

3. Assume the real rate of return in the economy is 2.5 percent, the expected rate of inflation is 6 percent and the risk premium is 5.5 percent. Compute the risk-free rate and required rate of return.

4. Assume the real return in the economy is 3.5 percent. It is anticipated that the Consumer Price Index will go from 320 to 334.4. Shares in common stock are assumed to have a required return ⅓ higher than the risk-free rate. Compute the required return on common stock.

5. A bond was originally purchased with a rate of return of 11 percent. The following year inflation caused the required rate of return to increase to 13 percent. Explain the effect of the required return change on the original bondholder.

SELECTED REFERENCES

Blume, Marshall E., and Irwin Friend. "Risk, Investment Strategy and the Long-Run Rates of Return." *The Review of Economics and Statistics,* August 1974, pp. 259–69.

The CFA Study Guide. Charlottesville, Va.: The Institute of Chartered Financial Analysts, 1984, pp. 6 and 7.

Editors of Consumer Guide with Peter A. Dickinson. *How to Make Money during Inflation Recession.* New York: Harper & Row, 1980.

Eilbott, Peter. "Trends in the Value of Individual Stockholdings." *Journal of Business,* July 1974, pp. 339–48.

Fisher, Lawrence, and James H. Lorie. *A Half-Century of Returns on Stocks and Bonds.* Chicago: The University of Chicago Graduate School of Business, 1977.

———. "Rates of Return on Investment in Common Stock: The Year-by-Year Record 1926–1965." *Journal of Business,* July 1968, pp. 219–316.

Ibbotson, Roger G., and Carol F. Fall. "The United States Wealth Portfolio." *The Journal of Portfolio Management,* Fall 1982, pp. 82–92.

Ibbotson, Roger G., and Lawrence B. Siegel. "The World Market Wealth Portfolio." *The Journal of Portfolio Management,* Winter 1983, pp. 5–17.

Ibbotson, Roger G., and Rex A. Sinquefield. "Stocks, Bonds, Bills, and Inflation: Year-by-Year Historical Returns (1926–1974)." *Journal of Business,* University of Chicago, January 1976, pp. 11–47.

Lease, Ronald C.; Wilbur G. Lewellen; and Gary G. Schlarbaum. "The Individual Investor: Attributes and Attitudes." *Journal of Finance,* May 1974, pp. 413–33.

Lorie, James H., and Lawrence Fisher. "Rates of Return on Investment in Common Stock." *Journal of Business,* January 1964, pp. 1–17.

"Ranking America's Biggest Brokers." *Institutional Investor,* April 1983, pp. 273–74.

Robichek, Alexander A.; Richard A. Cohn; and John J. Pringle. "Returns on Alternative Media and Implications for Portfolio Construction." *Journal of Business,* July 1972, pp. 427–43.

Stocks, Bonds, Bills and Inflation, 1984 Yearbook. Chicago: R. G. Ibbotson and Associates, Inc., 1984.

APPENDIX 1–A: Investor Profile

Profile Analysis: What Should You Invest in Now?

Directions: Circle the answer that most nearly applies to you. Write that number in the space at right. Then add up the numbers and divide by 9 to get a median score.

AGE—My age is closest to:

(9) 30   (7) 40   (5) 50   (3) 60   (1) 70   —————

INCOME—My present annual income from all sources is nearest to (in thousands):

(2) 10   (4) 20   (5) 30   (6) 40   (8) 50   _____

ANNUAL EXPENSES—In relation to income, my annual expenses approximate:

(1) 100%   (3) 90%   (5) 80%   (7) 70%   (9) 50%   _____

NUMBER OF DEPENDENTS—I presently have these dependents:

(0) 0   (8) 1   (6) 2–3   (4) 4–5   (1) 6 or   _____
                                                                    more

ESTIMATED VALUE OF ASSETS—My house, insurance, savings, and investments total (in thousands):

(1) 50   (3) 100   (5) 250   (7) 350   (9) 500 or   _____
                                                                    more

LIABILITIES—My bills, mortgages, installment payments, and debts in relation to assets approximate (in thousands):

(9) 30%   (7) 50%   (5) 75%   (3) 90%   (1) 100%   _____

SAVINGS—I have cash on hand in savings or other liquid assets to equal this amount of expenses:

(1) 1 month   (3) 2 months   (5) 3 months   (7) 4 months   (9) 6+   _____
                                                                    months

LIFE INSURANCE—My life insurance coverage equals (in thousands):

(9) 250   (7) 150   (5) 100   (3) 50   (1) 25 or   _____
                                                                    less

HEALTH INSURANCE—My health insurance coverage includes:

(9) Basic, major medical,   (5) Major medical plus   (1) Basic   _____
    catastrophic   basic

Add up your scores and divide by 9 to get the average. Then consider the investment strategies that follow.

The investment strategy rating numbers below correlate with the average score you got from the profile analysis. The investment strategy ratings indicate investment categories ranging from (1) ultraconservative to (9) highly speculative. By matching the profile score with the nearest investment strategy numbers, you get some feel for investments that may be appropriate for you. You would probably choose from two or three categories.

1. Insured savings accounts.
2. High-grade government securities.
3. High-quality corporate and municipal bonds, preferred stocks, investment trusts, and annuity income.
4. Lower-rated corporate and municipal bonds, preferred stocks, investment trusts, convertible bonds and preferred stocks, and variable insurance.
5. Higher-rated common stocks and investment trusts, and investment annuities.
6. Lower-rated common stocks and investment trusts.
7. Speculative bonds, stocks, and investment trusts.
8. Gold and silver-related investments, and foreign investment trusts.
9. Rare and exotic investments: stamps, rare coins, art, antiques, gems and jewelry, rare books, autographs, prints, and lithographs.

Source: The editors of *Consumer Guide,* with Peter A. Dickinson, *How to Make Money during Inflation Recession* (New York: Harper & Row, 1980).

APPENDIX 1–B: *Career Opportunities in Investments*

Career opportunities in the field of investments include positions as a stockbroker, security analyst or portfolio manager, investment banker, or financial planner.

Stockbroker

A stockbroker generally works with the public in advising and executing orders for individual or institutional accounts. Although he or she may have a salary base to cushion against bad times, most of the compensation is in the form of commissions. Successful brokers do quite well financially.

Most brokerage houses look for people who have effective selling skills as well as an interest in finance. In hiring, some (though not all) brokerage houses require prior business experience and a mature appearance. A listing of the 30 largest brokerage houses is presented in Table 1B–1. Further information on these firms (as well as others not included on the list) can be found in the Securities Industry Yearbook published by the Securities Industry Association, 10 Broad Street, New York, N.Y. 10005.

Security Analyst or Portfolio Manager

Security analysts study various industries and companies and provide research reports to their clientele. A security analyst might work for a brokerage house, a bank trust department, or any other type of institutional investor. Security analysts often specialize in certain industries, such as banking or the airlines. They are expected to have an in-depth knowledge of overall financial analysis as well as the variables that influence their industry.

The role of the financial analyst has been upgraded over the years through the establishment of a certifying program in which you can become a Chartered Financial Analyst (CFA). There are approximately 8,000 CFAs in the United States and Canada. To achieve this designation, there is a three-year minimum appropriate-experience requirement and extensive testing over a three-year period. Each of the annual exams is six hours long and costs approximately $200 (the fee changes somewhat from year to year). There is also an initial, one-time registration fee (currently, $100). You can actually begin taking the exams while still in school.

The six areas of coverage for the exams are:

1. Ethical and professional standards.
2. Financial accounting.
3. Economics.
4. Fixed income securities.
5. Equity securities.
6. Portfolio management.

TABLE 1B–1   30 Largest U.S. Brokerage Houses

1983	Name of firm	Total capital	Number of employees	Number of offices	Number of registered representatives
1	Merrill Lynch & Co.	$1,685,277,000	37,882	910	10,200
2	Salomon Brothers Holding Co.	1,091,600,000	2,478	9	727
3	Shearson/American Express	836,615,000	10,342	352	3,967
4	The E. F. Hutton Group	608,061,000	13,400	364	5,300
5	Goldman, Sachs & Co.	478,000,000	3,145	15	834
6	Prudential-Bache Securities	443,474,000	9,600	250	3,900
7	The First Boston Corp.	341,161,000	1,889	17	608
8	Paine Webber	313,738,000	9,642	234	3,557
9	Dean Witter Reynolds	300,875,000	12,000	345	4,800
10	Bear, Stearns & Co.	275,825,000	3,100	12	800
11	Donaldson, Lufkin & Jenrette	249,036,000	3,588	44	650
12	Stephens	248,268,788	146	1	82
13	Morgan Stanley & Co.	247,000,000	2,336	6	643
14	Drexel Burnham Lambert	241,307,000	4,561	52	1,400
15	Warburg Paribas Becker-A. G. Becker	225,840,000	2,732	20	320
16	Lehman Brothers Kuhn Loeb	201,599,000	2,534	10	510
17	Smith Barney	167,800,000	4,750	90	1,600
18	Kidder, Peabody & Co.	151,436,000	4,716	72	1,702
19	A. G. Edwards & Sons	143,015,000	3,484	206	1,738
20	Shelby Cullom Davis & Co.	140,263,644	12	2	5
21	Allen & Co.	130,663,000	n.a.	1	4
22	Thomson McKinnon Securities	126,079,211	3,620	107	1,600
23	Spear, Leeds & Kellogg	114,000,000	834	12	90
24	L. F. Rothschild, Unterberg, Towbin	102,633,000	1,424	9	528
25	The Securities Groups	90,025,000	115	3	n.a.
26	Neuberger & Berman	85,751,611	360	2	40
27	John Nuveen & Co.	81,307,000	412	15	128
28	Oppenheimer & Co.	79,665,826	1,600	6	365
29	Aubrey G. Lanston & Co.	67,500,000	57	3	n.a.
30	Alex. Brown & Sons	66,089,114	940	21	306

n.a. = Not available.
Source: "Ranking America's Biggest Brokers," *Institutional Investor,* April 1983, pp. 273–74.

Each exam covers all six topics, but the degree of difficulty increases as you progress from exam one through exam three. An undergraduate degree in business with a major in finance or accounting or an economics degree is quite beneficial to the exam process. (Though other degrees are also acceptable). Of course, educational background must be supplemented with additional study prescribed by the Institute of Chartered Financial Analysts. A detailed outline of CFA exam topical coverage is presented in Table 1B–2, with candidate level indicating the exam level. The bars show how much of the information is to be covered in exam I, II, or III. The address for more information is: The Institute of Chartered Financial Analysts, P.O. Box 3668, Charlottesville, VA 22903 (phone 804 977-6600).

TABLE 1B–2   Areas of Study for CFA Exams

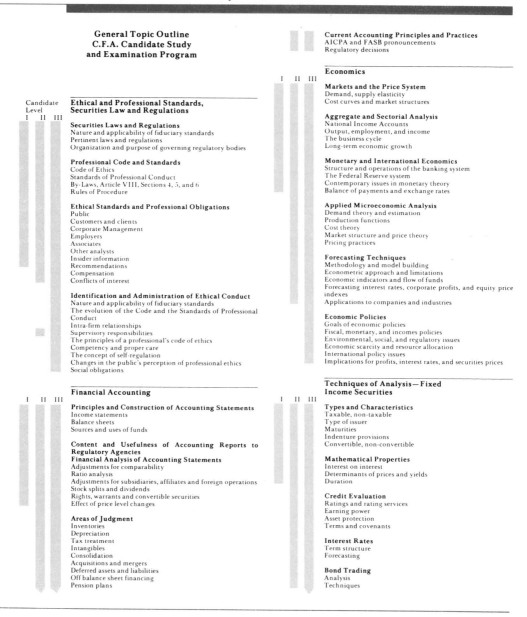

**General Topic Outline
C.F.A. Candidate Study
and Examination Program**

Candidate
Level
I   II   III

**Ethical and Professional Standards,
Securities Law and Regulations**

Securities Laws and Regulations
Nature and applicability of fiduciary standards
Pertinent laws and regulations
Organization and purpose of governing regulatory bodies

Professional Code and Standards
Code of Ethics
Standards of Professional Conduct
By-Laws, Article VIII, Sections 4, 5, and 6
Rules of Procedure

Ethical Standards and Professional Obligations
Public
Customers and clients
Corporate Management
Employers
Associates
Other analysts
Insider information
Recommendations
Compensation
Conflicts of interest

Identification and Administration of Ethical Conduct
Nature and applicability of fiduciary standards
The evolution of the Code and the Standards of Professional Conduct
Intra-firm relationships
Supervisory responsibilities
The principles of a professional's code of ethics
Competency and proper care
The concept of self-regulation
Changes in the public's perception of professional ethics
Social obligations

Financial Accounting

I   II   III

Principles and Construction of Accounting Statements
Income statements
Balance sheets
Sources and uses of funds

Content and Usefulness of Accounting Reports to Regulatory Agencies
Financial Analysis of Accounting Statements
Adjustments for comparability
Ratio analysis
Adjustments for subsidiaries, affiliates and foreign operations
Stock splits and dividends
Rights, warrants and convertible securities
Effect of price level changes

Areas of Judgment
Inventories
Depreciation
Tax treatment
Intangibles
Consolidation
Acquisitions and mergers
Deferred assets and liabilities
Off balance sheet financing
Pension plans

Current Accounting Principles and Practices
AICPA and FASB pronouncements
Regulatory decisions

Economics

I   II   III

Markets and the Price System
Demand, supply elasticity
Cost curves and market structures

Aggregate and Sectorial Analysis
National Income Accounts
Output, employment, and income
The business cycle
Long-term economic growth

Monetary and International Economics
Structure and operations of the banking system
The Federal Reserve system
Contemporary issues in monetary theory
Balance of payments and exchange rates

Applied Microeconomic Analysis
Demand theory and estimation
Production functions
Cost theory
Market structure and price theory
Pricing practices

Forecasting Techniques
Methodology and model building
Econometric approach and limitations
Economic indicators and flow of funds
Forecasting interest rates, corporate profits, and equity price indexes
Applications to companies and industries

Economic Policies
Goals of economic policies
Fiscal, monetary, and incomes policies
Environmental, social, and regulatory issues
Economic scarcity and resource allocation
International policy issues
Implications for profits, interest rates, and securities prices

Techniques of Analysis—Fixed Income Securities

I   II   III

Types and Characteristics
Taxable, non-taxable
Type of issuer
Maturities
Indenture provisions
Convertible, non-convertible

Mathematical Properties
Interest on interest
Determinants of prices and yields
Duration

Credit Evaluation
Ratings and rating services
Earning power
Asset protection
Terms and covenants

Interest Rates
Term structure
Forecasting

Bond Trading
Analysis
Techniques

While many security analysts are not CFAs, those that carry this designation tend to enjoy higher salary and prestige. The number of openings for security analysts has shrunk in recent times because of the tight research budgets of many brokerage houses. This came about in the mid–1970s when commission charges went from fixed to freely competitive, and fewer dollars were allocated to research.

TABLE 1B–2 (*concluded*)

Candidate Level			
I	II	III	**Risk Management**

Futures
Options

New Features
Contingent options and early redemptions
International bond investing

I	II	III	**Techniques of Analysis — Equity Securities**

Investment Context
Equity instruments (common stocks, convertible and
participating issues, rights, warrants, options and futures)
Development and application of equity instruments
Characteristics of equity markets: market indices,
relationship to economy, comparative risk and returns

Economic Framework
Industry Analysis and Evaluation
Identification of company's business(es)
External factors: political, regulatory, social
Demand analysis: end uses, growth (real and nominal),
cyclicality
Supply analysis: degree of concentration, ease of entry,
capacity
Profitability: demand/supply balance, pricing and costs

Company Analysis and Evaluation
Position(s) within industry(ies)
Sales Analysis: growth (real and nomial), cyclicality
Earnings analysis: earnings by business segment,
consolidated results, components of return on equity
Flow of funds analysis
Balance sheet analysis
Dividend analysis: payout policy, dividend growth
Management appraisal

Risk Analysis
Qualitative factors: external (political, social, environmental), company business (economic sensitivity, size,
growth, financial leverage), stock market (price volatility,
share characteristics, market sub-groups)
Quantitative measurements: capital asset pricing model
(beta, nonsystematic), factor analysis (identification, exposure)

Valuation
Earning multiples
Dividend discount and other valuation models
Technical analysis
Stock market perceptions
Valuation of equity instruments other than common stocks

Equity Analysis and the Efficient Markets
Weak, semi-strong and strong forms of efficient market
hypothesis
Implications relative to fundamental and technical analysis

Organization of the Equity Analysis Process
General investment philosophy
Techniques of information collection and processing
Analysts' interaction with other investment professionals
Communication of information inside and outside organ-
ization

Equity Analysis Performance Measurement
Criteria
Techniques
Evaluation process

I	II	III	**Objective of Analysis — Portfolio Management**

Principles of Financial Asset Management
Definition of portfolio management, basic concepts — return,
risk, diversification, portfolio efficiency
Evolution of portfolio management — traditional and recent
developments

Investor Objectives, Constraints and Policies
Liquidity requirement
Return requirement
Risk tolerance
Time horizon
Tax considerations
Regulatory and legal considerations
Unique needs, circumstances and preferences
Determination of portfolio policies

Expectational Factors
Social, political and economic
Capital markets
Individual financial assets

**Integration of Portfolio Policies and
Expectational Factors**
Portfolio construction — asset allocation, active/
passive strategies
Monitoring portfolio and responding to change —
objectives, constraints and policies, expectational factors
Execution — timing, commission costs, price effects

Portfolio Performance Appraisal
Performance criteria — absolute performance, relative to
portfolio objectives and risk level, relative to other portfolios
with similar objectives
Measurement of performance — valuation of assets, accounting for income, rates of return and volatility
Evaluation of results — relationship to performance criteria,
sources of results

Source: *The CFA Study Guide* (Charlottesville, Va.: The Institute of Chartered Financial Analysts, 1984), pp. 6 and 7.

In spite of this situation, really top analysts are still in strong demand. Six-figure salaries for top analysts are common. A magazine entitled the *Institutional Investor* actually picks an all-American team of security analysts, the best in energy, banking, and so on. As we will see later in the text, some academic researchers question the legitimacy of such designations.

Portfolio managers have the responsibility for managing large pools of

funds. They are generally employed by insurance companies, mutual funds, bank trust departments, pension funds, and other institutional investors. They often rely on the help of security analysts and brokers in designing their portfolios. They not only must decide which stocks to buy or sell, but also they must determine the risk level with the optimum trade-off between the common-stock and fixed-income components of a portfolio. Portfolio managers often rise through the ranks of stockbrokers and security analysts.

Investment Banker

Investment bankers are primarily involved in the distribution of securities from the issuing corporation to the public. Investment bankers also advise corporate clients on their financial strategy and may help to arrange mergers and acquisitions.

The investment banker is one of the most prestigious participants in the securities industry. Although the hiring of investment bankers was once closely confined to Ivy League graduates with the right family ties, such is no longer the case. Nevertheless, an MBA and top credentials are usually the first prerequisites.

Financial Planner

There is a new field of financial planning emerging to help solve the investment and tax problems of the individual investor. Financial planners may include specially trained representatives of the insurance industry, accountants who have expertise in this area, and Certified Financial Planners (actually an individual may fall into more than one of these categories).

Certified Financial Planners (CFPs) are so designated by the College for Financial Planning in Denver. The CFP program includes the following parts.

CFP I   Introduction to financial planning.
CFP II   Risk management.
CFP III Investments.
CFP IV   Tax planning and management.
CFP V   Employee benefits and retirement planning.
CFP VI   Estate planning.

Each part is concluded with a comprehensive written three-hour exam. The program normally takes 24 months to complete. The program participant may study on his or her own or attend formal classes. There are also appropriate experience requirements for final certification. Information on the CFP program can be obtained by contacting the College for Financial Planning, 9725 East Hampden Avenue, Denver, Colorado 80231 (phone 303 755 7101). There are also a number of other national and local groups offering programs in financial planning.

Chapter 2

SECURITY MARKETS— PRESENT AND FUTURE

Change in the securities markets that began in the 1970s has greatly accelerated in the 1980s. Deregulation of financial institutions created new competitors for retail brokerage houses and allowed banks and savings and loans to offer discount brokerage services and money market deposit accounts. Mergers continued to increase the consolidation of financial resources into well-capitalized financial-service-oriented companies, such as Merrill Lynch, Sears, Bank of America, and Shearson Lehman/American Express. One result is that investors probably have more alternative investments (securities) currently available to them than at any other time.

The market for stock options and financial futures has recently expanded to include options on futures and options on stock indexes. The popularity of individual retirement accounts (IRAs) has added to the demand for mutual funds, and these funds have increased the emphasis on traditional products as well as short-term money market funds, real estate investment trusts, and funds investing in international securities.

Even the traditional markets for common stocks have changed as the over-the-counter market through its NASDAQ automated quotation system has successfully increased its share of equity trades at the expense of the New York and American Stock Exchanges. Computer and communications technology is affecting the way securities are traded not only in the international market systems but also by the individual and institutional investors. As debt has become more widespread, markets for federal government securities, municipal bonds, and corporate debt have all expanded. The combined effects of all these events are still creating structural changes in the markets.

The impact of these changes as well as a complete discussion of securities available for investment will be presented in various chapters throughout the book. In this chapter we examine how the market system operates, with an eye toward efficiency, liquidity, and allocation of capital. We then look at the role of the secondary or resale market for stocks, bonds, and other securities. Finally, we examine some key protective legislation for the investor.

MARKET FUNCTIONS

Many times people will call their stockbroker and ask, How's the market? What they are referring to is usually the market for common stocks as measured by the Dow Jones Industrial Average, the New York Stock Exchange Index, or some other measure of common stock performance. The stock market is not the only market. There are markets for each different kind of investment that can be made.

A market is simply a way of exchanging assets, usually cash for something of value. It could be a used car, a government bond, gold, or diamonds. There doesn't have to be a central place where this transaction is consummated. As long as there can be communication between buyers and sellers, the exchange can occur. The offering party does not have to own what he sells. He can be an agent acting for the owner in the transaction. For example, in the sale of real estate, the owner usually employs a real estate broker/agent who advertises

and sells the property for a percentage commission. Not all markets have the same procedures, but certain trading characteristics are desirable for most markets.

Market Efficiency and Liquidity

In general, markets are efficient when prices respond quickly to new information, when each successive trade is made at a price close to the preceding price, and when the market can absorb large amounts of securities or assets without changing the price significantly. The more efficient the market, the faster prices react to new information, the closer in price is each successive trade, and the greater the amount of securities that can be sold without changing the price.

In order for markets to be efficient in this context, they must be liquid. Liquidity is a measure of the speed with which an asset can be converted into cash at its fair market value. Liquid markets exist when continuous trading occurs, and as the number of participants in the market becomes larger, price continuity increases along with liquidity. Transaction costs also affect liquidity. The lower the cost of buying and selling, the more likely it is that people will be able to enter the market.

Competition and Allocation of Capital

An investor must realize that all markets compete for funds; stocks against bonds, mutual funds against real estate, government securities against corporate securities, and so on. The competitive comparisons are almost endless. Because markets set prices on assets, investors are able to compare the prices against their perceived risk and expected return and thereby choose assets that enable them to achieve their desired risk-return trade-offs. If the markets are efficient, prices adjust rapidly to new information, and this adjustment changes the expected rate of return and allows the investor to alter his/her investment strategy. Without efficient and liquid markets, the investor would be unable to do this. This allocation of capital takes place on both secondary and primary markets.

Secondary Markets

Secondary markets are markets for existing assets which are currently traded between investors. It is these markets that create the prices and allow for liquidity. If secondary markets did not exist, investors would have no place to sell their assets. Without liquidity, many people would not invest at all. Would you like to own $10,000 of Eastman Kodak common stock but be unable to convert it into cash if needed? If there were no secondary markets, investors would expect a higher return to compensate for the increased risk of illiquidity and the inability to adjust their portfolios to new information.

Primary Markets

Primary markets are distinguished by the flow of funds between the market participants. Instead of trading between investors as in the secondary markets, participants in the primary market buy their assets directly from the source of the asset. A common example would be a new issue of corporate bonds sold by AT&T. You would buy the bonds through a brokerage firm acting as an agent for an investment banking firm or for AT&T. Your dollars would flow to AT&T rather than to another investor. The same would be true of buying a piece of art directly from the artist rather than from an art gallery. Primary markets allow corporations, government units, and others to raise needed funds for expansion of their capital base. Once the assets or securities are sold in the primary market, they begin trading in the secondary market. Price competition in the secondary markets between different risk-return classes enables the primary markets to price new issues at fair prices to reflect existing risk-return relationships. So far, our discussion of markets has been quite general but applicable to most free markets. In the following section, we will deal with the organization and structure of specific markets.

ORGANIZATION OF THE PRIMARY MARKETS—THE INVESTMENT BANKER

The most active participant in the primary market is the investment banker. Since corporations, states, and local governments do not sell new securities daily, monthly, or even annually, they rely on the expertise of the investment banker when selling securities.

Underwriting Function

The investment banker acts as a middleman in the process of raising funds, and in most cases, he takes a risk by *underwriting* an issue of securities. Underwriting refers to the guarantee the investment banking firm gives the selling firm to purchase its securities at a fixed price, thereby eliminating the risk of not selling the whole issue of securities and having less cash than desired. The investment banker may also sell the issue on a "best efforts" basis where the issuing firm assumes the risk and simply takes back any securities not sold after a fixed period of time.

We can see by inspecting Table 2–1 that on average the best-efforts offerings in recent years only equal about 20 percent of the total securities sold through public distribution, and the overwhelming majority of these issues were common stock. The more risk the investment banker takes, the higher the selling fee to the corporation. Some stock issues are so risky that the investment banker may charge too much of a fee for underwriting risk and distribution so the firm chooses the best-efforts method as a cheaper alternative. With underwriting, once the security is sold, the investment banker will usually make a market in the security, which means active buying and selling

TABLE 2–1 Corporate Issues by Method of Distribution and by Type of Security: 1981–1984 (Primary Issues Registered under the Security Act of 1933; in millions)

Year	Underwritten				Agency best-efforts				Direct by issuer			
	Total	Debt	Preferred	Common	Total	Debt	Preferred	Common	Total	Debt	Preferred	Common
1983	$40,826	$16,049	$4,918	$19,859	$ 8,454	$ 152	$16	$8,286	$2,543	$ 339	$28	$2,176
1982	36,674	21,570	4,558	10,546	9,935	1,305	10	8,620	4,138	2,589	6	1,542
1981	46,678	32,499	1,678	12,451	10,139	1,206	4	8,929	6,689	3,091	10	3,589

Source: Annual Report of the U.S. Securities and Exchange Commission, 1984.

to ensure a continuously liquid market and wider distribution. In the case of best efforts and for direct offerings, which are even smaller than best efforts, the firm assumes the risk of not raising enough capital and faces no guarantees that a continuous market will be made in the company's securities. Table 2–1 shows that most long-term capital raising efforts by corporations are through investment bankers and not directly by corporations.

Corporations may also choose to raise capital through private placements rather than through a public offering. With a private placement the company may sell its own securities to a financial institution such as an insurance company, pension fund, mutual fund, etc. or it can engage an investment banker to find an institution willing to buy a large block of stock or bonds. Most private placements involve bonds (debt issues) instead of common stock but, in general, as Table 2–2 demonstrates, private offerings of bonds have become less popular in recent years.

TABLE 2–2   Gross Proceeds of Corporate Bonds Publicly Offered and Privately Placed

Year	Publicly offered (in millions)	Privately placed (in millions)
1983	n.a.	n.a.
1982	$43,428	$ 7,748
1981	37,653	6,989
1980	41,587	11,619
1979	25,814	14,394
1978	19,815	17,057
1977	24,072	17,943
1976	26,453	15,927
1975	32,583	10,172
1970	25,384	4,931
1965	5,570	8,150
1960	4,806	3,275
1955	4,119	3,301
1950	2,360	2,560

n.a. = Not available.
Source: Selected issues of the *Federal Reserve Bulletin.*

Distribution

In a public offering, the distribution process is extremely important and on large issues an investment banker does not undertake this alone. More often, other investment banking firms will share the risk and the burden of distribution by forming a group called a syndicate. The larger the offering in dollar terms, the more participants there generally are in the syndicate. For example, the tombstone advertisement for Texaco Capital's issue of 13 percent notes due in 1991 shows 19 participating investment bankers (Figure 2–1). Texaco

FIGURE 2–1   Advertisement of Distribution

This announcement is neither an offer to sell nor a solicitation of an offer to buy these securities.
The offer is made only by the Prospectus Supplement and the related Prospectus.

New Issue / August 6, 1984

$500,000,000

Texaco Capital Inc.

13% Notes Due 1991

Unconditionally Guaranteed by

Texaco Inc.

Price 99.54% and accrued interest from August 1, 1984

Copies of the Prospectus Supplement and the related Prospectus may be obtained
in any State in which this announcement is circulated only from such of the
undersigned as may legally offer these securities in such State.

Merrill Lynch Capital Markets   **Salomon Brothers Inc**

PaineWebber Incorporated	**Atlantic Capital** Corporation	**Becker Paribas** Incorporated	**Daiwa Securities America Inc.**	**Dillon, Read & Co. Inc.**
Donaldson, Lufkin & Jenrette Securities Corporation	**E. F. Hutton & Company Inc.**		**Kidder, Peabody & Co.** Incorporated	**The Nikko Securities Co.** International, Inc.
Nomura Securities International, Inc.		**Prudential-Bache** Securities		**Swiss Bank Corporation International** Securities Inc.
Wertheim & Co., Inc.		**Dean Witter Reynolds Inc.**		**Yamaichi International (America), Inc.**
Thomson McKinnon Securities Inc.				**Wood Gundy Corp.**

Source: *The Wall Street Journal,* © Dow Jones & Company, Inc. (August 7, 1984).

Capital is a subsidiary of Texaco and the debt is fully guaranteed by the parent
company. Merrill Lynch Capital Markets and Salomon Brothers Inc. are the
managing underwriters, with the other 17 firms participating in the syndicate.
The firms are usually listed in the tombstone advertisement based on their
clout in the investment banking community. The firms at the top of the advertisement usually have taken the biggest dollar position and the firms at the
bottom, e.g., Thomson McKinnon Securities Inc., a relatively small position.

Each banker is responsible for selling the agreed-upon number of bonds or stock.

For most original offerings, the investment banker is extremely important as a link between the original issuer and the security markets. By taking much of the risk, the investment banker enables corporations and others to find needed capital and thus allows investors an opportunity to participate in the ownership of securities through purchase in the secondary markets. Notice that the bonds are priced at 99.54 percent of par value which means that the bonds are selling for $995.40 per $1,000 bond. In the case of the Texaco offering, the investment banker took some risk that interest rates would not rise during the offering period. Since rates did later rise, the price fell below par of $1,000 and the syndicate's profit was less than expected.

Investment bankers are in business to make a profit by selling new issues as quickly as possible so that they can use their capital for more offerings. The advantage of having a large number of investment bankers is that more potential public and institutional buyers are available to improve the liquidity and geographic distribution of the issue. Another advantage is that risk is reduced by spreading the selling effort between many investment bankers. The sale of bonds is primarily to large institutional investors in large blocks and so a large broker network is not as necessary as with common stock.

TABLE 2–3   Domestic Underwritings as Sole or Lead Manager

	1983			1982	
	Dollar volume (in billions)	Number of issues		Dollar volume (in billions)	Number of issues
Salomon Brothers	$15.76	176	Morgan Stanley	$10.62	108
Merrill Lynch Capital Markets	11.04	181	Merrill Lynch Capital Markets	9.42	136
Goldman Sachs	10.74	137	Salomon Brothers	9.34	107
First Boston	9.59	113	Goldman Sachs	6.88	83
Morgan Stanley	8.43	101	First Boston	5.74	65
Drexel Burnham Lambert	7.35	125	Lehman Brothers Kuhn Loeb	3.82	49
Lehman Brothers Kuhn Loeb	5.70	74	Blyth Eastman Paine Webber	3.01	54
Kidder Peabody	3.42	85	Drexel Burnham Lambert	2.16	48
Blyth Eastman Paine Webber	3.13	61	Kidder Peabody	2.01	46
E. F. Hutton	2.22	60	Shearson/American Express	1.10	30

Excludes all debt for equity swaps. Debt issues measured on net proceeds basis. Excludes issues done on a best-efforts basis.
Source: Reprinted by permission of *The Wall Street Journal,* © Dow Jones & Company, Inc. (January 6, 1984). All rights reserved.

A significant change that is taking place in the investment banking area can also be noted in previously discussed Figure 2–1. An offering of $500 million in the 1970s would have included at least twice as many investment bankers in the syndicate. As firms have merged, the financial strength of the investment bankers has increased to the point where they are able to assume more risk and thus larger dollar positions in new offerings.

Table 2–3 shows the top 10 lead underwriters for 1982 and 1983. The top few firms clearly consolidated their dominant position in this market. The rankings are used as a tool to convince clients that the investment banker can raise capital. The rise of shelf-registration under SEC Rule 415 (discussed in Chapter 9) increased the dominance of the large investment bankers specializing in bonds. A shelf registration allows firms to register their securities (mostly bonds and notes) with the Securities and Exchange Commission and then sell them at will as funds are needed. This allows investment bankers to buy portions of the shelf issue and immediately resell the securities to institutional clients without forming the normal syndicates or tying up capital for several weeks.

Some initial offerings, such as Treasury bills or other federal government securities, do not use investment bankers. They rely on Federal Reserve banks to auction the securities to government securities dealers who make markets by buying and selling to large financial institutions. Individuals desiring to buy initial offerings from the Treasury can place orders directly with the nearest Federal Reserve branch bank.

ORGANIZATION OF THE SECONDARY MARKETS

Once the investment banker or the Federal Reserve (for U.S. government securities) has sold a new issue of securities, it begins trading in secondary markets that provide liquidity, efficiency, continuity, and competition. The *organized exchanges* fulfill this need in a central location where trading takes place between buyers and sellers. The *over-the-counter markets* also provide markets for exchange but not in a central location. We will first examine the organized exchanges and then the over-the-counter markets.

Organized Exchanges

Organized exchanges are either national or regional, but both classifications are organized in a similar fashion. Exchanges have a central trading location where securities are bought and sold in an auction market by brokers acting as agents for the buyer and seller. Stocks usually trade at various trading posts on the floor of the exchange. Brokers are registered members of the exchanges, and their number is fixed by each exchange. The national exchanges are the New York Stock Exchange (NYSE) located at the corner of Broad and Wall Street in New York City and the American Stock Exchange (AMEX) located at the corner of Hanover and Wall Street, also in New York City. Both these

exchanges are governed by a board of directors consisting of one half exchange members and one half public members.

The regional exchanges began their existence trading securities of local firms. As the firms grew, they became listed on the national exchanges, but they also continued to trade on the regionals. Many cities, such as Chicago, Cincinnati, Baltimore, Detroit, Boston, and others, have regional exchanges. Today most of the trading on these exchanges is done in nationally known companies. Trading in the same companies is common between the NYSE and such regionals as the Midwest Exchange in Chicago, the Pacific Coast Exchange in San Francisco and Los Angeles, and the smaller regionals. In fact, about 90 percent of the companies traded on the Midwest and Pacific Coast Exchanges are also listed on the NYSE.

August 3, 1984, was the busiest day in the history of the New York Stock Exchange, and Table 2–4 shows that over 275 million shares of NYSE-listed stock was traded. Since some of these shares are dually listed on other exchanges and even traded over-the-counter, not all volume was transacted in

TABLE 2–4   Data on Trading Volume

NYSE-Composite Transactions

Friday, August 3, 1984

Quotations include trades on the Midwest, Pacific, Philadelphia, Boston and Cincinnati stock exchanges and reported by the National Association of Securities Dealers and Instinet

Friday's Volume
275,309,660 Shares; 649,000 Warrants

TRADING BY MARKETS

	Shares	Warrants
New York Exchange	236,570,000	648,000
Midwest Exchange	17,967,700	....
Pacific Exchange	7,331,100	....
Nat'l Assoc. of Securities Dealers ...	6,401,760	1,000
Philadelphia Exchange	4,607,700	....
Boston Exchange	1,917,700	....
Cincinnati Exchange	416,600	....
Instinet System	97,100	....

NYSE – Composite

Volume since Jan. 1:	1984	1983	1982
Total shares	16,202,304,430	15,172,333,820	9,131,951,746
Total warrants	56,607,800	98,163,900	22,587,150

New York Stock Exchange

Volume since Jan. 1:	1984	1983	1982
Total shares	13,664,668,450	13,018,334,165	7,851,651,596
Total warrants	54,697,800	97,683,100	22,558,800

New York. For example, the Midwest Exchange in Chicago accounted for almost 18 million shares of stock listed on the NYSE, while the NYSE traded 236 million shares in its own listed stocks.

Consolidated Tape

Although dual listing and trading has existed for some time, it was not until June 16, 1975, that a consolidated ticker tape was instituted. This allows brokers on the floor of one exchange to see prices of transactions on other exchanges in the dually listed stocks. Any time a transaction is made on a regional exchange or over-the-counter in a security listed on the NYSE, this transaction and any made on the floor of the NYSE are displayed on the composite tape. The composite price data keeps markets more efficient and prices more competitive between exchanges at all times.

The NYSE and AMEX are both national exchanges and for years did not allow dual listing of companies traded on their exchanges. As of August 1976, securities were able to be dually listed between these exchanges. There doesn't seem to be any advantage to this since both are located in New York City, and traditionally, shares traded on one exchange are not traded on the other.

Table 2–5 displays the number of trades (not number of shares) on all markets participating in the Consolidated Tape. We can see that trading volume has risen dramatically since 1976. However, the New York Stock Exchange is getting a smaller piece of the total number of trades in its own listed stock. Its percentage of trades in 1983 slipped to 77.68 percent, its lowest level since the inception of the Consolidated Tape.

During this same time the percentage of *shares* traded on the NYSE peaked in 1978 at 88.43 percent and declined to almost 82 percent by the end of 1983. Volume statistics on participating markets in NYSE listed stocks are shown in Table 2–6.[1] In general, the New York Stock Exchange is meeting tough competition from other exchanges and the over-the-counter NASDAQ system, but it is faced with a possible loss of prestige and profits during the rest of the 1980s as competition becomes even more intense.

Listing Requirements for Firms

Securities can only be traded on an exchange if they have met the listing requirements of the exchange and have been approved by the board of governors. All exchanges have minimum requirements that must be met before trading can take place in a company's common stock. Since the NYSE is the biggest exchange and generates the most dollar volume in large, well-known companies, it is not surprising that its listing requirements are the most restrictive.

---

[1] The NYSE has a larger percentage of the share volume (Table 2–6) than the trade volume (Table 2–5) because its average trade involves more shares than other exchanges.

TABLE 2–5 Number of Trades Shown on the Consolidated Tape

Consolidated tape trades by market, 1983

Year	NYSE	AMEX	PSE	MSE	PHLX	BSE	CSE	NASD	INST	Total
1983	15,050,791	43	1,661,907	1,318,868	751,002	241,520	94,171	248,820	7,250	19,374,372
1982	12,609,104	13	1,326,460	944,862	628,217	159,865	134,106	231,036	6,304	16,039,967
1981	11,701,098	673	910,634	644,176	547,219	129,593	123,911	136,519	3,329	14,197,152
1980	13,074,382	1,021	817,957	548,416	530,659	118,000	108,169	112,923	3,019	15,314,546
1979	10,442,237	244	665,073	402,196	333,805	78,087	63,689	71,858	4,123	12,061,312
1978	10,087,834	725	653,769	366,654	255,359	75,471	54,065	96,165	1,911	11,591,953
1977	8,264,036	1,982	548,507	328,653	150,234	74,263	155,804	178,020	2,062	9,703,561
1976	9,646,200	1,535	545,685	399,266	168,119	95,096	86,735	268,324	1,560	11,217,536

Distribution of consolidated tape trades, 1976–1983

Year	NYSE	AMEX	PSE	MSE	PHLX	BSE	CSE	NASD	INST	Total
1983	77.68%	0.00%	8.58%	6.81%	3.88%	1.25%	0.49%	1.28%	0.04%	100.00%
1982	78.61	0.00	8.27	5.89	3.92	1.00	0.84	1.44	0.04	100.00
1981	82.42	0.00	6.41	4.54	3.85	0.91	0.87	0.96	0.02	100.00
1980	85.37	0.01	5.34	3.58	3.47	0.77	0.71	0.74	0.02	100.00
1979	86.58	0.00	5.51	3.33	2.77	0.65	0.53	0.60	0.03	100.00
1978	87.02	0.01	5.64	3.16	2.20	0.65	0.47	0.83	0.02	100.00
1977	85.16	0.02	5.65	3.39	1.55	0.77	1.61	1.83	0.02	100.00
1976	85.99	0.01	4.86	3.56	1.50	0.85	0.77	2.39	0.01	100.00

Participating markets: NYSE, New York; AMEX, AMEX American; PSE, Pacific; MSE, Midwest; PHLX, Philadelphia; BSE,
Boston; CSE, Cincinnati; NASD, National Association of Securities Dealers; INST, Instinet.
Source: *New York Stock Exchange Fact Book* (New York: New York Stock Exchange, 1984).

TABLE 2–6 Share Volume Shown on the Consolidated Tape

Consolidated tape volume by market, 1983 (thousands of shares)

Year	NYSE	AMEX	PSE	MSE	PHLX	BSE	CSE	NASD	INST	Total
1983	21,589,577	188	802,012	1,634,760	416,206	182,812	51,325	649,261	36,320	25,362,458
1982	16,458,037	1	664,089	1,091,081	307,357	104,085	59,328	486,028	33,593	19,203,590
1981	11,853,740	194	451,591	700,830	215,000	74,406	47,226	319,081	17,125	13,679,194
1980	11,352,294	584	385,970	577,710	212,296	70,747	53,236	268,097	14,679	12,935,607
1979	8,155,914	76	297,379	359,615	160,550	54,711	34,148	180,297	11,357	9,254,044
1978	7,205,055	238	236,417	326,727	118,156	49,381	20,089	184,983	6,530	8,147,569
1977	5,273,767	771	201,841	267,189	80,208	40,054	49,126	234,413	5,803	6,153,173
1976	5,360,116	786	213,041	256,032	85,275	46,558	30,844	281,118	5,771	6,281,008

Distribution of consolidated tape volume, 1976–1983

Year	NYSE	AMEX	PSE	MSE	PHLX	BSE	CSE	NASD	INST	Total
1983	82.12%	0.00%	3.16%	6.45%	1.64%	0.72%	0.20%	2.56%	0.14%	100.00%
1982	85.70	0.00	3.46	5.68	1.60	0.54	0.31	2.53	0.17	100.00
1981	86.66	0.00	3.30	5.12	1.57	0.54	0.35	2.33	0.13	100.00
1980	87.76	0.00	2.98	4.47	1.64	0.55	0.41	2.07	0.11	100.00
1979	88.13	0.00	3.21	3.89	1.73	0.59	0.37	1.95	0.12	100.00
1978	88.43	0.00	2.90	4.01	1.45	0.61	0.25	2.27	0.08	100.00
1977	85.71	0.01	3.28	4.34	1.30	0.65	0.80	3.81	0.09	100.00
1976	85.34	0.01	3.39	4.08	1.36	0.74	0.49	4.48	0.09	100.00

Participating markets: NYSE, New York; AMEX American; PSE, Pacific; MSE, Midwest; PHLX, Philadelphia; BSE, Boston; CSE, Cincinnati; NASD, National Association of Securities Dealers; INST, Instinet.
Source: *New York Stock Exchange Fact Book* (New York: New York Stock Exchange, 1984).

Initial listing.   Although each case is decided on its own merits, according to the *NYSE Fact Book,* the minimum requirements for a company to be listed on the New York Stock Exchange for the first time are as follows:

1. Demonstrated earning power under competitive conditions of: *either* $2.5 million before Federal income taxes for the most recent year and $2 million pre-tax for each of the preceding two years, *or* an aggregate for last three fiscal years of $6.5 million *together with* a minimum in the most recent fiscal year of $4.5 million. (All three years must be profitable.)
2. Net tangible assets of $16 million, but greater emphasis is placed on the aggregate market value of the common stock.
3. Market value of publicly held shares, subject to adjustment depending on market conditions, within the following limits.

Maximum	$18,000,000
Minimum	$ 9,000,000
Present (2/13/84)	$18,000,000

    (The market value requirement is subject to adjustment, based on the NYSE Index of Common Stock Prices. The base in effect as of February 13, 1984, is the Index on July 15, 1971 (55.06). The Index as of January 15 and July 15 of each year (if lower than the base) is divided by the base, and the resulting percentage is multiplied by $18 million to produce the adjusted market value standard. The adjustment formula is used only when the current Index is below the base).
4. A total of 1,100,000 common shares publicly held.
5. *Either* 2,000 holders of 100 shares or more, *or* 2,200 total stockholders *together with* average monthly trading volume (for the most recent six months) of 100,000 shares.

The other exchanges have requirements covering the same areas, but the amounts are smaller.

Corporations desiring to be listed on exchanges have made the decision that public availability of the stock on an exchange will benefit their shareholders. The benefits will occur either by providing liquidity to owners or by allowing the company a more viable means for raising external capital for growth and expansion. The company must pay annual listing fees to the exchange and some fees based on the number of shares traded each year.

Delisting.   The New York Stock Exchange also has the authority to remove (delist) or suspend a security from trading when the security fails to meet certain criteria. There is much latitude in these decisions but generally a company's security may be considered for delisting if there are fewer than 1,200 round-lot (100 share owners), 600,000 shares or fewer in public hands and market value of the security is less than $5,000,000. A company that easily exceeded these standards on first being listed may fall below them during hard times.

Membership for Market Participants

We've talked about listing requirements for corporations on the exchange, but what about the investment houses or traders that service the listed firms; or trade for their own account on the exchanges? These privileges are reserved for a select number of people. The NYSE has 1,366 members who own "seats" which may be leased or sold with the approval of the NYSE. While the price of a seat was $425,000 in the mid-1980s, it could have been bought for a recent low of $35,000 in 1977. These 1,366 members can be divided into five distinct categories, each with a specific job.

Commission brokers.   Commission brokers represent commission houses, such as Merrill Lynch or E. F. Hutton, that execute orders on the floor of the exchange for customers of that firm. Many of the larger retail brokerage houses have more than one commission broker on the floor of the exchange. If I call my account executive (stockbroker) and place an order to buy 100 shares of Exxon, he will teletype my order to the NYSE where it will be transmitted to one of the firm's commission brokers who will go to the appropriate trading post and execute the order.

Floor brokers.   You can imagine that a commission broker could get very busy running from post to post on a heavy volume day. In times like these, he will rely on some help from a floor broker, who is registered to trade on the exchange but is not an employee of a member firm. Instead, the floor broker owns his own seat and charges a small fee for his services (usually around $4 per 100 shares).

Registered traders.   Registered traders own their own seat and are not associated with a member firm (such as Merrill Lynch). They are registered to trade for their own accounts and, of course, do so with the objective of earning a profit. Because they are members, they don't have to pay commissions on these trades; but in so trading, they help to generate a continuous market and liquidity for the market in general. There is always the possibility that these traders could manipulate the market if they acted in mass, and for that reason, the exchanges have rules governing their behavior and limiting the number of registered traders at one specific trading post.

Odd-lot dealers.   Odd lots (less than 100 shares) are not traded on the main floor of the exchange, so if a customer wants to buy or sell 20 shares of AT&T, the order will end up being processed by an odd-lot dealer. The dealer owns his own inventory of the particular security and buys and sells for his own account. If he accumulates 100 shares, he can sell them in the market, or if he needs 20 shares, he can buy 100 in the market and hold the other 80 shares in his inventory. A few very large brokerage firms, such as Merrill Lynch, have begun making their own odd-lot market in actively traded securities, and

it is expected that this trend will become common practice at the other large commission houses. Odd-lot trading on other exchanges is usually handled by the specialist in the particular stock.

Specialists.   Specialists are a very important segment of the exchange and make up about one fourth of total membership. Each stock traded has a specialist assigned to it, and most specialists are responsible for more than one stock. The specialist has two basic duties with regard to the stocks he supervises. First, he must handle any special orders that commission brokers or floor brokers might give him. For example, a special order could limit the price someone is willing to pay for General Telephone (GTE) stock at $40 per share for 100 shares. If the commission broker reaches the General Telephone trading post and GTE is selling at $41 per share, the broker will leave the order with the specialist to execute if and when the stock of GTE falls to $40 or less. The specialist puts these special limit orders in his "book" with the date and time entered so he can execute orders at the same price by the earliest time of receipt. A portion of the broker's commission is then paid to the specialist.

The second major function of specialists is to maintain continuous, liquid, and orderly markets in their assigned stocks. This is not a difficult function in the actively traded securities, such as General Motors, Du Pont, and American Telephone, but it becomes more difficult in those stocks where there are no large, active markets. For example, suppose you placed an order to buy 100 shares of Ametek at the market price. If the commission broker reaches the Ametek trading post and no seller is present, he can't wait for one to appear since he has other orders to execute. Fortunately, he can buy the shares from the specialist who acts as a dealer—in this case buying for and selling from his own inventory. To ensure his ability to maintain continuous markets, the exchange requires a specialist to have $500,000 or enough capital to own 5,000 shares of his assigned stock, whichever is greater. At times, specialists are placed under tremendous pressure to make a market for securities. A classic case occurred when President Eisenhower had a heart attack in the 1950s and specialists stabilized the market by absorbing wave after wave of "sell" orders.

The New York Stock Exchange actually keeps statistics on specialist performance and their ability to maintain price continuity, quotation spreads, market depth, and price stabilization. These data are given in Table 2–7. Price continuity is measured by the size of the price variation in successive trades. Column 1 is the percentage of transactions with no change in price or a minimum change of $1/8$ of a dollar. Column 2 presents the percentage of the quotes where the bid and asked price was equal to or less than $1/4$ of a point. Market depth (column 3) is displayed as a percentage of the time that 1,000 shares of volume failed to move the price of the stock more than $1/8$ of a point. Finally the NYSE expects the specialist to stabilize the market by buying and selling from his own account against the prevailing trend. This is measured in column 4 as the percentage of shares purchased below the last different price and the percentage of shares sold above the last different price. While these

TABLE 2-7   Market Quality and Specialists' Stabilization

	(1) Price continuity	(2) Quotation spreads	(3) Market depth	(4) Stabilization rate
1983	88.7%	60.7%	86.2%	90.0%
1982	89.5	65.1	85.2	88.9
1981	87.2	60.4	81.6	90.2
1980	86.4	60.6	80.4	90.9
1979	90.6	71.1	84.9	90.0
1978	90.8	72.9	84.4	90.0
1977	92.5	75.9	86.0	90.8
1976	90.3	71.0	—	92.5
1975	88.1	59.9	—	91.4
1974	84.3	44.9	—	91.1

Source: *New York Stock Exchange Fact Book* (New York Stock Exchange, 1984).

statistics are not 100 percent, it would be quite unreasonable for us to expect specialists to maintain that kind of a record in all types of markets. However, some critics of the specialist system on the NYSE think that these performance measures could be improved by having more than one specialist for each stock. Many market watchers feel that competing dealers on the over-the-counter market provide more price stability and fluid markets than the NYSE specialist system.

OTHER ORGANIZED EXCHANGES

The American Stock Exchange

The American Stock Exchange trades in smaller companies than the NYSE and, except for one dually listed company on the NYSE in 1983, the stocks traded on the AMEX are completely different from those on any other exchange. Because the small companies on the AMEX do not meet the liquidity needs of large institutional investors, the AMEX has been primarily a market for individual investors.

In an attempt to differentiate itself from the NYSE, the AMEX traded warrants in companies for many years before the NYSE allowed them. Even now, the AMEX has warrants listed for stocks trading on the NYSE, while the NYSE has very few warrants listed at all. The AMEX also trades put and call options in over 100 stocks, with most of the underlying common stocks being listed on the NYSE. This market has been a stabilizing force for the AMEX. The AMEX (as well as the NYSE) has also recently entered into commodity futures trading through interest rate futures. Although the AMEX also trades about 200 corporate bonds, this is not the major market for corporate bonds.

The Chicago Board Options Exchange

Trading in call options started on the Chicago Board Options Exchange (CBOE) in April of 1973 and proved very successful. The number of call options listed grew from 16 in 1973 to approximately 400 by 1985. A call option gives the owner the right to buy 100 shares of the underlying common stock at a set price for a certain period of time. The establishment of the CBOE standardized call options into three-month, six-month, and nine-month expiration periods on a rotating monthly series. For example, one series is January, April, July, October. A second series is December, March, June, September, and the last series is November, February, May, August. When the CBOE began, only the first series was traded, but the growth in the market dictated the need for other dates. The CBOE and the AMEX currently have many options that are dually listed, and the competition between them is fierce. The two exchanges also trade put options (options to sell). A number of smaller regional exchanges also provide for option trading, and the New York Stock Exchange began trading options in 1985.

A new wrinkle in the options game has been options on stock market indexes or industry groupings (called subindexes). The CBOE offers puts and calls on the Standard & Poor's 100 and 500 stock indexes; the NYSE has options on the NYSE Index; the AMEX has options on the AMEX Market Value Index and several options available on industry indexes such as the Computer Technology Index, the Oil and Gas Index, and the Transportation Index. Even the regional Philadelphia Exchange has options on a Gaming and Hotel Index and a Gold and Silver Index. More about these markets will be presented in Chapter 16.

Futures Markets

Futures markets have traditionally been associated with commodities but, more recently, also with financial instruments. Purchasers of commodity futures own the right to buy a certain amount of the commodity at a set price for a specified period of time. When the time runs out (expires), the futures contract will be delivered unless sold before expiration. One major futures markets is the Chicago Board of Trade, which trades corn, oats, soybeans, wheat, silver, plywood, Ginnie Mae futures, and Treasury bond futures. There are also other important futures markets in Chicago, Kansas City, Minneapolis, New York, and other cities. These markets are very important as hedging markets and help set commodity prices. They are also known for their wide price swings and volatile speculative nature.

In recent years trading volume has increased in foreign exchange futures such as the West German mark, Japanese yen and British pound as well as in Treasury bill and Treasury bond futures. One new product having a direct effect in the stock market is the development of futures contracts on stock market indexes. The Chicago Merchantile Exchange, Chicago Board of Trade, New York Futures Exchanges (a division of the NYSE) and the Kansas City Board of Trade have all developed contracts in separate market indexes such

as the Standard & Poor's 500 and the Value Line Index. Market indexes will be presented in the following chapter and we will spend more time discussing futures markets in Chapters 15 and 16.

OVER-THE-COUNTER MARKETS

Unlike the organized exchanges, the over-the-counter markets (OTC) have no central location where securities are traded. Being traded over-the-counter implies that the trade takes place by telephone or electronic device and that dealers stand ready to buy or sell specific securities for their own accounts. These dealers will buy at a bid price and sell at an asked price that reflects the competitive market conditions. The National Association of Securities Dealers (NASD), a self-policing organization of dealers, requires at least two market makers (dealers) for each security, but often there are 5 or 10 or even 20 for government securities. As previously mentioned, the multiple dealer function in the over-the-counter market is an attractive feature for many companies, in comparison to the single specialist arrangement on the NYSE and other organized exchanges.

OTC markets exist for stocks, corporate bonds, mutual funds, federal government securities, state and local bonds, commercial paper, negotiable certificates of deposits, and various other securities. Altogether these securities make the OTC the largest of all markets in the United States in dollar terms.

In the OTC market, the difference between the bid and asked price is the spread; it represents the profit the dealer earns by making a market. For example, if XYZ common stock is bid 10 and asked 10½, this simply means the dealer will buy at least 100 shares at $10 per share or will sell 100 shares at $10.50 per share. If his prices are too low, more buyers than sellers will appear, and he will run out of inventory unless he raises prices to attract more sellers and balances the supply and demand. If his price is at equilibrium, he will match an equal number of shares bought and sold, and for his market-making activities, he will earn 50 cents per share traded. Although in the future, many OTC stocks will no longer be reported on the basis of bid and ask prices, but simply a closing price, the concept of dealer spreads will remain.

There are actually several segments of the over-the-counter stock market, and the National Association of Securities Dealers divides the 5,000+ companies into the National Market System, the national list, and regional and local companies. Stocks in the National Market System receive the quickest and best reporting of their trading activity.

On the National Market System, stocks of companies such as Apple Computer, Coors Brewing, Intel and MCI Communications can be found. These companies all have a diversified geographical shareholder base,[2] while the national list and regional or local companies are usually smaller or closely held by management or the founding family. The small local stocks may not appear

---

[2] The standards for inclusion on the National Market System were reduced by the NASD in 1984 (with permission of the SEC). By early 1986, 2,500 OTC firms will be on the National Market System.

in *The Wall Street Journal,* but will be found on the financial pages of large city newspapers in Dallas, Cleveland, Chicago, Minneapolis, Los Angeles, and other major cities under the heading "Local Over-The-Counter Markets." OTC markets have always been very popular for bank stocks and insurance stocks because these stocks do not generate enough trading volume or have enough stockholders to merit their listing on the organized exchanges. Another reason is that many are small and have only local interest.

NASDAQ

NASDAQ stands for the National Association of Securities Dealers Automated Quotations System. This system is linked together by a computer network and provides up-to-the-minute quotations on over 4,000 of the OTC stocks traded on the NASDAQ system.

Table 2-8 presents the qualification standards for initial and continued listing on various OTC markets. The big difference between the OTC standards and the NYSE listing requirements are that the OTC requires fewer shareholders of record, smaller assets and less net income. While these qualifications allow many small companies to be included in the trading system, they do not preclude many large companies such as Apple Computer or Intel from trading. In fact the National Association of Securities Dealers estimates that over 600 companies on the National Market System would be eligible for listing on the New York Stock Exchange and many more would be eligible for the American Stock Exchange.

The OTC market used to be thought of as only an equity market for low-priced common stocks, but that is all changing with the advent of the National Market System. Table 2-9 depicts the OTC market and the most active stocks in dollar volume on August 3, 1984. On this day when the NYSE set a new trading high of 237 million shares, the OTC's volume was 122 million shares. Notice that some of the names of the most active stocks may be familiar to you. The prices range between $7.75 and $62.50 per share and the dollar volume is quite large. On August 3, 1984 the total number of issues traded was 4,157, which is more than the NYSE and AMEX combined.

During the mid-1980s many articles appeared comparing the New York Stock Exchange and the American Stock Exchange to the over-the-counter market and, in particular, to the inroads that the National Association of Securities Dealers had made in retaining companies on their automated quotation system. Traditionally companies that would reach listing qualifications would jump to the AMEX and then eventually to the NYSE. This cannot be assumed to happen any more. During the first half of 1984, NASDAQ's over-the-counter share volume amounted to about 65 percent of the volume on the NYSE and almost 10 times the volume on the AMEX. The AMEX seems to be suffering most of all in this battle, as the number of listings has fallen by about one third since 1974. The multiple dealer system as well as the enhanced reporting capability can be listed as reasons for the increased competitive nature of the OTC markets.

TABLE 2–8   NASDAQ, National List and NASDAQ NMS Qualification Standards

Standard	For initial NASDAQ inclusion (domestic common stocks)*	For continued NASDAQ inclusion (domestic common stocks)*	For newspaper national list inclusion — Alternative 1	Alternative 2	SEC criteria for mandatory NMS† inclusion‡	SEC criteria for voluntary NMS† inclusion‡
Registration under Section 12(g) of the Securities Exchange Act of 1934 or equivalent	Yes	Yes	Yes	Yes	Yes	Yes
Total assets	$2 million	$750,000	$2 million	$2 million	—	—
Tangible assets	—	—	—	—	$2 million	$2 million
Capital and surplus	$1 million	$375,000	$1 million	$8 million	$1 million	$1 million
Net income	—	—	$300,000 in latest or 2 of 3 last fiscal years	—	—	—
Operating history	—	—	—	4 years	—	—
Public float (shares)	100,000	100,000	350,000	800,000	500,000	250,000
Market value of float	—	—	$2 million	$8 million	$5 million	$3 million
Minimum bid	—	—	$3	—	$10 on 5 business days	$5 on 5 business days
Trading volume	—	—	—	—	Average 600,000 shares/month for 6 months	Average 100,000 shares/month for 6 months
Shareholders of record	300	300	300	300	300	300
Number of market makers	2	1	2	2	4 on 5 business days	4 on 5 business days

* Qualification standards for other types of securities are available upon request from the NASDAQ Operations Department in Washington, D.C.
† NMS—National Market System.
‡ A number of their standards were further reduced in 1984 to expand participation in the National Market System.
Source: *NASDAQ Fact Book* (Washington, D.C.: National Association of Securities Dealers, Inc., 1983).

Debt Securities Traded Over-the-Counter

Debt securities also trade over-the-counter. Actually, government securities of the U.S. Treasury provide the largest dollar volume of transactions on the OTC and account for billions of dollars in trades each week. These securities are traded by government securities dealers who are often associated with a

TABLE 2–9

Over-the-Counter Markets
Quotations From the Nasdaq System
4:00 p.m. Eastern Time Prices
Friday, August 3, 1984

Friday's Volume
All Issues, 122,230,800 Shares

| | SINCE JANUARY 1 | | |
	1984	1983	1982
Total sales	8,838,208,441	9,687,409,358	4,023,347,879

MARKET DIARY

	Fri	Thur	Wed	Tues	Mon
Issues traded	4,157	4,155	4,152	4,154	4,153
Advances	1,665	1,401	1,139	728	615
Declines	300	350	441	689	727
Unchanged	2,192	2,404	2,572	2,737	2,811
xNew highs	138	84	61	33	24
xNew lows	39	64	71	154	132

x-Based on 4 p.m. Eastern time bid quote.

ACTIVE STOCKS

	Dollar Volume	Close	Chg.
Apple Computer	71,386,000	27⅜	+ 3¼
Intel Cp	43,973,000	35¼	+ 2¼
MCI Commun	30,234,000	7¾	+ ¼
Digital Switch	27,255,000	27⅝	+ ⅛
American Intl Grp	24,127,000	62½	+ 2½
Tandem Computers	21,688,000	16⅝	+ 1⅜
Intergraph	20,878,000	53¼	+ 3¾
Tandon Cp	19,621,000	9⅝	+ ⅝
Apollo Computer	18,747,000	27½	+ 3
Convergent Tech	17,182,000	14⅛	+ ¼

division of a large financial institution, such as a New York, Chicago, or West Coast money market bank or a large brokerage house like Merrill Lynch. These dealers make markets in government securities, such as Treasury bills, Treasury bonds, or federal agency securities like Federal National Mortgage Association issues.

Municipal bonds of state and local governments are traded by specialized municipal bond dealers who, in most cases, work for large commercial banks. Commercial paper, representing unsecured, short-term corporate debt, is traded directly by finance companies, but a large portion of commercial paper sold by industrial companies is handled by OTC dealers specializing in this market. Every security has its own set of dealers and its own distribution

system. On markets where large dollar trades occur, the spread between bid and ask could be as little as $\frac{1}{16}$ or $\frac{1}{32}$ of $1 per $1,000 of securities.

The Third and Fourth Markets—Part of Over-the-Counter Trading

Prior to the mid-1970s, commissions on the NYSE were fixed. This meant that the same commission schedule applied to all transactions of a given size, and one broker could not undercut the other on the New York Stock Exchange. Several OTC dealers, most notably Weeden & Co., decided to make a market in about 200 of the most actively traded NYSE issues and to do this at a much smaller cost than the NYSE commission structure would allow. This trading in NYSE-listed securities in over-the-counter markets became known as the third market.

The third market diminished in importance for awhile as the NYSE became more price competitive. However, in the mid-80s this market made a comeback as OTC dealers accounted for 2.5 percent of the dollar volume in listed stocks for 1983. One advantage of the OTC market is that more than one specialist trades a security and there is greater flexibility in trading. During July of 1984, ITT Corporation reported a significant dividend cut and lower earnings after the NYSE was closed, but Jefferies Corporation, an over-the-counter trading firm, traded over 3 million shares by the time the NYSE opened the next morning. Another example occurred when the Justice department announced the breakup of AT&T on a Friday. MCI, a competitor in communications, traded OTC while AT&T traded on the NYSE. AT&T trading was halted until Monday because the specialist was unable to stabilize the market, whereas the 29 market makers in MCI stock transacted over $75 million dollars of securities before AT&T opened on Monday morning. It is the multimarket maker system that many people think makes the OTC market more competitive. At the time of this writing, much discussion is being held at the New York Stock Exchange about expanding trading hours, revising rules, and generally competing more effectively with the third market and the OTC.

The fourth market is that market in which institutions trade between themselves, bypassing the middleman broker altogether (replacing him with a computer). Much of the trading in this market is done through Instinet, Institutional Networks Inc. Instinet provides a low-cost automated stock trading system, with transactions available on over 3,500 securities, both listed and over-the-counter. The system allows banks, insurance companies, mutual and pension funds, etc. to enter an order over a computer terminal for up to 1,000 shares. The computer searches a nationwide trading network until it finds the trader with the best price, then the computer holds the order 30 seconds so that another trader may offer a better price. While Instinet is only a small trading system, Merrill Lynch bought 8 percent of the company and has plans to tie the trading system into the quote-terminal desktop computer that it is developing with IBM.

THE TRANSFORMATION AND FUTURE OF THE CAPITAL MARKETS

Financial institutions, such as banks, pension funds, insurance companies, and investment companies (mutual funds), have always invested and traded in securities. However, the growth of these institutions and their participation in the capital markets has increased dramatically in recent years. Part of the increased share activity can be found in the accelerated growth of pension plans during this period. Also, the rapid rise in stock prices during the post– World War II period attracted a lot of individual investors into mutual funds.

Table 2–10 on institutional activity shows that significant changes have taken place over the last two decades as institutional trading has accounted for a relatively larger percentage of total trading on the New York Stock Exchange. A block trade is a transaction of 10,000 shares or more and is almost always carried out by institutions rather than individuals. In 1965 block trades accounted for only 3.1 percent of the reported volume on the NYSE but by 1983 block trades increased to over 45 percent, an amount more than 14 times greater than that of two decades ago. This increased institutional activity is also evident by an examination of the second column of Table 2–10 which shows that between 1965 and 1983 the average number of block trades per day increased from 9 to 1,436.

TABLE 2–10   Institutional Activity on the New York Stock Exchange

Year	(1) Block trades as a percent of reported NYSE volume	(2) Average Number of block transactions per day	(3) Average Number of shares per trade
1965	3.1	9	224
1967	6.7	27	257
1969	14.1	61	356
1971	17.8	106	428
1973	17.8	116	449
1975	16.6	136	495
1977	22.4	215	641
1979	26.5	385	787
1981	31.8	575	1,013
1982	41.0	1,007	1,305
1983	45.6	1,436	1,434

Source: *New York Stock Exchange Fact Book* (New York: New York Stock Exchange, 1984).

Proof of the decreased importance of small investors and the increased importance of the institutional trader is seen in the average number of shares per trade, which soared more than 540 percent—from 224 shares in 1965 to 1,434 shares by 1983. These statistics do not necessarily mean that individual

investors are not getting a "piece of the action" in the stock market, but that many are investing indirectly in stocks through mutual funds, IRAs, and private pension plans at work.

In the early 1960s and before, the NYSE had been a market primarily for the individual investor. As this shift toward the institutions occurred, the market structure also changed. Because of fixed commissions on the NYSE, the third market and fourth market developed. The increased activity in these markets, and federal legislation, eventually forced the NYSE to eliminate its fixed commissions. When fixed commissions were replaced by negotiated rates, many smaller, research-oriented investment firms were unable to compete with the larger, retail brokerage houses. These firms eventually merged with other firms, went out of business, moved into portfolio management, or changed their emphasis toward a small market niche.

Competition in Financial Services

After negotiated commissions were in place, brokerage houses started charging individuals for research reports that previously had been distributed free of charge. This forced the individual to either buy research or simply take his or her account executive's advice. Under these conditions the individual investor started looking for services on a competitive fee basis and many ended up using brokers that only charged for making trades but gave no research advice. Because these brokers charged lower prices than the large retail brokerage firms, they became known as "discount brokers." This segment of the market is growing rapidly as many banks and savings and loans are now indirectly offering discount brokerage service to their customers. For example, many banks have simply linked up with the large discount brokers and are providing this investment service through trading desks located in their own buildings. This is an attempt to retain bank clients and their funds.

As previously mentioned, the rise of financial service companies has become commonplace. Starting in 1981, financial service firms purchased brokerage houses in order to diversify their consumer base. Prudential Insurance bought Bache Halsey Stuart Shields; Sears acquired Dean Witter; American Express bought Shearson and, later, Lehman Brothers; and Equitable Life purchased Donaldson, Lufkin and Jenrette. Most of these firms were adding brokerage houses to other financially-oriented companies. Sears, with its Allstate Insurance, Coldwell Banker real estate brokers, Sears Savings Bank, and Dean Witter brokerage services, now has financial service centers in many of its retail stores and is trying to take advantage of its relationship with 25 million Sears credit-card holders.

Shearson Lehman/American Express is a better example of a financial service company. Known world-wide for its card and travelers checks, it bought Fireman's Fund Insurance in 1968, a large casualty insurance company. In 1981 it acquired Shearson, the second largest retail brokerage firm; in 1983 it bought IDS, a Minneapolis-based life insurance company and one of the biggest mutual fund management companies; and in 1984 it purchased

Lehman Bros. Kuhn Loeb Inc., a prestigious investment banking house specializing in bonds. American Express International Banking Corporation bought the Swiss-based Trade Development Bank in 1984 and is now trying to combine its international banking firms. Shearson Lehman/American Express is currently attempting to integrate its operations to take advantage of the many services it offers. Shearson, perhaps more than any other company except Sears, has a huge client base that includes almost 18 million American Express cards. By crossing client lists from Shearson, IDS, and Fireman's Fund, the company hopes to develop a faithful group of customers taking advantage of all its many services, not to mention the new products it hopes to develop. The market has not seen the last of the changes brought about by deregulation and increased competition, but many observers feel that more firms like Shearson Lehman/American Express and Sears will be around by the end of the 1980s.

The National Market System

A national market system was mandated by Congress in the Securities Amendments Act of 1975. This is envisioned as a coordinated national system of security trading with no barriers between the various exchanges or the OTC market. There is sometimes confusion between the concept of a national market system and the National Market System listing segment of the OTC market. It is the former system that is the subject of the present discussion: The latter has already been discussed.

While there has been some delay in the implementation of a national market system due to industry foot-dragging and political changes in Washington, it is still a goal for the future. The implementation of the system is strongly supported by the SEC. No one knows exactly what form this national market might take, but there are several things that will be required. Some are easily achieved, while others are not. The first is already in place, and that is the composite tape that reflects trades on all exchanges for listed NYSE companies. There will also have to be competition between specialists and market makers. This is already occurring between the regional exchanges and the NYSE in dually listed securities. The prices seem to be more stable and the spreads between the bid and ask prices are closer for securities with competing market makers. A third occurrence is that the NYSE will most likely have to abolish Rule 390, which prohibits members of the NYSE from trading off the exchange in NYSE-listed securities.

Possibly the biggest dilemma in creating a national market system is fully developing a computerized system to execute limit orders. Currently, NYSE specialists execute most limit orders, which specify that a security must be bought or sold at a limited price or better. The national market system will need a computerized system to handle limit orders from all markets. Progress along these lines was being required by the SEC, and by the mid-1980s the NYSE had created several computer systems to aid in trading. The designated order turnaround system (Super DOT) allows members to transmit orders of

up to 599 shares directly to the correct trading post on the floor of the exchange. After the transaction, the execution report is returned back to the order origination point, and the NYSE states that 95 percent of the market orders are confirmed in two minutes. This electronic system transmits market and limit orders. In 1984 the AMEX announced that it had installed Autoper, an electronic order execution system that processes specialists' trades in a few seconds. This system uses a touch-screen that virtually eliminates clerical errors and allows market price trades of 300 shares or limit orders of up to 500 shares.

The national market system mandated by Congress could take the form of NASDAQ where several competing dealers make markets electronically. Clearly the National Association of Securities Dealers hopes that the national market system will follow its trading practices rather than the auction markets of the exchanges. The exchanges have complained to the SEC that the NASD's use of the term *National Market System* for its largest OTC companies should not be allowed because it gives the appearance that the OTC is *the* national market. Certainly the NYSE will not capitulate easily to an over-the-counter system of trading. The traditional exchange auction markets have been able to absorb block trades without difficulty and serve the needs of institutional customers and individuals. The NYSE does not want to give up its dominant market position, but it had better stop to look at who is catching up to it.

It is clear that any truly national market system will rely on computers more than ever and the trend seems to show no sign of ceasing. There are even systems in existence today that allow individual investors to use their personal computers to place stock market orders.

Expanded hours for trading is another issue. Charles Schwab, the largest discount broker and a subsidiary of Bank of America, takes orders 24 hours a day and orders received after the markets close are executed the next morning. Some envision an eventual 24-hour market. As the international markets link up to provide continuous trading in commodities such as gold, silver, and currencies, it has also been thought that continuous trading could exist in the common stock of multinational companies such as IBM, Sony, Royal Dutch Petroleum, Nestlé, and others. Speculating on the future of the markets may be foolish but we know they do not look like they did 10 years ago and we expect them to keep changing.

REGULATION OF THE SECURITY MARKETS

Organized securities markets are regulated by the Securities and Exchange Commission (SEC) and by the self-regulation of the exchanges. The OTC market is controlled by the National Association of Securities Dealers. There are three major laws governing the sale and subsequent trading of securities. The Securities Act of 1933 pertains to new issues of securities, while the Securities Exchange Act of 1934 deals with trading in the securities markets. The Securities Acts amendments of 1975 are the latest legislation, and their

main emphasis is on a national securities market. The primary purpose of these laws was to protect unwary investors from fraud and manipulation and to make the markets more competitive and efficient.

Securities Act of 1933

The Securities Act of 1933 was enacted after congressional investigations of the abuses present in the securities markets during the 1929 crash and again in 1931. The act's primary purpose was to provide full disclosure of all pertinent investment information whenever a corporation sold a new issue of securities. For this reason it is sometimes referred to as the "truth in securities" act. The Securities Act has several important features:

1. All offerings except government bonds and bank stocks that are to be sold in more than one state must be registered with the SEC.[3]
2. The registration statement must be filed 20 days in advance of the date of sale and include detailed corporate information. If the SEC finds the information misleading, incomplete, or inaccurate, they will delay the offering until the registration statement is corrected. The SEC in no way certifies that the security is fairly priced but only that the information seems to be factual and accurate. Under certain circumstances, the previously mentioned shelf registration is being used to modify the 20-day waiting period concept.
3. All new issues of securities must be accompanied by a *prospectus,* a detailed summary of the registration statement. Included in the prospectus is usually a list of directors and officers; their salaries, stock options, and shareholdings; financial reports certified by a CPA; a list of the underwriters; the purpose and use for the funds to be provided from the sale of securities; and any other reasonable information that investors may need to know before they can wisely invest their money. A preliminary prospectus may be distributed to potential buyers before the offering date, but it will not contain the offering price or underwriting fees. It is called a "red herring" because stamped on the front in red letters are the words "Preliminary Prospectus."
4. Officers of the company and other experts preparing the prospectus or registration statement can be sued for penalties and recovery of realized losses if any information presented was fraudulent, or factually wrong, or if relevant information was omitted.

Securities Exchange Act of 1934

This act created the Securities and Exchange Commission to enforce the securities laws. It was empowered to regulate the securities markets and those

---

[3] Actually the SEC did not come into existence until 1934. The Federal Trade Commission had many of these responsibilities prior to the formation of the SEC.

companies listed on the exchanges. Specifically, the major points of the 1934 Act are as follows:

1.   Guidelines for inside trading were established. Insiders must hold securities for at least six months before they can sell them. This is to prevent them from taking quick advantage of information which could result in a short-term profit. All short-term profits were payable to the corporation. Insiders were generally thought to be officers, directors, major stockholders, employees, or relatives. In the late 1960s the SEC widened its interpretation to include anyone having information that was not public knowledge. This could include security analysts, loan officers, large institutional holders, and many others who had business dealings with the firm.

2.   The Federal Reserve Board of Governors became responsible for setting margin requirements to determine how much credit one had available to buy securities.

3.   Manipulation of securities by conspiracies between investors was prohibited.

4.   The SEC was given control over the proxy procedures of corporations (a proxy is an absent stockholder vote).

5.   In its regulation of companies traded on the markets, it required certain reports to be filed periodically. Corporations must file quarterly financial statements with the SEC, send annual reports to stockholders, and file 10-K Reports with the SEC annually. The 10-K Report has more financial data than the annual report and can be very useful to an investor or loan officer. Most companies will now send 10-K Reports to stockholders on request.

6.   The act required all securities exchanges to register with the SEC. In this capacity, the SEC supervises and regulates many pertinent organizational aspects of exchanges, such as listing and trading mechanics.

The Securities Acts Amendments of 1975

The major focus of the Securities Acts amendments of 1975 was to direct the SEC to supervise the development of a national securities market. No exact structure was put forth, but the law did assume that any national market would make extensive use of computers and electronic communication devices. Additionally, the law prohibited fixed commissions on public transactions and also prohibited banks, insurance companies, and other financial institutions from buying stock exchange memberships to save commission costs for their own institutional transactions. This act is a worthwhile addition to the securities laws since it fosters greater competition and more efficient prices.

Other Legislation

In addition to these three major pieces of legislation, a number of other acts deal directly with investor protection. For example, The Investment Advisor Act of 1940 is set up to protect the public from unethical investment advisers.

Any adviser with over 15 public clients (excluding tax accountants and lawyers) must register with the SEC and file semiannual reports. The Investment Company Act of 1940 provides similar oversight for mutual funds and investment companies dealing with small investors. The act was amended in 1970 and currently gives the NASD authority to supervise and limit commissions and investment advisory fees on certain types of mutual funds.

Another piece of legislation dealing directly with investor protection is the Securities Investor Protection Act of 1970. The Securities Investor Protection Corporation (SIPC) was established to oversee liquidation of brokerage firms and to insure investors' accounts to a maximum value of $500,000 in case of bankruptcy of a brokerage firm. It functions much the same as the Federal Deposit Insurance Corporation (for banks) and the Federal Savings and Loan Insurance Corporation. SIPC resulted from the problems encountered on Wall Street during the period from 1967 to 1970. Share volume surged to then all-time highs, and many firms were unable to process orders fast enough. A back-office paper crunch caused Wall Street to shorten the hours the exchanges were formally open for new business but even this didn't help. Investors lost large sums, and for many months, they were unable to use or get possession of securities held in their names. Even though SIPC insures these accounts, it still does not cover market value losses suffered while waiting to get securities from a bankrupt brokerage firm.

Insider Trading

The Securities Exchange Act of 1934 established the initial restrictions on insider trading. However, over the years these restrictions have often proved to be inadequate. As previously indicated the definition of *insider* may go beyond officers, directors, and major stockholders to include anyone with special insider knowledge. Both the Congress and the Securities and Exchange Commission are attempting to grapple with the issue of making punitive measures severe enough to discourage the illegal use of nonpublic information for short-term profits.[4] Current and future legislation is likely to go beyond civil penalties to criminal prosecution. Also the penalties for improper action will expand beyond simple recovery of profits to a penalty three or more times the profits involved.

Regulators are also concerned about security analysts and financial writers who attempt to trade on the basis of their own analysis shortly before it is published. A classic case was the use of "Heard on the Street" material from *The Wall Street Journal* to achieve short-term profits. In this case, it was not so much the authors of the material, but friends of the authors who benefited. Federal regulators initiated quick and strong action to penalize the abuse.

On balance, all the legislation we have discussed has tended to increase the confidence of the investing public. In an industry where public trust is so critical, some form of supervision, whether public or private, is necessary and generally accepted.

---

[4] Insiders, of course, may make proper long-term investments in a corporation.

SUMMARY

A smoothly functioning market is one that is efficient and provides liquidity to the investor. The success of a primary market, in which new issues are generally underwritten by investment bankers, is highly dependent upon the presence of an active resale (secondary) market.

Secondary markets may be established in the form of an organized exchange or as an over-the-counter market. The predominant organized market is the New York Stock Exchange, but increasing attention is being directed to various other markets. The possibility of a true national market system looms as a consideration for the future, with the completed first step being the development of a consolidated tape among different markets. NASDAQ (National Association of Securities Dealers Automated Quotations System) has done much to improve the communications network in the over-the-counter market and bring competition to the organized exchanges. The first full year of trading under NASDAQ's National Market System began in 1983 and, by all accounts, more companies are remaining on the OTC market rather than being listed on the AMEX or NYSE.

The dominant role of the institutional investor has had an enormous impact on the markets. The push by large investors for lower commission rates first created a third market, in which NYSE-listed firms were traded over-the-counter by nonexchange members. This was ultimately followed by the elimination of the fixed commission system on the organized exchanges. Negotiated commissions have meant lower commissions for large institutional investors and thus less dollars to pay for organized research or to bankroll smaller brokerage firms. An enormous consolidation of market participants has taken place on Wall Street and the creation of financial service companies such as Shearson Lehman/American Express and Sears seems to be the wave of the future.

The term *market* seems to be broadening, with different types of new investment outlets as witnessed by the expansion of options, futures contracts on stock indexes, options on futures, and many other commodity trading mechanisms.

Finally, problems or imperfections in the marketplace during critical time periods have lead to a wide array of securities legislation. The legislation in the 1930s regulated the securities markets and created the SEC. Subsequent laws have dealt with restructuring the market and investor protection.

IMPORTANT WORDS AND CONCEPTS

Market	**Underwriting**
Primary market	**Best efforts**
Secondary market	**Public placement**
Third market	**Private placement**
Fourth market	**Organized exchange**
Investment banking	**OTC market**

Commission broker

Floor broker

Registered trader

Odd-lot dealer

Specialists

Options market

NASD

NASDAQ

OTC National Market System

SEC

Financial service companies

Securities Act of 1933

Prospectus

Red herring prospectus

Securities Exchange Act of 1934

Securities Acts Amendments of 1985

SIPC

DISCUSSION QUESTIONS

1. What is a market?
2. What is an efficient market?
3. What is the difference between primary and secondary markets?
4. What is the difference between an investment banker providing an underwriting function and a "best efforts" offering?
5. What is a private placement?
6. What generally determines how firms are listed in a tombstone advertisement for a security issue?
7. Why is a large network of investment bankers less necessary for a bond distribution than for a stock distribution?
8. How are organized exchanges and OTC markets related?
9. Briefly describe the participants on an exchange.
10. How do critics feel the specialist system on the NYSE might be improved?
11. What is the highest priority segment of the OTC market in terms of reporting of trading activity?
12. What is the NASDAQ and what service does it perform?
13. What are some differences between OTC standards for inclusion and NYSE listing requirements? (Suggest general categories of differences rather than actual numbers.)
14. Define a block trade. What does the increase in block trades since 1965 tend to indicate about the nature of investors in the market?
15. Why has the OTC market become more competitive in relation to the American Stock Exchange and other markets?
16. Name three finance service companies.
17. What is a discount broker?
18. List some factors that are required for the implementation of a national market system.
19. Indicate the primary purpose of the Securities Act of 1933. Why was it enacted? Does the SEC certify that a security is fairly priced?
20. Explain the purpose of the Securities Investor Protection Corporation (SIPC).

SELECTED REFERENCES

Dann, Larry Y.; David Myers; and Robert J. Raab. "Trading Rules, Large Blocks, and the Speed of Price Adjustment." *Journal of Financial Economics,* January 1977, pp. 3–22.

Eubank, Arthur E., Jr. "Risk/Return Contrast: NYSE, Amex, and OTC." *Journal of Portfolio Management,* Summer 1977, pp. 25–30.

Farrar, Donald E. "Toward a Central Market System: Wall Street's Slow Retreat into the Future," *Journal of Financial and Quantitative Analysis,* November 1974, pp. 815–27.

Feuerstein, Donald M. "Toward a National System of Securities Exchanges." *Financial Analysts Journal,* May–June 1972, pp. 28–34.

Freund, William C. "Issues Confronting the Stock Market in a Period of Rising Institutionalization." Supplement to *Journal of Financial and Quantitative Analysis,* March 1972, pp. 1687–90.

Friend, Irwin. "The Economic Consequences of the Stock Market." *American Economic Review,* May 1972, pp. 212–19.

Gillis, John G. "SEC Major Issues Conference—1984." *Financial Analysts Journal,* September–October 1984, pp. 10–12.

Henning, C. N.; W. Pigott; and R. H. Scott. *Financial Markets and the Economy.* Englewood Cliffs, N.J.: Prentice-Hall, 1975.

Hershman, Arlene. "Here Comes the New Stock Market." *Dun's Review,* April 1978, pp. 65–70.

Louis, Arthur M. "The Stock Market of the Future—Now." *Fortune,* October 29, 1984, pp. 105–16.

New York Stock Exchange Fact Book. New York: New York Stock Exchange, 1981.

Peake, Junius W. "The National Market System." *Financial Analysts Journal,* July–August 1978, pp. 25–33.

Roll, Richard. "A Simple Implicit Measure of the Effective Bid—Ask Spread in an Efficient Market." *Journal of Finance,* September 1984, pp. 1127–39.

Securities and Exchange Commission. *The Future Structure of the Securities Market.* Statement. Washington, D.C.: Securities and Exchange Commission, February 2, 1972. Also, *White Paper on the Structure of a Central Market System,* March 30, 1973.

Stoll, Hans R. "The Pricing of Security Dealer Service: An Empirical Study of NASDAQ Stocks." *Journal of Finance,* September 1978, pp. 1153–72.

Tinic, S. M., and R. R. West. "Competition and the Pricing of Dealer Service in the OTC Market." *Journal of Financial and Quantitative Analysis,* June 1972, pp. 1707–28.

Van Horne, James C. The Function and Analysis of Capital Market Rates. Englewood Cliffs, N.J.: Prentice-Hall, 1970.

Welles, Chris. "The Showdown over Rule 390." *Institutional Investor,* December 1977, pp. 33–38.

Chapter 3

Participating in the Market

There are many different kinds of investors participating in the market, from the individual to the professional, and each participant needs to know about the structure and mechanics of the market in which he or she might invest. In this chapter, we examine the use of indexes to gauge market performance, the rules and mechanics of opening and trading in an account, basic tax considerations for the investor, and the comparative features of investing individually or through mutual funds.

MEASURES OF PRICE PERFORMANCE— MARKET INDEXES

We first look at tracking market performance for stocks and bonds. Each market has several market indexes published by Moody's, Standard & Poor's, Dow Jones, and other financial services. These indexes allow investors to measure their portfolio's performance against an index which approximates their portfolio composition; thus different investors prefer different indexes. While a professional pension fund manager might use the Standard & Poor's 500 Stock Index, a mutual fund specializing in small, over-the-counter stocks might prefer the NASDAQ (National Association of Securities Dealers Automated Quotations) index, and a small investor might use the Value Line average as the best approximation of his or her portfolio.

STOCK MARKET INDEXES AND AVERAGES

Dow Jones Indexes

Since there are many stock market indexes, we will cover the most widely used ones. Dow Jones, the publisher of *The Wall Street Journal* and *Barron's,* publishes several indexes, of which the Dow Jones Industrial Average (DJIA) is the most popular. This average consists of 30 large industrial companies, and is considered a "blue chip" index (stocks of very high quality). Many people criticize the DJIA for being too selective and representing too few stocks. Nevertheless, the Dow Industrials do follow the general trend in the market, and these 30 common stocks comprise over 25 percent of the market value of the 1,550 firms listed on the New York Stock Exchange. Dow Jones also publishes an index of 20 transportation stocks, 15 utility stocks, and a 65-stock composite average. The companies that make up these Dow Jones averages are shown in Table 3–1, while the listing of indexes that appear in *The Wall Street Journal* are shown in Table 3–2.

The Dow Jones Industrial Average used to be a simple average of 30 stocks, but when a company splits its stock price, the average had to be adjusted in some manner. For the Dow Jones Industrials, the divisor in the formula has been adjusted downward from the original 30 to slightly more than 1. Each time a company splits its shares of stock (or pays a stock dividend), the divisor is reduced to maintain the average at the same level prior to the stock split. If this were not done, the lower-priced stock after the split

TABLE 3–1   Companies in the Dow Jones Averages

COMPONENTS
DOW JONES 65 STOCKS AVERAGES

The Dow Jones Stock Averages are compiled daily by using the New York Stock Exchange only closing prices and adjusting by the then current appropriate average divisor. The divisors appear in the second column of the Market Laboratory page under the data for the yearly Dow Jones Stock Average. A list of the stocks on which these averages are based follows:

INDUSTRIALS

Allied Corp.	General Electric	Owens–Illinois
Aluminum Co.	General Foods	Procter & Gamb
Amer Brands	General Motors	Sears Roebuck
Amer Can	Goodyear	Std Oil of Calif
Amer Express	Inco	Texaco
AT&T	IBM	Union Carbide
Bethlehem Steel	Inter Harvester	United Technologies
Du Pont	Inter Paper	US Steel
Eastman Kodak	Merck	Westinghouse El
Exxon	Minnesota M&M	Woolworth

TRANSPORTATION

AMR Corp.	Eastern Air Lines	Santa Fe So Pac
Burlington North	Federal Express	Transway Int'l
CSX Corp	Norfolk Southern	TWA
Canadian Pacific	Northwest Air	UAL Inc
Carolina Freight	Overnite Trans	Union Pac Corp
Consolid Freight	Pan Am World Air	USAir Group
Delta Air Lines	Rio Grande Indus	

UTILITIES

Am Elec Power	Consol Nat Gas	Panhandle E Cp
Cleveland E Ill	Detroit Edison	Peoples Energy
Colum-Gas Sys	Houston Indust	Phila Elec
Comwlth Edison	Niag Mohawk P	Pub Serv E&G
Consol Edison	Pacific Gas & El	Sou Cal Edison

would lower the average, giving the appearance that investors are worse off. Figure 3–1 depicts the daily graph that appears in *The Wall Street Journal* covering the Dow Jones Averages.

The Dow Jones Industrial Average is a *price-weighted average,* which means that each stock in the average is weighted by its price. To simplify the meaning of price-weighted: if you had three stocks in a price-weighted *index* that had values of 10, 40, and 100, you would add the prices and divide by three.[1] In this case you would get an average of 50 (150 divided by 3). A price-weighted index is similar to what you normally use in computing averages. Price-weighted *averages* tend to give a higher weighting bias to high-price stocks than to low-price stocks. For example, in the above analysis, if the $100 stock goes up by 10 percent, with all else the same, the average will go up over three points from 50 to 53.3. However, if the $10 stock goes up by 10 percent, with all else the same, the average will only go from 50 to 50.3. It is not necessary that you go back and do these computations, only that you understand the basic principle.

---

[1] This assumes there have been no prior stock splits affecting the denominator.

TABLE 3–2   Indexes and Averages Found in *The Wall Street Journal*

STOCK MARKET DATA BANK   January 3, 1985

Major Indexes

HIGH	LOW	(12 MOS)	CLOSE	NET CH	% CH	12 MO CH	%	FROM 12/31	%
DOW JONES AVERAGES									
1286.64	1086.57	30 Industrials	1189.82	− 9.95	− 0.76	− 92.42	− 7.21	−21.75	− 1.80
612.63	444.03	20 Transportations	555.58	+ 1.88	+ 0.34	− 53.89	− 8.84	− 2.55	− 0.46
149.93	122.25	15 Utilities	147.26	− 0.51	− 0.35	+ 13.06	+ 9.73	− 2.26	− 1.51
514.02	421.36	65 Composite	483.02	− 1.94	− 0.40	− 29.10	− 5.68	− 6.84	− 1.40
NEW YORK STOCK EXCHANGE									
98.12	85.13	Composite	95.05	− 0.38	− 0.40	− 2.29	− 2.35	− 1.33	− 1.38
114.40	99.73	Industrials	108.87	− 0.52	− 0.48	− 4.75	− 4.18	− 1.71	− 1.55
51.65	42.94	Utilities	51.17	− 0.04	− 0.08	+ 3.39	+ 7.10	− 0.40	− 0.78
100.46	73.11	Transportation	89.43	− 0.15	− 0.17	− 10.11	− 10.16	− 1.18	− 1.30
97.87	76.74	Finance	96.57	− 0.37	− 0.38	− 0.82	− 0.84	− 1.06	− 1.09
STANDARD & POOR'S AVERAGES									
169.28	147.82	500 Index	164.57	− 0.80	− 0.48	− 4.24	− 2.51	− 2.67	− 1.60
191.48	168.88	400 Industrials	183.14	− 0.96	− 0.52	− 7.01	− 3.69	− 3.22	− 1.73
161.64	117.21	20 Transportations	142.01	− 0.14	− 0.10	− 18.63	− 11.60	− 1.90	− 1.32
76.47	62.90	40 Utilities	75.21	− 0.25	− 0.33	+ 6.14	+ 8.89	− 0.68	− 0.90
18.88	14.09	40 Financials	18.56	− 0.09	− 0.48	− 0.22	− 1.17	− 0.24	− 1.28
NASDAQ									
287.90	225.30	OTC Composite	246.41	+ 0.50	+ 0.20	− 38.04	− 13.37	− 0.94	− 0.38
336.16	250.18	Industrials	259.40	+ 0.55	+ 0.21	− 72.01	− 21.73	− 1.33	− 0.51
283.91	226.87	Insurance	281.76	− 0.51	− 0.18	+ 19.67	+ 7.51	− 1.35	− 0.48
230.77	192.51	Banks	230.77	+ 0.54	+ 0.24	+ 25.94	+ 12.66	+ 1.00	+ 0.44
NASDAQ NATIONAL MARKET									
109.95	93.94	Composite	104.25	+ 0.30	+ 0.29			− 0.47	− 0.45
109.51	92.55	Industrials	97.47	+ 0.28	+ 0.29			− 0.56	− 0.57
OTHERS									
227.73	187.16	Amex	203.19	− 0.82	− 0.40	− 23.68	− 10.4	− 1.07	− 0.52
200.32	162.46	Value-Line	176.97	− 0.17	− 0.10	− 22.36	− 11.2	− 1.01	− 0.57
1766.132	1508.829	Wilshire 5000	1680.128	− 5.604	− 0.33	− 81.176	− 4.61	−21.87	− 1.29

In early-1985, Eastman Kodak was trading at 55, while International Harvester was trading at 6¾. Clearly an up or down 10 percent price movement in Eastman Kodak would have a greater impact on the Dow Jones Industrial Average than a 10 percent movement in International Harvester. Thus, we see the bias toward high-price stocks in the Dow Jones Industrial Average.

Barron's, which is also a publication of Dow Jones, publishes Barron's 50 Stock Average and an index of low-priced securities which meets the needs of many small investors. *Barron's* also publishes a weekly average called Barron's Group Stock Averages, covering 32 industry groups. These averages are especially useful to the analyst following the performance of a specific industry relative to the general market, and they are shown in Table 3–3.

FIGURE 3–1   Dow Jones Averages

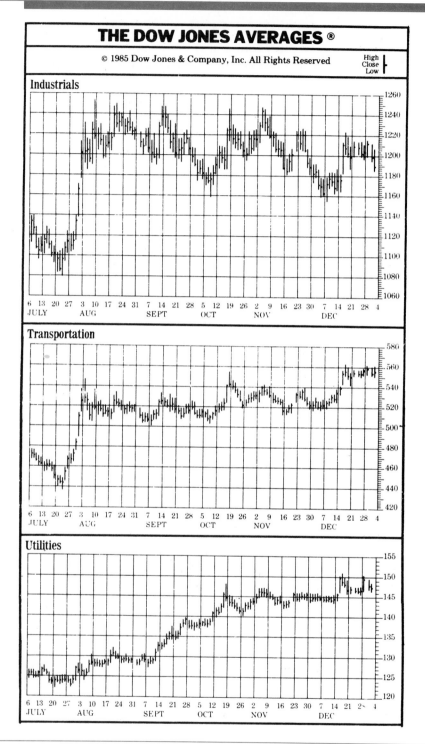

TABLE 3-3 Barron's Group Stock Averages

BARRON'S GROUP STOCK AVERAGES

1984 High-a	Low-a			May 31	May 24		% change
816.34	631.98	Aircraft manufacturing		667.56	657.01	+	1.61
247.91	181.45	Air transport		191.85	186.66	+	2.78
128.26	98.61	Automobiles		99.63	99.54	+	.09
324.19	244.16	Automobile equipment	L	243.79	244.16	−	.15
342.01	258.04	Banks	L	245.56	258.04	−	4.84
255.92	224.92	Bldg material, equipment		230.13	231.51	−	.60
475.85	393.25	Chemicals		414.85	412.08	+	.67
49.18	38.75	Closed-end invest	L	38.48	39.12	−	1.63
2,438.91	2,214.12	Drugs	L	2,210.00	2,234.38	−	1.09
929.75	756.74	Electrical equipment	L	743.26	756.74	−	1.78
542.21	389.62	Farm equipment		394.00	389.62	+	1.12
584.61	520.41	Foods and beverages		575.11	576.48	−	.24
933.24	723.77	Gold mining		816.67	794.62	+	2.77
475.31	404.73	Grocery chains	L	395.45	404.73	−	2.29
410.12	310.47	Installment financing	L	303.49	318.43	−	4.69
1,308.21	1,102.36	Insurance	L	1,071.20	1,102.36	−	2.83
1,351.50	1,160.51	Liquor		1,173.87	1,188.26	−	1.21
262.19	202.13	Machine tools		204.70	205.80	−	.54
194.75	150.49	Machinery (heavy)	L	144.89	150.49	−	3.72
896.06	726.90	Motion pictures		813.96	832.68	−	2.25
238.37	194.73	Non-ferrous metals	L	180.56	194.73	−	7.28
4,391.61	3,766.42	Office equipment		3,802.15	3,766.42	+	.95
760.76	621.26	Oil		716.02	724.47	−	1.17
594.39	442.21	Packing	L	435.63	452.88	−	3.81
428.72	352.93	Paper	L	347.19	352.93	−	1.63
341.04	216.42	Railroad equipment		217.59	225.11	−	3.34
1,344.96	1,004.56	Retail merchandise		1,062.23	1,084.37	−	2.04
442.22	337.69	Rubber	L	333.94	337.69	−	1.11
215.75	158.93	Steel and iron	L	157.82	158.93	−	.70
389.47	270.77	Television	L	261.06	270.77	−	3.59
351.64	281.21	Textiles	L	280.96	281.36	−	.14
407.65	351.77	Tobacco	L	349.78	351.77	−	.56
1,286.64	1,103.43	Dow-Jones Industrials		1,104.85	1,103.43	+	.13
612.63	461.32	Dow-Jones Transportation		467.08	461.32	+	1.25
134.83	123.55	Dow-Jones Utilities	L	122.69	123.55	−	.70
514.02	429.08	Dow-Jones Composite		430.32	429.08	+	1.29

a-1984 highs and lows through preceding week ended Thursday. In this table daily closings for trading week ended last Friday used in the range for the Dow Jones Averages. L-New low.

Change in Components: Chemicals: Allied Corp; 3-for-2 split, new multiplier is 12. Electrical Equipment: Westinghouse; 2-for-1 split, new multiplier is 32. Paper: Kimberly Clark; 2-for-1 split, new multiplier is 16.

Standard & Poor's Indexes

Standard & Poor's Corporation publishes several indexes, but two of the most important are the S&P 400 Industrials and the S&P 500 Stock Index. These indexes are followed by professional investors and others as measures of broad stock market activity. The S&P 400 consists of industrial common stocks and make up over 50 percent of the market value of NYSE-listed companies. The S&P 500 Stock Index includes the 400 industrials plus 20 transportation firms, 40 utilities, and 40 financial firms. The stocks in the Standard & Poor's 500 Stock Index are equivalent to 75 percent of the total value of the 1,550 firms listed on the New York Stock Exchange.[2]

These indexes are true indexes in that they are linked to some base value, in this case stock prices in the period from 1941 to 1943. The base period price in 1941 to 1943 was 10, so the S&P 500 Stock Index of 164.57 in early 1985 indicates that the index has increased by 1,545.7 percent over this period.

These indexes are *value-weighted,* which means that each company is weighted in the index by its own total market value as a percentage of the total market value for all firms. For example, in a value-weighted index comprising the following three firms, the weighting would be:

Stock	Shares	Price	Total market value	Weighting
A	150	$10	$ 1,500	12.0%
B	200	20	4,000	32.0
C	500	14	7,000	56.0
			$12,500	100.0%

In each case the weighting is determined by dividing the total market value of the stock by the total market value for all firms. In the case of stock A, that would be $1,500 divided by $12,500, or 12 percent. The same procedure is followed for stocks B and C.

Even though stock C has only the second highest price, it makes up 56 percent of the average because of its high total market value based on 500 shares outstanding. This same basic effect carries through in the Standard & Poor's Indexes, with large companies such as IBM, AT&T, and Exxon having a greater impact on the index than do small companies. For example, IBM makes up approximately 3.9 percent of the 500 company index, while Jonathan Logan Inc. makes up .01 percent. Value-weighted indexes do not require special adjustments for stock splits because the increase in the number of shares automatically compensates for the decline in the stock value caused by the split.

The Standard & Poor's 400 and 500 Stock Indexes provide a good measure of the direction of the market for large firms. Often the S&P 400 and S&P

---

[2] Actually there are also some large, over-the-counter firms in the S&P Indexes, though the indexes are predominantly made up of New York Stock Exchange firms.

500 are used as a proxy for market return when calculating the risk measures (betas) of individual stocks and portfolios.

Standard & Poor's also compiles value-weighted indexes for 90 different industries, and they are reported in the *Outlook,* a weekly Standard & Poor's publication.

Value Line Average

The Value Line Average represents 1,700 companies from the New York and American Stock Exchanges and the over-the-counter market. Some individual investors use the Value Line Average because it more closely corresponds to the variety of stocks the small investor may have in his or her portfolio.

Unlike the previously discussed price-weighted average (the Dow Jones Industrial Average) and value-weighted indexes (S&P 400 and 500), the Value Line Average is *equal-weighted.* This means that each of the 1,700 stocks, regardless of market price or total market value, is weighted equally. It is as if there were $100 to be invested in each and every stock. In this case IBM or Exxon is weighted no more heavily than Wendy's International or Mattel Inc. The equal-weighting characteristic also more closely conforms to the portfolio of individual investors.

Other Market Indexes

Indexes are also computed and published by the New York Stock Exchange, American Stock Exchange, and the National Association of Securities Dealers. Each index is intended to represent the performance of stocks traded in a particular exchange or market. As was seen in Table 3–2, the NYSE publishes a composite index as well as an industrial, utility, transportation, and financial index. Each index represents the stocks of a broad group or type of company. The American Exchange Market Value Index (AMEX) is composed of all stocks trading on the American Stock Exchange.

The National Association of Securities Dealers, which is the self-governing body of the over-the-counter markets, also constructs several indexes to represent the companies in their market. They publish the NASDAQ OTC composite, industrial, insurance, and banking indexes (which are also listed in Table 3–2). The NASDAQ also publishes subindexes for stocks listed in the National Market System.

The indexes of the New York Stock Exchange, American Stock Exchange, and NASDAQ are all *value-weighted* indexes.[3]

A relatively new index is the Wilshire 5000 Equity Index. It represents the *total dollar value* of 5,000 stocks, including all New York Stock Exchange and American Stock Exchange issues and the most active over-the-counter issues. By the very fact of including total dollar value, it is *value-weighted.* In

---

[3] Up until October 1973 the American Stock Exchange Index was price-weighted.

1984 the Wilshire Index had a range of $1,508 billion to $1,766 billion. The index literally tells you of the value of virtually all important equities daily. A typical daily change might be plus or minus $10 billion.

The direction of the indexes are all closely related, but they do not necessarily move together all the time. If a pension fund manager is trying to "outperform the market," then the choice of index may be crucial as to whether the fund manager maintains his or her accounts. The important thing for you, as well as a professional, when measuring success or failure of performance is to use an index that represents the risk characteristics of the portfolio being compared to the index. If you only want a general idea as to whether the market is going up or down over time, the choice of the average or index is not that critical since they all move fairly closely together.

Bond market averages.   Performance in the bond market is not widely followed by way of an index or average but usually is gauged by interest rate movements. Since rising interest rates mean falling bond prices and falling rates signal rising prices, investors can usually judge the bond market performance by yield curve changes or interest rate graphs. *Barron's* does publish an

TABLE 3–4   Lipper Mutual Fund Investment Performance Averages, Thursday, May 31, 1984

LIPPER MUTUAL FUND INVESTMENT PERFORMANCE AVERAGES

Thursday, May 31, 1984

LIPPER FUND INDICES	Close	Percentage Change Year to Date	Weekly		AVERAGE FUND PERFORMANCES		Percentage Change Year to Date	Weekly
				No.	Type of Fund			
Growth Funds	191.49	– 13.01	– 0.20	88	Capital Appreciation		– 14.28	– 0.13
				173	Growth Funds		– 12.34	– 0.17
Growth Income	301.57	– 8.55	– 0.32	23	Small Co. Growth Fds		– 14.11	– 0.70
				91	Growth & Income		– 7.84	– 0.26
Balanced Funds	245.54	– 9.14	– 0.86	33	Equity Income		– 5.31	– 0.68
				408	Average Performance		– 11.28	– 0.25
				24	Balanced Funds		– 6.71	– 0.42
				25	Income Funds		– 4.69	– 0.83
OTHER MARKET INDICATORS				8	Natural Resources		– 2.47	– 0.84
D. J. Industrial	1,104.84	– 12.22	+ 0.13	16	Specialty Funds		– 9.50	– 0.95
				17	Global Funds		– 7.80	– 1.12
S. & P. 500	150.55	– 8.72	– 0.45	10	International		– 6.55	– 2.41
				11	Gold Oriented		+ 5.75	+ 4.17
S. & P. 400	171.14	– 8.11	– 0.31	5	Option Growth		– 10.88	– 0.06
				10	Option Income		– 4.63	– 0.18
N.Y.S.E. Comp.	86.71	– 8.90	– 0.28	142	Fixed Income		– 3.20	– 0.69
				676	Average Performance		– 8.55	– 0.37
Amex Index	198.63	– 10.93	+ 0.34	676	Median Performance		– 7.33	– 0.43

Data supplied by Lipper Analytical Securities Corp. Year to date and weekly percentage changes on Thursday for mutual funds include reinvestment of income dividends and capital gains distributions, other market indicators do not. Only funds in existence for the entire period covered are included. Total number of funds, by objective, may include funds with net asset values unavailable at compilation time.
Source: Lipper Analytical Securities Corp.

index of 20 bonds (10 utility bonds and 10 industrial bonds), and other bond indexes are published by Salomon Brothers, and Lehman Brothers Kuhn Loeb (a part of Shearson Lehman/American Express).

Mutual fund averages.   Lipper Analytical Services publishes the Lipper Mutual and Investment Performance Averages shown in Table 3–4, taken from *Barron's.* Lipper publishes three basic fund indexes for growth funds, growth-with-income funds, and balanced funds. Additionally, the average performances on a year-to-date and weekly basis are provided for many other categories of funds in the right-hand portion of the table.

BUYING AND SELLING IN THE MARKET

Once you are generally familiar with the market and perhaps decide to invest directly in common stocks or other assets, you will need to set up an account with a retail brokerage house. Some of the largest and better-known retail brokers are Merrill Lynch; Shearson Lehman/American Express; Bache; and E. F. Hutton, but there are many other good houses, both regional and national. When you set up your account, the account executive (often called stockbroker) will ask you to fill out a card listing your investment objectives, such as: conservative, preservation of capital, income oriented, growth plus income, or growth. The account executive will also ask for your social security number for tax reporting, the level of your income, net worth, employer, and other basic information. Basically he or she needs to know the client's desire and ability to take risk in order to give good advice and proper management of the investor's assets.

Cash or Margin Account

The account executive will need to know if you want a cash account or margin account. Either account allows you five business days to pay for any purchase. A cash account requires full payment, while a margin account allows the investor to borrow a percentage of the purchase price from the brokerage firm. The percentage of the total cost the investor must pay is called the margin and is set by the Federal Reserve Board. During the great crash in the 1920s, margin on stock was only 10 percent, but it was as high as 80 percent in 1968. It has been at 50 percent since January 1974. The margin percentage is used to control speculation. When the Board of Governors of the Federal Reserve System thinks that the markets are being pushed too high by speculative fervor, they raise the margin requirement, which means that more cash must be put up.

Margin accounts are used mostly by traders and speculators or by investors who think their long-run return will be greater than the cost of borrowing. Most brokerage houses require a $2,000 minimum in an account before loaning out money, although many brokerage houses have higher limits. Here is

how a margin account works. Assume you purchased 100 shares of GE (General Electric) at $60 per share on margin and that margin is 50 percent.

Purchase: 100 shares of GE at $60 per share	$6,000
Borrow: Cost (1 − margin percentage)	−3,000
Equity contributed, cash or securities	$3,000

You can borrow $3,000 or the total cost times (1 − margin percentage). The percentage cost of borrowing is generally 1 to 2 percent above the prime rate, depending upon the size of the account. Rather than putting up $3,000 in cash, a customer could put $3,000 of other approved financial assets into the account to satisfy the margin. Not all stocks may be used for margin purchases. The Securities and Exchange Commission publishes a list of approved securities which may be borrowed against.

One of the reasons people buy on margin is to leverage their returns. Assume that GE rises to $80 per share. The account would now have $8,000 in stock and an increase in equity from $3,000 to $5,000.

100 shares of GE at $80	$8,000
Loan	−3,000
Equity	$5,000

This $2,000 increase in equity creates a 67 percent return on the initial $3,000 of equity. The 67 percent return was accomplished on the basis of only a 33 percent increase in the price of the stock ($60 to $80). With the increased equity in the account, the customer could now purchase additional securities on margin.

Margin is a two-edged sword however, and what works out to your advantage in up markets works to your disadvantage in down markets. If GE had gone to $40, your equity would decrease to $1,000.

100 shares of GM at $40	$4,000
Borrowed	−3,000
Equity	$1,000

There are minimum requirements for equity in a margin account called *minimum maintenance standards* (usually 25 percent). Your equity would now be at minimum maintenance standards where the equity of $1,000 equals 25 percent of the current market value of $4,000. A fall below $1,000 would bring a margin call for more cash or equity. Many brokerage firms have maintenance requirements above 25 percent, and when margin calls are made, the equity often needs to be increased to 35 percent or more of the portfolio value. Normally you must maintain a $2,000 minimum in your account, so you would have been called for more equity when the stock was at $50 even though the minimum maintenance requirement had not yet been reached.

An important feature of a margin account is that securities may not be delivered to the customer. In this case, the GE stock would be kept registered in the street name of your retail brokerage house (e.g., Shearson Lehman/

American Express), and your account would show a claim on 100 shares which are held as collateral for the loan. It is much like an automobile loan; you don't hold title to the car until you have made the last payment. In the use of margin, however, there is no due date on the loan. The use of margin increases risk and is not recommended for anyone who cannot afford large losses or who has no substantial experience in the market.

Long or Short?—That Is the Question

Once you have opened the account of your choice, you are ready to buy or sell. When investors establish a position in a security, they are said to be "long" if they purchase the security for their account. It is assumed that the reason they purchased the security was to profit on an increase in price over time and/or to receive dividend income. An investor who is long may take delivery of the securities (keep them in physical possession) if he or she has a cash account. An investor with a cash account may also choose to keep them on deposit in his/her brokerage account to facilitate bookkeeping, dividends, safe-keeping, and ease of sale. A margin account user has no choice but to keep them with the broker in "street name."

Sometimes investors anticipate that the price of a security may drop in value. If they are long in the stock, some may sell out their position. Those who have no position at all may wish to take a "short" position in order to profit from the expected decline. When you short a security, you are borrowing the security from your broker and selling it with the obligation to replace the security at a future time. How you can sell something you don't own is an obvious question. Your broker will simply loan you the security from the brokerage house inventory. If your brokerage house doesn't have an inventory of the particular stock you want to short, the firm will borrow the stock from another broker.

Once you go short, you begin hoping and praying that the price of the security will go down so that you can buy it back and replace the security that you sold at a lower price. In a perverse way, bad news starts to become good news. When you read the morning paper, you look for signs of unemployment, high inflation, and high interest rates in hopes of a stock market decline.

A short sale can only be made on a trade where the price of the stock advances (an uptick), or if there is no change in price, the prior trade must have been positive. These rules are intended to stop a snowballing decline in stock values caused by short sellers.

There is a margin requirement associated with short selling, and it is currently equal to 50 percent of the securities sold short. Thus if you were to sell 100 shares of Wrigley short at $70 per share, you would be required to put up $3,500 in margin (50 percent of $7,000). In a short sale, the margin is considered to be good-faith money and obviously is not a down payment toward purchase. The margin protects the brokerage house in case you start losing money on your account.

The way that you would lose money on a short sales position is if the

stock that you sold short starts going up. Assume that Wrigley goes from $70 to $80. Since you initially sold 100 shares short at $70 per share, you have suffered a $1,000 paper loss. Your initial margin or equity position has been reduced from $3,500 to $2,500.

Initial margin (equity)	$3,500
Loss	−1,000
Current margin (equity)	$2,500

We previously specified that there is a minimum 25 percent margin maintenance requirement in buying stock. There is a similar type requirement in selling short. The equity position must equal at least 30 percent of the *current* value of the stock that has been sold short. In the present example, the equity position is equal to $2,500, and the current market value of Wrigley is $8,000 ($80 × 100). Your margin maintenance percentage is 31.25 percent ($2,500 ÷ $8,000) or slightly above the minimum requirement. However, if the stock goes up another point or two and your losses increase, you will be asked to put up more margin to increase your equity position.

Of course, if the value of Wrigley stock goes down from its initial base of $70, you would be making profits off the bad news. A 20-point drop in Wrigley would mean a $2,000 profit on your 100 shares. Most market observers agree that it requires a "special breed of cat" to be an effective short seller. You often need nerves of steel and a contrariant outlook that can not be easily shaken by good news.

Aside from risk takers, some investors sell short to establish beneficial tax positions. For example, if you had bought Digital Equipment at $60 and five months later it was $100, you would have a $40 per share profit on paper. If you want to preserve the profit but wait until next year to pay the tax, you can "sell short against the box." This means you can short shares against those you already hold. Since you own the stock and also have a short position, you can neither gain nor lose by price movements in the stock. In the following tax year, you can deliver the shares you hold to cover your short position. At that point, you will incur the tax obligations associated with the transactions. The total net profit will still be $40.

TYPES OF ORDERS

When an investor places an order to establish a position, he or she has many different kinds of orders from which to choose. When the order is placed with the account executive on a NYSE-listed stock, it is teletyped to the exchange where it is executed by the company's floor broker in an auction market. Each stock is traded at a specific trading post on the floor of the exchange, so the floor broker knows exactly where to go to find other brokers buying and selling the same company's shares.

Most orders placed will be straightforward market orders to buy or sell. The market order will be carried by the floor broker to the correct trading post and will usually trade close to the last price or within ¼ of a point. For

example, if you wanted to sell 100 shares of AT&T at market, you would probably have no trouble finding a ready buyer, since AT&T may be trading 300,000 to 500,000 shares per day. On the other hand, if you wanted to sell 100 shares of Bemis, there might be as little as only 1,000 shares traded in a day, and no other broker would be waiting at the Bemis post to make a transaction with the floor broker. If the broker finds no one else wishing to buy the shares he is selling, he will transact the sale with the specialist who is always at the post ready to buy and sell 100-share "round lots." If the broker wants to sell, the specialist will either buy the shares for his own account at $\frac{1}{8}$ to $\frac{1}{4}$ less than the last trade or will buy out of his book in which special orders are kept.

There are two basic special orders, the "limit order" and the "stop order." A limit order limits the price at which you are willing to buy or sell and assures you that you will pay no more than the limit price on a buy or receive no less than the limit price on a sell. Assume you are trying to buy a thinly traded stock that fluctuates in value and you are afraid that with a market order you might risk paying more than you want. So, you would place a limit order to buy 100 shares of Bell Industries, as an example, at $16\frac{1}{2}$ or a better price. The order will go to the floor broker who goes to the post to check the price. The broker finds Bell Industries trading at its high for the day of $16\frac{7}{8}$, and so he leaves the limit order with the specialist who records it in his book. The entry will record the price, date, time, and brokerage firm. There may be other orders in front of yours at $16\frac{1}{2}$, but once these are cleared and assuming the stock stays in this range, your order will be executed at $16\frac{1}{2}$ or less. Limit orders are used by investors to buy or sell thinly traded stocks or to buy securities at prices thought to be at the low end of a price range and to sell securities at the high end of the price range. Investors who calculate fundamental values have a basic idea of what they think a stock is worth and will often set a limit to take advantage of what they view to be discrepancies in values.

Many traders are certain that they want their order to be executed if a certain price is reached. A limit order does not guarantee execution if orders are ahead of you on the specialist's book. In cases where you want a guaranteed "fill" of the order, a stop order is placed. A stop order is a two-part mechanism. It is placed at a specific price like a limit order, but when the price is reached, the stop turns into a market order which will be executed at close to the stop price but not necessarily at the exact price specified. Often there will be a common price that many short-term traders will view with optimism for a certain trading strategy. When the stock hits the price, it may pop up on an abundance of buy orders or decline sharply on a large volume of sell orders, and your "fill" could be several dollars away from the stop price. Assume that AXE Corporation stock has been trading between $25 and $40 per share over the last six months, reaching both these prices three times. A trader may follow several strategies. One strategy would be to buy at $25 and sell at $40 using a stop buy and a stop sell order. There may be some traders putting in a stop buy at $41 thinking that if the stock breaks through its peak trading range it will go

on to new highs, and finally some may put in a stop sell at $23 to either eliminate a long position or establish a short position with the assumption that the stock has broken its support and will trend lower. When used to eliminate a long position, a stop order is often called a stop-loss order.

Limit orders and stop orders can be "day orders" that expire at the end of the day if not executed, or they can be GTC (good till cancelled) orders. GTC orders will remain on the specialist's books until taken off by the brokerage house or executed. If the order remains unfilled for several months, most brokerage houses will send reminders that the order is still pending so that the client does not get caught buying stock for which he is unable to pay. Orders have been known to stay on the specialist's books for years.

COST OF TRADING

Since May 1, 1975, commissions have been negotiated between the broker and customer, with larger orders getting smaller percentage charges. Before "May Day" commissions were fixed, and all brokers charged the same fee out of a published table for a given size order. Now there are individual variations, so check with several brokers. If commissions are of concern, you may want to do business with a "discount" broker who charges a discount of up to 70 percent from the old fixed-commission schedule.

Discount brokers sprung up as bare-bones operators providing only transactions and no research. They have found a niche with those investors who make up their own minds and do not need advice or personal service. Discount brokers do not have many regional offices located around the country (but may be represented in some of the largest cities, such as New York, Chicago, and Los Angeles). Instead, they rely on toll-free, long-distance "WATS" lines for their customers. Many discount brokers advertise in *The Wall Street Journal* and other newspapers.

Regular brokerage houses still offer more personal service and more variety of services and are often part of a financial corporation involved in underwriting and investment banking, managing mutual funds, pension funds, economic advising, government bond dealings, and more. Unfortunately, you pay extra when dealing with a full-service broker. Table 3–5 sets forth the fees for one national brokerage house.

TABLE 3–5   Example of Round-Lot Commissions

Trades	Commissions
Under → $800	2.500% + $11
801–2,500	1.875 + 16
2,500–5,000	1.395 + 28
5,000–20,000	1.255 + 35
20,000–30,000	0.910 + 104
Over 30,000	0.560 + 209

Most full-service brokers still use a formula for computing commissions, but they also negotiate rates on large transactions, and are willing to give actively trading customers discounts from the formula if their business over the year makes them a large trader in volume.

The fees in Table 3–5 are not necessarily an industry standard, and you may find variations of these fees from broker to broker. However, most firms will have a similar structure, charging a commission based on the dollar value of the transactions and the number of shares purchased. Don't be embarrassed to ask your broker what the commission will be before you make any trades.

TAXES

In the previous sections, we discussed trading strategies and different types of orders that can be used to transact purchases and sales. In the brief example about selling short against the box, it was indicated that for tax reasons an investor would choose to defer taxes. As we go through this section, the basics of taxation on investment income will be considered.

Short-Term versus Long-Term Gains and Losses

There are different effective tax rates on short-term and long-term holdings. The Internal Revenue Service defines long-term as being over six months for stocks, bonds, and other assets. Up until June 22, 1984, the holding period for long-term capital gains was one year. However, the Deficit Reduction Act of 1984 reduced the time frame to six months.

Short-term gains are taxed as ordinary income, which is at the effective marginal tax rate of the investor. The marginal tax rate of the investor is the tax to be applied to each succeeding dollar of income. For example, a single investor who had $25,000 in salary would be in an approximate 30 percent marginal tax rate bracket. New income would be taxed at the marginal tax rate (though income between 0 and $25,000 had been taxed at a lower rate). A single individual with $85,000 of income would be in the 50 percent marginal tax bracket. For married couples filing joint returns, the marginal tax rate goes up at a slower pace.

Our initial comment was that short-term gains would be taxed at the marginal tax rate of the investor. What about short-term losses? Short-term losses may be used to offset short- or long-term gains. Any remaining short-term loss after the above deductions may be deducted from ordinary income—up to $3,000 per year. For example, if an investor had $10,000 in short-term losses beyond that written off against other gains, he could deduct $3,000 from salary and other income in 1985 and carry forward the $7,000 difference into 1986 to again be used to offset gains. Net short-term losses can be carried forward indefinitely until used up.

Long-term gains receive preferential tax treatment. The IRS allows 60 percent of long-term gains to be excluded from taxation so that the maximum tax an investor will pay is his or her marginal tax rate times $(1 - .6)$. If you are in the 40 percent marginal bracket your maximum tax would be $40\% \times (1 - $

.6), or 16 percent. This reduced rate maker long-term gains very advantageous and is one good reason to prefer long-term gains to short-term gains. Table 3–6 sets forth the tax liability of different gains, demonstrating the advantages of long-term gains.

TABLE 3–6   Short-Term versus Long-Term Gains

Short-term gain	$10,000	Long-term gain	$10,000
No exclusion	–0–	60% excluded	6,000
Taxable gain	$10,000	Taxable gain	$ 4,000
Marginal tax rate	40%	Marginal tax rate	40%
Tax	$ 4,000	Tax	$ 1,600
Effective tax rate	40%	Effective tax rate	16%

Note in Table 3–6 there would be a 40 percent marginal tax rate applied to short-term capital gains, but the effective tax on long-term capital gains is only 16 percent. This is because $6,000 of the $10,000 of gain was excluded from taxable income before the 40 percent tax was applied. The $1,600 in tax represents only 16 percent of $10,000. Once again, the effective tax rate to be applied to long-term capital gains is always the marginal tax rate times $(1 - .6)$. For an investor in a 50 percent tax bracket, the effective tax rate on long-term capital gains is 20 percent:

$$50\% \times (1 - .6) =$$
$$50\% \times .4 = 20\%$$

The investor is never required to pay more than 20 percent on long-term capital gains on stock transactions. Many years ago, the maximum long-term capital gains tax rate was 35 percent.

Long-term capital losses must first be written off against long-term gains and then short-term gains in a given year.[4] This is done on a dollar-for-dollar basis. Any remaining losses may be deducted from ordinary income to provide a write-off of $3,000 per year. However, long-term losses can only be written off against ordinary income at the rate of 50 cents on the dollar. Thus, $6,000 of long-term capital losses are necessary to provide a $3,000 deduction against ordinary income. You will recall that, in contrast, short-term losses can be deducted against ordinary income on a one-to-one basis. However, the maxi-

---

[4] As indicated above, any loss, such as a long-term loss, must be first written off against long-term gains and then against short-term gains. The same applies to short-term losses. They must first be written off against short-term gains and then long-term gains. Any unused losses are then written off against ordinary income to the extent allowable by law. Any loss that is carried forward to future years retains its original character. A short-term loss that is carried forward will be considered short-term in the next year, and a long-term loss will be considered long-term.

TABLE 3–7   Treatment of Capital Gains

Short-Term	
Gains	*Loss*
Taxed at marginal tax rate	After deductions against any short-term or long-term capital gains on a dollar-for-dollar basis, $3,000 may be written off against other ordinary income in a given year, also on a one-to-one basis. Additional losses may be carried forward.
Long-Term (over 6 months)	
Taxed at marginal tax rate times $(1 - .6)$	After deductions against any long-term or short-term capital gains on a dollar-for-dollar basis, a $3,000 deduction against ordinary income may be taken. However, long-term capital gains can only be deducted against ordinary income at the rate of 50 cents on the dollar, so $6,000 of long-term losses would be necessary to take the maximum $3,000 deduction against other ordinary income in a given year. Additional losses may be carried forward.

mum annual write-off is still only $3,000. In Table 3–7, we summarize the points related to short-term and long-term capital gains.

Timing of Gains and Losses

Because of the tax laws, the best kind of gain is long-term, which minimizes the tax, and the best kind of loss is short-term, because it maximizes your deductions. The worst tax combination would be to take long-term gains and short-term losses in the same year because they are netted out before the long-term gains receive any exclusion.

Investors should try to separate or combine short-term and long-term transactions in the appropriate year or year(s) for tax purposes. While this may not always be feasible because investments may move in unanticipated directions, it is still a worthwhile goal for which to strive. Examples of tax planning implications over two years are presented in Table 3–8.

In alternative A of Table 3–8, a $3,000 short-term capital loss is taken in the first year. This can be written off against ordinary income such as salary. Since the investor is in a 40 percent tax bracket, he or she will save $1,200 in other taxes on ordinary income. In the second year of alternative A, a $3,000 long-term capital gain is taken. Given the 60 percent exclusion on long-term capital gains, the tax is only $480. ($3,000 $\times$ $(1 - .6)$ $\times$ 40%).

TABLE 3–8   Short-Term Loss and Long-Term Gain—Implications for Tax Planning

Alternative A

Year 1

Short-term loss	($3,000)
Marginal tax rate, 40%	
Tax saving on ordinary income	$1,200

Year 2

Long-term gain	$3,000
Exclusion 60%	1,800
Taxable income	1,200
Marginal tax rate, 40%	
Tax	($ 480)
Net tax savings over 2 years ($1,200 − $480)	$ 720

Alternative B

Year 1 only

Short-term loss	($3,000)
Long-term gain	3,000
Net taxable gain or loss	0

Thus over the two-year time period in alternative A, there is a $1,200 tax savings and a $480 tax obligation. The net difference is $720 in tax savings.

Under alternative B, both the short-term loss and long-term gain are taken in the same year. All the benefits of the short-term loss are used up against the normally low-tax long-term capital gains. The net tax is 0. This figure represents $720 less than the tax savings in alternative A. The investor following alternative A has properly timed his transactions, while the investor in alternative B has not been so fortunate.

There are many other combinations that could be covered. In each instance, tax planners consider ways to match up various types of gains and losses and evaluate the impact. There are many other tax consequences an individual should be aware of, such as tax shelters, estate planning, and gift taxes. These will be covered more fully in later chapters. Also, there has been a strong tendency for tax laws to change rapidly in the 1980s. The basic rules presented in this section are valid as we go to press in late 1985. However, future changes are always possible. Nevertheless, the *basic principles* presented in this section will serve you well even if there are some future modifications to the capital gains tax laws.

INDIVIDUAL INVESTMENTS OR MUTUAL FUNDS

The investor must also determine whether he or she will participate in the market individually or through a mutual fund. We will explore the implications of investments through mutual funds.

A mutual fund or investment company professionally manages an investor's money in a portfolio consisting of many securities, sometimes numbering in the hundreds. The investor owns a share of the portfolio assets equal to his number of shares in the fund. There are several advantages to this approach. An investor with a small amount of money (under $1,000) can achieve diversification through the large number of securities in the portfolio. This diversification eliminates the risk of being concentrated in two or three securities. Other people may have larger sums of money to invest, but not have the time or skill to manage it as well as a professional.

In Chapter 20 we will do a thorough review of the performance of mutual funds in comparison to popular market indicators. For now, we would say that the long-term performance has not been particularly impressive, although some mutual funds have turned in good performances in the last few years, specifically the aggressive, growth-oriented funds. We now look at some important definitions and concepts associated with funds.

Closed versus Open-End Funds

A closed-end fund is similar to the common stock of corporations. The supply is fixed, and the only way an investor can purchase the fund shares is from another investor. Some closed-end funds trade on the New York Stock Exchange and others over-the-counter. Many are bond funds. Closed-end funds usually sell at a discount from the market value of assets held (net asset value) because they are not as liquid as open-end funds. Occasionally, a closed-end fund may sell at a premium over net asset value because one or more stocks in the portfolio is not publicly traded and is carried on an artificially low-cost basis. It is felt by the market that the true value of the shares is much greater than cost, so a premium in the portfolio occurs.

Open-end funds make up the majority of investment funds and allow investors to buy and sell shares at the net asset value (NAV) plus a possible commission for the trade. There is no limitation on the number of shares. The open-end mutual fund stands ready to redeem shares or sell new shares at the net asset value per share. This NAV per share is equal to the market value of the portfolio minus liabilities divided by the total shares outstanding in the mutual fund. If a mutual fund owner wants to sell his or her shares, the money is paid out, and the shares are retired. This does not cause any change in net asset value per share or penalize other investors in the fund. *The Wall Street Journal* lists the daily prices of open-end funds. An example appears in Figure 3–2.

Load versus No-Load Funds

Load and no-load funds both do the same thing in terms of managing an investor's money, but the load fund charges a commission (called a load) of between 7.25 and 8.5 percent on stock funds but occasionally as little as 2.5 percent on bond funds. According to *Forbes'* 1984 Annual Mutual Fund Survey, Investment Co. of America was the largest stock fund with $2.189 billion in assets and a load of 8.50 percent. Load funds are the predominant type of stock

FIGURE 3–2

Mutual Funds

Thursday, March 15, 1984

Price ranges for investment companies, as quoted by the National Association of Securities Dealers. NAV stands for net asset value per share; the offering includes net asset value plus maximum sales charge, if any.

	NAV	Offer NAV Price Chg.
DFA Small	157.34	N.L. – .58
Direct Cap	.94	N.L. – .01
D G DvSrs	22.34	N.L. + .04
DodgC Bal	25.52	N.L. + .11
DodgC Stk	23.27	N.L. + 16
Drx Burnh	16.47	17.07 – 05
Dreyfus Group:		
A Bonds	12.81	N.L.
CalT Ex	13.43	N.L. + .01
Drevf Fd	12.09	13.21 + 05
Dreyf Lv	15.95	17.43 – 04
Growth	11.42	N.L. + .01
Intrmd	12.42	N.L. + 01
NYT Ex	13.19	N.L. + .01
Spl Incm	7.80	N.L. + .11
Tax ExB	11.04	N.L. + 01
Third Cn	6.95	N.L. + .02
Eagle Gth	6.84	7.48 – .02
Eaton Vance Funds:		
EH Bal	7.32	7.89 + .03
EH Stk	10.85	11.70 + .02
Growth	6.31	6.90
High Yld	4.62	5.05
Inc Bost	8.57	9.37
Invests	7.48	8.17 + .03
Spc Eqty	17.29	18.64 + .02
Tax Mge	12.69	13.87 + .03
VS Specl	13.97	15.27 + .02
Eberstadt Group:		
Chem Fd	9.27	10.13 + .03
Enrgy R	12.01	13.13 + .08
Surveyr	13.18	14.40 + .13
Energy Utl	19.70	N.L. + .05
Evergrn r	36.57	N.L. + .12
Evrgrn TR	15.20	N.L. + .01
Farm B Gr	12.89	N.L + .04
Federated Group:		
Am Lead	10.97	11.73 + .02
Exch Fd	32.70	N.L. + 12
GNMA	10.35	N.L. + .02
Hi Incm	11.73	12.55 – .01
Incm Tr	10.11	N.L. – .01
Intrrnd	9.39	N.L. – 01
SIMT	10.10	N.L.
Stock Tr	14.40	N.L. + 03
ax Free	9.09	9.52 + .01
US Gvt S	8.35	8.74
Fidelity Group Funds:		
Bd Corp	6.51	N.L.
Congr St	50.60	N.L. + .25
Contra	9.63	N.L. + .04
Discovr	18.13	N.L. + .08
Eq Incm	22.16	22.61 + .04
Exch Fd	40.82	N.L. + .21
Fidel Fd	14.12	N.L. + .06
Freedm	11.33	N.L. + .03
Govt Sec	9.14	N.L.
Hi Incm	8.79	N.L.

	NAV	Offer NAV Price Chg.
I S I Group:		
Growth	6.36	6.95 + .01
Income	3.54	3.87
Trst Sh	10.05	10.98 + .01
Istel Fund	14.18	N.L. + .09
Ivy Grwth	12.47	N.L.
JP Growth	12.73	13.84 + .04
JP Income	7.71	8.38
Janus Fnd	12.53	N.L. + .03
John Hancock Funds:		
Bond Fd	13.62	14.80 – 01
Growth	11.59	12.60 + .08
US GvSc	8.26	8.98 + .01
Tax Ex	9.22	10.22
Kauf Fund	.10	N.L.
Kemper Funds:		
Cal Tax	12.07	12.64
Income	8.09	8.61
Growth	12.76	13.95 + .07
High Yld	10.12	10.85
Int'l Fd	15.92	17.40 + .03
Muni Bd	7.91	8.30
Optn Inc	11.76	12.85 + .03
Summit	22.46	24.55 + .13
Technol	11.51	12.58 + .07
Total R	12.70	13.88 – .05
US GvSc	8.65	9.01
Keystone Mass Group:		
Cust B1 r	15.53	N.L.
Cust B2 r	18.03	N.L. – .02
Cust B4 r	7.96	N.L. + .01
CustK1 r	6.65	N.L. + .01
CustK2 r	6.96	N.L. + .01
Cust S1 r	19.05	N.L. + .10
Cust S3 r	8.70	N.L. + .04
Cust S4 r	6.04	N.L. + .04
Intl Fd r	5.24	N.L. – .01
Tax Fr r	7.64	N.L.
Mass Fd	12.17	(z) + .03
Legg Masn	18.64	N.L. + .04
Lehm Cap	19.73	N.L. + .09
Leverage	7.43	N.L.
Lexington Group:		
Cp Ledrs	11.81	13.01 + .01
Gold Fd	4.46	N.L. – .04
Gnma	7.59	N.L. + .01
Growth	7.96	N L. + .02

	NAV	Offer NAV Price Chg.
Eq incm	7.34	8.02 + .01
Opp Fnd	8.44	9.22 + .06
Gold Spc	10.09	11.03 – .07
High Yld	18.24	19.56 – .01
Prm Inc	22.84	24.96 + .09
Regncy	13.26	14.49 + .11
Special	21.41	23.40 + .14
Target	16.15	17.18 + .14
Tax FrB	7.78	8.15 + .01
Time Fd	12.21	13.34 + .05
OTC SecFd	14.64	15.91 + .03
PW Atlas	9.25	10.11 + 04
PW Amer	x12.34	13.49 – .29
Paramnt	12.90	14.10 + .06
PaxWld Fd	10.69	N.L. + .03
Penn Mutl	6.28	N.L. + .01
Penn Squ	8.48	N.L. + .01
Permt Prtf	11.75	N.L.
Phila Fund	8.31	9.08 – 02
Phoenix Series Fund:		
Bal Ser	10.19	11.14 + 03
Conv Ser	15.98	17.46 – .01
Gwth Ser	11.99	13.10 + .04
High Yld	9.16	9.85 – .01
Stk Ser	10.35	11.31 + .06
PC CapF	12.11	(z) + .01
Pilgrim Group:		
Mag Cap	6.14	6.62 + .02
Mag Inc	7.74	8.35 + .03
Par Fnd	23.27	23.62 + .06
Pilgr Fd	11.97	12.91 + .04
Pioneer Funds:		
Bond Fd	8.68	9.49
Pionr Fd	19.81	21.65 + .08
Pionr II	15.47	16.91 + 02
Pionr III	12.61	13.78 + .03
Planned In	21.17	N.L. + .03
PLITRN	12.23	N.L. + .01
Prec Metl	21.74	N.L. – .24
Price Rowe:		
Growth	13.05	N.L. + .10
Grw Inc	12.57	N.L. + .03
Income	8.22	N.L.
Intl Fd	14.69	N.L. + .02
New Era	16.72	N.L. + .09
Nw Horz	12.37	N.L. + .11
TxF Inc	8.44	N.L.

	NAV	Offer NAV Price Chg.
State Bond Group:		
CmSt Fd	4.83	5.28 r .03
Diverst	5.73	6.26 - 02
Progrss	7.76	8.48 - .05
StateF Bal	12.68	N.L. - .03
State FrGr	9.24	N.L. - .05
StateSt r	68.19	68.46 + 43
StSt Grw r	50.01	N.L. + .78
StStExch r	76.79	N.L. + .30
Steadman Funds:		
Am Ind	3.28	N.L. + .05
Assoc Fd	.89	N.L.
Inves Fd	1.46	N.L. + .01
Oceang	6.49	N.L. + .10
Stein Roe Funds:		
Bond Fd	8.22	N.L.
Capit Op	19.84	N.L. + 13
Discvr	7.52	N.L. + .05
Specl Fd	13.23	N.L. + .07
Stock Fd	14.01	N.L. + .07
Total R	20.28	N.L. + .08
Univrse	15.59	N.L. + .07
Stratg Cap	7.13	7.79 – .03
Stratgc Inv	10.76	11.76 - .17
Strattn Gth	16.38	N.L. + .10
Strong Inv	15.98	N.L.
Strng TRF	14.70	N.L.
Tel Inc Sh	12.26	(z) – .09
Templeton Group:		
Foreign	11.71	12.80 + .02
Growth	9.60	10.49 + .02
World	11.99	13.10 + .02
Global I	32.85	(z) + .01
Global II	9.97	10.90 + .04
Thomson McKinnon:		
Growth	10.18	N.L. + .05
Income	9.95	N.L.
Opp Fnd	10.02	N.L. + .06
Trns Cap	10.68	11.61 + .05
Trns NInc	8.00	N.L.
Travl Equ	(z)	(z)
Tudor F	16.93	N.L. + .10
Twentieth Century:		
Giftrst r	4.14	4.16 + .02
Growth	12.21	N.L. + .03
Select	21.35	N.L. + .13
Ultra r	6.55	6.58 + .08
US Govt	96.45	N.L. + .02
VistaIn r	4.25	4.27 + .01
Unified Mgmt:		
Accum	8.03	N.L.
Growth	15.87	N.L. + .02
Income	12.37	N.L. - .01
Mutual	11.68	N.L + 04
United Funds:		
Accuml	7.01	7.66 + .02
Bond Fd	5.29	5.78
Cont Inc	12.85	14.04 + .04

Note: N.L. = No-load (no commissions).

fund, based on asset size and numbers of investment companies. There is a good reason for this—load funds are sold by salesmen who collect a portion of the commission. Many load funds have declining sales charges as larger amounts of money are invested.

No-load funds do not charge commissions and are sold directly by the investment company through advertisements, prospectus, and (800) WATS-line telephone orders. As of mid–1984, no-load funds made up about 25 percent of all stock fund assets but represented about half of the recently

started funds. The controversy for years has always been which type of fund performs better. Many feel that load funds, because of their larger size, have better management, while others feel that small funds have better potential to outperform the market. Actually, some of the no-load funds are not that small; T. Rowe Price New Horizons Fund had $1.179 billion in assets as of June 30, 1984. This popular no-load fund also has a fairly low annual expense per $100 of assets. In fact, notwithstanding size differences, both types of funds perform about the same—there is no significant statistical difference between them. Given that performance is approximately equal, most astute investors will shop around for a no-load fund to fit their needs rather than pay a commission.

If you reexamine Figure 3–2, you can distinguish between load and no-load funds. No-load funds have N.L. in the second column. Load funds give two prices. One is the current value and the other is the purchase price (which includes the load or commission).

Choosing a Fund to Meet Your Objectives

For years equity funds and bond funds have been the stable old favorites of mutual fund portfolios, but in recent years an emphasis on tax-free income funds and money market mutual funds have given new impetus to investment companies. Let's look at a number of different types of funds, moving from the stock funds to the less traditional areas. The reader may also wish to consult the Wiesenberger Financial Services *Investment Companies* guide for additional information on individual mutual funds (published annually by Warren, Gorham & Lamont, Boston).

Stock funds.   Investors can find any kind of stock fund to meet their needs for growth, income, high risk, high technology, natural resources, or other very specific investment strategies. For example, funds investing in international securities like the Templeton World Fund may provide an investor additional diversification as well as professional management. An investor is often unable to get research or to keep up with international securities because of the time and expense involved. Often mutual fund names indicate the emphasis or objectives of the fund. The following list of mutual funds will give you an idea of the variety (L = Load fund; NL = No-load fund):

American Insurance and Industrial Fund	L
Franklin Custodian Funds Utilities Series	L
ISI Income Fund	L
Over-the-Counter Securities Fund	L
Technology Fund	L
United Science & Energy Fund	L
Energy Fund	N.L.
Financial Industrial Income Fund	N.L.
Johnston Capital Appreciation Fund	N.L.
Rowe Price New Horizon Fund	N.L.
Steadman Oceanographic Technology & Growth Fund	N.L.

Index funds.   Many research studies have examined the ability of mutual fund managers to outperform the broad market as measured by the S&P 500. The findings indicate that some funds do outperform the market and some do not, but there is no statistical evidence to prove that professional managers can do better than the market year after year.

In response to these realities, some mutual funds have been started where the portfolio is weighted by company to be exactly equal to the S&P 500 Stock Index weights or any other index used for a market measure. This has stirred much controversy because it is a tacit admission that you can't outperform the market. The question is, should the manager of this kind of fund be paid when in fact there is no analysis or decision making necessary? Management fees should be at a minimum. If you believe that common stocks are good long-term investments but that you can't outperform the market on a consistent basis, maybe you could be comfortable with an index fund.

Balanced funds.   These funds combine investments in common stock and bonds and often preferred stock, and try to provide income plus some capital gains. But on the whole, they have not performed as well as the S&P 500 Stock Index. Funds that invest in convertible securities are also considered to be balanced, since the convertible security is a combination fixed-income security with the chance for appreciation if the underlying common stock rises.

Bond and preferred stock funds.   These funds invest in both bonds and preferred stock with the emphasis on income rather than growth. In the period of the late 1970s with interest rates reaching 20 percent on short-term securities and 14 to 15 percent on long-term bonds, many new mutual funds of this type were started.

Money market funds.   These funds have been the phenomenon of the late 1970s and the 1980s. *Forbes'* Mutual Fund Survey lists over 250 money market mutual funds, with the largest being the CMA Money Fund at over $13 billion. Money market mutual funds invest in short-term government securities, commercial paper, and repurchase agreements and have been very popular during periods of high short-term interest rates.

Money market funds are no-load, and most require a minimum deposit of $500 to $1,000. They also allow check-writing privileges, but usually the check must be for at least $500.

Length of time to maturity on money market portfolios averages between 20 and 50 days. These funds have definitely provided the small investor an opportunity to invest in securities that were once out of reach. Because of the initial drain of funds from banks and savings and loans occasioned by money market funds, these financial institutions now offer a "money market account," which pays competitive rates with money market funds, but has a slightly higher minimum deposit requirement ($1,000) than many funds. Also, there is a maximum number of checks that can be written per month.

Municipal bond funds. These provide the investor tax-free income, liquidity, and a diversified portfolio of municipal securities. Since municipal bonds can be somewhat illiquid when held in small amounts by individuals, municipal bond funds can overcome this deficiency. These funds are of greatest use to investors in high marginal tax brackets since the aftertax income on a tax-free portfolio may be better than the aftertax return on a taxable bond portfolio. For example, if an investor is in the 50 percent marginal tax bracket, he or she would be indifferent between an 8 percent tax-free yield and a 16 percent taxable yield. The funds may specialize in short-term (1–3 years), intermediate-term, or long-term municipals.

There are also tax-free money market funds. Technically, these funds fall into the previously discussed money market fund category because the funds' assets are very short-term in nature (20 to 50 days), and the funds offer check-writing privileges. Tax-free money market funds generally pay a lower yield than municipal bond funds, but they represent a good place for wealthy investors to park short-term funds.

Final Comment on Funds

An investment in mutual funds offers the investor the advantages of diversification and professional management, though mutual funds are unlikely to provide returns that are superior to the popular market averages over a long period of time. The individual must assess his or her own desires to determine if this is the optimum vehicle for market participation. Some individuals thrive on the idea of placing their own orders, charting their own performance, and generally determinating their own fate. For them, a mutual fund deprives them of these opportunities. However, there are others who wish to delegate the difficulties and time-consuming activities of money management to others, and mutual funds serve as an excellent outlet.

SUMMARY

The investor should have a basic understanding of measures of market performance, the rules and mechanics of opening and trading in an account, basic tax considerations, and the comparative advantages of investing individually or through mutual funds.

In gauging the movements in the market, the investor may view the Dow Jones Industrial Average, the Standard & Poor's 400 Industrials, the Standard & Poor's 500 Stock Index, the Value Line Average of 1,700 companies, or the NASDAQ averages (to name but a few). To evaluate various industry data, the investor may turn to *Barron's* Group Stock Averages or Standard & Poor's industry data, and for mutual funds to the Lipper Mutual Fund Investment Performance Averages. The investor will try to evaluate his or her performance in light of an index that closely parallels the makeup of his or her portfolio.

With some understanding of the various markets and the related means of measurements for those markets (such as the DJIA), the potential investor is now in a position to consider opening up an account. The investor may establish either a cash or margin account and use the account to buy securities or to sell short (in which case a margin account is necessary). The investor can also execute a number of different types of orders, such as a market order, a limit order, and a stop order. The latter two specify prices where the investor wishes to initiate transactions.

The investor must also consider the tax consequences of his or her actions. Important distinctions must be made between short-term and long-term capital gains and losses, with the latter representing a holding period in excess of six months. The IRS allows 60 percent of long-term capital gains to be excluded from taxation, so that the maximum the investor will have to pay on such a transaction is his or her marginal tax rate times 40 percent. Generally, it is best to establish long-term capital gains where possible and take losses short-term. If there are only short-term losses, $3,000 may be written off annually against ordinary income, with the balance carried forward.

While some investors prefer to directly manage their own financial resources, others look to the mutual fund industry for help. The fund may be either a closed-end investment company or an open-end mutual fund (with unlimited shares available). Mutual funds may be either loads (requiring commissions) or no-loads, and there is no discernible difference in performance between the two. Because of this, the investor is advised to consider going the no-load route and avoiding the commission. There are all types of funds available, including those that specialize in common stocks, corporate bonds, preferred stocks, and municipal bonds (and combinations thereof). Money market funds, which are no-load mutual funds specializing in short-term, high-yielding securities, have become particularly popular in the last few years.

IMPORTANT WORDS AND CONCEPTS

Dow Jones Industrial Average
***Barron's* Group Stock Averages**
Standard & Poor's 500 Stock
   Index
Value Line Average
NYSE Index
American Exchange
   Market Value Index
NASDAQ OTC Indexes
Wilshire 5,000
   Equity Index
Lipper Mutual Fund Investment
   Performance Averages

Price-weighted average
Value-weighted index
Equal-weighted index
Margin account
"Long position"
"Short position"
Sell short against the box
Limit order
Stop order
Long-term gains and losses
Short-term gains and losses
Investment company
Mutual fund

No-load fund   Index fund
Open-end fund   Balanced fund
Closed-end fund   Money market fund
Net asset value

DISCUSSION QUESTIONS

1. What four stock indexes make up the Dow Jones Averages?
2. How is the Dow Jones Industrial Average adjusted for stock splits?
3. What are criticisms and a defense of the Dow Jones Industrial Average?
4. Explain the price-weighted average concept as applied to the Dow Jones Industrial Average.
5. What categories of stocks make up the Standard & Poor's 500 Stock Index?
6. The Standard & Poor's 500 Stock Index represents 32 percent of the 1,550 firms listed on the New York Stock Exchange. What percent of the total value of the New York Stock Exchange does it represent?
7. What is a value-weighted index? Explain the impact that large firms have on value-weighted indexes such as the S&P 500.
8. What is an equal-weighted average? Which average has this characteristic?
9. Why might one say that the Wilshire 5000 Equity Index is the most comprehensive market measure?
10. Fill in the table below for the type of weighting system for the various indexes. Put an (x) under the appropriate weighting system.

	Price-weighted	Value-weighted	Equal-weighted
NYSE Composite Index	_____	_____	_____
Value Line Average	_____	_____	_____
S&P 500 Index	_____	_____	_____
Dow Jones Industrial Average	_____	_____	_____
NASDAQ OTC Composite	_____	_____	_____

11. If you did not wish a high-priced or heavily capitalized firm (one with high total market value) to overly influence your index, which of the weighting systems described in this chapter would you be likely to use?
12. Explain the difference between a cash and a margin account.
13. What is meant by the concept of minimum maintenance standards (or requirements) for margin?
14. Why is bad news "good news" to the short seller?
15. Explain how selling short against the box allows one to defer taxes until the following year.
16. Explain what is meant by a limit order. How does a stop order differ from a limit order?
17. What is the difference between day orders and GTC orders?

18. What do you give up and what do you gain when you use a discount broker in preference to a regular broker?

19. Explain how net short-term capital losses are applied against ordinary income.

20. Explain how net long-term capital losses are applied against ordinary income.

21. Contrast closed- and open-end investment funds.

22. Why might someone want to invest in a mutual fund? Does statistical evidence indicate that mutual funds tend to outperform the general market?

23. Contrast load and no-load funds. Does one tend to show superior performance over the other?

24. What are some of the different types of mutual funds?

25. Explain the difference between a money market fund and a money market account.

PROBLEMS

1. Assume the following five companies are used in computing an index.

Company	Shares outstanding	Base period Jan. 1, 1965 Market price	Current period Dec. 31, 1986 Market price
A	1,000	$ 4	$10
B	5,000	5	20
C	10,000	10	40
D	3,000	12	45
E	2,000	15	8

a. If the index is price-weighted, what will be the value of the index on December 31, 1986? (Take the average price on December 31, 1986, and divide by the average price on January 1, 1965, and multiply by 100.)

b. If the index is value-weighted, what will be the value of the index on December 31, 1986? (Take the total market value on December 31, 1986, and divide by the total market value on January 1, 1965, and multiply by 100.)

c. Explain why the answer in b is different from the answer in a.

2. Assume the following stocks make up a *value-weighted* index.

Corporation	Shares outstanding	Market price
Maris	6,000	$30
Mantle	14,000	5
Howard	4,000	8
Richardson	30,000	20

a. Compute the total market value and the weights assigned to each stock.

b. Assume the shares of the Howard Corporation go up by 50 percent,

while those of the Richardson Corporation go down by a mere 10 percent. The other two stocks remain constant. What will be the newly established value for the index?

    c. Explain why the index followed the pattern it did in part b.

3. Assume you buy 100 shares of stock at $50 per share on margin (50 percent). If the price rises to $60 per share, what is your percentage gain in equity?

4. In the problem above, what would the percentage loss be if the price had decreased to $35?

5. Assume you have a 25 percent minimum margin standard in Problems 3 and 4. With a price decline to $35, will you be called upon to put up more margin to meet the 25 percent rule? Disregard the $2,000 minimum margin balance requirement.

6. Recompute the answer to Problem 5 based on a stock decline to $32. Under this circumstance, will you be called upon to put up more margin?

7. You sell 100 shares of PIM Corporation short. The price of the stock is $80 per share.

    a. How much is your initial margin?

    b. If the stock goes down to $60, what is your percentage gain or loss on the initial margin (equity)?

    c. If stock goes up to $90, what is your percentage gain or loss on the initial margin (equity)?

    d. In part c, if the minimum margin standard is 30 percent, will you be required to put up more margin? (Do the additional necessary calculations to answer this question.)

    e. At what stock price (use a whole number) will you be required to put up more margin?

8. You are very optimistic about the home building industry so you buy 200 shares of Heavenly Homes at $65 per share. You are very pessimistic about the trucking industry so you short-sell 300 shares of Ace Trucking Corporation at $75. Each transaction requires a 50 percent margin balance.

    a. What is the initial equity in your account?

    b. Assume the price of each stock is as follows for the next three months (month-end). Compute the equity balance in your account for each month.

Month	Heavenly Homes	Ace Trucking
January	$68	$70
February	60	77
March	59	56

9. Assume an investor in a 45 percent tax bracket has a $6,000 long-term gain and a $3,000 short-term gain. How much total tax will be paid?

10. Mr. I. R. Ess has an $8,000 short-term loss in 1986.

    a. What is the maximum deduction he can take against ordinary income? How much will be carried forward to 1987?

    b.   Assume in 1987 Mr. Ess has a $16,000 short-term gain. If he is in a 40 percent marginal tax bracket, how much tax will he pay? Include the effect of the carry-over from part a in your answer.

11.   Will E. Sutton has a long-term capital loss of $10,000 in 1986.

    a.   What is the maximum deduction he can take against ordinary income? How much of the long-term capital loss must be utilized to take the maximum deduction against ordinary income? How much will be carried forward into 1987?

    b.   In 1987 Mr. Sutton had a $20,000 short-term capital gain. If he is in a 35 percent marginal tax bracket, how much tax will he pay? Include the effect of the carry-over from part a in your answer.

12.   Joan Sloan has a short-term capital loss of $3,000 in 1986. She is trying to decide whether to take a $5,500 long-term capital gain in the same year or wait until January of the following year to take the gain. She is in a 40 percent tax bracket. If she takes the gain and loss in the same year, how much total tax will she pay?

13.   Assume the investor in Problem 12 waits until 1987 to take the gain. Compare the tax savings in 1986 on the $3,000 write-off to the taxes paid in 1987 on the long-term capital gain. What is the net value? Comparing the answers in Questions 12 and 13, should the investor wait until January of 1987 to take her gain?

14.   Assume the same circumstances as in Problems 12 and 13, except that the investor is in a 50 percent tax bracket in 1987. Should she still wait until 1987 to take her long-term capital gain or take it in 1986?

15.   Joe Kline was very active in the market in 1986. His tax information is as follows:

Long-term capital gains	$2,000
Short-term capital gains	$7,500
Long-term capital losses	$7,000
Short-term capital losses	$6,000

By how much will his ordinary income be reduced in 1986 as a result of his stock transactions?

(Hint: You may wish to consult footnote 4 in the text.)

SELECTED REFERENCES

"A Brokerage that Plays by Its Own Rules." *Business Week,* September 24, 1984, pp. 119–20.

Branch, Ben, and Walter Freed. "Bid-Asked Spreads on the AMEX and the Big Board." *Journal of Finance,* March 1977, pp. 159–63.

Butler, Hartman, L., Jr., and J. Devon Allen. "The Dow Jones Industrial Average Reexamined." *Financial Analysts Journal,* November–December 1979, pp. 23–30.

Groth, John C.; Wilbur G. Lewellen; Gary G. Schlarbaum; and Ronald C. Lease. "An Analysis of Brokerage House Securities Recommendations." *Financial Analysts Journal,* January–February 1979, pp. 32–40.

Grube, R. Corwin; O. Maurice Joy; and Don B. Panton. "Market Response to Federal Reserve Changes in the Initial Margin Requirement. *Journal of Finance,* June 1979, pp. 659–74.

Hopewell, Michael H., and Arthur L. Schwartz, Jr. "Temporary Trading Suspensions in Individual NYSE Securities." *Journal of Finance,* December 1978, pp. 1355–73.

Latane, Henry A.; D. L. Tuttle; and W. E. Young. "Market Indices," *Financial Analysts Journal,* September–October 1971, pp. 75–85.

Lewellen, Wilber G.; Ronald C. Lease; and Gary G. Schlarbaum, "The Personal Investments of Professional Managers." *Financial Management,* Winter 1979, pp. 28–36.

Lorie, James H., and Mary T. Hamilton. "Stock Market Indexes." In *Modern Developments in Investment Management,* ed. James H. Lorie and Richard Brealey. New York: Praeger Publishers, 1972.

Mahon, Gigi. "Sunny Side of the Street: Discount Brokers Increase Share of Trade." *Barron's,* June 11, 1979, p. 11.

Molodovsky, Nicholas. "Building a Stock Market Measure." *Financial Analysts Journal,* May–June 1967, pp. 43–48.

Regan, Patrick J. "The 1976 BEA Pension Fund Survey." *Financial Management,* Spring 1977, pp. 48–65.

Reilly, Frank K. "Stock Price Changes by Market Segment." *Financial Analysts Journal,* March–April 1971, pp. 54–59.

Rudd, Andrew. "The Revised Dow Jones Industrial Average: New Wine in Old Bottles?" *Financial Analysts Journal,* November–December 1979, pp. 57–63.

Schultz, John W. "Misleading Averages." *Barron's,* July 7, 1977, p. 5.

Shepard, Lawrence. "How Good is Investment Advice for Individuals?" *Journal of Portfolio Management,* Winter 1977, pp. 32–36.

West, Richard R., and Seha M. Tinic. "Institutionalization: Its Impact on the Provision of Marketability Services and the Individual Investor." *Journal of Contemporary Business,* Winter 1974, pp. 25–48.

Chapter 4

SOURCES OF INVESTMENT INFORMATION

We are continually exposed to much information in this world of expanding and rapid communications. As the scope of investments has grown to include more than stocks and bonds, investment information has expanded to cover items such as gold and silver, diamonds, original art, antiques, stamps and coins, real estate, farm land, oil and gas, tax shelters, commodities, mutual funds, and other specialized assets. The problem investors are faced with is not only which investments to choose from the many available, but also where to find relevant information on specific investments.

First of all, the investor needs a basic knowledge of the economic environment. After determining the economic climate, the investor will proceed to a more detailed analysis of industries and unique variables affecting a specific investment. It is often said that the sign of an educated person is whether he or she knows where to find information to make an intelligent decision. The rest of this chapter will attempt to provide a list and description of the basic information sources for some of the more common forms of investments as well as sources for general economic data.

You may want to refer back to this chapter as you go through the chapters that follow. This chapter is not intended to be a guide for analysis—only an overview of what information is available. You may have heard the old phrase "a picture is worth a thousand words." You will find that is certainly true of the tables and figures in this chapter. It is virtually impossible to discuss each and every variable found in the figures and tables. To acquaint yourself more fully with information sources we suggest that you visit your college and local library and spend time browsing through their collection of economic and financial services. Appendix 4–A at the end of the chapter contains the addresses of a number of the sources mentioned in this chapter.

AGGREGATE ECONOMIC DATA

Economic data are necessary for analyzing the past and predicting future trends of the economy. The economic environment that exists today and the one expected in the future will bear heavily on the types of investments selected when creating or managing an investment portfolio. Information on inflation, wages, disposable income, economic growth rates, interest rates, money supply, demographic trends, and so on are important economic data that will influence investor decisions. This information is available in many publications from the government, commercial banks, and periodicals. What follows is a brief description of some of the major sources of economic data.

Federal Reserve Bulletin

The *Federal Reserve Bulletin* is published monthly by the Board of Governors of the Federal Reserve System, Washington D.C. It contains an abundance of monetary data, such as money supply figures, interest rates, bank reserves, and various statistics on commercial banks. Fiscal variables, such as U.S. budget receipts and outlays and federal debt figures are also found in the *Bulletin.*

This publication also contains data on international exchange rates and U.S. dealings with foreigners and overseas banks.

Since a complete description of the *Federal Reserve Bulletin* is outside the scope of this chapter, a partial listing of the table of contents should suffice to provide a better idea of what information it contains. Each heading may be divided into more detailed sections that provide information for the previous month, the current year on a monthly basis, and several years of historical annual data.

> Domestic Financial Statistics
> Federal Reserve Banks
> Monetary and Credit Aggregates
> Commercial Banks
> Financial Markets
> Federal Finance
> Securities Markets and Corporate Finance
> Real Estate
> Consumer Installment Credit
> Domestic Non Financial Statistics
> International Statistics
> Securities Holdings and Transactions
> Interest and Exchange Rates

The Federal Reserve Board also publishes a *Federal Reserve Quarterly Chart Book* and an annual *Historical Chart Book* depicting the data in the *Bulletin* in graphic form.

Federal Reserve Banks

There are 12 Federal Reserve Banks in the Federal Reserve System, representing different geographical areas (districts) of the United States. Each bank publishes its own monthly letter or review which includes economic data about its region and sometimes commentary on national issues or monetary policy. The 12 banks by district are as follows: Boston (1), New York (2), Philadelphia (3), Cleveland (4), Richmond (5), Atlanta (6), Chicago (7), St. Louis (8), Minneapolis (9), Kansas City (10), Dallas (11), and San Francisco (12).

Federal Reserve Bank of St. Louis

One district bank, the Federal Reserve Bank of St. Louis, publishes some of the most comprehensive economic statistics on a weekly and monthly basis. *U.S. Financial Data* is published weekly and includes data on the monetary base, bank reserves, money supply, a breakdown of time deposits and demand deposits, borrowing from the Federal Reserve Banks, and business loans from the large commercial banks. The publication also includes yields and interest rates

FIGURE 4–1

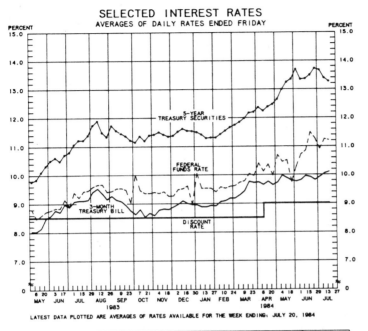

SELECTED INTEREST RATES
AVERAGES OF DAILY RATES ENDED FRIDAY

LATEST DATA PLOTTED ARE AVERAGES OF RATES AVAILABLE FOR THE WEEK ENDING: JULY 20, 1984

1984	FEDERAL FUNDS ■■	3-MONTH TREASURY BILL	6-MONTH TREASURY BILL ■■■	1-YEAR TREASURY BILL	5-YEAR TREASURY SECURITIES	LONG-TERM TREASURY SECURITIES
MAY 4	10.70	9.73	9.88	10.18	12.65	12.85
11	10.46	9.97	10.27	10.46	12.99	13.16
18	10.52	9.88	10.40	10.59	13.24	13.42
25	9.75	9.79	10.38	10.73	13.35	13.49
JUNE 1	10.30	9.76	10.62	10.94	13.69	13.71
8	10.72	9.81	10.57	10.80	13.34	13.38
15	10.85	9.95	10.66	10.87	13.36	13.35
22	11.49	9.91	10.49	10.97	13.49	13.41
29	11.27	9.81	10.49	11.09	13.72	13.62
JULY 6	10.91	9.92	10.54	11.01	13.67	13.65
13	11.25	10.04	10.52	10.94	13.39	13.51
20 ■	11.21	10.10	10.60	10.92	13.27	13.21
27						

■ AVERAGES OF RATES AVAILABLE.
■■ SEVEN-DAY AVERAGES FOR WEEK ENDING WEDNESDAY TWO DAYS EARLIER THAN DATE SHOWN.
CURRENT DATA APPEAR IN THE BOARD OF GOVERNORS' H.15 RELEASE.
■■■ NEW ISSUE RATE
RATES ON LONG-TERM TREASURY SECURITIES ARE COMPUTED BY THE FEDERAL RESERVE BANK OF ST. LOUIS.
TREASURY BILL YIELDS ON DISCOUNT BASIS.

PREPARED BY FEDERAL RESERVE BANK OF ST. LOUIS

on a weekly basis on selected short-term and long-term securities. An example of these published interest rates appears in Figures 4–1 and 4–2.

Monetary Trends is published monthly by the St. Louis Fed and includes charts and tables of monthly data. The information is similar to that found in *U.S. Financial Data* but covers a longer time period. The tables provide compound annual rates of change, while the graphs include the raw data with trend changes over time. Additional data are available on federal government debt and its composition by type of holder and on the receipts and expenditures of the government for both the National Income Account Budget and the High Employment Budget.

FIGURE 4–2

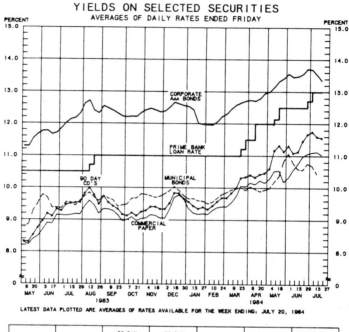

YIELDS ON SELECTED SECURITIES
AVERAGES OF DAILY RATES ENDED FRIDAY

LATEST DATA PLOTTED ARE AVERAGES OF RATES AVAILABLE FOR THE WEEK ENDING: JULY 20, 1984

1984	90 DAY CD'S	30-DAY COMMERCIAL PAPER	90-DAY BANKERS' ACCEPTANCES	CORPORATE AAA BONDS	CORPORATE BAA BONDS	MUNICIPAL BONDS ▬
MAY 4	10.60	10.28	10.42	13.00	14.46	9.99
11	11.17	10.52	10.98	13.15	14.61	10.19
18	11.32	10.54	11.07	13.33	14.75	10.36
25	11.14	10.19	10.93	13.42	14.91	10.83
JUNE 1	11.31	10.32	10.92	13.56	15.04	11.07
8	11.09	10.56	10.81	13.46	14.95	10.78
15	11.13	10.75	10.85	13.48	15.01	10.59
22	11.46	10.98	11.27	13.55	15.06	10.56
29	11.67	11.07	11.46	13.71	15.20	10.76
JULY 6	11.75	11.11	11.44	13.69	15.29	10.69
13	11.60	11.13	11.41	13.53	15.16	10.44
20 ▪	11.56	11.04	11.36	13.35	15.15	N.A.
27						

▪ AVERAGES OF RATES AVAILABLE.
▬ BOND BUYER'S AVERAGE INDEX OF 20 MUNICIPAL BONDS, THURSDAY DATA.
N.A. – NOT AVAILABLE

PREPARED BY FEDERAL RESERVE BANK OF ST. LOUIS

National Economic Trends is also published by the St. Louis Federal Reserve Bank and presents monthly economic data on employment, unemployment rates, consumer and producer prices, industrial production, personal income, retail sales, productivity, compensation and labor costs, gross national product, the implicit price deflator for the GNP, personal consumption expenditures, gross private domestic investment, government purchases of goods and services, disposable personal income, corporate profit after taxes, and inventories. This information is presented in graph form and in tables showing the compounded annual rate of change on a monthly basis. If raw data is needed, other economic publications are required.

Survey of Current Business

The *Survey of Current Business* is published monthly by the Bureau of Economic Analysis of the U.S. Department of Commerce. It contains monthly and quarterly raw data rather than compound annual growth rates as found in the St. Louis Federal Reserve's publications. The *Survey of Current Business* contains a monthly update and evaluation of the business situation, analyzing such data as GNP, business inventories, personal consumption, fixed investment, exports, labor market statistics, financial data, and much more. For example, if personal consumption expenditures are broken down into subcategories, one would find expenditures on durable goods, such as motor vehicles and parts, and furniture and equipment; nondurables, such as food, energy, clothing, and shoes; and services.

The *Survey* can be extremely helpful for industry analysis as it breaks down data into basic industries. For example, data on inventory, new plant and equipment, production, and more can be found on such specific industries as coal, tobacco, chemicals, leather products, furniture, paper, and many others. Even within industries, such as lumber, production statistics can be found on hardwoods and softwoods right down to Douglas fir trees, southern pine, and western pine. The Commerce Department publishes a weekly update to the *Survey* called *Weekly Business Statistics.* This publication updates the major series found in the *Survey of Current Business* and includes 27 weekly series and charts of selected series. To provide a more comprehensive view of what is available in the *Survey of Current Business* and *Weekly Business Statistics,* a list of the major series updates follows:

GNP	Housing Starts and Permits
National Income	Retail Trade
Personal Income	Labor Force, Employment and
Industrial Production	Earnings
Manufacturers Shipments, Inventories and Orders	Banking
Consumer Price Index	Consumer Installment Credit
Producer Price Index	Stock Prices
Construction Put in Place	Value of Exports and Imports
	Motor Vehicles

Business Conditions Digest

The *Business Conditions Digest* is published monthly by the Bureau of Economic Analysis of the U.S. Department of Commerce. The information differs from the other publications previously discussed in that its primary emphasis is on cyclical indicators of economic activity. The National Bureau of Economic Research (NBER) analyzes and selects the time series data, based on each series' ability to be identified as a leading, coincident, or lagging indicator over several decades of aggregate economic activity.

Over the years, the NBER has identified the approximate dates when aggregate economic activity reached its cyclical high or low point. Each time

FIGURE 4–3

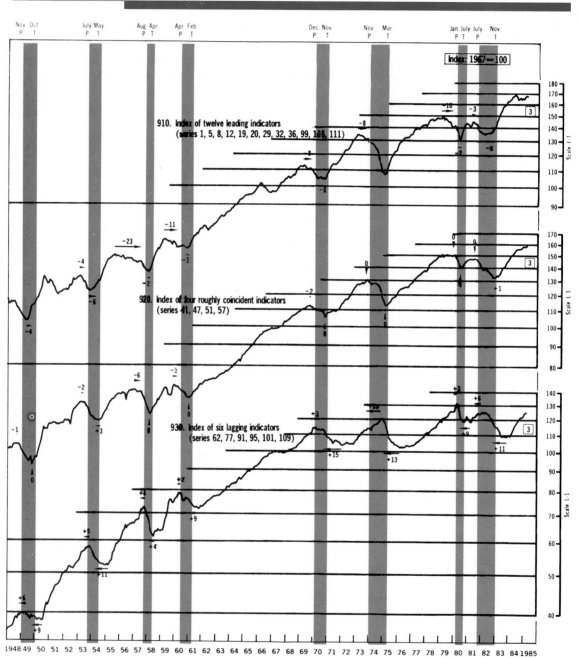

NOTE: Numbers entered on the chart indicate length of leads (−) and lags (+) in months from reference turning dates.
Current data for these series are shown on page 60.

Source: *Business Conditions Digest* (U.S. Department of Commerce, Bureau of Economic Analysis, April 1985).

series is related to the business cycle. Leading indicators are those that move prior to the business cycle, coincident indicators move with the business cycle, and lagging indicators follow directional changes in the business cycle. Figure 4–3 represents the composite index of 12 leading, 4 coincident, and 6 lagging indicators that have consistently performed well relative to the general swings in the economy. The 22 indicators were selected out of several hundred found in the *Business Conditions Digest* and time-tested by the NBER. This publication can be very helpful in understanding past economic behavior and in forecasting future economic activity with a higher degree of success.

Other Sources of Economic Data

So far, we have presented the basic sources of economic data. Much other data is available or duplicated in other publications. What is available to each investor may vary from library to library, so here are some brief notes on other sources of data.

Many universities have bureaus of business research that provide statistical data on a statewide or regional basis. Major banks, such as Citicorp, Morgan Guaranty Trust, Harris Trust, and Bank of America, publish monthly or weekly letters or economic reviews, including raw data and analysis. Several other government sources are available, such as *Economic Indicators* prepared by the Council of Economic Advisors and the *Annual Economic Report of the President.* Additionally, many periodicals, such as *Business Week, Fortune,* and *Barron's,* contain raw data as well as economic commentary. Moody's and Standard & Poor's Investment Services (introduced on the following pages) both publish economic data along with much other market-related information.

INVESTMENT ADVISORY SERVICES

Investment information and advice is available from many sources—from large corporate financial services to individuals writing investment letters. A look through such financial magazines as *Barron's, Forbes,* and *Financial World* will turn up hundreds of investment services charging fees large and small for the information they sell. Most public libraries and universities subscribe from several of the major publishers, such as Moody's, Standard & Poor's, or Value Line.

Moody's

Moody's is owned by Dun & Bradstreet and publishes several data bases for bonds and stocks. *Moody's Manuals* are widely used and present not only historical financial data on the companies listed but also on their officers and the companies' general corporate condition. The *Manuals* are divided into several categories (Banks and Finance, Industrial, Municipals and Government, OTC Industrial, Public Utility, and Transportation). Each manual has a bi-

weekly news supplement that updates quarterly earnings, dividend announcements, mergers, and other news of interest. *Moody's Manuals* are comprehensive, with each category taking up one or two volumes and over several thousand pages.

Moody's Bond Record contains data on corporates, convertibles, governments, municipals, and ratings on commercial paper and preferred stock. Corporate bond information includes the interest coupon, payment dates, call price, Moody's rating, and yield to maturity. The current price as well as the yearly and historical high-low price are presented. The total amount of the bond issue outstanding is given with a designation for a sinking fund and the original issue date. Data on convertible bonds also include the conversion price, conversion value, and conversion period. Information on industrial revenue and municipal bonds is usually limited to the Moody's rating. *Moody's Bond Record* also contains historical yield graphs for various types of bonds over at least 30 years. This is a monthly publication.

Moody's also publishes a weekly *Bond Survey* that reviews the week's activity in the bond market, rating changes, new issues, and bonds called for redemption. *Moody's Dividend Record* presents quarterly dividends and the date of declaration, date of record, date payable, and ex-dividend dates. This is an annual publication. *Moody's Handbook of Common Stock* is a quarterly reference guide that summarizes a company's 10-year historical financial data along with a discussion of corporate background, recent developments, and prospects. Approximately 1,000 companies are listed in the *Handbook*. *Moody's Stock Survey* is a weekly publication that discusses the weekly investment climate and market performance. This publication also presents some selected stocks for purchase. Only a brief description has been given for each Moody's publication, but enough has been presented for you to know whether a particular one may be worth looking at further.

Standard & Poor's

A second major source of information is the Standard & Poor's Corporation, a subsidiary of McGraw-Hill. Standard & Poor's has very comprehensive coverage of financial data. The following items will not all be discussed, but they provide a good look at what Standard & Poor's makes available to the investor.

Analysts Handbook	*Industry Survey*
Bond Guide	*International Stock Reports*
Called Bond Record	*Investment Advisory Survey*
Convertible Bond Reports	*Municipal Bond Selector*
Corporation Records	*Opportunities in Convertible*
Daily Stock Price Records	*Bonds*
Dividend Record	*The Outlook*
Earnings Forecaster	*Poor's Register of Corporations,*
Fixed Income Investor	*Directors and Executives*

Registered Bond Interest Record
The Review of Securities Regulation
Security Dealers Directory
Stock Guide
Stock Reports (A.S.E., N.Y.S.E., O-T-C and Regional Exchanges)

Stock Summary
Standard & Poor's Statistical Service
Transportation Service
Trendline Charts

Standard & Poor's Corporate Records are similar to *Moody's Manuals* except that they are organized alphabetically rather than by trade categories. The *Corporate Records* are published monthly, and the six volumes are updated by daily supplements. Information found in the volumes includes historical company background, financial statements, news announcements, earnings updates, and other news of general interest. Companies found in the *Corporate Records* are listed, and their subsidiary companies are cross-listed.

Something that may be overlooked when examining the *Corporate Records* is the statistical section found in the T–Z volume. The statistical section includes a mutual fund summary, an address list of many no-load mutual funds, and foreign bond statistics. Special tables contained in the T–Z volume list new stock and bond offerings on a monthly basis. This volume also presents a classified index of industrial companies listed by Standard Industrial Classification code numbers (SIC). For example, if you want to find out about cereal breakfast food companies, you would first find the corresponding SIC number for cereal breakfast foods which is listed in alphabetical order. The number, 2043, then leads you to the cross-listing of companies in the *Standard & Poor's Corporate Records*. These are the companies one would find listed under *2043 Cereal Breakfast Foods:*

Carnation Co.
The Clorox Company
General Foods Corp.
General Mills, Inc.
Gerber Products Co.
Iroquois Brands, Ltd.
Kellogg Company

Liggett Group Inc.
Nabisco, Inc.
Nestlé S.A.
The Quaker Oats Co.
Ralston Purina Co.
George Weston Limited

All of these companies make up an industry classification and may be found in the *Corporate Records*. This industry listing can certainly be helpful when trying to put together a list of companies for an industry analysis.

Several other Standard & Poor's publications are quite useful and present concise, thumbnail sketches of companies, common stock variables, and corporate bonds. Figure 4–4 depicts two pages from the *Stock Guide*. This is a monthly publication that enables investors to take a preliminary look at the common and preferred stock of several thousand companies and almost 200 mutual funds. The introduction to the *Stock Guide* presents recommendations

FIGURE 4–4   Sample pages, *Standard & Poor's Stock Guide*

214 Ten-Tho

Standard & Poor's Corporation

Index	Ticker Symbol	Name of Issue (Call Price of Pfd. Stocks)	Market	Com. Rank. & Pfd. Rating	Par Val.	Inst.Hold Cos	Inst.Hold Sha. (000)	Principal Business	Price Range 1971-83 High	Low	1984 High	Low	1985 High	Low	Mar. Sales in 100s	March, 1985 Last Sale Or Bid High	Low	Last	%Div. Yield	P-E Ratio
1	TNY	Tenney Engineering	AS	B+	10¢		467	Environmental test eq	6⅛	1⅞	¾	3½	6⅛	4⅜	625	6⅜	5⅜	5⅜		15
2	TEN	Tensor Corp	OTC	C	10¢	13	3	Hi-intensity lamps	14⅞	¾	5⅛	5⅛	5⅛	4⅜	129	5½	4⅜	4⅞		d
3	TRRA	TERA Corp	NR			1219	Computer sys/pkg software	39⅜	5¼	9¼	3½	9½	4⅜	950	5½	4⅜	4⅜		d
4	TER	Teradyne Inc	NY,M	B	12½	184	15662	Electr ind automatic test eq	39⅝	1¼	39¾	21¼	32⅜	22¾	32223	28⅜	21¼	23½		13
5	TERM	Terminal Data	OTC			9	942	Document microfilming sys	16½		8	6⅛	8	6⅜	1934	8	6¾	7⅛		13
6	TMEXF	Terra Mines Ltd	OTC,Vc	NR	50¢	6	231	Int'l silver producer	8⅝	1	4¾	1⅜	1⅞	1¼	3076	1⅞	1⅝	1⅞	s	d
7	TDSC	Tesdata Systems	OTC	C	1¢	2	148	Computer perf measure sys	25½	1	9¼	2	3	1½	515	2	1½	1⅜		d
8	TSO	Tesoro Petroleum	NY,B,M,P,Ph	B	16⅔¢	27	3759	Integrated oil company	32⅛	6¾	20⅝	9⅞	15	10⅜	16396	15	10½	12⅞	3.2	50
9	Pr	$2.16 cm Cv Pfd(25)vtg	OTC		33	4	605	Trinidad, Indonesia, U.S.	55½	2⅛	36⅜	20¾	27½	20¾	605	25⅝	22⅜	25	8.6	2
10	TEVIY	Teva Pharm Indus ADR§	OTC	NR		5	475	Pharmac'ls,veterinary prod	10¾	2½	3	1	2½	1½	475	2½	2½	2½	1.2	
11	TXC	Texaco Canada	AS,Ph,Mo,To	A	No	61	1352	Large factor in Canadian oil	38	5⅛	33	25½	27⅜	22½	331	25¼	22½	25¼	4.8	7
12	TX	Texaco Inc	NY,B,C,M,P,Ph,To	B+	6¼	587	76153	Major international oil co	54⅜	20	48⅜	31¼	36⅜	30⅞	135447	36¼	34⅜	36⅜	8.3	35
13	TXA	Texas Air	AS,M	C	1¢	48	3053	Multiple regional airlines	16⅜	8¾	49⅜	3¾	11⅞	3¾	11726	11⅞	10	10⅛		8
14	TXA	Texas Am'n Bancsh	N,M	A	5	8	3063	Multiple bank hldg,Ft Worth	45¾	8¾	42⅝	33¾	37½	33¾	2859	36½	32½	33¾	4.5	8
15	TAE	Texas Am'n Energy	AS	B	10¢	4	542	Hldg oil&gas prod'r:refinery	17	1⅛	10⅛	4⅞	10⅛	5⅝		7½	6	7	s	50
16	Pr	$2.575cm Cv¶¶Exch Pfd(**22.3175)		B+	No	4	127		46⅝	5⅛	22¼	16¼	20⅝	17⅛	432	20⅝	20	19¾	13.0	
17	TCB	Texas Commerce Bkshr	NY,M,P	A+	5	198	16508	Multiple bank hldg:Houston	44½	10	48¼	26½	44	32⅜	46838	43¾	32⅜	33⅜	4.7	8
18	TET	Texas East'n Corp	NY,B,C,M,P,Ph	A	10¢	250	24117	Gas P.L. sys:petrol mkt/distr	62⅝	10	35⅜	26¼	56	34¼	30542	34¼	30½	34⅛	6.4	8
19	TETPrA	Tex East Tr Adj Rt(**11.65% A Pfd)	NY		16⅜	20	272	Nat'l gas pipeline,Tex to N.Y	71	52⅜	39	32	56	55½	2071	56	55⅜	55⅜	10.4	
20	TXI	Texas Indus	NY,B,M,Ph	B+	1	46	1796	Concrete prod: constr: r.e.	36	14⅞	38⅞	20¾	34⅞	25¾	2361	33	25¼	27	2.9	13
21	TXN	Texas Instruments	NY,B,C,M,P,Ph	A	No	349	18051	Semiconductors:el'tronic eqp	176	39¾	149⅜	111¾	131¾	105½	17585	114	105½	111¼	1.8	9
22	TXO	Texas Oil & Gas	NY,M,P,Ph	C	10¢	450	3280	Crude oil & natural gas	46½	1	5⅜	3⅛	3	2¼	9207	2⅜	1⅞	1⅞		d
23	TPL	Texas Pac Ld Tr Ctfs	NY,M,P,Ph	B	16⅝	20	115229	Holds surface rights:royalties	71	4¾	32	17	21½	18¼	17027	19¾	16¼	17½	1.1	10
24	TXU	Texas Utilities	NY,B,C,M,P,Ph	A+	No	436	82741	Electric utility holding co.	36	14⅞	28½	20¾	28½	25⅛	89804	28⅜	26¼	26⅛	9.0	17
26	TXF	Texfi Indus	NY,M	C	20¢	5	490	Fabrics for apparel indus	67½	1⅜	8⅛	2	4¾	2½	1243	3⅞	3⅛	3½		d
27	TXON	Texon Energy	OTC	NR	20¢	5	1342	Oil & gas royalty interests	12½	⅛	6¾	1¾	1⅞	1⅜	922	1⅞	1¾	1⅛		d
28	TXS	Texscan Corp	AS	B	20¢	23	1667	CATV eq:radio freq,test'g eq	27½	⅜	20	3¼	7¾	3¼	7440	5⅞	3¾	3⅜		56
29	TXTN	Textone Inc§		B+	25¢	44	Wall paneling board:doors	29¼	¾	19¾	9¾	18¾	14¾	5667	18⅞	14⅜	16⅛	1.5	15
30	TXT	Textron, Inc	NY,B,C,M,P,Ph	A	25¢	140	11378	Aerosp:electr:consumer prod	38½	11¾	43¾	25¾	45¾	32¾	49995	45¾	39¾	45¾	4.0	15
31	Pr A	$2.08 cm Cv A Pfd(50)vtg	NY,B	BBB	No	14	233	outdoor ind'l prod:machine	46⅜	19	47½	28¾	49½	36	128	49½	43½	49½	4.2	
32	Pr B	$1.40 cm Cv B Pfd(45)vtg	NY,B	BBB	No	6	105	Deos.engineerd fasteners	32½	14	39	28½	40½	37	6524	40½	40½	40½	3.5	
33	THK	Thackeray Corp(**27.90:SF25)	NY,M	B	10¢	3	235	Textile,automotive	22½		38	25⅛	28	28¼	1366	28¼	26⅛	26½		d
34	Pr	$4.15 cm Pfd(**27.90:SF25)	OTC	CCC	1¢	2	114	hardware:RE	27	23¼	27	23⅛	26½	24⅞	30	26⅞	26⅛	26½	15.6	
35	THPR	Thermal Profiles	OTC	NR		12	323	Mfrs custom window units	13¼		15	7⅞	14⅜	12⅜	3033	14⅜	14	12¾		21
36	THMD	Thermedics Inc	OTC	NR	1	2	50	Mfrs biomedical prod & sys	8⅝	6½	10¼	6	17½	8	2923	17½	13	15⅝		d
37	TMO	Thermo Electron	NY,M	B	1¢	39	1659	Eng'd ind'l pr environ instr	26⅛	2¾	22½	13¾	26	18	5838	26	21	23¾		23
38	TDYN	Thermodynetics	OTC	NR	1¢		Mfr twisted metal tubing	2½	¼	1¾	1¼	¾	½	2382	¾	¾	⅜		37
39	THFR	Thetford Corp	OTC	B	25¢	11	403	Toilet sys:recreat veh,boat	29	6¼	15	6¾	10¾	7½	943	10⅝	9⅜	9⅜		7
40	TDAT	Third Nat'l	OTC	A	10	40	3721	Multi-bank hldg:Tennessee	26⅜	6¼	33½	21¼	37½	33	1171	37⅛	36⅛	36½	3.5	8
41	TCBY	This Can't' Be Yogurt	OTC	NR	10¢	128	9833	Franchises frozen yogurt strs	38¼	8¾	8¾	2⅛	27¼	8½	7967	27¼	19¾	19⅜		40
42	TNB	Thomas & Betts	NY,M,P	A+	50¢	126	2266	Elec connectors, accessories	19½	2¾	38	28¾	43¼	34¼	6524	36¾	36¾	36¾	3.4	15
43	TII	Thomas Indus	NY,M	A	1	16	984	Lighting fix:decor hm tools	19⅞	2¼	18¾	12¾	18	15%	947	18	15%	16⅛	4.2	79
44	TNEL	Thomas Nelson	OTC	B+	8¾	23	816	Book publ:prod'r,mktr-Bible	26	3¾	12¾	7¾	12	6⅝	1362	8	7¾	7⅞	2.8	6
45	TM	Thompson Medical	NY,M	B	No	63	1931	Mfr appetite suppressants	39	6¾	26½	13¾	18	13¼	4883	18⅜	13¼	14¼	2.1	19
46	THM.A	Thomson Newspaper A	To,M	A+	No			Large newspaper publisher		6	52¼	37	60	48	2048	60	54½	58¼		

Uniform Footnote Explanations—See Page 1. Other: ¹P:Cycle 1. ²P:Cycle 2. ³AS:Cycle 1. ⁴AS °AS °CBOE:Cycle 1. °Ph:Cycle 3. ¹Pr:Cycle 3. ²ADR's represent 12 Ord par IS1.
¹¹Pro forma,excl shrs held by co. ¹²○$0.98,'84. ¹⁴Incl reorg liab & new financing. ¹⁶○$1.20,'84. ¹⁷○$0.45,'85. ¹⁹Co opt fr 5-1-86exch for $20 amt 12⅞ Cv2014. ²¹To 4-30-85,scale to $20 in '94.
¹¹Com price equals 140%Cv price-20 trad'g days. ²³Subsid Pfd in M$. ²⁶○$4.00,'84. ²⁷○$0.14,'81. ²²Thru 5-31-85:min 7½%,max 15 1/2%. ²³Thru 11-30-92:then $50. ⁴⁴Stk dstr of Regal Int'l. ⁴⁷△$0.05,'80.
¹¹○$0.19,'82. ¹¹Nortek Inc plan acq 1.09 shrs. ²⁶○$1.87,'80. ⁷¹△$0.28,'82. ⁷⁷To 8-15-85,scale to $25 in '94. ⁷⁴□$0.50,'81. ⁸²○$0.36,'85. ⁸²○$1.01,'83. ³³ADR's represent 12 Ord par IS1.

FIGURE 4–4 *(concluded)*

Splits		Dividends						Financial Position				Capitalization			Earnings $ Per Shr.							Interim Earnings			
◆	Cash Divs.	Latest Payment			Total $			Mil-$			Balance	Lg Trm	Shs. 000		Years						Last 12		$ Per Shr.		
Index	Ea. Yr. Since	Per$	Date	Ex. Div.	So Far 1985	Ind. Rate	Paid 1984	Cash& Equiv.	Curr. Assets	Curr. Liab.	Sheet Date	Debt Mil-$	Pfd.	Com.	End	1980	1981	1982	1983	1984	Mos.	Period	1983	1984	Index
1◆	.....	None Paid			....	Nil	....	3.46	11.4	3.13	9-30-84	4.98	...	3484	Dc	0.21	0.24	0.19	0.22	P[51]0.39	0.39				1
2	.....	None Paid			....	Nil	....	0.03	2.05	4.69	9-30-84	2.58	...	546	Dc	•0.04	•0.21	d0.86	d2.84	....	d3.73	9 Mo Sep	d1.60	d2.49	2
3	.....	None Since Public			....	Nil	....	6.19	31.4	14.0	12-31-84	....	...	7507	Je	0.38	0.51	0.71	0.30	d0.48	d0.31	6 Mo Dec	d0.16	0.01	3
4◆	.....	None Paid			....	Nil	....	0.78	186.	46.7	9-29-84	58.7	...	22232	Dc	0.68	0.25	0.24	[52]1.08	P1.87	1.87				4
5◆	.....	None Since Public			....	Nil	....	1.21	26.4	13.4	12-31-84	7.38	...	4471	Sp	d0.18	0.39	0.55	0.44	0.68	0.56	3 Mo Dec	0.13	0.01	5
6◆	.....	5% Stk	1-28-85	1-8	5% Stk	Stk	5% Stk	...	3.57	5.59	9-30-84	0.92	...	9967	Dc	△d0.19	d0.22	△0.08	d0.30	Pd1.17	jd1.17				6
7	.....	None Since Public			....	Nil	....	0.26	5.34	1.80	9-30-84	0.01	...	1295	Dc	△0.53	d0.18	d0.92	▲d1.00	....	d2.49	9 Mo Sep	▲d0.65	■d2.14	7
8	1980	Q0.10	2-25-85	2-5	0.10	0.40	0.40	10.5	368.	328.	12-31-84	147.	4199	13731	Sp	7.15	■4.84	2.90	▲3.05	0.59	0.25	3 Mo Dec	0.40	0.06	8
9	1976	Q0.54	3-15-85	2-25	0.54	2.16	2.16	Cv into 1.7241 shr com:$14.50				....	1323	...	Sp	b5.11	b7.63	b6.24	b3.23	b1.56	....				9
10◆	1984	0.01½	1-29-85	1-7	0.01½	0.03	0.035	398.	5903	4519	j3-31-84	438.	...	[54]186848	Mr	0.89	0.71	0.56	[55]1.00	....	1.00				10
11◆	1944	gQ0.30	3-1-85	2-5	g0.30	1.20	g1.20	423.	1828	663.	j12-31-84	94.0	900	120768	Dc	2.92	2.45	2.15	2.74	3.41	j3.41				11
12	1903	Q0.75	3-8-85	1-30	0.75	3.00	3.00	1576	7501	6405	9-30-84	★11766	12627	237380	Dc	△8.31	8.75	■4.92	4.80	P■1.03	1.03	9 Mo Sep	3.80	3.39	12
13	.....	0.04	7-31-83	7-6	....	Nil	....	203.	448.	266.	9-30-84	[56]1113	4955	13015	Dc	0.55	d8.11	d7.27	d14.58	P•[57]1.24	1.24				13
14◆	1934	Q0.38	4-2-85	3-11	0.76	1.52	1.52	Book Value $31.68			12-31-84	128.	...	10604	Dc	■3.65	■4.52	■4.82	■3.66	▲4.06	4.06				14
15◆	.....	5% Stk	8-1-84	7-10	....	Stk	5% Stk	3.26	39.6	23.3	9-30-84	75.0	700	6719	Dc	0.67	d0.08	d0.33	□[58]0.84	P0.14	0.14				15
16	1984	Q0.64⅜	2-1-85	1-15	0.64⅜	2.57	0.987	Cv into 2.1 com shrs				....	700	...	Dc	....	....	....	....	....	....	Call restr to 5-1-86[61]			16
17◆	1920	Q0.39	4-1-85	3-4	0.78	1.56	1.42	Book Value $35.15			12-31-84	180.	...	32459	Dc	■3.48	■4.49	5.35	5.50	5.64	5.64				17
18◆	1950	Q0.55	3-1-85	2-5	0.55	2.20	2.16¼	180.	1341	2029	9-30-84	★1316	[62]323	52686	Dc	4.36	4.35	□3.54	2.97	P▲[63]4.04	4.04				18
19	1983	1.506	3-1-85	2-5	1.506	5.82	6.37½	Callable at $51.50 fr 12-1-87[65]				★926	±1835	1	Dc	....	....	b2.12	b2.22	b2.80	....				19
20◆	1962	Q0.20	2-28-85	1-28	0.20	0.80	s0.784	21.4	126.	50.1	11-30-84	137.	19	7517	My	5.16	3.76	2.28	2.34	1.54	2.06	9 Mo Feb△	0.36	0.88	20
21	1962	Q0.50	4-29-85	3-26	1.00	2.00	2.00	274.	1858	1412	12-31-84	388.	...	24616	Dc	9.22	4.62	6.10	■d6.09	▲13.05	13.05				21
22◆	.....	h[66]	5-28-82	6-1	....	Nil	....	12.2	55.0	54.5	9-30-84	346.	...	27458	Dc	△[67]0.76	□0.54	□[68]0.37	□d3.26	P△d0.85	d0.85				22
23◆	1965	Q0.04½	4-12-85	3-27	0.09	0.18	0.17	8.40	404.	373.	11-30-84	678.	...	210174	Au	0.67	0.91	1.17	1.40	1.65	1.67	3 Mo Nov	0.38	0.40	23
24◆	1956	A0.40	3-12-85	2-26	0.40	0.40	0.40	3.13	...	...	9-30-84	....	...	±4035	Dc	2.12	1.40	1.69	2.00	P1.77	1.77				24
25	1917	Q0.63	4-1-85	3-13	1.22	2.52	2.32	n/a	658.	832.	12-31-84	3340	[62]763	★133586	Dc	3.18	3.51	3.85	3.90	P4.21	4.21				25
26	.....	None Paid			....	Nil	....	n/a	20.8	15.5	2-1-85	26.4	...	3480	Oc	■d6.24	■▲0.09	▲d1.36	•0.51	d3.83	d3.82	3 Mo Jan△	•0.06	•0.05	26
27	.....	None Since Public			....	Nil	....	0.40	1.52	2.51	10-31-84	12.5	413	★7625	Ap	d0.05	d0.05	•0.03	d0.21	d0.24	d0.29	6 Mo Oct	d0.11	d0.16	27
28◆	.....	None Since Public			....	Nil	....	0.11	90.5	26.4	1-31-85	48.6	...	6721	Ap	0.26	0.46	0.68	0.89	0.70	0.06	9 Mo Jan△	0.48	d0.16	28
29	1983	0.25	1-16-85	12-24	0.25	0.25	0.25	5.67	13.7	1.43	9-30-84	2.53	...	p1169	Dc	0.28	0.71	1.03	2.11	P1.45	1.45				29
30	1942	Q0.45	4-1-85	3-11	0.90	1.80	1.80	42.9	1515	645.	12-29-84	200.	1994	33791	Dc	□[70]4.17	△[71]3.92	△[72]2.02	2.40	3.11	3.11				30
31	1968	Q0.52	4-1-85	3-11	1.04	2.08	2.08	Conv into 1.1 shrs common				....	1453	...	Dc	b4.55	b3.87	2.57	b3.11	b3.76	....				31
32	1968	Q0.35	4-1-85	3-11	0.70	1.40	1.40	Conv into 0.9 shrs common				....	541	...	Dc	b4.55	b3.87	b2.57	b3.11	b3.76	....				32
33	.....	0.30	6-5-74	5-6	....	Nil	....	1.71	35.7	10.1	9-30-84	34.3	730	5107	Dc	△•0.52	d0.81	d0.31	•Nil	P•d0.17	d0.17				33
34	1983	Q1.03¾	2-15-85	1-28	1.03¾	4.15	4.15	...	...	...		....	730	...	Dc	....	....	....	b0.98	....	....	Mand Red 10% fr 8-15-89			34
35	.....	None Since Public			....	Nil	....	1.45	10.1	4.83	12-31-84	7.16	...	2743	Mr	•0.03	d0.05	•0.18	0.50	....	0.60	9 Mo Dec	0.36	0.46	35
36◆	.....	None Since Public			....	Nil	....	4.52	5.60	0.42	9-29-84	....	...	6126	Dc	....	....	Nil	d0.01	Pd0.09	d0.09				36
37◆	.....	None Paid			....	Nil	....	9.52	95.3	46.2	9-29-84	47.1	...	6020	Dc	1.20	1.35	0.40	0.01	P1.01	1.01				37
38	.....	None Since Public			....	Nil	....	0.57	2.58	0.52	12-31-84	0.04	...	8113	Mr	•0.02	•0.01	•0.01	•0.03	....	0.02	9 Mo Dec	•0.02	•0.01	38
39	.....	None Since Public			....	Nil	....	0.80	10.4	3.56	12-31-84	2.21	...	1803	Sp	d0.56	[74]□d1.17	•0.06	•1.30	•1.43	1.37	3 Mo Dec	0.06	Nil	39
40◆	1929	Q0.32	4-1-85	3-7	0.59	1.28	1.046	Book Value $28.53			9-30-84	58.2	...	8661	Dc	■2.54	■3.02	■3.22	3.82	P4.46	4.46				40
41◆	.....	None Since Public			....	Nil	....	1.06	2.26	1.79	8-31-84	0.86	...	★2907	Nv	....	....	•0.13	0.09	P0.45	0.49	3 Mo Feb△	0.02	0.06	41
42◆	1934	Q0.31	4-1-85	3-4	0.62	1.24	1.17	53.0	190.	60.1	12-31-84	7.22	...	15534	Dc	2.11	2.15	1.52	1.74	2.51	2.51				42
43◆	1955	Q0.17	4-1-85	3-4	0.324	0.68	0.604	14.0	119.	32.2	12-31-84	43.1	...	8487	Dc	1.27	1.44	0.88	■1.09	1.87	1.87				43
44◆	1975	Q0.05	4-19-85	3-29	0.10	0.20	0.17	3.31	51.6	20.8	12-31-84	24.5	...	5126	Mr	0.41	0.49	0.57	0.68	....	0.10	9 Mo Dec	0.52	d0.06	44
45◆	1982	Q0.10	4-15-85	3-25	0.20	0.40	0.40	21.8	83.3	24.5	8-31-84	....	...	9560	Nv	1.00	1.03	1.16	1.65	P2.20	2.20				45
46	1966	gQ0.30½	3-15-85	2-25	g0.30½	1.22	g1.17½	68.7	171.	90.7	j12-31-83	97.8	155	±49236	Dc	□1.53	△1.96	□2.01	2.55	P3.11	3.11				46

◆ **Stock Splits & Divs By Line Reference Index** [1]4-for-3,'81,'82:5-for-4,'80,'83,'84. [4]2-for-1,'82,'83. [5]3-for-1,'81:5-for-4,'83,'84:10%,'81,'85. [6]10%,'80,'81(ex'80):Adj to 5%,'85. [10]7-for-5,'82. [11]4-for-1,'80. [14]10%,'80:5-for-4,'81. [15]Adj to 5%,'84. [17]2-for-1,'80. [18]2-for-1,'84. [20]Adj to 4%,'84. [22]2-for-1,'81. [23]10%,'80,'83:2-for-1,'81(wi'80)'84(wi'83). [24]3-for-1,'80. [28]6-for-5,'80:2-for-1,'81:5-for-4,'82. [36]5-for-4,'85. [37]3-for-2,'83. [40]6-for-5,'81,'82:3-for-2,'84. [41]3-for-2,'84,'85. [42]2-for-1,'84. [43]Adj for 5%,'83(ex'82):10%,'80,'81,'83,'84. [44]5-for-4,'80:2-for-1,'81:6-for-5,'82;3-for-2,'83. [45]5-for-4,'82:2-for-1,'83.

Source: *Standard & Poor's Stock Guide,* April 1985.

of common stock for price appreciation and income, and provides name changes, new exchange listings, common stock rating changes, and a graph of Standard & Poor's Stock Price Indexes.

The *Bond Guide* is of the same format as the *Stock Guide*. It is a monthly publication in booklet form that presents data on corporate and convertible bonds. Figure 4–5 shows one page on corporate bonds with a long list of Texas Electric Service bonds at the top. The Standard & Poor's rating is presented along with the bond form (either a coupon or registered bond), refunding dates, call prices, sinking funds, yields, prices, and other information. Figure 4–6 is one page of convertible bonds from the *Bond Guide*. Looking at Allied Stores, we see three convertible bonds having different coupons, interest payment dates, and maturity. Again, the Standard & Poor's rating is given. All the conversion data is presented with bond prices and common stock prices. Can you find how many shares of common stock an investor will receive for each $1,000 bond of Allied Stores having a 9½ percent coupon and a maturity of 2007?[1]

One of the more popularly used Standard & Poor's publications is the *Corporate Reports*. These reports are often mailed out from brokerage houses to customers who want basic information on a company. In Figure 4–7, Texas Instruments provides a good example of what one would expect to find in such reports. This information can be compared to the entry in Figure 4–4, line 21, for Texas Instruments to see the difference in the depth of coverage between the *Corporate Reports* and the *Stock Guide*. The *Corporate Reports* are contained in three separate multiple-volume sets, the New York Stock Exchange Stocks, American Stock Exchange Stocks, and Over-the-Counter and Regional Stocks. Each company is updated quarterly with new earnings, dividends, and recent developments. About 1,020 NYSE stocks are selected and bound in an annual publication called the Standard & Poor's *Stock Market Encyclopedia*, which contains end-of-the-year *Corporate Reports*. To develop an appreciation for the other Standard & Poor's services, try perusing this material at your library.

Value Line

Value Line Investment Survey is a publication of Arnold Bernhard & Co. It is one of the most widely used investment services by individuals, stockbrokers, and small bank trust departments. The *Value Line Investment Survey* follows 1,700 companies, and each common stock is covered in a one-page summary (see the one for Texas Instruments in Figure 4–8). Value Line is noted for its comprehensive coverage, which can be seen by comparing Figure 4–8 to Figures 4–4 and 4–7. Raw financial data is available as well as trendline growth rates, price history patterns in graphic form, quarterly sales, earnings and dividends, and a breakdown of sales and profit margins by line of business.

---

[1] The answer is 25 shares.

FIGURE 4–5 Page from *Standard & Poor's Bond Guide* (corporate bonds)

CORPORATE BONDS

Title-Industry Code & Co. Finances (In Italics) / Individual Issue Statistics — Exchange	Ind / Interest Dates	Chgs. 1982 / S&P Quality rating	Eligible	Times Earn. 1983 / Bond Form	Legality M a	Times Earn. 1984 / Legality N H	Yr. End / Legality N Y	Cash & Eqv / Redemption Provisions: Refund Earliest/Other	Current Assets, Liabs (Million $) / Call Price For S.F.	Date / Call Price Regular	L. Term Debt (Mil $) / Out-st'd'g (Mil $)	Debt % Prop / Underwriter Firm	Underwriter Year	Interim Times Earn. Period / Price Range 1972-83 High	1972-83 Low	Interim 1983 / 1984 High	Interim 1984 / 1984 Low	1985 High	1985 Low	Mo. End Price Sale(s) or Bid	Curr Yield	Yield to Mat.
Texas El Sv 1st 7½s 2001	Ao	A+	X	R	√	√	√	....	101.21	104.69	25.0		'71	102⅜	49⅝	68⅝	57⅜	69	64¼	64½	11.63	12.75
1st 7⅛s 2002	Jj	A+	X	R	√	√	√	....	±101.24	±104.50	30.0	K1	'72	101⅝	47⅛	65	54¼	65¾	61⅛	61⅜	11.61	12.76
1st 8⅝s 2004	Ao	A+	X	R	√	√	√	....	101.17	106.20	40.0	F2	'74	109⅝	55⅜	74½	62⅝	75⅜	70¼	70½	12.23	12.79
1st 9½s 2004	jD	A+	X	R	√	√	√	....	100	±106.07	60.0	B9	'74	116	60⅝	80¾	68	81¾	76⅛	76⅜	12.44	12.81
1st 8⅞s 2005	Jd	A+	X	R	√	√	√	....	z100	±105.78	50.0	B9	'75	112	56¾	75¾	63¾	76¾	71¼	71⅝	12.39	12.84
1st 8⅞s 2006	Ms	A+	X	R	√	√	√	....	±101.20	±107.04	100	F2	'76	112	56⅜	75½	63⅜	76⅜	71⅛	71⅜	12.43	12.84
1st 9½s 2009	Fa	A+	X	R	√	√	√	....	z100	±106.98	75.0	B9	'79	101¾	59⅝	79⅛	66⅝	80⅜	74⅝	74⅞	12.69	12.91
1st 14⅛s 2010	Ms	A+	X	R	√	√	√	....	z100	±111.28	75.0	S1	'80	121¼	83¼	114¾	97⅜	116¼	108¼	108⅝	13.00	12.95
1st 15⅞s 2011	jD	A+	X	R	√	√	√	[1]112.54	100	±113.80	50.0	B10	'81	121¾	95⅜	118¼	104	116⅛	112⅛	112⅞	14.06	14.01
1st 16s 2012	Ao	A+	X	R	√	√	√	[2]112.27	z100	113½	75.0	G2	'82	121⅞	97½	117½	104¾	116¼	111⅛	113⅛	14.14	14.10
1st 11⅝s 2012	jD	A+	X	R	√	√	√	[3]108¼	z100	±109.90	75.0	G2	'82	99⅜	89⅝	95⅛	80⅛	96¼	89⅜	89¾	12.95	12.99
SF Deb 6⅝s '93	Fa	A+	X	CR	√	√	√	....	±100.47	±102.20	7.65	K2	'68	99⅜	53½	74	63½	74⅝	71	71⅛	9.31	12.51
Texas Gas Transmission[4]	***73a***	***3.27***		***3.46***	....		***Dc***	***11.8***	***649 537***	***9-84***	***233***	***30.0***		***9 Mo Sep***		***3.35***	***4.33***					
• SF Deb 7⅞s '86	aO	A+	X	R	-	√	-	....	*100	100	30.0	D3	'76	102⅞	77¾	95½	91⅜	95	94	95⅛	8.28	11.50
SF Deb 6½s '87	[5]ao	A+	X	R	-	√	-	....	*100	±100.72	10.5	D3	'67	89⅛	62¾	90⅝	82⅞	91⅛	90¼	90⅜	7.19	11.66
SF Deb 9½s '90	[6]jd	A+	X	R	-	√	-	....	*100	101.92	15.9	D3	'70	110	69⅞	91¼	81¾	92½	90¾	91	10.44	11.94
SF Deb 12⅛s '90	fA15	A+	X	R	-	√	-	[7]101.57	[8]100	±104.71	75.0	D3	'80	103½	78¾	100½	92¾	100⅝	98½	98⅞	12.26	12.41
SF Deb 9¾s '90	[9]fa	A+	X	R	-	√	-	....	*100	±102.43	18.0	D3	'70	111⅜	70⅛	91¾	81½	93	90½	90⅝	10.76	12.13
SF Deb 8⅛s '91	[6]jj	A+	X	R	-	√	-	....	*100	102.01	16.9	D3	'71	105½	62	83⅝	73¾	84½	82½	82⅝	9.83	12.30
SF Deb 15s '92	Mn	A+	X	R	-	√	-	[10]100	[11]100	±110	100	D3	'81	114¾	93½	110⅛	101⅜	111⅜	108⅝	109	13.76	13.01
Texas Industries	***13a***	***1.66***		***2.13***		***1.77***	***My***	***21.4***	***126 50.1***	***11-84***	***137***	***64.0***		***6 Mo Nov***		***2.02***	***2.46***					
• Sub SF Deb 7¾s '92	mN15	B+	Y	R	-	-	-	....	100	±102.07	[12]15.0	D3	'72	91	50	76¾	72	75	72½	73⅛	10.60	13.50
Texas Instruments	***24b***	***5.35***		***d3.04***		***7.46***	***Dc***	***274***	***1858 1412***	***12-84***	***388***	***26.2***										
• SF Deb 4.80s '90	mN	AA-	X	R	√	√	-	....	100	±101	10.1	M8	'65	78	48½	68	64	71	71	70	6.86	12.40
• SF Deb 12.70s 2005	Fa	AA-	X	R	√	√	-	[13]102½	[14]100	±105¼	200	M8	'80	110	78⅛	101½	85	102⅝	98	100	12.70	12.70
Texas Intl Airlines[15]	***4***	***0.08***		***d1.66***	....		***Dc***	***File bankruptcy Chapt 11***			***[16]882***			***9 Mo Sep***		***d2.22***	***1.35***					
◆Sub SF Deb 10⅞s '98	§Ao15	D	Z	R	-	-	-	Default 10-15-83 int			17.6	S6	'78	100	35	57	38	71½	54½	69⅝	...	Flat
Texas International	***49b***	***1.27***		***d0.94***	....		***Dc***	***12.2***	***55.0 54.5***	***9-84***	***346***	***140***		***9 Mo Sep***		***d0.38***	***0.58***					
• Sr Sub Oil Ind Nt[19] 9s '95	aO	CCC	Y	R	-	-	-	[20]....	[21]....	[22]....	50.0	D7	'83	103	100	70	70	65	65	65	13.85	15.98
• Sr Sub Nts 13⅛s '93	jJ15	CCC	Y	R	-	-	-	[23]100	[24]100	100	[12]100	D7	'83	95½	85	90	79	65	61	62⅛	21.13	23.79
• SubSFDeb('77) 11½s '97	Ao	CCC	Y	R	-	-	-	[25]100	[25]100	102.30	[12]30.0	D7	'77	107¾	60	76	46	58	46	s52⅞	21.75	23.33
• SubSFDeb('78) 11½s '97	Ao	CCC	Y	R	-	-	-	....	[25]100	±102.30	20.0	D7	'78	97⅜	66	77⅜	49	57⅞	47½	s52⅞	21.75	23.33
Texas & New Orleans RR	***54***	***Assumed by Southern Pacific Trans., see***																				
• 1st & Ref C 3⅜s '90	Ao	BBB	X	CR	√	√	√	....	100⅛	100⅜	39.3	F2	'46	70	35	70	57¼	No Sale		69¼	4.87	11.66
Texas-New Mexico Pwr[26]	***72a***	***1.98***		***2.32***	....		***Dc***	***6.28***	***43.5 51.4***	***9-84***	***98.6***	***38.3***		***12 Mo Sep***		***2.28***	***2.36***					
1st G[27] 4.70s '93	jJ	A	X	CR	√	√	√	....	±100.74	±101.70	10.4	S1	'63	69¾	40⅝	61⅜	51⅝	62⅜	60	60⅛	7.82	12.61
1st H[28] 4.95s '95	fA	A	X	CR	√	√	√	....	±100.43	±101.92	4.10	S1	'65	70½	38¾	57¾	48⅛	58⅝	56	56¼	8.80	12.65
1st I[29] 6.075s '96	Mn	A	X	CR	√	√	√	....	±101.36	±103.09	4.13	S1	'66	82⅝	43⅜	63⅛	53	63⅞	61	61⅛	9.94	12.70
1st J 9s '99	aO	A	X	CR	√	√	√	....	±100.41	±104.59	8.58	S1	'69	110⅜	56½	78¼	66¼	79	75⅛	75⅜	11.94	12.77
1st K 8½s 2001	Mn	A	X	R	√	√	√	....	±101.35	±105.60	7.04	S1	'71	107⅜	52⅝	73⅜	62	74¼	70⅝	70⅞	11.99	12.81
1st M 8.70s 2006	mS	A	X	R	√	√	√	....	100	±106.30	9.30	S1	'76	104⅜	52⅜	71⅝	60¼	73⅛	69¼	69⅝	12.50	12.91
1st N 15¼s '91	mN	A	X	R	√	√	√	[30]100	100	±110.17	15.0	S1	'81	113⅝	94⅛	111	103¼	111¾	109⅞	110⅝	13.79	12.81
1st O 13¼s 2012	jD	A	X	R	√	√	√	[31]110.60	100	±111.66	14.9	S1	'82	104⅞	97⅛	102⅞	87⅛	104	100¼	102⅞	12.88	12.86
1st P 13s 2013	mS	A	X	R	√	√	√	[32]110.29	100	±112.46	15.0	S4	'83	100	96	101⅜	85⅝	103	99⅛	101⅜	12.82	12.81
Texas Oil & Gas	***73c***	***4.12***		***6.26***		***6.68***	***Au***	***8.40***	***404 373***	***11-84***	***678***	***22.2***										
• 1st C 7½s '92	Fa	AA	X	R	-	√	-	....	100	±101½	15.9	K2	'72	101	60	76⅝	73	81⅞	80	79½	9.43	11.97
• 1st D 7⅜s '92	mN15	NR	X	R	-	√	-	....	100	±101¾	1.54	K2	'72	No Sale		77	71⅞	77¾	77¾	76½	9.64	12.19
• 1st E 8¼s '94	Fa	AA	X	R	-	√	-	....	100	±102¾	19.0	K2	'74	102½	58⅛	78½	73	No Sale		79⅛	10.43	12.17
• 1st F 10¼s '95	Mn	AA	X	R	-	√	-	[33]104	100	±104.60	32.1	K2	'75	108¾	73⅞	86	78	88½	87⅛	90½	11.33	11.89

Uniform Footnote Explanations—See Page 1. Other: [1]Red rest'n(15.907%)to 12-1-86. [2]Red rest'n(16.109%)to 4-1-87. [3]Red rest'n(11.701%)to 12-1-87. [4]Subsid of Texas Gas Resources(CSX Corp). [5]Due Jun 1. [6]Due Apr 1. [7]Red rest'n(12.324%)to 8-15-88. [8]Fr 8-15-87. [9]Due Oct 1. [10]Red rest'n(15.184%)to 5-1-89. [11]Fr 5-1-90. [12]Incl disc. [13]Red rest'n(12.7%)to 2-1-90. [14]Fr 2-1-91. [15]Subsid of Continental Airlines Corp. [16]Incl Chapt 11 liabs. [17]Red rest'n(10 7/8%)to 4-15-88. [18]Fr 4-15-88. [19]Indexed Prin Amt(IPA)due 10-1-95,as defined. [20]Hldr's repyt opt on ea SF red date,as defined. [21]Red for SF fr 10-1-86 at IPA,as defined. [22]Red if IPA equals/exceeds $2,000,as defined. [23]Red rest'n(16 1/4%)to 7-15-88. [24]Fr 7-15-89. [25]Red rest'n(11 1/2%)to 4-1-87. [26]Subsid of TNP Enterprises. [27]Int incr fr 4 1/2%,7/1/74. [28]Int incr fr 4 3/4%,8/1/74. [29]Int incr fr 5 7/8%,11/1/74. [30]Red rest'n(15.4%)to 11-1-88. [31]Red rest'n(13 1/4%)to 12-1-87. [32]Red rest'n(13%)to 9-1-88. [33]Red rest'n(10.28%)to 5-1-85.

Source: *Standard & Poor's Bond Guide*, April 1985.

FIGURE 4–6 Page from *Standard & Poor's Bond Guide* (convertible bonds)

STANDARD & POOR'S CORPORATION

II

CONVERTIBLE BONDS — Issue, Rate, Interest Dates and Maturity	S&P Qual-ity Rating	B F o o d r m	Outstg. Mil.-$	Conv. Ex-pires	Shares per $1,000	Price per Share	Div. Income per Bond	1985 RANGE Hi	Lo	Curr Bid Sale(s) Ask(A)	Curr. Return	Yield to Mat	Stock Value of Bond	Conv. Parity	STOCK DATA Curr. Price	P/E Ratio	Yr. End	1983	1984	Last 12 Mos	1983 Dil u't'n
[1]Acapulco Y LA Rest...13⅜s QJul 1996	NR	R	9.99	1996	108.70	9.20	.....	84	83	84	16.0	16.6	47½	7%	4⅜	15	Dc	*d2.05	*0.25	[1]0.29	n/r
AccuRay Corp*...5½s Jd 1991	B-	R	11.2	1991	27.87	35.88	5.57	75	72	72	7.64	12.0	55%	25%	19%	12	Dc	1.31	P1.64	1.64	n/r
Action Indus...9s Ao 1998	NR	R	1.95	1998	101.32	9.87	.....	185	70	111½	8.07	7.59	111½	13%	◆11	20	Je	1.28	◇0.44	0.54	n/r
Advest Group...9s Ms15 2008	NR	R	27.5	2008	60.90	16.42	7.31	88¼	70	80¾	11.2	11.4	57%	13%	◆.9½	d	Sp	1.61	d0.10	d0.09	n/r
Aeroflex Labs...9¾s Ms15 2005	B-	R	25.0	2005	66.67	15.00	.....	100	99	99	9.47	9.48	79%	14%	.11%	11	Sp	0.91	0.96	1.04	n/r
Aeronca,Inc...12⅛s Fa 1993	NR	R	10.0	1993	170.21	5.875	.....	129½	112½	127½	9.79	7.73	127½	7½	◆7½	13	Dc	*d0.63	P0.58	0.58	*0.50
AFG Indus...8⅜s Ao 2005	BB-	R	40.0	2005	39.49	25.32	.....	100	100	100	8.38	8.38	84%	25%	21½	12	Dc	1.43	PA1.82	1.82	n/r
Alaska Airlines...9s mN15 2005	BBB-	R	25.0	2003	55.17	18.125	7.72	119	101	s118¾	7.58	7.16	108%	21%	19%	9	Dc	1.45	2.19	2.19	•1.93
Alaska Airlines'B...9s mN15 2003	BBB-	R	10.0	2003	55.17	18.125	7.72	117½	100¾	108¾	8.31	8.13	108%	19%	19%	9	Dc	1.45	2.19	2.19	•1.93
Alco Standard...9s mS30 2007	BBB+	R	50.0	2007	27.03	37.00	32.44	109¾	93	109	8.20	8.05	93%	40%	.34%	12	Sp	2.70	2.85	2.77	2.77
Alco Standard...8½s Ms31 2010	BBB+	R	60.0	2010	22.99	43.50	27.59	100¾	99%	99%	8.48	8.47	79%	43%	.34%	12	Sp	2.70	•NiP	d1.92	2.77
Alexander&Alex Sv...11s Ao15 2007	B	R	74.4	2007	25.64	39.00	25.64	83	91½	103	10.6	10.6	79%	40%	.31	19	Jl	1.03	△0.89	1.19	•0.88
Alexander's...5½s Jj 1996	NR	R	16.4	1996	31.01	32.25	.....	83	74½	74½	6.90	8.39	69%	25%	.22½	19	Jl	1.74	.....	1.03	1.67
Allegheny Beverage..6¾s fA 1988	NR	R	1.44	1988	190.11	5.26	76.04	430¾	309	373¾	1.68	.....	373%	19%	.57%	9	Ja	6.15	6.71	6.71	5.98
Allied Stores...4½s mS15 1992	NR	R	0.76	1992	44.94	22.25	95.27	256	231½	257	1.75	.....	257%	57%	.57%	9	Ja	6.15	P6.71	6.71	5.98
Allied Stores...9⅛s mN 2007	A-	R	124	2007	25.00	40.00	53.00	146½	125	143¾	6.64	5.99	143%	57%	.57%	9	Ja	6.15	P6.71	6.71	•5.98
Allied Stores...9⅛s jJ15 2009	A-	R	125	2009	18.31	54.625	38.82	116	104	s114½	7.64	7.44	104%	62%	.8%	9	Ja	1.32	2.31	2.41	•1.62
Amer Adventure*...10s Ao 1998	CCC	R	12.3	1998	86.96	11.50	.....	113	95	95	10.5	10.7	90%	10%	.10%	4	Sp	1.32	2.31	1.49	n/r
Amer Bkrs Ins Grp...8¼s	BBB	R	635.0	2004	73.26	13.65	36.63	113	102½	104	9.38	9.30	93%	14%	.12%	9	Dc	△1.42	P1.49	1.49	n/r
[7]Amer Can Int'l*...4⅞s Mn15 1988	NR	C	30.0	1988	717.76	56.30	51.50	108	No Sale	94¾	5.01	6.59	94%	53%	.53	11	Dc	△4.08	*4.74	4.74	4.50
Amer Cap Bd Fd(Ext)[10] ...11.35s[11]1990	AAA	R	50.0	1990	52.08	19.20	114.58	102⅝	100	97	11.7	12.2	97	18%	.18%	20	Je	△*1.10	*1.97	*1.97	*1.80
[12]Amer Century Corp*...7s Ao 1990	NR	R	61.67	1990	76.39	13.09	.....	77	65½	78	8.97	13.1	67%	10%	.8%	20	Je	*1.10	*1.97	*1.97	*1.80
[12]Amer Century Tr...6¾s Jd15 1991	NR	R	68.41	1991	39.87	25.08	39.78	88	64½	71	9.51	13.8	35%	17%	.8%	21	Dc	3.00	3.00	3.00	•2.90
Amer Gen'l...5¾s mS 1988	NR	R	1.90	1987	12.24	81.70	.....	88	88	s88	6.25	11.3	76%	71%	.62%	10	Dc	3.00	3.00	3.00	•2.90
Amer Gen'l...11s Fa8 2007	A+	R	128	2007	54.56	18.33	54.56	170¾	141½	158¾	6.95	6.12	158%	29	.29	11	Dc	△4.08	*4.74	4.74	4.50
Amer Gen'l...11s mN4 2008	A+	R	176	2008	54.56	18.33	54.56	170¾	140½	s163	6.75	5.98	158%	29%	.29	10	Dc	△3.00	3.00	*2.90	*2.90
Amer Hoist & Der...4¾s Jd 1992	NR	R	0.58	1992	63.86	15.66	.....	66½	66½	66½	7.14	11.8	65%	10%	.10%	d	Nv	d7.17	△d3.57	d3.57	n/r
Amer Hoist & Der...5¾s Jd 1993	NR	R	6.21	1993	50.25	19.90	16.12	65½	57½	s65	8.46	12.4	51%	12%	.10%	d	Nv	d7.17	△d3.57	d3.57	n/r
Amer Int'l Group...4s jJ 1997	AAA	R	6.64	1997	36.63	27.30	.....	285½	238	268¾	1.49	.....	268%	73%	.73%	17	Dc	□5.77	P4.27	4.27	n/r
Amer Israeli Paper...11s AuN15 1997	NR	R	13.3	1997	58.58	17.07	.....	78½	75	77¾	15.1	15.8	38%	13%	◆6%	4	Mr	1.73	.....	1.73	n/r
Amer Maize-Prod...11¾s fA 2000	BB+	R	25.0	2000	55.01	18.18	28.61	113	105	s106	11.0	10.9	86	19%	◆.15%	8	Dc	0.73	P1.92	1.92	n/r
Amer Medical Int'l...9½s mN15 2001	A-	R	125	2001	41.02	24.38	29.53	115	98½	s115	8.26	7.86	103%	28	.25%	12	Au	2.05	2.04	2.04	n/r
Amer Medical Int'l...8¼s Ao 2008	A-	R	63.6	2008	25.00	40.00	18.00	89½	78	s86¾	9.54	9.72	63%	34%	.25%	12	Au	2.05	1.64	2.04	n/r
American Motors...6s aO 1988	CCC	R	16.3	1988	133.69	7.48	.....	82½	81½	s79	7.59	13.7	43%	5%	.3%	d	Dc	d2.11	*Nil	Nil	n/r
[17]Amer Tobacco Int'l...5¾s fA 1988	NR	C	1.11	1988	55.56	18.00	216.68	No Sale		385½	1.36	.....	385%	69%	◆.69%	10	Dc	6.76	7.20	7.20	•7.03
Ames Dept Stores...8¼s aO 2009	BB+	R	40.0	2009	29.74	33.625	5.95	120	102	s119¾	7.11	6.84	105%	40%	.35%	18	Ja	1.53	2.00	2.00	n/r
Amfac...5s Mn 1989	B+	R	11.6	1989	28.00	35.714	.....	77	72¾	73½	6.80	14.0	73%	26%	.26%	d	Dc	d4.99	d0.93	d0.93	n/r
Amfac...5¼s Mn 1994	B+	R	24.3	1994	22.90	43.67	.....	82½	64	82½	6.36	.....	60%	36	.26%	d	Dc	d4.99	d0.93	d0.93	n/r
Anacomp,Inc(Sp)[18]...10s jJ 1995	NR	R	19.9	1995	250.00	4.00	.....	106¼	50	87½	.....	Flat	87%	3½	.3%	d	Sp	d0.38	d9.84	d7.07	n/r
Anacomp, Inc[20]...13⅞s Jj15 2002	CC	R	623.2	2002	57.14	17.50	.....	72	54½	s71	.....	Flat	20	12%	.3%	d	Sp	d0.38	d9.84	d7.07	n/r
◆Andal[21]Corp[22]...5⅜s mS15 1997	NR	R	2.27	1997	44.44	22.50	.....	47	44	46½	11.8	15.1	22½	10%	◆5	12	Dc	△1.35	P0.41	0.41	n/r
Andersen Group10⅛s aO15 2002	NR	R	9.98	2002	61.84	16.17	.....	97	81%	96	10.9	11.0	74%	15%	◆12	Fb	Fb	1.27	.....	1.04	1.16
Anixter Bros...8¼s Jj 2003	BBB	R	42.0	2003	36.43	27.45	10.20	93¾	83½	84¾	9.79	10.1	56%	23%	.15%	9	Jl	0.72	0.82	0.85	n/r
◆Anthony Indus...11¾s[23]jd15 2000	B-	R	622.0	2000	58.28	17.16	25.64	99¾	95	s97½	11.5	11.6	69%	16%	.12	6	Dc	△1.72	PA1.96	1.96	•1.73
[24]Apache Corp...6s jJ 1990	NR	R	2.40	1990	247.62	21.00	81.91	114¾	105¾	107¾	5.60	4.46	107%	22%	.22%	d	Dc	2.45	P2.67	*2.67	*2.65

Uniform Footnote Explanations—See Page XVI. Other: [1]Now Acapulco Restaurants. [2]Was Ind'l Nucleonics. [3]Plan fiscal chge to Mar. [4]Was Great Outdoor Amer Adventure. [5]Hldr's rept option on 12-1-91 at 110. [6]Incl disc. [7]Cv into & data of Amer Can. [8]Offered outside U.S. [9]P&I pay in U.S.$. [9]Hldr's rep't option on 1-1-90. [10]Int thru 12-31-89,adj aft as defined. [11]Due 1-1-95. [12]Was Amer Century Mtg Inv. [13]Now Amer Century Corp;was Amer Century Mtg Inv. [14]Was Lincoln Amer. [15]Cv into $3.25 Cv Jr pfd. [16]Into Cl'A'. [17]Cv into & data of Amer Brands. [18]Co option to pay int in cash/com,as defined. [19]Fiscal Jun'83 & prior. [20]Int:1-15-84,pd 3-21-84;7-15-84,pd 8-15-84. [21]Was Nat'l Kinney. [22]Int 5 1/4% to 3-9-82. [23]Due Jan 31. [24]Cv into & data of Continental Telecom.

Source: *Standard & Poor's Bond Guide*, April 1985.

FIGURE 4–7   Sample pages, *Standard & Poor's Corporate Reports*

Texas Instruments

2208

NYSE Symbol TXN   Options on CBOE (Jan-Apr-Jul-Oct)

Price	Range	P-E Ratio	Dividend	Yield	S&P Ranking
Mar. 29'85	1985				
111¼	131¾–105½	9	2.00	1.8%	A–

Summary

Texas Instruments is the leading producer of semiconductor products, and has important representation in other segments of the electronics industry, in geophysical exploration, and in specialty metal products. Following the strong gain in 1984, earnings for 1985 are expected to decline significantly, reflecting weakness in semiconductors in the first half of the year due to the recent industrywide slump. However, a pick-up in the semiconductor business is anticipated for the latter half of 1985.

Current Outlook

Earnings for 1985 are projected at $7.00 a share, down sharply from 1984's $13.05.

Dividends at $0.50 quarterly are the minimum expectation.

A modest sales decline is anticipated for 1985, reflecting a poor first half for semiconductors. That segment will continue to be affected by inventory adjustments by customers which has resulted in weak order levels. Profitability in semiconductors will be adversely affected by the lower sales volume and by declining prices. However, a much improved performance is seen for the second half. Digital products will be aided by new product introductions. Government electronics should benefit from a changing mix toward new weapons systems. Geophysical services are not expected to show much improvement, since that market has remained weak. Metallurgical materials should move with the economy. Long-term prospects appear favorable.

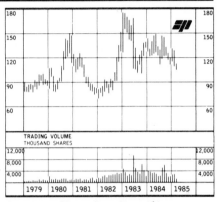

Net Sales (Million $)

Quarter:	1985	1984	1983	1982
Mar.	---	1,339	1,174	1,079
Jun.	---	1,464	1,100	1,093
Sep.	---	1,423	1,007	1,048
Dec.	---	1,516	1,299	1,107
	---	5,742	4,580	4,327

Sales for 1984 rose 25% from those of the preceding year, primarily reflecting strong gains in components. Results benefited from wider components margins and the absence of losses related to home computer operations. Net income equaled $316,000,000 ($13.05 a share), in contrast to a net loss of $145,400,000 ($6.09).

Common Share Earnings ($)

Quarter:	1985	1984	1983	1982
Mar.	E1.00	3.32	0.30	1.17
Jun.	E1.00	3.57	d5.00	1.56
Sep.	E2.25	3.54	d4.64	1.57
Dec.	E2.75	2.64	3.23	1.80
	E7.00	13.05	d6.09	6.10

Important Developments

Feb. '85—The company said that due to continued weakness in semiconductor markets worldwide, it would continue to reduced work schedules at its semiconductor plants through the first half of 1985. TXN added that the shortened work schedule would primarily affect overseas plants.

Next earnings report due in late April.

Per Share Data ($)

Yr. End Dec. 31[1]	1984	1983	1982	1981	1980	1979	1978	1977	1976	1975
Book Value	62.58	50.06	57.53	53.44	50.08	41.75	37.12	32.64	28.89	25.53
Earnings	13.05	d6.09	6.10	4.62	¹9.22	¹7.58	¹6.15	¹5.11	¹4.25	¹2.71
Dividends	2.00	2.00	2.00	2.00	2.00	2.00	1.76	1.41	1.08	1.00
Payout Ratio	16%	NM	33%	43%	22%	26%	29%	28%	25%	37%
Prices—High	149½	176	152½	126¼	150¾	101	92½	102¼	129¾	119⅜
Low	111¾	101	70½	75	78⅝	78	61⅜	68⅝	93⅛	61
P/E Ratio—	11–9	NM	25–12	27–16	16–9	13–10	15–10	20–13	31–22	44–23

Data as orig. reptd. 1. Ful. dil.: 9.04 in 1980, 7.52 in 1979, 6.12 in 1978, 5.10 in 1977, 4.23 in 1976, 2.70 in 1975. NM-Not Meaningful. d-Deficit. E-Estimated.

FIGURE 4–7   (concluded)

2208

Texas Instruments Incorporated

Income Data (Million $)

Year Ended Dec. 31	Revs.	Oper. Inc.	% Oper. Inc. of Revs.	Cap. Exp.	Depr.	Int. Exp.	Net Bef. Taxes	Eff. Tax Rate	Net Inc.	% Net Inc. of Revs.
1984	5,742	948	16.5%	¹705	423	48.9	487	35.0%	316	5.5%
1983	4,580	63	1.4%	¹454	351	36.0	d323	NM	d145	NM
1982	4,327	574	13.3%	¹329	339	33.1	213	32.4%	144	3.3%
1981	4,206	586	13.9%	¹341	333	41.3	175	38.0%	109	2.6%
1980	4,075	676	16.6%	548	257	44.3	379	44.0%	212	5.2%
1979	3,224	507	15.7%	435	187	19.5	309	44.0%	173	5.4%
1978	2,550	385	15.1%	311	131	8.4	257	45.5%	140	5.5%
1977	2,046	319	15.6%	200	108	9.2	211	44.7%	117	5.7%
1976	1,659	250	15.1%	138	87	8.3	178	45.3%	97	5.9%
1975	1,368	207	15.1%	71	92	10.8	116	46.4%	62	4.5%

Balance Sheet Data (Million $)

Dec. 31	Cash	Current Assets	Current Liab.	Ratio	Total Assets	Ret. on Assets	Long Term Debt	Common Equity	Total Cap.	% LT Debt of Cap.	Ret. on Equity
1984	274	1,858	1,412	1.3	3,423	10.2%	381	1,541	1,921	19.8%	22.8%
1983	185	1,452	1,231	1.2	2,713	NM	225	1,203	1,428	15.8%	NM
1982	420	1,527	959	1.6	2,631	5.8%	214	1,361	1,575	13.6%	11.0%
1981	150	1,197	765	1.6	2,311	4.6%	212	1,260	1,472	14.4%	8.9%
1980	140	1,299	971	1.3	2,414	9.7%	212	1,165	1,376	15.4%	19.9%
1979	117	1,083	882	1.2	1,908	10.1%	18	953	970	1.8%	19.2%
1978	115	915	637	1.4	1,518	10.1%	19	845	864	2.2%	17.7%
1977	257	815	467	1.7	1,255	9.8%	30	745	774	3.8%	16.6%
1976	294	783	418	1.9	1,128	9.4%	38	660	698	5.5%	15.7%
1975	267	663	302	2.2	941	6.5%	48	585	633	7.5%	11.0%

Data as orig. reptd. 1. Net of curr. yr. retirement and disposals. NM-Not Meaningful. d–Deficit.

Business Summary

Texas Instruments produces a variety of electrical and electronics products for industrial, consumer and government markets. Contributions by industry segment in 1984:

	Sales	Profits
Components	46%	79%
Digital products	19%	Nil
Government electronics.........	24%	24%
Metallurgical materials	3%	2%
Services	8%	−5%

Operations outside the U.S. accounted for 29% of sales and 48% of operating profits in 1984.

Components include semiconductor integrated circuits (microprocessors, memories and digital and linear circuits), semiconductor discrete devices (transistors, and optoelectronic products), assembled modules (microprocessor and memory printed circuit boards), and electrical and electronic control devices.

Digital products include minicomputers, electronic data terminals and peripherals, geophysical and scientific equipment, electronic calculators, learning aids and other products. In October, 1983 the company withdrew from the consumer home computer business.

Government electronics products include radar, infrared surveillance systems and missile guidance and control systems.

Metallurgical materials primarily involve clad metals which are used in variety of applications.

Services mainly consist of the collection and electronic processing of seismic data in connection with petroleum exploration.

Dividend Data

Dividends have been paid since 1962.

Amt. of Divd. $	Date Decl.	Ex-divd. Date	Stock of Record	Payment Date
0.50	Jun. 15	Jun. 19	Jun. 25	Jul. 30'84
0.50	Sep. 28	Oct. 2	Oct. 9	Oct. 29'84
0.50	Dec. 20	Dec. 26	Jan. 2	Jan. 28'85
0.50	Mar. 22	Mar. 26	Apr. 1	Apr. 29'85

Next dividend meeting: mid-Jun. '85.

Capitalization

Long Term Debt: $380,700,000.

Common Stock: 24,670,380 shs. ($1 par). Institutions hold about 74%. Shareholders of record: 30,701.

Office—13500 North Central Expressway, Dallas, Texas 75265. **Tel**—(214) 995-3773. **Chrmn**—M. Shepherd, Jr. **Pres & CEO**—J. F. Bucy. **VP-Secy**—R. J. Agnich. **VP-Treas**—W. A. Aylesworth. **Investor Contact**—M. Post. **Dirs**—H. W. Bell, J. F. Bucy, D. C. Garrett, Jr., S. T. Harris, D. C. Harvey, J. R. Junkins, E. R. Kane, P. F. Lorenz, P. W. McCracken, M. Shepherd, Jr., C. J. Thomsen, J. C. Toomay, J. M. Voss, W. P. Weber. **Transfer Agents & Registrars**—RepublicBank, Dallas; Morgan Guaranty Trust Co., NYC. **Incorporated** in Delaware in 1938.

FIGURE 4–8 *The Value Line Investment Survey*

TEXAS INSTR. NYSE-TXN	RECENT PRICE **129**	P/E RATIO **14.2** (Trailing: 10.1 / Median: 19.0)	RELATIVE P/E RATIO **1.27**	DIV'D YLD **1.6 %**	**1072**

| High | 70.1 | 67.3 | 64.5 | 95.0 | 138.9 | 115.8 | 119.4 | 129.8 | 102.2 | 92.5 | 101.0 | 150.8 | 126.3 | 152.5 | 176.0 | 149.5 | Target Price Range |
| Low | 47.4 | 30.7 | 39.8 | 58.7 | 74.4 | 58.8 | 61.0 | 93.1 | 68.6 | 61.4 | 78.0 | 78.6 | 75.0 | 70.5 | 101.0 | 111.8 | |

Insider Decisions 1984

	S O N D	J F M A M J	J A S O N
to Buy	0 2 0 0	0 1 0 0 1	0 2 3 0 0
to Sell	1 0 0 2	2 0 1 0 0	1 1 0 2 0 0

Options Trade On CBO

15.0× "Cash Flow" p sh

2 for 1 split

Relative Price Strength

Institutional Decisions

	3Q'83	4Q'83	1Q'84	2Q'84	3Q'84
to Buy	68	70	65	62	79
to Sell	91	80	79	83	80
Hldg's(000)	15516	16565	15994	15815	16088

Percent shares traded 12.0 / 8.0 / 4.0

February 8, 1985 Value Line

TIMELINESS **3** Average (Relative Price Performance Next 12 Mos.)
SAFETY **3** Average (Scale: 1 Highest to 5 Lowest)
BETA 1.05 (1.00 = Market)

1987-89 PROJECTIONS

	Price	Gain	Ann'l Total Return
High	580	(+350%)	46%
Low	390	(+200%)	33%

© Value Line, Inc. 87-89E

1968	1969	1970	1971	1972	1973	1974	1975	1976	1977	1978	1979	1980	1981	1982	1983	1984	1985		87-89E
30.68	37.69	37.50	34.58	42.55	56.54	68.76	59.66	72.58	89.70	110.67	141.25	175.22	178.37	182.92	190.61	233.21	**240.00**	Sales per sh	368.30
3.11	3.77	3.84	3.81	4.32	6.28	7.73	6.74	8.07	9.85	11.77	15.78	20.19	18.74	20.40	8.58	29.68	**27.40**	"Cash Flow" per sh	45.75
1.21	1.52	1.36	1.53	2.17	3.67	3.92	2.71	4.25	5.11	6.15	7.58	9.22	4.62	6.10	d6.09	12.72	**10.00**	Earnings per sh (A)	22.00
.40	.40	.40	.40	.42	.62	1.00	1.00	1.08	1.41	1.76	2.00	2.00	2.00	2.00	2.00	2.00	**2.00**	Div'ds Decl'd per sh (B)	4.00
2.21	3.90	1.97	1.54	2.15	5.48	6.46	2.86	5.97	8.73	13.44	18.71	23.32	14.48	13.92	18.90	29.33	**28.00**	Cap'l Spending per sh	40.00
11.59	12.76	13.74	14.87	16.67	20.62	23.67	25.53	28.89	32.64	36.69	41.75	50.08	53.44	57.53	50.06	62.57	**68.00**	Book Value per sh (C)	110.90
21.88	22.07	22.07	22.10	22.18	22.77	22.87	22.93	22.85	22.81	23.04	22.83	23.25	23.58	23.65	24.03	24.62	**25.00**	Common Shs Outst'g (C)	25.25
41.8	39.1	32.8	35.2	36.8	27.4	22.1	35.0	26.8	16.4	12.7	11.6	11.8	21.3	15.6	--	10.3		Avg Ann'l P/E Ratio	22.0
2.52	2.38	2.35	2.25	2.52	2.70	3.09	4.66	3.43	2.15	1.73	1.68	1.57	2.59	1.72	--	.96		Relative P/E Ratio	1.85
.8%	.7%	.9%	.8%	.5%	.6%	1.2%	1.1%	1.0%	1.7%	2.3%	2.3%	1.8%	2.0%	2.1%	1.5%	1.5%		Avg Ann'l Div'd Yield	.8%

CAPITAL STRUCTURE as of 12/31/84

Total Debt $427.0 mill. Due in 5 Yrs $80.0 mill.
LT Debt $380.7 mill. LT Interest $41.0 mill.
(LT interest earned: 12.9x; total interest coverage: 10.9x) (20% of Cap'l)

Leases, Uncapitalized Annual rentals $125.7 mill.

Pension Liability None in '84 vs. None in '83

Pfd Stock None

Common Stock 24,616,098 shs. (80% of Cap'l)

1572.5	1367.6	1658.6	2046.5	2549.9	3224.1	4074.7	4206.0	4326.6	4579.8	5741.6	**6000**	Sales ($mill)	9300
16.3%	15.1%	15.1%	15.6%	15.1%	15.7%	16.6%	13.9%	13.3%	1.4%	16.5%	**15.0%**	Operating Margin	16.5%
87.3	92.3	87.0	108.1	131.0	187.2	257.3	333.3	338.5	351.4	422.6	**435**	Depreciation ($mill) (D)	600
89.6	62.1	97.4	116.6	140.3	172.9	212.2	108.5	144.0	145.4	308.0	**250**	Net Profit ($mill)	555
45.0%	46.4%	45.3%	44.7%	45.5%	44.0%	44.0%	38.0%	32.4%	--	36.7%	**40.0%**	Income Tax Rate	40.0%
5.7%	4.5%	5.9%	5.7%	5.5%	5.4%	5.2%	2.6%	3.3%	NMF	5.4%	**4.2%**	Net Profit Margin	6.0%
314.4	360.8	364.8	348.3	278.3	200.7	327.9	432.1	568.2	221.2	446.2	**525**	Working Cap'l ($mill)	900
72.8	47.5	38.2	29.7	19.1	17.6	211.7	211.7	214.0	225.1	380.7	**375**	Long-Term Debt ($mill)	375
541.4	585.3	660.2	744.6	845.4	952.9	1164.5	1260.1	1360.8	1202.7	1540.5	**1700**	Net Worth ($mill)	2800
15.0%	10.2%	14.2%	15.2%	16.4%	17.9%	16.5%	8.3%	10.0%	NMF	17.1%	**15.0%**	% Earned Total Cap'l	18.0%
16.6%	10.6%	14.8%	15.7%	16.6%	18.1%	18.2%	8.6%	10.6%	NMF	20.0%	**17.0%**	% Earned Net Worth	20.0%
12.3%	6.7%	11.0%	11.3%	11.9%	13.4%	14.3%	4.9%	7.1%	NMF	16.8%	**14.5%**	% Retained to Comm Eq	16.5%
26%	37%	25%	28%	29%	26%	22%	43%	33%	NMF	16%	**20%**	% All Div'ds to Net Prof	18%

BUSINESS: Texas Instruments Incorporated is engaged in the development, manufacture, and sale of electronic equipment such as semiconductors, calculators, microprocessors, and small computers. Its equipment group fills military orders for missile guidance systems. International sales, about 29% of total; U.S. gov't, 15%. Employee costs, about 42% of sales; research and development, about 12%. Depreciation rate in 1984: 16.3%. Est'd plant age: 3 yrs. Has 86,500 employees, 30,700 shareowners. Insiders own 19% of outstanding stock. President: J. Fred Bucy. Chairman: Mark Shepherd, Jr. Incorporated: Delaware. Address: 13500 North Central Expressway (P.O. Box 225474), Dallas, TX 75265.

CURRENT POSITION	1982	1983	12/31/84
(SMILL.)			
Cash Assets	420.0	184.9	274.4
Receivables	641.7	664.6	793.7
Inventory(Avg Cst)	360.0	335.6	489.2
Other	105.2	266.6	301.1
Current Assets	1526.9	1451.7	1858.4
Accts Payable	784.0	1050.8	1122.6
Debt Due	49.5	37.3	46.3
Other	125.2	142.4	243.3
Current Liab.	958.7	1230.5	1412.2

ANNUAL RATES of change (per sh)	Past 10 Yrs	Past 5 Yrs	Est'd '82-'84 to '87-'89
Sales	14.0%	12.0%	13.0%
"Cash Flow"	12.5%	9.5%	18.5%
Earnings	2.5%	-8.0%	39.0%
Dividends	11.5%	3.0%	15.0%
Book Value	11.0%	9.0%	14.5%

Cal- endar	QUARTERLY SALES ($ mill.)				Full Year
	Mar. 31	June 30	Sept. 30	Dec. 31	
1981	1063.0	1055.6	1038.7	1048.7	4206.0
1982	1078.5	1092.9	1048.3	1106.9	4326.6
1983	1174.0	1099.8	1006.7	1299.3	4579.8
1984	1338.9	1464.2	1422.7	1515.8	5741.6
1985	*1350*	*1400*	*1550*	*1700*	*6000*

Cal- endar	EARNINGS PER SHARE (A)				Full Year
	Mar. 31	June 30	Sept. 30	Dec. 31	
1981	1.47	.44	1.15	1.56	4.62
1982	1.17	1.56	1.57	1.80	6.10
1983	.30	d5.00	d4.64	3.25	d6.09
1984	3.32	3.57	3.21	2.62	12.72
1985	*1.50*	*1.75*	*3.25*	*3.50*	*10.00*

Cal- endar	QUARTERLY DIVIDENDS PAID (B)				Full Year
	Mar. 31	June 30	Sept. 30	Dec. 31	
1981	.50	.50	.50	.50	2.00
1982	.50	.50	.50	.50	2.00
1983	.50	.50	.50	.50	2.00
1984	.50	.50	.50	.50	2.00
1985					

Profit margins are narrowing. Sales are slow and price competition is intense in semiconductors, Texas Instruments' largest business. Results are poor in two of TI's smaller operations—geophysical exploration services and data systems—as well. And margins in the company's big government electronics segment are also being squeezed somewhat by a buildup in production capacity for new weapons systems. As a result, we look for 1985 profits to come in below last year's record level. **But Texas Instruments is still well-placed for the pull to 1987-89.** TI's government electronics business should grow at a healthy rate during the second Reagan Administration. So should the company's semiconductor operations. Problems with the Department of Defense regarding testing procedures for semiconductors have been resolved. Texas Instruments is currently the worldwide leader in semiconductor sales, with a good position in Japanese and Far Eastern markets. The company is spending heavily to automate its manufacturing in order to remain a low-cost producer. (Texas Instruments laid off 2,000 workers in the December quarter and

charged off 27¢ a share against earnings to cover the associated costs.) Meanwhile, Texas Instruments is upgrading its product line to include programmable logic circuits, gate arrays, advanced memory devices, and, thanks to a long-term technical agreement with National Semiconductor, a 32-bit microprocessor with a family of related components. High technology products and low production costs are a good recipe for success in semiconductors, in our opinion. With TI's two largest business units (accounting for about two-thirds of sales and over three-quarters of profits) in such good shape, corporate profits could easily double by 1987-89, especially if some of today's laggard operations improve or get sold.
On a 3-to 5-year basis, the stock is valued modestly, we think, given TI's high earned returns on investment and its good growth prospects. Consequently, investors seeking large capital gains to 1987-89 will probably want to hold on to their positions. These shares are not timely now, however, given the lack of earnings progress presently. We advise investors to wait until TI's rank improves before making new commitments in this issue. *P.F./H.S.K.*

(A) Based on average shares outstanding. Excluding nonrecurring gain: '84, 33¢. Next earnings report due late Apr. Est'd current cost egs./sh.: '84, $11.65. **(B)** Next dividend meeting about Mar. 20. Goes ex about Apr. 5. Approximate dividend payment dates: Jan. 24, Apr. 25, July 25, Oct. 31. **(C)** In millions, adjusted for stock splits and dividends. **(D)** Depreciation on accelerated basis.

Company's Financial Strength	A
Stock's Price Stability	50
Price Growth Persistence	25
Earnings Predictability	5

Value Line contains 13 sections divided into several industries each. The first few pages beginning an industry classification are devoted to an overview of the industry, with the company summaries following. Each section is revised on a 13-week cycle.

Value Line has a unique evaluation system that is primarily dependent on historical relationships and regression analysis. From the valuation model, each company is rated 1 through 5, with 1 being the highest positive rating and 5 the lowest. Each company is rated on timeliness and safety. It should be noted that Value Line minimizes human judgment in making its evaluation, which is consistently mechanical from period to period.

The *Investment Survey* of Value Line also contains some information and advice on put and call options. This is updated weekly as are the stock rankings of the total sample. Data on options are presented in Figure 4–9. Value Line also publishes a separate *Options and Convertible Bond Survey,* which analyzes and recommends action on convertibles based on the underlying common stock, interest rate movements, and related market behavior. Other Value Line publications are *Special Situations, OTC Stocks,* and the *New Issue Service.*

Other Investment Services

Dun & Bradstreet publishes *Key Business Ratios* in bound form. This publication contains 14 significant ratios on 800 different lines of business listed by SIC (standard industrial classification) code. Examples of ratios included are current assets to current debt, net profits on net sales, and total debt to tangible net worth. This publication has replaced the old Dun & Bradstreet 11-page pamphlet on key business ratios for 125 lines of business. Another good source of ratios is Robert Morris Associates, which provides ratios on over 150 industry classifications.

Dun's Marketing Services division of Dun & Bradstreet also publishes the *Million Dollar Directory* and *Billion Dollar Directory.* Companies are listed in alphabetical order, by geographical location by city and state, and by product classification. The data provide names, addresses and phone numbers, and sales for each company. This could be helpful in identifying companies in the same industry or in writing to request such information as annual reports or product lists.

Another publication is the *Dow Jones–Irwin Business Almanac.* Almost everyone has looked through an almanac at some time and probably remembers being overwhelmed by all the facts and figures. This almanac is no exception. For our specific purposes, there is a section on finance and accounting which covers key business ratios, financial statement ratios by industry, and corporate profits and margins. A section on the stock market covers over 100 pages and includes market averages, mutual funds, dividends, common stock prices and yields, and much more. Information on commodities, banks, financial institutions, economic data, and a great deal more is contained in this 600-page business almanac.

FIGURE 4–9

OPTIONS—RELEVANT INFORMATION FOR BUYERS AND WRITERS

Ratings & Reports Page No.	Stock Name	Stock Ticker Symbol	Where Option Trades	Recent Stock Price	Time lines (3-6 mos.)	Technical	Safety	Stock Stability Index	Stock Beta	Est'd Current P/E Ratio	Est'd Div'd Yield (next 12 mos)	Industry Group	Industry Rank
980	Colgate-Palmolive	CL	CBO	25	▲3	3	1	85	0.80	12.6	5.1	Household Products	89
1310	Colt Ind., Inc.	COT	PHL	57	2	3	3	50	0.95	8.4	4.6	Machinery	43
1311	Combustion Eng.	CSP	PAC	33	4	3	3	55	1.15	14.7	5.6	Machinery	43
2050	Comdisco, Inc.	CDO	PAC	15	2	3	4	5	1.45	8.6	1.3	Financial Services (Div)	1
1090	Commodore Int'l	CBU	PHL	10	5	5	4	5	1.55	10.5	NIL	Computer And Peripherals	64
708	Commonwealth Edison	CWE	CBO	30	3	2	3	95	0.65	6.7	10.7	Electric Util. (Central)	37
763	Communic. Satellite	CQ	PHL	32	▲2	2	3	50	1.05	9.2	3.9	Telecommunications	36
1278	Community Psych Ctrs.	CMY	PHL	34	1	2	3	30	1.45	23.8	0.7	Medical Services	3
2105	Computer Sciences	CSC	CBO	15	3	3	3	30	1.00	9.4	NIL	Computer Software & Svcs	48
1092	Computervision Corp	CVN	PHL	16	5	3	3	15	1.60	16.0	NIL	Computer And Peripherals	64
188	Consol. Edison	ED	ASE	33	▼4	1	1	100	0.65	7.9	7.5	Electric Utility (East)	42
764	Cont'l Telecom Inc.	CTC	ASE	23	4	2	2	95	0.75	8.1	7.8	Telecommunications	36
1093	Control Data	CDA	CBO	30	4	4	3	40	1.45	16.0	2.4	Computer And Peripherals	64
1313	Cooper Ind.	CBE	ASE	31	3	3	3	45	1.25	13.5	4.3	Machinery	43
224	Coopervision Inc.	EYE	ASE	22	—	—	3	NMF	NMF	14.7	1.8	Medical Supplies	50
1006	Corning Glass Works	GLW	CBO	38	3	3	2	80	1.05	14.3	3.4	Electrical Equipment	44
1095	Cray Research	CYR	PAC	73	▲1	3	3	15	1.45	17.9	NIL	Computer And Peripherals	64
933	Crown Zellerbach	ZB	ASE	42	—	3	3	50	1.20	13.0	2.4	Paper & Forest Products	57
2106	Cullinet Software	CUL	CBO	27	1	3	3	20	1.60	28.4	NIL	Computer Software & Svcs	48
1469	Dart & Kraft Inc.	DKI	ASE	93	3	2	1	100	0.75	9.5	4.9	Food Processing	35
1096	Data General Corp.	DGN	PAC	39	4	3	3	15	1.40	18.5	NIL	Computer And Peripherals	64
1097	Datapoint Corp.	DPT	CBO	14	4	5	4	5	1.45	NMF	NIL	Computer And Peripherals	64
1098	Dataproducts Corp.	DPC	PAC	12	5	4	3	15	1.70	9.6	1.3	Computer And Peripherals	64
1650	Dayton Hudson Corp.	DH	PAC	40	3	2	2	70	1.05	13.6	1.9	Retail Store	16
1433	Deere & Co.	DE	ASE	28	3	3	3	70	1.05	22.4	3.6	Agricultural Equip./Div	55
257	Delta Air Lines	DAL	CBO	42	▼2	3	3	40	1.15	7.0	1.9	Air Transport	28
410	Diamond Shamrock	DIA	PAC	19	3	4	3	50	1.05	10.7	9.3	Petroleum (Integrated)	79
1125	Diebold, Inc.	DBD	CBO	40	3	3	3	55	1.00	8.5	2.6	Office Equipment&Supply	8
1099	Digital Equipment	DEC	ASE,CBO	103	3	3	2	50	1.25	14.3	NIL	Computer And Peripherals	64
1756	Disney (Walt) Prod.	DIS	ASE,CBO	79	2	3	3	60	0.90	16.6	1.5	Recreation	65
1221	Dome Mines	DM	PHL	9¼	5	4	4	10	1.35	33.2	2.2	Gold (No. American)	91
190	Dominion Resources	D	PHL	30	3	3	2	100	0.60	8.5	9.3	Electric Utility (East)	42
1242	Dow Chemical	DOW	CBO	30	3	4	2	80	1.20	12.6	6.0	Chemical (Basic)	76
1846	Dresser Ind.	DI	PHL	21	3	4	3	40	1.20	12.7	4.3	Oilfield Services	87
191	Duke Power	DUK	PHL	33	3	1	2	100	0.60	8.0	7.7	Electric Utility (East)	42
1791	Dun & Bradstreet	DNB	ASE	76	2	2	2	90	0.90	20.4	2.9	Publishing	6
1243	Du Pont	DD	ASE,CBO	58	▼4	3	2	80	1.15	11.6	5.3	Chemical (Basic)	76
154	EG & G, Inc.	EGG	PHL	38	2	3	3	55	1.30	17.8	1.3	Precision Instrument	25
557	E-Systems	ESY	PAC	30	2	3	3	40	1.20	14.7	1.9	Aerospace/Diversified	18
1877	Eastern Gas & Fuel	EFU	PHL	22	4	3	3	55	0.95	13.7	5.9	Coal & Uranium	80
155	Eastman Kodak	EK	CDO	67	3	3	1	95	0.85	11.3	5.6	Precision Instrument	25
785	Eckerd (Jack) Corp.	ECK	CBO	27	3	3	3	65	1.00	10.7	3.9	Drug Store	11
1183	Edwards (A.G.) Inc.	AGE	CBO	31	3	3	3	20	1.70	14.8	2.7	Securities Brokerage	30
1009	Emerson Electric	EMR	ASE	72	2	3	1	95	0.90	12.0	3.6	Electrical Equipment	44
259	Emery Air Freight	EAF	PHL	16	▼4	3	3	25	1.30	10.3	3.1	Air Transport	28
1894	Engelhard Corp.	EC	CBO	27	4	3	3	55	0.95	12.0	2.7	Chemical/Diversified	66
453	ENSERCH Corp.	ENS	PAC	26	3	3	3	55	1.10	15.8	6.2	Natural Gas(Diversified)	75
411	Exxon Corp.	XON	CBO	52	3	1	1	100	0.85	7.5	6.8	Petroleum (Integrated)	79
260	Federal Express	FDX	CBO	38	4	2	3	35	1.40	24.2	NIL	Air Transport	28
1156	Federal Nat'l Mtg.	FNM	PHL	16	3	4	4	20	1.45	NMF	1.0	Savings & Loan	10
1157	Fin'l Ccrp. Of America	FIN	PHL	6½	5	5	5	5	1.85	NMF	NIL	Savings & Loan	10
130	Firestone Tire	FIR	ASE	20	3	3	3	60	0.95	10.0	4.0	Tire & Rubber	58
1184	First Boston Inc.	FBC	CBO	68	2	2	3	30	1.35	8.7	3.4	Securities Brokerage	30
650	First Chicago Inc.	FNB	CBO	25	4	3	3	50	1.05	6.7	5.3	Bank (Midwest)	13
1896	First Mississippi	FRM	ASE	9⅛	▼3	3	5	20	1.45	8.5	3.0	Chemical/Diversified	66
1560	Fleetwood Enterprises	FLE	ASE	22	3	3	3	20	1.35	10.4	1.7	Manu Housing/Rec Veh	31
870	Fluor Corp.	FLR	CBO	19	▲3	3	3	35	1.35	NMF	2.1	Building	32
105	Ford Motor	F	CBO	43	3	3	3	45	1.15	3.0	5.8	Auto & Truck	9
1367	Foster Wheeler	FWC	PAC	14	▲3	3	3	35	1.20	13.9	3.1	Machinery(Const.&Mining)	53
1223	Freeport McMoRan	FTX	CBO	21	3	4	3	25	1.40	13.5	2.9	Metals & Mining(General)	62
1897	GAF Corp.	GAF	PHL	32	1	2	3	35	1.00	10.6	0.6	Chemical/Diversified	66
158	GCA Corp.	GCA	ASE	25	3	4	4	10	1.60	10.7	NIL	Precision Instrument	25
766	GTE Corp.	GTE	ASE	41	3	3	1	95	0.90	7.8	7.6	Telecommunications	36
561	Gen'l Dynamics	GD	CBO	70	▼2	3	1	40	1.30	7.1	1.6	Aerospace/Diversified	18
1015	Gen'l Electric	GE	CBO	61	3	3	1	95	1.00	11.2	3.8	Electrical Equipment	44
1475	Gen'l Foods	GF	CBO	64	4	1	1	95	0.80	10.4	4.1	Food Processing	35
1052	Gen'l Instrument	GRL	PHL	17	▼5	4	3	25	1.40	NMF	1.5	Electronics	84
107	Gen'l Motors	GM	CBO	70	3	3	2	80	1.10	6.0	7.1	Auto & Truck	9
1053	GenRad	GEN	PHL	17	5	4	4	10	1.45	17.0	0.6	Electronics	84
117	Genuine Parts Co.	GPC	PAC	33	3	3	1	80	0.90	14.0	3.6	Auto Parts (Rep)	82
1850	GEO Int'l	GX	ASE	4⅞	4	4	4	10	1.45	NMF	NIL	Oilfield Services	87
937	Georgia-Pacific	GP	ASE	23	3	3	3	50	1.40	8.9	3.5	Paper & Forest Products	57
1103	Gerber Scientific	GRB	PHL	18	▼2	3	4	5	1.85	11.3	0.7	Computer And Peripherals	64
818	Gillette	GS	ASE	62	3	2	1	90	0.80	11.5	4.2	Toiletries/Cosmetics	33
1851	Global Marine	GLM	ASE	4⅛	5	5	5	10	1.55	NMF	6.0	Oilfield Services	87
1774	Golden Nugget	GNG	ASE	12	2	3	4	25	1.05	16.7	NIL	Hotel/Gaming	41
1160	Golden West Fin'l	GDW	PHL	30	1	2	4	10	1.50	6.2	0.8	Savings & Loan	10
133	Goodyear Tire	GT	ASE	27	4	3	3	75	1.05	8.0	5.9	Tire & Rubber	58
1054	Gould Inc.	GLD	ASE	22	4	4	3	40	1.15	11.2	3.1	Electronics	84
1898	Grace (W. R.)	GRA	ASE	41	4	3	2	90	0.95	13.8	6.8	Chemical/Diversified	66
1161	G't Western Fin'l	GWF	CBO	27	2	3	3	20	1.50	8.0	3.3	Savings & Loan	10
1391	Greyhound Corp.	G	ASE	28	3	3	2	75	1.10	9.2	4.3	Multiform	38
438	Gulf Canada Ltd.	GOC	PHL	15	▲2	3	3	25	1.30	11.3	2.9	Canadian Energy	67
1392	Gulf & Western Ind.	GW	CBO	38	4	3	3	70	1.10	10.7	2.4	Multiform	38
2076	Hall (Frank B.) & Co.	FBH	ASE	26	3	3	3	55	0.70	14.7	3.8	Insurance (Diversified)	69
1852	Halliburton Co.	HAL	CBO	32	5	4	3	40	1.35	11.6	6.0	Oilfield Services	87
1055	Harris Corp.	HRS	CBO	25	▼4	4	3	55	1.10	10.8	3.5	Electronics	84
626	Hecla Mining	HL	ASE	17	4	4	4	10	1.30	NMF	1.2	Lead. Zinc & Mining	71
1245	Hercules Inc.	HPC	ASE	33	3	3	3	60	1.10	9.6	4.8	Chemical (Basic)	76
1104	Hewlett-Packard	HWP	CBO	34	3	3	2	55	1.30	13.9	0.7	Computer And Peripherals	64
1775	Hilton Hotels	HLT	PAC	68	—	2	3	75	1.00	16.0	2.6	Hotel/Gaming	41
1571	Hitachi Ltd. (ADR)	HIT	CBO	32	3	4	3	55	0.90	10.6	1.0	Foreign Stocks/Japanese	22
1776	Holiday Inns Inc.	HIA	CBO	54	▲1	3	3	55	1.20	13.5	1.9	Hotel/Gaming	41
1226	Homestake Mining	HM	CBO	25	4	3	3	25	1.20	46.3	0.8	Gold (No. American)	91
1105	Honeywell, Inc.	HON	CBO	57	3	3	2	65	1.20	8.7	3.6	Computer And Peripherals	64
1280	Hospital Corp Of Amer	HCA	PAC	42	2	3	3	55	1.25	10.9	1.4	Medical Services	3
2053	Household Int'l Inc.	HI	ASE	36	3	3	2	75	0.90	8.1	4.9	Financial Services (Div)	1

ASE—American Stock Exchange　　　　PAC—Pacific Stock Exchange
CBO—Chicago Board Options Exchange　　　PHL—Philadelphia Stock Exchange

Source: "Summary of Advices and Index," *The Value Line Investment Survey*, May 3, 1985.

Weisenberger Services, Inc., publishes one of the best-known sources of information on mutual funds. The annual issue covers a 10-year statistical history (a sample page appears in Chapter 20) and is updated quarterly. Another publication which is like an investment service is the annual issue of The Individual Investor's Guide to No-Load Mutual Funds published by the American Association of Individual Investors.

Retail stockbrokers have long provided information to their clients. Of course, the more you can afford to pay and the bigger your account, the more research you may receive. Most large brokers, such as Merrill Lynch; Shearson Lehman/American Express; Bache; and E. F. Hutton, will provide investors information free and for a fee. You name what you want, and they have it—industry-company analysis, bond market analysis, futures and commodities, options advice, tax shelters in oil and gas and real estate, and so on. The brokerage industry provides much more sophisticated coverage of investments outside of stocks and bonds than they have in the past. This is partly because investors themselves have become more sophisticated in response to inflation and partly because of the increasing numbers and complexity of alternative investments.

INDEXES, SEC FILINGS, PERIODICALS, AND JOURNALS

Indexes

One way to find relevant articles in periodicals and journals is to use indexes. There are many that will lead an analyst to useful information. The *Business Periodicals Index* references subjects in approximately 170 periodicals in the fields of accounting, advertising, banking, communications, economics, finance, insurance, investments, labor management, marketing, taxation, and other specific topics. The *Funk and Scott Index of Corporations and Industries* indexes articles from over 750 publications in two volumes. Each article covered includes a brief description of the article's contents. The articles are taken from business, financial, and trade magazines, major newspapers, bank newsletters, and investment advisory services. One very popular index is *The Wall Street Journal Index,* which identifies the date, page, and column of articles appearing in *The Wall Street Journal.* The index is presented in two parts—corporate news and general news. Many libraries have several years of *The Wall Street Journal* on microfiche or microfilm. There are many other indexes, such as *Who's Who in Finance and Industry,* Dun & Bradstreet's *Reference Book of Corporate Management,* and Standard & Poor's *Register of Corporations, Directors and Executives.* These last three focus on people and can provide important qualitative information about management.

Securities and Exchange Commission Filings

As discussed in Chapter 2, the Securities and Exchange Commission (SEC) was established by the Securities Exchange Act of 1934 and has the power to

regulate trading on the exchanges and to require corporate disclosure of information relevant to the stockholders of publically traded companies. The SEC even has the power to dictate accounting conventions such as the mandatory inflation-adjusted accounting statements required in corporate annual reports.

Information available through the SEC consists primarily of corporate income statements, balance sheets, detailed support of accounting information, and internal data not always found in a company's annual report. There are specific reports that companies are required to file with the SEC. The annual 10-K report is perhaps the most widely known and can usually be obtained free of charge directly from the company rather than paying the SEC a copying charge. This report should be read in combination with the firm's annual report as it contains the same type of information, but in greater detail. The 8-K report must be filed when the corporation undergoes some important event that stockholders would be interested in knowing about, such as: changes in control, bankruptcy, resignation of officers or directors, and other material events. 10-Q statements are filed quarterly no later than 45 days after the end of the quarter. This report includes quarterly financial statements, changes in stockholdings, legal procedings, and other matters.

There are many other SEC reports. The most common are proxy statements which disclose information relevant to stockholders' votes; a prospectus which must be issued whenever a new offering of securities is made to the public, and a registration trading statement which is required for new issues by firms trading on an organized exchange or over-the-counter. Figure 4–10 presents a detailed listing of information available from SEC filings, including reports required for tender offers and acquisitions. This table is taken from Disclosure Inc., a firm providing on-line computer access to SEC filings and other information sources to subscribers. These reports can be obtained from the Disclosure retrieval system at 37¢ a page with a one-business-day turnaround, or they can be ordered from the Securities and Exchange Commission at 10¢ per page with a seven-business-day turnaround.[2] They can also be read at the SEC regional office, where the corporation is headquartered, or in the SEC's regional New York, Chicago, or Los Angeles offices. A list of SEC addresses is given in Appendix 4–B at the end of this chapter.

Periodicals and Newspapers

After using the *Business Periodical Index,* an investor will most likely be referred to several of the most popular business periodicals, such as *Fortune, Business Week, Forbes, Dun's Business Month, Financial World,* and others. *Fortune* is published biweekly and is known for its coverage of industry problems and specific company analysis. *Fortune* has several regular features that make interesting reading. One, called "Business Roundup," usually deals with a major business concern, such as the federal budget, inflation, productivity, etc.

---

[2] The costs will obviously change over time.

FIGURE 4–10 Securities Exchange Commission Filings

REPORT CONTENTS	10-K	19-K 20-F	10-Q	8-K	10-C	6-K	Proxy Statement	Prospectus	Registration Statements '34 Act F-10 8-A 8-B	Registration Statements '33 Act "S" Type	ARS	Listing Application	N-1R	N-1Q
Auditor														
Name	A	A	■				■		A	A	A	■	A	
Opinion	A	A					■			A	A		A	
Changes				A				■						
Compensation Plans														
Equity	■		■				F	F	A		F	■	■	
Monetary							F	F	A		F		■	
Company Information														
Nature of Business	A	A				F		A	A		A	■	■	
History	F	A						A		A		■		
Organization and Change	F■	F		A	■	F	■	A		F	A			
Debt Structure	A					F		A	A		A	A		A
Depreciation & Other Schedules	A	A				F		A	A		A			
Dilution Factors	A	A	F			F		A	A		A	A		
Directors, Officers, Insiders														
Identification	F	A				F	A	A	A		A	F		
Background	■	A				F	F	A	■		A	■		
Holdings		A		■			A	A	A		A			
Compensation		A					A	A	A		A			
Earnings Per Share	A	A	A			F			A		A		A	
Financial Information														
Annual Audited	A	A							A		A		A	
Interim Audited		A					■	■	■					
Interim Unaudited	■		A			F		F		F	F			
Foreign Operations	A							A	A		A	■	F	
Labor Contracts		■		■					F		F			
Legal Agreements	F	■		■					F		F			
Legal Counsel								A			A	■		
Loan Agreements	F		F	■					F		F	■		
Plants and Properties	A	F		■				F	A		F			
Portfolio Operations														
Content (Listing of Securities)														A
Management														A
Product-Line Breakout	A							A			A	■		
Securities Structure	A	A			■			A	A		A			
Subsidiaries	A	A					■	A	A		A	■		
Underwriting				■				A	A		A			
Unregistered Securities	■							F			F			
Block Movements			F					■	A			■		

TENDER OFFER ACQUISITION REPORTS	13D	13 G	14D-1	14D-9	13E-3	13E-4
Name of Issuer (Subject Company)	A	A	A	A	A	A
Filing Person (or Company)	A	A	A	A	A	A
Amount of Shares Owned	A	A				
Percent of Class Outstanding	A	A				
Financial Statements of Bidders			F		F	F
Purpose of Tender Offer			A	A	A	A
Source and Amount of Funds	A		A		A	
Identity and Background Information			A	A	A	
Persons Retained, Employed or to be Compensated			A	A	A	A
Exhibits	F		F	F	F	F

Legend

A-always included - included-if occured or significant

F-frequently included

■ special circumstances only

Source: "A Guide to SEC Corporate Filings," (Bethesda, Md.: Disclosure, Inc. April 1983), pp. 12–13.

Another feature, "Personal Investing," is always a thought-provoking article presenting ideas and analysis for the average investor.

Forbes is also a biweekly publication featuring several company-management interviews. This management-oriented approach points out various management styles and provides a look into the qualitative factors of security analysis. There are several regular columnists who discuss investment topics from a diversified perspective. *Business Week* is somewhat more general in nature than *Forbes.* It includes a weekly economic update on such economic variables as interest rates, electricity consumption, and market prices while also featuring articles on industries and companies. Many other periodicals, such as *The Harvard Business Review,* and *Money Magazine,* are helpful to the financial manager or personal investor. Unfortunately, space limits describing very many.

Most major city newspapers (Chicago, Dallas, and Cleveland, to name a few) have good financial sections. The *New York Times* has an exceptional financial page. However, the most widely circulated financial daily is *The Wall Street Journal,* published by Dow Jones. This is the paper that is read by millions of investors in order to keep up with the economy and business environment. Feature articles on labor, business, economics, personal investing, technology, and taxes appear weekly. Corporate announcements of all kinds are published. Figure 4–11, "Digest of Earnings Reports," is a daily feature that updates quarterly and annual earnings of firms.

New offerings of stocks and bonds are also advertised by investment bankers in the *Journal.* Prices of actively traded securities are presented by market. Common stock prices are organized by exchange and over-the-counter markets. Figure 4–12 is an example of common stock prices on the New York Stock Exchange. Along with the prices, notice that trading volume by markets is presented, and that the most active securities for the day are listed.

Many other prices are printed in *The Wall Street Journal.* An investor will find prices of mutual funds, government Treasury bills, notes and bonds, put and call prices from the option exchanges, government agency securities, foreign exchange prices, and commodities future prices. Figure 4–13 is an example of the future prices from the *Journal.* The prices are listed by category and exchange. Because of the comprehensive price coverage on a daily basis and other features, it is hard to believe that an up-to-date intelligent investor would be able to function without *The Wall Street Journal.* Each Fall *The Wall Street Journal* publishes an educational edition which explains how to read *The Wall Street Journal* and interpret some of the data presented.

Barron's National Business and Financial Weekly is also published by Dow Jones (every Monday). It contains regular features on dividends, put and call options, international stock markets, commodities, a review of the stock market, and many pages of prices and financial statistics. *Barron's* takes a weekly perspective and summarizes the previous week's market behavior. It also has regular analysis of several companies in its section called "Investment News and Views." The common stock section of *Barron's* not only

FIGURE 4–11

Digest of Earnings Reports

ADVANCED MICRO DEVICES (N)

13 wk June 24:	1984	1983
Sales	$234,266,000	$108,034,000
Net income ...	38,202,000	8,124,000
Avg shares	58,038,000	a57,048,000
Shr earns (com & com equiv):		
Net income	.66	a.14

a-Adjusted for a two-for-one stock split paid in August 1983.

AMERICAN ECOLOGY CORP. (O)

Quar June 30:	1984	1983
Sales	$10,656,000	$10,403,000
Net income ...	1,341,000	930,000
Shr earns:		
Net income .	.46	.32
6 months:		
Sales	19,202,000	20,217,000
Net income .	1,940,000	1,507,000
Shr earns:		
Net income .	.67	.52

AMERICAN SECURITY CORP. (O)

Quar June 30:	1984	1983
Net income ...	$4,594,000	$7,405,000
Shr earns:		
Net income .	.40	a.67
6 months:		
Net income .	11,768,000	15,089,000
Shr earns:		
Net income .	1.04	a1.36

a-Adjusted to reflect a three-for-two stock split paid in May 1984.

ASTROSYSTEMS INC. (O)

9 mo May 31:	1984	1983
Sales	$6,413,000	$6,831,000
Net income	2,063,000	2,241,000
Shr earns (primary):		
Net income .	.39	.41
Shr earns (fully diluted):		
Net income .	.39	.40

BANCO DE PONCE (O)

Quar June 30:	1984	1983
Income	$3,017,494	$2,747,338
Extrd cred ...	2,488,458	
Net income ..	5,505,953	2,747,338
Shr earns:		
Income	1.86	1.69
Net income .	3.39	1.69
6 Months:		
Income	6,029,506	5,670,166
Extrd cred ...	2,488,458	
Net income .	8,517,964	5,670,166
Shr earns:		
Income	3.72	3.49
Net income .	5.25	3.49

BEECHAM GROUP PLC (O)

Year Mar 31:	1984	1983
Sales	$2,560,200,000	$2,242,100,000
Net inco	213,100,000	200,100,000

The above results have been computed at the pound's current rate.

BINKS MANUFACTURING CO. (A)

Quar May 31:	1984	1983
Sales	$41,012,000	$29,718,000
Net income ...	1,764,000	1,228,000
Shr earns:		
Net income .	.57	.40
6 months:		
Sales	67,572,000	55,543,000
Net income .	2,945,000	2,120,000
Shr earns:		
Net income .	.96	.69

BLUESKY OIL & GAS LTD. (O)

Year Apr 30:	1984	a1983
Revenues	$23,735,936	$17,854,336
Net income ..	9,213,072	5,344,693
Shr earns:		
Net income .	.34	.20

a-Restated.

Amounts in Canadian dollars.

CHEMFIX TECHNOLOGIES (O)

Quar May 31:	1984	1983
Sales	$253,832	$1,456,260
Net loss	518,620	b128,731
Shr earns:		
Net loss	....	c.03
9 months:		
Sales	3,059,890	4,332,485
Net loss	649,976	b316,965
Shr earns:		
Net loss	....	c.06

b-Income. c-Income; adjusted for a three-for-one stock split paid in July 1983.

COMPACT VIDEO INC. (O)

Year Apr 30:	1984	f1983
Revenues ....:	$35,741,000	$29,024,000
Loss cnt op ..	a1,686,000	b720,000
Inco dis op ..		c677,000
Net loss	a1,686,000	b1,397,000
Shr earns:		
Loss cnt op .	....	e.22
Net loss	....	e.43
Quarter:		
Revenues	10,852,000	7,937,000
Loss cnt op ..	a1,795,000	e188,000
Inco dis op ...		c196,000
Net loss	a1,795,000	e384,000
Shr earns:		
Loss cnt op .	....	e.06
Net loss	....	e.12

a-Includes charge of $1,438,000 primarily from writedown of assets and certain assessments. b-Income; includes gain of $908,000 from sale and leaseback of real estate. c-From gain on disposal of discontinued operations. e-Income. f-Restated.

FEDERAL CO. (N)

Year June 2:	1984	1983
Revenues .	$1,303,754,000	$1,122,844,000
Net income ..	41,367,000	25,707,000
Shr earns:		
Net income .	5.03	3.13
Quarter:		
Revenues .	377,011,000	295,568,000
Net income .	13,304,000	3,467,000
Shr earns:		
Net income .	1.62	.42

FLAGLER BANK CORP. (O)

Quar June 30:	1984	1983
Net income ..	$473,088	$318,077
Shr earns:		
Net income .	.37	a.25
6 months:		
Net income .	901,128	595,802
Shr earns:		
Net income .	.71	a.47

a-Adjusted for a four-for-one stock split paid in January 1984 and a 10% stock dividend paid in December 1983.

GENERAL MILLS INC. (N)

Year May 27:	1984	1983
Sales	$5,600,800,000	$5,550,800,000
Net income ..	233,400,000	245,100,000
Avg shrs	46,900,000	50,100,000
Shr earns:		
Net income .	4.98	4.89
13 weeks:		
Sales	1,361,100,000	1,341,300,000
Net income ..	40,500,000	55,100,000
Avg shrs	45,700,000	49,200,000
Shr earns:		
Net income .	.90	1.13

GENERAL MICROWAVE CORP. (O)

Quar June 2:	1984	1983
Sales	$3,173,694	$2,594,054
Net income .	368,472	225,633
Avg shares ..	1,329,312	917,367
Shr earns:		
Net income .	.28	.25

H & H OIL TOOL CO. (O)

Quar May 31:	1984	1983
Revenues	$4,207,000	$3,406,000
Net loss	34,000	318,000

HADRON INC. (O)

Year Mar 31:	1984	a1983
Revenues	$29,554,000	$28,263,000
Inco cnt op ..	156,000	1,232,000
Loss dis op ..	2,882,000	859,000
Loss	2,726,000	c373,000
Extrd cred ...	b23,000	b129,000
Net loss	2,703,000	c502,000
Shr earns:		
Inco cnt op ..	.01	.10
Loss	....	c.03
Net loss	....	c.04

a-Restated to reflect discontinued operations. b-Tax-loss carry-forward. c-Income.

HIGHWOOD RESOURCES (O)

Year Jan 31:	1984	1983
Revenues	$167,025	$275,967
Net loss	a561,333	80,431

a-Includes a $366,513 write-down of non-productive Canadian petroleum and natural gas properties. Amounts in Canadian dollars.

KOGER PROPERTIES INC. (N)

Year Mar 31:	1984	1983
Revenues	$41,760,000	$37,675,000
Net income ..	3,876,000	4,185,000
Shr earns (com & com equiv):		
Net income .	.61	.68

NATIONAL ENVIRON CNTRLS (O)

Quar May 1:	1984	1983
Sales :..........	$2,315,939	$1,996,271
Net loss	187,640	c81,748
Shr earns:		
Net loss	....	c.02
9 months:		
Sales	6,634,888	5,771,564
Net loss	142,734	c307,788
Shr earns:		
Net loss	....	c.09

c-Income.

SCHULMAN (A.) INC. (O)

Quar May 31:	1984	1983
Sales	$87,371,000	$72,409,000
Net income ...	3,148,000	2,764,000
Shr earns:		
Net income .	.60	a.52
9 months:		
Sales	238,541,000	197,084,000
Net income .	8,155,000	6,335,000
Shr earns:		
Net income .	1.54	a1.20

a-Adjusted for a two-for-one stock split paid in November 1983.

TRECO INC. (O)

Year Mar 31:	1984	1983
Revenues	$29,044,139	$29,576,764
Income	2,766,564	2,044,141
Extrd cred ...	b1,889,000	a6,265,689
Net income ...	4,655,564	8,309,830
Shr earns (primary):		
Income	.56	.41
Net income .	.95	1.67
Shr earns (fully diluted):		
Income	.35	.26
Net income .	.60	.98
Quarter:		
Revenues	10,445,312	8,158,493
Income	414,147	2,713,966
Extrd cred ...	b639,000	b1,784,000
Net income .	1,053,147	4,497,966
Shr earns (primary):		
Income	.05	.61
Net income .	.17	1.01
Shr earns (fully diluted):		
Income	.05	.31
Net income .	.15	.55

a-Consists of a $2,420,689 gain from early extinguishment of debt and a $3,845,000 tax-loss carry-forward. b-Tax-loss carry-forward.

VALLEY NATIONAL BANCORP (O)

Quar June 30:	1984	1983
Net income ..	$4,128,551	$3,554,434
Shr earns:		
Net income .	1.74	1.50
6 months:		
Net income .	8,173,522	7,012,922
Shr earns:		
Net income .	3.45	2.96

VYQUEST INC. (O)

Quar May 31:	1984	a1983
Inco cnt op	$944,000	$13,000
Loss dis op		65,000
Net income	944,000	d52,000
Shr earns (primary):		
Inco cnt op ..	.25	....
Net income .	.25	....
Shr earns (fully diluted):		
Net income .	.24	....
6 months:		
Inco cnt op	1,346,000	326,000
Loss dis op	22,000	168,000
Net income ..	1,324,000	158,000
Shr earns (primary):		
Inco cnt op ..	.35	b.08
Net income .	.34	b.04
Shr earns (fully diluted):		
Inco cnt op ..	.34	b.08
Net income .	.33	b.04

a-Restated to reflect discontinued operations. b-Adjusted for a two-for-one stock split paid in January 1984. d-Loss.

(N) New York Stock Exchange
(A) American Exchange (O) Over-the-Counter (Pa) Pacific (M) Midwest (P) Philadelphia (B) Boston (T) Toronto (Mo) Montreal (F) Foreign.

FIGURE 4–12 Common Stock Prices

40 THE WALL STREET JOURNAL
Friday, July 20, 1984

Thursday's Volume

100,777,200 Shares; 180,200 Warrants

TRADING BY MARKETS

	Shares	Warrants
New York Exchange	85,230,000	180,200
Midwest Exchange	6,171,800	....
Pacific Exchange	3,317,900	....
Nat'l Assoc. of Securities Dealers	3,434,940	....
Philadelphia Exchange	1,438,100	....
Boston Exchange	844,700	....
Cincinnati Exchange	174,400	....
Instinet System	165,400	....

NYSE – Composite

Volume since Jan. 1:	1984	1983	1982
Total shares	14,778,612,529	14,069,232,820	8,484,830,046
Total Warrants	52,416,500	91,296,400	21,308,850

New York Stock Exchange

Volume since Jan. 1:	1984	1983	1982
Total shares	12,454,764,269	12,076,685,005	7,296,119,596
Total warrants	50,521,100	90,845,300	21,282,500

ACTIVE STOCKS

	Open	High	Low	Close	Chg.	Volume
ITT Corp	22 1/8	24	22	23 5/8	+ 1 3/8	2,703,500
Amer T&T n	17 3/4	18	17 3/4	17 7/8	+ 1/4	1,855,500
Unocal	35 1/4	38 3/8	35 1/4	38	+ 2 1/8	1,451,000
ContIllCp	4 1/8	4 1/8	3 1/4	3 3/8	− 1	1,388,400
Ramada Inn	6	6 1/8	5 3/4	5 3/4	− 3/4	983,700
StRegisCp	46 1/2	47 3/8	43 3/4	44	− 2 3/4	970,800
AMD s	29 1/4	29 1/4	26 3/8	26 5/8	− 2 7/8	966,400
Phila Elec	11 1/4	11 1/4	9	10 3/8	− 1	912,000
IBM	107 3/8	107 3/8	106 1/4	107	− 1/2	895,900
Pfizer	30 3/4	30 7/8	29 3/4	30 1/4	− 5/8	889,500
Revlon	39	39 3/4	38 7/8	39 1/4	+ 1/8	887,700
FordMot s	38 1/2	39 3/8	38 1/4	38 5/8	.....	872,300
Comdreint	22 5/8	22 5/8	19 3/4	20	− 2 3/4	821,000
LTV Corp	10 1/4	10 3/8	10 1/8	10 1/4	− 1/4	820,000
Colg Palm	23	23	22 1/2	22 3/4	− 1/4	792,700

52 Weeks High	Low	Stock	Div.	Yld %	P-E Ratio	Sales 100s	High	Low	Close	Net Chg.

NYSE-Composite Transactions

Thursday, July 19, 1984

Quotations include trades on the Midwest, Pacific, Philadelphia, Boston and Cincinnati stock exchanges and reported by the National Association of Securities Dealers and Instinet

FIGURE 4–13

Futures Prices

Thursday, July 19, 1984.

Open Interest-Reflects Previous Trading Day.

Col. headers (repeated throughout): Open | High | Low | Settle | Change | Lifetime High | Low | Open Interest

GRAINS AND OILSEEDS

- CORN (CBT) 5,000 bu.; cents per bu.
- CORN (MCE) 1,000 bu.; cents per bu.
- OATS (CBT) 5,000 bu.; cents per bu.
- SOYBEANS (CBT) 5,000 bu.; cents per bu.
- SOYBEANS (MCE) 1,000 bu.; cents per bu.
- SOYBEAN MEAL (CBT) 100 tons; $ per ton.
- SOYBEAN OIL (CBT) 60,000 lbs.; cents per lb.
- WHEAT (CBT) 5,000 bu.; cents per bu.
- WHEAT (KC) 5,000 bu.; cents per bu.
- WHEAT (MPLS) 5,000 bu.; cents per bu.
- WHEAT (MCE) 1,000 bu.; cents per bu.
- BARLEY (WPG) 20 metric tons; Can. $ per ton
- FLAXSEED (WPG) 20 metric tons; Can. $ per ton
- RAPESEED (WPG) 20 metric tons; Can. $ per ton
- RYE (WPG) 20 metric tons; Can. $ per ton

- COTTON (CTN) 50,000 lbs.; cents per lb.
- ORANGE JUICE (CTN) 15,000 lbs.; cents per lb.
- SUGAR—WORLD (CSCE) 112,000 lbs.; cents per lb.
- SUGAR—DOMESTIC (CSCE) 112,000 lbs.; cents per lb.

METALS & PETROLEUM

- COPPER (CMX) 25,000 lbs.; cents per lb.
- GOLD (CMX) 100 troy oz.; $ per troy oz.
- GOLD (IMM) 100 troy oz.; $ per troy oz.
- PLATINUM (NYM) 50 troy oz.; $ per troy oz.
- PALLADIUM (NYM) 100 troy oz.; $ per troy oz.
- SILVER (CMX) 5,000 troy oz.; cents per troy oz.

WOOD

- LUMBER (CME) 130,000 bd. ft.; $ per 1,000 bd. ft.

FINANCIAL

- BRITISH POUND (IMM) 25,000 pounds; $ per pound
- CANADIAN DOLLAR (IMM) 100,000 dlrs.; $ per Can $
- JAPANESE YEN (IMM) 12.5 million yen; $ per yen (.00)
- SWISS FRANC (IMM) 125,000 francs-$ per franc
- W. GERMAN MARK (IMM) 125,000 marks; $ per mark
- EURODOLLAR (LIFFE) $1 million; pts of 100%
- STERLING DEPOSIT (LIFFE) £250,000; pts of 100%
- LONG GILT (LIFFE) £50,000; pts of 100%
- EURODOLLAR (IMM) $1 million; pts of 100%
- GNMA 8% (CBT) $100,000 prncpl.; pts. 32nds. of 100%
- TREASURY BONDS (CBT) $100,000; pts. 32nds of 100%
- TREASURY NOTES (CBT) $100,000; pts. 32nds of 100%
- TREASURY BILLS (IMM) $1 mil.; pts. of 100%
- BANK CDs (IMM) $1 million; pts. of 100%

FIGURE 4–14 Market Transactions from *Barron's*

INDEX TO STATISTICS

WEEK'S MARKET TRANSACTIONS

NYSE COMPOSITE

[Dense stock quotation tables with columns: 52-Weeks High Low, Name and Dividend, Sales 100s, Yield Pct, P-E Ratio, Week's High Low Last, Net Chg., Interim or Fiscal Year (Earnings), Year ago, Latest divs, Record date, Payment date (Dividends) — listing securities A–B–C–D–E... including AAR, AMCA, AMF, AMR Cp, APL, ARA, ASA, AVX, AbtLab, AccoWd, AcmeC, AcmeE, AdamDg, AdaEX, AdmMl, AdvSys, Advest, Aetna, Aileen, AirbFrt, AirPrd, AlMoa, AlaP, Alagco, and many others.]

a Also extra or extras
b Annual rate plus stock dividend
c Liquidating dividend
d New 52-week low
e Declared or paid in preceding 12 months
g Dividend or earnings in Canadian money. Stock trades in U.S. dollars. No yield or PE shown unless stated in U.S. money
i Declared or paid after stock dividend or split up

j Paid this year, dividend omitted, deferred or no action taken at last dividend meeting
k Declared or paid this year, an accumulative issue with dividend in arrears
m Months for which share results are given
n New issue in the past 52 weeks. The high-low range begins with the start of trading in the new issue and does not cover the entire 52-week period

q Quarterly
r Declared or paid in preceding 12 months plus stock dividend
rt Rights
s Stock split or stock dividend amounting to 25 per cent or more in the past 52 weeks. The high-low range is adjusted from the old stock. Dividend begins with the date of split or stock dividend.
sa Semi-annual
t Paid in stock in preceding 12 months, estimated cash value on ex-dividend or ex-distribution date

u New 52-week high
un Units
v Trading halted on primary market
w When issued
wd When distributed
wi When issued
wt Warrants
x Ex-dividend or ex rights
x-dis Ex-distribution
xw Without warrants

y Ex-dividend and sales in full
z Sales in full
cld Called
vj In Bankruptcy or receivership or being reorganized under the Bankruptcy act, or securities assumed by such companies
D Deficit per share
Def Deficit
E Estimated
I Includes non-recurring loss

M Monthly
S Payments in stock
X Includes non-recurring profit
Y Latest dividend paid on date indicated
♦ Dividend declared
⊙ Dividend omitted or deferred
▲ New earnings

provides weekly high-low-close prices and volume, but also informs investors as to the latest earnings per share, dividends declared, and the dividend record and payable dates. This can be seen in the middle portion of Figure 4–14.

One unique feature of *Barron's* is the "Market Laboratory" covering the last five pages of each issue. Weekly data on major stock indexes are presented with the week's market statistics. Special weekly tables also include: Pulse of Industry and Trade and Economic and Financial Indicators. Figures 4–15 and 4–16 show some of the tables from *Barron's* Market Laboratory. Careful reading of this publication will turn up useful data in a compact summary form not found in other publications.

Other major papers would be *The Wall Street Transcript* (weekly) and the *Commercial and Financial Chronicle* (weekly). *The Media General Financial Weekly* is an exceptional source of fundamental and technical indicators for the professional manager. Over 3,400 common stocks are divided into 60 industrial groups and analyzed based on relative strength (whether they are leading or lagging the market), trends, earnings, and other variables that may be useful to the analyst.

Journals

Most journals are academic and, because of this, are more theoretical than practical or trade oriented. However there are several that are industry oriented, such as the *Financial Analysts Journal,* which is a publication of the Financial Analysts Federation. This journal has both academic and practitioner articles that deal mainly with analytical tools, new laws and regulations, and financial analysis. *The Journal of Portfolio Management* and the *Institutional Investor* are also well read by the profession. The more scholarly, research-oriented academic journals would include the *Journal of Finance, Journal of Financial Economics, Financial Management,* and the *Journal of Financial and Quantitative Analysis.* These journals include information on the development and testing of theories, such as the random walk and efficient market hypothesis, capital asset pricing model, portfolio theories, and much empirical research on a variety of financial topics. Lastly, the *Journal of Financial Education* includes articles on classroom topics and computer applications.

COMPUTER DATA BASES

More computer-accessible data bases have become available in the last several years as home computer usage has increased and data-based storage management has improved. Currently, there are several major sources of data that are available for use in large mainframe computers on magnetic tapes, or that are accessible on an interactive, time-sharing basis. Many of these data bases are now accessible from a personal computer.

FIGURE 4–15

BARRON'S MARKET LABORATORY

Dow Jones Hourly Averages

30 Industrials

	May 6	7	8	9	10
Open	1246.91	1248.23	1248.67	1251.88	1268.99
11:00	1250.77	1252.21	1251.10	1254.09	1268.11
12:00	1249.45	1257.73	1250.33	1253.86	1272.75
1:00	1250.55	1256.29	1246.80	1253.64	1273.30
2:00	1249.56	1255.08	1247.35	1255.30	1275.84
3:00	1249.89	1251.88	1247.78	1259.05	1275.18
Close	1247.79	1252.76	1249.78	1260.27	1274.18
High	1256.40	1261.37	1258.94	1265.57	1282.46
Low	1241.39	1243.15	1239.51	1246.58	1261.59
Change	+0.55	+4.97	−2.98	+10.49	+13.91
Advances	16	21	10	22	26
Declines	9	6	18	5	0
Unchanged	5	3	2	3	4

Intra-day range: High 1282.46 Low 1239.51

20 Transportation Cos.

	May 6	7	8	9	10
Open	585.25	586.47	588.80	595.22	610.27
11:00	587.58	586.80	588.24	597.43	610.94
12:00	586.47	588.68	589.90	597.21	612.05
1:00	587.36	587.91	590.35	598.10	614.04
2:00	588.35	587.80	591.78	598.65	617.91
3:00	588.13	586.47	591.78	602.30	617.21
Close	587.36	588.46	594.66	604.30	617.03
High	592.01	591.23	597.54	606.51	621.46
Low	582.04	584.15	584.48	592.34	607.06
Change	+2.88	+1.10	+6.20	+9.64	+12.73
Advances	12	10	12	17	18
Declines	7	4	6	1	1
Unchanged	1	6	2	2	1

Intra-day range: High 621.46 Low 582.04

15 Utilities

	May 6	7	8	9	10
Open	154.75	155.42	157.57	157.98	159.31
11:00	154.90	156.34	158.03	158.39	159.26
12:00	155.06	156.39	157.78	158.65	159.47
1:00	155.42	156.24	157.57	158.75	159.42
2:00	155.21	156.19	157.88	158.34	159.98
3:00	154.90	156.29	158.03	158.85	159.83
Close	155.47	157.67	157.83	159.11	159.73
High	155.98	158.14	159.62	159.73	160.60
Low	153.93	154.75	156.24	157.06	158.19
Change	+0.52	+2.20	+0.16	+1.28	+0.62
Advances	7	10	7	10	12
Declines	3	1	6	2	3
Unchanged	5	4	2	3	0

Intra-day range: High 160.60 Low 153.93

65 Stocks Composite

	May 6	7	8	9	10
Open	507.12	508.05	509.78	512.24	520.45
11:00	508.64	509.52	510.46	513.48	520.37
12:00	508.15	511.28	510.53	513.51	521.82
1:00	508.80	510.69	509.70	513.72	522.39
2:00	508.70	510.35	510.33	514.03	524.17
3:00	508.57	509.34	510.48	516.02	523.78
Close	508.18	510.71	511.54	516.90	523.45
High	511.54	513.61	515.27	518.97	526.86
Low	504.66	505.98	505.95	509.86	517.39
Change	+1.06	+2.53	+0.83	+5.36	+6.55
Advances	35	41	29	49	56
Declines	19	11	30	8	4
Unchanged	11	13	6	8	5

Intra-day range: High 526.86 Low 504.66

Shares Traded on N.Y. Exchange

	May 6	7	8	9	10
10-11	23,290	23,580	27,080	26,480	44,730
11-12	13,010	19,910	17,140	16,430	24,270
12- 1	12,530	15,690	15,660	13,390	20,680
1- 2	9,900	9,270	11,020	9,900	18,700
2- 3	10,370	13,900	10,820	16,700	15,350
3- 4	16,550	17,800	19,550	28,090	16,530
Total, ths	85,650	100,150	101,270	110,990	140,260
Dow Jones Stock Averages					
30 Ind	7,100.7	9,141.1	9,708.6	16,318.6	16,462.4
20 Tran	3,701.1	3,780.1	3,873.2	3,635.7	7,913.4
15 Util	2,928.6	3,362.8	3,102.0	2,067.0	2,635.7
65 Stock	13,730.4	16,284.0	16,683.8	22,021.3	27,011.5
Ratio of 10 Most Active Stocks (Composite) to total trading:	13.57	11.52	10.25	13.09	9.89
Average closings (Composite) of 10 Most Active Stocks:	43.36	32.22	43.12	46.74	38.35

Dow Jones Bond Averages

	May 6	7	8	9	10
20 Bonds	75.19	75.40	75.35	75.46	75.75
10 Util	72.12	72.62	72.55	72.45	72.90
10 Ind	78.26	78.18	78.15	78.45	78.61

NYSE Odd-Lot Trading

	May 3	6	7	8	9
Purch th shs	188.7	183.6	195.5	186.9	180.0
Sales, th shs	398.4	438.0	418.5	363.2	414.8
Short sales, sh	17,043	4,654	2,753	695	1,741

Dow Jones Weekly Averages

Dow Jones Stock Averages

	First	High	Low	Last	Chg.
Indus	1247.79	1274.18	1247.79	1247.18	+ 26.94
Trans	587.36	617.03	587.36	617.03	+ 32.55
Utils	155.47	159.73	155.47	159.73	+ 4.78
Comp	508.18	523.45	508.18	523.45	+ 16.33

Dow Jones Stock Diary

	Advances	Declines	Unchanged
Indus	24	5	1
Trans	20	0	0
Utils	13	0	2
Comp	57	5	3

Dow Jones Bond Averages

	First	High	Low	Last	Chg.
20 Bonds	75.19	75.75	75.19	75.75	+ 0.69
10 Util	72.12	72.90	72.12	72.90	+ 0.93
10 Ind	78.26	78.61	78.15	78.61	+ 0.45

Dow Jones Averages for 1985

Dow Jones Stock Averages

	First	High	Low	Last	Chg	%
Ind	1198.87	1299.36	1184.96	1274.18	+ 62.61	+ 5.17
Trp	553.70	635.30	553.03	617.03	+ 58.90	+ 10.55
Util	147.77	159.73	146.54	159.73	+ 10.21	+ 6.83
Cmp	484.96	528.78	480.93	523.45	+ 33.59	+ 6.86

Stock averages are compiled daily by using the following divisors: Industrials, 1.132; Transports, 1.129; Utilities, 2.437; 65 Stks Comp., 4.830.

Dow Jones Bond Averages

	First	High	Low	Last	Chg	%
20 Bds	72.64	75.75	72.27	75.75	+ 3.30	+ 4.55
10 Util	68.75	72.90	68.62	72.90	+ 4.07	+ 5.91
10 Ind	76.53	78.61	75.61	78.61	+ 2.54	+ 3.34

Dow Jones Price-Earnings Ratio

	May 10 1985	April 10 1985	May 10 1984	May 10 1983
Industrials	11.2	11.1	16.1	134.4
Trnsprt Cos	9.9	9.5	13.1	18.7
Utilities	7.6	7.4	6.6	7.0

Per share earnings for 12 months ended Dec. 31.

Standard & Poor's Price-Earnings Ratio

	Last Week	Prev. Week	Last Year
500 Composite	10.80	10.66	11.38
400 Industrials	11.14	11.04	12.28

Based on week ended Wednesday. Per share earnings for 12 months ended Dec. 31.

NASDAQ OTC Indexes

Index	5/10/85	% Chg.
Industrial	299.58	+ 2.66
Composite	287.46	+ 2.55
Bank	270.61	+ 1.23
Insurance	345.00	+ 3.27
Other Finance	354.55	+ 2.22
Transportation	360.61	+ 3.33
Utilities	277.05	+ 2.44

(February 5, 1971, equals 100.00)

Other Market Indicators

	May 6	7	8	9	10
NYSE Comp.	104.18	104.59	104.56	105.31	106.64
Ind.	118.90	119.32	119.15	119.93	121.40
Util.	55.72	55.98	56.09	56.41	56.94
Tran.	95.68	96.10	96.62	97.97	99.58
Fin.	111.22	111.85	112.23	113.67	115.98
Amex Index	225.78	226.04	225.07	226.64	228.17
OTC-a Comp.	279.85	280.89	281.07	283.27	287.46
Ind.	290.82	291.91	291.65	294.38	299.58
Insur.	334.84	336.41	338.13	340.92	345.00
Banks	267.22	268.14	268.77	270.07	270.61
NMS-b Comp.	118.01	118.47	118.60	119.58	121.45
NMS-b Ind.	108.00	108.41	108.39	109.48	111.52
S&P 500 Comp.	179.99	180.76	180.62	181.92	184.28
S&P 400 Ind.	199.63	200.44	200.08	201.45	203.95
Value Line	191.10	191.74	191.86	193.29	195.60

a-NASDAQ. b-National Market System.

Week's Market Statistics

	Last week	Prev. week	Last year
Sales NYSE, th sh	538,475	504,642	439,565
Sales AMEX, th sh	36,640	34,100	27,840
Sales OTC, th sh-a	383,140	347,220	285,896
Sales Dow Indus, th sh	58,731	50,094	42,814
Sales Dow Transp, th sh	22,904	24,937	15,269
Sales Dow Utils, th sh	14,096	12,540	10,949
Sales Dow Comp, th sh	95,731	87,571	69,032
Bond offerings, th $-v	2,693,460	2,826,800	1,047,031
Stock offerings, th $-v	383,044	544,995	219,950
Low Price Stk. Index-v	245.12	241.31	247.75
Volume, th sh	674.6	1,077.8	1,450.7
%vol to DJI vol	1.32	2.14	3.09
20 Most Active Stocks:			
Average price	43.22	47.20	42.49
% vol to total vol	14.34	20.77	15.61
NYSE volume report, Apr. 26:			
Buy/sell, th sh-w	484,712	459,017	431,889
Total shorts, th sh	37,304.6	37,277.2	41,129.2
Public shorts, th sh	7,710.6	7,279.6	8,514.9
Member trading, Apr. 26:			
Member shrt, th sh-x	29,594.0	29,997.6	32,614.3
Speclst shrt, th sh	14,180.8	15,316.9	13,648.9
Purchases, th sh	128,378.0	120,984.0	118,952.4
Sales, th sh-z	125,829.0	127,039.8	121,139.3
Net buy/sell, th sh	+2,549.0	−6,055.8	−2,186.9
% vol to NYSE vol	26.22	27.02	27.80
Odd-lot trading, Apr. 26:			
Purchases, th sh	1,564	1,827	1,526
Purchases, th $	58,459	64,550	52,353
Sales, th sh-z	3,417	3,748	3,367
Sales, th $	134,557	136,786	124,187
Short sales, actual	33,447	43,813	12,409
Bond vol, NYSE, th $	182,380	144,627	163,318
Best Grade Bonds %-y	11.58	11.61	12.39
Intrm Grade Bonds %-y	12.42	12.54	13.85
Confidence Index-c	93.2	92.6	89.5
T-Bill/Eurodollar Futures Spread, %	+0.88	+0.94	+1.80
Saloman Govt./Corp. Yield Spread, %	−1.58	−1.59	N.A.
Stock/Bond Yield Gap-s	−6.77	−6.71	−7.61
Yield Returns on Dow-Jones Averages:			
30 Industrials, %	4.81	4.90	4.78
20 Transports, %	2.38	2.50	2.71
15 Utilities, %	8.67	8.92	10.18
20 Bonds, %-y	12.04	12.14	13.51
10 Utils, %-y	12.46	12.58	14.64
10 Indus, %-y	11.61	11.71	12.38
Bond Buyers' 20 Muni Bond Index, %-y	9.11	9.37	10.19

a-NASDAQ. c-Ratio best grade to intermediate grade bonds. r-Revised. s-Spread between dividend yield on DJI and yield to maturity on best grade bonds. v-Week ended Thursday. w-Shares and warrants. x-Includes specialists short sales. y-Yield to maturity week ended Thursday. z-Includes short sales.

NYSE Most Active Stocks

High	Low		Sales	High	Low	Last	Chg.
64¼	40⅝	AtlRich	11,348,600	64¼	61⅛	62⅛	− ⅝
22½	15	AT&T	7,570,000	22½	21	22¼	+ 1⅛
34⅜	23⅛	Mobil	6,485,100	34⅜	30¼	30½	− 2⅝
24	14¼	BethStl	5,840,500	16⅞	16⅜	16⅝	+ ¼
138¼	99	IBM	5,495,300	130⅞	124¾	130⅛	+ 5⅛
44¼	31¼	HewlPk	4,118,000	34⅜	32⅛	34	+ 1⅝
36	17⅝	USFG	4,012,800	34½	32⅞	34¼	+ 1⅜
16⅜	9½	NtSemi	3,946,500	11⅝	10½	11⅝	+ 1
54⅛	38	Exxon	3,774,100	52¾	49¼	50	− ⅞
85	61	GMot	3,772,800	69½	67¾	68⅞	+ 2⅝
32½	25¾	DowCh	3,765,200	31½	30	31⅛	+ ⅞
51⅜	34	FordM	3,721,600	43⅞	41	43	+ 2
6⅛	4	PanAm	3,588,900	5⅝	4⅞	5⅝	+ ½
20⅞	9¾	Uniroyl	3,576,400	20½	19⅜	19¾	+ ⅞
46	25	AmExp	3,552,800	46	42⅞	45⅝	+ 2⅞
95⅛	62½	PhilMr	3,536,400	86	81½	84¼	+ 1⅜
30½	17	WrnCm	3,504,800	30½	28¼	28⅞	− ⅛
24⅛	16	Arkla	3,253,200	24⅛	21¼	23	+ 1¼
65¼	48¼	GenEl	3,215,200	60⅜	58⅜	60½	+ 1⅞
66⅞	37	Boeing	3,169,400	62¾	57⅜	62¼	+ 4⅜

STOCK EXCHANGE VOLUME TRENDS

(Volume, th shs)

		NYSE Up	NYSE Down	NYSE (%) QCHA	Amex Up	Amex Down	Amex (%) QCHA	NASDAQ Up	NASDAQ Down
May	6	39,556	34,265	+ .10	2,217	2,747	− .04	16,218	18,655
	7	60,086	25,649	+ .25	3,953	1,530	+ .19	30,440	15,284
	8	45,985	42,905	+ .07	2,482	2,580	− .12	26,825	23,076
	9	81,106	18,271	+ .61	3,980	1,080	+ .06	41,701	15,077
	10	114,047	17,473	+ .98	6,119	1,961	+ .82	50,680	9,087

Supplied by QUOTRON, th. of shares. "QCHA" is the average percentage movement for all exchange listed stocks each day on an unweighted basis.

Weekly Composite Diary

Week ended May 10, 1985

	NYSE	AMEX	NASDAQ
Total	2,235	910	4,131
Advances	1,469	456	1,629
Declines	546	290	981
Unchanged	220	164	1,521
New Highs	341	76	
New Lows	58	36	

NYSE Common Stock Diary

	May 6	7	8	9	10
Total	1,492	1,486	1,500	1,495	1,497
Advances	603	722	565	843	995
Declines	525	419	581	335	262
Unchanged	364	345	354	317	240

NYSE Composite Diary

	May 6	7	8	9	10
Total	2,001	2,013	2,010	2,027	2,008
Advances	815	907	764	1,078	1,233
Declines	688	608	765	498	393
Unchanged	498	498	481	451	382
New Highs	81	81	91	114	196
New Lows	17	13	23	12	11
Sales ths shs	101,955	119,181	122,290	130,287	162,510

AMEX Composite Diary

	May 6	7	8	9	10
Total	747	765	768	785	809
Advances	264	266	255	317	399
Declines	275	247	274	213	203
Unchanged	208	252	239	255	207
New Highs	19	15	22	36	34
New Lows	11	7	11	14	7
Sales ths shs	7,486	8,162	7,765	7,729	10,867

NASDAQ OTC Market Diary

	May 6	7	8	9	10
Total	4,131	4,130	4,133	4,136	4,131
Advances	765	1,005	828	1,123	1,329
Declines	871	713	835	631	491
Unchanged	2,495	2,412	2,470	2,382	2,311
New Highs	122	158	145	181	233
New Lows	76	71	75	57	39
Sales ths shs	59,314	70,938	76,848	80,740	95,508

New York Exchange Bond Diary

	May 6	7	8	9	10
Total	885	965	944	957	1,013
Advances	393	508	378	467	670
Declines	286	263	358	275	181
Unchanged	206	194	208	215	162
New Highs	83	103	79	80	176
New Lows	2	3	8	4	7
Sales ths $	29,630	36,810	35,730	34,610	45,600

Sales ths $ May 2 corrected to 27,390.

AMEX Bond Diary

	May 6	7	8	9	10
Total	55	64	71	63	82
Advances	26	20	33	27	52
Declines	17	24	23	17	17
Unchanged	12	20	15	19	13
New Highs	3	5	6	6	12
New Lows	3	1	0	2	0
Sales ths $	1,670	3,550	3,300	2,270	2,510

Weekly Trading by Markets in NYSE Listed Stocks

	Last Week	Prev. Week	Last Year
NYSE	538,475	504,642	439,565
Midwest	41,329	37,036	38,810
Pacific	20,514	21,657	17,825
NASDAQ	18,129	19,753	15,238
Phila.	9,317	10,494	9,438
Boston	6,682	7,770	5,094
Cincinnati	1,131	1,052	917
Instinet	800	1,337	565
Total	636,377	603,74[1]	527,452

FIGURE 4–16   From *Barron's* Market Laboratory—Trade and Foreign Data

PULSE OF INDUSTRY AND TRADE

	Latest date	Latest period	Preceding period	Year ago
Production—What They Make:				
Autos, U.S. domestic units	May 11	e178,652	r181,029	170,699
Electric power, mil kw hrs	May 4	43,927	44,467	43,008
Paper, th tons	May 4	651	r656	692
Paperboard, th tons	May 4	626.7	r611.9	681.9
Petroleum, daily runs, th bbls	May 3	11,604	11,692	11,631
Petroleum, rated capacity, %	May 3	75.9	76.7	73.0
Rotary rigs running (Hughes)	May 6	1,950	1,962	2,317
Steel production, th tons	Apr. 27	1,823	1,841	2,128
Steel, rated capacity, % (AISI)	Apr. 27	71.1	71.8	81.9
GNP (adjusted annual rate)	1st qtr.	+1.3	+4.3	+10.1
Factory operating rate, %	Feb.	80.7	81.4	80.1
Industrial Production (FRB)	Mar.	165.4	r164.9	160.8
Manufacturing a	Mar.	p167.1	r166.5	162.1
Durable Mfg a	Mar.	p158.5	r157.7	151.4
Non-durable Mfg a	Mar.	p179.5	r179.1	177.6
Mining a	Mar.	p123.5	r123.1	123.8
Utilities a	Mar.	p184.7	r184.8	180.0
Newsprint, U.S. & Can., th metric tons	Mar.	1,244	1,147	1,100
Distribution—What They Sell:				
Business sales, bil $	Feb.	419.21	r418.21	401.78
Autos, U.S. domestic units	Apr.	788,281	768,927	721,091
Autos, imports	Apr.	196,000	198,040	171,000
Retail store sales, bil $	Mar.	110.54	r112.74	103.87
Factory Shipments, bil $	Feb.	192.03	r192.71	185.00
Durable goods, bil $	Mar.	101.83	r101.72	96.99
Machine tools, mil $	Mar.	227.7	166.2	189.3
Inventories—What's Left on Hand:				
Business inventories, bil $	Feb.	576.89	r574.79	531.90
Domestic crude oil, th bbls	May 3	349,244	342,075	347,191
Gasoline, th bbls	May 3	214,981	214,339	249,216
Factory Inventories, bil $	Feb.	285.70	r284.79	246.07
Newsprint, U.S. & Can., th metric tons	Mar.	1,372	r1,373	1,146
New Orders Received:				
New Factory Orders, bil $	Mar.	191.61	193.44	196.48
Durable goods, bil $	Mar.	99.74	102.85	105.18
Non-durable goods, bil $	Mar.	91.87	90.59	91.29
Machine tools, mil $	Mar.	297.3	r237.5	208.5
Unfilled Orders:				
Factory orders backlog	Mar.	348.65	r350.05	348.71
Failures (D. & B.)				
Business Failures b	Apr. 26	10/.0	109.4	96.5
Business Incorporations (D. & B.)				
New Incorporations	Nov.	53,490	r52,587	51,642
Purchasing Power:				
Whlesle Food Price Index (D&B) $	Apr. 30	16.39	16.38	17.25
Leading Indicators Composite Index a	Mar.	167.1	167.5	165.5
Consumer Price Index a	Mar.	318.8	317.4	307.3
Producer Price Index Finished Goods a	Apr.	293.1	292.4	291.6
Inventory-to-sales ratio	Feb.	1.38	1.37	1.32
Employment:				
Civil labor force, th	Apr.	115,370	r115,510	113,202
Employed, th	Apr.	106,950	r107,120	104,402
Unemployed, th	Apr.	8,430	r8,390	8,800
Unemployment Rate, %	Apr.	7.3	7.3	7.7
Construction:				
Advance Planning (ENR), mil $	May 9	3,153.4	3,444.1	3,636.5
Bldg contracts, (Dodge), bil $	Mar.	227.75	204.15	
Construction Spending, bil $	Mar.	324.2	r323.8	309.7
Private Spending, bil $	Mar.	265.6	r265.7	254.9
Public Spending, bil $	Mar.	58.6	r58.1	54.8
Lumber production, mil bd ft	Jan.	2,727	2,295	2,740
Lumber shipments, mil bd ft	Jan.	2,666	2,411	2,589
New housing starts, th units	Mar.	1,895	r1,631	1,645

a–1967 equals 100. b-5 week moving average. e-Estimate. p-Preliminary. r-Revised.

THE WILSHIRE 5000 EQUITY INDEX				
(Published by Wilshire Associates, Santa Monica, California)				
	Current (5/10/85)	Last Week (5/3/85)	Last Month (4/16/85)	Last Year (5/18/84)
Wilshire Index, Bil $	1,899.715	1,852.921	1,849.821	1,641.335
Net Change, Bil $		46.794	49.895	258.380
Percent Change		2.53	2.70	15.74

The Wilshire 5000 Equity Index is the total market value of all stocks listed on the New York Stock Exchange and American Stock Exchange as well as those actively traded over-the-counter.

FOREIGN

SOUTH AFRICAN ADR's

Closing prices of selected issues in U.S currency.
May 10. 1985

	Week's		Week's
Name of Stock	Close		Change
Bracken	.88	+	.30
Consol. Modderfontein	7.40	+	.275
Deelkraal	3.125	+	.375
Doornfontein	18.75	+	1.75
Durban Deep	14.75	+	1.75
ERPM	8.00	+	.50
Elandsrand	8.75	+	.375
Elsburg	2.75	+	.35
ERGO	5.25	+	.125
Gen Mining	xd14.75	+	1.00
Grootvlei	8.625	+	1.00
Harmony	15.75	+	1.875
Hartesbeestfontein	5.625	+	.375
Impala Platinum	10.625	+	.25
Kinross	20.00	+	.50
Leslie	13.25	+	.75
Libanon	24.75	+	2.00
Loraine	4.875	+	.875
Lydenburg Platinum	7.50	+	1.00
Randfontein	10.90	+	.70
Rustenburg Platinum	8.375	+	.375
So. African Breweries	3.75	+	.25
So. A. Manganese Amcor	xd2.875	+	.125
Southvaal	47.00	+	3.00
Stilfontein	8.125	+	.875
Unisel	10.625	+	1.125
Venterspost	9.00	+	1.00
West Rand Cons	4.50	+	.25
Western Areas	4.25	+	.25
Winkelhaak	33.00	+	2.00
Zandpan	.95	+	.10

Source: S.G. Warburg, Rowe & Pitman. Akroyd. Inc.

STOCK INDEXES

	-1984-'85-		May 7	Week's
	High	Low	Close	Change
Australia	889.90	646.30	884.70 +	18.90
Belgium	2,309.65	1,817.31	2,220.45 +	14.75
Canada	2,657.78	2,175.58	N.A.	N.A.
France	211.36	165.49	211.36 +	2.85
Hong Kong	1,621.45	746.02	1,613.36 +	62.56
Italy	1,870.00	1,086.00	1,363.00 +	53.00
Japan	12,683.36	9,897.15	12,526.31 +	74.52
Netherlands	213.00	149.70	209.1 -	3.00
Singapore	1,071.01	764.38	798.14 -	2.37
Sweden	484.80	367.20	399.40 +	1.00
Switzerland	353.30	293.30	353.30 +	5.90
U.K.	1,308.40	790.30	1,001.90 +	12.00
W.Germany	1,244.50	932.60	1,244.50 +	21.90

GOLD COINS

		Premium Over the Value of the Gold Contained in Coin	
		In $	As a % of Gold
NAME OF COIN	Price	Per Coin	Value
Krugerrand	326.75	10.50	3.32
Maple Leaf	326.75	10.50	3.32
Mexican 1 oz	326.75	10.50	3.32
Mexico Peso	394.00	12.73	3.34
Austria crown	309.50	-.49	-.16
Sovereign	77.00	2.56	3.44

MOCATTA'S spot Gold price $316.25.
Wholesale dealer offering price on Friday.
Source: Mocatta Metals Corp.

GOLD AND SILVER PRICES

Handy & Harman's base for pricing gold content of shipments and for making refining settlements was $314.50 a troy ounce Friday. The company's silver price was $6.32 a troy ounce.

ECONOMIC AND FINANCIAL INDICATORS

	Latest period	Preceding period	Year ago
Fed Reserve Condition Report, Mil $, Apr. 24			
Loans, leases, securities, net	834,776	r-837,989	761,052
US Treasury agency securities, total	85,471	86,882	80,927
Other securities, total	48,785	48,792	49,774
Other loans and leases, gross	661,752	r-663,493	598,597
Commercial & industrial, total	253,744	254,780	237,045
Commercial & industrial, adjusted	251,088	251,727	233,907
Real estate	165,653	165,218	150,017
Depository, financial institutions	39,661	r39,396	40,289
Nonbank depository & others	23,723	23,968	24,439
Total Assets	1,053,277	1,067,064	990,626
Deposits, total	685,110	r698,086	633,683
Demand deposits, total	182,808	r193,048	181,288
Domestic depository institutions	20,893	r23,570	19,547
Transaction balances, total	37,676	r40,518	34,031
Nontransaction balances, total	464,626	r464,520	418,364
Liabilities for borrowed money	198,514	r200,800	191,054
Total Liabilities	979,450	r993,194	923,721
Federal Reserve Bank Changes, Mil $, May 8:			
Gov't. securities bought outright	168,164	167,089	154,534
Federal agency issues bought outright	8,371	8,372	8,556
Borrowings from Fed	634	1,272	1,098
Seasonal Borrowings	164	172	161
Extended credit	119	672	52
Float	743	r120	892
Total reserve bank credit	195,663	r195,059	175,410
Treasury gold stock-z	11,091	11,091	11,107
Currency in circulation	181,965	180,477	171,473
Treasury deposits with Fed banks	12,557	16,463	5,651
Total	203,766	r206,115	185,764
Fed Monetary & Reserve Aggregates			
Daily Average, Mil $; Two Weeks Ended May 8:			
Total Reserves (sa)	40,962	r41,352	36,230
Nonborrowed Reserves (sa)	40,009	r40,194	35,166
Required Reserves (sa)	40,155	r40,470	35,639
Excess Reserves	807	r882	591
Free Reserves (nsa)	557	392	52
Monetary Base, Bil $	205,058	r203,842	190,581
Money Supply (M1) Bil $, sa Apr. 29:	575.2	r576.1	541.0
Federal Reserve Interest Rates, % May 3:			
Federal Funds	8.35	7.69	10.70
Treasury bill (90 day)	7.78	7.77	9.99
Commercial paper (dealer, 90 day)	8.19	8.08	10.33
Certfs of Deposit (resale, 90 day)	8.29	8.20	10.60
Eurodollar (90 days)	8.58	8.49	10.99
Money Market Funds, bil $, May 8:			
Total Assets	210.13	208.3	171.6
Treasury Statement, bil $, May 8:			
Total Public Debt Outstanding	1,744.6	1,744.0	1,489.3
Total Subject to Limit	1,745.2	1,744.7	1,490.0

a-Excluding extended credit. r-Revised. nsa-Not seasonally adjusted. sa-Seasonally adjusted. z-Actual. NA-Not available; Fed monetary and reserve aggregates released by Fed only every other week.

Monthly Economic And Financial Indicators

	Latest period	Preceding period	Year ago
Bank Debits, bil $, sa, Feb.:			
All Banks	143,281.5	140,678.6	126,749.9
New York City	63,157.0	64,474.7	55,776.7
Other Banks	80,124.5	76,203.9	70,973.1
Avg. Deposits Outstanding, bil $, sa, Feb.:			
All Banks	303.9	300.2	291.6
New York City	33.2	32.1	31.9
Other Banks	270.7	268.1	259.7
Velocity Rate of Deposit Turnover, Feb.:			
All Banks	471.4	468.6	434.7
New York City	1,902.2	2,008.6	1,747.7
Other Banks	295.9	284.2	273.3
Money Supply, bil $, sa, Mar.:			
Total (M1)	r572.0	569.3	537.3
Total (M2)	r2429.3	r2420.9	2229.1
Total (M3)	r3055.4	r3041.4	2765.4
Currency	r161.3	160.5	151.2
Travelers Checks	r5.4	5.3	5.0
Demand Deposits	251.9	251.7	245.5
Other Checkable Deposits	r153.4	151.7	135.6
Savings Deposits, total	288.9	r289.6	302.9
Small Time Deposits, total	r878.5	r877.2	802.3
Large Time Deposits, total	r423.5	419.7	349.7
sa-Seasonally adjusted.			

The Use of Mainframe Computers

The following data bases are all made to be used on large mainframe computers. *Compustat* is published by Investors Management Science Company, a subsidiary of Standard & Poor's Corporation. The Compustat tapes are very comprehensive, containing 20 years of annual financial data for over 3,000

companies. Each year's data for the industrial companies include over 120 balance sheet, income statement, and market-related items. Compustat has an industrial file that includes company data from the New York and American Stock Exchanges and the over-the-counter market. There is also a file on utilities and banks. Besides the annual file, which is updated weekly, users can order tapes with quarterly data also updated weekly.

A second data base created by Compustat is called the Price-Dividend-Earnings tape (PDE) which contains monthly data on per-share performance. These tapes are leased to financial institutions for a fairly large sum or to nonprofit educational institutions at a significant discount. The tapes may be paid for in cash or in soft dollars (commissions funneled through an S&P brokerage subsidiary).

These tapes are useful for the analysis of large numbers of companies in a short time period. Ratios can be created, analyzed, and compared. Trends and regression analysis can be performed. Searches can be implemented for specific kinds of companies. For example, one could read through the tapes and sort out companies meeting certain parameters, such as:

1. Dividend yield greater than 6 percent.
2. Earnings growth greater than 15 percent per year.
3. Price–earnings ratio less than the Standard & Poor's 500 Index.
4. Market price less than book value.

It should be noted that Interactive Data Corporation also provides the same information as the Compustat tapes on a time-sharing basis.

The *CRSP Tapes* are maintained by the University of Chicago in the Center for Research in Security Prices. The information provided is oriented to earnings, dividends, stock prices, and dates of mergers, stock splits, stock dividends, etc. The tapes are extremely useful (data begin in 1926) for historical research on stock performance. They are widely used in academia for research on the efficient market hypothesis, the capital asset pricing model, and other portfolio questions.

Value Line also has made computer tapes of its 1,700 companies available. Again these would have market price data as well as financial statement items. The Federal Trade Commission has industry trade topics available on aggregate industry data and the Federal Reserve Bank of St. Louis has been known to make tapes of monetary data available for academic researchers.

The Use of Personal Computers

During the last few years there has been a proliferation of data bases for the personal computer. The owner of a personal computer with communications ability and a modem (phone hook-up), can now dial up a data base such as the Dow Jones News Retrieval System. This data base is oriented to the business user and includes financial data, current and historical information on stock quotes, commodity quotes, access to Disclosure's SEC reports mentioned pre-

viously and much more.[3] Other information outlets, such as The Source and CompuServe, also provide financial data, general information, government statistics, and electronic mail. Chase Econometrics and Nite-Line specialize in financial, business, and economic data, while Citishare Corporation offers U.S. economic statistics. Many old line financial companies such as Value Line (Value/Screen, and ValuePak) and Standard & Poor's (Stockpak II) are offering their financial data on micro-computer floppy disks with monthly updates. One good place to look for more complete information on these sources is in a computer magazine such as *Personal Computing* or *Byte.*

In addition to the data bases available for the personal computer, new software to access and analyze the data is being created at an extremely rapid pace. The raw data can either be "downloaded" (quickly transferred) onto a floppy disk or into your computer memory to save time and analyzed later, or it can be read directly into a software program which is designed to perform calculations on the raw data.

There are programs that analyze and create charts of the technical behavior of price movements, and others that evaluate the financial data from income statements and balance sheets. Using the Dow Jones Investment Evaluator, you can access the Dow Jones News Retrieval System to obtain information for stocks, bonds, warrants, options, mutual funds, or treasury issues. Information related to 10K statements, ratios, earnings growth rates, earnings per share forecasts, etc. are available on 2400 companies. The Dow Jones Market Analyzer, The Dow Jones Microscope, and the Dow Jones Investor Workshop all allow access to the Dow Jones information network. Once the correct data is entered into these software programs, they then create standardized analysis from preprogrammed instructions. Also, new programs are now able to transfer data from a news retrieval service straight into a spread sheet program such as Lotus 1-2-3 or SuperCalc. This saves time and money and allows the individual flexibility to create his or her own financial analysis. Not all these programs are available for every personal computer. Most programs are for the IBM personal computer and compatible systems, or for the Apple computer. Before buying one, check to make sure which software programs run on your computer.

INFORMATION ON NONTRADITIONAL MARKETS

For the purposes of this section, we define nontraditional as being out of the realm of stocks, bonds, and government securities. A major area that received increased attention during the last decade has been commodities and financial futures. A major source of information on commodities is the *Commodity Yearbook.*

Commodity Yearbook

This is a yearly publication which can be supplemented by the *Commodity Yearbook Statistical Abstract* three times per year. The *Commodity Yearbook*

---

[3] There is generally a monthly subscription fee associated with this and other such services.

runs several feature articles of educational interest, covering commodities or situations that are currently in the forefront of commodity trading. For 1984, the articles included such items as, "the Petroleum Futures Complex: Factors Affecting Supply/Demand and Prices," and "Understanding the Aluminum Futures Market."

In addition to the featured articles, the *Yearbook* covers each traded commodity from alcohol to zinc. For example, corn is covered in six pages. The first page is a description of the corn crop and occurrences for the 1983–84 year. The next five pages cover much data in tabular form for the last 13 years. The tables show world production of corn, acreage, and supply of corn in the United States, corn production estimates and disposition by value in the United States, corn supply and disappearance, distribution of corn in the United States, corn price support data, average price received by farmers for corn in the United States, and of course, weekly high-low-close of the nearest month's futures price. Each commodity has a similarly detailed evaluation and statistical summary.

There are other publications about commodities from main-line brokerage houses and specialty commodity brokers. In addition, the commodities exchanges publish educational booklets and newsletters. The International Monetary Market publishes the *I.M.M. Weekly Report,* which discusses the interest rate markets, the foreign exchange markets, and gold. It also presents weekly prices for all interest rate futures, foreign exchange markets, gold, and selected cash market information, such as the federal funds rate and the prime rate. The Chicago Board of Trade publishes the *Interest Rate Futures Newsletter.* As investors continue to become active in these markets, an investor (speculator) can be sure to find more available data.

Scott Publishing Company

The Scott Publishing Company has long been involved in the philatelic (stamp) market. They turn out annual catalogues with price data and pictures with descriptions. Recently, Scotts has added a *Stamp Market Update,* which is a quarterly report on current trends and prices. It features prices of major U.S. stamps and popular foreign stamps, information for specialized collectors, investment opportunities and strategies as stated by recognized experts, and special articles, statistical tables, and graphs.

SUMMARY

In summary, we can say that information is easy and yet difficult to find. The problem that beginners have is knowing where to look and what to look for, and this chapter has attempted to provide some guidance and sample data. The problem that advanced investors have is knowing what data is usable. This may also haunt beginners once they find the sources. To become proficient in finding data, spend a day in your library just looking through the volumes. This will increase your awareness of the types of information available. Then do

some of the exercises at the end of this chapter to see if you can find specific data. As for the problem of knowing what information is useful, the authors hope to shed some light on that as we proceed through the rest of the book.

IMPORTANT WORDS AND CONCEPTS

Federal Reserve Bulletin
Survey of Current Business
Business Conditions Digest
Moody's Manuals
Standard & Poor's publications
Value Line Investment Survey
Business Periodicals Index

Funk and Scott Index of
*   Corporations and Industries*
The Wall Street Journal Index
Disclosure Journal
Data base
Compustat tapes
CRSP tapes

DISCUSSION QUESTIONS

1.   What type of information is part of aggregate economic data?
2.   The Federal Reserve Bank of St. Louis has a number of comprehensive economic publications. What are they?
3.   What is one of the major benefits provided by the *Survey of Current Business* in regard to industry data?
4.   What makes *Business Conditions Digest* unique among publications of economic data?
5.   Of the major advisory services for investors, which ones would likely be found in most libraries?
6.   What is special about the T–Z volume of Standard & Poor's *Corporate Records?*
7.   What is the Standard & Poor's *Stock Guide?* What is included in the introduction.
8.   Briefly describe the Value Line evaluation system.
9.   Assume one needs information about an industry or company. Suggest three types of indexes for periodicals or journals that can be used.
10.   What type of information is contained in the following three filings with the SEC: 10-K, 8-K, 10-Q?
11.   Under what category in *Barron's* would weekly data on stock market indexes and general market statistics be found?
12.   Who publishes *Compustat?* What type of information is available on *Compustat?*
13.   What information is available through the Dow Jones News Retrieval System? Can you access this service with a personal computer?
14.   Suggest some sources for information about commodities.
15.   Choose a company and look it up in *Moody's, Standard & Poor's,* and *Value Line* to see the information provided and compare the data.
16.   Select an industry and find the SIC code. Then look up all firms listed in

this business. (Suggestion—the SIC code can be found in the T–Z volume of *Standard & Poor's Corporate Records,* which will also provide the list of firms by the SIC number.)

17. Look up the implicit price deflator for the GNP (one source is the St. Louis Federal Reserve Bank's *National Economic Trends*) and total corporate profits after taxes (same source). This data can be useful for current projects and will expose you to a good source for this type of information.

18. Select a company, go to *The Wall Street Journal Index* for the previous year, and identify the dates of all news stories about the company.

APPENDIX 4–A: *Names and Addresses of Important Data Sources*

Federal Reserve Bank of:
  Atlanta, Ga. 30301
  Boston, Mass. 02106
  Chicago, Ill. 60690
  Cleveland, Ohio 44101
  Dallas, Tex. 75222
  Kansas City, Kans. 64198
  Minneapolis, Minn. 55480
  New York, N.Y. 10045
  Philadelphia, Pa. 19105
  Richmond, Va. 23219
  San Francisco, Calif. 94120
  St. Louis, Mo. 63166

Federal Reserve Bulletin
  Board of Governors of the
  Federal Reserve System
  Washington, D.C. 20551

Stock and commodity exchanges:
  American Stock Exchange
  86 Trinity Place
  New York, N.Y. 10006

  Chicago Board of Trade
  LaSalle at Jackson
  Chicago, Ill. 60604

  Chicago Mercantile Exchange
  444 West Jackson Blvd.
  Chicago, Ill. 60606

  New York Stock Exchange
  11 Wall Street
  New York, N.Y. 10005

The following U.S. government publications can be requested from the:
Superintendent of Documents
U.S. Government Printing Office
Washington, D.C. 20402
Survey of Current Business
Weekly Business Statistics
Business Conditions Digest
Economic Indicators
Economic Report of the President
Statistical Abstract of the United States
Statistical Bulletin
Periodicals:
  The Wall Street Journal and *Barron's*
  Dow Jones & Company
  Subscriptions Office
  200 Burnett Rd.
  Chicopee, Mass. 01021

  Changing Times
  The Kiplinger Magazine
  1729 H St., N.W.
  Washington, D.C. 20006

  Disclosure Journal
  Disclosure Inc.
  1450 Broadway
  New York, N.Y. 10018

Forbes
60 5th Avenue
New York, N.Y. 10011

Financial World
Macro Communications Inc.
150 East 58th Street
New York, N.Y. 10155

Business Week
1221 Avenue of the Americas
New York, N.Y. 10020

Money Magazine
Fortune
Time Inc.
3435 Wilshire Blvd.
Los Angeles, Calif. 90010

Media General Financial
   Services, Inc.
P.O. Box 26991
Richmond, Va. 23261

Financial Analysts Journal
1633 Broadway
New York, N.Y. 10019

Investment services:
   Moody's Investors Service
   99 Church Street
   New York, N.Y. 10007

Standard & Poor's Corporation
345 Hudson Street
New York, N.Y. 10014

Value Line Services
Arnold Bernhard and Company
5 East 44th Street
New York, N.Y. 10017

Dun & Bradstreet
99 Church Street
New York, N.Y. 10007

Dun's Marketing Division
3 Century Drive
Parsippany, N.J. 07054

Computer data bases:
   Compustat
   P.O. Box 239
   Denver, Colo. 80201
   CRSP Tapes
   Center for Research in Security
      Prices
   University of Chicago
   Graduate School of Business
   Chicago, Ill. 60637
   Interactive Data Corporation
   122 East 42nd Street
   New York, N.Y. 10017

APPENDIX 4–B: Regional and Branch Offices of the SEC

Where You Can Find the Reports: A Directory

Financial and other data included in registration statements, reports, applications, and similar documents filed with the commission are available for study in the public reference room in the main office in Washington, D.C. Copies of these documents may be obtained for 10¢ per page, with a $5.00 minimum. Cost estimates are available by writing to Public Reference Room, Securities and Exchange Commission, Washington, D.C. 20549.

   Current annual reports and other periodic reports filed by companies whose securities are listed on the national exchanges are also available for study in the SEC's New York, Chicago, and Los Angeles regional offices.

   Registration statements and subsequent reports filed by those companies whose securities are traded over-the-counter and that register under the Secu-

rities Exchange Act are also available at the New York, Chicago, and Los Angeles offices.

SEC filings can also be examined at the regional office serving the area in which the issuer's principal office is located. These regional offices are located in Atlanta, Boston, Denver, Fort Worth, and Seattle.

Prospectuses covering recent public offerings of securities registered under the Securities Act may be examined in all regional offices.

Broker-dealer and investment adviser registrations, as well as Regulation A notifications and offering circulars, may be examined in the particular regional office in which they were filed.

Regional and Branch Offices

Region 1 – New York Regional Office
      26 Federal Plaza
      New York, NY 10278
      (212)/264-1636
      Region: New York and New Jersey

Region 2 – Boston Regional Office
      150 Causeway Street
      Boston, MA 02114
      (617)/223-2721
      Region: Maine, New Hampshire, Vermont, Massachusetts, Rhode Island and Connecticut

Region 3 – Atlanta Regional Office
      1375 Peachtree Street, N.E.
      Suite 788
      Atlanta, GA 30367
      (404)/881-4768
      Region: Tennessee, Virgin Islands, Puerto Rico, North Carolina, South Carolina, Georgia, Alabama, Mississippi, Florida and Louisiana east of the Atchafalays River

      Miami Branch Office
      Dupont Plaza Center
      300 Biscayne Blvd. Way, Suite 1114
      Miami, FL 33131
      (305)/350-5765

Region 4 – Chicago Regional Office
      Everett McKinley Dirksen Bldg.
      219 South Dearborn Street, Room 1204
      Chicago, IL 60604
      (312)/353-7390
      Region: Michigan, Ohio, Kentucky, Wisconsin, Indiana, Iowa, Minnesota, Missouri, and Kansas City (Kansas) and Illinois

Detroit Branch Office
1044 Federal Bldg.
Detroit, MI 48226
(313)/226-6070

Region 5 — Fort Worth Regional Office
411 W. Seventh St.
Fort Worth, TX 76102
(817)/334-3821
Region: Oklahoma, Arkansas, Texas, Louisiana west of the Atchafa-
laya River and Kansas (except Kansas City)

Houston Branch Office
Federal Office and Courts Bldg.
515 Rusk Avenue, Room 5615
Houston, TX 77002
(713)/226-4986

Region 6 — Denver Regional Office
410 17th Street
Suite 700
Denver, CO 80202
(303)/837-2071
Region: North Dakota, South Dakota, Wyoming, Nebraska, Colorado, New Mexico, and Utah

Salt Lake Branch Office
Boston Bldg. Suite 810
Nine Exchange Place
Salt Lake City, UT 84111
(801)/524-5796

Region 7 — Los Angeles Regional Office
10960 Wilshire Blvd.
Suite 1710
Los Angeles, CA 90024
(213)/473-4511
Region: Nevada, Arizona, California, Hawaii, and Guam

San Francisco Branch Office
450 Golden Gate Avenue, Box 36042
San Francisco, CA 94102
(415)/556-5264

Region 8 — Seattle Regional Office
3040 Federal Building
915 Second Avenue
Seattle, WA 98174
(206)/442-7990
Region: Montana, Idaho, Washington, Oregon, and Alaska

Region 9 – Washington Regional Office
   Ballston Center Tower 3
   4015 Wilson Blvd.
   Arlington, VA 22203
   (703)/557-8201
   Region: Pennsylvania, Delaware, Maryland, Virginia, West Virginia, and District
      of Columbia

   Philadelphia Branch Office
   William J. Green, Jr. Federal Bldg.
   600 Arch Street, Room 2204
   Philadelphia, PA 19106
   (215)/597-2278

U.S. Securities and Exchange Commission Washington, D.C. 20549

For	*Call*
General information	Office of Public Affairs 202/272-2650
Investor complaints	Office of Consumer Affairs 202/523-5516
Filings by registered companies	Public Reference Room 1100 L Street, N.W. 202/523-5360
Forms and publications	202/523-3761

For the Official Summary, $70 a year, $6.50 per issue, contact: Superintendent of Documents, Government Printing Office, Washington, D.C. 20402. Phone: (202)/783-3238.

Source: John Markese, 'Culling Information from the SEC," *American Association of Individual Investors Journal,* January 1984, pp. 31–34.

Part Two

ANALYSIS AND VALUATION OF EQUITY SECURITIES

While we often praise the investor who is fortunate enough to receive a hot tip and capitalize on it, in the real world, events do not normally follow this course. In the second section of the text, we examine the in-depth analytical process that the typical security analyst must pursue.

Initially, we look at key variables influencing the economy. The security analyst must consider the role of fiscal and monetary policy, and their impact on economic conditions in the near term and over a long period of time. The security analyst also should examine business cycles, their length, and causation. An understanding of leading indicators and their ability to provide warnings about peaks and troughs in the economy is also important. We take a look at many of these items, although clearly we are drawing from a vast body of knowledge (exact and inexact) from which we can only consider the most relevant material.

As part of the consideration of economic movements, we also evaluate industry patterns. What industries peak with the economy, which go against the grain? Not only are industries influenced by the business cycle, but also by their own life cycle which is related to the ability to adjust to technological change.

The evaluation of the individual firm is the next logical step in the valuation process. We first examine valuation procedures based on the present value of future dividends and earnings of the firm. The widely used concept of the price–earnings ratio (earnings multiplier) is also a major item for consideration.

In assessing value, the security analyst also devotes much time and attention to the examination of the financial statements of the firm. Key ratios must

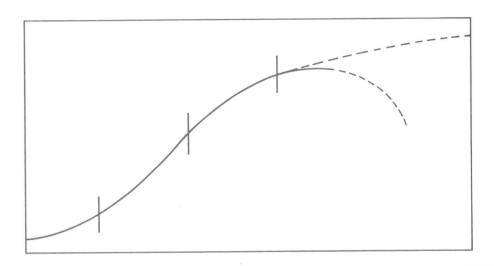

be computed and additional analysis done. Very little on the financial statements should be accepted at face value.

Finally, a key question for any security analyst is whether the security markets are assumed to be "efficient." In an efficient market environment, securities are assumed to be correctly priced at any point in time. All relevant information is thus presumed to be impounded into the value of the security at a given point in time. At the end of this section, we will consider the pros and cons of the arguments related to this·efficient market hypothesis. We also present a discussion of technical analysis (the use of charting and key indicator series to predict stock prices) and its role in investment analysis.

Chapter 5

ECONOMIC AND INDUSTRY ANALYSIS

Chapter 6

VALUATION OF THE INDIVIDUAL FIRM

Chapter 7

FINANCIAL STATEMENT ANALYSIS

Chapter 8

A BASIC VIEW OF TECHNICAL ANALYSIS AND MARKET EFFICIENCY

Chapter 5

ECONOMIC AND INDUSTRY ANALYSIS

To determine the value of the firm, the process of fundamental analysis relies on long-run forecasts of the economy, the industry, and the company's financial prospects. Short-run changes in business conditions are also important in that they influence investors' required rates of return and expectations of corporate earnings and dividends. This chapter presents the basic information for analysis of the economy and industry, while the next chapter focuses specifically on the valuation of the individual firm. In Chapter 7, we extend our discussion to include financial statement and ratio analysis for the firm.

Figure 5–1 presents an overview of the valuation process as an inverted triangle. The process starts with a macro analysis of the economy and then moves into industry variables. Next, common stocks are individually screened out according to expected risk-return characteristics, and finally the surviving stocks are combined into portfolios of assets (portfolio management is discussed in Part Five). This figure is not inclusive of all variables considered by an analyst, but is intended to indicate representative areas applicable to most industries and companies.

ECONOMIC ACTIVITY AND THE BUSINESS CYCLE

An investor begins the valuation process with an economic analysis. The hope is that an accurate forecast and examination of economic activity will provide the basis for accurate stock market predictions and indicate which industries may prosper. The analyst needs information on present and expected interest rates, monetary and fiscal policy, government and consumer spending patterns, and other economic data. To be successful, investors must understand business cycles and be able to forecast accurately. Unfortunately, these are not easy tasks, but the rewards can be significant if the timing is right.

Whether or not an analyst uses statistical methods, such as regression analysis and probability theory, or simply seat-of-the-pants judgment, he or she is still basing the forecast on expectations related to past data and experiences. Past information usually is not extrapolated into the future without being adjusted to conform with the subjective beliefs of the decision maker. Even when highly sophisticated statistical methods are used, subjectivity enters into the decision in some fashion.

Most likely, past knowledge will be helpful, but modifications for the present effects of worldwide currency fluctuations, international debt obligations and other factors, which were not so important previously, need to be included in any forecast now. Since most companies are influenced to some degree by the general level of economic activity, a forecast will usually start with an analysis of the government's economic program.

FEDERAL GOVERNMENT ECONOMIC POLICY

Government economic policy is guided by the Employment Act of 1946 and subsequent position statements by the Federal Reserve Board, the President's Council of Economic Advisors, and other acts of Congress. The goals estab-

FIGURE 5–1   Overview of the Valuation Process

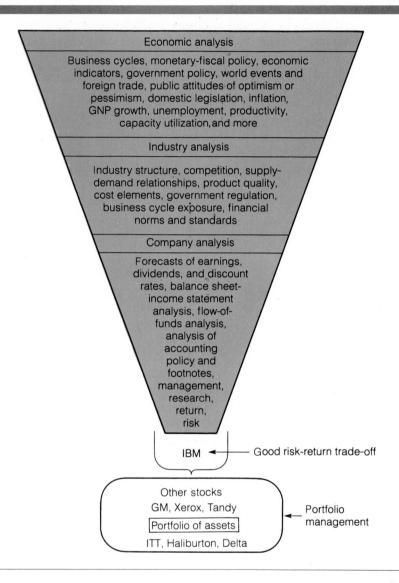

lished by the Employment Act still hold and cover four broad areas. These goals are the focus of monetary and fiscal policy, and they are as follows:

1. Stable prices.
2. Business stability at high levels of production and employment.
3. Sustained economic growth.
4. A balance in international payments.

These goals are often conflicting in that they do not all respond favorably to the same economic stimulus. Therefore, goal priorities and economic policies change to reflect current economic conditions. In the 1950s and early 1960s, the United States did not have an international trade problem or spiraling inflation, so the focus of economic policy was on employment and economic growth. The economy grew rapidly between 1961 and 1969, and because of the Vietnam War, unemployment reached very low levels. The demand for goods and competition for funds was very high during the war, and eventually war expenditures, large budget deficits, full employment, and large increases in the money supply caused many problems. Inflation accelerated to high levels, interest rates reached record heights, and an imbalance of international payments finally resulted in two devaluations of the U.S. dollar in the early 1970s.

By the time Jimmy Carter took office in January 1977, it was recognized that the primary goals were once again to reduce unemployment, control inflation, and create a moderate level of economic growth that could be sustained without causing more inflation (a very difficult task indeed!). The achievement of these goals was thrown into the hands of the Federal Reserve Board. The Fed's tight money policy caused a rapid increase in interest rates in order to control inflation. These high rates depressed common stock prices as the required rate of return by investors reached record levels. Ronald Reagan inherited most of the same problems as Carter but tried new ways of reaching the goals. As the 1980s began, Reagan relied more on fiscal policy than previous administrations in his desire to control inflation and increase economic growth. He instituted a three-year tax cut to increase disposable income and stimulate consumption and thus economic growth, and at the same time he negotiated reductions in government spending. These policies were successful in sharply reducing inflation and creating strong growth in the gross national product (GNP), but they were accomplished with record government deficits and high interest rates. While the Reagan administration's economic policies have been the object of praise in some quarters, many others have expressed concern that continuation of these policies could cause renewed government stimulus of inflation.

Fiscal Policy

Fiscal policy can be described as the government's taxing and spending policies. These policies can have a great impact on economic activity. One must realize at the outset that fiscal policy is cumbersome. It has a long implementation lag and is often motivated by political rather than economic considerations since Congress must approve budgets and develop tax laws. Figure 5–2 presents a historical picture of government income and expenditures. When the government spends more than it receives, it runs a deficit which must be financed by the Treasury.

A forecaster must pay attention to the size of the deficit and how it is financed in order to measure its expected impact on the economy. If the deficit

FIGURE 5–2   Federal Budget Seasonally Adjusted Annual Rates (quarterly)

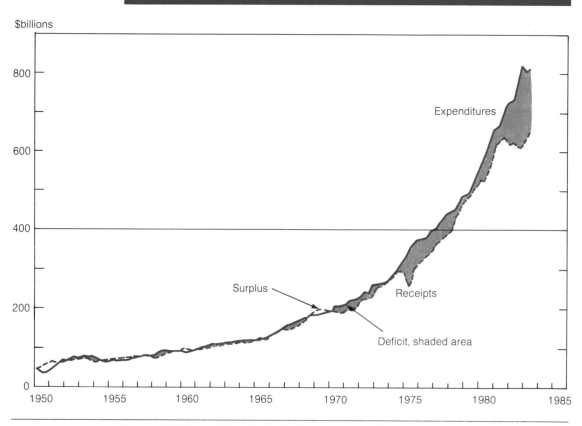

Source: *1983 Historical Chart Book* (Washington, D.C.: Board of Governors of the Federal Reserve System, 1983).

is financed by the Treasury selling securities to the Federal Reserve, it is very expansive. The money supply will increase without having any significant short-run effects on interest rates. If the deficit is financed by selling securities to individuals, there is not the same expansion in the money supply, and short-term interest rates will rise unless the Federal Reserve intervenes with open-market trading.

A look at Figure 5–2 shows that surpluses have occurred very infrequently from 1950 to 1983, and that the annual deficit increased dramatically in the early 1980s. Surpluses have a tendency to reduce economic growth as the government slows its demand for goods and services relative to its income. In an analysis of fiscal policy, the important consideration for the investor is the determination of the flow of funds. In a deficit economy, the government usually stimulates GNP by spending on socially productive programs or by increasing spending on defense, education, highways, or other government programs. The Reagan administration instituted budget cuts in education, rev-

enue sharing, and a rash of social programs at the same time that it reduced tax revenues through tax cuts. This strategy was one that attempted to shift GNP growth from the government sector into the private sector.

Monetary Policy

Monetary policy is conducted by the Federal Reserve Board of Governors through several methods of controlling the money supply and interest rates. There are lags in the effectiveness of monetary policy, but it can be implemented very quickly to reinforce fiscal policy or, when necessary, to offset the effects of fiscal policy.

The Federal Reserve has several ways to influence economic activity. First of all, it can raise or lower the reserve requirements on commercial bank time deposits or demand deposits. An increase in reserve requirements would contract the money supply. Why? The banking system would have to hold larger reserves for each dollar deposited and would not be able to loan as much money on the same deposit base. A reduction in reserve requirements would have the opposite effect. The Fed also changes the discount rate periodically to reflect its attitude toward the economy. This discount rate is the interest rate the Federal Reserve charges commercial banks on very short-term loans. The Fed does not make a practice of loaning funds to a single commercial bank for more than two or three weeks, and so this charge can influence an individual bank's willingness to borrow money for expansionary loans to industry. The Fed can also influence bank behavior by issuing policy statements, or jawboning.

Beyond these monetary measures, the tool most widely used is open-market operations in which the Fed buys and sells securities for its own portfolio. When the Fed sells securities in the open market, purchasers write checks to pay for their securities, and demand deposits fall, causing a contraction in the money supply. At the same time, the increase in the supply of Treasury bills sold by the Fed will force prices down and interest rates up to entice buyers to part with their money. The Fed usually accomplishes its adjustments by selling securities to commercial banks, government securities dealers, or individuals. If the Fed buys securities, exactly the opposite occurs; the money supply increases, and interest rates go down. As you will see in the next chapter on stock valuation, the interest rate is extremely important in determining the required rate of return, or discount rate for a stock. Many economists feel that Federal Reserve open-market activity and the resultant changes in the money supply and interest rates are good indicators of the policy position taken by the Fed. If the money supply increases and interest rates fall, the general consensus is that the Fed is encouraging economic expansion. As the money supply decreases or increases slowly and interest rates rise, the expectation is that the Fed is "tightening up" monetary policy to restrict economic growth and inflation. It should be pointed out that the Federal Reserve can not totally control the money supply. Money market funds, the resultant monetary expansion created by banks lending money, and

changing spending patterns by the population all contribute to the difficulty in controlling the money supply.

In the early 1980s, the Federal Reserve began to direct substantially more attention to controlling steady growth in the money supply rather than attempting to control interest rates. Historically, the policy has been the opposite. Thus the Fed, in recent times, has attempted to control the growth rate in the monetary aggregates of M1 (currency in circulation plus private checking deposits, including those in interest-bearing NOW accounts) and M2 (M1 plus savings accounts and money market mutual funds).

Many "pure monetarists" (those who think that money growth is the major economic driving force) think that the desired growth rates for the monetary aggregates should be 3 to 5 percent for M1 and 8 to 10 percent for M2. This is a very narrow range. Politicians often argue for much greater flexibility. The Fed has taken a middle ground by allowing for moderate

FIGURE 5–3   Gross National Product Seasonally Adjusted Annual Rates (quarterly)

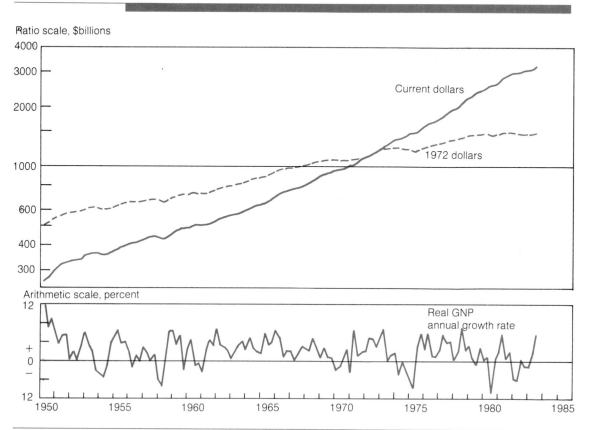

Source: *1983 Historical Chart Book* (Washington, D.C.: Board of Governors of the Federal Reserve System, 1983).

growth ranges. For example, in 1984 the desired annual target growth in M1 was 4 to 8 percent but the M2 target was 6 to 9 percent, which was 1 percent lower than the range in 1983. Because the Fed places more emphasis on controlling the growth rate in the money supply as opposed to simply stabilizing interest rates, investors can continue to expect more volatile interest rates than those experienced during most of the post–World War II period.

Government Policy, Real Growth, and Inflation

There is always the danger that fiscal or monetary policy can be too stimulative. This can cause rapid economic growth, demand for goods greater than supply, rising inflation, and eventually an economy that ends up in a recession.

Figure 5–3 depicts over 30 years of GNP in current dollars and in inflation-adjusted 1972 dollars. In the bottom portion of the figure, we see changes in the annual growth rate for real GNP.

Figure 5–4 shows the annual percentage change in the consumer price index and is used as a proxy for inflation. Notice the inverse relationship between real GNP in the bottom half of Figure 5–3 and inflation in Figure 5–4.

FIGURE 5–4 Consumer Price Index Change in Annual Rates, Seasonally Adjusted (quarterly)

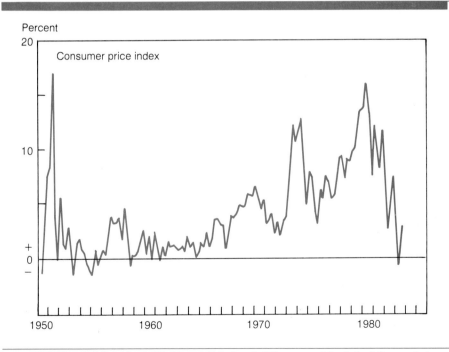

Source: *1983 Historical Chart Book* (Washington, D.C.: Board of Governors of the Federal Reserve System, 1983).

(For example, observe the 1960 and 1980 periods.) Since real GNP is the "nominal" GNP adjusted for inflation, it stands to reason that the change in real GNP is inversely related to the rate of inflation. As inflation rises, real GNP falls (as indicated in 1980) and as inflation subsides, as in 1981–83, real GNP rises. Since real GNP is the measure of economic output in real physical terms, it does not do any good to stimulate the economy only to have all the gains eroded by inflation.

BUSINESS CYCLES AND CYCLICAL INDICATORS

The economy expands and contracts through a cyclical process, and by measuring GNP and other economic data we can develop a statistical picture of the economic growth pattern. The National Bureau of Economic Research (NBER) is the final authority in documenting cyclical turning points. The NBER defines recessions as two or more quarters of negative real GNP growth and documents the beginning and end of a recession. Table 5–1 presents an historical picture of business cycle expansions and contractions in the United States. While the modern day data may be more relevant, it is interesting to see that economic cycles have existed and been defined for over 130 years.

Table 5–1 measures each contraction and expansion and then presents summary data for all business cycles and for cycles in peacetime only. A trough represents the end of a recession and the beginning of an expansion, and a peak represents the end of an expansion and the beginning of a recession. In general, we see on page 143 that during peacetime cycles between 1945 and 1982 contractions (recessions) have lasted an average of 11 months, while

TABLE 5–1   Business Cycle Expansions and Contractions in the United States

Business cycle reference dates		Contraction (trough from previous peak)	Expansion (trough to peak)	Cycle	
				Trough from previous trough	Peak from previous peak
Trough	Peak				
December 1854	June 1857	—	30	—	—
December 1858	October 1860	18	22	48	40
June 1861	April 1865	8	<u>46</u>	30	<u>54</u>
December 1867	June 1869	<u>32</u>	18	<u>78</u>	50
December 1870	October 1873	18	34	36	52
March 1879	March 1882	65	36	99	101
May 1885	March 1887	38	22	74	60
April 1888	July 1890	13	27	35	40
May 1891	January 1893	10	20	37	30
June 1894	December 1895	17	18	37	35

TABLE 5–1   (concluded)

Business cycle reference dates		Duration in months			
		Contraction (trough from previous peak)	Expansion (trough to peak)	Cycle	
Trough	Peak			Trough from previous trough	Peak from previous peak
June 1897	June 1899	18	24	36	42
December 1900	September 1902	18	21	42	39
August 1904	May 1907	23	33	44	56
June 1908	January 1910	13	19	46	32
January 1912	January 1913	24	12	43	36
December 1914	August 1918	23	44	35	67
March 1919	January 1920	7	10	51	17
July 1921	May 1923	18	22	28	40
July 1924	October 1926	14	27	36	41
November 1927	August 1929	13	21	40	34
March 1933	May 1937	43	50	64	93
June 1938	February 1945	13	80	63	93
October 1945	November 1948	8	37	88	45
October 1949	July 1953	11	45	48	56
May 1954	August 1957	10	39	55	49
April 1958	April 1960	8	24	47	32
February 1961	December 1969	10	106	34	116
November 1970	November 1973	11	36	117	47
March 1975	January 1980	16	58	52	74
July 1980	July 1981	6	12	64	18
November 1982		16	—	28	—
Average, all cycles:					
1854–1982 (30 cycles)		18	33	51	51*
1854–1919 (16 cycles)		22	27	48	49†
1919–1945 (6 cycles)		18	35	53	53
1945–1982 (8 cycles)		11	45	56	55‡
Average, peacetime cycles:					
1854–1982 (25 cycles)		19	27	46	46‡
1854–1919 (14 cycles)		22	24	46	47§
1919–1945 (5 cycles)		20	26	46	45
1945–1982 (6 cycles)		⑪	㉞	46	44

Note: Underscored figures are the wartime expansions (Civil War, World Wars I and II, Korean war, and Vietnam war), the postwar contractions, and the full cycles that include the wartime expansions.
* 29 cycles.
† 15 cycles.
‡ 24 cycles.
§ 13 cycles.
Source: *Business Conditions Digest* (U.S. Department of Commerce Bureau of Economic Analysis, July 1984).

FIGURE 5–5 Cross-Classification of Cyclical Indicators by Economic Process and Cyclical Timing

A. Timing at business cycle peaks

Cyclical timing \ Economic process	(1) Employment and unemployment (18 series)	(2) Production and income (10 series)	(3) Consumption, trade, orders, and deliveries (13 series)	(4) Fixed capital investment (18 series)	(5) Inventories and inventory investment (9 series)	(6) Prices, costs, and profits (17 series)	(7) Money and credit (26 series)
Leading (L) indicators (62 series)	Marginal employment adjustments (6 series); Job vacancies (2 series); Comprehensive employment (1 series); Comprehensive unemployment (3 series)	Capacity utilization (2 series)	New and unfilled orders and deliveries (6 series); Consumption (2 series)	Formation of business enterprises (2 series); Business investment commitments (5 series); Residential construction (3 series)	Inventory investment (4 series); Inventories on hand and on order (1 series)	Stock prices (1 series); Commodity prices (1 series); Profits and profit margins (7 series); Cash flows (2 series)	Money flows (3 series); Real money supply (2 series); Credit flows (4 series); Credit difficulties (2 series); Bank reserves (2 series); Interest rates (1 series)
Roughly coincident (C) indicators (23 series)	Comprehensive employment (1 series)	Comprehensive output and real income (4 series); Industrial production (4 series)	Consumption and trade (4 series)	Backlog of investment commitments (1 series); Business investment expenditures (5 series)			Velocity of money (2 series); Interest rates (2 series)
Lagging (Lg) indicators (18 series)	Duration of unemployment (2 series)			Business investment expenditures (1 series)	Inventories on hand and on order (4 series)	Unit labor costs and, labor share (4 series)	Interest rates (4 series); Outstanding debt (3 series)
Timing unclassified (U) (8 series)	Comprehensive employment (3 series)		Trade (1 series)	Business investment commitments (1 series)		Commodity prices (1 series); Profit share (1 series)	Interest rates (1 series)

B. Timing at business cycle peaks

Economic process / Cyclical timing	(1) Employment and unemployment (18 series)	(2) Production and income (10 series)	(3) Consumption, trade, orders, and deliveries (13 series)	(4) Fixed capital investment (18 series)	(5) Inventories and inventory investment (9 series)	(6) Prices, costs, and profits (17 series)	(7) Money and credit (26 series)
Leading (L) indicators (47 series)	Marginal employment adjustments (3 series)	Industrial production (1 series)	New and unfilled orders and deliveries (5 series) Consumption and trade (4 series)	Formation of business enterprises (2 series) Business investment commitments (4 series) Residential construction (3 series)	Inventory investment (4 series)	Stock prices (1 series) Commodity prices (2 series) Profits and profit margins (6 series) Cash flows (2 series)	Money flows (2 series) Real money supply (2 series) Credit flows (4 series) Credit difficulties (2 series)
Roughly coincident (C) indicators (23 series)	Marginal employment adjustments (2 series) Comprehensive employment (4 series)	Comprehensive output and real income (4 series) Industrial production (3 series) Capacity utilization (2 series)	Consumption and trade (3 series)	Business investment commitments (1 series)		Profits (2 series)	Money flow (1 series) Velocity of money (1 series)
Lagging (Lg) indicators (40 series)	Marginal employment adjustments (1 series) Job vacancies (2 series) Comprehensive employment (1 series) Comprehensive and duration of unemployment (5 series)		Unfilled orders (1 series)	Business investment commitments (2 series) Business investment expenditures (6 series)	Inventories on hand and on order (5 series)	Unit labor costs and labor share (4 series)	Velocity of money (1 series) Bank reserves (1 series) Interest rates (8 series) Outstanding debt (3 series)
Timing unclassified (U) (1 series)							Bank reserves (1 series)

Source: *Business Conditions Digest* (U.S. Department of Commerce Bureau of Economic Analysis, 1981).

expansions have averaged 34 months. Thus, one *complete* business cycle during modern *peacetimes* lasts almost four years whether measured from trough to trough or peak to peak. This has led many to call the cycle politically induced by the four-year presidential elections. While there may be some truth in this statement, there are many other theories about what causes the economy to cycle. However, if investors can make some forecast concerning the beginning and ending of the business cycle, they will be better able to choose what types of investments to hold over the various phases of the business cycle.

So far we have discussed the government's impact on the economy. Fiscal policy and monetary policy both provide important clues to the direction and magnitude of economic expansions and contractions. There are other measures used to evaluate the direction of the business cycle. These measures are called economic indicators, and they are divided into leading, lagging, and coincident indicators. The National Bureau of Economic Research classifies indicators relative to their performance at economic peaks and troughs.

Leading indicators change direction in advance of general business conditions and are of prime importance to the investor who wants to anticipate rising corporate profits and possible price increases in the stock market. Coincident indicators move roughly with the general economy, and lagging indicators usually change directions after business conditions have turned around.

The National Bureau of Economic Research publishes its indicators in the monthly publication, *Business Conditions Digest* (BCD). This publication includes moving averages, turning dates for recessions and expansions, cyclical indicators, composite indexes and their components, diffusion indexes,[1] and information on rates of change. Many of the series are seasonally adjusted and are maintained on a monthly or quarterly basis.

Figure 5–5 on page 144 and 145 presents a summary of cyclical indicators by economic process and cyclical timing with the first half (part A) of the figure presenting timing at business cycle peaks and the second half (part B) showing timing at business cycle troughs. Thus, in the first part we see the leading, coincident, and lagging indicators for business cycle peaks and in the second part, similar indicators for the bottoming out of business cycles (troughs). While we would not expect you to study or learn all the leading or lagging indicators for a cyclical peak or trough, it is important that you know that they are heavily relied upon by economists and financial analysts. Let's look more specifically at how they are used.

Leading Indicators

Of the 109 leading indicators shown in parts A and B of Figure 5–5, 62 lead at peaks and 47 lead at troughs. Of these, 12 basic indicators have been reasonably consistent in their relationship to the business cycle. These 12 leading

---

[1] A diffusion index shows the pervasiveness of a given movement in a series. If 100 units are reported in a series, the diffusion index will indicate what percentage followed a given pattern.

FIGURE 5–6   Composite Indexes (leading, lagging, and coincident indexes)

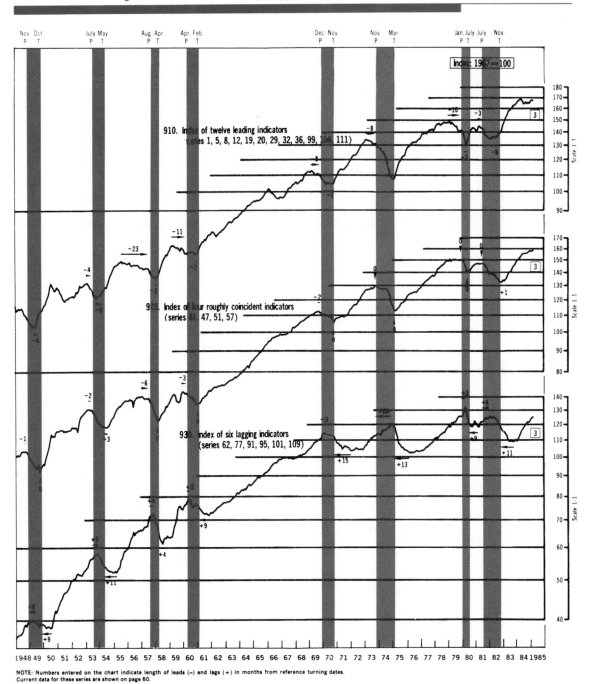

NOTE: Numbers entered on the chart indicate length of leads (–) and lags (+) in months from reference turning dates.
Current data for these series are shown on page 60.

Source: *Business Conditions Digest* (U.S. Department of Commerce Bureau of Economic Analysis, April 1985).

indicators have been standardized and used to compute a composite index that is widely followed. It is a much smoother curve than each individual component since erratic changes in one indicator are offset by movements in other indicators. The same can be said for a similar index of 4 coincident indicators and 6 lagging indicators.

Figure 5–6 shows the performance of the composite index of leading, lagging, and coincident indicators over several past business cycles. The bracketed areas are recessions as defined by the NBER. The minus figures indicate how many months the index preceded the economy. (For lagging indicators there are plus signs.)

TABLE 5–2   Components of the Leading, Coincident, and Lagging Indicators (series title and unit of measure)

LEADING INDICATORS

1.	Average workweek, production workers, manufacturing (hours)
5.	Average weekly initial claims, State unemployment insurance (thousands)
8.	New orders for consumer goods and materials in 1972 dollars (billion dollars)
32.	Vendor performance, companies receiving slower deliveries (percent)
12.	Net business formation (index: 1967 = 100)
20.	Contracts and orders for plant and equipment in 1972 dollars (billion dollars)
29.	New building permits, private housing units (index: 1967 = 100)
36.	Change in inventories on hand and on order in 1972 dollars, smoothed (annual rate, billion dollars)
99.	Change in sensitive materials prices, smoothed (percent)
19.	Stock prices, 500 common stocks (index: 1941–43 = 10)
106.	Money supply (M2) in 1972 dollars (billion dollars)
111.	Change in credit—business and consumer borrowing (annual rate, percent)
910.	Composite index of 12 leading indicators' (index: 1967 = 100)

COINCIDENT INDICATORS

41.	Employees on nonagricultural payrolls (thousands)
51.	Personal income less transfers in 1972 dollars (annual rate, billion dollars)
47.	Industrial production, total (index: 1967 = 100)
57.	Manufacturing and trade sales in 1972 dollars (million dollars)
920.	Composite index of 4 roughly coincident indicators (index: 1967 = 100)

LAGGING INDICATORS

91.	Average duration of unemployment (weeks)
77.	Ratio, constant-dollar inventories to sales, manufacturing and trade (ratio)
62.	Labor cost per unit of output, manufacturing—actual data as a percent of trend (percent)
109.	Average prime rate charged by banks (percent)
101.	Commercial and industrial loans outstanding in 1972 dollars (million dollars)
95.	Ratio, consumer installment credit to personal income (percent)
930.	Composite index of 6 lagging indicators (index: 1967 = 100)

Source: *Business Conditions Digest* (U.S. Department of Commerce Bureau of Economic Analysis, July 1984).

While the composite index of leading indicators (top of Figure 5–6) has been a better predictor than any single indicator, it has varied widely at peaks, with the longest lead time being 23 months before the peak in 1957 and the shortest being 3 months in 1981. At troughs, the longest lead has been 8 months before the bottom in 1982 and the shortest, one month in 1974–75. Table 5–2 presents the components for the 12 leading, 4 roughly coincident, and 6 lagging indicators.

Studies have found that the 12 leading indicators do not exhibit the same notice at peaks as they do at troughs. The notice prior to peaks is quite long, but the warning prior to troughs is very short, which means that it is very easy to miss a turnaround to the upside, but on the downside, you can be more patient waiting for confirmation from other indicators. It should also be noted that the indicators occasionally give false signals. Sometimes the indicators give no clear signal at all, and with the large variability of leads and lags versus the average lead time, an investor is lucky to get close to predicting economic activity within three or four months of peaks and troughs. It becomes clear that despite economic indicators and forecasting methods, investors cannot escape uncertainty in an attempt to manage their portfolios of assets.

One very important fact is that the stock market is the most reliable and accurate of the 12 leading indicators. This, of course, presents a very real problem for us because our initial objective is to forecast (as well as we are able) changes in common stock prices. In order to do this, we are constrained by the fact that the stock market is anticipatory and, in fact, has worked on a lead time of nine months at peaks and five months at troughs. Clearly, we need to find some variables that give longer leads than the stock market.

MONEY SUPPLY AND STOCK PRICES

One variable that has been historically popular as an indicator of the stock market is the money supply. The money supply is supposed to influence stock prices in several ways. Studies of economic growth and the money supply from 1867 to 1960 by Milton Friedman and Anna Schwartz found a long-term relationship between these two variables.[2]

Why does money matter? If you are a monetarist, money explains much of economic behavior. The quantity theory of money holds that as the supply of money increases relative to the demand for money, people will make adjustments in their portfolios of assets. If they have too much money, they will first buy bonds (a modification of the theory would now include Treasury bills or other short-term monetary assets), stocks, and, finally, real assets. This is the direct effect of money on stock prices sometimes referred to as the liquidity effect.

The indirect effect of money on stock prices would flow through the GNP's impact on corporate profits. As money influences economic activity, it

---

[2] Milton J. Friedman and Anna J. Schwartz, "Money and Business Cycles," *Review of Economics and Statistics,* Supplement, February 1963.

**FIGURE 5–7   Money Supply, Stock Prices, and Corporate Profits
Cyclical Indicators**

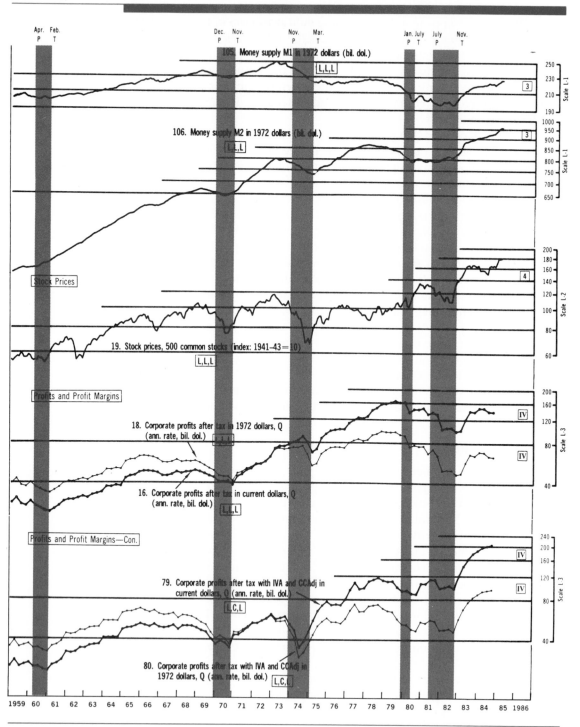

Source: *Business Conditions Digest* (U.S. Department of Commerce Bureau of Economic Analysis, April 1985).

will eventually influence corporate earnings and dividends and, thus, returns to the investors. Many studies have found that a significant relationship exists between the money supply variable and stock prices, but unfortunately, money supply growth and stock prices have turning points that are too similar to be really helpful to the investor.

Observe Figure 5–7, which includes the money supply, stock prices, and corporate profits on the same graph. It can be noted that in the 1969–70 and 1974–75 periods, the drop in the money supply did not lead the decline in stock prices enough to be helpful. In fact, during 1978–79 when the money supply began declining, stock prices continued to rise. This pattern of contrary movements is one that was of great interest to economists and financial analysts.

We question whether investors should react to short-term changes in the money supply. Present wisdom would suggest that the most positive long-term sign may simply be a *slow,* steady, predictable growth in the money supply— which will tend to moderate inflationary influences through restricted growth in the available dollars to purchase a limited supply of goods.

BUSINESS CYCLES AND INDUSTRY ANALYSIS

Each industry may be affected by the business cycle differently. Industries where the underlying demand for the product is consumer oriented will quite likely be sensitive to short-term swings in the business cycle. These industries would include durable goods, such as washers and dryers, refrigerators, electric and gas ranges, and automobiles. Changes in the automobile industry will also be felt in the tire and rubber industry as well as by auto glass and other automobile component suppliers. Figure 5–8 shows the automobile industry's sales from 1973 to mid-1984 relative to the real GNP's growth rate. Notice the similarity of the pattern. From the beginning of 1973 to the beginning of 1975, both GNP and automobile sales show steep declines. A recovery begins in 1975 and peaks in 1978 before declining again. This same type of pattern also continues into the 1980s. This close relationship is why it is often said that the United States lives in an automobile economy.

Not all industries are so closely related to the business cycle. Necessity-oriented industries, such as food and pharmaceuticals, are consistent performers since people do have to eat, and illness is not dependent upon the economy. Industries that have products with low price elasticities[3] that are habitual in nature, such as cigarettes and alcohol, do not seem to be much affected by business cycles either. In fact, there are some industries that do better during a recession. The movie industry prospers during a recession as more people substitute low-cost entertainment for more expensive forms. This is one pattern that may not remain the same, however. As cable television and pay TV come into their own with satellite hookups, people may find it even more convenient to stay at home than go to the movies when money is tight.

---

[3] Price elasticity represents the sensitivity of quantity purchased to price.

FIGURE 5–8   New Auto Sales and Real GNP, 1973–1984

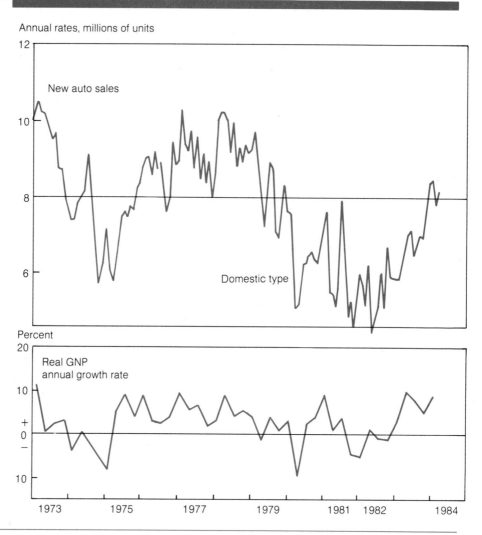

Source: *Federal Reserve Quarterly Chart Book* (Washington, D.C.: Board of Governors of the Federal Reserve System, July 1981 and May 1984).

This is one thing that makes investments exciting—the ever changing environment.

Housing is another example of an industry that historically has done well in recessionary environments. As the economy comes to a standstill, interest rates tend to come down, and prospective home purchasers are once again able to afford mortgage rates on a home. In the period of extremely high mortgage rates in the early 1980s, it was felt that a precipitous drop in mort-

gage rate would be necessary to once again stimulate growth in the housing market.

The Federal Reserve tracks data on various types of consumer expenditures. In Figure 5–9, we see the pattern for personal consumption expenditures on durable goods, nondurables, and services. Durable goods have fared relatively poorly during this period (1976–84) and have been the most susceptible to downturns, while nondurables have done quite well, with services leading the growth for personal expenditures.

FIGURE 5–9   Personal Consumption Expenditures (services, nondurable goods, and durable goods)

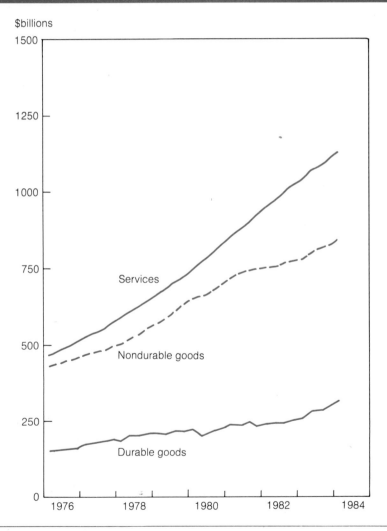

Source: *Federal Reserve Quarterly Chart Book* (Washington, D.C.: Board of Governors of the Federal Reserve Systems, May 1984).

Sensitivity to the business cycle may also be evident in industries which produce *capital* goods for other business firms (rather than consumer goods). Examples would be manufacturers of business plant and equipment, machine tools, or pollution control equipment. There often is a lag between the recovery from a recession and the increased purchase of capital goods, so that recoveries within these industries may be delayed. Computers and other high-technology industries tend to be less cyclical in nature and not as sensitive to the ups and down of the economy.

We do not mean to imply that cyclical industries are bad investments or that they should be avoided. We merely point out the cyclical influence of the economy. Often cyclical industries are excellent buys in the stock market because the market does not look far enough ahead to see a recovery and its impact on cyclical profits.

INDUSTRY LIFE CYCLES

Life cycles are created because of economic growth, competition, availability of resources, and the resultant market saturation by the particular goods and services offered. Life-cycle growth influences many variables considered in the valuation process. The particular phase of the life cycle that an industry or company is at determines the growth of earnings, dividends, capital expenditures, and market demand for products.

Figure 5–10 shows an industry life cycle (although it could very well be a company life cycle) and the corresponding dividend policy that is most likely to be found at each stage. A small firm in the initial stages of development (Stage I) pays no dividends because it needs all of its profits (if there are any) for reinvestment in new productive assets. If the firm is successful in the marketplace, the demand for its products will create growth in sales, earnings, and assets, and the industry will move into Stage II. At this stage, sales and returns on assets will be growing at an increasing rate, and earnings will still be reinvested. In the early part of Stage II, stock dividends (distributions of additional shares) may be instituted, and in the latter part of Stage II, *low* cash dividends may be started to inform investors that the firm is profitable.

Obviously, industries in Stage I or early Stage II are very risky, and the investor does not really know if growth objectives will be met or dividends will ever be paid. But if you want to have a chance to make an investment (after careful research) in a high-growth industry with large potential returns, then Stage I or II industries will provide you with opportunities for gains or losses. Since actual dividends are irrelevant in these stages, an investor will be purchasing shares for capital gains based on expected growth rather than current income. As the industry enters Stage III, the growth rate is still positive, but the rate of change starts declining. This is often the point where investors do not recognize that the growth rate has begun to decline, and they still pay large premiums over the regular market for stocks in these industries. However, when the market does realize that the growth rate in fact is diminishing, stock prices can take a sizable tumble.

FIGURE 5–10   Industry Life Cycle

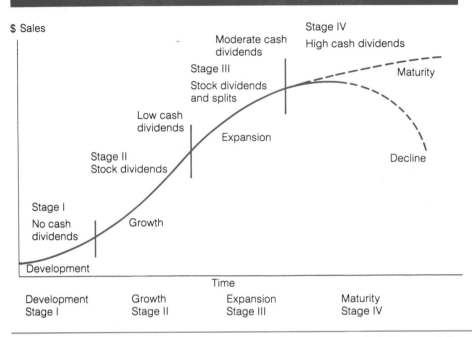

Source: Stanley Block and Geoffrey Hirt, *Foundations of Financial Management,* 3d ed. (Homewood, Ill.: Richard D. Irwin, 1984).

In Stage III, the expansion of sales continues but at a decreasing rate, and returns on investment may decline as more competition enters the market and attempts to take away market share from existing firms. The industry has expanded to the point where asset expansion slows in line with production needs, and the firms in the industry are more capable of paying cash dividends. Stock dividends and stock splits are still common in Stage III, and the dividend payout ratio usually increases from a low level of 5 to 15 percent of earnings to a moderate level of 25 to 40 percent of earnings. Finally, at Stage IV, maturity, the firm maintains a stable growth rate in sales similar to that of the economy as a whole, and when risk premiums are considered, its returns on assets level out to those of the economy. Automobiles might be a good example of a mature industry.

In unfortunate cases, industries suffer declines in sales (passenger railroads) if product innovation has not increased the product base over the years. In Stage IV, assuming maturity rather than decline, dividends might range from 40 to 60 percent of earnings. Of course, these percentages will be different from industry to industry depending on individual characteristics.

It is also important to realize that growth companies can exist in a mature industry and that not all companies within an industry experience the same growth path in sales, earnings, and dividends. Some companies are simply

better managed, have better people, more efficient assets, and have put more money into productive research and development that has created new products or improved products.

For example, electric utilities are generally considered mature, but some utilities exist in states like Florida, Texas, and California that have undergone rapid population explosions over the last decade. These utilities would still have higher growth rates than the industry in general. Computer companies, such as IBM, were fast approaching maturity until technical innovations created new markets. Now personal computers and word processors have not only added vitality to older markets, but also created new industries of their own. You can trace the histories of many industries to see that this pattern repeats itself over and over.

The warning to the investor is to not become too enamored with a company just because it is in a "growth industry." Its time of glory may have passed. Other investors improperly ignore companies that are in the process of revitalization because they no longer carry the growth-stock tag. More will be said about growth stocks in the next chapter.

Other Industry Factors to Consider

There are other significant factors that a financial analyst may wish to evaluate for a given industry. For example, is the industry structure monopolistic like a regulated utility, oligopolistic like the automobile or steel industry, partially competitive like the drug industry, or very competitive like the market for farm commodities? Questions of industry structure are very important in analyzing pricing structures and price elasticities that exist because of competition or lack of it.

Questions of supply and demand relationships are very important as they affect the price structure of the industry and its ability to produce quality products at a reasonable cost. The cost variable can be affected by many factors. For example, high relative hourly wages in basic industries, such as steel, autos, rubber, and others, are somewhat responsible for the inability of the United States to compete in the world markets of these products. Availability of raw material is also an important cost factor. Industries like aluminum and glass have to have an abundance of low-cost bauxite and silicon to produce their products. Unfortunately, the aluminum industry uses very large amounts of electricity in the production process, and so the low cost of bauxite may be offset by the high cost of energy. Energy costs are of concern to all industries, but the availability of reasonably priced energy sources is particularly important to the airline and trucking industries. The list could go on and on, but as an analyst becomes familiar with a specific industry, he or she learns the crucial variables.

Most industries are also affected by government regulation. This applies to the automobile industry where safety and exhaust emmissions are regulated and to all industries where air, water, and noise pollution are of concern. Many industries engaged in interstate commerce, such as utilities, railroads, and

telephone companies, are strongly regulated by the government. On the other hand, many industries, such as airlines, trucking, and natural gas production companies, are being deregulated, and these industries will be facing a new climate where the old game plan may no longer prove successful. Most industries are also affected by government expenditures; this is especially true for industries involved in defense, education, and transportation.

These are but a few examples to alert you to the importance of having a thorough understanding of your industry. This is why in many large investment firms, trust departments, and insurance companies, analysts are assigned to only one industry or to several related industries so that they may concentrate their attention on a given set of significant factors.

SUMMARY

The primary purpose of this chapter is to provide you with a process of valuation and an appreciation of some of the variables that should be considered. The valuation process is based upon fundamental analysis of the economy, industry, and company. This method assumes decisions are made based on economic concepts of value over the long-term trend of the stock market. The purpose of the process is to eliminate losers from consideration in your portfolio and to thereby provide you with a good opportunity to build a sound portfolio.

The first step in the valuation process is an analysis of the economy and long-term economic trends. The difficulties of attaining government policy goals are discussed as a trade-off between conflicting objectives (high growth versus low inflation). Fiscal and monetary policy are discussed as the primary tools used to stimulate economic activity. Interest rates are influenced by inflation, with the end result being a higher required rate of return for the investor.

Business cycles are short-term swings in economic activity; they have impacts on stock prices because they change investor expectations of risk and return. In order to forecast economic activity, cyclical indicators are presented as leading, lagging, and coincident indexes. The one index potentially most valuable to an investor is the composite index of 12 leading indicators. Unfortunately, stock prices are one of the most accurate leading indicators, and we must try to find another indicator that leads stock prices. The most popular and economically rational leading indicator is the money supply. The money supply influences economic activity by increasing or decreasing interest rates and corporate profits, which in turn eventually affect corporate dividends. Money also has a direct effect on stock prices by changing liquidity. An investor cannot escape risk, however, and the money supply is no sure way to forecast stock prices. The leads are too similar, and many factors have clouded the effect of changes in the money supply on the economy and stock prices.

The sensitivity of various types of industries to the business cycle is also examined. Firms in consumer durable goods as well as those in heavy capital

goods manufacturing (plant and equipment) are perhaps most vulnerable to the business cycle. Industries are also examined from the standpoint of their life-cycle growth path. This growth path affects earnings, dividends, and market valuation and provides a perspective on the valuation process which will be discussed further in the next chapter.

IMPORTANT WORDS AND CONCEPTS

Fundamental analysis
Valuation
Monetary policy
Fiscal policy
Federal deficit and surplus
Business cycles
Fed
Reserve requirements
Discount rate
Nominal GNP

Real GNP
Open-market operations
Cyclical indicators
Peaks and troughs
Monetarist
Money supply
Industry factors
Cyclical industries
Industry life cycle

DISCUSSION QUESTIONS

1. As depicted in Figure 5–1, what are the three elements in the valuation process?
2. What are the four goals under the Employment Act of 1946?
3. What is fiscal policy? Did Reagan or Carter place more emphasis on fiscal policy?
4. What is monetary policy?
5. How specifically can the Fed influence economic activity?
6. In regard to Federal Reserve open-market activity, if the Fed buys securities, what is the likely impact on the money supply? Is this likely to encourage expansion or contraction of economic activity?
7. In the early 1980s, how did the Federal Reserve redirect policy in regard to the money supply and interest rates?
8. What is the historical relationship between real GNP and inflation? What lesson might be learned from observing this relationship?
9. What is the advantage of using a composite of indicators (such as the 12 leading indicators) over simply using an individual indicator?
10. Do leading indicators tend to give longer warning before peaks or before troughs? What is the implication for the investor?
11. Give some examples of how different types of industries would relate to the business cycle.
12. Why do industry life cycles exist? How does the dividend policy generally relate to the life cycle of the firm or industry?

13. How has the computer industry avoided moving into Stage IV of maturity?

14. Develop a list of industries in each phase of the life cycle, and look up their dividend record to see if they correspond to the general view of the chapter.

15. Observe the performance of the 12 leading indicators for the next month. Compare this to changes in stock prices and interest rates.

SELECTED REFERENCES

Cairncross, Alec. "Economic Forecasting," *Economic Journal,* December 1969, pp. 797–812.

Elliott, J. W. "A Direct Comparison of Short-Run GNP Forecasting Models." *Journal of Business,* January 1973, pp. 33–60.

Federal Reserve Historical Chart Book and *Federal Reserve Quarterly Chart Book.* Washington, D.C.: Federal Reserve Board of Governors, selected issues.

Friedman, Milton J., and Anna J. Schwartz. "Money and Business Cycles." *Review of Economics and Statistics,* supplement, February 1963.

Gray, William. "The Stock Market and the Economy in 1988." *The Journal of Portfolio Management,* September 1984, pp. 73–80.

Heathcotte, Bryan, and Vincent P. Apilado. "The Predictive Content of Some Leading Economic Indicators for Future Stock Prices." *Journal of Financial and Quantitative Analysis,* March 1974, pp. 247–58.

Herbst, Anthony F. and Craig W. Slinkman. "Political-Economic Cycles in the U.S. Stock Market." *Financial Analysts Journal,* March–April 1984, pp. 38–44.

Hickman, B. G., ed. *Econometric Models of Economic Behavior.* New York: National Bureau of Economic Research, 1971.

Kenan, Michael W. "Expectations, Money, and the Stock Market." *Federal Reserve Bank of St. Louis Review,* January 1971, pp. 16–31.

Latane, Henry A., and Donald L. Tuttle. "Profitability in Industry Analysis." *Financial Analysts Journal,* July–August 1968, pp. 51–61.

Livingston, Miles. "Industry Movements of Common Stocks." *Journal of Finance,* June 1977, pp. 861–74.

Mennis, Edmund A. "The Practical Use of Economic Analysis in Investment Management." *The Economic Framework for Investors.* Charlottesville, Va.: The Financial Analysts Research Foundation, 1975.

Moor, Roy E. "The Use of Economics in Investment Analysis." *Financial Analysts Journal,* November–December 1971, pp. 63–69.

Nelson, Charles R. "Rational Expectations and the Predictive Efficiency of Economic Models," *Journal of Business,* July 1975, pp. 331–43.

Reilly, Frank K., and Eugene Drzycimski. "Alternative Industry Performance and Risk." *Journal of Financial and Quantitative Analysis,* June 1974, pp. 423–46.

Rozeff, Michael S. "Money and Stock Prices: Market Efficiency and the Lag in Effect on Monetary Policy." *Journal of Financial Economics,* September 1974, pp. 245–302.

Rogalski, Richard J., and Joseph D. Vinso. "Stock Returns, Money Supply and the Direction of Causality." *Journal of Finance,* September 1977, pp. 1017–30.

Spiro, Harvey M. "The Use of Economics in Portfolio Decisions." *Journal of Portfolio Management,* Spring 1976, pp. 34–38.

Sprinkel, Beryl W. *Money and Markets: A Monetarist View.* Homewood, Ill.: Richard D. Irwin, 1971.

Tysseland, Milford S. "Further Tests of the Validity of the Industry Approach to Investment Analysis." *Journal of Financial and Quantitative Analysis,* March 1971, pp. 835–47.

Wenglowski, Gary M. "Industry Profit Analysis—A Progress Report and Some Predictions." *The Economic Framework for Investors.* Charlottesville, Va.: The Financial Analysts Research Foundation, 1975.

Chapter 6

VALUATION OF THE INDIVIDUAL FIRM

The analysis in Chapter 5 centered on economic activity and the resultant swings in the business cycle which affected industries and corporate profitability and influenced the purchase of common stocks. The valuation of the individual firm was depicted as the last major step of the valuation process (Figure 5–1).

Valuation is based upon economic factors, industry variables, and an analysis of the financial statements and the outlook for the individual firm. The purpose of valuation is to determine the long-run fundamental economic value of a specific company's common stock. In the process, we try to determine whether a common stock is undervalued, overvalued, or fairly valued relative to its market price. As will be indicated in Chapter 8, there is a continuing controversy in academic circles over the ability of security markets to correctly price securities. This has led to debate over the efficient market hypothesis, which states that all securities are correctly priced at any point in time (there is no secret information to be uncovered by the enterprising analyst). For purposes of this chapter, we shall not be fully bound by the limiting assumptions of the efficient market hypothesis—though they are carefully considered in Chapter 8. Furthermore, most of the orientation in this chapter is to long-run concepts of valuation rather than to the determination of short-term market pricing factors.

BASIC VALUATION CONCEPTS

There are several ways to approach the valuation of common stock. Some models rely solely on dividends expected to be received during the future, and these are usually referred to as dividend valuation models. A variation on the dividend model is the earnings model, which substitutes earnings as the main income stream for valuation. Earnings valuation models may also call for the determination of a price–earnings ratio, or multiplier of earnings, to determine value. Other methods may include the market value of assets, such as cash and liquid assets, replacement value of plant and equipment, and other hidden assets, such as undervalued timber holdings. For the first part of our discussion, we develop the dividend valuation model and then move to earnings-related approaches. We conclude with a consideration of asset values.

DIVIDEND VALUATION MODELS

The value of a share of stock may be interpreted by the shareholder as the present value of an expected stream of future dividends. Although in the short run, stockholders may be influenced by a change in earnings or other variables, the ultimate value of any holding rests with the distribution of earnings in the form of dividend payments. Though the stockholder may benefit from the retention and reinvestment of earnings by the corporation, at some point the

earnings must generally be translated into cash flow for the stockholder.[1] While dividend valuation models are theoretical in nature and subject to many limitations, they are the most frequently used models in the literature of finance.

General Dividend Model

A generalized stock valuation model based on future expected dividends can be stated as follows:

$$P_0 = \frac{D_1}{(1 + K_e)^1} + \frac{D_2}{(1 + K_e)^2} + \frac{D_3}{(1 + K_e)^3} + \cdots + \frac{D_\infty}{(1 + K_e)^\infty} \quad (6\text{--}1)$$

where:

P_0 = Present value of the stock price.
D_i = Dividend for each year.
K_e = Required rate of return (discount rate).

This model is a very general model and assumes that the investor can, in fact, determine the right dividend for each and every year as well as the annualized rate of return that an investor requires.

Constant Growth Model

Rather than predict the actual dividend each year, a more widely used model includes an estimate of the growth rate in dividends. This model assumes a constant growth rate in dividends to infinity.

If a constant growth rate in dividends is assumed, Formula (6–1) can be expressed as:

$$P_0 = \frac{D_0(1 + g)^1}{(1 + K_e)^1} + \frac{D_0(1 + g)^2}{(1 + K_e)^2} + \frac{D_0(1 + g)^3}{(1 + K_e)^3} + \cdots + \frac{D_0(1 + g)^\infty}{(1 + K_e)^\infty} \quad (6\text{--}2)$$

where:

$D_0(1 + g)^1$ = Dividends in the initial year.
$D_0(1 + g)^2$ = Dividends in year 2, and so on.
g = Constant growth rate in the dividend.

The current price of the stock should equal the present value of the expected stream of dividends. If we can correctly predict the growth of future dividends and determine the discount rate, we can ascertain the value of the stock.

For example, assume that we wanted to determine the present value of ABC Corporation common stock based on this model. We shall assume that ABC anticipates an 8 percent growth rate in dividends per share, and we use a

---

[1] Some exceptions to this principle are noted later in the chapter.

12 percent discount rate as the required rate of return. The required rate of return (discussed in Chapter 1) is intended to provide the investor with a minimum real rate of return, compensation for expected inflation, and a risk premium. Twelve percent is sufficient to fulfill that function in this example.

Rather than project out the dividends for an extremely long period of time and then discount them back to the present, we can reduce Formula (6–2) to a more usable form:

$$P_0 = D_1/(K_e - g) \tag{6–3}$$

This formula is appropriate as long as two conditions are met. The first is that the growth rate must be constant in nature. For the ABC Corporation, we are assuming that to be the case. It is a constant 8 percent. Secondly, K_e (the required rate of return) must exceed g (the growth rate). Since K_e is 12 percent and g is 8 percent for the ABC Corporation, this condition is also met. Let's further assume D_1 (the dividend at the end of period 1) is $3.38.

Using Formula (6–3), we determine a stock value of:

$$P_0 = D_1/(K_e - g)$$
$$= \$3.38/(.12 - .08)$$
$$= \$3.38/.04$$
$$P_0 = \$84.50$$

This value, in theory, represents the present value of all future dividends. The meaning is further illustrated in Table 6–1, in which we take the present value of the first 20 years of dividends ($43.71) and then add in a figure of $40.79 to arrive at the present value of all future dividends of $84.50 as determined by Formula (6–3). The $40.79 value represents the present value of dividends occuring between 2006 and infinity (that is after the 20th year).

We must be aware that there are several things that could be wrong with our analysis. First, our expectations of dividend growth may be too high for an infinite period of time. Perhaps 6 percent is a more realistic estimate of expected dividend growth. If we substitute our new estimate into Formula (6–3), we can measure the price effect as dividend growth changes from an 8 percent rate to a 6 percent rate.

$$P_0 = \$3.38/(.12 - .06)$$
$$= \$3.38/.06$$
$$= \$56.33$$

A 6 percent growth rate cuts the present value down substantially from the prior value of $84.50.

We could also misjudge our required rate of return, K_e, which could be higher or lower. A lower K_e would increase the present value of ABC Corporation, whereas a higher K_e would reduce its value. We have made these points to show how sensitive stock prices are to the basic assumptions of the model. Even though you may go through the calculations, the final value is only as accurate as your inputs. This is where a security analyst's judgment and expertise are important—in justifying the growth rate and required rate of return.

TABLE 6–1   Present Value Analysis of ABC Corporation

Year	Expected dividends g = 8%	Present value factor $K_c = 12\%$ *	Present value of dividends
1986	$ 3.38	.893	3.02
1987	3.65	.797	2.91
1988	3.94	.712	2.81
1989	4.26	.636	2.71
1990	4.60	.568	2.61
1991	4.97	.507	2.52
1992	5.37	.453	2.43
1993	5.80	.404	2.34
1994	6.26	.361	2.26
1995	6.76	.322	2.18
1996	7.30	.288	2.10
1997	7.88	.257	2.03
1998	8.51	.229	1.95
1999	9.19	.204	1.87
2000	9.93	.182	1.81
2001	10.72	.163	1.75
2002	11.58	.146	1.69
2003	12.51	.130	1.63
2004	13.51	.116	1.57
2005	14.59	.104	1.52

PV of dividends for years 1986–2005	43.71
PV of dividends for years 2006 to infinity	40.79
Total present value of ABC Common Stock	$84.50

* Figures are taken from Appendix B at the end of this book.

A Nonconstant Growth Model

Many analysts do not accept the premise of a constant growth rate in dividends or earnings. As we examined in Chapter 5, industries go through a life cycle in which growth is nonlinear. Growth is usually highest in the infancy and growth phases of the life cycle, and as expansion is reached, the growth rate slows until the industry reaches maturity. At maturity, a constant, long-run growth rate that approximates the long-run growth of the macro economy may be appropriate for a particular industry.

It should be remembered that some companies in an industry may not behave like the industry in general. Companies constantly try to avoid maturity or decline, and so they strive to develop new products and markets to maintain growth.

In situations where the analyst wants to value a company without the constant growth assumption, a variation on the constant growth model is possible. Growth is simply divided into several periods with each period hav-

ing a present value. The present value of each period is summed to attain the
total value of the firm's share price. An example of a two-period model may
illustrate the concept. Assume that JAYCAR Corporation is expected to have
the growth pattern shown in Figure 6–1.

FIGURE 6–1   JAYCAR Growth Pattern

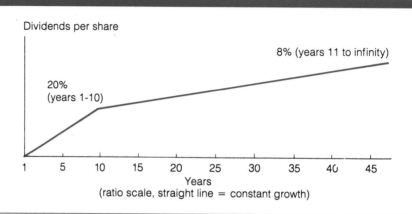

It is assumed that JAYCAR will have a dividend growth rate of 20 percent
for the next 10 years of its life and an 8 percent perpetual growth rate after
that. JAYCAR's dividend is expected to be $1 next year, and the appropriate
required rate of return (discount rate) is 12 percent. Taking the present value
for the first 10 years of dividends, and then applying the constant dividend
growth model for years 11 through infinity, we can arrive at an answer. First,
we find the present value of the initial 10 years of dividends.

Year	Dividends (20 percent growth)	PV factor (12 percent)*	Present value of dividends first 10 years
1	$1.00	.893%	$ .89
2	1.20	.797	.96
3	1.44	.712	1.03
4	1.73	.636	1.10
5	2.07	.567	1.17
6	2.48	.507	1.26
7	2.98	.452	1.35
8	3.58	.404	1.45
9	4.29	.361	1.55
10	5.15	.322	1.66
			$12.42

* Figures are taken from Appendix B at the end of this book.

We then determine the present value of dividends after the tenth year. The dividend in year 11 is expected to be $5.56 or $5.15 (for year 10) compounded at the new, lower 8 percent growth rate ($5.15 $\times$ 1.08). Since the rest of the dividend stream will be infinite, Formula (6–3) can provide the value of JAYCAR at the end of year 10, based on a discount rate of 12 percent and an expected growth rate of 8 percent.

$$P_{10} = D_{11}/(K_e - g)$$
$$P_{10} = \$5.56/(.12 - .08)$$
$$= \$5.56/.04$$
$$= \$139$$

An investor would pay $139 at the end of the 10th year for the future stream of dividends from year 11 to infinity. To get the present value of the 10th-year price, the $139 must be discounted back to the present by the 10-year PV factor for 12 percent from Appendix B (.322). This part of the answer is $139.00 $\times$ .322 or $44.76. The two parts of this analysis can be combined to get the current valuation per share of $57.18.

Present value of the dividends from years 1 to 10	$12.42
Present value of 10th year price ($139.00 $\times$ .322)	44.76
Total present value of JAYCAR common stock	$57.18

Do Dividends Really Matter?

Dividend valuation models estimate the present value from an expected future stream of dividends. If the predictions are correct, the valuation will probably be reasonably accurate, but if the forecast is off its target, such would not be the case.

If a firm fails to pay dividends, then dividend valuation makes little sense. If a firm were never to pay a dividend, would the company cease to have value? Probably not! As long as the expectation existed (borne out by reality) that retained earnings were being reinvested to increase the asset base of the company, the firm would have some value.

Dividends are currently taxed at 2½ times the rate for long-term capital gains. In this environment, many investors prefer to have capital gains from appreciating stock prices rather than dividends. Nevertheless, there has always been the "bird-in-the-hand theory" that dividends are worth more than earnings because, once paid to the stockholder, the company cannot take them away. While it is true that dividends do have information content and thus influence expectations, rising dividends are no guarantee that the common stock will also rise in the short run.

Fortune magazine compiled a list of companies with no dividends and with rising dividends for the period from 1970 to 1980. The results are not necessarily what one might expect. Table 6–2 shows 12 companies that paid no dividends over the entire 10-year period. The median annual return for these companies was 18.7 percent versus 9.4 percent for the Fortune 500 as a whole.

TABLE 6-2   A Dozen That Paid No Dividends

| Company | Total return to investors, 1970-80 | |
	Annual average compounded (percent)	Rank in Fortune 500
NVF	41.7%	2
National Semiconductor*	33.3	7
Teledyne*	32.2	9
Tosco*	28.9	17
Data General*	25.3	34
Penn Central	19.9	78
Digital Equipment*	17.4	96
Lockheed	13.9	143
Median for 500	9.4	
LTV	6.9	284
Crown Cork & Seal	4.6	342
DPF*	(5.7)	451
Memorex*	(13.9)	463

* Company has never paid a cash dividend.
Source: "Fresh Evidence that Dividends Don't Matter," *Fortune*, May 4, 1981, p. 351. *Fortune* Magazine Art Department. © 1981 Time Inc. All rights reserved.

Table 6-3 presents 19 companies with rising dividends over this decade. The 19 companies with rising dividends performed rather poorly on the basis of total return because of declining stock prices.

While increased dividends generally increase common stock value, we see that this is not always the case. If a company's overall performance is questionable, then raising dividends may not encourage investors. Although the examples in Table 6-3 represent exceptions to the rule, they occur frequently enough to deserve investor caution.

EARNINGS VALUATION MODELS

Dividend valuation models are best suited for those companies that are in the expansion or maturity phase of their life cycle. Dividends of these companies are more predictable and usually make up a larger percentage of the total return than capital gains. Earnings-per-share models are also used for valuation. For example, the investor may take the present value of all future earnings to determine a value. This might be particularly appropriate where the firm pays no cash dividend and has no intention of paying one.

The Combined Earnings and Dividend Model

Another, more comprehensive valuation model relies on earnings per share (EPS) and a price-earnings ratio (earnings multiplier) combined with a finite

TABLE 6–3   Growing Dividends Didn't Save These Stocks

Company	Growth in cash dividends, average annual rate, compounded 1971–80 (percent)	Decline in stock price 1970–80 (percent)	Total return to investors, 1970–80	
			Annual average return, compounded (percent)	Rank in Fortune 500
Burroughs	26.6%	(1.4%)	1.2%	398
Brunswick	24.7	(17.3)	1.3	396
Economics Laboratory	16.7	(13.2)	.8	404
Jim Walter	16.3	(16.4)	1.9	386
Georgia-Pacific	14.0	(4.1)	2.4	381
Nashua	13.5	(16.8)	1.5	392
Coca-Cola	11.8	(21.2)	1.0	402
Brockway Glass	10.4	(36.4)	.7	411
Avon Products	10.0	(61.4)	(5.2)	449
Colgate-Palmolive	9.9	(8.1)	3.0	375
Quaker Oats	9.0	(6.4)	2.9	376
Warner-Lambert	8.7	(41.2)	(1.8)	432
ITT	8.5	(40.7)	.5	413
Owens-Illinois	8.4	(10.5)	3.3	370
Champion Spark Plug	8.0	(11.5)	4.2	350
Heublein	7.7	(38.3)	(1.3)	428
National Service Industries	7.3	(9.3)	5.0	324
Sybron	6.8	(45.4)	(1.7)	431
Squibb	4.9	(17.9)	.8	405

Source: "Fresh Evidence that Dividends Don't Matter" *Fortune*, May 4, 1981, p. 354. *Fortune* Magazine Art Department. © 1981 Time Inc. All rights reserved.

dividend model. The value of a common stock can be viewed as a dividend stream plus a market price at the end of the dividend stream. Using Procter & Gamble as an example, we develop a present value for the stock at the beginning of 1986 (the numbers are shown in Table 6–4).

The total present value (stock price) for Procter & Gamble is shown at the bottom of Table 6–4 to be $79.38. Note that Part A of Table 6–4 describes the present value of future dividends, while Part B is used to determine the present value of the future stock price. These are assumed to be the two variables that determine the current stock price under this model.

In Part A, earnings per share are first projected for the next five years. The earnings are then multiplied by the company's estimated payout ratio of 45 percent to determine anticipated dividends per share for the next five years. In this example, we are assuming investors have a 13 percent required rate of return, so that is used as the discount rate. The present value of five years of dividends is shown in column (5) of Part A of Table 6–4 as $13.11.

In Part B of the table, we multiply 1990 earnings per share of $10.17 by

TABLE 6–4   Procter & Gamble Present Value Analysis at Beginning of 1986

Part A: Present value of dividends for 5 years

Year	(1) Estimated earnings per share (growth = 10%)	×	(2) Estimated payout ratio	=	(3) Estimated dividends per share	×	(4) PV factor (13%)	=	(5) Present value
1986	$ 6.95		.45		3.13		.885		$ 2.77
1987	7.64		.45		3.44		.783		2.69
1988	8.41		.45		3.78		.693		2.62
1989	9.25		.45		4.16		.613		2.55
1990	10.17		.45		4.58		.543		2.48
									$13.11

Part B: Present value of common stock price

Year	EPS	×	P/E	=	Price	×	PV factor	
1990	$10.17		12.0		$122.04		.543	66.27

A + B = Total present value of Procter & Gamble
common stock at the beginning of 1986 $79.38

the P/E multiple (earnings multiple) of 12 to arrive at an anticipated price five years into the future. This price of $122.04 is then discounted back for five years at 13 percent to arrive at a present value of $66.27.

The present value of the stock is equal to the present value of the dividend stream for five years ($13.11) plus the present value of the future stock price of ($66.27) for a total current value of $79.38 at the beginning of 1986.

The Pure, Short-Term Earnings Model

Often, investors/speculators take a very short-run view of the market and simply ignore using present value analysis with its associated long-term forecasts of dividends and earnings per share. Instead they only use earnings per share and apply an appropriate multiplier to compute the estimated value.

Applying this approach to Procter & Gamble's financial data initially presented in Table 6–4, we arrive at a value of $83.40, based on 1986 earnings and a price–earnings multiplier of 12.

$$P_0 = EPS \times P/E$$
$$= \$6.95 \times 12$$
$$P_{1986} = \$83.40$$

Of course, every method of valuation has its limitations. Although this method is simplified by ignoring dividends and present value calculations,

earnings need to be correctly estimated, and the appropriate price–earnings (P/E) multiplier must be applied. Unfortunately, just as in the dividend models, even if the estimated EPS is correct, there is no assurance that the market will agree with your P/E ratio.

THE PRICE–EARNINGS RATIO

The price–earnings ratio is simply the price per share divided by earnings per share. The price–earnings ratio is ultimately set by investors in the market-place. In the previous section, we attempted to determine the value of a share of Procter & Gamble at the end of the year by estimating earnings per share and the likely P/E ratio. The P/E ratio may or may not turn out to equal our estimate. Any stock that has positive earnings may have its P/E ratio computed at any point in time. The current price of the stock is simply divided by 12 months of earnings per share.

Even though the current P/E ratio for a stock in the market is known, investors may or may not agree that it is appropriate. In fact, stockbrokers and investors probably spend more time examining P/E ratios and assessing their appropriate level than any other variable. Although the use of P/E ratios in valuation approaches lacks the theoretical underpinning of the present value-based dividend and earnings valuation models previously discussed in the chapter, P/E ratios are equally important. The well-informed student of investments should have a basic understanding of both the theoretically based present-value approach and the more pragmatic, frequently used P/E ratio approach.

What determines whether a stock should have a high or low P/E ratio? Let's first talk about the market for stocks in general, and then we will look at individual securities.

Stocks generally trade at a relatively high P/E ratio (perhaps 13 or greater) when there are strong growth prospects in the economy. However, inflation also plays a key role in determining P/E ratios for the overall market.

It is interesting to note that the market was generally rising between 1973 and January of 1981 while price-earnings ratios were falling. This can be seen in Figure 6–2, in which stock prices are graphed on the upper portion of the figure and measured along the left-hand axis, and the range of annual P/E ratios is shown on the bottom portion of the figure, with values presented on the right-hand axis.

Why were P/E ratios declining between 1973 and early 1981? The year 1973 was the start of particularly high inflation, which continued into 1981 and finally was significantly reduced by 1984. To further illustrate the point, Figure 6–3 presents the relationship between the year-end Standard & Poor's 500 composite P/E ratio and the annual rate of inflation measured by the change in the consumer price index (CPI). The graphical relationship between these two variables shows that they are inversely related. The price–earnings ratio goes down when the change in the CPI goes up and the reverse is also true.

FIGURE 6–2   Standard & Poor's 500 Stock Index and Price–Earnings Ratios

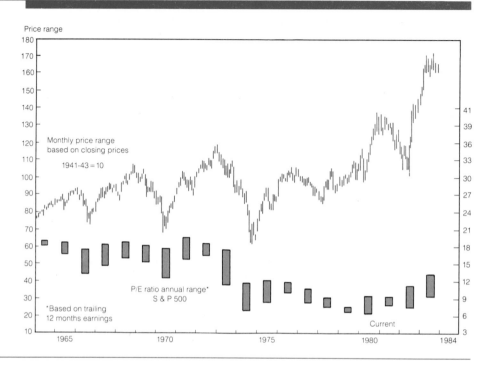

The dramatic drop in the P/E ratio in 1973–74 can be attributed to a large degree on the rate of inflation increasing from 3.41 percent in 1972 to 12.2 percent in 1974, or a change of more than three times its former level. For a brief period (1976) inflation decreased to an annual rate of less than 5 percent, only to soar to 13.3 percent by 1979. The average rate of inflation for 1982–83 was reduced to 3.84 percent and the market responded by paying higher share prices for one dollar of earnings (that is, higher P/E ratios). Perhaps if investors can be convinced that inflation will average less than 5 percent over the coming years, P/E ratios may again reach their former high levels. As was pointed out in Chapter 1, required rates of return are directly influenced by the rate of inflation. As inflation increases, the required rate of return on common stocks, K_e, rises, and prices decline. This is the basic mechanism that causes inflation to indirectly influence P/E ratios.

Of course, other factors besides the previously mentioned growth factor and the heavily emphasized inflationary considerations influence the P/E ratio for the market in general. Federal Reserve policy and interest rates, federal deficits, the government's leading indicators, the political climate, the mood and confidence of the population, international considerations, and many other factors have an influence on the P/E ratio for the overall market. The astute analyst is constantly studying a multitude of variables in analyzing the future outlook for P/E ratios.

FIGURE 6–3   Inflation and Price–Earnings Ratios

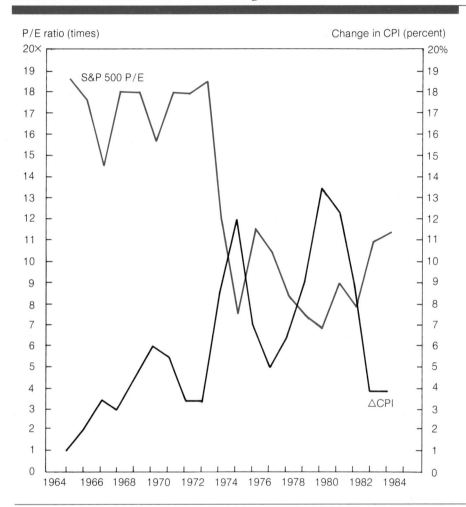

The P/E Ratio for Individual Stocks

Although the overall market P/E ratio is the collective average of individual P/Es, those factors that influence the market P/E do not necessarily impact P/E ratios of individual companies consistently from one industry to another. An individual firm's P/E ratio is heavily influenced by its growth prospects and the risk associated with its future performance. In Table 6–5, we see examples of growth rates and P/E ratios for different industries and firms. Generally, a strong future growth rate for 1984–89 (column 4) is associated with a reasonably high P/E for mid-1984 (column 6). Obviously the relationship can be complicated by other considerations. For example, the brokerage firm, Merrill Lynch, shows an inordinately high P/E ratio of 60x in mid–1984. This is associated with a mere 7.0 percent expected growth rate for EPS in 1984–89.

TABLE 6–5   P/E and Growth in EPS

(1) Industry	(2) Company	(3) 5-year EPS growth 1979–83	(4) Expected growth EPS 1984–89	(5) 1979–83 median P/E	(6) P/E Mid-1984	(7) Expected normal P/E
Appliances	Maytag	5.0%	8.2%	9.8×	8.7×	10.0×
Newspaper	Dow Jones	19.0	19.5	14.0	19.5	27.0
Railroads	CSX	9.5	15.5	6.5	6.0	9.5
Drugs	Bristol Myers	13.5	15.0	12.0	13.7	15.0
Fast Foods	McDonald's	17.5	15.0	12.0	11.5	13.0
Trucking	Roadway	11.5	13.0	13.0	9.3	13.0
Tobacco	Reynolds	10.5	9.5	6.5	7.6	8.0
Brokerage	Merrill Lynch	26.0	7.0	7.5	60.0	10.0

Source: *Value Line Investment Survey,* selected issues (Value Line Inc.)

The reason behind this inconsistency is that Merrill Lynch's recent earnings are down sharply. Their slightly reduced price over an *unusually* low earnings base gives the appearance of a high P/E ratio. This high P/E ratio is phantom in nature and will work itself down as earnings improve, even if the stock price increases somewhat. Highly cyclical firms, such as those in the brokerage, auto, or housing industries, have temporarily misleading P/E ratios from time to time when their earnings are very low.

In addition to the future growth of the firm and the risk associated with that growth, investors and analysts also consider a number of other factors that influence a firm's P/E ratio. These cannot be easily quantified; nevertheless they have an impact on a broad range of stocks. Included in this category are the debt-to-equity ratio and the dividend policy of the firm. All things being equal, the less debt that a firm has, the more likely it is to be highly valued in the marketplace.

The dividend policy is a more elusive matter. For firms that show superior internal reinvestment opportunities, low cash dividends may be acceptable. On the other hand, maturing companies may be expected to pay a high cash dividend. For the latter group, a reduction in cash dividends may be associated with a lower P/E ratio.

Certain industries also traditionally command higher P/E ratios than others. Over the years, it would appear that investors have some preference for industries that have a high technology and research emphasis. Thus firms in computers, medical research and health care, and sophisticated telecommunications often have higher P/E ratios than the market in general. This does not mean that firms in these industries represent superior investments, but merely that investors value their earnings more highly.[2] There are also fads and other

---

[2] William Kittrell, Geoffrey A. Hirt, and Roger Potter, "Price-Earnings Multiples, Investors' Expectations, and Rates of Return: Some Analytical and Empirical Findings," paper presented at the 1984 Financial Management Association meeting.

factors that cause a shift in industry popularity from time to time. For example, because Ronald Reagan has emphasized military strength, defense-oriented stocks have been popular during his administration. Jimmy Carter stressed the need for environmental control, and stocks dealing in air and water pollution control traded at high P/E ratios during his tenure in office.

Another factor that influences a firm's P/E ratio is the quality of management as perceived by those in the marketplace. To the extent that management is viewed as being highly capable, clever, or innovative, the firm may carry a higher P/E ratio. Investors may look to magazines such as *Forbes* or *Business Week,* which highlight management strategies by various companies, or to management-oriented books such as *In Search of Excellence.*[3] Of course, it is entirely possible that today's trend setters may represent tomorrow's failures.

Not only is the quality of management important to investors in determining the firm's P/E ratio, but so is the quality of earnings. As, perhaps, you have studied in accounting and will observe further in the next chapter on financial statement analysis, there are many interpretations of a dollar's worth of earnings. Some companies choose to use very conservative accounting practices so that their reported earnings can be interpreted as being very solid by investors (in fact they may even be understated). Other companies use more liberal accounting interpretations in order to report maximum earnings to their shareholders, and they, at times, overstate their true performance. It is easy to see that a dollar's worth of conservatively reported earnings may be valued at a P/E ratio of 13 to 15 times, whereas a dollar's worth of liberally reported earnings should be valued at a much lower multiple.

All of these factors impact a firm's P/E ratio. Thus, investors will consider growth in sales and earnings, future risk, the debt position, the dividend policy, the quality of management and earnings, and a multitude of other factors in eventually arriving at the P/E ratio. The P/E ratio, like the price of the stock, is set by the interaction of the forces of demand and supply for the security. Those firms which are expected to provide returns greater than the overall economy, with equal or less risk, generally have superior P/E ratios.

Relating an Individual Stock's P/E Ratio to the Market—the General Signal Corporation

The General Signal Corporation is a leading producer of electronic and hydraulic control devices (pumps, valves, etc.). Table 6–6 provides a summary of earnings per share (EPS), the high-low stock price, and high-low P/E ratio for the company. Also shown is the average P/E ratio for the Standard & Poor's 500 Stock Index over a similar time period. In the last three columns, the high, average, and low P/E ratio for General Signal Corporation is compared to the average P/E ratio for the Standard & Poor's 500 Stock Index. For example, in 1976, General Signal's high P/E ratio is 14.20. The Standard & Poor's 500 Stock

---

[3] Thomas J. Peters and Robert H. Waterman, Jr., *In Search of Excellence* (New York: Harper & Row, 1982).

TABLE 6–6   General Signal Corporation—EPS, Price, P/E, and P/E Relative

	General Signal EPS	General Signal price		General Signal P/E			Standard & Poor's 500 P/E	General Signal's P/E relative to S&P 500		
Year	EPS	High	Low	High	Average	Low	Average*	High	Ave.	Low
1976	2.00	28.40	17.10	14.20	11.36	8.6	11.25	1.26	1.01	.76
1977	2.43	29.50	22.70	12.14	9.28	9.3	9.28	1.31	1.16	1.00
1978	2.93	33.70	23.50	11.50	9.75	8.0	8.33	1.38	1.17	.96
1979	3.52	39.10	25.00	11.11	9.14	7.1	7.43	1.50	1.23	.96
1980	4.01	54.20	28.20	13.52	10.26	7.0	8.02	1.69	1.28	.87
1981	4.23	51.38	33.38	12.15	9.99	7.9	8.47	1.43	1.18	.93
1982	3.85	47.00	28.00	12.21	9.79	7.3	8.82	1.38	1.11	.83
1983	3.16	52.38	40.50	16.58	14.72	12.8	12.69	1.31	1.16	1.01
1984	4.15e									
Average high P/E for last five years for General Signal							13.11			
Average low P/E for last five years for General Signal							8.42			
Average P/E for last five years for General Signal							10.77			
S&P's average P/E for last five years							9.09			
Average P/E relative to S&P's 500 for last five years							1.19			

e = Estimated.
* Quarterly average based on 12-month moving average EPS.

Index value is 11.25, and the relative (or ratio between the two) is 1.26. The same relationship can be derived for General Signal's average and low P/E ratios.

The second part of Table 6–6 provides average values over the last five years; for example, the average high P/E ratio over the last five years for General Signal is 13.11, the average low P/E is 8.42, etc.

Using the information from Table 6–6, we can derive a range of reasonable price predictions for General Signal based upon our estimates of future earnings per share. We indicate the following:

	Estimated	P/E*			Anticipated stock price		
Year	EPS	High	Ave.	Low	High	Ave.	Low
1984e	$4.15	13.11	10.77	8.42	$54.41	$44.70	$34.94
1985e	4.73	13.11	10.77	8.42	62.01	50.94	39.83
1986e	5.39	13.11	10.77	8.42	70.66	58.05	45.38
1987e	6.15	13.11	10.77	8.42	80.63	66.24	51.78
1988e	7.01	13.11	10.77	8.42	91.90	75.50	59.02

e = Estimated.
* Taken from the second part of Table 6–6.

The earnings forecasts are based on an analysis of historical growth and future prospects. In September of 1984 General Signal was actually trading at

$48.75 per share. This price is a little higher than the average value of $44.70 shown above for 1984, but seems reasonable, given our analysis of historical P/E ratios. Furthermore, if earnings projections come through, higher stock values may be expected in the future.

What about a comparison of General Signal's P/E ratio to the Standard & Poor's 500? As indicated in the last line of the second part of Table 6–6, General Signal's average P/E carries a premium multiple of 1.19 times the average S&P 500. The Standard & Poor's Index was actually selling at 10.3 times earnings per share in late 1984. Based on the normal relationship to the S&P Index, General Signal should have a P/E ratio of 12.26 (10.3 × 1.19). This would imply a stock price of $50.88 (12.26 × $4.15) which is $2 higher than its current price. Whether this is reasonable or not would require much further analysis. The assumption of this kind of analysis is that by picking stocks selling at the low end of their P/E relative you have a better chance of outperforming the overall market.

FORECASTING EARNINGS PER SHARE

The other side of choosing an appropriate P/E is forecasting the earnings per share of a company with the proper growth rate. There are several ways investors can get earnings forecasts. They can rely on professional brokerage house research, investment advisory firms such as Value Line, financial magazines such as *Forbes* or *Business Week,* or they can do it themselves.

Investment Advisory Services

Standard & Poor's Earnings Forecaster is a service that provides estimated earnings per share data from several different sources. Table 6–7 shows a few forecasts from this S&P publication for GEO International and for Georgia Pacific. The company providing the forecast is listed as well as the date the forecast was made (i.e., Advest, September 15 for GEO International). There can be a wide difference of opinion for some companies, such as Georgia Pacific in the lumber-housing industry. The estimates for 1982 vary from $2.25 per share to $3.75 per share. Obviously, Bache has a different concept of interest rates and the housing industry than the other forecasters.

Least Squares Trendline

One of the most common ways of forecasting earnings per share is to use regression or least squares growth analysis. This involves a statistical method whereby a trendline is fitted to a time series of historical earnings. This trendline, by definition, is a straight line which minimizes the distance of the individual observations from the line. Figure 6–4 depicts a scattergram for the earnings per share of XYZ Corporation. The earnings of this company have been fairly consistent, and so we get a good trendline with a minimum of variation. The compounded growth rate for the whole 10-year period was 16.5

TABLE 6–7   Sample data from *Standard & Poor's Earnings Forecaster*

Company and fiscal year ending date	Stock price	Estimated date	P/E ratio	Earnings per share		
				1980*	1981	1982
GEO International (September)	34		8×	2.31		
Advest		September 15			4.00–4.25	—
Bacon, Whipple		September 16			4.20	—
A. G. Edwards		October 7			4.10	5.70
Howard, Weil, Labouisse, Freidrichs		October 14			4.00	5.75
Georgia Pacific (December)	20		9×	2.34		
Bache		September 3			1.65†	2.25
E. F. Hutton & Co.		September 20			1.60†	2.50
Shearson		August 1			2.75†	3.75
United Business Service		October 5			2.10†	—

* Actual.
† Fully diluted.
Source: *Standard & Poor's Earnings Forecaster,* October 23, 1981.

percent, with 9.8 percent for the first 5 years and 20.4 for the last 5 years. This shows up in Figure 6–4 as two distinct five-year trendlines. Most universities have statistical programs that run regression analysis, and even handheld calculators have the ability to compute a growth rate from raw data.

Whenever a mechanical forecast is made, subjectivity still enters the decision in choosing the data which will be considered in the regression plot.

FIGURE 6–4   Least Squares Trendline for EPS of XYZ Corporation

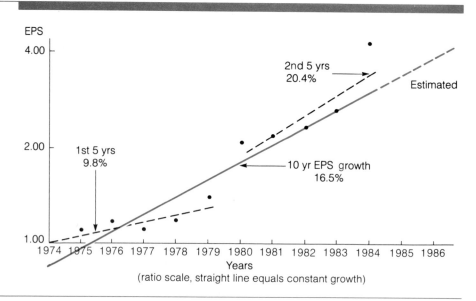

The analyst should be careful not to extrapolate a trend from a peak to a trough (bottom) or a trough to a peak. This can be extremely misleading for a cyclical industry. The analyst should also be sure to use enough data points to get a good line, and in cyclical industries, plot out the line for several business cycles to get a long-run average. Let's examine two actual companies to contrast different patterns of growth and the implications for forecasting.

Using Allied Corporation, a cyclical chemical stock, and Merck & Company, a consistently growing drug company, we compare earnings per share trends in Table 6–8. Both companies have achieved a similar overall growth over the time frame, but Allied Corporation is much more subject to ups and downs in the economy.

TABLE 6–8   Growth in Earnings per Share

Year	Earnings per share Allied Corporation (past 10-year EPS growth equals 12%)	Earnings per share Merck & Co. (past 10-year EPS growth equals 12%)
1972	1.59	1.99
1973	2.30	2.40
1974	3.62	2.79
1975	2.78	3.03
1976	3.01	3.38
1977	3.29	3.85
1978	2.83	4.07
1979	.13	5.06
1980	5.43	5.54
1981	6.11	5.36
1982	3.68	5.61
1983	4.17	6.10
1984e	5.20e	6.75e

e = Estimated.

The values are plotted in Figure 6–5. From that figure, it is clear that Merck & Company would provide the more reliable forecast based on past data. Its trendline is very consistent. While Merck has basically the same growth rate as Allied Corporation, it is much more stable with less deviation. In order to forecast Allied Corporation you would not start in 1982 and end in 1984 (trough to peak). Starting in 1977 would probably also not provide a "true" trendline because the line would begin at a cyclical peak. Clearly an Allied Corporation forecast based on 10 or 12 years of data is more reliable than a three- or five-year (based) forecast. With companies that follow economic cycles, the best forecasting period encompasses at least two peaks and two troughs or several business cycles. Remember that trendline earnings projected into the future, especially in the case of Allied Corporation, represent an average estimate and not an annual forecast.

FIGURE 6–5   Allied Corporation and Merck & Company EPS Trendlines

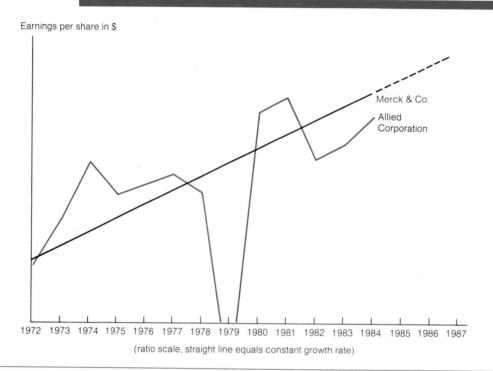

Earnings per share in $

Merck & Co.

Allied
Corporation

1972 1973 1974 1975 1976 1977 1978 1979 1980 1981 1982 1983 1984 1985 1986 1987

(ratio scale, straight line equals constant growth rate)

The Income Statement Method

A more process-oriented method of forecasting earnings per share is to start
with a sales forecast and create a standardized set of financial statements based
on historical relationships. Of course, the sales forecast must be accurate if the
earnings estimates are to have any significance. This method can be involved
and provides a student with a very integrated understanding of the relationships that go into the creation of earnings. For a firm such as Merck & Co. there
would not be much gained from an income statement forecast, but for Allied
Corporation the cyclical nature of profitability would be brought out.

Several important factors are included in this method of forecasting. The
analyst is forced to examine profitability and the resultant fluctuations in profit
margins before and after taxes. The impact of short-term interest expense and
any new bond financing can be factored into the analysis as well as any increase in shares of common stock from new equity financing.

Most analysts use an abbreviated method of forecasting earnings per
share. They use a sales forecast combined with aftertax profit margins. For
example, let us assume that the Hutchins Corporation has a sales and profit
margin history as set forth in Table 6–9. The sales have been growing at a 10
percent growth rate, and so the forecast is a simple extrapolation. However,

TABLE 6–9   Abbreviated Income Statement Method—Hutchins Corporation

Year	Sales ($000s)	Aftertax profit margin	Earnings ($000s)	Shares (000s)	Earnings per share
1980	$1,250,000	7.9%	$ 98,750	30,000	$3.29
1981	1,375,000	9.1	125,125	31,500	3.97
1982	1,512,500	8.5	128,562	33,200	3.87
1983	1,663,750	6.5	108,143	35,000	3.08
1984	1,830,125	8.3	151,900	35,200	4.31
1985	2,013,137	8.7	175,142	37,000	4.73
1986e	2,214,452	8.2	173,958	38,400	4.53
1987e	2,435,896	9.0	219,230	39,800	5.50

e = Estimated.

the profit margin has fluctuated between 6.5 percent and 9.1 percent, with 8.2 percent being the average. Common stock outstanding has also grown consistently by an average of 1.4 million shares per year. Given the cyclical nature of the profit margin, 8.2 percent was used for 1986, which is expected to be an average year. Nine percent was used for 1987, a year expected to be economically more robust. Multiplying the profit margin times the estimated sales produced an estimate of earnings which was divided by the number of shares outstanding to find the earnings per share. Once the EPS is found, it still must be plugged into a valuation model to determine a normal value.

GROWTH STOCKS AND GROWTH COMPANIES

In assessing the worth of an investment, stockbrokers, analysts, and investors often make reference to such terms as *growth stock* and *growth companies.* As part of the process of improving your overall valuation skills, you should have some familiarity with these terms.

A *growth stock* may be defined as the common stock of a company generally growing faster than the economy or market norm. These companies are usually predictable in their earnings growth. Many of the more popular growth stocks, such as 3M, Eastman Kodak, and McDonald's, are really in the middle-to-late stages of the expansion phase. They tend to be fully valued and recognized in the marketplace.

Growth companies, on the other hand, are those companies that exhibit rising returns on assets each year and sales that are growing at an increasing rate (growth phase of the life-cycle curve). Growth companies may not be as well known or recognized as growth stocks. Companies that may be considered to be growth companies might be in such industries as cable television, word processors, personal computers, medical electronics, and so on. These companies are growing very rapidly, and extrapolations of growth trends can be very dangerous if you guess incorrectly. There are many things that growth

companies have in common. Usually, they have developed a proprietary product that is patented and protected from competition like the Xerox process (now other companies can use the dry process). This market protection allows a high rate of return and generates cash for new-product development.

One of the things that growth stocks and growth companies have in common is good research and development (R&D). Each company tries to prolong the growth and expansion phase of its life cycle as long as possible with new products or improved products. Value Line's November 13, 1981, issue of *Selection and Opinion* featured an article entitled "R&D: Key to Growth." Value Line took 409 companies over the 1978–80 period and measured research and development expenditures as a percentage of sales. They then ranked these 409 companies from the highest to lowest (R&D/sales) ratio. The top 10 R&D companies' average spending was 11 percent of sales dollars on research and development, which generated an earnings per share growth of 33.7 percent over the 10-year period. The bottom 10 companies spent less than .12 percent on average, and EPS grew at only 8.3 percent. A further test with the top 100 companies showed R&D/sales averaged 5.6 percent with a resultant 15.2 percent growth in EPS, while the bottom 100 companies' R&D/sales averaged .44 percent and increased earnings 11.3 percent.

Besides research and development, there are other indicators of growth potential. Companies should have sales growth greater than the economy by a reasonable margin. Increasing sales should be translated into similar earnings growth, which means consistently stable and high profit margins. Additionally, the earnings growth should show up in earnings per share growth (no dilution of earnings through unproductive stock offers). The firm should have a low labor cost as a percentage of total cost, since wages are prone to be inflexible on the downside but difficult to control on the upside.

The biggest error made in searching for growth-oriented companies is that the price may already be too high. By the time you identify the company, so has everyone else, and the price is probably inflated. If the company has one quarter where earnings do not keep up with expectations, the stock price could tumble. The trick, of course, is to find growth companies before they are generally recognized in the market, and this requires taking more risk in small companies trading over-the-counter.

ASSETS AS A SOURCE OF STOCK VALUE

Up until now, our emphasis has been primarily on earnings and dividends as the source of value. However, in certain industries, asset values may have considerable importance. These assets may take many forms—cash and marketable securities, buildings, land, timber, old movies, oil, and other natural resources. At times, any one of these assets may dominate a firm's value. Furthermore, companies with heavy cash positions are attractive merger and acquisition candidates because there is a possibility that a firm with highly

TABLE 6–10 Value from Energy Reserves

Company (1980 revenues in $ millions)	(1) Operating income (percent) Pipelines	(2) Operating income (percent) Oil and gas production	(3) Present value of proven reserves on 12/31/80 (per share)	(4) Stock price (early March)	(5) Price as multiple of estimated 1981 earnings*	(6) Yield (percent)
Interstate transmission:						
Texas Eastern ($4,272)	35%	54%	$178.17	$57.00	6.1	5.6%
United Energy Resources ($4,135)	91	9	14.49	42.75	6.3	3.6
Transco Companies ($2,628)	85	15	43.19	47.00	9.4	3.1
Panhandle Eastern Pipe Line ($2,472)	56	44	25.17	42.00	6.7	4.1
Southern Natural Resources ($1,798)	58†	8†	16.21	67.25	8.9	2.8
Intrastate transmission:						
ENSERCH ($2,695)	41	35	27.06‡	50.25	10.1	3.4
Houston Natural Gas ($2,358)	54	18	12.49§	49.50	8.5	2.6
Texas Oil & Gas ($1,191)	40‡	55‡	15.02 ‖	37.25	19.4	.5

* Source for earnings: Institutional Brokers Estimate System.
† Percent of net income.
‡ Estimate.
§ On July 31, 1980.
‖ On August 31, 1980.
Source: "There is Still a Glow in Gas Pipelines," *Fortune*, April 6, 1981, p. 96. *Fortune* Magazine Art Department.

liquid assets could be taken over and its own cash used to pay back debt incurred in the takeover.

In the 1970s and 1980s, natural resources have also had an important influence on value. Let's briefly examine this topic.

Natural Resources

Natural resources, such as timber, copper, gold, and oil, often give a company value even if the assets are not producing an income stream. This is because of the present value of the future income stream that is expected as these resources are used up. Companies like International Paper, Weyerhaeuser, and other forest-product companies have timberlands with market values far in excess of their book values and, in some cases, in excess of their common stock prices.

Oil companies with large supplies of oil under the ground may have to wait 20 years before some of it is pumped, but there may be substantial value there. In the case of natural-gas pipeline companies, increasing reserves have changed the way these companies are viewed by the market. They used to be considered similar to utilities because of their natural gas transmission system, but now they are also being valued based on their hidden assets (called energy reserves). Table 6–10 gives a list of pipeline companies and the present value of their proven reserves compared to the common stock price (in the third and fourth columns).

Investors should not overlook hidden assets because of naive extrapolation of past data or failure to understand an industry or company. Furthermore, assets do not always show up on the books of a company. They may be fully depreciated, like the movies *Sound of Music, Jaws,* or *Star Wars,* but still have substantial value in the television market.

SUMMARY

This chapter presents several common stock valuation models that rely on dividends and earnings per share. The point is made in all of them that in order for the valuation to be accurate, the forecast of earnings and dividends needs to be correct.

Firms can be valued in many ways, and an analyst may choose to use several methods to substantiate his or her estimates. Valuation models based primarily on dividends look at future projections of dividends and the associated present values of the dividends. Assumptions must be made as to whether the dividend growth pattern is constant, accelerating, or decreasing.

Valuation using the earnings method requires that a price–earnings ratio be used as a multiplier of EPS. Price–earnings ratios are influenced by many variables, such as growth, risk, capital structure, dividend policy, level of the market in general, industry factors, and more. A careful study of each situation must be concluded before choosing the appropriate P/E. The price–earnings ratio is a function of two fluctuating variables—earnings and price. The two

variables combine together to form a ratio that is primarily future oriented. High price–earnings ratios usually indicate positive expectations of the future, whereas low price–earnings ratios connote negative expectations.

In order to choose a P/E that is reasonable, the analyst must have some idea about the expected growth rate in earnings per share. Investors may find earnings estimates in investment advisory services, in statistical forecasts by brokerage houses, through their own time series statistical regression analysis, or by using the income statement method. Growth stocks were discussed more with the view of alerting the student of what to look for when trying to identify a growth stock or company than with the concept of valuation. The previously developed methods of valuation can be used on growth stocks as long as care is taken to evaluate the duration and level of growth.

We also presented some basic ideas about the value of companies based not on their earnings or dividend stream but on their assets, such as cash or natural resources. Throughout the chapter, it was pointed out that every industry and company is unique. Management, products, organization structure, accounting systems, and philosophy are different for each. The role of an analyst is to understand the intricacies of several related industries and companies so as to enlighten the investing public.

An example of a sophisticated company analysis prepared by the research department of Kidder, Peabody & Company, is shown in the appendix at the end of this chapter.

IMPORTANT WORDS AND CONCEPTS

Valuation
Fundamental analysis
Valuation models
Dividend valuation models
Earnings valuation models
P/E ratio
Income statement method
Growth stock

Growth company
Hidden asset values
Constant growth model
Nonconstant growth model
Combined earnings and
    dividend model
Least squares trendline

DISCUSSION QUESTIONS

1. How is value interpreted under the dividend valuation model?
2. The discount rate in the dividend valuation model is referred to as the required rate of return. What three factors make up the required rate of return?
3. What two conditions are necessary to use Formula (6–3)?
4. Is there any conflict between the assumption of constant growth (g) in Formula (6–3) and the industry life cycle?
5. How can companies with nonconstant growth be analyzed?

6. Give a reason why a stockholder may prefer the potential for capital gains to current dividends. Likewise, give a reason why dividends may be preferred to retaining the earnings.

7. In considering P/E ratios for the overall market, what was the relationship between price–earnings ratios and inflation in the 1970s and early 1980s?

8. What other factors beside inflation influence P/E ratios for the general market?

9. What two factors are probably most important in influencing the P/E ratio for an *individual stock?* Suggest a number of other factors as well.

10. What type of industries tend to carry the highest P/E ratios?

11. What is the essential characteristic of a least squares trendline?

12. What two elements go into an abbreviated income statement method of forecasting?

13. What is the difference between a growth company and a growth stock? What are some industries in which there are growth companies?

14. How should a firm with natural resources be valued?

15. What is an example of a valuable asset that might not show any "value" on a balance sheet?

PROBLEMS

1. Assume D_1 = $1.80, k_e = 13 percent, g = 9 percent. Using Formula (6–3) for the constant growth dividend valuation model, compute P_0.

2. Using the data from Problem 1:
   a. If D_1 and k_e remain the same, but g goes up to 10 percent, what will the new stock price be? Briefly explain the reason for the change.
   b. If D_1 and g retain their original value ($1.80 and 9 percent), but k_e goes up to 15 percent, what will the new stock price be? Briefly explain the reason for the change.

3. Using the original data from Problem 1, find P_0 by following the steps described below:
   a. Project dividends for years one through three (the first year is already given). Round all values that you compute to two places to the right of the decimal point.
   b. Find the present value of the dividends in part a.
   c. Project the dividend for the fourth year (D_4).
   d. Use Formula (6–3) to find the present value of all future dividends, beginning with the fourth year's dividend. The present value you find will be at the end of the third year (the equivalent of the beginning of the fourth year).
   e. Discount back the value found in part d for three years at 13 percent.
   f. Observe that in part b you determined the percent value of dividends for the first three years and, in part e, the present value of an

infinite stream after the first three years. Now add these together to get the total present value of the stock.

    g.   Compare your answers in part f to your answer to Problem 1. Comment on the relationship.

4. Nonconstant-growth model problem. The Haltom Corporation anticipates a nonconstant growth pattern for dividends. Dividends at the end of year one are $2.40 per share and are expected to grow by 15 percent per year until the end of year five (that's four years of growth). After year five, dividends are expected to grow at 5 percent as far as the company can see into the future. All dividends are to be discounted back to the present at a 9 percent rate ($k_e = 9$ percent).

    a.   Project dividends for years one through five (the first year is already given). Round all values that you compute to two places to the right of the decimal point.

    b.   Find the present value of the dividends in part a.

    c.   Project the dividend for the sixth year (D_6).

    d.   Use Formula (6–3) to find the present value of all future dividends, beginning with the sixth year's dividend. The present value you find will be at the end of the fifth year.

        Use Formula (6–3) as follows: $P_5 = D_6/(k_e - g)$.

    e.   Discount back the value found in part d for five years at 9 percent.

    f.   Add together the values from part b and part e to determine the present value of the stock.

    g.   Explain how the two elements in part f go together to provide the present value of the stock.

5. Rework Problem 4 with a new assumption, that dividends at the end of the first year are $1.60 and that they will grow at 18 percent per year until the end of the fifth year, at which point they will grow at 6 percent per year for the foreseeable future. Use a discount rate of 12 percent throughout your analysis. Round all values that you compute to two places to the right of the decimal point.

6. R. L. Lynch investment bankers will use a combined earnings and dividend model to determine the value of the Pierce Corporation. The approach they take is basically the same as that in Table 6–4 in the chapter. Estimated earnings per share for the next five years are:

1986	$4.00
1987	4.40
1988	4.84
1989	5.32
1990	5.85

    a.   If 35 percent of earnings are paid out in dividends, and the discount rate is 14 percent, determine the present value of dividends.

    b.   If it is anticipated that the stock will trade at a P/E of 10 times 1990 earnings, determine the stock's price at that point in time and discount back the stock price for five years at 14 percent.

    c.   Add together part a and part b to determine the stock price under this combined earnings and dividend model.

7.   Mr. Brown of Northwest Investment Company is evaluating the P/E ratio of Alaska Consumer Electronics (ACE). The firm's P/E is currently 13. With earnings per share of $2, the stock price is $26.

    The average P/E ratio in the consumer electronics industry is presently 12. However, Ace has an anticipated growth rate of 15 percent versus 10 percent for the industry norm, so 2 will be added to the industry P/E by Mr. Brown. Also, the operating risk associated with ACE is less than that for the industry because of their long-term contract with Sears. For this reason, Mr. Brown will add another factor of 1 to the industry P/E ratio.

    The debt to total asset ratio is not as encouraging. It is 50 percent, while the industry ratio is 40 percent. In doing his evaluation, Mr. Brown decides to subtract a factor of ½ from the industry P/E ratio. Other ratios, including dividend payout, appear to be in line with the industry, so Mr. Brown will make no further adjustments along these lines.

    However, he is somewhat distressed by the fact that the firm only spent 3 percent of sales on R&D last year, when the industry norm is 5 percent. For this reason he will subtract a factor of 1 from the industry P/E ratio.

    In spite of the relatively low research budget, Mr. Brown observes that the firm has just hired two of the top executives from a competitor in the industry. He decides to add a factor of ½ to the industry P/E ratio because of this.

    a.   Determine the P/E ratio for ACE, based on Mr. Brown's analysis.

    b.   Multiply this times earnings per share and comment on whether you think the stock might possibly be under- or overvalued in the marketplace at its current P/E and price.

8.   Refer to Table 6–6 in the chapter. Assume that analysts determine that General Signal's P/E ratio in 1984 should be 15 percent higher than the S&P average P/E ratio or the last five years. (Carry your calculation of the P/E ratio two places to the right of the decimal point in this problem.) What would the stock price be, based on earnings per share of $4.15?

9.   In Problem 8, if analysts determine that because of unusually favorable conditions, the P/E ratio should be equal to the average high P/E ratio for the last five years for General Signal Corporation, what would the stock price be, based on earnings per share of $4.15?

10.   Security analysts following Wolfson Corporation use a simplified income statement method of forecasting. Assume that 1985 sales are $20 million and are expected to grow by 12 percent in 1986 and 1987. The aftertax profit margin is projected at 6.1 percent in 1986 and 5.9 percent in 1987. The number of shares outstanding is anticipated to be 500,000 for 1986 and 510,000 for 1987. Project earnings per share for 1986 and 1987.

11. The average price–earnings ratio for the industry that the Wolfson Corporation is in is 8×. If the company has a P/E ratio 20 percent higher than the industry of 8 in 1986 and 25 percent higher than the industry ratio also of 8 in 1987, (*a*) indicate the appropriate P/Es for the firm in 1986 and 1987; (*b*) combine this with the earnings per share data in Problem 10 to determine the anticipated stock price for 1986 and 1987.

12. Relating to Problems 10 and 11, assume that you wish to determine the probable price range in 1987 if the P/E ratio is between 9.5 and 11. What is this price range?

SELECTED REFERENCES

Basu, S. "Investment Performance of Common Stocks in Relation to Their Price–Earnings Ratios: A Test of the Efficient Market Hypothesis." *Journal of Finance,* June 1977, pp. 663–82.

Beaver, William, and Dale Morse. "What Determines Price–Earnings Ratios?" *Financial Analysts Journal,* July–August 1978. pp. 65–76.

Benishay, Haskell. "Market Preferences for Characteristics of Common Stocks." *Economic Journal,* March 1973, pp. 173–91.

Black, Fischer. "The Dividend Puzzle." *Journal of Portfolio Management,* Winter 1976, pp. 5–8.

Chung, Peter S. "An investigation of the Firms Effect Influence in the Analysis of Earnings to Price Ratios of Industrial Common Stocks." *Journal of Financial and Quantitative Analysis,* December 1974, pp. 1009–29.

Friend, Irwin, and Marshall Puckett. "Dividends and Stock Prices." *American Economic Review,* September 1964, pp. 656–82.

Goodman, David A., and John W. Peavy III. "Industry Relative Price–Earnings Ratios As Indicators of Investment Returns." *Financial Analysts Journal,* July–August 1983, pp. 60–66.

Graham, Benjamin. "The Future of Common Stocks." *Financial Analysts Journal,* September–October 1974, pp. 20–30.

Kittrell, William; Geoffrey A. Hirt; and Roger Potter. "Price–Earnings Multiplier, Investors' Expectations, and Rates of Return: Some Analytical and Empirical Findings." Paper presented at the 1984 Financial Management Association meeting.

Latane, Henry A.; O. Maurice Joy; and Charles P. Jones. "Quarterly Data, Sort-Rank Routines, and Security Evaluation." *Journal of Business,* October 1970, pp. 427–38.

Litzenberger, Robert H., and O. Maurice Joy. "Further Evidence on the Persistence of Corporate Profitability Rates." *Western Economic Journal,* June 1970, pp. 209–12.

Mao, James C. T. "The Valuation of Growth Stocks: The Investment Opportunities Approach." *Journal of Finance,* March 1966, pp. 95–102.

Miller, Merton, and Franco Modigliani. "Dividend Policy, Growth, and the Valuation of Shares." *Journal of Business,* October 1961, pp. 411–33.

Peters, Thomas J., and Robert H. Waterman, Jr. *In Search of Excellence.* New York: Harper & Row, 1982.

Reilly, Frank. "The Misdirected Emphasis on Security Evaluation," *Financial Analysts Journal,* January–February 1973, pp. 54–60.

Robichek, Alexander A., and Marcus C. Bogue, "A Note on the Behavior of Expected Price/Earnings Ratios Over Time." *Journal of Finance,* June 1971, pp. 731–35.

Walter, James E. "Dividend Policy: Its Influence on the Value of the Enterprise." *Journal of Finance,* May 1963, pp. 280–91.

Wendt, Paul F. "Current Growth Stock Valuation Models," *Financial Analysts Journal,* March–April 1965, pp. 91–103.

Wippern, Ronald F. "Financial Structure and the Value of the Firm" *Journal of Finance,* December 1966, pp. 615–33.

APPENDIX: Kidder, Peabody & Co. Research Report on
General Electric Company

The Research Department

Company Follow-Up

June 5, 1984

General Electric Company¶
(NYSE-GE)

52-Week Range	Recent Price	Earnings Per Share (a)			P/E Ratio		Dividend Rate	Current Yield
		1983	1984(E)	1985(E)	1984(E)	1985(E)		
59-46	54	$4.45	$5.10	$5.70	10.6	9.5	$2.00	3.7%

(E) Kidder, Peabody & Co. Incorporated estimate.
(a) Fiscal year-end December 31.

- GE is currently the most dynamic company in the electrical equipment industry; major restructuring continues.

- The 1984 and 1985 earnings outlooks are good, but the real challenge is to increase earnings in the next downward phase of the economic cycle, as GE did in 1982 and early 1983.

- GE foresees 5%-to-6 1/2% real GNP growth in 1984; 2 1/2%-to-3% in 1985; and no recession in 1985.

- Our 1985 earnings estimate revised to $5.70 from $6.00 a share.

- We continue to recommend purchase. GE is a Current Recommendation on the Kidder, Peabody Selected Stock List.

POINT OF VIEW

At a recent analyst meeting Jack Welch, Chairman, presented an update on GE's progress in restructuring and realigning of its present businesses, divestitures and acquisitions, operating margin improvement despite the sale of Utah, and new products. *The overall impression is that GE is in great shape under the strong leadership of Mr. Welch and an impressive and deep management team.*

The GE story has become somewhat simpler. The company now has *three main thrusts: High Technology, Services, and Core.* There are fifteen major businesses in these three areas, and there are three support businesses. There is a very clear strategy for each business, enunciated by Mr. Welch at the meeting. We were impressed by his grasp of even the smallest details in all his businesses and also by his ability to address the big picture questions with insight.

The real challenge is not to increase earnings each year in the current business expansion but *to keep earnings up in the next recession,* as GE did in 1982 and early 1983. The large reduction in salaried and blue collar employment was a one-shot benefit, but the big investments being made in productivity improvements should cushion an economic downturn so that GE should continue to increase earnings.

As for the economy, Mr. Welch was bullish in December 1983, and the company was driving to build inventory. Now the outlook is very gray. GE expects that in 1984 as a whole there should be 5%-to-6 1/2% real GNP growth. The momentum is there; the personal income is there; the economy is not going to shut down with an interest rate

Electrical Equipment —————————————

Robert W. McCoy, Jr.
(212) 747-2522

APPENDIX (continued)

Kidder, Peabody & Co.
Incorporated

bulge. Inflation will come in at 4% to 5 1/2%. 1985 should be a year of growth, but much slower than 1984's, maybe 2 1/2% to 3%. That would be a fairly good range for GE, although not good for the third year of a recovery. GE thinks the government will come to grips with the deficit problem immediately after the election. Inflation will go up by a percentage point to the 5 1/2%-to-7% range. *GE does not expect a recession to develop in 1985.*

Inflation is not being driven by the manufacturing sector because the manufacturing industries are not being driven by commodity prices. Manufacturing companies have little ability to raise prices because the environment is very competitive; everyone is afraid to lose even a single percentage point of market share. The heat is good for American industry because it forces companies to concentrate on productivity to increase earnings.

In the current depressed stock market GE stock at 54 has held up reasonably well because of the market's preference for strong blue chips. The stock is selling at 10.6 times our 1984 earnings-per-share estimate of $5.10. This is a relative multiple premium of 16% to the *S&P 500*, and the stock appears slightly undervalued on the basis of the Kidder, Peabody Investment Strategy benchmark of 0.8 times the next-five-year earnings growth rate (14% x 0.8 = 11.2). Our long-term growth rate projection for GE is 13% to 15%. However, it is our opinion that, because of the progress being made at GE, the relative multiple premium should be at least 30% and possibly 50%; hence *we continue to recommend purchase and retain the stock as a Current Recommendation on the Kidder, Peabody Selected Stock List.*

THE EVOLVING COMPANY

GE is now structured into three major categories: High Technology, Services, and Core, and fifteen businesses (see table). In High Technology are five businesses: Industrial Electronics, Medical Systems, Materials, Aerospace, and Aircraft Engines. In Services are four businesses: Financial, Information, Construction and Engineering, and Nuclear. The core has six businesses: Lighting, Major Appliances, Motors, Turbines, Transportation, and Construction Equipment.

These fifteen businesses are supported by three other businesses: One is Oil and Gas, which is a backup source of feedstock to GE's $2-billion-a-year materials business and is a very big part of GE's owned and operated cogeneration activities.

General Electric Company
GE's Principal Business Categories
(As percentages of 1983 net earnings)

Major Businesses

High Technology (29%)	Services (31%)	Core (32%)
Industrial Electronics	Financial	Lighting
Medical Systems	Information	Major Appliance
Materials	Construction and Engineering	Motor
Aerospace	Nuclear	Turbine
Aircraft Engines		Transportation
		Construction Equipment

Support Businesses

Oil and Gas	Semiconductor	Trading

Another is Semiconductors, which are critical to almost every business in all three categories as GE changes from an electromechanical company to an electronic company. The importance of the third, the trading company, is ever more critical in obtaining foreign orders for GE products by countertrade and even barter.

In its three categories GE is either dominant today or has a clear-cut shot at becoming dominant. It is not dominant, nor does it intend to be, in the three support areas. GE thinks it has a very good handle on most of its businesses, a reasonable handle on some, and a few problems that have yet to be solved.

ORDER OUTLOOK

New orders in the first four months of 1984 were up more than 10% year to year. In High Technology all five businesses had strong order gains. Orders of Medical Systems were up 10% without booking the 135 orders for magnetic resonance units that have been obtained up to now. Orders of Materials were up 20%. Those of Industrial Electronics were off the chart — only because its business was so bad last year. For Aerospace and Aircraft Engines, as for everyone else in that industry, rates of new orders were strong.

In Services, GE Credit sets a monthly record every month. Even though GE Credit has sold off

APPENDIX (continued)

Kidder, Peabody & Co.
Incorporated

$600 million of second mortgage businesses, its earning assets will be up 20% in 1984 to $16 billion. Construction and Engineering Services is showing strong growth, as is Nuclear Services. Information Services is flat as GE goes from one strategy to another (from a remote computing service business to a solution business).

In the Core, business for Major Appliances continues to be strong. Lighting is up 15%. Motors are strong. Construction Equipment continues to pick up. Turbines are very weak, as is Transportation. The backlog of stored locomotives is dropping off significantly, and proposal activity is picking up. Transportation orders should be up in the second half of the year, but Turbines' business will remain dead. Cogeneration is the only exciting area for Turbines.

DIVESTITURES AND ACQUISITIONS

GE has had a very active year so far in divestitures and acquisitions. The sale of Utah was closed in April; GE got $2 billion in cash. The sale of Housewares was closed for $300 million. Family Financial, the second mortgage company, was sold for $660 million. Employers Reinsurance (ERC) was purchased for $1.075 billion and the assets of Patrick Petroleum for $200 million, and GE established a joint-venture laser company with *Coherent (25)*.

The ERC acquisition was a straight purchase from *Texaco¶ (35)* with no tender fight and no dilution of 1984 earnings. ERC should contribute to earnings next year.

ERC has six key people in Kansas City, Missouri, who have been with the organization for most of their careers. They are good, solid people. GE has signed employment contracts and feels very good about the people and the culture.

ERC is a good risk-assessment business. It will provide positive cash flow to help fund GECC's growth. It will provide good earnings growth. GE paid a fair price [*General Reinsurance's (54)* multiple] without any premium. The transaction provided good value for both Texaco and GE. GE thinks it can manage 300-people operations very nicely.

In Patrick GE is buying assets that will increase Ladd Petroleum's reserves by 26%, at $8 a barrel of oil, and will double acreage from 1 million to 2 million.

Through Coherent GE has 40% of a joint venture in lasers called General Laser, which Coherent will manage.

North American Car was an asset play. GE Credit had a credit problem with *Tiger International (5 5/8)*. GE was able to buy, at a very low price, the rail cars and the servicing business while at the same time providing liquidity to Tiger International.

In Guiness Peat GE has 18% of an aviation company that as a worldwide airplane broker is proving valuable. GE and Guiness Peat have been able to move airplanes from one airline to another.

In ceramics, GE bought a business from ▶*3M (76)*. Sales should go from $40 million in 1983 to an $80-million-to-$90-million rate by the end of 1984.

AMIC (mortgage insurance) and GECAL (automobile leasing) were both new areas to GE two years ago. In 1984 they will account for 10% of GECC's earnings.

These examples of small acquisitions represent an underlying culture of activity.

Buying back GE stock remains an option. There is a time to sell, and there is a time to buy; a number of companies that GE has looked at at higher prices in the past are now more interesting.

Progress in divestitures will be slower for a while because market demand for properties is weak. GE will continue to work on its problem businesses, improving the fundamentals. GE has given three-year commitments to young, aggressive management teams to fix the video and mobile radio businesses. Video and Mobile Radio are now in the black.

OPERATING MARGIN

GE bought Utah at the peak of its operating margin (35%). Over the next eight years Utah's operating margin dropped 9 points to 26% — still very high for a part of a company with an overall operating margin of 9%. The question now is what will happen to GE with the elimination of this $1.8-billion-a-year, 26%-margin company.

In 1972 GE had an operating margin of around 8%. In the 1975 recession the margin dropped to 7%; after Utah was included it rose to 10%. As Utah eroded, the overall margin went to 9%, but GE was not standing by idle; it cut base costs dramatically over the past three and a half years. Salaried employment is down by 25,000, and hourly employment is down by 60,000. GE has put $2.5 billion into rationalization of Major Appliance, Motors, Lighting, and other businesses. More recently the state of the economy has been reasonably good. *In 1984, without Utah, GE should have a 9.4% margin, and there is a chance the*

APPENDIX (continued)

Kidder, Peabody & Co.
Incorporated

margin could exceed 10% (GE's highest margin without Utah in recent history).

STRATEGY UPDATE

In High Technology GE has four clear-cut businesses where it knows what it is doing and where it is and is on the way to fulfilling the whole story. In Medical the question is whether GE can duplicate its success in computerized temography (CT), where GE's share went from nothing to 50% of the world market. Can the company do the same thing in magnetic resonance (MR)? The jury is still out. In the past 12 months GE has received 135 commitments for these $2-million machines, that is, 65% of the domestic market. GE has the only machine with a magnet power of 1.5 Tesla. When the machine is approved by the Food and Drug Administration GE will be in a clear-cut leadership position in the worldwide market.

CT scanner sales will be up in 1984, but orders will be down. The number of units shipped will be over 1,000, and orders will be about 900. Orders in 1983 were about 980. The CT market is clearly being affected by the availability of funds because everyone wants an MR machine. There is a drive to lower costs through simpler CT machines such as those produced by a GE joint venture in Japan, which will ship 80 units in 1984 (versus 20 in 1983) to third world countries and the Middle East.

In Materials GE knows where it is. It has a 70% leadership position in the market for poly-carbonate and 100% in Noryl. This is going to be an increasingly competitive market. But GE has a business that is really profitable. Dow Chemical (29) is entering the market in 1985 with 30 million pounds of engineered plastics (a very small part of the total industry). To become a major competitor Dow must spend hundreds of millions of dollars. (A new plant costs $3 per pound of capacity.) Thus, GE with its economies of scale and dominant market position should be able to withstand the increasing competition, at least through the 1980s.

In Aircraft Engines the question is whether there will be a viable, long-term commercial engine business in terms of profitability. GE feels fairly good about the commercial engine business. The Boeing 737-300 with the CFM56 engine is using Rolls Royce's marketing strength for GE's big engines. The CFM56-4 will have a real run at the United Technologies consortium's new engine (the 2500). GE looks at its engine business as a unit and does not draw an artificial demarcation line between commercial and military. It builds cores and common technology and gets economies of scale. Having the CFM56 enabled GE to bid the F110 the way it did.

In Aerospace the question is: Can GE broaden the niches so that it can compete successfully in a broader range of the same type of product (be a bigger player in the same niche, like radar)?

In Industrial Electronics, the product strategy (programmable and numerical control) is coming along well. GE's real strategy, though, is to develop a full-system business in which margins are much higher and there is less competition. Customers do want one-stop shopping, and plant managers want solutions rather than a bunch of products. GE can deliver total systems because it is making them internally. The question is whether the system business will come along fast enough in this cycle to make it. Progress is beginning to be made. Currently GE has $80 million of system jobs; the goal this year is $400 million. However, GE will lose another $40 million after taxes in 1984 on industrial electronics. GE will continue to spend, and it has the resources and the muscle to win, but maybe not in this cycle.

In Services, there was some concern that with further deregulation GE Credit would have some problems. The answer is absolutely no. GE Credit is in the risk-assessment business, and it understands that business better than anybody. It understands collateral as well as technology better than anyone else. It understands money and is not simply in the "money over money" business. (That is, it does not just lend at a spread but adds value to a transaction.) That is why Family Financial (fixed-rate second mortgages with rising interest rates currently) was sold. GE is going after niches and not playing in a variety of games. ERC has had a sustained ROE of over 20%. Financial Services will account for 15% of total GE net income in 1984. The maximum GE wants is 18% to 20%. As long as GE Financial Services can maintain high profitability, assess risk, employ few people, and remain consumer-oriented, GE will be successful in financial services.

In Construction and Engineering GE is having a problem because it is fighting employees' and customers' long entrenched component (versus systems) mentality. The business is profitable and growing (although it has less than $100 million in annual net profit). GE must build its engineering capability to compete with Bechtel and others. It must take advantage of its leadership position in turbines to do a total system job.

In Nuclear GE has a clear-cut winning play but in a game that may not be big enough to make the

APPENDIX (concluded)

win exciting. GE is going to supply services and reload fuel for boiling water reactors only.

In Information Services there is a revolution going on. It is a big game, and GE has a lot of talent. The company is confident that it can make the transition from raw power to a solution business.

In the Core GE is number one or two in every business. These businesses are big and profitable; the challenge is to keep them very profitable a decade from now. Some of the best reinvestment stories are in Major Appliances and Lighting. In Dishwashers, GE has gone from a 31% share to 45% in an old business with leading quality and lowest cost. In Lighting, GE is in the process of closing 12 plants and taking lines that make 4,000 bulbs an hour up to 8,000 bulbs an hour. It took 26 years to go from 3,000 to 4,000 bulbs an hour. Now GE is trying to double the output rate in 26 months.

The point is that GE is after quantum changes, not incremental changes. GE is out to *radically restructure* businesses like Lighting and Motors. The 1984 theme at GE is to ask whether every act is just incremental or is quantum.

NEW PRODUCTS

Modicom [*Gould*¶† *(27)*] and *Allen Bradley* dominate the market for programmable controllers. GE's sales were zero in 1981 and will be $80 million in 1984. Sales are doubling every month, and the production line is full. GE thinks it will be number two within five years.

In magnetic resonance GE received $260 million of commitments over the past 12 months.

In cogeneration GE will do $300 million in volume in 1984. GE has three roles: 1) financing entrepreneurs; 2) equipment sales; and 3) owning and operating.

Xenoy, the new engineered material, in its third year will have sales of $55 million.

The Trading Company will do $600 million in countertrade in 1984. It has made possible the sale of turbines in Rumania and has undertaken big obligations in Sweden and Spain to facilitate the sale of large orders.

In China the outlook is very exciting, but time will tell. GE has a $225-million locomotive order and just got a big CT scanning order. It also has a letter of intent to form a joint venture lighting company.

1984 AND 1985 OUTLOOK

We think GE will earn $5.10 a share in 1984, up 15% from 1983's $4.45. Our estimate includes a 25% net earnings gain for Services and Materials, a 10% gain for GE Credit, a 25% increase for Consumer Products, a 10% increase for Power Systems, a 25% gain for Aircraft Engines, and a 42% increase for Technical Systems. The only real drag on 1984 performance centers on the divestiture of Utah and the inability to immediately reinvest the proceeds at the high return that Utah was earning. Thus we estimate that earnings of Natural Resources will be down 19% in 1984.

With the publication of this report we are lowering our 1985 earnings-per-share estimate from $6.00, up 18%, to $5.70, up 12%. The reason for the modest revision is a slightly less positive economic environment than previously forecasted. We estimate earnings increases for Services and Materials of 10%, GE Credit of 12%, Consumer Products of 8%, Power Systems of 10%, and Aircraft Engines and Technical Systems of 30% each. Earnings of Natural Resources should be down 16% because Utah will be missing for the full year, while it was included for one quarter of 1984.

Robert W. McCoy, Jr. (212) 747-2522
Alan M. Mark, Research Assistant

Dow Jones Industrial Average (6/4/84): 1131.57
Standard & Poor's 500 Index (6/4/84): 154.34

Chapter 7

FINANCIAL STATEMENT ANALYSIS

Financial statements present a numerical picture of a company's financial and operating health. Since each company is different, an analyst needs to examine the financial statements for industry characteristics as well as for differences in accounting methods. The major financial statements are the balance sheet, income statement, and the sources-and-uses-of-funds statements. A very helpful long-term financial overview is usually provided by a 5- or 10-year summary statement found in the corporate annual report. One must remember that the footnotes to these statements are an integral part of the statements and provide a wealth of in-depth explanatory information. More depth can often be found in additional reports such as the 10K filed with the Securities and Exchange Commission and obtainable on request (free of charge) from most companies.

Fundamental analysis depends on variables internal to the company, and the corporate financial statements are one way of measuring fundamental value and risk. Financial statement analysis should be combined with economic and industry analysis before a final judgment is made to purchase or sell a specific security. Chapter 6 presented methods of valuation that used forecasts of dividends and earnings per share. Earnings per share combined with an estimated price–earnings ratio was also used to get a future price. Careful study of financial statements provides the analyst with much of the necessary information to forecast earnings and dividends, to judge the quality of earnings, and to determine financial and operating risk.

THE MAJOR FINANCIAL STATEMENTS

In the first part of this chapter, we examine the three basic types of financial statements—the income statement, the balance sheet, and the sources-and-uses-of-funds statement—with particular attention paid to the interrelationships among these three measurement devices. In the rest of the chapter, ratio analysis is presented in detail, and deficiencies of financial statements are discussed along with the impact of inflation and the role of the security analyst in interpreting financial statements.

Income Statement

The income statement is the major device for measuring the profitability of a firm over a period of time. An example of the income statement is presented in Table 7–1 for The Coca-Cola Company. First of all, note that the income statement is for a defined period of time, whether it be one month, three months, or a year. The statement is presented in a stair-step, or progressive, fashion so that we may examine the profit or loss after each type of expense item is deducted.

For 1983, The Coca-Cola Company had net operating revenues (sales) of $6,828,992,000. After subtracting the cost of goods sold and selling, administrative, and general expenses, the firm's operating income was $992,625,000. Because of a high level of cash and marketable securities during 1983, Coca-Cola had more interest income than interest expense (not a common occur-

TABLE 7–1   The Coca-Cola Company Income Statement

Consolidated Statements of Income (In thousands except per share data)	The Coca-Cola Company and Subsidiaries		
Year Ended December 31,	1983	1982	1981
Net Operating Revenues	$6,828,992	$6,021,135	$5,698,901
Cost of goods and services	3,772,741	3,310,847	3,187,924
Gross Profit	3,056,251	2,710,288	2,510,977
Selling, administrative and general expenses	2,063,626	1,830,527	1,724,925
Operating Income	992,625	879,761	786,052
Interest income	82,912	106,172	70,604
Interest expense	72,677	74,560	38,301
Other income (deductions)—net	(2,528)	6,679	(23,211)
Income From Continuing Operations Before Income Taxes	1,000,332	918,052	795,144
Income taxes	442,072	415,076	355,221
Income From Continuing Operations	558,260	502,976	439,923
Discontinued operations: Income from discontinued operations (net of applicable income taxes of $414 in 1983, $4,683 in 1982 and $12,234 in 1981)	527	9,256	12,788
Gain on disposal of discontinued operations (net of applicable income taxes of $13,274)	—	—	29,071
Net Income	$ 558,787	$ 512,232	$ 481,782
Per Share: Continuing operations	$ 4.10	$ 3.88	$ 3.56
Discontinued operations	—	.07	.34
Net income	$ 4.10	$ 3.95	$ 3.90
Average Shares Outstanding	136,222	129,793	123,610

Source: The Coca-Cola Company Annual Report, 1983.

ance) and reported income from continuing operations before taxes of slightly over $1.0 billion. Income after taxes from continuing operations is $558,260,000. Notice that The Coca-Cola Company has been disposing of some assets for the last three years and that income from discontinued operations is listed separately. While income from discontinued operations was not material in all years, the analyst still needs this information. The income statement shows two earnings-per-share patterns. It is the earnings per share from continuing operations that are relevant in making forecasts of expected growth.

Are these good income figures or bad? As we shall see later, the analyst's interpretation of the numbers will depend on historical figures, industry data, and on the relationship of income to balance sheet items such as assets and net worth.

Balance Sheet

The balance sheet indicates what the firm owns, and how these assets are financed in the form of liabilities or ownership interest. While the income

statement purports to show the profitability of the firm, the balance sheet delineates the firm's holdings and obligations. Together these statements are intended to answer two questions: How much did the firm make or lose, and what is a measure of its worth? A balance sheet for The Coca-Cola Company is presented in Table 7–2.

TABLE 7–2   The Coca-Cola Company Consolidated Balance Sheet

Consolidated Balance Sheets	The Coca-Cola Company and Subsidiaries	
(In thousands except per share data)	December 31.	
Assets	1983	1982
Current		
Cash	$ 319,385	$ 177.530
Marketable securities, at cost (approximates market)	292,084	83.381
Trade accounts receivable, less allowances of		
$20,160 in 1983 and $21,336 in 1982	779,729	751.775
Inventories and unamortized film costs	744,107	808.799
Prepaid expenses and other assets	195,009	255.080
Total Current Assets	2,330,314	2.076.565
Investments, Film Costs and Other Assets		
Investments, at cost	241,780	221.909
Unamortized film costs	252,612	211.460
Other assets	240,880	241.395
	735,272	674.764
Property, Plant and Equipment		
Land	128,642	126.201
Buildings and improvements	618,586	602.475
Machinery and equipment	1,412,697	1.383.668
Containers	341,597	333.472
	2,501,522	2.445.816
Less allowances for depreciation	940,716	907.250
	1,560,806	1.538.566
Goodwill and Other Intangible Assets	601,430	633.415
	$5,227,822	$4.923.310
Liabilities and Shareholders' Equity	1983	1982
Current		
Loans and notes payable	$ 85,913	$ 70.561
Current maturities of long-term debt	20,783	50.623
Accounts payable and accrued expenses	910,951	792.250
Participations and other entertainment obligations	154,213	154.803
Accrued taxes—including income taxes	219,240	258.574
Total Current Liabilities	1,391,100	1.326.811
Participations and Other Entertainment Obligations	226,129	190.408
Long-Term Debt	513,202	462.344
Deferred Income Taxes	176,635	165.093
Shareholders' Equity		
Common stock, no par value—		
Authorized: 180,000,000 shares		
in 1983 and 140,000,000 shares		
in 1982;		
Issued: 136,653,676 shares in 1983		
and 136,099,741 shares in 1982	68,704	68.427
Capital surplus	500,031	478.308
Retained earnings	2,494,215	2.300.217
Foreign currency translation adjustment	(130,640)	(54.486)
	2,932,310	2.792.466
Less treasury stock, at cost (300,588 shares		
in 1983; 359,338 shares in 1982)	11,554	13.812
	2,920,756	2.778.654
	$5,227,822	$4.923.310

Source: The Coca-Cola Company Annual Report, 1983.

Note that the balance sheet is given at one point in time, in this case December 31, 1983. It does not represent the result of transactions for a specific month, quarter, or year, but rather is a cumulative chronicle of all transactions that have affected the corporation since its inception. This is in contrast to the income statement, which measures results only over a short, quantifiable period of time. Generally, balance sheet items are stated on an original cost basis rather than at market value.

The Coca-Cola Company was chosen for analysis because of its product diversification, international scope, and its well-known soft drinks such as Coca-Cola, Tab, Sprite, Diet Coke, etc. Its food division accounted for almost 19 percent of sales and 12 percent of operating income in 1983. This division includes Minute Maid orange juice, Hi-C fruit drinks, Maryland Club and But-ter-Nut coffees, Ronco household consumer products, and Presto pasta products as well as institutional food service products.

During 1982 Coca-Cola purchased Columbia Pictures Industries as a diversification move. In 1983 this division accounted for 12.5 percent of revenues and 9 percent of operating income. Columbia produces the television series "Fantasy Island," and the daytime "soaps" "Days of Our Lives" and "The Young and the Restless." Some of the big-name movies produced by Columbia were *Tootsie, The Big Chill, The Natural, The Karate Kid,* and one of the biggest movies of all time, *Ghostbusters.*

Sources-and-Uses-of-Funds Statements

The third major financial statement is the sources-and-uses-of-funds statement (statement of changes in financial position). This statement supplements the income statement and balance sheet. As indicated in Figure 7–1, the sources-and-uses-of-funds statement allows us to measure how changes in the balance sheet were financed over a period of time. While the balance sheet is nothing more than a snapshot of the firm at a point in time, if we put together two such snapshots, we can ascertain significant changes.

In the case of Coca-Cola's sources-and-uses-of-funds statement (Table 7–3), the emphasis is on changes in the amount of working capital available to the firm. Working capital represents net short-term assets (current assets minus current liabilities). Only the *noncurrent* changes in the balance sheet are listed individually in the major portions of Table 7–3. If we look at the difference between long-term sources of funds and long-term uses of funds, the difference will tell us by how much working capital went up or down.[1]

Sources of working capital include increases in stockholders' equity, decreases in long-term assets, and increases in long-term liabilities. Applications or uses of working capital include decreases in stockholders' equity, increases in long-term assets, and decreases in long-term liabilities. Changes in

---

[1] Other firms may use a cash approach, where the emphasis is on changes in every single account, rather than merely net working capital.

FIGURE 7–1   Relationship of Funds Statement to Balance Sheet

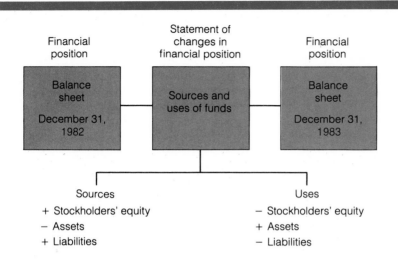

stockholders' equity are caused by profits or losses, cash dividends, and the retirement of securities, as well as accounting adjustments.

In the Coca-Cola example, sources of working capital totaled $1,107,027,000 in 1983. The primary contributions came from income from continuing operations ($558 million) and the adding back of depreciation, amortization, and deferred income tax charges that represented noncash deductions on the income statements. There were also contributions from the reduction of assets from discontinued operations, the sale of stock, the increases in long-term debt, and a number of other items.

The applications or uses of working capital were primarily in the form of cash dividends ($365 million), additions to property plant and equipment ($376 million), and additions to noncurrent film costs ($115 million). The total applications of working capital were $917,567,000.

Sources of working capital exceeded the *applications* of working capital by $189,460,000.

Source	$1,107,027,000
Application	917,567,000
Difference	$ 189,460,000

The allocation of the increased working capital is shown in the bottom part of Table 7–3.

In analyzing a sources and uses statement, the analyst must examine how the buildup (or reduction) in long-term assets was accomplished. For example, are increases in long-term assets being supported by profits and long-term borrowing, or are they being financed by the more dangerous route of short-term borrowing? Also, what is the source of funding for cash dividends? In the

TABLE 7–3   The Coca-Cola Company Sources and Uses of Funds

Consolidated Statements of Changes in Financial Position (In thousands)			*The Coca-Cola Company and Subsidiaries*	
Year Ended December 31,		**1983**	1982	1981
Source of Working Capital				
From operations:				
Income from continuing operations		$ **558,260**	$ 502,976	$439,923
Add charges not requiring outlay of working capital during the year:				
Depreciation		**153,655**	143,549	132,713
Amortization:				
Goodwill		**16,468**	10,101	3,796
Noncurrent film costs		**57,167**	43,495	—
Deferred income taxes		**12,220**	48,702	23,169
Other		**25,460**	24,111	57,134
Total From Continuing Operations		**823,230**	772,934	656,735
Discontinued operations (excludes provisions for depreciation, amortization and deferred income taxes of $8,219 in 1983, $7,504 in 1982 and $7,186 in 1981)		**8,746**	16,760	49,045
Total From Operations		**831,976**	789,694	705,780
Net long-term assets of discontinued operations (including property, plant and equipment)		**89,990**	1,851	8,303
Common stock issued		**22,000**	370,152	1,090
Increase in long-term debt		**50,398**	249,392	4,057
Increase in participations and other entertainment obligations		**35,721**	—	—
Transfer of noncurrent film costs to current		**16,987**	93,909	—
Disposals of property, plant and equipment		**34,972**	44,467	64,023
Decrease in investments and other assets		**—**	21,836	—
Decrease in goodwill (purchase accounting adjustment)		**20,547**	—	—
Other		**4,436**	3,302	—
		1,107,027	1,574,603	783,253
Application of Working Capital				
Cash dividends		**364,789**	321,557	286,787
Acquisitions of purchased companies excluding net current assets:				
Property, plant and equipment—net		**7,439**	56,739	9,814
Other assets net of other liabilities		**(583)**	89,693	103
Goodwill		**7,480**	516,115	10
Additions to property, plant and equipment		**376,197**	325,016	319,792
Additions to noncurrent film costs		**115,306**	95,804	—
Increase in investments and other assets		**19,361**	—	86,284
Foreign currency translation		**27,299**	21,693	—
Other		**279**	28,153	11,215
		917,567	1,454,770	714,005
Increase in Working Capital		$ **189,460**	$ 119,833	$ 69,248
Increase (Decrease) in Working Capital by Component				
Cash and marketable securities		$ **350,558**	$ (78,631)	$108,456
Trade accounts receivable		**27,954**	268,284	(39,632)
Inventories and unamortized film costs		**(64,692)**	58,080	(59,516)
Prepaid expenses and other current assets		**(60,071)**	192,586	4,685
Loans and notes payable		**(15,352)**	19,086	(2,060)
Current maturities of long-term debt		**29,840**	(45,108)	2,013
Accounts payable and accrued expenses		**(118,701)**	(120,201)	60,974
Participations and other entertainment obligations		**590**	(154,803)	—
Accrued taxes—including income taxes		**39,334**	(19,460)	(5,672)
Increase in Working Capital		$ **189,460**	$ 119,833	$ 69,248

Source: The Coca-Cola Company Annual Report, 1983.

case of Coca-Cola, there was strong funding from profits and depreciation/ amortization add-back to help meet these needs. Many companies are not so fortunate. For example, a number of hard-pressed firms in the energy industry in the 1980s had insufficient earnings to pay dividends or maintain or expand long-term asset commitments. In such cases short-term borrowing is required to meet long-term needs. This leads to a reduction in working capital and a dangerous operating position.

KEY FINANCIAL RATIOS FOR THE SECURITY ANALYST

We have just summarized the three major financial statements that will be the basis of your analysis in this section emphasizing financial ratios. Ratio analysis brings together balance sheet and income statement data to permit a better understanding of the firm's past and current health which will aid you in forecasting the future outlook.

Ratio Analysis

Ratios are used in much of our daily life. We buy cars based on miles per gallon; we evaluate baseball players by earned run averages and batting averages; basketball players by field goal and foul-shooting percentages, and so on. These are all ratios constructed to judge comparative performance. Financial ratios serve a similar purpose, but you must know what is being measured in order to construct a ratio and to understand the significance of the resultant number.

Financial ratios are used to weigh and evaluate the operating performance and capital structure of the firm. While an absolute value such as earnings of $50,000 or accounts receivable of $100,000 may appear satisfactory, its acceptability can only be measured in relation to other values.

For example, are earnings of $50,000 actually good? If a company earned $50,000 on $500,000 of sales (10 percent "profit margin" ratio), that might be quite satisfactory, whereas earnings of $50,000 on $5,000,000 could be disappointing (a meager 1 percent return.) After we have computed the appropriate ratio, we must compare our firm's results to the achievements of similar firms in the industry as well as to our own firm's past performance. Even then, this "number crunching" process is not always adequate because we are forced to supplement our financial findings with an evaluation of company management, physical facilities, and numerous other factors.

Ratio analysis will not discover "gold mines" for the analyst. It is more like a physical exam at the doctor's office. You hope you are all right but if not, you may be content to know what is wrong and what to do about it. Just as with medical illness some diseases are easier to cure than others, the same is true of financial illness. The analyst is the doctor. He or she determines the illness and keeps track of management to see if they can administer the cure. Sometimes ailing companies can be very good values. Penn-Central went into bankruptcy and its common stock could have been purchased at $2 per share

for several years. In 1984, Penn Central stock traded in the $35–50 range. Chrysler and Lockheed were both on the brink of bankruptcy until the government made guaranteed loans available. Chrysler could have been bought at $3 per share and Lockheed at $1 per share, but by 1984 Chrysler traded in a price range of $20–32 and Lockheed $30–47. These were sick companies that got repaired, and any investor willing to take a risk would have profited nicely but albeit at great risk.

Bankruptcy Studies

In a sense, ratio analysis protects an investor from picking losers more so than it guarantees picking winners. Several studies have used ratios as predictors of financial failure. The most notable studies are by William Beaver and Edward Altman. Beaver found that ratios of failing firms signal failure as much as five years ahead of bankruptcy, and as bankruptcy approaches, the ratios deteriorate more rapidly, with the greatest deterioration in the last year. The Beaver studies also found that (*a*) "Investors recognize and adjust to the new solvency positions of failing firms and (*b*) the price changes of the common stocks act as if investors rely upon ratios as a basis for their assessments, and impound the ratio information in the market prices."[2]

The first Altman[3] research study indicated that five ratios combined were 95 percent accurate in predicting failure one year ahead of bankruptcy and were 72 percent accurate two years ahead of failure, with the average lead time for the ratio signal being 20 months. Altman developed a Z score which was an index developed through multiple discriminate analysis that could predict failure. Altman modified and improved his model's accuracy even further by increasing the number of ratios to seven.[4] This service is currently sold to institutional investors by Zeta Services Inc. The Z (zeta) score relies upon the following variables:

1. Retained earnings/total assets (cumulative profitability).
2. Standard deviation of operating income/total assets (measure of earnings stability during last 10 years).
3. Earnings before interest and taxes/total assets (productivity of operating assets).
4. Earnings before interest and taxes/Interest (leverage ratio, interest coverage).
5. Current assets/current liabilities (liquidity ratio).
6. Market value of common stock/book value of equity (a leverage ratio).
7. Total assets (proxy for size of the firm).

---

[2] Beaver, William H. "Market Prices, Financial Ratios, and the Prediction of Failure," *Journal of Accounting Research,* Autumn 1968, p. 192.

[3] Altman, Edward I. "Financial Ratios, Discriminant Analysis and the Prediction of Corporate Bankruptcy," *Journal of Finance,* September 1968, pp. 589–609.

[4] Altman, Edward I. *Corporate Financial Distress,* New York: John Wiley & Sons, 1983.

The greater the firm's bankruptcy potential, the lower its Z score. The ratios were not equally significant, but together they separated the companies into a correct bankruptcy group and nonbankruptcy group a high percentage of the time. Retained earnings/total assets has the heaviest weight in the analysis and leverage is also very important. In the next section we present six classifications of ratios that ought to be helpful to the analyst. Many more could be used, but these represent the most widely used measures.

Classification System

We divide 20 significant ratios into six primary groupings:

A. Profitability ratios: *EBIT/sales*
  1. Operating margin.
  2. Aftertax profit margin.   *ATE/sale*
  3. Return on assets.   *Assets/sale*
  4. Return on equity.
B. Asset utilization ratios:
  5. Receivables turnover.
  6. Inventory turnover.
  7. Fixed asset turnover.
  8. Total asset turnover.
C. Liquidity ratios:
  9. Current ratio.
  10. Quick ratio.
  11. Net working capital to total assets.
D. Debt utilization ratios:
  12. Long-term debt to equity.
  13. Total debt to total assets.
  14. Times interest earned.
  15. Fixed charge coverage.
E. Price ratios:
  16. Price to earnings.
  17. Price to book value.
  18. Dividends to price (dividend yield).
F. Other ratios:
  19. Average tax rate.
  20. Dividend payout.

The interpretation of ratios is as much a science as an art, and one can compare ratio analysis to putting together a puzzle. It takes all the pieces of a puzzle to make a complete picture, but a skillful analyst can often get a good picture of the company with only 5 or 10 ratios. Whether the picture is in focus depends upon the interpretive skill of the analyst.

The users of financial statements will attach different degrees of importance to the six categories of ratios. To the potential investor, the critical consideration is profitability and debt utilization. For the banker or trade credi-

tor, the emphasis shifts to the firm's current ability to meet debt obligations. The bondholder, in turn, may be primarily influenced by debt to total assets— while also eyeing the profitability of the firm in terms of its ability to cover interest payments in the short term and principal payments in the long term. Of course, the shrewd analyst looks at all the ratios, with different degrees of attention.

A. Profitability ratios.   The profitability ratios allow the analyst to measure the ability of the firm to earn an adequate return on sales, total assets, and invested capital. The profit margin ratios (1, 2) relate to income statement items, while the two return ratios (3, 4) relate the income statement (numerator) to the balance sheet (denominator). Many of the problems related to profitability can be explained, in whole or in part, by the firm's ability to effectively employ its resources. We shall apply these ratios to Coca-Cola's income statement and balance sheet for 1983 which were previously presented in Tables 7–1 and 7–2. The values are further rounded for ease of computation (dollars in millions).

Profitability ratios (Coca-Cola, 1983; in millions)

1. Operating margin $= \dfrac{\text{Operating income}}{\text{Sales (revenue)}} = \dfrac{\$\ 993}{\$6,829} = 14.54\%$

2. Aftertax profit margin $= \dfrac{\text{Net income}}{\text{Sales (revenue)}} = \dfrac{\$\ 559}{\$6,829} = 8.19\%$

3. Return on assets

   (*a*) $\dfrac{\text{Net income}}{\text{Total assets}} \qquad\qquad = \dfrac{\$\ 559}{\$5,228} = 10.69\%$

   (*b*) $\dfrac{\text{Net income}}{\text{sales}} \times \dfrac{\text{Sales}}{\text{Total assets}}$

   $\qquad\quad 8.19\% \quad \times \quad\quad 1.306 \qquad\qquad\qquad = 10.69\%$

4. Return on equity

   (*a*) $\dfrac{\text{Net income}}{\text{Stockholder's equity}^{5}} \qquad = \dfrac{\$\ 559}{\$2,921} = 19.14\%$

   (*b*) $\dfrac{\text{Return on assets}}{(1 - \text{Debt/Assets})} \qquad = \dfrac{10.69\%}{1 - .441} = 19.14\%$

The profitability ratios indicate that Coca-Cola's aftertax profit margin, in comparison to the operating margin, is slightly higher than one would expect, given a 46 percent corporate tax rate for the year. This leads us to suspect that investment tax credits or other tax benefits reduced the tax rate.

---

[5] A working definition of stockholders' equity is the common stock accounts plus retained earnings. Coca-Cola also has a few other adjustments.

Du Pont Analysis—Notice that the return on assets and return on equity have parts (*a*) and (*b*), or two ways to determine the ratio. The methods employed in (*b*), which arise from the Du Pont Company's financial system, help the analyst see the relationship between the income statement and the balance sheet. The return on assets is generated by multiplying the aftertax profit margin (income statement) by the asset turnover ratio (combination income statement–balance sheet ratio).

The Du Pont Company was a forerunner in stressing that satisfactory return on assets may be achieved through high profit margins or rapid turnover of assets, or a combination of both. The Du Pont system causes the analyst to examine the sources of a company's profitability. Since the profit margin is an income statement ratio, a high profit margin indicates good cost control, whereas a high asset turnover ratio demonstrates efficient use of the assets on the balance sheet. Different industries have different operating and financial structures. For example, in the heavy capital goods industry the emphasis is on a high profit margin with a low asset turnover—while in food processing the profit margin is low and the key to satisfactory returns on total assets is a rapid turnover of assets.

Du Pont analysis further stresses that the return on equity stems from the return on assets adjusted for the amount of financial leverage by using the total debt-to-asset ratio. About 44 percent of The Coca-Cola Company's assets are financed by debt, and the return on equity reflects a high level of debt financing because return on equity (19.14 percent) is almost twice as large as return on assets (10.69 percent). As a detective, the financial analyst can judge how much debt a company employs by comparing these two measures of return. Of course, you will want to check this clue with the debt utilization ratios. The total relationship between return on assets and return on equity under the Du Pont system is depicted in Figure 7–2.

FIGURE 7–2   Du Pont Analysis

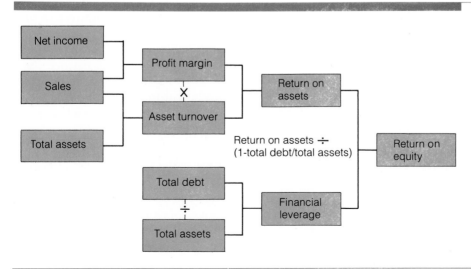

In computing return on assets and equity, the analyst must also be sensitive to the age of the assets. Plant and equipment purchased 15 years ago may be carried on the books far below its replacement value in an inflationary economy. A 20 percent return on assets that were purchased in the late 60s or early 70s may be inferior to a 15 percent return on newly purchased assets.

B. Asset utilization ratios.   Under this heading, we measure the speed at which the firm is turning over accounts receivable, inventory, and longer-term assets. In other words, asset utilitization ratios measure how many times per year a company sells its inventory or collects its accounts receivable. For long-term assets, the utilization ratio tells us how productive the fixed assets are in terms of sales generation.

Asset utilization ratios (Coca-Cola, 1983; in millions)

$$5. \quad \text{Receivables turnover} = \frac{\text{Sales}}{\text{Receivables}} = \frac{\$6,829}{\$\ \ 780} = 8.76\times$$

$$6. \quad \text{Inventory turnover} \quad = \frac{\text{Sales}}{\text{Inventory}} = \frac{\$6,829}{\$\ \ 744} = 9.18\times$$

$$7. \quad \text{Fixed asset turnover} = \frac{\text{Sales}}{\text{Fixed assets}} = \frac{\$6,829}{\$1,561} = 4.37\times$$

$$8. \quad \text{Total asset turnover} \quad = \frac{\text{Sales}}{\text{Total assets}} = \frac{\$6,829}{\$5,228} = 1.30\times$$

The asset utilization ratios relate the income statement (numerator) to the various assets on the balance sheet. Given that Coca-Cola's primary products are soft drinks and food, the receivable turnover and inventory turnover ratios reflect high turnover. Since most of the company's consumable products are not perishable, these ratios seem satisfactory. However the large amount of cash and marketable securities, as seen on the balance sheet, reduces the total asset turnover. We can also tell from comparing fixed asset turnover to total asset turnover that a sharp reduction in the ratios occurs. This does not seem to be totally warranted with such high receivables and inventory turnover even in light of the high cash position. Closer scrutiny of the balance sheet shows that the Investments, Film Costs, and Other Assets category accounts for $735 million in assets not included in fixed asset turnover, and the same is true of $600 million of goodwill. These factors create a lower total asset turnover without directly influencing fixed asset turnover.

C. Liquidity ratios.   The primary emphasis of the liquidity ratios is a determination of the firm's ability to pay off short-term obligations as they come due. These ratios can be related to receivables and inventory turnover in that a faster turnover creates a more rapid movement of cash through the company and improves liquidity. Again remember that each industry will be different. A jewelry store chain will have much different ratios than a grocery store chain.

Liquidity ratios (Coca-Cola, 1983; in millions)

9. Current ratio $= \dfrac{\text{Current assets}}{\text{Current liabilities}} = \dfrac{\$2,330}{\$1,391} = 1.675$

10. Quick ratio

$\dfrac{\text{Current assets} - \text{inventories}}{\text{Current liabilities}} = \dfrac{\$2,330 - \$744}{\$1,391} = 1.14$

11. Net working capital to total assets

$\dfrac{\text{Current assets} - \text{Current liabilities}}{\text{Total assets}} = \dfrac{\$2,330 - \$1,391}{\$5,228} = .180$

The first two ratios (current and quick) indicate whether the firm can pay off its short-term debt in an emergency by liquidating its current assets. The quick ratio looks only at the most liquid assets which include cash, marketable securities, and receivables. Cash and securities are already liquid but receivables usually will be turned into cash during the collection period. If there is concern about the firm's liquidity, the analyst will want to cross check the liquidity ratios with receivable turnover and inventory turnover to determine how fast the current assets are turned into cash during an ordinary cycle.

The last liquidity ratio is a measure of the percentage of current assets (after short-term debt has been paid) to total assets. This indicates the liquidity of the assets of the firm. The higher the ratio, the greater the short-term assets relative to fixed assets and the safer a creditor.

Coca-Cola seems to be in reasonable shape. Coke syrup is not that perishable and the raw ingredients such as sugar are readily marketable. This makes the current ratio of 1.675 quite safe when compared to a quick ratio of over 1.1.

D. Debt utilization ratios. The debt utilization ratios provide an indication of the way the firm is financed between debt (lenders) and equity (owners) and therefore helps the analyst determine the amount of financial risk present in the firm. Too much debt can not only impair liquidity with heavy interest payments but can also damage profitability and the health of the firm during an economic recession or industry slowdown.

Debt utilization ratios (Coca-Cola, 1983; in millions)

12. Long-term debt to equity

$\dfrac{\text{Long-term liabilities}}{\text{Stockholder's equity}} = \dfrac{\$\,513}{\$2,921} = .176$

13. Total debt to total assets

$\dfrac{\text{Total debt}}{\text{Total assets}} = \dfrac{\$2,307}{\$5,228} = .441$

14. Times interest earned

$\dfrac{\text{Income before interest and taxes}}{\text{Interest}} = \dfrac{\$\,993}{\$\,73} = 13.60\times$

15. Fixed charge coverage[6]

$$\frac{\text{Income before fixed charges and taxes}}{\text{Fixed charges}} = \frac{\$\ 993}{\$\ \ 73} = 13.60\times$$

We have already discussed the impact of financial leverage on return on equity, and the first two ratios in this category indicate to the analyst how much financial leverage is being used by the firm. The more debt, the greater the interest payments and the more volatile the impact on the firm's earnings. Companies with stable sales and earnings, such as utilities, can afford to employ more debt than those in cyclical industries, such as automobiles or airlines. Ratio 12, long-term debt to equity, provides information concerning the long-term capital structure of the firm. In the case of Coca-Cola, long-term liabilities represent 17 percent of the stockholders' equity base provided by the owners of the firm. Ratio 13, total debt to total assets, looks at the total assets and the use of borrowed capital. Each firm must consider its optimum capital structure, and the analyst should be aware of industry fluctuations in assessing the firm's proper use of leverage. Coca-Cola seems quite safe, given that its business is not subject to large swings in sales.

The last two debt utilization ratios indicate the firm's ability to meet its cash payments due on fixed obligations such as interest, leases, licensing fees, or sinking fund charges. The higher these ratios, the more protected the creditor's position. Use of the fixed charge coverage is more conservative than interest earned since it includes all fixed charges. Now that leases are capitalized and show up on the balance sheet it is easier to understand that lease payments are similar in importance to interest expense. Charges after taxes such as sinking fund payments must be adjusted to before-tax income. For example, if a firm is in the 40 percent tax bracket and must make a $60,000 sinking fund payment, the firm would have had to generate $100,000 in before-tax income to meet that obligation. The adjustment would be as follows:

$$\text{Before-tax income required} = \frac{\text{Aftertax payment}}{1\ -\ \text{tax rate}}$$

$$= \frac{\$60,000}{1\ -\ .40}$$

$$= \$100,000$$

Coca Cola's fixed charge coverage is the same as its interest earned ratio because it has no fixed charges other than interest expense.

E. Price ratios.   Price ratios relate the internal performance of the firm to the external judgment of the marketplace in terms of value. What is the firm's

---

[6] Coca-Cola had no lease expense or sinking fund payments in 1983; therefore ratios 14 and 15 are the same.

end result in market value? The price ratios indicate the expectations of the market relative to other companies. For example, a firm with a high price-to-earnings ratio has a higher market price relative to $1 of earnings than a company with a lower ratio.

Price ratios (Coca-Cola, March 26, 1984; in millions)

16. Price to earnings
$$\frac{\text{Common stock price}}{\text{Earnings per share}} = \frac{\$54.375}{\$4.10} = 13.26\times$$
(fully diluted)

17. Price to book value
$$\frac{\text{Common stock price}}{\text{Book value per share}} = \frac{\$54.375}{\$21.55} = 2.52\times$$

18. Dividends to price (dividend yield)[7]
$$\frac{\text{Dividends per share}}{\text{Common stock price}} = \frac{\$2.68}{\$54.375} = 4.93\%$$

Coca-Cola's price–earnings ratio indicates that the firm's stock price represents $13.26 for every $1 of earnings. This number can be compared to that of other companies in the soft-drink industry and/or related industries. As indicated in Chapter 6, the price–earnings ratio (or P/E ratio, as it is commonly called) is influenced by the earnings and the sales growth of the firm; also, the risk (or volatility in performance), the debt–equity structure of the firm, the dividend payment policy, the quality of management, and a number of other factors. The P/E ratio indicates expectations about the future of a company. Firms which are expected to provide greater returns than those for the market in general, with equal or less risk, often have P/E ratios higher than the overall market P/E ratio.

Expectations of returns and P/E ratios do change over time, as Table 7–4 illustrates. Price–earnings ratios for a selected list of U.S. firms in 1975, 1981, and 1984 show that during this nine-year period price–earnings ratios fell for those companies during the first two periods and recovered for most between 1981 and 1984. A change in investor philosophy may have substantially lowered the P/E ratio of many of the traditional growth stocks, such as IBM, Upjohn, McDonald's, and Texas Instruments from their high values in 1975.

The price-to-book-value ratio relates the market value of the company to the historical accounting value of the firm. In a company that has old assets this ratio may be quite high, but in one with new, undepreciated fixed assets the ratio might be lower. This information needs to be combined with your knowledge of the company's assets and of industry norms.

---

[7] Dividends annualized at most recent quarterly rate.

TABLE 7–4   Price–Earnings Ratios for Selected U.S. Corporations

Corporation	Industry	P/E ratio		
		December 31, 1975	December 10, 1981	September 28, 1984
Exxon	International oil	8	5	7
Texas Utilities	Public utility	9	6	6
Union Carbide	Chemical	9	5	17
Bank America	Banking	10	7	10
CBS	Broadcasting	11	7	11
Halliburton	Oil service	12	11	11
Winn-Dixie	Retail	14	8	11
IBM	Computers	17	9	13
Upjohn	Ethical drugs	18	10	9
McDonald's	Restaurant franchises	26	10	12
Texas Instruments	Semiconductors	34	15	23
S&P 500	Market index	11	8	11

The dividend yield is part of the total return that an investor receives along with capital gains or losses. It is usually calculated by annualizing the current quarterly dividend, since that is the cash value a current investor would receive over the next year.

F. Other ratios.   The other ratios presented in category F are to help the analyst spot special tax situations that impact the profitability of an industry or company, and to determine what percentage of earnings are being paid to the stockholder and what is being reinvested for internal growth.

Other ratios (Coca-Cola, 1983; in millions)

19.   Average tax rate

$$\frac{\text{Income tax}}{\text{Taxable income}} = \frac{\$\ 442}{\$1000} = 44.2\%$$

20.   Dividend payout*

$$\frac{\text{Dividends per share}}{\text{Earnings per share}} = \frac{\$2.68}{\$4.10} = 65.4\%$$

These other ratios are calculated to provide the analyst with information that may indicate unusual tax treatment or reinvestment policies. For example, the tax ratio for forest products companies will be low because of the capital gains treatment given timber cuttings. A company's tax rate may decline in one year due to heavy capital expenditures and the resultant investment tax credits. Earnings per share may rise, but we need to know if it is from operations or from favorable tax treatment. If it is from operations, we will be more

sure of next year's forecast, but if it is from tax benefits we can not normally count on the benefits being continued into the future.

The dividend payout ratio provides data concerning the firm's reinvestment strategies. A high payout ratio tells the analyst that the stockholder is receiving a large part of the earnings and that the company is not retaining much income for investment in new plant and equipment. High payouts are usually found in industries that do not have great growth potential, while low payout ratios are associated with firms in growth industries.

USES OF RATIOS

The previous section presented 20 ratios that may be helpful to the analyst in evaluating a firm. How can we further use the data we have gathered to check the health of companies we are interested in analyzing?

One way is to compare the company to the industry. This is becoming more difficult as companies diversify into several industries. Twenty years ago firms competed in one industry and ratio comparisons were more reliable. Now companies have a wide range of products and markets. Coca-Cola is becoming more diversified all the time. Table 7–5 presents the business segments in which Coca-Cola operates.

Coca-Cola has three principal business segments: Soft Drinks, Entertainment, and Foods. This additional data adds a new dimension to our analysis. The soft-drink segment is by far the largest segment, accounting for almost 69 percent of total revenues and 86.5 percent of operating income. This is accomplished with only 51 percent of the firm's assets. Entertainment (Columbia Pictures) has almost 27 percent of the assets and yet produces the smallest percentage of revenues (12.4 percent) and even less operating profit (9 percent). We know from previous reading that Coca-Cola is redeploying its assets by selling off certain operations and acquiring new ones such as Columbia. The analyst must be able to forecast Coca-Cola with Columbia Pictures as an integral part. By looking at the business segments, we can tell that recently acquired Columbia Pictures does not match Coca-Cola's traditional return requirements or its asset turnover ratio. Is this because of poor management at Columbia or simply industry characteristics? More comments about this a bit later in the chapter.

Other data drawn from Table 7–5 are summarized in Table 7–6. In the first line of Table 7–6, we see that each dollar invested in assets in the food segment produces the most revenue ($2.97), with the soft-drink division in second place ($1.76) and the entertainment segment well behind ($.61). The ratio of operating income to assets places the soft drink division in first place, with the food segment close behind. The entertainment division is once again a distant third. It is only in the area of operating income to sales that the entertainment division is able to achieve a second-place finish.

After examining Table 7–5 and Table 7–6, an analyst realizes that Coca-Cola's ratios reflect a composite of several industries. Familiarity with all seg-

TABLE 7–5 Business Segments for the Coca-Cola Company

Notes to Consolidated Financial Statements (continued)

13. Lines of Business (1). The Company operates principally in the soft drink industry. In June 1982, the Company acquired Columbia Pictures Industries, Inc., which operates in the entertainment industry. Citrus, Hi-C fruit drinks, coffee and pasta products are included in the Foods Business Sector. Plastic products are not material and are also included in the Foods Business Sector. Inter-company transfers between Sectors are not material. Information concerning operations in different lines of business is as follows (in millions):

Year Ended December 31,	1983	1982	1981
Net operating revenues:			
Soft drinks	$4,694.6	$4,413.8	$4,558.6
Entertainment	849.5	457.3	—
Foods	1,284.9	1,150.0	1,140.3
Consolidated net operating revenues	$6,829.0	$6,021.1	$5,698.9
Operating income:			
Soft drinks	$ 858.6	$ 800.0	$ 752.0
Entertainment	90.6	35.8	—
Foods	121.3	117.9	106.7
General expenses	(77.9)	(73.9)	(72.6)
Consolidated operating income	$ 992.6	$ 879.8	$ 786.1
Identifiable assets at year-end:			
Soft drinks	$2,670.6	$2,521.4	$2,472.5
Entertainment	1,394.0	1,309.8	—
Foods	431.9	380.4	379.0
Corporate assets (principally marketable securities, investments and fixed assets)	731.3	476.2	452.7
Discontinued operations	—	235.5	260.6
Consolidated assets	$5,227.8	$4,923.3	$3,564.8
Capital expenditures (including fixed assets of purchased companies):			
Soft drinks	$ 237.6	$ 249.5	$ 251.5
Entertainment	72.9	53.9	—
Foods	45.1	53.7	58.4
Corporate	28.0	24.6	19.6
Consolidated capital expenditures	$ 383.6	$ 381.7	$ 329.5
Depreciation and amortization of goodwill:			
Soft drinks	$ 120.4	$ 117.6	$ 109.0
Entertainment	15.7	7.6	—
Foods	25.2	20.8	18.7
Corporate	8.8	7.6	8.8
Consolidated depreciation and amortization of goodwill	$ 170.1	$ 153.6	$ 136.5

(1) Operating results for 1982 and 1981 have been restated to exclude the results of the Company's wine business, which was sold in 1983 and has been accounted for as a discontinued operation. In addition, certain amounts for 1982 and 1981 have been reclassified on a comparable basis with 1983.

Source: The Coca-Cola Company Annual Report, 1983.

TABLE 7–6 Selected Values by Industry Segment, The Coca-Cola Company

	Soft drink	Entertainment	Food
Revenue/Assets	1.76×	.61×	2.97×
Operating income/Assets	32.2%	6.5%	28.1%
Operating income/Sales	18.3%	10.7%	9.4%

ments makes the analyst more capable of interpreting the significance of these ratios. It may be that the analyst will compare the Coca-Cola ratios with two or three industries rather than one. Table 7–7 compares selected Coca-Cola ratios with the soft drink, recreation, and food industries.

Table 7–7 Selected Ratio Comparisons for the Coca-Cola Company, 1983

	Coca-Cola	Industries		
		Soft drinks	Recreation	Food
Operating margin	14.54%	14.5%	15.0%	9.5%
Aftertax profit margin	8.19%	5.6%	.6%	3.6%
Return on equity	19.14%	17.5%	1.5%	13.5%
Long-term debt to equity	17.60%	30.5%	42.0%	33.3%
Price to earnings	13.26×	10.9×	12.1×	9.0×
Dividend yield	4.93%	5.2%	2.5%	5.1%
Average tax rate	44.2%	40.0%	38.0%	44.0%
Dividend payout	65.4%	54.0%	35.0%	45.0%

Industry source: *Value Line Investment Survey* (Arnold Bernhard & Co., March 1984).

In comparing Coca-Cola with the industry ratios in Table 7–7, it is important to know that five companies (Coca-Cola, Pepsi, Dr Pepper, MEI, and Royal Crown) make up the soft drinks industry ratios and by the time you read this page, Dr Pepper will be privately held and Royal Crown will be merged. Secondly, the recreation industry ratios include manufacturing companies such as Brunswick and AMF as well as firms like Disney and MGM. Additionally, the 1983 data is not fully representative because MGM took a large loss write-off ($418 million) on its Atari division, which distorted the whole industry picture. So you see, even with industry ratios, truth is hard to find and the analyst must have a perspective on the industry over time.

The most important set of ratios is for the soft drink industry, since that is Coca-Cola's major market. Coca-Cola's operating profit margins are on the same level as its competitors, but its aftertax margins are superior. This, most likely, is because Coca-Cola has relatively little long-term debt (17.6 percent) compared to the rest of the soft drink industry. This allows the firm to bring more operating profit down to aftertax income.

Return on equity is the highest of all three industries. The company does seem to be retaining less income than other companies (dividend payout of 65.4%), but it did note in its annual report that investors should expect slower growth in dividends as the company increases its internal spending. This reflects an unwillingness on management's part to expand by increasing the amount of debt in the firm's capital structure. Evidently the market thinks that Coca-Cola's earnings merit a higher value compared to the three industries since it has a superior price–earnings ratio.

TABLE 7–8   International Diversification

Notes to Consolidated Financial Statements (continued)

---

14. Operations in Geographic Areas (1). Information about the Company's operations in different geographic areas is presented below (in millions). Inter-company transfers between geographic areas are not material.

Year Ended December 31,	1983	1982	1981
Net operating revenues:			
United States	$4,071.4	$3,351.5	$3,048.5
Latin America	401.3	516.3	608.1
Europe and Africa	1,225.6	1,155.6	1,096.3
Canada and Pacific	1,130.7	997.7	946.0
Consolidated net operating revenues	$6,829.0	$6,021.1	$5,698.9
Operating income:			
United States	$ 498.7	$ 403.2	$ 322.3
Latin America	69.4	123.2	156.1
Europe and Africa	295.4	249.5	235.6
Canada and Pacific	207.0	177.8	144.7
General expenses	(77.9)	(73.9)	(72.6)
Consolidated operating income	$ 992.6	$ 879.8	$ 786.1
Identifiable assets at year-end:			
United States	$2,996.5	$2,773.2	$1,431.5
Latin America	420.9	435.9	436.2
Europe and Africa	606.5	582.0	583.0
Canada and Pacific	472.6	420.5	400.8
Corporate assets (principally marketable securities, investments and fixed assets)	731.3	476.2	452.7
Discontinued operations	—	235.5	260.6
Consolidated assets	$5,227.8	$4,923.3	$3,564.8

(1) Operating results for 1982 and 1981 have been restated to exclude the results of the Company's wine business, which was sold in 1983 and has been accounted for as a discontinued operation.

Identifiable liabilities of operations outside the United States were $652 million, $627 million and $637 million at December 31, 1983, 1982 and 1981, respectively.

Source: The Coca-Cola Company Annual Report, 1983.

In general one could conclude that Coca-Cola is in good shape, but that the profitability of its entertainment division could be increased with more productive use of Columbia's assets. Movie companies have a low, distorted, balance sheet figure for assets since most of their films are fully depreciated after a three-year run. This should inflate returns on assets so we can assume that Columbia, with its *low* returns, has had some problems and expect that Coca-Cola will turn the company around over time. That is certainly Coca-Cola's intention.

It is important to realize that Coca-Cola is an international company that may be impacted by political and economic events abroad. Devaluation of the Mexican peso, revolts, and the rising dollar can all have an impact on Coca-Cola's reported earnings. Table 7–8 shows the breakdown of the company's worldwide sales and profitability by region. While the United States accounts for about 60 percent of sales, the two regions "Europe and Africa," and "Canada and Pacific" account for 18 and 16 percent of sales, respectively, but a

much larger share of income. Europe and Africa account for almost 30 percent of income while Canada and Pacific account for 20 percent. We can see that the trouble spot is Latin America. Sales and profits have been declining for three years, while assets have stayed about the same. High inflation and deflating currencies in Latin America are part of the problem. Just a return to 1982 profitability for Latin America would boost earnings per share $.40 and have a significant positive effect on the profitability ratios.

COMPARING LONG-TERM TRENDS

Over the course of the business cycle, sales and profitability may expand and contract, and ratio analysis for any one year may not present an accurate picture of the firm. Therefore, we look at trend analysis of performance over a number of years.

First examine the 10-year summary of selected financial data for Coca-Cola in Table 7–9. One can see the overall growth in net operating revenues since 1974. The firm has a higher level of cash and marketable securities than usual. An increase in the amount of long-term and total debt over the last two years is apparent, but the level is still not high. Over the last two years the company has issued common stock, which combined with the increased debt, shows up in a large increase in total capital since 1981. In terms of income from continuing operations to net operating revenues, the years 1980 and 1981 seem to have been low points for the company due to competition from Pepsi and the effects of the recession. 1982 and 1983, however, indicate that Coca-Cola is back to its historical average performance. The payout ratio has been rising, but management intends to reduce this ratio.

A GENERAL STUDY OF INDUSTRY TRENDS

In this section we expand the horizon by shifting our attention to four very different industries, and look at their comparative trends over time based on the ratios of return on equity and long-term debt to equity. The specially picked industries are airlines, brewing, chemicals, and drugs. By studying these important industries, the analyst develops a feel for comparative performance in our economy.

The return on equity for the four separate industries shown in Table 7–10 exhibits some wide differences in profitability. Table 7–10 is graphed in Figure 7–3 and the trends are more visible. It is clear that the drug industry has the highest and most consistent returns on equity, with very little variation due to industry or economic effects. The brewing industry has the next highest returns but more volatility than drugs. The chemical industry is next, followed by airlines, which show a cyclical character and very low returns.

Although it may be easy to generalize about industries and their relationship to economic cycles, individual companies within each industry seem to stand out. The benefit of looking at companies in the industry together is that the best and worst become apparent to the trained analyst.

TABLE 7–9

Selected Financial Data
(In millions except per share data)

Year Ended December 31.	1983	1982	1981
Summary of Operations (a,b)			
— Net operating revenues	$6,829	$6,021	$5,699
Cost of goods and services	3,773	3,311	3,188
Gross profit	3,056	2,710	2,511
Selling, administrative and general expenses	2,063	1,830	1,725
Operating income	993	880	786
Interest income—net	10	31	32
Other income (deductions)—net	(3)	7	(23)
Income from continuing operations before income taxes	1,000	918	795
Income taxes	442	415	355
Income from continuing operations	$ 558	$ 503	$ 440
Year-End Position			
— Cash and current marketable securities	$ 611	$ 261	$ 340
Property, plant and equipment—net	1,561	1,539	1,409
Total assets	5,228	4,923	3,565
— Long-term debt	513	462	137
— Total debt	620	583	232
Shareholders' equity	2,921	2,779	2,271
— Total capital (c)	3,541	3,362	2,503
Per Share Data (e)			
Income from continuing operations	$ 4.10	$ 3.88	$ 3.56
Net income	4.10	3.95	3.90
Dividends	2.68	2.48	2.32
Financial Ratios			
— Income from continuing operations to net operating revenues	8.2%	8.4%	7.7%
Income from continuing operations to average shareholders' equity	19.6%	19.9%	20.2%
Long-term debt to total capital	14.5%	13.7%	5.5%
Total debt to total capital	17.5%	17.3%	9.3%
— Dividend payout	65.3%	62.8%	59.5%
Other Data			
Average shares outstanding (e)	136	130	124
Capital expenditures	$ 384	$ 382	$ 330
Depreciation	154	144	133

Notes:
(a) Operating results for 1974-1982 have been restated to exclude the results of the Company's wine business which was sold in November 1983 and accounted for as a discontinued operation.
(b) In June 1982, the Company acquired Columbia Pictures Industries, Inc. in a purchase transaction.

In 1982, the Company adopted Statement of Financial Accounting Standards No. 52, "Foreign Currency Translation." See Note 10 to the Consolidated Financial Statements.

In the brewing industry, Heileman stands head and shoulders over the others in terms of return on equity even though it uses very little long-term debt. Pabst was recently acquired, and Coors has been struggling in this very competitive industry. The chemical industry had a difficult time dealing with the recession in 1981–82 and the effects lingered into 1983. Monsanto is perhaps the most consistent company in terms of profitability and the industry on the whole seems not to have any real losers. Again, the drug industry has consistent winners changing positions from year to year. Historically, Lilly Pfizer, and Merck have been the premier companies in the industry for high returns. The airline industry truly lacks any consistent performers among the major carriers.

				The Coca-Cola Company and Subsidiaries		
1980	1979	1978	1977	1976	1975	1974
$5,475	$4,588	$4,013	$3,328	$2,928	$2,773	$2,425
3,103	2,521	2,203	1,836	1,614	1,633	1,462
2,372	2,067	1,810	1,492	1,314	1,140	963
1,635	1,378	1,167	922	806	693	616
737	689	643	570	508	447	347
5	26	28	23	23	16	15
(9)	(3)	(14)	(9)	(4)	(8)	5
733	712	657	584	527	455	367
329	318	300	268	245	218	170
$ 404	$ 394	$ 357	$ 316	$ 282	$ 237	$ 197(d)
$ 231	$ 149	$ 321	$ 350	$ 364	$ 389	$ 241
1,341	1,284	1,065	887	738	647	601
3,406	2,938	2,583	2,254	2,007	1,801	1,610
133	31	15	15	11	16	12
228	139	69	57	52	42	69
2,075	1,919	1,740	1,578	1,434	1,302	1,190
2,303	2,058	1,809	1,635	1,486	1,344	1,259
$ 3.27	$ 3.18	$ 2.89	$ 2.56	$ 2.29	$ 1.93	$ 1.60(d)
3.42	3.40	3.03	2.68	2.38	2.02	1.65(d)
2.16	1.96	1.74	1.54	1.325	1.15	1.04
7.4%	8.6%	8.9%	9.5%	9.6%	8.5%	8.1%
20.2%	21.5%	21.6%	21.0%	20.6%	19.0%	17.1%
5.8%	1.5%	.8%	.9%	.7%	1.2%	1.0%
9.9%	6.8%	3.8%	3.5%	3.5%	3.1%	5.5%
63.2%	57.6%	57.4%	57.5%	55.7%	56.9%	63.0%
124	124	124	123	123	123	123
$ 293	$ 381	$ 306	$ 264	$ 191	$ 145	$ 154
127	106	88	77	67	64	57

(c) Includes shareholders' equity and total debt.
(d) In 1974, the Company adopted the last-in, first-out (LIFO) accounting method for certain major categories of inventories. This accounting change caused a reduction in net income of $31.2 million ($.25 per share) in 1974.
(e) Adjusted for a two-for-one stock split in 1977.

Source: The Coca-Cola Company Annual Report, 1983.

In Table 7–11 and Figure 7–4 the same four industries' long-term debt to equity ratios are given, which might explain the impact of financial leverage on the return on equity and possibly explain why some companies and industries are more volatile than others. In general the airline industry has the most debt, followed by the chemical, brewing, and drug industries.

The basic business of airlines requires a large capital commitment in terms of airplanes, and therefore a large amount of debt is needed to finance them because profitability is not sufficient to provide enough internal funds. Delta traditionally has had a low level of long-term debt but in 1983 the firm increased its borrowing dramatically. Currently, Northwest is the only airline that is almost entirely without long-term debt (in 1983 long-term debt was 11

TABLE 7–10   Return on Equity (selected companies; in percent)

	1974	1975	1976	1977	1978	1979	1980	1981	1982	1983
Airline (industry)	6.6	NMF	7.3	11.9	16.6	6.8	1.0	NMF	NMF	NMF
AMR (American)	3.6	NMF	9.2	10.2	16.2	9.8	NMF	2.0	NMF	14.9
Delta	20.4	10.2	13.0	14.9	17.8	16.0	10.1	14.1	2.0	NMF
Eastern	2.3	NMF	10.4	9.1	15.3	11.8	NMF	NMF	NMF	NMF
Northwest	11.0	7.0	7.8	12.4	7.8	8.5	.8	1.3	.6	5.9
UAL (United)	12.7	NMF	2.4	0.1	25.6	NMF	1.8	NMF	1.0	8.9
Brewing (industry)	10.0	8.8	11.7	11.1	10.3	12.7	12.8	11.6	11.9	15.6
Anheuser-Busch	11.9	4.3	9.0	13.5	14.7	15.8	16.6	18.0	15.1	17.0
Carling O'Keefe	NMF	NMF	3.1	1.2	8.8	10.4	10.4	11.1	16.1	19.5
Coors	11.3	4.1	15.4	12.2	9.2	10.4	9.1	6.9	5.1	10.4
Heileman	12.3	3.3	21.7	22.8	23.2	27.4	27.3	25.3	23.5	23.8
Pabst	8.2	8.8	12.6	8.1	4.1	3.5	4.5	NMF	1.1	ACQ
Chemical (industry)	16.9	3.2	14.1	12.9	13.6	15.0	13.0	11.9	7.1	8.5
Allied	14.9	1.1	11.3	11.6	9.5	.8	15.0	14.0	6.6	13.1
Dow	29.8	5.1	21.4	17.8	16.9	20.1	18.1	11.5	4.4	5.8
Du Pont	10.8	7.1	11.4	12.8	16.5	17.7	12.6	10.3	8.5	9.3
Monsanto	18.4	5.5	16.3	11.5	11.7	11.9	5.3	13.4	9.4	10.6
Union Carbide	21.2	3.9	14.4	11.3	10.8	13.8	14.1	12.3	6.0	4.3
Drug (industry)	19.4	8.5	18.1	16.6	19.2	20.0	19.5	17.9	19.0	19.7
Lilly	21.1	8.9	18.6	18.1	20.1	21.0	19.7	19.8	20.0	21.6
Merck	25.6	4.1	23.2	22.8	21.1	22.9	22.3	19.9	18.8	18.5
Pfizer	15.9	5.9	15.7	25.6	16.5	16.8	16.2	13.0	16.9	20.5
Searle(G.D)	21.3	0.2	14.1	NMF	16.9	18.0	17.9	18.2	21.1	16.2
Upjohn	17.1	5.1	15.8	16.7	20.2	20.1	19.7	18.8	13.0	15.2

NMF = not meaningful due to loss; ACQ = Acquired.
Source: *Value Line Investment Survey* (Arnold Bernhard & Co, selected issues).

FIGURE 7–3   Return on Equity—Airlines, Brewing, Chemicals and Drugs

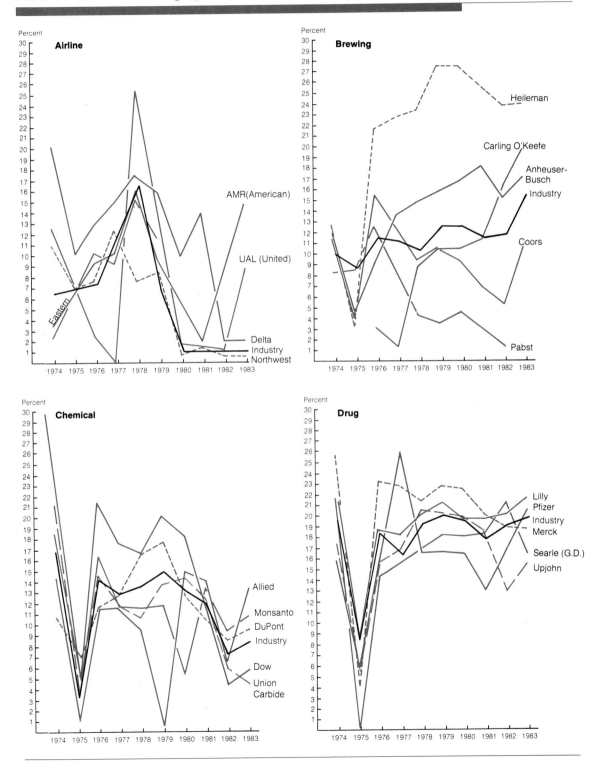

TABLE 7–11   Long-Term Debt to Equity (selected companies; in percent)

	1974	1975	1976	1977	1978	1979	1980	1981	1982	1983
Airline (industry)	130.3	136.0	111.0	91.4	106.0	118.6	140.0	150.8	180.2	139.2
AMR (American)	84.3	83.4	68.2	59.7	119.3	131.0	158.2	180.3	160.2	98.8
Delta	77.7	82.2	64.7	38.3	22.7	14.7	16.0	19.1	35.5	121.8
Eastern	204.0	214.5	167.0	116.0	213.0	256.6	250.9	340.7	484.0	732.3
Northwest	36.3	39.4	18.3	13.4	12.6	11.8	7.5	1.5	0.0	11.7
UAL (United)	117.7	125.8	116.6	89.6	97.2	106.3	100.0	107.35	160.1	82.1
Brewing (industry)	29.5	39.0	35.5	31.7	32.0	32.7	39.4	37.0	38.7	35.6
Anheuser-Busch	35.9	57.6	53.7	48.6	55.7	55.2	71.0	67.7	53.5	46.8
Carling O'Keefe	19.1	17.9	15.1	17.1	13.3	10.9	7.7	5.2	3.3	2.9
Coors	—	—	—	—	—	—	—	—	—	—
Heileman	38.2	40.2	29.0	22.2	21.2	31.5	35.8	33.9	87.8	40.0
Pabst	—	—	—	7.3	9.5	7.	5.2	5.2	15.3	ACQ
Chemical (industry)	38.3	43.2	44.7	51.2	50.0	46.6	45.3	56.3	47.4	42.6
Allied	43.3	59.0	57.3	69.4	74.6	66.7	46.0	34.4	18.5	42.2
Dow	66.2	63.8	65.6	76.1	86.5	78.6	77.7	81.3	69.5	55.5
Du Pont	21.1	23.2	31.7	30.0	23.1	20.8	19.4	70.1	54.1	41.3
Monsanto	33.4	42.8	40.6	42.9	47.4	43.2	48.8	33.3	28.7	25.6
Union Carbide	35.7	46.5	51.5	47.0	40.7	43.9	38.9	39.9	47.1	48.4
Drug (industry)	16.6	24.9	25.8	23.8	22.5	20.2	18.9	18.3	17.1	15.7
Lilly	.6	1.2	1.8	—	.3	.2	1.9	2.8	2.4	4.3
Merck	5.2	23.0	19.7	16.7	14.5	12.8	11.3	12.0	15.3	15.8
Pfizer	29.9	50.7	45.7	41.2	42.8	40.0	37.1	40.7	26.3	22.2
Searle(G.D)	60.5	87.0	78.8	90.2	80.2	50.3	16.5	33.3	30.8	24.4
Upjohn	14.3	41.0	46.0	41.2	33.6	29.8	35.3	47.5	47.4	51.9

— = No long-term debt.
Source: *Value Line Investment Survey* (Arnold Bernhard & Co., selected issues).

FIGURE 7–4   Total Debt to Equity—Airlines, Brewing, Chemicals, and Drugs

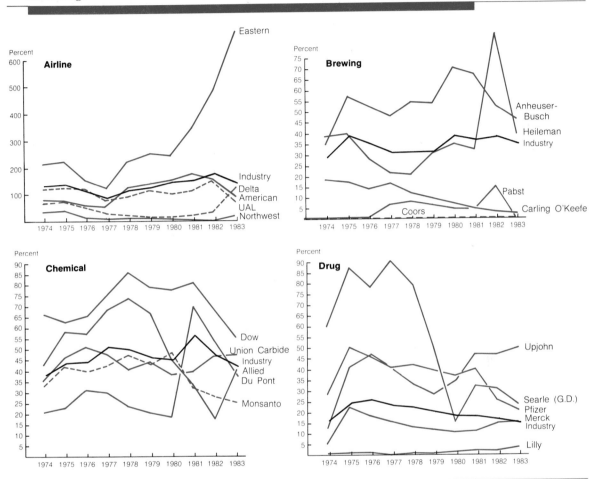

percent of equity). This industry in general is burdened with debt and the cyclical nature of the industry compounds earnings swings.

All the other industries are in safe territory. Coors has no long-term debt while Anheuser-Busch is declining after having a rising debt ratio during its rapid expansion in the last half of the 1970s. Dow leads chemicals with the highest long-term debt to equity ratio but has made a concerted effort to reduce its debt load over the last three years. Du Pont traditionally Had the lowest debt ratio, but the purchase of Conoco Oil in 1981 caused long-term debt to rise significantly. The company has been reducing its debt burden. The drug industry, in general, has low levels of debt, mostly because their consistently high returns allow internal generation of funds and little reliance on the debt markets.

These tables only cover two ratios but they should get across the point that industry comparisons allow one to pick the quality companies and find the potential losers. These two ratios can be extremely important when making risk-return choices between common stocks.

DEFICIENCIES OF FINANCIAL STATEMENTS

Several differences occur between companies and industries, and inflation has additionally clouded the clarity of accounting statements. Some of the more important difficulties occur in the area of inflation-adjusted accounting statements, inventory valuation, depreciation methods, pension funds liabilities, research and development, deferred taxes, and foreign exchange accounting. We do not have space to cover all of them, but we will touch on the most important ones.

Inflation

Inflation causes phantom sources of profit that may mislead even the most alert analyst. The major problem is that revenue is almost always stated in current dollars, whereas plant and equipment or inventory may have been purchased at lower price levels. Thus, profit may be more a function of increasing prices than of satisfactory performance.

Much of the distortion of inflation shows up on the balance sheet since most of the values on the balance sheet are stated on a historical or original cost basis. This may be particularly troublesome in the case of plant and equipment and inventory, which may now be worth two or three times the original cost or—from a negative viewpoint—may require many times the original cost for replacement.

The accounting profession has been groping with this problem for decades, and the discussion becomes particularly intense each time inflation rears its ugly head. In October 1979, the Financial Accounting Standards Board (FASB) issued a ruling that required about 1,300 large companies to disclose inflation-adjusted accounting data in their annual reports. The ruling was extended for five more years in 1984. This information is disclosed in addition to the traditional historical cost data.

Inflation-adjusted accounting is a relatively new concept in accounting practice, and most likely it will undergo many modifications over time. Initially, the FASB required the use of two separate methods. The first, called the constant-dollar method, adjusts statements by using the consumer price index. The second, called the current-cost method (sometimes referred to as replacement cost), requires assets to be revalued at their current cost. It now appears that the second method is the most widely accepted, and in 1984 the FASB said that the constant-dollar reporting requirement will be dropped for those companies using current-cost information. Overall, these adjustments will affect inventory and plant and equipment the most, thus affecting overall balance

sheet accounts and the total asset value of the firm. The revaluation will also affect inflation-adjusted profits through adjustments to depreciation expense and cost of goods sold, and profits will be smaller than they would be on a historical-cost basis. The appendix at the end of this chapter presents The Coca-Cola Company's 1983 inflation-adjusted data provided to the stockholders in the annual report.

Many financial executives think that the new data will simply confuse most investors, but others see benefits. One problem seems to be that many analysts do not know exactly how to use these statements for comparative purposes, and the SEC and FASB hope that another five years will increase use and the analysts' adaptability to these statements. The most important benefit could be the ability to determine if a company is generating enough cash flow from internal operations to replace worn-out equipment and maintain the existing level of production. Another benefit to investors will come from being able to measure dividends, income, and stock prices in dollars adjusted for inflation.

From a study of 10 chemical firms and 8 drug companies using current-cost (replacement-cost) data found in the financial 10K statements that these companies filed with the Securities and Exchange Commission, it was found that the changes shown in Table 7–12 occurred in their assets, income, and other selected ratios.

The comparison of replacement-cost and historical-cost accounting methods shows that replacement cost increases assets but at the same time reduces income. This increase in asset lowers the debt-to-assets ratio, since debt is a monetary asset that is not revalued because it is paid back in nominal dollars.

TABLE 7–12   Comparison of Replacement-Cost Accounting to Historical-Cost Accounting

	Ten chemical companies		Eight drug companies	
	Replacement cost	Historical cost	Replacement cost	Historical cost
Increase in assets	28.4%	—	15.4%	—
Decrease in net income before taxes	(45.8%)	—	(19.3%)	—
Return on assets	2.8%	6.2%	8.3%	11.4%
Return on equity	4.9%	13.5%	12.8%	19.6%
Debt-to-assets ratio	34.3%	43.8%	30.3%	35.2%
Interest coverage ratio (times interest earned)	7.1×	8.4×	15.4×	16.7×

Note: Replacement cost is but one form of current cost. Nevertheless, it is widely used as a measure of current cost.
Source: Jeff Garnett and Geoffrey A. Hirt, "Replacement Cost Data: A Study of the Chemical and Drug Industry for Years 1976 through 1978" (working paper).

The decreased debt-to-assets ratio would indicate that the financial leverage of the firm is decreased, but a look at the interest coverage ratio tells a different story. Because the interest coverage ratio measures the operating income available to cover interest expense, the declining income penalizes the ratio, and the firm shows a decreased ability to cover its interest cost.

As long as prices continue to rise in an inflationary environment, profits appear to feed on themselves. The main objection is that when prices do level off, there is a rude awakening for management and unsuspecting stockholders as expensive inventory is charged against softening retail prices. A 15 to 20 percent growth rate in earnings may be little more than an "inflationary illusion." Industries most sensitive to inflation-induced profits are those with cyclical products, such as lumber, copper, rubber, and food products, as well as those in which inventory is a significant percentage of sales and profits. Reported profits for the lumber industry have been influenced as much as 50 percent by inventory pricing, and a number of other industries' profits have been influenced by 15 to 20 percent.[8]

Inventory Valuation

The income statement can show considerable differences in earnings, depending upon the method of inventory valuation. The two basic methods are FIFO (first-in, first-out) and LIFO (last-in, first-out). In an inflationary economy, a firm could be reporting increased profits even though no actual increase in physical output took place. The example of the Rhoades Company will illustrate this point. We first observe their income statement for 1985 in Table 7–13. They sold 1,000 units for $20,000 and show earnings after taxes of $4,200 and an operating margin and aftertax margin of 35 percent and 21 percent, respectively.

Assume that in 1986 the number of units sold remains constant at 1,000 units. However, inflation causes a 10 percent increase in price, from $20 to $22 per unit. Total sales will go up to $22,000, but with no actual increase in physical volume. Further assume the firm uses FIFO inventory pricing, so that inventory first purchased will be written off against current sales. We will assume that 1,000 units of 1985 inventory at a cost of $10 per unit are written off against 1986 sales revenue. If Rhoades used LIFO inventory, and cost of goods sold went up 10 percent also, to $11 per unit, income will be less than under FIFO. Table 7–14 shows the 1986 income statement of Rhoades under both inventory methods.

Table 7–14 demonstrates the difference between FIFO and LIFO inventory methods. Under FIFO, Rhoades Corporation shows higher profit margins and more income even though no physical increase in sales occurs. This is because FIFO costing lags behind current prices, and the company generates

[8] Ronald M. Copeland, Joseph F. Wojdak, and John K. Shank, "The Use of LIFO to Offset Inflation," *Harvard Business Review,* May–June 1971, pp. 91–100.

TABLE 7–13

RHOADES CORPORATION
First-Year Income Statement
Net income for 1985

Sales	$20,000	(1,000 units at $20)
Cost of goods sold	10,000	(1,000 units at $10)
Gross profit	10,000	
Selling and administrative expense	2,000	
Depreciation	1,000	
Operating profit	7,000	
Taxes (40 percent)	2,800	
Earnings after taxes	$ 4,200	
Operating margin	$7,000/20,000 = 35%	
Aftertax margin	$4,200/20,000 = 21%	

"phantom profits" due to capital gains on inventory. Unfortunately, this inventory will need to be replaced next period at higher costs. When and if prices turn lower in a recessionary environment, FIFO will have the opposite effect and show a more negative performance. LIFO inventory costing, on the other hand, relates current costs to current prices, and although profits rise in dollar terms from 1985, the margins stay basically the same. The only problem with LIFO inventory accounting is that low-cost layers of inventory build up on the balance sheet of the company and understate inventory. This will cause inventory turnover to appear higher than under FIFO.

TABLE 7–14

RHOADES CORPORATION
Second-Year Income Statement Using FIFO and LIFO
Net income for 1986

	FIFO		LIFO	
Sales	$22,000	(1,000 at $22)	$22,000	(1,000 at $22)
Cost of goods sold	10,000	(1,000 at $10)	11,000	(1,000 at $11)
Gross profit	12,000		11,000	
Selling and administrative expense	2,200	(10% of sales)	2,200	(10% of sales)
Depreciation	1,000		1,000	
Operating profit	8,800		7,800	
Taxes (40 percent)	3,520		3,120	
Earnings after taxes	$ 5,280		4,680	
Operating margin	$8,800/22,000 = 40%		$7,800/22,000 = 35.4%	
Aftertax margin	$5,280/22,000 = 24%		$4,680/22,000 = 21.2%	

Extraordinary Gains and Losses

Nonrecurring gains or losses may occur from the sale of corporate fixed assets, lawsuits, or similar events that would not be expected to occur often, if ever again. Some analysts argue that such extraordinary events should be included in computing the current income of the firm, while others would leave them off in assessing operating performance. The choice can have a big impact on ratios that rely on earnings or earnings per share. Extraordinary gains can inflate returns and lower payout ratios if they are included in earnings. The analyst concerned about forecasting should only include those earnings from continuing operations; otherwise, the forecast will be seriously off its mark. Unfortunately, there is some inconsistency in the manner in which nonrecurring losses are treated in spite of determined attempts by the accounting profession to ensure uniformity of action.

Pension Fund Liabilities

One area of increasing concern among financial analysts is the unfunded liabilities of corporate pension funds. These funds eventually will have to pay workers their retirement income from the pension fund earnings and assets. If the money is not available from the pension fund, the company is liable to make the payments. These unfunded pensions may have to come out of earnings in future years, which would penalize shareholders and limit the corporation's ability to reinvest in new assets.

Other Distortions

There are other problems in accounting statements and methods of reporting earnings. Space does not permit us to cover each and every area of potential earnings distortion, but a mention of some of them might provide you with areas that require further investigation. Some other areas for detective work are in accounting methods for the following: research and development expenditures, deferred taxes, investment tax credits, foreign exchange currency translations, merger accounting, intangible drilling and development costs, and percentage depletion allowances. As you can see, there are many issues that cause analysts to dig further and to be cautious about accepting bottom-line earnings per share.

SUMMARY

Chapter 7 presents the basics of accounting statements and ratio analysis. After going through an income statement, balance sheet, and the source-and-uses-of-funds statements, ratios are presented that help tie together these statements.

    Ratio analysis is used to evaluate the operating performance and capital structure of a firm. Ratios will not help you find a gold mine, but they can help you avoid the trap of buying sick companies. Using ratio analysis, a brief

description of two bankruptcy studies was given which emphasized the ability of ratios to spot troubled firms with a potential for failure.

Twenty ratios were classified into six categories which measured profitability, asset utilization, liquidity, debt utilization, relative prices, and taxes and dividend policy. The Coca-Cola Company was used as an example as we went through the computation of each ratio. The Du Pont method was presented to demonstrate the relationship between assets, sales, income, and debt for creating returns on assets and equity.

Ratios are best used when compared to industry norms, company trends, and economic and industry cycles. It is becoming more difficult to use ratio analysis on an industry basis as firms become more integrated and diversified into several industries. Four industries were used—airlines, brewing, chemicals, and drugs—to examine industry trends and differences. Each company was compared to industry norms, and the difference between companies and industries was easily seen.

Finally, the deficiencies of financial statements were discussed with an emphasis on inflation. Accounting statements adjusted for inflation appear in the appendix at the end of the chapter. The effect on ratios was examined for replacement-cost versus historical-cost data. Other distortions were discussed, such as extraordinary gains and losses and pension fund liabilities.

Financial analysis is a science as well as an art, and experience certainly sharpens the skills. It would be unrealistic for someone to pick up all the complex relationships involved in ratio analysis immediately. This is why analysts are assigned industries which they learn inside and out. After much practice, the analytical work is easier, and the true picture of financial performance becomes focused.

IMPORTANT WORDS AND CONCEPTS

Income statement
Balance sheet
Sources and uses of funds
    statement
Net working capital
Profitability ratios
Du Pont analysis
Asset utilization ratios
Liquidity ratios
Debt utilization ratios
Price ratios

Dividend yield
Payout ratio
Trend analysis
Inflation-adjusted accounting
Constant-dollar method
Current-cost method
Extraordinary gains and losses
Operating margin
Return on equity
Current ratio
Quick ratio

DISCUSSION QUESTIONS

1. Does a balance sheet that is dated year-end 1986 only reflect transactions for that year?

2. In the sources-and-uses-of-funds statement, suggest some factors that can cause changes in stockholders' equity.

3. What is a dangerous way to finance a build-up in long-term assets?

4. What ratios are likely to be of greatest interest to the banker or trade creditor? To the bondholder?

5. If a firm's operating margin and aftertax margin are almost the same (an unusual case), what can we say about the firm?

6. If a firm has a high return on assets and a low net-income-to-sales margin, what can the analyst infer about the firm?

7. Contrast the capital goods industry and the food processing industry, using ratio 3b as shown in the profitability ratios. (You need only to provide comments—no numbers are expected.)

8. In computing return on assets and return on equity, how does the age of the assets influence the interpretation of the values?

9. If a firm's return on equity is substantially higher than the firm's return on assets, what can the analyst infer about the firm?

10. How do the asset utilization ratios relate to the liquidity ratios?

11. Can public utility firms better justify the use of high debt than firms in the automobile or airline industry? Comment.

12. Suggest a reason why a firm may have a high price-to-book-value ratio, but not necessarily be a strong performer.

13. Why would a forest products company generally have a low effective tax rate?

14. What might a high dividend-payout ratio suggest to an analyst about a company's growth prospects?

15. In what way does the general trend to corporate diversification over the last 20 years make ratio comparison more difficult?

16. Comment on the relative profitability of Coca-Cola's soft drink and entertainment segments (refer to Table 7–5). Has moving into the entertainment area enhanced Coca-Cola's reported earnings?

17. Using Table 7–7, comment on Coca-Cola's position relative to the industries listed in terms of operating margin and dividend yield.

18. Why is the airline industry so much more subject to the effects of a recession than the drug industry?

19. Select the industry in Table 7–10 with the highest return on equity. Was this high return accomplished as a result of high profitability, high debt utilization, or both?

20. Explain the probable impact of replacement-cost accounting on the ratios of return on assets, debt to total assets, and times interest earned for a firm that has substantial old fixed assets.

21. In examining Table 7–13 and the first column of Table 7–14, explain why earnings after taxes, and the ratios, have improved in spite of a constant unit sales volume.

22. Explain why unfunded pension obligations may impair future performance.

PROBLEMS

Look for on exam

1. Given the following financial data: net income/sales = 5 percent; sales/ total assets = 2.5; debt/total assets = 60 percent; compute:
   a. Return on assets.
   b. Return on equity.
2. Explain in Problem 1 why return on equity was so much higher than return on assets.
3. A firm has a return on assets of 10 percent and a return on equity of 15 percent. What is the debt-to-total-assets ratio?
4. Given the following financial data:

Assets:	
Cash	$ 1,000
Accounts receivable	3,500
Inventory	1,500
Fixed assets	4,000
Total assets	$10,000
Liabilities and stockholders' equity:	
Short-term debt	$ 2,000
Long-term debt	1,000
Stockholders' equity	7,000
Total liabilities and stockholders' equity	$10,000
Income before fixed charges and taxes	$3,000
Interest payments	500
Lease payment	700
Taxes (40 percent tax rate)	720
Net income (after taxes)	$ 1,080

Compute:
   a. Return on equity.
   b. Quick ratio.
   c. Long-term debt to equity.
   d. Fixed charge coverage.
5. Assume in part d of Problem 4 that the firm had a sinking fund payment obligation of $100. How much before-tax income is required to cover the sinking fund obligation? Would higher tax rates increase or decrease the before-tax income required to cover the sinking fund?
6. In Problem 4, if total debt were increased to 50 percent of assets and interests payments went up by $200, what would be the new value for return on equity?
7. Assume the following financial data:

Short-term assets	$200,000
Long-term assets	300,000
Total assets	$500,000

Short-term debt	$100,000
Long-term debt	50,000
Total liabilities	150,000
Common stock	100,000
Retained earnings	250,000
Total liabilities and stockholders' equity	$500,000
Total earnings (aftertax)	$ 48,000
Dividends per share	$1.00
Stock price	$27
Shares outstanding	16,000

    a. Compute the P/E ratio (stock price to earnings per share).

    b. Compute the ratio of stock price to book value per share (note that book value equals stockholders' equity).

    c. Compute the dividend yield.

    d. Compute the payout ratio.

8. Referring to Problem 7:

    a. If the tax rate were 40 percent, what could you infer the value of before-tax income was?

    b. Compute aftertax return on equity.

    c. Now assume the same before-tax income computed in part a, but a tax rate of 25 percent; recompute aftertax return on equity (using the simplifying assumption that equity remains constant).

    d. Assume the taxes in part c were reduced largely as a result of one-time, nonreoccuring tax credits. Would you expect the stock value to go up substantially as a result of the higher return on equity?

9. The Multi-Corporation has three different operating divisions. Financial information for each is as follows:

	Bowling	Machine Tools	Toys
Sales	$2,000,000	$10,000,000	$16,000,000
Operating income	220,000	800,000	2,000,000
Net income (A/T)	100,000	600,000	900,000
Assets	1,000,000	8,000,000	6,000,000

    a. Which division provides the highest operating margin?

    b. Which division provides the lowest aftertax profit margin?

    c. Which division has the lowest aftertax return on assets?

    d. Compute net income (aftertax) to sales for the entire corporation.

    e. Compute net income (aftertax) to assets for the entire corporation.

    f. The vice president of finance suggests that the assets in the Machine Tool division be sold off for $8,000,000 and redeployed in Toys. The new $8,000,000 in Toys will produce the same aftertax return on assets as the current $6,000,000 in that division. Recompute net income to total assets for the entire corporation assuming the above suggested change.

   g. Explain why Toys, which has a lower return on sales than Machine Tools, has such a positive effect on return on assets. Try to use numbers to support your answer.

10. Security Analyst A thinks that the Oliver Corporation is worth 12 times current earnings. Security Analyst B has a different approach. He assumes that 40 percent of earnings (per share) will be paid out in dividends and the stock should provide a 4 percent current dividend yield. Assume total earnings are $10,000,000 and that there are 5,000,000 shares outstanding.

   a. Compute the value of the stock based on Security Analyst A's approach.

   b. Compute the value of the stock based on Security Analyst B's approach.

   c. Security Analyst C uses the constant-dividend-valuation model approach presented in Chapter 6 as Formula (6–3). She uses Security Analyst B's assumption about dividends (per share), and assigns a growth rate (g) of 9 percent and a required rate of return (K_e) of 12 percent. Is her value higher or lower than that of the other security analysts?

SELECTED REFERENCES

Backer, Morton, and Martin L. Gosman. "The Use of Financial Ratios in Credit Downgrade Decisions." *Financial Management,* Spring 1980, pp. 53–56.

Barefield, Russell M., and Eugene E. Comiskey. "The Smoothing Hypothesis: An Alternative Test." *Accounting Review,* April 1972, pp. 291–98.

Bernstein, Leopold A., and Joel G. Siegel. "The Concept of Earnings Quality." *Financial Analysts Journal,* July–August 1979, pp. 72–75.

Chen, Kung H., and Thomas A. Shimerda. "An Empirical Analysis of Useful Financial Ratios." *Financial Management,* Spring 1981, pp. 51–60.

Copeland, Ronald M.; Joseph F. Wojdak and John K. Shank. "The Use of Lifo to Offset Inflation." *Harvard Business Review,* May–June 1971, pp. 91–100.

Edwards, James Don, and John B. Barrack. "Last-In, First-Out Inventory Valuation As a Way to Control Illusory Profits." *MSU Business Topics,* Winter 1975, pp. 19–27.

Fabozzi, Frank J., and Robert Fonfeder. "Have You Seen Any Good Quarterly Statements Lately?" *The Journal of Portfolio Management,* Winter 1983, pp. 71–74.

Horngren, Charles T. "Accounting Principles: Private or Public Sector?" *Journal of Accountancy,* May 1972, pp. 37–41.

Hunter, John E., and T. Daniel Coggin. "Measuring Stability and Growth in Annual EPS." *The Journal of Portfolio Management,* Winter 1983, pp. 75–78.

Joy, O. Maurice; Robert H. Litzenberger; and Richard W. McEnally. "The Adjustment of Stock Prices to Announcements of Unanticipated Changes in Quarterly Earnings." *Journal of Accounting Research,* Autumn 1977, pp. 207–25.

Modak, N. D. "Corporate Planning and the Securities Analyst." *Financial Analysts Journal,* September–October 1974, pp. 51–54.

"Pension Liabilities: Improvement is Illusory." *Business Week,* September 14, 1981, pp. 114–18.

Stauffer, Thomas R. "The Measurement of Corporate Rate of Return: A Generalized Formulation." *Bell Journal of Economics and Management Science,* Autumn 1971, pp. 434–69.

Terborgh, George. "Inflation and Profits." *Financial Analysts Journal,* May–June 1974, pp. 19–23.

Walker, Ernest W., and J. William Petty II. "Financial Differences between Large and Small Firms." *Financial Management,* Winter 1978, pp. 61–68.

APPENDIX: *The Coca-Cola Company Inflation-Adjusted Financial Data*

As required by Standards numbers 33 and 70 of the Financial Accounting Standards Board, The Coca-Cola Company is presenting supplementary information designed to represent the effect of inflation on its operations.

Certain amounts appearing in the primary financial statements (inventories, property, plant, and equipment, cost of goods and services, and depreciation and amortization expenses) have been adjusted to reflect "current costs." The restatement of current costs is intended to reflect changes in specific prices. The use of various indexes measuring price changes for specific types of assets was the principal technique used in estimating current costs. These costs are meant to indicate the amount needed to replace existing inventories and production facilities at current prices. Since motion picture films are unique and unable to be duplicated exactly, it is not possible to estimate the current cost of film inventories, therefore, based on FASB Standard No. 46, film inventories are based on constant-dollar equivalents.

Depreciation and amortization expenses are adjusted by restating the historical cost of property, plant, and equipment to show current costs for 1983. These restated costs become the base from which depreciation and amortization are calculated utilizing the same methods and asset lines used in historical-cost statements. The last line on Table 7A–1 (Statement of Income Adjusted for Changing Prices) shows that property plant and equipment net of depreciation would have a replacement cost of $2,174.6 million versus $1,560.8 million on the historical-cost statement. This $613.8 million increase is the reason the depreciation expense jumps from $156.1 million to $226.2 million in the third line of Table 7A–1.

Cost of goods and services is adjusted by restating part of the historical cost of inventories to current costs. No adjustment has been made for that portion of the company's inventories valued by the LIFO method, since these amounts already approximate average fiscal 1983 dollars. The inflation adjustment to cost of goods and services (excluding depreciation) caused a $7.3 million increase in these costs under the current-cost method as indicated in the second line of Table 7A–1.

In accordance with Standard No. 33, no adjustments to income tax expense reported in the primary financial statements have been made in determining net income in the restated replacement-cost column. This provision is

TABLE 7A–1

Statement of Income Adjusted for Changing Prices (In millions except per share data) Year Ended December 31, 1983	As Reported in the Primary Statements	Adjusted for Changes in Specific Prices (Current Costs)
Net operating revenues	$6,829.0	$6,829.0
Cost of goods and services (excluding depreciation)	3,709.2	3,716.5
Depreciation and amortization	156.1	226.2
Other operating expenses	1,973.0	1,973.0
Net of other (income) and deductions	(9.6)	(13.9)
Income from continuing operations before income taxes	1,000.3	927.2
Income taxes	442.0	442.0
Income from continuing operations	$ 558.3	$ 485.2
Income per share from continuing operations	$ 4.10	$ 3.57
Effective income tax rate	44.2%	47.7%
Purchasing power gain from holding net monetary liabilities in the year		$ 27.8
Increase in specific prices of inventories and property, plant and equipment held in the year		$ 184.1
Less effect of increase in general price level		273.9
Increase in specific prices over increase in the general price level		$ (89.8)
Estimated translation adjustment		$ (80.0)
Inventory and film costs	$ 996.7	$1,198.4
Property, plant and equipment—net	$1,560.8	$2,174.6

A significant part of the Company's operations are measured in functional currencies other than the United States dollar. Adjustments to reflect the effects of general inflation were determined on the translate-restate method using the U.S. CPI(U).

Source: The Coca-Cola Company Annual Report, 1983.

consistent with present tax laws which do not allow deduction for inflation-adjusted costs. As a result, the consolidated effective income tax rate rises from 44.2 percent on the historical cost basis to 47.7 percent on the current-cost basis.

For Coca-Cola, the net impact of these inflation adjustments is to reduce income from continuing operations from $558.3 million to $485.2 million and to reduce earnings per share from $4.10 to $3.57. The changes can be seen in the middle of Table 7A–1.

Monetary assets such as cash, marketable securities, and accounts receivables lose purchasing power during periods of inflation whereas monetary liabilities, such as accounts payable, accruals, and debt due in the current year, increase in purchasing power because cheaper dollars will be used to repay these obligations. Coca-Cola held net monetary liabilities during 1983 and as a result the company experienced a gain of $27.8 million. It should be noted that this purchasing power gain on net monetary liabilities does not represent receipt of cash and should not be considered as providing funds for subsequent reinvestment in the company.

TABLE 7A–2

Five-Year Comparison of Selected Supplemental Financial Data
Adjusted for Effects of Changing Prices (In Average 1983 Dollars)
(In millions except per share data)

Year Ended December 31,	1983	1982	1981	1980	1979
Net operating revenues	$6,829.0	$6,214.7	$6,242.9	$6,619.7	$6,297.4
Current cost information:					
Income from continuing operations	485.2	409.0	376.3	317.7	378.8
Income per share from continuing operations	3.57	3.16	3.04	2.55	3.05
Increase in specific prices over (under) increase in the general price level, including translation adjustments	(169.8)	(191.0)	(226.7)	26.7	220.3
Net assets at year-end	3,748.0	3,732.9	3,435.5	3,846.7	3,882.9
Purchasing power gain on net monetary items	27.8	18.2	26.8	52.1	28.4
Cash dividends declared per share:					
As reported	2.68	2.48	2.32	2.16	1.96
Adjusted for general inflation	2.68	2.56	2.54	2.61	2.69
Market price per common share at year-end:					
Historical amount	53.50	52.00	34.75	33.375	34.50
Adjusted for general inflation	53.50	53.67	38.07	40.35	47.35
Average Consumer Price Index—Urban	298.4	289.1	272.4	246.8	217.4

Source: The Coca-Cola Company Annual Report, 1983.

Both general and specific inflation adjustments involve estimates, assumptions, and subjective judgments which should be viewed only as an attempt to approximate the effects of inflation.

Five years of inflation-adjusted data is also presented in Table 7A–2. It can be seen that income per share adjusted for inflation has shown a positive trend, going from $3.05 to $3.57 (the third row in the table). However, cash dividends per share adjusted for inflation have shown a slight decline, from $2.69 to $2.68 (fourth line from the bottom).

Chapter 8

A Basic View of Technical Analysis and Market Efficiency

In the preceding three chapters, we have followed a fundamental approach to security analysis. That is, we have examined the fundamental factors that influence the business cycle, the performance of various industries, and the operations of individual firms. We have further examined the financial statements and tools of measurement that are available to the security analyst. In following a fundamental approach, one attempts to evaluate the appropriate worth of a security and perhaps ascertain whether it is under- or overpriced.

In this chapter, we shall examine a technical approach to investment timing. In this approach, analysts and market technicians examine prior price and volume data, as well as other market-related indicators, to determine past trends in the belief that they will help forecast future ones. Technical analysts place much more emphasis on charts and graphs of *internal market data* than on such fundamental factors as earnings reports, management capabilities, or new product development. They believe that even when important fundamental information is uncovered, it may not lead to profitable trading because of timing considerations and market imperfections.

We shall also devote much time and attention in this chapter to the concept of market efficiency; that is, the ability of the market to adjust very rapidly to the supply of new information in valuing a security. This area of study has led to the efficient market hypothesis, which states that all securities are correctly priced at any point in time.

At the outset, be aware that there are many disagreements and contradictions in the various areas that we will examine. As previously implied, advocates of technical analysis do not place much emphasis on fundamental analysis, and vice versa. Even more significant, proponents of the efficient market hypothesis would suggest that neither technical nor fundamental analysis is of any great value in producing superior returns.

In light of the various disagreements that exist, we feel it is important that the student be exposed to many schools of thought. For example, we devote the first part of the chapter to technical analysis and then later offer research findings that relate to the value of the technical approach as well as the fundamental approach. Our philosophy throughout the chapter is to recognize that there is a gap between practices utilized by brokerage houses (and on Wall Street) and beliefs held in the academic community, yet the student should be exposed to both.

TECHNICAL ANALYSIS

Technical analysis is based on a number of basic assumptions:

1.   Market value is determined solely by the interaction of demand and supply.
2.   Demand and supply are governed by both rational and irrational factors.
3.   It is assumed that though there are minor fluctuations in the market, stock prices tend to move in trends that persist for long periods of time.
4.   Reversals of trends are caused by shifts in demand and supply.

5. Shifts in demand and supply can be detected sooner or later in charts.

6. Many chart patterns tend to repeat themselves.[1]

For our purposes, the most significant items to note are the assumptions that stock prices tend to move in trends that persist for long periods and that these trends can be detected in charts. The basic premise is that past trends in market movements can be used to forecast or understand the future. The market technician generally assumes that there is a lag between the time he perceives a change in the value of a security and when the investing public ultimately assesses this change.

In developing the tools of technical analysis, we shall divide our discussion between the *(a)* use of charting, and *(b)* key indicator series to project future market movements.

THE USE OF CHARTING

Charting is often linked to the development of the Dow theory in the late 1890s by Charles Dow.[2] Mr. Dow was the founder of the Dow Jones Company and editor of *The Wall Street Journal.* Many of his early precepts were further refined by other market technicians, and it is generally believed that the Dow theory was successful in signaling the market crash of 1929.

Essential Elements of the Dow Theory

The Dow theory maintains that there are three major movements in the market: daily fluctuations, secondary movements, and primary trends. According to the theory, daily fluctuations and secondary movements (covering two weeks to a month) are only important to the extent that they reflect on the long-term primary trend in the market. Primary trends may be characterized as either bullish or bearish in nature.

In Figure 8–1 we look at the use of the Dow theory to analyze a market trend. Note that the primary movement in the market is positive in spite of two secondary movements that are downward. The important facet of the secondary movements is that each low is higher than the previous low and each high is higher than the previous high. This tends to confirm the primary trend, which is bullish.

Under the Dow theory, it is assumed that this pattern will continue for a long period, and the analyst should not be confused by secondary movements. However, the upward pattern must ultimately come to an end. This is indicated by a new pattern in which a recovery fails to exceed the previous high (abortive recovery) and a new low penetrates a previous low as indicated in the top part of Figure 8–2. For a true turn in the market to take place, the new

---

[1] R. D. Edwards and John Magee, Jr., *Technical Analysis of Stock Trends* (Springfield, Mass: John Magee, 1958).

[2] *The Wall Street Journal,* December 19, 1900.

FIGURE 8–1   Presentation of the Dow Theory

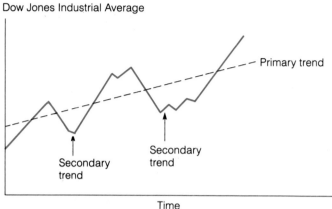

pattern of movement in the Dow Jones Industrial Average must also be confirmed by a subsequent movement in the Dow Jones Transportation Average as indicated on the bottom part of Figure 8–2.

A subsequent change from a bear to a bull market would require similar patterns of confirmation. While the Dow theory has proved helpful to market technicians, there is always the problem of false signals. For example, not

FIGURE 8–2   Market Reversal and Confirmation

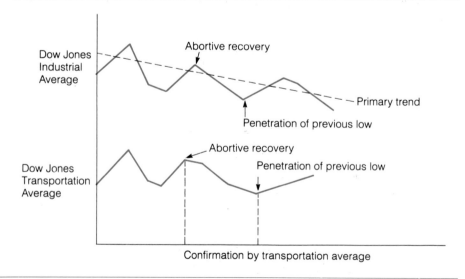

every abortive recovery is certain to signal the end of a bull market. Further-more, the investor may have to wait a long time to get full confirmation of a change in a primary trend. By the time the Transportation Average confirms the pattern in the Industrial Average, important market movements may have already taken place.

Support and Resistance Levels

Chartists attempt to define trading levels for individual securities (or the market) where there is a likelihood that price movements will be challenged. Thus, in the daily financial press or on television, the statement is often made that the next barrier to the current market move is at 1350 (or some other level). This assumes the existence of support and resistance levels. As indicated in Figure 8–3, a support level is associated with the lower end of a trading range and a resistance level with the upper end.

FIGURE 8–3   Support and Resistance

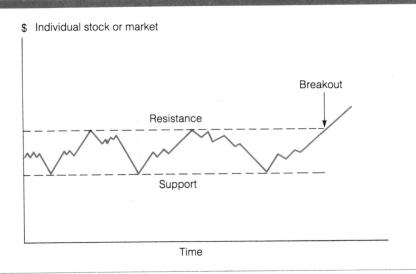

Support may develop each time a stock goes down to a lower level of trading because investors who previously passed up a purchase opportunity may now choose to act. It is a signal that new demand is coming into the market. When a stock reaches the high side of the normal trading range, resistance may develop because some investors who bought in on a previous wave of enthusiasm (on an earlier high) may now view this as a chance to get even. Others may simply see this as an opportunity to take a profit.

A breakout above a resistance point (as indicated in Figure 8–3) or below a support level is considered significant. The stock is assumed to be

trading in a new range, and higher (lower) trading values may now be expected.

Volume

The amount of volume supporting a given market movement is also considered significant. For example, if a stock (or the market in general) makes a new high on heavy trading volume, this is considered to be bullish. Conversely, a new high on light volume may indicate a temporary move that is likely to be reversed.

A new low on light volume is considered somewhat positive because of the lack of investor participation. On the other hand, when a new low is established on the basis of heavy trading volume, this is considered to be quite bearish.

In the mid-1980s, the New York Stock Exchange has been averaging a volume of 80 to 90 million shares daily. When the volume jumps to 130 to 140 million shares, analysts take a very strong interest in the trading pattern of the market.

Types of Charts

Up until now, we have been using typical line charts to indicate market patterns. Technicians also use bar charts and point and figure charts. We shall examine each.

Bar chart.   A bar chart shows the high and low price for a stock with a dash along the line to indicate the closing price. An example is shown in Figure 8–4.

FIGURE 8–4   Bar Chart

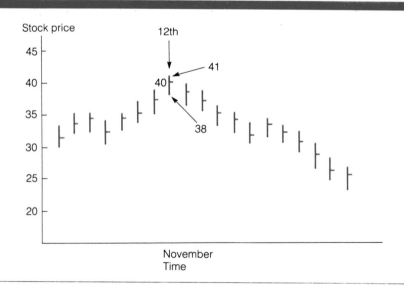

FIGURE 8–5   Bar Chart of Market Averages

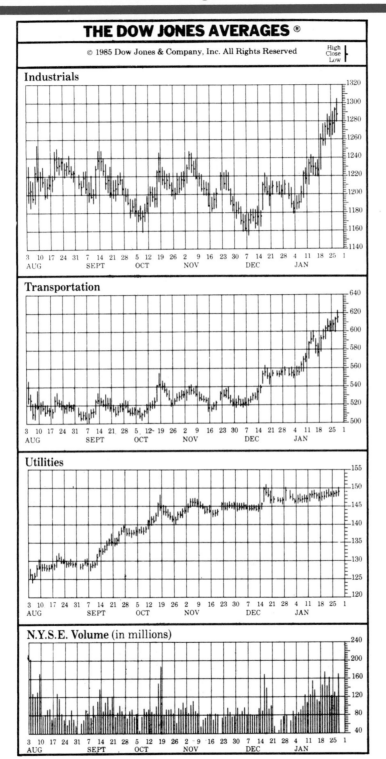

FIGURE 8–6   Chart Representation of Market Bottoms and Tops

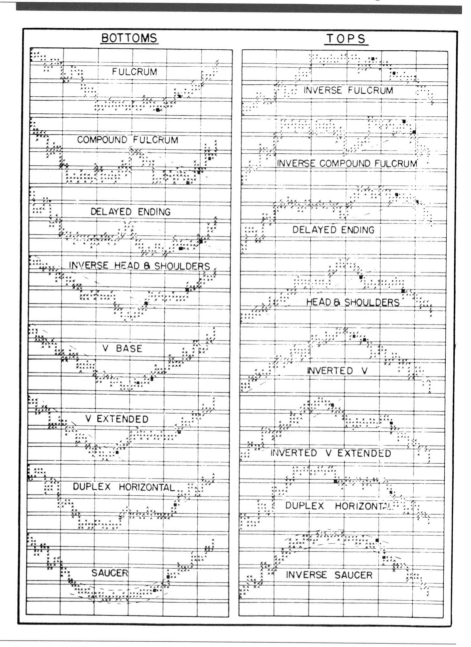

Source: Irwin Shishko, "Techniques of Forecasting Commodity Prices," *Commodity Yearbook* (New York: Commodity Research Bureau, 1965), p. 4.

We see on November 12 the stock traded between a high of 41 and a low of 38 and closed at 40. Daily information on the Dow Jones Averages are usually presented in the form of a bar chart, with daily volume shown at the bottom as indicated in Figure 8–5.

Trendline, published through a division of Standard & Poor's, provides excellent charting information on a wide variety of securities traded on the major exchanges and is available at many libraries and brokerage houses. Market technicians carefully evaluate the charts, looking for what they perceive to be significant patterns of movement. For example, the pattern in Figure 8–4 on page 242 might be interpreted as a head and shoulder pattern (note the head in the middle) with a lower penetration of the neckline to the right indicating a sell signal. In Figure 8–6, we show a series of price movement patterns presumably indicating market bottoms and tops.

Though it is beyond the scope of this book to go into interpretation of chart formations in great detail, special books on the subject are suggested at the end of our discussion of charting.

Point and Figure Chart

A point and figure chart (PFC) emphasizes significant price changes and the reversal of significant price changes. Unlike a line or bar chart, there is no time dimension. An example of a point and figure chart is presented in Figure 8–7.

FIGURE 8–7   Point and Figure Chart

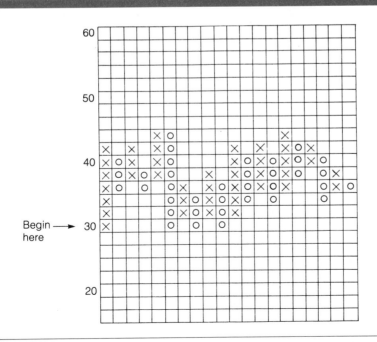

The assumption is that the stock starts out at 30. Only moves of two points or greater are plotted on the graph (some may prefer to use one point). Advances are indicated by X's and declines are shown by O's. A reversal from an advance to a decline or vice versa calls for a shift in columns. Thus, the stock initially goes from 30 to 42 and then shifts columns in its subsequent decline to 36 before moving up again in column 3. A similar pattern persists throughout the chart.

Chartists carefully read point and figure charts to observe market patterns (where there is support, resistance, breakouts, congestion, etc.). Students with a strong interest in charting may consult such books as Edwards and Magee, *Technical Analysis of Stock Trends*[3] and Zweig, *Understanding Technical Forecasting*.[4] The problem in reading charts has always been to analyze patterns in such a fashion that they truly predict stock market movements before they unfold. In order to justify the effort, one must assume that there are discernible trends over the long term.

KEY INDICATOR SERIES

In the television series, "Wall Street Week," host Louis Rukeyser has a number of technical indicators that he watches on a weekly basis. He refers to them as his elves and compares the bullish and bearish indicators to determine what the next direction of the market might be.

In this section, we will examine similar bullish and bearish technical indicator series. We will first look at contrary opinion rules, then smart money rules, and finally overall market indicators.

Contrary Opinion Rules

The essence of a contrary opinion rule is that it is easier to figure out who is wrong than who is right. If you know your neighbor has a terrible sense of direction and you spot him taking a left at the intersection, you automatically take a right. In the stock market, there are similar guidelines.

Odd-lot theory.   An odd-lot trade is one of less than 100 shares, and only small investors tend to engage in odd-lot transactions. The odd-lot theory suggests that you watch very closely what the small investor is doing and then do the opposite. *The Wall Street Journal* reports odd-lot trading on a daily basis, and *Barron's* reports similar information on a weekly basis. It is a simple matter to construct a ratio of odd-lot purchases to odd-lot sales. For example, on July 18, 1984, 195,357 odd-lot shares were purchased, and 392,164 shares were sold, indicating a ratio of .498. The ratio generally fluctuates between .40 and 1.60.

---

[3] R. D. Edwards and John Magee, Jr., *Technical Analysis of Stock Trends*, 5th ed. (Springfield, Mass: Stock Trends Service, 1966).

[4] Matin E. Zweig, *Understanding Technical Forecasting* (Princeton, N.J.: Dow Jones, 1978).

The odd-lot theory actually suggests that the small trader does all right most of the time but badly misses on key market turns. As indicated in Figure 8–8, the odd-lot trader is on the correct path as the market is going up; that is, selling off part of the portfolio in an up market (the name of the game is to buy

FIGURE 8–8 Comparing Standard & Poor's 500 Index and the Odd-lot Index

low and sell high). This net selling posture is reflected by a declining odd-lot index (purchase/sales ratio). However, as the market continues upward, the odd-lot trader suddenly thinks he or she sees an opportunity for a killing in the market and becomes a very strong net buyer. This precedes a fall in the market.

The odd-lot trader is also assumed to be a strong seller right before the bottom of a bear market. Presumably, when the small trader finally gets grandfather's 50 shares of AT&T out of the lockbox and sells them in disgust, it is time for the market to turn upward.

As if to add injury to insult, there is a corollary to the odd-lot theory that says one should be particularly sensitive to what odd-lot traders do on Monday because odd-lotters tend to visit with each other over the weekend, confirm each others opinions or exchange hot tips, and then call their brokers on Monday morning. The assumption is that their chatter over the barbeque pit or in the bowling alley is even more suspect than their own individual opinions.

While the odd-lot theory appeared to have some validity in the 1950s and 1960s, it has not been a particularly valuable tool in the 1970s and early 1980s. For one thing, the odd-lotters outguessed many of the professional money managers in selling off before the stock market debacle of the mid-1970s, and they began buying in advance of a recovery. Another problem is that odd-lotters have been fairly consistent net sellers since the late 1960s, so there is not a balanced movement in the index.

Short sales position.   A second contrary opinion rule is based on the volume of short sales in the market. As you will recall from Chapter 3, a short sale represents the selling of a security you do not own with the anticipation of purchasing the security in the future to cover your short position. An investor would only engage in a short sale transaction if he believed the security would, in fact, be going down in price in the near future so that he could buy back the security at a lower price to cover his short sale. When the aggregate number of short sellers is large (that is they are bearish), this is thought to be a bullish signal.

The contrary opinion stems from two sources: first, that short sellers are sometimes emotional and may overreact to the market; second and more important, that there now is a built-in demand for stocks that have been sold short by investors who will have to repurchase the shares to cover their short positions.

Daily short sale totals for the New York Stock Exchange are recorded in *The Wall Street Journal.* Also once a month (around the 20th), *The Wall Street Journal* provides a report on total short sale figures for the two major exchanges, as well as securities traded on those exchanges (based on mid-month data). This feature usually contains comments about current trends in the market.

Technical analysts compute a ratio of the total short sales positions on an exchange to average daily exchange volume for the month. The normal ratio is between 1.00 and 1.75. A ratio of 1.00 would indicate that the current short sales position is equal to one day's average trading volume.

As the short sales ratio (frequently called the short interest ratio) approaches the higher end of the normal trading range, this would be considered bullish (remember this is a contrary opinion trading rule). As is true with many other technical trading rules, its use in predicting future performance has produced mixed results.[5]

Investment advisory recommendations.   A further contrary opinion rule states that you should watch the predictions of the investment advisory services and do the opposite. This has been formalized by Investors Intelligence (an investment advisory service itself) into the Index of Bearish Sentiment. Abraham W. Cohen, president of Investors Intelligence, suggests that when 42 percent or more of the advisory services are bearish, you should expect a market upturn. Conversely, when only 17 percent or fewer are bearish, you should expect a decline.[6]

Lest one take investment advisory services too lightly, however, observe the market impact of a recommendation by Joseph Granville, publisher of the *Granville Market Letter.* On Tuesday, January 6, 1981, Mr. Granville issued a late evening warning to his subscribers to "sell everything." He helped cause a

---

[5] Randall Smith, "Short Interest and Stock Market Prices," *Financial Analysts Journal,* November–December, 1968, pp. 151–54. Barton M. Briggs, "The Short Interest—A False Proverb," *Financial Analysts Journal,* July–August, 1966, pp. 111–16.

[6] How to Read Stock Market Indicators," *Business Week,* December 8, 1980, p. 14.

next-day decline in the Dow Jones Industrial Average of 23.80 points. Forty billion ($40,000,000,000) in market value was chopped off the total value of stocks traded on U.S. security exchanges and the over-the-counter market.

Although market events did not immediately confirm Mr. Granville's pessimism (and brought much criticism), the fact that one man could trigger such a reaction is an indication of the number of people that are influenced by the suggestion of an advisory service.

Greed Index.   A final contrary opinion rule is represented by the Greed Index. The index measures how greedy investors are, and is prepared by Lee H. Idleman, research director at Neuberger and Berman. Greed, as measured by the index, is synonymous with bullish sentiment, or optimism. The more greedy or optimistic investors are, the more likely the market is to fall under this contrary opinion rule. The Greed Index comprises 10 different factors that are assigned a value from 1 to 10. Among these factors are portfolio aggressiveness (high technology versus defensive stocks), acceptance of new ideas, ratio of positive to negative comments by investment analysts, willingness to invest in untested issues and so on.

When the Greed Index exceeds 60, this is considered to be bearish. It got up to 69 in March 1983 before a market sell-off began. It got to an all-time high of 89 in December 1968 during the go-go days of a long-forgotten bull market. When the Greed Index goes below 30, this is interpreted as a buy signal. For example, the index was at 28 before the great market upturn of June 1982. While the Greed Index may provide some market clues, it is less than exacting. For example, the investor who began to go short when the index hit 60 in 1968, would have suffered large losses before the index got up to 89.

Smart Money Rules

Market technicians have long attempted to track the pattern of sophisticated traders in the hope that they might provide unusual insight into the future. We shall briefly observe theories related to bond market traders and stock exchange specialists.

Barron's Confidence Index.   The *Barron's* Confidence Index is used to observe the trading pattern of investors in the bond market. The theory is based on the premise that bond traders are more sophisticated than stock traders and will pick up trends more quickly. The theory would suggest that if one can figure out what bond traders are doing today, he may be able to determine what stock market investors will be doing in the near future.

Barron's Confidence Index is actually computed by taking the yield on 10 top-grade corporate bonds and dividing by the yield on 10 intermediate grade bonds, and multiplying by 100.

$$\begin{array}{c} Barron's \\ \text{Confidence} \\ \text{Index} \end{array} = \frac{\text{Yield on 10 top grade corporate bonds}}{\text{Yield on 10 intermediate grade bonds}} (100) \qquad (8\text{--}1)$$

The bonds in this index are presented in Table 8–1.

TABLE 8–1   Issues in *Barron's* Confidence Index

Best (Top) Grade

Industrials

AT&T 3⅞s 90
Exxon 6s 97
Gen. Elec. 8½s 04
U.S. Steel 4½s 86

Transports

Atchison 4s 95
Ches. and Ohio 4½s 92
Nort. and Western 4s 96
Union Pac. 2½s 91

Utilities

Consumer Pwr. 5⅞s 96
Ill. Bell 2¾s

Intermediate Grade

Industrials

Beth. Steel 6⅞s 99
Ford Motor 8⅛s 90
Pfizer 9¼s 00

Transports

Louis. Nash. 7⅜s 93
Missouri Pac. 4¼s 05
St. L. SF. 4s 97

Utilities

Alabama Pwr. 9¾s 04
Detroit Ed. 9s 99
Pacific G.&E. 7¼s 05
Phil. Elec. 7⅜s 01

The index is published weekly in the "Market Laboratory" section of *Barron's* magazine. What does it actually tell us? First of all, we can observe that the top-grade bonds in the numerator will always have a smaller yield than the intermediate grade bonds in the denominator. The reason is that the higher-quality issues can satisfy investors with smaller returns. The bond market is very representative of a risk-return trade-off environment in which less risk requires less return and higher risk necessitates a higher return.

With top-grade bonds providing smaller yields than intermediate-grade bonds, the Confidence Index will always be less than 100 (percent). The normal trading range is between 80 and 95, and it is within this range that technicians look for signals on the economy. If bond investors are bullish about future economic prosperity, they will be rather indifferent between

holding top-grade bonds and intermediate-grade bonds, and the yield differences between these two categories will be relatively small. This would indicate that the Confidence Index may be close to 95. An example is presented below in which top-grade bonds are providing 11.4 percent and intermediate-grade bonds are yielding 12 percent.

$$\begin{array}{c}\textit{Barron's}\\ \text{Confidence}\\ \text{Index}\end{array} = \frac{\text{Yield on 10 top-grade corporate bonds}}{\text{Yield on 10 intermediate-grade bonds}}(100)$$

$$= \frac{11.4\%}{12\%}(100) = 95(\%)$$

Now let us assume that investors become quite concerned about the outlook for the future health of the economy. If events go poorly, some weaker corporations may not be able to make their interest payments, and thus, bond market investors will have a strong preference for top-quality issues. Some investors will continue to invest in intermediate- or lower-quality issues but only at a sufficiently high yield differential to justify the risk. We might assume that the *Barron's* Confidence Index will drop to 84 because of the increasing spread between the two yields in the formula.

$$\begin{array}{c}\textit{Barron's}\\ \text{Confidence}\\ \text{Index}\end{array} = \frac{\text{Yield on 10 top grade corporate bonds}}{\text{Yield on 10 intermediate grade bonds}}(100)$$

$$= \frac{11.6\%}{13.8\%}(100) = 84(\%)$$

The yield on the intermediate-grade bonds is now 2.2 percent higher than that on the 10 top-grade bonds, and this is reflected in the lower Confidence Index reading. Of course, as confidence in the economy is once again regained, the yield spread differential will narrow, and the Confidence Index will go up.

Market technicians assume that there is a few months of lead time between what happens to the Confidence Index and what happens to the economy and stock market. As is true with other such indicators, it has a mixed record of predicting future events. One problem is that the Confidence Index is only assumed to consider the impact of investors' attitudes on yields (their demand pattern). We have seen in the late 1970s and 1980s that the supply of new bond issues can also influence yields. Thus, a very large bond issue by AT&T or General Motors may drive up high-grade bond yields even though investor attitudes indicate they should be going down.

Short sales by specialists.   Another smart money index is based on the short sales positions of specialists. Recall from Chapter 2 that one of the roles that specialists perform is to make markets in various securities listed on the organized exchanges. Because of the uniquely close position of specialists to the action on Wall Street, market technicians ascribe unusual importance to their decisions. One measure of their activity that is frequently monitored is

the ratio of specialists' short sales to the total amount of short sales on an exchange.

When we previously mentioned short sales in this chapter, we suggested that a high incidence of short selling might be considered bullish because short sellers often overreact to the market and provide future demand potential to cover their short position. In the case of market specialists, this is not necessarily true. These sophisticated traders keep a book of limit orders on their securities so that they have a close feel for market activity at any given point in time, and their decisions are considered important.

The normal ratio of specialist short sales to short sales on an exchange is about 55 percent. When the ratio goes up to 65 percent or more, market technicians interpret this as a bearish signal. A ratio under 40 percent is considered bullish.

Overall Market Rules

Our discussion of key indicator series has centered on both contrary opinion rules and smart money rules. We now briefly examine two overall market indicators; the breadth of the market indicator series and the cash position of mutual funds.

Breadth of the market. A breadth of the market indicator attempts to measure what a broad range of securities are doing as opposed to merely examining a market average. The theory is that market averages, such as the Dow Jones Industrial Average of 30 stocks or the Standard & Poor's 500 Stock Average, are weighted toward large firms and may not be representative of the entire market. In order to get a broader perspective of the market, an analyst may examine all stocks on an exchange. In Figure 8–9, we see an example of daily advances and declines for all stocks on the New York Stock Exchange.

The technician often compares the advance-declines with the movement of a popular market average to determine if there is a divergence between the two. Advances and declines usually move in concert with the popular market averages but may move in the opposite direction at a market peak or bottom.

FIGURE 8–9 Advance–Decline Data on the New York Stock Exchange

MARKET DIARY

	Tue.	Mon.	Fri.	Thu.	Wed.	Tue.
Issues traded	1,977	1,945	1,965	1,950	1,967	1,994
Advances	884	705	887	502	421	694
Declines	628	790	625	942	1,098	796
Unchanged	465	450	453	506	448	504
New highs	16	8	11	4	4	15
New lows	98	99	104	140	99	70

Source: Reprinted by permission of *The Wall Street Journal,* Dow Jones & Company, Inc. (July 18, 1984). All rights reserved.

One of the possible signals for the end of a bull market is when the Dow Jones Industrial Average is moving up but the number of daily declines consistently exceeds the number of daily advances. This indicates that conservative investors are investing in blue chip stocks but that there is a lack of broad-based confidence in the market. In Table 8–2, we look at an example of divergence between the advance–decline indicators and the Dow Jones Industrial Average (DJIA).

TABLE 8–2   Comparing Advance–Decline Data and the Dow Jones Industrial Average

	(1)	(2)	(3)	(4)	(5)	(6)
					Cumulative	
				Net advances	advances or	
Day	Advances	Declines	Unchanged	or declines	declines	DJIA
1	850	750	350	+100	+100	+7.09
2	800	810	340	− 10	+ 90	+4.52
3	792	821	337	− 29	+ 61	+3.08
4	780	828	342	− 48	+ 13	+5.21
5	719	890	341	−171	−158	−2.02
6	802	812	336	− 10	−168	+5.43
7	783	824	343	− 41	−209	+3.01
8	692	912	340	−226	−435	+ .52

In column 4, we see the daily differences in advances and declines. In column 5, we look at the cumulative pattern by adding or subtracting each new day's value from the previous total. We then compare the information in column 4 and column 5 to the Dow Jones Industrial Average (DJIA) in column 6. Clearly, the strength in the Dow Jones Industrial Average is not reflected in the advance-decline data, and this may be interpreted as signaling future weakness in the market.

Breadth of the market data can also be used to analyze upturns in the market. When the Dow Jones Industrial Average is going down but advances consistently lead declines, the market may be positioned for a recovery. Some market technicians develop sophisticated weighted averages of the daily advance-declines to go along with the data in Table 8–2.

While a comparison of advance-decline data to market averages can provide important insights, there is also the danger of false signals. Not every divergence between the two signals a turn in the market, so the analyst must be careful in his or her interpretation. The technical analyst generally looks at a wide range of variables.

Mutual fund cash position.   Another overall market indicator is the cash position of mutual funds. This measure indicates the buying potential of mutual funds and is generally representative of the purchasing potential of other

large institutional investors. The cash position of mutual funds, as a percentage of their total assets, generally varies between 5 percent and 20 to 25 percent.[7]

At the lower end of the boundary, it would appear that mutual funds are fully invested and can provide little in the way of additional purchasing power. As their cash position goes to 15 percent or higher, market technicians assess this as representing significant purchasing power that may help to trigger a market upturn. While the overall premise is valid, there are problems in identifying just what is a significant cash position for mutual funds in a given market cycle. It may change in extreme market environments.

EFFICIENT MARKET HYPOTHESIS

We shift our attention from technical analysis to that of examining market efficiency. As indicated at the beginning of the chapter, we shall now view any contradictions between the assumptions of fundamental or technical analysis and findings of the efficient market hypothesis.

We previously said that an efficient market is one in which new information is very rapidly processed so that securities are properly priced at any given point in time. An important premise of an efficient market is that there are a large number of profit-maximizing participants concerned with the analysis and valuation of securities. This would seem to describe the security market environment in the United States. Any news on IBM, AT&T, an oil embargo, or tax legislation is likely to be absorbed and acted upon very rapidly by profit-maximizing individuals. For this reason, the efficient market hypothesis (EMH) assumes that no stock price can be in disequilibrium or improperly priced for very long. There is almost instantaneous adjustment to new information. The efficient market hypothesis applies most directly to large firms trading on the major security exchanges.

The efficient market hypothesis further assumes that information travels in a random, independent fashion and that prices are an unbiased reflection of all currently available information.

More generally, the efficient market hypothesis is stated and tested in three different forms: the weak form, the semi-strong form, and the strong form. We shall examine each of these and the related implications for technical and fundamental analysis.

WEAK FORM OF THE EFFICIENT MARKET HYPOTHESIS

The weak form of the efficient market hypothesis suggests that there is no relationship between past and future prices of securities. They are presumed to be independent over time. Because the efficient market hypothesis maintains that current prices reflect all available information and that information

---

[7] The cash dollars are usually placed in short-term credit instruments, as opposed to stocks and bonds.

travels in a random fashion, it is assumed that there is little or nothing to be gained from studying past stock prices.

The weak form of the efficient market hypothesis has been tested in two different ways. First, researchers have attempted to determine the actual independence of price changes over time.

Tests of Independence

Tests of independence have examined the degree of correlation between stock prices over time and have found the correlation to be consistently small (between $+.10$ and $-.10$) and not statistically significant. This would indicate stock price changes are independent.[8] A further test is based on the frequency and extent of runs in stock price data. A run occurs when there is no difference in direction between two or more price changes. An example of a series of data and some runs is presented below.

Runs can be expected in any series of data through chance factors, but an independent data series should not produce an unusual amount of runs. Statistical tests have indicated that security prices generally do not produce any more runs that would be expected through the process of random number generation.[9] This would also tend to indicate that stock price movements are independent over time.

Trading Rule Tests

A second method of testing the weak form of the efficient market hypothesis (that past trends in stock prices are not helpful in predicting the future) is through trading rule tests. Because practicing market technicians maintain that tests of independence (correlation studies and runs) are too rigid to test the assumptions of the weak form of the efficient market hypothesis, additional tests by academic researchers have been developed. These are known as trading rule or filter tests. The purpose of these tests is to determine whether a given trading rule based on past price data, volume figures, etc. can be used to beat a naive buy-and-hold approach. The intent is to simulate the conditions under which a given trading rule is used and then determine if superior returns were produced after consideration of transaction costs and the risks involved.

---

[8] Sidney S. Alexander, "Price Movements in Speculative Markets: Trends or Random Walks," *Industrial Management Review,* May 1961, pp. 7–26. Eugene F. Fama, "The Behavior of Stock Market Prices," *Journal of Business,* January 1965, pp. 34–105.

[9] Sidney S. Alexander, "Price Movements in Speculative Markets: Trends or Random Walks," *Industrial Management Review,* May 1961, pp. 7–26. Eugene F. Fama, "The Behavior of Stock Market Prices," *Journal of Business,* January 1965, pp. 34–105.

As an example of a trading rule, if a stock moves up 5 percent or more, the rule might be to purchase it. The assumption is that this represents a breakout and should be considered bullish. Similarly, a 5 percent downward movement would be considered bearish and call for a sell strategy (rather than a buy-low/sell-high strategy, this is a follow-the-market-trend strategy). Other trading rule tests might be based on advance-decline patterns, short sales figures, and similar technical patterns. Research results have indicated that in a limited number of cases, trading rules may produce slightly positive returns, but after commission costs are considered, the results are neutral and sometimes negative in comparison to a naive buy-and-hold approach.[10]

Implications for Technical Analysis

The results of the *tests of independence* and *trading rules* would seem to uphold the weak form of the efficient market hypothesis. Security prices do appear to be independent over time or, more specifically, move in the pattern of a random walk.

Some challenge the research on the basis that academic research in this area does not capture the personal judgment that an experienced technician brings forward in reading his charts. There is also the fact that there are an infinite number of trading rules, and not all of them can or have been tested.[11] Nevertheless, research on the weak form of the efficient market hypothesis would seem to suggest that prices move independently over time, that past trends cannot be used to predict the future, and that charting and technical analysis may have limited value.

SEMI-STRONG FORM OF THE EFFICIENT MARKET HYPOTHESIS

The semi-strong form of the efficient market hypothesis maintains that all public information is already impounded into the value of a security, and therefore, one cannot use fundamental analysis to determine whether a stock is under- or overvalued.

Basically, the semi-strong form of the efficient market hypothesis would support the notion that there is no learning lag in the distribution of public information. When a company makes an announcement, investors across the country assess the information with equal speed. Also, a major firm listed on the New York Stock Exchange could hardly hope to utilize some questionable accounting practice that deceptively leads to higher reported profits and not

---

[10] Eugene F. Fama and Marshall Blume, "Filter Rules and Stock Market Trading Profits," *Journal of Business,* supplement, January 1966, pp. 226–41. George Pinches, "The Random Walk Hypothesis and Technical Analysis," *Financial Analysts Journal,* March–April 1970, pp. 104–10.

[11] It has even been suggested that an investor observe the winning team in the Super Bowl and invest accordingly. If a National Football Conference team (or an original National Football League team such as the Steelers) wins, this is assumed to be bullish. If an American Football Conference team wins, this is considered bearish.

expect sophisticated analysts to pick it up. (This may not be equally true for a lesser known firm that trades over-the-counter and enjoys little investor attention.)

Researchers have tested the semi-strong form of the efficient market hypothesis by determining whether investors who have acted on the basis of newly released public information have been able to enjoy superior returns. If the market is efficient in a semi-strong sense, this information is almost immediately impounded in the value of the security, and there would be little or no trading profits available. The implications would be that one could not garner superior returns by trading on public information about stock splits, earnings reports, or other similar items.

Tests on the semi-strong form of the efficient market hypothesis have generally been on the basis of risk-adjusted returns. Thus, the return from a given investment strategy must be compared to the performance of popular market indicators with appropriate risk adjustments. As will be described in Chapter 19, the risk measurement variable is usually the beta. After such adjustments are made, the question becomes, Are there abnormal returns that go beyond explanations associated with risk? If the answer is yes and can be shown to be statistically significant, then the investment strategy may be thought to refute the semi-strong form of the efficient market hypothesis. The investor must also cover transaction costs in determining that a given strategy is superior.

The risk adjustment measure may be viewed as:

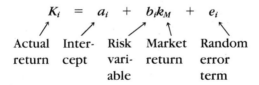

$$K_i \;=\; a_i \;+\; b_i k_M \;+\; e_i$$

| Actual return | Inter-cept | Risk vari-able | Market return | Random error term |

Each of these items will receive further attention in Chapter 19. For now, our concern is whether our investment strategy can produce consistently superior, abnormal returns.

Tests examining the impact of such events as stock splits and stock dividends, earnings announcements, and changes in accounting policy have generally indicated that the market is efficient in a semi-strong sense. For example, a study by Fama, Fisher, Jensen, and Roll indicated that almost all of the market impact of a stock split takes place before public announcement.[12] There is little to be gained from acting on the announcement.

Other studies have indicated that favorable or unfavorable earnings reports have generally been considered prior to public announcement, and there is little or no price change after announcement (unless there is a very large deviation from expected results).[13]

---

[12] Eugene F. Fama, Lawrence Fisher, Michael G. Jensen, and Richard Roll, "The Adjustment of Stock Prices to New Information," *International Economic Review,* February 1969, pp. 2–21.

[13] Ray Ball and Philip Brown, "An Empirical Evaluation of Accounting Income Numbers," *Journal of Accounting Research,* Autumn 1968, pp. 159–78.

According to the semi-strong form of the efficient market hypothesis, investors not only digest information very quickly, but they are able to see through mere changes in accounting information that do not have economic consequences. For example, the switching from accelerated depreciation to straight-line depreciation for financial reporting purposes (but not tax purposes) would tend to make earnings per share look higher but would provide no economic benefit for the firm. Research studies indicate this would have no positive impact on valuation.[14]

Similarly, investors are not deceived by mere accounting changes related to inventory policy, reserve accounts, exchange translations, or other items that appear to have no economic benefits. The corporate treasurer who switches from LIFO to FIFO accounting to make earnings look better in an inflationary economy will probably not see his or her firm's stock price rise as investors look at the economic consequences of higher taxes associated with the action and disregard the mere financial accounting consequences of higher reported profits.[15] Under this circumstance, the effect on stock may be neutral or negative.

Implications for Fundamental Analysis

If stock values are already based on the analysis of all available public information, it may be assumed that there is little to be gained from additional fundamental analysis. Under the semi-strong form of the efficient market hypothesis, if General Motors is trading at $70, the assumption is that every shred of public information about GM has been collected and evaluated by thousands of investors, and they have determined an equilibrium price of $70. The assumption is that anything you read in *The Wall Street Journal* or *Standard & Poor's* publications has already been considered many times over by others and is currently impounded in the value of the stock. If you were to say that you think GM is really worth $73 because of some great new product, proponents of the semi-strong form of the efficient market hypothesis would suggest that your judgment cannot be better than the collective wisdom of the marketplace in which everyone is trying desperately to come out ahead.

Ironically, although many would suggest that fundamental analysis may not lead to superior profits in an efficient market environment, it is fundamental analysis itself which makes the market so efficient. Because everyone is doing fundamental analysis, there is little in the way of unabsorbed or undigested information. Therefore, one extra person doing fundamental analysis is unlikely to achieve superior insight.

---

[14] T. Ross Archibald, "Stock Market Reaction to Depreciation Switch-Back," *Accounting Review,* January 1972, pp. 22–30. Robert S. Kaplan and Richard Roll, Investor Evaluation of Accounting Information: Some Empirical Evidence," *Journal of Business,* April 1972, pp. 225–57.

[15] Shyam Sunder, "Stock Price and Risk Related to Accounting Changes in Inventory Valuation," *Accounting Review,* April 1975, pp. 305–15.

Although the semi-strong form of the efficient market hypothesis has strong research support and would generally be considered valid, there are exceptions. For example, Basu has found that stocks with low P/E ratios consistently provide better returns than stocks with high P/E ratios on both a nonrisk-adjusted and risk-adjusted basis.[16] Since a P/E ratio is publicly available information that may be used to generate superior returns, this flies in the face of the more common conclusions on the semi-strong form of the efficient market hypothesis. Banz[17] and Reinganum's[18] research indicates that small firms tend to provide higher returns than larger firms even after considering risk. Perhaps fewer institutional investors in smaller firms make for a less efficient market and superior potential opportunities. Oppenheimer and Schlarbaum have also shown that investors can generate superior risk-adjusted returns by following widely disseminated rules by Graham and Dodd on such factors as dividends, capitalization, firm size and P/E ratios, and by using only public information.[19] Additional evidence of this nature continues to accumulate, and in Chapter 14, on special situations, we present an extended discussion of some of the above items and other possible contradictions to the majority viewpoint of the semi-strong version of the efficient market hypothesis. We also comment on measurement problems in that chapter.

Thus, even if the semi-strong form of the efficient market hypothesis appears to be generally valid, exceptions can be noted. Also, there is the possibility that while most analysts may not be able to add additional insight through fundamental analysis, there are exceptions to every rule. It can be assumed that some analysts have such *extraordinary* insight and capability in analyzing publicly available information that they can perceive what others cannot. Also, if you take a very long-term perspective, the fact that a stock's value is in short-term equilibrium may not discourage you from taking a long-term position or attempting to find long-term value.

STRONG FORM OF THE EFFICIENT MARKET HYPOTHESIS

The strong form of the efficient market hypothesis goes beyond the semi-strong form to state that stock prices reflect not only all public information,

---

[16] S. Basu, "Investment Performance of Common Stocks in Relation to Their Price-Earnings Ratios: A Test of the Efficient Market Hypothesis," *Journal of Finance,* June 1977, pp. 663–82. Also, S. Basu, "The Information Content of Price-Earnings Ratios," *Financial Management,* Summer 1975, pp. 53–64.

[17] Rolf W. Banz, "The Relationship between Returns and Market Value of Common Stocks," *Journal of Financial Economics,* March 1981, pp. 3–18.

[18] Marc R. Reinganum, "Misspecification of Capital Asset Pricing—Empirical Anomalies Based on Earnings Yield and Market Values," *Journal of Financial Economics,* March 1981, pp. 19–46.

[19] Henry Oppenheimer, R. Oppenheimer, and Gary G. Schlarbaum, "Investing with Ben Graham: An Ex Ante Test of the Efficient Markets Hypothesis," *Journal of Financial and Quantitative Analysis,* September 1981, pp. 341–60.

but *all* information. Thus, it is hypothesized that insider information is also immediately impounded into the value of a security. In a sense, we go beyond the concept of a market that is highly efficient to one that is perfect.

The assumption is that no group of market participants or investors has monopolistic access to information. If this is the case, then no group of investors can be expected to show superior risk-adjusted returns under any circumstances.

Unlike the weak and semi-strong form of the efficient market hypothesis, major test results are not generally supportive of the strong form of the hypothesis. For example, specialists on security exchanges have been able to earn superior rates of return on invested capital.[20] The book they keep on unfilled limit orders would appear to provide monopolistic access to information. An SEC study actually found that specialists typically sell above their latest purchase 83 percent of the time and buy below their latest sell 81 percent of the time.[21] This implies wisdom that greatly exceeds that which would be available in a perfect capital market environment. Likewise, an institutional investor study, also sponsored by the SEC, indicated that specialists average return on capital was over 100 percent.[22]

Another group that appears to use nonpublic information to garner superior returns is corporate insiders. As previously described, an insider is considered to be a corporate officer, member of the board of directors, or substantial stockholder. The SEC requires that insiders report their transactions to that regulatory body. A few weeks after reporting to the SEC, the information becomes public. Researchers can then go back and determine whether investment decisions made by investors appeared, on balance, to be wise. Did heavy purchases by insiders precede strong upward price movements, and did sell-offs precede poor market performance? The answer appears to be yes. Research studies indicate insiders consistently achieve higher returns than would be expected in a perfect capital market.[23] Although inside traders are not allowed to engage in short-term (of six months or less) or illegal transactions to generate trading profits, they are allowed to take longer-term positions, which may well prove to be profitable. It has even been demonstrated that investors who follow the direction of inside traders after information on their

---

[20] Victor Niederhoffer and M. F. M. Osborne, "Market-Making and Reversal on the Stock Exchange," *Journal of the American Statistical Association,* December 1966, pp. 897–916.

[21] Securities and Exchange Commission, *Report of the Special Study of the Security Markets,* part 2 (Washington, D.C.: U.S. Government Printing Office, 1965).

[22] Securities and Exchange Commission, *Institutional Investor Study Report* (Washington D.C.: U.S. Government Printing Office, 1971).

[23] James H. Lorie and Victor Niederhoffer, "Predictive Statistical Properties of Insider Trading," *Journal of Law and Economics,* April 1966, pp. 35–53. Joseph E. Finnerty, "Insiders and Market Efficiency," *Journal of Finance,* September 1976, pp. 1141–48. Jeffrey Jaffe, "Special Information and Insider Trading," *Journal of Business,* July 1974, pp. 410–28. Shannon P. Pratt and Charles W. DeVere, "Relationship between Insider Trading and Rates of Return for NYSE Common Stocks, 1960–1966," in *Modern Developments in Investment Management,* ed. James H. Lorie and Richard Beasley (New York: Praeger Publishers, 1972), pp. 268–79.

activity becomes public may enjoy superior returns.[24] (This, of course, represents contrary evidence to the semi-strong form of the efficient market hypothesis as well.)

Even though there is evidence on the activity of specialists and insiders that would cause one to reject the strong form of the efficient market hypothesis (or at least not to accept it), the range of participants with access to superior information is not large. For example, tests on the performance of mutual fund managers have consistently indicated that they are not able to beat the market averages over the long term.[25] Although mutual fund managers may get the first call when news is breaking, that is not fast enough to generate superior returns.

While the strong form of the efficient market hypothesis suggests more opportunity for superior returns than the weak or semi-strong form, the premium is related to monopolistic access to information rather than other factors.

SUMMARY

Following the discussion of fundamental analysis in Chapters 5 through 7, we examined technical analysis in this chapter and, more significantly, the impact of the efficient market hypothesis on both fundamental and technical analysis.

While fundamental analysis deals with financial analysis and determinants of valuation, technical analysis is based on the study of past price and volume data as well as associated market trends to predict future price movements. Technical analysis relies heavily on charting and the use of key market indicators to make forecasts.

Charting came into prominence with the development of the Dow theory in the late 1800s by Charles Dow. The theory stresses the importance of primary trends that may be temporarily obscured by daily and secondary movements. In order for a long-term, bullish trend to be reversed, there must be an abortive recovery followed by penetrations of previous lows, and patterns in the Dow Jones Industrial Average must be ultimately confirmed by the Dow Jones Transportation Average. Similar patterns of movement in the opposite direction would signal the end of a bear market.

Technical analysts also observe support and resistance levels in the market as well as data on volume. Line, bar, and point and figure charts are used to determine turns in the market.

Market technicians also follow a number of key indicator series to predict the market. There are contrary opinion indicators, smart money indicators, and general market indicators.

---

[24] Pratt and DeVere, "Relationship," pp. 268–79.

[25] Michael Jensen, "The Performance of Mutual Funds in the Period 1945–1964," *Journal of Finance,* May 1968, pp. 389–416.

Although there have been traditional arguments about whether fundamental or technical analysis is more important, a great deal of current attention is directed to the efficient market hypothesis and its implications for all types of analysis.

The efficient market hypothesis (EMH) maintains that the market adjusts very rapidly to the supply of new information, and because of this, securities tend to be correctly priced at any given time (or very rapidly approaching this equilibrium value). The EMH further assumes that information travels in a random, independent fashion and that prices are an unbiased reflection of all currently available information. Furthermore, past trends in prices mean little or nothing.

The efficient market hypothesis has been stated and tested in three different forms.

a.   The weak form states that there is no relationship between past and future prices (they are independent over time).

b.   The semi-strong form suggests that all public information is currently impounded in the price of a stock and there is no concept of under- or over-valuation based on publicly available information.

c.   The strong form suggests that *all* information, public or otherwise, is included in the value of a security. The implication of the strong form is that security prices are not only highly efficient, they are perfect.

Substantial research tends to support the weak form of the efficient market hypothesis, which causes many researchers to seriously question the overall value of technical analysis. However, many on Wall Street would vigorously debate this position. The semi-strong form of the efficient market hypothesis is also well supported by research, and this fact would tend to question the value of fundamental analysis by the individual investor. (It is, however, the collective wisdom of all fundamental analysis that leads to the efficient market hypothesis in the first place.) There are a few contradictions to the semi-strong form of the efficient market hypothesis, and much research is aimed at supplying additional contradictory data. The semi-strong form probably does not apply with equal emphasis to smaller firms that are not in the institutional investor's limelight.

The strong form of the efficient market hypothesis is not generally accepted. Thus, the market does not perfectly adjust to all information (insider as well as public). Evidence suggests that stock exchange specialists and corporate insiders may be able to achieve superior returns based on the monopolistic use of nonpublic data. However, there are very few groups who demonstrate successful access or use of nonpublic information.

IMPORTANT WORDS AND CONCEPTS

Technical analysis	Dow theory
Charting	Support and resistance levels
Key indicators	Contrary opinion rules

Odd-lot theory
Short sales position
Smart money rules
Barron's **Confidence Index**
Greed Index
Overall market rules
Breadth of market

Advances and declines
Efficient market hypothesis
Mutual fund cash position
Weak form of EMH
Semi-strong form of EMH
Strong form of EMH

DISCUSSION QUESTIONS

1. What is technical analysis?
2. What are the views of technical analysts toward fundamental analysis?
3. Outline the basic assumptions of technical analysis.
4. Under the Dow theory, if a recovery fails to exceed the previous high and a new low penetrates a previous low, what does this tell us about the market?
5. Also under the Dow theory, what other average is used to confirm movements in the Dow Jones Industrial Average?
6. What is meant by a support level for a stock or a market average? When might a support level exist?
7. In examining Figure 8–7, if the next price movement is to 34, will a shift to a new column be indicated? (Assume the current price is 36.)
8. What is the logic behind the odd-lot theory? If the odd-lot index starts to move higher in an up market, what does the odd-lot theory indicate the next movement in the market will be?
9. How reliable has the odd-lot theory been in recent times?
10. What is the logic behind *Barron's* Confidence Index?
11. If the advance-decline movement in the market is weak (more declines than advances) while the DJIA is going up, what might this indicate to a technician about the market?
12. Categorize the following as either contrary opinion or smart money indicators (as viewed by technicians).
    a. Short sales by specialists.
    b. Odd-lot positions.
    c. Short sales positions.
    d. *Barron's* Confidence Index.
    e. Investment advisory recommendations.
    f. Greed Index
13. Under the efficient market hypothesis, what is the assumption about the processing of new information, and what effect does this have on security pricing?
14. What does the weak form of the efficient market hypothesis suggest? What are the two major ways in which it has been tested?
15. Would low correlation coefficients over time between stock prices tend to prove or disprove the weak form of the efficient market hypothesis?

16. What is the essence of the semi-strong form of the efficient market hypothesis?

17. Under the semi-strong form of the efficient market hypothesis, is there anything to be gained from a corporate treasurer changing accounting methods to increase earnings per share when there is no associated true economic benefit or gain?

18. Why does fundamental analysis tend to make the market efficient?

19. Suggest some studies that would indicate that the market is not completely efficient in the semi-strong form.

20. What does the strong form of the efficient market hypothesis suggest? Are major test results generally supportive of the strong form?

21. How do specialists, insiders, and mutual fund managers fare in terms of having access to superior information to generate large returns? (Comment on each separately.)

22. Project: Follow a number of technical indicators over the next few weeks, and compare actual market performance to suggested market performance (by the indicators).

SELECTED REFERENCES

Alexander, Sidney S. "Price Movements in Speculative Markets: Trends or Random Walks." *Industrial Management Review,* May 1961, pp. 7–26.

Archibald, Ross T. "Stock Market Reaction to Depreciation Switch-Back." *Accounting Review,* January 1972, pp. 22–30.

Ball, Roy, and Phillip Brown. "An Empirical Evaluation of Accounting Income Numbers." *Journal of Accounting Research,* Autumn 1968, pp. 159–78.

Banz, Rolf W. "The Relationship between Returns and Market Value of Common Stocks." *Journal of Financial Economics,* March 1981, pp. 3–18.

Basu, S. "Investment Performance of Common Stocks in Relation to Their Price-Earnings Ratios: A Test of the Efficient Market Hypothesis." *Journal of Finance,* June 1977, pp. 663–82.

————. "The Information Content of Price-Earnings Ratios." *Financial Management,* Summer 1975, pp. 53–64.

Boldt, Bob L., and Hal L. Arbit. "Efficient Markets and the Professional Investor." *Financial Analysts Journal,* July–August 1984, pp. 22–34.

Edwards, R. D., and John Magee, Jr. *Technical Analysis of Stock Trends,* 5th ed. Springfield, Mass: Stock Trends Service, 1966.

Fama, Eugene F. "The Behavior of Stock Market Prices." *Journal of Business,* January 1965, pp. 34–105.

Fama, Eugene F., and Marshall Blume. "Filter Rules and Stock Market Trading Profits." *Journal of Business,* supplement, January 1966, pp. 226–41.

Fama, Eugene F.; Lawrence Fisher; Michael G. Jensen; and Richard Roll. "The Adjustment of Stock Prices to New Information." *International Economic Review,* February 1969, pp. 1–21.

Finnerty, Joseph E. "Insiders and Market Efficiency." *Journal of Finance,* September 1976, pp. 1141–48.

Jaffe, Jeffrey. "Special Information and Insider Trading." *Journal of Business,* July 1974, pp. 410–28.

Jensen, Michael, "The Performance of Mutual Funds in the Period 1945–1964." *Journal of Finance,* May 1968, pp. 389–416.

Kaplan, Robert S., and Richard Roll. "Investor Evaluation of Accounting Information: Some Empirical Evidence." *Journal of Business,* April 1972, pp. 225–57.

Lorie, James H., and Victor Niederhoffer. "Predictive Statistical Properties of Insider Trading." *Journal of Law and Economics,* April 1966, pp. 35–53.

Niederhoffer, Victor, and M. F. M. Osborne. "Market-Making and Reversal on the Stock Exchange." *Journal of the American Statistical Association,* December 1966, pp. 897–916.

Oppenheimer, Henry R., and Gary G. Schlarbaum. "Investing with Ben Graham: An Ex Ante Test of the Efficient Market Hypothesis." *Journal of Financial and Quantitative Analysis,* September 1981, pp. 341–60.

Pinches, George. "The Random Walk Hypothesis and Technical Analysis." *Financial Analysts Journal,* March–April 1970, pp. 104–10.

Pratt, Shannon P., and Charles H. DeVere. "Relationship beween Insider Trading and Rate of Return for NYSE Common Stocks, 1960–1966," In *Modern Developments in Investment Management,* ed. James H. Lorie and Richard Beasley. New York: Praeger Publishers, 1972, pp. 268–79.

Reinganum, Marc R. "Misspecification of Capital Asset Pricing—Empirical Anomalies Based on Earnings Yield and Market Values." *Journal of Financial Economics,* March 1981, pp. 19–46.

Shishko, Irwin. "Techniques of Forecasting Commodity Prices." *Commodity Yearbook.* New York: Commodity Research Bureau, Inc., 1965, pp. 30–41.

Smith, Randall. "Short Interest and Stock Market Prices." *Financial Analysts Journal,* November–December 1968, pp. 151–54.

Sunder, Shyam. "Stock Price and the Risk Related to Accounting Changes in Inventory Valuation. *Accounting Review,* April 1975, pp. 305–15.

Securities and Exchange Commission. *Institutional Investor Report.* Washington D.C.: U.S. Government Printing Office, 1971.

Zweig, Martin E. *Understanding Technical Forecasting.* Princeton, N.J.: Dow Jones & Company, Inc., 1978.

Part Three

FIXED INCOME AND LEVERAGED SECURITIES

We now shift our attention from stocks to fixed-income and leveraged securities. Fixed-income securities include bonds, preferred stock, certificates of deposit, and even money market funds. In the high interest rate environment of the last decade, many investors have increased their emphasis on fixed-return investments. However, we shall see that fixed-income securities are not without risk or uncertainty as to outcome.

In Chapter 9 we look at the organization of the debt markets and the elements that define the basic debt instrument. The functions of the bond rating agencies are also explored, along with the perceived efficiency of the bond market. In Chapter 10 we assume the role of the bond investor and examine a number of strategy considerations for optimizing return on investment. Chapter 11 moves to a discussion of duration, or weighted average life, of a bond. Since professional investors use duration concepts in designing their strategies, the student is given a basic description of these considerations. (The chapter is optional in nature and may be skipped without loss of continuity.)

The second half of this section covers leveraged securities, that is, securities in which there is a magnified return or loss potential for a given level of investment ("maximum bang for the buck"). The discussion begins with convertibles and warrants in Chapter 12. We examine the valuation of these securities and the existence of speculative premiums (the difference between market value and intrinsic value). We also look at the advantages and disadvantages of convertibles and warrants to the investor as well as to the corporation. A recurring question is, are we dealing with fool's gold? While the answer is no, it is a qualified no that can only be fully understood after you have examined the ins and outs of investing in these securities.

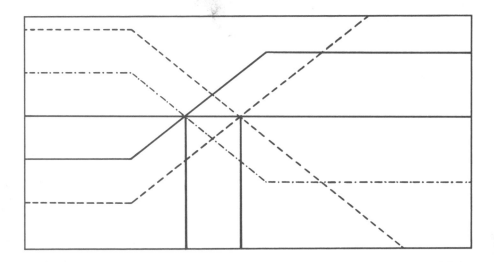

The stock option became highly popular with the founding of the Chicago Board Options Exchange in 1973. Options allow the investor to buy and sell stock at a specified future price, and they may be used as a form of speculation or as a defensive tool. In Chapter 13, we examine the basic types of options (puts and calls), the operations of the options market, how option prices are established, and the use of leverage in the option contract. We also examine how "option plays" can be tailored to the overall objectives of the portfolio. We conclude with a discussion of some of the more sophisticated option strategies.

Chapter 9

BOND AND FIXED-INCOME FUNDAMENTALS

As the reader will observe in various sections of this chapter, bonds actually represent a more substantial portion of new offerings in the capital markets than common stock. Some of the most financially rewarding jobs on Wall Street go to sophisticated analysts and dealers in the bond market.

In this chapter, we will examine the fundamentals of the bond instrument for both corporate and government issuers, with an emphasis on the debt contract and security provisions. We will also look at the overall structure of the bond market and the ways in which bonds are rated. The question of bond market efficiency is also considered. While most of the chapter deals with corporate and government bonds, other forms of fixed-income securities also receive attention. Thus, there is a brief discussion of short-term, fixed-income investments (such as certificates of deposit and commercial paper) as well as preferred stock.

In Chapter 10 we will shift the emphasis to actually evaluating fixed-income investments and devising strategies that attempt to capture profitable opportunities in the market. In Chapter 11 we will look at the interesting concept of *duration.* We begin our present discussion by considering the key elements that go into a bond contract.

THE BOND CONTRACT

A bond normally represents a long-term contractual obligation of the firm to pay interest to the bondholder as well as the face value of the bond at maturity. The major provisions in a bond agreement are spelled out in the *bond indenture,* a complicated legal document often over 100 pages in length, administered by an independent trustee (usually a commercial bank). We shall examine some important terms and concepts associated with a bond issue.

Par value—the face value of a bond. Most corporate bonds are traded in $1,000 units, while many federal, state, and local issues trade in units of $5,000 or $10,000.

Coupon rate—the actual interest rate on the bond, usually payable in semiannual installments. To the extent that interest rates in the market go above or below the coupon rate after the bond is issued, the market price of the bond will change from the par value. A bond initially issued at a rate of 8 percent will sell at a substantial discount from par value when 14 percent is the currently demanded rate of return. We will eventually examine how the investor makes and loses substantial amounts of money in the bond market with the swings in interest rates. A few corporate bonds are termed *variable rate notes* or *floating rate notes,* meaning that the coupon rate is only fixed for a short period of time and then varies with a stipulated short-term rate, such as the rate on U.S. government Treasury bills. In this instance, the interest payment varies up and down rather than the price of the bond, and most of the bonds can be redeemed at par early in the life of the issue at the option of the holder. This type of issue is likely to become increasingly popular in the future. In recent times, zero-coupon bonds have also been issued at values substan-

tially below maturity value. The investor receives his or her return in the form of capital appreciation over the life of the bond since no semiannual cash interest payments are received.

Maturity date—the date on which final payment is due at the stipulated par value.

Methods of repayment—repayment of the bond can take place under many different arrangements. Some bonds are never paid off, such as selected *perpetual* bonds issued by the Canadian and British governments, in which there are no maturity dates. A more normal procedure would simply call for a single-sum lump payment at the end of the obligation. Thus, the issuer may make 40 semiannual interest payments over the next 20 years plus one lump-sum payment of the par value of the bond at maturity. There are three other significant means of repayment.

The first is the *serial* payment, in which bonds are paid off in installments over the life of the issue. Each serial bond has its own predetermined date of maturity and receives interest only to that point. Although the total bond issue may span over 20 years, 15 to 20 maturity dates are assigned. Municipal bonds are often issued on this basis. Second, there may be a *sinking fund* provision in which semiannual or annual contributions are made by a corporation into a fund administered by a trustee for purposes of debt retirement. The trustee takes the proceeds and goes into the market to purchase bonds from willing sellers. If no sellers are available, a lottery system may be used to repurchase the required number of bonds from among outstanding bondholders.

Finally, debt may be retired under a *call provision.* A call provision allows the corporation to call or force in all of the debt issue prior to maturity. The corporation usually pays a 5 percent to 10 percent premium over par value as part of the call provision arrangement. The ability to call is often *deferred* for the first five years of an issue (it can only take place after this time period). There are exceptions. An investor recently related buying a Michigan-Wisconsin Pipeline bond in 1981 having a 17.75 percent coupon with a deferred call to November 1, 1988. To his surprise the bond was called in less than three years when rates declined substantially. The fine print stated that the bond could not be called by a refunding (selling a new issue to replace the old bond) but could be retired at any time before maturity with cash from other sources. It pays to read the fine print rather than taking your broker's word for it.

SECURED AND UNSECURED BONDS

We have discussed some of the important features related to interest payments and retirement of outstanding issues. At least of equal importance is the nature of the security provision for the issue. Bond market participants have a long-standing practice of describing certain issues by the nature of asset claims in liquidation. In actuality, only infrequently are pledged assets sold off and the proceeds distributed to bondholders. Typically, the defaulting corporation is reorganized, and existing claims are partially satisfied by issuing new securities

to the participating parties. Of course, the stronger and *better secured* the initial claim, the higher the quality of the security to be received in a reorganization.

There are a number of terms used to denote collateralized or secured debt. Under a *mortgage* agreement, real property (plant and equipment) is pledged as security for a loan. A mortgage may be *senior* or *junior* in nature, with the former requiring satisfaction of claims before payment is given to the latter. Bondholders may also attach an *after-acquired property clause* requiring that any new property be placed under the original mortgage.

A very special form of a mortgage or collateralized debt instrument is the *equipment trust certificate.* It is used by firms in the transportation industry (railroads, airlines, etc.). Proceeds from the sale of the certificate are used to purchase new equipment, and this new equipment in turn serves as collateral for the trust certificate.

Not all bond issues are secured or collateralized by assets. Certainly, most federal, state, and local government issues are unsecured. A wide range of corporate issues also are unsecured. There is a set of terminology referring to these unsecured issues. A corporate debt issue that is unsecured is referred to as a *debenture.* Even though the debenture is not secured by a specific pledge of assets, there may be priorities of claims among debenture holders. Thus, there are senior debentures and junior, or subordinated, debentures.

If liquidation becomes necessary because all other avenues for survival have failed, secured creditors are paid off first out of the disposition of the secured assets. The proceeds from the sale of the balance of the assets are then distributed among unsecured creditors, with those holding a senior ranking being satisfied before those holding a subordinate position (subordinated debenture holders).[1]

Unsecured corporate debt may provide slightly higher yields because of the greater suggested risk. However, this is partially offset by the fact that many unsecured debt issuers have such strong financial statements that security pledges may not be necessary.

Companies with less favorable prospects may issue *income bonds.* These bonds specify that interest is to be paid only to the extent that it is earned in current income. There is no legally binding requirement to pay interest on a regular basis, and failure to make interest payments cannot trigger bankruptcy proceedings. These issues appear to offer the corporation the unusual advantage of paying interest as a tax-deductible expense (as opposed to dividends) combined with freedom from the binding contractual obligation of most debt issues. But any initial enthusiasm for these issues is quickly reduced by recognition of the fact that they have very limited appeal to investors. The issuance of income bonds is usually restricted to circumstances where new corporate debt is issued to old bondholders or preferred stockholders to avoid bankruptcy or where a troubled corporation is being reorganized.

---

[1] Those secured creditors that are not fully satisfied by the disposition of secured assets may also participate with the unsecured creditors in the remaining assets.

THE COMPOSITION OF THE BOND MARKET

Having established some of the basic terminology relating to the bond instrument, we now are in a position to take a more comprehensive look at the bond market.

While there may be a tendency to think of corporate issues as making up a large percentage of the bond market, this is simply not the case. Corporate issues must vie with offerings from the U.S. Treasury, federally sponsored credit agencies, and state and local governments (municipal offerings). The relative importance of the four types of issues is indicated in Figure 9–1. Over

FIGURE 9–1   Long-Term Funds Raised by Business and the Government

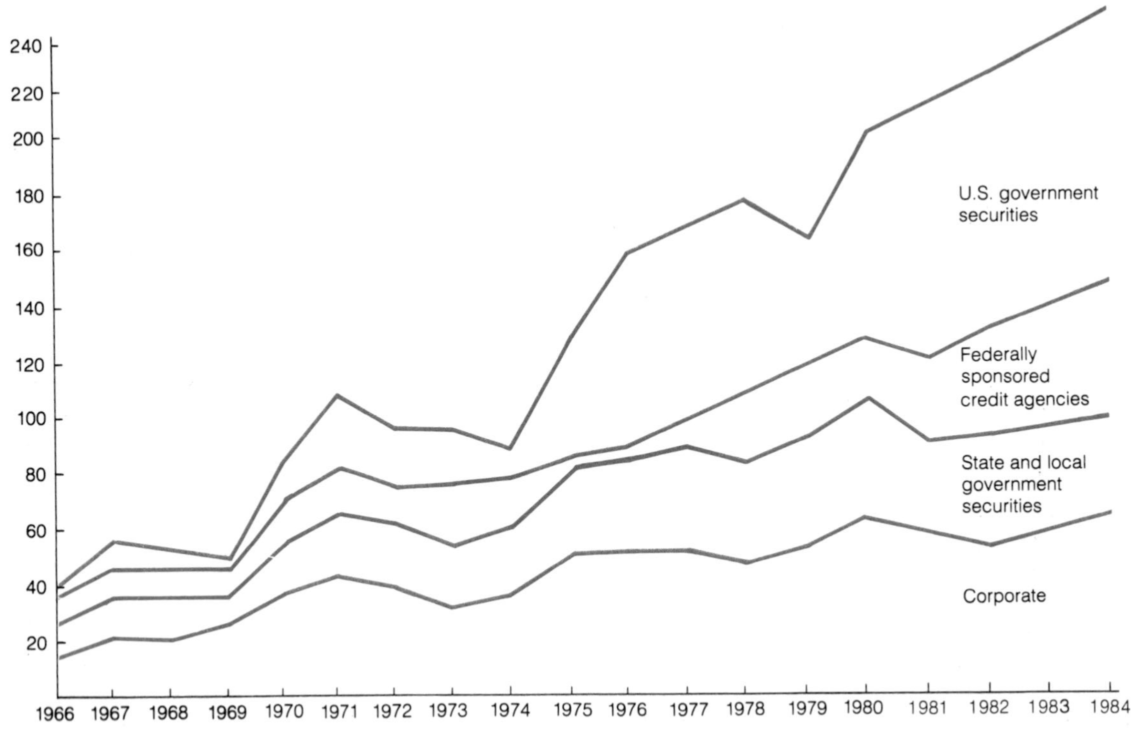

Source: *Federal Reserve Bulletin* (Washington D.C.: Federal Reserve Board of Governors, selected issues).

the 18-year period, new issues of corporate securities averaged only 30 percent of the total, while government securities (federal, state, and local) made up the other 70 percent. It is interesting to note the dramatic recent rise in long-term U.S. government securities (top portion of Figure 9–1). Large deficits, beginning in the mid-1970s, have steadily increased the U.S. government's portion of new financing. In the 1984 fiscal year, the U.S. deficit was in excess of $200 billion and economists were concerned that the U.S. government's

need for funds would "crowd out" smaller corporate borrowers, keeping them from being able to raise capital for needed plant and inventory expansion.

In the following section, we will briefly discuss the various forms of debt instruments available to the investor.

U.S. Government Securities

U.S. government securities take the form of Treasury bills, Treasury notes, and Treasury bonds (only the latter two are considered in the top part of Figure 9–1). The distinction between the three categories relates to the life of the obligation.

Treasury bills (T-bills) are short-term in nature, with a maximum maturity of one year and common maturities of 91 and 182 days. Treasury bills are unique in that they trade on a discount basis meaning that the yield the investor receives takes place as a result of the difference between the price paid and the maturity value (and no actual interest is paid). Thus, a $10,000 Treasury bill quoted to pay 10 percent annualized interest over a six-month period will initially sell for $9,500. The investor receives $500 on the $10,000 face amount, or 5 percent for six months, which is translated into a 10 percent annualized rate. Actually, the true rate is slightly higher than the 10 percent quoted rate. The investor is receiving $500 interest on the $9,500 discounted price ($500/% 9,500) or 5.26 percent, which translates into 10.52 percent.

Treasury bills trade in minimum units of $10,000, and there is an extremely active secondary, or resale, market for these securities. Thus, an investor buying a Treasury bill from the government with an initial life of approximately six months would have no difficulty in selling it to another investor after two or three weeks. Since the T-bill now has a shorter time to run, its market value would be a bit closer to par.

A second type of U.S. government security is the *Treasury note,* which is considered to be of intermediate term and generally has a maturity of 1 to 7 years. Finally, *Treasury bonds* are long-term in nature and mature in 7 to 25 years or longer. Unlike Treasury bills, Treasury notes and bonds provide direct interest and trade in units of $1,000 and higher. Because there is no risk of default (unless the government stops printing money or the ultimate bomb explodes), U.S. government securities provide lower returns than other forms of credit obligations. Interest on U.S. government issues is fully taxable for IRS purposes but is exempt from state and local taxes.

Some Treasury notes and bonds have been repackaged into zero-coupon bonds by major brokerage firms and investment bankers such as Merrill Lynch, Goldman Sachs, A. G. Becker, and others. These firms buy U.S. "governments" and put these securities in trust (usually a commercial bank acts as trustee). A security is divided into two parts—one generating a cash flow from the interest payments and the other providing principal at maturity. These two parts are then sold separately to investors with specific needs. The principal payment part is generically called a "zero-coupon Treasury bond" but each investment banker labels their own product, with names such as TIGRs (for Merrill Lynch's Treasury Investment Growth Receipts); COUGARs (for A. G. Becker's

Zero-Coupon Certificates on Government Receipts); and RATs, CATs, and GATORs for other firms. For example, Merrill Lynch's TIGRs are called Principal TIGRs (the zero-coupon part) and Serial TIGRs, which pay interest at six-month intervals for 40 payments. Serial TIGRs are annuities with, of course, no principal at maturity. In 1985, the U.S. treasury also began trading zero-coupon bonds directly on its own.

Since zero-coupon bonds pay no interest, all returns to the investor come in the form of increases in the value of the investment. For example, 15-year zero-coupon bonds might initially sell for 18 percent of par value. You might buy a $1,000 instrument for $180.[2]

The Internal Revenue Service taxes zero-coupon bonds as if interest were paid semi-annually even though no cash flow is received until maturity. The tax is based on amortizing the built-in gain over the life of the instrument. For tax reasons, zero-coupons are usually only appropriate for nontaxable accounts such as Individual Retirement Accounts, Keogh plans or other nontaxable pension funds.

Federally Sponsored Credit Agency Issues

Referring back to Figure 9–1, observe the rapid growth in securities issued by federal agencies. New issues have been running at the rate of approximately $20–$30 billion per year. These issues represent obligations of various agencies of the government, such as the Federal Home Loan Bank, the Federal National Mortgage Association (FNMA), and the Federal Housing Administration (FHA). Although these issues are authorized by an act of Congress and are used to finance federal projects, they are not direct obligations of the Treasury but rather of the agency itself.

Though the issues are essentially free of risk (there is always the implicit standby power of the government behind the issues), they carry a slightly higher yield than U.S. government securities simply because they are not directly issued by the Treasury. Agency issues have been particularly active as a support mechanism for the housing industry. The issues generally trade in denominations of $5,000 and up. They have varying maturities of from 1 to 40 years, with an average life of approximately 15 years. Examples of some agency issues are presented below.

	Minimum denomination	Life of issue
Federal Home Loan Bank	$10,000	12–25 years
Federal Intermediate Credit Banks	5,000	Up to 4 years
Federal Housing Administration	50,000	1–40 years
Export-Import Bank	5,000	Up to 7 years
U.S. Postal Service	10,000	25 years

[2] On zero-coupon bonds the yield to maturity is a true rate over the life of the security, since the price paid includes the assumption of continuous compounding at the yield to maturity. Zero-coupon securities are the most price-sensitive to a change in interest rates of any bond having the same maturity. This is fine when interest rates decline, but can be disasterous when rates rise. A good deal more will be said about zero-coupon bonds in Chapter 11.

Interest on agency issues is fully taxable for IRS purposes and is generally taxable for state and local purposes although there are exceptions. (For example, interest on obligations issued by the Federal Housing Administration are subject to state and local taxes, but those of the Federal Home Loan Bank are not.)

One agency issue that is of particular interest to the investor because of its unique features is the GNMA ("Ginnie Mae") pass-through certificate. These certificates represent an undivided interest in a pool of federally insured mortgages. Actually, GNMA, the Government National Mortgage Association, buys a pool of mortgages from various lenders at a discount and then issues securities to the public against these mortgages. Security holders in GNMA certificates receive monthly payments that essentially represent a pass through of interest and principal payments on the mortgages. These securities come in minimum denominations of $25,000, are long-term in nature, and are fully taxable for federal, state, and local income tax purposes. A major consideration in this investment is that the investor has fully consumed his or her capital at the end of the investment. (Not only has interest been received monthly, but all principal has been returned over the life of the certificate, and therefore there is no lump-sum payment at maturity.)

State and Local Government Securities

Debt securities issued by state and local governments are referred to as municipal bonds. Examples of issuing agencies include states, cities, school districts, toll roads, or any other type of political subdivision. The most important feature of a municipal bond is the tax-exempt nature of the interest payment. Dating back to the United States Supreme Court opinion of 1819 in *McCullough* v. *Maryland*, it was ruled that the federal government and state and local governments do not possess the power to tax each other. An eventual by-product of the judicial ruling was that income from municipal bonds cannot be taxed by the IRS. Furthermore, income from municipal bonds is also exempt from state and local taxes if bought within the locality in which one resides. Thus, a Californian buying municipal bonds in that state would pay no state income tax on the issue. However, the same Californian would have to pay state or local income taxes if the originating agency were in Texas or New York.

We cannot overemphasize the importance of the federal tax exemption that municipal bonds enjoy. The consequences are twofold. First of all, individuals in high tax brackets may find highly attractive investment opportunities in municipal bonds.[3] Some have referred to municipal bond investments as "welfare for the rich." The formula used to equate interest on municipal bonds to other investments is:

---

[3] It should be noted, however, that any capital gain on a municipal bond is taxable as would be the case with any investment.

$$Y = \frac{i}{(1 - t)} \qquad\qquad (9-1)$$

where:

y = Equivalent before-tax yield on a taxable investment.
i = Yield on the municipal obligation.
t = Marginal tax rate of the investor.

If an investor has a marginal tax rate of 45 percent and is evaluating a municipal bond paying 10 percent interest, the equivalent before-tax yield on a taxable investment would be:

$$\frac{10\%}{(1 - .45)} = \frac{10\%}{.55} = 18.18\%$$

Thus, the investor could choose between a *non*-tax-exempt investment paying 18.18 percent and a tax-exempt municipal bond paying 10 percent and be indifferent between the two. Table 9–1 presents examples of trade-offs between tax-exempts and non-tax-exempt (taxable) investments at various interest rates and marginal tax rates. Clearly, the higher the marginal tax rate, the greater the advantage of tax-exempt municipal bonds.

TABLE 9–1   Marginal Tax Rates and Return Equivalents

Yield on municipal (percent)	Comparable yield on taxable investment (in percent for each marginal tax bracket)			
	35 percent bracket	40 percent bracket	45 percent bracke	50 percent bracket
8.0%	12.3%	13.3%	14.5%	16.0%
9.0	13.8	15.0	16.4	18.0
10.0	15.4	16.6	18.2	20.0
11.0	16.9	18.3	20.0	22.0
12.0	18.5	20.0	21.8	24.0
13.0	20.0	21.7	23.6	26.0
14.0	21.5	23.3	25.5	28.0

A second significant feature of municipal bonds is that the yield that the issuing agency pays on municipal bonds is lower than the yield on taxable instruments. Of course, a municipal bond paying 10 percent may be quite competitive with taxable instruments paying considerably more. Average differentials are presented in Table 9–2.

TABLE 9–2 Comparable Yields on Long-Term Municipals and Taxable Corporates (yearly averages)

Year	Municipals Aa	Corporates Aa	Yield difference
1984	9.95	12.25	2.30
1983	9.20	12.42	3.22
1982	11.39	14.41	3.02
1981	10.89	14.75	3.86
1980	8.06	12.50	4.44
1979	6.12	9.94	3.82
1978	5.68	8.92	3.24
1977	5.39	8.24	2.85
1976	6.12	8.75	2.63
1975	6.77	9.17	2.40
1974	6.04	8.84	2.80
1973	5.11	7.66	2.55
1972	5.19	7.48	2.29
1971	5.36	7.78	2.42

Sources: *Moody's Municipal & Government Manual, Moody's Industrial Manual, Moody's Bond record* (published by Moody's Investors Service, Inc., New York, N.Y., selected issues).

The difference is of a 2 to 4.5 percent magnitude, and this is extremely important to issuing agencies. The ability of a city, state, or political subdivision to save 2 to 4.5 percent from normal bond market yields is critically important to municipal issuers. During those time periods when an overly aggressive Congress has attempted to propose legislation that might overturn the tax-exempt features of municipals, the cries of anger from mayors and governors is loud and clear. A major distinction that is also important to the bond issuer and investor is whether the bond is of a general obligation or revenue nature.

General obligation versus revenue bonds.   A general obligation issue is backed by the full faith, credit, and "taxing power" of the governmental unit. For a revenue bond, on the other hand, the repayment of the issue is fully dependent on the revenue-generating capability of a specific project or venture, such as a toll road, bridge, or municipal colosseum.

Because of the taxing power behind most general obligation (GO) issues, they tend to be of extremely high quality. Approximately three fourths of all municipal bond issues are of the general obligation variety, and very few failures have taken place in the post–World War II era. Revenue bonds tend to be of more uneven quality, and the economic soundness of the underlying revenue-generating project must be carefully examined (though most projects are quite worthwhile).

One special form of revenue bond that has gained popularity in the late 1970s and 80s is the pollution and environmental control revenue bond. A political subdivision offers the issue with the backing of a long-term pledge or

guarantee from an industrial firm that will use the proceeds. Essentially, the political subdivision serves as a funneling device for the corporate entity and, through this approach, allows for the utilization of tax-exempt funds by the corporation. Well over 1,000 such issues are currently in existence. Examples of pollution and environmental control bonds are presented in Table 9–3.

TABLE 9–3   Pollution and Environmental Control Revenue Bonds

Amount	State/municipality	Lessee/guarantor
$ 35,000,000	Escambia County, Fla.	St. Regis Paper Co.
60,000,000	Gary, Ind.	Standard Oil of Indiana
110,000,000	East Baton Rouge, La.	Exxon Corp.
40,000,000	Ohio Air Quality Authority	Republic Steel Corp.
60,000,000	Gulf Coast Waste Disposal	Shell Oil Co.
75,000,000	Allegeheny County—Pennsylvania	U.S. Steel Corp.

Source: *Moody's Bond Record* (published by Moody's Investors Service, Inc., New York, N.Y., selected issues).

Congress has been generally supportive of this activity as a means of providing less expensive financing for low-dollar return projects that provide benefits to society. In an earlier era, industrial revenue bonds (tax-exempt issues used to attract industry into a given area through low-cost financing) enjoyed a similar popularity. However, since the net benefit to society of one city stealing another city's factory and payroll is nil, many restrictions have been put on industrial revenue bonds.

Municipal bond guarantee.   A growing factor in the municipal bond market is the third-party guarantee. Whether dealing with a general obligation or revenue bond, a fee may be paid by the originating governmental body to a third party insurer to guarantee that all interest and principal payments will be made. A number of states, including California and Michigan, now have provisions to guarantee payments on selected issues. There are also two large private insurers. The first is a consortium of four insurance companies that market their product under the name of the Municipal Bond Insurance Association (MBIA). The second is the American Municipal Bond Assurance Corporation (AMBAC). Both will insure general obligation or revenue bonds.

A bond that carries a guarantee will have a slightly lower yield and a better secondary, or resale, market. This may be important because municipal bonds, in general, do not provide as strong a secondary market as U.S. government issues. The market for a given municipal issue is often small and fragmented, and there are high indirect costs associated with reselling the issue.

Corporate Securities

While corporate bonds represent only 30 percent of the total bond market (which also includes U.S. government securities, federally sponsored credit

agencies, and municipal bonds), they are still the dominant source of new financing for the U.S. corporation. That is, corporate bonds have been the most significant form of new financing for U.S. corporations, as indicated in Figure 9–2.

FIGURE 9–2   Long-Term Corporate Financing, 1964–1983

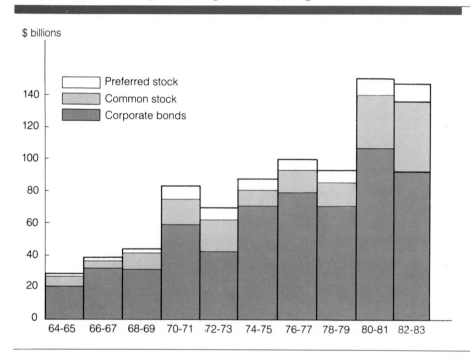

Source: *Federal Reserve Bulletin* (Washington, D.C.: Federal Reserve Board of Governors, *SEC Monthly Statistical Review* (U.S. Securities and Exchange Commission, selected issues).

Between 1964 and 1983, corporate bonds represented 77 percent of the total volume of long-term corporate securities sold. In tight money periods, such as 1974–75, the ratio approached 87 percent. However, during 1982–83 when the stock market reached new highs, corporations took advantage of lofty stock prices, using common stock to raise 29 percent of external funds. Bond financing was only 62.5 percent during this period.

The corporate market may be broken down into a number of subunits, including *industrials, public utilities, rails* and *transportation,* and *financial issues* (banks, finance companies, etc.). The industrials are a catchall category that includes everything from high technology companies to discount chain stores. Public utilities represent the largest segment of the market and have issues that run up to 40 years in maturity. Because public utilities are in constant need of funds to meet ever expanding requirements for power generation, telephone services, and other essentials, they are always in the bond market to raise new funds. The needs associated with rails and transportation

as well as financial issues tend to be less than those associated with public utilities or industrials. In Table 9–4, we see the comparative yields from three of the categories and for all corporations.[4]

TABLE 9–4   Comparative Yields on Aa Bonds among Corporate Issuers (percent)

(January)	Industrial	Public utility	Rails and transportation	All corporations
1984	12.39%	13.02%	12.22%	12.71%
1983	11.94	12.74	11.24	12.35
1982	15.01	16.48	13.52	15.75
1981	13.01	14.03	11.40	13.52
1980	11.16	11.95	9.99	11.56
1979	9.24	9.70	8.33	9.48
1978	8.42	8.76	7.93	8.59
1977	7.90	8.41	7.52	8.16
1976	8.87	9.39	8.45	9.13
1975	8.81	9.45	8.70	9.13
1974	7.85	8.15	7.92	8.00

Source: *Moody's Bond Record* (published by Moody's Investors Service, Inc., New York, N.Y., selected issues).

The higher yields on public utility issues represent a supply–demand phenomenon more than anything else. A constant stream of new issues to the market can only be absorbed by a higher yield pattern. In other cases the higher required return also may be associated with quality deterioration as measured by profitability and interest coverage. During 1983–84, the default of the Washington State Power Authority on bonds issued to construct power-generating facilities sent waves through the bond market. Again in 1984 when Public Service of Indiana canceled construction of a partially complete nuclear power plant, nuclear utility issues (both stocks and bonds) suffered severe price erosion and the bond market demanded high risk premiums on bonds of almost all nuclear utilities.

Corporate bonds of all types generally trade in units of $1,000, and this is a particularly attractive feature to the smaller investor who does not wish to purchase in units of $5,000 to $10,000 (which is necessary for many Treasury, federally sponsored credit agency issues, and municipals). Because of higher risk relative to government issues, the investor will generally receive higher yields on corporates as well. All income from corporates is taxable for federal, state, and local purposes. Finally, corporate issues have the disadvantage of being subject to calls. When buying a bond during a period of high interest rates, the call provision must be considered a negative feature because the

---

[4] Financial issues are generally not broken out of the published data.

high-yielding bonds may be called in for early retirement as interest rates go down.

BOND MARKET INVESTORS

Having considered the issuer or supply side of the market, we now comment on the investor, or demand, side. The bond market is dominated by large institutional investors (insurance companies, banks, pension funds, mutual funds) even more than the stock market. Institutional investors account for 90 to 95 percent of the trading in key segments of the bond market.[5] However, the presence of the individual investor is partially felt in the corporate and municipal bond market where the incentives of low denomination ($1,000) corporate bonds or tax-free municipal bonds have some attraction.

Institutional investors' preferences for various sectors of the bond market are influenced by their tax status as well as the nature of their obligations or liabilities to depositors, investors, or clients. For example, banks traditionally have been strong participants in the municipal bond market because of their substantial tax obligations. Their investments tend to be in short- to intermediate-term assets because of the short-term nature of their deposit obligations (the funds supplied to the banks). One problem that banks find in their bond portfolios is that such investments are often preferred over loans to customers when the economy is weak and loan demand is sluggish. Not so coincidentally, this happens to be the time period when interest rates are low. When the economy improves, interest rates go up, and so does loan demand. In order to meet the loan demand of valued customers, banks liquidate portions of their bond portfolio. The problem with this recurring process is that banks are buying bonds when interest rates are *low* and selling them when interest rates are *high.* This can cause losses in the value of the bank portfolio.

The bond market investor must be prepared to deal in a relatively strong primary market (new issues market) and a relatively weak secondary market (resale market). While the secondary market is active for many types of Treasury and agency issues, such is not the case for corporate and municipal issues. Thus, the investor must look well beyond the yield, maturity, and rating to determine if a purchase is acceptable. The question that must be considered is: How close to the going market price can I dispose of the issue if that should be necessary? If a 5 or 10 percent discount is involved, that might be unacceptable. Unlike the stock market, the secondary market in bonds tends to be dominated by over-the-counter transactions (although there are listed bonds traded as well).

In February of 1982, the Securities and Exchange Commission began allowing a process called shelf registration under SEC Rule 415. Shelf registration permits large companies to file one comprehensive registration statement, which outlines the firm's plans for future long-term financing. Then, when

---

[5] Sidney Homer, "Historical Evolution of Today's Bond Market," *Journal of Portfolio Management,* Spring 1975, pp. 6–11.

market conditions seem appropriate, the firm can issue the securities without further SEC approval. Future issues are said to be sitting on the shelf, waiting for the most advantageous time to appear. Shelf registration has been most frequently used with debt issues and other fixed income securities. Table 9–5 from *Moody's Bond Survey* of May 1984 shows a sample of the various shelf offerings outstanding at that time. The largest is the $2 billion offering of notes by Citicorp. While only 30–40 percent of corporate bonds are sold through shelf registration, this process is becoming increasingly popular in the 1980s.

TABLE 9–5   Prospective Offerings—Shelf Registrations under SEC Rule 415

Date of registration	Original amount ($millions)	Registrants	Types of securities	Prospective ratings
6/07/1982	150.0	ACF Industries, Inc.	Equity Trust Certificates	A2
2/17/1984	1,000.0	Alliance Mortgage Acceptance Corp.	GNMA Obligations	—
10/11/1983	500.0	American Express Credit Corp.	Senior Unsecured Debt Securities	Aa2
1/17/1983	250.0	Carolina Power & Light	First Mortgage Bonds	A2
3/14/1983	50.0	Central Power & Light	Cumulative Preferred Stock	"aa3"
3/09/1983	2,000.0	Citicorp	Notes	Aa1
8/04/1983	150.0	Continental Illinois Corp.	Adjusted Rate Preferred Stock	"ba2"

Private Placement.   A number of bond offerings are sold to investors as a private placement. That is, they are sold privately to investors rather than through the public markets. Historically, private placements have equaled 30 to 35 percent of new debt issues. Private placements are most popular with such investors as insurance companies and pension funds. They are primarily offered in the corporate sector by industrial firms rather than public utilities. The lender can generally expect to receive a slightly higher yield than on public issues to compensate for the extremely limited or nonexistent secondary market and the generally smaller size of the borrowing firm in a private placement.

BOND RATINGS

Bond investors tend to place much more emphasis on independent analysis of quality than do common stock investors. For this reason, both corporate financial management and institutional portfolio managers keep a very close eye on bond rating procedures. The difference between an AA and an A rating may mean the corporation will have to pay ¼ percent more interest on the bond

issue (perhaps 12½ percent rather than 12¼ percent). On a $100 million, 20-year issue, this represents $250,000 per year (before tax), or a total of $5 million over the life of the bond.

The two major bond rating agencies are Moody's Investors Service (a subsidiary of Dun & Bradstreet, Inc.) and Standard & Poor's (a subsidiary of McGraw-Hill, Inc.). They rank thousands of corporate and municipal issues as well as a limited number of private placements, commercial paper, and preferred stock issues, and offerings of foreign companies and governments. U.S. government issues tend to be free of risk and therefore are given very little attention by the bond rating agencies. Moody's, founded in 1909, is the older of the two bond rating agencies and covers twice as many securities as Standard & Poor's (particularly in the municipal bond area). Other less well-known bond rating agencies include Fitch Investors Service, Inc. (an old-line rating agency that specializes in bank securities), and Duff & Phelp, Inc.

The bond ratings, generally ranging from an AA to a D category, are decided on a committee basis at both Moody's and Standard & Poor's.[6] There are no fast and firm quantitative measures that specify the rating that a new issue will receive. Nevertheless, measures pertaining to cash flow and earnings generation in relationship to debt obligations are given strong consideration. Of particular interest are coverage ratios that show the number of times that interest payments, as well as all annual contractual obligations, are covered by earnings. A coverage of two or three may contribute to a low rating, while a ratio of 5 to 10 may indicate the possibility of a strong rating. Operating margins, return on invested capital, and returns on total assets are also evaluated along with debt-to-equity ratios.[7] Financial ratio analysis makes up perhaps 50 percent of the evaluation. Other factors of importance are the nature of the industry in which the firm operates, the relative position of the firm within the industry, the pricing clout that the firm has, and the quality of management.

Decisions are not made in a sterile, isolated environment. Thus, it is not unusual for corporate management or the mayor to make an actual presentation to the rating agency, and on-sight visitations to plants or cities may take place. Corporations or municipalities have been known to change their operating or financial policies in order to satisfy people at the rating agencies. Perhaps the size of the issue will be pared down to provide for better interest coverage, or an increase in cash dividends will be delayed to strengthen the internal financing position of the firm.

The overall quality of the work done by the bond rating agencies may be judged by the agencies' acceptance in the business and academic community. In truth, their work is very well received. Although Paine, Webber and some other investment houses have established their own analysts to shadow the activities of the bond rating agencies and look for imprecisions in their classifi-

---

[6] Irwin Ross, "Higher Stakes in the Bond Rating Game," *Fortune*, April 1976, pp. 133–42.

[7] Similar appropriate measures can be applied to municipal bonds, such as debt per capita or income per capita within a governmental jurisdiction.

cations (and thus potential profits), the opportunities are not great. Academic researchers have generally found that accounting and financial data were well considered in the bond ratings and that rational evaluation appeared to exist.[8]

One item lending credibility to the bond rating process is the frequency with which the two major rating agencies arrive at exactly the same grade for a given issue (and this occurs well over 50 percent of the time). When "split ratings" do occur (different ratings by different agencies), they are invariably of a small magnitude. A typical case might be AAA versus AA rather than AAA versus BBB. While one can question whether one agency is looking over the other's shoulder or "copying its homework," this is probably not the case in this skilled industry.

Nevertheless, there is room for criticism. While initial evaluations are quite thorough and rational, the subsequent monitoring process may not be wholly satisfactory. Subsequent changes in corporate or municipal government events may not trigger a rating change quickly enough in all cases. One sure way that a corporation or municipal government will get a reevaluation is for them to come out with a new issue. This tends to generate a review of all existing issues.

Actual Rating System

In Table 9–6, we see an actual listing of the designations used by Moody's and Standard & Poor's. Note that Moody's combines capital letters and small *a*'s, and Standard & Poor's uses all capital letters.

The first four categories are assumed to represent investment-grade quality (high or medium grades). Large institutional investors (insurance companies, banks, pension funds) generally confine their activities to these four categories. The next two B grades are considered speculative in nature, while C and D rated issues are generally in default and may trade flat (without interest). Moody's also modifies their basic ratings with numerical values for categories Aa through B: 1 is the highest in a category, 2 is the mid-range, and 3 is the lowest. Thus a Aa2 rating means the bond is in the mid-range of Aa. Standard & Poor's has a similar modification process with plusses and minuses applied. Thus AA+ would be on the high end of a AA rating, AA would be in the middle and AA− would be on the low end.

It is also possible for a corporation to have issues outstanding in more than one category. For example, highly secured mortgage bonds of a corporation may be rated AA, while unsecured issues carry an A rating.

The level of interest payment on a bond is inverse to the quality rating. If a bond rated AAA by Standard & Poor's pays 12 percent, an A-quality bond

[8] James O. Horrigan, "The Determination of Long-Term Credit Standing with Financial Ratios," *Empirical Research in Accounting: Selected Studies,* supplement to *Journal of Accounting Research,* 4 (1966), pp. 44–62. Thomas F. Pogue and Robert M. Soldofsky, "What's in a Bond Rating?" *Journal of Financial and Quantitative Analysis,* June 1969, pp. 201–8. George E. Pinches and Kent A. Mingo, "A Multivariate Analysis of Industrial Bond Ratings," *Journal of Finance,* March 1973, pp. 1–18.

TABLE 9–6   Description of Bond Ratings

Quality	Moody's	Standard & Poor's	Description
High-grade	Aaa	AAA	Bonds that are judged to be of the best quality. They carry the smallest degree of investment risk and are generally referred to as "gilt edge." Interest payments are protected by a large or exceptionally stable margin, and principal is secure.
	Aa	AA	Bonds that are judged to be of high quality by all standards. Together with the first group, they comprise what are generally known as high-grade bonds. They are rated lower than the best bonds because margins of protection may not be as large.
Medium-grade	A	A	Bonds that possess many favorable investment attributes and are to be considered as upper medium-grade obligations. Factors giving security to principal and interest are considered adequate.
	Baa	BBB	Bonds that are considered as medium-grade obligations, i.e., they are neither highly protected nor poorly secured.
Speculative	Ba	BB	Bonds that are judged to have speculative elements; their future cannot be considered as well assured. Often the protection of interest and principal payments may be very moderate.
	B	B	Bonds that generally lack characteristics of the desirable investment. Assurance of interest and principal payments or of maintenance of other terms of the contract over any long period of time may be small.
Default	Caa	CCC	Bonds that are of poor standing. Such issues may be in default, or there may be elements of danger present with respect to principal or interest.
	Ca	CC	Bonds that represent obligations which are speculative to a high degree. Such issues are often in default or have other marked shortcomings.
	C		The lowest rated class in Moody's designation. These bonds can be regarded as having extremely poor prospects of attaining any real investment standing.
		C	Rating given to income bonds on which interest is not currently being paid.
		D	Issues in default with arrears in interest and/or principal payments.

Sources: *Moody's Bond Record* (published by Moody's Investors Service, Inc., New York, N.Y.) and *Bond Guide* (Standard & Poor's).

might pay 13 percent; a BB, 13.75 percent; and so on. The spread between these yields changes from time to time and is watched closely by the financial community as a barometer of future movements in the financial markets. A relatively small spread between two rating categories would indicate investors generally have confidence in the economy. As the yield spread widens between higher and lower rating categories, this may indicate some loss of confidence. Investors are demanding increasingly higher yields for lower-rated bonds. Their loss of confidence indicates they will demand progressively higher returns for taking risks.

The relative positioning of different types of corporate bonds within the various rating categories is presented in Table 9–7. We see the predominance of bonds ranked in the top four categories, with one exception being the transportation industry (rails, airlines).

TABLE 9–7   Percentage Distribution of Corporate Bonds by Rating Categories (based on par value outstanding)

	Total corporate	Utilities	Industrial	Finance	Transportation
AAA	23%	26%	21%	19%	7%
AA	26	25	26	33	10
A	33	32	34	34	27
BBB	13	16	10	5	18
BB	2	1	3	1	8
B	1	—	2	1	8
CCC and lower	2	—	4	7	22
	100%	100%	100%	100%	100%

Source: Salomon Brothers.

BOND QUOTES

The Wall Street Journal and a number of other sources publish bond values on a daily basis. In Table 9–8, we see an excerpt from the daily quote sheet for corporate bonds.

In the first column, note the company name followed by the annual coupon rate and the maturity date. For example, the sixth entry in the Table shows Alabama Power with a coupon rate of 7¾ percent maturing in 02 (the year 2002). The current yield (Cur Yld) represents the annual interest or coupon payment divided by the price and is 12 percent (rounded). The volume (Vol) is indicated to be 3 bonds traded, and the closing price is 64-⅞. The bond quote does not represent actual dollars, but percent of par value. Since corporate bonds trade in units of $1,000 par value, 64.875 percent represents $648.75. Other issues of Alabama Power also trade at different prices.

A student interested in further information on a bond could proceed to *Moody's Bond Record,* published by Moody's Investors Service, or the *Bond Guide,* published by Standard & Poor's. For example, using the aforementioned *Moody's Bond Record,* the reader could determine, in Table 9–9, that the Avco 7½s of 1993 are subordinated debentures with a Moody's bond rating of Ba2 and a current call price of 100 percent of par, or $1,000 (no premium in this case). The *Moody's Bond Record* further indicates that the bonds were initially issued on January 1, 1969, and interest is payable on March 31 and November 30 of each year (first column, Interest Dates).

In Table 9–10 we turn our attention to quotes on U.S. government securities (as opposed to corporate issues). Treasury notes and bonds are traded on a price basis as a percentage of par value, similar to corporate bonds. Historically, price changes in the market have been rather small and bonds are quoted in ¹⁄₃₂ of a percentage point. For example, the price for the 10½

TABLE 9–8 Daily Quotes on Corporate Bonds

CORPORATION BONDS
Volume, $23,510,000

Bonds	Cur Yld	Vol	High	Low	Close	Net Chg.
AbbtL 9.2s99	11.	10	82	82	82	+1⅞
Advst 9s08	cv	4	83	83	83	−1
AetnLf 8⅛07	12.	6	68¼	68¼	68¼	−2¼
AlaP 9s2000	12.	22	73⅝	73⅝	73⅝	+ ¼
AlaP 8½s01	12.	7	70½	69⅝	69¾	+ ¼
AlaP 7⅞s02	12.	13	66⅛	66⅛	66⅛	− ⅛
→ AlaP 7¾s02	12.	3	64⅞	64⅞	64⅞	+ ⅞
AlaP 8⅞s03	12.	15	72	71¼	71½	− ½
AlaP 8¼s03	12.	3	66⅜	66⅜	66⅜	− ⅝
AlaP 9¾s04	13.	30	76¾	76¾	76¾	+ ⅝
AlaP 10⅞05	13.	4	85¾	85¾	85¾	− ¼
AlaP 10½05	13.	28	81⅞	81⅝	81⅞	+ ⅜
AlaP 8¾07	13.	25	69¼	69¼	69¼	.....
AlaP 8⅝87	9.1	4	94⅞	94⅞	94⅞	+ ¾
AlaP 9¼07	13.	4	72⅞	72⅞	72⅞	− ⅛
AlaP 9½08	13.	44	75½	74¾	75½	+ ¾
AlaP 15¼10	14.	19	107½	107¼	107¼	.....
AlaP 17⅜11	15.	40	114¾	113⅛	114¾	+ ¾
AlaP 18¼89	17.	122	110⅛	109½	110	+ ¾
AlskA 9s03	cv	22	118½	118½	118½	+ ½
AlskH 16¼99	15.	1	110	110	110	−1
AlskH 17¾91	16.	25	114½	114	114	.....
AlskH 18⅜01	17.	99	111⅜	111	111	.....
AlskH 15s92	15.	26	102⅜	101⅝	102⅜	+ ⅞
AlldC zr87	..	25	77¼	77¼	77¼	+ ¼
AlldC zr92	..	40	41½	40⅝	41	.....
AlldC zr96s	..	13	26⅜	26⅜	26⅜	−1½
AlldC zr98s	..	15	20¼	19½	19½	− ¾
AlldC zr2000s	..	23	16¾	16½	16¾	.....
AlldC d6s88	7.3	23	82¼	82	82	+ ⅛
AlldC d6s90	8.2	10	74	73⅜	73½	− ½
AlldC zr87t a	..	60	76¾	76¾	76¾	+ ¾
AlldC zr95t	..	10	28¾	28¾	28¾	+ ¼
AlldC zr03t	..	20	10⅞	10⅞	10⅞	.....
AlldSt 8¾09	cv	10	115	115	115	−1
AlsCha 12s90	14.	39	84¾	84¼	84¼	− ½
AlsCha 16s91	16.	20	97¾	97⅝	97¾	+ ⅛
Alcoa 6s92	8.8	5	68	68	68	−3⅝
Alcoa 7.45s96	11.	1	69¼	69¼	69¼	− ¾
AMAX 9⅜00	14.	1	65⅝	65⅝	65⅝	−4⅜
Amax 14¼90	14.	34	100½	100¼	100½	+1
Amax 14½94	15.	22	98	97½	98	.....
AFoP 4.8s87	5.4	2	89⅛	89⅛	89⅛	+1⅛
AForP 5s30	12.	7	41½	39¾	41½	+1¼
AAirl 4¼92	7.0	22	61	61	61	+1½
ABrnd 11⅛89	11.	15	98⅞	98⅞	98⅞	+ ⅛
ACan 13¼93	13.	1	103¼	103¼	103¼	− ¾
AExC 7.7s87	8.2	10	94⅛	94⅛	94⅛	− ½
AmGn 11s07	cv	5	156	156	156	−4
AmGn 11s08	cv	11	156	155½	156	−4
AHoist 5½93	cv	10	65	65	65	.....
AmMed 9½01	cv	17	111½	111	111	+1
AmMed 8¼08	cv	38	86	84¾	86	+1
AmMed 11¾99	13.	5	88½	88½	88½	+ ⅜
ATT 2⅝s86	2.8	32	93½	93	93½	+ ⅞
ATT 2⅞s87	3.3	14	86¾	86½	86¾	+ ⅛
ATT 3⅞s90	5.2	205	73⅞	73¼	73⅞	+ ⅝
ATT 8¾00	12.	168	74¾	74½	74½	.....
ATT 7s01	11.	119	62⅞	62⅜	62⅞	+ ½
ATT 7⅛s03	11.	160	62	61¼	62	+ ¾
ATT 8.80s05	12.	88	73	72⅝	73	+ ⅜
ATT 8⅝s07	12.	67	71	70⅝	70⅞	− ⅜
Burlind 8¾08	cv	102	81½	81½	81½	....
Butte 10¼97	20.	71	53	52	52¼	.....
CIGNA 8s07	cv	37	102	102	102	−1½
CIT 9s91	11.	5	85¼	85¼	85¼	+ ¼
CIT 15½87	14.	3	108½	108½	108½	−1¼
Caesr 12½90	13.	24	97¼	97⅛	97⅛	− ⅝
Caesr 11¼97	13.	20	84	83½	84	+1⅜
Caesr 12½00	14.	8	92	92	92	−8
Campbl 9⅞90	10.	5	94⅜	94⅜	94⅜	− ⅜
CPc4s perp	12.	5	34	34	34	− ¼
CastlC 5⅜94f	cv	53	77½	74	74	−2
CatTr 5½00	cv	23	77	77	77	− ½
CatTr 12½90	12.	4	100¾	100¾	100¾	+ ¾
Cave 11½00N	15.	2	77⅛	77⅛	77⅛	.....
Celanse 4s90	cv	5	97½	97½	97½	+ ¼
Celanse 9¾06	cv	38	124⅜	124	124⅛	+ ⅛
CtrlTel 8s96	11.	5	72¼	72¼	72¼	− ⅛
Cessna 8s08	cv	30	88½	88	88½	.....
CATS zr88	..	14	68⅞	68⅞	68⅞	+1⅞
CATS zr91	..	46	48¼	46⅝	47½	+ ⅛
CATS zr92	..	8	47	47	47	.....
CATS zr94	..	2	37⅜	37⅜	37⅜	− ½
CATS zr95	..	10	35	35	35	− ½
CATS zr96	..	32	28	27½	27⅝	−1⅜
CATS zr97	..	33	27	26¼	27	.....
CATS zr99	..	4	25	25	25	+ ½
CATS zr03	..	53	14¾	14	14	− ¾
CATS zr06-11	..	45	9	8¾	8⅞	.....
vjChtCo 10⅝98f	..	5	33⅛	33⅛	33⅛	−1⅜
vjChtC d14¾02f	..	50	35¾	35	35	− ¾
ChsBk 8¾86	9.0	15	97⅜	97⅜	97⅜	+ ⅛
ChsCp 10.20s99t	10.	5	99⅞	99⅞	99⅞	.....
ChsCp 11.3s09t	13.	2	89	89	89	− ½
Chmtrn 9s94	12.	24	77⅛	77	77	+ ⅜
C&O 4½92	7.0	1	64	64	64	.....
CPoV 8⅝09	12.	3	71	71	71	− ⅛
CPoV 9¼15	13.	24	73⅞	73⅞	73⅞	− ¼
CPWV 7¼13	12.	22	58¼	58¼	58¼	+ ⅛
ChvrnC 12¾87	12.	6	103	103	103	− ⅛
ChvrnC 11¾88	12.	37	100⅜	100¼	100⅜	...
ChvrnC 12s94	12.	134	99⅜	99¼	99⅜	+ ⅛
ChvrnC 11s90	11.	35	97⅛	97⅛	97⅛	+ ⅛
Chvrn 7s96	10.	4	69⅞	69⅞	69⅞	.....
Chvrn 8¾05	12.	11	72¾	72¾	72¾	+ ⅛
ChCft 15s99t	14.	25	105¼	105¼	105¼	.....
Chrysl 8⅞95	11.	18	80	79¾	79¾	− ⅜
Chryslr 8s98	11.	25	70⅝	70⅝	70⅝	− ⅛
Chryslr 12¾92	13.	10	99¾	99¾	99¾	.....
ChryF 7⅜86	7.7	45	96	96	96	.....
ChryF 9s86	9.3	14	96½	96⅜	96½	+ ⅛
ChryF 9⅜87	9.7	11	97¼	96⅜	96⅜	− ⅝
ChryF 13¼88	13.	3	103¾	103¾	103¾	+ ¾
ChryF 13½91	13.	4	103	103	103	.....
Citicp 8.45s07	12.	16	68¾	67⅝	67¾	+ ¾
Citicp 9.65s98t	10.	5	92½	92½	92½	−1
Citicp 11¾04t	13.	50	94	94	94	+ ¼
Citicp 12¼93	12.	71	99½	99⅜	99½	.....
Citicp 12s90	12.	43	99⅞	99½	99⅞	+ ½
Citicp 11⅞88	12.	50	100⅜	100⅜	100⅜	+ ⅝
Citicp 13.60s99	13.	5	102	102	102	− ⅜
CitSv 6⅛97	11.	5	54¾	54⅝	54⅝	−1⅛
CitSv 6⅝99	12.	10	55⅛	55⅛	55⅛	−1⅜
CitSv 9¾00	12.	3	80	79¾	80	+5¼
CitSv 13⅞11	14.	74	100¾	100¾	100¾	− ¼
CnNG 8⅛97	10.	20	80	80	80	+4
CnPw 4⅝89	6.5	5	70⅞	70⅞	70⅞	+ ⅞
CnPw 5⅞96	12.	8	51	50⅝	51	+ ⅜
CnPw 7⅝99	14.	1	55⅝	55⅝	55⅝	− ½
CnPw 8⅝00	14.	50	61½	61½	61½	− ⅛
CnPw 8⅛01	14.	11	57½	57	57	− ½
CnPw 7½02J	14.	5	53½	53½	53½	+ ¼
CnPw 7½02O	14.	17	53⅜	53	53	− ½
CnPw 9¾06	15.	20	66¼	65¼	65¼	− ⅞
CnPw 9s06	15.	10	61⅜	61⅜	61⅜	+ ⅜
CnPw 8⅞07	15.	2	60	60	60	+ ½
CnPw 8⅝07	15.	73	59	58¾	58¾	− ⅛
CnPw 9s08	15.	6	60½	60⅜	60½	− ¾
Ct IICp 8.9s89	2.2	5	97	97	97	−2⅝
Ct IC 8½85	8.7	25	98 5-32	98 5-32	98 5-32	+13-32
Ct IC zr89	..	11	55⅜	55	55⅜	+ ⅛
Coopvsn 8⅝05	cv	20	102	102	102	− ¾
CornG 8¼07	8.2	33	101	100¼	100¼	− ½
Crane 7s94	11.	36	63	62¼	62¼	− ¾
CrdF 9s86	9.2	2	97⅜	97⅜	97⅜	+1⅛
CrdF 8¾88	9.5	5	91⅞	91⅞	91⅞	+ ⅛
CrdF 10¼89	11.	5	93⅛	93⅛	93⅛	− ⅞
CritAc 11⅞14	..	50	97½	97	97½	+ ½
CrocN 5¾96	cv	7	62½	62½	62½	− ⅛
CrwnZ 9¼05	13.	3	73¾	73¾	73¾	.....
CrwnZ 9¼09	cv	4	113	109	112	−1
Culb 11½05	13.	1	86	86	86	.....
Dana d5⅞06	cv	5	68½	68½	68½	−1
Datpnt 8⅞06	cv	55	65	64½	64½	.....
Dayc 6s4	cv	14	94¼	94¼	94¼	.....
DaytP 10.7s05	13.	1	82	82	82	+1
DaytP 17s91	16.	15	109½	108¾	109½	+ ¾
Deere 7.9s87	8.4	62	94	94	94	+ ¼
Deere 10½85	11.	25	100	100	100	.....
Deere 11½89	12.	10	97½	97½	97½	− ⅜
Deere 9s08	cv	26	100¾	100¾	100¾	.....
DeereCr 9.35s03	13.	3	70⅝	70⅝	70⅝	− ¾
DelPw 6⅜97	10.	10	61⅜	61⅜	61⅜	− ⅝
DetEd 6.4s98	11.	24	58⅞	58⅝	58⅞	+1
DetEd 9s99	12.	41	74⅝	74	74⅝	+ ⅝
DetEd 9.15s00	12.	15	74⅛	74⅛	74⅛	− ¼
DetEd 8.15s00	12.	5	66¾	66¾	66¾	− ⅝
DetEd 8⅛01	12.	15	68⅛	66⅝	66⅝	.....
DetEd 9⅞04	13.	26	77⅞	77⅜	77⅜	− ⅝
DetEd 11⅞00	13.	23	91	90⅞	91	+1
DetEd 10⅝06	13.	12	82⅛	82⅛	82⅛	− ⅛
Digit 8s09	cv	117	111	109¼	109¼	−2¼
Divers 10½91	12.	20	88	88	88	+1½
Dow 4.35s88	5.4	2	81¼	81¼	81¼	.....
Dow 8⅞2000	12.	3	75⅞	75⅞	75⅞	+ ¾
Dow 8.92000	12.	9	74⅞	74⅞	74⅞	.....
Dreyfs 7⅜08	cv	1	126½	126½	126½	−2
duPnt 8.45s04	12.	5	71⅞	71⅞	71⅞	− ½
duPnt 8½06	12.	8	72¼	72¼	72¼	+ ½
duPnt 14s91	13.	40	107¾	107	107¾	+ ⅞
duPnt d6s01	11.	124	55⅛	54⅝	55	+ ¼
DukeP 7⅜02	12.	15	63⅞	63¼	63⅞	+ ⅜
DukeP 7¾03	12.	6	65⅝	65⅝	65⅝	+ ⅛
DukeP 8⅛03	12.	31	68⅝	67¾	68⅝	+1¼
DukeP 9¾04	12.	32	79¼	79	79⅛	+ ⅛
DukeP 10⅛09	13.	15	81½	80	80	− ⅜
DuqL 8¾00	12.	4	70⅛	70⅛	70⅛	+ ⅜
DuqL 9s06	13.	10	69	69	69	

Source: Reprinted by permission of *The Wall Street Journal*, © Dow Jones & Company, Inc. (March 26, 1985).

TABLE 9–9 Background Data on Bond Issues

Issue	Interest Dates	Current Call Price	Moody's Rating	Current Price		Yield to Mat	Price 1984 High	Price 1984 Low	Range 1946-83 High	Range 1946-83 Low	Amt Outst Mil $	Sink Fund Prov	Legal Status	Fed Tax	Issued	Price	Yld
Autotote Systems Inc. sr.deb.11.50 1996	J&D1	100.00	— r	80	bid	15.20	81	50	84	53	13.6	Yes	——	N	6-2-81		
• AVCO CORP. sr.nts.12.00 1990	J&D15	• 100.00	Baa3 r	90⅛	sale	14.58	97⅜	85⅛	102	72⅞	75.0	No	——	N	6-19-80	100.00	12.00
• do sub.deb. 7.50 1993 "	M31&N30	100.00	Ba2 r	64	bid	14.76	71	61⅜	94½	30½	66.8	No	——	N	Jan.1969		
• Avco Finan. Ser.Inc. sr.nts.14.125 1985	J&D15	N.C.	A3 r	100	sale	14.12	104⅛	100	107	99⅝	100	No	1	N	8-17-82	99.63	14.25

Source: *Moody's Bond Record*, September 1984 (published by Moody's Investors Service, Inc., New York, N.Y.)

TABLE 9–10 Daily Quotes on Government Issues

Treasury Issues/*Bonds, Notes & Bills*

Thursday, May 31, 1984

Representative mid-afternoon Over-the-Counter quotations supplied by the Federal Reserve Bank of New York City, based on transactions of $1 million or more.

Decimals in bid-and-asked and bid changes represent 32nds; 101.1 means 101 1/32. a-Plus 1/64. b-Yield to call date. d-Minus 1/64. n-Treasury notes.

Treasury Bonds and Notes

Rate	Mat.	Date	Bid	Asked	Bid Chg.	Yld.
8⅞s,	1984	Jun n	99.27	99.31	+ .1	8.97
14⅜s,	1984	Jun n	100.6	100.10	− .1	9.39
13⅛s,	1984	Jul n	100.13	100.17		9.25
6⅜s,	1984	Aug	99.4	99.20		8.14
7¼s,	1984	Aug n	99.10	99.14		9.93
11⅝s,	1984	Aug n	100.6	100.10		9.97
13¼s,	1984	Aug n	100.17	100.21		9.49
12⅛s,	1984	Sep n	100.8	100.12	− .1	10.69
9¾s,	1984	Oct n	99.10	99.14	− .1	11.10
12⅝s,	1987	Nov n	97.31	98.3	+ .5	13.33
11¼s,	1987	Dec n	94.1	94.5	+ .9	13.36
12⅜s,	1988	Jan n	97.2	97.6	+ .7	13.38
10⅛s,	1988	Feb n	90.11	90.15	+ .10	13.48
12s,	1988	Mar n	95.15	95.17	+ .7	13.52
13¼s,	1988	Apr n	99.14	99.18	+ .13	13.40
8¼s,	1988	May n	84.14	84.22	+ .11	13.37
9⅞s,	1988	May n	89	89.4	+ .9	13.52
14s,	1988	Jul n	101.16	101.24	+ .9	13.43
10½s,	1988	Aug n	90.5	90.9	+ .7	13.61
15⅜s,	1988	Oct n	105.18	105.26	+ .2	13.56
8¾s,	1988	Nov n	84.18	84.26	+ .12	13.39
11¾s,	1988	Nov n	93.26	93.30	+ .10	13.61
14⅝s,	1989	Jan n	102.30	103.2	+ .11	13.71
11⅜s,	1989	Feb n	92.3	92.7	+ .10	13.67
14⅜s,	1989	Apr n	102.3	102.7	+ .9	13.73
9¼s,	1989	May n	84.26	85.2	+ .10	13.49
11¾s,	1989	May n	93.2	93.6	+ .9	13.69
14½s,	1989	Jul n	102.17	102.21	+ .7	13.76
11⅞s,	1989	Oct n	93.2	93.10	+ .9	13.68
10¾s,	1989	Nov n	88.19	88.23	+ .7	13.76
→ 10½s,	1990	Jan n	87.9	87.17	+ .9	13.76
3½s,	1990	Feb	89.8	90.8	+ .2	5.51
10½s,	1990	Apr n	86.31	87.7	+ .11	13.75
8¼s,	1990	May	78.20	79.4	+ .12	13.46
10¾s,	1990	Jul n	87.14	87.18	+ .9	13.84
10¾s,	1990	Aug n	87.13	87.21	+ .9	13.77
11½s,	1990	Oct n	90.13	90.17	+ .10	13.78
13s,	1990	Nov n	96.21	96.25	+ .9	13.77
11¾s,	1991	Jan n	91	91.4	+ .10	13.84
12⅜s,	1991	Apr	93.18	93.22	+ .11	13.83
14½s,	1991	May n	102.27	103.3	+ .6	13.79
14⅞s,	1991	Aug n	104.16	104.24	+ .8	13.81
14¼s,	1991	Nov n	101.20	101.28	+ .8	13.84
14⅝s,	1992	Feb n	103.8	103.16	+ .9	13.87
13¾s,	1992	May n	99.9	99.17	+ .12	13.85
4¼s,	1987-92	Aug	89.18	90.18	+ .2	5.71
7¼s,	1992	Aug	68.19	69.3	+ .8	13.62
10½s,	1992	Nov n	83.14	83.18	+ .10	13.86
4s,	1988-93	Feb	89.16	90.16		5.38
6¾s,	1993	Feb	66.6	66.22	+ .14	13.34
7⅞s,	1993	Feb	70.8	70.16	+ .16	13.81
10⅞s,	1993	Feb n	85	85.4	+ .12	13.87

U.S. Treas. Bills

Mat. date	Bid (Discount)	Asked (Discount)	Yield
-1984-			
6- 7	8.39	8.29	8.41
6-14	9.65	9.57	9.73
6-21	10.17	10.11	10.30
6-28	7.74	7.58	7.72
7- 5	9.22	9.16	9.36
7-12	9.48	9.40	9.63
7-19	9.43	9.37	9.61
7-26	9.31	9.23	9.49
8- 2	9.77	9.69	9.98
8- 9	9.76	9.70	10.01
8-16	9.73	9.67	10.00
8-23	9.71	9.65	10.00
8-30	9.75	9.73	10.10
9- 6	9.82	9.78	10.18
9-13	9.70	9.64	10.05
9-20	9.96	9.90	10.35
9-27	9.95	9.89	10.35
10- 4	10.16	10.10	10.60
10-11	10.25	10.21	10.75
10-18	10.32	10.28	10.84
10-25	10.33	10.27	10.86
11- 1	10.59	10.55	11.19
11- 8	10.58	10.52	11.18
11-15	10.41	10.35	11.01
11-24	10.58	10.52	11.23
11-29	10.58	10.54	11.27
12-27	10.58	10.52	11.31
-1985-			
1-24	10.39	10.33	11.14
2-21	10.79	10.73	11.60
3-21	10.86	10.80	11.74
4-18	10.96	10.90	11.93
5-16	10.99	10.97	12.09

Source: Reprinted by permission of *The Wall Street Journal,*

Treasury note due January 1990 is quoted at 87.9 bid and 87.17 asked. These prices translate into 87-9/32 and 87-17/32 percent of $1,000. The bid price on a $1,000 bond would be $872.8125 and the asked price $875.3125, for a total spread between the bid and asked price of $2.50 per $1,000 bond. This small spread is customary in the very liquid government bond market. Note that while Treasury notes and bonds are quoted on the basis of price, Treasury bills are quoted on the basis of yield. Looking at the Treasury bills in the right-hand

part of Table 9–10, notice that the bid and asked prices are quoted as a discount from the $10,000 par value. A $10,000 Treasury bill quoted at 10 percent, with one year to maturity, would provide $1,000 in interest and would sell on a discount basis for $9,000. The effective yield would be 11.1 percent ($1,000/$9,000). The same 10 percent bond with six months to maturity would provide $500 in interest and sell for $9,500. The effective yield would be 10.53 percent ($500/$9,500 times 2).

BOND MARKETS, CAPITAL MARKET THEORY, AND EFFICIENCY

In many respects, the bond market appears to demonstrate a high degree of rationality in recognition of risk and return. Corporate issues promise a higher yield than government issues to compensate for risk, and furthermore, federally sponsored credit agencies pay a higher return than Treasury issues for the same reason. Also, lower-rated bonds consistently trade at higher yields than quality bonds, to provide a risk premium.

Taking this logic one step further, bonds should generally pay a lower return than equity investments. Why? The reason is that the equity holder is in a riskier position because of the absence of a contractual obligation to receive payment. As was pointed out in Chapter 1, Ibbotson and Sinquefield[9] and Fisher and Lorie[10] have attributed superior returns to equity investments relative to debt over the long term.

However, in the highly inflationary, high-interest rate periods of the 1970s and 80s the aforementioned researchers as well as others have indicated a reversal of this pattern; that is, "lower-risk" debt investments have at times provided a higher return (for example, virtually riskless bank CDs have paid as much as 18 percent).

A number of studies have also investigated the efficiency of the bond market. A primary item under investigation was the extent of price change that was associated with a change in a bond rating. If the bond market is efficient, much of the information that led to the rating change was already known to the public and should have been impounded into the value of the bond before the rating change. Thus, the rating change should not have led to major price movements. Major research has generally been supportive of this hypothesis.[11]

---

[9] *Stocks, Bonds, Bills and Inflation, 1984 Yearbook,* (Chicago: R. G. Ibbotson and Associates, Inc., 1984).

[10] Lawrence Fisher and James H. Lorie, *A Half Century of Returns on Stocks and Bonds,* (Chicago: University of Chicago Graduate School of Business, 1977). Also, James H. Lorie and Lawrence Fisher, "Rates of Return on Investment in Common Stock," *Journal of Business,* January 1964, pp. 1–17. Lawrence Fisher and James H. Lorie, "Rates of Return on Investment in Common Stock: The Year-by-Year Record 1926–1965," *Journal of Business,* July 1968, pp. 219–316.

[11] Steven Katz, "The Price Adjustment Process of Bonds to Rating Classifications: A Test of Bond Market Efficiency," *Journal of Finance,* May 1974, pp. 551–59. George W. Hettenhouse and William S. Sartoris, "An Analysis of the Informational Content of Bond Rating Changes," *Quarterly Review of Economics and Business,* Summer 1976, pp. 65–78.

Nevertheless, there is evidence that the bond market may still be less efficient than the stock market (as viewed in terms of short-term trading profits).[12] The reason behind this belief is that the stock market is heavily weighted toward being a secondary market in which *existing* issues are constantly traded back and forth between investors. The bond market is more of a primary market, with the emphasis on new issues. Thus, bond investors are not constantly changing their portfolio with each new action of the corporation. Many institutional investors, such as insurance companies, are not active bond traders in existing issues but instead buy and hold bonds to maturity.

OTHER FORMS OF FIXED-INCOME SECURITIES

Our interest so far in this chapter has been on fixed-income securities, primarily in the form of bonds issued by corporations and various sectors of the government. There are other significant forms of debt instruments from which the investor may choose, and they are primarily short-term in nature.

Certificates of deposit (CDs).   These instruments are used by commercial banks and savings and loans (or other thrift institutions) and have traditionally been issued in small amounts such as $1,000 or $10,000, or large amounts such as $100,000 (jumbo CDs). The procedure is that the investor provides the funds and receives an interest-bearing certificate in return. The smaller CDs usually have a maturity of anywhere from six months to five years, and the jumbo CDs 30 to 90 days.

The jumbo CDs are usually sold to corporate investors, money market funds, pension funds, etc., while the small CDs are sold to individual investors. One main difference between the two CDs, besides the dollar amount, is that there is a secondary market for the jumbo CDs which allows these investors to maintain their liquidity without suffering an interest penalty. Investors in the small CDs have no such liquidity. Their only option is to redeem the certificate before maturity to the borrowing institution and suffer the interest penalty.

Small CDs have been traditionally regulated by the government, with federal regulatory agencies specifying the maximum interest rate that can be paid and the life of the CD. By 1986, all such interest rate regulations and ceilings will be phased out, and the free market will determine return. Any financial institution will be able to offer whatever it desires.

Commercial paper.   Another form of a short-term credit instrument is commercial paper, which is issued by large business corporations to the public. Commercial paper usually comes in minimum denominations of $25,000 and represents an unsecured promissory note. Commercial paper will carry a higher yield than small CDs or government Treasury bills and will be in line

---

[12] George E. Pinches and Clay Singleton, "The Adjustment of Stock Prices to Bond Rating Changes," *Journal of Finance,* March 1978, pp. 29–44.

with the yield on jumbo CDs. The maturity is usually 30, 60, or 90 days (though up to six months is possible).

Bankers' acceptance. This instrument often arises from foreign trade. The acceptance is a draft which is drawn on a bank for approval for future payment and is subsequently presented to the bank for payment. The investor buys the bankers' acceptance from an exporter (or other third party) at a discount with the intention of presenting it to the bank at face value at a future date. Bankers' acceptances provide yields comparable to commercial paper and jumbo CDs and have an active secondary or resale market.

Money market funds. These funds, previously discussed in Chapter 3, are not a direct form of fixed-income security, but rather represent a vehicle for individuals to buy short-term fixed-income securities through a mutual fund arrangement. An individual with a small amount to invest may pool his or her funds with others to buy high-yielding jumbo CDs and other similar instruments indirectly through the fund. There is a great deal of flexibility in withdrawing funds through check-writing privileges (usually in minimums of $500). As also mentioned in Chapter 3, individuals may get money market returns by depositing funds at a bank or savings and loan into a money market account. This account allows the individual to write three checks per month without penalty and presently requires a minimum balance of $1,000.

PREFERRED STOCK AS AN ALTERNATIVE TO DEBT

Finally, we look at preferred stock as an alternative to debt because some investors may elect to purchase preferred stock to satisfy their fixed-income needs. A $50 par value preferred stock issue paying $6.40 in annual dividends would provide an annual yield of 12.80 percent.

Preferred stock as an investment falls somewhere between bonds and common stock as far as protective provisions for the investor. In the case of debt, the bondholders have a contractual claim against the corporation and may force bankruptcy proceedings if interest payments are not forthcoming. Common stockholders have no such claim but are the ultimate owners of the firm and may receive dividends and other distributions after all prior claims have been satisfied. Preferred stockholders, on the other hand, are entitled to receive a stipulated dividend and must receive the dividend prior to any payment to common stockholders. However, the payment of preferred stock dividends is not compelling to the corporation as is true in the case of debt. In bad times, preferred stock dividends may be omitted by the corporation.

While preferred stock dividends are not tax deductible to the corporation, as would be true with interest on bonds, they do offer certain investors unique tax advantages. The tax law provides that any corporation which receives *preferred* or common stock dividends from another corporation must add only 15 percent of such dividends to its taxable income. Thus, if a $5

dividend is received, only 15 percent of the $5, or 75 cents, would be taxable to the corporate recipient.[13]

Because of this tax feature, preferred stock may carry a slightly lower yield than corporate bond issues of similar quality. As indicated in Table 9–11 (since the early 1960s) preferred stock has actually carried a yield of ¼ to 1 percent below comparable corporate bond issues. As interest rates rose in the late 1970s and 1980s, the spread in favor of corporate bonds became even larger, peaking at over 3 percent.

TABLE 9–11   Yields on Corporate Bonds and High-Grade Preferred Stock

Year	(1) High-grade bonds (percent)	(2) High-grade preferred stock (percent)	(2) – (1) Spread
1983	12.42%	10.55%	–1.87%
1982	14.41	11.68	–2.73
1981	14.75	11.64	–3.11
1980	12.50	10.11	–2.39
1979	9.94	8.54	–1.40
1978	8.92	7.76	–1.16
1977	8.24	7.12	–1.12
1972	7.49	6.56	–.93
1967	5.66	5.13	–.53
1962	4.47	4.21	–.26
1957	4.03	4.36	.33
1952	3.04	3.75	.71
1947	2.70	3.51	.81

Source: *Moody's Industrial Manual* and *Moody's Bond Record* (published by Moody's Investor Service, selected issues).

Features of Preferred Stock

Preferred stock may carry a number of features that are similar to a debt issue. For example, a preferred stock issue may be *convertible* into common stock. Also, preferred stock may be *callable* by the corporation at a stipulated price, generally slightly above par. The call feature of a preferred stock issue may be of particular interest in that preferred stock has no maturity date as such. If the corporation wishes to take preferred stock off the books, it must call in the issue or purchase the shares in the open market at the going market price.

---

[13] An individual investor does not enjoy the same tax benefit. The purpose of the corporate exemption is to avoid triple corporate taxation (that is, the issuing corporation is taxed once, and the receiving corporation's stockholders are taxed on subsequent dividend distributions, but the receiving corporation itself is only lightly taxed).

An important feature of preferred stock is that the dividend payments are usually *cumulative* in nature. That is, if preferred stock dividends are not paid in any one year, they accumulate and must be paid before common stockholders can receive any cash dividends. If preferred stock carries a $6.40 dividend and dividends are not paid for three years, the full $19.20 must be paid before any dividends go to common stockholders. This provides a strong incentive for the corporation to meet preferred stock dividend obligations on an annual basis even though preferred stock does not have a fixed, contractual obligation as is true of bonds. If the corporation gets behind in preferred stock dividends, it may create a situation that is quite difficult to get out of in the future. Being behind or in arrears on preferred stock dividends can make it almost impossible to sell new *common stock* because of the preclusion of common stock dividends until the preferred stockholders are satisfied.

An example of existing preferred stock issues is presented in Table 9–12. The issues are listed in *Moody's Bond Record,* and the daily price quotes may be found in the NYSE Composite Stock Transactions section of the *The Wall Street Journal* or other newspapers.

TABLE 9–12   Examples of Outstanding Preferred Stock Issues, August 1984

Issuer	Moody's rating*	Par value	Call price	Market price	Yield (percent)
American Telephone & Telegraph $3.64 cumulative preferred	aa1	$ 50	$102.50	33⅞	10.8
Gulf States Utilities Co. $8.80 cumulative preferred	baa3	100	105.88	62	13.0
Tenneco $7.40 cumulative preferred	baa2	100	101.00	66½	11.1

* Lowercase letters are used by Moody's to rate preferred stock.
Sources: *Moody's Bond Record* (Moody's Investor Service, Inc., New York, N.Y.) and *The Wall Street Journal.*

SUMMARY

Debt continues to play an important role in our economy from both the issuer's and investor's viewpoints. The primary fund raisers in the bond market are the U.S. Treasury, federally sponsored credit agencies, state and local governments, and corporations. The corporate sector is made up of industrials, public utilities, rails and transportation, as well as financial issues. The amount of new, long-term debt financing in the United States greatly exceeds the volume of equity financing.

Bond instruments are evaluated on the basis of a number of factors, including yield, maturity, method of repayment, security provisions, and tax treatment. The greater the protection and privileges accorded the bondholder,

the lower the yield. Thus, U.S. Treasury securities generally provide a lower yield than federally sponsored credit agency issues, and corporate securities provide a higher yield than governmental offerings. Because interest received on municipal bonds is tax-exempt to the recipient, they provide the lowest promised yield. However, when one converts this figure to an equivalent before-tax return on a taxable investment, the return may be quite attractive. Preferred stock also offers some unique tax advantages in the form of an 85 percent tax exemption on dividends paid to corporate purchasers.

A significant feature for a bond issue is the rating received by Moody's Investors Service, or Standard & Poor's. The ratings generally range from AAA to D and determine the required yield to sell a security in the marketplace. Although there are no firm and fast rules to determine a rating, strong attention is given to such factors as cash flow and earnings generation in relation to interest and other obligations (coverage ratios) as well as to operating margins and return on invested capital and total assets. Financial ratio analysis makes up perhaps 50 percent of the evaluation, with other factors of importance including the nature of the industry, the relative position of the firm within the industry, the pricing ability of the firm, and the overall quality of management (similar criteria have also been developed for municipal bonds).

The bond market appears to be reasonably efficient in terms of absorbing new information into the price of existing issues. Some researchers have suggested that the bond market may be slightly less efficient than the stock market in pricing outstanding issues because of the lack of a highly active secondary, or resale, market for certain issues. Insurance companies, pension funds, and bank trust departments are not normally active traders in their bond portfolios.

Short-term investors with a need for fixed income may look to certificates of deposit, commercial paper, bankers' acceptances, money market funds (and, of course, the previously discussed government securities) as sources of investment. Such factors as maturity, yield, and minimum amount must be considered.

Finally, preferred stock may also be thought of as an alternative form of a fixed-income security. Although dividends on preferred stock do not represent a contractual obligation to the firm as would be true of interest on debt, they must be paid before common stockholders can receive any payment. The preferred stock alternative may be important to the issuing firm because it provides some balance to the corporate capital structure.

IMPORTANT WORDS AND CONCEPTS

Indenture	**Call provision**
Par value	**Secured bond**
Coupon rate	**After-acquired property clause**
Maturity date	**Debenture**
Perpetual bonds	**Equipment trust certificate**
Serial bonds	**Subordinated debenture**
Sinking fund	**Income bonds**

Zero-coupon bonds

Municipal bonds

General obligation bonds

Revenue bonds

Government securities

Treasury bill, note, bond

Agency issues

Municipal securities

General obligation bonds

Revenue bonds

Private placements

CDs

Commercial paper

Certificates of deposit

Commercial paper

Bankers's acceptances

Money market funds

Preferred stock

DISCUSSION QUESTIONS

1. What are some of the major provisions found in the bond indenture?
2. What are four common means of repaying the principal of a bond issue?
3. Explain how a sinking fund works.
4. Why do you think the right to call a bond is often deferred for a period of time?
5. What is the nature of a mortgage agreement?
6. What is a senior security?
7. Discuss the statement, "A debenture may not be more risky than a secured bond."
8. How do zero-coupon bonds provide returns to investors? How is the return taxed?
9. Explain the concept of a pass-through certificate.
10. What is an agency issue? Are they direct obligations of the U.S. Treasury?
11. What tax advantages are associated with municipal bonds?
12. Distinguish between general obligation and revenue bonds.
13. How might an investor reduce the credit risk in buying a municipal bond issue?
14. What is an industrial bond?
15. What is shelf registration? Comment on its popularity.
16. What is meant by the private placement of a bond issue?
17. What is a split bond rating?
18. What does a bond quote of 72¼ represent in dollar terms?
19. Why might the bond market be considered less efficient than the stock market?
20. What is a jumbo CD? Comment on the secondary market for a jumbo CD.
21. Why would a corporate investor consider preferred stock over a bond? What is meant by the cumulative feature in preferred stock issues?

PROBLEMS

1. If an investor is in the 42 percent marginal tax bracket and can purchase a municipal bond paying 9.6 percent, what would the equivalent before-tax return from a nonmunicipal bond have to be to equate the two?

2.   Assume a $10,000 Treasury bill is quoted to pay 12 percent interest over a six-month period.
   a.   How much interest would the investor receive? 600
   b.   What will be the price of the Treasury bill?   9400
   c.   What will be the effective yield?   0.382
3.   In Problem 2, if the Treasury bill had only three months to maturity:
   a.   How much interest would the investor receive?
   b.   What will be the price of the Treasury bill?
   c.   What will be the effective yield?
4.   A corporation buys $100 par value preferred stock of another corporation. The dividend payment is 10.2 percent of par. The corporation is in a 40 percent tax bracket.
   a.   What will be the aftertax return on the dividend payment? (Show in dollars and percent).
   b.   Assume a second investment in a corporate bond pays 12 percent interest. What will be the aftertax return on the interest payment? (Show in percent).
   c.   Should the corporation choose the corporate bond over the preferred stock because it has a higher quoted yield (12.0 percent versus 10.2 percent)?

SELECTED REFERENCES

Ang, James S., and K. A. Patel, "Bond Rating Methods: Comparison and Validation." *Journal of Finance,* May 1975, pp. 631–40.

Bond Guide. Standard & Poor's Corporation, selected issues.

Fisher, Lawrence, and James H. Lorie. *A Half Century of Returns on Stocks and Bonds.* Chicago: University of Chicago Graduate School of Business, 1977.

Grier, Paul, and Steven Katz. "The Differential Effects of Bond Rating Changes among Industrial and Public Utility Bonds by Maturity." *Journal of Business,* April 1976, pp. 226–39.

Hettenhouse, George W., and William S. Sartoris. "An Analysis of the Informational Content of Bond Rating Changes." *Quarterly Review of Economics and Business,* Summer 1976, pp. 65–78.

Homer, Sidney. "Historical Evolution of Today's Bond Market." *Journal of Portfolio Management,* Spring 1975, pp. 6–11.

Horrigan, James O. "The Determination of Long-Term Credit Standing with Financial Ratios." *Empirical Research in Accounting.* Supplement to *Journal of Accounting Research,* 1966, pp. 44–62.

Ibbotson, Roger G., and Rex A. Sinquefield. "Stocks, Bonds, Bills, and Inflation: Year-by-Year Historical Returns (1926–1974)." *Journal of Business,* January 1976, pp. 11–47.

Katz, Steven. "The Price Adjustment Process of Bonds to Rating Classifications: A Test of Bond Market Efficiency." *Journal of Finance,* May 1974, pp. 551–59.

Moody's Bond Record. Moody's Investors Service, selected issues.

Pinches, George E., and Kent A. Mingo. "A Multivariate Analysis of Industrial Bond Ratings." *Journal of Finance,* March 1973, pp. 1–18.

Pinches, George E.; Kent A. Mingo; and Clay Singleton. "The Adjustment of Stock Prices to Bond Rating Charges." *Journal of Finance,* March 1978, pp. 29–44.

Pogue, Thomas F., and Robert M. Soldofsky. "What's in a Bond Rating?" *Journal of Financial and Quantitative Analysis,* June 1969, pp. 201–8.

Reilly, Frank K., and Michael D. Joehnk. "The Association between Market-Determined Risk Measures for Bonds and Bond Ratings." *Journal of Finance,* December 1976, pp. 1387–1403.

Ross, Irwin. "Higher Stakes in the Bond Rating Game." *Fortune,* April 1976, pp. 133–42.

Stocks, Bonds, Bills, and Inflation, 1984 Yearbook. Chicago: A. G. Ibbotson and Associates, Inc., 1984.

Yawitz, Jess B. "Risk Premia on Municipal Bonds." *Journal of Financial and Quantitative Analysis,* September 1978, pp. 475–85.

Yawitz, Jess B., and William J. Marshall. "Risk and Return in the Government Bond Market." *Journal of Portfolio Management,* Summer 1977, pp. 48–52.

Yawitz, Jess B.; George H. Hepel; and William J. Marshall. "A Risk-Return Approach to the Selection of Optimal Government Bond Portfolios." *Financial Management,* Autumn 1976, pp. 36–45.

Chapter 10

PRINCIPLES OF BOND VALUATION AND INVESTMENT

The old notion that a bond represents an inherently conservative investment can be quickly dispelled. A $1,000, 10 percent coupon rate bond with 25 years to maturity could rise $214.80 or fall $157.60 in response to a 2 percent change in interest rates in the marketplace. According to a study by Ibbotson and Sinquefield, investors enjoyed a total return of 43.79 percent on long-term corporate bonds in 1982 and a return of over 18 percent in 1970 and 1976. By contrast, the same investor would have lost 8.09 percent on his bond portfolio in 1969.[1] While bond prices may not normally be as volatile as those of stocks, there are still many opportunities for wide fluctuations in value.

In this chapter, we will examine the valuation process for bonds, the relationship of interest rate changes to the business cycle, and various investment and speculative strategies related to bond maturity, quality, and pricing.

FUNDAMENTALS OF THE BOND VALUATION PROCESS

The price of a bond at any point in time represents the present value of future interest payments plus the present value of the par value of the bond at maturity. We say that:

$$V = \sum_{t=1}^{n} \frac{C_t}{(1 + i)^t} + \frac{P_n}{(1 + i)^n} \qquad (10\text{--}1)$$

where:

V = Market value or price of the bond.
n = Number of periods.
t = Each period.
C_t = Coupon or interest payment for each period, t.
P_n = Par or maturity value.
i = Interest rate in the market.

We can use logarithms and various mathematical calculations to find the value of a bond or simply use Table 10–1 and Table 10–2 to determine the present value of C_t and P_n and add the two together. (Expanded versions of these two tables are presented in appendixes at the end of the text.)

Assume a bond pays 10% interest or $100 ($C_t$) for 20 years ($n$) and has a par ($P_n$) or maturity value of $1,000. The interest rate (i) in the marketplace is assumed to be 12 percent. The present value of the bond, using annual compounding, is shown to be $850.90 as follows:

Present value of coupon payments (C_t) *(from Table 10–1)*	*Present value of maturity value* (P_n) *(from Table 10–2)*
n = 20, i = 12%	n = 20, i = 12%
$100 × 7.469 = $746.90	$1,000 × .104 = $104.00

Present value of coupon payments	= $746.90
Present value of maturity value	= 104.00
Value of bond	= $850.90

---

[1] *Stocks, Bonds, Bills and Inflation, 1984 Yearbook* (Chicago: A. G. Ibbotson and Associates, Inc., 1984).

TABLE 10–1   Present Value of an Annuity of $1 (coupon payments ($C_t$)

Number of periods (*n*)	Interest rate (*i*)					
	4 percent	*5 percent*	*6 percent*	*8 percent*	*10 percent*	*12 percent*
1	.962	.952	.943	.926	.909	.893
2	1.886	1.859	1.833	1.783	1.736	1.690
3	2.775	2.723	2.673	2.577	2.487	2.402
4	3.630	3.546	3.465	3.312	3.170	3.037
5	4.452	4.329	4.212	3.993	3.791	3.605
10	8.111	7.722	7.360	6.710	6.145	5.650
20	13.590	12.462	11.470	9.818	8.514	7.469
30	17.292	15.373	13.765	11.258	9.427	8.055
40	19.793	17.160	15.046	11.925	9.779	8.244

Because the bond pays 10 percent of the par value when the competitive market rate of interest is 12 percent, investors will only pay $850.90 for the issue. This bond is said to be selling at a discount of $149.10 from the $1,000 par value. The discount is determined by several factors, such as the years to maturity, spread between the coupon and market rates, and the level of the coupon. While the $850.90 price was calculated using annual compounding, coupon payments on most bonds are paid semiannually. To adjust for this, we *divide* the annual coupon payment and required interest rate in the market by two and *multiply* the number of periods by two. Using the same example as before but with the appropriate adjustments for semiannual compounding, we show a slightly lower price of $849.30 as follows:

Present value of coupon payments (C_t) *(from Table 10–1)*	*Present value of maturity value (P_n)* *(from Table 10–2)*
$n = 40, i = 6\%$	$n = 40, i = 6\%$
$50 \times 15.046 = $752.30	$1,000 \times .097 = $97.00

Present value of coupon payments	= $752.30
Present value of maturity value	= 97.00
Value of bond	= $849.30

We see a minor adjustment in price as a result of using the more exacting process. To check our answer, in Table 10–3 we present an excerpt from a bond table indicating prices for 10 percent and 12 percent annual coupon rate bonds at various market rates of interest (yields to maturity) and time periods. Though the values are quoted on an annual basis, the assumption is that semiannual discounting, such as that shown in our second example, was utilized. Note that for a bond with a 10 percent coupon rate, a 12 percent market rate (yield to maturity), and 20 years to run, the value in the table is 84.93. This is assumed to represent 84.93 percent of par value. Since the par value of the bond in our example was $1,000, the answer would be $849.30 ($1,000 × 84.93%). This is precisely the answer we got in our second example. A typical

TABLE 10–2   Present Value of a Single Amount of $1 (par or maturity value P_n)

Number of periods (n)	Interest rate (i)					
	4 percent	*5 percent*	*6 percent*	*8 percent*	*10 percent*	*12 percent*
1	.962	.952	.943	.926	.909	.893
2	.925	.907	.890	.857	.826	.797
3	.889	.864	.840	.794	.751	.712
4	.855	.823	.792	.735	.683	.636
5	.822	.784	.747	.681	.621	.567
10	.676	.614	.558	.463	.386	.322
20	.456	.377	.312	.215	.149	.104
30	.308	.231	.174	.099	.057	.033
40	.208	.142	.097	.046	.022	.011

modern bond table may be 1,000 pages long and cover time periods up to 30 years and interest rates from ¼ to 30 percent. For professionals working with bonds on a continual basis, financial calculators and computers are replacing these tables, with quicker response time.

TABLE 10–3   Excerpts from Bond Value Table

Yield to maturity (percent)	Coupon rate (10 percent)				Coupon rate (12 percent)				Yield to maturity (percent)
	1 year	*5 years*	*10 years*	*20 years*	*1 year*	*5 years*	*10 years*	*20 years*	
8%	101.89%	108.11%	113.50%	119.79%	103.77%	116.22%	127.18%	139.59%	8%
9	100.94	103.96	106.50	109.20	102.81	111.87	119.51	127.60	9
10	100.00	100.00	100.00	100.00	101.86	107.72	112.46	117.16	10
11	99.08	96.23	94.02	91.98	100.92	103.77	105.98	108.02	11
12	98.17	92.64	88.53	84.93	100.00	100.00	100.00	100.00	12
13	97.27	89.22	83.47	78.78	99.09	96.41	94.49	92.93	13
14	96.38	85.95	78.81	73.34	98.19	92.98	89.41	86.67	14

Source: Reprinted by permission from the *Thorndike Encyclopedia of Banking and Financial Tables*, 1981, Copyright © 1981, Warren Gorham and Lamont Inc., 210 South Street, Boston, Mass. All rights reserved.

RATES OF RETURN

Bonds are evaluated on a number of different types of returns, including current yield, yield to maturity, yield to call, and anticipated realized yield.

Current Yield

The current yield, which is shown in *The Wall Street Journal* and many daily newspapers, is the annual interest payment divided by the price of the bond.

An example might be a 12 percent coupon rate $1,000 par value bond selling for $900. The current yield would be:

$$\frac{\$120}{\$900} = 13.3\%$$

The 13.3 percent indicates the annual cash rate of return an investor would receive in interest payments on the $900 investment, but does not include any adjustments for capital gains or losses as bond prices change in response to new market interest rates. Another problem with current yield is that it does not take into consideration the maturity date of a debt instrument. A bond with 1 year to run and another with 20 years to run would have the same current yield quote if interest payments were $120 and the price were $900. Clearly, the one-year bond would be preferable under this circumstance because the investor would not only get $120 in interest, but also a gain in value of $100 ($1000 − $900) within a one-year time period.

Yield to Maturity

Yield to maturity takes into consideration annual interest received, the difference between the current bond price and its maturity value, and the number of years to maturity. Returning to our earlier example, if a bond pays $100 in annual interest and sells for $849.30 with 20 years to maturity, the investor would be receiving $100 annually plus the $150.70 differential, spread over 20 years, or $7.54 per year. This would indicate a total annual return of $107.54. We would also think of the investor's average investment as being approximately the mid-point between the initial investment of $849.30, and the ending value of $1,000. Thus, the average investment would be $924.65. The yield to maturity is the total return an investor would receive from income plus capital appreciation assuming the bond is held to maturity. The *approximate* yield to maturity would be:

$$\frac{\$107.54}{\$924.65} = 11.63\%$$

The preceding calculations can be summarized into a formula in which we show:

$$Y' = \frac{\text{Coupon payment } (C_t) + \dfrac{\text{Par value } (P_n) - \text{Market value } (V)}{\text{Number of periods } (n)}}{\dfrac{\text{Market value } (V) + \text{Par value } (P_n)}{2}} \qquad (10\text{--}2)$$

On an annual basis, we indicate:

Y' = Approximate yield to maturity.
Coupon payment = $100.
Par or maturity value = $1,000.

Market value = $849.30.
Number of periods = 20.

$$Y' = \frac{\$100 + \dfrac{\$1,000 - \$849.30}{20}}{\dfrac{\$849.30 + \$1,000}{2}}$$

$$= \frac{\$100 + \dfrac{\$150.70}{20}}{\$924.65}$$

$$= \frac{\$107.54}{\$924.65}$$

$$= 11.63\%$$

This answer is merely an approximation of exact yield to maturity. The precise answer can only be found mathematically by returning to Formula (10–1) and determining the precise interest rate (i) that allows us to discount back all future coupon payments (C_t) and the par or maturity value (P_n) at the end of n periods to arrive at the current price. The yield to maturity may be thought of as the internal rate of return or yield on the bond. Since computing the exact yield to maturity is a very involved, trial-and-error process, bond tables are readily available to allow us to determine this value. As a matter of fact, all we have to do is return to Table 10–3, the bond value table, and use it in a slightly different fashion. We pick our coupon rate, read across the table for number of years, into the table for price, and then read to the outside column to determine yield. A 10 percent coupon rate bond with 20 years to run, selling at $849.30 (84.93 in the table), provides the investor with a yield to maturity of 12 percent.[2]

Note the exact answer in this case is .37 percent above the approximation (12 percent versus 11.63 percent). In the jargon of bond trading, each 1/100th of 1 percent is referred to as a basis point, so we say the difference is 37 basis points. The approximate-yield-to-maturity method tends to understate exact yield to maturity for issues trading at a discount (in this case, the bond is priced at $849.30). The opposite effect takes place for bonds trading at a premium (above par value). The extent of the discrepancy is directly related to the magnitude of the discount or premium and the life span on the bond. For a $950 bond with five years to maturity, the difference between approximate yield and exact yield is a mere .03 percent, or three basis points.[3]

The concept of *yield to maturity* is used interchangeably with the term *market rate of interest*. When we say the market rate of interest is 12 percent, it is the equivalent of saying the required yield to maturity is 12 percent.

---

[2] Interpolation may also be used to find intermediate values in the table.

[3] It should be pointed out that in all our bond problems, we are assuming that we are buying the bond at the beginning of an interest payment period. To the extent there is accrued interest, we would have to modify our calculations slightly.

Yield to Call

As discussed in the preceding chapter on bond fundamentals, not all fixed-income securities are held to maturity. To the extent a debt instrument may be called in prior to maturity, a separate calculation is necessary to determine yield to the call date. Assume a 20-year bond was initially issued at a 13.5 percent interest rate, and after two years, rates have dropped. Let us assume the bond is currently selling for $1,180 and the yield to maturity on the bond is 11.15 percent. However, the investor who purchases the bonds for $1,180 may not be able to hold the bonds for the remaining 18 years because the issue can be called. Under these circumstances yield to maturity may not be the appropriate measure of return over the expected holding period.

In the present case we shall assume the bonds can be called in five years after issue at $1,090. Thus, the investor who buys the bonds two years after issue can have his bonds called back after three more years at $1,090. To compute yield to call, we determine the approximate interest rate that will equate an $1,180 investment today with $135 (13.5 percent) per year for the next three years plus a payoff or call price value of $1,090 at the end of three years. We can adjust Formula (10–2) (approximate yield to maturity) to Formula (10–3) (approximate yield to call).

$$Y'_c = \frac{\text{Coupon payment } (C_t) + \dfrac{\text{Call price } (P_c) - \text{Market price } (V)}{\text{Number of periods to call } (n_c)}}{\dfrac{\text{Market value } (V) + \text{Call price } (P_c)}{2}} \quad (10\text{–}3)$$

On an annual basis, we show:

Y'_c = Approximate yield to call.
Coupon payment = $135.
Call price = $1,090.
Market value = $1,180.
Number of periods to call = 3.

$$Y'_c = \frac{\$135 + \dfrac{\$1,090 - \$1,180}{3}}{\dfrac{\$1,180 + \$1,090}{2}}$$

$$= \frac{\$135 + \dfrac{-\$90}{3}}{\$1,135}$$

$$= \frac{\$135 - \$30}{\$1,135}$$

$$= \frac{\$105}{\$1,135}$$

$$= 9.25\%$$

The yield to call figure of 9.25 percent is 238 basis points less than the yield to maturity figure of 11.63 percent. Clearly, the investor needs to be

aware of the differential. Generally speaking, any time the market price of a bond is equal to or greater than the call price, the investor should do a separate calculation for yield to call.[4]

In the case where market interest rates are much lower than the coupon, there is always the chance that the company will call the bond. Because of this possibility, the call price often serves as an upper price limit and further reductions in market interest rates will not cause this callable bond to increase in price. In other words, investors' capital gain potential may be quite limited with bonds selling at a premium.

Anticipated Realized Yield

Finally, we have the case where the investor purchases the bond with the intention of holding the bond for a period that is different from either the call date or the maturity date. Under this circumstance, we examine the anticipated realized yield for the holding period.

Assume an investor buys a 12.5 percent coupon bond for $900. Based on his forecasts of lower interest rates, he anticipates the bond will go to $1,050 in three years. The formula for the approximate realized yield is:

$$Y'_r = \frac{\text{Coupon payment } (C_t) + \dfrac{\text{Realized price } (P_r) - \text{Market price } (V)}{\text{Number of periods to realization } (n_r)}}{\dfrac{\text{Market value } (V) + \text{Realized price } (P_r)}{2}}$$

(10–4)

The terms are:

Coupon payment = $125.
Realized price = $1,050.
Market price = $900.
Number of periods to realization = 3.

$$Y'_r = \frac{\$125 + \dfrac{\$1,050 - \$900}{3}}{\dfrac{\$900 + \$1,050}{2}}$$

$$= \frac{\$125 + \dfrac{\$150}{3}}{\$975}$$

$$= \frac{\$125 + \$50}{\$975}$$

$$= \frac{\$175}{\$975}$$

$$= 17.95\%$$

---

[4] Bond tables may also be used to find the exact value for yield to call. A source is *Thorndike Encyclopedia of Banking and Financial Tables* (Boston: Warren, Gorham & Lamont, 1981).

The anticipated return of 17.95 percent would not be unusual in periods of falling interest rates such as 1970, 1976, and 1982.

Reinvestment Assumption

Throughout our analysis, when we have talked about yield to maturity, call, or realization, we have assumed that the determined rate also represents an appropriate rate for reinvestment of funds. If yield to maturity is 11 percent or 12 percent, then it is assumed that coupon payments, as they come in, can also be reinvested at that rate. To the extent that this is an unrealistic assumption, the investor will wish to temper his thinking. For example, if it is anticipated that returns can be reinvested at a higher rate in the future, this increases true yield, and the opposite effect would be present for a decline in interest rates.

The reinvestment topic is more fully developed in Chapter 11, and the interested student can also consult *Inside the Yield Book: New Tools for Bond Market Strategy*[5] for a more complete development of the reinvestment assumption.

THE MOVEMENT OF INTEREST RATES

In developing our discussion of bond valuation and investments, we have observed that lower interest rates bring higher bond prices and profits. A glance back at Table 10–3 (right-hand portion) indicates that a 20-year, 12 percent coupon bond will sell for $1,171.60 if yields to maturity on competitive bonds decline to 10 percent and to $1,276.00 when yields decline to 9 percent. The maturity of the bond is also important, with the impact on price being much greater for longer-term obligations.

The investor who wishes to make a substantial profit in the bond market must make an attempt to anticipate the turns and directions of interest rates. While much of the literature on efficient markets would indicate this is an extremely difficult task,[6] Wall Street economists, bank economists, and many others rely upon interest rate forecasts to formulate financial strategies. The fact that short-term and long-term rates do not necessarily move in the same direction or move with the same magnitude makes the task even more formidable. Nevertheless, some historical analysis and knowledge of interest rate patterns over the business cycle is useful in making investment decisions.

Interest rates have long been viewed as a coincident indicator in our economy; that is to say, they are thought to move in concert with industrial

---

[5] S. Homer and M. L. Leibowitz, *Inside the Yield Book: New Tools for Bond Market Strategy* (Englewood Cliffs, N.J.: Prentice-Hall, 1972).

[6] Michael J. Prell, "How well do the Experts Forecast Interest Rates?" Federal Reserve Bank of Kanses City, *Monthly Review,* September–October, 1973, pp. 3–13. Oswald D. Bowlin and John D. Martin, "Extrapolations of Yields over the Short Run: Forecast or Folly?" *Journal of Monetary Economics* (1975), pp. 275–88. Richard Roll. *The Behavior of Interest Rates* (New York: Basic Books, 1970).

production, gross national product, and similar measures of general economic health. This is generally true, although in the recessions of 1969–70, 1973–75, and 1980–81 interest rates actually lagged behind the decline in industrial production.

This pattern of lag between interest rate changes and the business cycle, witnessed since the mid-1960s, can be explained in terms of inflationary expectations. In earlier time periods, the occurrence of a recession tended to immediately break off inflationary expectations. Since the mid-60s, a decline in inflationary rates has only taken place well into the recession, deferring the drop-off of interest rates.

While inflationary expectations have their greatest influence on long-term rates, a number of other factors also influence overall interest rates. The demand for funds by individuals, business, and the government represent one side of the equation, with the desire for savings and Federal Reserve policy influencing the supply side. A classic study by Feldstein and Eckstein found that bond yields were inversely related to the money supply (the slower the growth, the higher the interest rates) and directly related to economic activity, the demand for loanable funds by the government, the level of inflation, and changes in short-term interest rate *expectations*.[7]

Term Structure of Interest Rates

Of general importance to understanding the level of interest rates is the development of an appreciation for the relationship between the level of interest rates and the maturity of the debt obligation. There is no one single interest rate, but rather a whole series of interest rates associated with the given maturity of bonds.

The term structure of interest rates depicts the relationship between maturity and interest rates. It is sometimes called a yield curve because yields on existing securities having maturities from 3 months to 30 years are plotted on a graph to develop the curve. In order to eliminate any business risk consideration, the securities analyzed are usually U.S. Treasury issues. Examples of four different types of term structures are presented in Figure 10–1.

In panel (a) we see an ascending term structure pattern in which interest rates increase with the lengthening of the maturity dates. When the term structure is in this posture, it is a general signal that interest rates will rise in the future. In panel (b) we see a descending pattern of interest rates, with this pattern generally predictive of lower interest rates. Panel (c) is a variation of panel (b), with the hump indicating intermediate-term interest rates. This particular configuration is an even stronger indicator that interest rates may be declining in the future. Finally, in panel (d) we see a flat-term structure indicating investor indifference between debt instrument maturity. This generally indicates there is no discernible pattern for the future of interest rates. There

[7] Martin Feldstein and Otto Eckstein, "The Fundamental Determinants of the Interest Rate," *The Review of Economics and Statistics,* November 1970, pp. 363–75.

FIGURE 10–1   Term Structure of Interest Rates

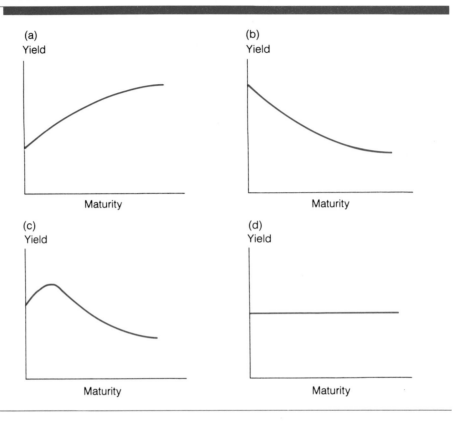

are several theories of interest rates that are used to explain the particular shape of the yield curve. We shall review three of these theories.

Expectations hypothesis.   The dominant rationale for the shape of the term structure of interest rates rests on a phenomenon called the expectations hypothesis. The hypothesis is that any long-term rate is an average of the expectations of future short-term rates over the applicable time horizon. Thus, if lenders expect short-term rates to be continually increasing in the future, they will demand higher long-term rates. Conversely, if they anticipate short-term rates to be declining, they will accept lower long-term rates. An example may be helpful. Suppose that the interest rate on a one-year Treasury bill is 10 percent, and that after one year it is assumed a new one-year Treasury bill may be bought to yield 12 percent. At the end of year two it is assumed that a third one-year Treasury bill may be bought to yield 14 percent. In other words, the investor can buy (this is sometimes called "roll over") three one-year Treasury bills in yearly succession, each with an expected one-year return.

But what about the investor who buys a one-, two-, or three-year security today? The yield he will require will be based on expectations about the future. For the one-year security, there is no problem. The 10 percent return will be acceptable. But the investor who buys a two-year security now will want the average of the 10 percent he could expect in the first year and the 12 percent expected in the second year, or 11 percent.[8] An investor who buys a three-year security will demand an average of 10, 12, and 14 percent, or a 12 percent return. Higher expected interest rates in the future will mean that longer maturities will carry higher yields than will shorter maturities. The reverse would be true if interest rates were expected to go down.

The expectations hypothesis tends to be reinforced by lender/borrower strategy. If investors (lenders) expect interest rates to increase in the future, they will attempt to lend short-term and avoid long-term obligations so as to diminish losses on long maturity obligations when interest rates go up. Borrowers have exactly the opposite incentive. When interest rates are expected to go up, they will attempt to borrow long-term now to lock in the lower rates. Thus the desire of lenders to lend short term (and avoid the long-term) and the desire of borrowers to borrow long-term (and avoid short-term) accentuates the expected pattern of rising interest rates. The exact opposite motivations are in effect when interest rates are expected to decline.

Liquidity preference theory.   The second theory used to explain the term structure of interest rates is called the liquidity preference theory. The shape of the term structure curve tends to be upward sloping more than any other pattern. This reflects a recognition of the fact that long maturity obligations are subject to greater price change movements when interest rates change. Because of the increased risk of holding longer-term maturities, investors demand a higher return to hold long-term securities relative to short-term securities. This is called the liquidity preference theory of interest rates. Since short-term securities are more easily turned into cash without the risk of large price changes, investors will pay a higher price for short-term securities and thus receive a lower yield.

Market segmentation theory.   The third theory related to the term structure of interest rates is called the market segmentation theory and focuses on the demand side of the market. There are several large institutional participants in the bond market, each with his own maturity preferences. Banks tend to prefer short-term liquid securities to match the nature of their deposits, whereas life insurance companies prefer long-term bonds to match their long-run obligations. The behavior of these two institutions, as well as of savings and loans, often creates pressure on short-term or long-term rates but very little in the intermediate market of 5–7 year maturities. This theory helps to focus on

---

[8] The expectations hypothesis actually uses the geometric mean (compound growth rate) rather than the arithmetic mean (simple average) used in the example. For a short number of years, the two means would be quite similar.

the accumulation or liquidation of securities by institutions during the different phases of the business cycle and the resultant impact on the yield curve.

As stated earlier, the expectations hypothesis is probably the most dominant theory, but all three theories have some part in the creation of the term structure of interest rates. Also, as we discussed, the curve takes on many different shapes over time. For example, in May of 1981 the yield curve had reached new high levels and was steeply downsloping in anticipation of lower interest rates, as viewed in Figure 10–2. Lower rates came, and by May of

FIGURE 10–2   Yield Curve Patterns

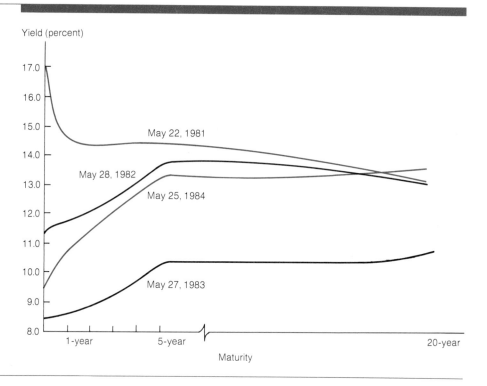

1982, short-term rates had fallen sharply, but long-term rates were still relatively high, as investors had fears of high continued inflation. The term structure at this point was slightly humped, but by May 1983 the curve had shifted down significantly for all maturities, and was now presenting a more normal upsloping yield curve. Over the two-year period from May of 1981 to May of 1983, three-month Treasury bills dropped from 16.99 percent to 8.48 percent, for a total decline of 851 basis points. Long-term Treasuries went from 13.26 percent to 10.75 percent over the same two-year period, for a decline of only

251 basis points. One year later, by May 25, 1984, interest rates had started to rise on fears that large government deficits would rekindle rampant inflation. What happened between May 1983 and May 1984 was that long-term rates rose to 13.49 percent, or a change of 274 basis points, more than wiping out the previous decrease since 1981. Obviously, investors in long-term bonds suffered large capital losses between May 1983 and May 1984. This pattern of interest rate advances and declines and yield curve changes no doubt will take place many times throughout the 1980s.

Before concluding our discussion of the term structure of interest rates and proceeding to the development of investment strategies, one final observation is significant. Short-term rates, which are most influenced by Federal Reserve policy in attempting to regulate the money supply and economy, are much more volatile in nature than long-term rates. An examination of Figure 10–3 indicates that *short-term* prime commercial paper rates move much more widely than *long-term,* high-grade corporate bond rates.

FIGURE 10–3   Relative Volatility of Short-Term and Long-Term Interest Rates

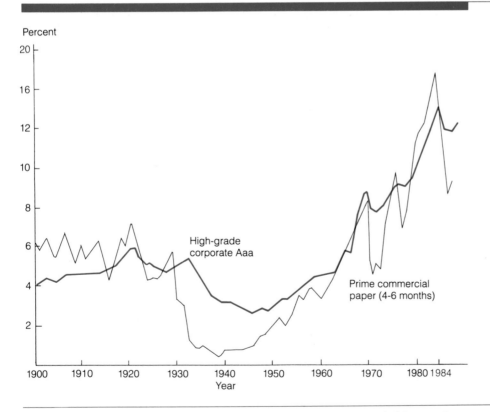

Source: *Federal Reserve Historical Chart Book* (Washington, D.C.: Federal Reserve Board of Governors).

INVESTMENT STRATEGY—INTEREST RATE CONSIDERATIONS

Thus far in this chapter, we have examined the different valuation procedures for determining the price or yield on a bond and the methods for evaluating the future course of interest rates. We now bring this knowledge together in the form of various investment strategies.

When the bond investor believes that interest rates are going to fall, he will take a long position in the market by buying long-term bonds and try to maximize the price movement pattern associated with a change in interest rates. He can do this by considering the *maturity, coupon rate,* and *quality* of the issue.

Because the impact of an interest rate change is much greater on long-term securities, the investor will generally look for extended maturities. The impact of various changes in yields on bond prices for a 12 percent coupon rate bond can be examined in Table 10–4. For example, looking at the second line from the bottom, we see a 2 percent drop in interest rates would cause a 1.86 percent increase in value for a bond with one year to maturity, but an 18.93 percent increase in value for a bond with 30 years to maturity.

TABLE 10–4   Change in Market Prices of Bonds for Shifts in Yields to Maturity (12 percent coupon rate)

Yield change (percent)	Maturity (years)				
	1	5	10	20	30
+3%	−2.69%	−10.30%	−15.29%	−18.89%	−19.74%
+2	−1.81	− 7.02	−10.59	−13.33	−14.04
+1	− .91	− 3.57	− 5.01	− 7.08	− 7.52
−1	+ .92	+ 3.77	+ 5.98	+ 8.02	+ 8.72
−2	+1.86	+ 7.72	+12.46	+17.16	+18.93
−3	+2.81	+11.87	+19.51	+27.60	+30.96

We can also observe that the effect of interest rate changes is not symmetrical. Drops in interest rates will cause proportionally greater gains than increases in interest rates will cause losses, particularly as we expand the maturity. An evaluation of the 30-year column running from −19.74 percent to +30.96 percent will confirm this point.[9]

---

[9] A sophisticated investor would also consider the concept of *duration.* Duration is defined as the weighted average time to recover interest and principal. For a bond that pays interest (which includes most cases except zero-coupon bonds), duration will be shorter than maturity, in that interest payments start almost immediately. Portfolio strategy may call for maximizing duration rather than maturity in order to achieve maximum movement.

Though we have emphasized the need for long maturities in maximizing price movement, the alert student will recall that short-term interest rates generally move up and down more than long-term interest rates as was indicated in Figure 10–3. What if short-term rates are more volatile—even though long-term rates have a greater price impact—which then do we choose? The answer is fairly direct. The mathematical impact of long maturities on price changes far outweighs the more volatile feature of short-term interest rates. A one-year debt instrument would need to have an interest rate *change* of almost *10 percent* to have the equivalent impact of a 1 percent change in a 30-year debt obligation.

Another consideration in maximizing price movement is the coupon rate level of the bond. Assume two bonds have "roughly" the same yield to maturity and that one possesses a 13.5 percent coupon rate and is trading well above par while the other has a 5 percent coupon rate and is trading substantially below par. The price of the lower coupon rate bond is more sensitive to interest rate changes. For example, a 5 percent coupon rate, 30-year bond will advance 30.42 percent as a result of a 2 percent decline in interest rates, whereas the 13.5 percent coupon rate bond will move only 16.71 percent.[10] This is an important point if the investor expects to trade bonds actively over the interest rate cycle. The next chapter on duration provides a more comprehensive analysis of price sensitivity, coupon rates, maturity, market rates, and their combined impact on bond prices.

A final consideration is the quality of the offering. High-quality securities are more sensitive to *pure* interest rate changes than are lower-quality issues. Most of the movement in Treasury securities or Aaa utilities is a function of interest rates, whereas lower-grade corporates may also be influenced by GNP, industry projections, and corporate profits. To take advantage of a perceived interest rate move, quality should be stressed. For other investment strategies related to a perceived improvement in business conditions, lower-quality corporates may be an ideal investment outlet.

Actually some investment managers put together portfolios of high-risk, low-grade bonds. The headline in a *Wall Street Journal* article of May 16, 1984, read "Merrill Lynch Seeks 'Junk-Bond' Buyers for Cash to Finish Seabrook Nuclear Unit." These so-called junk bonds are extremely speculative and carry high yields with a relatively high risk of default. These bonds may behave more like common stock than bonds and rally on good news, actual interest payments, or improving business conditions. Several institutions such as Merrill Lynch, Fidelity Investments, and Drexel Burnham Lambert Inc. manage a mutual fund with a junk-bond emphasis. One such manager is James R. Caywood of Security Pacific Corporation. He uses a large amount of junk-bonds, a small amount of convertible bonds, and financial futures or options to hedge his funds risk.[11] During the last half of 1983 and first half of 1984 his

---

[10] Tax benefits and protection from call provisions are other advantages of low coupon rate bonds and are discussed in a subsequent section.

[11] Financial futures and bond options are covered in Chapter 15.

fund increased by over 8 percent while the Salomon Bros. High-Grade Bond Index fell 6.8 percent. Junk bonds can be fun to play with, but for now let's return to a more conventional approach.

Example of Interest Rate Change

Let's look at an actual example of an interest rate change. Assume we buy 20-year, Aaa utility bonds at par providing a 12 percent coupon rate. Further assume that interest rates on these bonds in the market fall to 10 percent.[12] Based on Table 10–5, the new price on the bonds would be $1,171.60 ($1,000 × 117.16).

TABLE 10–5   Bond Value Table (coupon rate 12 percent)

Yield to maturity (percent)	Number of years		
	10	20	30
8%	127.18%	139.59%	145.25%
10	112.46	117.16	118.93
12	100.00	100.00	100.00
14	89.41	86.55	85.96

Source: Reprinted by permission from the *Thorndike Encyclopedia of Banking and Financial Tables,* 1981, copyright © 1981, Warren, Gorham and Lamont Inc., 210 South Street, Boston, Mass. All rights reserved.

Though we have assumed the gain in price from $1,000 to $1,171.60 took place very quickly, even if the time horizon were one year, the gain is still 17.16 percent annually. This is only part of the picture. An integral part of many bond interest rate strategies is the use of margin or borrowed funds. For government securities, it is possible to margin as low as 5 percent, and on high-quality utility or corporate bonds, the requirement is generally 30 percent. In the above case, if we had put down 30 percent and borrowed the balance, the rate of return on invested capital would have been 57.2 percent.

$$\frac{\text{Return}}{\text{Investment}} = \frac{\$171.60}{\$300.00} = 57.2\%$$

Though we would have had to pay interest on the $700 we borrowed, the interest on the bonds (which belongs to the borrower/investor) would have partially or fully covered this expense. Also if interest rates drop down further to 8 percent, our leveraged return could be over 100 percent on our original investment.

---

[12] Buying bonds at a lower coupon rate, that are trading at a discount from par, would provide greater price volatility as previously indicated, but would complicate our analysis unnecessarily. We will also not worry about calls for now; this matter will be given attention in the next section.

Lest the overanxious student sell all his or her worldly possessions to participate in this impressive gain, there are many admonitions. Even though we think interest rates are going down, they may do quite the opposite. A 2 percent *increase* in interest rates would cause a $134.50 loss or a negative return on a leveraged investment of $300 of 44.8 percent. At the very time it appears that interest rates should be falling due to an anticipated or actual recession, the Federal Reserve may generate the opposite effect by tightening the money supply as an anti-inflation weapon as it did in 1970, 1974, 1979, and 1981. Having now given adequate warning, the authors would summarize the discussion of interest rate plays by saying there are opportunities for unusually large profits with the anticipated risks.

INVESTMENT STRATEGY—DEEP DISCOUNT VERSUS PAR BONDS

Another feature in analyzing a bond is the current pricing of the bond in regard to its par value. Bonds that were previously issued at interest rates significantly lower than current market levels may trade at deep discounts from par. The long-term secular upward trend in interest rates since World War II has made the deep discount bond very common. As an example, consider the pricing pattern for a number of American Telephone and Telegraph bonds in mid-1984.

Coupon rate (percent)	Maturity year	Price
3.875%	1990	$718.75
7.000	2001	562.50
7.125	2003	558.75
8.800	2005	661.25
8.625	2007	642.50

Deep discount bonds generally trade at a lower yield to maturity than bonds selling at close to par. There are two reasons for this. One is that a deep discount bond has almost no chance to be called away. Even if prices go up because of falling interest rates, the price is still likely to be below par value. Because of this protection against a caller and the associated risk of having to reinvest principal at a lower interest rate, the investor in deep discount bonds accepts a lower yield. Secondly, the deep discount bond offers the investor certain tax advantages; namely, that part of the return will represent capital gains as opposed to being subject to the ordinary income tax provision associated with pure interest income. We are assuming that the capital gain is long-term (bond owned for more than six months) and therefore is taxed at a maximum of 20 percent. For this reason, also, the investor is willing to accept a lower yield to maturity on a before-tax basis.[13]

---

[13] Zero-coupon bonds, discussed in Chapter 10, do not ordinarily receive favorable capital gains treatment. The investor's ordinary income tax rate is applied to the annual amortized increase in value over the life of the bond.

Let us examine how the tax feature might influence an investment decision. Assume we are evaluating three bonds that each have 20 years to run. Their coupon rates, price, and yield to maturity are presented in Table 10–6.

TABLE 10–6   Characteristics of Potential Bond Investments

Bond	Coupon rate (percent)	Price	Yield to maturity (percent)
A	6%	$ 612.60	10.75%
B	10	866.20	11.75
C	12	1,000.00	12

Our first inclination may be to invest in bond C because it provides the highest yield to maturity. But in bonds A and B, we get both interest income and capital appreciation by holding the bond to maturity. As an approximate measure, in bond A we are getting 6 percent per year in interest and the balance in capital gains. Let us assume that interest on ordinary income is taxed at 50 percent and capital gains at 20 percent. In Table 10–7, we evaluate each bond on an aftertax basis to see which provides the highest yield.

TABLE 10–7   Total Aftertax Yield (percent)

	(1)	(2)	(3) (1) − (2)	(4)	(5)	(6) (4) + (5)
Bond	Yield to maturity	Coupon portion of yield	Capital gains portion of yield	Aftertax yield on coupon (50% tax)	Aftertax yield on capital gains (20% tax)	Total aftertax yield
A	10.75%	6.00%	4.75%	3.00%	3.80%	6.80%
B	11.75	10.00	1.75	5.00	1.40	6.40
C	12.00	12.00	–0–	6.00	–0–	6.00

As indicated in the table, we have divided the yield to maturity (1) between the coupon portion (2) and the capital gains portion (3) and then examined aftertax return in columns 4 and 5. The coupon payment in column 2 is assumed to be taxed at 50 percent, providing the value in column 4, while the capital gains portion in column 3 is assumed to be taxed at 20 percent, providing the figures in column 5. Total aftertax return is presented in column 6. In the measures utilized, the lowest yield-to-maturity bonds actually provide the highest aftertax yields.

INVESTMENT STRATEGY—YIELD SPREAD CONSIDERATIONS

As discussed in the previous chapter, different types or grades of bonds provide different yields. For example, the yield on Baa corporate bonds is always above that of corporate Aaa obligations, to compensate for risk. Similarly, Aaa corporates pay a higher yield than long-term government obligations. In Figure 10–4, we observe the actual yield spread between Moody's corporate Baa's, Moody's Corporate Aaa's, and long-term government securities.

Let's direct our attention to total spread between corporate Baa bonds and government securities (corporate Aaa's fall somewhere in between). Over the long term, the spread appears to be between 75 and 100 basis points. For example, in 1973, corporate Baa's were yielding 8 percent, while government

FIGURE 10–4   Yield Spread Differentials on Long-Term Bonds

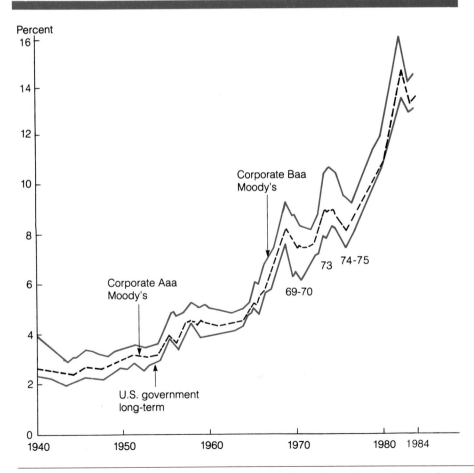

Source: *Federal Reserve Historical Chart Book* (Washington, D.C.: Federal Reserve Board of Governors).

securities provided a return of 7.25 percent. Nevertheless, at certain phases of the business cycle, the yield spread changes. For example, in the early phases of a recession, confidence tends to be at a low ebb, and as a consequence, investors will attempt to shift out of low-grade securities into stronger instruments. The impact on the yield spreads can be observed in the recessions of 1969–70, 1974–75, and 1981–82. In all cases, the yield spread between corporate Baa's and government securities went over 200 basis points, only to narrow again during the recovery. Remember that in Chapter 8, on technical analysis, one of the market indicators was the Barron's Confidence Index which measured the ratio of high-grade bonds to medium-grade bonds. The closer the confidence index is to 1.00, the smaller the spread between rates and the more optimistic investors are about the economy. The further the index is below 1.00, the greater the spread in yields and the less the confidence.

The individual investor must determine how the yield spread affects his strategy. If he does not need to increase the quality of his portfolio during the low-confidence periods of a recession, he can enjoy unusually high returns on lower-grade instruments relative to higher grades.

INVESTMENT STRATEGY—SWAPS

The term swap refers to the procedure of selling out of a given bond position and immediately buying into another one with similar attributes in an attempt to improve overall portfolio return or performance.

Often there are bonds that appear to be comparable in every respect with the exception of one characteristic. For example, newly issued bonds that are the equivalent in every sense to outstanding issues generally trade at a slightly higher yield. The rationale behind this phenomenon is discussed further in Chapter 14 under a general discussion of special situations.

Swaps may also be utilized for tax adjustment purposes and are very popular at the end of the year. Assume that you own a AAA rated AT&T bond that you bought five months ago and are currently sitting on a 20 percent capital loss because of rising interest rates. You can sell the bond and claim the loss (up to $3,000) against ordinary income.[14] This will save you taxes equal to the loss times your marginal tax rate. You can then take the proceeds from the sale and reinvest in a bond of equal risk, and you will have increased your total cash returns because of tax benefits. If interest rates turn down, you may be able to eventually claim a long-term capital gain.

Another common swap is the pure pickup yield swap where a bond owner thinks that he can increase the yield to maturity by selling a bond and buying a different bond of equal risk. The key to this swap is that the bond price of one or both bonds has to be in disequilibrium. This, of course, assumes the market is less than totally efficient. By selling the bond that is overpriced and purchasing the bond that is underpriced the investor is increasing the yield on his investment. If by chance the true quality and risk of the two bonds

---

[14] Losses above $3,000 can be carried forward to future years.

are different, the bond trader may have swapped for nothing or may even end up losing on the trade. Other types of swaps exist for arbitrages associated with interest payment dates, call transactions, conversion privileges, or any quickly changing factor in the market.

SUMMARY

The price of a bond is based on the concept of the present value of future interest payments plus a single-sum payment at maturity. The true return on a bond investment may be measured by yield to maturity, yield to call, or anticipated realized yield. A study of interest rates in the business cycle indicates that while interest rates were at one time a coincident indicator, their movement has tended to lag behind the drop in business activity during recent recessions.

The term structure of interest rates depicts the relationship between maturity and interest rates over a long time horizon. The slope of the curve gives some indication as to future movements, with an ascending pattern generally followed by higher interest rates and a descending pattern associated with a possible decline in the future. While these movements hold true in the long run, it is somewhat difficult to project interest movements in the short run.

An investor who wishes to capture maximum gains from an anticipated interest rate decline should maximize the length of his portfolio while investing in low coupon, interest-sensitive securities. Deep discount bonds also offer some protection from call provisions and a lower tax obligation associated with capital gains.

A complete analysis of a bond portfolio will also include a consideration of the yield spreads between low- and high-quality issues. The spread between long-term U.S. government bonds and corporate Baa's has been as high as 200 basis points during periods in the 1970s and early 1980s. Investors with different quality requirements should consider new portfolio strategies during such changes in the market.

IMPORTANT WORDS AND CONCEPTS

Current yield
Yield to maturity
Coupon rate
Basis point
Market rate
Yield to call
Anticipated realized yield
Term structure of interest rates
Liquidity preference theory
Market segmentation theory

Yield curve
Expectations hypothesis
Duration
Deep discount bond
Par bonds
Junk bonds
Bond swaps
Tax swaps
Pure pickup yield swap

DISCUSSION QUESTIONS

1. Why are bonds not necessarily a conservative investment?
2. How can the market price of a bond be described in terms of present value?
3. Why does a bond price change when interest rates change?
4. Why is current yield not a good indicator of bond returns? (Relate your answer to maturity considerations).
5. What is the significance of the yield-to-call calculation?
6. What is the bond reinvestment assumption? Is this necessarily correct?
7. What is the meaning of term structure of interest rates?
8. What does an ascending-term structure pattern tend to indicate?
9. Explain the general meaning of the expectations hypothesis as it relates to the term structure of interest rates.
10. Explain the liquidity preference theory as it relates to the term structure of interest rates.
11. How might the market segmentation theory help to explain why short-term rates on government securities increase when bank loan demand becomes high?
12. Under what circumstances would the yield spread on different classes of debt obligations tend to be largest?
13. In preparing a strategy to invest in bonds, what variables should be considered to maximize return? Assume that a decline in interest rates is anticipated.
14. How do margin requirements affect investor strategy for bonds?
15. Explain the benefits derived from investing in deep discount bonds.
16. What is another name for a high-risk, low-grade bond that behaves very much like common stock in terms of performance?

PROBLEMS

1. Given a 15-year bond that originally sold for $1,000 with an 11 percent coupon rate, what would be the price of the bond if interest rates in the marketplace on similar bonds are now 12 percent? Interest is paid semi-annually. (Do the two-step calculation.)
2. Given the facts in Problem 1, what would be the price if interest rates go down to 8 percent? (Once again, do a semiannual analysis and use two steps).
3. What is the current yield of a 10 percent coupon rate bond priced at $880?
4. a. What is the approximate yield to maturity of a 10 percent coupon rate, $1,000 par value bond priced at $880 if it has eight years to maturity? Use Formula (10–2).
   b. Explain why the answer in Problem 4a is different from that in Problem 3.

5. What is the approximate yield to maturity of a 14 percent coupon rate ($1,000) par value bond priced at $1,150 if it has 15 years to maturity? Use Formula (10–2).

6. a. Using the facts given in Problem 5, what would be the yield to call if the call can be made in four years at a price of $1,060? Use Formula (10–3).

   b. Explain why the answer is lower in Problem 6a than in Problem 5.

   c. Given a call value of $1,060 in four years, is it likely that the bond price would actually get to $1,150?

7. a. Using the facts given in Problem 5, what would be the anticipated realized yield if the forecast is that the bond can be sold in three years for $1,240? Use Formula (10–4). That is, assume the bond has a 14 percent coupon rate ($140) and a current price of $1,150.

   b. Now break down the anticipated realized yield between current yield and capital appreciation. (Hint: Compute current yield and subtract this from anticipated realized yield to determine capital appreciation.)

8. Expectations hypothesis problem. The following pattern for one-year Treasury bills is expected over the next four years.

Year 1	8%
Year 2	9%
Year 3	11%
Year 4	13%

   a. What return would be necessary to induce an investor to buy a two-year security?

   b. What return would be necessary to induce an investor to buy a three-year security?

   c. What return would be necessary to induce an investor to buy a four-year security?

   d. Diagram the term structure of interest rates for years one through four.

9. An investor places $600,000 in 20-year bonds (12 percent coupon rate) and interest rates decline by 3 percent. Use Table 10–4 to determine the current value of the portfolio.

10. Assume an investor purchases a 20-year, $1,000 bond with a coupon rate of 10 percent. The market rate falls to 8 percent. What would be the return on the investment if the buyer borrowed part of the funds with a 25 percent margin requirement? Assume the interest payments on the bond cover the interest expense on the borrowed funds. (You can use Table 10–3 in this problem to determine the new value of the bond.)

11. a. Assume that a 4.5 percent coupon rate deep discount bond provides an 11.5 percent yield to maturity to the investor. Further assume the investor pays a 50 percent tax on ordinary income (such as interest) and a 20 percent tax on capital gains. Use the methodology in Table 10–7 to determine the total aftertax yield to the investor.

b. If, instead of buying the deep discount bond, the investor had bought a par value bond yielding 12.5 percent, what would be his aftertax return based on the ordinary income tax rate specified above?

c. If the investor is primarily interested in aftertax return, should he buy the 12.5 percent par value bond or the 4.5 percent deep discount bond?

d. If interest rates are likely to decline sharply in the future, how might that influence the decision?

12. Tax swap problem. Mr. Goldfarb bought $8,000 of bonds four months ago. The bonds were purchased at par with a 10 percent coupon rate. Now interest rates in the market are 13 percent for similar obligations with 10 years to maturity. The rapid rise in interest rates was caused by an unexpected increase in inflation.

a. Determine the current value of Mr. Goldfarb's portfolio. Use Table 10–3 to help accomplish this.

b. How large a deduction from ordinary income can Mr. Goldfarb take if he sells the bonds?

c. If he is in a 40 percent tax bracket, what is the tax write-off worth to him?

d. Assume he will replace the old 10 percent par value bonds with 12.3 percent par value bonds selling at $954. Based on your answer in part *a*, how many new bonds can be purchased? Round to the nearest whole number.

SELECTED REFERENCES

Barnes, Tom; Keith Johnson; and Don Shannon. "A Test of Fixed-Income Strategies." *The Journal of Portfolio Management,* Winter 1984, pp. 60–65.

Cohen, Kalman J.; Robert L. Kramer; and W. Howard Waugh. "Regression Yield Curves for U.S. Government Securities." *Management Science,* December 1966, pp. 68–175.

Dann, Larry Y., and Wayne H. Mikkelson. "Convertible Debt Issuance, Capital Structure Change and Financing—Related Information: Some New Evidence." *Journal of Financial Economics,* June 1984, pp. 155–186.

Feldstein, Martin, and Otto Eckstein. "The Fundamental Determinants of the Interest Rate." *The Review of Economics and Statistics,* November 1970, pp. 363–75.

Ferri, Michael G. "How Do Call Provisions Influence Bond Yields?" *Journal of Portfolio Management,* Winter 1979, pp. 55–57.

Hastie, K. Larry. "Determinants of Municipal Bond Yields." *Journal of Financial and Quantitative Analysis,* June 1972, pp. 1729–48.

Homer, S., and M. L. Leibowitz. *Inside the Yield Book: New Tools for Book Market Strategy.* Englewood Cliffs, N.J.: Prentice-Hall, 1972.

Jen, Frank C., and James E. Wert. "The Effect of Call Risk on Corporate Bond Yields." *Journal of Finance,* December 1967, pp. 637–52.

Joehnk, Michael D., and James F. Nielsen. "Return and Risk Characteristics of Speculative Grade Bonds." *Quarterly Review of Economics and Business,* Spring 1975, pp. 27–46.

Leibowitz, Martin L. "Goal Oriented Bond Portfolio Management." *Journal of Portfolio Management,* Summer 1979, pp. 13–18.

McCulloch, J. Huston. "Measuring the Term Structure of Interest Rates." *Journal of Business,* January 1971, pp. 19–31.

Malkiel, Burton. "Expectations, Bond Prices, and the Term Structure of Interest Rates." *Quarterly Journal of Economics,* May 1962, pp. 197–218.

Prell, Michael J. "How Well Do The Experts Forecast Interest Rates?" Federal Reserve Bank of Kansas City, *Monthly Review,* September–October, 1973, pp. 3–13.

Roll, Richard. *The Behavior of Interest Rates.* New York: Basic Books, 1970.

Schaefer, Stephen M. "The Problem With Redemption Yields." *Financial Analysts Journal,* July–August 1977, pp. 29–35.

Thorndike Encyclopedia of Banking and Financial Tables. Boston: Warren, Gorham & Lamont, 1981.

Zaentz, Neil. "Relative Price Performance among Coupon Areas in Corporate Bonds." *Financial Analysts Journal,* July–August 1969, pp. 146–55.

Chapter 11

DURATION AND REINVESTMENT CONCEPTS

REVIEW OF BASIC BOND VALUATION CONCEPTS

In Chapter 10 we discussed the principles of bond valuation. The value of a bond was established in Formula (10–1) as follows:

$$V = \sum_{t=1}^{n} \frac{C_t}{(1 + i)^t} + \frac{P_n}{(1 + i)^n} \qquad (10\text{–}1)$$

where:

V = Market value or price of the bond.
n = Number of periods.
t = Each period.
C_t = Coupon or interest payment for each period, t.
P_n = Par or maturity value.
i = Interest rate in the market.

Based on this equation, as interest rates in the market rise the price of the bond will decline, because the present value of the cash flows is worth less at a higher discount rate. The opposite is true if interest rates decline. We also demonstrated in Table 10–4 that bonds with long-term maturities were generally more sensitive to changes in interest rates than were short-term bonds. In the reproduction of Table 10–4 below, it can be seen that a 30-year bond

(Reproduction of Table 10–4)   **Change in Market Prices of Bonds for Shifts in Yields to Maturity (12 percent coupon rate)**

Yield change (percent)	Maturity (years)				
	1	5	10	20	30
+3%	−2.69%	−10.30%	−15.29%	−18.89%	−19.74%
+2	−1.81	− 7.02	−10.59	−13.33	−14.04
+1	− .91	− 3.57	− 5.01	− 7.08	− 7.52
−1	+ .92	+ 3.77	+ 5.98	+ 8.02	+ 8.72
−2	+1.86	+ 7.72	+12.46	+17.16	+18.93
−3	+2.81	+11.87	+19.51	+27.60	+30.96

exhibits larger price changes in response to a change in yield than do shorter-term obligations. For example, a 2 percent drop in interest rates would cause a 1.86 percent increase in value for a bond with one year to maturity, but an 18.93 percent increase in value for a bond with 30 years to maturity. Given the relationship between the life of a bond and the price sensitivity just described, it is particularly important that we have an appropriate definition of the life or term of a bond.

The first inclination is to say the term of a bond is an easily determined matter. One supposedly merely needs to look up the maturity date (such as

1995 or 2004) in a bond book and the matter is settled. However, the notion of effective life of a bond is more complicated than this. The situation is somewhat analogous to the quoted coupon rate on the bond not really conveying the true yield on the obligation. Similarly, the maturity date on a bond may not convey all important information about the life of a bond.

In studying the true characteristics about the life of a bond, not only must the final date and amount of the maturity payment be considered, but also the pattern of coupon payments that take place in the interim. If you were to receive $1,000 after 20 years and no interest payments during the term of the obligation, clearly the effective life is 20 years. But suppose in addition to the $1,000, you were also to receive $100 per year for the next 20 years. Part of the payment is coming early and part of the payment is coming late, and the weighted average term of the payout is certainly less than 20 years. The higher the coupon payments relative to the maturity payment, the shorter the weighted average life of the payout. In the next section, we shall go through the simple mathematics of computing the weighted average life of the payout; for now it is enough to know that such a concept exists.

The important consideration is that bond price sensitivity can be more appropriately related to weighted average life than to just the maturity date. While many bond analysts simply relate price sensitivity to maturity, (and we did that also in Chapter 10), there is a more sophisticated approach related to weighted average life.

Before we move on to determining weighted average life, there is an investment decision we wish you to consider. Assume you have to decide whether to invest in an 8 percent coupon rate bond with a 20-year maturity or a 12 percent coupon rate bond with a 25-year maturity. Which bond will have the larger increase in price if interest rates decline? You may choose the 25-year, 12 percent coupon rate bond because it has the longer maturity, but don't answer too quickly on this. Let's consider weighted average life, and then eventually come back to this question of price sensitivity.

DURATION

The concept of weighted average life of a bond falls under the general topic of duration. We shall first of all do a simple example of weighted average life, and then more formally look at duration. Assume that we have a five-year bond that provides $80 per year for the next five years, plus $1,000 at the end of five years. For ease of calculation, we are using annual coupon payments in our analysis. Semiannual analysis would change the answer only slightly. An approach to computing weighted average life is presented in Table 11–1.

First of all, we see the weighted average life of the bond, based on the annual cash flows, is 4.4290 years. Let's see how this is calculated. In column *(1)* is the year in which each cash flow falls, and in column *(2)* is the size of the cash flow for each year plus the total cash flow. Column *(3)* calls for dividing the annual cash flow in column *(2)* by the total cash flow at the bottom of column *(2)* to determine what percentage of the total it represents. For example, the annual cash flow of $80 on the first line of column *(2)* represents .0571

TABLE 11–1   Simple Weighted Average Life

(1) Year, t	(2) Cash flow	(3) Annual cash flow (2) ÷ by total cash flow	(4) Year × weight (1) × (3)
1	$ 80	.0571	.0571
2	80	.0571	.1142
3	80	.0571	.1713
4	80	.0571	.2284
5	80	.0571	.2855
5	1,000	.7145	3.5725
Total cash → flow	$1,400	1.0000	4.4290

of the total cash flow of $1,400. ($80 ÷ $1,400 = .0571.) The same basic procedure is followed for all subsequent years. In column *(4)*, each year is multiplied by the weights (percentages) developed in column *(3)*. For example, year 1 is multiplied by .0571 to arrive at .0571 in column *(4)*. Year 2 is multiplied by .0571 to arrive at .1142 in column *(4)*. This procedure is followed for each year and each weight. The final answer is 4.4290 for the weighted average life of the bond.

If you can understand the approach presented in Table 11–1, you should have no difficulty in following a more formal and appropriate definition of weighted average life called duration. Duration represents the weighted average life of a bond where the weights are based on the *present value* of the individual cash flows relative to the *present value* of the total cash flows (previously we did not discount the cash flows in determining weights, but merely used stated values). An example of duration is presented in Table 11–2. Present value calculations are based on the market rate of interest (yield to maturity) for the bond, which in this case, we shall assume to be 12 percent.

The only difference between Table 11–1 and Table 11–2 is that in Table 11–2 the cash flows are present valued before the weights are determined. Thus the cash flows *(2)* are multiplied by the present value factors at 12 percent *(3)* to arrive at the present value of cash flows *(4)*. The total present value of cash flows at the bottom of column *(4)* is also the same concept as the price of the bond. In column *(5)*, weights for each year are determined by dividing the present value of each annual cash flow *(4)* by the total present value of cash flows (bottom of column *4*). For example in year 1, the present value of the cash flow is $71.44, and this is divided by the total present value of cash flows of $855.40 to arrive at .0835 in column *(5)*. Similarly, the weight in year 2, as shown in column *(5)*, is determined by dividing $63.76 by $855.40 to arrive at .0745. In column *(6)*, each year is multiplied by the weights developed in column *(5)*. For example, year 1 is multiplied by .0835 to arrive at .0835 in column *(6)*. Year 2 is multiplied by .0745 to arrive at .1490. This procedure is followed for each year, and the values are then summed. The final

TABLE 11-2   Duration Concept of Weighted Average Life

(1)	(2)	(3)	(4)	(5)	(6)
				PV of annual cash flow (4)	Year ×
		PV *factor*	PV *of cash*	÷ *by total* PV	*weight*
Year, t	Cash flow (CF)	at 12 percent	flow (CF)	of cash flows	(1) × (5)
1	$ 80	.893	$ 71.44	.0835	.0835
2	80	.797	63.76	.0745	.1490
3	80	.712	56.96	.0666	.1998
4	80	.636	50.88	.0595	.2380
5	80	.567	45.36	.0530	.2650
5	$1,000	.567	567.00	.6629	3.3145
		Total PV of → cash flows (V)	$855.40	1.0000	4.2498 ↑ Duration

answer for duration (the weighted average life based on present value) is 4.2498. Duration, once determined, is the most representative value for effective bond life, and the measure against which bond price sensitivity should be evaluated.

The formula for duration can be formally stated as:

$$\text{Duration} = \underbrace{\frac{PV\,CF}{V}}_{\text{Weight}}\underbrace{(1)}_{\text{Year}} + \underbrace{\frac{PV\,CF}{V}}_{\text{Weight}}\underbrace{(2)}_{\text{Year}} + \underbrace{\frac{PV\,CF}{V}}_{\text{Weight}}\underbrace{(3)}_{\text{Year}}$$

$$+ \cdots + \underbrace{\frac{PV\,CF}{V}}_{\text{Weight}}\underbrace{(n)}_{\text{Year}} \quad (11\text{-}1)$$

where:

PV = The present value factor for each time period (from Appendix B at the end of the book).
CF = The yearly cash flow for each time period.
V = The total present value or market price of the bond.
n = number of periods to maturity.[1]

---

[1] Using the symbols from Formula (10-1), duration can also be stated as:

$$\text{Duration} = \sum_{t=1}^{n} \frac{C_t \dfrac{1}{(1+i)^t}}{V}(t) + \frac{P_n \dfrac{1}{(1+i)^n}}{V}(n)$$

If semiannual analysis is used throughout the calculation, the answer should be divided by two to convert the figure to annual terms.

**TABLE 11–3   Duration for an 8 Percent Coupon Rate Bond with Maturities
of 1, 5, and 10 Years Discounted at 12 Percent**

1-Year bond

(1)	(2)	(3)	(4)	(5)	(6)
				PV of annual cash flow (4) ÷ by total PV	Year × weight
		PV factor	PV of cash	÷ by total PV	weight
Year, t	Cash flow (CF)	at 12 percent	flow (CF)	of cash flows	(1) × (5)
1	$ 80	.893	$ 71.44	.0741	.0741
2	1,000	.893	893.00	.9259	.9259
		Total PV of → cash flows	$964.44	1.0000	1.0000 ↑ Duration

5-Year bond

(1)	(2)	(3)	(4)	(5)	(6)
				PV of annual cash flow (4) ÷ by total PV	Year × weight
		PV factor	PV of cash	÷ by total PV	weight
Year, t	Cash flow (CF)	at 12 percent	flow (CF)	of cash flows	(1) × (5)
1	$ 80	.893	$ 71.44	.0835	.0835
2	80	.797	63.76	.0745	.1490
3	80	.712	56.96	.0666	.1998
4	80	.636	50.88	.0595	.2380
5	80	.567	45.36	.0530	.2650
5	1,000	.567	567.00	.6629	3.3145
		Total PV of → cash flows	$855.40	1.0000	4.2498 ↑ Duration

10-Year bond

(1)	(2)	(3)	(4)	(5)	(6)
				PV of annual cash flow (4) ÷ by total PV	Year × weight
		PV factor	PV of cash	÷ by total PV	weight
Year, t	Cash flow (CF)	at 12 percent	flow (CF)	of cash flows	(1) × (5)
1	$ 80	.893	$ 71.44	.0923	.0923
2	80	.797	63.76	.0824	.1648
3	80	.712	56.96	.0736	.2208
4	80	.636	50.88	.0657	.2628
5	80	.567	45.36	.0586	.2930
6	80	.507	40.56	.0524	.3144
7	80	.452	36.16	.0467	.3269
8	80	.404	32.32	.0418	.3344
9	80	.361	28.88	.0373	.3357
10	80	.322	25.76	.0333	.3330
10	1,000	.322	322.00	.4160	4.1600
		Total PV of → cash flows	$774.08	1.0000	6.8381 ↑ Duration

In Table 11–3 on page 329, we observe durations for an 8 percent coupon rate bond with maturities of 1, 5, and 10 years. The discount rate is 12 percent. The procedure used to compute duration in Table 11–3 is precisely the same as that employed in Table 11–2. Although many calculations are involved, you should primarily direct your attention to the last value presented in the last column (6) for each of the three bonds. This value, of course, represents the duration of the issue.

We see in Table 11–3 that the duration for a one-year bond is 1.0. Since all cash flows are paid at the end of year 1, duration equals the maturity.[2] As maturity increases (to 5 and 10 years) duration increases but less than the maturity of the bond. With a 5-year bond, duration is 4.2498, and with a 10-year bond, duration is 6.8381. Duration is increasing at a decreasing rate because the principal repayment in the last year becomes a smaller percentage of the total present value of cash flow, and the annual coupon payments become more important.[3]

DURATION AND PRICE SENSITIVITY

Once duration is computed, its most important use is in determining the price sensitivity of a bond. In Table 11–4, we consider the maturity, duration, and percentage price change for an 8 percent coupon rate bond based on a 2 percent decrease and of a 2 percent increase in interest rates. The *market* rate of interest for computing duration in Table 11–4 is 8 percent. One quick point before examining Table 11–4. Duration is related not only to maturity, but also to coupon rate and market rate of interest. For example, in Table 11–3, the coupon rate of interest was 8 percent and the market rate of interest was 12 percent. In the calculations in Table 11–4, the coupon rate is 8 percent and the market rate of interest is assumed to be 8 percent. Because of the different market rates of interest in Tables 11–3 and 11–4, the duration for a given maturity (such as 5 and 10 years) will be different. The point just discussed will be further clarified later in the chapter, so even if you do not fully understand it, you should still continue to read on.

We see in Table 11–4 that the longer the maturity or duration, the greater the impact of a 2 percent change in interest rates on price. However, we shall also observe how much more closely the percentage change in price parallels the change in duration as compared to maturity. For example, between 25 and 50 years, duration increases very slowly (column 2) and the same can be said for the increase in the percentage impact that a 2 percent decline in interest rates has on price (column 3). This is true in spite of the fact that the maturity period has increased by 100 percent, from 25 to 50 years.

As a rough measure of price sensitivity, one can multiply duration times

---

[2] If semiannual analysis were used, the duration would be slightly less than the maturity in the first year.

[3] A sinking fund provision can also have an effect on duration, causing the weighted average life of the bond to be shorter.

TABLE 11–4   Duration and Price Sensitivity (8 percent coupon rate bond)

(1) Maturity	(2) Duration	(3) Impact of a 2 percent decline in interest rates on price	(4) Impact of a 2 percent increase in interest rates on price
1	1.0000	+ 1.89%	− 1.81%
5	4.3121	+ 8.42	− 7.58
10	7.2470	+14.72	−12.29
20	10.6038	+22.93	−17.03
25	11.5290	+25.57	−18.50
30	12.1585	+27.53	−18.85
40	12.8787	+30.09	−19.55
50	13.2123	+31.15	−19.83

the change in interest rates to determine the percentage change in the value of a bond.

$$\text{Percentage change in the value of a bond} \quad \overset{\text{Approximately}}{\underset{\text{equals}}{\cdots}} \rightarrow \text{Duration} \times \text{Change in interest rates}$$

The sign in the final answer is reversed because interest rate changes and bond prices move in opposite directions. For example, if a bond has a duration of 7.2470 years, and interest rates go down by 2 percent, a rough measure of bond value appreciation is +14.494 percent (7.2470 × 2). Columns (2) and (3) in Table 11–4, across from 10 years maturity, indicate that this is a reasonably good approximation. That is, when duration was 7.2470, a 2 percent drop in interest rates produced a 14.72 percent increase in bond prices (not too many basis points away from our projected value of +14.494 percent). The approximation gets progressively rougher as the term of the bond is extended.[4] It is also a less valid measure for interest rate increases (and the associated price decline). Even with these qualifications, one can observe a more useful relationship between price changes and duration than between price changes and maturity.

It is for this reason that the analyst must have a reasonable feel for the factors that influence duration. It is apparent that the length of the bond affects duration, but, as previously mentioned, it is not the only variable. Duration is

---

[4] The approximation can be slightly improved by using modified duration instead of actual duration. Modified duration is defined as: Duration ÷ (1 + market rate of interest/the number of coupon payments per period). For more information, see Michael H. Hopewell and George C. Kaufman, "Bond Price Volatility and Term to Maturity: A Generalized Respecification," *American Economic Review,* September 1973, pp. 749–53.

also influenced by market rate of interest and the coupon rate on the bond. In fact, it is theoretically possible for these two factors to outweigh maturity in determining duration. That is to say, it is possible that a bond with a shorter maturity than another bond may actually have a longer duration and be more price-sensitive to interest rate changes.

Duration and Market Rates

Market rates of interest (yield to maturity) and duration are inversely related. The higher the market rate of interest, the lower the duration. This is because of the present valuing effect that is part of duration. Higher market rates of interest mean lower present values. For example, in Table 11–2, if the market rate of interest in column (3) had been 16 percent instead of 12 percent, the final answer for duration would have been 4.1859. The new value is actually computed in Table 11–5. Clearly, it is less than the 4.2498 duration value in Table 11–2.

TABLE 11–5   Duration of an 8 Percent Coupon Rate Bond with a 16 Percent Market Rate of Interest

(1)	(2)	(3)	(4)	(5)	(6)
				PV of annual cash flow (4)	Year ×
		PV factor	PV of cash	÷ by total PV	weight
Year, t	Cash flow (CF)	at 16 percent	flow (CF)	of cash flows	(1) × (5)
1	$ 80	.862	$ 68.96	.0935	.0935
2	80	.743	59.44	.0806	.1612
3	80	.641	51.28	.0695	.2085
4	80	.552	44.16	.0598	.2392
5	80	.476	38.08	.0516	.2580
5	1,000	.476	476.00	.6451	3.2255
		Total PV of → cash flows	$737.92	1.0000	4.1859 ↑ Duration

To expand our analysis, in Table 11–6 we see the duration values for an 8 percent coupon rate bond at different market rates of interest. As market rates of interest increase, duration decreases. This can be easily seen in the 20-year row (reading across). At a 4 percent market rate of interest, duration for the 8 percent coupon rate bond is 12.3995. At 8 percent it is 10.6038, and at 12 percent, 8.9390.

Also note in Table 11–6 that an equal change in market rates of interest will have a bigger impact on duration when rates move down than when they move up. For example, in the 50-year row, a 4 percent decrease in market rates of interest (say, from 8 percent to 4 percent) causes duration to increase by

TABLE 11–6   Duration Values at Varying Market Rates of Interest (based on 8 percent coupon rate bond)

Maturity (years)	Market rates of interest				
	4 percent	6 percent	8 percent	10 percent	12 percent
1	1.00	1.00	1.00	1.00	1.00
5	4.3717	4.3423	4.3121	4.2814	4.2498
10	7.6372	7.4450	7.2470	7.0439	6.8381
→20	12.3995	11.4950	10.6038	9.7460	8.9390
25	14.2265	12.8425	11.5290	10.3229	9.2475
30	15.7935	13.8893	12.1585	10.6472	9.3662
40	18.3274	15.3498	12.8787	10.9176	9.3972
50	20.2481	16.2494	13.2123	10.9896	9.3716

7.0358 years, from 13.2123 to 20.2481 years. A similar increase of 4 percent from 8 percent to 12 percent would only cause duration to decrease by 3.8407 years, from 13.2123 to 9.3716 years.

Duration and Coupon Rates

In the previous section, we learned that duration is inversely related to market rate of interest. We now look at the relationship between duration and the coupon rate on a bond. As the coupon rate rises, duration decreases. Why? The answer is that high coupon rate bonds tend to produce higher annual cash flows prior to maturity, and thus tend to weight duration toward the earlier to middle years. On the other hand, low coupon rate bonds produce less annual cash flows prior to maturity and have less influence on duration. Duration is weighted more heavily toward the final payment at maturity, and duration tends to be somewhat closer to the actual maturity on the bond. At the extreme, on a zero-coupon bond, maturity and duration are the same.

The relationship between duration and coupon rates can be seen in Table 11–7. Here three different coupon rate bonds are presented. Each bond

TABLE 11–7   Duration and Coupon Rates (25-year bonds)

Market rate of interest	Coupon rates		
	4 percent	8 percent	12 percent
4%	16.2470	14.2265	13.3278
6	14.7455	12.8425	12.0407
8	13.2459	11.5290	10.8396
10	11.8112	10.3229	9.7501
12	10.4912	9.2475	8.7844

is assumed to have a maturity of 25 years. The best way to read the table is to pick a market rate of interest in the first column and then read across the table to determine the duration at various coupon rates. For example, at an 8 percent market rate of interest, duration is 13.2459 at a 4 percent coupon rate, 11.5290 at an 8 percent coupon rate, and 10.8396 at a 12 percent coupon rate. Clearly, the higher the coupon rate, the lower the duration (and vice versa).

The impact of coupon rates on duration is also demonstrated in Figure 11–1. Note that with a zero-coupon bond the line is at a 45-degree angle; that is, duration and years to maturity are always the same value. There is only one payment, and it is at maturity.

FIGURE 11–1   The Effect of Coupon Rates on Duration

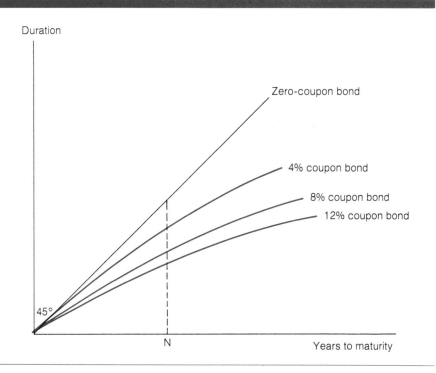

You can also observe in Figure 11–1 that progressively higher coupon rates lead to a lower duration. As an example, go to point N on the horizontal axis, and observe duration for 4 percent, 8 percent, and 12 percent interest. Clearly the higher the coupon rate, the lower the duration value.

Because the higher the duration the greater the price sensitivity, it follows that an investor desiring maximum price movements will look toward lower coupon rate bonds. As previously demonstrated, low coupon rate and

high duration go together, and high duration leads to maximum price sensitivity. The relationship of low coupon rates to price sensitivity was briefly discussed in Chapter 10 under investment strategy. We now see that the un-named explanatory variable at that point was duration.

BRINGING TOGETHER THE INFLUENCES ON DURATION

The three factors that determine the value of duration are maturity of the bond, market rate of interest, and the coupon rate. Duration is positively correlated with maturity, but moves in the opposite direction of market rates of interest and coupon rates, i.e., the higher the coupon rate, the lower the duration. Earlier in this chapter, you were asked to consider whether you should invest in an 8 percent coupon rate, 20-year bond or a 12 percent coupon rate, 25-year bond. Since we were assuming interest rates were going to go down, you were looking for maximum price volatility. Had you not studied duration, you probably would have selected the bond with the longest maturity. This would generally be a valid assumption as indicated in Chapter 10. However, the primary emphasis to the sophisticated bond investor when assessing price volatility, or sensitivity, is duration.

Note that the bond with the longer maturity (25 years versus 20 years) also has a higher coupon rate (12 percent versus 8 percent). The first factor (longer maturity) would indicate higher duration, but the second factor (higher coupon rate) would indicate a lower duration. What is the net effect? The answer can be found in earlier tables in this chapter. Let's assume that the market rate of interest is 12 percent for both bonds. Table 11–6 presented information on 8 percent coupon rate bonds for varying maturities and market rates of interest. To determine the duration on the 8 percent coupon rate, 20-year bond, assuming a 12 percent market rate of interest, we read across the 20-year row to the last column in the table and see the answer is 8.9390. (Note that all bonds in Table 11–6 have an 8 percent coupon rate, so we must identify the value associated with 20 years and a 12 percent market rate of interest.)

To determine the duration for the 12 percent coupon rate, 25-year bond with a 12 percent market rate of interest, we must go to Table 11–7. Note that all bonds in this table have a 25-year maturity, so read down to a market rate of interest of 12 percent and across to a coupon rate of 12 percent. The value for duration on this bond is 8.7844.

Based on the above analysis, the answer to the question posed earlier in the chapter is that the bond with the shorter maturity (8 percent coupon rate for 20 years) has a longer duration than the bond with the greater maturity (12 percent for 25 years), and thus is the most price-sensitive.[5]

---

[5] As previously indicated, if we vary the market rate of interest, we can also influence the outcome to our question.

Bond	Duration
8%, 20 years	8.9390 ← greater price sensitivity
12%, 25 years	8.7844

In actuality, if interest rates went down by 2 percent, the 8 percent, 20-year bond would go up by 18.5 percent, while the 12 percent, 25-year bond would only increase by 17.9 percent.

DURATION AND ZERO-COUPON BONDS

Characteristics of zero-coupon bonds were briefly described in Chapter 9. As previously mentioned, Figure 11–1 depicts the duration of zero-coupon bonds as a 45-degree line relative to years to maturity. This graphically indicates that the duration of a zero-coupon bond equals the number of years it has to maturity. For all bonds of equal risk and maturity, the zero-coupon bond has the greatest duration and therefore the greatest price sensitivity. This price risk is one that is often lost in the image of safety that CATs, RATs, TGRs, COUGARs, and other zero-coupons have when backed by U.S. government securities.

A headline in *The Wall Street Journal* on June 1, 1984, appeared as follows: "Zero-Coupon Bonds' Price Swings Jolt Investors Looking for Security."[6] It was reported that between March 31, 1983, and March 31, 1984, Salomon Brothers' 30-year CATs declined 25 percent in price, while returns on conventional 30-year government bonds declined only a few percentage points. The article cited one client buying $100,000 of zero coupons, thinking they were similar to short-term Treasury bill investments, only to find out four weeks later that his zero-coupon bonds had declined in value by $24,000.

To put the volatility of a zero-coupon bond into better perspective, we compare the duration of a zero-coupon bond to that of an 8 percent coupon bond for several maturities in Table 11–8.

The far right column in Table 11–8 indicates the ratio of duration between zero-coupon and 8 percent coupon rate bonds. As stressed throughout the chapter, duration represents a measure of price sensitivity. Thus for a 10-year maturity period, a zero-coupon bond is almost 1½ times as price sensitive as an 8 percent coupon rate bond (the ratio in the last column is 1.4625). For a 20-year maturity period, it is over two times more price-sensitive (2.2374), and for 50 years the duration, or price sensitivity, ratio is over 5 times greater (5.3353). This might explain why zero-coupons were much more sensitive to rising interest rates during 1983–84 as described in the story in *The Wall Street Journal*. Of course, tremendous profits can be made in zero-coupon bonds when there is a sharp drop in interest rates as in early 1985.

---

[6] Randall Smith, "Zero-Coupon Bonds' Price Swings Jolt Investors Looking for Security," *The Wall Street Journal*, June 1, 1984, p. 19.

TABLE 11–8   Duration of Zero-Coupon versus 8 Percent Coupon Bonds (market rate of interest is 12 percent)

Years to maturity	Duration of zero-coupon bond	Duration of 8 percent coupon bond	Relative duration of zero-coupon to 8 percent coupon bonds
10	10	6.8374	1.4625
20	20	8.9390	2.2374
30	30	9.3662	3.2030
40	40	9.3972	4.2566
50	50	9.3716	5.3353

THE USES OF DURATION

Duration is primarily used as a measure to judge bond price sensitivity to interest rate changes. Since duration includes information on several variables (maturity, coupon rate, and market rate of interest), it captures more information than any one of them. It therefore allows more accurate decisions for complex bond strategies. One such strategy involves the timing of investment inflows to provide a needed cash outlay at a known future date. Perhaps $1,000,000 is needed after five years. Everything is tailored to this five-year time horizon. If interest rates go up, there will be a decline in the value of the portfolio, but a higher reinvestment rate opportunity for inflows. Similarly, if interest rates go down, there will be capital appreciation for the portfolio, but a lower reinvestment rate opportunity. By tying all the investment decisions to a duration period, the portfolio manager can take advantage of these counter forces to ensure a necessary outcome. This strategy is called immunization, and is used by insurance companies, pension funds, and other institutional money managers to protect their portfolios against swings in interest rates. For a more comprehensive discussion of immunization strategies, an article by Fisher and Weil is an appropriate source.[7] For an excellent criticism of duration and immunization strategy, see Yawitz and Marshall.[8] One of the problems with duration analysis is that it often assumes a parallel shift in yield curves. Although long-duration bonds are clearly more price-sensitive than shorter-duration bonds, there is no assurance that long- and short-term interest rates will move by equal amounts.

---

[7] Lawrence Fisher and Roman L. Weil, "Coping with Risk of Interest Rate Fluctuations: Returns to Bondholders from Naive and Optimal Strategies," *Journal of Business,* October 1971, pp. 408–31.

[8] Jess B. Yawitz and William J. Marshall, "The Shortcomings of Duration as a Risk Measure for Bonds," *The Journal of Financial Research,* Summer 1981, pp. 91–101.

BOND REINVESTMENT ASSUMPTIONS AND TERMINAL WEALTH ANALYSIS

Reinvestment Assumptions

As indicated in the previous section, one concern an investor may have when purchasing bonds is that the interest income will not be reinvested to earn the same return that the coupon payment represents. This may not be a problem for an individual consuming the interest payments, but it could be a serious concern for individuals building a retirement portfolio or a pension fund manager accumulating funds for future payout to retirees. The crucial issue is the amount of money accumulated at the time the retirement fund will be used to cover living expenses. And, of course, one major determinant of the ending value of a retirement fund is the rate of return on coupon payments as they are reinvested.

Since the late 1960s, interest rates have been much higher and more volatile than during the previous 30 years. This has caused more emphasis on the management of fixed-income securities, not only in the selection of maturity but also in the switching from short- to long-term securities. These volatile high rates have caused more emphasis on concepts like duration to measure bond price sensitivity and on total return as a measure of bond management success. Given that interest rates change daily and by large amounts over the period of a year, what impact would a lower or higher reinvestment assumption have on the outcome of your retirement nest egg?

First let us look at a small part of Appendix A (reproduced in Table 11–9 for compound sums). Appendix A assumes that all interest is reinvested at the same rate as the coupon rate in order to find the ending value of one dollar invested at a given rate for a set maturity. For our current analysis, we are assuming annual interest (though the answer only changes slightly if we use semiannual interest).

TABLE 11–9   Compound Sum of $1.00 (from Appendix A)

Period	7 percent	8 percent	9 percent	10 percent	11 percent	12 percent
10	1.967	2.159	2.367	2.594	2.839	3.106
20	3.870	4.661	5.604	6.727	8.062	9.646
30	7.612	10.063	13.268	17.449	22.892	29.960
40	14.974	21.725	31.409	45.259	65.001	93.051

The table values are given in $1 amounts, so for a $1,000 bond we would just move the decimal three places to the right. A $1,000 bond having a 12 percent coupon rate with interest being reinvested at 12 percent would compound to $93,051 over 40 years, while a 7 percent coupon bond reinvested at

7 percent would only compound to $14,974 over a similar time period. A difference of 5 percent in the rates creates a total difference of $78,077. This is quite a large difference. Notice that the longer the compounding period, the larger the difference. From further inspection of Table 11–9, other comparisons can be made between years and total ending values.

The importance of the reinvestment assumption can also be viewed from the perspective of its contribution to total wealth. For example, an investor in a 40-year bond at a 12 percent coupon rate and assumed reinvestment rate of 12 percent will have an accumulated value of $93,051. In terms of payout, $4,800 (40 × $120) comes directly from 40 years of 12 percent interest payments, $1,000 comes from principal, and the balance of $87,251 comes from interest that is earned on the annual interest payments. In this case, interest on interest represents 93.8 percent of the overall return ($87,251/ $93,051).

Terminal Wealth Analysis

Now we will assume a reinvestment assumption different from the coupon rate. Take the two extreme values from Table 11–9 of 12 percent and 7 percent. Assume that you buy a bond having a 12 percent coupon rate, but that the interest can only be reinvested at 7 percent. To find the ending value of this investment we will need to use a terminal wealth table.

Table 11–10 is called a terminal wealth table because it generates the ending value of the investment at the end of each year, assuming that the bond has a *maturity* date corresponding to that year. Let's use 10 years as an example in examining Table 11–10. If the bond matures in 10 years, the $1,000 principal in column *(2)* will be recovered. Also the investor will receive $120 in annual interest (12 percent of $1,000) in year 10 as indicated in column *(3)*. In column *(4)* the accumulated interest up to the beginning of year 10 is shown. The reinvestment rate on this previously accumulated interest is a mere 7 percent as indicated in column *(5)*. The interest on the previously accumulated interest is $100.62 (.07 × $1,437.38). Finally, the total interest for year 10 is shown in column *(7)*. This consists of the coupon interest of $120 and the interest on interest of $100.62 and totals to $220.62. The total ending value of the portfolio is shown in column *(8)*. The ending value consists of the recovered principal of $1,000, plus the accumulated interest of $1,437.38 up to the beginning of year 10, plus the total interest paid in year 10 of $220.62. The ending wealth value (portfolio sum) thus shown in column *(8)* is $2,658.00. The value is summarized below.

–Recovered principal	$1,000.00	Column *(2)*
–Accumulated interest (beginning of year 10)	1,437.38	Column *(4)*
–Total annual interest (during year 10)	220.62	Column *(7)*
Ending wealth value (portfolio sum)	$2,658.00	Column *(8)*

TABLE 11–10   Terminal Wealth Table (12 percent coupon with 7 percent reinvestment rate on interest)

(1)	(2)	(3)	(4)	(5)	(6)	(7)	(8)	(9)	(10)
Years to maturity	Principal	Annual coupon interest	Accum- ulated interest*	Reinvest- ment rate on interest	Interest on interest	Total annual interest	Portfolio sum	Compound sum factor	Annual percentage return
0.0	$1,000.00								
1.0	1,000.00	$120.00	$ 0.00			$ 120.00	$ 1,120.00	1.12000	12.00
2.0	1,000.00	120.00	120.00	.07	$ 8.40	128.40	1,248.40	1.24840	11.73
3.0	1,000.00	120.00	248.40	.07	17.39	137.39	1,385.79	1.38579	11.48
4.0	1,000.00	120.00	385.79	.07	27.01	147.01	1,532.80	1.53280	11.26
5.0	1,000.00	120.00	532.80	.07	37.30	157.30	1,690.10	1.69010	11.06
6.0	1,000.00	120.00	690.10	.07	48.31	168.31	1,858.41	1.85841	10.86
7.0	1,000.00	120.00	858.41	.07	60.09	180.09	2,038.50	2.03850	10.71
8.0	1,000.00	120.00	1,038.50	.07	72.70	192.70	2,231.20	2.23120	10.55
9.0	1,000.00	120.00	1,231.20	.07	86.18	206.18	2,437.38	2.43738	10.40
10.0	1,000.00	120.00	1,437.38	.07	100.62	220.62	2,658.00	2.65800	10.26
11.0	1,000.00	120.00	1,658.00	.07	116.06	236.06	2,894.06	2.89406	10.14
12.0	1,000.00	120.00	1,894.06	.07	132.58	252.58	3,146.64	3.14664	10.02
13.0	1,000.00	120.00	2,146.64	.07	150.26	270.26	3,416.90	3.41690	9.91
14.0	1,000.00	120.00	2,416.90	.07	169.18	289.18	3,706.08	3.70608	9.80
15.0	1,000.00	120.00	2,706.08	.07	189.43	309.43	4,015.51	4.01551	9.71
16.0	1,000.00	120.00	3,015.51	.07	211.09	331.09	4,346.60	4.34660	9.61
17.0	1,000.00	120.00	3,346.60	.07	234.26	354.26	4,700.86	4.70086	9.54
18.0	1,000.00	120.00	3,700.86	.07	259.06	379.06	5,079.92	5.07992	9.44
19.0	1,000.00	120.00	4,079.92	.07	285.59	405.59	5,485.51	5.48551	9.37
20.0	1,000.00	120.00	4,485.51	.07	313.99	433.99	5,919.50	5.91950	9.29
21.0	1,000.00	120.00	4,919.50	.07	344.37	464.37	6,383.87	6.38387	9.22
22.0	1,000.00	120.00	5,383.87	.07	376.87	496.87	6,880.74	6.88074	9.16
23.0	1,000.00	120.00	5,880.74	.07	411.65	531.65	7,412.39	7.41239	9.09
24.0	1,000.00	120.00	6,412.39	.07	448.87	568.87	7,981.26	7.98126	9.04
25.0	1,000.00	120.00	6,981.26	.07	488.69	608.69	8,589.95	8.58995	8.98
26.0	1,000.00	120.00	7,589.95	.07	531.30	651.30	9,241.25	9.24125	8.92
27.0	1,000.00	120.00	8,241.25	.07	576.89	696.89	9,938.14	9.93814	8.87
28.0	1,000.00	120.00	8,938.14	.07	625.67	745.67	10,683.81	10.68381	8.82
29.0	1,000.00	120.00	9,683.81	.07	677.87	797.87	11,481.68	11.48168	8.78
30.0	1,000.00	120.00	10,481.68	.07	733.72	853.72	12,335.40	12.33540	8.73
31.0	1,000.00	120.00	11,335.40	.07	793.48	913.48	13,248.88	13.24888	8.69
32.0	1,000.00	120.00	12,248.88	.07	857.42	977.42	14,226.30	14.22630	8.65
33.0	1,000.00	120.00	13,226.30	.07	925.84	1,045.84	15,272.14	15.27214	8.61
34.0	1,000.00	120.00	14,272.14	.07	999.05	1,119.05	16,391.19	16.39119	8.57
35.0	1,000.00	120.00	15,391.19	.07	1,077.38	1,197.38	17,588.57	17.58857	8.53
36.0	1,000.00	120.00	16,588.57	.07	1,161.20	1,281.20	18,869.77	18.86977	8.50
37.0	1,000.00	120.00	17,869.77	.07	1,250.88	1,370.88	20,240.65	20.24065	8.46
38.0	1,000.00	120.00	19,240.65	.07	1,346.85	1,466.85	21,707.50	21.70750	8.43
39.0	1,000.00	120.00	20,707.50	.07	1,449.53	1,569.53	23,277.03	23.27703	8.40
40.0	1,000.00	120.00	22,277.03	.07	1,559.39	1,679.39	24,956.42	24.95642	8.37

* At beginning of year.

A $1,000 investment that grows to $2,658.00 after 10 years is the equivalent of a $1 investment that grows to 2.65800 as indicated in column *(9)*. The annual percentage return for a $1 investment that grows to 2.65800 after 10 years is 10.26 percent as indicated in column *(10)*.

A similar analysis can be done for all other maturity periods running from 1 to 40 years. One thing to notice from Table 11–10 is that the longer the maturity period of the bond, the greater the effect the low 7 percent reinvestment rate has on the bond. For 5 years, the annual percentage return (column 10) is 11.06 percent, for 15 years 9.71 percent, and for 40 years 8.37 percent.

What is the actual difference between the ending value for a 40-year, 12 percent coupon rate bond assuming a *12 percent* reinvestment rate and the 40-year, 7 *percent* reinvestment rate just presented in Table 11–10? Earlier in this section we saw in Table 11–9 that a 12 percent coupon rate bond with an assumed 12 percent reinvestment rate for 40 years would grow to $93,051. In Table 11–10, we see a 12 percent coupon rate bond with a 7 percent reinvestment rate will only grow to $24,956.42 after 40 years. It should be evident that it is not only the coupon rate that matters, but the reinvestment rate as well.

If the bond were not held to maturity in our analysis, then we would have to rely upon the realized rate of return analysis developed in Chapter 10. The realized rate of return approach would assume that the bond is not held to maturity and that it is sold at either a gain or loss. In the case of the bond analyzed in the terminal wealth table (11–10), we know that since interest rates declined, any sale of the bond before maturity should result in a capital gain. How large that capital gain would be will be dependent upon its duration. Terminal wealth analysis is a way of analyzing the reinvestment assumption when bonds are held to maturity, while the realized yield approach assumes that bonds are actively traded to take advantage of interest rate swings.

Zero-Coupon Bonds and Terminal Wealth

One of the benefits of zero-coupon bonds is that they lock in a compound rate of return (or reinvestment rate) for the life of the bond *if held to maturity.* There are no coupon payments during the life of the bond to be reinvested, so the originally quoted rate holds throughout if held to maturity. If a $1,000 par value, 15-year zero-coupon bond is quoted at a price of $183 to yield 12 percent, you truly have locked in a 12 percent reinvestment rate. Some would say you have not only locked in 12 percent, but have thrown away the key. In any event, zero-coupon bonds allow you to predetermine your reinvestment rate.

Of course, if a zero-coupon bond is sold before maturity, there could be large swings in the sales price of the bond because of its high duration characteristics. Under this circumstance, the locked-in reinvestment concept for the zero-coupon bond loses much of its meaning. It is only valid when the zero-coupon bond is held to maturity.

SUMMARY

In Chapter 11 we have taken the concepts developed in Chapter 10 and expanded on the principles of bond price volatility and total return. We developed the concept of duration so that the student has a basic understanding of what it means and some of its applications. In general, we have shown that duration is the number of years, on a present-value basis, that it takes to recover an initial investment in a bond. More specifically, each year is weighted by the present value of the cash flow as a proportion to the present value of the bond, and is then summed. The higher the duration, the more sensitive the bond price is to a change in interest rates. Duration as one number captures the three variables—maturity, coupon rate, and market rate of interest—to indicate the price sensitivities of bonds with unequal characteristics. Generally, bond duration increases with the increase in number of years to maturity. Duration also increases as coupon rates decline to zero, and finally, duration declines as market interest rates increase.

Zero-coupon bonds are highlighted as the most price-sensitive of bonds to a change in interest, and comparisons are made between zero-coupon bonds and coupon bonds. Duration's primary use is in explaining price volatility, but it also has applications in the insurance industry and other areas of investments where interest rate risk can be reduced by matching duration with predictable cash outflows in a process called immunization.

An important concept has to do with the reinvestment of interest at rates other than the coupon rate. The method used to explain the effect on the total return is terminal wealth analysis, which assumes that the investment is held to maturity and all proceeds over the life of the bond are reinvested at the reinvestment rate. In general, the longer the maturity, the more total annualized return approaches the reinvestment rate. If the reinvestment rate is significantly different from the coupon rate, the annualized return can differ greatly from the coupon rate in as little as five years.

IMPORTANT WORDS AND CONCEPTS

Zero-coupon bond	**Immunization**
Duration	**Terminal wealth table**
Reinvestment assumption	**Bond price-sensitivity**

DISCUSSION QUESTIONS

1. Why is the weighted average life of a bond less than the maturity date?
2. Define duration.
3. How can duration be used to determine a rough measure of the percentage change in the price of a bond as a result of interest rate changes?
4. Comment on the statement, "It is possible that a bond with a shorter

maturity than another bond may actually have a longer duration and be more price-sensitive to interest rate changes." Explain why a bond with a shorter maturity than another bond could actually have a longer duration.

5. As market rates of interest become higher, what impact does this have on duration?

6. What happens to duration as the coupon rate on a bond issue declines from 12 percent to 0 percent with the maturity date remaining constant?

7. Why is the maturity date and duration the same for a zero-coupon bond?

8. Should an investor who thinks interest rates are going down seek low or high coupon rate bonds? Relate your answer to duration and price sensitivity.

9. Why are zero-coupon bonds the most price-sensitive of any type of bond issue?

10. Why is the reinvestment rate assumption critical to bond portfolio management?

11. What is a terminal wealth table? How is terminal wealth analysis different from the realized yield approach in Chapter 10?

12. Why is it said that zero-coupon bonds lock in the reinvestment rate?

13. Is the locked-in reinvestment assumption valid for zero-coupon bonds if they are sold before maturity? Explain.

PROBLEMS

1. Compute the simple weighted average life for the following data. Use an approach similar to that in Table 11–1.

Year	Cash flow
1	$ 115
2	115
3	115
4	115
5	115
5	1,000

2. Compute the duration for the data in Problem 1. Use an approach similar to that in Table 11–2. A discount rate of 14 percent should be applied.

3. As part of the your answer to Problem 2, you computed the price of the bond (column 4).

   a. Recompute the price of a bond based on a 12 percent discount rate (market rate of interest).

   b. What is the percentage change in the price of the bond as interest rates decline by 2 percent from 14 percent to 12 percent?

   c. Approximate this same value by multiplying the duration computed in Problem 2 times the change in interest rates (2 percent). The answer in part c should come reasonably close to the answer in part b. However, they will not be exactly the same.

4. a. Compute the duration for the following data. Use a discount rate of 14 percent.

Year	Cash flow
1	$ 60
2	60
3	60
4	60
5	60
5	1,000

b. Explain why the answer to 4a is higher than the answer to Problem 2.

c. If in part 4a, the discount rate were 10 instead of 14 percent, would duration be longer or shorter? You do not need to actually compute a value; merely indicate an answer based on the discussion material in the text.

5. You are considering the purchase of two $1,000 bonds, both issued by Lotus Incorporated. Your expectation is that interest rates will drop and you want to buy the bond which provides the maximum capital gains potential. The first Lotus bond has a coupon rate of 5 percent with four years to maturity, while the second has a coupon rate of 14 percent and comes due six years from now. The market rate of interest (discount rate) is 10 percent. Which bond has the best price movement potential? Use duration to answer the question.

6. Assume you desire maximum duration to take advantage of anticipated interest rate declines. Answer the following questions based on information taken from Table 11–6 and Table 11–7.

a. Would you prefer an 8 percent coupon rate bond with a 20-year maturity or a 4 percent coupon rate bond with a 25-year maturity? The market rate of interest is 10 percent.

b. Would you prefer an 8 percent coupon rate bond with a 20-year maturity or a 12 percent coupon rate bond with a 25-year maturity? The market rate of interest is 12 percent.

c. Would you prefer an 8 percent coupon rate bond with a 20-year maturity or a 12 percent coupon rate bond with a 25-year maturity? The market rate of interest is 6 percent.

7. A 25-year, $1,000 par value zero-coupon bond provides a yield of 12 percent.

a. Compute the current price of the zero-coupon bond. (Hint: simply take the present value of the ending $1,000 payment).

b. What is the duration of the bond?

c. Does the bond have a longer or shorter duration than a 50-year, 8 percent coupon rate bond, where the duration on the latter bond is based on a 10 percent market rate of interest (consult Table 11–6).

d. Assume you were going to put the zero-coupon bond(s) in a non-taxable Investment Retirement Account (IRA). If you wish to have $30,000 after 25 years, how much would you need to invest today?

e. If a $1,000 par value zero-coupon rate bond had a 40-year maturity and provided a yield of 12 percent, what would be the current price of the zero-coupon bond?

8. Assume you buy a 15-year, $1,000 par value zero-coupon bond that provides a 12 percent yield. Almost immediately after you buy the bond, yields go down to 11 percent. What will be your gain on the investment?

9. You have invested $1,000 in a 14 percent coupon bond that matures in five years. This bond is held in your Individual Retirement Account, and you are not concerned about tax consequences. You are investing the interest income in a money market fund earning 9 percent. At the end of five years, what will be your portfolio sum? Follow the procedure in Table 11–10.

10. In Problem 9, what is the annual percentage return? Use Appendix A at the end of the book to help you find the answer. An approximation will be sufficient.

SELECTED REFERENCES

Fabozzi, Frank J., and Irving M. Pollack, eds. "Bond Yield Measures and Price Volatility Properties." Chap. 4, *The Handbook of Fixed Income Securities,* Homewood, Ill.: Dow-Jones Irwin, 1983, pp. 53–90.

Fisher, Lawrence, and Roman L. Weil. "Coping with the Risk of Interest Rate Fluctuations: Returns to Bondholders from Naive and Optimal Strategies." *Journal of Business,* October 1971, pp. 408–31.

Haugen, Robert A., and Dean Wichern. "The Elasticity of Financial Assets." *Journal of Finance,* September 1974, pp. 1229–40.

Hessel, Christopher A., and Lucy T. Huffman. "Incorporation of Tax Considerations into the Computation of Duration." *The Journal of Financial Research,* Fall 1983, pp. 213–15.

Hopewell, Michael H., and George G. Kaufman. "Bond Price Volatility and Term to Maturity: A Generalized Respecification." *American Economic Review,* September 1973, pp. 749–53.

Macaulay, F. R. *Some Theoretical Problems Suggested by the Movement of Interest Rates, Bond Yields, and Stock Prices in the United States Since 1856.* New York: National Bureau of Economic Research, 1938.

Malkiel, B. G. "Expectations, Bond Prices, and the Term Structure of Interest Rates." *Quarterly Journal of Economics,* May 1962, pp. 197–218.

Reilly, Frank K., and Rupindner S. Sidha. "The Many Uses of Bond Duration." *Financial Analysts Journal,* July–August 1980, pp. 58–72.

Smith, Randall, "Zero-Coupon Bonds' Price Swings Jolt Investors Looking for Security." *The Wall Street Journal,* June 1, 1984, p. 19.

Yawitz, Jess B.; George H. Hempel; and William J. Marshall. "The Use of Average Maturity as a Risk Proxy in Investment Portfolios." *Journal of Finance,* May 1975, pp. 325–35.

Yawitz, Jess B., and William J. Marshall, "The Shortcomings of Duration As a Risk Measure for Bonds." *The Journal of Financial Research,* Summer 1981, pp. 91–101.

Chapter 12

CONVERTIBLE SECURITIES AND WARRANTS

An investment in convertible securities or warrants offers the market participant special opportunities to meet investment objectives. For conservative investors, convertible securities can offer regular income and potential downside protection against falling stock prices. Convertibles also offer capital gains opportunities for an investor desiring the appreciation potential of an equity investment. Warrants are more speculative securities and offer the chance for leveraged returns.

These securities have been used as financing alternatives for corporations in periods of high interest rates or tight money. Also, convertibles have been utilized as a medium of exchange for acquiring other companies' stock in mergers and acquisitions. Convertibles and warrants have advantages to the corporation and to the owner of the security. It is important to realize as we go through this chapter that what is an advantage to the corporation is often a disadvantage to the investor, and vise versa. These securities involve trade-offs between the buyer and the corporation that are taken into consideration in the pricing of each security.

CONVERTIBLE SECURITIES

A convertible security is a bond or share of preferred stock that can be converted into common stock at the option of the holder. Thus, the owner has a fixed-income security that can be transferred to common stock if and when the affairs of the firm indicate that such a conversion is desirable. For purposes of our discussion, we will use a Tandy Corporation 6½ percent convertible bond (debenture) rated Aa by Moody's.

While this bond was called for redemption on September 10, 1980, it still serves as one of the best examples of the benefits and perils of owning convertible bonds. In general, the best time to buy convertible bonds is when interest rates are high (bond prices are depressed) and when stock prices are relatively low. Purchase at times like these increases the probability of a successful investment because rising stock prices and falling interest rates both exert upward pressure on the price of a convertible security. This will become more apparent as we proceed through the chapter.

CONVERSION PRICE AND CONVERSION RATIO

The following quote from the footnotes to Tandy's 1979 Annual Report indicates the kind of information available to the bond- or stockholder.

> On October 31, 1978, the Company issued $100,000,000 of 6½ percent convertible subordinated debentures due 2003. These debentures are convertible at the option of the holder into common stock of the Company at $29 per share, unless previously redeemed. The debentures may be redeemed, at the Company's option, at any time in whole or in part on not less than 30 nor more than 60 days notice at 106.50 percent of their principal amount on or before December 31, 1979. The redemption price declines annually to 100.00 in 1998. Mandatory sinking fund payments are required, beginning in 1989, sufficient to redeem on December 31 of each year $5,000,000 principal amount of debentures at par.

Most of the terms contained in the quote are simply a review of your knowledge on bonds. However, one question is not answered directly. How many shares of common stock are you entitled to receive upon conversion? Notice that the debentures are convertible at $29 per share. This is called the *conversion price.* The face value ($1,000) or par value never changes (the market price does), so by dividing the face value by the conversion price, we get the number of shares received upon conversion of one $1,000 bond. This is called the *conversion ratio.*

$$\frac{\text{Face value}}{\text{Conversion price}} = \text{Conversion ratio} \qquad (12\text{--}1)$$

For the Tandy convertible bond, an investor would receive 34.4827 shares for each bond.

$$\frac{\$1000\ (\text{face value})}{\$29/\text{share}\ (\text{conversion price})} = \frac{34.4827\ \text{shares}}{(\text{conversion ratio})}$$

Value of the Convertible Bond

Let us follow the October 31, 1978, issue of Tandy's 6½ percent convertible bond through conversion on September 10, 1980. The bond was originally sold at $1,000, and the common stock price on the day of this offering closed at 23⅛ on the New York Stock Exchange. If the bondholder converted the bond into 34.48 shares of common stock, what would be the market value of the common stock received? We can find this by multiplying the conversion ratio by the market price per share of the common stock, and we get a value of $797.35.

$$\text{Conversion ratio} \times \text{Common stock price} = \text{Conversion value} \qquad (12\text{--}2)$$
$$34.48\ \text{shares} \quad \times \quad \$23.125 \quad = \$797.35\ (\text{round to }\$797)$$

This value is called the *conversion value* and represents the value of the underlying shares of common stock each bond represents.

The convertible bond also has what is called a *pure bond value.* This represents its value as a straight bond (nonconvertible). In the case of Tandy Corporation there was also a straight debenture outstanding, carrying a coupon rate of 10 percent and a market price of $960. Based on this information, the yield to maturity on a nonconvertible Tandy bond would be 10.45 percent at the time the convertible bond was issued. If the 6½ percent Tandy bond were valued as a straight debenture at this 10.45 percent yield to maturity, it would have a pure bond value of $654.[1] This is considered the floor price or minimum value of the bond. The conversion value and the pure bond value can be seen in Figure 12–1, which depicts the Tandy convertible bond. As a

---

[1] Using present value procedures from Chapter 10, the interest payment of $65 per year for 25 years would have a present value at 10.45 percent of $570.17, and the principal of $1,000 would have a present value of 83.34 for a total value of $653.51. We round to $654.

FIGURE 12–1 Tandy Convertible Bond on Day of Issue, October 31, 1978

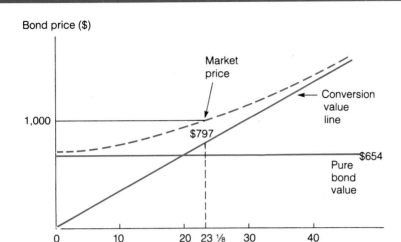

side point, the reader should be aware that it is possible for the pure bond value to change if interest rates in the market change. This point, of course, is not reflected in Figure 12–1.

Bond Price and Premiums

You may wonder how a company can originally sell a bond for $1,000 when the conversion value is $797 and the pure bond value is $654. Let's examine these values. The difference between the bond's market price ($1,000) and the conversion value ($797) is a premium of $203; it is usually expressed as a percentage of the conversion value and thus is called the *conversion premium*. In this case, the conversion premium at issue was 25.47 percent.

$$\text{Conversion premium} = \frac{\text{Market price of bond} - \text{Conversion value}}{\text{Conversion value}} \qquad (12\text{–}3)$$

$$= \frac{\$1000 - \$797}{\$797} = \frac{\$203}{\$797}$$

$$= 25.47 \text{ percent}$$

The $203 premium indicates the extra amount paid for the 34.48 shares of stock. Remember, in essence you paid $29 per share for 34.48 shares by purchasing the bond, but you could have had the same number of shares purchased on the NYSE for 23⅛.

There are several reasons why people pay the conversion premium. In the case of Tandy's bond, the premium is somewhat larger than the usual 15 to

20 percent. First, Tandy common stock pays no dividend, while the bond pays $65 per year in interest. If the bondholder owns the bond for a little over three years, he recovers almost all the premium through the $65 yearly differential between dividend and interest income. Many companies do pay dividends on their common stock, and an analysis of interest income versus dividend income is always important in comparing a stock purchase to a convertible bond purchase.

Additionally, the bond price will rise as the stock price rises because of the convertible feature, but there is a downside limit if the stock should decline in price. This downside limit is established by the pure bond value, which in this case is $654. This downside protection is further justification for the conversion premium. One way to compute this downside protection is to calculate the difference between the market price of the bond and the pure bond value as a percentage of the market price.

$$\text{Downside risk} = \frac{\text{Market price of bond} - \text{Pure bond value}}{\text{Market price of bond}} \qquad (12\text{--}4)$$

$$= \frac{\$1000 - \$654}{\$1000} = \frac{\$346}{\$1000}$$

$$= 34.6 \text{ percent}$$

In the case of Tandy, there is a downside limit of 34.6 percent. This is the maximum percentage the bond will decline in value if the stock price falls. One important warning is necessary—the pure bond value is sensitive to market interest rates. As competitively rated Aa bond interest rates rise, the pure bond value will decline. Therefore, downside risk can vary with changing interest rates.

The conversion premium is also affected by several other variables. The more volatile the stock price as measured by beta or standard deviation of returns, the higher the conversion premium. This occurs because the potential for capital gains is larger than on less volatile stocks. The longer the term to maturity, the higher the premium—because there is a greater chance that the stock price could rise, making the bond more valuable.

Figure 12–2 presents a graph of the Tandy convertible bond and depicts the conversion premium in Panel (a) and the downside risk in Panel (b). Point *P* in both panels represents the parity point where the conversion value equals the pure bond value. Notice that the market price follows the conversion value to the right of point *P* and is more influenced by the pure bond value to the left of point *P*. As the common stock price rises, the conversion value rises accordingly, and the bond market price also rises. Furthermore, the conversion premium shrinks and the downside risk increases, which gives the bondholder less downside protection should the stock decline. As the stock declines, the conversion value falls and the conversion premium increases, but the downside risk declines as the pure bond value acts as a "floor value."

Let us track the Tandy bond from issue to conversion. As previously mentioned, Tandy Corporation also had a debenture (nonconvertible) out-

FIGURE 12–2   Tandy Convertible Bond—6½ Percent, 2003 Maturity (convertible into 34.4827 shares of common stock as of October 31, 1978)

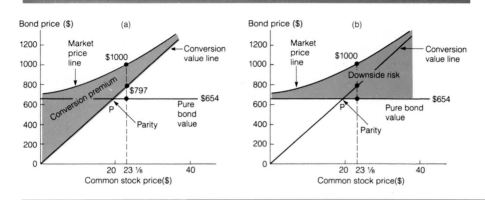

standing with a 10 percent coupon. The debenture maintained a relatively stable price, and the yield to maturity hovered around 10.45 percent during the 22 months the convertible bond was outstanding. Given that the convertible bond would have approximately the same yield to maturity as the debenture, we assume that the pure bond value of the convertible bond stayed the same in all three panels in Figure 12–3. In Panel (a) we see the original information on the convertible issue. Approximately seven months later, as

FIGURE 12–3   Tandy 6½ Convertible Bond Closing Prices

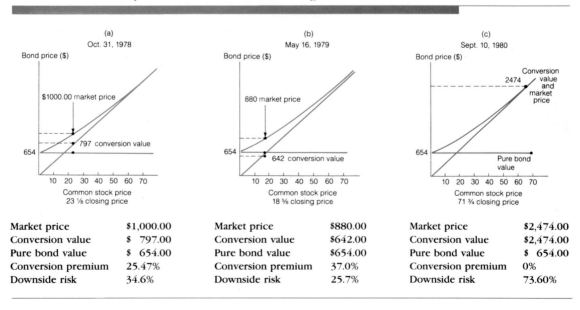

	(a)	(b)	(c)
	Oct. 31, 1978	May 16, 1979	Sept. 10, 1980
Market price	$1,000.00	$880.00	$2,474.00
Conversion value	$ 797.00	$642.00	$2,474.00
Pure bond value	$ 654.00	$654.00	$ 654.00
Conversion premium	25.47%	37.0%	0%
Downside risk	34.6%	25.7%	73.60%

shown in Panel (b), Tandy common stock had declined to 18⅝ and the bond to $880, creating a conversion value of $642 and a conversion premium of 37 percent. The downside risk had declined from 34.6 percent on October 31, 1978, to 25.7 percent by May 16, 1979. In retrospect, this would have been a good price at which to buy the bond. By September 10, 1980, we see in Panel (c) that the stock skyrocketed to 71¾ and the bond had a conversion value of $2,474. This was exactly equal to the market price, as there was no conversion premium. On this date, the Tandy Corporation also called the bond at $1,061.60. Thus, the investor could allow the bond to be redeemed at a mere $1,061.60 or convert it into common shares worth $2,474.[2]

Comparison to Common Stock

Would you have been better off putting $1,000 in Tandy stock on October 31, 1978, or $1,000 into the convertible bond? One thousand dollars in Tandy stock at 23⅛ would have purchased 43.24 shares, while $1,000 invested in the bond got the investor 34.48 shares. On the day of redemption (September 10, 1980), a stock investment would have been worth $3,103 and the convertible bond, $2,474 plus $128 in interest over the life of the issue, or $2,602. The common stock investor would have been better off, but if the stock had gone down sharply, then the convertible with its floor value would have been the better investment. Table 12–1 shows the comparison between a stock investment and a convertible bond investment.

TABLE 12–1   Comparative Tandy Corporation Investments

	Amount invested, October 31, 1978	Shares	Stock prices, September 10, 1980	Ending value	Total dividends	Total interest	Total value
Stock	$1,000	43.24	71¾	$3,103	$0	—	$3,103
Convertible bond	1,000	34.48	71¾	2,472	—	$128	2,602

Actually, we have picked one of the more successful convertible bond offerings in recent years. If the convertible bondholder had taken common shares on the call date, these 34.48 shares would have increased to 137.93 shares by June 1981, through several 2-for-1 stock splits. During 1983 Tandy common stock reached $64.50 per share, which would have created a total value of $8,896.00 on the original $1,000 investment. However, by July of 1984 the shares fell to $25.25 ($3,482), which shows that timing is important. The danger in using such a good example is that you may think convertible bonds are always a good investment.

---

[2] As the third alternative, the investor might immediately sell the bonds and allow another investor to convert.

Table 12–2 is a page from the Shearson/American Express January 1984 issue of *Selected Convertibles*. A glance down the fourth column of the top portion of the table for bond prices will point out that many bonds were above $1,000.00 (remember that bond prices are quoted in percentages of par value). Examples include American General, Bank of New York, and Barnett Banks. Notice that the conversion premiums (seventh column) for these bonds are quite low, which would indicate that the stock price is close to the conversion price. However, several of the convertibles, such as Burnup & Sims, Digicon, Hughes Tool, Oak Industries, and Storage Technology have conversion premiums of 100 percent, which means that the bond price is twice the conversion value. This indicates that these bonds are selling based on their interest-paying ability rather than on the underlying stock price. Notice that most of the bonds and preferred stock listed in Table 12–2 have ratings below an S&P category of A. This is quite common for convertibles.

Disadvantages to Convertibles

It has been said that everything has a price, and purchasing convertible securities at the wrong price can eliminate one of its main advantages. For example, once convertible debentures begin going up in value, the downside protection becomes pretty meaningless. In the case of Tandy Corporation, in our earlier example, the floor price is at $654. If an investor were to pay $1,400 for the convertible bond, he or she would be exposed to $746 in potential losses (hardly adequate protection for a true risk averter). Also, don't forget if interest rates in the market rise, the floor price, or pure bond value, could fall, thus creating greater downside risk.

Another drawback with convertible bonds is that the purchaser is invariably asked to accept below-market rates on the debt instrument. The interest rate on convertibles is generally one third below that for instruments in a similar risk class (e.g., 8 percent instead of 12 percent). In the sophisticated environment of the bond and stock markets, one seldom gets an additional benefit without having to suffer a corresponding disadvantage.

The student will also recall that the purchaser of a convertible bond pays a premium over the conversion value. For example, if a $1,000 bond were convertible into 20 shares of common at $45 per share, a $100 conversion premium would be involved initially. If the same $1,000 were invested directly in common stock at $45 per share, 22.2 shares could be purchased. If the shares go up in value, we have 2.2 more shares on which to garner a profit.

From the institutional investor's standpoint many convertible securities lack liquidity because of small trading volume or even the small amount of convertibles issued by one company. The institutions tend to stick with convertible issues of $100 million or more when they can be found.

When to Convert into Common Stock

Convertible securities generally have a call provision, such as the Tandy bond had (see earlier description), which gives the corporation the option of re-

TABLE 12–2

Selected Convertible Bonds–January 1984

Issue	Coupon	Maturity	S&P Rating	Approx. Price	Current Yield	Conversion $ PX/#Shs.	Conv. Prem.	Yield Advan. Over Common	Call Price	Quotron Symbol
Amer General	11%	2/ 8/07	A+	133	8.2%	$18.3/54.6	6.0%	4.7%	110.0	AGW.F
American Medical Int'l*	8¼	4/ 1/08	A–	88	9.4	40.0/25.0	47	7.4	107.4	AMV.F
Avnet*	8	10/ 1/13	A+	111	7.2	52.0/19.2	25	6.1	106.4	AVI.F
Bank of New York	12	12/ 1/06	A	132	10.0	24.6/40.6	1	4.4	109.6	BKQ.F
Barnett Banks†	12¼	12/15/06	A–	140	8.8	31.0/32.3	11	5.7	108.6	BBF.F
Big Three Ind.	8½	4/15/06	A	82	10.4	43.5/23.0	61	6.7	106.7	BIH.F
Boeing Co.*	8⅞	6/15/06	A	123	7.2	42.2/23.7	18	4.0	106.5	BAH.F
Burnup & Sims	12	11/15/01	B+	80	15.0	19.3/52.0	100	14.0	107.2	—
Comserv (OTC)†† †	11	7/ 1/02	CCC	65	16.9	14.5/69.0	55	16.9	108.8	—
Digicon†	10½	11/15/01	B	67	15.7	32.8/30.5	100	15.7	107.4	DGCA.A
Dreyfus Corp.	7⅜	6/1/08	BBB+	83	8.9	37.0/27.0	28	6.8	105.9	DRY.F
Eastman Kodak*	8¼	12/15/07	AAA	101	8.2	102.3/9.8	35	4.3	107.4	EKA.F
General Cinema (RJR)*	10	3/15/08	BBB	112	8.9	62.8/15.9	14	3.4	107.0	GCN.F
Graphic Scanning	10	12/ 1/01	B	82	12.2	10.6/94.1	33	12.2	107.0	—
Great Western Fincl.*	8⅞	12/01/07	BBB–	99	9.0	30.5/32.8	37	5.0	107.7	GWF.F
GTE Corp.*	10½	11/ 1/07	BBB	117	8.9	46.0/21.7	21	2.0	107.6	GTV.F
Hughes Tool*	9½	12/15/06	A	86	11.0	47.2/21.2	100	7.0	107.8	HTB.F
InterNorth(MOB)*	10½	6/ 1/08	BBB+	101	10.4	40.0/25.0	39	3.4	100.0	INZ.F
LIN Broadcasting (OTC)††	8¾	12/15/07	BB–	122	7.2	20.3/49.4	11	7.2	107.9	LINB.G
M/A Com*	9¼	5/15/06	BB+	92	10.1	36.5/27.4	67	9.0	107.4	MAI.F
Mapco*	10	5/15/05	BBB–	88	11.4	45.7/21.9	63	7.3	107.3	MDX.F
MCI Comm.†† †	7¾	3/15/03	BB+	82	9.5	26.1/38.4	46	9.5	106.2	MCICG
Oak Industries*	10½	2/15/02	B	66	15.9	33.7/29.7	100	15.9	108.4	OAB.F
Pacific Scientific	7¾	6/15/03	B	75	10.3	38.0/26.3	60	8.0	106.2	PSX.F
PNC Financial (OTC)†† †	8¼	5/15/08	AA	106	7.8	46.0/21.7	17	2.9	106.6	—
Pogo Producing*	8	12/31/05	BB–	74	10.8	39.5/25.3	40	7.9	106.8	PPP.F
Quaker State	8⅞	3/15/08	BBB+	100	8.9	20.8/48.2	19	4.3	107.1	KSG.F
Research Cottrell	10½	10/31/06	BBB–	106	9.9	17.0/58.8	19	7.8	108.9	RCT.F
Seagram Co.*	8¼	6/ 1/08	A	107	7.7	37.8/26.5	11	5.8	106.6	SEG.F
Storage Technology*	9	5/15/01	BBB–	72	12.5	36.8/27.2	100	12.5	106.3	STV.F
Storer Communications*	8½	12/31/05	BB–	108	7.9	40.0/25.0	14	6.8	107.2	SCII.F
Sun Co. (BDX)*	10¾	4/ 1/06	AA–	97	11.1	59.9/16.7	56	8.0	109.1	SUU.F
Texas Industries	9	1/15/08	B+	99	9.1	43.1/23.2	22	6.8	107.2	TXP.F
Wang Lab*	7¾	6/ 1/08	BBB	97	8.0	52.2/19.2	41	7.7	106.7	WANI.A

Selected Convertible Preferred Stocks–January 1984

Issue	Dividend	S&P Rating	Approx. Price	Current Yield	Conversion Ratio	Conversion Premium	Yield Advan. Over C/S	Call Price	Quotron Symbol	Ex-Div Schedule
Allied Corp*	6.74	BBB	64	10.5%	.786	45%	6.2%	57.0	ALD.PrC	JAJO
Anheuser Busch*	3.60	NR	49	7.4	.645	22	4.7	40.0	BUD.PrA	FMAN
Barnett Banks†	2.375	NR	42	5.7	1.042	2	2.6	25.0	BBF.PrA	MJSD
Castle & Cooke	2.50	NR	32	7.8	1.553	14	7.8	27.5	CKEPr	FMAN
Cigna*	2.75	NR	29	9.5	.422	52	3.9	27.1	CIPrA	MJSD
City Investing*	2.875	BB–	25	11.5	.500	32	6.5	27.9	CNVPrE	MJSD
Crown Zellerbach*	4.625	BBB–	50	9.3	1.058	28	6.7	53.2	ZBPrA	MJSD
Fruehauf	2.00	BB–	37	5.4	.758	6	4.5	27.0	FTRPr	JAJO
Georgia Pacific*	2.24	BBB+	35	6.4	1.00	45	4.0	39.0	GPPrA	FMAN
LTV Corp*	3.06	BB–	30	10.2	1.3	25	8.8	28.1	LTVPrB	FMAN
RCA Corp*	2.125	BB	28	7.6	.714	12	5.1	26.1	RCAPrC	MJSD
Signal Co.*	4.125	A+	57	7.2	1.471	18	4.5	53.3	SGNPrA	JAJO
UAL Inc.*	2.40	BB–	28	8.6	.585	29	8.6	26.1	UALPrB	FMAN
United Technologies*	2.55	A	33	7.7	.393	15	4.1	29.0	UTXPrD	FMAN
Weyerhaeuser*	4.50	A	49	9.2	1.111	30	5.3	53.0	WYPrA	FMAN

**Listed Options Available*
†Shearson/American Express has an investment banking relationship.
††Shearson/American Express maintains an Over-the-Counter market in the underlying common stocks.

Special Note: The call provisions of convertible bonds and preferreds can be very complex. When in question, please call for complete details. The call price and date may not be complete as described in a summary guide.

Source: Shearson/American Express *Selected Convertibles,* January 1984.

deeming the bond at a specified price before maturity. The call price is usually at a premium over par value ($1,000) in the early years of callability, and it generally declines over time to par value. We know that as the price of the common stock goes up, the convertible security will rise along with the stock so that the investor has no incentive to convert his bonds into stock. However, the corporation may use the call privilege to force conversion before maturity. Companies usually force conversion when the conversion value is well above the call price, like the Tandy offer which forced conversion on September 10, 1980, when the conversion value was $2,474 and the call price was $1,061.60. Investors will take the shares rather than the call price since the shares are worth more. This enables the company to turn debt into equity on its balance sheet and makes new debt issues a better risk for future lenders because of higher interest coverage and a lower debt-to-equity ratio.

Corporations may also encourage voluntary conversion by using a step-up in the conversion price over time. When the bond is issued, the contract may specify the following conversion provisions.

	Conversion price	Conversion ratio
First five years	$40	25.0 shares
Next three years	45	22.2 shares
Next two years	50	20.0 shares
Next five years	55	18.2 shares

At the end of each time period, there is a strong inducement to convert rather than accept an adjustment to a higher conversion price and a lower conversion ratio. This is especially true if the bond's conversion value is the dominating influence on the market price of the bond. In the case where the conversion value is below the pure bond value and where the interest income is greater than the dividend income, an investor will most likely not be induced to convert through the step-up feature.

About the only other reason for voluntarily converting is if the dividend income received on the common stock is greater than the interest income on the bond. Even in this case, investors who are risk-averse may want to hold the bond because interest is guaranteed, whereas dividends may be reduced. As with most investment decisions, investors must consider their expectations of future corporate and market conditions. Hard and fast rules are difficult to find, and different investors may react according to their own risk aversion and objectives.

ADVANTAGES AND DISADVANTAGES TO THE ISSUING CORPORATION

Having established the fundamental characteristics of the convertible security from the investor viewpoint, let us now turn the coin over and examine the

factors a corporate financial officer must consider in weighing the advisability of a convertible offer for the firm.

Not only has it been established that the interest rate paid on convertible issues is lower than that paid on a straight debt instrument, but also the convertible feature may be the only device for allowing smaller corporations access to the bond market. In this day of debt-ridden corporate balance sheets, investor acceptance of new debt may be contingent upon a special sweetener, such as the ability to convert to common stock.

Convertible debentures are also attractive to a corporation that feels its stock is currently undervalued. For example, assume a corporation's $1,000 bonds are convertible into 20 shares of common stock at a conversion price of $50. Also assume the company's common stock has a current price of $45, and new shares of stock might be sold at only $44.[3] Thus, the corporation will effectively receive $6 over current market price, assuming future conversion. Of course, one can also argue that if the firm had delayed the issuance of common stock or convertibles for a year or two, the stock might have gone up from $45 to $60 or $65, and new common stock might have been sold at this lofty price.

To translate this to overall numbers for the firm, if a corporation needs $10 million in funds and offers straight stock now at a new price of $44, it must issue 227,272 shares ($10 million/$44). With convertibles, the number of shares potentially issued is only 200,000 shares ($10 million/$50). Finally, if no stock or convertible bonds are issued now and the stock goes up to a level at which new shares can be offered at a price of $60, only 166,667 will be required ($10 million/$60).

Another matter of concern to the corporation is the accounting treatment accorded to convertibles. In the funny-money days of the 1960s conglomerate merger movement, corporate management often chose convertible securities over common stock because the convertibles had a nondilutive effect on earnings per share. As is indicated in the following section on reporting earnings for convertibles, the rules were changed in 1969, and this practice is no longer followed.

ACCOUNTING CONSIDERATIONS WITH CONVERTIBLES

Prior to 1969, the full impact of the conversion privilege as it applied to convertible securities, warrants (long-term options to buy stock), and other dilutive securities was not adequately reflected in reported earnings per share. Since all of these securities may generate additional common stock in the future, the potential effect of dilution should be considered. Let us examine the unadjusted (for conversion) financial statements of the XYZ Corporation in Table 12–3.

---

[3] There is always a bit of underpricing to ensure the success of a new offering.

TABLE 12-3   XYZ Corporation

1. Capital section of balance sheet
   Common stock (1 million shares at $10 par) $10,000,000
   4.5% convertible debentures (10,000 deben-
   tures of $1,000; convertible into 40 shares
   per bond, or a total of 400,000 shares)   10,000,000
   Retained earnings   20,000,000
   Net worth $40,000,000

2. Condensed income statement
   Earnings before interest and taxes $ 2,450,000
   Interest (4.5% of $10 million of convertibles)   450,000
   Earnings before taxes   2,000,000
   Taxes (50%)   1,000,000
   Earnings after taxes $ 1,000,000

3. Earnings per share (unadjusted)
   $$\frac{\text{Earnings after taxes}}{\text{Shares of common stock}} = \frac{\$1,000,000}{1,000,000} = \$1$$

An analyst would hardly be satisfied in accepting the unadjusted earnings per share figure of $1 for the XYZ Corporation. In computing earnings per share, we have not accounted for the 400,000 additional shares of common stock that could be created by converting the bonds. How then do we make this full disclosure? According to Accounting Principles Board *Opinion No. 15,* issued by the American Institute of Certified Public Accountants in 1969, we need to compute earnings per share using two different methods when there is potential dilution of a material nature.

1. Primary earnings per share

$$= \frac{\text{Adjusted earnings after taxes}}{\text{Shares outstanding} + \text{Common stock equivalents}} \qquad (12\text{-}5)$$

Common stock equivalents include warrants, other options, and any convertible securities that paid less than two thirds of the going interest rate at time of issue.[4]

2. Fully diluted earnings per share

$$= \frac{\text{Adjusted earnings after taxes}}{\substack{\text{Shares outstanding} + \text{Common stock equivalents} \\ + \text{All convertibles regardless of the interest rate}}} \qquad (12\text{-}6)$$

The intent in computing both primary and fully diluted earnings per share is to consider the effect of potential dilution. Common stock equivalents

---

[4] The going interest rate was initially defined as the prime interest rate in Accounting Principles Board *Opinion No. 15* (1969). In 1982 the Financial Accounting Standards Board defined the going interest rate as the average Aa bond yield at the time of issue.

represent those securities that are capable of generating new shares of common stock in the future. Note that convertible securities may or may not be required in computing primary earnings per share depending on rates, but they must be included in computing fully diluted earnings per share.

In the case of the XYZ Corporation in Table 12–3 the convertibles pay 4.5 percent interest. We assume that the going interest rate was 9 percent at the time they were issued, so they are considered as common stock equivalents and are included in both primary and fully diluted earnings per share.

We get new earnings per share for the XYZ Corporation by assuming that 400,000 new shares will be created from potential conversion, while at the same time allowing for the reduction in interest payments that would take place as a result of the conversion of the debt to common stock. Since before-tax interest payments on the convertibles are $450,000, the aftertax interest cost ($225,000) will be saved and can be added back to income. Making the appropriate adjustments to the numerator and denominator, we show adjusted earnings per share.

$$\frac{\text{Primary earnings}}{\text{per share}^5} = \frac{\text{Adjusted earnings after taxes}}{\text{Shares outstanding} + \text{Common stock equivalents}}$$

$$= \frac{\overset{\substack{\text{Reported} \\ \text{earnings}}}{\$1,000,000} + \overset{\substack{\text{Interest} \\ \text{savings}}}{\$225,000}}{1,000,000 + 400,000} = \frac{\$1,225,000}{1,400,000} = \$.875$$

We see a 12½-cent reduction from the earnings per share figure of $1 in Table 12–4. The new figure is the value that a sophisticated security analyst would utilize.

SPECULATING THROUGH WARRANTS

A warrant is an option to buy a stated number of shares of stock at a specified price over a given time period. For example, Eastern Airlines has a number of issues of warrants outstanding. One warrant due in the late 1980s, allows the holder to buy one share of common stock at $10 per share. Eastern has been struggling to stay alive in the airline competition and the stock price as of July 23, 1984, was $4.125. If Eastern Airlines can return to profitability, the common stock could rise above $10 per share and the warrants could become quite valuable. If the stock does not eventually rise to $10 per share, it is possible that Eastern Airlines could extend the expiration date of the warrant. One advantage of the warrants to the company is that when exercised, they bring in cash for new shares of common stock. A firm like Eastern might want to increase equity under its current heavy debt load.

Warrants are usually issued as a sweetener to a bond offering, and they may enable the firm to issue debt when this would not be feasible otherwise.

---

[5] Same as fully diluted in this instance.

TABLE 12–4   Selected Warrants as of July 23, 1984

(1) Firm, warrant, listing, stock listings	(2) Warrant price	(3) Per share stock price	(4) Per share option price	(5) Intrinsic value (3) – (4)	(6) Premium (2) – (5)	(7) Percent stock must rise to break even	(8) Number of shares per warrant	(9) Due date
American General, NY, NY	6.25	20.125	24.25	–4.125	10.375	52%	1.00	1/4/89
Atlas Corp., AM;, NY	3.75	15.25	31.25	–16.00	19.75	130%	1.00	Perpetual
Computers Horizons, OTL, OTL	1.75	6.50	15.25	–4.375*	6.125	168%	.5	9/20/88
Eastern Airlines, NY, NY	1.50	4.125	10.00	–5.875	7.375	179%	1.00	6/1/87
Fuqua Industries, OTL, NY	30.00	25.00	11.75	30.34*	–.34	–1%	2.29	6/30/88
International Harvester, NY, NY	4.75	6.50	5.00	1.50	3.25	50%	1.00	12/15/93
Kidde, AM, NY	3.375	29.125	40.00	–10.875	14.25	49%	1.00	11/15/87

* For these two companies, we use column (3) – column (4) times the value in column (8).

AM = American Stock Exchange, NY = New York Stock Exchange, OTL = Over-the-Counter. The first abbreviation indicates where the warrant trades, and the second abbreviation indicates where the common stock trades.

The warrants allow the bond issue to carry a lower coupon rate and are usually detachable from the bond after the issue date. After being separated from the bond, warrants have their own market price and are primarily traded on the American Stock Exchange or over-the-counter, with a few issues traded on the New York Stock Exchange. After the warrants are exercised, the initial debt with which they were sold remains in existence.

The financial company Bache Group (Bache Halsey Stuart Shields), which is known for its retail brokerage business, had a bond offering October 30, 1980. They offered 35,000 units of $1,000 debentures due in the year 2000 with a coupon interest rate of 14 percent. To each bond, 30 warrants were attached. Each warrant allowed the holder to buy one share of stock at $18.50 until November 1, 1985. At the time of issue, the warrant had no true value since the common stock was selling below $18.50. During 1981, however, the stock went up as several merger offers were made for retail brokerage companies.[6] On May 29, 1981, Bache common stock was selling at 31½, and each warrant traded at 13⅝. The 30 warrants received with each bond were now worth $408.75 and provided the sweetener every bondholder had hoped for.

Because a warrant is dependent on the market movement of the underlying common stock and has no "security value" as such, it is highly speculative in nature. If the common stock of the firm is volatile, the value of the warrants may change dramatically.

Tri-Continental Corporation warrants went from 1/32 to 75¾ between 1942 and 1969, while United Airlines warrants moved from 4½ to 126 in the 1962–66 time span. Of course, this is not a one-way street, as holders of LTV warrants will attest when they saw their holdings dip from 83 to 2¼ in the 1968–70 bear market.

Valuation of Warrants

Because the value of a warrant is closely tied to the underlying stock price, we can develop a formula for the minimum or intrinsic value of a warrant.

$$I = (M - OP) \times N \qquad\qquad (12\text{--}7)$$

where:

I = The intrinsic or minimum value of the warrant.
M = The market value of the common stock.
OP = The option or exercise price of the warrant.
N = The number of shares each warrant entitles holder to purchase.

Assume that the common stock of the Graham Corporation is $25 per share, and each warrant carries an option to purchase one share at $20 over the next 10 years. Using Formula (12–7) the minimum value is $5. [($25 − $20) × 1]. Since the warrant has 10 more years to run and is an effective vehicle for speculative trading, it may well trade for over $5. If the warrant

---

[6] Bache was subsequently acquired by Prudential Insurance Company.

were selling for $9, we would say that it had an intrinsic or formula value of $5 and a premium of $4.

Even if the stock were trading at less than $20 (the option price on the warrant), the warrant might still have some value in the market. Speculators might purchase the warrant in the hope that the common stock value would increase sufficiently in the future to make the option provision valuable. If the common stock were selling for $15 per share, thus giving the warrant a negative intrinsic value of $5, the warrant might still command a value of $1 or $2 in anticipation of increased common stock value. In Table 12–4 on page 359, we see warrant prices in column (2) and intrinsic values in column (5) for a number of warrants. In column (6) we see the premium (warrant price minus intrinsic value).

In several cases the intrinsic value is negative according to the formula but in practice when the intrinsic value is negative, we generally say it is zero or has no value. Since the owner of the warrant has the option to purchase stock at a set price, the only money the warrant holder can lose is the purchase price of the warrant. Therefore, a negative intrinsic value is meaningless except for determining the premium in column (6) and the break-even percentage in column (7).

As an example of an extreme case, Atlas Corporation's common stock was trading $16.00 below the exercise price on the warrant, and yet the warrant still traded for $3.75. Atlas warrants are perpetual, however, and even though the stock had to increase 130 percent for a warrant purchaser to break even, there is no expiration date to worry about. Actually the Eastern Airlines warrant is even more speculative than Atlas, which can be seen by its high break-even percentage and short time to expiration.

The typical relationship between the market price and the intrinsic value of a warrant is depicted in Figure 12–4. We assume the warrant entitles the holder to purchase one new share of common stock at $20.

Although the intrinsic value of the warrant is theoretically negative at a common stock price between 0 and $20, the warrant still carries some value in the market. Also, observe that the difference between the market price of the warrant and its intrinsic value is diminished at the upper ranges of value. Two reasons may be offered for the declining premium.

First, the speculator loses the ability to use leverage to generate high returns as the price of the stock goes up. When the price of the stock is relatively low, say, $25, and the warrant is in the $5 to $10 range, a 10-point movement in the stock could mean a 200 percent gain in the value of the warrant, as indicated in Part (A) of Table 12–5. At the upper levels of stock value, much of this leverage is lost, as indicated in Part (B) of the same table. At a stock value of $50 and a warrant value of approximately $30, a 10-point movement in the stock would produce only a 33 percent gain in the warrant.

Another reason why speculators pay a very low premium at higher stock prices is that there is less downside protection. A warrant selling at $30 when the stock price is $50 is more vulnerable to downside movement than is a $5 to $10 warrant when the stock is in the 20s.

FIGURE 12–4   **Market Price Relationships for a Warrant**

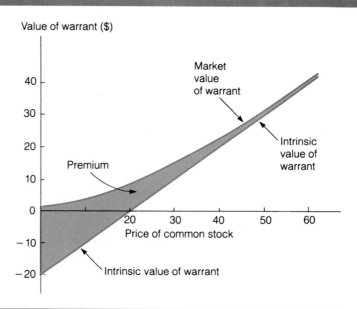

Premiums are also influenced by the same factors that affect convertible bond premiums. More volatile common stocks will have greater potential to create short-run profits for warrant speculators, so the higher the price volatility the greater the premium. Also, the longer the option has before expiration, the higher the premium will be. This "time premium" is worth more the longer the common stock has to reach and surpass the option price of the warrant.

Use of Warrants by Corporations

As previously indicated, warrants may allow for the issuance of debt under difficult circumstances. While a straight debt issue may not be acceptable or may be accepted only at extremely high rates, the same security may be well received because detachable warrants are included. Warrants may also be included as an add-on in a merger or acquisition agreement. A firm might offer $20 million in cash plus 10,000 warrants in exchange for all the outstanding shares of the acquisition candidate.

The use of warrants has traditionally been associated with such aggressive, "high-flying" firms as real estate investment trusts, airlines, and conglomerates. However, in 1970, American Telephone and Telegraph came out with a $1.57 billion debt offering sweetened by the use of warrants.

As a financing device for creating new common stock, warrants may not be as desirable as convertible securities. A corporation with convertible debentures outstanding may force the conversion of debt to common stock through a call, while no similar device is available to the firm with warrants.

TABLE 12–5   Leverage in Valuing Warrants

(A)	(B)
Stock price, \$25; warrant price, \$5* + 10-point movement in stock price. New warrant price, \$15 (10-point gain)	Stock price, \$50; warrant price, \$30 + 10-point movement in stock price. New warrant price, \$40 (10-point gain)

$$\text{Percentage gain in warrant} = \frac{\$10}{\$5} \times 100 = 200\% \qquad \text{Percentage gain in warrant} = \frac{\$10}{\$30} \times 100 = 33\%$$

* The warrant price would, of course, be greater than \$5 because of a premium. Nevertheless, we use \$5 for ease of computation.

The only possible inducement might be a step-up in the option price—whereby the warrant holder may pay a progressively higher option price if he does not exercise by a given date.

The capital structure of the firm after the exercise of a warrant is somewhat different from that created after the conversion of a debenture. In the case of a warrant, the original debt outstanding remains in existence after the detachable warrant is exercised, whereas the conversion of a debenture extinguishes the former debt obligation.[7]

ACCOUNTING CONSIDERATIONS WITH WARRANTS

As with convertible securities, the potential dilutive effect of warrants must be considered. Warrants are generally included in computing both primary and fully diluted earnings per share.[8] The accountant must compute the number of new shares that could be created by the exercise of all warrants, with the provision that the total can be reduced by the assumed use of the cash proceeds to purchase a partially offsetting amount of shares at the market price. Assume that warrants to purchase 10,000 shares at \$20 are outstanding and that the current price of the stock is \$50. We show the following:

1. New shares created	10,000
2. Reduction of shares from cash proceeds (computed below)	4,000

Cash proceeds—10,000 shares at \$20 = \$200,000
Current price of stock—\$50
Assumed reduction in shares outstanding from cash proceeds =
  \$200,000/\$50 = 4,000

3. Assumed net increase in shares from exercise of warrants (10,000 − 4,000)	6,000

[7] It should be pointed out that a number of later financing devices can blur this distinction. See Jerry Miller, "Accounting for Warrants and Convertible Bonds," *Management Accounting,* January 1973, pp. 36–38.

[8] Under most circumstances, if the market price is below the option price, dilution need not be considered (APB *Opinion No. 15*).

In computing earnings per share, we will add 6,000 shares to the denominator with no adjustment to the numerator, which will lower earnings per share. If earnings per share had previously been $1 based on $100,000 in earnings and 100,000 shares outstanding, EPS would now be reduced to $.943.

$$\frac{\text{Earnings}}{\text{Shares}} \frac{\$100,000}{106,000} = \$.943$$

With warrants included in computing both primary and fully diluted earnings per share, their impact on reported earnings is important from both the investor and corporate viewpoints.

SUMMARY

Convertible securities and warrants offer the investor an opportunity for participating in increased common stock values without owning common stock directly. Convertible securities may be in the form of debt or preferred stock, though most of our examples refer to debt.

Convertible securities provide a guaranteed income stream and a floor value based on required yield on the investment. At the same time, they have an established conversion ratio to common stock (par value/conversion price). The conversion value of an issue is equal to the conversion ratio times the current value of a share of common stock. The conversion value is generally less than the current market price of the convertible issue. Actually, the difference between the market price of the convertible issue and the conversion value is referred to as the conversion premium. The conversion premium is influenced by the volatility of the underlying common stock, the time of maturity, the dividend payment on common stock relative to the interest rate on the convertibles, and other lesser factors. Generally, when the common stock price has risen well above the conversion price (and the convertible is trading well above par), the conversion premium will be quite small, as indicated in the left-hand portion of Figure 12–2. The small premium is attributed to the fact that the investor no longer enjoys significant downside protection.

A convertible issue is considered to be potentially dilutive to the reported earnings of the corporation, and since 1969, primary and/or fully diluted earnings per share must consider the impact of potential conversion. Actually, the corporation may ultimately have the opportunity to force conversion through calling the issue at slightly over par when in fact it is selling at a substantially higher price. In the absence of a call, there is generally little incentive to convert since the convertible security will move up and down with the common stock issue.

A warrant is an option to buy a stated number of shares of stock (usually one) at a specified price over a given time period. Warrants are often issued as a sweetener to a bond issue and may allow the firm to issue debt where it would not normally be feasible. The warrants are generally detachable from the bond issue. Thus, if the warrants are exercised, the bond issue still remains

in existence (this is clearly different from a convertible security). The difference between the market price of a warrant and its minimum or intrinsic value represents a premium that the investor is willing to pay. This premium represents the speculative potential in the warrant. Warrants are dilutive to earnings and must generally be considered in computing primary and fully diluted earnings per share.

IMPORTANT WORDS AND CONCEPTS

Convertible securities
Warrants
Conversion price
Conversion ratio
Conversion value
Pure bond value
Conversion premium
Downside protection
Downside risk
Floor value

Dilution
Primary earnings per share
Fully diluted earnings per
  share
Intrinsic value (of warrant)
Speculative premium
Option price (of warrant)
Exercise price (of warrant)
Warrant break-even

DISCUSSION QUESTIONS

1. Why would an investor have an interest in convertible securities? (What do they offer to the investor?)
2. What are the disadvantages of investing in convertible securities?
3. When is the best time to buy convertible bonds?
4. How can you determine the conversion ratio from the conversion price?
5. How do you determine the conversion value?
6. What is meant by the pure bond value?
7. In Figure 12–2, what does point P represent? What is the most important influence on the market price of the convertible to the right of point P? What is the most important influence to the left of point P?
8. When the Tandy convertible bond described in this chapter was called at $1,061.60, what was the most likely course for investors to take?
9. For bonds that have conversion premiums in excess of 100 percent, what can you generally infer about the stock price?
10. How does the volatility of a stock influence the conversion premium?
11. How might a step-up in the conversion price force conversion?
12. Why do corporations use convertible bonds?
13. What is meant by the dilutive effect of convertible securities?
14. What is a warrant?
15. For what reasons do firms issue warrants?
16. Why are warrants highly speculative?
17. Why do investors tend to pay less premium for a warrant as the price of the stock goes up?

18. If warrants were initially a detachable part of a bond issue, will the amount of debt be reduced if the warrants are eventually exercised? Contrast this with a convertible security.

19. What type of firms generally issue warrants?

PROBLEMS

1. A convertible bond has a face value of $1,000 and the conversion price is $40 per share. The stock is selling at $33 per share. The bond pays $70 per year interest and is selling in the market for $960. It matures in 10 years. Market rates are 12 percent per year.
   a. What is the conversion ratio?
   b. What is the conversion value?
   c. What is the conversion premium (in dollars and percent)?
   d. What is the floor value or pure bond value? (You may wish to review material in Chapter 10 for computing bond values.)

2. Compute the downside risk as a percentage in Problem 1. What does this mean?

3. Under what circumstances might the downside risk increase? Relate your answer to interest rates in the market.

4. Alvin Motor Corporation has a $1,000 face value convertible bond outstanding that has a market value of $1,030. It has a coupon rate of 6 percent and matures in five years. The conversion price is $50. The common stock currently is selling for $44.
   a. What is the conversion premium (in percentage)?
   b. At what price does the common stock need to sell for the conversion value to be equal to the current bond price?

5. In Problem 4, market rates of interest for comparable bonds are 10 percent and the pure bond value is $845.66. What will happen to the pure bond value if market rates of interest go to 12 percent? (Once again, you may wish to consult Chapter 10 for computing bond values.)

6. Given the following data, compute unadjusted earnings per share and fully diluted earnings per share. There are no other potentially dilutive securities outstanding, and the 8 percent interest is greater than two thirds of the going interest rate at time of issue.

Common stock (500,000 shares at $5 par) =	$2,500,000
Eight percent convertible debentures (5,000 bonds at $1,000 each; convertible into 50 shares per bond)	5,000,000
Retained earnings	5,000,000
Earnings before interest and taxes	2,800,000
Interest	400,000
Earnings before taxes	$2,400,000
Earnings after taxes (50 percent)	$1,200,000

7. Assume you bought a convertible bond two years ago for $900. The bond has a conversion ratio of 32. At the time the bond was purchased the stock was selling for $25 per share. The bond pays $75 in annual

interest. The stock pays no cash dividend. Assume after two years the stock price rises to $35 and the firm forces investors to convert to common stock by calling the bond (there is no conversion premium at this point in time).

Would you have been better off if you (a) had bought the stock directly or (b) bought the convertible bond and eventually converted it to common stock? Assume you would have invested $900 in either case. Disregard taxes, commissions, etc. Hint: consider appreciation in value plus any annual income received. See Table 12–1 for an example.

8. Assume a firm has warrants outstanding that permit the holder to buy one new share of stock at $30 per share. The market price of the stock is now $36.
   a. What is the intrinsic value of the warrant?
   b. Why might the warrant sell for $2 on the market even if the stock price is $28?

9. Morgan Donuts has warrants outstanding which allow the holder to purchase 1.85 shares of stock per warrant at $18 per share (option price). The common stock is currently selling for $21. The warrant has a market value of $7.
   a. What is the intrinsic value of the warrant?
   b. If the stock sold for $16.50, how large would the negative intrinsic value be?

10. Assume in Table 12–4 that International Harvester had a warrant price of $5.50 instead of $4.75 in column (2). The per share stock price in column (3) remains at $6.50 and per share option price is still $5 in column (4). Based on the new information, compute:
   a. Intrinsic value (does it change?)
   b. Premium (warrant price minus intrinsic value).
   c. Percent the stock must rise to break even (first determine what price the stock must go to for the warrant to equal $5.50; then determine how large a growth that is from the current stock value). This assumes no premium.

11. Assume a corporation has $300,000 in earnings and 150,000 shares outstanding ($2 in earnings per share). Also assume there are warrants outstanding to purchase 25,000 shares at $30 per share. The stock is currently selling at $50 per share. In considering the effect of the warrants outstanding, what would revised earnings per share be?

12. Assume a firm has warrants outstanding that allow the holder to buy one share of stock at $30 per share. Also assume the stock is selling for $35 per share, and the warrants are now selling for $7 per warrant (this, of course, is above intrinsic value). You can invest $1,000 in the stock or the warrants (for purposes of the computation, round to two places to the right of the decimal point). Assume the stock goes to $42, and the warrants trade at their intrinsic value when the stock goes to $42. Would you have a larger total dollar profit by initially investing in the stocks or the warrants?

SELECTED REFERENCES

Alexander, Gordon J., and Roger D. Stover. "Pricing in the New Issue Convertible Debt Market." *Financial Management,* Fall 1977, pp. 35–39.

Bierman, Harold J., Jr., "The Cost of Warrants." *Journal of Financial and Quantitative Analysis,* June 1973, pp. 499–504.

Brennan, M. J., and E. S. Schwartz. "Convertible Bonds; Valuation and Optimal Strategies for Call and Conversion." *Journal of Finance,* December 1977, pp. 1699–1715.

Brigham, Eugene F. "An Analysis of Convertible Debentures." *Journal of Finance,* March 1966, pp. 35–54.

Jennings, Edward H. "An Estimate of Convertible Bond Premiums." *Journal of Financial and Quantitative Analysis,* January 1974, pp. 33–56.

Hayes, Samuel L. III, and Henry B. Reiling. "Sophisticated Financing Tool: The Warrant." *Harvard Business Review,* January–February 1969, pp. 137–50.

Ingersoll, Jonathan. "An Examination of Corporate Call Policies on Convertible Securities." *Journal of Finance,* May 1977, pp. 463–78.

Kassouf, Sheen T. "Warrant Price Behavior 1945–1964." *Finance Analysts Journal,* January–February 1968, pp. 123–26.

Miller, Jerry D., "Effects of Longevity on Values of Stock Purchase Warrants." *Financial Analysts Journal,* November–December 1971, pp. 78–85.

———. "Accounting for Warrants and Convertible Bonds." *Management Accounting,* January 1973, pp. 36–38.

Parkinson, Michael. "Empirical Warrant-Stock Relationships." *Journal of Business,* October 1972, pp. 563–69.

Noddings, Thomas C. *The Dow Jones-Irwin Guide to Convertible Securities.* Homewood, Ill.: Dow Jones-Irwin, 1973.

Rush, David F., and Ronald W. Melicher. "An Empirical Examination of Factors which Influence Warrant Prices." *Journal of Finance,* December 1974, pp. 1449–66.

Stone, Bernell K., "Warrant Financing." *Journal of Financial and Quantitative Analysis,* March 1976, pp. 143–53.

Water, James E., and Agustin V. Que. "The Valuation of Convertible Bonds." *Journal of Finance,* June 1973, pp. 713–32.

Chapter 13

PUT AND CALL OPTIONS

The word *option* has many different meanings, but most of them include the ability or right to choose a certain alternative. One definition provided by *Webster's* is "the right, acquired for a consideration, to buy or sell something at a fixed price within a specified period of time." This definition is very general and applies to puts, calls, warrants, real estate options, or any other contracts entered into between two parties where a choice of action or decision can be put off for a limited time at a cost. The person acquiring the option pays an agreed-upon sum to the person providing the option. For example, someone may want to buy your house for its sale price of $75,000. The buyer does not have the money but will give you $2,000 in cash if you give him the right to buy the house for the next 60 days at $75,000. If you accept, you have given the buyer an option and have agreed not to sell the house to anyone else for the next 60 days. If the buyer raises $75,000 within the 60-day limit, he may buy the house, giving you the $75,000. Perhaps he finds the $75,000 but also finds another house he likes better for $72,000. He will not buy your house, but you have $2,000 and must now find someone else to buy your house. By selling the option, you tied up the sale of your house for 60 days, and if the option is unexercised, you have foregone an opportunity to sell the house to someone else.

Puts and calls are options on common stock. A put is an option to sell 100 shares of common stock at a specified price for a given period of time. Calls are the opposite of puts and allow the owner the right to buy 100 shares of common stock from the option seller (writer). Contracts on listed puts and calls have been standardized at date of issue for periods of three, six, and nine months, although as these contracts approach expiration, they may be purchased with a much shorter life.

OPTIONS MARKETS

Before the days of options trading on exchanges, puts and calls were traded over-the-counter by the Put and Call Dealers Association. These dealers would buy and sell puts and calls for their own accounts for stocks traded on the New York Stock Exchange and then try to find an investor, hedger, or speculator to take the other side of the option. For example, if you owned 1,000 shares of General Motors and you wanted to write a call option giving the buyer the right to buy 1,000 shares of General Motors at $70 per share for six months, the dealer might buy the calls and look for someone who would be willing to buy them.

There were several disadvantages to this system. Dealers had to have contact with the buyers and sellers, and the financial stability of the option writer had to be endorsed (guaranteed) by a brokerage house. The option writer either had to keep the shares on deposit with the brokerage firm or put up a cash margin. Options in the same stock could exist in the market at various strike prices (price at which the option could be exercised) and scattered expiration dates. This meant that when an option buyer wanted to exercise or terminate the contract before expiration, he or she would have to deal directly with the option writer. This does not make for an efficient, liquid

market. Unlisted options also reduced the striking price of a call by any dividends paid during the option period, which did not benefit the writer of the call.

Listed Options Exchanges

The Chicago Board Options Exchange was established in 1973 as the first exchange for call options. The market response was overwhelming, and within three years, the American, Pacific, and Philadelphia exchanges were also trading call options. By 1984, the list of stocks with available option contracts increased dramatically from the original list of 20 companies to 390 companies, and puts as well as calls were traded for many companies. Appendix 13A at the end of the chapter presents a comprehensive list of available options as well as the principal trading exchange for the option. On many days the number of underlying shares of stock represented by options traded on the option exchanges is greater than the number of actual shares traded on the NYSE in those same issues.

Table 13–1, from the *Chicago Board Option Exchange's 1983 Fact Book,* shows the growth in options trading since 1973. Besides the Chicago Board Options Exchange (CBOE), the American Exchange (AMEX), the Philadelphia Exchange (PHLX), and the Pacific Coast Exchange (PSE) all continue to trade options. The New York Stock Exchange began trading options in 1985.

The options market has recently been expanded to include options not only on individual stocks, but options on stock market indexes as well. Thus, by the mid-1980s one could buy an option to purchase the equivalent of the Standard & Poor's 500 Stock Index or other indexes. This, of course, is different from the traditional option to purchase options on individual stocks such as General Motors. This chapter will concentrate on options on individual stocks, while Chapter 16 will cover stock index options and futures.

There are several reasons why the listed options markets are so desirable compared to the previous method of over-the-counter trading for options. The contract period was standardized with three-, six-, and nine-month expiration dates on three calendar cycles.

Cycle 1: January/April/July/October.
Cycle 2: February/May/August/November.
Cycle 3: March/June/September/December.

As one month's expiration date comes up, another month in the cycle is added. For example, as the January option expires, the October nine-month option is added, and the cycle is continued. The use of three cycles spreads out the expiration dates for the options so that not all contracts come due on the same day. Each contract expires at 11:59 P.M. Eastern time on the Saturday immediately following the third Friday of the expiration month. For all practical purposes, any closing out of positions must be done on that last Friday while the markets are open.

The exercise price (striking price) is also standardized. This is the price at which the contract specifies for a buy or sell. For all stocks under $100 per

TABLE 13–1 Historical Stock Options Contract Volume on All Exchanges (for individual stocks)

Time period	CBOE	AMEX	PHLX	PSE	MSE*	Total	CBOE share of options contract volume	Reported NYSE volume (millions of shares)	Options volume in shares as % of NYSE volume	
									CBOE	All options
1983	71,695,563	36,199,701	16,607,806	11,155,906	—	135,658,976	52.8	21,589.6	33.2	62.8
1982	75,721,605	38,766,996	13,466,652	9,309,563	—	137,264,816	55.2	16,458.0	46.0	83.4
1981	57,584,175	34,859,475	10,009,565	6,952,567	—	109,405,782	52.6	11,853.7	48.6	92.3
1980	52,916,921	29,048,323	7,758,101	5,486,590	1,518,611	96,728,546	54.7	11,352.3	46.6	85.2
1979	35,379,600	17,467,018	4,952,737	3,856,344	2,609,164	64,264,863	55.1	8,155.9	43.4	78.8
1978	34,277,350	14,380,959	3,270,378	3,289,968	2,012,363	57,231,018	59.9	7,205.1	47.6	79.4
1977	24,838,632	10,077,578	2,195,307	1,925,031	600,780	39,637,328	62.7	5,273.8	47.1	75.2
1976	21,498,027	9,035,767	1,274,702	550,194	15,237	32,373,927	66.4	5,360.1	40.1	60.4
1975	14,431,023	3,530,564	140,982	—	—	18,102,569	79.7	4,693.4	30.7	38.6
1974	5,682,907	—	—	—	—	5,682,907	100.0	3,517.7	16.2	16.2
1973	1,119,177	—	—	—	—	1,119,177	100.0	4,053.2	2.8	2.8

* The Midwest Stock Exchange options program was consolidated with the CBOE on June 2, 1980.

Source: *Chicago Board Options Exchange Fact Book* (Chicago: Chicago Board Options Exchange, 1983).

share, the striking price changes by $5 intervals, and for stocks selling over $100 per share, the strike price changes by $10 a share. As the underlying stocks change prices in the market, options with new striking prices are added. For example, a stock selling at $30 per share when the January option is added will have a striking price of $30, but if the stock gets to 32½ (half way to the next striking price), the exchange may add another option (to the class of options) with a $35 strike price.

An example of an actual call option is presented in Table 13–2 for Exxon. Note the different strike prices (35, 40, 45, 50) and expiration months (January, April, July). Exxon common stock is selling for 44¼. The values within the table, such as 9⅜ or 4⅜, reflect the price of the various option contracts. Much of this type of information will take on greater meaning as we go through the chapter.

TABLE 13–2   November 1, 1984, Exxon Calls

Stock price close Exxon	Strike price	Calls—last		
		January	April	July
44¼	35	9⅜	9⅝	Not traded
44¼	40	4⅜	4⅞	5
44¼	45	⅞	1⁹⁄₁₆	2
44¼	50	⅛	⁵⁄₁₆	Not traded

This standardization of expiration dates and strike prices creates more certainty when buying and selling options in a changing market and allows more efficient trading strategies because of better coordination between stock prices, strike prices, and expiration dates. Dividends no longer affect the option contract as they did in the unlisted market. Transactions occur at arm's length between buyer and seller without any matchmaking needed on the part of the broker. The ultimate result of these changes in the option market is a highly liquid, efficient market where speculators, hedgers, and arbitrageurs all operate together.

THE OPTIONS CLEARING CORPORATION

Much of the liquidity and ease of operation of the option exchanges is due to the role of the Options Clearing Corporation, which functions as the issuer of all options listed on the five exchanges—the CBOE, the AMEX, the Pacific Coast Exchange, the Philadelphia Exchange, and the NYSE. Investors who want to trade puts and calls need to have an approved account with a member brokerage firm; upon opening an account, they receive a prospectus from the Options Clearing Corporation detailing all aspects of option trading.

Options are bought and sold or written through a member broker the same as other securities. The exchanges allow special orders, such as limit, market, and stop orders, as well as orders used specifically in options trading, like spread orders and straddle orders. The order process originates with the broker and is transacted on the floor of the exchange. Remember that for every order there must be a buyer and seller (writer) so that the orders can be "matched." Once the orders are matched, they are filed with the Options Clearing Corporation, which then issues the necessary options or closes the position. There are four basic transactions handled:

Opening purchase transaction—A transaction in which an investor intends to become the holder of an option.

Opening sale transaction—A transaction in which an investor intends to become the writer of an option.

Closing purchase transaction—A transaction in which an investor who is obligated as a writer of an option intends to terminate his obligation as a writer. This is accomplished by "purchasing" an option in the same series as the option previously written. Such a transaction has the effect, upon acceptance by the Options Clearing Corporation, of canceling the investor's preexisting position as a writer.

Closing sale transaction—A transaction in which an investor who is the holder of an outstanding option intends to liquidate his position as a holder. This is accomplished by "selling" an option in the same series as the option previously purchased. Such a transaction has the effect, upon acceptance by the Options Clearing Corporation, of liquidating the investor's preexisting position as a holder of the option.

What occurs in a transaction is that holders and writers of options are not contractually linked together but are committed to the Options Clearing Corporation. Since there are no certificates issued for options, a customer must maintain a brokerage account as long as he or she holds an option position and must liquidate the option through the broker originating the transaction unless a brokerage transfer is completed before an ensuing transaction. If an option is traded on more than one exchange, it may be bought, sold, or closed out on either exchange and cleared through the Options Clearing Corporation. Basically, the aggregate obligation of the option holders is backed up by the aggregate obligation of the option writers. If holders choose to exercise their options, they must do so through the Clearing Corporation, which randomly selects a writer from all Clearing member accounts in the same option series.[1]

---

[1] Actually very few option holders choose to exercise their option and take possession of securities. Data for 1983 indicate that only 15.1 percent of all call options were exercised while only 6.9 percent of all put options were exercised. Assuming that the option holder does not want to exercise her option, she may choose to close her position on the open market through a closing sale transaction. An investor would do this whenever the value of the option after commissions is positive. During 1983, 63 percent of all call contracts were closed out (not necessarily at a profit) and 22 percent of call contracts expired worthless.

This would be true whether the holder chooses to exercise early or at expiration. Upon notice from the Options Clearing Corporation, a call writer must sell 100 shares of the underlying common stock at the exercise price, while the put writer must buy 100 shares from the holder exercising the put.

All option contracts are adjusted for stock splits, stock dividends, or other stock distributions. For example, a 2-for-1 stock split for a stock selling at 60, with options available at 70, 60, and 50 strike prices, would cause the stock to trade at 30 and the strike prices to be 35, 30, and 25. Now the option holder would have two puts or calls at the adjusted price.

OPTION PREMIUMS

Before one can understand various option strategies, an investor or speculator must be able to comprehend what creates option premiums (prices). Look at Table 13–3. Using Eastman Kodak (EK) as an example, we can see that the common stock closed at $70 per share on the NYSE and that puts and calls are available at the following strike prices—55, 60, 65, 70, 75, 80. The October 70 call closed at 3¾ ($375.00 for one call on 100 shares), while the October 80 call closed at 9/16. The 65 call is said to be "in-the-money" because the market price (70) is above the strike (or purchase) price (65), but the 80 call is "out-of-the-money" since the strike price is above the market price. The 70 call is said to be "at-the-money" because the strike price and the market price are equal.

In-the-money options have an intrinsic value equal to the market price minus the strike price. In the case of the EK October 65 call, the intrinsic value is $5 as indicated by Formula (13–1). Options that are out of the money have no positive intrinsic value.

$$\text{Intrinsic value}_{call} = \text{Market price} - \text{Strike price} \quad (13\text{–}1)$$
$$\text{Intrinsic value}_{EK\ 65\ October\ call} = \$70 - \$65$$
$$= \$5$$

The EK October 80 call would have a negative $10 intrinsic value derived by Formula (13–1). When the market price minus the strike price is negative, the negative value represents the amount the stock price must increase to have the option at-the-money where the strike price and market price are equal.

Returning to the Eastman Kodak 65 October call, we see in Table 13–3 that the total premium is 7⅛, while the previously computed intrinsic value is $5. This call option has an additional premium of 2⅛ due to other factors. The total premium (option price) is a combination of the intrinsic value plus a *speculative premium* which is a function of common stock volatility and risk, time to expiration, dividend yield on the underlying common stock, potential leverage, and market expectations.

$$\text{Total premium} = \text{Intrinsic value} + \text{Speculative premium} \quad (13\text{–}2)$$
$$\$7⅛ = \$5 + \$2⅛$$

TABLE 13–3

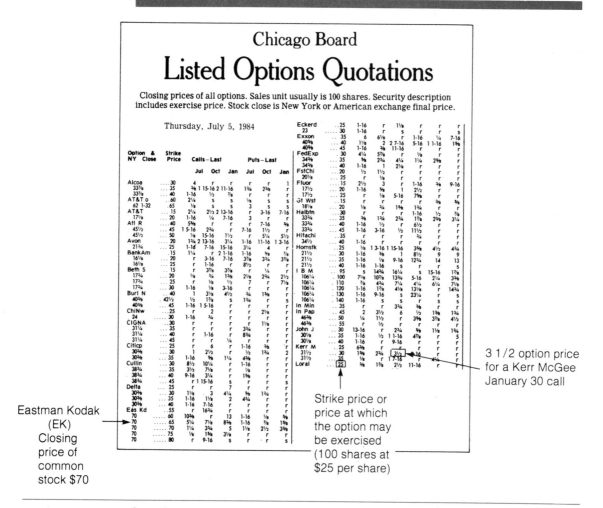

Eastman Kodak (EK) Closing price of common stock $70

Strike price or price at which the option may be exercised (100 shares at $25 per share)

3 1/2 option price for a Kerr McGee January 30 call

Generally, the higher the volatility of the common stock—as measured by its stock price's standard deviation or by its beta—and the lower the dividend yield, the greater the speculative premium. The longer the exercise period, the higher the speculative premium, especially if market expectations over the duration of the option are positive. Finally, the deeper the option is in-the-money, the smaller the leverage potential and therefore the smaller the speculative premium. Most often, we examine the speculative premium separately to see if it is a reasonable premium to pay for the possible benefits.

The speculative premium can be expressed in dollars or as a percentage of the common stock price. A speculative premium expressed in percent

TABLE 13–4   Speculative Premiums on July 5, 1984, for Eastman Kodak Options

Market price	Eastman Kodak strike price	Total premium	–	Intrinsic value	=	Speculative premium	Speculative premium as % of common stock price
$70	$55 October call	$16¾		$15		$ 1¾	2.50%
70	65 October call	7⅛		5		2⅛	3.03
70	70 October call	3¾		0		3¾	5.35
70	75 October call	1⅝		(5)		6⅝	9.46
70	80 October call	9⁄16		(10)		10⁹⁄16	15.09

indicates the increase in the stock price needed for the purchaser of a call option to break even on the expiration date. Table 13–4 shows this point. Notice that the Eastman Kodak October 55 call option, which is deep in-the-money, has the lowest speculative premium, while the 80 option has the highest. Realize that the 80 option only has a cash value of 9⁄16 (the total premium) and that the other $10 represents the required increase in the stock price for the strike price and market price to be equal. The 14.08 percent premium, however, does represent the percentage movement in stock price by the expiration date for a break-even position. Remember that at expiration there will be no speculative premium. The option will only reflect the intrinsic value and possibly even a discount because of commission expenses incurred upon exercise.

Table 13–5 provides a look at premiums for in-the-money and out-of-the-money options with varying times to expiration. Since the quotes are as of July 5, the July options will expire first, then the October options and finally the January options. You should notice how the option premiums increase with more time to expiration.

Eastman Kodak's speculative premiums are not very high due to a low beta, high dividend yield, and an uninspired stock market in July 1984. Several relationships in Table 13–5 are evident, however. The speculative premiums increase with time for all strike prices but are very low for the 55 and 60 calls because of low leverage potential and a chance of being exercised on the expiration date. The 75 and 80 calls have high speculative premiums, but an option writer would *not reap much cash inflow*. Generally speaking, out-of-the-money call options have high speculative premiums, but little of the premium may be in the form of cash. A $50 stock with a $55 strike price may have a $2 total premium and a speculative premium of $7. Note that only a small part of the speculative premium is in cash. This, or course, is an important consideration for an option writer.

Table 13–6 demonstrates the relationship of betas and dividend yields to the speculative premium. The three options listed are all October calls from Table 13–3, and they are either at-the-money or slightly in-the-money. Notice that the speculative premiums (in percent) rise as the betas increase and

TABLE 13–5 Speculative Premiums over Time (Eastman Kodak calls, July 5, 1984, Beta .85)

Market price	Strike price	July total premium*	Speculative premium		October total premium†	Speculative premium		January total premium‡	Speculative premium	
			Dollars	Percent		Dollars	Percent		Dollars	Percent
$70	$55	Not traded	—	—	$16¾	$ 1¾	2.50	Not traded	—	—
70	60	$10⅜	$ ⅜	.54%	Not traded	—	—	$13	$3	4.29%
70	65	5¼	¼	.36	7⅛	2⅛	3.04	8⅜	3⅜	4.82
70	70	1¼	1¼	1.79	3¾	3¾	5.36	5	5	7.14
70	75	⅛	5⅛	7.32	1⅝	6⅝	9.46	3⅛	8⅛	11.61
70	80	Not traded	—	—	9/16	10 9/16	15.09	Not offered	—	—

* July—16 days to expiration.

† October—107 days to expiration.

‡ January—198 days to expiration.

TABLE 13–6   Speculative Premiums Related to Betas and Dividend Yields

Stock	October strike	Market price	Total premium	Speculative premium Dollars	Speculative premium Percent	Beta	Expected dividend yield
Eastman Kodak	$70	$70	$3¾	$3¾	5.36%	.85	5.6%
Citicorp	30	30⅜	2½	2⅛	7.00	1.05	6.1
Delta Airlines	30	30⅜	3	2⅝	8.64	1.10	1.8

dividend yields fall. This, of course, is not always true since other factors, such as market attitudes, can have a strong bearing on the speculative premium in addition to other influences mentioned previously. In fact, Citicorp's higher dividend yield is associated with a higher speculative premium relative to Eastman Kodak because the banking industry was considered to be quite risky with the Continental Illinois Bank's loan loss problems and Citicorp's large international loan portfolio. Normally, higher dividend yields are associated with lower speculative premiums.

Premiums can be deceiving. The novice may attempt to write the options with the highest total premium or speculative premium, while the buyer may think the smallest investment provides the greatest leverage. These are not usually true if we look at speculative premiums on a per-day basis. For example, the EK 70 calls have the following speculative premiums per day. Note the speculative premium (in percent) is divided by the number of days to expiration.

Speculative premiums until expiration

July	70	1.79%/16 days	=	.1119% per day
October	70	5.36%/107 days	=	.0501% per day
January	70	7.14%/198 days	=	.0361% per day

An examination of daily premiums would suggest that call writers should write short-lived calls and then roll them over if they don't get exercised. On the other hand, call buyers get more time for less premium by purchasing long-lived calls.

Although this section has examined call premiums, puts have most of the same relationship except for the definitions of in-the-money and out-of-the-money. Since puts allow the owner to sell stock at the strike price, in-the-money put options exist where the strike price is above the market price of the stock. Out-of-the-money puts have market values for common stock above the strike price. Since the owner of the stock can sell the stock for more in the market than by exercising a put, the put has no intrinsic value. The speculative

premium of a put as a percentage of the stock price then represents the percentage decline in the stock price necessary to break even.

Understanding option premiums is important in order to make sense out of options strategies. Various strategies involving puts and calls are covered in the next section. Do not go on unless you are reasonably comfortable with this section on option premiums. Appendix 13–B presents the Black-Scholes option pricing model, a much more sophisticated way of analyzing option prices and their time premiums and speculative premiums. This model puts all the variables together in a model to demonstrate the relationships and determinants of option prices. This appendix is primarily designed for those who wish to achieve a more advanced understanding of the theoretical basis for option pricing and is not essential for the standard reading of the text.

BASIC OPTION STRATEGIES

Option strategies can be very aggressive and risky, or they can be quite conservative and used as a means of reducing risk. Option buyers and writers both attempt to take advantage of the option premiums discussed in the preceding section. In theory many option strategies can be created, but in practice the market must be liquid in order to execute these strategies. After a decade of explosive growth, option volume declined slightly in 1984–85 while trading on the underlying stocks went up. Because of the introduction of index options, trading in individual equity options may have been affected. A reduction of individual option trading reduces the ability to create workable strategies for specific companies. For example, the lack of a liquid market can keep institutional investors from executing hedging strategies involving several hundred thousand shares. Even with these limitations in mind, the average investor can still find many opportunities for option strategies. In this section, we discuss the possible uses of puts and calls to achieve different investment goals. Table 13–7 provides option quotes at three separate time periods for our examples. We have ignored commissions in most examples, but we do advise that commissions can be a significant hidden cost in some types of option strategies.

Buying Call Options

The leverage strategy.   Leverage is a very common reason for buying call options when the market is expected to rise during the exercise period. The use of calls in this way is similar to warrants discussed in Chapter 12, but calls have shorter lives and lower premiums. The call option is priced much lower than the common stock, and the leverage is derived from a small percentage change in the price of the common stock that can cause a large percentage change in the price of the call option. For example, on July 5, 1984, Federal Express common stock closed at 34⅜, and the 40 October call closed at 1 (see Table 13–7). Two months later in September, the stock closed at 42⅞ for an 8½ point gain of 24.7 percent. The 40 October call option closed at 4¼ for

TABLE 13–7

Chicago Board

Listed Options Quotations

Closing prices of all options. Sales unit usually is 100 shares. Security description includes exercise price. Stock close is New York or American exchange final price.

Thursday, July 5, 1984

Option & NY Close	Strike Price	Calls—Last Jul	Calls—Last Oct	Calls—Last Jan	Puts Last Jul	Puts Last Oct	Puts Last Jan
Alcoa	30	4	r	r	r	r	1
33 7/8	35	3/8	1 15-16	2 11-16	1 3/4	2 3/8	r
33 7/8	40	1-16	1/2	1/8	r	r	r
AT&T o	60	2 1/4	s	s	1/8	s	s
62 1-32	65	1/8	s	s	3	s	s
AT&T	15	2 1/4	2 1/2	2 13-16	r	3-16	7-16
17 1/8	20	1-16	1/4	7-16	3	r	r
Atl R	40	5 5/8	r	r	r	7-16	5/8
45 1/2	45	1 5-16	2 3/4	r	7-16	1 1/2	r
45 1/2	50	1/8	15-16	1 1/2	r	5 1/4	5 1/2
Avon	20	1 3/4	2 13-16	3 1/4	1-16	11-16	1 3-16
21 3/4	25	1-16	7-16	15-16	3 1/4	4	r
BankAm	15	1 1/4	r	2 1-16	1-16	5/8	7/8
16 1/8	20	r	3-16	7-16	3 7/8	3 3/4	3 7/8
16 1/8	25	r	1-16	r	8 1/2	r	r
Beth S	15	r	3 7/8	3 7/8	r	1/4	r
17 3/4	20	1/8	3/4	1 3/8	2 1/8	2 3/4	2 1/2
17 3/4	25	r	1/8	1/2	7	r	7 1/8
17 3/4	30	1-16	1/8	3-16	r	r	r
Burl N	40	1	3 1/8	4 1/2	3/4	1 5/8	r
40 3/8	42 1/2	1/2	1 7/8	s	1 3/4	r	s
40 3/8	45	1-16	1 5-16	r	r	r	r
ChiNw	25	r	2	r	r	2 1/8	r
24	30	1-16	3/4	r	r	r	r
CIGNA	30	r	r	r	r	1 1/8	r
31 1/4	35	r	r	r	3 3/4	r	r
31 1/4	40	r	1-16	r	8 3/4	r	r
31 1/4	45	r	r	1/4	r	r	r
Citicp	25	r	6	r	1-16	3/8	r
30 3/8	30	1	2 1/2	r	1/2	1 3/4	2
30 3/8	35	1-16	5/8	1 1/4	4 3/8	r	r
Cullin	30	8 1/2	10 1/4	r	1-16	r	r
38 3/4	35	3 1/2	7 1/8	r	1/8	r	r
38 3/4	40	9-16	3 1/4	r	1 5/8	r	r
38 3/4	45	r	1 15-16	s	r	r	s
Delta	25	r	r	7	r	r	r
30 3/8	30	1 1/8	3	4 1/4	5/8	1 3/4	r
30 3/8	35	1-16	1 1/8	2	4 3/4	r	r
30 3/8	40	1-16	7-16	r	r	r	r
Eas Kd	55	r	16 3/4	r	r	r	r
70	60	10 3/8	r	13	1-16	1/8	5/8
70	65	5 1/4	7 1/8	8 3/8	1-16	7/8	1 5/8
70	70	1 1/4	3 3/4	5	1 1/8	2 1/2	3 3/8
70	75	1/8	1 5/8	3 1/8	r	r	r
70	80	r	9-16	s	r	r	s
Eckerd	25	1-16	r	1 1/8	r	r	r
23	30	1-16	r	s	r	r	s
Exxon	35	6	6 1/8	r	1-16	1/4	7-16
40 5/8	40	1 1/8	2	2 7-16	5-16	1 1-16	1 5/8
40 5/8	45	1-16	3/8	11-16	r	r	r
FedExp	30	4 1/4	5 7/8	r	1/8	r	r
34 3/8	35	5/8	2 3/4	4 1/4	1 1/4	2 5/8	r
34 3/8	40	1-16	1	2 1/8	r	r	r
FstChi	20	1/2	1 1/2	r	r	r	r
20 1/8	25	r	1/8	r	r	r	r
Fluor	15	2 1/2	3	r	1-16	3/8	9-16
17 1/2	20	1-16	5/8	1	2 1/2	r	r
17 1/2	25	r	1/8	5-16	7 5/8	r	r
Gt Wst	15	r	r	r	r	3/8	5/8
18 1/8	20	1/8	3/4	1 5/8	1 3/4	r	r
Halbtn	30	r	r	r	1-16	1/2	7/8
33 3/4	35	3/8	1 3/4	2 3/4	1 7/8	2 3/8	3 1/4
33 3/4	40	1-16	1/2	r	6 1/2	r	r
33 3/4	45	1-16	3-16	1/2	11 1/2	r	r
Hitachi	35	r	r	r	3/4	r	r
34 1/2	40	1-16	r	r	r	r	r
Homstk	25	1/8	1 3-16	1 15-16	3 5/8	4 1/2	4 3/4
21 1/2	30	1-16	3/8	1	8 1/2	9	9
21 1/2	35	1-16	1/8	9-16	12 3/4	14	13
21 1/2	40	1-16	1-16	s	r	r	s
B M	95	s	14 3/4	16 1/4	s	15-16	1 7/8
106 1/4	100	7 1/8	10 7/8	13 3/4	5-16	2 1/4	3 3/8
106 1/4	110	7/8	4 3/4	7 1/4	4 1/4	6 1/4	7 1/8
106 1/4	120	1-16	1 7/8	4 1/8	13 1/8	r	14 3/4
106 1/4	130	1-16	9-16	s	23 1/4	r	s
106 1/4	140	1-16	s	s	r	s	s
In Min	35	r	r	3 3/4	3/8	r	r
In Pap	45	2	3 1/2	6	1/2	1 3/8	1 3/4
46 3/8	50	1/4	1 1/2	r	3 5/8	3 7/8	4 1/2
46 3/8	55	r	1/2	r	r	r	r
John J	30	13-16	r	2 3/4	5/8	1 1/8	1 3/4
30 1/8	35	1-16	1/2	1 1-16	4 7/8	r	5
30 1/8	40	1-16	r	9-16	r	r	r
Kerr M	25	6 3/8	r	r	r	r	r
31 1/2	30	1 5/8	2 3/4	3 1/2	3-16	r	r
31 1/2	35	1/8	r	1 7-16	r	4 1/4	r
Loral	25	3/8	1 7/8	2 1/2	11-16	r	r

Thursday, September 6, 1984

Option & NY Close	Strike Price	Calls Last Oct	Calls Last Jan	Calls Last Apr	Puts Last Oct	Puts Last Jan	Puts Last Apr
Alcoa	30	5 1/2	6 1/2	r	1/8	1/2	3/4
34 7/8	35	1 1/2	2 15-16	r	1 1/4	1 3/4	2 3/8
34 7/8	40	1/4	1 3-16	2	r	r	r
34 7/8	45	1/8	s	s	r	s	s
AT&T	15	4	4 1/4	4 1/2	1-16	3-16	r
18 7/8	20	3/8	7/8	1 3/8	1 1/4	1 3/4	1 3/4
Atl R	40	r	r	r	r	3-16	r
49 7/8	45	5 3/8	6 1/2	r	3-16	7/8	1 1/2
49 7/8	50	1 1/2	3	4	1 5-16	2 1/4	r
49 7/8	55	1/4	1	2	r	r	r
Avon	20	3 3/4	4 1/2	r	r	3/8	r
23 1/2	25	7-16	1 1/4	1 3/4	1 5/8	2	2 5/8
23 1/2	30	1-16	1/4	7-16	r	r	r
BankAm	15	2	2 1/2	r	3-16	1/2	3/4
16 5/8	20	1-16	5-16	5/8	r	r	r
Beth S	15	4 1/8	r	r	r	r	r
18 7/8	20	11-16	1 1/2	2 1/8	r	r	r
Burl N	40	7	r	8 3/4	r	1	r
46 1/8	45	2 9-16	4 3/4	6	1 1/4	r	3
46 1/8	47 1/2	1 9-16	s	s	2 1/4	s	s
46 1/8	50	13-16	2 1/4	3 1/2	r	r	r
ChiNw	15	r	13 3/8	r	r	r	r
28	20	8 3/8	9	r	r	r	r
28	25	4	5 1/2	r	r	r	r
28	30	1 5-16	3	r	r	r	4
28	35	5/8	r	r	r	r	r
CIGNA	30	r	r	r	3-16	r	r
35 1/2	35	2 1/8	r	r	1	2	r
35 1/2	40	5-16	1 1/8	1 13-16	r	r	r
Citicp	25	r	r	r	1/8	r	r
34 1/4	30	4 1/2	5	5 3/4	7-16	r	1 1/2
34 1/4	35	1	2 1/4	2 3/4	2	2 3/4	r
34 1/4	40	1/8	9-16	1 1-16	6 1/8	r	6 3/8
Cullin	40	r	7 5/8	r	3/4	2 1/2	r
44 3/4	45	3	4 3/4	r	r	r	6 1/8
44 3/4	50	1	3 1/4	r	r	r	r
Delta	30	2 7/8	4	6	9-16	1 1/2	1 3/4
31 3/4	35	9-16	1 5/8	2 1/2	3 3/4	3 5/8	r
31 3/4	40	3-16	3/4	1 1/2	r	r	r
31 3/4	45	1-16	s	s	r	s	s
Dig Eq	90	7 1/8	r	r	1 5/8	r	r
Eas Kd	60	r	17 1/2	s	1-16	3-16	s
75 3/4	65	11 3/4	r	r	1-16	3/8	11-16
75 3/4	70	7	8 3/8	r	3-16	1	1 1/2
75 3/4	75	2 13-16	4 3/4	6 5/8	1 1/4	2 1/2	3 1/8
75 3/4	80	11-16	2 1/2	3 7/8	4 1/2	r	r
Eckerd	20	4 3/4	r	r	r	r	r
24 3/8	25	11-16	1 3/8	r	r	r	r
Engelh	30	3/4	1 5/8	2	r	r	r
Exxon	35	9	9 1/4	r	r	3-16	r
43 3/4	40	4 1/4	4 3/4	5 1/4	1/8	9-16	7/8
43 3/4	45	9-16	1 7-16	2	1 1/2	r	2 7/8
FedExp	35	8 3/8	9 1/8	r	1/4	3/4	r
42 7/8	40	4 1/4	6	r	1	1 7/8	2 9-16
42 7/8	45	1 9-16	3 7/8	5 1/8	3 1/4	4	r
FstChi	20	r	3 3/8	r	r	r	r
22 5/8	25	5-16	3/4	r	r	r	r
Fluor	10	r	r	r	r	r	3-16
16 3/8	15	r	2 5/8	3 1/4	7-16	7/8	1
16 3/8	20	1/8	5/8	r	r	r	r
16 3/8	25	1-16	r	s	r	r	s
Gt Wst	15	r	r	r	1-16	r	r
19 7/8	20	1 1/4	2 1/8	r	1 1/4	r	r
19 7/8	25	3-16	3/4	r	r	r	r
Halbtn	30	3 1/2	4 1/4	5 1/4	5-16	1	1 3/4
32 1/4	35	11-16	1 3/4	2 1/2	3 1/4	r	r
32 1/4	40	1/8	3/8	1 1/8	r	r	r
32 1/4	45	r	r	s	r	12 1/4	s
Homstk	20	r	6 3/4	r	1/4	5/8	1
25 1/2	25	2	3 1/4	4 1/2	1 1/4	2 1-16	2 1/2
25 1/2	30	3/8	1 3/8	2 5/8	4 1/2	5	r
25 1/2	35	1/8	5/8	s	r	r	s
25 1/2	40	1-16	s	s	r	s	s
I B M	95	r	r	s	r	3-16	s
123 1/4	100	24 3/4	r	29 1/2	1-16	7-16	13-16
123 1/4	110	15 1/8	17 1/2	19 7/8	3-16	1 3/8	1 15-16
123 1/4	120	6 1/2	10 1/2	13 1/4	1 13-16	3 7/8	4 3/4
123 1/4	130	1 7/8	5 1/4	8	7 1/8	8 1/2	9 1/2
In Min	35	r	5 3/4	r	1/4	r	r
41 1/4	40	1 7/8	2 15-16	3 1/2	r	r	r
41 1/4	45	1/2	1 1/4	1 3/4	r	r	r
In Pap	45	11	r	r	r	r	r
55 1/2	50	6 1/2	r	8	5-16	r	r
55 1/2	55	2 7/8	4 1/4	5 1/2	1 3/4	r	r
55 1/2	60	7/8	2 1/4	3 5/8	r	r	r
John J	25	9 1/2	10 1/2	r	r	r	r
34 3/8	30	5 1/8	5 7/8	6 3/4	1/8	1/2	11-16
34 3/8	35	1	2 1/8	2 3/4	1 1/8	1 3/4	r
34 3/8	40	3-16	9-16	s	r	r	s
Kerr M	25	5 3/4	r	r	r	r	r
30 3/8	30	1 5/8	2 3/4	3 3/4	3/4	r	1 7/8
30 3/8	35	5-16	1	r	r	r	r
Loral	20	8 1/8	r	r	r	r	r
27 7/8	25	3 1/2	r	r	3/8	r	r

Thursday, November 1, 1984

Option & NY Close	Strike Price	Calls Last Jan	Calls Last Apr	Calls Last Jul	Puts Last Jan	Puts Last Apr	Puts Last Jul
Alcoa	30	7 1/2	7 1/2	r	3-16	r	r
36 7/8	35	3 1/2	4	4 3/4	3/4	r	r
36 7/8	40	13-16	1 15-16	2 3/4	4	r	r
AT&T	10	8 1/2	s	s	r	s	s
18 5/8	15	3 7/8	4 1/8	4 3/8	1-16	r	5-16
18 5/8	20	3/8	13-16	1 1/8	1 5/8	2	2 1/4
18 5/8	25	r	3-16	s	r	6 1/4	s
Atl R	40	r	r	r	3-16	r	r
47 1/8	45	3 1/2	4 3/8	r	3/4	1 5/8	r
47 1/8	50	1	1 3/4	2 1/2	3 1/4	r	r
47 1/8	55	r	5/8	s	r	r	s
Avon	20	r	3 3/4	r	1/4	r	r
23	25	9-16	1 1-16	1 1/2	r	3	r
23	30	1-16	r	r	r	r	r
BankAm	15	r	3 7/8	r	1/8	r	r
18 3/4	20	7-16	3/4	1	1 3/4	r	r
Beth S	15	2	r	r	7-16	7/8	r
16 5/8	20	5-16	13-16	1 1/4	3 7/8	4	3 3/4
16 5/8	25	1-16	1/4	s	r	r	s
Burl N	35	11	r	s	r	r	s
45 3/4	40	r	r	s	r	1	s
45 3/4	45	3 1/4	4 7/8	r	1 3/4	r	3 1/8
45 3/4	50	1 1/4	2 1/2	r	5 1/8	r	r
45 3/4	55	r	1 3/8	r	r	r	r
ChiNw	20	6 3/4	r	s	r	r	s
CIGNA	35	3 1/8	r	r	7/8	r	1 7/8
37 5/8	40	r	1 7-16	2 1/2	r	r	r
Citicp	25	10 3/8	r	s	r	3-16	s
35 3/4	30	6 1/2	r	r	3/8	r	r
35 3/4	35	2 1/2	3 1/4	4	1 5-16	r	r
35 3/4	40	1/2	1 1/8	1 5/8	4 7/8	r	r
Cullin	30	r	r	s	1/8	1/2	s
43 1/2	40	r	r	r	1 1/2	r	3 1/4
43 1/2	45	2 3/4	r	r	3 5/8	r	r
43 1/2	50	r	r	4 1/4	r	r	r
Delta	30	9 3/4	r	s	r	r	s
39 1/8	35	5 1/4	6 1/4	r	1/2	1 1/4	1 7/8
39 1/8	40	2 3-16	3 5/8	4 1/4	2 1/2	r	r
39 1/8	45	3/4	1 1/2	2 1/8	r	r	r
Eas Kd	65	7 5/8	r	r	7-16	r	1 7-16
71 1/4	70	3 1/2	5 5/8	r	1 7/8	2 3/8	r
71 1/4	75	1 3/8	3	4	4 3/4	5	r
71 1/4	80	3/8	1 3/8	2 1/8	9 1/8	r	r
Eckerd	20	8 3/4	r	s	r	r	s
28 1/2	25	4 1/8	4 3/8	r	r	3/8	r
28 1/2	30	13-16	1 1/2	r	r	r	r
Engelh	20	7 3/4	r	s	r	r	s
27 7/8	25	r	4 5/8	r	r	r	r
27 7/8	30	1/2	1 1/4	r	r	r	r
27 7/8	35	r	r	5/8	r	r	r
Exxon	35	9 3/8	9 5/8	s	r	r	s
44 1/4	40	4 3/8	4 7/8	5	1/4	1/2	1
44 1/4	45	7/8	1 9-16	2	1 3/4	2 3/8	2 13-16
44 1/4	50	1/8	5-16	s	r	r	s
FedExp	30	r	r	s	r	1/2	s
38 1/2	35	5 1/4	r	r	1 1/8	1 3/4	r
38 1/2	40	2 1/4	3 3/4	5	3 1/2	3 3/4	r
38 1/2	45	3/4	1 3/4	r	r	r	r
38 1/2	50	3-16	r	s	r	r	s
FstChi	15	r	r	r	1/8	r	r
20 7/8	20	1 5/8	r	r	1 1-16	2	r
20 7/8	25	r	11-16	1	r	r	r
Fluor	10	6 3/4	r	s	r	r	s
16 1/2	15	2	2 1/2	2 1/2	3/8	5/8	3/4
16 1/2	20	3-16	1/2	3/4	r	r	3 1/2
Gt Wst	20	5 1/4	5 3/4	r	r	5/8	r
24 3/4	25	1 9-16	2 3/8	3	r	r	r
24 3/4	30	r	r	1 1/4	r	r	r
Halbtn	30	2 1/2	r	4	1	r	2 1/4
31 1/4	35	7-16	1 1/4	1 7/8	r	r	r
31 1/4	40	1-16	r	s	r	r	s
Hitachi	35	2 1/2	r	r	r	r	r
Homstk	20	5 3/4	6 1/4	7 1/4	3/8	3/4	1
25 1/8	25	2 1/8	3 3/8	4 1/8	1 5/8	2 1/8	2 5/8
25 1/8	30	5/8	1 7-16	2 1/4	5	5 5/8	r
25 1/8	35	3-16	s	s	r	s	s
I B M	95	33 1/2	s	s	r	s	s
126	100	28 3/4	29 1/4	s	r	3-16	s
126	110	18 3/4	21 1/2	22	5-16	15-16	1 5/8
126	120	9 7/8	13 1/4	15 5/8	1 3/8	2 7/8	4
126	130	3 3/4	7 3/8	9 1/4	5 3/8	6 1/2	7 1/2
126	140	7/8	2 15-16	5 1/4	14 1/2	r	15
In Min	40	1	r	r	r	r	r
38 1/4	45	3/8	5/8	r	r	r	r
In Pap	45	r	r	r	1/2	1 1/8	r
50 7/8	50	3	r	r	1 7/8	r	r
50 7/8	55	1	2 3-16	3	r	r	r
50 7/8	60	1/4	1	s	r	r	s
John J	30	4	4 1/2	r	7-16	7/8	r
33 1/8	35	7/8	1 3/4	2 1/4	r	r	r
33 1/8	40	1/8	s	s	r	s	s
Kerr M	25	r	r	r	1/4	r	r
29 1/8	30	1 1/4	2	2 5/8	1 7/8	r	r
29 1/8	35	1/4	r	1	r	r	r
Loral	25	3 3/8	r	r	r	r	r
27 3/8	30	1	r	r	r	r	r

Source: Reprinted by permission of *The Wall Street Journal,* (July 6, 1984; September 7, 1984; and November 2, 1984).

a 3¼ point gain of 325 percent. The option increased by more than 13 times the percentage move in the common stock. The relationship is indicated below.

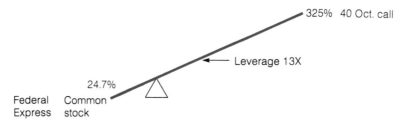

325% 40 Oct. call

Leverage 13X

24.7%

Federal   Common
Express   stock

Figure 13–1 depicts the relationship between profit and loss opportunities for the Federal Express 40 October call option, given the market price at expiration (no speculative premium exists at expiration).

As long as the common stock closes under 40, the call buyer loses the whole premium of 1 (or 100 times $1 equals $100). At a price of 41, the call buyer breaks even as the option is worth an intrinsic value of 1. As the stock increases past 41, the profit starts accumulating. If the option is sold before expiration, a speculative premium may alter the profit potential.

FIGURE 13–1   Federal Express 40 October Call Buy 1 Option (excludes commissions)

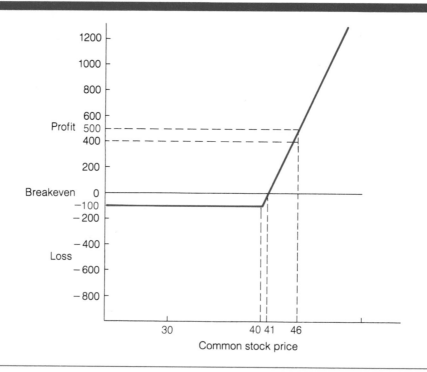

An investor striving for maximum leverage will generally buy options that are out-of-the-money or only slightly in-the-money. Buying high-priced options for $10 or $15 that are well in-the-money definitely limits the potential for leverage. You may have to invest almost as much in the options as you would have in the stocks.

Playing the leverage game doesn't always work out. If a speculator had assumed that Federal Express would continue its rapid price rise, he might have purchased an in-the-money January 40 call on September 6, 1984 for 6. While the stock declined 4⅜ from 42⅞ to 38½ by November 1, 1984, the call option declined from 6 to 2¼ (−62.5 percent). Since the stock decline from 42⅞ to 38½ represents only a 10.2 percent loss, the 62.5 percent loss on the option is significant. It is not hard to lose all your money under these circumstances—leverage works in reverse too.

Call options instead of stock. Many people do not like to risk losing large amounts of money and view call options as a way of controlling 100 shares of stock without a large dollar commitment. For example, using Table 13–7 for the September 6, 1984, prices, International Paper common stock could have been purchased at 55½ or $5,550 plus commission for 100 shares. A January 55 call could also be bought for 4¼ ($425), which would leave $5,125 leftover cash ($5,550 − $425) for an investment elsewhere while still maintaining the opportunity to buy 100 shares at 55.

Assume the call is purchased for $425 and $5,125 is left to be invested in a money market fund at 10 percent until November 1, 1984. The interest income would be about $85 for two months.

During this time the stock declined from 55½ to 50⅞. That's a loss of 4⅝, or $462.50. This was partially offset by a $60 dividend payment, for a net loss of $402.50 on the 100 shares of stock. As would be expected, the call option also went down from 4¼ ($425) to 1 ($100). That's a loss of $325, which was partially offset by the $85 of interest income from the investment of leftover cash in a money market fund. The net loss associated with the call option is $240 ($325 − $85). The net loss on the call option of $240 is certainly less than the net loss of $402.50 on the stock purchase. The overall effect is demonstrated in Table 13–8. An additional unspecified, cost consideration is that the investor probably saved another $25 to $50 in commissions since stock trading is more expensive than option trading.

Had the stock really declined in value, say, to $30, the advantage of the limited dollar loss exposure of the option would be even more apparent. The purchaser of 100 shares of stock would have lost $2,550 as the stock declined from 55½ to 30. This loss is only slightly reduced by the receipt of $60 in dividends. On the other hand, the purchaser of the option cannot lose more than the initial purchase price of $425 (100 × 4¼). Even this loss is slightly offset by the $85 of interest from the investment of leftover cash in a money market account.

Of course, if the stock does the opposite and goes way up to $70 or $80, both the stock purchaser and option buyer will show substantial profits.

TABLE 13–8   Comparison of Call Option to Stock Purchase (International Paper)

Buy call; Draw interest	*Buy stock*
September 6, 1984	September 6, 1984
$425.00 (100 × 4¼)	$5,550.00 (100 × 55½)
November 1, 1984 value	November 1, 1984 value
$100.00 (100 × 1)	$5,087.50 (100 × 50⅞)
+ 85.00 Interest income	+ 60.00 Dividend income
$185.00	$5,147.50
$240.00 Loss	$402.50 Loss

Protecting a short position.   Calls are often used to cover a short sale against the risk of rising stock prices. This is called hedging your position; by purchasing a call, the short seller guarantees a loss of no more than a fixed amount while at the same time reducing any potential profit by the total premium paid for the call. Again refer to Table 13–7 and assume you had sold 100 shares of Delta Airlines short at 30⅜ on July 5, 1984, and had bought a January 30 call for 4¼ as protection against a rise in the price of the stock. By November 1, the stock has risen to 39⅛ for an 8¾ loss on the short position. This loss has been partially offset by an increase in the call option price to 9¾, or a 5½ gain. Instead of losing 8¾, the short position is only out 3¼ so far (8¾ − 5½). This is the loss of 8¾ on the short position less the gain of 5½ on the call option. This strategy has locked in a maximum loss potential of 3⅞ plus commissions. The 3⅞ is the *speculative* premium paid for the January 30 call; as the stock rises, the speculative premium evaporates at expiration, but otherwise the call goes up dollar for dollar with the stock. If the investor thinks Delta is a good short at 39⅛ on November 1, he may sell the call for 9¾ on November 1 and be left with an unprotected short position with the stock at 39⅛, hoping for an eventual decline in the stock price.

Consider the initial 4¼ call premium insurance. If the stock goes up, it limited your loss, but if the stock goes down, your profit on the short position is reduced by the call premium. In the case of Delta, the stock would have to reach 26⅛ (30⅜ − 4¼) before the short seller with call protection would break even. A decline of more than 14 percent in the stock price would have to occur before the short seller would begin to profit, and this ignores commissions. As is true of most option plays, there are advantages and disadvantages to most strategies.

Guaranteed price.   Often an investor thinks a stock will rise over the short-term and long-term, but does not currently have the cash available to purchase the stock. The important point for this strategy is that the investor wants to own this stock eventually but does not want to miss out on a good

buying opportunity now (based on his or her expectations). Perhaps the oil stocks are depressed or semiconductors have hit bottom. A call option can be utilized. The investor could be anticipating a cash inflow at a specific time in the future when he plans to exercise the call option with a tax refund, a book royalty, or even the annual Christmas bonus.

For example, on July 5, 1984, Mrs. Harris buys a January 70 Eastman Kodak call option for 5, which is a 5 speculative premium since Eastman Kodak is selling at 70 per share. By September, she has received her $7,000 anticipated check and exercises the option when the stock is selling at 75¾. For tax purposes, the cost or basis of this 100 shares of Eastman Kodak is the strike price (70) plus the option premium (5), or 75 per share. Since most investors will not pursue this strategy if they expect prices to fall, they will usually seek out the deepest in-the-money option that they can afford because it is likely to have the lowest speculative premium. For example, Mrs. Harris could have used a January 60 call with a price of 13 and the final cost would be 73 rather than 75 per share. If she does not initially have the $1,300 for the 60 call, she might consider the 65 call for 8⅜ as the next best alternative.

Writing Call Options

Writers of call options take the opposite side of the market from the buyers. The writer is similar to a short seller in that he or she expects the stock to decline or stay the same. In order for short sellers to profit, prices must decline, but since writers of call options receive a premium, they can make a profit if prices stay the same or even rise less than the speculative premium. Option writers can write covered options, meaning they own the underlying common stock, or they can write naked call options, meaning they do not own the underlying stock.

Writing covered call options is often considered a hedged position because, if the stock price declines, the writer's loss on the stock is partially offset by the option premium. A writer of a covered call must decide if he is willing to sell the underlying stock if it closes above the strike price and the option is exercised. He also must consider any adverse tax consequences, such as short-term capital gains.

Returning to Table 13–7 for another set of option quotes, find Atlantic Richfield (Atl R) options. The market price of the common stock is 49⅞ on September 6 (middle of table), and the writer for an October call option can choose from the strike prices reprinted in Table 13–9.

TABLE 13–9   Atlantic Richfield October Strike Prices

September 6, 1984	Strike	October premiums	Market price
Atl R	45	5⅜	49⅞
Atl R	50	1½	49⅞
Atl R	55	¼	49⅞

Remember, the writer agrees to sell 100 shares at the strike price for the consideration of the premium. The 45 strike price has the highest premium and would be a good write if the stock closed at less than 45 because the call would not get exercised and the writer would profit by the amount of the premium, 5⅜. If the stock closed above 45, then the call could get exercised, and the writer would have to deliver 100 shares at 45. More likely, the option writer would buy back the option for its price in the market to avoid having the option exercised. For example, if the ending value of the stock were 48, the option writer could buy back the 45 option for 3. If the stock closed at more than 50⅜, the call writer would be at a loss and could buy back the option at a loss. Figure 13–2 shows this relationship between profit and loss and the common stock price.

By October 20, the date of expiration, Atlantic Richfield stock closed at 46⅜, and the option was worth 1⅜. Both a covered writer and a naked writer would have made a profit. The covered writer would have collected a dividend, repurchased the call option at 1⅜ and still have had possession of 100

FIGURE 13–2   Atlantic Richfield October Calls Write 1 Call (excludes commissions)

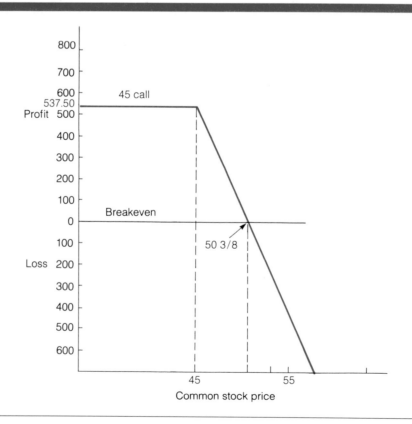

shares of stock now valued at $4,637.50 instead of $4,987.50. The following is an analysis of how the two types of call writers fared.

Covered writer		Naked writer	
−Initial investment			
(100 @ 49⅞)	($4,987.50)	−Margin (30 percent of	
+Option premium (5⅜)	537.50	stock price)	($1,496.25)
+Dividend	75.00	+Option premium (5⅜)	537.50
+Ending value stock	4,637.50	+Ending value margin	1,496.25
−Repurchase of option (1⅜)	(137.50)	−Repurchase of option (1⅜)	(137.50)
Profit	$ 125.00	Profit	$ 400.00
Percent return on		Percent return on	
initial investment	2.55%	initial margin investment	26.7%

The covered writer hedged the losses on his stock by collecting an option premium. In spite of a declining stock price, he still managed a positive return. Our naked writer was required to put up margin on 30 percent of the value of the stock to ensure her ability to close out the option write if the stock should rise significantly. The capital was returned to her when it was no longer needed as collateral, and she profited with almost a 27 percent return. To avoid exercise of the option, the call writer in both cases is assumed to enter the market with a closing transaction to repurchase the 45 call at 1⅜ before expiration. If the stock price had risen, the naked writer was exposed to unlimited risk as she either had to close out her position at a loss or purchase the stock above the strike price and deliver it at a loss. The covered writer had limited risk because he locked in the cost of his stock and can deliver it or close out his position before it is called.

Another critical decision for a call writer is the choice of months. In the section on option premiums, we examined percentage premiums per day and found that the shortest expiration dates provided the highest daily speculative premium. In most cases, the call writer will choose the shorter-term options and, as they expire, write another short-term option. Annualized returns of 20 percent are not uncommon for continuously covered writing strategies.

Buying Put Options

The owner of a put may sell 100 shares of stock to the put writer at the strike price. The strategy behind a put is similar to selling short or writing a call except losses are limited to the total investment (premium), and no more risk exposure is possible if the stock rises. Buying a put in anticipation of a price decline is one method of speculating on market price changes. The same factors influencing call premiums also apply to put premiums except that expectations for the direction of the market are the opposite.

On September 6, 1984, Eastman Kodak's common stock price was 75¾, and a 75 January put could be purchased for 2½ (see Table 13–7 and remember to look for put prices rather than call prices). The put was out-of-the-money by ¾. Four and one half months remained until expiration. The buyer of the put would expect a price decline with the idea that the intrinsic value of

the put would increase. By November 1, 1984, Eastman Kodak had declined to 71¼ with the 75 January put at 4¾. The intrinsic value was now 3¾ (75 − 71¼) and the speculative premium was 1. At this point in time, the owner of the put had a 2¼ gain on a 2½ investment or a 90 percent return while the stock was declining only 6 percent.

Puts can make money in a down market and also possibly help offset a large loss in the value of the common stock. In the latter case, an owner of 100 shares of Eastman Kodak could have bought a put to hedge against a loss in the value of the stock. Eastman Kodak dropped 4½ (74¾ − 71¼), and the gain of 2¼ on the put offset some of the loss suffered on the common stock.

Hedges do not always work out as expected. For example, on September 6, 1984, assume the owner of 100 shares of IBM anticipated a price decline because of expectations of rising interest rates, but he did not want to sell the stock and pay a capital gains tax on these shares held for many years. Instead he bought a January 120 put for 3⅞ when the stock was at 123¼. By November 1, 1984, IBM stock was up 2¾ (the decline never materialized), and the January 120 put was worth 1⅜, providing a loss of $250 on the put. Of course, one can think of the $250 loss as insurance against a price decline that never happened—much like auto insurance, we pay a premium for something we hope never happens.

USING OPTIONS IN COMBINATIONS

Spreads

Now that you have a basic understanding of puts and calls from both the buyer's and writer's perspective, we proceed with a discussion of spreads. Most combinations of options are called spreads and consist of buying one option (going long) and writing an option (going short) on the same underlying stock. Spreads are for the sophisticated investor and involve many variations on a theme. Vertical spreads involve buying and writing two contracts at different striking prices with the same month of expiration. Horizontal spreads consist of buying and writing two options with the same strike price but different months, and a diagonal spread is a combination of the vertical and horizontal spread. These spreads are constructed using call options. Table 13–10 presents an example of XYZ Corporation demonstrating the options, months, and strike prices involved in each type of spread. There are more complicated spreads than these, such as the butterfly spread, variable spread, and domino spread. We cannot attempt to explain all of these spreads in the space available and so we will concentrate on vertical bull spreads and vertical bear spreads.

Since spreads require the purchase of one call and the sale of another call, a speculator's account will have either a debit or credit balance. If the cost of the long call is greater than the revenue from the short position, the speculator has a net cash outflow and a debit in his account. When your spread is put on with a debit, it is said that you have "bought the spread." You have "sold the

TABLE 13–10   Spreads (call options)

Vertical Spreads   Option Prices

	Mkt. Price	Strike Price	Oct.	Jan.	April
XYZ	36⅜	35	4	6	6½
	36⅜	40	2	3⅜	4
	36⅜	45	1¹¹⁄₁₆	1½	6

Horizontal Spread (Time Spread)

	Mkt. Price	Strike Price	Oct.	Jan.	April
XYZ	36⅜	35	4	6	6½
	36⅜	40	2	3⅜	4
	36⅜	45	¹¹⁄₁₆	1½	6

Diagonal Spread

	Mkt. Price	Strike Price	Oct.	Jan.	April
XYZ	36⅜	35	4	6	6½
	36⅜	40	2	3⅜	4
	36⅜	45	¹¹⁄₁₆	1½	6

spread" if the receipt from writing the call is greater than the cost of the long call and you have a credit balance. For example, the difference between the option prices for a vertical spread on XYZ Corporation in Table 13–10 with October strike prices of 35 and 40 is $2 ($4 − $2). The $2 difference between these two option prices is sometimes called the price spread and could be either a debit or credit, depending on whether a bull or bear spread is used. In either case, the profit or loss from a spread position results in the change between the two option prices over time as the price of the underlying stock goes up or down.

Vertical bull spread.   Being a bull spread, the expectation is that the common stock price will rise. The speculator can buy the common stock outright, or if he wants to profit from an expected price increase but reduce his risk of loss, he can enter into a bull spread. Vertical bull spreads limit both the maximum gain and maximum loss available. They are usually debit positions because the spreader buys the higher-priced, in-the-money option and shorts (writes) an inexpensive, out-of-the-money option. Using Table 13–10 for an

XYZ October bull spread, we would buy the October 35 at 4 and sell the October 40 at 2 for a debit of 2 (price spread). This represents a $200 investment. Assume that three weeks later, XYZ stock rises from 36⅜ to 42 with the October 35 selling at 7½ (previously purchased at 4) and the October 40 at 4½ (previously sold at 2). Table 13–11 shows the result of closing out the spread.

TABLE 13–11   Profit on Vertical Bull Spread

XYZ October 35		XYZ October 40		Price spread
Bought at	4	Sold at	2	2
Sold at	7½	Bought at	4½	3
Gain	3½	(Loss)	(2½)	1
	Net gain	$100		
	Investment	$200		
	Return	50%		

Because the investment was only $200, the total return of $100 provided a 50 percent return. However, returns on spreads can be greatly altered by commissions. If the following spread incurred commissions of $50 in and out, the percentage return could be cut in half to 25 percent.

The maximum profit at expiration is equal to the difference in strike prices ($5 in this case) minus the initial price spread ($2 in this case). For the XYZ bull spread, the maximum profit is $300, and the maximum loss is the original debit of $200. At expiration, all speculative premiums are gone, and each option sells at its intrinsic value. Table 13–12 shows maximum profit and loss at various closing market prices at expiration. Remember, our initial investment is $200.

TABLE 13–12   XYZ Vertical Bull Spread

XYZ stock price at expiration 35				XYZ stock price at expiration 40				XYZ stock price at expiration 45			
October 35		October 40		October 35		October 40		October 35		October 40	
Bought at	4	Sold at	2	Bought at	4	Sold at	2	Bought at	4	Sold at	2
Expired at*	0	Expired at*	0	Sold at*	5	Expired at*	0	Sold at*	10	Bought at*	5
(Loss)	(4)	Gain	2	Gain	1	Gain	2	Gain	6	Loss	(3)
(Net loss) (2)				Net gain 3				Net gain 3			
$(200) 100 percent loss				$300 150 percent gain				$300 150 percent gain			

* All call options on date of expiration equal their intrinsic value.

As Table 13–12 shows, profit does not increase after the stock moves through the $40 call price. The stock price must increase from 36⅜ to 40 (10 percent) to generate a 150 percent spread profit. Every dollar of increased profit on the long position is offset by $1 of loss on the short position after the stock passes a price of 40. One of the important but difficult aspects of spreading is forecasting a range of prices rather than just the direction prices will move. If a speculator is bullish, he or she may buy a call instead of spreading. The potential loss is higher with the call but still limited, while the possible gain is unlimited. The relationship between long calls and bull spreads starts in the bottom of Figure 13–3. Note the maximum loss with the bull spread is

FIGURE 13–3   Profit and Loss Relationships on Spreads and Calls

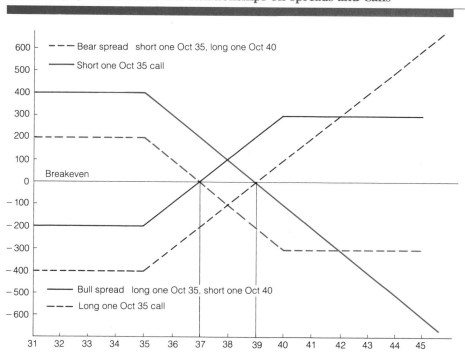

$200 and $400 with a long call. The break-even point is also $2 less for the bull spread ($37 versus $39). However, the long call has unlimited profit potential, and the bull spread is locked in at $300 at a stock price of $40 or higher. The spread position lowers the break-even point by $2 per share but also limits potential returns—a classic case of risk-return trade-off.

Vertical bear spread. The speculator enters a bear spread anticipating a decline in stock prices. Instead of selling short or writing a call with both

having unlimited risk, he spreads by selling short the call with the lower strike price (highest premium) and covers the upside risk with the purchase of a call having a higher strike price. This creates a credit balance. In a sense, the bear spread does the opposite of the vertical bull spread as seen in Table 13–13, in which we show profits and losses from the strategy if XYZ ends up at $35 or at $40. With a bear spread, the price spread of 2 is the maximum gain if the stock closes at $35 or less at expiration, while the maximum loss equals 3, the difference between the exercise prices minus the price spread. The relationships between bear spreads and writing a call option was also demonstrated in Figure 13–3 (the comparison starts at the top of the figure).

TABLE 13–13   XYZ Vertical Bear Spread

XYZ stock price at expiration 35				XYZ stock price at expiration 40			
October 35		October 40		October 35		October 40	
Sold at	4	Bought at	2	Sold at	4	Bought at	2
Expired at	0	Expired at	0	Bought at	5	Expired at	0
Gain	4	(Loss)	(2)	(Loss)	1	(Loss)	2
	Net gain 2				(Net loss) (3)		
	$200				$(300)		

Straddles

A straddle is a combination of a put and call on the same stock with the same strike price and expiration date. It is used to play wide fluctuations in stock prices and is usually applied to individual stocks with high betas and a history of large, short-term fluctuations in price. The speculator using a straddle may be unsure of the direction of the price movement but may be able to make a large enough profit on one side of the straddle to cover the cost of both options even if one option expires worthless.

For example, assume a put and a call can be bought for $5 apiece on an ABC October 50 when ABC Corporation is selling at 50 with six months to expiration. The total investment is 10 ($1,000). If the stock should rise from 50 to 65 at expiration, the call would provide a profit of 10 (15 value − 5 cost), and the put would be left to expire worthless for a loss of 5. This would provide a net gain of 5, or $500. The same type of example can be drawn if the price goes way down. Some who engage in spreads or straddles might attempt to close out one position before the other. This expands the profit potential but also increases the risk.

OTHER OPTION CONSIDERATIONS

Many factors have not been covered in detail because of their changing nature over time. Tax laws relating to options are constantly changing, and some

items, such as capital gains holding periods for determination of long-term and short-term tax treatment, have been revised several times in the last several years. We do know that tax laws have a significant impact on spread positions and also on the long-term tax treatment where put options are involved. The best advice we can give is to check the tax consequences of any option strategy with your accountant or stockbroker.

Commissions vary between different brokerage houses and are not easy to pinpoint for option transactions since quantity discounts exist. We can assure you that because many option positions involve small dollar outlays, commissions of $25 to $50 for buying and selling can significantly alter your returns and even create losses. Commissions on exercising common stock through options are higher than the transaction costs of options, and these are a motivating force in causing closing option transactions before expiration. Overall, commissions on options tend to be more significant than commissions on commodities or other highly leveraged investments.

SUMMARY

Put and call options are an exciting area of investment and speculation. We have discussed the past history of over-the-counter options trading and more recent trading of options on the listed options exchanges, such as the CBOE. The markets are more efficient, and the standardized practices of the listed exchanges have made options more usable for many investors and widened the number of options strategies that can be employed.

Option premiums (option prices) are affected by many variables, such as time, market expectations, stock price volatility, dividend yields, and in-the-money, out-of-the-money relationships. The total premium consists of an intrinsic value plus a speculative premium which declines to zero by the expiration date. Calls are options to buy 100 shares of stock, while puts are options to sell 100 shares of stock.

Understanding the benefits and risks of trading options is complicated. Options can be risky or used to reduce risk. Calls can be bought for leverage, to cover a short position, or as an alternative to investing in the underlying common stock while buying time to purchase the stock (waiting for the financial resources to exercise the call). Calls are written either as a hedge on a long position in the underlying stock or to speculate on a price decline. Puts are bought to hedge a long position against a price decline or as an alternative to selling short. A writer of a put may speculate on a price increase or use the write as a hedge against a short position (if the price goes up, he will come out ahead on the writing of the put to partially offset the loss on the short sale).

Spreads are combinations of buying and writing the same options for an underlying common stock. In general, spreads reduce the risk of loss while at the same time limiting the gain. Spreads can be created to profit from rising prices, falling prices, or no price change at all. The important part is having the correct expectations. Straddles are a combination of a put and a call in a stock

at the same exercise date and strike price. They are used to profit from stocks showing large, short-term price fluctuations.

Other factors affect option profitability, such as taxes and commissions, and in general, each investor or speculator should check out his or her own situation and factor in the appropriate information with regard to taxes and commissions.

IMPORTANT WORDS AND CONCEPTS

Bull spread	**Intrinsic value**
Buying-the spread	**Opening purchase transaction**
Call	**Opening sale transaction**
CBOE	**Option**
Closing purchase transaction	**Option premium**
Closing sale transaction	**Options Clearing Corporation**
Covered writer	**Put**
Diagonal spreads	**Spreads**
Exercise price	**Straddle**
In-the-money	**Vertical spread**

DISCUSSION QUESTIONS

1. What exchanges trade in stock options?
2. How has the option market been expanded recently?
3. What is the exercise or strike price on an option?
4. Explain how the Options Clearing Corporation operates.
5. Approximately what percent of call options get exercised? What percent of put options? (Consult text footnote 1.)
6. What are factors that influence a speculative premium on an option?
7. Why might an option price reflect a discount at expiration?
8. Why does an option that is deep in-the-money often have a low speculative premium?
9. Why would a high-beta stock often have a greater speculative premium than a low-beta stock?
10. Comment on the statement, "the novice may attempt to write the options with the highest total premium or speculative premium, while the buyer may think the smallest investment provides the greatest leverage."
11. What does the speculative premium as a percent of stock price indicate for a call option?
12. Do call options or warrants normally have shorter lives?
13. Comment on how leverage works in purchasing a call option.
14. Assume you wish to control the price movement of 100 shares of stock. You may buy 100 shares of stock directly or purchase a call option on the 100 shares. Which strategy is likely to expose you to the larger

potential dollar amount of loss? Which strategy is likely to expose you to the larger potential percentage loss on your investment?

15. Explain how options can be used to protect a short position.

16. What are two option strategies to take advantage of an anticipated decline in stock prices? (Relate one to call options and the other to put options.)

17. What is the difference between a covered and naked call option write?

18. In general, if the price of the underlying stock is going up, what will happen to the price of a put option? Briefly explain.

19. What is a vertical spread; a horizontal spread; a diagonal spread?

20. Is a vertical bear spread likely to be more or less risky than selling short or writing a naked call option?

21. What is a straddle? Why is it used?

22. Why might small commissions of $25 to $50 be important in option trades?

PROBLEMS

1. Look at the option quotes in Table 13–3. **(a)** What is the closing price of the common stock of Delta? **(b)** What is the highest strike price listed? **(c)** What is the price of an October 30 call option? **(d)** What is the price of an October 30 put option? **(e)** Explain the reason for the difference between the prices of the put and the call.

2. Assume that a stock is selling for $51.50 with options available at 40, 50, and 60 strike prices. The 50 call option price is at 4½.
   a. What is the intrinsic value of the 50 call?
   b. Is the 50 call in-the-money?
   c. What is the speculative premium on the 50 call option?
   d. What percent does the speculative premium represent of common stock price?
   e. Are the 40 and 60 call options in-the-money?

3. In the case of Bank America in Table 13–3, **(a)** What is the intrinsic value of the January 15 call? **(b)** What is the total premium? **(c)** How much is the speculative premium?

4. In the case of Alcoa in Table 13–3, **(a)** What is the intrinsic value of the January 40 call? **(b)** How much is the speculative premium? **(c)** By what percent does the stock need to go up by expiration to break even on the call option?

5. Assume on May 1, you are considering a stock with three different expiration dates for the 60 call options. The percentage speculative premium for each date is as follows:

May	2.6%
August	6.9%
November	11.2%

Each contract expires at 11:59 P.M. Eastern time on the Saturday immediately following the third Friday of the expiration month. For purposes of this problem, assume the May option has 21 days to run, the August option has 112 days, and the November option has 203 days.

   a.   Compute the percentage speculative premium per day for each of the three dates.

   b.   From the viewpoint of a call option purchaser, which expiration date appears most attractive? (all else being equal).

   c.   From the viewpoint of a call option writer, which expiration date appears most attractive? (all else being equal).

6.   In Table 13–7, calculate the leverage from holding a Citicorp option (October 30 call) from July 5 until September 6. (The best approach for doing this is to compute the percentage gain from holding the option, then compute the percentage gain from holding the stock, and finally divide the first value by the second value.)

7.   Assume that a party writes a call option for 100 shares at a strike price of 40 for a premium of 6½. This is a naked option. **(a)** What would his gain or loss be if the stock closed at 35? **(b)** What would the break-even point be in terms of the closing price of the stock?

8.   Assume you purchase 100 shares of stock at $73 per share and wish to hedge your position by writing a 100-share call option on your holdings. The option has a $70 strike price and a premium of $8. If the stock is selling at $68 at the time of expiration, what will be the overall gain or loss on this covered option play? (Consider the change in stock value as well as the gain or loss on the option.) Note that the stock does not pay a cash dividend.

9.   In Problem 8, what would be the overall gain or loss if the stock ended up at **(a)** $70, **(b)** $48, **(c)** $85, **(d)** $100 (disregard the stock being called away in **(a)** and **(c)**.

10.   Though commissions are not explicitly considered in Problems 7 through 9, might they be significant?

11.   Assume a 40 July put option is purchased for 5½ on a stock selling at $36 per share. If the stock ends up on expiration at $29½, what will be the value of the put option?

12.   In Problem 11, at what ending stock price would the investor break even?

13.   Vertical bull spread: a stock is selling for $57. You buy a July 55 call option for 3¼ and a short (write) a July 60 call option for 1. If the stock is $64 at expiration, what will your profit or loss be on the spread? (Note: you do not own any stock directly.)

14.   Assume you sell 100 shares of Bowie Corporation short at $61. You also buy a 60 call option for 3½ to protect against the stock price going up.

   a.   If the stock ends up at $80, what will be your overall gain or loss?

   b.   If the stock ends up at $40, what will be your overall gain or loss?

   c.   What is the most you can lose under this short sale-call option plan?

    d.   If you had an unprotected short sale position (no call option), what is the most you could lose?

15.   Refer to Table 13–7. Assume on September 6, you turn negative on the shares of Eastman Kodak. You are considering two different bearish strategies on 100 shares of Eastman Kodak: (1) Write a January 75 call option. (2) Buy a January 75 put option.

    a.   Assume you initiate these actions on September 6, which will offer the larger dollar gain by November 1? Once again, refer to Table 13–7.

    b.   Generally speaking, which of these two strategies is the riskier?

    c.   If the stock price is way down at expiration, which strategy will allow you the larger profit opportunity?

    d.   Finally, if Eastman Kodak's stock does not change in price at all and ends up at 75¾ (its value on September 6), which strategy will produce the better results for the investor?

SELECTED REFERENCES

Black, Fisher. "Fact and Fantasy in the Use of Options." *Financial Analysts Journal,* July–August 1975, pp. 36–41.

Black, Fisher, and Myron Scholes. "The Valuation of Option Contracts and a Test of Market Efficiency." *Journal of Finance,* May 1972, pp. 399–417.

————. "The Pricing of Options and Corporate Liabilities." *Journal of Political Economy,* May–June 1973, pp. 637–54.

Chicago Board of Options Exchange. Selected material.

Clasing, Henry. *The Dow Jones-Irwin Guide to Put and Call Options.* Homewood, Ill.: Dow Jones-Irwin, 1975.

Dawson, Frederic S. "Risk and Returns in Continuous Option Writing." *Journal of Portfolio Management,* Winter 1979, pp. 58–63.

Finnerty, Joseph E. "The Chicago Board Options Exchange and Market Efficiency." *Journal of Financial and Quantitative Analysis,* March 1978, pp. 29–38.

French, Dan W. "The Weekend Effect on the Distribution of Stock Prices: Implications for Option Pricing." *Journal of Financial Economics,* forthcoming.

French, Dan W., and Glenn V. Henderson. "Substitute Hedged Option Portfolios: Theory and Evidence." *Journal of Financial Research,* Spring 1981, pp. 21–31.

Galai, Dan. "Tests of Market Efficiency of the Chicago Board Options Exchange." *Journal of Business,* April 1977, pp. 167–97.

Gastineau, Gary L. "An Index of Listed Option Premiums." *Financial Analysts Journal,* May–June 1977, pp. 70–75.

Gambola, Michael J.; Rodney L. Roenfeldt; and Philip L. Cooley. "Spreading Strategies in CBOE Options: Evidence on Market Performance." *Journal of Financial Research,* Winter 1978, pp. 35–44.

Hettenhouse, George W., and Donald J. Puglisi. "Investor Experience with Put and Call Options." *Financial Analysts Journal,* July–August 1975, pp. 53–58.

"How to Play the Option Game." *Business Week,* December 22, 1980, p. 88.

Malkiel, Burton, and Richard Quandt. *Strategies and Rational Decisions in the Securities Option Market.* Cambridge, Mass.: MIT Press, 1969.

Merton, Robert C.; Myron S. Scholes; and Mathew L. Gladstein. "The Returns and Risk of Alternative Call Option Investment Strategies." *Journal of Business,* April 1978, pp. 183–242.

"Options—A Pension Management Tool for Controlling Risk and Return." *Financial Executive,* March 1979, pp. 37–43.

Reback, Robert. "Risk and Return in Option Trading." *Financial Analysts Journal,* July–August 1975, pp. 42–52.

Rendleman, Richard J., Jr. "Optimal Long-Run Option Investment Strategies." *Financial Management,* Spring 1981, pp. 61–76.

Scholes, Myron. "Taxes and the Pricing of Options." *Journal of Finance,* May 1976, pp. 319–32.

Smith, Clifford W., Jr. "Option Pricing: A Review." *Journal of Financial Economics,* January–March 1976, pp. 3–51.

Stoll, Hans R. "The Relationship between Put and Call Option Prices." *The Journal of Finance,* December 1969, pp. 801–24.

APPENDIX 13–A: Options Available on Companies' Common Stock

Company Name/Ticker Symbol/Exchange

Company	Exch	Company	Exch	Company	Exch
Abbott Labs (ABT)	PH	Chemical New York (CHL)	A	First Chicago (FBC)	C
Advanced Micro Devices (AMD)	P	Chevron Corp. (CHV)	A	First Mississippi (FRM)	A
Aetna Life (AET)	A	Chicago & Northwestern (CNW)	C	Fleetwood Ent. (FLE)	A
Air Products & Chemicals (APD)	PH	Chrysler (C)	C	Fluor (FLR)	C
Alcan Aluminum (AL)	A	Church's Fried Chicken (CHU)	PH	Ford Motor (F)	C
Alexander & Alexander Srv.(AAL)	C	CIGNA (CI)	C	Foster Wheeler (FWC)	P
Allied (ALD)	PH	Cincinnati Milacron (CMZ)	PH	Freeport-McMoRan (FTX)	C
Allied Stores (ALS)	C	Citicorp (FNC)	C	GAF (GAF)	PH
Allis-Chalmers (AH)	PH	City Investing (CNV)	PH	GCA (GCA)	A
Aluminum Co. of America (AA)	C	Clorox (CLX)	PH	General Dynamics (GD)	C
Amax (AMS)	A	Coastal (CGP)	C,A	General Electric (GE)	C
Amdahl (AMH)	C	Coca-Cola (KO)	C	General Foods (GF)	C
Amerada Hess (AHC)	PH	Coleco (CLO)	PH	General Instrument (GRL)	PH
American Brands (AMB)	A	Colgate Palmolive (CL)	C	General Motors (GM)	C
American Broadcasting (ABC)	P	Colt Industries (COT)	PH	Genuine Parts (GPC)	P
American Can (AC)	A	Combustion Eng. (CSP)	P	Genrad (GEN)	PH
American Cyanamid (ACY)	A	Comdisco (CDO)	P	GEO International (GX)	A
American Electric Power (AEP)	C	Commodore Intl. (CBU)	PH	Georgia-Pacific (GP)	PH
American Express (AXP)	C,A	Commonwealth Edison (CWE)	C	Gerber Scientific (GRB)	AH
American Home Products (AHP)	A	Communication Satellite (CQ)	PH	Gillette (GS)	A
American Hospital Supply (AHS)	C	Community Psych. Ctrs. (CMY)	PH	Global Marine (GLM)	A
American Intl. Group (AIG)	C	Computer Sciences (CSC)	C	Golden Nugget (GNG)	A
American Medical Intl. (AMI)	C	Computervision (CVN)	PH	Golden West Fin. (GDW)	PH
AT&T (T)	C	Consolidated Edison (ED)	A	Goodyear Tire (GT)	A
AMF (AMF)	A	Continental Telecom (CTC)	A	Gould (GLD)	A
AMP (AMP)	C	Control Data (CDA)	C	Grace W.R. (GRA)	A
AMR (AMR)	A	Cooper Industires (CBE)	A	Great Western Fin. (GWF)	C
Anheuser-Busch (BUD)	PH	CooperVision (EYE)	A	Greyhound (G)	A
Apache (APA)	C	Corning Glass (CLW)	C	GTE (GTE)	A
Archer-Daniels-Midland (ADM)	PH	Cray Research (CRY)	P	Gulf + Western (GW)	C
Arkla (ALG)	A	Crown Zellerbach (ZB)	A	Gulf Canada Ltd. (GOC)	PH
Armco (AS)	PH	CSX (CSX)	P	Frank B. Hall & Co. (FBH)	A
ASA, Ltd. (ASA)	A	Cullinet (CUL)	C	Halliburton (HAL)	C
Asarco (AR)	A	Dart & Kraft (DK)	A	Harris (HRS)	C
Ashland Oil (ASH)	PH	Data General (DGN)	P	Hecla (HL)	A
Atlantic Richfield (ARC)	C	Datapoint (DPT)	C	Hercules (HPC)	A
Automatic Data Proc. (AUD)	PH	Dataproducts (DPC)	P	Hewlett-Packard (HWP)	C
Avco (AV)	PH	Dayton-Hudson (DH)	C	Hilton Hotels (HLT)	P
Avnet (AVT)	A	Deere (DE)	A	Hitachi (HIT)	C
Avon (AVP)	C	Delta Air Lines (DAL)	C	Holiday Inns (HIA)	C
Baker International (BKO)	P	Denny's (DEN)	P	Homestake Mining (HM)	C
Bally Mfg. (BLY)	C,A	Diamond Shamrock (DIA)	P	Honeywell (HON)	C
Bank America (BAC)	C	Diebold (DBD)	C	Hospital Corp. of Amer. (HCA)	P
Bard C.R. (BCR)	PH	Digital Equipment (DEC)	C,A	Household International (HI)	A
Bausch & Lomb (BOL)	P	Disney (DIS)	C,A	Houston Natural Gas (HNG)	P
Baxter Travenol Labs (BAX)	C	Dome Mines (DM)	PH	Hughes Tool (HT)	C
Beatrice Foods (BRY)	A	Dominion Resources (D)	PH	Humana (HUM)	C
Becton Dickinson (BDX)	PH	Dow Chemical (DOW)	C	Hutton E.F. (EFH)	A
Bell South Corp. (BLS)	A	Dresser (DI)	PH	Inexco Oil (INX)	PH
Bethlehem Steel (BS)	C	Duke Power (DUK)	PH	IBM (IBM)	C
Beverly Enterprises (BEV)	P	Dun & Bradstreet (DNB)	A	Intl. Flavors & Frag. (IFF)	C
Black & Decker (BDK)	C	duPont (DD)	C,A	Intl. Minerals & Chem. (IGL)	C
Boeing (BA)	C	E-Systems (ESY)	P	International Paper (IP)	C
Boise Cascade (BCC)	C	Eastern Gas & Fuel (EFU)	PH	ITT (ITT)	C
Bristol-Myers (BMY)	C	Eastman Kodak (EK)	C	Johnson & Johnson (JNJ)	C
Browning Ferris Ind. (BFI)	A	Eckerd, Jack (ECK)	C	Joy Manufacturing (JOY)	PH
Brunswick (BC)	C	Edwards A.G. (AGE)	C	Kaneb Services (KAB)	A
Bucyrus-Erie (BY)	A	EG & G (EGG)	PH	Kerr-McGee (KMG)	C
Burlington Northern (BN)	C	Emerson Electric (EMR)	A	Key Pharmaceuticals (KPH)	P
Burroughs (BGH)	C,A	Emery (EAF)	PH	K Mart (KM)	C
Campbell Red Lake (CRK)	PH	Engelhard (EC)	C	Lear Siegler (LSI)	PH
Capital Cities Comm. (CCB)	C	Enserch (ENS)	P	Lehman (LEM)	PH
Carter Hawley Hale (CHH)	P	Enstar (EST)	PH	Levi Strauss (LVI)	P
Caterpillar (CAT)	A	Exxon (XON)	C	Lilly, Eli (LLY)	A
CBS (CBS)	C	Federal Express (FDX)	C	Limited (LTD)	C
Celanese (CX)	C	Fed. Natl. Mort. Assoc. (FMN)	PH	Litton Industries (LIT)	C
Cessna Aircraft (CEA)	C	Financial Corp. (FIN)	PH	Lockheed (LK)	P
Champion Intl. (CHS)	C	Firestone (FIR)	A	Loews Corp. (LTR)	C
Chase Manhattan (CNB)	A	First Boston (FBC)	C	Loral (LOR)	C

A – AMEX;   C – CBOE;   P – Pacific;   PH – Philadelphia

March 1, 1985

Company Name/Ticker Symbol/Exchange

Louisiana Land & Expl. (LLX)	PH	Quaker Oats (OAT)	PH	Trans World (TW)	P
Louisiana Pacific (LPX)	A	Ralston Purina (RAL)	C	Travelers (TIC)	P
LTV (LTV)	A	Raychem Corp. RYC)	P	Tri-Continental (TY)	PH
M/A Com (MAI)	A	Raytheon (RTN)	C	TRW (TRW)	A
R.H. Macy (MZ)	A	RCA (RCA)	C	UAL (UAL)	C
Manufacturers Hanover (MHC)	A	Reading & Bates (RB)	P	Union Carbide (UK)	A
MAPCO (MDA)	P	Resorts Intern'l Cl. A (RT.A)	P	Union Pacific (UNP)	PH
Marriott (MHS)	PH	Revco D.S. (RDS)	A	United States Steel (X)	A
Martin Marietta (ML)	PH	Revlon (REV)	C	United Technologies (UTX)	C
Mary Kay Cosmetics (MKY)	C	Reynolds Metals (RLM)	P	Unocal (UCL)	P
MCA (MCA)	PH	Reynolds R.J. Ind. (RJR)	C	Upjohn (UPJ)	C
McDermott (MDR)	PH	Rockwell International (ROK)	C	U.S. Air (U)	P
McDonald's (MDC)	C	Rowan (RDC)	PH	Valero Energy (VLO)	A
McDonald Douglas (MD)	P	Royal Dutch Petroleum ((RD)	A	Varian (VAR)	A
Medtronic (MDT)	C	Ryder Systems (RDR)	P	Veeco (VEE)	A
Merck (MRK)	C	Sabine (SAB)	C	Verbatim (VRM)	P
Merrill Lynch (MER)	C,A	Safeway Stores (SA)	C	Viacom International (VIA)	C
Mesa Petroleum (MSA)	A	St. Regis Corp. (SRT)	PH	Wal-Mart Stores (WMT)	C
MGM/UA (MGM)	P	Sanders Associates (SAA)	PH	Walter, Jim (JWC)	C
Middle South Utilities (MSU)	C	Santa Fe Southern Pac. (SFX)	A	Wang Labs B (WAN.B)	P
Minnesota Mining & Mfg. (MMM)	C	Schering-Plough SGP)	P	Warner Communications (WCI)	C
Mitchell Energy & Devel. (MND)	P	Schlumberger Ltd. (SLB)	C	Warner-Lambert (WLA)	A
Mobil (MOB)	C	Scientific Atlanta (SFA)	P	Waste Management (WMX)	PH
Mohawk Data Sciences (MDS)	P	Scott Paper (SPP)	PH	Wendy's International (WEN)	P
Monsanto (MTC)	C	Seagram (VO)	P	Western Co. of N. Amer. (WSN)	A
Morgan J.P. (JPM)	PH	Searle G.D. (SRL)	A	Western Union (WU)	PH
Motorola (MOT)	A	Sears & Roebuck (S)	C	Westinghouse (WX)	C
Murphy Oil (MUR)	P	Security Pacific (SPC)	PH	Weyerhaeuser (WY)	C
National Distillers (DR)	A	SEDCO (SED)	A	Whittaker (WKR)	A
National Medical Ent. (NME)	A	Shaklee (SHC)	A	Williams (WMB)	C
National Patent (NPD)		Shell Oil (SUO)	P	Winnebago (WGO)	P
National Semiconductor (NSM)	C,A	Signal Cos. (SGN)	P	Woolworth F.W. (Z)	PH
NBI (NBI)	C	Singer (SMF)	A	Xerox (XRX)	C,P
Newmont Mining (NEW)	PH	Skyline (SKY)	C	Zapata (ZOS)	P
NL Industries (NL)	PH	Smith International (SII)	P	Zenith Radio (ZE)	A
Noble Affiliates (NBL)	A	Smith Kline (SKB)	P		
Norfolk Southern (NSC)	C	Sony (SNE)	P		
Northern Telecom (NT)	C	Southern Co. (SO)	C	Index Options	
Northrop (NOC)	C	Southland (SLC)	PH		
Northwest Airlines (NWA)	C	Southland Royalty (SRO)	P	S & P 100 Index (OEX)	C
Northwest Industires (NWT)	C	Southwest Airlines (LUV)	C	S & P 500 Index (SPX)	C
Novo Industry A/S (NVO)	A	Sperry (SY)	C	S & P Trans. Index (OTN)	C
Occidental Petroleum (OXY)	C	Squibb (SQB)	C	AMEX Market Value Ind. (XAM)	A
Ocean Drilling & Expl. (ODR)	A	Standard Oil of Ind. (SN)	C	Computer Tech. Index (XCI)	A
Owens-Corning Fiber (OCF)	PH	Standard Oil of Ohio (SOH)	A	Gold/Silver Index (XAU)	PH
Owens-Illinois (OI)	C	Sterling Drug (STY)	A	Major Market Index (XMI)	A
Paine Webber (PWJ)	C	Storage Technology (STK)	C	NYSE Double Index (NDX)	NY
Paradyne (PDN)	C	Storer Communications (SCI)	A	NYSE Options Index (NYA)	NY
Parker Drilling (PKD)	P	Sun Co. (SUN)	PH	NYSE Telephone Index (NTI)	NY
Penn Central (PC)	PH	Sybron (SYB)	A	Oil Index (XOI)	A
Penney J.C. (JCP)	A	Syntex (SYN)	C	Oil & Gas Index (XOZ)	A
Pennzoil (PZL)	C	Tandy (TAN)	C,A	Technology Index (PSE)	P
Pepsi Co. (PEP)	C	Tektronix (TEK)	C	Transportation Index (XTI)	A
Perkin-Elmer (PKN)	P	Teledyne (TDY)	C,P	Value Line Comp. Index (XVL)	PH
Pfizer (PFE)	A	Telex (TC)	A		
Phelps Dodge (PD)	A	Tenneco (TGT)	A		
Phibro-Salomon (PSB)	PH	Teradyne (TER)	P		
Philip Morris (MO)	A	Tesoro Petroleum (TSO)	PH		
Phillips Petroleum (P)	A	Texaco (TX)	A		
Pioneer (PNA)	PH	Texas Instruments (TXN)	C		
Pitney Bowes (PBI)	A	Texas Oil & Gas (TXO)	PH		
Pittston (PCO)	PH	Textron (TXT)	PH		
Pogo Producing (PPP)	P	Thrifty (TFD)	A		
Polaroid (PRD)	C,P	Tidewater (TDW)	C		
PPG Industries (PPG)	PH	TIE Communications (TIE)	P		
Prime Computer (PRM)	A	Time (TL)	PH		
Procter & Gamble (PG)	A	Toys "R" Us (TOY)	C		
Pulte Homes (PHM)	PH	Transamerica (TA)	PH		

A - AMEX;   C - CBOE;   P - Pacific;   PH - Philadelphia;   NY - NYSE

APPENDIX 13–B: *The Black-Scholes Option Pricing Model**

Theory

In 1973 Fischer Black and Myron Scholes published their derivation of a theoretical option pricing model. They started with three securities: riskless bonds, shares of common stock, and call options. The shares of common stock and call options were combined to form a riskless hedge, which by definition, had to duplicate the return of a discount bond with the same maturity length as the option. Using the riskless hedge concept as a basis, Black and Scholes then proceeded with their model derivation.

Black and Scholes made the following assumptions:

1. Markets are frictionless. This means that there are no taxes or transactions costs; all securities are infinitely divisible; all market participants may borrow and lend at the known and constant riskless rate of interest; there are no penalties for short selling.
2. Stock prices are lognormally distributed, with a constant variance for the underlying returns.
3. The stock neither pays dividends nor makes any other distributions.
4. The option may be exercised only at maturity.

Given the above assumptions and the riskless hedging strategy, Black and Scholes derived a call option pricing model which may be expressed as:

$$c = (S)(N(d_1)) - (X)(e^{-rt})(N(d_2)) \qquad (13B-1)$$

where:

$$d_1 = \frac{1n(S/X) + (r + (\sigma^2/2))(T)}{(\sigma)(\sqrt{T})} \qquad (13B-2)$$

$$d_2 = d_1 - (\sigma)(\sqrt{T}) \qquad (13B-3)$$

The terms are defined as follows:

c = The price of the call option.
S = The prevailing market price of a share of common stock on the date the call option is written.
X = The call option's striking price (exercise price).
r = The annualized prevailing short-term riskless rate of interest.
T = The length of the option's life expressed in annal terms.
σ^2 = The annualized variance associated with the underlying security's price changes.
$N(\cdot)$ = The cumulative normal density function.

---

* This appendix was developed by Professor Carl Luft of DePaul University in consultation with the authors.

At maturity $(T = 0)$, so the call option must sell for either its intrinsic value, or zero, whichever is greater. This boundary condition may be expressed mathematically as:

$$c = \text{Max}(0, S - X) \qquad (13B\text{-}4)$$

It can be shown that given a put option and a call option, with the same striking price, and one share of the underlying stock, one can form a portfolio which will earn an amount equal to the option's striking price no matter what value the stock takes at expiration. From this relationship the value of a put option can be determined mathematically as:

$$p = (X)(e^{-rt}) - S + c \qquad (13B\text{-}5)$$

with the boundary condition,

$$p = \text{Max}(0, X - S) \qquad (13B\text{-}6)$$

Equation 13B–5 is known as the put-call parity relationship, and Equation 13B–6 shows that at maturity the put must sell for either its intrinsic value or zero.

Inspection of Equations (13B–1) through (13B–6) reveals that both the call and put option prices are a function of only five variables: S, the underlying stock's market price; X, the striking price; T, the length of the option's life; σ^2, the volatility of the stock price changes, and r, the riskless rate of interest. All of these variables are easily observed or estimated. Previously developed option pricing models relied on variables that were based on individual investor risk preferences, or on expected values of the stock price. Since the Black-Scholes model does not rely on such variables, it is superior to prior models.

To understand the behavior of options it is necessary to examine the relationship of the option price to each of the five inputs. For call options the price is positively related to the stock's price, the riskless rate of interest, the volatility, and the time to maturity, whereas an inverse relationship exists between the call option price and the striking price. Put options exhibit positive relationships with the striking price and volatility, negative relationships with the underlying stock price and riskless rate, and either a positive or negative relationship with time.

These relationships are easy to grasp if one realizes that options will not be exercised unless they have an intrinsic value. Consider first the price of the underlying stock. As it increases, calls go in-the-money and gain intrinsic value while puts fall out-of-the-money and lose intrinsic value. If the stock price declines, then the reverse is true. This explains the positive relationship between the call price and the stock price, and the inverse relationship between the put price and stock price. Higher striking prices cause lower intrinsic values for call options, but result in greater intrinsic values for put options. In this case, the loss of intrinsic value causes the inverse relationship between the call option and striking price, while the gain in intrinsic value causes the positive relationship between the put price and the striking price. The positive relationship of both put and call prices to the volatility can be explained by the

fact that options written on higher volatility stocks have a relatively better chance of being in-the-money at expiration than do options written on lower volatility stocks. The positive relationship of the call price to the risk-free rate reflects the fact that the intrinsic value increases because the present value of the exercise price decreases as the risk-free rate rises. For put options, such rate increases and declining present values of exercise prices cause a loss of intrinsic value and account for the inverse relationship between the put option price and risk-free rate. Finally, the positive relationship of the call price to time is caused by an increasing intrinsic value due to lower present values of the exercise price for longer time periods. A more complex relationship exists for put options.

Intuitively one might expect a strictly positive relationship between the put option price and time. Such a relationship will occur if the put is at- or out-of-the-money, while a negative relationship can exist for deep in-the-money puts. The reason for this inverse relationship lies embedded in the stock's price behavior. Since stock prices cannot be less than zero, the put option has a maximum value which equals the strike price. Investors who own deep in-the-money put options which are close to their maximum value because of extremely low stock prices are prohibited from exercising these options by assumption 4. Thus, time is working against these investors since they run the risk of losing intrinsic value if the stock price rises prior to expiration.

After deriving the model, Black and Scholes subjected it to empirical testing. They implemented the riskless hedging strategy by combining options and stock in proportions dictated by the model, and comparing these hedge returns to observed Treasury bill returns. They hypothesized that if the model provided equilibrium, or fair option prices, then the hedge returns should equal the returns generated by the investment in riskless securities. In effect, they attempted to create a synthetic Treasury bill by combining options and stock. If the returns from the option-stock hedge were not equal to the Treasury bill return, it meant that the model was unable to provide equilibrium option prices. On the other hand, if there was no significant difference between the hedge and Treasury bill returns, then it could be concluded that the model did indeed provide equilibrium prices. The results of the Black-Scholes empirical test showed no significant difference between the option-stock hedge returns and the Treasury bill returns. Thus, Black and Scholes concluded that the model did provide equilibrium prices.

The theoretical derivation and empirical justification of an option pricing model by Black and Scholes was an extremely important accomplishment with far reaching implications. Basically it meant that model-generated prices could be considered being the equilibrium, or correct, prices. Thus, an investor could use the model to determine whether or not the market had mispriced an option. Mispriced options spawn arbitrage opportunities. Given such an opportunity, the most obvious way to benefit is to form a riskless hedge by combining options and stock and then maintaining the hedge until the option's market price adjusts to the equilibrium model price. This strategy will provide arbitrage profits since the level of risk that is being assumed equals that of a

Treasury bill, but the profits earned when the mispriced option adjusts to the equilibrium, or model price, will exceed the profits earned from investing in a Treasury bill.

Application

The data in Table 13B–1 are used to illustrate the mechanics of the Black and Scholes Option Pricing Model.

TABLE 13B–1   Illustrative Data for Black-Scholes Option Model

(1)	(2)	(3)	(4)	(5)	(6)	(7)
	(S)	(X)	(T)	(r)	(σ)	(σ^2)
			Days to		Standard	Variance
Stock	Stock	Strike	maturity divided	Risk-free	deviation	of stock
symbol	price	price	by days in year	rate	of returns	returns
CFL	33	35	180/365	.09	.20	.04
GAH	42	40	50/365	.10	.23	.0529

Column (1) simply denotes the stock's ticker symbol, while columns (2) through (7) provide the required inputs for the model. Notice that the option maturity is expressed in calendar days, and that the volatility is given as the standard deviation of returns. The call and put option prices (for both stocks) implied by the data will now be computed.

When the values from Table 13B–1 for CFL stock are used in equations 13B–2 and 13B–3, we obtain the following answers for d_1 and d_2:

$$d_1 = \frac{\ln(33/35) + (.09 + (.04/2))(.4932)}{(.2)(\sqrt{.4932})}$$

$$= \frac{-.0588 + .0543}{.1405}$$

$$= -.032$$

$$d_2 = -.032 - .1405$$

$$= -.1725$$

To obtain values for $N(d_1)$ and $N(d_2)$, the Standard Normal Distribution Function Table (Table 13B–2) at the end of this appendix must be used. The $N(d_1)$ and $N(d_2)$ values are found by first locating the row and column entries in the table which correspond to the computed d_1 and d_2 values. For CFL stock, the row entry is −.0, and the column entry is 3. This value of −.03 approximates the computed d_1 value of −.032. For d_2, the row entry is −.1, and the column entry is 7, yielding a value of −.17, approximating the computed value of −.1725 for d_2.

Locating the d_1 and d_2 values yield the table entries which define the values of $N(d_1)$ and $N(d_2)$. For CFL stock, the $N(d_1)$ value is .4880, while the $N(d_2)$ value is .4325. In this example these values are only approximations, since $-.03$ and $-.17$ are approximations. If one desires more precise $N(d_1)$ and $N(d_2)$ values, they can be obtained through interpolation. For these examples, the approximations are sufficient.

At this point all the necessary values for computing the option price have been found. Determining the options' prices via Equations 13B–1 and 13B–5 is all that remains to be done. Thus, the CFL call option price is:

$$
\begin{aligned}
c &= (33)(.4880) - (35)(e^{-(.09)(.4932)})(.4325) \\
&= 16.1040 - (35)(.9566)(.4325) \\
&= 16.1040 - 14.4805 \\
&= 1.6235
\end{aligned}
$$

and the CFL put option price is:

$$
\begin{aligned}
p &= (35)(e^{-(.09)(.4932)}) - 33 + 1.6235 \\
&= (35)(.9566) - 33 + 1.6235 \\
&= 2.1045
\end{aligned}
$$

Since each option controls 100 shares of stock, the theoretical call price is $162.35 while the put's theoretical price is $210.45.

A second example (using GAH stock) again uses the variables from Table 13B–1 and substitutes them into Equations (13B–2) and (13B–3) to derive d_1 and d_2 as follows:

$$
\begin{aligned}
d_1 &= \frac{\ln(42/40) + (.10 + (.0529/2))(.1370)}{(.23)(\sqrt{.1370})} \\
&= \frac{.0488 + .0173}{.0851} \\
&= .7767
\end{aligned}
$$

$$
\begin{aligned}
d_2 &= .7767 - .0851 \\
&= .6916
\end{aligned}
$$

The $N(d_1)$ and $N(d_2)$ values from the Standard Normal Distribution Table (13B–2) are .7823 and .7549 respectively. As mentioned in the previous example, greater precision is possible through interpolation.

Given the above values, the GAH call and put prices are computed as:

$$
\begin{aligned}
c &= (42)(.7823) - (40)(e^{-(.10)(.1370)})(.7549) \\
&= 32.8566 - (40)(.9864)(.7549) \\
&= 32.8566 - 29.7853 \\
&= 3.0713
\end{aligned}
$$

$$
\begin{aligned}
p &= (40)(e^{-(.10)(.1370)}) - 42 + 3.0713 \\
&= (40)(.9864) - 42 + 3.0713 \\
&= .5273
\end{aligned}
$$

TABLE 13B–2 Standard Normal Distribution Function

t	0	1	2	3	4	5	6	7	8	9
.0	.5000	.5040	.5080	.5120	.5160	.5199	.5239	.5279	.5319	.5359
.1	.5398	.5438	.5478	.5517	.5557	.5596	.5636	.5675	.5714	.5753
.2	.5793	.5832	.5871	.5910	.5948	.5987	.6026	.6064	.6103	.6141
.3	.6179	.6217	.6255	.6293	.6331	.6368	.6406	.6443	.6480	.6517
.4	.6554	.6591	.6628	.6664	.6700	.6736	.6772	.6808	.6844	.6879
.5	.6915	.6950	.6985	.7019	.7054	.7088	.7123	.7157	.7190	.7224
.6	.7257	.7291	.7324	.7357	.7389	.7422	.7454	.7486	.7517	.7549
.7	.7580	.7611	.7642	.7673	.7704	.7734	.7764	.7794	.7823	.7852
.8	.7881	.7910	.7939	.7967	.7995	.8023	.8051	.8079	.8106	.8133
.9	.8159	.8186	.8212	.8238	.8264	.8289	.8315	.8340	.8365	.8189
1.0	.8413	.8438	.8461	.8485	.8508	.8531	.8554	.8577	.8599	.8621
1.1	.8643	.8665	.8686	.8708	.8729	.8749	.8770	.8790	.8810	.8830
1.2	.8849	.8869	.8888	.8907	.8925	.8944	.8962	.8980	.8997	.9015
1.3	.9032	.9049	.9066	.9082	.9099	.9115	.9131	.9147	.9162	.9177
1.4	.9192	.9207	.9222	.9236	.9251	.9265	.9279	.9292	.9306	.9319
1.5	.9332	.9345	.9357	.9370	.9382	.9394	.9406	.9418	.9429	.9441
1.6	.9452	.9463	.9474	.9484	.9495	.9505	.9515	.9525	.9535	.9545
1.7	.9554	.9564	.9573	.9582	.9591	.9599	.9608	.9616	.9625	.9633
1.8	.9641	.9649	.9656	.9664	.9671	.9678	.9686	.9693	.9700	.9706
1.9	.9713	.9719	.9726	.9732	.9738	.9744	.9750	.9756	.9761	.9767
2.0	.9773	.9778	.9783	.9788	.9793	.9798	.9803	.9808	.9812	.9817
2.1	.9821	.9826	.9830	.9834	.9838	.9842	.9846	.9850	.9854	.9857
2.2	.9861	.9864	.9868	.9871	.9875	.9878	.9881	.9884	.9887	.9890
2.3	.9893	.9896	.9898	.9901	.9904	.9906	.9909	.9911	.9913	.9916
2.4	.9918	.9920	.9922	.9925	.9927	.9929	.9931	.9932	.9934	.9936
2.5	.9938	.9940	.9941	.9943	.9945	.9946	.9948	.9949	.9951	.9952
2.6	.9953	.9955	.9956	.9957	.9959	.9960	.9961	.9962	.9963	.9964
2.7	.9965	.9966	.9967	.9968	.9969	.9970	.9971	.9972	.9973	.9974
2.8	.9974	.9975	.9976	.9977	.9977	.9978	.9979	.9979	.9980	.9981
2.9	.9981	.9982	.9982	.9983	.9984	.9984	.9985	.9985	.9986	.9986
3.	.9987									

t	0	1	2	3	4	5	6	7	8	9
-3.	.0013									
-2.9	.0019	.0018	.0017	.0017	.0016	.0016	.0015	.0015	.0014	.0014
-2.8	.0026	.0025	.0024	.0023	.0023	.0022	.0021	.0021	.0020	.0019
-2.7	.0035	.0034	.0033	.0032	.0031	.0030	.0029	.0028	.0027	.0026
-2.6	.0047	.0045	.0044	.0043	.0041	.0040	.0039	.0038	.0037	.0036
-2.5	.0062	.0060	.0059	.0057	.0055	.0054	.0052	.0051	.0049	.0048
-2.4	.0082	.0080	.0078	.0075	.0073	.0071	.0069	.0068	.0066	.0064
-2.3	.0107	.0104	.0102	.0099	.0096	.0094	.0091	.0089	.0087	.0084
-2.2	.0139	.0136	.0132	.0129	.0125	.0122	.0119	.0116	.0113	.0110
-2.1	.0179	.0174	.0170	.0166	.0162	.0158	.0154	.0150	.0146	.0143
-2.0	.0227	.0222	.0217	.0212	.0207	.0202	.0197	.0192	.0188	.0183
-1.9	.0287	.0281	.0274	.0268	.0262	.0256	.0250	.0244	.0239	.0233
-1.8	.0359	.0351	.0344	.0336	.0329	.0322	.0314	.0307	.0300	.0294
-1.7	.0446	.0436	.0427	.0418	.0409	.0401	.0392	.0384	.0375	.0367
-1.6	.0548	.0537	.0526	.0516	.0505	.0495	.0485	.0475	.0465	.0455
-1.5	.0668	.0655	.0643	.0630	.0618	.0606	.0594	.0582	.0571	.0559
-1.4	.0808	.0793	.0778	.0764	.0749	.0735	.0721	.0708	.0694	.0681
-1.3	.0968	.0951	.0934	.0918	.0901	.0885	.0869	.0853	.0838	.0823
-1.2	.1151	.1131	.1112	.1093	.1075	.1056	.1038	.1020	.1003	.0985
-1.1	.1357	.1335	.1314	.1292	.1271	.1251	.1230	.1210	.1190	.1170
-1.0	.1587	.1562	.1539	.1515	.1492	.1469	.1446	.1423	.1401	.1379
-.9	.1841	.1814	.1788	.1762	.1736	.1711	.1685	.1660	.1635	.1611
-.8	.2119	.2090	.2061	.2033	.2005	.1977	.1949	.1921	.1894	.1867
-.7	.2420	.2389	.2358	.2326	.2297	.2266	.2236	.2206	.2177	.2148
-.6	.2743	.2709	.2676	.2643	.2611	.2578	.2546	.2514	.2483	.2451
-.5	.3085	.3050	.3015	.2981	.2946	.2912	.2877	.2843	.2810	.2776
-.4	.3446	.3409	.3372	.3336	.3300	.3264	.3228	.3192	.3156	.3121
-.3	.3821	.3783	.3745	.3707	.3669	.3632	.3594	.3557	.3520	.3483
-.2	.4207	.4168	.4129	.4090	.4052	.4013	.3974	.3936	.3897	.3859
-.1	.4602	.4562	.4522	.4483	.4443	.4404	.4364	.4325	.4286	.4247
-.0	.5000	.4960	.4920	.4880	.4840	.4801	.4761	.4721	.4681	.4641

These calculations indicate that the theoretically correct price (for 100 shares) for the call is $307.13 and that $52.73 is the theoretically correct price for the put.

Suppose the market had priced the GAH call at $262.50. How would you be able to earn arbitrage profits? According to Black and Scholes, you would buy the undervalued calls at $262.50 and sell shares of GAH stock at $42 per share to form a riskless hedge and thus obtain arbitrage profits when equilibrium is established. However, to implement such a strategy an investor must know how many shares to combine with each option in order to form the riskless hedge. This information is provided by $N(d_1)$ and is known as the hedge ratio or delta.

Since each option controls 100 shares of stock, the appropriate arbitrage activity in this example is to sell .7823 shares of GAH stock for every option purchased. Practically speaking, one cannot buy and sell fractional shares. Thus, 78 shares should be sold for each option that is purchased. If the market had overpriced the option, then the arbitrageur would sell options and purchase 78 shares for each option sold. In either case, the hedge's risk level will equal that of a Treasury bill, but the hedge's returns will exceed the Treasury bill's return, thus generating arbitrage profits.

Part Four

BROADENING THE
INVESTMENT PERSPECTIVE

In this section, we expand the investment horizon to consider many different types of investment strategies.

We begin in Chapter 14 with a consideration of "special situations" that at times exist in the stock and bond markets. Empirical research has indicated that some of these investment alternatives may provide superior returns on a risk-adjusted basis. Topics for consideration include investing in mergers and acquisitions, in new stock or bond issues, in securities that are initially listed on major exchanges, and in firms that are repurchasing their own shares in the market. Also, the possible advantage of investing in small firms or those with low P/E ratios is considered.

Another consideration for the investor expanding the investment horizon is that of commodity and financial futures (discussed in Chapter 15). Commodities include such items as wheat, copper, and pork bellies, whereas financial futures include such categories as currencies and Treasury securities. In the chapter, we consider the mechanics of various trading and hedging strategies and the risks that are involved.

As a follow-up to Chapter 15, we expand the discussion to stock index futures and options in Chapter 16. It is currently possible to hedge the risk of an entire stock portfolio by going short (selling futures or writing options) on such indexes as the S&P 500, S&P 100, NYSE Index, etc. Speculative strategies for upward markets are also considered.

The emphasis in Chapter 17 is on real assets, which include real estate, gold and silver, precious gems, collectibles, and many other forms of tangible assets. Real assets are thought to represent a strong inflation hedge; however, they also have drawbacks in terms of illiquidity and high transaction costs. In

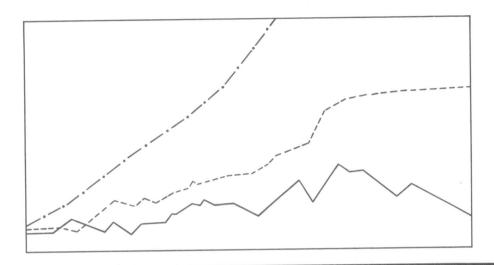

this chapter, we also go through a detailed analysis of a real estate investment project.

For those who might wish to add an international dimension to their investment strategy, Chapter 18 may be of interest. Not only are there risk reduction benefits through international diversification, but, in some cases, superior return potential as well. After pointing out some of the difficulties of foreign investments, the authors indicate how most of these can be overcome by investing in internationally oriented mutual funds or in securities called ADR's (American Depository Receipts).

Chapter 14
INVESTMENTS IN SPECIAL SITUATIONS

Chapter 15
COMMODITIES AND FINANCIAL FUTURES

Chapter 16
STOCK INDEX FUTURES AND OPTIONS

Chapter 17
INVESTMENTS IN REAL ASSETS

Chapter 18
INTERNATIONAL SECURITIES MARKETS

Chapter 14

INVESTMENTS IN SPECIAL SITUATIONS

In a previous discussion of market efficiency in Chapter 8, we suggested that while the security markets were generally efficient in the valuing of securities, there were still opportunities for special returns in a limited number of circumstances. Just what these circumstances are is subject to debate as not all researchers agree.

In most instances, special or abnormal returns refer to gains beyond what the market would normally provide after adjustment for risk. In this chapter, we will explore such topics as market movements associated with mergers and acquisitions, the underpricing of new stock issues, the impact of an exchange listing on a stock's valuation, the stock market impact of a firm repurchasing its own shares, and the small-firm effect. Additionally, in the bond market, we will look at a special situation associated with interest rate premiums on new bond issues.

We will attempt to separate some of the market folklore from significant analysis. Furthermore, when a valid investment opportunity is perceived to exist, we attempt to suggest under what circumstances it is most likely to prove profitable. Let's begin our analysis with a discussion of investment opportunities in mergers and acquisitions.[1]

MERGERS AND ACQUISITIONS

Many stocks that were leaders in daily volume and price movement in the late 1970s and 1980s represented firms that were merger candidates; that is, companies that were being acquired or anticipated being acquired by other firms. The stocks of these acquisition candidates often increased by 60 percent or more over a relatively short period of time. The list of acquired companies included such well-known names as Conoco, Gulf Oil, Avis, EDS, Seven-Up, and Anaconda Copper.

Premiums for Acquired Companies

The primary reason for the upward market movement in the value of the acquisition candidate is the high premium that is offered over current market value in a merger or acquisition. The premium represents the difference between the offering price per share and the market price per share for the candidate (before the impact of the offer). For example, a firm that is selling for $25 per share may attract a purchase price of $40 per share. Quite naturally, the stock will go up in response to the offer and the anticipated consummation of the merger.

As expected, researchers have consistently found that there are abnormal returns for acquisition candidates.[1] A study has indicated that the aver-

---

[1] Gershon Mandelker, "Risk and Return: The Case of Merging Firms," *Journal of Financial Economics,* December 1974, pp. 303–35; Donald R. Kummer and J. Ronald Hoffmeister, "Valuation Consequences of Cash Tender Offers," *Journal of Finance,* May 1978, pp. 505–16; and Peter Dodd, "Merger Proposals, Management Discretion and Stockholder Wealth," *Journal of Financial Economics,* December 1980, pp. 105–38.

age premium paid in a recent time period was approximately 60 percent, and there was an associated upward price movement of a similar magnitude.[2] This is a much larger average premium than in prior time periods and may be attributed to the recognition of high replacement value in relationship to current market value. The premium was based on the difference between the price paid and the value of the acquisition candidate's stock *three months* before announcement of the merger. Some examples of premiums paid are presented in Table 14–1.

TABLE 14–1   Premiums Paid in Mergers and Acquisitions

Acquiring firm	Acquired firm	Price paid in cash for acquiring company's stock	Value of acquired firm three months before announcement	Premium paid (percent)
Beatrice Food Co	Harmon International Industries	$35.25	$20.00	76.25%
Parker Pen Co.	Manpower, Inc.	15.20	11.50	32.18
Colt Industries	Menaso Man.	26.60	15.00	77.33
Pepsico, Inc.	Pizza Hut, Inc.	38.00	22.375	69.83
Walter Kidde & Co.	Victor Comptometer	11.75	7.375	59.32
Dana Corporation	Weatherford Co.	14.00	9.375	49.33
Allis Chalmers Corporation	American Air Filter	34.00	19.50	74.36
Time, Inc.	Inland Containers	35.00	20.75	68.67

The only problem from an investment viewpoint is that approximately two thirds of the price gain related to large premiums takes place before public announcement. It is clear that people close to the situation are trading on information leaks. The highly prestigious investment banking house of Morgan Stanley was actually embarrassed by charges brought by the U.S. Attorney's Office that two of its former merger and acquisition specialists were conspiring to use privileged information on takeovers to make profits on secret trading accounts.[3]

Those who attempt to legitimately profit by investing in mergers and acquisitions can follow a number of routes. First of all, there are investors who try to identify merger candidates before public announcement to capture maximum profits. This is a difficult process. While researchers have attempted to identify financial and operating characteristics of acquisition candidates, the

---

[2] Henry Oppenheimer and Stanley Block, "An Examination of Premiums and Exchange Ratios Associated with Merger Activity during the 1975–78 Period" (Financial Management Association Meeting, 1980).

[3] "Two Former Morgan Stanley Executives Accused of Plot Involving Takeover Data," *The Wall Street Journal,* February 4, 1981, p. 2.

information is often contradictory and may even change over time.[4] In prior time periods (such as the 1960s), aquisition candidates were often firms with sluggish records of performance, whereas many of the current acquirees are high-quality companies that have unusually good records of performance (Alcon Labs, Coca Cola Bottling of Los Angeles, Steak and Ale, EDS).

Some alert analysts do keep a close eye on such sources as the *Financial Weekly's* "Stocks in the Spotlight," which pinpoints securities that are undergoing unusual volume or pricing patterns (of course, this could be for any number of reasons). Other investors identify industries where companies are being quickly absorbed and attempt to guess which firm will be the next to be acquired. Prime examples of such industries in recent times were natural resource firms being acquired by multinational oil companies, and brokerage houses being absorbed by insurance companies or other firms in the financial services industry.

While trying to guess an acquisition candidate prior to public announcement can be potentially profitable, it requires that an investor tie up large blocks of capital in betting on an event that may never come to pass. Others prefer to invest at the time of announcement of a merger or acquisition. A gain of the magnitude of 20 percent or more may still be available (over a few months' time period). Perhaps a stock that was $25 before any consideration of merger is up to $34 on announcement. If the actual purchase price is $40, there may still be a nice profit to be made. The only danger is that the announced merger may be called off, in which case the stock may sharply retreat in value, perhaps all the way back down to $25 (that is, assuming another potential acquiring company does not come into the picture). Examples of price drops associated with merger cancellations are shown in Table 14–2.

The wise investor must carefully assess the likelihood of cancellation. Special attention must be given to such factors as the possibility of antitrust action, the attitude of the target company's management toward the merger,

TABLE 14–2 Stock Movement of Potential Acquirees in Cancelled Mergers

Acquirer-potential acquiree	Preannouncement	One day after announcement	One day after cancellation
Mead Corporation—Occidental Petroleum	20⅜	33¼	23¼
Olin Corp.—Celanese	16	23¾	16¾
Chicago Rivet—MITE	20¾	28⅛	20¾

---

[4] Robert J. Monroe and Michael A. Simkowitz, "Investment Characteristics of Conglomerate Targets: A Discriminant Analysis," *Southern Journal of Business,* November 1971, pp. 1–15. Donald J. Stevens, "Financial Characteristics of Merger Firms: A Multivariate Analysis," *Journal of Financial and Quantitative Analysis,* March 1973, pp. 149–58.

the possibility of unhappy stockholder suits, and the likelihood of poor earnings reports or other negative events. In a reasonably efficient market environment, the potential price gain that exists at announcement may be well correlated with the likelihood of the merger being successfully consummated. That is to say, if it appears that the merger is almost certain to go through, the stock may be up to $37.50 at announcement based on an anticipated purchase price of $40. If a serious question remains, the stock may only be at $31. When a merger becomes reasonably certain, arbitrageurs come in and attempt to lock in profits by buying the acquisition candidate at a small spread from the purchase price.

One of the most interesting features of the current merger movement has been the heavy incidence of unfriendly takeovers; that is, the bidding of one company for another against its will. This strategy has occurred in 20 to 25 percent of announced mergers.[5] Such events often lead to the appearance of a third company on the scene, referred to as a "white knight," whose function is to save the target company by buying them out, thus thwarting the undesired suitor. The new suitor is generally deemed to be friendly to the interests of the target company and may be specifically invited by it to partake in the process. Examples of white knights occurred when Gulf Oil thwarted an offer from Mesa Petroleum and went with Standard Oil of California (renamed Chevron) in 1984. Similarly, Marathon Oil rejected an offer from Mobil to merge with U.S. Steel in 1982, and Babcock and Wilcox rejected an offer from United Technologies, choosing to go with J. Ray McDermott in the late 1970s.

As one might guess, these multiple-suitor bidding wars often lead to unusually attractive offers. A 40 to 60 percent premium may ultimately parlay into an 80 to 100 percent gain or more. For example, the bidding for Gulf Oil sent the stock from 38 to 80.

Acquiring Company Performance

What about the acquiring company's stock in the merger and acquisition process? Is this a special situation; that is, does this stock also show abnormal market gains associated with the event? A study by Mandelker has indicated that it does not.[6] Long-term economic studies have indicated that many of the anticipated results from mergers may be difficult to achieve.[7] There is often an initial feeling of optimism that is not borne out in reality. The synergy, or "2 + 2 = 5," effect associated with broadening product lines or eliminating overlapping functions may be offset by the inability of management to mesh divergent

[5] Anna Merjos, "Costly Propositions—Some Big Mergers Have Lately Fallen Through," *Barron's,* May 14, 1979, p. 9.

[6] Gershon Mandelker, "Risk and Return: The Case of Merging Firms," *Journal of Financial Economics,* December 1974, pp. 303–35.

[7] T. Hogarty, "The Profitability of Corporate Managers," *Journal of Business,* July 1970, pp. 317–27.

philosophies. However, companies do appear to be more adept at the process than in prior time periods; now conservatively managed firms, such as General Motors, Du Pont, and Atlantic Richfield, are replacing the funny-money conglomerate gunslingers of the 1960s. Nevertheless, most investors would prefer to position themselves with the acquired firm, which is certain to receive a high premium, rather than with the acquiring firm, which has to pay it.

Form of Payment

A final consideration in a merger is the form of payment. Cash offers usually carry a slightly higher premium than stock offers because of the immediate tax consequences to the acquired firm's shareholders. When stock is offered, the tax obligation usually may be deferred by the acquired company's stockholders until the stock of the acquiring firm is actually sold. This may occur relatively soon or many years in the future.

The merger movement of the late 1970s and the 1980s has seen a much heavier utilization of cash as a medium of payment than in prior time periods (in the 50 percent range as opposed to 25 percent in the 1960s).[8] Many of the old accounting advantages associated with stock or residual stock items (convertibles, warrants) in mergers have been diminished by accounting rule changes. Most financial management texts have whole chapters covering mergers and acquisitions, which could further expand your knowledge of the subject.

NEW STOCK ISSUES

Another form of a special situation is the initial issuance of stock by a corporation. There is a belief in the investment community that securities may be underpriced when they are issued to the public for the first time. That is to say, when a company goes public by selling formerly privately held shares to new investors in the over-the-counter market, the price may not fully reflect the value of the security.

Why does this so-called underpricing take place, and what is the significance to the investor? The underpricing may be the result of the firm commitment to buy the shares that an investment banker makes in distributing the issue. That is, the investment banker agrees to buy the stock from company A at a set price and then resells it to the public (along with other investment bankers, dealers, and brokers). The investment banker must be certain that the issue will be fully subscribed to at the initial public market price or he (and others) will absorb losses or build up unwanted inventory. In order to protect his position, the investment banker may underprice the issue by 5 to 10 percent to ensure adequate demand.

---

[8] 1978 Merger Survey (Chicago: W. T. Grimm and Co., 1978).

Studies by Reilly,[9] McDonald and Fisher,[10] and Ibbotson[11] have indicated there are positive abnormal returns in the new issues market for one week and one month after issue. Reilly, for example, observed positive excess returns of 10.9 percent one week after issue and 11.6 percent one month after issue. However, the efficiency of the market comes into play after the stock is actively trading on a regular basis, and any excess returns begin to quickly disappear. The lesson to be learned here is that, on average, the best time to buy a new, unseasoned issue is on initial distribution from the underwriting syndicate (investment bankers, dealers, brokers), and the best time to sell is in the first few weeks of trading.

Participating in the distribution of a new issue is not always as easy as it sounds. A really hot new issue may be initially oversubscribed, and only good customers of a brokerage house may be allocated shares. Such was the case in the feverish atmosphere that surrounded the initial public trading of Apple Computer and Genentech. Genentech actually went from $35 to $89 in the first 20 minutes of trading (only to quickly come back down). For the most part, customers with a regular brokerage account and a desire to participate in the new-issues market can find adequate opportunities for investment, though perhaps in less spectacular opportunities than those described above.

Performance of Investment Bankers

Research studies indicate that large, prestigious investment banking houses do not generally provide the highest initial returns to investors in the new issues they underwrite.[12] The reason for this is that the upper tier investment bankers tend to underwrite the issues of the strongest firms coming into the market. These firms generally shop around among the many investment bankers that are interested in their business and eventually negotiate terms that would allow for very little underpricing when they reach the market. (They want most of the benefits to go to the corporation, not to the initial stockholders.)

Factors to Consider in a New Issue

First of all, the investor should consider the management of the firm and their prior record of performance. In most cases, a firm that is going public will have

[9] Frank K. Reilly, "New Issues Revisited," *Financial Management,* Winter 1977, pp. 28–42.

[10] J. G. McDonald and A. K. Fisher, "New Issue Stock Price Behavior," *Journal of Finance,* March 1974, pp. 97–102.

[11] Roger G. Ibbotson, "Price Performance of Common Stock New Issues," *Journal of Financial Economics,* September 1975, pp. 235–72.

[12] Brian M. Neuberger and Carl T. Hammond, "A Study of Underwriters' Experience with Unseasoned New Issues," *Journal of Financial and Quantitative Analysis,* March 1974, pp. 165–74. Also, see Dennis E. Logue, "On the Pricing of Unseasoned New Issues, 1965–1969," *Journal of Financial and Quantitative Analysis,* January 1973, pp. 91–103, and Brian M. Neuberger and Chris A. La Chapelle, "Unseasoned New Issue Price Performance on Three Tiers: 1975–1980," *Financial Management,* Autumn 1983, pp. 23–28.

past sales and profit figures that can be compared to others in the industry. In one study the average sales volume for a firm approaching the new issues market was $22.9 million with $1.8 million in aftertax profits and $14.6 million in assets.[13]

The investor also should take a close look at the intended use of funds from the public distribution. There are many legitimate purposes, such as the construction of new plant and equipment, the expansion of product lines, or the reduction of debt. The investor should be less enthusiastic about circumstances in which funds are being used to buy out old stockholders or to acquire property from existing shareholders.

The investor should also be sensitive to the industry and nature of the product involved. Examples of changing industry patterns for new issues are presented in Table 14–3.

TABLE 14–3   Industry Groupings for New Public Issues (based on samples)

Lines of business	1969–1972	1974–1978
Computers	8	18
Electronics	5	9
Retailing	7	3
Wholesaling	2	0
Financial services	11	11
Energy	3	9
Health care	6	8
Light manufacturing	21	6
Heavy manufacturing	7	12
Entertainment	4	1
Restaurants	1	1
Construction	7	1
Transportation	0	2
Food processing	4	4
Other	16	17
	102	102

Source: Stanley Block and Marjorie Stanley, "The Financial Characteristics and Price Movement Patterns of Companies Approaching the Unseasoned Securities Market in the Late 1970's," *Financial Management*, Winter 1980, p. 36.

Wall Street West

A discussion of the market for new issues would not be complete without a few comments on the "Denver Stock Exchange." This is a special market for low-priced, untested securities that are somewhat different in character from

---

[13] Stanley Block and Marjorie Stanley, "The Financial Characteristics and Price Movement Patterns of Companies Approaching the Unseasoned Securities Market in the Late 1970's," *Financial Management*, Winter 1980, pp. 30–36.

the issues previously discussed. They are often referred to as "penny" stocks. Investors may be looking for a gamble here, and there is plenty of opportunity. Of the 270 new issues taking place between January 1, 1979, and January 30, 1980, 199 were initially offered for $1 or less.[14] Many of these infant, wildcatter companies provided astronomical returns for investors shortly after trading, while others were hardly ever heard of again.

EXCHANGE LISTINGS

A special situation of some interest to investors is an exchange listing, in which a firm trading over-the-counter now lists its shares on an exchange (such as the American or New York Stock Exchange). Another version of a listing is for a firm to step up from an American Stock Exchange listing to a New York Stock Exchange listing.

An exchange listing may well generate interest in a security (particularly in reference to moving up from the over-the-counter market to an organized exchange). The issue will now be assigned a specialist who has responsibility for maintaining a continuous and orderly market.[15] Furthermore, there may be greater marketability for the issue as well as more readily available price quotes (particularly in small-town newspapers). An exchange listing may also make the issue more acceptable for margin trading and short selling. Large institutional investors and foreign investors may also consider a listed security more appropriate for inclusion in their portfolio.

Listed firms must meet certain size and performance criteria provided in Table 14–4 (and previously mentioned in Chapter 2 for the NYSE). Although the criteria are not highly restrictive, meeting these standards may still signal a favorable message to investors.

A number of research studies have specifically examined the stock market impact of exchange listings. As might be expected, there is a strong upward movement associated with securities that are to be listed, but there is also a strong sell-off after the event has taken place. Research by Van Horne,[16] Fabozzi,[17] and others[18] indicates that the total effect may be neutral. Research by

---

[14] Penny Stocks, "New Issues Are Still the Rage; Risks, Fraud Charges Don't Deter Investors," *The Wall Street Journal,* March 30, 1981, p. 42.

[15] This is not always a superior arrangement to having multiple market makers in the over-the-counter market. It depends on how dedicated the specialist is to maintaining the market. Some banks and smaller industrial firms may choose the competitive dealer system in the over-the-counter market in preference to the assigned specialist.

[16] James C. Van Horne, "New Listings and Their Price Behavior," *Journal of Finance,* September 1970, pp. 783–94.

[17] Frank J. Fabozzi, "Does Listing on the AMEX Increase the Value of Equity?" *Financial Management,* Spring 1981, pp. 43–50.

[18] Richard W. Furst, "Does Listing Increase the Market Value of Common Stock?" *Journal of Business,* April 1970, pp. 174–80. Waldemar M. Goulet, "Price Changes, Managerial Accounting and Insider Trading at the Time of Listing," *Financial Management,* Spring 1974, pp. 303–6.

TABLE 14–4   Minimum Requirements for Exchange Listing

1. Demonstrated earning power under competitive conditions of: *either* $2.5 million before Federal income taxes for the most recent year and $2 million pre-tax for each of the preceding two years, *or* an aggregate for last three fiscal years of $6.5 million *together with* a minimum in the most recent fiscal year of $4.5 million. (All three years must be profitable.)

2. Net tangible assets of $16 million, but greater emphasis is placed on the aggregate market value of the common stock.

3. Market value of publicly held shares, subject to adjustment depending on market conditions, within the following limits:

   Maximum $18,000,000
   Minimum $ 9,000,000
   Present (2/13/84) $18,000,000

4. A total of 1,100,000 common shares publicly held.

5. *Either* 2,000 holders of 100 shares or more, *or* 2,200 total stockholders *together with* average monthly trading volume (for the most recent six months) of 100,000 shares.

Ying, Lewellen, Schlarbaum, and Lease (YLSL) would tend to indicate an overall gain.[19]

The really significant factor is that regardless of whether a stock has a higher net value a few months after listing as opposed to a few months before listing, there still may be profits to be made. This would be true if the investor simply bought the stock four to six weeks before listing and sold it upon listing. Because an application approval for listing is published in the weekly bulletin of the American Stock Exchange or the New York Stock Exchange well before the actual date of listing, this is often possible. The study by YLSL, sighted above, indicates there may be an opportunity for abnormal returns on a risk-adjusted basis in the many weeks between announcement of listing and actual listing (between 4.40 percent and 16.26 percent over normal market returns, depending on the time period involved). In this case, YLSL actually reject the semi-strong form of the efficient market hypothesis by suggesting there are substantial profits to be made even after announcement of a new listing. The wise investor may wish to sell on the eventual date of listing because sometimes a loss in value may take place at that point.

The reader should also be aware of the potential impact of delisting on a security; that is, the formal removal from New York Stock Exchange or American Stock Exchange listing, and a resumption of trading over-the-counter. This may take place because the firm has fallen substantially below the require-

---

[19] Louis K. W. Ying, Wilbur G. Lewellen, Gary G. Schlarbaum, and Ronald C. Lease, "Stock Exchange Listing and Securities Returns," *Journal of Financial and Quantitative Analysis,* September 1977, pp. 415–32.

ments of the exchange.[20] As you would expect, this has a large negative effect on the security. Merjos found that 48 of the 50 firms in her study declined between the last day of trading on an exchange and the resumption of trading over-the-counter.[21] The average decline was 17 percent. While the value was not risk adjusted, it is large enough to indicate the clear significance of the event.

STOCK REPURCHASE

The repurchase by a firm of its own shares provides for an interesting special situation. The purchase price is generally over current market value and tends to increase the demand for the shares while decreasing the effective supply. Before we examine the stock market effects of a repurchase, we will briefly examine the reasons behind the corporate decisions.

Reasons for Repurchase

In some cases, management believes their stock is undervalued in the market. Prior research studies have indicated that repurchased securities have generally underperformed the popular market averages before announcement of repurchase.[22] Thus, management or the board of directors may perceive this to be an excellent opportunity because of depressed prices. Others, however, might see the repurchase as a sign that management is not creative or that it lacks investment opportunities for the normal redeployment of capital.[23] Empirical study indicates that firms that engage in repurchase transactions often have lower sales and earnings growth and lower return on net worth than other, comparable firms.[24] There also tends to be a concentration of these firms in the lower-growth areas, such as apparels, steel, food products, tobacco, and aerospace.

Tax factors may also play a role in the repurchase decision. In the literature of finance, it is suggested that a stock repurchase will put a stockholder in a better aftertax position than the direct payment of cash dividends.[25] Assume a corporation has $2 million in excess cash, with 1 million shares of stock

---

[20] Firms may also be delisted because they have been acquired in a merger or acquisition, in which case the shares are no longer traded.

[21] Anna Merjos, "Stricken Securities," *Barron's*, March 4, 1963, p. 9.

[22] Richard Norgaard and Connie Norgaard, "A Critical Evaluation of Share Repurchase," *Financial Management*, Spring 1974, pp. 44–50. Larry Y. Dann, "Common Stock Repurchases: An Analysis of Returns to Bondholders and Stockholders," *Journal of Financial Economics*, June 1981, pp. 113–38.

[23] Charles D. Ellis and Allen E. Young, *The Repurchase of Common Stock* (New York: The Ronald Press, 1971), p. 61.

[24] Norgaard and Norgaard, "A Critical Evaluation."

[25] Harold Bierman, Jr., and Richard West, "The Acquisition of Common Stock by the Corporate Issuer," *Journal of Finance*, December 1966, pp. 687–96.

outstanding. One strategy would be to pay the stockholders a \$2 cash dividend. An alternate strategy, however, would be to repurchase a portion of the outstanding shares in the market. Through reducing the shares outstanding, earnings per share would increase, and with an assumed constant P/E ratio, the market price would increase. Thus, corporate management may determine that stockholders could receive additional value either in the form of dividends, which are taxable as ordinary income, or appreciation in value, which is taxable at a lower capital gains tax rate. The lower capital gains rate may therefore provide support for a repurchase strategy. This line of reasoning is largely theoretical; the market may or may not provide the appreciation in value associated with an increase in earnings per share in each individual case.

Another reason for the repurchase of shares is the acquisition of treasury stock to be used in future mergers and acquisitions or to fulfill obligations under an employee stock option plan. Shares may also be acquired to reduce the number of voting shares outstanding and thus diminish the vulnerability of the corporation to an unwanted or unsolicited takeover attempt by another corporation. Finally, the repurchase decision may be closely associated with a desire to reduce stockholder servicing cost; that is, to eliminate small stockholder accounts that are particularly unprofitable for the corporation to maintain.

Actual Market Effect

From the viewpoint of a special situation, the key question is, What is the stock market impact of the repurchase? Is there money to be made here or not? Much of the earlier research said no.[26] However, recent research would tend to indicate there might well be positive returns to investors in a repurchase situation.[27] Most of the higher returns are confined to formal tender offers to repurchase shares (perhaps 10 to 20 percent of the shares outstanding) rather than the use of informal, unannounced, open-market purchases. Under a formal tender offer, the corporation will specify the purchase price, the date of purchase, and the number of shares it wishes to acquire.

Of particular interest is the fact that most of the positive market movement comes *on* and *after* the announcement rather than before it. The implications are that there may be trading profits to be made here.

---

[26] A good example is Charles D. Ellis and Allen E. Young, *The Repurchase of Common Stock* (New York: Ronald Press, 1971), p. 156.

[27] Terry E. Dielman, Timothy J. Nantell, and Roger L. Wright, "Price Effects of Stock Repurchasing: A Random Coefficient Regression Approach," *Journal of Financial and Quantitative Analysis,* March 1980, p. 175–89. Larry Y. Dann, "Common Stock Repurchases: An Analysis of Returns to Bondholders and Stockholders," *Journal of Financial Economics,* June 1981, pp. 113–38. Theo Vermaelen, "Common Stock Repurchases and Market Signaling: An Empirical Study," *Journal of Financial Economics,* June 1981, pp. 139–83. R. W. Masulis, "Stock Repurchase by Tender Offer: An Analysis of the Causes of Common Stock Price Changes," *Journal of Finance,* May 1980, pp. 305–19.

TABLE 14–5   Summary Statistics for the Tender Offer Sample, 1962–1976 (143 observations)

Characteristic of offers	Mean (percent)	Median (percent)
Tender offer premium relative to closing market price one *day* prior to announcement	22.46%	19.40%
Tender offer premium relative to closing market price one *month* prior to announcement	20.85	18.83
Percentage of outstanding shares sought	15.29	12.57
Percentage of outstanding shares acquired	14.64	11.93
Percentage of outstanding shares tendered	18.04	14.27
Number of shares tendered ÷ number of shares sought	142.30	115.63
Number of shares acquired ÷ number of shares sought	111.35	100.00
Value of proposed repurchase relative to pre-offer market value of equity	19.29	15.28
Value of actual repurchase relative to pre-offer market value of equity	18.63	13.90
Duration of offer	22 days	20 days

Source: Larry Y. Dann, "Common Stock Repurchases: An Analysis of Returns to Bondholders and Stockholders," *Journal of Financial Economics,* June 1981, p. 122.

Dann determined that the average premium paid over the stock price (the day prior to announcement) was 22.46 percent as indicated on the top line of Table 14–5.

This high premium helps to generate a return of 8.946 percent on the day of announcement and 6.832 percent one day after announcement. This represents a two-day return of approximately 15.8 percent.[28] Dann further indicated that the price movements shortly *before* announcement were negligible, as indicated in Table 14–6.

The predominant argument for the beneficial effects of the repurchase is that management knows what they are doing when they purchase their *own* shares. In effect, they are acting as insiders for the benefit of the corporation, and we previously observed in Chapter 8 that insiders tend to be correct in their investment decisions. This factor, combined with the high premium, may provide positive investment results. Of course, these are merely average results over many transactions, and not all tender offers will prove to be beneficial events. The investor must carefully examine the premium offered, the number of shares to be repurchased, the reasons for repurchase, and the future impact on earnings and dividends per share.

---

[28] Professor Dann's observations are based on raw data rather than normalized returns. However, they are of sufficient magnitude to be important.

TABLE 14–6   Common Stock Rates of Return over a 121-Day Period Around Announcement of Common Stock Repurchase Tender Offer

Trading day	Mean rate of return (percent)	Trading day	Mean rate of return (percent)
−60	.217%	0	8.946%
−50	−.034	1	6.832
−40	.058	2	.908
−30	−.562	3	−.041
−25	−.125	4	.133
−20	−.071	5	.158
−19	.026	6	.230
−18	−.346	7	.129
−17	−.317	8	.051
−16	−.413	9	−.211
−15	.377	10	.213
−14	−.228	11	.172
−13	−.738	12	−.024
−12	.051	13	.181
−11	−.424	14	−.143
−10	−.578	15	.497
− 9	.188	16	−.105
− 8	−.391	17	−.236
− 7	.107	18	.148
− 6	.417	19	.141
− 5	−.169	20	−.057
− 4	.943	25	−.003
− 3	.239	30	−.025
− 2	.490	40	.133
− 1	.959	50	−.069
		60	.161

Source, Larry Y. Dann, "Common Stock Repurchases: An Analysis of Returns to Bondholders and Stockholders," *Journal of Financial Economics,* June 1981, p. 124.

THE SMALL-FIRM EFFECT

Two University of Chicago doctoral studies in the early 1980s have contended that a true key to superior risk-adjusted rates of return rests with investing in firms with small market capitalizations. (Market capitalization refers to shares outstanding times stock price.) In a study of New York Stock Exchange firms, covering from 1936 to 1975, Banz indicates that the lowest quintile (one fifth) firms in terms of market capitalization provide the highest returns even after adjusting for risk. Banz suggests that, "on average, small NYSE firms have had significantly larger risk-adjusted returns than larger NYSE firms over a 40-year period."[29]

---

[29] Rolf W. Banz, "The Relationship between Returns and Market Value of Common Stocks," *Journal of Financial Economics,* March 1981, pp. 3–18.

Some criticized Banz for using only NYSE firms in his analysis and for using a time period that included the effects of both a depression and a major war. Small firms had incredibly high returns following the depression. A similar type study, produced by Reinganum[30] at about the same time, overcame these criticisms. Reinganum examined 2,000 firms that were traded on the New York Stock Exchange or American Stock Exchange between 1963 and 1980. He annually divided the 2,000 firms up into 10 groupings based on size, with the smallest category representing less than $5 million in market capitalization and the largest grouping representing a billion dollars or more.

A synopsis of the results from the Reinganum study are presented in Table 14–7.

TABLE 14–7   Synopsis of Results—Reinganum Study

(1)	(2) Median market value (capitalization, in millions)	(3) Median share price	(4) Average annual return
Grouping*			
MV 1	$ 4.6	$ 5.24	32.77%
MV 2	10.8	9.52	23.51
MV 3	19.3	12.89	22.98
MV 4	30.7	16.19	20.24
MV 5	47.2	19.22	19.08
MV 6	74.2	22.59	18.30
MV 7	119.1	26.44	15.64
MV 8	209.1	30.83	14.24
MV 9	434.6	34.43	13.00
MV 10	1,102.6	44.94	9.47

* MV = market value.
Source: Marc R. Reinganum, "Portfolio Strategies Based on Market Capitalization," *The Journal of Portfolio Management,* Winter 1983, pp. 29–36.

Column *(2)* indicates the median value of the market capitalization for the firms in each group. Column **(3)** is the median stock price for firms in each group, while column *(4)* indicates average annual return associated with that category.

As observed in column *(4)*, the smallest capitalization group (MV 1)

[30] Marc R. Reinganum, "Misspecification of Capital Asset Pricing—Empirical Anomalies Based on Earnings Yield and Market Values," *Journal of Financial Economics,* March 1981, pp. 19–46. Also, "A Direct Test of Roll's Conjecture on the Firm Size Effect," *Journal of Finance,* March 1982, pp. 27–35, and "Portfolio Strategies Based on Market Capitalization," *The Journal of Portfolio Management,* Winter 1983, pp. 29–36.

outperformed the largest capitalization group (MV 10) by over 23 percent per year. Although not included in the table, in 14 out of the 18 years under study, the MV 1 group showed superior returns to the MV 10 group. In a similar analysis, Reinganum found that $1 invested in the smallest capitalization group would have grown to $46 between 1963 and 1980, while the same dollar invested in the largest capitalization group would have only grown to $4. As did Banz, Reinganum adjusted his returns for risk and continued to show superior risk-adjusted returns.

Such superior return evidence drew criticisms from different quarters. Roll sugested that small-capitalization studies underestimate the risk measure (beta) by failing to account for the infrequent and irregular trading patterns of stocks of smaller firms.[31] Stoll and Whaley maintained that transaction costs associated with dealing in smaller capitalization firms might severely cut into profit potential.[32] They indicated that the average buy-sell spread on small capitalized, low-priced stocks might be four or five times that of large capitalization firms. Reinganum has maintained that even after accounting for these criticisms, small capitalization firms continue to demonstrate superior risk-adjusted returns.[33]

Given that there might be advantages to investing in smaller firms, why haven't professional money managers picked up on the strategy. This, in part, is a Catch-22. Part of the reason for the inefficiency in this segment of the market that allows for superior returns is the absence of institutional traders. This absence means that there is less information generated on the smaller firms, and the information that is generated is reacted to in a less immediate fashion. Studies suggest there is an important linkage between the absence of organized information and superior return potential.[34]

For the institutional investor who wishes to participate in the small-firm segment of the market there is, of course, the problem of positioning. A large purchase may only be possible at well in excess of the current market price and a sell at well below the market. While market critics may well have us believe that it is the smaller investor who has difficulty in competing with the large, market-dominating institutional investor, the opposite may, in fact, be true. Historically, the 100 share investor has been able to explore segments of the market that are effectively closed to the institutional money manager.

In response to the small-firm effect, indirect doors are being opened up

---

[31] Richard Roll, "A Possible Explanation of the Small Firm Effect," *Journal of Finance,* September 1981, pp. 879–88.

[32] H. A. Stoll and R. E. Whaley, "Transaction Costs and the Small Firm Effect," Working paper, Owen Graduate School of Management, Vanderbilt University, January 1982.

[33] Marc R. Reinganum, "A Direct Test of Roll's Conjecture on the Firm Size Effect," *Journal of Finance,* March 1982, pp. 27–35, and "Portfolio Strategies Based on Market Capitalization," *The Journal of Portfolio Management,* Winter 1983, pp. 29–36.

[34] Avner Arbel and Paul Strebel, "Pay Attention to Neglected Firms," *The Journal of Portfolio Management,* Winter 1983, pp. 37–42.

to institutional investors through newly formed money management groups. The institutional investor can place his money with these groups. An example is Dimensional Fund Advisors (DFA). Market Researcher Rex Sinquefield serves as executive vice president of the fund, which specializes in investments in small capitalization firms. The fund only invests in the fifth quintile (lowest 20 percent) of NYSE firms in terms of market capitalization. DFA buys stocks without engaging in significant analysis, but rather relies on the small-firm effect to hopefully produce long-term positive effects.

Advocates of the small-firm effect argue that it is this phenomenon alone, rather than others, such as the low P/E ratio effect, that leads to superior risk-adjusted returns. Peavy and Goodman would argue that the low P/E ratio effect is also important,[35] and others maintain that the dividend yield must also be taken into consideration.[36] No doubt debate will continue on these points for many years to come.

A SPECIAL SITUATION IN THE BOND MARKET—NEW BOND ISSUES

The student should be aware of the situation that exists in the new issues market for bonds. As indicated in Figure 14–1, new bond issues are often priced to provide higher yields than existing (seasoned) issues of the same quality, maturity, and other similar features. The lines descending from the dots on the graph represent the difference between the yield on old issues and new issues. This yield differential provides a special-situation opportunity for higher returns to the investor.

What is the reason for the gap in yields between new and seasoned issues? It could be that investment bankers choose to overprice the yield (underprice the bond) in order to ensure the successful distribution of the issue and reduce the risk. Investment bankers are particularly vulnerable to taking losses on new bond issues when interest rates are rising rapidly. A new issue they thought was attractively priced when interest rates were 12 percent may prove to be almost unmarketable if interest rates shoot up. For this reason, it is hypothesized that investment bankers may garner an extra margin of protection by overpricing yields on new issues in relation to seasoned issues, particularly when interest rates are moving upward. The danger of getting trapped into too low a rate is illustrated by what happened to the securities firm of Salomon Brothers in its distribution of a high-quality IBM offering in October of 1979. Federal Reserve Board Chairman Paul Volcker announced an unexpected, extreme credit tightening policy during the distribution process, and bond prices fell dramatically, leaving Salomon Brothers and other investment bankers with approximately $10 million in losses.

---

[35] John W. Peavy III and David A. Goodman, "The Significance of P/Es for Portfolio Returns," *The Journal of Portfolio Management,* Winter 1983, pp. 43–47.

[36] Solveig Jansson, "The Big Debate over Little Stocks," *Institutional Investor,* June 1982, pp. 141–48.

FIGURE 14–1   Yields on Corporate Bonds—New Issues versus Seasoned Issues

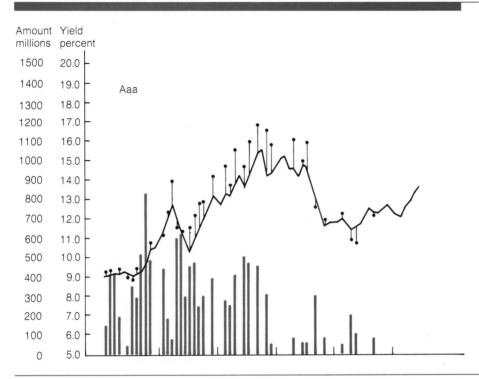

Source: *Moody's Bond Record* (New York: Moody's Investor's Service, Inc., July 1984).

One important piece of research has taken a slightly different approach to explain the gap between yields on new and existing issues of the same quality. Lindvall has suggested that dealers or market makers in the existing bond market are slow to change the value of their inventory to reflect current market conditions.[37] Because trading in existing bond issues is not as intense as similar trading in the stock market, dealers are more arbitrary in setting prices. This may be particularly true when interest rates are going up and dealers do not wish to mark down the value of their inventory. The essence of the Lindvall argument is that, in the bond market, new offerings may come closer to reflecting current market conditions than seasoned issues do.

Regardless of the reasoning, it is clear that new issues tend to carry a higher yield than existing issues of the same quality most of the time. The consequences are twofold. First, investors should prefer new issues to seasoned issues, other things being equal. Second, there may be short-term arbitrage or swap possibilities between old and new issues.

---

[37] John R. Lindvall, "New Issue Corporate Bonds, Seasoned Market Efficiency and Yield Spreads," *Journal of Finance,* September 1977, pp. 1057–67.

SUMMARY

In this chapter we examined various forms of special situations for the investor. Perhaps none has gotten more attention than the great wave of mergers and acquisitions in the late 1970s and 1980s. Because of the premiums paid by the acquiring companies, there is substantial upward potential in the stocks of the acquired firms. However, two-thirds of the gain comes before public announcement, and for that reason, some analysts attempt to identify potential target companies before announcements are made. One of the problems of investing in mergers and acquisitions is that announced plans may be called off, and there may be substantial retractions in value for the stock of the target company. A final point of observation is that stocks of acquiring firms generally do no better than the market in general.

Next we observe the price patterns of firms going public (selling their stock to the general public for the first time). There appears to be abnormal returns for the first week and month after issue, and then the efficiency of the market comes strongly into play. The reason for the initial excess returns is the underpricing by investment bankers to ensure a good reception for the new issue. Stocks of firms underwritten by prestigious underwriters may show smaller returns because of the bargaining power of the issuing firm.

Exchange listings may or may not provide higher values for the securities involved; the research is somewhat contradictory in this regard. However, the interesting feature suggested by the Ying, Lewellen, Schlarbaum, and Lease research is that there may be excess returns between point of announcement and listing (regardless of whether or not there is a sell-off after listing). This is somewhat at variance with the semi-strong form of the efficient market hypothesis.

There is also conflicting evidence on the impact of a firm's repurchase of its own shares in the marketplace. Recent research, however, does indicate that the high premiums paid (22.46 percent) on cash tender offers may provide upward market movement at and immediately after the point of announcement.

Studies of the "small-firm effect" indicate there may be superior return potential in investing in smaller capitalization firms. One justification for the "effect" is that there is less efficiency in this segment of the market due to minimal institutional participation. Others suggest the results may be attributed to poor measurement techniques.

Finally, new bond issues may be considered for purchase on the premise that they provide higher yields than equivalent existing securities. The gap in yield may be explained by either the underpricing (over-yielding) activities of investment bankers to ensure the success of a distribution or by the hesitancy of dealers in the bond market to mark down seasoned issues to reflect current interest rate conditions.

IMPORTANT WORDS AND CONCEPTS

Abnormal return

Unfriendly takeover

White knight

Synergy

Batting average

Trading range

After-market performance

Market capitalization

Merger price premium

Going public

Unseasoned issue

Exchange listing

Ying, Lewellen, Schlarbaum, and Lease study

Stock repurchase

Underpricing

Small-firm effect

DISCUSSION QUESTIONS

1. Define special or abnormal returns.
2. What is the basis for upward movement in the stock of an acquisition candidate?
3. What is an unfriendly takeover?
4. What is the primary danger in investing in merger and acquisition candidates?
5. What factor(s) will determine the extent of upward price potential for an acquisition candidate at the time of merger announcement?
6. Do the stocks of acquiring companies tend to show strong upward market movement as a result of the merger process? Comment on the reasoning behind your answer.
7. Why do cash tender offers frequently carry a higher premium than stock offers?
8. Why does abnormal return potential sometimes exist in the new-issues market?
9. What are some factors to consider before buying a new issue?
10. Why might firms that are underwritten by large, prestigious, investment banking houses not necessarily provide the highest initial returns to investors in the new-issues market?
11. What are some reasons why a firm may wish to have its security listed on an exchange?
12. What was the major finding of the Ying, Lewellen, Schlarbaum, and Lease study? How does this relate to the semi-strong form of the efficient market hypothesis?
13. What are some reasons a firm may repurchase its own stock?
14. What are some negative connotations associated with a firm repurchasing its own shares?
15. Indicate how the repurchase of shares may increase the stock price if the P/E ratio remains constant.
16. Relate the existence of positive returns on stock repurchases to the type of offer (formal versus informal).

17. According to researchers such as Banz and Reinganum, what is the general performance of small firms relative to larger firms?

18. What does the term *market capitalization* mean?

19. What criticisms of the small-firm effect were offered by Roll, and Stoll and Whaley? Were these considered valid by Reinganum?

20. What explanation might be offered for the possible market inefficiency in the small-firm segment of the market?

21. What problem does an institutional investor have when he or she tries to purchase shares of a "small firm?" How can this be partially overcome?

22. Advocates of the small-firm effect argue that it is this factor *alone* that leads to superior risk-adjusted returns. Is there complete agreement on this point?

23. What is the Lindvall reasoning as to why the interest rate on new bond issues may be higher than the interest rate on comparable, outstanding, old bond issues.

24. Project: Identify a recently announced merger or acquisition. Determine the price of the acquisition candidate's stock three months before announcement. Compare this to the actual offer by the acquiring company in terms of cash or stock. Also compare this to the acquisition candidate's stock price at point of announcement. Determine the percentage premium over the acquisition candidate's stock value in each case. Do these premiums seem reasonable in light of the quality of the companies involved and the likelihood of the merger going through? (Note: You can use old issues of *The Wall Street Journal* to determine the first date of announcement and the stock prices.)

SELECTED REFERENCES

Arbel, Auner, and Paul Strebel. "Pay Attention to Neglected Firms." *The Journal of Portfolio Management,* Winter 1983, pp. 37–42.

Banz, Rolf W. "The Relationship between Returns and Market Value of Common Stocks." *Journal of Financial Economics,* March 1981, pp. 3–18.

Bierman, Harold J., and Richard West. "The Acquisition of Common Stock by the Corporate Issuer." *Journal of Finance,* December 1966, pp. 687–96.

Block, Stanley, and Marjorie Stanley. "The Financial Characteristics and Price Movement Patterns of Companies Approaching the Unseasoned Securities Market in the Late 1970's." *Financial Management,* Winter 1980, pp. 30–36.

————. "An Analysis of Structural Differences between Industries in the Unseasoned Securities Market." *The Financial Review,* June 1984, p. 9.

Dann, Larry Y. "Common Stock Repurchases: An Analysis of Returns to Bondholders and Stockholders." *Journal of Financial Economics,* June 1981, pp. 113–38.

Dielman, Terry E.; Timothy J. Nantell; and Roger L. Wright. "Price Effects of Stock Repurchasing: A Random Coefficient Regression Approach." *Journal of Financial and Quantitative Analysis,* March 1980, pp. 175–89.

Dodd, Peter. "Merger Proposals, Management Discretion and Stockholder Wealth." *Journal of Financial Economics,* December 1980, pp. 105–38.

Ellis, Charles D., and Allen E. Young. *The Repurchase of Common Stock.* New York: The Ronald Press, 1971.

Fabozzi, Frank J. "Does Listing Increase the Market Value of Common Stock?" *Journal of Business,* April 1970, pp. 174–80.

Fama, Eugene F.; Lawrence Fisher; Michael G. Jensen; and Richard Roll. "The Adjustment of Stock Prices to New Information." *International Economic Review,* February 1969, pp. 1–21.

Furst, Richard W. "Does Listing Increase the Market Value of Common Stock?" *Journal of Business,* April 1970, pp. 174–80.

Goulet, Waldemar. "Price Changes, Managerial Accounting and Insider Trading at the Time of Listing." *Financial Management,* Spring 1974, pp. 303–6.

Hausman, W. H., R. R. West; and J. A. Largay. "Stock Splits, Price Changes and Trading Profits: A Synthesis." *Journal of Business,* January 1971, pp. 69–77.

Hogarty, T. "The Profitability of Corporate Mergers." *Journal of Business,* July 1970, pp. 317–27.

Ibbotson, Roger G. "Price Performance of Common Stock New Issues." *Journal of Financial Economics,* September 1975, pp. 235–72.

Jansson, Solveig. "The Big Debate Over Little Stocks." *Institutional Investor,* June 1982, pp. 141–48.

Kummer, Donald R., and J. Ronald Hoffmeister. "Valuation Consequences of Cash Tender Offers." *Journal of Finance,* May 1978, pp. 505–16.

Lindvall, John R. "New Issue Corporate Bonds, Seasoned Market Efficiency and Yield Spreads." *Journal of Finance,* September 1977, pp. 1057–67.

Logue, Dennis E. "On the Pricing of Seasoned New Issues, 1965–1969." *Journal of Financial and Quantitative Analysis,* January 1973, pp. 91–103.

Mandelker, Gershon. "Risk and Return: The Case of Merging Firms." *Journal of Financial Economics,* December 1974, pp. 303–35.

Masulis, R. W. "Stock Repurchase by Tender Offer: An Analysis of the Causes of Common Stock Price Changes." *Journal of Finance,* May 1980, pp. 305–19.

————. "Costly Propositions—Some Big Mergers Have Lately Fallen Through." *Barron's,* May 14, 1979, pp. 9–16.

Monroe, Robert J., and Michael A. Simkowitz. "Investment Characteristics of Conglomerate Targets: A Discriminant Analysis." *Southern Journal of Business,* November 1971, pp. 1–15.

Neuberger, Brian M., and Carl T. Hammond. "A Study of Underwriters' Experience with Unseasoned New Issues, 1965–1969." *Journal of Financial and Quantitative Analysis,* January 1973, pp. 91–103.

Neuberger, Brian M., and Chris A. La Chapelle. "Unseasoned New Issues Price Performance on Three Tiers: 1975–1980." *Financial Management,* Autumn 1983, pp. 23–28.

Norgaard, Richard, and Connie Norgaard. "A Critical Evaluation of Share Repurchase." *Financial Management,* Spring 1974, pp. 44–50.

Oppenheimer, Henry, and Stanley Block. "An Examination of Premiums and Exchange Ratios Associated with Merger Activity during the 1975–78 Period." Financial Management Association Meeting, 1980.

Peavy, John W. III, and David A. Goodman. "The Significance of P/Es for Portfolio Returns." *The Journal of Portfolio Management,* Winter 1983, pp. 43–47.

"Penny Stocks, New Issues Are Still the Rage; Risks, Fraud Charges Don't Deter Investors." *The Wall Street Journal,* March 30, 1981, p. 42.

Reilly, Frank K. "New Issues Revisited." *Financial Management,* Winter 1977, p. 28–42.

Reinganum, Marc R. "Misspecification of Capital Asset Pricing—Empirical Anomalies Based on Earnings Yield and Market Values." *Journal of Financial Economics,* March 1981, pp. 19–46.

————. "A Direct Test of Roll's Conjecture on the Firm Size Effect." *Journal of Finance,* March 1982, pp. 27–35.

————. "Portfolio Strategies Based on Market Capitalization." *The Journal of Portfolio Management,* Winter 1983, pp. 29–36.

Roll, Richard. "A Possible Explanation of the Small Firm Effect." *Journal of Finance,* September 1981, pp. 879–88.

Stevens, Donald J. "Financial Characteristics of Merger Firms: A Multivariate Analysis." *Journal of Financial and Quantitative Analysis,* March 1973, pp. 149–58.

Stoll, H. A., and R. E. Whaley. "Transaction Costs and the Small Firm Effect." Working paper, Owen Graduate School of Management, Vanderbilt University, January 1982.

"Two Former Morgan Stanley Executives Accused of Plot Involving Takeover Data." *The Wall Street Journal,* February 4, 1981, p. 2.

Van Horne, James C. "New Listings and Their Price Behavior." *Journal of Finance,* September 1970, pp. 783–94.

Vermaelen, Theo. "Common Stock Repurchases and Market Signaling: An Empirical Study." *Journal of Financial Economics,* June 1981, pp. 139–83.

Ying, Louis K. W.; Wilbur G. Lewellen; Gary G. Schlarbaum; and Ronald C. Lease. "Stock Exchange Listing and Securities Returns." *Journal of Financial and Quantitative Analysis,* September 1977, pp. 415–32.

Chapter 15

COMMODITIES AND FINANCIAL FUTURES

What do pork bellies, soybeans, Japanese yen, and Treasury bills have in common? They are all items on which contracts may be traded in the commodities and financial futures markets.

Def →

A futures contract is an agreement that provides for the delivery of a specific amount of a commodity at a designated time in the future at a given price. An example might be a contract to deliver 5,000 bushels of corn in September of 1985 at $3.00 per bushel. The person who sells the contract does not need to have actual possession of the corn, nor does the purchaser of the contract need to plan on taking possession of the corn. Almost all commodity futures contracts are closed out or reversed before the actual transaction is to take place. Thus, the seller of a futures contract for the delivery of 5,000 bushels of corn may simply buy back a similar contract for the purchase of 5,000 bushels and close out his position. The initial buyer also reverses his position. Over 97 percent of all contracts are closed out in this fashion rather than through actual delivery.[1] The commodities futures market is similar to the options market in that there is a tremendous volume of activity but very few actual items ever change hands.

The futures markets were originally set up to allow grain and livestock producers and processors to hedge their positions in a given commodity. For example, a wheat producer might have a five-month lead time between the planting of his crop and the actual harvesting and delivery to the market. While the current price of wheat might be $4.00 a bushel, there is a tremendous risk that the price might change before delivery to the market. The wheat producer can hedge his position by offering to sell futures contracts for the delivery of wheat. Even though he will probably close out or reverse these futures contracts prior to the call for actual delivery, he will still have effectively hedged his position. Let's see how this works. If the price of wheat goes down, he will have to sell his crop for less than he anticipated when he planted the wheat, but he will make up the difference on the wheat futures contracts. That is, he will be able to buy back the contracts for less than he sold them. Of course, if the price of the wheat goes up, the extra profit he makes on the crop will be lost on the futures contracts as he now has to buy back the contracts at a higher price.[2]

A miller who uses wheat as part of his processing faces the opposite dilemma in terms of pricing. The miller is afraid the price of wheat might go up and ultimately cut into his profit margin when he takes actual delivery of his product. He can hedge his position by buying futures contracts in wheat. If the actual price of wheat does go up, the extra cost of producing his product will be offset by the profits he makes on his futures contracts.

---

[1] "Speculating on Inflation: Futures Trading in Interest Rates, Foreign Currencies and Precious Metals," Merrill Lynch, Pierce, Fenner & Smith, July 1979.

[2] The hedger not only reduces risk of loss but also eliminates additional profit opportunities. This may be appropriate for farmers since they are not in the risk-taking business but rather in agriculture.

FIGURE 15–1

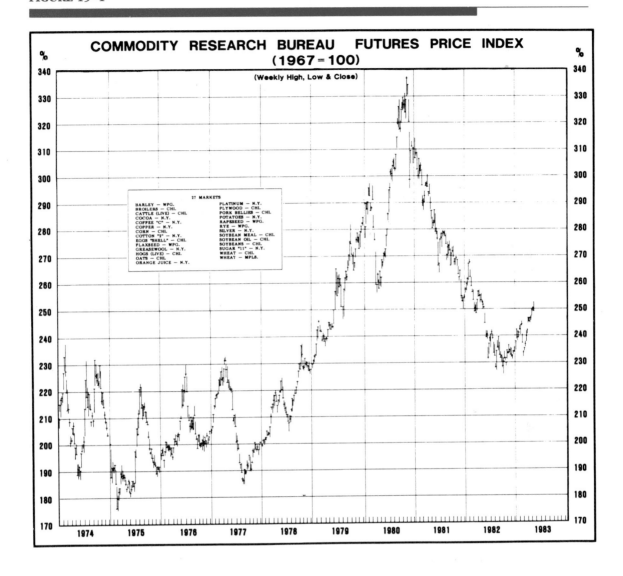

COMMODITY RESEARCH BUREAU FUTURES PRICE INDEX
(1967 = 100)
(Weekly High, Low & Close)

CRB Futures Price Index, Monthly High, Low & Close 1967 = 100

Year		Jan.	Feb.	Mar.	Apr.	May	June	July	Aug.	Sept.	Oct.	Nov.	Dec.	Range
1980	High	290.4	297.4	296.9	263.7	271.8	286.4	303.2	308.4	329.0	329.9	337.6	329.0	337.6
	Low	276.8	287.5	258.0	256.3	259.4	269.4	289.5	301.9	310.4	316.8	321.8	295.1	256.3
	Close	289.6	288.4	258.0	258.1	270.1	286.4	302.3	308.4	319.4	327.1	334.8	308.5	—
1981	High	314.5	306.9	298.4	300.7	290.0	286.0	279.7	279.7	276.0	274.0	269.8	264.8	314.5
	Low	299.2	296.7	287.5	287.7	280.7	263.9	266.6	268.1	266.8	266.6	260.7	250.5	250.5
	Close	300.1	296.7	298.4	289.1	287.5	263.9	279.3	269.4	268.6	268.9	262.2	254.9	—
1982	High	267.2	268.6	257.5	257.3	253.3	242.0	242.4	238.4	239.8	234.3	236.3	235.7	268.6
	Low	256.0	256.5	248.7	252.5	244.9	231.5	233.2	227.1	227.9	225.8	231.2	231.1	225.8
	Close	267.2	256.5	250.1	253.1	244.9	239.3	233.7	235.4	227.9	229.9	235.7	234.0	—
1983	High	242.7	245.1	242.1	247.3									
	Low	234.8	232.1	232.8	244.7									
	Close	242.7	232.1	242.1	246.7									

Source: *Commodity Yearbook* (New York: Commodity Research Bureau, 1983), p. 6.

The commodities market allows the many parties in need of hedging opportunities to acquire contracts. While some of this could be accomplished on a private basis (one party in Kansas City calls another party in Chicago on the advice of his banker), this would be virtually impossible to handle on a large-scale basis. Liquid, fluid markets, such as those provided by the commodity exchanges, are necessary to accomplish this function.

While the hedgers are the backbone and basic reason for existence of the commodity exchanges, they are not the only significant participants. We also have the speculators who take purely long or short positions without any intent to hedge actual ownership. Thus, there is the speculator in wheat or silver who believes that the next major price move can be predicted to such an extent that a substantial profit can be made. Because commodities are purchased on the basis of a small investment in the form of margin (usually running 5 to 10 percent of the value of the contract), there is substantial leverage on the investment, and percentage returns and losses are greatly magnified. The typical commodities trader often suffers many losses with the anticipation of a few very substantial gains. Commodities speculation, as opposed to hedging, represents somewhat of a gamble, and stories have been told of reformed commodities speculators who gave up the chase to spend the rest of their days merely playing the slot machines.

The volatility of commodity prices can be seen in Figure 15–1 on page 435. While the price trend for the 27 commodities in the index has been upward, note the up and down patterns, particularly in the mid-1970s and early 1980s.

TYPES OF COMMODITIES AND EXCHANGES

Commodities and financial futures can be broken down into a number of categories based on their essential characteristics. As indicated in Table 15–1, there are six primary categories. In each case, we show representative items that fall under the category.

The first five categories represent traditional commodities, but category 6 came into prominence in the 1970s, with foreign exchange futures originating in 1972, interest rate futures beginning in 1975, and stock index futures in 1982. Because financial futures have tremendous implications for financial managers, we will give them special attention in a later section of this chapter. We will defer discussion of stock index futures to Chapter 16, so that they can be given complete coverage as a separate topic.

The commodities listed in Table 15–1 trade on various commodity exchanges in the United States and Canada (see Table 15–2). While the exchanges are well organized and efficient in their operation, they are still run by an open auction complete with outcries of bids and various hand-signal displays.

The largest commodity exchange is the Chicago Board of Trade (CBT) with the Chicago Mercantile Exchange (CME) in second place. While some exchanges are highly specialized, such as the New York Cotton Exchange,

TABLE 15–1   Categories of Commodities and Financial Futures

(1)	(2)	(3)
Grains and oilseeds:	Livestock and meat:	Food and fiber:
Corn	Cattle—feeder	Cocoa
Oats	Cattle—live	Coffee
Soybeans	Hogs—live	Cotton
Wheat	Pork bellies	Orange juice
Barley	Turkeys	Potatoes
Rye	Broilers	Sugar
		Rice
		Butter

(4)	(5)	(6)
Metals and petroleum:	Wood:	Financial futures:
Copper	Lumber	*a.* Foreign exchange
Gold	Plywood	(pound, yen, franc, etc.)
Platinum		*b.* Interest rate futures
Silver		GNMA certificates
Mercury		Treasury bonds
Heating oil no. 2		Treasury bills
		Certificates of deposit
		Commercial paper
		Eurodollars
		c. Stock index futures
		S&P 500
		Value Line

TABLE 15–2   Major United States and Canadian Commodity Exchanges

American Commodities Exchange (ACE)
Chicago Board of Trade (CBT)
Chicago Mercantile Exchange (CME)
    Also controls International Monetary Market (IMM)
Commodity Exchange (CMX)
Kansas City Board of Trade (KC)
Minneapolis Grain Exchange (MPLS)
New Orleans Commodity Exchange
New York Coffee, Sugar, and Cocoa Exchange (CSCE)
New York Cotton Exchange (CTN)
New York Futures Exchange (NYFE)
    Subsidiary of the New York Stock Exchange
New York Mercantile Exchange (NYM)
Pacific Commodities Exchange (PCE)
Winnipeg Grain Exchange (WPG)

most exchanges trade in a wide number of securities. For example, the Chicago Board of Trade deals in such diverse products as corn, oats, soybeans, wheat, plywood, GNMA certificates, and Treasury bonds.

The American Commodities Exchange (ACE), part of the American Stock Exchange, and the New York Futures Exchange (NYFE), part of the New York Stock Exchange, are rather new in the game and specialize in financial futures. As the Chicago Board of Trade and Chicago Mercantile Exchange moved into this territory with financially oriented securities (such as GNMA futures and Treasury bill futures), members of Wall Street felt compelled to get into the financial futures game as well.

The activities of the commodity exchanges are primarily regulated by the Commodity Futures Trading Commission (CFTC), a federal regulatory agency established by Congress in 1975. The CFTC has had a number of jurisdictional disputes with the SEC over the regulation of financial futures.

Types of Commodities Contracts

The commodity contract lists the type of commodity and the denomination in which it is traded (bushels, pounds, troy ounces, metric tons, percentage points, etc.). The contract will also specify the standardized unit for trade (5,000 bushels, 30,000 pounds, etc.). A further designation will indicate the month in which the contract ends, with most commodities having a whole range of months from which to choose. Typically, contracts run as far as a year into the future, but some interest rate futures contracts extend as far as three years.

Examples of the sizes of futures contracts are presented in Table 15–3. Be aware that there may be many different forms of the same commodity (such as spring wheat or amber/durum wheat).

TABLE 15–3   Size of Commodity Contracts

Contract	Trading units	Size of contract based on mid-1984 prices
Corn	5,000 bushels	$ 16,200
Oats	5,000 bushels	9,500
Wheat	5,000 bushels	20,000
Pork bellies	38,000 pounds	26,500
Coffee	37,500 pounds	53,250
Cotton	50,000 pounds	42,500
Sugar	112,000 pounds	6,720
Copper	25,000 pounds	17,500
Gold	100 troy ounces	35,000
Silver	5,000 troy ounces	40,000
Treasury bonds	$100,000	59,150
Treasury bills	$1,000,000	878,200

ACTUAL COMMODITIES CONTRACT

To examine the potential gain or loss in a commodities contract, let's go through a hypothetical investment. Assume we are considering the purchase of a December wheat contract (it is now May 1). The price on the futures contract is $4.00 per bushel. Since wheat trades in units of 5,000 bushels, the total price is $20,000. As we go through our example, we will examine many important features associated with commodity trading—beginning with margin requirements.

Margin Requirements

Commodity trading is based on the use of margin rather than on actual cash dollars. Margin requirements are typically 5 to 10 percent of the value of the contract and may vary over time or even from exchange to exchange for a given commodity. For our example, we will assume a $1,500 margin requirement. This would represent 7.5 percent of the value of the contract ($20,000).

Margin requirements on commodities contracts are much lower than those on stock transactions, where 50 percent of the purchase price has been the requirement since 1974. Furthermore, in the commodities market, the margin payment is merely considered to be a good-faith payment against losses. There is no actual borrowing or interest to be paid.[3]

In addition to the initial margin requirements, there are also margin maintenance requirements (minimum maintenance standards) that run 70 to 80 percent of the value of the initial margin. In the case of the wheat contract, the margin maintenance requirement might be $1,200 (80% × $1,500). If our initial margin of $1,500 is reduced by $300 due to losses on our contract, we will be required to replace the $300 to cover our margin position. If we do not do so, our position will be closed out and we will take our losses.

The margin requirement, relative to size, is even less for financial futures. For example, on a $1 million Treasury bill contract, the investor generally must only post an initial margin of $1,500. Similar requirements exist for other types of financial futures.

Note that the high risk inherent in a commodities contract is not so much a function of volatile price movements as it is the impact of high leverage made possible by the low initial margin requirements. A 10 percent price move may equal or exceed the size of our initial investment in the form of the margin deposit. This is similar to the type of leverage utilized in the options market as described in Chapter 13. However, the action in the commodities market is much quicker. You can be asked to put up additional margin within hours after you establish your initial position.

---

[3] It should also be pointed out that we may need a minimum account balance of $5,000 or greater to open a commodity account.

Market Conditions

Because the price of every commodity moves in response to market conditions, each investor must determine the key market variables that influence the value of his or her contract. In the case of wheat, the investor may be particularly concerned about such factors as weather and crop conditions in the Midwest, the price of corn as a substitute product, the carryover of wheat supply from the previous year, and the potential wheat sales to the Soviet Union and other foreign countries. A rumor about an impending transaction with the Soviet Union has often caused market prices to change radically.

Gains and Losses

In the present example, assume we guessed right in our analysis of the wheat market; we purchased a December futures contract for $4.00 per bushel, and the price goes to $4.35 per bushel (recall that the contract was for 5,000 bushels). With a 35-cent increase per bushel, we have established a dollar gain of $1,750 (5,000 bushes × $.35 per bushel profit). With an initial margin requirement of $1,500, we have made a percentage profit of 116.7 percent.[4]

$$\frac{\text{Dollar gain}}{\text{Amount of margin deposit}} = \frac{\$1,750}{\$1,500} \times 100 = 116.7\%$$

If this transaction took place over a one-month time period, the annualized gain would be 1,400 percent (116.7% × 12 = 1,400.4%). Note that this was all accomplished by a 35-cent movement in the price of a December wheat contract from $4.00 to $4.35, a percentage change of 8.7 percent ($.35/$4.00).

Actually, the investor may choose to close out his contract or attempt to let his profits run. He also may use his profits to establish the basis for margin on additional futures contracts. A paper gain of $1,750 is more than enough to provide the $1,500 margin on another wheat contract. Actually, a gain of only 30 cents per bushel would have accomplished this by providing $1,500 in profits (5,000 bushels × $.30).

The investor is now in a position to use an inverse pyramid to expand his position. With two contracts outstanding, a mere 15-cent price change will provide $1,500 in profits.

$$\begin{array}{rl} \$ & .15 \text{ Price change} \\ \times & 10,000 \text{ Bushels (two contracts)} \\ \hline & \$1,500 \text{ Profits (can be applied} \\ & \text{to third contract)} \end{array}$$

The $1,500 in profits can be used to purchase a third contract, and now with 15,000 bushels under control, a 10-cent price change will generate enough profits for a fourth contract.

---

[4] This does not include commissions, which are generally less than $60 to $70 for a complete transaction (buy and sell).

$ .10 Price change
× 15,000 Bushels (three contracts)
$1,500 Profits (can be applied
to fourth contract)

The process of inverse pyramiding begins to sound astounding since eventually a 1-cent or ½-cent change in the price of wheat will trigger off enough profits for a new contract. Of course, there are great risks associated with such a process. It is like building a house with playing cards. If one card tumbles, the whole house comes down. The investor can become so highly leveraged that any slight reversal in price can trigger off tremendous margin calls. While it is often wise to let profits run and perhaps do some amount of pyramiding, prudence must be exercised.

Our primary attention up to this point has been on contracts that are making money. What are the implications if there is an immediate price reversal after we have purchased our December wheat contract? You will recall there was a margin maintenance requirement of $1,200 based on our initial margin of $1,500. In this case, a $300 loss would call for an additional deposit to bring our margin position up to $1,500. How much would the price of wheat have to decline for us to get this margin call to increase our deposit? With a 5,000-bushel contract, we are talking about a mere decline of 6 cents per bushel.

$$\frac{\$300 \text{ loss}}{5,000 \text{ bushels}} = \$.06 \text{ per bushel}$$

This could happen in a matter of hours or days after our initial purchase. When we get the margin call, we can either elect to put up the additional $300 and continue with the contract or tell our commodities broker to close out our contract and take our losses. If we put up the $300, our broker could still be on the phone two hours later asking for more margin because the price has shown further deterioration. Because investors often buy multiple contracts, such as 10 December wheat contracts, the process can be all the more intense. In the commodities market, the old adage of "cut your losses short and let your profits run" probably has its greatest significance. Even a seasoned commodities trader might determine that he is willing to lose 80 percent of the time and only win 20 percent of the time, but those victories will represent home runs and the losses mere outs.

Price Movement Limitations

Because of the enormous opportunities for gains and losses in the commodities markets, the commodity exchanges do place some broad limitations on maximum daily price movements in a commodity. Some examples are shown in Table 15–4.

These daily trading limits obviously must affect the efficiency of the market somewhat. If market conditions indicate the price of wheat should

TABLE 15–4   Maximum Daily Price Changes

Commodity	Exchange	Normal price range	Maximum daily price change (from previous close)*
Corn	CBT	$2.30–$4.00	$.10 per bushel
Oats	CBT	$1.25–$2.40	$.06 per bushel
Wheat	CBT	$3.00–$5.50	$.20 per bushel
Pork bellies	CBT	$.40–$.80	$.02 per pound
Copper	CME	$.60–$1.50	$.03 per pound
Silver	CMX	$6.00–$50.00	$.50 per ounce
Treasury bills	IMM of CME	85% of par and up	50 basis points

* These values may change slightly from exchange to exchange and are often temporarily altered in response to rampant speculation.

decline by 30 cents and the daily limit is 20 cents, then obviously the price of wheat is not in equilibrium as it opens the following morning. However, the desire to stop market panics tends to override the desire for total market efficiency in the commodity markets. Nevertheless, the potential intraday trading range is still large. Recall, for example, that a 20-cent change in the price of wheat, which is the daily limit, is more than enough to place tremendous pressure on the investor to repeatedly increase his margin position. On the typical 5,000-bushel contract, this would represent a daily loss of $1,000.

READING MARKET QUOTES

We now turn our attention to interpreting market quotes in the daily newspaper. In Figure 15–2, we show an excerpt from the June 1, 1984, edition of *The Wall Street Journal* covering 18 different types of contracts (this represents about one third of the contracts reported for that day).

In each case, we see there is a wide choice of months for which a contract may be purchased. For example, oats, which trade on the Chicago Board of Trade (CBT), have futures contracts for July, September, December, and March. Some commodities offer a contract for virtually every month. In order to directly examine some of the terms in Figure 15–2, we reproduce the portion related to the oats contract (CBT) in Table 15–5.

We initially read the second line in the table that indicates we are dealing in oats traded on the Chicago Board of Trade (CBT). We then note that oats are traded in 5,000-bushel units and quoted in cents per bushel. Quotations in cents per bushel require some mental adjustment. For example, 200 cents per bushel would actually represent two dollars ($2) per bushel. We generally move the decimal point two places to the left and read the quote in terms of dollars. For example, the July 1984 opening price was 188, or $1.88 per bushel.

FIGURE 15–2 Examples of Price Quotes on Commodity Futures

Futures Prices

Thursday, May 31, 1984

Open Interest Reflects Previous Trading Day.

–GRAINS AND OILSEEDS–

CORN (CBT) 5,000 bu.; cents per bu.

	Open	High	Low	Settle	Change	Lifetime High	Lifetime Low	Open Interest
July	353¾	354¼	349¾	350½	− 3¼	388	288¼	81,567
Sept	328	329¼	325½	325¾	− 2¾	356½	295½	23,685
Dec	304¼	306¼	303	303	− 2	330	279¾	41,936
Mar85	313	314½	312	312¼	− 1¼	319	289¾	7,188
May	317¼	319	316¼	316½	− 1	322	295½	1,498
July	320¼	320½	318½	318½	− 1	323¼	307½	603
Sept	311½	311½	311½	311½	− 1	315	311	8

Est vol 35,900; vol Wed 34,771; open int 156,486, +807.

CORN (MCE) 1,000 bu.; cents per bu.

	Open	High	Low	Settle	Change	Lifetime High	Lifetime Low	Open Interest
July	354	354¼	349⅝	350½	− 3¼	388⅛	288½	6,092
Sept	327¾	329	325¾	325¾	− 2¾	355	298½	1,019
Dec	304¼	306	302¾	303	− 2	330	281¼	5,428
Mar85	313	313¾	312½	312¼	− 1¼	319	292¼	303
May	.	..	.	316½	− 1	321	292	46
July	320	320	320	318½	− 1	323¼	309¾	21

Est vol 1,150 vol Wed 1,123; open int 12,909, +89.

OATS (CBT) 5,000 bu.; cents per bu.

	Open	High	Low	Settle	Change	Lifetime High	Lifetime Low	Open Interest
July	188	188½	187	188½	+ 1½	226	166¼	2,017
Sept	183¾	184	182	182½	− ½	219	164¾	915
Dec	187½	187½	186	186¼	− ¾	193¼	168½	906
Mar85	189¼	189¾	189¼	189¾	− 1½	196½	181¾	267

Est vol 600; vol Wed 864; open int 4,105, +236.

SOYBEANS (CBT) 5,000 bu.; cents per bu.

	Open	High	Low	Settle	Change	Lifetime High	Lifetime Low	Open Interest
July	867	868¼	846	847	− 19	992½	639½	58,102
Aug	861	863	842	843	− 17½	956¾	640	15,846
Sept	791	798½	786	786¼	− 5	860	705½	8,980
Nov	745	755	742	745½	+ 1	772¼	661	24,609
Jan85	756	765½	753	754¼	− 1¼	765½	676	5,698
Mar	767	776	764	766¾	+ ¼	776	692	1,916
May	775	784	773	777	+ 2	784	729½	608
July	781½	781½	781½	781½	+ 2	784	742	111

Est vol 85,300; vol Wed 67,668; open int 115,870, −79.

SOYBEANS (MCE) 1,000 bu.; cents per bu.

	Open	High	Low	Settle	Change	Lifetime High	Lifetime Low	Open Interest
July	886	867	845	847	− 19	992½	645	20,291
Aug	861	863	841	843	− 17½	955	646	2,061
Sept	801	797½	784½	786¼	− 5	853	708	560
Nov	746	755	742	745½	+ 1	772¼	661	4,181
Jan85	753	766	752½	754¼	− 1¼	766	678	747
Mar	767	776	763	766¾	+ ¼	776	722	386
May	773	783	772	777	+ 2	783	733	92
July	777	777	777	781½	+ 2	777	754	30

Est vol 5,280; vol Wed 5,513; open int 28,348, −5.

SOYBEAN MEAL (CBT) 100 tons; $ per ton.

	Open	High	Low	Settle	Change	Lifetime High	Lifetime Low	Open Interest
July	200.50	200.90	195.20	195.40	− 4.70	267.50	188.00	30,597
Aug	202.50	203.00	197.50	197.80	− 4.40	251.00	190.30	10,866
Sept	200.00	200.00	196.50	196.50	− 3.20	243.00	188.00	6,674
Oct	190.00	192.50	189.00	189.50	− .30	240.00	182.00	9,680
Dec	191.50	194.00	190.50	192.50	+ 1.30	227.00	182.50	13,197
Jan85	193.00	196.10	192.50	194.30	+ 1.60	208.00	184.00	2,645
Mar	195.80	198.00	194.00	195.70	+ 2.20	209.00	188.50	750
May	....	....	....	198.00	− 2.50	205.00	191.00	63

Est vol 27,600; vol Wed 14,330; open int 74,473, −29.

SOYBEAN OIL (CBT) 60,000 lbs.; cents per lb.

	Open	High	Low	Settle	Change	Lifetime High	Lifetime Low	Open Interest
July	37.10	37.70	36.75	36.90	− .38	39.75	20.00	26,429
Aug	36.15	36.80	35.90	35.95	− .35	38.45	20.30	10,398
Sept	34.50	34.75	34.10	34.15	− .52	36.15	23.45	6,680
Oct	31.55	31.85	31.15	31.18	− .62	33.05	23.50	10,637
Dec	29.70	29.85	29.30	29.33	− .58	30.80	23.45	8,804
Jan85	29.55	29.55	29.00	29.05	− .45	30.25	24.05	2,213
Mar	29.10	29.10	28.90	28.90	− .30	30.25	25.25	864
May	....	....	....	28.88	− .30	29.90	28.20	4
July	....	....	....	28.88	− .30	30.25	29.50	0

Est vol 24,200; vol Wed 28,307; open int 66,029, −932.

WHEAT (CBT) 5,000 bu.; cents per bu.

	Open	High	Low	Settle	Change	Lifetime High	Lifetime Low	Open Interest
July	363	363¾	356	356	− 7½	427	322	25,380
Sept	367	367¾	360	360¼	− 7¼	432	325	11,966
Dec	382½	383¾	375½	375¾	− 7¾	418	337½	12,395
Mar85	393	393¾	386	386¼	− 8	404	344	3,032
May	396	396	390½	390½	− 7¼	405	367¼	119
July	382	382	376	376	− 7	390	376	12

Est vol 20,400; vol Wed 14,168; open int 52,904, −359.

WHEAT (KC) 5,000 bu.; cents per bu.

	Open	High	Low	Settle	Change	Lifetime High	Lifetime Low	Open Interest
July	370	370¼	365½	365½	− 5	419	339¾	9,212
Sept	376	376	371½	371½	− 4¾	417	343½	5,100
Dec	388	388¼	383½	383½	− 5	397	355	2,501
Mar85	392½	392½	392½	392½	− 6	407½	377¼	173

Est vol 4,379; vol Wed 3,383; open int 16,986, +52.

WHEAT (MPLS) 5,000 bu.; cents per bu.

	Open	High	Low	Settle	Change	Lifetime High	Lifetime Low	Open Interest
July	413¾	414	409	409¼	− 4½	430	372½	2,342
Sept	405	405¼	400	400¼	− 4¾	408½	364½	1,915
Dec	410½	410¾	405½	406	− 5	414	366½	798
Mar85	....	....	....	409	− 3¼	413½	392½	168

Est vol 1,080; vol Wed 1,212; open int 5,222, −47.

WHEAT (MCE) 1,000 bu.; cents per bu.

	Open	High	Low	Settle	Change	Lifetime High	Lifetime Low	Open Interest
July	362½	363½	355	356	− 7½	428	322⅜	14,186
Sept	367	367	359½	360¼	− 7¼	430	327	232
Dec	383	383¼	375	375¾	− 7¾	408¾	340	3,015
Mar85	392½	392½	392½	386¼	− 8	397⅞	348	88
May	....	....	....	390½	− 7¼	401½	368	5
July	381	381	381	376	− 7	387	381	2

Est vol 680; vol Wed 450; open int 17,528, +106.

COTTON (CTN)–50,000 lbs.; cents per lb.

	Open	High	Low	Settle	Change	Lifetime High	Lifetime Low	Open Interest
July	84.96	85.17	84.50	84.62	− .34	86.25	71.50	10,416
Aug	....	....	....	81.00	− 1.25	80.80	79.90	1
Oct	80.96	80.96	80.21	80.25	− .89	82.09	72.19	3,556
Dec	77.66	77.75	77.05	77.08	− .61	78.40	70.72	14,623
Mar85	78.75	78.75	78.20	78.15	− .70	79.35	72.50	1,996
May	....	....	....	78.60	− .70	79.20	73.74	128
July	79.32	79.32	79.32	78.71	− .70	79.85	75.75	146
Oct	....	....	....	76.60	− .70	77.50	77.00	7

Est vol 6,000; vol Wed 5,883; open int 30,873, −86.

ORANGE JUICE (CTN)–15,000 lbs.; cents per lb.

	Open	High	Low	Settle	Change	Lifetime High	Lifetime Low	Open Interest
May	....	....	....	....	....	....	....	64
July	179.25	181.90	178.50	181.55	+ 1.30	190.50	101.00	3,484
Sept	179.10	180.25	177.50	180.10	+ .10	188.90	103.80	3,008
Nov	178.25	178.95	177.10	178.50	− .65	185.65	107.50	1,387
Jan85	178.50	179.05	178.00	179.00	− .40	183.60	109.00	1,639
Mar	178.50	179.00	178.50	178.75	− .35	182.70	118.50	1,124
May	179.00	179.00	178.50	178.65	− .35	181.50	151.00	168
July	177.25	177.25	177.25	178.50	....	181.00	155.00	156
Sept	178.25	178.50	178.25	178.50	....	181.00	171.50	12

Est vol 1,500; vol Wed 546; open int 11,042, +38.

SUGAR–WORLD (CSCE)–112,000 lbs.; cents per lb.

	Open	High	Low	Settle	Change	Lifetime High	Lifetime Low	Open Interest
July	5.72	5.88	5.70	5.88	+ .13	14.95	5.48	27,239
Sept	5.99	6.14	5.97	6.14	+ .14	14.93	5.80	3,829
Oct	6.17	6.35	6.16	6.35	+ .16	15.30	6.03	41,855
Jan85	6.77	6.90	6.77	6.85	+ .07	13.10	6.60	535
Mar	7.32	7.51	7.31	7.45	+ .09	13.60	7.19	12,433
May	7.59	7.76	7.57	7.71	+ .10	10.50	7.54	3,591
July	7.87	8.00	7.86	8.00	+ .12	9.95	7.86	1,646
Sept	8.20	8.20	8.20	8.26	+ .07	9.75	8.10	84
Oct	8.40	8.48	8.40	8.47	+ .07	9.05	8.30	67

Est vol 6,066; vol Wed 4,045; open int 91,289, +747.

SUGAR–DOMESTIC (CSCE)–112,000 lbs.; cents per lb.

	Open	High	Low	Settle	Change	Lifetime High	Lifetime Low	Open Interest
July	22.10	22.10	22.05	22.05	− .02	22.65	21.35	3,770
Sept	22.10	22.14	22.05	22.08	− .04	22.58	21.50	2,063
Nov	21.80	21.83	21.80	21.82	+ .02	22.19	21.65	2,399
Jan85	21.76	21.76	21.76	21.76	− .07	22.20	21.66	477
Mar	21.86	21.86	21.85	21.85	− .02	22.30	21.70	2,066
May	21.90	21.90	21.90	21.90	− .02	22.40	21.75	996
July	21.98	21.98	21.98	21.98	....	22.43	21.90	617

Est vol 438; vol Wed 215; open int 12,388, −36.

–METALS & PETROLEUM–

COPPER (CMX)–25,000 lbs.; cents per lb.

	Open	High	Low	Settle	Change	Lifetime High	Lifetime Low	Open Interest
June	63.25	63.25	63.25	63.35	− .15	72.10	63.25	1
July	63.80	64.20	63.35	63.95	− .20	89.80	62.35	39,985
Aug	....	....	....	64.65	− .20	....	....	0
Sept	65.25	65.55	64.70	65.35	− .20	90.80	63.75	21,530
Dec	67.40	67.60	66.80	67.45	− .15	92.70	65.70	13,212
Jan85	....	....	....	68.15	− .15	92.00	66.55	257
Mar	69.35	69.60	69.20	69.55	− .10	93.20	67.50	7,352
May	70.65	70.65	70.60	70.95	− .10	92.50	69.10	4,444
July	72.10	72.10	72.10	72.40	− .10	88.25	70.35	2,268
Sept	73.50	73.50	73.50	73.80	− .10	82.10	72.25	957
Dec	75.60	75.60	75.60	76.00	....	84.25	74.05	1,514
Jan86	....	....	....	76.75	....	84.20	70.00	56
Mar	....	....	....	78.30	+ .05	80.00	76.55	424

Est vol 9,000; vol Wed 9,747; open int 92,000, +451.

GOLD (CMX)–100 troy oz.; $ per troy oz.

	Open	High	Low	Settle	Change	Lifetime High	Lifetime Low	Open Interest
June	383.00	388.50	383.00	386.80	+ 2.30	580.00	370.00	8,281
July	387.00	391.00	387.00	390.10	+ 2.10	388.80	378.80	7
Aug	390.50	395.50	390.30	393.60	+ 2.00	588.00	377.00	42,102
Oct	399.00	403.50	399.00	401.70	+ 1.90	597.00	385.50	12,165
Dec	408.00	412.50	407.00	410.40	+ 2.00	608.00	386.80	20,184
Feb85	416.00	420.50	416.00	419.30	+ 2.00	522.00	402.50	22,028
Apr	426.00	429.50	425.80	428.30	+ 1.90	514.50	410.00	20,816
June	436.50	439.50	436.20	437.90	+ 1.80	510.00	415.50	13,960
Aug	447.00	447.00	447.00	447.90	+ 1.70	485.00	422.00	3,019
Oct	455.50	455.50	455.50	457.80	+ 1.60	493.00	434.00	703
Dec	466.50	470.00	466.50	468.40	+ 1.50	489.50	450.00	1,589
Feb86	....	....	....	478.70	+ 1.50	479.00	459.00	168
Apr	....	....	....	489.10	+ 1.40	....	....	0

Est vol 34,000; vol Wed 43,629; open int 145,022, +101.

GOLD (IMM)–100 troy oz.; $ per troy oz.

	Open	High	Low	Settle	Change	Lifetime High	Lifetime Low	Open Interest
June	383.00	386.20	383.00	386.20	+ 3.40	574.60	372.00	287
Sept	394.70	397.50	394.70	397.50	+ 3.60	436.00	386.00	27
Dec	406.50	409.50	406.50	409.50	+ 4.70	444.50	397.20	181

Est vol 25; vol Wed 211; open int 495, −61.

Source: Reprinted by permission of *The Wall Street Journal,*

TABLE 15–5   Price Quotes for Oat Contracts

(1)	Open	High	Low	Settle	Change	Lifetime high	Low	Open interest
(2) **Oats (CBT)—5,000 bu.; cents per bu.**								
July	188	188½	187	188½	+1½	226	166¼	2,017
Sept	183¾	184	182	182½	− ½	219	164¾	915
Dec	187½	187½	186	186¼	− ¾	193¼	168½	906
Mar 85	189¼	193¾	189¼	193¾	−1½	196½	181¾	267

Source: *Reprinted by permission of The Wall Street Journal.* © Dow Jones & Company, Inc., June 1, 1984, p. 25.

Across the top of the table we observe that we are given information on the open, high, low, settle (close), and change from the previous day's close as well as the lifetime high and low for that particular contract. The last column represents the open interest, or the number of actual contracts presently outstanding for that delivery month.

THE CASH MARKET AND THE FUTURES MARKET

Many commodity futures exchanges provide areas where buyers and sellers can negotiate cash (or spot) prices. The cash price is the actual dollar value paid for the immediate transfer of a commodity. Unlike a futures contract, there must be a transfer of the physical possession of the goods. Prices in the cash market are somewhat dependent on prices in the futures market. Thus, it is said that the futures markets (12 in the United States and 1 in Canada) provide an important service as a price discovery mechanism. By cataloging price trends in everything from corn to cattle, the producers, processors, and handlers of over 40 commodities are able to observe price trends in categories of interest.

THE FUTURES MARKET FOR FINANCIAL INSTRUMENTS

The major event in the commodities markets for the last decade has been the development of financial futures contracts. With the great volatility in the foreign exchange markets and in interest rates, corporate treasurers, investors, and others have felt a great need to hedge their positions. Financial futures also have an appeal to speculators because of their low margin requirements and wide swings in value.

Financial futures may be broken down into three major categories, currency futures, interest rate futures, and stock index futures (the latter is covered in Chapter 16). Trading in currency futures began in May of 1972 on the International Monetary Market (part of the Chicago Mercantile Exchange).

Interest rate futures started trading on the Chicago Board of Trade in October of 1975 with the GNMA certificate.[5] Trading in financial futures, regardless of whether they are currency or interest rate futures, is very similar to trading in traditional commodities, such as corn, wheat, copper, or pork bellies. There is a stipulated contract size, month of delivery, margin requirement, and so on. We will first look at currency futures and then shift our attention to interest rate futures.

CURRENCY FUTURES

These futures are generally available in eight different currencies. They include the following:

British pound	West German mark
Canadian dollar	French franc
Japanese yen	Mexican peso
Swiss franc	Dutch guilder

The futures market in currencies provides many of the same functions as the older and less formalized market in "foreign exchange" operated by banks and specialized brokers, who maintain communication networks throughout the world. In either case, one can speculate or hedge. The currency futures market, however, is different in that it provides standardized contracts and a strong secondary market.

Let's examine how the currency futures market works. Assume you wish to purchase a currency futures contract in Japanese yen. The standardized contract is 12.5 million yen. The value of the contract is quoted in cents per yen. Assume that you purchase a December futures contract in May, and the price on the contract is .4342 cents per yen. The total value of the contract is $54,275 (12.5 million yen × $.004342). The typical margin on a yen contract is $3,000.

We will assume that the yen strengthens relative to the dollar. This might happen because of decreasing U.S. interest rates, declining inflation in Japan, or any number of other reasons. Under these circumstances, the currency might rise to .4530 cents per yen (the yen is now equivalent to more cents than it was previously). The value of the contract has now risen to $56,625 (12.5 million × $.004530). This represents an increase in value of $2,350.

$$\begin{array}{r} \$56,625 \\ -54,275 \\ \hline \$\ 2,350 \end{array}$$

---

[5] A GNMA (Ginnie Mae) certificate represents an interest in a pool of federally insured mortgages. Actually, GNMA (the Government National Mortgage Association) buys a pool of mortgages from various lenders at a discount and then issues securities to the public against the mortgages. They are pass-through in nature in that the holder of a GNMA certificate receives the interest and principal payment on the mortgages on a monthly basis.

With an original margin requirement of $3,000, this represents a return of 78.3 percent.

$$\frac{\$2,350}{\$3,000} \times 100 = 78.3\%$$

On an annualized basis, it would even be higher. Of course, the contract could produce a loss if the yen weakens against the dollar as a result of higher interest rates in the United States or increasing inflation in Japan. With a normal margin maintenance requirement of $2,400, a $600 loss on the contract will call for additional margin beyond the original $3,000.

Corporate treasurers often try to hedge an exposed position in their foreign exchange dealings through the currency futures market. Assume a treasurer closes a deal today to receive payment in two months in Japanese yen. If the yen goes down relative to the dollar, he will have less value than he anticipated. One solution would be to sell a yen futures contract (go short). If the value of the yen goes down, he will make money on his futures contract that will offset the loss on the receipt of the Japanese yen in two months.

In Table 15–6, we see the typical size of contracts for four other foreign currencies that trade on the International Monetary Market (part of the Chicago Mercantile Exchange).

TABLE 15–6   Contracts in Currency Futures

Currency	Trading units	Size of contract based on mid-1984 prices
British pound	25,000	$35,000
Canadian dollar	100,000	77,250
Swiss franc	125,000	56,250
West German mark	125,000	46,300

INTEREST RATE FUTURES

Since the inception of the interest rate futures contract with GNMA certificates in October of 1975, the market has been greatly expanded to include Treasury bonds, Treasury bills, Treasury notes, commercial paper, certificates of deposits, and Eurodollars. There is almost unlimited potential for futures contracts on interest-related items.

Interest rate futures trade on a number of major exchanges, including the Chicago Board of Trade, the International Monetary Market of the Chicago Mercantile Exchange, the New York Futures Exchange, and the American Commodities Exchange. As we mentioned earlier, there is competition between Chicago and New York on interest rate futures. Among the most popularly traded contracts in the 1980s were Treasury bonds and GNMA certificates traded on the Chicago Board of Trade, and Treasury bills traded on the

International Monetary Market of the Chicago Mercantile Exchange. The New York Futures Exchange was coming on strong with their Treasury bond and certificates of deposit futures, and the American Commodities Exchange was also moving into various Treasury futures, such as Treasury bonds and Treasury bills.

Figure 15–3 shows examples of quotes on interest rate futures. Direct your attention to the second category, Treasury bonds (CBT), trading on the Chicago Board of Trade.

FIGURE 15–3   Examples of Price Quotes on Interest Rate Futures

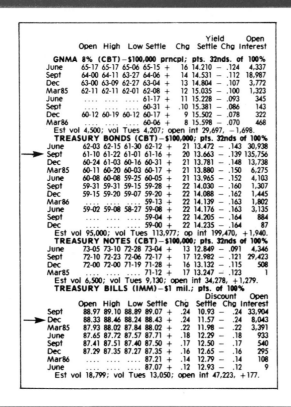

The bonds trade in units of $100,000, and the quotes are in percent of par taken to 32ds of a percentage point. Although it is not shown in this data, the bonds on which the futures are based are assumed to be new, 15-year instruments paying 8 percent interest. Since long-term rates tend to be above 8 percent, the quoted price is usually at a discount from $100,000. In the first column for the September contract for Treasury bonds, we see a price of 61–

10. This indicates a value of $61^{10}/_{32}$ percent of par. We thus show a contract value of $61,312.50 ($61^{10}/_{32} \times 100,000$). This represents the opening value. The entire line in Figure 15–3 would read as follows:

	Open	High	Low	Settle	Chg.	Yield Settle	Chg.	Open Interest
Sept	61–10	61–22	61–01	61–16	+20	13.663	−.139	135,756

We see the settle, or closing, price is 61–16, which represents a change (chg.) of $^{20}/_{32}$ from the close from the previous day. The reader should be aware that the close for the previous day is not necessarily the same as the open for the current day.[6] We also see what yield the settle (closing) price represents on a 15-year bond paying an 8 percent coupon rate. In this case, it is 13.663 percent, which is a decline in yield from the previous day of .139 percent. The decline in yield is consistent with the increase in settle price (and vice versa). Finally, we see there is an open interest of 135,756 indicating the number of contracts that are presently outstanding for September.

Assume we buy a September futures contract for 61–16 or $61,500 ($61^{16}/_{32} \times 100,000$). The margin requirement for this contract on the Chicago Board of Trade is $2,000 with a $1,600 margin maintenance requirement. In this case, it may be that we have bought the futures contract because we anticipate easier monetary policy by the Federal Reserve, which will trigger a decline in interest rates and an increase in bond prices. If interest rates decline by .3 percent (30 basis points), Treasury bond prices will increase by approximately $1^{30}/_{32}$.[7] On a $100,000 par value futures contract, this would represent a gain of $1,937.50 as indicated below.

$$\begin{array}{r} \$100,000 \\ \times \quad \underline{1^{30}/_{32}\% \ (1.9375\%)} \\ \$1,937.50 \end{array}$$

With a $2,000 initial margin, the $1,937.50 profit represents an attractive return. Note, however, that if interest rates go up by even a small amount, our Treasury bond futures contract value will fall, and there will be a margin call.

As is true of other commodities, when we trade in interest rate futures, we do not take actual title or possession of the commodity unless we fail to reverse our initial position. The contract merely represents a bet or hedge on the direction of future interest rates and bond prices.

Quotes on Treasury Bill Futures

One type of interest rate future that requires special attention is the Treasury bill future. Particular reference in this case is made to the 90-day, $1 million, T-bill futures contract that trades on the International Monetary Market of the

---

[6] A number of overnight events can cause the difference. In this case, we can assume the close for the previous day was 60–96 based on the change of +20.

[7] This is derived from a standard bond table and not explicitly calculated in their example.

Chicago Mercantile Exchange and is shown on the bottom portion of Figure 15–3 on page 447. We reproduce the second line below.

	Open	High	Low	Settle	Chg.	Yield Settle	Chg.	Open Interest
Dec	88.33	88.46	88.24	88.43	+.24	11.57	−.24	8,043

The items of particular interest are the settle price of 88.43 and the settle discount of 11.57 percent. Unlike other interest rate futures, such as Treasury bonds or GNMA certificates, we cannot simply multiply the settle price of 88.43 (percent) times par value of $1 million to get the value of the contract. Why? Because this Treasury bill represents a 90-day instrument, and the annual yield of 11.57 percent must be converted to a 90-day rate in order to determine value. We thus take the annual rate of 11.57 percent and multiply it by $90/360$ to get an equivalent 90-day yield of 2.89%.

$$11.57 \times \frac{90}{360} = 2.89\%$$

We then subtract this value from 100 percent to get the appropriate percentage to multiply times par value to get the value of the contract. For the $1 million Treasury bill, the actual converted price is:

$$(100\% - 2.89\%) \times \$1,000,000$$
$$97.11\% \times \$1,000,000 = \$971,100$$

Each time the yield on a Treasury bill changes by .01 percent ($1/100$ of 1 percent or 1 basis point), the price of the T-bill future will change by $25 as indicated in the two steps below:

$$.01\% \text{ of } \$1,000,000 = \$100$$

we convert this from an annual rate to a 90-day rate by multiplying by $90/360$.

$$\$100 \times 90/360 = \$25$$

Thus, if you buy a Treasury bill futures contract and interest rates on Treasury bills change by .50 percent (50 basis points), you will gain or lose $1,250.

$$\begin{aligned} &\$25 \text{ For each .01\% or basis points} \\ &\underline{\times\ 50 \text{ Basis points}} \\ &\$1,250 \end{aligned}$$

The initial margin requirement for a $1 million Treasury bill on the International Monetary Market of the Chicago Mercantile Exchange is only $1,500, with a $1,200 margin maintenance requirement. The daily trading limit is 50 basis points, so a $1,250 change in value is possible in one day.[8]

---

[8] The American Commodity Exchange and other markets have even smaller margin requirements and larger daily limits for price movements, so there is plenty of opportunity for action.

Hedging with Interest Rate Futures

Interest rate futures have opened up opportunities for hedging that can only be compared to the development of the traditional commodities market over a century ago. Consider the following potential hedges against interest rate risks.

a. A corporate treasurer is awaiting a new debt issue that will take place in 60 days. The underwriters are still putting the final details together. The great fear is that interest rates will rise between now and then. The treasurer could hedge his or her position in the futures market by selling a Treasury bond, Treasury bill, GNMA certificate, or other similar security short. If interest rates go up, the price to buy back the interest rate futures will go down, and a profit will be made on the short position. This will partially or fully offset the higher interest costs on the new debt issue.

b. A corporate treasurer is continually reissuing commercial paper at new interest rates or borrowing under a floating prime agreement at the bank. He or she fears that interest rates will go up and make a big dent in projected profits. By selling (going short) on commercial paper, certificates of deposit, or other interest rate futures, the corporate treasurer can make enough profit on interest rate futures if interest rates go up to compensate for the higher costs of money.

c. A mortgage banker has made a forward commitment to provide a loan at a set interest rate one month in the future. If interest rates go up, the resale value of the mortgage in the secondary market will go down. He or she can hedge the position by selling or going short on a GNMA certificate futures contract or other interest rate futures contract.

d. A pension fund manager has been receiving a steady return of 12.5 percent on his short-term portfolio in 90-day Treasury bills. He is afraid that interest rates will go down and he will have to adjust to receiving lower returns on the managed funds. His strategy might be to buy (go long) on a Treasury bill futures contract. If interest rates go down, he will make a profit on his futures contract that will partially or fully offset his decline in interest income. Of course, if he is heavily invested in long-term securities and fearful of an interest rate rise, a sell or short position that would provide profits on an interest rate rise would be advisable. This, of course, would offset part of the loss in the portfolio value due to increasing interest rates.

e. A commercial banker has most of his loans on a floating prime basis, meaning that the rate that he charges will change with the cost of funds. However, some of the loans have a fixed rate associated with them. If the cost of funds go up, the fixed-rate loans will become unprofitable. By selling or going short in interest rate futures, the danger of higher interest rates can be hedged away by the profits he will make on the interest rate futures. Similarly, a banker may make a commitment to pay a set amount of interest on certificates of deposit for the next six months. If interest rates go down, the banker may have to loan the funds at a lower rate than he is currently paying. If he buys a futures contract in certificates of

deposit, then lower interest rates will increase the value of the contract and provide a profit. This will offset the possible negative profitability spread described above.

An Actual Example

Assume an industrial corporation has a $10 million, 15-year bond to be issued in 60 days. Long-term rates for such an issue are currently 12.75 percent, and there is concern that interest rates will go up by ¼ percent by the time of the issue. The corporate treasurer has figured out that the extra ¼ percent would have a present value cost of $161,550 over the life of the issue (on a before-tax basis).

$10,000,000
 ¼%
───────
 $25,000
   6.462 Present value factor for 15 years at 13 percent
───────
 $161,550 Present value of futures costs

To establish a hedge position, he sells 154 Treasury bond futures short. We assume they are currently selling at 65 (65 percent of $100,000), equaling $65,000 each. The total value of the hedge would be $10,010,000. This is roughly the equivalent to the $10 million size of the corporate bond issue. If interest rates go up by ¼ percent, the profit on the Treasury bond futures contract (due to falling prices with a short position) will probably offset the present value of the increased cost of the corporate bond issue.

Of course, we do not suggest that both rates (on Treasury bonds and corporate bonds) would move exactly together. However, the general thrust of the example should be apparent. We are actually establishing a *cross-hedging* pattern by using one form of security (Treasury bonds) to hedge another form of security (corporate bonds). This is often necessary. Even when the same security is used, there may be differences in maturity dates or quality characteristics so that a perfect hedge is difficult to establish.

Many financial managers prefer partial hedges to complete hedges. They are willing to take away part of the risk but not all of it. Others prefer no hedge at all because it locks in their position. While a hedge ensures them against loss, it precludes the possibility of an abnormal gain.

Nevertheless, in a risk-averse financial market environment, most financial managers can gain by hedging their position as described in the many examples in this section. Companies such as Burlington Northern, Esmark, and Stauffer Chemical have established reputations for just such actions.[9] Others have not yet joined the movement because of a lack of appreciation or understanding of the highly innovative financial futures market. Much of this will change with the passage of time.

---

[9] "Hedging with Interest Rate Futures," *Business Week,* December 8, 1980, p. 96.

OPTIONS AS WELL AS FUTURES

In late 1982 many exchanges began offering options on financial instruments and commodities. For example, the Chicago Board Options Exchange began listing put and call options on Treasury bonds. Also, the American Stock Exchange started trading options on Treasury bills and Treasury notes, and the Philadelphia Exchange offered foreign currency options. The Chicago Board of Trade, the Chicago Mercantile Exchange and the Comex have also attached options to commodity plays. The relationship, similarities, and dissimilarities between option contracts and futures contracts is given much greater attention in the following chapter, Stock Index Futures and Options. For now it will suffice to say that the futures contract requires an initial margin, which can be parlayed into large profits or immediately wiped out, whereas an option requires the payment of an option premium, which represents the full extent of an option purchaser's liability.

SUMMARY

In this chapter we broke down the commodities future markets into traditional commodities (such as grains, livestock, and meat) and financial futures primarily in currencies and interest rates.

A commodities futures contract is an agreement that provides for the delivery of a specific amount of a commodity at a designated time in the future. It is not intended that the purchaser of a contract take actual possession of the goods, but rather that he or she reverse or close out the contract before delivery is due. The same is true for the seller.

Primary participants in the commodities market include both speculators and hedgers. We first examine speculators. A speculator buys a commodities contract (goes long) or sells a commodities contract (goes short) because he believes he can effectively anticipate the direction in which the market is going to move. Because of low margin (initial deposit) requirements of 5 to 10 percent, large profits or losses are possible with small price movements. If the market moves against someone who has a commodity contract, they may be asked to put up additional margin.

A hedger buys or sells a commodities futures contract to protect an underlying position he or she might have in the actual commodity. For example, a wheat farmer may sell (go short) on a futures contract in wheat to protect against a price decline. If prices go down, he can buy back his contract at a lower price than he sold it and record a profit on the transaction. This may offset any losses he incurs as a result of selling wheat at a lower price to its intended user. Of course, if the price goes up, he will lose on his futures contract but make up the difference on the actual sale of wheat. Millers or bakers who know they will have to purchase wheat in the future may buy (go long) on a futures contract. If the price goes up, they will make money on the contract, and this will offset the added production costs.

Many commodity futures exchanges provide areas where buyers and sellers can negotiate cash (or spot) prices. The cash price is the actual dollar paid for the immediate delivery of the goods. Near-term futures prices and cash prices tend to approximate each other.

Currency and interest rate futures represent important financial futures. Although these markets only came into existence in the 1970s, they have seen explosive growth. The contract on financial futures is very similar to that on basic, traditional commodities; only the items traded and units of measurement are different.

Currency futures relate to eight different currencies and enable the financial manager to hedge his position in foreign markets. There is also active participation by the speculators.

Interest rate futures cover Treasury bonds, Treasury bills, GNMA certificates, Treasury notes, commercial paper, and certificates of deposit. Many other items are on the drawing board. Interest rate futures generally trade in units of $100,000 or $1 million with extremely low margin requirements. There is a battle between the traditional commodity exchanges in Chicago and the New York Futures Exchange (part of the New York Stock Exchange) and the Amex Commodity Exchange (part of the American Stock Exchange) to see who will ultimately have a dominant position in the financial futures markets.

In the current environment of volatile interest rates, interest rate futures offer an excellent opportunity to hedge dangerous interest rate risks. Possible hedgers include corporate financial officers, pension fund managers, mortgage bankers, and commercial bankers. As sophistication and understanding in the use of these hedging techniques increase, the market in financial futures will continue to expand. In Chapter 16 we expand the discussion of futures to include stock index futures and options.

IMPORTANT WORDS AND CONCEPTS

Futures contract	**Spot market**
Commodity markets	**Currency futures**
Hedging	**Interest rates futures**
Margin requirement	**Settle price**
Margin maintenance	**Basis point**
requirement	**Cross hedge**
Inverse pyramiding	**Partial hedge**

DISCUSSION QUESTIONS

1. What is a futures contract?
2. Do you have to take delivery or deliver the commodity if you are a party to a futures contract?
3. Explain what hedging is.

4. Why is there substantial leverage in commodity investments?
5. What are the basic categories of items traded on the commodities exchanges?
6. What group has primary regulatory responsibility for the activities of the commodity exchanges?
7. How does the concept of margin on a commodities contract differ from that of margin on a stock purchase?
8. Indicate some factors that might influence the price of wheat in the commodities market.
9. What is meant by a daily trading limit on a commodities contract?
10. Refer to Figure 15–2, and explain the quotation for December corn on the Chicago Board of Trade (CBT).
11. How does the cash market differ from the futures market for commodities?
12. What are the three main categories of financial futures? Which two are discussed in this chapter?
13. How does the currency futures market differ from the foreign exchange market?
14. Describe the Treasury bonds that are part of the futures contract that trades on the Chicago Board of Trade (size of units, maturity, assumed initial interest rate).
15. If you purchase a Treasury bill futures contract and interest rates change by 25 basis points, how much does this represent in dollars?
16. How can using the financial futures markets for interest rates and foreign exchange help financial managers through hedging? Briefly explain and give one example.

PROBLEMS

1. You purchase a 5,000-bushel contract for corn at $3.20 per bushel with an initial margin requirement of 5 percent. The price goes up to $3.32 in one month. What is your percentage profit and the annualized gain?
2. Farmer Aggie Bryan anticipates taking 80,000 bushels of oats to the market in three months. The current cash price for oats is $1.88. He can sell a three-month futures contract for oats at $1.90. He decides to sell ten 5,000-bushel futures contracts at that price. Assume in three months, when Farmer Bryan takes the oats to market and also closes out the futures contracts (buys them back), the price of oats has tumbled to $1.77.
   a. What is his total loss in value over the three months on the actual oats he produced and took to market?
   b. How much did his hedge in the futures market generate in gains?
   c. What is his overall net loss considering the answer in a and the partial hedge in part b?
3. The Grain Miller's Corporation anticipates the need to purchase 60,000

bushels of wheat in six months to use in their products. The current cash price for wheat is $3.75 a bushel. A six-month futures contract for wheat can be purchased at $3.78.

a. Explain why Grain Miller's Corporation might need to purchase futures contracts to hedge their position.

b. To attempt to completely hedge their exposure, how many contracts will they need to purchase? (Consult Table 15–3 for the size of a contract.)

c. If the price of wheat ends up at $3.94 per bushel after six months, by how much will the cost of 60,000 bushels of wheat have gone up?

d. After the futures contracts are closed out (sold) at $3.94 also, what will be the gain on the futures contracts?

e. Considering the answers to parts c and d, what is their net position?

f. Given the number of wheat futures contracts they control, what is the most they can lose in the futures markets on any given day?

4. With a 5,000-bushel contract for $30,000, assume the margin requirement is $2,500 and maintenance margin is 80 percent of the margin requirement. How much would the price per bushel have to fall before additional margin is required?

5. If contracts are written on a 5,000-bushel basis requiring $2,000 of margin and you control 10 contracts, how much would the price per bushel have to change to generate enough profit to purchase an additional contract?

6. Referring to Problem 5, how many contracts would need to be controlled to generate enough profit for a new margin contract if the price changed by only 1 cent per bushel?

7. You purchase a futures contract in German marks for $45,000. The trading unit is 125,000 marks.

a. What is ratio of cents to marks in this contract? (Divide dollar contract size by the size of the trading unit.)

b. Assume you are required to put up 6 percent margin, and the mark increases by 4 cents (per mark). What will be your return as a percentage of margin?

8. Hartford Securities buys a $100,000 par value, March 1985 Treasury bond contract at the quoted settle price in Figure 15–3.

a. What is the dollar value of the contract?

b. With a $2,000 margin requirement, what is the margin requirement as a percent of the contract value?

c. Assume there is a $1,600 margin maintenance requirement. If an interest rate increase causes the bond to go down by .5 percent of par value, will Hartford be called upon to put up more margin?

d. Assume Hartford's investment is for six months. In order to have a 100 percent annualized return on the initial $2,000 margin, by what percent of par value must the bond increase to achieve this?

9. What is the value of the June 1985 Treasury bill contract in Figure 15–3?

Remember to convert settle yield (12.29 percent) from an annual basis to a 90-day basis as the first step in the calculation.

10. Assume a Treasury bill futures contract is up the limit for five straight days. What will be the dollar return to the investor?

11. The treasurer of Convex Corporation is going to bring a $5,000,000 issue to the market in 45 days. It will be a 30-year issue. The interest rate environment is highly volatile, and even though interest rates are currently 12¼ percent, there is a fear that interest rates will be up to 13 percent by the time the bonds get to the market.

    a. If interest rates go up by ¾ percent, what is the present value of the extra interest this increase will cost the corporation? Use a 13 percent discount rate and disregard tax considerations.

    b. Assume the corporation is going to short September 1984 Treasury bonds as quoted in Figure 15–3. Based on the settle price, how many contracts must they sell to equal the $5,000,000 exposed position? Round to the nearest whole number.

    c. Based on your answer in b, if Treasury bond prices increase by 2.8 percent of par value in each contract in response to a ½ percent decline in interest rates over the next 45 days, what will be the total loss on the futures contracts?

12. Should the treasurer of Convex Corporation feel that he has failed in his tasks if the circumstance in part c of Question 11 takes place?

SELECTED REFERENCES

Angell, George. *Winning in the Commodities Market.* New York: Doubleday & Co., 1979.

Bacon, Peter W., and Richard Williams. "Interest Rate Futures Trading: New Tool for the Financial Manager." *Financial Management,* Spring 1976, pp. 32–38.

Bear, Robert M. "Margin Levels and the Behavior of Futures Prices." *Journal of Financial and Quantitative Analysis,* September 1972, pp. 1907–30.

Biger, Nahum, and John Hull. "The Valuation of Currency Options." *Financial Management,* Spring 1983, pp. 24–28.

Dusak, Katherine. "Futures Trading and Investor Returns: An Investigation of Commodity Market Risk Premiums." *Journal of Political Economy,* November–December 1973, pp. 1387–1406.

Harlow, Charles V., and Richard J. Teweles. "Commodities and Securities Compared." *Financial Analysts Journal,* September–October 1972, pp. 64–70.

"Hedging with Interest Rate Futures." *Business Week,* December 8, 1980, p. 96.

Peterson, Richard L. "Investor Preferences for Futures Straddler." *Journal of Financial and Quantitative Analysis,* March 1977, pp. 105–20.

Powers, Mark J. "Does Futures Trading Reduce Price Fluctuations in the Cash Markets?" *American Economic Review,* June 1970, pp. 460–64.

Robichek, Alexander; Richard Cohn; and John Pringle. "Returns on Alternative Investment Media and Implications for Portfolio Construction." *Journal of Business,* July 1972, pp. 427–43.

Senchach, Andrew J., Jr., and Donald M. Heep. "Auction Profits in the Treasury Bill Market." *Financial Management,* Summer 1975, pp. 45–52.

Shellenbarger, Susan. "Boom in Financial Futures Trading Transforms Commodities Markets." *The Wall Street Journal,* March 23, 1981, p. 25.

"Speculating on Inflation: Futures Trading in Interest Rates, Foreign Currencies and Precious Metals." Merrill Lynch, Pierce, Fenner & Smith, July 1979.

Stevenson, Richard A., and Robert M. Bear. "Commodity Futures: Trends or Random Walks." *Journal of Finance,* March 1970, pp. 65–82.

Telser, Lester G., and Harlow N. Higinbotham. "Organized Futures Markets: Costs and Benefits." *Journal of Political Economy,* October 1977, pp. 969–1000.

"The Zooming Futures Market." *Business Week,* June 11, 1979, pp. 62–73.

Chapter 16

STOCK INDEX FUTURES AND OPTIONS

In February of 1982, the Kansas City Board of Trade began trading futures on a stock index, the Value Line Index. This event ushered in a whole new era of futures and options trading.

A future or option on an index allows the investor to participate in the movement of an entire index rather than an individual security. There are currently futures and options relating to such indexes as the Standard & Poor's 500 Stock Index, the New York Stock Exchange Composite Index, the American Stock Exchange Index, the Value Line Index, and many other old and new market measures.[1]

If an investor purchases a futures contract on a stock market index, he puts down the required margin, and gains or losses on the transaction based on the movement of the index. For example, an investor may purchase a futures contract on the Standard & Poor's 500 Stock Index with $6,000 in margin. The actual contract value is based on the index value times 500. If the S&P 500 Futures Index were at 160, the initial contract value would be $80,000 (500 × 160). If the index went up or down by 2 points, the investor would gain or lose $1,000 (500 × ±2). Since the initial investment is only $6,000 in margin, we see a fairly large percentage gain or loss for a small movement in the index (16.7% = $1,000/$6,000).

An "option" on the Standard & Poor's 500 Stock Index can also be purchased. Such an option is traded on the Chicago Board Options Exchange. If the S&P 500 Stock Index were 161 at a given point in time, an option to purchase the index at a strike price of 160, may carry a premium (price) of $3. The premium is multiplied by 100 to get a total value for the option of $300 (100 × $3). If the Standard & Poor's 500 Stock Index closed out at 167 at expiration, the premium value will be $7 and a profit of $400 will be achieved.

Final value	100 × $7 = $700
Purchase price	100 × $3 = $300
Profit	$400

As we go further into the chapter, you will see there are not only futures and options on stock market indexes, but also "options to purchase futures" on stock market indexes.

Stock index futures have grown faster than any new futures trading outlet in history. In their first six months of trading, the average daily volume was 4.5 times as great as the volume on Treasury bill and Treasury bond futures during a comparable period of infancy. Volume figures on the Standard & Poor's 500 Futures Index are presented in Figure 16–1. While stock index futures in general only began trading in 1982, they now make up over 10 percent of the total volume on the 135-year-old U.S. commodity futures markets.[2] The under-

---

[1] To date, there is no contract on the Dow Jones Industrial Average because Dow Jones & Company has resisted having their venerable index used for this purpose.

[2] This market is composed of traditional commodities futures, financial futures, and stock index futures. It should be noted that the term *financial futures* is sometimes considered to be a very broad term, covering currency, interest rate, and stock index futures.

FIGURE 16–1

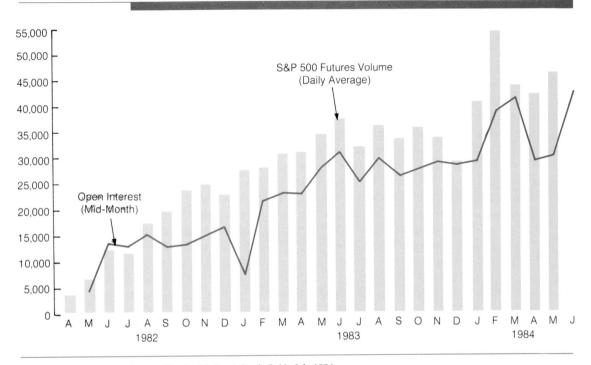

Source: *Standard & Poor's Stock Guide,* July 1984.

lying value of the stocks traded in index futures often equals the entire volume on the New York Stock Exchange on a daily basis. Stock index options are enjoying a similar popularity. In time, they may equal or exceed stock index futures in investor acceptance.

Before we go into a deeper discussion of futures and options on stock market indexes, the student should have read Chapter 13 on put and call options and Chapter 15 on Commodities and Financial Futures.

TRADING STOCK INDEX FUTURES

As indicated in Table 16–1, there are four key stock index futures contracts. The S&P (Standard & Poor's) 500 Futures Index traded on the Chicago Mercantile Exchange (CME), the S&P 100 Futures Index traded on the same exchange, the NYSE (New York Stock Exchange) Composite Futures traded on the New York Futures Exchange (NYFE),[3] and the KC Value Line Futures traded on the Kansas City Board of Trade.

―――――――――
[3] The NYFE is a division of the New York Stock Exchange.

TABLE 16-1   Stock Index Futures (April 19, 1984, prices)

```
                                      Lifetime    Open
                Open High Low Settle Change High Low Interest

   S&P 500 FUTURES INDEX (CME) 500 Times Index
 June   158.45 159.85 158.40 159.20 +  .10 177.10 155.00 27,779
 Sept   160.90 162.15 160.85 161.55 +  .10 178.15 156.80  1,689
 Dec    163.30 164.15 163.15 163.95 +  .30 179.20 158.60    155
 Mar85 165.90 165.90 164.85 165.70 +  .35 180.25 160.50     19
 June   167.60 167.60 166.50 167.40 +  .35 180.70 161.75      6
 Sept   169.30 169.30 168.25 169.70 +  .35 171.75 165.70      5
   Est vol 33,741; vol Wed 43,480; open int 29,653, +159.
       S&P 500 STOCK INDEX (Prelim)
       157.30 158.02 157.10 158.02 +  .12
   S&P 100 FUTURES INDEX (CME) 200 Times Index
 Apr    154.80 155.40 154.60 155.78 +  .78 158.90 151.00    841
 May    155.30 155.60 155.25 155.95 +  .40 158.65 153.10      1
 June   155.70 157.00 155.55 156.60 +  .40 177.80 152.20  2,473
 July    ...   ...    ...   157.10 +  .40 157.90 154.05      1
 Sept    ...   ...    ...   158.85 +  .30 162.00 154.30      6
   Est vol 399; vol Wed 755; open int 3,322, -224.
       S&P 100 STOCK INDEX (Prelim)
       154.60 155.78 154.35 155.78 +  .58  ...    ...

   NYSE COMPOSITE FUTURES (NYFE) 500 Times Index
 June    91.45  92.15  91.30  91.80 +  .15 103.00  82.30  6,419
 Sept    92.60  93.25  92.60  93.00 +  .15 103.10  89.25    999
 Dec     93.75  93.90  93.75  94.15 +  .15 103.55  91.35    637
 Mar85   94.90  95.10  94.90  95.30 +   15 103.80  93.00    208
 June    96.05  96.05  96.05  96.45 +  .15 105.00  94.25     65
 Sept    97.20  97 20  97.20  97.60 +  .15  99.00  96.00     14
   Est vol 8,299; vol Wed 13,794; open int 8,342, +277.
       NYSE COMPOSITE STOCK INDEX
       90.83  90.92  90.44  90.89 +  .06
   KC VALUE LINE FUTURES (KC) 500 Times Index
 June   179.60 181.10 179.35 180.45 +  .60 212.00 176.15  3,442
 Sept   181.70 183.40 181.70 182.80 +  .80 213.50 178.45     99
 Dec     ...   ...    ...   185.10 +  .80 210.00 182.20      4
   Est vol 2,825; vol Wed 3,422; open int 3,545, -88.
       KC VALUE LINE COMPOSITE STOCK INDEX
       179.05 179.05 178.54 179.02 +  .04
```

You will note in Table 16-1 that the title line for each contract (such as S&P 500 Futures Index) indicates an appropriate multiple times the index. For example, 500 times the index for the S&P 500, NYSE Composite Futures, and KC Value Line Futures. For the S&P 100 Futures Index, the multiplier is 200 times. Looking at the June settle prices in each of the four indexes, we see the value of the contracts in Table 16-2.

TABLE 16-2   Value of Contracts

	June settle price	*Multiplier*	*Contract value*
S&P 500 Futures	159.20	500	$79,600
S&P 100 Futures	156.60	200	31,320
NYSE Composite Futures	91.80	500	45,900
KC Value Line Futures	180.45	500	90,225

With a margin of from 5 to 10 percent of the value of the contract, the investor can establish a position. If the investor thinks the market is going up, he will purchase a futures contract. If he thinks the market is going down, he will sell a futures contract and hope that the market will decline so that the contract can be closed out (repurchased) at a lower value than the sales price. Selling futures contracts can also be used to hedge a large stock portfolio. If the market goes down, what you lose on your portfolio you recoup in your futures contract.

In the example in Table 16–2, the investor has four indexes from which to choose. (Stock market indexes were covered in Chapter 3). You should be aware that the S&P 500, S&P 100, and NYSE indexes are heavily influenced by large corporations (IBM, Exxon, etc.). The indexes are weighted in proportion to the total market values of the firms in the index. The larger the firm, the more heavily it is weighted. The Value Line Index is an equal-weighted index, which means that IBM has no greater price influence than a smaller firm trading on the American Stock Exchange or over-the-counter.

Also note the relative size of the contracts in Table 16–2. If you wish to deal in smaller values, you may prefer the S&P 100 contract. If you are attempting to hedge a large dollar portfolio, however, your preference might be for the S&P 500 contract or the KC Value Line contract (which you might use in multiples).

We shall direct our attention for now to the S&P 500 Futures Index contract (though the same basic principles would apply to other contracts). Part of the material from Table 16–1 that pertains to the S&P 500 Futures Index is reproduced in Table 16–3 so that we can examine a number of key features related to the contract.

TABLE 16–3   S&P 500 Futures Index (CME) 500 Times Index (April 19, 1984, prices)

Contract month	Open	High	Low	Settle	Change
June 84	158.45	159.85	158.40	159.20	+.10
Sept	160.90	162.15	160.85	161.55	+.10
Dec	163.30	164.15	163.15	163.95	+.30
March 85	165.90	165.90	164.85	165.70	+.35
June	167.60	167.60	166.50	167.40	+.35
Sept	169.30	169.30	168.25	169.70	+.35

Value of S&P 500 Stock Index (April 19, 1984) = 158.02

Trading Cycle

The trading cycle is made up of the four months of June, September, December, and March. The last day of trading for a contract is the third Thursday of the ending month. The reader will observe that the contracts in Table 16–3 extend out nearly a year and a half in the future.

Margin Requirement

As previously mentioned, the basic margin requirement for buying or selling an S&P 500 Futures Index contract is $6,000. Based on the June 1984 contract settle value of $79,600 (found in Table 16–2), this represents a margin requirement of 7.54 percent ($6,000 ÷ $79,600). There is also a margin maintenance requirement of $2,500. Thus if the initial margin or equity in the account falls to this level, the investor will be required to supply sufficient cash or securities to bring the account back up to the $6,000 level. Since the contract trades at 500 times the index, a decline of 7 points in the S&P contract value would cause a loss of $3,500. In this instance, the margin position would be reduced from $6,000 to $2,500, and the investor would be called upon to supply $3,500 in funds to bring the margin up to the initial $6,000 balance.

Actually, if the investor can prove that he is hedging a long position, the margin requirement will be less. For example, if an investor owns a portfolio of stocks that roughly equates the value of the index futures contract ($79,600 in this case), the initial margin requirement is only $2,500 and the margin maintenance requirement is $1,500. Since a hedged position is not as risky as a speculative position, less margin is required. Of course, it is sometimes difficult to prove that a truly hedged position is in place.[4]

Minimum Price Change

The minimum price change for the S&P 500 Futures Index contract is .05. Thus if the June futures contract is at 159.20, the smallest possible price move would be down to 159.15 or up to 159.25. Since the index is multiplied times 500 to determine value, an index movement of .05 represents $25 (500 × .05 = $25). Thus the smallest possible price change is $25. Unlike many traditional commodities, there is no limit to daily price movements on the S&P Futures Index contract (or any other of the stock index futures contracts).

Cash Settlement

In traditional commodity futures markets, the potential for physical delivery exists. One who is trading in wheat or Treasury bonds could actually decide to deliver the commodity to close out the contract. As discussed in Chapter 15, this only happens a very small percentage of the time, but it is possible. The stock index futures market, on the other hand, is purely a cash settlement market. There is never the implied potential for future delivery of the Standard & Poor's 500 Stock Index. An investor simply closes out (or reverses) his position prior to the settlement date. If he does not, his account is automati-

---

[4] For an investor initiating a spread position (buying and selling comparable but somewhat different contracts at the same time), the margin requirement is even lower ($400 initial, $200 maintenance).

cally credited with his gains or debited with his losses and the transaction is completed.[5]

One of the advantages of a cash settlement arrangement is that it makes it impossible for a "short squeeze" to develop. A short squeeze takes place when one attempts to corner a market in a commodity, such as silver, so that it is not possible for those who have short positions to make physical delivery. Clearly, with a cash settlement position, this can never happen.

Basis

The term *basis* represents the difference between the stock index futures price and the value of the actual underlying index.[6] We can now turn back to Table 16–3 to see a numerical example of basis. On April 19, 1984, the S&P 500 Futures contract for June was quoted at a settle (closing) price of 159.20 (2d item from the right in the first row). The actual S&P 500 Stock Index, as shown at the bottom of Table 16–3, closed at 158.02. The basis, or difference, between the futures price and the actual underlying index was 1.18.

Stock index futures price	159.20
Actual underlying index	158.02
Basis	1.18

Moving to the December 1984 contract in Table 16–3, the basis is the difference between the December contract settle value of 163.95 and the value of the underlying index which, of course, is still 158.02. The difference is 5.93. For the data in Table 16–3, the basis indicates a premium is being paid over the actual underlying index value and, furthermore, the premium expands with the passage of time. This is generally thought to be a positive sign. If the index futures price is below the actual underlying index, there is a negative basis.

For an excellent discussion of the ability of stock index futures to forecast the actual underlying index, the reader may wish to consult an article by Zeckhauser and Niederhoffer in the January–February 1983 issue of the *Financial Analysts Journal*.[7] A part of their thesis is that futures contracts move instantaneously to reflect market conditions, whereas the actual underlying index moves more slowly. If the market makes an important move, some of the stocks that are part of the actual underlying index will not yet have traded. Thus, initial, significant, and potentially predictive information may be found in the futures market quotes.

Also, at times, futures or options markets stay open later or begin trading earlier than the actual underlying stock markets. For example, stock futures

---

[5] Actually the account is adjusted daily to reflect the gains and losses. This is known as marking the customer's position to market.

[6] The same concept can be applied to other types of futures contracts.

[7] Richard Zeckhauser and Victor Niederhoffer, "The Performance of Market Index Futures Contracts," *Financial Analysts Journal*, January–February 1983, pp. 59–65.

trade for three minutes after the Federal Reserve releases money supply data at 4:12 P.M. Eastern time. The stock market has already closed at 4 P.M. Eastern time. Market watchers pay particular attention to what happens in the futures market in anticipation of what might happen in the stock market the next day. Also, in July of 1984, the Chicago Board of Trade began trading options on the American Exchange Major Market Index 15 minutes before the actual stock market opened.[8]

Overall Features

Many of the important features related to stock index futures on the various exchanges are presented in Table 16–4. This table can serve as a ready reference guide to trading commodities in various markets.

TABLE 16–4　Specifications for Stock Index Futures Contracts

NYSE Composite Index

Exchange	Trading hours	Index	Trading symbol	Contract size and value	Contract months
New York Futures Exchange (NYFE) of the New York Stock Exchange	10:00 AM to 4:15 PM (NYT)*	Total Value of NYSE Market: 1505 listed common stocks, weighted to reflect market value of issues	YX	$500 X the NYSE Composite Index	March, June, September, December

S&P 500 Index

Index and Options Market (IOM) of Chicago Mercantile Exchange (CME)	10:00 AM to 4:15 PM (NYT)*	Value of 500 selected stocks traded on NYSE, AMEX and OTC, weighted to reflect market value of issues	SP	$500 X the S&P 500 Index	March, June, September, December

Value Line Index

Kansas City Board of Trade (KCBT)	10:00 AM to 4:15 PM (NYT)*	Equally weighted average of 1683 NYSE, AMEX, OTC and Regional stock prices expressed in index form	KV	$500 X the VLA Index	March, June, September, December

* NYT = New York time.

---

[8] A brief description of this index is given in the stock index options section of this chapter.

USE OF STOCK INDEX FUTURES

There are a number of actual and potential users of stock index futures. As is true of most commodity futures contracts, the motivation may be either speculation or the opportunity to hedge.

Speculation

The speculator may use stock index futures in an attempt to profit from major movements in the market. He or she may have developed a conviction about the next move in the market through utilizing fundamental or technical analysis. For example, those who utilize fundamental analysis may determine that P/E ratios are at a 10-year low or that earnings performance should be extremely good in the next two quarters, so they wish to bet on the market moving upward. Market technicians might observe that a resistance or support position in the market is being penetrated, and that it is time to take a position based on the anticipated consequences of that penetration.

While the market participant could put his or her money in individual stocks, it might be more efficient and less time-consuming to simply invest in stock index futures. In buying futures on the S&P 500 Index, you are capturing the performance of 500 securities, with the New York Stock Exchange Index over 1,500 securities, and with the Value Line Index approximately 1,700 securities.

As discussed in Chapter 1, there are two types of risks associated with investments: systematic, or market-related, risks and unsystematic, or firm-related, risks. Since only systematic risk is assumed to be rewarded in an efficient capital market environment (unsystematic risk can be diversified away), the investor may only wish to be exposed to systematic risk. Stock index futures represent an efficient approach to only taking systematic, market-related risk.

Another advantage of stock index futures is that there is less manipulative action and insider trading than with individual securities. While it is possible (though not legal) for "informed" insider trading to cause an individual stock to move dramatically in the short-term, such activity is not as likely for an entire index. This advantage, however, should not be overstated. Trading activity on the S&P 100 Index did come under scrutiny of the major exchanges in April of 1984.[9]

Stock index futures also offer maximum leverage potential. As previously indicated, the margin is only 5 to 10 percent of the investment that is being controlled. An $80,000 S&P index futures contract can be established for $6,000 in margin, and there is no interest on the balance.[10] If you were invest-

---

[9] "CBOE, Big Board Join to Formally Probe Unusual Trading in Stock-Index Option," *The Wall Street Journal,* April 26, 1984, p. 3.

[10] As mentioned in Chapter 15, margin on futures contracts merely represents good-faith money and there is never any interest on the balance.

ing $80,000 in actual stocks through margin, you would have to put up a minimum of $40,000 (50%) in margin and pay interest on the balance. Also, the commissions on a stock index futures contract are miniscule in comparison to commissions on securities of comparable value.

One of the key questions an investor must consider is the relative volatility of the various indexes. This will give him some feel for the profit or wipeout potential for a given investment. In Table 16–5, you can observe the mean (average) daily price movements on the Standard & Poor's 500 Stock Index over a number of years. The mean appears to be approximately .50 (½ of a point) per day. Since stock index futures contracts trade in multiples of 500, a .50 movement would lead to a profit or loss of $250. With a margin requirement of $6,000, that's a fairly good daily move on your money. By contrast, if $6,000 were invested in a certificate of deposit at a 10 percent annualized return, only $1.67 in interest would accrue on a daily basis. The difference here, of course, is that the $250 related to the index may be up or down, whereas the $1.67 is only up.

TABLE 16–5   Absolute Values of Daily Changes* in the S&P 500 Stock Index (by year)

Year	Mean	Maximum
1968	.32	1.71
1969	.37	1.90
1970	.44	3.48
1971	.35	1.73
1972	.36	2.26
1973	.65	3.07
1974	.69	3.27
1975	.54	2.14
1976	.47	1.60
1977	.37	1.72
1978	.47	3.70
1979	.41	3.25
1980	.74	3.63
1981	.64	3.24
1982†	.59	3.18

* Daily changes are defined as the difference between the closing price for the S&P 500 Index on one day and the closing price on the next day.
† Through March 31, 1982.
Source: *Inside S&P 500 Stock Index Futures* (Chicago: Index and Option Market Division of Chicago Mercantile Exchange, 1983).

As further indicated in the last column of Table 16–5, the maximum (largest) *daily* price change taking place in any given year is in the 2 to 3.5 point range, indicating maximum potential daily moves of $1,000 to $1,750 (2 × 500 to 3.5 times 500).

The reader should be aware that the price moves reported in Table 16–5 relate to the actual underlying index rather than to the index futures contract. Nevertheless, one tends to move parallel to the other, so the approximations are reasonably valid.

A more detailed presentation of movements in the major indexes can be seen in Figure 16–2. Panel (a) shows price changes for the S&P 500 Index, Panel (b) for the Value Line Index, and Panel (c) for the NYSE Composite Index. Each line represents the high and low for a month with the dot along the middle representing the closing price for that period. For example, as indicated in Panel (a), the S&P 500 in January of 1978 (first observation on the graph) had a high of approximately 94, a low of approximately 88½ and a close of 89. You should note that the year is set at the middle of the time period rather than at the beginning.

Let's examine the consequences of some of the price movements in Figure 16–2. In looking at the S&P 500 Index in Panel (a), for 1982, we see the index was as low as 102 in mid-1982 and as high as 143 in late 1982. Assuming the price of the index futures contract parallels that of the underlying index, a

FIGURE 16–2   Movements in Stock Market Indexes

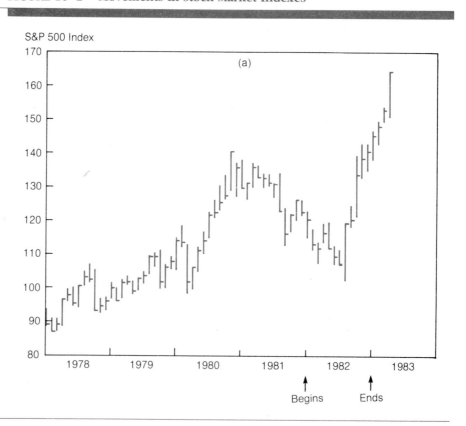

FIGURE 16–2 (*concluded*)

Value Line Index

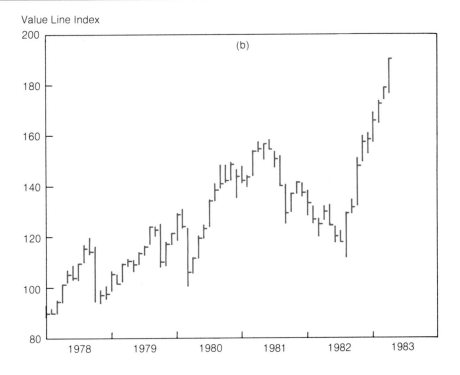

(b)

NYSE Composite Index

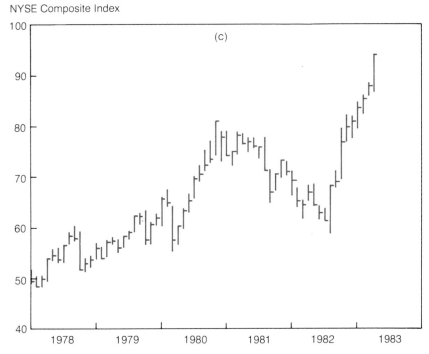

(c)

Source: These charts are reprinted from *The Merrill Lynch Guide to Stock Index Futures* by permission of Merrill Lynch, Pierce, Fenner & Smith Incorporated. © Copyright 1983 Merrill Lynch, Pierce, Fenner & Smith Incorporated.

41 point increase would translate into a $20,500 gain ($41 \times 500$). On an initial margin of $6,000, this represents a 342 percent gain ($20,500/$6,000). If you had merely held a portfolio of stocks that performed as well as the S&P 500 Index, your return would be 40.2 percent (a gain of 41 on a base value of 102). The gain on the index futures was over eight times greater.

As is true of all leveraged investments, this is a two-edged sword. You may recall from our earlier discussion that if your margin declines from $6,000 to $2,500 on an S&P index futures contract, you will be required to put up more margin to cover your position. This $3,500 decline in margin would occur if the value of your contract went down by seven points (500×7). The call for more margin puts tremendous pressure on the investor. One must decide whether to liquidate a position and close out a $3,500 loss or put up an additional $3,500 in cash (which could possibly generate another $3,500 loss). In once again examining Panel (a) of Figure 16–2, you can see many time periods where seven-point declines were commonplace.

The investment strategy we have discussed up to this point was in anticipation of an upward market. Quite obviously, you can also speculate that the market will go down. You simply sell a contract with the anticipation of repurchasing it at a lower price at a later point in time. There are similar margin requirements, and gains come from a declining market and losses from an increasing market. If the index futures price goes up by seven points, you will be called upon to put up more margin.

Hedging

Up to now our discussion of stock index futures has mainly related to speculating (or anticipating the next major move in the market). Perhaps the most important use of stock index futures is for hedging purposes. One who has a large diversified portfolio may feel the market is about to decline. A portfolio manager who suffers a 20 percent decline in his or her portfolio actually requires a 25 percent gain from the newly lower base just to break even.

A portfolio manager faced with the belief that a declining market is imminent may be inclined to sell off part or all of the portfolio.[11] The question becomes, is this realistic? First of all, there are large transaction costs associated with selling off part or all of a portfolio and then repurchasing it at a later point in time. Secondly, it may be difficult to liquidate a position in certain securities that are thinly traded. For example, a mutual fund or pension fund that tries to sell 10,000 shares of a small over-the-counter stock may initially find a price quote of $25, but only be able to close out its relatively large position at $23.50. A $15,000 loss would be suffered. Furthermore, there may be the same type of problem in reacquiring the stock after the overall market decline is over. This problem could be multiplied by 25 or 50 times, depending on the number of securities in the portfolio. Though larger, more liquid,

---

[11] While the authors are not necessarily recommending this as a prudent strategy, it is often a way of life among money managers.

holdings would be easier to trade there are still significant transactions costs involved.

A more easily executed defensive strategy would be to sell one or more stock index futures as a hedge against the portfolio. If the stock market does go down, the loss on the portfolio will be partially or fully offset by the profit on the stock index futures contract(s) because they are bought back at a lower price than the initial sales price.

As an example, assume a corporate pension fund has $20,000,000 in stock holdings. The investment committee for the fund is very bearish in its outlook. There is a fear that the overall market could go down by 20 percent in the next few months and a $4,000,000 loss would be suffered. The pension fund decides to fully hedge its position.

The fund is going to use S&P Index futures for the hedge. We shall assume the futures can be sold for 162, with a settlement date in three months. Before the number of contracts for execution is determined, the portfolio manager must consider the relative volatility of his portfolio. If the portfolio is more volatile than the market, this must be factored into the decision-making process. As discussed in Chapter 1, the beta coefficient indicates how volatile a stock is relative to the market. If a stock has a beta of 1.20, it is 20 percent more volatile than the market (or market index). We shall assume the $20,000,000 portfolio discussed above has a weighted average beta of 1.15 (that is, the portfolio is 15 percent more volatile than the market).

In order to determine the number of contracts necessary to hedge the position, we use the following formula:

$$\frac{\$ \text{ Value of portfolio}}{\$ \text{ Value of contract}^{12}} \times \frac{\text{Weighted beta}}{\text{of portfolio}} = \frac{\text{Number of}}{\text{contracts}} \qquad (16\text{--}1)$$

In the example under discussion, we would show:

$$\frac{\$20,000,000}{162 \times 500} \times 1.15 = \frac{\text{Number of}}{\text{contracts}}$$

In the first term, the numerator is the size of the portfolio being hedged. The denominator is the size of each contract. It is found by multiplying the S&P futures contract value of 162 by 500. The first term is then multiplied by the beta value of 1.15. The answer works out as:

$$\frac{\$20,000,000}{\$81,000} \times 1.15 = 246.91 \times 1.15 = 284 \text{ contracts}$$

The portfolio can be effectively hedged with 284 contracts.

Assume the market does go down, but only by 10 percent instead of the 20 percent originally anticipated. Let's demonstrate that the hedge has worked. Since the portfolio has a beta of 1.15, its decline would be 11.5 percent (10 percent × 1.15). With a $20,000,000 portfolio, the loss would be

_____

[12] Based on the particular contract being analyzed.

$2,300,000. To offset this loss, we will have a gain on 284 contracts. The gain is shown as follows:

S&P Index futures contract (sales price)	= 162.0
Decline in price on the futures contract[13] (10% × 162)	16.2
Ending value (purchase price)	= 145.8

The 16.2 point decline on the index futures indicates the profit made on each contract. They were sold for 162.0 and repurchased for 145.8. With 284 contracts, the profit on the stock index futures contracts comes out as $2,300,400.

Profit per contract (16.2 × 500) =	$8,100
Number of contracts	284
Total profit	= $2,300,400

The gain of $2,300,400 on the stock index futures contracts offsets the loss of $2,300,000 on the portfolio. The difference of $400 between the two values represents a rounding procedure. Actually executing a perfect hedge may be further complicated by a number of other factors such as the lack of an appropriate index to match against the portfolio and the change in basis over time. Also, the portfolio may not move exactly in accordance with the beta. There are no doubt many real-world factors that can complicate any hedge.

While a stock index futures hedge offers the advantage of protecting against losses, it, of course, takes away the upside potential. If the market goes up by 10 percent instead of down, the gain on the portfolio may be wiped out by the loss on the stock index futures contracts. The investor could be forced to buy back the futures for 10 percent more than the selling price. Because some portfolio managers are afraid of losing all their upside potential in a hedged position, they may only wish to hedge a fourth or a half of their position.

Other uses of hedging.   There are a number of other uses of hedging with stock index futures besides protecting the position of a long-term investment portfolio. These include:

Underwriter hedge.   As described in Chapter 14, the investment banker or underwriter has a risk exposure from buying stock from the issuing corporation with the intention of reselling it in the public markets. If there is weakness during the distribution period, the potential resale price could fall below the purchase price, and the underwriter's profit would be wiped out. In order to protect against this market risk, the underwriter could sell stock index futures contracts. If the market goes down, presumably the loss on the stock will be compensated for by the gain on the stock index futures contract as a result of

---

[13] Note that the futures contract is assumed to move on a one-to-one basis with the market. The actual relationship may not be this precise.

being able to repurchase it at a lower price. This, of course is not a perfect hedge. It is entirely possible that the stock could go down while the market is going up, and losses on both the stock and stock index futures contract would take place (writing options directly against the stock might be more efficient, but in many cases such options are not available).

Specialist or dealer hedge.   As indicated in Chapter 2, a specialist on an exchange or a dealer in the over-the-counter market buys and sells stocks for his own inventory for temporary holding. He may, at times, assume a larger temporary holding than desired, with all the risks associated with that exposure. Stock index futures can reduce the market (or systematic) risk, although the futures can not reduce the specific risk associated with a security.

Retirement or estate hedge.   As we move into the next two or three decades, large retirement funds will be accumulated from voluntary retirement plans. A retirement plan participant who has accumulated a large sum in an equity fund may feel a need to hedge his or her position in certain time periods in the economy (where liquidation is either not legal or possible). A futures contract may provide that hedge. Also, one with responsibility for an estate may be locked into a portfolio during the period of probate (validation of the will process), and wish to hedge his or her position with a stock index futures contract.

Tax hedge.   An investor may have accumulated a large return on a diversified portfolio in a given year. In order to maintain the profitable position, but defer the taxable gains until the next year, futures contracts may be employed.

TRADING STOCK INDEX OPTIONS

Stock index options also allow the market participant to speculate or hedge against major market movements. Stock index options are similar in many respects to the standard put and call options on individual stocks discussed in Chapter 13. The purchaser of an option pays an initial premium, and then closes out the option at a given price in the future. One essential difference between stock index options and options on individual securities is that in the former case there is only a cash settlement of the position, whereas in the latter case (individual securities), you can force the option writer to deliver the securities.

Examples of stock index options are presented in Table 16–6.

The major option contracts are the S&P 100 Index and S&P 500 Index (traded on the Chicago Board Options Exchange), the American Exchange Major Market Index (a price-weighted index of 20 large firms),[14] the Amex

---

[14] Somewhat surprising is the fact that 15 out of 20 firms in the Index are part of the Dow Jones Industrial Average. The index is not meant to represent the American Stock Exchange, but large firms. An option contract on the American Exchange Major Market Index also began trading on the Chicago Board of Trade in July of 1984.

TABLE 16–6   Stock Index Options (April 19, 1984)

Index Options

Chicago Board

S&P 100 INDEX

Strike Price	Calls–Last Apr	May	June	Puts–Last Apr	May	June
140	....	....	¼	....	1/16	....
145	10	10½	10⅞	....	3/16	⅝
150	5¾	6⅝	7⅜	1/16	⅞	1½
155	¾	3¼	4½	1/16	2⅜	3⅛
160	1/16	1⅛	2¼	4⅛	5⅜	6
165	1/16	¼	¾	10	10½	10¾
170	....	1/16	¼	15	15¼	....
175	....	1/16	⅛	20½		

Total call volume 106,701. Total call open int. 358,892.
Total put volume 76,071. Total put open int. 415,339.
The index: High 155.78; Low 154.34; Close 155.78, +0.58.

S&P 500 INDEX

Strike Price	Calls–Last June	Sept	Puts–Last June	Sept
155	....	....	1½	....
160	2 13/16	....	....	....
165	1⅛	....	....	....

Total call volume 12.   Total call open int. 122.
Total put volume 2.   Total put open int. 219.
The index: High 158.02; Low 157.10; Close 158.02, +0.12.

COMPUTER/BUSINESS EQUIPMENT INDEX
(No Trades)

Total call volume 0.   Total call open int. 1353.
Total put volume 0.   Total put open int. 29.
The index: High 162.09; Low 160.80; Close 161.79, +0.23.

American Exchange

MAJOR MARKET INDEX

Strike Price	Calls–Last Apr	May	June	Puts–Last Apr	May	June
105	....	....	....	....	⅛	7/16
110	2 7/16	3⅞	4⅜	1/16	¾	1 5/16
115	1/16	1 1/16	1 13/16	2⅛	3⅛	3⅜
120	....	⅛	½	7¾		

Total call volume 7029   Total call open int. 41,812
Total put volume 5343   Total put open int. 42,389
The index: High 112.84; Low 111.63; Close 112.84, +0.52

AMEX MARKET VALUE INDEX

Strike Price	Calls–Last Apr	May	June	Puts–Last Apr	May	June
200	8¼	8¾	....	....	¾	1¼
205	2⅞	....	6⅞	....	1⅞	2⅝
210	....	2⅜	4⅛	2⅛	....	4⅞
215	....	¾	....	....		

Total call volume 199   Total call open int. 2435
Total put volume 233   Total put open int. 2447
The index: High 208.21; Low 207.58; Close 207.93, −0.18

N.Y. Stock Exchange

NYSE OPTIONS INDEX

Strike Price	Calls–Last Apr	May	Jun	Puts–Last Apr	May	Jun
85	5⅝	5⅝	6½	....	⅛	¼
90	⅞	2 1/16	2 13/16	1/16	1	1¼
95	....	¼	11/16	4⅜	4¼	4¾
100	....	....	⅛	....		

Total call volume 7631.   Total call open int. 67,933.
Total put volume 3,397.   Total put open int. 68,917.
The index: High 90.92; Low 90.44; Close 90.89, +0.06

The multiplier times the premium is 100.

Market Value Index (based on that exchange's index), and the NYSE Options Index (based on the New York Stock Exchange Composite Index). For closer inspection, we reproduce part of the Chicago Board Options Exchange S&P 100 Index quotations in Table 16–7.

TABLE 16–7   S&P 100 Index Stock Options (Chicago Board Options Exchange) (April 19, 1984, prices)

Strike price	Calls			Puts		
	April	May	June	April	May	June
140	—	—	1/4	—	1/16	—
145	10	10 1/2	10 7/8	—	3/16	5/8
150	5 3/4	6 5/8	7 3/8	1/16	7/8	1 1/2
155	3/4	3 1/4	4 1/2	1/16	2 3/8	3 1/8
160	1/16	1 1/8	2 1/4	4 1/8	5 3/8	6
165	1/16	1/4	3/4	10	10 1/2	10 3/4
170	—	1/16	1/4	15	15 1/4	—
175	—	1/16	1/8	20 1/2	—	—

The multiplier times the premium is 100.
Value of the S&P 100 Index (April 19, 1984) = 155.78.

Options related to the S&P 100 Index have been the most popular of the stock index options. The S&P 100 Index represents a market-value-weighted index of 100 of the stocks currently listed for option trading on the Chicago Board Options Exchange (CBOE). The movement of the S&P 100 Index closely parallels that of the S&P 500 Index.

Note at the bottom of Table 16–7 that the S&P 100 Index closed on April 19, 1984, at 155.78. With this value in mind, we can examine the strike price and premiums for the various contracts. The premium in each case is multiplied times 100 to determine the total cash involved.[15] Let's read down to the 150 strike price and across to the June call option (3rd month column). The premium is 7⅜ (7.375).

Assume an investor bought a June 150 contract for a 7.375 premium on April 19, 1984, and that when the June contract expired, the S&P 100 Index was 165 under our optimistic assumption; and that under our pessimistic assumption it was 145. At a value of 165, the option valve is 15 (165 − 150). The ending or expiration price is 15 points higher than the strike price. Keep in mind the option cost 7.375. The profit is shown to be $762.50. At an ending value of 145, the option is worthless, and there is a loss of $737.50.

---

[15] The 100 multiplier applies to all the other option contracts listed in Table 16–6 as well.

	165 Optimistic Assumption	145 Pessimistic Assumption
Final value (100×15) =	1,500.00	0
Purchase price (100×7.375) =	737.50	737.50
Profit or loss =	+ $762.50	− $737.50

We have been working with call options; let's shift our attention to put options. If a 150 June put option (the option to sell at 150 rather than buy at 150) had been purchased on April 19th, we can see in the third row of the last *put* column of Table 16–7 that the initial price of the June put option would have been 1½. Let's assume that when the June put contract expired, the S&P 100 Index was 165 under what is now our pessimistic assumption and 145 under what is now our optimistic assumption.

At a final value of 165, there is no value associated with a put option that allows you to sell at 150. Since the put option costs 1½, there is a $150 loss. At a final value of 145, the put option to sell at 150 has a value of 5. With a cost of 1½, a $350 profit takes place.

The profits and losses are indicated below:

	165 Pessimistic Assumption	145 Optimistic Assumption	
Final value (0) =	0	(100×5) =	500
Purchase price ($100 \times 1\frac{1}{2}$) =	150	($100 \times 1\frac{1}{2}$) =	150
Profit or loss =	− $150		+ $350

Hedging with Stock Index Options

The discussion of stock index options thus far has pertained to straight investments. Stock index options can also be used for hedging. Like stock index futures, stock index options can be used to protect a portfolio, or for special purposes by underwriters, specialists, dealers, tax planners, and others.

At times options may offer a hedging advantage over futures to investors who are limited by law from purchasing futures contracts. On the other hand, futures generally allow for a more efficient hedge than options. If the market goes down by 20 or 25 percent, chances are good that a completely hedged short futures position (selling futures contracts) will compensate fully, or to a reasonable degree, losses in a portfolio. An option write, used to hedge a portfolio, may prove to be inadequate. Perhaps the option premium income represents 10 percent of the portfolio, but the market goes down by 25 percent. Fifteen percent of the loss will be unprotected. Buying a put option may overcome this problem, but the cash outflow to purchase the put option could involve substantial funds. Clearly, both futures and options have their advantages and disadvantages.

STOCK INDEX OPTIONS FOR INDUSTRIES

There are also option contracts tailor-designed for industries. Thus, one who wishes to speculate on a given industry's performance, or hedge against hold-

ings in that industry, can use industry index options. The options are similar to those previously discussed in that put and call options are traded at various strike prices. The industry index options trade at a value equal to 100 times the premium.

Examples of industry index options are presented in Table 16–8. We will briefly examine the first two industry indexes.

TABLE 16–8   Industry Index Options

Index	Exchange
1. S&P Computer and Business Equipment Index	Chicago Board Options Exchange
2. S&P Integrated International Oil Index	Chicago Board Options Exchange
3. S&P Telephone Index	Chicago Board Options Exchange
4. S&P Transportation Index	Chicago Board Options Exchange
5. NY Telephone Index	New York Stock Exchange
6. Computer Technology Index	American Stock Exchange
7. Oil and Gas Index	American Stock Exchange
8. Transportation Index	American Stock Exchange
9. Gaming/Hotel Index	Philadelphia Stock Exchange
10. Technology Index	Pacific Stock Exchange

S&P Computer and Business Equipment Index.   This S&P industry index is made up of 12 firms. It is a market-value-weighted index. The participating firms and weights in 1983 are shown in Table 16–9.

TABLE 16–9   S&P Computer and Business Equipment Index

Company	Weight
Burroughs Corporation	2.3
Control Data	2.1
Data General	.8
Datapoint	.5
Digital Equipment	5.8
IBM	73.0
NCR Corporation	3.3
Pitney-Bowes	.9
Sperry Corporation	2.3
Storage Technology	.7
Wang Labs	4.2
Xerox Corporation	4.2
	100.0

Source: *S&P Computer and Business Equipment Index (OBE): A Preview* (Chicago: Chicago Board Options Exchange, 1983).

FIGURE 16–3

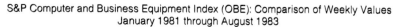

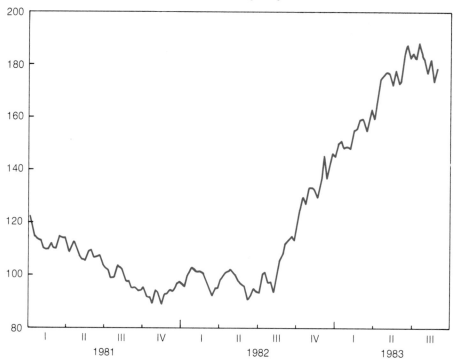

S&P Computer and Business Equipment Index (OBE): Comparison of Weekly Values
January 1981 through August 1983

Source: *S&P Computer and Business Equipment Index (OBE): A Preview* (Chicago: Chicago Board Options
Exchange, 1983).

.A three-year history of the index is presented in Figure 16–3. As you can
see, the price movements are quite volatile.

The S&P Integrated International Oil Index.   This market-value-
weighted index comprises six firms. The firms and their weights in 1983 are
shown in Table 16–10.

In Figure 16–4, we can observe a three-year history of the index that
indicates even greater price volatility than that shown in Figure 16–3 for the
Computer and Business Equipment Index.

A purchaser of an S&P Integrated International Oil Index option might
buy an option with a 120 strike price for a premium of 3 ($300 in total). The
option will move up and down in value with the underlying index just as all
other options do.

TABLE 16–10   S&P Integrated International Oil Index

Company	Weight
Exxon Corporation	37.3
Gulf Oil	8.0
Mobil Corporation	15.1
Royal Dutch Petroleum	14.3
Standard Oil of California	14.4
Texaco, Inc.	10.9
	100.0

Source: *S&P Integrated International Oil Index (OIO): A Preview* (Chicago: Chicago Board Options Exchange, 1983).

FIGURE 16–4

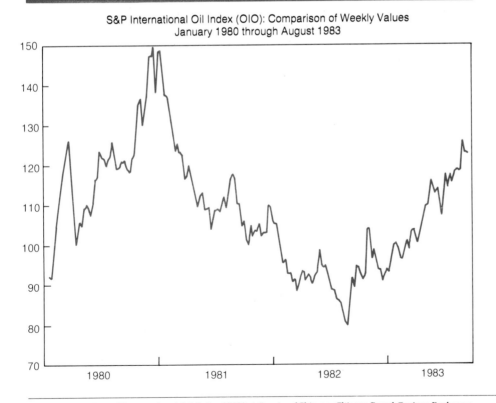

S&P International Oil Index (OIO): Comparison of Weekly Values
January 1980 through August 1983

Source: *S&P Integrated International Oil Index (OIO): A Preview* (Chicago: Chicago Board Options Exchange, 1983).

OPTIONS ON STOCK INDEX FUTURES

We have discussed *stock index futures* and *stock index options,* so a natural extension of our discussion is to consider the third form of stock index trading, *options on stock index futures.* The three forms of index trading are listed below for future reference.

a. Stock index futures.
b. Stock index options.
c. Options on stock index futures.

An option on a stock index future (item c) gives the holder the right to purchase the *stock index future* at a specified price over a given time period. This is slightly different from the stock index option (item b) that gives the holder the right to purchase the *underlying index at a specified price over a given time period.*[16] *The contrast is shown in Figure 16–5.*

The primary topic for discussion in this section is represented by the left-hand column in Figure 16–5, an option on a stock index future. The value of an option to purchase a stock index future will depend on the outlook for the

FIGURE 16–5   Comparison of Option Contracts

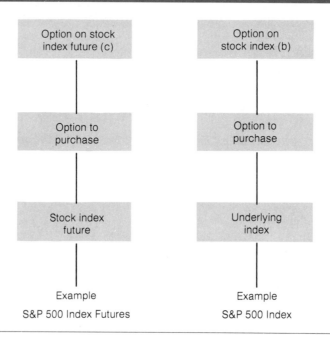

---

[16] Because of cash settlement procedures, the actual index will never actually be purchased, and the gain or loss will be settled for cash.

TABLE 16–11 Options on Stock Index Futures (April 19, 1984)

Chicago Mercantile Exchange

S&P 500 STOCK INDEX – Price = $500 times premium.

Strike Price	Calls – Settle			Puts – Settle		
	Jun	Sep	Dec	Jun	Sep	Dec
135	....	....	....	....	....	
140	....	....	....	....	....	
145	....	....	....	.15	....	
150	9.60	....	....	.50	1.50	
155	5.60	....	....	1.45	2.70	
160	2.65	5.85	....	3.40	4.55	
165	1.00	3.80	....	6.70	7.00	7.50
170	.30	2.15	....	11.00	....	
175	.10	1.25	....	....	....	
180	.05	.70	....	....	....	
185	.05	....	....	....	....	

Estimated total vol. 1,268
Calls: Wed. vol. 426; open int. 11,456
Puts: Wed. vol. 547; open int. 13,326

N.Y. Futures Exchange

NYSE Composite Index – Price = $500 times premium.

Strike Price	Calls – Settle			Puts – Settle		
	Jun	Sep	Dec	Jun	Sep	Dec
88	4.40	6.25	8.05	.60	1.25	1.90
90	2.95	4.85	6.60	1.15	1.85	2.45
92	1.85	3.65	5.35	2.05	2.65	3.20
94	1.10	2.60	4.20	3.30	3.60	4.05
96	.55	1.90	3.30	4.75	4.90	5.15
98	.25	1.30	2.55	6.45	6.30	6.40
100	.10	.85	1.90	8.30	7.85	7.75
102	.05	.55	....	10.20	9.55	....
104	.05	.35	....	12.20	11.35	....

Estimated total vol. 122
Calls: Wed. vol. 85; open int. 4611
Puts: Wed. vol. 75; open int. 1565

futures contract. Quotes on options to purchase stock index futures are shown in Table 16–11.[17]

As indicated in Table 16–11, options on stock index futures trade on the Chicago Mercantile Exchange (based on S&P 500 stock index futures) and the New York Futures Exchange (based on NYSE composite index futures). Let's look at sample quotes on the Chicago Mercantile Exchange at the top of the table. A call option to buy a June S&P 500 stock index futures contract at a strike price of 160 has a premium of 2.65. On these option contracts, the premium is multiplied times *500* to get the value of the contract. Thus the cost of the contract is $1,325 (500 × 2.65).

In examining Table 16–11, note that the premiums on the call options increase substantially with the passage of time from June to September. This gain in value is not only a function of the extended time period associated with the option, but also of the fact that the S&P 500 futures contract has a higher

---

[17] These quotes generally appear in the futures section of *The Wall Street Journal* rather than the options section. This can be potentially confusing to the reader.

value in September than June. On April 19, 1984, the June S&P 500 futures contract traded at 159.20, while the September contract traded at 161.55. Thus options on stock index futures not only have a time premium (as all options do), but may also have an additional premium (or discount) depending on the relationship of the far-term futures market to the near-term futures market.

Options on stock index futures may be settled on a cash basis, or the holder of a call option may actually exercise the option and force the option writer to produce a specified futures contract.

Although options on *stock index futures* preceded options on *stock indexes* in the marketplace, they are not currently as popular, Nevertheless, they continue to trade on major exchanges in Chicago and New York.

SUMMARY

For the investor who wishes to trade in stock indexes, there are three basic types of securities: stock index futures, stock index options, and options on stock index futures. With stock index options, there is also the opportunity to purchase the indexes of various industries. These include such industries as computers, international oils, transportation, and technology.

Stock index futures and options offer the potential for speculation as well as for hedging. With stock index futures, the margin is relatively low, which allows for a strong leverage potential. In hedging a portfolio position, the investor should take into consideration the beta of his or her portfolio, and adjust the number of contracts accordingly. Basis in the futures market represents the difference between the stock index futures price and the value of the actual underlying index. Basis may present the investor with a potential clue about the future direction of the market. The stock index futures market and stock index option market trade on a cash settlement basis. No securities ever change hands, as the settlement is always in cash.

The stock index option contract is generally similar to the option contract on individual securities. There is the opportunity to buy puts and calls, and the premium is related to the future prospects for the index.

The third form of stock index contracts, an option on stock index futures, combines the option concept with the futures market. Instead of an option on an actual index, you have an option on a stock index futures contract. The contract may be settled either with cash or with securities.

The two forms of option contracts have the advantage of offering an investment outlet to some investors who are constrained by law from investing in commodity contracts, and thus can not participate in stock index futures. On the other hand, stock index futures do provide a more efficient hedging device in that the gain on the futures contract may offset the loss on the portfolio. On an option play, this may be more difficult or expensive to establish.

In terms of actual popularity of the indexes, the S&P 500 is the dominant

contract for stock index futures, the S&P 100 Index is the most widely traded stock index option, and the New York Stock Exchange Composite Index represents the most popular option on a stock index futures contract. The actual firms, the percentage composition, and other characteristics of the S&P 500 Index are presented in the appendix at the end of this chapter.

IMPORTANT WORDS AND CONCEPTS

Stock index futures	**Basis**
Stock index options	**Efficient hedge**
Options on stock index futures	**Beta-related hedge**
Options on industry indexes	**Underwriter hedge**
Cash settlement	**Specialist or dealer hedge**
S&P International Oil Index	**Tax hedge**

DISCUSSION QUESTIONS

1. Why is there less margin required for a hedged position than a speculative position?

2. What is meant by the concept of cash settlement?

3. Why does cash settlement make a "short squeeze" impossible?

4. What does the term *basis* mean in the futures market? If there is a premium and it expands with the passage of time, what is the general implication?

5. If you speculate in stock index futures, will you be exposed to unsystematic risk?

6. Explain why stock index futures provide much greater leverage than the outright purchase of a portfolio of securities on margin.

7. Why is it unrealistic for a portfolio manager to sell off a large portion of his portfolio if he thinks the market is about to decline?

8. How does the beta of a portfolio influence the number of contracts that must be used in the hedging process?

9. What are some complicating factors in attempting to hedge a portfolio?

10. Why might stock index futures be used to hedge a retirement fund?

11. What is an essential difference between stock index options and options on individual securities in terms of settlement procedures?

12. If you were using stock index options to hedge a portfolio and you thought the stock market was going to go down dramatically, why might purchasing put options be more effective than selling call options?

13. In the S&P Computer and Business Equipment Index presented in Table 16–9, if IBM comes out with a new mainframe computer that increases its market value by 10 percent and causes other computer firms in the index to decline by 10 percent on average, what will be the general direction of move in the index?

14. Explain the difference between a stock index option and an option on stock index futures.

15. Suggest two reasons why an option on a stock index futures contract that has a distant expiration date might have a high premium.

PROBLEMS

1. Based on the information in Table 16–1, what is the total value of a S&P 500 Futures Index contract for March 1985? Use the settle price and the appropriate multiplier. Also, if the required margin is $6,000, what percent of the contract value does margin represent?

2. In Problem 1, if the S&P 500 Futures Index goes up to 169.10, what will be the total dollar profit on the contract? What is the percent return on the initial margin? If this price change took place over four months, what is the annualized return?

3. Return to Problem 1 and assume that margin must be maintained at a minimum level of $2,500. If the S&P 500 Futures Index goes from its initial value to 158.65, will there be a call for more margin?

4. Examine Table 16–3, and using settle prices, what is the value of the basis for the September 1984 and June 1985 contracts?

5. Northeastern Mutual Life Insurance Company has a $10 million stock portfolio. The company is very aggressive and the portfolio has a weighted beta of 1.25.

    a. Assume they use S&P 500 Futures contracts to hedge the portfolio for the next 60 days and the contracts can be sold at 165. With the appropriate beta adjustment factor, how many contracts should be sold? Round your final answer to the nearest whole number.

    b. If S&P 100 Futures contracts selling at 162 were used instead, how many contracts should be sold? Once again, consider the appropriate beta adjustment factor and round your final answer to the nearest whole number.

6. The Twenty-First Century Pension Fund decides to hedge its $15 million stock portfolio on September 15. The portfolio has a beta of 1.10. They will use NYSE Composite Futures contracts selling at 94. They intend to hedge the portfolio for the next 90 days.

    a. With the appropriate beta adjustment factor and rounding the final answer to the nearest whole number, how many contracts should be sold?

    b. Assume by December 15 the market has gone down by 20 percent and the stock portfolio moves in accordance with its beta, what will be the total dollar decline in the portfolio?

    c. Assume the NYSE Composite Futures contract value also declines by 20 percent. What will be the total dollar gain on the futures contract?

    d. Now assume that because of changing basis, the stock index futures

contract does not move exactly in parallel with the market (as described by the NYSE Composite Index in this case). Although the market goes down by 20 percent, the stock index futures only decline by 15 percent. What will be the gain on the futures contracts? How does that compare to the loss in portfolio value in part b?

7. The following problem relates to data in Table 16–7. Assume you purchase a June 145 S&P Index call option. Compute your total dollar profit or loss if the index has the following values at expiration.
   a. 165.
   b. 145.
   c. 105.

8. Once again using the data from Table 16–7, assume you purchase a May 160 S&P Index put option. Compute your total dollar profit or loss if the index has the following values at expiration.
   a. 165.
   b. 145.
   c. 105.

9. The J. R. Oil Company has a $1 million funded pension plan for its employees. The portfolio beta is equal to 1.14. Assume the company sells (writes) a total of 75 June 110 call option contracts on the American Exchange Major Market Index as shown in Table 16–6. (Each contract trades in units of 100). At the time the options were written, the index had a value of 112.84.
   a. What are the proceeds from the sale of the call options?
   b. Assume the market goes down by 10 percent. Considering the portfolio beta, what will be the total dollar decline in the portfolio?
   c. Assume that the American Exchange Major Market Index also goes down by 10 percent at expiration, what will be the value of the index at that point in time?
   d. Based on your answer to part c, what will be your profit on the option writes?
   e. Considering your answers to parts b and d, what is your net gain or loss?

10. Assume that in Problem 9 you had purchased a total of 75 June 110 *put* option contracts on the American Exchange Major Market Index listed in Table 16–6 instead of the call options. If the American Exchange Major Market Index goes down by 10 percent at expiration:
    a. What will be your profit on the puts? Comparing that to your loss on the stock portfolio in Problem 9b, what is your net overall gain or loss?
    b. Compare the protection afforded by the call writing hedge in Problem 9 to the protection afforded by the put purchase in this problem.
    c. Suggest any modifications to the put writing strategy that would allow you to increase your protection.

11. Lerner Money Manager Incorporated runs a $2 million portfolio. Its beta is equal to the market. In order to hedge its position, it sells (writes) a total of 50 May 110 call option contracts on the American Exchange Major Market Index as shown in Table 16–6. It also buys 60 May 115 put option contracts on the same American Major Market Index shown in Table 16–6. Instead of going down, the market goes up by 10 percent (as does the portfolio), and the American Major Market Index ends up at 124.

   Consider the change in the portfolio value and the gains or losses on the call and put options. What is the overall net gain or loss to Lerner Money Managers as a result of the changes in the market?

12. The California School Retirement Fund purchases a call option on a stock index futures contract. The quote can be found in Table 16–11. The option is on the N.Y. Futures Exchange. It is at a strike price of 90 for December.

   a. What is the quoted option premium (price)?

   b. Refer to Table 16–1, what was the quote of the December contract for the NYSE Composite Futures? (Use the settle price).

   c. Also referring to Table 16–1, what was the actual quote (value) for the NYSE Composite Stock Index? (Use the settle price).

   d. By how much does the futures quote (part b) exceed the actual index quote (part c)? That is, how much is the basis?

   e. By how much does the quoted option premium (part a) exceed the basis (part d)?

   f. If the basis were to suddenly go to zero, and the option declined by a similar amount, what would the new option premium be?

SELECTED REFERENCES

Fabozzi, Frank J., and Gregory M. Kipnis. *Stock Index Futures.* Homewood, Ill.: Dow Jones-Irwin, 1984.

Gastineau, Gary, and Albert Madansky. "S&P 500 Stock Index Futures Evaluation Tables." *Financial Analysts Journal,* November–December 1983, pp. 68–76.

Inside S&P 500 Stock Index Futures. Chicago: Chicago Mercantile Exchange, 1983.

Kamara, Avraham. "The Behavior of Futures Prices: A Review of Theory and Evidence." *Financial Analysts Journal,* July–August 1984, pp. 68–75.

Kawaller, Ira. "Options Beat Futures?" *Commodities,* July 1983, p. 98.

Maidenberg, N. J. "Whirlwind CBOE-CME Romance Puts New Slant on Options Race." *Commodities,* June 1983, pp. 54–55.

Markets for Today's Investors. Chicago: Chicago Mercantile Exchange, 1983.

Merrill Lynch Guide to Stock Index Futures. New York: Merrill Lynch Futures, Inc., 1983.

Modest, D. M., and M. Sundaresan. "The Relation between Spot and Futures Prices in Stock Index Futures Markets: Some Preliminary Evidence." *Journal of Futures Markets,* Spring 1983, pp. 15–41.

Niederhoffer, Victor, and Richard Zeckhauser. "Market Index Futures Contracts." *Financial Analysts Journal,* January–February 1980, pp. 45–50.

Nix, William E., and Susan W. Nix. *The Dow Jones-Irwin Guide to Stock Index Futures and Options.* Homewood, Ill.: Dow Jones-Irwin, 1984.

Nordhauser, Fred. "Using Stock Index Futures to Reduce Market Risk." *Journal of Portfolio Management,* Spring 1984, pp. 56–69.

S&P Computer and Business Equipment Index (OBE): A Preview. Chicago: Chicago Board Options Exchange, 1983.

S&P Integrated International Oil Index (OIO): A Preview. Chicago: Chicago Board Options Exchange, 1983.

"Stock Futures: A Hot New World." *Business Week,* August 22, 1983, pp. 58–66.

Zeckhauser, Richard, and Victor Niederhoffer. "The Performance of Market Index Futures Contracts." *Financial Analysts Journal,* January–February 1983, pp. 59–65.

APPENDIX: S&P 500 Index (1983)

Ticker	Name	Percent of S&P 500	Beta
AA	ALUMINUM CO AMER	0.220	0.911
ABC	AMERICAN BROADCASTING COS	0.110	0.691
ABT	ABBOTT LABS	0.380	0.889
AC	AMERICAN CAN CO	0.080	0.756
ACCOB	COORS ADOLPH CO	0.040	1.118
ACF	ACF INDS INC	0.040	1.213
ACK	ARMSTRONG WORLD INDS INC	0.050	1.013
ACB	ALBERTO CULVER CO	0.010	1.644
ACY	AMERICAN CYANAMID CO	0.160	1.138
AD	AMSTED INDS INC	0.040	1.372
ADM	ARCHER DANIELS MIDLAND CO	0.150	1.523
AEP	AMERICAN ELEC PWR INC	0.300	0.283
AET	AETNA LIFE & CAS CO	0.410	0.721
AGC	AMERICAN GEN CORP	0.120	1.073
AGM	AMALGAMATED SUGAR CO	0.010	1.179
AH	ALLIS CHALMERS CORP	0.020	1.016
AHM	AHMANSON H F & CO	0.040	1.231
AHP	AMERICAN HOME PRODS CORP	0.660	0.551
AHS	AMERICAN HOSP SUPPLY CORP	0.190	0.987
AIGR	AMERICAN INTL GROUP INC	0.430	0.860
AL	ALCAN ALUM LTD	0.220	1.271
ALD	ALLIED CORP	0.170	1.489
ALS	ALLIED STORES CORP	0.060	0.586
AMB	AMERICAN BRANDS INC	0.230	0.421
AMF	AMF INC	0.070	1.013
AMI	AMERICAN MED INTL INC	0.100	2.021
AMO	AMERICAN MTRS CORP	0.020	0.859
AMP	AMP INC	0.210	0.960
AMR	AMERICAN AIRLS INC	0.040	1.198
AMT	ACME CLEVELAND CORP	0.010	1.289
AMX	AMAX INC	0.340	1.760
ANR	AMERICAN NAT RES CO	0.110	1.041
APC	ALPHA PORTLAND INDS INC	0.000	1.356
AR	ASARCO INC	0.080	2.036
ARA	ARA SVCS INC	0.030	0.764
ARC	ATLANTIC RICHFIELD CO	1.310	1.318
AS	ARMCO INC	0.200	1.469
ASA	ASA LTD	0.050	0.942
ASC	AMERICAN STORES CO NEW	0.030	0.846
ASR	AMSTAR CORP	0.030	1.138
AST	AMERICAN STD INC	0.090	1.005
AUD	AUTOMATIC DATA PROCESSING	0.100	0.841
AVP	AVON PRODS INC	0.210	0.691
AXO	AKZONA INC	0.010	1.057
AXP	AMERICAN EXPRESS CO	0.470	0.692
BA	BOEING CO	0.250	1.326
BAC	BANKAMERICA CORP	0.360	0.536
BAX	BAXTER TRAVENOL LABS INC	0.270	0.764
BBL	BLUE BELL INC	0.040	0.641
BC	BRUNSWICK CORP	0.040	1.134
BCC	BOISE CASCADE CORP	0.110	1.384
BCR	BARD C R INC N J	0.030	1.404
BDK	BLACK & DECKER MFG CO	0.070	1.237
BDX	BECTON DICKINSON & CO	0.110	1.073
BFI	BROWNING FERRIS INDS INC	0.070	1.529
BG	BROWN GROUP INC	0.040	0.733
BGE	BALTIMORE GAS & ELEC CO	0.090	0.368
BGG	BRIGGS & STRATTON CORP	0.040	0.700
BGH	BURROUGHS CORP	0.170	0.926
BKI	BEKER INDS CORP	0.010	1.664
BKO	BAKER INTL CORP	0.300	1.834
BMS	BEMIS INC	0.010	0.750
BMY	BRISTOL MYERS CO	0.410	0.812
BN	BORDEN INC	0.100	0.371
BNI	BURLINGTON NORTHN INC	0.260	2.083
BNL	BENEFICIAL CORP	0.050	0.897
BNS	BROWN & SHARPE MFG CO	0.010	1.400
BOR	BORG WARNER CORP	0.130	0.919
BRY	BEATRICE FOODS CO	0.210	0.544
BS	BETHLEHEM STL CORP	0.120	1.264
BT	BANKERS TR N Y CORP	0.100	0.682
BU	BROOKLYN UN GAS CO	0.020	0.283

Ticker	Company		
BUD	ANHEUSER BUSCH COS INC	0.220	0.704
BUR	BURLINGTON INDS INC	0.080	0.795
BX	BENDIX CORP	0.130	0.987
BY	BUCYRUS ERIE CO	0.040	1.038
C	CHRYSLER CORP	0.030	1.186
CAF	CNA FINL CORP	0.080	1.805
CAT	CATERPILLAR TRACTOR CO	0.560	1.098
CBE	COOPER INDS INC	0.260	1.128
CBM	CHESEBROUGH PONDS INC	0.130	0.670
CBS	CBS INC	0.150	0.871
CCB	CAPITAL CITIES COMMUNICATNS	0.110	0.989
CCC	CONTINENTAL GROUP INC	0.130	0.924
CCK	CROWN CORK & SEAL INC	0.050	0.916
CDA	CONTROL DATA CORP DEL	0.150	1.519
CFD	CONSOLIDATED FOODS CORP	0.100	0.408
CG	COLUMBIA GAS SYS INC	0.120	0.656
CGG	CHICAGO PNEUMATIC TOOL CO	0.010	0.731
CGN	CONNECTICUT GEN CORP	0.240	0.953
CHA	CHAMPION INTL CORP	0.130	1.222
CHH	CARTER HAWLEY HALE STORES	0.050	0.770
CHL	CHEMICAL NEW YORK CORP	0.100	0.600
CHM	CHAMPION SPARK PLUG CO	0.030	0.945
CHU	CHURCHS FRIED CHICKEN INC	0.040	1.022
CHUB	CHUBB CORP	0.070	0.616
CIC	CONTINENTAL CORP	0.160	0.761
CIL	CONTINENTAL ILL CORP	0.150	0.652
CKL	CLARK EQUIP CO	0.040	0.742
CL	COLGATE PALMOLIVE CO	0.160	0.690
CLU	CLUETT PEABODY & CO INC	0.020	1.069
CLX	CLOROX CO CALIF	0.030	0.901
CMB	CHASE MANHATTAN CORP	0.200	0.766
CMK	CARNATION CO	0.120	0.746
CMZ	CINCINNATI MILACRON INC	0.070	1.967
CNF	CONSOLIDATED FREIGHTWAYS INC	0.060	1.285
CNG	CONSOLIDATED NAT GAS CO	0.120	1.089
COE	CONE MLS CORP	0.020	0.854
COX	COX BROADCASTING CORP	0.120	0.665
CPB	CAMPBELL SOUP CO	0.110	0.211
CPC	CPC INTL INC	0.200	0.651
CPH	CAPITAL HLDG CORP DEL	0.070	0.585
CPS	COLUMBIA PICTURES INDS INC	0.040	1.655
CR	CRANE CO	0.040	1.324

Ticker	Company		
CRK	CAMPBELL RED LAKE MINES LTD	0.080	0.968
CS	CITIES SVC CO	0.450	1.534
CSC	COMPUTER SCIENCES CORP	0.020	1.394
CSP	COMBUSTION ENGR INC	0.140	1.604
CSR	CENTRAL & SOUTH WEST CORP	0.130	0.352
CSX	C S X CORP	0.280	NA
CTC	CONTINENTAL TEL CORP	0.120	0.459
CTU	CENTRAL TEL & UTILS CORP	0.100	0.301
CTX	CENTEX CORP	0.040	2.312
CUM	CUMMINS ENGINE INC	0.030	1.094
CWE	COMMONWEALTH EDISON CO	0.280	0.295
CZ	CELANESE CORP	0.100	0.915
DAL	DELTA AIR LINES INC	0.110	0.928
DCN	DANA CORP	0.120	0.455
DD	DU PONT E I DE NEMOURS & CO	1.020	0.924
DE	DEERE & CO	0.280	1.019
DEC	DIGITAL EQUIP CORP	0.150	1.250
DEN	DENNYS INC	0.030	0.645
DG	ASSOCIATED DRY GOODS CORP	0.040	0.835
DGN	DATA GEN CORP	0.170	1.605
DH	DAYTON HUDSON CORP	0.170	0.690
DI	DRESSER INDS INC	0.300	1.184
DIS	DISNEY WALT PRODTNS	0.200	1.237
DJ	DOW JONES & CO INC	0.180	0.990
DKI	DART & KRAFT INC	0.320	0.187
DM	DOME MINES LTD	0.120	1.170
DN	DIAMOND INTL CORP	0.060	1.095
DNB	DUN & BRADSTREET CORP	0.210	0.991
DOC	DR PEPPER CO	0.030	1.220
DOW	DOW CHEM CO	0.580	1.123
DPT	DATAPOINT CORP	0.120	2.068
DR	NATIONAL DISTILLERS & CHEM	0.090	0.919
DTE	DETROIT EDISON CO	0.120	0.326
DUK	DUKE PWR CO	0.210	0.075
EAF	EMERY AIR FGHT CORP	0.020	0.964
ECH	ECHLIN INC	0.030	0.907
ECK	ECKERD JACK CORP	0.110	0.979
ED	CONSOLIDATED EDISON CO N Y	0.240	0.301
EDS	ELECTRONIC DATA SYS CORP	0.080	1.261
EFU	EASTERN GAS & FUEL ASSOC	0.060	1.831
EK	EASTMAN KODAK CO	1.330	0.938
ELG	EL PASO CO	0.140	1.474

APPENDIX: (continued)

Ticker	Name	Percent of S&P 500	Beta	Ticker	Name	Percent of S&P 500	Beta
EMR	EMERSON ELEC CO	0.340	0.741	GEB	GERBER PRODS CO	0.030	0.729
ENS	ENSERCH CORP	0.160	1.328	GET	GETTY OIL CO	0.620	1.612
ESM	ESMARK INC	0.070	1.098	GF	GENERAL FOODS CORP	0.180	0.584
ETN	EATON CORP	0.100	0.818	GID	GIDDINGS & LEWIS INC	0.030	1.955
EVY	EVANS PRODS CO	0.030	1.179	GIS	GENERAL MLS INC	0.210	0.319
F	FORD MTR CO DEL	0.230	0.511	GLD	GOULD INC	0.100	0.908
FB	FIRST NATL BOSTON CORP	0.070	0.613	GLM	GLOBAL MARINE INC	0.080	2.722
FBG	FABERGE INC	0.010	1.678	GLW	CORNING GLASS WKS	0.110	0.990
FBO	FEDERAL PAPER BRD INC	0.020	1.171	GM	GENERAL MTRS CORP	1.350	0.509
FCF	FIRST CHARTER FINL CORP	0.040	1.501	GO	GULF OIL CORP	0.780	1.244
FDS	FEDERATED DEPT STORES INC	0.200	0.578	GP	GEORGIA PAC CORP	0.230	1.139
FDX	FEDERAL EXPRESS CORP	0.140	2.225	GPC	GENUINE PARTS CO	0.100	0.678
FG	USF&G CORP	0.140	0.692	GQ	GRUMMAN CORP	0.030	1.438
FIR	FIRESTONE TIRE & RUBR CO	0.080	0.985	GR	GOODRICH B F CO	0.050	1.083
FJQ	FEDDERS CORP	0.010	1.724	GRA	GRACE W R & CO	0.250	1.241
FLE	FLEETWOOD ENTERPRISES INC	0.020	1.654	GS	GILLETTE CO	0.120	0.722
FLR	FLUOR CORP DEL	0.270	1.704	GSX	GENERAL SIGNAL CORP	0.120	0.998
FMC	FMC CORP	0.100	1.195	GT	GOODYEAR TIRE & RUBR CO	0.160	0.771
FNB	FIRST CHICAGO CORP	0.090	1.002	GTE	GENERAL TEL & ELECTRS CORP	0.600	0.437
FNC	CITICORP	0.360	0.859	GW	GULF & WESTN INDS INC	0.140	1.247
FPA	FIRST PA CORP	0.010	0.525	GWF	GREAT WESTN FINL CORP	0.040	1.465
FPL	FLORIDA PWR & LT CO	0.140	0.338	GWW	GRAINGER W W INC	0.060	0.740
FRM	FIRST MISSISSIPPI CORP	0.040	2.022	HAL	HALLIBURTON CO	0.710	1.559
FTR	FRUEHAUF CORP	0.030	0.792	HBJ	HARCOURT BRACE JOVANOVICH	0.020	1.078
FWC	FOSTER WHEELER CORP	0.060	1.716	HBL	HEUBLEIN INC	0.090	0.762
GAO	GENERAL AMERN OIL CO TEX	0.110	1.881	HCA	HOSPITAL CORP AMER	0.210	1.254
GAP	GREAT ATLANTIC & PAC TEA INC	0.020	1.209	HD	HUDSON BAY MNG & SMLT LTD	0.020	1.181
GCI	GANNETT INC DEL	0.220	0.647	HDL	HANDLEMAN CO DEL	0.010	1.488
GCN	GENERAL CINEMA CORP	0.050	1.419	HI	HOUSEHOLD INTL INC	0.080	0.792
GCO	GENESCO INC	0.010	1.335	HIA	HOLIDAY INNS INC	0.100	1.736
GD	GENERAL DYNAMICS CORP	0.150	1.778	HLR	HELLER WALTER E INTL CORP	0.030	1.126
GE	GENERAL ELEC CO	1.520	0.854	HLT	HILTON HOTELS CORP	0.120	1.556
				HLY	HOLLY SUGAR CORP	0.010	1.847

Ticker	Company		
JPM	MORGAN J P & CO INC	0.240	0.412
JWC	WALTER JIM CORP	0.040	1.180
JWL	JEWEL COS INC	0.050	0.665
K	KELLOGG CO	0.200	0.705
KB	KAUFMAN & BROAD INC	0.010	1.925
KCC	KAISER CEMENT CORP	0.020	1.581
KFM	KROEHLER MFG CO	0.000	0.719
KLU	KAISER ALUM & CHEM CORP	0.080	1.144
KM	K MART CORP	0.230	0.521
KMB	KIMBERLY CLARK CORP	0.170	0.663
KO	COCA COLA CO	0.500	0.548
KR	KROGER CO	0.080	1.039
KRN	KNIGHT RIDDER NEWSPAPERS INC	0.110	1.051
LCE	LONE STAR INDS INC	0.040	1.203
LIT	LITTON INDS INC	0.260	1.502
LKS	LUCKY STORES INC	0.080	0.666
LLX	LOUISIANA LD & EXPL. CO	0.130	1.426
LLY	LILLY ELI & CO	0.490	0.723
LNC	LINCOLN NATL CORP IND	0.100	0.981
LOF	LIBBEY OWENS FORD CO	0.030	0.700
LPX	LOUISIANA PAC CORP	0.070	1.438
LST	LOWENSTEIN M CORP	0.010	1.053
LVI	LEVI STRAUSS & CO	0.130	0.950
MA	MAY DEPT STORES CO	0.090	0.808
MAI	M A COM INC	0.110	2.224
MAN	MANVILLE CORP	0.040	1.148
MAS	MASCO CORP	0.110	1.686
MAT	MATTEL INC	0.020	1.662
MB	MILTON BRADLEY CO	0.020	1.511
MCA	MCA INC	0.110	1.097
MCD	MCDONALDS CORP	0.310	0.580
MD	MCDONNELL DOUGLAS CORP	0.130	1.714
MDC	MARYLAND CUP CORP	0.030	1.203
MDE	MCDERMOTT INC	0.160	2.052
MDP	MEREDITH CORP	0.020	1.324

Ticker	Company		
HM	HOMESTAKE MNG CO	0.070	1.498
HNZ	HEINZ H J CO	0.150	0.685
HON	HONEYWELL INC	0.180	1.285
HPC	HERCULES INC	0.110	0.977
HR	INTERNATIONAL HARVESTER CO	0.030	1.213
HRS	HARRIS CORP DEL	0.150	1.472
HSM	HART SCHAFFNER & MARX	0.020	1.137
HSY	HERSHEY FOODS CORP	0.070	0.547
HT	HUGHES TOOL CO	0.260	1.620
HUM	HUMANA INC	0.150	1.693
HWP	HEWLETT PACKARD CO	0.560	1.356
HWR	WALKER HIRAM RES LTD	0.160	0.298
HYST	HYSTER CO	0.020	0.996
I	FIRST INTST BANCORP	0.160	1.005
IAD	INLAND STL CO	0.060	0.772
IBM	INTERNATIONAL BUSINESS MACHS	3.900	0.725
ICX	IC INDS INC	0.070	1.315
ID	IDEAL TOY INC DEL	0.000	1.187
IDL	IDEAL BASIC INDS INC	0.030	1.500
IFC	INTERFIRST CORP	0.140	0.743
IFF	INTL FLAVORS & FRAGRANCES	0.080	0.787
IGL	INTL MINERALS & CHEM CORP	0.100	1.122
IK	INTERLAKE INC	0.030	1.092
INA	INA CORP	0.200	0.971
INI	INTERNORTH INC	0.160	1.347
INTC	INTEL CORP	0.110	1.531
IP	INTERNATIONAL PAPER CO	0.230	1.467
IQ	QUESTOR CORP	0.010	1.493
IR	INGERSOLL RAND CO	0.130	0.984
ISS	INTERCO INC	0.080	0.641
ITT	INTERNATIONAL TEL & TELEG CO	0.440	1.150
JCP	PENNEY J C INC	0.230	0.561
JNJ	JOHNSON & JOHNSON	0.800	0.681
JOL	JONATHAN LOGAN INC	0.010	1.307
JOY	JOY MFG CO	0.080	1.235
JP	JEFFERSON PILOT CORP	0.070	0.660

Ticker	Name	Percent of S&P 500	Beta	Ticker	Name	Percent of S&P 500	Beta
MEA	MEAD CORP	0.070	1.514	N	INCO LTD	0.130	1.180
MEL	MELLON NATL CORP	0.080	0.670	NAC	NATIONAL CAN CORP	0.020	1.433
MES	MELVILLE CORP	0.110	0.648	NB	NABISCO BRANDS INC	0.230	0.210
MET	METROMEDIA INC	0.070	1.160	NC	NORTH AMERN COAL CORP	0.010	1.488
MF	MARSHALL FIELD & CO	0.020	1.094	NCB	NCNB CORP	0.030	1.068
MGM I	METRO GOLDWYN MAYER FILM CO	0.050	0.157	NCR	NCR CORP	0.140	1.223
MGR	MCGRAW EDISON CO	0.070	1.264	NEM	NEWMONT MNG CORP	0.130	1.679
MHC	MANUFACTURERS HANOVER CORP	0.140	0.570	NES	NEW ENGLAND ELEC SYS	0.060	0.475
MHP	MCGRAW HILL INC	0.150	1.042	NFK	NORFOLK & WESTN RY CO	0.200	1.314
MHS	MARRIOTT CORP	0.110	1.435	NG	NATIONAL GYPSUM CO	0.040	1.180
MIS	MISSOURI PAC CORP	0.150	1.488	NL	NL INDS INC	0.310	1.792
ML	MARTIN MARIETTA CORP	0.160	1.338	NLT	NLT CORP	0.090	1.413
MLL	MACMILLAN INC	0.020	1.146	NME	NATIONAL MED ENTERPRISES INC	0.090	1.760
MLN	MCLEAN TRUCKING CO	0.000	0.274	NMK	NIAGARA MOHAWK PWR CORP	0.120	0.287
MMM	MINNESOTA MNG & MFG CO	0.740	0.668	NOB	NORTHWEST BANCORPORATION	0.070	0.628
MMO	MONARCH MACH TOOL CO	0.010	1.597	NS	NATIONAL STL CORP	0.050	0.625
MNC	MASONITE CORP	0.040	1.213	NSI	NORTON SIMON INC	0.090	0.877
MO	PHILIP MORRIS INC	0.710	0.655	NSM	NATIONAL SEMICONDUCTOR CORP	0.050	2.014
MOB	MOBIL CORP	1.200	1.135	NSP	NORTHERN STS PWR CO MINN	0.080	0.328
MOH	MOHASCO CORP	0.010	1.136	NT	NORTHERN TELECOM LTD	0.200	1.079
MOT	MOTOROLA INC	0.210	1.314	NWA	NORTHWEST AIRLS INC	0.070	1.731
MRK	MERCK & CO INC	0.730	0.628	NWT	NORTHWEST INDS INC	0.210	1.315
MSA	MESA PETE CO	0.160	2.537	OAT	QUAKER OATS CO	0.080	0.701
MSE	MASSEY FERGUSON LTD	0.010	0.874	OCF	OWENS CORNING FIBERGLAS CORP	0.080	0.898
MSU	MIDDLE SOUTH UTILS INC	0.180	0.223	OEC	OHIO EDISON CO	0.110	0.369
MTC	MONSANTO CO	0.320	1.079	OI	OWENS ILL INC	0.100	1.041
MYG	MAYTAG CO	0.040	0.520	OKE	ONEOK INC	0.030	1.391
MZ	MACY R H & CO INC	0.100	0.996	OM	OUTBOARD MARINE CORP	0.020	1.622

Ticker	Company		
P	PHILLIPS PETE CO	0.720	1.257
PABT	PABST BREWING CO	0.010	1.168
PB	PHIBRO CORP	0.200	0.349
PBD	PEABODY INTL CORP	0.010	1.607
PBI	PITNEY BOWES INC	0.050	1.049
PCAR	PACCAR INC	0.080	1.388
PCG	PACIFIC GAS & ELEC CO	0.310	0.081
PCH	POTLATCH CORP	0.050	1.331
PCO	PITTSTON CO	0.110	1.707
PD	PHELPS DODGE CORP	0.080	2.063
PE	PHILADELPHIA ELEC CO	0.170	0.292
PEG	PUBLIC SVC ELEC & GAS CO	0.180	0.402
PEL	PANHANDLE EASTN CORP	0.170	1.345
PEP	PEPSICO INC	0.390	0.637
PFE	PFIZER INC	0.460	0.749
PG	PROCTER & GAMBLE CO	0.770	0.523
PGL	PEOPLES ENERGY CORP	0.030	1.152
PIN	PUBLIC SVC CO IND INC	0.090	0.264
PKN	PERKIN ELMER CORP	0.130	1.615
PLT	PACIFIC LTG CORP	0.080	0.341
PN	PAN AMERN WORLD AWYS INC	0.020	1.450
PPG	PPG INDS INC	0.150	0.893
PRD	POLAROID CORP	0.080	1.358
PRX	PUREX INDS INC	0.030	0.659
PSY	PILLSBURY CO	0.100	0.662
R	UNIROYAL INC	0.020	1.184
RAD	RITE AID CORP	0.050	1.396
RAL	RALSTON PURINA CO	0.150	0.750
RAM	RAMADA INNS INC	0.020	1.535
RB	READING & BATES CORP	0.080	2.601
RCA	RCA CORP	0.160	1.003
RCC	ROYAL CROWN COS INC	0.010	0.464
RD	ROYAL DUTCH PETE CO	1.090	0.898
RDS	REVCO D S INC	0.060	0.956
RE	REDMAN INDS INC	0.010	2.079
REV	REVLON INC	0.110	0.879

Ticker	Company		
REX	REXNORD INC	0.040	0.870
RJR	REYNOLDS R J INDS INC	0.570	0.670
RLM	REYNOLDS METAL CO	0.050	1.189
RM	ROLM CORP	0.060	1.797
ROAD	ROADWAY EXPRESS INC	0.090	1.832
ROK	ROCKWELL INTL CORP	0.290	1.214
ROP	ROPER CORP	0.000	0.999
RS	REPUBLIC STL CORP	0.050	0.881
RTN	RAYTHEON CO	0.370	1.553
RVS	REEVES BROS INC	0.010	0.390
S	SEARS ROEBUCK & CO	0.590	0.688
SA	SAFEWAY STORES INC	0.080	0.558
SAFC	SAFECO CORP	0.090	0.817
SCE	SOUTHERN CALIF EDISON CO	0.290	0.271
SD	STANDARD OIL CO CALIF	1.700	1.409
SED	SEDCO INC	0.140	2.031
SFA	SCIENTIFIC ATLANTA INC	0.070	1.658
SFF	SANTA FE INDS INC	0.220	1.665
SFN	SFN COS INC	0.030	0.955
SGN	SIGNAL COS INC	0.210	1.793
SGP	SCHERING PLOUGH CORP	0.170	0.759
SHW	SHERWIN WILLIAMS CO	0030	1.414
SKL	SMITHKLINE BECKMAN CORP	0.520	0.863
SKY	SKYLINE CORP	0.020	1.403
SLB	SCHLUMBERGER LTD	1.880	1.238
SLZ	SCHLITZ JOS BREWING CO	0.040	0.963
SMF	SINGER CO	0.030	1.132
SMI	SPRINGS MLS INC	0.020	1.189
SN	STANDARD OIL CO IND	1.790	1.377
SNT	SONAT INC	0.160	1.071
SO	SOUTHERN CO	0.260	0.321
SOC	SUPERIOR OIL CO	0.540	1.499
SOH	STANDARD OIL CO OHIO	1.180	1.592
SPP	SCOTT PAPER CO	0.080	1.050
SQB	SQUIBB CORP	0.190	0.655
SQD	SQUARE D CO	0.090	1.057
SR	SOUTHERN RY CO	0.170	1.000

APPENDIX: (concluded)

Ticker	Name	Percent of S&P 500	Beta	Ticker	Name	Percent of S&P 500	Beta
SRL	SEARLE G D & CO	0.190	1.218	TGR	TIGER INTL INC	0.030	1.715
SRT	ST. REGIS PAPER CO	0.130	1.110	TGT	TENNECO INC	0.500	1.313
STF	STAUFFER CHEM CO	0.110	0.781	TIC	TRAVELERS CORP	0.220	0.657
STK	STORAGE TECHNOLOGY CORP	0.120	1.860	TKA	TONKA CORP	0.010	1.546
STN	STEVENS JP & CO INC	0.030	0.934	TKR	TIMKEN CO	0.080	1.046
STPL	ST PAUL COS INC	0.120	0.725	TL	TIME INC	0.210	1.137
STY	STERLING DRUG INC	0.160	0.716	TMC	TIMES MIRROR CO	0.180	1.157
SUN	SUN INC	0.630	1.944	TNB	THOMAS & BETTS CORP	0.050	1.002
SUO	SHELL OIL CO	1.580	1.558	TRA	TRANE CO	0.030	1.090
SVC	STOKELY VAN CAMP INC	0.010	0.517	TRW	TRW INC	0.210	1.283
SX	SOUTHERN PAC CO	0.130	1.238	TX	TEXACO INC	0.990	1.277
SY	SPERRY CORP	0.170	1.561	TXB	TEXAS GAS TRANSMISSION CORP	0.080	1.643
T	AMERICAN TEL & TELEG CO	5.560	0.132	TXN	TEXAS INSTRS INC	0.220	1.362
TA	TRANSAMERICA CORP	0.170	1.161	TXO	TEXAS OIL & GAS CORP	0.390	1.747
TAN	TANDY CORP	0.400	2.026	TXT	TEXTRON INC	0.110	1.233
TDY	TELEDYNE INC	0.330	1.923	TXU	TEXAS UTILS CO	0.240	0.315
TEK	TEKTRONIX INC	0.120	1.182	TYM	TYMSHARE INC	0.040	1.856
TET	TEXAS EASTERN CORP	0.160	1.438	UAL	UAL INC	0.060	1.167
TFB	TAFT BROADCASTING CO	0.040	1.088	UCC	UNION CAMP CORP	0.140	1.058

UCL	UNION OIL CO CALIF	0.760	1.570	WLA	WARNER LAMBERT CO	0.210	0.787
UH	U S HOME CORP	0.020	2.233	WMB	WILLIAMS COS	0.090	1.624
UK	UNION CARBIDE CORP	0.410	0.791	WMOR	WESTMORELAND COAL CO	0.020	1.159
UN	UNILEVER N V	0.220	0.579	WMX	WASTE MGMT INC	0.170	1.509
UNP	UNION PAC CORP	0.580	1.598	WPC	WISCONSIN ELEC PWR CO	0.070	0.198
UPJ	UPJOHN CO	0.190	0.951	WPM	WEST POINT PEPPERELL INC	0.030	0.515
USG	UNITED STATES GYPSUM CO	0.060	0.937	WSN	WESTERN CO NORTH AMER	0.120	2.145
UT	UNITED TELECOMMUNICATIONS	0.190	0.583	WSW	WHITE CONS INDS INC	0.040	0.678
UTX	UNITED TECHNOLOGIES CORP	0.250	1.391	WWY	WRIGLEY WM JR CO	0.030	0.431
				WX	WESTINGHOUSE ELEC CORP	0.250	1.447
VEL	VIRGINIA ELEC & PWR CO	0.140	0.253	WY	WEYERHAEUSER CO	0.430	1.357
VFC	V F CORP	0.040	1.024				
VO	SEAGRAM LTD	0.230	1.317	X	UNITED STATES STL CORP	0.310	1.103
				XLO	EX CELL O CORP	0.040	1.763
W	WESTVACO CORP	0.070	1.124	XON	EXXON CORP	3.120	0.980
WAG	WALGREEN CO	0.040	1.058	XRX	XEROX CORP	0.400	0.936
WAN B	WANG LABS INC	0.230	2.489				
WCI	WARNER COMMUNICATIONS INC	0.390	1.401	YELL	YELLOW FGHT SYS INC	0.030	0.773
WEN	WENDYS INTL INC	0.040	1.731				
WFI	WHEELABRATOR FRYE INC	0.090	1.361	Z	WOOLWORTH F W CO	0.060	0.920
WHR	WHIRLPOOL CORP	0.110	0.851	ZB	CROWN ZELLERBACH CORP	0.090	1.234
WHX	WHEELING PITTSBURGH STL CORP	0.010	1.670	ZE	ZENITH RADIO CORP	0.020	1.304
WIN	WINN DIXIE STORES INC	0.090	0.196	ZRN	ZURN INDS INC	0.020	1.181

Source: *Inside S&P 500 Stock Index Futures* (Chicago: Chicago Mercantile Exchange, 1983).

Chapter 17

INVESTMENTS IN REAL ASSETS

In this chapter, we turn our attention to real assets; that is, tangible assets that may be seen, felt, held, or collected. Examples of such assets are real estate, gold, silver, diamonds, coins, stamps, and antiques. This is no small area from which to consider investments. For example, the total market value of all real estate holdings in the United States in the mid-1980s was in excess of $4.5 trillion as compared to $3 trillion in stocks and bonds.

As further evidence of value, in the 1980s, Rubens's painting, *Samson and Delilah,* sold for $5.4 million, and a 132-carat diamond earring set sold for $6.6 million. Coins and stamps also sold for values well into the hundreds of thousands.

A number of the traditional stock brokerage houses have moved into the area of real assets with such firms as Merrill Lynch participating in real estate and Thomson McKinnon Securities managing a diamond fund. Likewise, Citicorp of New York has an art investment program. No less than 25 million people in the United States are stamp collectors, and 8 million collect and invest in coins.

As was pointed out in Chapter 1, in inflationary environments, real assets have at times outperformed financial assets (such as stocks and bonds). With this in mind, the reader is well advised to become familiar with these investment outlets—not only to take advantage of the investment opportunities, but to be well aware of the pitfalls. A money manager who is challenged by clients to include real assets in a portfolio (such as real estate or precious metals) must be conversant not only with the opportunities, but also with the drawbacks.

ADVANTAGES AND DISADVANTAGES OF REAL ASSETS

As previously mentioned, real assets may offer an opportunity as an inflation hedge. This is because inflation means higher replacement costs for real estate, precious metals, and other physical items. Real assets also serve as an investment hedge against the unknown and feared. When people become concerned about world events, gold and other precious metals may be perceived as the last, safe haven for investments.

Real assets also may serve as an effective vehicle for portfolio diversification. Since financial and real assets at times move in opposite directions, some efficient diversification may take place. A study by Robichek, Cohn, and Pringle in the *Journal of Business* actually indicates that movements between various types of real and monetary assets are less positively correlated than are those for monetary assets alone.[1] The general findings indicate that enlarging the universe of investment alternatives would benefit the overall portfolio construction in terms of risk-return alternatives. The reader who wishes to follow the performance of a wide range of investments can consult the monthly investment scorecard of *Money* magazine as a source. An example for mid-1984 is presented in Table 17–1.

---

[1] Alexander A. Robichek, Richard A. Cohn, and John J. Pringle, "Return on Alternative Media and Implications for Portfolio Construction," *Journal of Business,* July 1972, pp. 427–43.

TABLE 17–1   Investment Scorecard

	Mid-May	A month earlier	A year earlier	One-month change (percent)	12-month change (percent)
Stocks					
Dow Jones Industrial Average	1157	1157	1214	0%	− 4.7%
Over-the-counter Index	251	243	302	+3.3	−16.9
Semiconductor stocks	56	51	46	+9.8	+21.8
Construction machinery stocks	338	369	319	−8.4	+ 6.0
Interest-bearing securities (prices)					
Long-term corporate	63.1	64.6	74.5	−2.3	−15.3
Long-term Treasury	63.65	65.0	75.7	−2.2	−16.0
Interest-bearing securities (yields)					
Long-term corporate	13.9%	13.6%	11.5%	+2.2	+20.9
Long-term Treasury	12.8%	12.5%	10.5%	+2.4	+21.9
Municipal bonds	10.0%	9.9%	8.9%	+1.0	+12.4
Money market certificates	10.1%	10.1%	8.6	0	+ 1.7
Money market funds	9.3%	9.0%	7.9%	+3.3	+17.7
Metals and gems					
Gold (ounce)	$372	$382	$440	−2.6	−15.5
Silver (ounce)	$8.63	$9.10	$12.90	−5.2	−33.1
Diamond (one-carat D-flawless)	$14,500	$14,500	$17,000	0	−14.7
Real estate					
Median single-family house	$72,400	$71,800	$68,900	+0.8	+ 5.1
REIT index	3.68	3.59	3.94	+2.5	− 6.6
Collectibles					
Sotheby art index	289	—	257	—	+12.5
Coin portfolio	$24,735	—	$19,910	—	+24
U.S. stamp index	568.6	—	628.3	—	− 9.5

Notes and cautions: House price is for March. Sources: National Association of Securities Dealers, Standard & Poor's, Shearson Lehman/American Express, the Bond Buyer, Federal Reserve, Donoghue's Money Fund Report, Handy & Harman, the Diamond Registry, National Association of Realtors, Numismatic Professionals, Linn's Stamp News.

A final advantage of an investment in real assets is the psychic pleasure that may be provided. One can easily relate to a beautiful painting in the living room, a mint gold coin in a bank lockbox, or an attractive real estate development.

There are many disadvantages to consider as well. Perhaps the largest drawback is the absence of large, liquid, and relatively efficient markets. Whereas stocks or bonds can generally be sold in a few minutes at a value close

to the latest quoted trade, such is not likely to be the case for real estate, diamonds, art, and other forms of real assets. It may take many months to get the desired price for a real asset, and even then, there is an air of uncertainty about the impending transaction until it is consummated.

Furthermore, there is the problem of dealer spread or middleman commission. Whereas in the trading of stocks and bonds, spreads or commissions are very small (usually 1 or 2 percent), dealer spreads for real assets can be as large as 20 to 25 percent or more. This is particularly true for small items that do not have great value. On more valuable items, such as rare paintings, valuable jewels, or mint gold coins, the dealer spread tends to be smaller (perhaps 5 to 10 percent) but still more than that on securities.

The investor in real assets generally receives no current income (with the possible exception of real estate) and may in fact incur storage and insurance costs. Furthermore, there may be the problem of high unit cost for investments. You cannot easily acquire multiple art masterpieces.

A final drawback or caveat in real assets is the hysteria or overreaction that tends to come into the marketplace from time to time. Gold, silver, diamonds, and coins may be temporarily bid all out of proportion to previously anticipated value. The last buyer, who arrives too late, may end up owning a very unprofitable investment. The trick is to get into the recurring cycle early enough to take advantage of the large capital gains opportunities that regularly occur for real assets. Also, you should buy items of high enough quality so that you can ride out the setbacks if your timing is incorrect.

In the remainder of this chapter, we will examine real estate, gold, silver, diamonds, and other collectibles as investment outlets. Because real estate lends itself more directly to analytical techniques familiar to students of finance, it will receive a proportionately larger share of our attention.

REAL ESTATE AS AN INVESTMENT

Approximately one half of the households in the United States own real estate as a home or investment. Also, many firms in the brokerage and investment community have also moved into the real estate sector. As examples, Merrill Lynch and Shearson Lehman/American Express have acquired real estate affiliates to broker property, conduct mortgage banking activities, or package real estate syndications. While only 2.3 percent of pension fund assets are currently in real estate, predictions indicate that the number may grow to 10 percent by the end of the current decade.[2]

Some insight into changing real estate values may be gained from viewing Figure 17–1. We see the gain for a dollar invested in 1946 (as compared to fixed-income investments).

---

[2] "Soaring Real Estate Values Are Enticing Big Securities Concerns into the Field," *The Wall Street Journal,* August 6, 1980, p. 32.

FIGURE 17–1   Growth in Value, 1946–1980 ($1 of investment)

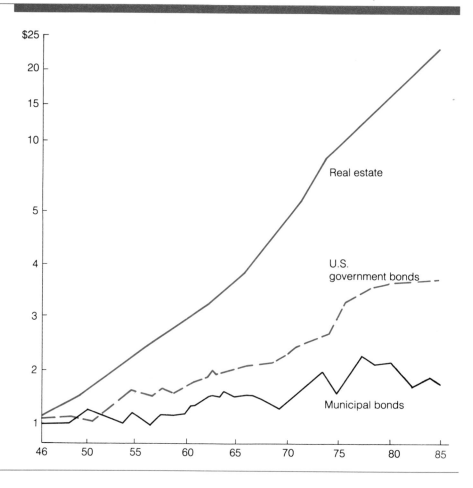

In Table 17–2, we see the change in conventional mortgage rates and median home prices in the United States. The gain in home prices is well over threefold.

Real estate investments may include such outlets as your own home, duplexes and apartment buildings, office buildings, shopping centers, industrial buildings, hotels and motels, as well as raw land. The investor may participate as an individual, as part of a limited partnership real estate syndicate, or through a real estate investment trust. These forms of ownership will receive further coverage toward the end of this section.

We have already talked generally about the advantages and disadvantages of real assets (on the positive side, an inflation hedge and the associated psychic value, and on the negative side, illiquidity and high transaction costs).

TABLE 17–2   Mortgage Rates and Home Prices

Year	*Average conventional mortgage rate*	*Median price of a new home**
1970	8.40	$23,258
1971	7.71	24,998
1972	7.56	27,110
1973	7.98	30,823
1974	8.97	34,055
1975	9.11	37,237
1976	9.05	42,200
1977	8.80	47,900
1978	9.30	55,100
1979	10.48	64,000
1980	12.25	72,700
1981	14.16	78,000
1982	14.47	80,400
1983	12.20	82,500
1984	13.75	86,300

* There are a number of different definitions of "average new home." The value may change somewhat between data collectors.
Sources: Federal Home Loan Bank Board (Washington, D.C.); National Association of REALTORS® (Chicago); Moody's (New York), Jim Kaden, economist; U.S. League of Savings Associations (Chicago); and Federal Reserve System (Washington, D.C.).

Over and above these considerations, real estate also has some unique features of its own. A major advantage of real estate relates to tax considerations. Accelerated depreciation and interest payments can provide substantial tax benefits.[3] Also, real estate provides for a high degree of leverage with a cash down payment of 20 to 25 percent supporting a large asset base. Most other forms of real assets do not serve so readily as collateral. An issue associated with real estate is the high degree of government regulation (particularly at the local level). Thus, the investor must be prepared to deal with zoning regulations, building codes, and the incidence of relatively high property taxes. On the other hand, the government also serves in a positive role by providing guarantees for FHA and VA loans and a secondary market for mortgages (the original lender can dispose of the initial mortgage).

Throughout the rest of this section on real estate, we will evaluate a typical real estate investment and the related tax aspects, consider new methods of real estate financing, and examine limited partner syndicates and real estate investment trusts.

[3] In the tax reform package developed by the Treasury Department in 1984–85, the tax benefits related to real estate would be reduced somewhat by extending the depreciation period. It is still problematical as to whether the proposed reform package will become law. The examples in this chapter are based on the tax laws in existence in mid-1985.

INVESTMENT EXAMPLE

Assume we are considering investing $170,000 in a new fourplex (four-unit apartment housing project). Our land costs will be $30,000, and the actual physical structure will cost $140,000. This latter amount will be the value to be depreciated. Though we are dealing with relatively small numbers for ease of computation, the same types of considerations would apply to a multimillion-dollar shopping center or office building. Before we actually evaluate our cash inflows and outflows, we will consider tax and accounting factors related to depreciation in real estate.

Depreciation Effects

In the present case, we can write off depreciation on real estate over 18 years. The appropriate annual depreciation schedule is presented in Table 17–3.[4]

Applying the depreciation schedule in Table 17–3 to our $140,000 physical structure (fourplex building), we show the depreciation schedule in Table 17–4. The $30,000 land value cannot be written off for depreciation purposes.

TABLE 17–3   Accelerated Depreciation Allowance on Real Estate under the 1981 Economic Recovery Tax Act and 1984 Deficit Reduction Act (approximates 175 percent declining balance depreciation with an eventual shift to straight-line)

Year of depreciation	Percentage depreciation
1–2	9%
3	8
4–5	7
6	6
7–12	5
13–18	4

Most real estate investors prefer the most rapid depreciation possible in the early years because it provides a tax shelter for other income. However, there are two issues here. One is that a rapid rate of depreciation in the early life of the asset dictates a slower rate in the later years as depreciation runs out.

A second issue related to accelerated depreciation is that of *recaptured depreciation,* which can take place upon selling the property. When accelerated depreciation is taken and the property is sold at a profit, part of the profit may be taxed as ordinary income rather than capital gains. This part of the profit is considered to be recaptured depreciation.

---

[4] Low-income rental property can be written off over 15 years. The present project would not qualify for such treatment.

TABLE 17–4   Accelerated Depreciation Schedule for Investment

Year	Percentage depreciation	Initial unit value	Dollar depreciation
1	9%	$140,000	$12,600
2	9		12,600
3	8		11,200
4	7		9,800
5	7		9,800
6	6		8,400
7	5		7,000
8	5		7,000
9	5		7,000
10	5		7,000
11	5		7,000
12	5		7,000
13	4		6,600
14	4		5,600
15	4		5,600
16	4		5,600
17	4		5,600
18	4		5,600

Cash Flow Considerations

The only aspect of our investment we have considered so far is depreciation. We have established the fact that on a $170,000 investment with $30,000 in land and $140,000 in the building, we could take 9 percent in first-year depreciation or $12,600 (see Table 17–4).[5] Depreciation is a noncash, tax-deductible item. We now must consider various cash flow items, such as the receipt of rent and the payment of interest, property taxes, insurance, maintenance expenses, and so on. An example of overall cash flow analysis is presented in Table 17–5.

We see in Table 17–5 that we have a loss of $12,270 for federal income tax purposes and that this provides a tax shelter benefit of $6,135 against other income. We also add depreciation back in to get cash flow because it was previously subtracted out but is really a noncash item. The negative and two positive values provide a positive cash flow figure of $6,465 at the bottom of Table 17–5.

We should point out that in considering the cost of the loan in Table 17–5, we have only evaluated interest payments. We might wish to consider repayment of principal as well. In the present case, we are assuming that in the first year we are paying 12 percent interest on a loan balance of $127,500, or $15,300 (as shown in Table 17–5). Assuming a 20-year loan (it is not unusual

---

[5] We are assuming the real estate is purchased at the first of the year so that the full 9 percent depreciation can be taken.

TABLE 17–5   Cash Flow Analysis for an Apartment (Fourplex) Investment

Gross annual rental (4 units at $425 per month/$5,100 per year each)		$20,400
Less 5 percent vacancy		1,020
Net rental income		$19,380
Interest expense on a loan of 75 percent of property value at 12 percent interest:		
(75%) × $170,000 = $127,500		
(12%) × $127,500 = $15,300	$15,300	
Property taxes	2,000	
Insurance	750	
Maintenance	1,000	
Depreciation	$12,600	
Total expenses		$31,650
Before-tax income or (loss)		(12,270)
Tax shelter benefit assumes 50 percent tax rate		6,135
Depreciation		12,600
Cash flow		$6,465

for the life of the loan to be different from the depreciation period), the total first-year payment for interest and principal is actually $17,070, indicating that $1,770 is applied toward the repayment of principal.

$$\text{Payment} - \text{Interest} = \text{Repayment of principal}$$
$$\$17,070 - \$15,300 = \$1,770$$

On this basis, our cash flow figure will be reduced to $4,695.

$$\text{Cash flow} - \text{Repayment of principal} = \text{Net cash flow}$$
$$\$6,465 - \$1,770 = \$4,695[6]$$

Of course, this value only applies to the first year. Rental income, interest, depreciation, and many other expense items will change each year. (For example, we will eventually run out of depreciation.)

In terms of investor return in the first year, the initial cash investment is $42,500. This is based on the total value of the property of $170,000 minus the initial loan amount of $127,500, requiring the investor to put up $42,500 in cash. With a *net* cash inflow of $4,695 in the first year, the cash on cash investor return in the first year is 11.05% ($4,695/$42,500). This represents the cash return on the investment divided by the actual "cash" investment.

---

[6] One could argue that we are building up equity or ownership interest through the repayment of principal. However, our focus for now is simply on the amount of cash flow going in and out. We will consider buildup in equity in a subsequent discussion.

The investor will also build up his or her equity or ownership interest by the amount of repayment toward principal as well as any increase in property value resulting from inflation. If the property increases by 8 percent in the first year, this represents an added benefit of $13,600 (8 percent times the $170,000 value of the property). Actually, return benefits associated with price appreciation may exceed all other considerations. An investor may be willing to accept little or no cash flow if he or she can enjoy inflation-related gains. Note that in the present case, the $13,600 gain from price appreciation alone would represent a first-year return on cash investment of 32 percent ($13,600/$42,500).

You can readily see the twin factors that make real estate attractive are depreciation write-off and appreciation in value due to price appreciation. Apartments, office buildings, warehouses, and shopping centers have served particularly well as good performers in inflationary environments. In low-inflationary environments, the benefits of real estate are substantially reduced as there is less price appreciation potential. The investor must also be sensitive to the possibility of new tax legislation that could reduce early depreciation write-off benefits. Nevertheless, the previous example clearly shows some of the key factors to examine in real estate investments.

FINANCING OF REAL ESTATE

One of the essential considerations in any real estate investment analysis is the cost of financing. In the prior example, we said a loan for $127,500 over 20 years at 12 percent interest would have yearly payments of $17,070. Note, in Table 17–6, the effects of various interest rates on annual payments.

TABLE 17–6   Interest Rates and Annual Repayment Obligations for a 20-Year Loan (principal amount equals $127,500)

	8 percent	10 percent	12 percent	14 percent	16 percent
Annual payment	$ 12,986	$ 14,975	$ 17,070	$ 19,251	$ 21,504
Total interest over the life of the loan	132,220	172,000	213,900	257,520	302,580

We see the difference in annual payments ranges from $12,986 at 8 percent up to $21,504 at 16 percent. Even more dramatic is the increase in total interest paid over the life of the loan; it goes from $132,220 at 8 percent to $302,580 at 16 percent. (Keep in mind that the total loan was only $127,500.)

An investor who has the unlikely opportunity to shift out of the loan at 16 percent into one at 8 percent might be willing to pay as much as $83,692.72 for the privilege. (Tax effects are not specifically considered here.)

16 percent interest − 8 percent interest = Dollar difference in annual payments

$21,504   − $12,986   = $8,518

Present value of $8,518 over 20 years assuming an 8 percent discount rate (see Appendix D at the end of the book):

$$\$8,518 \times 9.818 = \$83,629.72$$

Thus, it is easy to appreciate the role of interest rates in a real estate investment decision. No industry is more susceptible to the impact of changing interest rates than real estate. Each time the economy overheats and interest rates skyrocket, the real estate industry comes to a standstill. With the eventual easing of interest rate pressures, the industry once again enjoys a recovery.

This pattern has continued into the 1980s. It is within this environment that many traditional lenders have hesitated to commit themselves to long-term lending on a fixed interest rate basis. A 20-year loan commitment at a fixed rate of 10 percent can be both embarrassing and expensive to the lender when interest rates advance to 14 or 15 percent.

New Types of Mortgages

In actuality, a whole new set of mortgage arrangements have appeared as alternatives to the fixed interest rate mortgage (particularly for home mortgages). The borrower must now be prepared to consider such alternative lending arrangements as the *variable rate mortgage,* the *graduated payment mortgage,* and the *shared appreciation mortgage.*

Adjustable rate mortgage (ARM).   Under an adjustable rate mortgage, the interest rate is adjusted regularly. Recent pronouncements by federal regulatory authorities have indicated a tendency to allow the rate to *float* more and more with market conditions (originally there were many restrictions). If interest rates go up, borrowers may either increase their normal payments or extend the maturity date of the loan at the same, fixed-payment level to fully compensate the lender. Similar downside adjustments can also be made if interest rates fall. Generally, adjustable rate mortgages are initially made at rates 1 to 2 percent below fixed-interest rate mortgages because the lender enjoys the flexibility of changing interest rates and is willing to share the benefits with the borrower. Adjustable rate mortgages currently account for over half of the residential mortgage market. Although adjustable rate mortgages usually have an upper boundary (such as 15 or 18 percent), there is a real possibility of default for many borrowers if interest rates reach high levels.

Graduated payment mortgage (GPM).   Under this type of financial arrangement, the payments start out on a relatively low basis and increase over the life of the loan. This type of mortgage may be well suited to the young borrower who has an increasing repayment capability over the life of the loan.

An example would be a 30-year, $50,000 loan at 12 percent which would normally require monthly payments of $503.20 under a standard fixed-payment mortgage. With a graduated payment mortgage, monthly payments might start out as $350 or $400 and eventually progress to over $600. The GPM plan has been referred to by a few of its critics as the "gyp em" plan, in that early payments may not be large enough to cover interest and therefore later payments must cover not only the amortization of the loan, but also interest on the accumulated, unpaid, early interest. This is not an altogether fair criticism but merely an interpretation of what the graduated payment stream represents.

Shared appreciation mortgage (SAM). Perhaps the newest and most innovative of the mortgage payment plans is the shared appreciation mortgage. This provides the lender with a direct hedge against inflation because he directly participates in any increase in value associated with the property being mortgaged. The lender may enjoy as much as 30 to 40 percent of the appreciation in value over a specified time period, such as 10 years. The lender may take his return from the selling of the property or from the refinancing of the appreciated property value with a new lender. In return for this appreciation potential privilege, the lender may advance funds at well below current market rates (perhaps at three quarters of current rates). The shared appreciation mortgage is not yet legal in all states.

Other forms of mortgages. Somewhat similar to the shared appreciation mortgage is the concept of *equity participation* that is popular in commercial real estate. Under an equity participation arrangement, the lender not only provides the borrowed capital, but part of the equity or ownership funds as well. A major insurance company or savings and loan thus may acquire an equity interest of 10 to 25 percent (or more). This financing arrangement becomes popular each time inflation rears its head. Some lenders are simply unwilling to commit capital for long time periods without a participation feature.

Borrowers may also look toward a *second mortgage* for financing. Here a second lender provides additional financing beyond the first mortgage in return for a secondary claim or lien. The second mortgage is generally for a shorter period of time than the initial mortgage. Primary suppliers of second mortgages in the 1980s have been sellers of property. Quite often, in order to consummate a sale, it is necessary for the seller to supplement the financing provided by a financial institution. Sellers providing second mortgages generally advance the funds at rates below the first mortgage rate to facilitate the sale, whereas other second mortgage lenders (nonsellers) will ask for a few percentage points above the first mortgage rate to compensate for the extra risk of being in a secondary claim position.

In some cases, sellers may actually provide all the financing to the buyer. Usually the terms of the mortgage are for 20–30 years, but the seller has the right to call in the loan after three to five years if he so desires. The assumption

is that the buyer may have an easier time finding his own financing at that point in time. This may or may not turn out to be true.

FORMS OF REAL ESTATE OWNERSHIP

Ownership of real estate may take many forms. The investor may participate as an individual, in a regular partnership, through a real estate syndicate (generally a limited partnership), or through a real estate investment trust (REIT).

Individual or Regular Partnership

Investing as an individual or with two or three others in a regular partnership offers the simplest way of getting into real estate from a legal viewpoint. The investors pretty much control their own destinies and can take advantage of personal knowledge of local markets and changing conditions to enhance their returns.

As is true with most smaller and less complicated business arrangements, there is a well-defined center of responsibility that often leads to quick corrective action. However, there may be a related problem of inability to pool adequate capital to engage in large-scale investments as well as the absence of expertise to develop a wide range of investments. Furthermore, there is unlimited liability to the investor(s).

Syndicate or Limited Partnership

In order to expand the potential for investor participation, a syndicate or limited partnership may be formed.[7] The purpose of the limited partnership is to combine the limited liability protection of a *corporation* with the tax provisions of a *regular partnership*. The limited partnership works as follows: a general partner forms the limited partnership and has unlimited liability for the partnership liabilities. The general partner then sells participation units to the limited partners whose liability is generally limited to the extent of their initial investment (such as $5,000 or $10,000). Limited liability is particularly important in real estate because mortgage debt obligations may exceed the net worth of the participants.

The other significant feature of the limited partnership (or any partnership) is that all profits or losses are directly assigned to the partners rather than accounted for in the business unit. Thus, there is avoidance of double taxation as would be true in a corporation. The direct assignment of tax losses in the early years of a project may be particularly attractive as a tax shelter device for a wealthy individual. As we showed in Table 17–5, a typical investment might be an apartment project that has a $12,270 first-year tax loss, in spite of the fact that there was a positive cash flow of $6,465 and perhaps another $13,600

---

[7] A syndicate may take the form of a corporation, but this is not common. The term *real estate syndicate* has become virtually synonymous with the limited partnership form of operation.

appreciation in value due to inflation. Investors can claim the tax losses directly rather than have them go through business or corporate taxation first. Thus, we see the limited partnership offers the dual benefits of (a) limited liability to limited partners (similar to a corporation) as well as (b) the avoidance of double taxation and therefore the direct assignment of losses as tax shelters (similar to individuals or regular partnerships).

As previously indicated, the limited partnership allows the investor to participate in much larger, more diversified holdings than the individual or normal partnership could hope to achieve. A wealthy investor in Connecticut can acquire an interest in apartments in Dallas, shopping centers in Phoenix, and so on. Furthermore, he or she will have full-time managers to look after the holdings.

As is true in almost any form of investment, there are also drawbacks to the limited partnership. As implied by the title, the *limited* partner has very little to say in the operations of the partnership. It is the general partner who represents the operation and makes the day-to-day decisions. This is fine as long as the general partner is operating in a prudent and effective manner. However, it is quite difficult for limited partners to replace the general partner when other forms of behavior appear.

Furthermore, the limited partners must be particularly sensitive to the front-end fees and commissions that the general partner might charge. These can vary anywhere from 5 to 10 percent to as large as 20 to 25 percent.[8] The investor must also be sensitive to any double-dealing that the general partner might be doing. An example would be selling property back and forth between different syndicates that the general partner has formed and taking a commission each time. The inflated paper profits may prove quite deceptive and costly to the uninformed limited partner.

In assessing a general partner and his associated real estate deal, the investor should look at a number of items. First of all, prior record of performance should be reviewed. Is this the 1st or 10th deal that the general partner has put together? The investor will also wish to be sensitive to any lawsuits against the general partner that might exist. The investor might also wish to ascertain whether he or she is investing in a *blind pool* arrangement where funds are provided to the general partner to ultimately select properties for investment or if specific projects have already been identified and analyzed.

Finally the investor may have to decide whether to invest in a limited partnership/syndication that is either *public* or *private* in nature. A public offering generally involves much larger total amounts and has gone through the complex and rigorous process of SEC registration. Of course, SEC registration only attempts to ensure that full disclosure has taken place—it does not judge the prudence of the venture. A private offering of a limited partnership syndication is usually local in scope and restricted to a maximum of 35 investors.

---

[8] Kenneth R. Harvey, *Beating Inflation with Real Estate* (New York: Random House, 1980), p. 230.

FIGURE 17–2   Data Sheet for an REIT

SOUTHMARK CORP. NYSE-SM RECENT PRICE **10** P/E RATIO **6.7** (Trailing: 5.7 / Median: NMF) EARN'S YLD **15.0%** DIV'D YLD **1.6%** **675**

High	16.8	30.8	31.1	32.9	26.3	5.0	4.1	1.5	1.3	2.1	3.9	4.8	6.5	12.5
Low	14.5	18.6	23.2	21.9	1.6	0.9	1.0	NA	NA	0.9	1.0	2.8	3.7	5.1

Insider Decisions 1983
A S O N D J F M A M J J A S O
to Buy 0 0 0 0 0 1 0 0 0 0 2 0 2 0
to Sell 0 0 2 2 1 1 0 0 0 0 0 0 0 0

10
(Continued from Capital Structure)
Common Stock 29,062,450 shs (34% of Cap'l)
Warrants
3.21 mill. Series C warrants each exercisable until 2-1-87 for 1.21 common share for a total price of $7.50, callable at $2.50. (Called effective 2-1-84).

Institutional Decisions
	3Q'82	4Q'82	1Q'83	2Q'83	3Q'83
to Buy	3	2	3	1	11
to Sell	4	5	4	1	
Hldg's(000)	1341	1338	1433	1329	3656

Percent 15.0
shares 10.0
traded 5.0

TIMELINESS 1 Highest — Relative Price Performance Next 12 Mos. 5 Lowest
SAFETY 3 (Scale: 1 Highest to 5 Lowest)
BETA 1.15 (1.00 = Market)

1986-88 PROJECTIONS
	Price	Gain	Ann'l Total Return
High	30	(+200%)	32%
Low	17	(+ 70%)	16%

© Value Line, Inc. 86-88E

1968	1969	1970	1971	1972	1973	1974	1975	1976	1977	1978	1979	1980	1981	1982	1983	1984	1985		86-88E
--	--	--	15.11	15.35	16.19	15.75	2.73	d6.97	d2.98	d1.25	1.69	1.88	3.26	5.47	8.32	10.25		Book Value per sh (A)	18.00
--	--	--	1.50	2.20	2.51	1.78	d12.59	d10.75	d7.68	d1.06	d.02	.35	.32	1.83	1.81	2.00		"Cash Flow" per sh	2.30
--	--	--	1.52	2.15	2.56	1.71	d12.85	d10.79	d.77	d1.53	d.31	.04	.19	1.19	1.34	1.50		Earnings per sh (B)	2.00
--	--	--	1.51	2.05	2.50	2.15	.37	--	--	--	--	--	.04	.05	.16		Div'ds Decl'd per sh (C)	.50
--	--	--	35.83	54.63	82.94	93.18	103.70	108.91	61.29	38.72	15.65	13.08	6.77	21.61	31.50	22.85		Loans & Real Est per sh	29.35
--	--	--	3.40	4.11	4.62	4.63	4.63	4.63	d4.63	7.79	8.31	18.17	18.10	19.63	35.00		Common Shs Outst'g	37.50
--	--	--	43%	74%	82%	7%	-72%	205%	--	--	10%	-10%	-30%	-5%	--		Premium over Book	35%
--	--	--	14.5	12.7	11.3	10.0	--	--	--	--	--	NMF	16.0	3.4	4.2		Avg Ann'l P/E Ratio	12.0
--	--	--	6.9%	7.9%	8.9%	10.0%	--	--	--	--	--	NMF	6.2%	3.0%	24.0%		Avg Ann'l Earn's Yield	8.3%
--	--	--	6.9%	7.5%	8.6%	12.5%	11.3%	--	--	--	--	--	1.0%	.8%			Avg Ann'l Div'd Yield	2.1%

CAPITAL STRUCTURE as of 9/30/83
ST Debt $53.5 mill. (7% of Cap'l)
LT Debt $381.3 mill. (49% of Cap'l)
Due in 5 Yrs 240.0 mill. LT Interest $45.0 mill.
(Total long-and short-term interest coverage in fiscal 1983: 2.4x)
Pfd Stock $80.3 mill. **Pfd Div'd** See below
1,606,024 shs. Series D cum. adj. rate dividend (floats at 175 basis points above the highest rate on three Treasury securities, between 8% and 17%) with $50 liq. value.
(Continued on Chart) (10% of Cap'l)

60.2	39.8	25.2	19.0	28.5	20.5	23.0	26.1	99.1	161.6	240	Gross Income ($mill) (A)	350
7.9	d58.6	d50.0	d35.8	d7.1	d2.5	.4	35.4	26.4	37.7	75.0	Net Profit ($mill)	95.0
13.2%	NMF	NMF	NMF	NMF	NMF	1.7%	13.4%	26.7%	23.3%	31.0%	Net Profit Margin	27.0%
431.7	480.5	504.6	284.0	179.4	121.8	108.6	123.1	391.0	618.5	800	Loans & Real Est ($mill)	1100
5.7	53.9	91.4	55.0	33.5	21.0	15.3	12.4	1.8	1.8	1.5	Loss Reserve ($mill)	1.0%
11.3%	9.3%	1.8%	1.2%	2.1%	2.1%	2.2%	5.5%	13.1%	13.2%	11.5%	Avg Interest Paid	11.0%
303.5	365.9	361.4	193.0	157.6	76.7	63.3	1.8	31.9	61.9	35.0	Short-Term Debt ($mill)	50.0
85.0	56.6	91.0	62.6	28.9	19.4	17.7	54.5	241.3	311.1	380	Long-Term Debt ($mill)	300
73.0	12.7	d32.3	d13.8	d5.8	13.2	15.6	59.3	149.8	293.1	490	Net Worth ($mill)	875
25.6%	13.3%	3.0%	6.4%	9.0%	14.2%	19.4%	51.9%	45.0%	53.9%	61.5%	% Cap Funds to Tot Cap	75.0%
.8%	7%	1.1%	1.5%	2.6%	4.4%	2.9%	3.5%	4.9%	3.8%	3.0%	% Expenses to Assets	2.5%
11.2%	NMF	NMF	NMF	NMF	NMF	1.3%	5.9%	15.3%	11.3%	11.0%	% Earned Total Cap'l	9.5%
10.3%	NMF	NMF	NMF	NMF	NMF	2.8%	11.3%	27.1%	19.3%	15.5%	% Earned Net Worth	11.0%

FUNDS FLOW
	1981	1982	1983
Net Profit Plus Noncash Charges	6.7	50.9	48.3
Investments Repaid	17.0	86.3	192.7
Net New Debt	(14.1)	32.7	(15.5)
New Equity	23.0	47.8	79.3
Investments Funded	35.8	219.8	281.3
Dividends Declared	--	2.2	8.6

FINANCIAL POSITION
	9/30/82	9/30/83
Senior Debt	$284.4 mill.	$368.8 mill.
Subordinated Debt	$40.8 mill.	$66.0 mill.
Sr Debt/Cap'l Funds	1.3:1	.9:1
Total Debt/Equity	2.7:1	1.3:1

PORTFOLIO CONDITION
	Year Ago	Latest
Mtges Repaid in Quarter	$28.2 mill.	$47.4 mill.
Loss Reserve—% of Invests	4%	2%
Non-Earn Assets—% of Invests	NA	NA

LOANS & REAL ESTATE ($mill.) (A)
Fiscal Year Ends	Sept. 30	Dec. 31	Mar. 31	June 30
1980	120.9	120.3	112.8	108.6
1981	105.8	104.2	102.1	123.1
1982	141.8	225.0	234.5	391.0
1983	449.1	476.0	473.8	618.5
1984	730.9	750	775	800

EARNINGS PER SHARE (A) (B)
Fiscal Year Ends	Sept. 30	Dec. 31	Mar. 31	June 30	Full Fiscal Year
1980	.01	--	.03	--	--
1981	--	--	.06	.11	.19
1982	.30	.37	.47	.05	1.19
1983	.06	.18	.38	.72	1.34
1984	.26	.40	.40	.44	1.50

QUARTERLY DIVIDENDS PAID (C)
Calendar	Mar. 31	June 30	Sept. 30	Dec. 31	Full Year
1980	NO DIVIDENDS PAID 1976-80				
1981	--	--	.04	--	.04
1982	--	--	--	.05	.05
1983	--	--	.04	.04	.08
1984					

(A) Fisc. yr. ends June 30th of cal. yr. Ended Sept. 30 thru fiscal '76. Fiscal '77 = 9 mos. Portfolio growth from June quarter '81 mostly from acquisitions. (B) Fully-diluted egs. beg. in '81, primary in '80 and before. Next egs. rep'l due late Jan. Excl. extra. gains: '76, $1.09; 9 mos. to 6/30/77, $11.71; '78, $3.41; '79, $1.95; '80, 9c; '81, 9c; '82. $1.04; '83, 96c; '84, 26c. (C) Next div'd meet'g about Feb. 1. Goes ex about Feb. 13. Div'd paym'ts: 3/15, 6/15, 9/15, 12/15.

BUSINESS: Southmark Corp. (formerly Citizens and Southern Realty Investors) acquires real estate assets, seeks to enhance their value, and then to realize a profit on their disposition. At 6/30/83, 34% of investments were in real estate of which apartments comprised 33%; shopping centers, 11%; condominiums, 9%; land, 24%; office buildings, 6%; hotels/motels, 7%; other, 10%. Owns 92% of North American Mortgage, 60% of American Realty Trust and interests in other real estate cos. Has 5,719 shareholders. Chrmn. & Pres. Gene E. Phillips and William S. Friedman have 41% of voting control. Inc.: Ga. Address: 1601 LBJ Fwy., Park West, Suite 800, Dallas, TX 75234.

The Series C warrants have been called, effective February 1st. Each warrant can be exchanged for 1.21 Southmark common shares until January 25th upon payment of $7.50 per warrant. At the recent common stock quotation of $10, the warrants have a value of $4.60, well above the $2.50 call price. As long as the common price remains above 8¼, the warrants should be exercised rather than permitted to be called. **Common shares outstanding will have increased by more than 75% in fiscal '84**, which ends June 30th. The call for redemption and subsequent conversion of the Series A preferred stock added 10.5 million shares in the September and December periods. And warrant exercise will add another 4.8 million shares in the March quarter. In order to give more meaningful year-to-year comparisons, the accompanying statistics now show fully diluted earnings from '81 forward. **Earnings comparisons remain strong, but the stock's price has weakened.** The weakness relates in part to a negative article on real estate syndications, which appeared in a national magazine. Such syndications are Southmark's bread and butter business (probably 35% or more of combined

September- and December-quarter profits). Management reports that its syndication business is strong and that it has never had a syndication go awry. But when the bubble bursts, Southmark could experience negative fallout. There's also a measure of uncertainty that stems from the ambitious pace of acquisitions in '81-'83 and from the complexity that's been introduced into financial reporting by the resulting rapid growth of disparate financial entities. Thus, only venturesome investors will want to hold these shares on the expectation that fundamentals will be strong enough to support superior relatively price action over the next year. **Most future acquisitions will be designed to fill out present business lines.** As the life insurance business and the S&L operations grow, they will reduce the relative importance of real estate transactions and thereby tend to smooth the income statement's bottom line. The lower interest rates that we think will unfold over the 3- to 5-year pull will be conducive to profitable growth of both of these new activities. Lower rates will also help contain the cost of the $130 million floating rate preferred.   D.L.H/N.R.W

Company's Financial Strength C+
Stock's Price Stability 5
Price Growth Persistence 60
Earnings Predictability 30

Source: *The Value Line Investment Survey,* © 1984 Value Line, Inc., January 20, 1984, p. 675.

Real Estate Investment Trusts

Another form of real estate investment is the real estate investment trust (REIT). REITs are similar to mutual funds or investment companies and trade on organized exchanges or over-the-counter. They pool investor funds, along with borrowed funds, and invest them directly in real estate or use them to make construction or mortgage loans to investors.

The advantage to the investor of an REIT is that he or she can participate in the real estate market for as little as $5 to $10 per share. Furthermore, this is the most liquid type of real estate investment because of the large secondary market for the shares.

REITs were initiated under the Real Estate Investment Trust Act of 1960. Like other investment companies, they enjoy the privilege of single taxation of income (only the stockholder pays and not the trust). In order to qualify for the tax privilege of a REIT, a firm must pay out at least 90 percent of its income to shareholders, have no less than 75 percent of its assets in real estate, and concurrently obtain at least 75 percent of its income from real estate.

REITs may take any of three different forms or combinations thereof. *Equity trusts* buy, operate, and sell real estate as an investment; *construction and development trusts* make short-term loans to developers during their construction period; and *mortgage trusts* make long-term loans to real estate investors. REITs are generally formed and advised by affiliates of commercial banks, insurance companies, mortgage bankers, and other financial institutions. Representative issues include Bank America Realty, Continental Illinois Property, and Connecticut General Mortgage.

Although REITs were enormously popular investments during the 1960s and early 1970s, the bottom fell out of the REIT market in the mid-1970s. Many had made questionable loans that came to the surface in the tight money, recessionary period of 1973–75. Nevertheless, REITs have now regained some of their earlier popularity. Many investors look at the equity trust, which owns real estate directly, as a hedge against inflation. Somewhat less popular are the construction and development trusts and mortgage trusts (many REITs combine these various functions). The investor in REITs hopes to receive a reasonably high yield because 90 percent of income must be paid out in the form of dividends plus a modest capital appreciation in stock value. In some cases, outside investors have taken over REIT's with the intention of liquidating assets at higher than current stock market values.

There are over 200 REITs from which the investor may choose. Further information on REITs may be acquired from the National Association of Real Estate Investment Trusts, 1101 17th St., N.W., Washington, D.C. 20036. In Figure 17–2, a Value Line data sheet is presented for Southmark Corporation, an example of a reasonably successful REIT.

GOLD AND SILVER

We now examine a number of other forms of real asset investments. Precious metals represent the most volatile of the investment alternatives. Gold and

FIGURE 17–3   Dollar per Troy Ounce

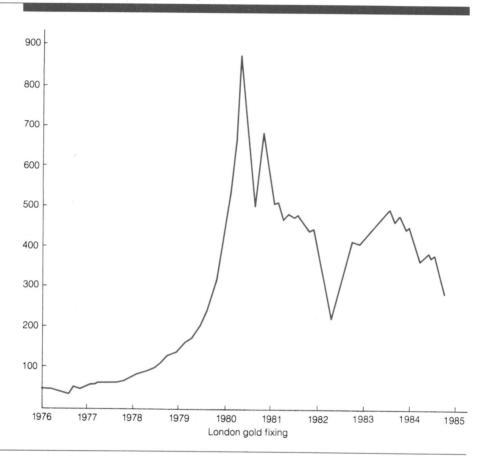

London gold fixing

silver tend to move up in troubled times and show a decline in value during stable, predictable periods. Observe the movement in the price of gold between January 1976 and December 1984 in Figure 17–3.

Gold

Major factors that tend to drive up gold prices are fear of war, political instability, and inflation (these were particularly evident in 1979 with the takeover of U.S. embassies and double-digit inflation). Conversely, moderation in worldwide tensions and lower inflation cause a decline in gold prices. High interest rates are also a negative influence on gold prices. When interest rates are high, it may be very expensive to carry gold as an investment.

Gold may be owned in many different forms, and a survey by *Changing Times* indicated that 30 percent of the United States population with incomes

over $30,000 per year owned gold or other forms of precious metals. Let's examine the different forms of gold ownership.

Gold bullion. Gold bullion includes gold bars or wafers. The investor may own anywhere from 1 troy ounce to 10,000 troy ounces (valued at approximately $3 million in 1985). Smaller bars generally trade at a 6 to 8 percent premium over pure gold bullion value, with larger bars trading at a 1 to 2 percent premium. Gold bullion may provide storage problems, and unless the gold bars remain in the custody of the bank or dealer who initially sells them, they must be reassayed before being sold.

Gold coins. Many of the storing and assaying costs associated with gold bullion can be avoided by investing directly in gold coins. There are three basic outlets for investing in gold coins. First, there are *gold bullion coins,* such as the South African Kruggerand, the Mexican 50 peso, and the Austrian or Hungarian 100 korona. These coins trade at a small premium of 2 to 3 percent over pure bullion value and afford the investor an excellent outlet for taking a position in the market. A second form is represented by *common date gold coins* that are no longer minted, such as the United States double eagle, the British sovereign, or the French Napoleon. These coins may trade at as much as 50 to 100 times their pure gold bullion value. Finally, there are gold coins that are *old* and *rare* and that may trade at a numismatic value into the thousands or hundreds of thousands of dollars.

Gold stocks. In addition to gold bullion and gold coins, the investor may choose to take a position in gold by simply buying common stocks that have heavy gold mining positions. Examples of companies listed on U.S. exchanges include Campbell Red Lake (Canadian based), Dome Mines (Canadian based), and Homestake Mining (U.S. based). Because these securities often move in the opposite direction of the stock market as a whole, they may provide excellent portfolio diversification. The investor may also examine closed-end investment companies with heavy gold mining positions (such as ARA Limited).

Gold futures contracts. Finally, the gold investor may consider trading in futures contracts. Gold futures are traded on five different U.S. exchanges and on many foreign exchanges.[9]

Silver

Silver has many of the same investment characteristics as gold in terms of being a hedge against inflation and a safe haven for investment during troubled times. Silver has moved from $4 a troy ounce in 1976 to over $50 an ounce in early 1980 and then back to $6 an ounce in 1985.

---

[9] There are also options on gold futures on the Comex.

More so than gold, silver has heavy industrial and commercial applications. Areas of utilization include photography, electronic and electrical manufacturing, electroplating, dentistry, and silverware and jewelry. It is estimated that industrial uses of silver exceed annual production by 150 million ounces per year. Furthermore, supply of silver does not necessarily increase with price because silver is a byproduct of copper, lead, zinc, and gold. Because of the undersupply factor, many consider silver to be appropriate for long-term holding.

Investment in silver can also take many different forms. Some may choose to buy *silver bullion* in the form of silver bars. Because the price of silver generally is 1/20th to 1/40th the price of gold and larger bulk is involved for an equivalent dollar size investment, the storage and carrying costs can be quite high. Secondly, *silver coins* may be bought in large bags or as rare coins for their numismatic value. Keep in mind that dimes, quarters, and half-dollars minted during and prior to 1965 were 90 percent pure silver. As a third outlet, the investor may wish to consider *silver futures contracts.* Finally, the investor may purchase *stocks* of firms that have interests in silver mining, such as Callahan Mining, Hecla Mining, or Rosario Resources.

PRECIOUS GEMS

Precious gems include diamonds, rubies, sapphires, and emeralds. Diamonds and other precious gems have appeal to investors because of their small size, easy concealment, and great durability. They are particularly popular in Europe because of a long-standing distrust of paper currencies as a store of value.

The reason diamonds are so valuable can be best understood by considering the production process. It is estimated that 50 to 200 *tons* of rock or sand is required to uncover one carat (1/142 of an ounce) of quality diamonds.

The distribution of diamonds is under virtual monopolistic control by De Beers Consolidated Mines of South Africa, Ltd. They control the distribution of approximately 80 percent of the world's supply and have a stated policy of maintaining price control. Diamonds have generally enjoyed a steady, somewhat spectacular movement in price. For example, the price of a "D" color, one-carat, flawless, polished diamond increased over 10-fold between 1974 and 1980.

Of course, not all diamonds have done so well. Furthermore, there have been substantial breaks in the market, such as in 1974 and 1980–82 when diamond prices declined by one fourth and more. Even with large increases in value, the diamond investor does not automatically come out ahead. There may be dealer markups anywhere from 10 percent to 100 percent so that three to five years of steady gain may be necessary to show a substantial profit.

In no area of investment is product and market knowledge more important. Either you must be an expert yourself or know that you are dealing with an "honest" expert. Diamonds are judged on the basis of the four c's (color, clarity, carat weight, and cut), and the assessment of any stone should be certified by the Gemological Institute of America. As is true of most valuable

items, the investor is well advised to purchase the highest quality possible. You are considerably better off using the same amount of money to buy a higher-quality, smaller-carat diamond than a lesser-quality, high-carat diamond.

OTHER COLLECTIBLES

A listing of other collectibles for investment might include art, antiques, stamps, Chinese ceramics, rare books, sports memorabilia, and other items that appeal to various sectors of our society. Each offers psychic pleasure to the investor as well as the opportunity for profit.

Anyone investing in a collectible should have some understanding of current market conditions and of the factors that determine the inherent worth of the item. Otherwise, you may be buying someone else's undesirable holding at a premium price. It is important not to get swept away in a buying euphoria. The best time to buy art, antiques, or stamps is when the bloom is off the market and dealers are overburdened with inventory, not when there is a weekly story in *The Wall Street Journal* or *Business Week* about overnight fortunes being made. There seems to be a pattern or cycle in the collectibles market the same as in other markets (arts, antiques, and stamps actually do move together). The market was very strong in the 1970s with a pause in the mid-1970s caused by the recession. The market gained tremendous momentum from 1975 to 1980, with a sell-off in late 1980 and early 1981. Only a moderate recovery has taken place in the mid-1980s.

As is true of other markets, the wise investor in the collectibles market must be sensitive to dealer spreads. A price guide that indicates a doubling in value every two or three years may be meaningless if the person with whom you are dealing sells for $100 and buys back for $50. The wise investor/collector can best maintain profits by dealing with other collectors or investors and eliminating the dealer or middleman from the transaction where possible.

Such periodicals as *Money* magazine and the *Collector/Investor* provide excellent articles on the collectibles market. Specialized periodicals, such as *American Arts and Antiques, Coin World, Linn's Stamp News, The Sports Collectors Digest,* and *Antique Monthly,* also are helpful. The interested reader can find books on almost any type of collectible in a public library or large bookstore.

SUMMARY

Investments in real assets have gained increasing popularity in the last decade. They offer a measure of inflation protection, an opportunity for efficient portfolio diversification, and psychic pleasure to the investor.

A disadvantage is the absence of a large, liquid market, such as that provided by the securities markets. There also may be a large dealer or middleman spread, and the investor may have to forgo current income.

The hysteria that grips these markets from time to time not only creates substantial opportunities for profit, but also dictates that the investor must be particularly cautious about market timing. It can be quite expensive to be the last buyer in a gold or silver boom.

Investors in real estate must be sensitive to tax aspects related to the investment, particularly the impact of accelerated depreciation in the early years of the investment and the associated effect of recaptured depreciation when the property is sold. Although real estate may show a loss for federal income tax purposes, related tax savings and the adding back of depreciation may well create a positive cash flow. Real estate also may enjoy substantial appreciation benefits in an inflationary economy.

The financing of real estate is becoming increasingly complicated as lenders seek alternatives to fixed-rate mortgages. Thus, we have seen the creation of the adjustable rate mortgage (ARM) and other floating-rate plans, the graduated payment mortgage (GPM), and the shared appreciation mortgage (SAM).

Gold and silver represent two highly volatile forms of real assets in which price movements often run counter to events in the economy and the world. Bad news is good news (and vice versa) for precious metal investors. Gold and silver may generally be purchased in bullion or bulk form, as coins, in the commodities futures market, or indirectly through securities of firms specializing in gold or silver mining.

Precious gems and other collectibles, such as art, antiques, stamps, Chinese ceramics, and rare books, have caught the attention of investors in recent times. Although there are many warning signs, the wise and patient investor can do well over the long run. The investor should understand the factors that determine value before taking a serious investment position.

IMPORTANT WORDS AND CONCEPTS

Real assets	**Limited partnership**
REIT	**Blind pool**
Straight-line depreciation	**Equity trust**
Recaptured depreciation	**Construction and development**
Adjustable rate mortgage	**trust**
Graduated payment mortgage	**Mortgage trust**
Shared appreciation mortgage	**Equity participation**

DISCUSSION QUESTIONS

1. Why might real assets offer an opportunity as an inflation hedge?
2. Explain why real assets might add to effective portfolio diversification.
3. What are some disadvantages of investing in real estate?

4. In what way does real estate provide for a high degree of leverage?
5. In what ways does real estate provide substantial tax benefits?
6. What is an adjustable rate mortgage?
7. For what type of borrower is the graduated payment mortgage best suited?
8. Explain a shared appreciation mortgage.
9. What is meant by a seller loan with a call privilege?
10. How is liability handled in a limited partnership?
11. What are REITs? What are the various types of REITs?
12. What are some factors that drive up the price of gold? What are factors that drive it down?
13. What are three different ways to invest in gold coins?
14. Suggest some commercial and industrial uses of silver. What forms can silver investments take?
15. Explain how the dealer spread can affect the rate of return on a collectible item.

PROBLEMS

1. There is a strip shopping center with land valued at $200,000 and buildings valued at $1 million. The depreciation schedule in Table 17–3 will apply.
   a. What is the first-year depreciation deduction?
   b. Assume revenue minus all other expenses besides depreciation equals minus $10,000. Now, considering depreciation, how much will the before-tax loss be in the first year? How much will the cash flow be in the first year? Use a tax rate of 50 percent.
   c. Assume a 20-year loan equal to 75 percent of the total value of the property at 14 percent interest. Annual payments will be $135,890. How much of the annual payment will go toward interest and how much toward repayment of principal in the first year?
   d. Based on information in b and c, compute *net* cash flow (cash flow minus repayment of principal).
   e. What is the ratio of net cash flow to initial cash investment? Initial cash investment equals total investment minus the loan.
   f. If there is 7 percent inflation related to the total property value in the first year, what will be the ratio of inflationary gains to initial cash investment?
2. If straight-line depreciation over 18 years had been used in Problem 1 (with all else equal), how much cash flow would there be in the first year? Recompute parts a and b.
3. If there is only 1 percent inflation gain in Problem 1, what will the ratio of inflation gains to initial cash investment be? Comment on the importance of inflation to real estate investments.

SELECTED REFERENCES

Bleck, Erich K. "Real Estate Investments and Rates of Return." *The Appraisal Journal,* October 1973, pp. 535–47.

Cooper, James R., and Stephen A. Pyhrr. "Forecasting the Rates of Return on an Apartment Investment: A Case Study." *The Appraisal Journal,* July 1973, pp. 312–37.

The editors of *Consumer Guide,* with Peter A. Dickinson. *How to Make Money During Inflation/Recession.* New York: Harper & Row, 1980.

Folger, H. Russell. "20% in Real Estate: Can Theory Justify It?" *The Journal of Portfolio Management,* Winter 1984, pp. 6–13.

Freedman, Michael. *The Diamond Book.* Homewood, Ill.: Dow Jones-Irwin, 1980.

Harvey, Kenneth R. *Beating Inflation with Real Estate.* New York: Random House, 1980.

Lipscomb, Joseph. "Discount Rates for Cash Equivalent Analysis." *The Appraisal Journal,* January 1981, pp. 23–33.

McQuade, Walter. "Invest in the Art Market? Soybeans Might Be Safer." *Fortune,* May 1974, pp. 201–6.

Robichek, Alexander A.; Richard A. Cohn; and John J. Pringle. "Return on Alternative Media and Implications for Portfolio Construction." *Journal of Business,* July 1972, pp. 427–43.

Rosen, Lawrence R. *When and How to Profit from Buying and Selling Gold.* Homewood, Ill.: Dow Jones-Irwin, 1975.

Roulac, Stephen E. "Can Real Estate Returns Outperform Common Stocks?" *Journal of Portfolio Management,* Winter 1976, pp. 26–43.

Rush, Richard H. *Antiques as an Investment.* New York: Bonanza Books, 1968.

"Soaring Real Estate Values Are Enticing Big Securities Concerns into the Field." *The Wall Street Journal,* August 6, 1980, p. 32.

Shenkel, William M. *Modern Real Estate Principles.* Rev. ed. Plano, Tex.; Business Publications, 1980.

Van Caspel, Venita. *Money Dynamics in the 1980's.* Reston, Va.: Reston Publishing, 1980.

Wendt, Paul F., and Alan R. Cerf: *Real Estate Investment Analysis and Taxation.* New York: McGraw-Hill, 1979.

Chapter 18

INTERNATIONAL SECURITIES MARKETS

In Chapter 1, we discussed the advantage of diversification in terms of risk reduction. In order to reduce risk exposure, the investor may desire a broad spectrum of securities from which to choose. An investor who lives in California would hardly be expected to limit all his investments to that geographic boundary. The same might be said for an investor living in the United States or Germany or Japan. The advantages of crossing international boundaries may be substantial in terms of diversification benefits. While energy-importing nations such as France or Japan may temporarily suffer from high energy prices, energy-exporting nations are benefiting. The same can be said about the effects of crop failures, wars, tariffs, and many other factors. Furthermore, in spite of the alternating up and down markets in the United States, there is almost certain to be a bull market somewhere in the world for the investor who likes to keep his chips on the table at all times.

The main drawback to investing in international securities would appear to be the more complicated nature of the investment. Currently, one cannot simply pick up the phone and ask his broker to buy 100 shares of Banco Bilbao on the Spanish Stock Exchange (this may change some day in the future). Nevertheless, the difficulties of participating in international securities are not as great as one might initially expect. As will be later suggested in this chapter, there are a number of feasible and easily executed routes to follow in participating in the international markets.

The primary attention in this chapter is in international equities, although investments may certainly include fixed-income securities and real assets.

In the chapter, we shall examine the composition of world equity markets, the diversification and return benefits that can be derived from foreign investments, the obstacles that are present, and finally, the methods of participating in foreign investments, directly and indirectly.

THE WORLD EQUITY MARKET

In the early 1970s, U.S. securities represented 75 percent of the total market value of equities around the world. In the 1980s that value has declined to close to 50 percent as security markets in other countries have become more important. In Figure 18–1 we see a percentage breakdown of approximately a trillion dollars of equity securities in major exchanges outside of the United States. One can quickly see the importance of the Tokyo Stock Exchange in Japan as well as of a number of other key exchanges. The U.S. equity market, of course, is equal to the full size of this graph.

DIVERSIFICATION BENEFITS

As previously mentioned, not all foreign markets move in the same direction at any point in time. In Table 18–1, we see the stock market movements for a number of key countries over a 21-year period. Sharply contrasting movements are noted in such years as 1973 and 1977. In 1973 U.S. equities were

FIGURE 18–1   Market Values of Non-U.S. Equities at the End of 1980 (in billions of U.S. dollars; non-U.S. equity total = $1,049.3 billion)

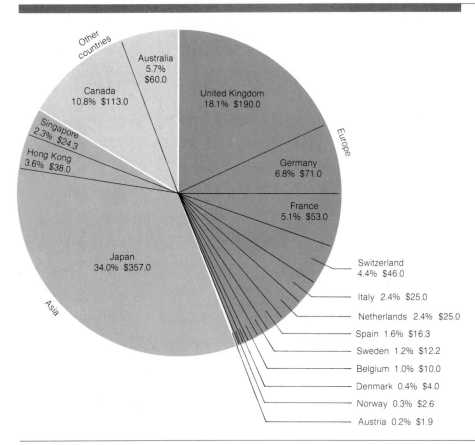

Source: Roger G. Ibbotson, Richard C. Carr, and Anthony W. Robinson, "International Equity and Bond Returns," *Financial Analysts Journal,* July–August 1982, p. 63.

down by 18.68 percent, while equities in Norway gained 128.52 percent, those in Austria appreciated by 25.09 percent, and those in Spain gained 24.03 percent. In 1977 U.S. equities showed a slightly bearish posture with a 3.03 percent decline, while equities in the United Kingdom were up 56.49 percent and stocks in Switzerland appreciated 25.49 percent.

Another way to consider diversification benefits is to measure the extent of correlation of stock movements. Such a measure is presented in Table 18–2, in which stock movements of a number of foreign countries are compared to those of the United States.

The average correlation is approximately .30, which is low. The best risk reduction benefits can be found by combining U.S. securities with those from such countries as Spain (−.115), Austria (−.076), and Norway (.009); and the least benefits can be found in combinations with Hong Kong (.814), the Neth-

TABLE 18–1   World Equities: Year-by-Year Adjusted Total Returns (in percent)*

Year	US total	Austria	Belgium	Denmark	France	Germany	Italy	Netherlands	Norway	Spain	Sweden	Switzerland	United Kingdom	Hong Kong	Japan	Singapore	Canada	Australia
								Europe										
1960	0.83	52.28	-7.99	3.77	6.72	42.32	46.18	3.24	12.24	10.14	5.51	43.82	0.13		38.50		-1.16	-0.07
1961	27.52	41.14	22.84	3.81	13.62	2.14	14.73	12.49	18.14	36.42	5.57	54.89	12.56		-13.03		39.03	14.86
1962	-9.29	-12.76	-1.99	8.12	11.38	-21.70	-10.44	-5.39	-15.43	19.65	12.47	-8.51	4.76		4.68		-6.84	0.95
1963	21.04	-4.28	18.06	17.77	-14.77	14.87	-12.71	17.71	0.42	0.15	12.92	-14.49	22.80		8.78		14.39	24.92
1964	16.71	3.78	8.04	11.88	-1.17	4.70	-26.43	9.61	10.22	10.44	23.17	-7.16	-5.14		10.93		24.36	5.17
1965	15.26	-1.16	-2.65	11.93	-4.10	-12.63	30.16	-10.00	0.37	16.12	11.00	-11.74	12.66		21.39		4.81	-9.75
1966	-8.21	-4.88	-15.82	5.63	-8.18	-15.06	8.89	-14.54	-7.61	11.87	-23.93	-12.91	-2.07		9.04		-9.24	4.87
1967	30.45	0.97	13.35	-11.88	0.46	51.80	-2.51	38.97	1.09	-8.48	7.69	52.39	16.57		-4.85		7.18	44.70
1968	14.95	2.95	13.63	17.81	14.81	13.61	4.23	37.58	21.55	31.42	45.52	30.44	51.34		26.43		26.61	28.62
1969	-9.86	6.90	7.18	3.36	18.39	23.42	15.19	-4.42	24.75	46.87	1.75	5.05	-12.52		34.15		3.21	16.10
1970	-1.00	13.49	9.66	-6.47	-5.14	-23.76	-17.52	-6.50	39.53	-3.68	-18.92	-13.17	-5.72	21.31	-6.35	-5.43	15.81	-19.14
1971	18.16	8.44	25.00	10.18	1.66	24.61	-12.34	1.76	14.13	26.26	36.12	27.41	47.99	59.52	46.55	65.52	14.13	-1.59
1972	17.71	37.65	32.69	112.20	24.83	18.54	15.33	29.56	9.03	42.30	16.82	28.61	3.93	161.66	126.56	211.04	33.12	21.06
1973	-18.68	25.09	18.16	5.44	3.83	-4.44	10.18	-4.74	28.52	24.03	2.86	-3.75	-23.44	-39.01	-20.13	-34.58	-3.11	-12.06
1974	-27.77	15.00	-11.74	-10.74	-22.43	17.20	-33.43	-15.56	-39.98	-8.49	11.72	-12.37	-50.33	-60.33	-15.65	-46.69	-26.52	-32.97
1975	37.49	-2.90	17.45	23.96	45.08	30.09	-8.69	50.23	-15.14	0.05	21.00	41.18	115.06	99.56	19.84	63.57	15.07	50.71
1976	26.68	15.58	13.00	7.23	-20.03	6.57	-26.55	16.94	14.98	-36.00	6.37	10.42	-12.55	40.55	25.80	13.83	9.71	-10.00
1977	-3.03	-3.76	11.02	1.74	5.07	23.08	-18.92	14.65	-23.83	-19.66	-21.64	25.49	56.49	-11.58	15.70	4.60	-1.37	11.25
1978	8.53	15.68	33.27	9.47	73.19	26.96	46.37	20.83	6.81	7.86	23.96	21.82	14.63	18.61	53.33	45.31	20.55	22.24
1979	24.18	19.43	21.08	-2.18	28.90	-1.93	17.39	19.95	183.01	5.51	2.64	12.21	22.20	83.50	-11.69	28.58	52.26	43.44
1980	33.22	-11.90	-11.40	15.80	-1.30	-8.20	78.40	11.90	-17.30	4.60	21.00	-7.10	38.80	69.90	29.70	61.20	22.00	52.20

* U.S.-dollar-adjusted.

Source: Roger G. Ibbotson, Richard C. Carr, and Anthony W. Robinson, "International Equity and Bond Returns," *Financial Analysts Journal,* July–August 1982, p. 69.

TABLE 18–2   Correlation of Foreign Stock Movements with U.S. Stock
Movement (1960–1980)

U.S.	1.000
Hong Kong	.814
Netherlands	.730
Canada	.710
Australia	.699
United Kingdom	.617
Singapore	.579
Switzerland	.454
Sweden	.398
Belgium	.389
Denmark	.243
Japan	.216
France	.214
Germany	.210
Italy	.208
Norway	.009
Austria	−.076
Spain	−.115

Source: Roger G. Ibbotson, Richard C. Carr, and Anthony W. Robinson, "International Equity and Bond Returns,"
Financial Analysts Journal, July–August 1982, p. 71.

erlands (.730), and Canada (.710). Somewhat attractive is the relatively low
correlation with Japan (.216). According to one researcher, a well-diversified
international portfolio can achieve the same risk reduction benefits as a pure
U.S. portfolio that is twice the size in terms of securities.[1] In Chapter 19, there
is a much more detailed discussion on the importance of correlation considerations to risk reduction. We have merely touched the surface for now.

RETURN POTENTIAL IN INTERNATIONAL MARKETS

Actually, risk reduction through effective international diversification is only
part of the story. Not only does the investor have less risk exposure, but there
is also the potential for higher returns in many foreign markets. Why? A number of countries have had superior growth rates to that of the United States in
terms of real GNP. These would include Japan, Norway, Singapore, and Hong
Kong. Secondly, many countries have become highly competitive in traditional
U.S. products such as automobiles, steel, and consumer electronics. A classic
example is, once again, Japan. Thirdly, many nations (Germany, Japan, France,
Canada) enjoy higher individual savings than does the United States and this
leads to capital formation and potential investment opportunity. This, of
course, is not to imply that the United States does not have the strongest

---

[1] Bruno H. Solnik, "Why Not Diversify Internationally Rather than Domestically?" *Financial
Analysts Journal,* July–August 1974, pp. 48–54.

security markets in the world. It clearly does. However, it is a more mature market than many others, and there may be abundant opportunities for superior returns in a number of foreign markets.

In Table 18–3 we can see the compound rate of return for 18 different countries over a long time period. While the return for U.S. equities during this time frame was 8.7 percent (column one, second item from the bottom), Hong Kong, Japan, and Singapore enjoyed annualized returns of between 15 and 25 percent. If you examine the next to last column in Table 18–3, you can observe the value that a one-unit investment would have grown to over this

TABLE 18–3   World Equities: Summary Statistics, 1960–1980

| | Annual returns in U.S. dollars | | | | 1980 |
Asset	Compound return (percent)	Arithmetic mean (percent)	Standard deviation (percent)	Year-end wealth index (1959 = 1.00)	Year-end value in billions U.S. $
Non-U.S. equities:					
Europe					
Austria	9.1%	10.3%	16.9%	6.23	$ 1.9
Belgium	9.2	10.1	13.8	6.39	10.0
Denmark	9.5	11.4	24.2	6.72	4.0
France	6.2	8.1	21.4	3.56	53.0
Germany	8.3	10.1	19.9	5.32	71.0
Italy	2.4	5.6	27.2	1.63	25.0
Netherlands	9.3	10.7	17.8	6.45	25.0
Norway	10.3	17.4	49.0	7.81	2.6
Spain	8.4	10.4	19.8	5.49	16.3
Sweden	8.4	9.7	16.7	5.40	12.2
Switzerland	10.2	12.5	22.9	7.74	46.0
United Kingdom	10.0	14.7	33.6	7.39	190.0
Europe total	8.4	9.6	16.2	5.47	457.0
Asia					
Hong Kong*	24.6	40.3	61.3	11.24	38.0
Japan	15.6	19.0	31.4	20.86	357.0
Singapore*	23.2	37.0	66.1	9.96	24.3
Asia total	15.9	19.7	33.0	22.29	419.3
Other					
Australia	9.8	12.2	22.8	7.12	60.0
Canada	10.7	12.1	17.5	8.47	113.0
Other total	10.6	11.9	17.1	8.24	173.0
Non-U.S. total equities	10.6	11.8	16.3	8.23	1049.3
U.S. total equities	8.7	10.2	17.7	5.78	1380.6
World total equities	9.3	10.5	15.8	6.47	2429.9

* 1970–1980.
Source: Roger G. Ibbotson, Richard C. Carr, and Anthony W. Robinson, "International Equity and Bond Returns," *Financial Analysts Journal,* July–August 1982, p. 65.

21-year period. If it had been invested in U.S. equities, the ending value would be 5.78. The same one-unit investment in Asian securities (referred to as "Asia total," and including Hong Kong, Japan, and Singapore) would have grown to 22.29. If invested in the category of "Other" securities (including Australia and Canada), the accumulation is to 8.24.

It should be pointed out that Table 18–3 represents a relatively long-term prospective. There are, of course, time periods when the United States outperforms foreign markets. A diagram of the accumulated values previously discussed is presented in Figure 18–2.

We bring together two main points of this chapter in Table 18–4 on p. 526. Here we see a listing of a number of foreign countries whose returns are superior to those of the United States and whose correlation values with U.S. equity markets are less than .5 (providing high returns and risk reduction at

FIGURE 18–2   U.S.-Dollar-Adjusted Cumulative Wealth Indexes of World Equities, 1960–1980 (year-end 1959 = 1.00)

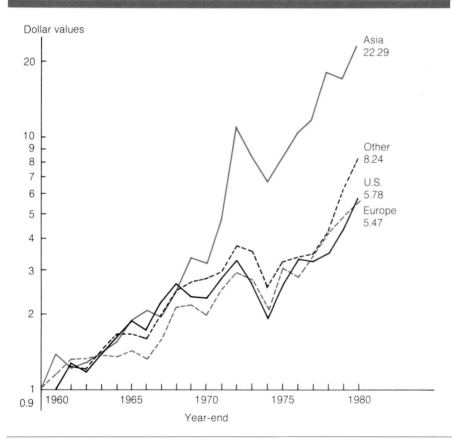

Source: Roger C. Ibbotson, Richard C. Carr, and Anthony W. Robinson, "International Equity and Bond Returns," *Financial Analysts Journal,* July–August 1982, p. 66.

TABLE 18–4   Annual Compound Returns and Correlation Values with U.S. Security Markets (1960–1980)

Country	Compound (percent) return	Correlation with U.S. security market
Japan	15.6%	.216
Norway	10.3	.009
Switzerland	10.2	.454
Denmark	9.5	.243
Belgium	9.2	.389
Austria	9.1	−.076
United States	8.7	1.000

the same time). Japan with its strong returns and low correlation appears particularly attractive.

Current Quotations on Foreign Market Performance

In order to track the current performance of selected world markets, *The Wall Street Journal* provides daily quotes of price movement activity. The closing quotes of May 23, 1984, are presented in Table 18–5.

TABLE 18–5   Daily *Wall Street Journal* Quote

	May 23	May 22	% This Year
U.S.	143.7	144.4	− 8.1
Britain	305.6	308.2	+ 8.4
Canada	242.5	243.5	−12.6
Japan	452.2	453.2	+ 7.5
France	183.8	184.5	+11.2
Germany	124.6	125.1	− 2.4
Hong Kong	617.4	620.3	+ 6.4
Switzerland	114.7	116.3	− 1.7
Australia	125.9	126.9	−13.1
World Index	177.6	177.9	− 3.4

The quotes assume a base period value of each country's index of 100 for 1969. As reflected in the index quotes of May 23, it is plain that Hong Kong (617.4) and Japan (452.2) have substantially outperformed the United States (143.7) over the 15-year period. Also in the year-to-date performance for 1984 (last column), Hong Kong and Japan are up while the United States is down. Of the 9 countries shown in Table 18–5, 4 have an increase in value for the year,

while 5 have a decline. This once again provides evidence of the differing movements in foreign markets.

The last item at the bottom of Table 18–5, the World Index, is a value-weighted index of the performance in 19 major countries as compiled by Capital International, S.A., of Geneva, Switzerland. The United States alone makes up approximately 50 percent of the index because it is value-weighted by market size. Similar type information on global stock markets can also be found in the "International Trades" section of *Barron's*.

The *Institutional Investor,* a magazine used by professional portfolio managers, also tracks the performance of world markets on a regular basis. Quotes for December 31, 1983 (from the February 1984 issue) are shown in Table 18–6.

Table 18–6 is of interest because it shows price–earnings ratios and yields, as well as price changes, for foreign markets. Note the extremes in

TABLE 18–6   World Stock Markets

Here's a recap of the performance of 19 stock markets in leading countries around the world as of December 30, 1983, based upon data supplied by Capital International Perspective of Geneva. It should be noted that the percentage changes are in local currencies and are calculated from Capital International's market indexes.

Rank		3 Months % change	6 Months % change	9 Months % change	12 Months % change	Price–earnings ratio	Yield
1	Mexico	16.2%	56.4%	125.0%	188.1%	4.8	5.5%
2	Hong Kong	16.0	−9.0	−12.1	9.7	9.0	5.8
3	Switzerland	14.8	15.8	19.5	26.7	12.6	2.5
4	Germany	11.4	9.7	15.8	38.3	15.0	3.7
5	France	10.4	23.4	33.1	58.4	63.8	4.7
6	Australia	9.3	28.9	51.9	63.0	15.1	3.6
7	Japan	6.3	12.2	18.3	21.3	25.1	1.3
8	United Kingdom	4.9	1.6	15.2	24.5	10.4	4.8
9	Belgium	4.6	7.7	19.3	36.1	10.4	10.6
10	Singapore/Malaysia	4.2	0.5	11.0	30.1	28.2	1.8
11	Norway	4.2	19.3	49.5	91.5	12.9	3.3
12	Netherlands	4.0	7.6	22.4	52.1	6.4	5.0
13	Denmark	3.6	29.8	48.3	95.5	17.2	1.7
14	Austria	2.2	0.4	3.7	9.5	272.2	2.7
15	Canada	2.0	4.2	19.0	29.5	27.5	3.2
16	United States	−0.6	−1.6	7.4	16.6	12.2	4.5
17	Sweden	−1.5	6.9	15.6	61.2	15.2	2.1
18	Italy	−2.2	0.5	−8.8	22.3	Loss	3.1
19	Spain	−4.0	−7.7	−3.2	4.1	7.0	14.2
	The World Index	2.2	2.7	11.7	21.6	13.9	3.8

Source: *Institutional Investor,* February 1984, p. 50.

price–earnings ratios for certain countries such as Austria (272.2) and France (63.8). Also note in the price-earning ratio column that the average firm in Italy actually had a loss.

Less Developed Countries

Our discussion thus far has primarily centered on what are considered as developed countries (DCs). While many of these countries are considerably smaller than the United States, they still have reasonably well-organized economies and financial markets. There are also potential investment opportunities in less developed countries that have not been previously mentioned. These include such nations as Chile, Jordan, Korea, Thailand, and Zimbabwe. A number of these less developed countries may represent superior investment opportunities in terms of return and risk reduction opportunities. In fact, most have low or negative correlations with the U.S. While this chapter will not explicitly cover the less developed markets, the reader who has an interest in this subject is encouraged to read an article by Vihang Errunza in the September–October 1983 issue of the *Financial Analysts Journal*—"Emerging Markets: A New Opportunity for Improving Global Portfolio Performance."[2]

CURRENCY FLUCTUATIONS AND RATES OF RETURN

Up until now, we have been talking about rates of returns in foreign countries without specifying whether they were in terms of foreign exchange of that country or of U.S. dollars. For example, assume an investment in France produces a 10 percent return. But suppose at the same time the French franc declines in value by 5 percent against the U.S. dollar. The French franc profits are thus worth less in dollars. In the present case, the gain on the investment would be shown as follows:

110%	(Investment with 10% profit)
× .95	(Adjusted value of French franc relative to U.S. dollar)
104.5%	Percent of original investment

The actual return in U.S. dollars would be 4.5 percent instead of 10 percent. Of course, if the French franc appreciated by 5 percent against the dollar, the French franc profits converted to dollars would be worth considerably more than 10 percent. The values are indicated below.

110%	(Investment with 10% profit)
× 1.05	(Adjusted value of French franc relative to U.S. dollar)
115.5%	Percent of original investment

---

[2] Vihang R. Errunza, "Emerging Markets: A New Opportunity for Improving Global Portfolio Performance," *Financial Analysts Journal,* September–October 1983, p. 51–58.

The 10 percent gain in the French franc investment has produced a 15.5 percent gain in U.S. dollars. It is apparent that a U.S. investor in foreign securities must not only consider the potential trend of security prices, but also the trend of foreign currencies against the dollar. A consideration of this point becomes more apparent in examining Table 18–7.

TABLE 18–7   Return on World Stock Markets (through March 1983)

	Return in each currency (percent)			Currency valuation (percent)			Return in U.S. dollars (percent)		
	3-month	*1-year*	*5-year*	*3-month*	*1-year*	*5-year*	*3-month*	*1-year*	*5-year*
New York	8.8%	36.6%	11.4%	0.0%	0.0%	0.0%	8.8%	36.6%	11.4%
Tokyo	4.0	15.7	8.7	−2.0	3.5	−1.7	1.9	19.8	6.8
London	9.8	15.2	7.2	−8.3	−16.9	−4.5	0.6	−4.3	2.4
Toronto	10.1	36.6	15.2	−0.7	−0.8	−1.7	9.3	35.5	13.2
Frankfurt	19.1	26.5	2.7	−2.2	−0.7	−3.9	16.5	25.6	−1.3
Sydney	5.6	11.0	10.8	−11.9	−17.7	−5.4	−6.9	−8.7	4.8
Paris	20.5	10.8	8.6	−7/4	−13.9	−9.1	11.6	−4.5	−1.3
Zurich	9.0	22.4	1.3	−3.7	−7.2	−2.6	5.0	13.7	−1.3
Hong Kong	27.1	14.6	17.3	−3.7	−13.0	−7.2	22.4	−25.7	8.8
Milan	28.5	4.8	28.5	−5.3	−8.4	−10.1	21.7	−4.0	15.6
Amsterdam	29.4	49.9	7.1	4.0	−2.0	−4.6	24.1	47.0	2.2
Singapore	18.5	19.3	24.9	1.1	2.3	2.1	19.8	22.0	27.5

Although the foreign exchange impact in Table 18–7 is not significant in some countries, its effect can be clearly seen for London. In this instance, the one-year return in the local currency was 15.2 percent (column 2), but the currency (British pound) declined 16.9 percent against the U.S. dollar for the one-year period, causing an overall *loss* on the investment of 4.3 percent (second column from the right for London). The values are computed as follows:

115.2%	(Investment with 15.2% profit)
	Adjusted value of British pound to the U.S. dollar
× .831	(1.000 − .169 decline in currency)
95.7%	Percent of original investment

The ending value of 95.7 percent indicates a loss of 4.3 percent from the initial value of 100 percent.[3] If one were to merely subtract the foreign cur-

---

[3] Due to rounding and other statistical adjustments, not all values adjusted to U.S. dollars come out as precisely as this.

rency loss of 16.9 percent from the 15.2 percent profit, the answer would be a loss of 1.7 percent, but this is not the correct procedure. The reason is that the gain of 15.2 percent was on an initial base of 100 percent, but the foreign currency loss of 16.9 percent was on an ending value of 115.2 percent (which comes out to an actual loss in currency value of 19.5 percent). The difference between 19.5 percent and 15.2 percent is 4.3 percent.

Actually those who track the performance in foreign markets usually make adjustments so that the reported returns are in U.S. dollars that have already been adjusted for foreign currency effects. For example, all the returns in Tables 18–1, 18–3, and 18–4 of this chapter have already been adjusted for the foreign currency effect. However, the material in Table 18–6 is an example of returns specifically reported in unadjusted local currencies.

One might justifiably ask, how important is the foreign currency effect in relation to the overall return performance in the foreign currency? Do events in foreign exchange markets tend to overpower actual returns achieved in specific investments in foreign countries? Normally, the foreign currency effect is only about 10–20 percent as significant as the actual return performance in the foreign currency.[4] However, when the dollar is rising or falling rapidly over a short period of time, the impact can be much greater.

In a well-diversified international portfolio, the changes in foreign currency values in one part of the world normally tend to cancel out changes in other parts of the world. Also, those who do not wish to have foreign currency exposure of any sort may use forward exchange contracts, futures market contracts, or put options on foreign currency to hedge away the risk. Finally, there are those who believe in parity theories that suggest that one should get additional compensation in local returns to make up for potential losses in foreign currency values. This latter point is a purely theoretical matter that provides little comfort in the short run.

The authors would suggest that those considering international investments be sensitive to the foreign currency effect, but not be overly discouraged by it. The superior return potential from foreign investments shown in Figure 18–2 (and most other places in this chapter) are constructed *after* taking into consideration the foreign exchange effect on U.S. dollar returns. While foreign currency swings have been *wider* in recent times, they are still not a major deterrent to an internationally diversified portfolio.

OTHER OBSTACLES TO INTERNATIONAL INVESTMENTS

There are some other problems that are peculiar to international investments. Let us consider some of these.

---

[4] Betrand Jacquillat and Bruno Solnik, "Multinationals are Poor Tools for Diversification," *Journal of Portfolio Management,* Winter 1978, pp. 8–12.

Political Risks

Many firms operate in foreign political climates that are more volatile than that of the United States (such as Mexico). There is the danger of nationalization of foreign firms or the blockage of capital flows to investors. There also may be the danger of a violent overthrow of the political party in power. Furthermore, many countries have been unable to meet their foreign debt obligations, and this has important political implications.

The informed investor must have some feel for the political/economic climate of the foreign country in which he or she invests. Of course, problems sometimes create opportunities. It is entirely possible that local investors may overreact to political changes that are taking place in their environment. Because all their eggs are in one basket, they may engage in an "overkill" or oversell in regard to political changes. It is possible that a less impassioned outside investor may actually identify an opportunity for profit.

Nevertheless, political risk represents a potential deterrent to foreign investment. The best solution for the investor is to be sufficiently diversified around the world so that a political or economic development in one foreign country does not have a major impact on his or her portfolio (this can be accomplished through a mutual fund or through other means discussed later in the chapter).

Tax Problems

Many major foreign countries may impose a 7.5 percent to 15 percent withholding tax against the dividends or interest paid to nonresident holders of equity or debt securities. However, it is often possible for *tax-exempt* U.S. investors to secure an exemption or rebate on part or all of the withholding tax. Also, taxable U.S. investors can normally claim a U.S. tax credit for taxes paid in foreign countries. The problem is more likely to be one of inconvenience and paper shuffling rather than loss of funds.[5]

Lack of Market Efficiency

U.S. capital markets tend to be the most liquid and efficient in the world. Therefore, an investor who is accustomed to trading on the New York Stock Exchange may have some difficulties in adjusting to foreign markets. There is likely to be a larger spread between the bid (sell) and ask (buy) price in foreign countries. Also, there may be more difficulty in handling a large transaction (the seller may have to absorb a larger discount in executing the trade). Furthermore, as a general rule, commission rates are higher in foreign markets than in the United States.

---

[5] Gary L. Bergstrom, John K. Koeneman, and Martin J. Siegel, "International Securities Market" in *Readings in Investment Management,* ed. Frank J. Fabozzi (Homewood, Ill.: Richard D. Irwin, 1983).

Administrative Problems

There can also be administrative problems in dealing in foreign markets in terms of adjusting to the various local systems. For example, in the Hong Kong, Swiss, and Mexican stock markets, you must settle your account one day after the transaction; in London there is a two week settlement procedure; and in France there are different settlement dates for cash and forward markets. The different administrative procedures of foreign countries simply add up to an extra dimension of difficulty in executing trades (as implied throughout this chapter, there are ways to avoid most of these difficulties by going through mutual funds and other investment outlets).

Information Difficulties

The U.S. security markets are the best in the world at providing investment information. The Securities and Exchange Commission, with its rigorous requirements for full disclosure, is the toughest national regulator of investment information. Also, the United States has the Financial Accounting Standard Board (FASB) continually providing pronouncements on generally accepted accounting principles for financial reporting. Publicly traded companies are required to provide stockholders with fully audited annual reports. In the United States we are further spoiled by the excellent evaluative reports and ratings generated by Moody's, Standard & Poor's, Value Line, and other firms. We also have extensive economic data provided by governmental sources such as the Department of Commerce and the Federal Reserve System.

Many international firms, trading in less sophisticated foreign markets, simply do not provide the same quantity or quality of data. This would be particularly true of firms trading in some of the smaller foreign markets. Even when the information is available, there may be language problems for the analyst who does not speak German, French, Portuguese, etc.

Also, the analyst must be prepared to analyze the firm in light of the standards that are generally accepted in the foreign market in which the company operates. For example, Japanese companies often have much higher debt ratios than U.S. firms. A debt-to-equity ratio of three times is not unusual in Japan, whereas in the United States the standard is closer to one to one. The uninformed analyst may be inclined to "mark down" the Japanese firm for high debt unless he or she realizes the different features at play in the Japanese economy. For example, in Japan there are normally very close relationships between the lending bank and the borrower, with the lender perhaps having an equity position in the borrower and with interlocking boards between the two. This diminishes the likelihood of the lender calling in the loan in difficult economic periods. Also, the Japanese make extensive use of reserve accounts which tend to give the appearance of a smaller asset or equity base than actually exists. This pattern of understatement is further aided by a strict adherence to historical cost valuation even though Japanese land values have increased more rapidly than almost anywhere else in the world. When appropriate adjustments are made for these effects on financial reporting, a Japanese

debt-to-equity ratio of three to one may not be a matter of any greater concern than a U.S. debt-to-equity ratio of one to one.

METHODS OF PARTICIPATING IN FOREIGN INVESTMENTS

The avenues to international investment include investing in firms in their own foreign markets, purchasing the shares of foreign firms trading in the United States, investing in mutual funds and closed-end funds with a global orientation, buying the shares of multinational corporations, and entrusting funds to private money managers who specialize in international equities. We shall examine each of these alternatives.

Direct Investments

The most obvious, but least likely alternative, would be to directly purchase the shares of a firm in its own foreign market through a foreign broker or an overseas branch of a U.S. broker. The investor might consider such firms as Toshiba or Fanuc on the Tokyo Stock Exchange, Consolidated Rutile on the Sydney Stock Exchange, or Hoechst on the Frankfort Stock Exchange. This approach is hampered with all the difficulties and administrative problems associated with international investments. There could be information-gathering problems, tax problems, stock delivery problems, capital transfer problems, and communication difficulties in executing orders. Only the most sophisticated money manager would probably follow this approach (though this may change somewhat in the future as foreign markets become better coordinated).

A more likely route to direct investment would be to purchase the shares of foreign firms that actually trade in U.S. security markets. There are actually hundreds of foreign firms that actively trade their securities in the United States. A listing of some key participants is presented in Table 18–8.

TABLE 18–8   Foreign Firms Trading on the New York Stock Exchange

Country	Company	Industry
Bahamas	Commodore International Ltd.	Integrated microcomputer systems
Bermuda	Sea Containers Ltd. (3 Pfd. issues)	Cargo container leasing
Canada	Alcan Aluminum Ltd.	Aluminum
	AMCA International Limited	Industrial prods.; construct.; engineer.
	Bell Canada Enterprises Inc.	Telecommunication services & equip.
	Campbell Red Lake Mines Ltd.	Gold mining
	Campbell Resources Inc. (2 issues)	Holding co.—coal; oil & gas interests
	Canadian Pacific Enterprises Ltd.	Iron & steel production; mining
	Canadian Pacific Limited	Integrated transportation system
	Carling O'Keefe Limited	Breweries

TABLE 18–8   *(concluded)*

Country	Company	Industry
	Dome Mines Limited	Gold mining
	Genstar Limited (2 issues)	Land, building development
	Hiram Walker Resources Ltd.	Distilleries; gas utility
	Inco Ltd.	Nickel & copper production
	Inspiration Resources Corporation	Metals mining; petroleum
	MacMillan Bloedel Ltd.	Forest products, pulp & paper
	Massey-Ferguson Ltd.	Farm equipment
	McIntyre Mines Ltd.	Coal mining
	Mitel Corporation	Electronic telecomm. equip.
	Moore Corporation Ltd.	Business forms
	Northern Telecom Ltd.	Telecommunications equip.
	Northgate Exploration Limited	Holding co.—explor.; mining; invest.
	Ranger Oil Limited	Oil & gas exploration, production
	Seagram Co. Ltd.	Distilleries
	Westcoast Transmission Co., Ltd.	Natural gas transmission
Denmark	Novo Industri A/S	Industrial enzymes; drugs
Great Britain	British Petroleum Company Ltd.	Holding co.—integrated oil company
	Imperial Chemical Industries PLC	Diversified chemicals
	Plessey Company Ltd.	Telecommun. and electronic equip.
	"Shell" Transport and Trading Public Ltd. Co.	Holding co.,—integrated oil company
	Tricentrol PLC	Oil & gas prod., oil trading
	Unilever PLC	Foods; consumer goods
Japan	Hitachi, Ltd.	Indust. equip., consumer products
	Honda Motor Co., Ltd.	Motor vehicles and parts
	Kubota, Ltd.	Agricultural equipment; piping
	Kyocera Corp.	Ceramic electronic products
	Matsushita Electric Industrial Co., Ltd.	Consumer electronic products
	Pioneer Electronic Corporation	Consumer electronic products
	Sony Corporation	Consumer electronic products
	TDK Corporation	Electronic components; magnetic tapes
Netherlands	KLM Royal Dutch Airlines	Air transportation
	Royal Dutch Petroleum Co.	Holding company-integrated oil co.
Netherlands Antilles	Erbamont N.V.	Pharmaceuticals
	Schlumberger, Ltd.	Oilfield serv.; electronics
	Unilever, N.V.	Foods; consumer goods
Panama	Norlin Corporation	Organs, pianos, guitars
	Syntex Corporation	Pharmaceuticals
Philippines	Benguet Corporation	Mining; construction
South Africa	ASA Limited	Investment company
Spain	Banco Central, S.A.	Holding company—bank

Source: *New York Stock Exchange Fact Book* (New York: New York Stock Exchange, 1984), p. 40.

Firms such as Alcan Aluminum Ltd., Massey-Ferguson Ltd., and Hitachi, Ltd., trade their stocks directly on the New York Stock Exchange. Most of the other firms on the list (as well as other large foreign firms) trade their shares in the United States through American Depository Receipts (ADRs). These ADRs represent the ownership interest in a foreign company's common stock. The process is as follows: The shares of the foreign company are purchased and put in trust in a foreign branch of a New York bank. The bank, in turn, receives and can issue depository receipts to the American shareholders of the foreign firm. These ADRs (i.e., depository receipts) allow foreign shares to be traded in the United States.

When you call your broker and ask to purchase Sony Corporation or Honda Motor Co., Ltd. (which are represented by ADRs), you will notice virtually no difference between this transaction and buying shares of General Motors or Eastman Kodak. You can receive a certificate that looks very much like a U.S. stock certificate. You'll receive your dividends in dollars and get your reports about the company in English. Generally, you will pay your normal commission rates.

In Table 18–9, you see a page from *Standard & Poor's Stock Guide* that includes Sony Corporation's ADRs. Note the financial information is basically the same as that for other U.S. corporations trading on a major exchange or over-the-counter. The Sony ADRs also receive coverage from *Value Line* and other reporting services. There are daily quotes in *The Wall Street Journal* just as there would be for any company. Since these ADRs trade on the New York Stock Exchange, the quote would be found in that section of the paper.

The *Standard & Poor's Stock Guide* is a good place to start in determining whether a foreign company has ADRs trading in the United States or not. As previously indicated, there are hundreds of ADRs trading in U.S. markets.

Indirect Investments

The forms of indirect investments in the international securities include *(a)* purchasing shares of multinational corporations, *(b)* purchasing mutual funds or closed-end investment funds specializing in worldwide investments, and *(c)* engaging the services of a private firm specializing in foreign investment portfolio management.

Purchasing shares of multinational corporations.   Multinational corporations, that is, firms with operations in a number of countries, represent an opportunity for international diversification. For example, the major oil companies have investments and operations throughout the world. The same can be said for large banking firms and mainframe computer manufacturers. When one buys Exxon, to some extent he or she is buying exposure to the world economy (71.4 percent of sales are foreign for this firm). A list of the 20 largest U.S. multinational firms is presented in Table 18–10. Of particular interest is the second column from the left, which represents foreign revenue as a percentage of total revenue, and the fourth column from the right, which represents foreign profit as a percentage of total profit.

TABLE 18–9   Sample Page from Standard & Poor's Stock Guide

200 Smu-Sou

Standard & Poor's Corporation

Index	Ticker Symbol	Name of Issue (Call Price of Pfd. Stocks)	Market	Com. Rank. & Pfd. Rating	Inst. Hold Cos	Inst. Hold Sha. (000)	Par Val.	Principal Business	Price Range 1971-82 High	1971-82 Low	1983 High	1983 Low	1984 High	1984 Low	Apr. Sales in 100s	April 1984 Last Sale Or Bid High	Low	Last	%Div. Yield	P-E Ratio
1	SJM	Smucker (J.M.)	NY,M	A	22	1084	No	Preserves; jellies & fillings	37⅛	4³/₁₆	46¼	30¾	44½	36¼	483	38¼	36½	37⅝	2.5	11
2	SNA	Snap-On Tools	NY,M	A	127	8995	No	Hand tools; auto/ind'l maint	31⅞	7⅜	34¼	24½	33¾	27	4604	31	28½	29¾	3.1	13
3	SOL	Snyder Oil Partners	AS	NR	4	82		Mgmt of oil & gas prop			16¼	14¾	16¼	14¾	303	15¾	15	15	13.3	14
4	SOCI	Society Corp	OTC	A	21	1084	10ₐ	Multi-bank hldg;Cleveland	24½	8½	30¾	21½	33	28	686	31	29¾	30⅝	5.7	7
5	SOFT	SofTech Inc	OTC	NR	13	412	10ₐ	Devel software svcs & prod		7	25⅛	13	15¾	7	1284	8¼		7⅛/8		15
6	SAGA	Software AG Sys Gr	OTC	NR	14	864	1ₐ	Computer sys software pkgs	22¼	5½	13	7⅞	14	10¾	3502	14	11¾	12¼/8		15
7	SOD	Solid State Scien't		C	13	137	40ₐ	Semiconductor devices	26	3	11½	5⅞	8¾	6⅜	1711	9¼	8¾	8⅝		d
8	SNT	Soltron Devices	AS,B,M,P,Ph	B	4			Nat'l conductors-microwave	19½	¾	12⅛	6¾	8¾	6¾	1334	9¾	6⅞	7⅛		26
9	SNT	Sonat, Inc.	NY,B,C,M,P,Ph	B+	270	17873	3¾	Nat'l gas P.L. drill'g o&g	30¼	6¾	39⅝	23½	46½	30½	10091	37⅜	34½	36¾	4.9	7
10	SONO	Sonoco Products	OTC	A+	53	2339	No	Industrial paper products	32¾	4¾	47½	28¾	46½	39½	1879	43¾	39½	43¼/8	12.9	12
11	SNMA	Sonoma Vineyards	OTC	C	6		25ₐ	Premium wines; mach tools	41	3¾	11⅜	5⅛	7⅜	5⅛	2586	6⅞	5⅛	5¼/8		d
12	SNE	Sony Corp ADR	NY,B,C,M,P,Ph,To,M	NR	153	31246	50ₐ	Color TV sets,tape rec,radio	33⅜	3⅜	16¾	12⅜	16¾	14⅛	80878	17	15¾	16¼/8	1.0	21
13	SOO	Soo Line RR	NY,M	B+	26	1022	3⅓	Railroad contr by Canad Pac	17¾	5⅞	35¼	26⅝	29½	23¾	470	25¾	23¾	25¼/8	4.8	11
14	SOK	Sooner Fed'l Sv & Ln	NY,M	B	10	472	1ₐ	Savings & loan in Oklahoma	15½	4	24½	16¾	34½	23¾	3679	27½	23¾	27¼/8		7
15	SORG	Sorg Printing	OTC				No	Fin'l & corporate printing				10	16	10	906	12½	10	11⅛		42
16	SOR	Source Capital	NY,M	NR	14	191	1ₐ	Closed-end invest:divers	30	5⅞	33	27¼	31⅞	28¾	608	31⅛	28⅜	30¾	10.2	
17	Pr	$2.40 cm Pfd(27.50)vtg	NY,M				1ₐ		26½	16	21½	17¼	20½	17½	140	20⅝	19½	19⅞	12.3	…
18	SCG	South Carolina E&G	NY,B,C,M,P,Ph	A-	140	9144	4½	Utility; electric & gas	31⅛	8⅛	21¼	17¾	22	19¾	9907	20⅜	19½	20⅝	12.5	8
19	Pr	5% cm Pfd (52½)	NY				50ₐ	Charleston,Columbia areas	39½	16¼	24	20¾	22½	19⅜	7	20	20	20⅝	12.3	…
20	SCNC	South Carolina Nat'l	OTC	A-	36	1447	5ₐ	Bank hldg: South Carolina	33½	9¾	45	30¾	43	39	454	43	40	43⅜	4.1	7
21	SJIR	South Jersey Indus	NY,M,Ph	A-	14	287	2½	Hldg co, gas, fuel oil, sand	29	9⅛	25%	19¾	26¼	22	430	25	22½	24½	10.0	7
22	SDR	Sea Drill'g & Ex	AS	B+				On shore contract drill'g o&g	43¾	2¾	4¾	2⅜	4½	3⅛	686	4½	4⅛	4⅛		10
23	SDW	Southdown Inc	NY,M	A	27	1110	3½	Cement mfr & dstr:oil & gas	37¼	4¾	39⅝	28¾	42¾	31¾	5042	42½	40½	41½	s1.2	9
24	STB	Southeast Banking	NY,B,M,Ph	A-	68	4555	2	Multiple bank hldg:Miami	13¾	6	13¾	9	26	18¾		24¾	24¼	24½	4.9	7
25	SOE	Southeastern Capital	AS	NR			5	Hldg co. SBIC: invest					11	10	35	10½	10	10¾	10.4	33
26	SMGS	Southeast'n Mich Gas Ent.	OTC	B+	7	84	10	Integrated natural gas sys	13¾	7⅞	14½	10⅞	14¼	13½	235	14¼	13¾	14¼/8s1	0.7	6
27	SPV	Southeast'n Pub Sv	NY,M	B	2	181	1ₐ	Utility/town sv:ref'n,LP	10	1¾	14	6⅜	12¾	11½	255	11	11	11⅞	s4.3	9
28	STBN	Southern Bancorp S.C.	OTC	A	12	300	2½	Bank hldg:South Carolina	18¾	6½	42¾	34	20¾	15½	961	20¼	18¼	19½	10.1	12
29	SE A	5% Orig Ptc Pfd (NC) vtg	AS(M),P	AA	414	47007	8⅓	Utility: primar'ly engaged	34½	16½	39½	32	38½	33	28000	37¾	34¾	34¾	11.1	6
30						57		in supply electric energy							55					
31	Pr D	4.32% cm Pfd (28¼)vtg	AS,P	AA			25	in portions of central&south-	16	6½	9%	8	9⅝	8⅛	177	8¾	8⅛	8⅛	12.2	
32	Pr C	4.24% cm Pfd (25.80)vtg	AS,P	AA			25	ern California, excluding the	16⅛	6½	10	8	9⅝	7¾	841	8¾	8	8⅛	12.7	
33	Pr G	4.08% cm Pfd (25.80)vtg	AS,B,P	AA		2	25	City of Los Angeles & certain	18⅛	6¾	9½	8	9¼	8	1518	8½	7¾	8	13.0	
34	Pr B	4.78% cm Pfd (25¼)vtg	AS,P	AA			25	other cities. Fuel mix:oil	18⅜	7	11%	9	10⅜	9¾	79	9¼/8	9¾	9¼/8	12.9	
35	Pr G	5.80% cm Pfd (25¼)vtg	AS,P	AA		4	25	& gas 32%,coal 15%,renew-	22¼	7¾	13¼	11¾	12¾	11	349	11	11	11	13.2	
36	Pr J	8.96% cm Pfd (**107)vtg	AS,P	AA	1		100	ables includ'g all hydro 10%,	117	56¾	82½	69¾	77	66¾	129	74	66½	65⅝/8	13.7	
37	Pr K	7.58% cm Pfd (**102)vtg	AS,P	AA	1		100	nuclear 1%,purchased power-	105¼	54¾	90½	68	62½	65	52	79¾	65	65⅝	13.4	
38	Pr L	8.85% cm Pfd (**25.75)vtg	AS,B,P	AA	1	6	25	42%	28½	14½	23¾	19¾	21¾	16¾	301	19¾	18½	18⅝	12.9	
39	Pr M	9.20% cm Pfd (**26½)vtg	AS,P	AA	1	4	25		28¾	14¼	21	18¾	20	17¼	1215	18%	17¼	17%	13.0	
41	Pr Op	8.54% cm Pfd(**108.54:SF100)vtg		AA	2	19	100		100	59	88½	73	77½	70	271	75¾	73¾	73½/8	11.6	8
42	Pr H	12% cm Pfd(**112:SF100)vtg	AS,P	AA	3	30	100		106⅛	89	109	105⅜	105⅜	99½	203	99½	99½	99⅞	12.1	
43	Pr I	5.20% cm Cv Pref (25)vtg	AS,B,P	AA		2	25	Subsid of Pacific Lighting	29	12⅜	33½	27	30⅜	27¼	102	28⅛	27¼	28⅝	4.4	
44	SWTR	South'n Cal Gas cm6%PfdA(NC)vtg	AS,P	A-	9	167	25	Water supply: some elec	16¾	8¾	13¾	11¾	11⅜	11¾	47	11⅛	11¾	11⅝	10.6	9
45	SO	Southern Co	NY,B,C,M,P,Ph	1 A-	260	38115	5	Elec util hldg:Southeast	28¾	7¼	17%	14¾	16½	15¼	58885	16	15¼	15½/8	11.6	5

TABLE 18–10   Large U.S. Multinational Corporations

Rank	Company	Foreign revenue (millions)	Total revenue (millions)	Foreign as % of total	Foreign operating profit* (millions)	Total operating profit* (millions)	Foreign as % of total	Foreign assets (millions)	Total assets (millions)	Foreign as % of total
1	Exxon	$69,386	$97,173	71.4%	$2,208	$4,343	50.8%	$29,914	$62,289	48.0%
2	Mobil	37,778[1]	60,969[1]	62.0	880[2]	1,380[2]	63.8	18,802	36,439	51.6
3	Texaco	31,118	46,986	66.2	833[2]	1,281[2]	65.0	12,956	27,114	47.8
4	Standard Oil California	16,957	34,362	49.3	404[2]	1,377[2]	29.3	8,861	23,465	37.8
5	Phibro-Salomon	16,600	26,703	62.2	218[2]	337[2]	64.7	4,600	39,669	11.6
6	Ford Motor	16,526	37,067	44.6	460[2]	−658[2]	P/D	14,327	21,956	65.3
7	IBM	15,336	34,364	44.6	1,646[2]	4,409[2]	37.3	14,122	32,541	43.4
8	General Motors	14,376	60,026	23.9	−107[2]	963[2]	D/P	12,288	41,363	29.7
9	Gulf Oil	11,513	28,427	40.5	300[2]	900[2]	33.3	7,625	20,436	37.3
10	E I du Pont de Nemours	11,057	33,223	33.3	488[6]	1,491[6]	32.7	5,911	24,343	24.3
11	Citicorp	10,865	17,814	61.0	448[2]	723[2]	62.0	73,316[4]	121,482[4]	60.4
12	Intl Tel & Tel[3]	9,824	21,922	44.8	851	1,194	71.3	9,914	29,172	34.0
13	BankAmerica	8,051	14,955	53.8	253[5]	389[5]	65.0	54,847[4]	119,869[4]	45.8
14	Chase Manhattan	6,207	10,171	61.0	215[2]	307[2]	70.0	41,387	80,863	51.2
15	Dow Chemical	5,544	10,618	52.2	143	356	40.2	5,260	11,807	44.5
16	General Electric	5,490[1]	27,192[1]	20.2	395[2]	1,817[2]	21.7	5,373	21,615	24.9
17	Sun Co	4,901[1]	15,739[1]	31.1	54[6]	706[6]	7.7	2,399	12,019	20.0
18	Standard Oil Indiana	4,862[1]	28,389[1]	17.1	618[2]	1,826[2]	33.8	6,470	24,289	26.6
19	Occidental Petroleum	4,715[1]	18,527[1]	25.4	345[6]	548[6]	63.0	3,502	15,773	22.2
20	Safeway Stores	4,380	17,633	24.8	84[2]	160[2]	52.5	1,052	3,891	27.0

* Unless otherwise indicated. [1] Includes other income. [2] Net income. [3] Includes proportionate interest on unconsolidated subsidiaries or investments. [4] Average assets. [5] Income before security gains or losses. [6] Profit before interest and after taxes.

Source: Excerpt from "100 Largest Multinationals," *Forbes*, July 4, 1983, p. 114.

Although buying shares in a U.S. multinational firm is an easy route to take in order to experience worldwide economic effects, some researchers maintain that multinationals do not provide the major *investment* benefits that are desired. Jacquillat and Solnik found that multinationals provide very little risk reduction over and above purely domestic firms (perhaps only 10 percent).[6] The prices of multinational shares tend to move very closely with U.S. financial markets in spite of their worldwide investments. Thus U.S. multinationals may not do well in a U.S. bear market even if they have investments in strong markets in other countries. This leaves us to turn to mutual funds and closed-end investment companies as potential international investments.

Mutual funds and closed-end investment companies.   As previously described in Chapter 3, mutual funds offer the investor an opportunity for diversification as well as professional management. Nowhere is the mutual fund concept more important than in the area of international investments. Those who organize the funds usually have extensive experience in investing overseas and are prepared to deal with the administrative problems. This, of course, does not necessarily lead to superior returns, but the likelihood for inexperienced blunders is reduced. An example of an international fund, the Scudder International Fund, Inc., is presented in Table 18–11. A description of the fund's international holdings is presented in the upper part of the table.

The Scudder Fund is an open-end mutual fund and trades at its net asset value. The net asset value is equal to the market value of the portfolio minus liabilities divided by the total number of shares outstanding in the mutual fund. It is also a no-load fund.

One may also invest in closed-end investment companies specializing in international equity investments. As described in Chapter 3, a closed-end investment company has a fixed supply of shares outstanding and trades on a national exchange or over-the-counter, much as an individual company does. It may trade at a premium or discount from its net asset value. An example is the Japan Fund.

A listing of internationally oriented funds is provided in Table 18–12. The address for these funds can be found in *Wiesenberger Investment Companies Service,* a publication found in most libraries.

Specialists in international securities.   The large investor may consider the option of engaging the services of selected banks and investment counselors with specialized expertise in foreign equities. Major firms include Morgan Guaranty Trust Co., State Street Bank and Trust Co., Batterymarch Financial Management, and Fidelity Trust Company of New York. These firms provide a total range of advisory and management services. However, they often require a minimum investment well in excess of $100,000 and are tailored to the needs of the large institutional investor.

---

[6] Bertrand Jacquillat and Bruno Solnik, "Multinationals Are Poor Tools for Diversification," *Journal of Portfolio Management,* Winter 1978, pp. 8–12.

TABLE 18–11

SCUDDER INTERNATIONAL FUND, INC.

The primary objective of the fund is long-term growth of capital, through investments in companies which, without limitation to any particular country, have their principal activities and interests outside the United States. Under normal conditions, the fund expects to maintain a portfolio consisting primarily of a diversified list of equity securities. The fund may purchase restricted issues up to five percent of invested assets.

At the end of 1983, the fund had 81% of its assets in common stocks, of which the substantial proportion was in five industrialized countries: Japan (20.1% of assets), Netherlands (11.8%), Germany (8.9%), Canada (7.9%) and Switzerland (6.7%). The five largest individual common stock investments were Siemens, A.G. (2.6% of assets), Philips Glocilampenfabricken (2.3%), Société Générale de Surveillance and Daimler Benz (2.2% each) and Ciba-Geigy (2%). The rate of portfolio turnover in the latest fiscal year was 38.9% of average assets. Unrealized appreciation at the calendar year-end was 27% of total net assets.

Statistical History

	AT YEAR-ENDS							ANNUAL DATA					
Year	Total Net Assets ($)	Number of Share-holders	Net Asset Value Per Share ($)	Yield (%)	Cash & Equiv-alent	Bonds & Pre-ferreds	Com-mon Stocks	Income Div-idends ($)	Capital Gains Distribu-tion ($)	Expense Ratio (%)	Offering Price ($) High	Low	
1983	133,482,471	6,578	22.15	1.4	8	11	81	0.31	—	1.13	22.15	17.10	
1982	79,112,561	3,940	17.33	3.1	12	22	66	0.54	—	1.16	17.92	14.06	
1981	59,814,118	3,233	17.84	2.3	18	18	64	0.404	0.034	1.10	19.26	15.78	
1980	49,088,930	2,773	18.81	2.9	18	11	71	0.572	1.231*	1.15	19.32	14.80	
1979	25,927,381	2,184	16.35	2.8	18	12	70	0.493	1.356*	1.25	17.00	14.78	
1978	18,058,078	2,108	15.37	1.8	2	—	98	0.286	0.497*	1.41	16.69	12.95	
1977	14,454,457	2,175	13.30	2.1	9	—	91	0.277	—	1.28	13.72	12.72	
1976	16,157,645	2,462	13.65	1.1	10	—	90	0.148	—	1.35	13.65	12.22	
1975	17,992,758	2,725	13.01	2.7	12	2	86	0.35	—	1.48	13.14	10.33	
1974	15,527,507	2,943	10.33	1.5	30	1	69	0.156	0.257	1.26	14.40	9.56	
1973	24,012,278	3,136	13.89	0.1	21	—	79	0.022	1.757	1.38	19.42	13.16	

* Includes $0.008 short-term capital gains in 1978; $0.303 in 1979; $0.104 in 1980.

An assumed investment of $10,000 in this fund, with capital gains accepted in shares and income dividends reinvested, is illustrated below. The explanation on Page 163 must be read in conjunction with this illustration.

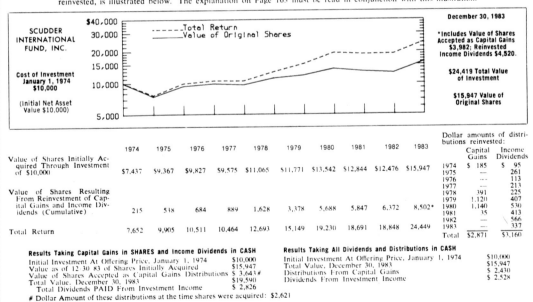

SCUDDER INTERNATIONAL FUND, INC.

Cost of Investment January 1, 1974 $10,000

(Initial Net Asset Value $10,000)

------ Total Return
——— Value of Original Shares

December 30, 1983

*Includes Value of Shares Accepted as Capital Gains $3,982; Reinvested Income Dividends $4,520.

$24,419 Total Value of Investment

$15,947 Value of Original Shares

	1974	1975	1976	1977	1978	1979	1980	1981	1982	1983
Value of Shares Initially Acquired Through Investment of $10,000	$7,437	$9,367	$9,827	$9,575	$11,065	$11,771	$13,542	$12,844	$12,476	$15,947
Value of Shares Resulting From Reinvestment of Capital Gains and Income Dividends (Cumulative)	215	538	684	889	1,628	3,378	5,688	5,847	6,372	8,502*
Total Return	7,652	9,905	10,511	10,464	12,693	15,149	19,230	18,691	18,848	24,449

Dollar amounts of distributions reinvested:

	Capital Gains	Income Dividends
1974	$ 185	$ 95
1975	—	261
1976	—	113
1977	—	213
1978	391	225
1979	1,120	407
1980	1,140	530
1981	35	413
1982	—	566
1983	—	337
Total	$2,871	$3,160

Results Taking Capital Gains in SHARES and Income Dividends in CASH

Initial Investment At Offering Price, January 1, 1974	$10,000
Value as of 12 30 83 of Shares Initially Acquired	$15,947
Value of Shares Accepted as Capital Gains Distributions	$ 3,643#
Total Value, December 30, 1983	$19,590
Total Dividends PAID From Investment Income	$ 2,826

Dollar Amount of these distributions at the time shares were acquired: $2,621

Results Taking All Dividends and Distributions in CASH

Initial Investment At Offering Price, January 1, 1974	$10,000
Total Value, December 30, 1983	$15,947
Distributions From Capital Gains	$ 2,430
Dividends From Investment Income	$ 2,528

TABLE 18–12   Internationally Oriented Funds

Name of fund	Open- or closed-end	Load (L) no-load (NL)	Where invested
Canadian Fund, Inc.	Open	L	Canada
International Investors Incorporated	Open	L	Gold mines
G. T. Pacific Fund, Inc.	Open	NL	Asia (Japan, Hong Kong, etc.)
Kemper International Fund, Inc.	Open	L	Worldwide
Merrill Lynch Pacific	Open	L	Far East
Merrill Lynch International Holdings	Open	L	Worldwide
Putnam International Equities Fund	Open	L	Worldwide
Research Capital Fund, Inc.	Open	L	Foreign mining
T. Rowe Price International Fund, Inc.	Open	NL	Worldwide
Scudder International Fund, Inc.	Open	NL	Worldwide
Strategic Investments Fund, Inc.	Open	L	South African gold mines
Templeton World Fund, Inc.	Open	L	Worldwide
Transatlantic Fund, Inc.	Open	NL	Worldwide
United International Growth Fund	Open	L	Worldwide
ASA Limited	Closed	Commission	South African gold mines
Japan Fund	Closed	Commission	Japan
U.S. and Foreign Securities	Closed	Commission	Worldwide

The average investor, with an international interest, is probably better-advised to consider the ADR alternative or the mutual fund or closed-end investment company.

SUMMARY

Investments in international securities allow the investor to diversify his or her portfolio beyond the normal alternatives. Because different foreign markets are influenced by varying and often contradictory factors, effective risk reduction can be provided. An example might be a sharp and unexpected increase in energy prices. The negative impact on oil importers will likely be offset by the positive impact on oil exporters.

Investments in selected foreign equity markets may also provide excellent return opportunities. A number of countries have had superior real GNP growth performance in comparison to the United States. They may also have greater savings rates and higher capital formation. Furthermore, a number of countries are becoming more competitive in traditional U.S. products such as

automobiles, steel, and consumer electronics. Less developed countries, such as Chile, Jordan, Korea, Thailand, and Zimbabwe, may offer even greater return and risk reduction benefits than investments in better established markets (e.g., France, Germany). However, many of the problems of international investments can surface in these less developed countries.

The impact of currency fluctuations on returns is an added dimension to international investments. Not only must the investor determine whether the security will provide a positive return, but he or she must also evaluate the possibility of the return being enhanced or diminished by changes in currency relationships with the U.S. dollar.

Other obstacles to foreign investment include political risks associated with foreign nations, tax problems, market efficiency and liquidity concerns, administrative problems, and gaps in information transference. The latter issue draws attention because of the comprehensive reporting system in the United States compared to the rest of the world. Also the analyst must evaluate a security within the norms of the country in which the firm resides. This can be a problem for the uninitiated investor.

Fortunately, most of these obstacles can be overcome by appropriate investment routes into foreign markets. ADRs (American Depository Receipts) represent the ownership interest in a foreign company's common stock. The shares of the foreign company are put in trust in the foreign branch of a New York bank. The bank, in turn, receives and can issue depository receipts to the American shareholders of the foreign firm. These ADRs (depository receipts) allow foreign shares to be traded in the United States.

Indirect means of participation include the purchase of shares in multinational firms or, more importantly, investing in mutual funds or closed-end investment companies specializing in foreign securities. An international fund offers the advantages of partial or comprehensive worldwide diversification, and the removal of administrative and information-gathering problems.

The reader can readily observe that one who wishes to participate in foreign equities has many feasible alternatives.

IMPORTANT WORDS AND CONCEPTS

Diversification benefits	International tax problems
World Index	American Depository Receipts
Currency fluctuations	(ADRs)
Foreign currency effects	Multinational corporations
Less developed countries	Internationally oriented funds
Foreign political-risks	

DISCUSSION QUESTIONS

1. According to Table 18–2, what two countries provided the best risk reduction benefits in comparison to the United States? Which two countries provided the least risk reduction benefits?

2. Why does Canada represent a relatively poor outlet for achieving risk reduction for U.S. investors? (Merely use your own judgment in answering this question).

3. Explain the general nature of the World Index. What percentage does the U.S. comprise? If it were equal-weighted instead of value-weighted, what percentage would the U.S. comprise?

4. Explain how currency fluctuations impact on the return on foreign investments.

5. Refer to Table 18–7, describe the change in currency values between the British pound (London) and the U.S. dollar over three months, one year, and five years. What was the likely pattern between one and five years?

6. Suggest two types of strategies to reduce or neutralize the impact of currency fluctuations on portfolio returns.

7. Suggest how foreign political risk may create a potential investment opportunity.

8. Are foreign markets likely to be more or less efficient than U.S. markets? What effect does this have on bid-ask spreads and the ability to absorb large transactions?

9. Explain why high debt ratios in Japan may not be as great a problem as one might first assume.

10. What are some of the key problems in investing directly in foreign securities?

11. Explain the concept of an ADR.

12. Why did Jacuillat and Solnik indicate that multinational firms may provide very little risk reduction benefits in comparison to domestic firms?

13. Why might mutual funds be particularly beneficial in the international area?

14. Suggest the names of three investment funds that are open-end, no load, and trade worldwide.

PROBLEMS

1. Assume you invest in the German equity market and have a 15 percent return (quoted in German marks).
   a. If during this period the mark appreciated by 10 percent against the dollar, what would be your actual return translated into U.S. dollars?
   b. What if the mark declined by 10 percent against the dollar, what would your actual return be translated into dollars?
   c. Recompute the answer based on a 25 percent decline in the mark against the dollar.

2. Assume you invest in the Japanese equity market and you have a 12 percent return (quoted in yen). However, during the course of your investment, the yen declines versus the dollar. By what percent could the yen decline relative to the dollar before all your gain is eliminated?

3. You invest in the French equity market and you lose 15 percent (quoted in francs). In the meantime, the dollar declines by 8 percent against the franc. What is your percentage gain or loss translated into dollars?
4. Assume you invest in the Italian equity market and your return is 28.5 percent over three months. However, the Italian lira declines by 5.3 percent. What is your return translated to U.S. dollars? After you have computed your answer, check it out by going to Table 18–7, and comparing your answer to the three-month figure under Return in U.S. Dollars (%) for Milan, Italy.

SELECTED REFERENCES

Bergstrom, Gary L. "A New Route to Higher Returns and Lower Risks." *The Journal of Portfolio Management,* Fall 1975, pp. 30–38.

Bergstrom, Gary L.; John K. Koeneman; and Martin J. Siegel. "International Security Market" in *Readings in Financial Management,* ed. Frank J. Fabozzi. Homewood, Ill.: Richard D. Irwin, 1983.

Errunza, Vihang R. "Emerging Markets: A New Opportunity for Improving Global Portfolio Performance." *Financial Analysts Journal,* September–October 1983, pp. 51–58.

Hughes, John G.; Dennis E. Logue; and Richard James Sweeney. "Corporate International Diversification and Market Assigned Measures of Risk and Diversification." *Journal of Financial and Quantitative Analysis,* November 1975, pp. 627–83.

Ibbotson, Roger G.; Richard C. Carr; and Anthony W. Robinson. "International Equity and Bond Returns." *Financial Analysts Journal,* July–August 1982, pp. 61–83.

Ibbotson, Roger G., and Laurence B. Siegel. "The World Market Wealth Portfolio." *The Journal of Portfolio Management,* Winter 1983, pp. 5–17.

Jacquillat, Bertrand, and Bruno Solnik. "Multinationals Are Poor Tools for Diversification." *The Journal of Portfolio Management,* Winter 1978, pp. 8–12.

Lessard, Donald R. "World, Country and Industry Relationships in Equity Returns." *Financial Analysts Journal,* January–February 1976, pp. 32–38.

Logue, Dennis E. "An Experiment in International Diversification." *The Journal of Portfolio Management,* Fall 1982, pp. 22–27.

Maldanado-Bear, Rita, and Anthony Sanders. "International Portfolio Diversification and the Stability of International Stock Market Relationships, 1957–1980." *Financial Management,* Autumn 1981, pp. 54–63.

Solnik, Bruno. "Why Not Diversify Internationally Rather than Domestically?" *Financial Analysts Journal,* July–August 1974, pp. 48–54.

Stanley, Marjoviet. "Capital Structure and Cost of Capital for the International Firm." *Journal of International Business Studies,* Spring–Summer 1981, pp. 103–20.

Part Five

INTRODUCTION TO PORTFOLIO MANAGEMENT

The contemporary portfolio manager is continually called upon to assess the nature of his or her performance over a period of time. A couple of decades ago, an analysis that merely indicated the extent of gains and losses would have been sufficient. This is no longer the case. There are at least two dimensions to every modern portfolio evaluation: the rate of return that was earned and the amount of *risk* that was taken. Many of the earlier concepts related to risk (introduced in Chapter 1) will now be more formally developed.

In Chapter 19 we evaluate the risk measurement tools for an individual asset as well as a portfolio of assets. We also review the concept that most investors are risk-averse (dislike risk) and will therefore require proportionally higher returns as risk increases.

If we accept the concept of a premium return for risk, we must then consider what type of risk should be rewarded. Portfolio theory suggests that much of the risk in individual assets can be diversified away in a cross section or portfolio of investments, and that only risk which cannot be diversified is likely to receive a higher return in a competitive marketplace. This topic is developed in the first of the two chapters on portfolio management.

In Chapter 20 we examine empirical studies of portfolio managers and the nature of their performance. A typical question for consideration is, "Have mutual fund or pension fund managers actually provided superior investment returns on a risk-adjusted basis? We also evaluate how effective they have been in pursuing investment policies that are consistent with their stated objectives. Finally, we consider the various types of investors that are part of the category of institutional investors (as opposed to individual investors) and some of the investment management characteristics of each.

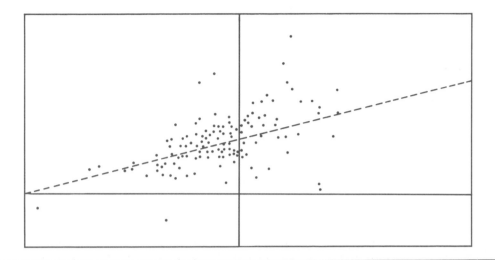

Chapter 19
A BASIC LOOK AT PORTFOLIO MANAGEMENT AND CAPITAL MARKET THEORY

Chapter 20
MEASURING RISKS AND RETURNS OF PORTFOLIO MANAGERS

Chapter 19

A BASIC LOOK AT PORTFOLIO MANAGEMENT AND CAPITAL MARKET THEORY

In this chapter, we develop a more complete understanding of how the investor perceives risk and demands compensation for it. We eventually build toward a theory of portfolio management that incorporates many of these concepts. While the use of mathematical terms is an essential ingredient to a basic understanding of portfolio theory, more involved or complicated concepts are treated in appendixes at the end of the chapter.

As indicated in Chapter 1, risk is generally associated with uncertainty about future outcomes. The greater the range of possible outcomes, the greater the risk. We also observed in Chapter 1 that most investors tend to be risk-averse; that is, all things being equal, investors prefer less risk to more risk and will only increase their risk-taking position if a premium for risk is involved. Each investor has a different attitude toward risk. The inducement necessary to cause a given investor to withdraw his funds from a savings account to drill an oil well may be quite different from yours. For some, only a very small premium for risk is necessary, while others may not wish to participate unless there are exceptionally high rewards. We begin the chapter with a more formal approach toward the measurement of risk.

FORMAL MEASUREMENT OF RISK

Having defined risk as uncertainty about future outcomes, how do we actually measure risk? The first task is to design a probability distribution of anticipated future outcomes. This is no small task. The possible outcomes and associated probabilities are likely to be based on economic projections, past experience, subjective judgments, and many other variables. For the most part, we are forcing ourselves to write down what already exists in our head. Having established the probability distribution, we then determine the *expected value* and the *dispersion* around that expected value. The greater the dispersion, the greater the risk.

Expected Value

To determine the expected value, we multiply each possible outcome by its probability of occurrence. Assume we are considering two investment proposals where K represents a possible outcome and P represents the probability of that outcome based on the state of the economy. If we were dealing with stocks, K would represent the price appreciation potential plus the dividend yield (total return). Assume that for our first investment (investment i) the following data are indicated.

Investment i

K	P	*Based on the state of the economy*
5%	.20	Recession
7	.30	Slow growth
13	.30	Semi-strong economy
15	.20	Strong economy

We will say that $\bar{K}_i$ (the expected value of investment i) equals ΣKP. In this case, our answer would be 10.0 percent.

$$\bar{K}_i = \Sigma KP \qquad (19\text{--}1)$$

K	P	KP
5%	.20	1.0%
7	.30	2.1
13	.30	3.9
15	.20	3.0
		10.0% $= \Sigma KP$

$\bar{K}_i$ (or the expected value for investment i) equals 10.0 percent.

Standard Deviation

The commonly used measure of dispersion is the standard deviation, which is a measure of the spread of the outcomes around the expected value.[1] The formula for the standard deviation is:

$$\sigma_i = \sqrt{\Sigma(K - \bar{K}_i)^2 P} \qquad (19\text{--}2)$$

Let's determine the standard deviation for investment i around the expected value ($\bar{K}_i$) of 10 percent.

K	$\bar{K}_i$	P	$(K - \bar{K}_i)$	$(K - \bar{K}_i)^2$	$(K - \bar{K}_i)^2 P$
5%	10%	.20	-5%	25%	5.0%
7	10	.30	-3	9	2.7
13	10	.30	$+3$	9	2.7
15	10	.20	$+5$	25	5.0
					15.4% $= \Sigma(K - \bar{K}_i)^2 P$

$$\sigma_i = \sqrt{\Sigma(K - \bar{K}_i)^2 P} = \sqrt{15.4\%} = 3.9\%$$

The standard deviation of investment i is 3.9 percent (rounded). In order to have some feel for the relative risk characteristics of this investment, we compare it to a second proposal, investment j.

We assume that investment j is a countercyclical investment. It does well during a recession and poorly in a strong economy. Perhaps it represents a firm in the housing industry that is most profitable when the economy is sluggish and interest rates are low. Under these circumstances, people will avail themselves of low-cost financing to purchase a new home, and the stock of the firm will do well. In a booming economy, interest rates will advance rapidly, and the financing of housing will become quite expensive. Thus, we have a coun-

---

[1] Rather than being the average difference of each K value from $\bar{K}_i$, it is the quadratic mean of the difference; that is, we square the differences, average these squared differences, and then reverse the process by taking the square root.

tercyclical investment. The outcomes and probabilities of outcomes for investment j are as follows:

Investment j

K	P	Based on the state of the economy
20%	.20	Recession
8	.30	Slow growth
8	.30	Semi-strong economy
6	.20	Strong economy

The expected value for investment j is:

$$\bar{K}_j = \Sigma KP$$

K	P	KP
20%	.20	4.0%
8	.30	2.4
8	.30	2.4
6	.20	1.2
		$\bar{K}_j = 10.0\%$

The standard deviation for investment j is:

$$\sigma_j = \sqrt{\Sigma(K - \bar{K}_j)^2 P}$$

K	$\bar{K}_j$	P	$(K - \bar{K}_j)$	$(K - \bar{K}_j)^2$	$(\bar{K}_j)^2 P$
20%	10%	.20	+10%	100%	20.0%
8	10	.30	−2	4	1.2
8	10	.30	−2	4	1.2
6	10	.20	−4	16	3.2
					25.6% $= \Sigma(K - \bar{K}_j)^2 P_j$

$$\sigma_j = \sqrt{\Sigma(K - \bar{K}_j)^2 P} = \sqrt{25.6\%} = 5.1\% \text{ (rounded)}$$

We now see we have two investments, each with an expected value of 10 percent but with varying performances in different types of economies and different standard deviations (3.9 percent versus 5.1 percent).

PORTFOLIO EFFECT

An investor who is holding only investment i may wish to consider bringing investment j into the portfolio. If the stocks are weighted evenly, the new portfolio's expected value will be 10 percent. We define K_p as the expected value of the portfolio.

$$K_p = X_i \overline{K_i} + X_j \overline{K_j} \tag{19-3}$$

The X values represent the weights assigned by the investor to each component in the portfolio and are 50 percent for both investments in this example. The K_i and K_j values were previously determined to be 10 percent. Thus we have:

$$K_p = .5(10\%) + .5(10\%) = 5\% + 5\% = 10\%$$

What about the standard deviation for the combined portfolio (σ_p)? If a weighted average were taken of the two investments, the new standard deviation would be 4.5 percent.

$$X_i \sigma_i + X_j \sigma_j$$
$$.5(3.9\%) + .5(5.1\%) = 1.95\% + 2.55\% = 4.5\%$$

The interesting element is that the investor in investment i would appear to be losing from the combined investment. His expected value remains at 10 percent, but his standard deviation has increased from 3.9 percent to 4.5 percent. Given that he is risk-averse, he appears to be getting more risk rather than less risk by expanding his portfolio.

There is one fallacy in the analysis. The standard deviation of a portfolio is not based on the simple weighted average of the individual standard deviations (as the expected value is). Rather, it takes into consideration significant interaction between the investments. If one investment does well during a given economic condition while the other does poorly and vice versa, there may be significant risk reduction from combining the two, and the standard deviation for the portfolio may be less than the standard deviation for either investment (this is the reason we do not simply take the weighted average of the two).

Note in Figure 19-1 the risk reduction potential from combining the two investments under study. Investment i alone may produce outcomes anywhere from 5 to 15 percent and investment j from 6 to 20 percent. By combining the two, we narrow the range for investment (i, j) to from 7.5 to 12.5 percent. Thus, we have reduced the risk while keeping the expected value constant at 10 percent. We now examine the appropriate standard deviation formula for the two investments.

Standard Deviation for a Two-Asset Portfolio

The standard deviation for a two-asset portfolio (Formula 19-4 on p. 551) appears complicated but is actually quite easy to calculate.[2]

---

[2] For a multiple asset portfolio, the expression is written as:

$$\sigma_p = \sqrt{\sum_{i=1}^{N} X_i^2 \sigma_i^2 + 2 \sum_{i=1}^{N-1} \sum_{j=i+1}^{N} X_i X_j r_{ij} \sigma_i \sigma_j}$$

N is the number of securities in the portfolio.

FIGURE 19–1   Investment Outcomes under Different Conditions

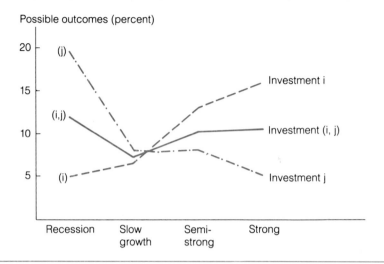

$$\sigma_p = \sqrt{X_i^2\sigma_i^2 + X_j^2\sigma_i^2 + 2X_iX_jr_{ij}\sigma_i\sigma_j} \qquad (19-4)$$

The only new term in the entire expression is r_{ij}, which represents the correlation coefficient or measurement of joint movement between the two variables. If two variables move in completely opposite directions, the coefficient correlation has a maximum negative value of -1. If two variables move in precisely the same direction, the maximum positive correlation coefficient is $+1$. For most variables, the coefficient correlation falls somewhere in between. The actual computation of the correlation coefficient for investments i and j is covered in Appendix 19–A. It is *not* necessary to go through Appendix 19–A before proceeding with our discussion, though some readers may wish to do so. As indicated there, the correlation coefficient (r_{ij}) between investment i and investment j is $-.70$. This indicates that the investments show a high degree of negative correlation. Plugging this value into Formula 19–4, along with other previously determined values, the standard deviation (σ_p) for the two-asset portfolio can be computed.[3]

$$\sigma_p = \sqrt{X_i^2\sigma_i^2 + X_j^2\sigma_j^2 + 2X_iX_jr_{ij}\sigma_i\sigma_j}$$

---

[3] Note that the squared values, such as $(3.9)^2 = 15.4$, are the reverse of earlier computations. Previously we found the square root of 15.4 to be 3.9 (see computation under Formula 19–2). The use of rounding introduces slight discrepancies where we square numbers for which we previously found the square root.

where:

$$X_i = .5, \sigma_i = 3.9$$
$$X_j = .5, \sigma_j = 5.1$$
$$r_{ij} = -.70$$

$$\sigma_p = \sqrt{(.5)^2(3.9)^2 + (.5)^2(5.1)^2 + 2(.5)(.5)(-.7)(3.9)(5.1)}$$
$$= \sqrt{(.25)(15.4) + .25(25.6) + 2(.25)(-.7)(19.9)}$$
$$= \sqrt{3.85 + 6.4 + (.5)(-13.93)}$$
$$= \sqrt{3.85 + 6.4 - 6.97}$$
$$= \sqrt{3.28} = 1.8\%$$

The interesting factor is that the newly computed standard deviation of the portfolio of 1.8 percent is less than the standard deviation of either investment i or j (3.9 percent or 5.1 percent) or the weighted average of the individual investments (4.5 percent). Any time two investments have a correlation coefficient (r_{ij}) less than $+1$ (perfect positive correlation), the standard deviation of the portfolio (σ_p) will be less than the weighted average of the standard deviation for the individual investments and some risk reduction will be possible. In the real world most items are positively correlated; to the extent that we can still get risk reduction from positively correlated items gives extra meaning to portfolio management. Note the impact of various assumed correlation coefficients for the two investments previously described in terms of individual standard deviations.[4]

r_{ij}	σ_p
$+1.0$	4.5
$+.5$	3.9
0	3.2
$-.5$	2.3
$-.7$	1.8
-1.0	0

The conclusion to be drawn from our portfolio analysis discussion is that the most significant risk factor associated with an individual investment may not be its own standard deviation but how it affects the standard deviation of a portfolio through correlation. As we shall later see in this chapter, there is not considered to be a risk premium for the total risk or standard deviation of an individual security, but only for that risk component which can not be eliminated by various portfolio diversification techniques.

DEVELOPING AN EFFICIENT PORTFOLIO

We have seen how the combination of two investments has allowed us to maintain our return of 10 percent, but reduce the portfolio standard deviation to 1.8 percent. We also saw in the preceding table that different coeffi-

---

[4] Each is assumed to represent 50 percent of the portfolio.

cient correlations produce many different possibilities for portfolio standard deviations. A shrewd portfolio manager may wish to consider a large number of portfolios, each with a different expected value and standard deviation, based on the expected values and standard deviations of the individual securities and, more importantly, on the correlations between the individual securities. Though we have been discussing a two-asset portfolio case, our example may be expanded to cover 5-, 10- or even 100-asset portfolios.[5] The major tenets of portfolio theory that we are currently examining were developed by Professor Harry Markowitz in the 1950s, and so we refer to them as Markowitz portfolio theory.

Assume we have identified the following risk-return possibilities for eight different portfolios (there may also be many more, but we will restrict ourselves to this set for now).

Portfolio number	K_p	σ_p
1.	10%	1.8%
2.	10	2.1
3.	12	3.0
4.	13	4.2
5.	13	5.0
6.	14	5.0
7.	14	5.8
8.	15	7.2

In diagramming our various risk-return points, we show the values in Figure 19–2.

Though we have only diagrammed eight possibilities, we see an efficient set of portfolios would lie along the ABCD line. That is, along this *efficient frontier,* we can receive a maximum return for a given level of risk or a minimum risk for a given level of return. Points above this line are assumed not to exist (they are not part of the feasible set of investment alternatives). Points below this line do not offer acceptable alternatives to points along the line. As an example of maximum return for a given level of risk, consider point C. Along the efficient frontier, we are receiving a 14 percent return for a 5 percent risk level, whereas directly below point C, we are only receiving a return of 13 percent for a 5 percent risk level.

To demonstrate that we also are getting minimum risk for a given return level, we can examine point A in which we receive a 10 percent return for a 1.8 percent risk level, whereas to the right of point A, we get the same 10 percent return but a less desirable 2.1 percent risk level. Though we have

---

[5] The incremental benefit from reduction of the portfolio standard deviation through adding securities appears to diminish fairly sharply with a portfolio of 10 securities and is quite small with a portfolio as large as 20. A portfolio of 12 to 14 securities is generally thought to be of sufficient size to enjoy the majority of desirable portfolio effects. See W. H. Wagner and S. C. Lau, "The Effect of Diversification on Risk," *Financial Analysts Journal,* November–December 1971, pp. 48–53.

FIGURE 19–2   Diagram of Risk-Return Trade-Offs

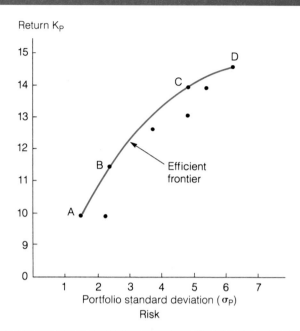

shown but eight points, a fully developed efficient frontier may be based on a virtually unlimited number of observations as is presented in Figure 19–3.

In Figure 19–3, we once again view the efficient frontier in relationship to the feasible set and note certain risk-return possibilities are not attainable (and should be disregarded). At this point in the analysis, we can stipulate that the various points along the efficient frontier are all considered potentially optimal and that a given investor must choose the most appropriate single point based on his or her individualized risk-return trade-off desires. We would say that a low-risk-oriented investor might prefer point A or B in Figure 19–2, whereas a more-risk-oriented investor would prefer point C or D. At each of these points, the investor is getting the best risk-return trade-off for his or her own particular risk-taking propensity.

Risk-Return Indifference Curves

To actually pair up an investor with an appropriate point along the efficient frontier, we look at his or her indifference curve as illustrated in Figure 19–4.

The indifference curves show the investor's trade-off between risk and return. The steeper the slope of the curve, the more risk-averse the investor is. For example, in the case of investor B (I_B in Figure 19–4), the indifference curve has a steeper slope than that for investor A (I_A). This means that investor B will require more incremental return (more of a risk premium) for each

FIGURE 19–3   Expanded View of Efficient Frontier

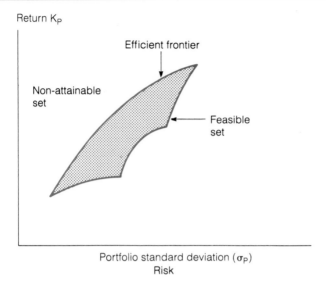

Return K_P

Efficient frontier

Non-attainable
set

Feasible
set

Portfolio standard deviation (σ_P)
Risk

FIGURE 19–4   Risk-Return Indifference Curves

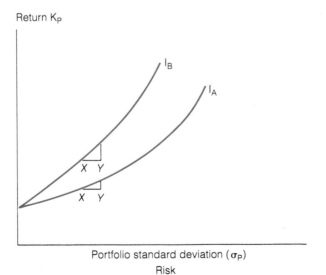

Return K_P

I_B

I_A

X Y

X Y

Portfolio standard deviation (σ_P)
Risk

additional unit of risk. Note that to take risks, investor B requires approximately twice as much incremental return as investor A between points X and Y. Investor A is still somewhat risk-averse and perhaps represents a typical investor in the capital markets.

Once the shape of an investor's indifference curve is determined, a second objective can be established—to attain the highest curve possible. For example, investor A, initially shown in Figure 19–4, would have a whole set of similarly shaped indifference curves as presented in Figure 19–5.

FIGURE 19–5   Indifference Curves for Investor A

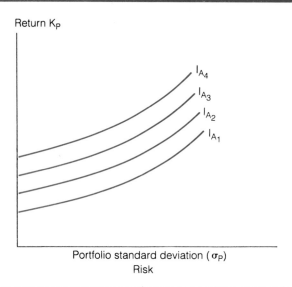

While he is indifferent to any point along a given curve (such as I_{A4}), he is not indifferent to achieving the highest curve possible (I_{A_4} is clearly superior to I_{A_1}). It provides more return at all given risk levels. The only limitation to achieving the highest possible indifference curve is the feasible set of investments that are available.

Optimum Portfolio

The investor must theoretically match his own risk-return indifference curve with the best investments that are available in the market as represented by points on the efficient frontier. We see in Figure 19–6 that investor A will achieve the highest possible indifference curve at point C along the efficient frontier.

FIGURE 19–6   Combining the Efficient Frontier and Indifference Curves

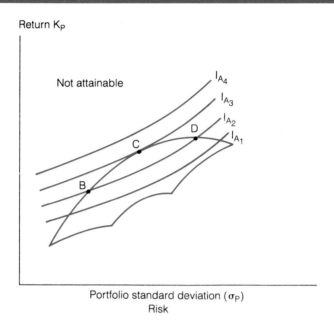

Return K_P

Not attainable

I_{A_4}

I_{A_3}

I_{A_2}

I_{A_1}

D

C

B

Portfolio standard deviation (σ_P)
Risk

This is the point of tangency between his own indifference curve (I_{A_3}) and the efficient frontier. Both curves have the same slope or risk-return characteristics at this point. While a point along indifference curve (I_{A_4}) might provide a higher level of utility, it is not attainable in relationship to the efficient frontier. Also, any other point along the efficient frontier would cross a lower level indifference curve and be inferior to point C. For example, points B and D cross I_{A_2}, providing less return for a given level of risk than I_{A_3}. Investors must relate the shape of their *own* risk-return indifference curves to the efficient frontier to determine that point of tangency providing maximum benefits.

CAPITAL ASSET PRICING MODEL

The development of the efficient frontier in the previous section gives insight into optimum portfolio mixes in an appropriate risk-return context. Nevertheless, the development of multiple portfolios is a rather difficult and tedious task. Professors Sharpe, Lintner, and others have allowed us to take the philosophy of efficient portfolios into a more generalized and meaningful context through the capital asset pricing model. Under this model, we examine the theoretical underpinnings through which assets are valued based on their risk characteristics.

The capital asset pricing model (CAPM) takes off where the efficient frontier concluded through the introduction of a new investment outlet, the risk-free asset *(R_F)*. A risk-free asset has a standard deviation of 0 ($\sigma_{RF} = 0$) and is the lowest assumed safe return that can be earned. A U.S. Treasury bill or Treasury bond is often considered representative of a risk-free asset. Under the capital asset pricing model, we introduce the notion of combining the risk-free asset and the efficient frontier with the development of the *R_F MZ* line as indicated in Figure 19–7.

FIGURE 19-7   Basic Diagram of the Capital Asset Pricing Model

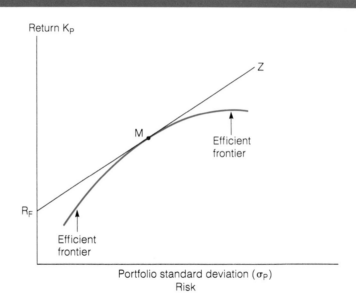

The *R_F MZ* line opens up the possibility of a whole new set of superior investment opportunities. That is, by combining some portion of the risk-free asset (R_F) with M (a point along the efficient frontier), we create new investment opportunities that will allow us to reach higher indifference curves than would be possible simply along the efficient frontier. We see in Figure 19–8 that points O and P provide higher utility than points on the efficient frontier. The only point along the efficient frontier that now has significance is point M, where the straight line from R_F is tangent to the old efficient frontier.

We can reach points along the *R_F MZ* line in a number of different ways. To be at point R_F, we would simply buy a risk-free asset. To be at a point between R_F and M, we would buy a combination of R_F and the M portfolio along the efficient frontier. To be at a point between M and Z, we buy M with our available funds and then borrow additional funds to further increase our

purchase of the M portfolio (an example of this would be to be at point P in Figure 19–8). To the extent that M is higher than R_F and we can borrow at a rate equal to R_F or slightly higher, we can get larger returns with a combination of buying M and borrowing additional funds to buy M. (Of course, this calls for greater risk as well.)

FIGURE 19–8   The CAPM and Indifference Curves

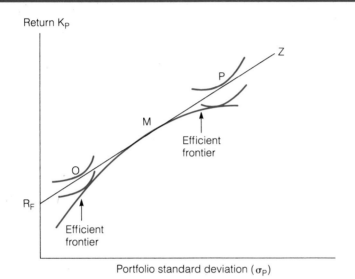

We also note that point M is considered the optimum "market basket" of investments that is available (though you may wish to combine this market basket with risk-free assets or borrowing). If you took all the possible investments that investors could acquire and determined the optimum basket of investments, you would come up with point M (because it is along the efficient frontier and tangent to the R_F line). Point M can be measured by the total return on the Standard & Poor's 500 Stock Average, the Dow Jones Industrial Average, the New York Stock Exchange Index, or similar measures. If point M or the market were not represented by the optimum risk-return portfolio for all investments at a point in time, then it is assumed there would be an instantaneous change and the market measure (point M) would once again be in equilibrium (be optimal).

Capital Market Line

The previously discussed R_FMZ line is called the capital market line (CML) and is once again presented in Figure 19–9.

FIGURE 19–9   Illustration of the Capital Market Line

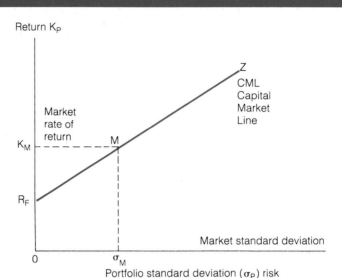

The formula for the capital market line in Figure 19–9 may be written as:

$$K_P = R_F + \left(\frac{K_M - R_F}{\sigma_M - 0} \right) \sigma_P \qquad (19\text{–}5)$$

We indicate that the expected return on any portfolio (K_P) is equal to the risk-free rate of return (R_F), plus the slope of the line times a value along the horizontal axis (σ_P), indicating the amount of risk undertaken. We can relate the formula for the capital market line to the basic equation for a straight line as follows:

Straight line $Y = a + b \cdot X$

Capital market line $K_P = R_F + \left(\dfrac{K_M - R_F}{\sigma_M - 0} \right) \cdot \sigma_P$

In using the capital market line, we start with a minimum rate of return of R_F and then say any additional return is a reward for risk. The reward for risk or risk premium is equal to the market rate of return (K_M) minus the risk-free rate (R_F) divided by the market standard deviation (σ_M). If the market rate of return (K_M) is 9 percent and the risk-free rate of return (R_F) is 6 percent, with a market standard deviation (σ_M) of 10 percent, there is a risk premium of .3. Then if the standard deviation of our portfolio (σ_P) is 14 percent, we can expect a return of 10.2 percent along the CML as computed on p. 561.

$$K_P = R_F + \left(\frac{K_M - R_F}{\sigma_M - 0}\right)\sigma_P$$

$$K_P = 6\% + \left(\frac{9\% - 6\%}{10\% - 0}\right)14\%$$

$$= 6\% + \left(\frac{3\%}{10\%}\right)14\%$$

$$= 6\% + (.3)\,14\%$$

$$= 6\% + 4.2\% = 10.2\%$$

The essence of the capital market line is that the way to get larger returns is to take increasingly higher risks. Thus, the only way to climb up the K_P *return* line in Figure 19–9 is to extend yourself out on the σ_P *risk* line. Portfolio managers who claim highly superior returns may have taken larger than normal risks and thus may not really be superior performers on a risk-adjusted basis. We shall see in the following chapter that the best way to measure a portfolio manager is to evaluate his returns relative to the risks taken. Average to slightly above average returns on low risk may be superior to high returns on high risk. One does not easily exceed market-dictated constraints for risk and return.

RETURN ON AN INDIVIDUAL SECURITY

We have been examining return expectations for a portfolio; we now turn our attention to an individual security. Once again, the return potential is closely tied to risk. However, when dealing with an individual security, the premium return for risk is not related to *all* the risk in the investment as measured by the standard deviation (σ).[6] The reason for this is that the standard deviation is made up of two types of risks, but only one is accorded a premium return under the capital asset pricing model.

We now begin an analytical process that allows us to get at the two forms of risk in an individual security. The first form of risk is measured by the beta coefficient.

Beta coefficient.   In analyzing the performance of an individual security, it is first important to measure its relationship to the market through the beta coefficient. Let us lay the groundwork for understanding beta. In the case of a potential investment, stock i, we can observe its relationship to the market by tracing its total return performance relative to market total return over the last five years.[7]

---

[6] Actually, rather than use the standard deviation, we often use its squared value, termed the *variance,* to describe risk. That is, we may use σ^2 (the standard deviation squared) to describe risk in an individual security.

[7] Though monthly or quarterly calculations would be desirable, we can satisfy our same basic objectives with annual data.

	Stock i return (K)	Market return (K$_M$)
1982	4.8%	6.5%
1983	14.5	11.8
1984	19.1	14.9
1985	3.7	1.1
1986	15.6	12.0

We see that stock i moves somewhat with the market. Plotting the values in Figure 19–10, we observe a line that is upward sloping at slightly above a 45-degree angle.

FIGURE 19–10   Relationship of Individual Stock to the Market

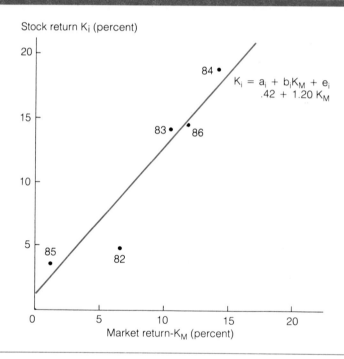

A straight line of best fit has been drawn through the various points representing the following formula:

$$K_i = a_i + b_iK_M + e_i \qquad (19\text{–}6)$$

K_i represents the anticipated stock return based on the formula; a_i (alpha) is the point at which the line crosses the vertical axis; b_i (beta) is the slope of the line; K_M is the independent variable of market return; and e_i is the random error term. The $a_i + b_iK_M$ portion of the formula describes a straight

line, and e_i represents deviations or random, nonrecurring movements away from the straight line. In the present example, the formula for the straight line is $K_i = .42 + 1.20\ K_M$ (indicating a beta or line slope of 1.2). These values can be approximated by drawing a line of best fit as indicated in Figure 19–10 or through the use of least squares regression analysis presented in Appendix 19–B. Basically, the equation tells us how volatile our stock is relative to the market through the beta coefficient. In the present case, if the market moves up or down by a given percent, our stock is assumed to move by 1.2 times that amount. With a beta of 1.2, our stock is considered to be 20 percent more volatile than the market. A stock with average volatility would have a beta of 1.

Systematic and Unsystematic Risk

Previously, we mentioned that there are two major types of risk associated with a stock. One is the market movement or beta (b_i) risk. If the market moves up or down, a stock is assumed to change in value. This type of risk is referred to as *systematic* risk and was first introduced in Chapter 1. The second type of risk is represented by the error term (e_i) and indicates changes in value not associated with market movement. It may represent the temporary influence of a competitor's new product, changes in raw material prices, or unusual economic and government influences on a given firm. These changes are peculiar to an individual security or industry at a given point in time and are not directly correlated with the market. This second type of risk is referred to as *unsystematic* risk.

Recall that one type of risk is assumed to be compensated for under the capital asset pricing model, while another is not. The investor is presumed to receive a risk premium for the beta (or systematic) risk but not for unsystematic risk. Since the latter is associated with an individual company or industry, it may be diversified away in a large portfolio and is not a risk inherent in investing in common stocks. Thus, by picking stocks that are less than perfectly correlated, unsystematic risk may be eliminated. For example, the inherent risks of investing in semiconductor stocks may be diversified away by investing in the countercyclical housing stocks. Researchers have indicated that all but 15 percent of unsystematic risk may be eliminated with a carefully selected portfolio of 10 stocks and all but 11 percent with a portfolio of 20 stocks.[8] We thus can describe total risk as:

$$\text{Total risk} = \text{Systematic risk} + \text{Unsystematic risk}$$

But unsystematic risk can be diversified away, so that systematic risk (b_i) is the only relevant risk under the capital asset pricing model for which the investor can expect to receive compensation.

---

[8] Wagner and Lau, "The Effect of Diversification on Risk."

Security Market Line

We actually express the trade-off between risk and return for an *individual stock* through the security market line (SML) in Figure 19–11. Whereas in Figure 19–10 we graphed the relationship that allowed us to compute the *beta (b₁)* for a security, in Figure 19–11 we now take that *beta* and show what the

FIGURE 19–11   Illustration of the Security Market Line

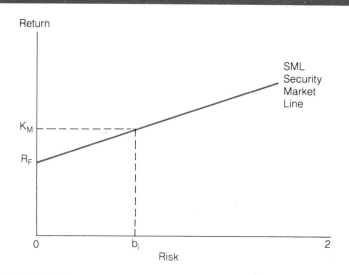

anticipated or required return in the marketplace is for a stock with that characteristic. The security market line (SML) is a generalized concept to show the risk-return trade-off for an individual stock just as the capital market line (CML) accomplished that same objective for a portfolio (in Figure 19–9).

Once again, we stress that the return is not plotted against the total risk (σ) for the individual stock, but only that part of the risk that can not be diversified away, commonly referred to as the systematic or beta risk. The actual formula for the security market line (SML) is:

$$K_i = R_F + b_i(K_M - R_F) \tag{19–7}$$

The mathematical derivation of the formula is presented in Appendix 19–C. As we did with the capital market line for portfolio returns, with the security market line we start out with a basic rate of return for a risk-free asset (R_F) and add a risk premium. In this case, the premium is equal to the beta on the stock times the difference between the market rate of return (K_M) and the risk-free rate of return (R_F). If $R_F = 6\%$, $K_M = 9\%$, and the stock has a beta (b_i) of 1, the anticipated rate of return, using Formula 19–7, would be the same as that in the market, or 9 percent.

$$K_i = 6\% + 1(9\% - 6\%) = 6\% + 3\% = 9\%$$

Since the stock has the same degree of risk as the market in general, this would appear to be logical. If the stock has a beta of 1.5, the added systematic risk would call for a return of 10.5 percent, whereas a beta of .5 would indicate the return should be 7.5 percent.

Beta = 1.5
$$K_i = 6\% + 1.5(9\% - 6\%) = 6\% + 1.5(3\%) = 6\% + 4.5\% = 10.5\%$$
Beta = .5
$$K_i = 6\% + .5(9\% - 6\%) = 6\% + .5(3\%) = 6\% + 1.5\% = 7.5\%$$

Since the beta factor is deemed to be important in analyzing potential risk and return, there is much emphasis placed on knowing the beta for a given security. Merrill Lynch, Value Line, and various brokerage houses and investment services publish information on beta for a large number of securities. A representative list is presented in the table below.

Corporation	Beta (August 1984)
Georgia-Pacific	1.40
Digital Equipment	1.25
Ford Motor	1.05
Eli Lilly	.90
Colgate-Palmolive	.80
Cincinnati Gas and Electric	.60

ASSUMPTIONS OF THE CAPITAL ASSET PRICING MODEL

Having evaluated some of the implications of the CAPM, it is important that the student be aware of some of the assumptions that go into the model.

1. All investors can borrow or lend an unlimited amount of funds at a given risk-free rate.
2. All investors have the same one-period time horizon.
3. All investors wish to maximize their expected utility over this time horizon and evaluate investments on the basis of means and standard deviations of portfolio returns.
4. All investors have the same expectations—that is to say, all investors estimate identical probability distributions for rates of return.
5. All assets are perfectly divisible—it is possible to buy fractional shares of any asset or portfolio.
6. There are no taxes or transactions costs.
7. The market is efficient and in equilibrium or quickly adjusting to equilibrium.

The purpose of listing these assumptions is to indicate some of the necessary conditions to create the CAPM. While at first they may appear to be severely limiting, they are similar to those often used in the standard economic theory of the firm and in other basic financial models.

The primary usefulness in examining this model or similar risk-return trade-off models is to provide some reasonable basis for relating return opportunity with risk on the investment. Portfolio managers find risk-return models helpful in explaining their performance or the performance of their competitors to clients. A competitor's portfolio that has unusually high returns may have been developed primarily on the basis of high-risk assets. To the extent that this can be explained on the basis of capital market theory, the competitor's performance may look less like superior money management and more like a product of high risk taking. As we shall see in Chapter 20, Measuring Risk and Returns of Portfolio Managers, many of the techniques for assessing portfolio performance on Wall Street are explicitly or implicitly related to the risk-return concepts discussed in this chapter.

Though empirical tests have somewhat supported the capital asset pricing model, a number of testing problems remain. In order to develop the SML in which stock returns (vertical axis) can be measured against beta (horizontal axis), an appropriate line must be drawn. Researchers have some disagreement about R_F. (Is it represented by short-term or long-term Treasury rates?) There is also debate about what is the appropriate K_M, or market rate of return. Some suggest the market proxy variable will greatly influence beta and that difficulties in dealing with this problem can bring the whole process under attack.[9]

When empirical data is compared to theoretical return expectations, there is some discrepancy in that the theoretical SML may have a slightly greater slope than the actual line fitted on the basis on real-world data as shown in Figure 19–12.[10]

There may also be a possible problem in that betas for individual securities are not necessarily stable over time (rather than remaining relatively constant at 1.3 or perhaps .7, they tend to approach 1 over time). Thus, a beta based on past risk may not always reflect current risk.[11] Because the beta for a portfolio may be more stable than an individual stock's beta, portfolio betas are also used as a systematic risk variable. A portfolio beta is simply the weighted average of the betas of the individual stocks. We can say:

$$b_P \text{ (portfolio beta)} = \Sigma Xb \qquad (19\text{--}8)$$

and

$$K_P = R_F + b_P(K_M - R_F) \qquad (19\text{--}9)$$

---

[9] Richard Roll, "A Critique of the Asset Pricing Theory's Test," *Journal of Financial Economics,* March 1977, pp. 129–76. Also, "Ambiguity When Performance is Measured by the Securities Market Line," *Journal of Finance,* September 1978, pp. 1051–69.

[10] Franco Modigliani and Gerald A. Pogue, "An Introduction to Risk and Returns," *Financial Analysts Journal,* March–April 1974, pp. 68–86, and May–June 1974, pp. 69–86.

[11] Robert A. Levy, "On the Short-Term Stationary of Beta Coefficients," *Financial Analysts Journal,* November–December 1971, pp. 55–62. Also Marshall E. Blume, "Beta and Their Regression Tendencies," *Journal of Finance,* June 1975, pp. 785–95.

FIGURE 19–12   Test of the Security Market Line

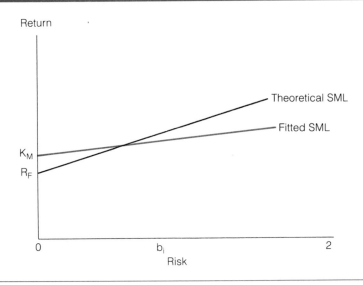

By examining portfolio betas rather than individual stock betas, we overcome part of the criticism leveled at the instability of betas in the capital asset pricing model. Many of the other criticisms have also evoked new research that may provide different approaches or possible solutions to past deficiencies in the model. In any event, the capital asset pricing model is likely to remain relatively important in the future.

ARBITRAGE PRICING THEORY

Another theory for explaining stock prices and stock returns is known as arbitrage pricing theory. While the capital asset pricing model bases return solely on one form of systematic risk (market risk), arbitrage pricing theory (APT) accommodates several sources of systematic risk. For example, it may be hypothesized that a security's required return beyond the risk-free rate is based on GNP, unemployment, the value of the dollar, inflation and long-term interest rates. We shall refer to each of these factors as F_1, F_2, F_3, F_4 and F_5. In comparing two securities or portfolios in a hypothetical analysis, we will assume that factors F_4 and F_5 may be diversified away so that only factor F_1, F_2, and F_3 remain. These factors represent systematic, nondiversifiable risk.

Each of the three factors will have an influence on the expected return of the two securities or portfolios we are examining. You will recall the first three factors are GNP (F_1), unemployment (F_2), and value of the dollar (F_3). Let's discuss the causal relationship of these three factors to the expected return on a security or portfolio. We will refer to this relationship by the symbol β (also

called beta).[12] Keep in mind that we are dealing with two securities (or portfolios) and three factors *(F)* that influence rates of return. In order to clarify statements about β, we will add the subscripts i and j to it. The first subscript refers to the security number ($i = 1$ or 2), and the second subscript refers to the factor number ($j = 1, 2,$ or 3). Thus β_{13} would refer to the first security and the third factor.

The β indicates the influence that a factor has on expected return. For example, if β_{13} were .25, a 6 percent increase in factor 3 would add 1.5 percent to the expected return of security 1. The expected return for security 1 can be generally stated as:

$$E_1 = a + \beta_{11}F_1 + \beta_{12}F_2 + \beta_{13}F_3 \qquad (19\text{--}10)$$

where:

E_1 = Expected return on security 1
a = Risk-free rate *(R_F)*
β_{11} = Relationship between F_1 (factor 1) and E_1 (expected return on security 1)
F_1 = Factor 1 (GNP)
β_{12} = Relationship between F_2 (factor 2) and E_1 (expected return on security 1)
F_2 = Factor 2 (unemployment)
β_{13} = Relationship between F_3 (factor 3) and E_1 (expected return on security 1)
F_3 = Factor 3 (value of the dollar)

Without going through all the numbers, we shall assume that Equation 19–10 provides an expected return of 11 percent for security 1. We shall also assume that a similar analysis of security 2, based on the same economic factors (GNP, unemployment, and value of the dollar) but different β values, will provide an expected return of 12 percent. Suppose both securities are trading for $10 and pay no cash dividends. Now assume that security 1's price changes by more than is indicated by the expected return factors in relation to the second security. Suppose security 1 goes up by 15 percent while security 2 only goes up by 8 percent. Market participants will trade back and forth between the two securities until the appropriate relationship between expected returns is achieved. This is deemed to be a form of arbitraging, thus the term *arbitrage pricing theory.* The notion is that you cannot earn returns that exceed those allowed by the various forms of systematic risk.

Unlike the capital asset pricing model, there is no necessity to define K_M (the market rate of return or market proxy variable), and this is an advantage of arbitrage pricing theory. On the other hand, there is some difficulty in arbitrage pricing theory with properly defining the F and β factors and their relationship. While arbitrage pricing theory may offer some conceptual and

---

[12] This, of course, is not the same concept as systematic, market-related, risk used previously. More generally, beta describes the effect of one variable on another.

empirical (testing) advantages over the capital asset pricing model, it is less widely used. In Chapter 20, Measuring Risks and Returns of Portfolio Managers, our emphasis will be on the capital asset pricing model.

SUMMARY

The investor is basically risk-averse and therefore will demand a premium for incremental risk. In an efficient market context, the ability to achieve high returns may be more directly related to absorption of additional risk than superior ability in selecting stocks (this remains a debatable point which proponents of fundamental and technical analysis would argue).

Risk for an individual stock is measured in terms of the standard deviation (σ_i) around a given expected value $(\overline{K}_i)$. The larger the standard deviation, the greater the risk. For a portfolio of stocks, the expected value (K_P) is the weighted average of the individual returns; but this is not true for the portfolio standard deviation (σ_P). The portfolio standard deviation is also influenced by the interaction between the stocks. To the extent the correlation coefficient (r_{ij}) is less than $+1$, there will be some reduction from the weighted average of the standard deviation of the individual stocks that we are combining. A negative correlation coefficient will provide substantial reduction in the portfolio standard deviation.

Under classic Markowitz portfolio theory we look at a large array of possible portfolios in an attempt to construct an efficient frontier that represents the best possible risk-return trade-off at different levels of risk. Individuals then match their own risk-return indifference curves with the efficient frontier to determine where they should be along this optimal scale.

This was the prevailing theory until the capital asset pricing model (CAPM) was developed in the 1960s and 70s. The CAPM supersedes some of the findings of classic portfolio theory with the introduction of the risk-free asset (R_F) into the analysis. The assumption is that an individual can choose an investment combining the return on the risk-free asset with the market rate of return, and this will provide superior returns to the efficient frontier at all points except M, where they are equal. The investor may invest in any combination of R_F and M to achieve the risk-return positions described by the capital market line in Figure 19–9.

The capital market line describes the general trade-off between risk and return for portfolio managers in the economy. Any attempt to get higher portfolio returns must be matched by higher portfolio risks. Although the portfolio manager is investing in stocks and bonds, the general pattern set out for the risk-free asset and market combination is perceived to establish the limits for investment performance of any nature. Any increase in portfolio returns (K_P) must be associated with an increase in the portfolio standard deviation (σ_P).

The capital asset pricing model also calls for an evaluation of individual assets (rather than portfolios). The security market line in Figure 19–11 shows

the same type of risk-return trade-off for individual securities as the capital market line did for portfolios. Investors in individual assets are only assumed to be rewarded for systematic, market-related risk, known as the beta (b_i) risk. All other risk is assumed to be susceptible to diversification.

There are a number of assumptions associated with the capital asset pricing model that are subject to close review and challenge. Furthermore, there is some question about the appropriate measure for R_F and K_M as well as the stability of beta and the appropriate slope of the SML line. Nevertheless, the capital asset pricing model represents a generally useful device for portraying the relationship of risk and return in the capital markets over the long term.

Arbitrage pricing theory allows for several sources of systematic risk as opposed to one measure under the capital asset pricing model. It further assumes that investors will appropriately hedge or arbitrage between securities and portfolios to establish expected returns. While arbitrage pricing theory offers some conceptual and empirical advantages over the capital asset pricing model, it is less widely used.

IMPORTANT WORDS AND CONCEPTS

Risk	**Capital asset pricing model**
Expected value	**(CAPM)**
Dispersion	**Capital market line (CML)**
Standard deviation	**Beta coefficient**
Portfolio effect	**Systematic risk**
Correlation coefficient	**Unsystematic risk**
Efficient portfolio	**Security market line (SML)**
Efficient frontier	**Arbitrage pricing theory (ATP)**

DISCUSSION QUESTIONS

1. Define risk.
2. How is risk measured?
3. What is an expected value?
4. What is the most commonly used measure of dispersion?
5. In a two-asset portfolio, is the portfolio standard deviation a weighted average of the two individual stocks' standard deviation? Explain.
6. What is the efficient frontier?
7. What does the steepness of the slope of the risk-return indifference curve indicate?
8. Describe the optimum portfolio for an investor in terms of indifference curves and the efficient frontier.
9. What new investment variable or outlet allowed market researchers to

go from Markowitz portfolio theory (including the efficient frontier) to the capital asset pricing model?

10. In examining the capital market line as part of the capital asset pricing model, in order to increase portfolio return (K_P) what other variable must you increase?

11. In terms of the capital asset pricing model:
   a. Indicate the two types of risks associated with an individual security.
   b. Which of these two is the beta risk?
   c. What risk is assumed not to be compensated for in the marketplace under the capital asset pricing model. Why?

12. What does the security market line indicate? In general terms, how is it different from the capital market line?

13. In regard to the capital asset pricing model, comment on disagreements or debates related to R_F (the risk-free rate) and K_M (market rate of return).

14. Are betas of individual stocks necessarily stable (constant) over time? What about portfolio betas?

15. How does arbitrage pricing theory differ from the capital asset pricing model in regard to systematic risk?

16. Is APT or the CAPM more widely used?

PROBLEMS

1. An investment has the following range of outcomes and probabilities.

Outcomes (percent)	Probability of outcomes
6%	.30
9	.40
12	.30

Calculate the expected value and the standard deviation (round to two places after the decimal point where necessary).

2. Given another investment with an expected value of 13 percent and a standard deviation of 3.1 percent that is counter-cyclical to the investment in Problem 1, what is the expected value of the portfolio and its standard deviation if both are combined into a portfolio with 40 percent invested in the first investment and 60 percent in the second? Assume the correlation coefficient (r_{ij}) is $-.40$.

3. What would be the portfolio standard deviation if the two investments in the Problem 2 had a correlation coefficient (r_{ij}) of $+.40$?

4. Assume the following risk-return possibilities for 10 different portfolios. Plot the points in a manner similar to Figure 19–2 and indicate the approximate shape of the efficient frontier.

Portfolio number	K_p	σ_p
1	10%	1.5%
2	10	2.5
3	9	3.0
4	12	4.0
5	11	4.0
6	12	5.0
7	12	6.0
8	13.5	6.5
9	13	6.5
10	14	7.0

5.   Using the formula for the capital market line (Formula 19–5), if the risk-free rate (R_F) is 7 percent, the market rate of return (K_M) is 12 percent, the market standard deviation (σ_M) is 10 percent, and the standard deviation of the portfolio (σ_p) is 13 percent, compute the anticipated return (K_p).

6.   Recompute the answer to Question 5 based on a portfolio standard of 16 percent. In terms of capital market theory, explain why K_p has increased.

7.   Using the formula for the security market line (Formula 19–7), if the risk-free rate (R_F) is 7 percent, the beta (b_i) is 1.15, and the market rate of return (K_M) is 12 percent, compute the anticipated rate of return (K_i).

8.   If another security had a lower beta than indicated in Question 7, would K_i be lower or higher? What is the logic behind your answer in terms of risk?

9.   Assume the following values for a stock's return and the market return.

Year	Stock i return (K)	Market return (K_M)
1980	15.5	14.9
1981	2.8	1.1
1982	17.7	12.0
1983	15.1	10.1
1984	6.0	3.2

Plot the date and draw a line of best fit similar to that in Figure 19–10.

10. Using the formulas in Appendix 19–B, compute a least squares regression equation for problem 9. (Round beta and alpha to two places after the decimal point).

SELECTED REFERENCES

Baker, H. Kent; Michael B. Hargrove; and John A. Haslem. "An Empirical Analysis of the Risk-Return Preferences of Individual Investors." *Journal of Financial and Quantitative Analysis,* September 1977, pp. 377–89.

Black, Fischer. "Capital Market Equilibrium with Restricted Borrowing." *Journal of Business,* July 1972, pp. 444–54.

Blume, Marshall E. "Betas and Their Regression Tendencies." *Journal of Finance,* June 1975, pp. 785–95.

————. "Betas and Their Regression Tendencies: Some Further Evidence." *Journal of Finance,* March 1979, pp. 265–67.

Blume, Marshall E., and Irwin Friend. "The Asset Structure of Individual Portfolios and Some Implications for Utility Functions." *Journal of Finance,* May 1975, pp. 585–603.

Dhymes, Phoebus J. "The Empirical Relevance of Arbitrage Pricing Models." *Journal of Portfolio Management,* Summer 1984, pp. 35–44.

Elgers, Pieter T.; James R. Haltiner; and William H. Hawthorne. "Beta Regression Tendencies: Statistical and Real Causes." *Journal of Finance,* March 1979, pp. 261–63.

Elton, Edwin J.; Martin J. Gruber; and Thomas J. Ulrich. "Are Betas Best?" *Journal of Finance,* December 1978, pp. 1375–84.

Fabozzi, Frank J., and Jack Clark Francis. "Stability Tests for Alphas and Betas over Bull and Bear Market Conditions." *Journal of Finance,* September 1977, pp. 1093–99.

Friend, Irwin; Randloph Westerfield; and Michael Granito. "New Evidence on the Capital Asset Pricing Model." *Journal of Finance,* June 1978, pp. 903–17.

Hill, Joanne M. "Reducing Forecast Error in Portfolio Management: Sample Clustering and Alternative Risk Specifications." *Financial Management,* Winter 1980, pp. 42–50.

Jensen, Michael C., ed. *Studies in the Theory of Capital Markets.* New York: Praeger Publishers, 1972.

Levy, Robert A. "On the Short-Term Stationarity of Beta Coefficients." *Financial Analysts Journal,* November–December 1971, pp. 55–62.

Linter, John. "The Evaluation of Risk Assets and the Selection of Risky Investments in Stock Portfolios and Capital Budgets." *Review of Economics and Statistics,* February 1965, pp. 13–37.

Martin, John D., and Arthur Keown. "A Misleading Feature of Beta for Risk Measurement." *Journal of Portfolio Management,* Summer 1977, pp. 31–34.

Markowitz, Harry H. "Portfolio Selection." *Journal of Finance,* March 1952, pp. 77–91.

————. *Portfolio Selection: Efficient Diversification of Investments.* New York: John Wiley & Sons, 1959.

Modigliani, Franco, and Gerald A. Pogue. "An Introduction to Risk and Returns." *Financial Analysts Journal,* March–April 1974, pp. 68–80, and May–June 1974, pp. 69–86.

Roll, Richard. "Ambiguity When Performance is Measured by the Securities Market Line." *Journal of Finance,* September 1978, pp. 1051–70.

————. "A Critique of the Asset Pricing Theory's Test." *Journal of Financial Economics,* March 1977, pp. 129–76.

Roll, Richard, and Stephen A. Ross. "An Empirical Investigation of the Arbitrage Pricing Theory." *The Journal of Finance,* December 1980, pp. 1073–1103.

Ross, Stephen A. "The Current Status of the Capital Asset Pricing Model." *Journal of Finance,* June 1978, pp. 885–901.

————. "The Arbitrage Theory of Capital Asset Pricing." *Journal of Economic Theory,* December 1976, pp. 314–360.

Sharpe, William F. "A Simplified Model for Portfolio Analysis." *Management Science,* January 1963, pp. 277–93.

————. "Capital Asset Prices: A Theory of Market Equilibrium under Conditions of Risk." *Journal of Finance,* September 1964, pp. 425–42.

————. "Bonds versus Stocks: Some Lessons from Capital Market Theory." *Financial Analysis Journal,* November–December 1973, pp. 74–80.

Wagner, W. H., and S. C. Lau. "The Effect of Diversification on Risk." *Financial Analysts Journal,* November–December 1971, pp. 48–53.

Weston, J. Fred. "Investment Decisions Using the Capital Asset Pricing Model." *Financial Management,* Spring 1973, pp. 25–33.

————. "Developments in Financial Theory." *Financial Management,* 10th anniversary issue, 1981, pp. 5–22.

Yawitz, Jess B.; George H. Hempel; and William J. Marshall. "A Risk-Return Approach to the Selection of Optimal Government Bond Portfolios." *Financial Management,* Autumn 1976, pp. 36–47.

APPENDIX 19–A: *The Correlation Coefficient*

There are a number of formulas for the correlation coefficient. We shall use the statement:

$$r_{ij} = \frac{\text{cov}_{ij}}{\sigma_i \sigma_j} \qquad (19A-1)$$

Cov$_{ij}$ (covariance) is an *absolute* measure of the extent to which two sets of variables move together over time. Once we have determined this value, we simply divide by $\sigma_i \sigma_j$ to get a relative measure of correlation (r_{ij}). The formula for the covariance is:

$$\text{cov}_{ij} = \Sigma(K - \bar{K_i})(K - \bar{K_j})P \qquad (19A-2)$$

We take our K and P values from investment i and investment j in Chapter 19 to compute the following:

K	$\bar{K_i}$	$(K - \bar{K_i})$	K	$\bar{K_j}$	$(K - \bar{K_j})$	$(K - \bar{K_i})(K - \bar{K_j})$	P	$(K - \bar{K_i})(K - \bar{K_j})P$
5%	10%	−5%	20%	10%	+10%	−50%	.20	−10.0%
7	10	−3	8	10	−2	+6	.30	+1.8
13	10	+3	8	10	−2	−6	.30	−1.8
15	10	+5	6	10	−4	−20	.20	−4.0
								−14.0%

$$\text{cov}_{ij} = \Sigma(K - \bar{K_i})(K - \bar{K_j})P = -14.0\%$$

Using the values in the chapter for σ_i and σ_j, we determine:

$$r_{ij} = \frac{\text{cov}_{ij}}{\sigma_i \sigma_j} = \frac{-14.0}{(3.9)(5.1)} = \frac{-14.0}{19.9} = -.70$$

APPENDIX 19–B: *Least Squares Regression Analysis*

We shall show how least squares regression analysis can be used to develop a linear equation to explain the relationship between the return on a stock and return in the market.

We will develop the terms in the expression:

$$K_i = a_i + b_i K_M + e_i$$

(e_i is the random error term and will not be quantified in our analysis).
Using the data from the chapter,

Year	K	K_M
1982	4.8%	6.5%
1983	14.5	11.8
1984	19.1	14.9
1985	3.7	1.1
1986	15.6	12.0

The normal or mathematical equation to solve for b_i is:

$$b_i = \frac{N\Sigma KK_M - \Sigma K\Sigma K_M}{N\Sigma K_M^2 - (\Sigma K_M)^2} \qquad (19B–1)$$

For a_i, we use the following formula (which is dependent on prior determination of b_i).

$$a_i = \frac{\Sigma K - b_i \Sigma K_M}{N} \qquad (19B–2)$$

We compute four columns of data and plug the values into our formulas.

K	K_M	KK_M	K_M^2
4.8	6.5	31.20	42.25
14.5	11.8	171.10	139.24
19.1	14.9	284.59	222.01
3.7	1.1	4.07	1.21
15.6	12.0	187.20	144.00
$\Sigma K = 57.7$	$\Sigma K_M = 46.3$	$\Sigma KK_M = 678.16$	$\Sigma K_M^2 = 548.71$

Also N (number of observations) = 5.

$$b_i = \frac{N\Sigma KK_M - \Sigma K\Sigma K_M}{N\Sigma K_M^2 - (\Sigma K_M)^2}$$

$$b_i = \frac{5(678.16) - 57.7(46.3)}{5(548.71) - (46.3)^2}$$

$$= \frac{3390.80 - 2671.51}{2743.55 - 2143.69} = \frac{719.29}{599.86} = 1.20$$

Using our beta value, we now compute alpha:

$$a_i = \frac{\Sigma K - b_i \Sigma K_M}{N}$$

$$a_i = \frac{57.7 - 1.2(46.3)}{5}$$

$$= \frac{57.7 - 55.6}{5} = \frac{2.1}{5} = .42$$

In summary:

$$K_i = a_i + b_iK_M$$

$$K_i = .42 + 1.20\ K_M$$

APPENDIX 19–C: Derivation of the Security Market Line (SML)

First of all, we graph the SML based on covariance (Figure 19C–1).[13]
Along the vertical axis we show return, and along the horizontal axis, covariance of return with the market.[14] We can describe our equation for the SML in terms of the slope of the line.

FIGURE 19C–1   Derivation of the SML

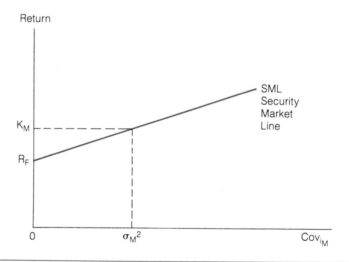

$$K_i = R_F + \frac{(K_M - R_F)}{(\sigma_M{}^2 - 0)}\text{cov}_{iM} \qquad (19C-1)$$

We then rearrange our terms:

$$K_i = R_F + \left[\frac{\text{cov}_{iM}}{\sigma_M{}^2}\right](K_M - R_F) \qquad (19C-2)$$

---

[13] The concept of covariance is described in Appendix 19–A.

[14] Actually, $\sigma_M{}^2$ represents the covariance of the market with the market (a bit redundant). The cov_{MM} equals $\sigma_M{}^2$. The covariance of a variable with itself is equal to the variance.

The systematic risk of an individual asset is measured by its covariance with the market (cov_{iM}). We can convert this to a relative measure by dividing through by the market variance (σ_M^2). The *relative* systematic movement of an individual asset with the market is referred to as the beta regression coefficient. Thus, we show in Formula 19C–3.

$$b_i = \frac{\text{cov}_{iM}}{\sigma_M^2} \qquad\qquad (19C\text{–}3)$$

Plugging this in to equal Formula 19C–2, we show:

$$K_i = R_F + b_i(K_M - R_F) \qquad\qquad (19C\text{–}4)$$

Chapter 20

Measuring Risks and Returns of Portfolio Managers

In the bull market days of the 1950s and part of the 1960s, many portfolio managers turned in performances that were vastly superior to the market averages. These high returns were often achieved by taking larger than normal risks through investing in small, growth companies or concentrating in a limited number of high-return industries. These portfolio managers or their representatives proclaimed their superior ability in managing money and often extrapolated past returns into the future to indicate the potential returns to the investor. A typical statement might be: "The Rapid Growth Fund has earned 20 percent per year over the past 10 years. The investor who places his or her funds with us has the possible opportunity to see the funds grow from a $100 investment today to $672.70 in 10 years at this historical growth rate of 20 percent." There was very little attempt to relate rate of return directly to risk exposure or to provide caveats about the likelihood of replicating past performance. In terms of generating returns, people were simply superior money managers or they were not.

Nevertheless, with the end of the bull market era of the 1960s, a new mentality developed. Many of the gunslinging super performers of the past were the worst performers in a bear market. It could be reasonably inferred that their high returns of the past were not so much a function of unusual insight, but rather the utilization of unusually high risk. Actually, some portfolio managers began to welcome the notion of risk-adjusted returns. A mutual fund manager or bank trust department head could rationally explain to a client, "although a competitor had a 2 percent higher return, it was actually inferior to our performance on a risk-adjusted basis."

In this chapter, we will examine actual studies of risk-return performance for professional money managers. We will evaluate the setting of objectives, the achievement of efficient diversification, and the measurement of return related to risk. In some of this discussion, we will relate back to the capital asset pricing model developed in Chapter 19.

Though the majority of comments in this chapter relate to mutual funds, there are many other important participants among professional money managers. These include pension funds, life insurance companies, property and casualty insurance companies, and endowments and foundations. These institutional investors are examined in a later section of this chapter, particularly in light of earlier comments on risk-return characteristics.

STATED OBJECTIVES AND RISK

A first question to be posed to a professional money manager is, Have you followed the basic objectives that were established? These objectives might call for maximum capital gains, a combination of growth plus income, or simply income (with many variations in between). The objectives should be set with an eye toward the capabilities of the money managers and the financial needs of the investors. The best way to measure adherence to these objectives is to evaluate the risk exposure that the fund manager has accepted. Anyone who aspires to maximize capital gains must, by nature, absorb more risk. An income-oriented fund should have a minimum risk exposure.

A study by John McDonald published in the *Journal of Financial and Quantitative Analysis* indicates that mutual fund managers generally follow the objectives they initially set out. As indicated in Figure 20–1, he measured the betas and standard deviations for 123 mutual funds and compared these to the funds' stated objectives. In Panel (a), we see the fund's beta dimension

FIGURE 20–1   Risk and Fund Objectives for 123 Mutual Funds, 1960–1969

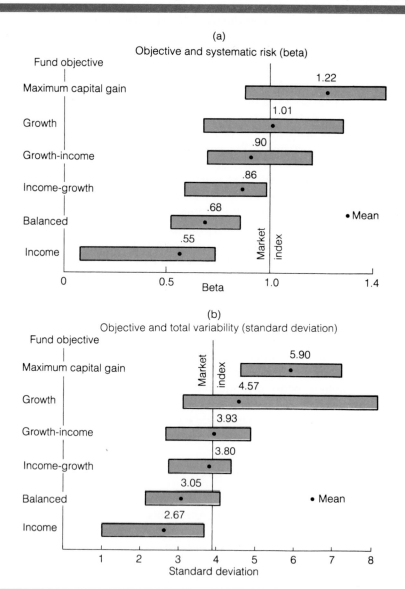

Source: John G. McDonald, "Objectives and Performance of Mutual Funds, 1960–1969," *Journal of Financial and Quantitative Analysis,* June 1974, p. 316.

along the horizontal axis and the fund's stated objective along the vertical axis. Inside the panel, we see the association between the two. For example, funds with an objective of maximum capital gains had an average beta of 1.22, those with a growth objective had an average beta of 1.01, and so on all the way down to an average beta of .55 for income oriented funds. In Panel (b) of Figure 20–1, a similar approach was used to compare the fund's objective to the portfolio standard deviation

In both cases of using betas and portfolio standard deviations, we see that the risk absorption was carefully tailored to the fund's stated objectives. Funds with aggressive capital gains and growth objectives had high betas and portfolio standard deviations, while the opposite was true of balanced and income-oriented funds.

Adherence to objectives as measured by risk exposure is important in evaluating a fund manager because risk is one of the variables a money manager can directly control. While short-run return performance can be greatly influenced by unpredictable changes in the economy, the fund manager has almost total control in setting the risk level. He can be held accountable for doing what was specified or promised in regard to risk. Most lawsuits brought against money managers are not for inferior profit performance but for failure to adhere to stated risk objectives. Though it may be appropriate to shift the risk level in anticipation of changing market conditions (lower the beta at a perceived peak in the market), long-run adherence to risk objectives is advisable.

MEASUREMENT OF RETURN IN RELATION TO RISK

In examining the performance of fund managers, the return measure commonly used is "excess returns." Though the term excess returns has many definitions, the one most commonly used is: total return on a portfolio (capital appreciation plus dividends) minus the risk-free rate.

Excess returns = Total portfolio return − Risk-free rate

Thus excess returns represents returns over and above what could be earned on a riskless asset. The rate on U.S government Treasury bills is often used to represent the risk-free rate of return in the economy (though other definitions are possible). Thus a fund that earns 12 percent when the Treasury bill rate is 6 percent has excess returns of 6 percent.

Once computed, excess returns are then compared to risk. We look at three different approaches to comparing excess returns to risk: the Sharpe approach, the Treynor approach, and the Jensen approach

Sharpe Approach

In the Sharpe approach,[1] the excess returns on a portfolio are compared to the portfolio standard deviation.

---

[1] William F. Sharpe, "Mutual Fund Performance," *The Journal of Business,* January 1966, pp. 119–38.

$$\text{Sharpe measure} = \frac{\text{Total portfolio return} - \text{Risk-free rate}}{\text{Portfolio standard deviation}} \quad (19\text{--}1)$$

The portfolio manager is thus able to view his or her excess returns per unit of risk. If a portfolio has a total return of 10 percent, and the risk-free rate is 6 percent, and the portfolio standard deviation is 18 percent, the Sharpe measure is .22.

$$\text{Sharpe measure} = \frac{10\% - 6\%}{18\%} = \frac{4\%}{18\%} = .22$$

This measure can be compared to other portfolios or to the market in general to assess performance. If the market return per unit of risk is greater than .22, then the portfolio manager has turned in an inferior performance. Assume there is a 9 percent total market return, a 6 percent risk-free rate, and a market standard deviation of 12 percent. Then the Sharpe measure for the overall market is:

$$\frac{9\% - 6\%}{12\%} = \frac{3\%}{12\%} = .25$$

The portfolio measure of .22 is less than the market measure of .25 and represents an inferior performance. Of course, a portfolio measure above .25 would have represented a superior performance.

Treynor Approach

The formula for the second approach for comparing excess returns to risk (developed by Treynor[2]) is:

$$\text{Treynor measure} = \frac{\text{Total portfolio return} - \text{Risk-free rate}}{\text{Portfolio beta}} \quad (19\text{--}2)$$

The only difference between the Sharpe and Treynor approach is in the denominator. While Sharpe uses the portfolio standard deviation—Formula (19–1), Treynor uses the portfolio beta—Formula (19–2). Thus, one can say that Sharpe uses total risk, while Treynor uses only the systematic, or beta, risk. Implicit in the Treynor approach is the assumption that portfolio managers have diversified away unsystematic risk and only systematic risk remains.

If a portfolio has a total return of 10 percent, and the risk-free rate is 6 percent, and the portfolio beta is .9, the Treynor measure would be:

$$\frac{10\% - 6\%}{.9} = \frac{4\%}{.9} = \frac{.04}{.9} = .044$$

This measure can be compared to other portfolios or to the market in general to determine whether there is a superior performance in terms of

---

[2] Jack L. Treynor, "How to Rate Management of Investment Funds," *Harvard Business Review,* January–February 1965, pp. 63–74.

return per unit of risk. Assume that the total market return is 9 percent, and the risk-free rate is 6 percent, and the market beta (by definition) is 1; then the Treynor measure as applied to the market is .03.

$$\frac{9\% - 6\%}{1.0} = \frac{3\%}{1.0} = \frac{.03}{1.0} = .03$$

This would imply that the portfolio has turned in a superior return to the market (.044 versus .03). Not only is the portfolio return higher than the market return (10 percent versus 9 percent), but the beta is less (.9 versus 1.0). Clearly, there is more return per unit of risk.

Jensen Approach

In the third approach, Jensen also emphasizes using certain aspects of the capital asset pricing model to evaluate portfolio managers.[3] He compares their actual excess returns (total portfolio return − risk-free rate) to what should be required in the market, based on their portfolio beta.

The required rate of excess returns in the market for a given beta is shown in Figure 20–2 as the market line. If the beta is 0, the investor should expect to earn no more than the risk-free rate of return since there is no systematic risk. If the portfolio manager earns only the risk-free rate of return, the excess returns will be 0. Thus with a beta of 0, the expected excess returns on the market line is 0. With a portfolio beta of 1, the portfolio has a systematic risk equal to the market, and the expected portfolio excess returns should be equal to market excess returns. If the market return (K_M) is 9 percent and the risk-free rate (R_F) is 6 percent, the market excess returns are 3 percent. A portfolio with a beta of 1 should expect to earn the market rate of excess returns $(K_M - R_F)$, equal to 3 percent. Other excess returns expectations are shown for beta ranging from 0 to 1.5. For example, a portfolio with a beta of 1.5 should provide excess returns of 4.5.

Adequacy of Performance

Using the Jensen approach, the adequacy of a portfolio manager's performance can be judged against the market line. Did he fall above or below the line? While it would appear that portfolio manager Y in Figure 20–2 had inferior excess returns in comparison to portfolio manager Z (2.1 percent versus 3.9 percent), this notion is quickly dispelled when one considers risk. Actually, portfolio manager Y performed above risk-return expectations as indicated by the market line, while portfolio manager Z was below his risk-adjusted expected level. The vertical difference from a fund's performance point to the

[3] Michael C. Jensen, "The Performance of Mutual Funds in the Period 1945–1964," *Journal of Finance,* May 1968, pp. 389–416.

FIGURE 20–2   Risk-Adjusted Portfolio Returns

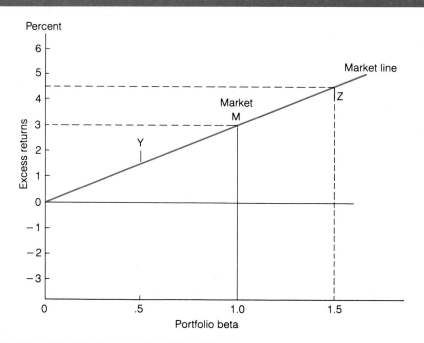

market line can be viewed as a measure of performance. This value, termed *alpha* or *average differential return,* indicates the difference between the return on the fund and a point on the market line that corresponds to a beta equal to the fund. In the case of fund Z, the beta of 1.5 indicated an excess return of 4.5 percent along the market line, and the actual excess return was only 3.9 percent. We thus have a negative alpha of .6 percent (3.9% − 4.5%). Clearly, a positive alpha indicates a superior performance, while a negative alpha leads to the opposite conclusion.

A key question for portfolio managers in general is, Can they consistently perform at positive alpha levels? Can they generate returns better than those that are available along the market line, which are theoretically available to anyone? The results of a study conducted by John McDonald on 123 mutual funds are presented in Figure 20–3.

The upward-sloping line is the market line, or anticipated level of performance based on risk. The small dots represent performance of the funds. About as many funds underperformed (negative alpha below the line) as overperformed (positive alpha above the line). Although a few high-beta funds had an unusually strong performance on a risk-adjusted basis, there is no consistent pattern of superior performance.

FIGURE 20–3   Empirical Study of Risk-Adjusted Portfolio Returns—Systematic Risk and Return

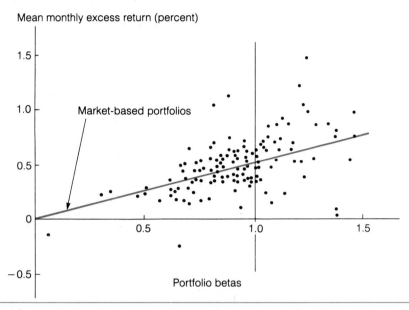

Source: John G. McDonald, "Objectives and Performance of Mutual Funds, 1960–1969," *Journal of Financial and Quantitative Analysis,* June 1974, p. 321.

Other Studies

There are many other studies of a similar nature. In Figure 20–4, we see the results of a landmark study by Michael Jensen in which he computed the alpha values of 115 mutual funds between 1945 and 1964. The average alpha value was −1.1 percent per year, and only 39 out of 115 funds had a positive alpha.

A number of other important studies have been conducted by the Securities and Exchange Commission, Merrill Lynch, and various professors throughout the country (Friend, Blume, Mains, Gentry, Schlarbaum, Williamson, etc.).[4] Although they worked with different data bases over varying time periods, their general results were similar. Professional money managers have generally not outperformed the market over the long term on a risk-adjusted basis.

Those portfolio managers that do produce superior results (positive alphas) may attribute their performance to either superior market timing or excellence in security analysis and selection. As indicated in a subsequent section of this chapter, even when superior performance is achieved, it is not necessarily continued into the future.

---

[4] Complete citations for these sources are presented under Selected References at the end of this chapter.

FIGURE 20–4   Frequency Distribution of Estimated Alphas

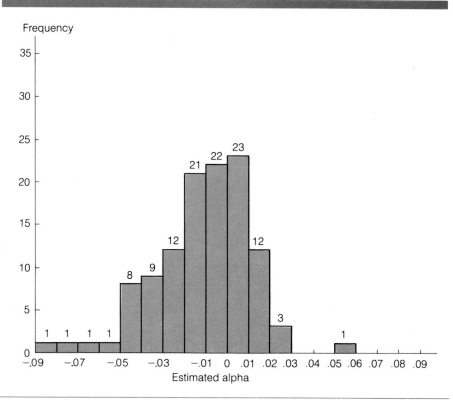

Source: Michael C. Jensen, "The Performance of Mutual Funds in the Period 1945–1964," *Journal of Finance,* May 1968, p. 404.

Transaction Costs

One frequently cited reason for no better than average performance over the long term is the potentially high transaction costs associated with fund management. A study by the Securities and Exchange Commission indicated that fund performance could not be positively correlated with the size of the fund, the method of selling the fund (load or no-load), or size of assets managed. However, performance was negatively correlated with rate of portfolio turnover. On average, a 10 percent increase in portfolio turnover was associated with a .3 percent to .6 percent reduction in net return per year.[5] Although some portfolio managers thought they were improving their returns by active trading, in most instances, this was simply not the case.

[5] *Institutional Investor Study Report of the Securities and Exchange Commission* (Washington, D.C.: U.S. Government Printing Office, 1971).

Performance Reviews

Each year *Forbes* magazine publishes a list of mutual funds and their average returns over a 10- to 15-year period as well as in the last 12 months. An excerpt from this survey is presented in Table 20–1.

In examining the *Forbes* data, the reader may also compare the fund's

TABLE 20–1 *Forbes* **Mutual Fund Performance Review, 1984**

Performance in UP markets	Performance in DOWN markets		Average annual total return 1974-84	Latest 12 months total return	Latest 12 months return from income dividends	Total assets 6/30/84 (millions)	Total assets % change '84 vs '83	Maximum sales charge	Annual expenses per $100
		Standard & Poor's 500 stock average	14.9%	−4.8%	4.8%				
		FORBES stock fund composite	17.5%	−10.8%	3.0%				
		FORBES balanced fund composite	13.9%	−2.1%	8.3%				
		FORBES bond and preferred stock fund composite	10.2%	−0.1%	12.6%				
		Stock funds (load) Group averages	17.2%	−11.5%	3.1%				
B	B	Fidelity Equity-Income Fund (800-225-6190)	24.3%	−2.3%	8.0%	$ 841.6	29.9%	2.00%	$0.80
A+	B	Fidelity Magellan Fund (800-225-6190)	34.7	−12.8	1.2	1,613.7	17.9	3.00	1.04
B	C	First Investors Discovery Fund (212-825-7900)	20.4	−31.0	0.6	40.5	47.3	8.50	1.21
B	F	First Investors Fund for Growth (212-825-7900)	15.6	−26.6	1.9	75.8	−30.1	8.50	0.95
D	F	First Investors Natural Resources Fund (212-825-7900)	8.1	−18.9	0.6	12.5	−11.4	8.50	1.24
D	B	First Investors Option Fund (212-825-7900)	11.3	−1.0	2.2	127.9	7.4	7.25	0.94
D	F	FPA Capital Fund⁴ (800-237-0738)	10.2	−13.3	4.1	35.7	−19.2	8.00	0.92
C	A	FPA Paramount Fund⁵ (800-421-4374)	21.0	2.3	4.2	108.2	51.3	8.50	1.09
A	D	Franklin Custodian Dynatech Ser (800-632-2350)	19.1	−17.7	1.2	39.4	−3.0	7.25	0.91
D	D	Franklin Custodian Growth Ser (800-632-2350)	12.3	−12.3	1.9	18.1	12.4	7.25	1.01
D	A	Franklin Custodian Utilities Ser (800-632-2350)	15.0	4.2	9.8	26.4	20.6	7.25	0.92
A+	C	Franklin Gold Fund⁶ (800-632-2350)	17.6	−4.8	4.6	139.4	25.1	7.25	0.96
C	C	Franklin Option Fund (800-632-2350)	17.7	−3.8	0.2	6.4	−3.0	7.25	1.20
B	C	Fund of America (800-231-3638)	19.2	0.9	4.4	137.3	6.8	8.50	0.78
A	D	Fund of the Southwest (800-231-0808)	21.2	−24.4	0.6	7.2	−10.0	7.50	1.05
D	C	Fundamental Investors (800-421-0180)	14.6	−5.8	3.8	349.5	−17.0	8.50	0.64
•B	•F	The Greenway Fund (713-626-1919)	—*	−19.4	0.1	3.6	−28.0	6.50	1.83
B	A	Growth Fund of America (800-421-9900)	22.2	−10.9	3.3	434.6	6.6	8.50	0.68
C	C	The Guardian Park Avenue Fund (212-598-8259)	19.2	−3.7	3.0	51.4	2.2	8.50	0.71
C	F	Hamilton Funds (800-525-7048)	12.0	−19.4	4.2	190.3	−27.4	8.50	0.98
A	F	John Hancock Growth Fund (617-421-2909)	14.1	−12.6	1.7	52.2	4.8	8.00	1.06
A+	D	IDS Growth Fund (800-328-8300)	23.3	−30.1	0.1	608.8	−10.8	5.00	0.75
D	D	IDS Stock Fund⁷ (800-328-8300)	13.8	−8.2	4.1	1,291.1	−18.1	5.00	0.60
C	D	IDS Variable Payment Fund⁸ (800-328-8300)	13.9	−18.2	3.5	322.3	−26.4	5.00	0.59
A	D	IDS New Dimensions Fund (800-328-8300)	20.1	−18.0	1.4	337.0	−12.4	5.00	0.82
C	C	IDS Progressive Fund (800-328-8300)	18.1	−3.9	3.5	155.5	−0.3	5.00	1.00
D	A	Income Fund of America (800-421-9900)	15.4	2.1	8.5	267.9	−5.2	8.50	0.66
C	C	The Investment Co of America (800-421-9900)	17.4	−4.4	4.2	2,189.4	−7.2	8.50	0.44
C	F	Investment Trust of Boston (617-542-0213)	12.5	−17.3	2.8	51.8	−25.3	7.25	0.92
A	D	Investors Research Fund (800-328-8300)	17.8	−22.4	none	36.3	−10.6	8.50	0.86
D	A	ISI Growth Fund (415-832-1400)	11.3	−0.8	7.4	13.3	−9.5	8.50	1.32
D	A	ISI Income Fund (415-832-1400)	9.1	1.0	10.1	6.9	−16.9	8.50	1.52
D	A	ISI Trust Fund (415-832-1400)	8.5	7.5	8.8	103.0	−3.7	8.50	1.06
D	C	JP Growth Fund (919-378-2448)	16.2	−7.2	4.7	17.3	−6.5	8.00	0.84
A+	F	Kemper Growth Fund (800-621-1048)	20.7	−12.4	2.2	215.1	−15.7	8.50	0.69
•C	•B	Kemper Option Income Fund (800-621-1048)	—*	1.4	4.0	192.6	101.7	8.50	0.82
A+	C	Kemper Summit Fund (800-621-1048)	24.6	−17.0	1.6	150.0	7.9	8.50	0.47
•A	•D	Lord Abbett Develop Growth (212-425-8720)	—*	−28.4	0.7	300.4	−11.6	8.50	0.73
D	C	MagnaCap Fund (800-526-0475)	16.5	4.5	5.3	7.3	−22.3	7.25	1.50
A+	D	Mass Capital Development Fund (800-343-2829)	23.7	−18.5	2.2	577.8	2.3	7.25	0.67
B	B	Mass Finl Development Fund (800-343-2829)	17.7	−20.0	2.9	181.9	−19.3	7.25	0.82
C	F	Mass Investors Growth Stock (800-343-2829)	14.2	−15.8	2.9	796.4	−25.4	7.25	0.56
C	F	Massachusetts Investors Trust (800-343-2829)	13.5	−7.7	4.5	985.3	−17.8	7.25	0.53
•B	•C	Merrill Lynch Basic Value Fund (800-631-0749)	—*	−0.5	4.7	269.3	14.6	6.50	0.89

•Fund rated for two periods only; maximum allowable rating A. *Fund not in operation for full period. ⁴Formerly Transamerica Capital Fund. ⁵Formerly Paramount Mutual Fund. ⁶Formerly Research Capital Fund. ⁷Formerly Investors Stock Fund. ⁸Formerly Investors Variable Payment Fund.

Source: "1984 Fund Ratings," *Forbes,* August 27, 1984, p. 77.

TABLE 20–2   Sample Data from *Wiesenberger Investment Companies Service*

T. ROWE PRICE NEW ERA FUND, INC.

The investment objective of the fund is long-term growth of capital. It may seek this in any industry, but its current portfolio consists largely of securities of companies in the energy sources area, forest products, precious metals and other metals and minerals; other basic commodities, and companies which own or develop land. Investments in companies which provide consumer products and services are included, as well as companies operating in technological areas, such as the manufacture of labor-saving machinery and instruments.

At the 1983 year-end, the fund had 81.9% of its assets in common stocks, of which the major proportion was concentrated in five industry groups: science & technology (11.2% of assets), integrated petroleum (10.2%), diversified resources (9.1%), and forest products and diversified metals (each 7.4%). The four largest individual common stock investments were Phibro-Salomon (3.9% of assets), IBM (3.5%), and Kaiser Aluminum & Chemical and Champion International (each 3.0%). The rate of portfolio turnover during the year was 37.2% of average assets. Unrealized appreciation was 22.8% of year-end assets.

Statistical History

	AT YEAR-ENDS				% of Assets in			ANNUAL DATA				
Year	Total Net Assets ($)	Number of Share-holders	Net Asset Value Per Share ($)	Yield (%)	Cash & Equiv-alent	Bonds & Pre-ferreds	Com-mon Stocks	Income Div-idends ($)	Capital Gains Distribu-tion ($)	Expense Ratio (%)	Offering Price ($) High	Low
1983	485,072,775	47,214	18.44	4.4	12	6	82	0.81	0.072	0.68	18.60	14.97
1982	411,506,259	46,422	15.53	4.6	11	—	89	0.863	3.045	0.71	19.35	11.38
1981	436,197,041	44,712	19.34	3.4	20	—	80	0.672	1.489	0.64	25.53	17.87
1980	571,568,790	41,463	25.27	1.9	10	1*	89	0.47	0.362	0.63	27.23	14.58
1979	330,817,793	30,172	17.45	2.3	15	—	85	0.38	0.388	0.67	17.45	11.15
1978	189,827,658	28,600	11.66	2.7	7	—	93	0.316	0.254	0.73	12.79	9.66
1977	198,186,550	32,680	11.00	2.2	8	—	92	0.244	0.03	0.67	11.66	10.25
1976	245,158,364	35,574	11.74	2.4	6	3*	91	0.279	—	0.68	11.74	10.00
1975	220,394,522	38,659	9.94	2.9	8	1	91	0.286	—	0.71	11.64	8.29
1974	190,040,724	38,505	8.47	2.2	18	—	82	0.184	0.105	0.72	12.13	7.78
1973	230,930,308	35,682	11.79	0.9	15	—	85	0.105	0.138	0.72	12.63	10.55

* Includes a substantial proportion in convertible issues.

An assumed investment of $10,000 in this fund, with capital gains accepted in shares and income dividends reinvested, is illustrated below. The explanation on Page 163 must be read in conjunction with this illustration.

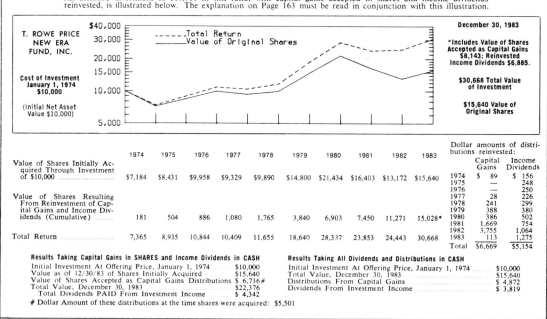

T. ROWE PRICE NEW ERA FUND, INC.

Cost of Investment January 1, 1974 $10,000

(Initial Net Asset Value $10,000)

- - - - - Total Return
———— Value of Original Shares

December 30, 1983

*Includes Value of Shares Accepted as Capital Gains $8,143; Reinvested Income Dividends $6,885.

$30,668 Total Value of Investment

$15,640 Value of Original Shares

	1974	1975	1976	1977	1978	1979	1980	1981	1982	1983
Value of Shares Initially Acquired Through Investment of $10,000	$7,184	$8,431	$9,958	$9,329	$9,890	$14,800	$21,434	$16,403	$13,172	$15,640
Value of Shares Resulting From Reinvestment of Capital Gains and Income Dividends (Cumulative)	181	504	886	1,080	1,765	3,840	6,903	7,450	11,271	15,028*
Total Return	7,365	8,935	10,844	10,409	11,655	18,640	28,337	23,853	24,443	30,668

Dollar amounts of distributions reinvested:

	Capital Gains	Income Dividends
1974	$ 89	$ 156
1975	—	248
1976	—	250
1977	28	226
1978	241	299
1979	388	380
1980	386	502
1981	1,669	754
1982	3,755	1,064
1983	113	1,275
Total	$6,669	$5,154

Results Taking Capital Gains in SHARES and Income Dividends in CASH

Initial Investment At Offering Price, January 1, 1974	$10,000
Value as of 12/30/83 of Shares Initially Acquired	$15,640
Value of Shares Accepted as Capital Gains Distributions	$ 6,736#
Total Value, December 30, 1983	$22,376
Total Dividends PAID From Investment Income	$ 4,342

Results Taking All Dividends and Distributions in CASH

Initial Investment At Offering Price, January 1, 1974	$10,000
Total Value, December 30, 1983	$15,640
Distributions From Capital Gains	$ 4,872
Dividends From Investment Income	$ 3,819

Dollar Amount of these distributions at the time shares were acquired: $5,501

performance to the Standard & Poor's 500 Stock Average and the *Forbes* Stock Fund Composite Average as well as other averages. On the left-hand margin are listed performance ratings for the funds in up and down markets. For example, IDS Growth Fund is shown as having an A+ rating in an up market and a D rating in a down market. In terms of grading, the top 12.5 percent get an A+; the next 12.5 percent, an A; the next 25 percent, a B; and so on. The *Forbes* survey comes out in August of each year.

Wiesenberger Investment Companies Service also provides excellent information on mutual funds as indicated by the excerpt in Table 20–2 for the T. Rowe Price New Era Fund, Inc. In the section on statistical history, we see the total net assets managed and other important data. In the box inside the table we see what would have happened to a $10,000 investment in the T. Rowe Price New Era Fund over a 10-year time period. While the original investment of $10,000 would have grown to $15,640, if we add in shares accepted as capital gains and reinvested dividend income, the total is $30,668. As indicated in the right-hand portion of the box in Table 20–2, the $30,668 is composed of the $15,640 current value of the original shares, plus $8,143 in shares distributed as capital gains, plus reinvested dividend income of $6,885.

Current value of original shares	$15,640
Capital gains distribution	8,143
Reinvested dividends	6,885
Total	$30,668

The Wiesenberger survey book, from which Table 20–2 is drawn, comes out annually and covers virtually every mutual fund.

PAST PERFORMANCE AND FUTURE PERFORMANCE

Even with this wealth of data available to investors, a key question that must be considered is, How well does past performance indicate future performance? Will a fund that has provided high positive alphas or A's on the *Forbes* scale necessarily do the same in the future? Will a fund that has the most impressive record in the Wiesenberger survey necessarily do the best in the future?

Substantial research by the SEC and Jensen found that this is not necessarily the case. In Table 20–3, we observe results from the Jensen study of 115 mutual funds from 1955 through 1964.

In the left-hand column of Table 20–3, we see the number of years that selected funds beat a passive (unmanaged) portfolio with equal market risk. In the right-hand column, we see the percent of those funds that beat the same measure in the next year. Even for funds with good prior year's performance, the odds on beating the control group in the next year was not particularly high.

Though past performance does not offer significant promise for the future, historical perspective does take on some importance. Clearly, you would not wish to buy a fund that has had consistently negative alphas or performance below the norm measured on some other basis. They may be overtrad-

ing the portfolio or inefficiently diversifying. By the same token, you should be most hesitant about paying any kind of premium sales commission or high management fee purely on the basis of a fund's strong past performance, which may or may not be replicated in the future. A good rule to follow is to go for the best past performance, but pay no extra premium for it. This is often possible because money managers with prior success may have large asset bases and low percentage management fees.

TABLE 20–3   Relating Past and Future Performance

Number of consecutive years funds' performance exceeded that of a passive portfolio with similar risk	Percentage of group with performance exceeding that of a passive portfolio with similar market risk in the next year
1	50.4%
2	52.0
3	53.4
4	55.8
5	46.4
6	35.3
7	25.0

Source: Michael C. Jensen, "Risk, Capital Assets, and Evaluation of Portfolios," *The Journal of Business,* April 1969, p. 239.

DIVERSIFICATION

An important service that a money manager can provide is effective diversification of asset holdings. Once we at least partially accept the fact that superior performance on a risk-adjusted basis is a difficult achievement, we begin to look hard at other attributes that money managers may possess. We can ask, Are mutual fund managers effective diversifiers of their holdings?

As previously discussed in Chapter 19 and in this chapter, there are two measures of risk: systematic and unsystematic. Systematic risk is measured by the portfolio (or individual stock's) beta. Under the capital asset pricing model, higher betas are rewarded with relatively high returns, and vice versa. As the market goes up 10 percent, our portfolio might go up 12 percent (beta of 1.2), and a similar phenomenon may occur on the downside. Unsystematic risk is random or nonmarket related and may be generally diversified away by the astute portfolio manager. Under the capital asset pricing model, there is no market reward for unsystematic risk since it can be eliminated through diversification.

The question for a portfolio manager then becomes, How effective have you been at diversifying away the nonrewarded, unsystematic risk? Put another way, to what extent can a fund's movements be described as market-related rather than random in nature? If we plot a fund's excess returns over an

extended period of time against market excess returns, we can determine the joint movement between the two as indicated in Figure 20–5. In Panel (a) we plot our basic points. In Panel (b) we draw a regression line through these points. Of importance to the present discussion is the extent to which our line fits the data. If the points of observation fall very close to the line, the independent variable, excess market returns, is largely responsible for describing the dependent variable, excess returns for fund X.

FIGURE 20–5   Relationship of Fund's Excess Returns to Market Excess Returns

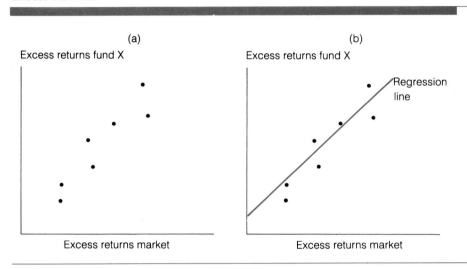

The degree of association between the independent and dependent variables is measured by R^2 (coefficient of determination).[6] R^2 may take on a value anywhere between 0 and 1. A high degree of correlation between the independent and dependent variables will produce an R^2 of .7 or better. In Panel (b) it is assumed to be .90.

In Figure 20–6 the points do not fall consistently close to the regression line, and the R^2 value is assumed to be only .55. In this instance, we say that the independent variable (excess market returns) was not the only major variable in explaining changes in the dependent variable (excess returns for fund Y).

---

[6] R^2 also represents the correlation coefficient squared. Thus, we can square Formula (19A–1) in Chapter 19. Another statement is

$$R^2 = 1 - \frac{\Sigma(y - y_c)^2/n}{\Sigma(y - \bar{y})^2/n}$$

where y_c represents points along the regression line and y is the average value of the independent variable.

FIGURE 20–6   Example of Lower Correlation

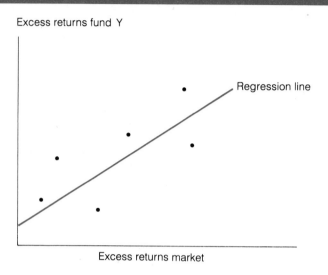

The points in Figure 20–6 imply that the portfolio manager for fund Y may have not been particularly effective in his diversification efforts. Many other factors besides market returns appear to be affecting the portfolio returns of fund Y, and these could have been diversified away rather than allowed to influence returns. In this instance, we say there is a high degree of unsystematic, or nonmarket-related, risk. Since unsystematic risk is presumed to go unrewarded in the marketplace under the capital asset pricing model, there is evidence of inefficient portfolio diversification.

What does empirical data tell us about the effectiveness of portfolio managers in achieving diversification. How have they stacked up in terms of R^2 values for their portfolios? As indicated in Figure 20–7, their record is generally quite good.

The Merrill Lynch study of 100 mutual funds between 1970 and 1974 shows an average R^2 value of approximately .90 with very few funds falling below .70. The actual range is between .66 and .98. Studies by McDonald, Jensen, Gentry, and Williamson have led to similar conclusions (see Selected References for complete citations).

Although many mutual funds invest in 80 to 100 securities to achieve effective diversification, this is often more than is necessary. A high degree of diversification can be achieved with between 10 and 20 efficiently selected stocks, as is indicated in Table 20–4. The Wagner and Lau study shows the number of securities in the portfolio, the portfolio standard deviation, and correlation with return on the market index (R^2).

FIGURE 20–7   Quarterly Returns Attributable to Market Fluctuations: 100 Mutual Funds, 1970–1974

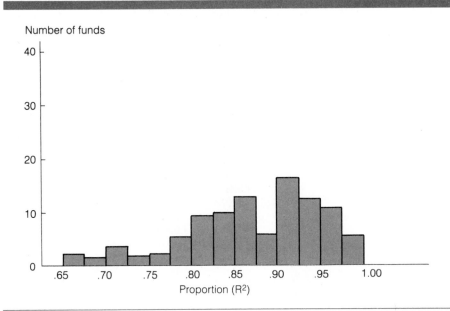

Source: Merrill Lynch, Pierce, Fenner & Smith, *Investment Performance Analysis, Comparative Survey, 1970–1974.*

TABLE 20–4   Reduction in Portfolio Risk through Diversification

Number of securities in portfolio	Standard deviation of portfolio returns, σ_p (percent per month)	Correlation with return on market index*
1	7.0	0.54
2	5.0	0.63
3	4.8	0.75
4	4.6	0.77
5	4.6	0.79
10	4.2	0.85
15	4.0	0.88
20	3.9	0.89

* The market here refers to an unweighted index of all NYSE stocks.
Source: W. H. Wagner and C. S. Lau, "The Effect of Diversification on Risk," *Financial Analysts Journal,* November–December 1971, p. 53.

STABILITY OF BETAS

In Chapter 19 the lack of stability of the beta coefficient of an individual security was mentioned as a possible drawback to the use of the capital asset pricing model. Instability means prior beta values may not be reflective of future beta values. If this is the case, then use of a beta based on prior performance may not be entirely accurate in reflecting future return potential. Since

TABLE 20–5   Industry Beta Values 1951–1970

	1951–55	1956–60	1961–65	1966–70
Aerospace	.96247	.66585	.72409	1.31815
Agricultural machinery	.78687	.90875	.81422	1.14613
Aluminum	1.18617	1.60756	1.13980	1.21376
Apparel manufacturing	.50733	.47428	1.23344	1.52437
Auto parts and accessories	.87577	1.03116	.84302	1.17786
Autos	1.21383	1.00899	.87593	1.00869
Auto tires and rubber goods	1.18350	1.20016	1.16497	.97226
Auto trucks and parts	.96299	1.24551	1.21358	1.24255
Biscuit bakers	.34377	.18935	.76037	.68711
Bituminous coal	1.02612	1.14341	1.11203	.80200
Bread and cake bakers	.35396	.35301	.93734	1.91074
Brewers	.18364	.56817	.74847	1.03782
Business and office equipment	1.12362	1.12134	1.44912	1.09700
—Canned foods	.65238	.55939	1.04155	1.01861
Cement	1.01518	.87642	.82306	1.53511
Chemicals	1.06482	1.04785	.94006	.85256
Cigarettes	.29077	.23970	1.29410	.55432
Confectionery	.35793	.35514	1.04756	.59934
Construction and material handling machinery	1.14771	1.18300	.91518	1.19976
Copper	1.17911	.97515	.94643	1.08206
Corn refiners	.32177	.44286	1.02606	.93099
Crude oil producers	.69844	1.03158	1.12971	.95093
Dairy products	.40212	.35200	.98700	1.04501
—Department stores	.60589	.53718	.66176	1.21765
Distillers	.74801	.79331	.86246	.90287
Drugs	.54110	1.05861	1.29238	.95521
Electrical equipment	.96542	1.25540	1.04542	1.19990
Electrical household appliances	.76593	1.01648	.91009	1.15041
Electronics	.90328	1.31251	1.55722	1.56784
Food chain stores	.38349	.51301	1.00418	.73317
Gold mining	.54291	.63910	.06125	.07090
Heating and plumbing	.64976	.86583	.95464	1.27624
Home furnishings	.45473	.76023	1.18308	1.60301
Industrial machinery	.81678	1.18670	1.03285	1.33398
Integrated domestic oil companies	.79546	1.09107	.82772	.96288
Integrated international oil companies	1.05360	.98599	.70443	.73875
Lead and zinc	.91563	.99167	1.07584	.72259

Source: Jerome L. Valentine, "Investment Analysis and Capital Market Theory," *Occasional Paper No. 1* (Charlottesville, Va.: The Financial Research Foundation, 1975), p. 34.

the beta coefficient is such an integral part of our analysis in Chapters 19 and 20, we must address ourselves to this issue.

We break down our discussion on beta stability as it relates to individual stocks, industry groupings, and portfolios. In regard to individual stocks, a study by Blume provided evidence that the betas of individual stocks tend to regress or approach 1 over time.[7] That is, a stock with a beta of 1.5 may tend to have a beta of 1.4 in the next period, 1.3 in a subsequent period, and so on. Stocks with betas below 1 also tend to approach 1 over time. While this is not an automatic occurrence, there is a tendency to follow this pattern.

The same pattern of instability would apply to betas for various industry groupings, as indicated in Table 20–5. The Valentine study shows the changing betas for different industry groupings over time. The pattern of typical change can be found in such industries as canned goods and department stores.

While betas of individual stocks and industries may not be particularly stable over time, there is some evidence that portfolio betas are stable. This stability can be achieved with reasonably sized diversified portfolios of 10 to 20 stocks. We look to the research of Marshall Blume.

As indicated in Table 20–6, he measured the correlation between portfolio betas during different time periods. In each case, he compared one period

TABLE 20–6   Correlation Coefficients of Betas for Portfolios of N Securities

Number of securities per portfolio	7/26–6/33 and 7/33–6/40	7/33–6/40 and 7/40–6/47	7/40–6/47 and 7/47–6/54	7/47–6/54 and 7/54–6/61	7/54–6/61 and 7/61–6/68
1	0.63	0.62	0.59	0.65	0.60
2	0.71	0.76	0.72	0.76	0.73
4	0.80	0.85	0.81	0.84	0.84
7	0.86	0.91	0.88	0.87	0.88
10	0.89	0.94	0.90	0.92	0.92
20	0.93	0.97	0.95	0.95	0.97
35	0.96	0.98	0.95	0.97	0.97
50	0.98	0.99	0.98	0.98	0.98

Source: Abstracted from Marshall Blume, "On the Assessment of Risk," *Journal of Finance,* March 1971, p. 7.

to the next and determined the extent of correlation for different size portfolios. A high degree of correlation would indicate a stable beta as the past would be correlated with the future. For example, the last column shows the correlation of betas between the seven-year time periods of July 1954 to June 1961 and July 1961 to June 1968. With only one security, there was a correlation coefficient of .60; with 10 securities, .92; with 20 securities, .97; and finally

---

[7] Marshall E. Blume, "Betas and Their Regression Tendencies," *Journal of Finance,* June 1975, pp. 785–95.

with 50 securities, .98. The presumption is that reasonably large portfolios have stable betas over time, and this may be useful in assessing future risk considerations.

THE MAKEUP OF INSTITUTIONAL INVESTORS

Having discussed measurement and portfolio management techniques for institutional investors, we will now take a more specific look at the participants. Institutional investors (as opposed to individual investors) represent organizations that are responsible for bringing together large pools of capital for purposes of reinvestment. Our coverage will center on investment companies (including mutual funds), pension funds, life insurance companies, bank trust departments, and endowments and foundations.

Investment Companies (Including Mutual Funds)

Investment companies take the proceeds of individual investors and reinvest them in other securities according to their specific objectives. Income and capital gains are generally distributed to stockholders and are subject to single taxation under Subchapter M of the Internal Revenue Code. Investment companies were discussed at some length in Chapter 3.

Other Institutional Investors

Other institutional investors (along with investment companies) and their extent of market participation are presented in Table 20–7. Total institutional holdings are approximately 1.5 trillion dollars. We will briefly comment on

TABLE 20–7   Percentage of Institutional Market Held by Institutional Investors

		Percent
1.	Private noninsured pension funds	26.2%
2.	Open-end investment companies	15.5
3.	Other investment companies	2.0
4.	Life insurance companies	6.1
5.	Property-liability insurance companies	4.9
6.	Personal trust funds	27.8
7.	Common trust funds	1.7
8.	Mutual savings banks	1.1
9.	State and local retirement funds	4.6
10.	Foundations	7.4
11.	Educational endowments	2.7
		100.0%

Source: Compiled from a review of annual reports from the Securities and Exchange Commission and the New York Stock Exchange.

pension funds, insurance companies, bank trust departments, and foundations and endowments.

Pension funds.   Pension funds represent an important and growing sector of the institutional market. Pension funds may be private or public in nature. Private funds represent well over 50 percent of the total. The benefits that accrue under private pension funds may be insured or uninsured, with the latter arrangement occurring most frequently. Public pension funds are run for the benefit of federal, state, or local employees.

Insurance companies.   Insurance companies may be categorized as either "life" or "property and casualty." Life insurance companies must earn a minimum rate of return assumed in calculating premiums, and public policy places great emphasis on safety of assets. Approximately 70 percent of life insurance company assets are in privately placed debt or mortgages, with the balance in bonds and stocks. Property and casualty insurance companies enjoy more lenient regulation of their activities and generally have a larger percentage of their assets in bonds and stocks.

Bank trust departments.   The emphasis in bank trust departments is on managing other people's funds for a fee. Banks may administer individual trusts or commingled (combined) funds in a common trust fund. Often a bank will establish more than one common trust fund to serve varying needs and objectives. The overall performance of bank trust departments has been mixed, with the usual number of leaders and laggards. Bank trust management is highly concentrated with a relatively small number of trust departments holding the majority of funds. Out of approximately 4,000 bank trust departments, the top 10 hold one third of all assets, and the largest 60 hold two thirds.

Foundations and endowments.   Foundations represent nonprofit organizations set up to accomplish social, educational, or charitable purposes. They are often established through the donation of a large block of stock in which the donor was one of the corporate founders. Examples include the Ford, Carnegie, and Rockefeller Foundations. Endowments, on the other hand, represent permanent capital funds that are donated to universities, churches, or civic organizations. The management of endowment funds is often quite difficult because of the pressure for current income to maintain operations (perhaps the university library), while at the same time there is a demand for capital appreciation. Measurement of performance for foundations and endowments has gone much more to a total-return basis (dividends plus capital appreciation) rather than the traditional interest-earned or dividend-received basis.

COMMENTS ON INSTITUTIONAL PERFORMANCE

Performance studies similar to those presented earlier in the chapter on mutual funds have been conducted on other institutional portfolios by Gentry,

Schlarbaum, Williamson, and others.[8] The conclusion of this research is very similar to that reached on mutual funds; that is, on a risk-adjusted basis, they have not provided performance superior to a generally accepted market average or a randomly selected portfolio.

Another question that frequently arises in regard to institutional investors is whether they effectively control the movements in the market due to their large size. Although they represent approximately 35 percent of equity wealth and conduct 75 to 85 percent of the daily trading volume, empirical research indicates they do not control the market for their own purpose. Researchers Kraus and Stoll found little evidence to support a market dominance theory.[9] While there is a tendency for *similar* institutions to follow a given pattern, there is a compensating tendency for *different* institutions to take offsetting positions. This, of course, does not guarantee the absence of problems in the future as increased concentration continues.

SUMMARY

The ability of portfolio managers to meet various goals and objectives is considered in this chapter. Many portfolio managers appeared to demonstrate superior performances during the market boom years of the 1950s and part of the 1960s. However, when this performance is adjusted for risk, any perceived superiority quickly vanishes.

Some concepts related to the capital asset pricing model may be used to evaluate the performance of money managers. Portfolio beta values are shown along the horizontal axis, while the market line indicates expected returns. Portfolio managers that are able to operate above the line (positive alphas) are thought to be superior managers, while the opposite would be true of those falling below the line. Research by McDonald, Jensen, and others indicates that, on average, portfolio managers do not beat the popular averages or random portfolios on a risk-adjusted basis. One possible reason is the high transaction costs involved in active portfolio management. Some portfolio managers have even set up index funds in which they directly replicate the performance of the Standard & Poor's 500 Stock Average to minimize transaction costs or to ensure that they will not underperform the averages.

Empirical research has also indicated that those funds that have done well in the past do not necessarily promise superior returns in the future. Although it may be helpful to examine past records to eliminate clearly unsatisfactory performers, the stars of the past may not necessarily be the stars of the future. Nevertheless, mutual funds (or other managed portfolios) do have some desirable attributes. As indicated by a Merrill Lynch study (and others as

---

[8] Complete citations are provided under Selected References at the end of the chapter.

[9] Alan Kraus and Hans K. Stoll, "Parallel Trading by Institutional Investors," *Journal of Financial and Quantitative Analysis,* December 1972, pp. 2107–38. Also, Frank K. Reilly, "Institutions on Trial: Not Guilty!" *Journal of Portfolio Management,* Winter 1977, pp. 5–10.

well), mutual funds tend to be very efficient diversifiers. Their average correlation with the market (R^2) tends to be approximately 90 percent, indicating only 10 percent unsystematic, or nonrewarded, risk. In general, mutual fund managers also do a good job of constructing portfolios that are consistent with their initially stated objectives (i.e., maximum capital gains, growth, income, etc).

The beta for a diversified portfolio also tends to be more stable than that for a given stock or group of stocks within an industry. Thus, the historical portfolio beta may be more reflective of current and future risk than would be the case with individual securities.

The market of institutional investors is made up of investment companies (closed-end and mutual funds), pension funds, insurance companies, foundations, endowments, and other participants. Although the great weight of empirical research has dealt with mutual funds, the same basic conclusions about risk-adjusted returns can be applied to other institutional investors. Research also indicates that large institutional investors do not control the market. While there is a tendency for similar institutions to follow a given pattern, there is also a compensating tendency for other institutions to follow an offsetting pattern.

IMPORTANT WORDS AND CONCEPTS

Risk-adjusted return	**Investment companies**
Excess returns	**Efficient diversification**
Alpha	**Average differential return**
Market line	**Wiesenberger Financial Services**
Beta stability	**Sharpe Measure**
Institutional investors	**Treynor Measure**
R^2	**Jensen Measure**
Excess returns	

DISCUSSION QUESTIONS

1. What is a risk-adjusted return?
2. In evaluating a mutual fund manager, what would be the first point to analyze?
3. How can adherence to portfolio objectives be measured?
4. How can risk exposure be measured?
5. How are excess returns defined?
6. What is the Sharpe approach to measuring portfolio risk? If a portfolio has a higher measure than the market in general under the Sharpe approach, what is the implication?
7. How does the Treynor approach differ from the Sharpe approach? Which of the two measures assumes that unsystematic risk will be completely diversified away?

8. Under the Jensen approach, how is the market line related to the beta?
9. Explain alpha as a measure of performance.
10. What conclusions can be drawn from the empirical studies of portfolio (fund) managers' performances?
11. Is the past performance of portfolio managers of any significance?
12. What is the meaning of beta instability versus stability? Relate this to individual firms, industries, and portfolios.
13. If investment companies do not offer returns which are, on average, any better than the market in general, why would someone invest in them?
14. "The vast holdings of institutions and their large trading volume could mean they effectively control the market." Do you agree, based on the discussion in the latter part of the chapter?
15. Examining the information in Table 20–1 for the Kemper Growth Fund, would you think it has a high or low beta?
16. What is meant by an institutional investor? Give some examples.

PROBLEMS

1. A firm that evaluates portfolios uses the Sharpe approach to measuring performance. How would it rank the following three portfolios?

	Portfolio return	Risk-free rate	Portfolio standard deviation
Bowman Money Managers	11%	7%	20%
Donruss Group	15	7	25
Fleer Investment Company	10	7	14

2. Assume a second firm that evaluates portfolios uses the Treynor approach to measuring performance. The firm is also evaluating the three portfolios in Problem 1. The portfolio betas are as follows:

	Portfolio beta
Bowman Money Managers	1.08
Donruss Group	1.20
Fleer Investment Company	1.10

a. Using the Treynor approach, how would the second firm rank the three portfolios?
b. Explain why any differences have taken place in the rankings between Problem 1 and Problem 2a.
c. If the Treynor approach is utilized, and the market return is 10 percent (with a risk-free rate of 7 percent), which of the portfolios outperformed the market?

3. Assume the Jensen approach to portfolio valuation is being used.
a. Draw a market line similar to that in Figure 20–2 (i.e., show 0 excess returns at a 0 portfolio beta and 3 percent (10 percent − 7 percent) at a portfolio beta of 1).

b. Now graph the three portfolios. Which portfolio(s) over or under-performed the market?

SELECTED REFERENCES

Altman, Edward I., and Robert A. Schwartz. "Common Stock Price Volatility Measures." *Journal of Financial and Quantitative Analysis,* January 1970, pp. 603–25.

Blume, Marshall E. "Betas and Their Regression Tendencies." *Journal of Finance,* June 1975, pp. 785–95.

————. "On the Assessment of Risk." *Journal of Finance,* March 1971, pp. 1–10.

Fielitz, Bruce D. "Indirect vs. Direct Diversification." *Financial Management,* Winter 1974, pp. 54–62.

"Forbes 1981 Mutual Fund Survey." *Forbes,* August 31, 1981, pp. 58–87.

Friend, Irwin, Marshall Blume, and Jean Crockett. *Mutual Funds and Other Institutional Investors.* New York: McGraw-Hill, 1970.

Gentry, James A. "Capital Market Line Theory, Insurance Company Portfolio Performance, and Empirical Anomalies." *Quarterly Review of Economics and Business,* Spring 1975, pp. 8–16.

Institutional Investor Study Report of the Securities and Exchange Commission. Washington D.C.: U.S. Government Printing Office, 1971.

Jensen, Michael C. "The Performance of Mutual Funds in the Period 1945–1964." *Journal of Finance,* May 1968, pp. 389–416.

————. "Risk, Capital Assets, and Evaluation of Portfolios." *Journal of Business,* April 1969, pp. 167–247.

Kraus, Alan, and Hans K. Stoll. "Parallel Trading by Institutional Investors." *Journal of Financial and Quantitative Analysis,* December 1972, pp. 2107–38.

McDonald, John G. "Objectives and Performance of Mutual Funds, 1960–1969." *Journal of Financial and Quantitative Analysis,* June 1974, pp. 311–33.

Mains, Norman. "Risk, the Pricing of Capital Assets, and the Evaluation of Investment Portfolios: Comment." *Journal of Business,* July 1977, pp. 371–84.

Pinches, George E., and William R. Kinney, Jr. "The Measurement of the Volatility of Common Stock Prices." *Journal of Finance,* March 1971, pp. 119–25.

Reilly, Frank K. "Institutions on Trial: Not Guilty." *Journal of Portfolio Management,* Winter 1977, pp. 5–10.

Schlarbaum, Gary G. "The Investment Performance of the Common Stock Portfolios of Property-Liability Insurance Companies." *Journal of Financial and Quantitative Analysis,* January 1974, pp. 89–106.

Sharpe, William F. "Mutual Fund Performance." *Journal of Business,* January 1966, pp. 119–38.

Treynor, Jack L. "How to Rate Management of Investment Funds." *Harvard Business Review,* January–February 1965, pp. 63–74.

Valentine, Jerome L. "Investment Analysis and Capital Market Theory." Occasional Paper No. 1., Charlottesville, Va.: The Financial Research Foundation, 1975.

Wagner, W. H., and S. C. Lau. "The Effect of Diversification on Risk." *Financial Analysts Journal,* November–December 1971, pp. 48–53.

Wiesenberger Investment Companies Service. Boston: Warren, Gorham & Lamont, 1983.

Williamson, J. Peter. "Measuring Mutual Fund Performance." *Financial Analysts Journal,* November–December 1972, pp. 78–84.

Part Six

LIFELONG PLANNING CONCEPTS

The emphasis in the final chapter is on lifelong planning with special attention devoted to retirement and estate considerations. Not only is the material potentially important to an individual's planning (whether or not to have an IRA), but also to a future financial adviser who may be expected to address many of these issues in dealing with his or her clientele.

In this section, the authors consider the role of social security as well as the use of corporate pension plans and individual pension plans. It is not that difficult for persons who are currently in their 20s to accumulate a million dollars or more at retirement, but there are no assurances as to what the future purchasing power may be.

A final consideration is estate planning and estate taxes. By having an understanding of the basic nature of the estate tax structure under the 1981 Economic Recovery Tax Act, the student may be able to provide useful input to family members. Also, more meaningful conversations can take place with lawyers, CPAs and financial planners.

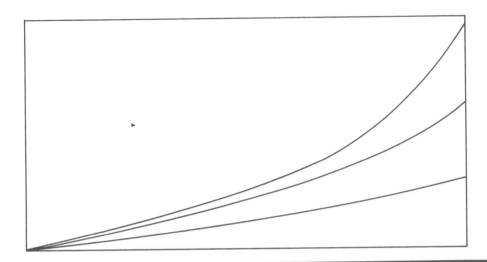

Chapter 21
RETIREMENT AND ESTATE PLANNING FOR YOURSELF AND OTHERS

Chapter 21

RETIREMENT AND ESTATE PLANNING FOR YOURSELF AND OTHERS

The various investment outlets described in the text may be related to investment for immediate income and capital gains or to retirement and estate planning needs; indeed, the concepts of current and future needs are closely related. However, because most of the text has dealt with current investment strategy, in this chapter we will focus on retirement and estate planning. You will be asked to make many decisions that can affect your retirement and estate planning when you accept your first full-time job, so this is not a topic solely for middle-aged investors. For example, should you open an Investment Retirement Account (IRA), and how much should you place in it? Some of you may be making this decision now. Also, if you go into the investments or financial planning area, you will be called upon to advise others on their retirement and estate planning needs.

FINANCIAL NEEDS

Planning is a difficult task, and the unpredictability and uncertainty of politics and economics in recent years has made financial planning and forecasting even more difficult. Of course, these conditions make careful financial planning, especially retirement planning, critical to the accomplishment of lifelong goals.

Even though the future is uncertain and returns from various investments may fluctuate greatly, future time is as much a benefit as it is a detriment to investments. Over time, unusual variations tend to smooth out and follow long-term trends that override short-term aberrations. This will be helpful when analyzing specific strategies for building retirement funds.

Assume that someone wishes to retire at age 65 and anticipates a 10-year retirement period to age 75 based on life expectancy tables. Further assume that the individual will need $18,000 for the first year and that this requirement will go up by 8 percent per year based on inflation and higher medical expenses. We will assume that the individual can earn 10 percent on investments, and this will be the discount rate to equate the future with the present.[1] The future needs and associated present values are presented in Table 21–1.

The present value factors are found in Appendix B at the end of the book. We see in Table 21–1 that the individual will need to accumulate $150,872 for retirement. We further assume the individual is 48 years old, so that he or she has 17 years to accomplish this goal. If we once again assume a 10 percent discount rate, a current investment of $29,872.66 will allow the investor to achieve this objective.

$$\$150,872 \times .198 = \$29,872.66$$

$$\uparrow$$

Present value factor
for 17 years at 10 percent

---

[1] Taxes are not explicitly considered at this point.

TABLE 21–1   Financial Needs at Retirement

Year	Annual requirement (assumes 8 percent increase)	Present value factor (10 percent)	Present value
1	$18,000	.909	$ 16,362
2	19,440	.826	16,057
3	20,995	.751	15,767
4	22,675	.683	15,487
5	24,489	.621	15,208
6	26,448	.564	14,917
7	28,564	.513	14,653
8	30,849	.467	14,406
9	33,317	.424	14,126
10	35,982	.386	13,889
Financial needs at retirement =			$150,872

This analysis assumes that the proceeds from the investment are being reinvested on a tax-free basis. This is somewhat difficult to accomplish on a lump-sum investment of this nature. On the other hand, the individual may wish to set aside an annual annuity contribution that will grow to $150,872 if invested at 10 percent for 17 years. Employing various tax deferral devices discussed later in this chapter (such as pension plan contributions, Keogh plans, IRAs, and other forms of annuities), this may be possible to accomplish with little or no tax liability as the funds are accumulating. Using Appendix C for the compound sum of an annuity, we see the annual annuity contribution would be $3,719.99 in order to accumulate $150,872 in 17 years at 10 percent.

$$\frac{\$150,827}{40.545} = \$3,719.99$$

$\uparrow$

Compound sum factor
for 17 years at 10 percent

Note that a relatively small contribution will accomplish the objective of raising $150,872 because of the time horizon involved and the relatively high reinvestment rate of 10 percent. At 6 percent, we must contribute $7,640.11 annually and at 13 percent, $2,807.49.

$$\frac{\$150,872}{20.213} = \$7464.11 \qquad \frac{\$150,872}{53.739} = \$2807.50$$

$\uparrow$ $\uparrow$

Compound sum factor   Compound sum factor
for 17 periods at 6   for 17 periods at 13
percent   percent

Also consider that social security benefits will reduce the need for accumulated funds or, conversely, that a desire to leave a lump sum in a final estate will increase the need for annual payments.

As previously specified, one of the advantages of long-term planning is the ability to smooth out short-term variations in investment returns. For example, if we make an annual purchase of a diversified common stock portfolio to achieve part of our investment objectives, we may have some years in which stock values are up or down, but over the long run, we should receive a normal return of perhaps 10–12 percent.

Of course, this smoothing out principle is not true for all investments. Who can say what the price of gold or silver will be 17 years from now? We can retire as millionaires or in poverty if all our holdings are in precious metals. For this reason, it is generally advisable that an individual who is doing retirement planning attempt to achieve a sufficiently diversified portfolio so that long-term returns are reasonably predictable. For example, gold or silver may represent an important inflation hedge in a retirement portfolio but should generally represent a relatively small percentage because of the impact of price volatility.

DOLLAR-COST AVERAGING

In building a portfolio over the long term, we may also wish to utilize dollar-cost averaging in purchasing stocks or other assets. Under dollar-cost averaging, we place a fixed-dollar investment in a given security each year regardless of its price or the current market outlook. The use of dollar-cost averaging is a concession to the principle that most investors cannot outsmart the market (at least in the short run). All too often, investors buy when a stock is high on a wave of good news only to find themselves with a desire to liquidate when the stock is low due to negative events. A recent example of this was the boom in energy stocks in 1979–80 due to a belief in an energy shortage and the need for domestic oil production. In 1981, the tables turned. An oil glut was present in world markets, and energy issues were under sharp selling pressure.

The intent with dollar-cost averaging is to avoid the common practice of buying high and selling low. In fact, you are forced to do the opposite. Why? You are committing a fixed dollar amount each year (or month) and buying the stock at the current market price regardless of what it is. When the price is high, you will be buying relatively fewer shares. When the price is low, your fixed-dollar investment will allow you to accumulate more shares. An example is presented in Table 21–2, in which we are purchasing $1,000 of stock each year over a five-year time period. The price is assumed to reach a low of $97 and a high of $130 a share. To facilitate the analysis, a purchase of fractional shares is assumed possible (such as 8.3 shares in 1983).

Note that when the stock price is relatively low, such as in 1984 or 1986, we purchase relatively more shares. When it is high, such as 1987, we purchase fewer shares. On balance, we are buying more shares at lower prices. In this case, there is a happy ending in that the stock ends up at $130 in 1987.

TABLE 21–2   Dollar-Cost Averaging

(1)	(2)	(3)	(4)
			Shares
Year	*Investment*	*Stock price*	*purchased*
1983	$1,000	120	8.3
1984	1,000	100	10.0
1985	1,000	118	8.5
1986	1,000	97	10.3
1987	1,000	130	7.7
	$5,000	565	44.8

What would happen if the price merely ended up at the average price over the five-year time period? The values in column 3 total to 565, so that the average price over five years is $113 (565/5). Actually, we would still make money under this assumption because the average *cost* is less than this amount. Consider that we invested $5,000 and purchased 44.8 shares. This translates to an average cost of only $111.61.

$$\frac{\text{Investment}}{\text{Shares}} = \frac{\$5,000}{44.8} = \$111.61$$

The reason that the average cost ($111.61) is less than the average price ($113) is that we bought relatively more shares at the lower price levels and they weigh more heavily in our calculations. Thus, under dollar-cost averaging, we have shown that you can make money if the stock ends up at a relatively high level ($130) or even at the average price over the time horizon of $113.[2]

The only time you would lose money is if the eventual price falls below the average cost ($111.61) and you sell at that point in time. While dollar-cost averaging has its advantages, it is not without criticism. Clearly, if a stock continues to go down over a long period of time, it is hard to convince yourself that you are doing the right thing to continue buying. For example, Polaroid stock fell from 149½ to 25½ between 1972 and 1977. To continue with dollar-cost averaging may have been too painful or foolish to endure. Also, one of the advantages of dollar-cost averaging is a disadvantage as well; namely, that you are removing all human judgment from the decision-making process. You simply buy x dollars worth when it's time to buy. The plan could be carried out by a computer or robot. Many investors are uncomfortable with this approach.

Of course, you could arrange various alterations or modifications to basic dollar-cost averaging by saying, "I will only follow the plan if such and such happens to the stock." This altered version may dilute some of the presumed

---

[2] This, of course, does not consider commissions, which could be important.

advantages of dollar-cost averaging. It is like a person on a diet outlining the circumstances when they will or will not eat chocolate.

ELEMENTS OF RETIREMENT PLANS

In examining actual retirement plans, we look at government-sponsored social security as well as private sector plans. In both cases, we will examine costs and benefits involved as well as other features of the programs. Let's first look at social security.

Social Security

Ninety percent of those employed in the United States participate in the social security system, which provides not only retirement benefits, but also payments for dependents of the deceased, disability income for workers and their dependents, and health care expenses for elderly and low-income families. Those exempt from participation in the social security program are employees of state and local governments, employees of tax-exempt charities or service institutions, civilian employees of the federal government, and other less important categories. Many of these people participate in similar programs outside of the social security system.

When social security was initiated under the Social Security Act in 1935, the social security tax was levied against 1 percent of wages up to $3,000. Thus, the maximum payment into the program was $30 per year. In 1986, the employee's share of the annual contribution (to be added with similar payments by the employer) is stipulated as 7.15 percent on a maximum base of $37,800. Thus, someone making $37,800 or higher will pay $2,702.70 in social security taxes. The tax is currently scheduled to go up each year into the next century. Since the social security tax is not a tax-deductible item for federal income purposes, it is a heavy burden to the payer. Many of the tax reduction benefits of the Reagan Administration will be offset by increased social security taxes to those in the work force.

What are the benefits of social security and how do they influence retirement planning? In the mid-1980s, one retiring at age 65 could expect to receive a maximum monthly base of $750–800 per month. The amount tends to be adjusted upward annually. The monthly payment is based on prior earnings history, but does not go up proportionally for high wage earners. One who had average lifetime earnings of $150,000 per year would not be compensated more than one who had earned 1/5th this much on an annual basis. For those who wish to retire at age 62, the monthly benefits would be approximately 20 percent less. Also, a dependent spouse may collect benefits equal to approximately half that of a retired working spouse. Because there are so many variations and exceptions in computing benefits, the Social Security Administration no longer publishes a formal table showing monthly retirement benefits. However, a useful guide to determining retirement benefits is *Estimating Your*

Social Security Retirement Check—Using the Indexing Method, issued by the Social Security Administration.[3]

Prior to 1984, social security benefits were not taxable. However, presently up to one half of a person's benefits may be subject to federal income taxes if adjusted gross income, plus nontaxable interest, plus one half of social security benefits exceed $25,000 for an individual, or $32,000 for a couple filing jointly.[4]

Those receiving benefits can continue to work without losing benefits if annual earnings do not exceed $5,160 for those between ages 62 and 64 and $6,960 for those between 65 and 69 years. At age 70, earnings restrictions are removed. The penalty for exceeding the maximum allowable earnings prior to age 70 is 50 cents on the dollar. If a person age 65 earns $1,000 over the $6,960 maximum, $500 in benefits will be lost.[5]

While the social security system has faced many financial problems in the past, most experts agree that the system will not be permitted to falter or disintegrate. A number of changes have been made in the 1980s to help the operation of the system. These changes include better defined standards for receiving benefits and ultimately delaying the age at which one can receive maximum benefits.[6]

Nevertheless, if we have 6 percent inflation over the next 25 years and social security benefits are adjusted accordingly, total social security benefits could be at least four times higher than they are today. This is a heavy burden for the system to bear. Social security operates on a current-funding basis. That is, taxes that are paid into the system now are used to fund the retirement benefits of workers who have worked in the past. Each current generation pays the benefits of past generations. Although there is a social security trust fund, it merely serves as a short-term cushion in periods when revenues are not sufficient to meet expenses. Those who plan to retire 40 to 50 years from now can only hope that their children and grandchildren are prepared to work hard enough to support their social security payments.

PRIVATE PENSION PLANS

Clearly, there is a need to supplement social security benefits for many in the population. About 60 percent of nongovernmental employees are also covered by private pension plans.

---

[3] *Estimating Your Social Security Retirement Check—Using the Indexing Method* (Washington, D.C.: U.S. Government Printing Office, 1984).

[4] The amount of benefits subject to the tax is equal to either one half of social security benefits or one half of income in excess of the base amount (such as $25,000), whichever is less.

[5] Only earnings from employment or self-employment are counted in this test. No penalty applies to income from pensions, dividends, interest, or sale of assets. The amount of allowable maximum income can be expected to change over time.

[6] Between the years 2000 and 2027, maximum benefits will be deferred until age 67. However, one can still retire at age 62.

In the discussion of private pension plans, we will consider plans that apply to employees of business firms as well as individual plans. We first examine employee pension plans.

Legal Considerations

No employer is required to have a pension plan. However, if a plan exists, it is regulated by law.

Several major features of the law protect those covered by a pension. The law having the most impact on pensions is the Employee Retirement Income Security Act of 1974 (ERISA), commonly called the Pension Reform Act of 1974, which requires that vesting must take place after a period of time. Vesting means that pension benefits or rights cannot be taken away. Typically, vesting occurs after 10 years of service or is based on a formula. The law requires full vesting after 10 years if there is no partial vesting prior to that; or if graduated vesting occurs after 4 years of service, full vesting must take effect after 15 years.

ERISA also prescribes minimum standards of eligibility for participation in plans, required disclosure to participants, and employer fiscal responsibility. All newly initiated *private* pension plans by firms engaged in interstate commerce are covered by ERISA (most older plans are covered as well). ERISA does not regulate plans sponsored by governmental bodies, charitable organizations, or those involved in intrastate commerce (other regulatory organizations are generally responsible).

Understanding Benefits and Contributions

Understanding the features of a plan is critical to good retirement planning. Some plans base the pension on average earnings over a period of years, often the two to five years prior to retirement. Others use formulas based on such things as years of service, age, or job class. Knowledge of the way contributions and benefits are calculated and of the options available can have a significant effect on retirement income.

The law does not attempt to specify the features of a pension plan; it only requires that they be fully disclosed and meet minimum standards. A first question to be considered is whether the plan is *contributory* or *noncontributory*. Many private pension plans are noncontributory, meaning the employer makes the full contribution and the employee does not have to contribute. In a contributory plan, both the employer and employee contribute. Contributory plans are common for federal, state, and local governments and in many colleges and universities. Under a contributory plan, the employer might pay in 50 or 60 percent of the annual contribution with the balance coming from the employee through payroll deductions.

If an employee leaves a job covered by a contributory plan before retirement, he usually receives his contribution plus interest. In some cases, the funds may be left in the plan, and a pension is paid when a particular age is

reached. The noncontributory plans usually pay only a pension that is based on the vested rights of the employee if vesting has occurred when the employee leaves.

We've been discussing methods of contribution into a plan, but what about the receipt of benefits? There are two different approaches that may be applied. The first is called a *defined benefit plan.* Under a defined benefit plan, the employee can calculate his pension based on a formula using years of service and average earnings. Thus, the employee might be assured of receiving 1½ percent of the average of his last two year's salary for each year of service. If the average is $30,000 and the employee has been with the firm 20 years, the annual retirement benefit will be $9,000.

$$\text{Percentage} \times \text{Salary} \times \text{Number of years} = \text{Yearly benefit}$$
$$1\tfrac{1}{2}\% \quad \times \ 30,000 \ \times \qquad 20 \qquad = \$9,000$$

The second type of benefit plan is *the defined contribution plan.* Under this arrangement, retirement benefits are a function of total contributions over the life of the plan. The responsibility for those contributions are defined between employer and employee. Needless to say, large contributions will lead to substantial retirement benefits, with the opposite outcome for meager contributions. Conditions in the financial markets over the life of the contributions will also influence the total payoff.

The previously described *defined benefit plan* generally allows for greater predictability in planning. Many retirement plans combine elements of both the defined benefit plan and defined contribution plan, in which retirement benefits are based on annual contributions, years of service, average earnings, and a number of other factors.

Impact of Changing Employers

One of the major errors that occur in retirement planning is to overlook the effect of changing jobs. The present law requiring vesting of benefits has eliminated some of the problem by permitting employees to retain some pension rights if they leave a firm *after* vesting has taken place. Of course, if no vesting has occurred, then all benefits may be lost. Even if rights have been vested, a financial loss may occur because most plans pay benefits based on the salary earned at the time of employment. This means that with inflation and normally greater salaries just prior to retirement, benefits based on a job that was left, say, 20 years ago, will probably be so small in terms of today's needs that they are nearly worthless. This is particularly true if you have not built up similar benefits in a new job because of employment shifts.

The uninitiated might believe that being in three different plans (due to changing jobs) each for 10 years would give the same total pension income as being in one plan for 30 years. However, this is not true. Most plans base benefits on the salary earned in the last few years of employment or on some average of earnings as well as years of service. To receive a reasonable retirement benefit, most plans require at least 20 years of service—more for a really

good pension. Thus, it is sad but true that most people cannot really afford to change jobs after age 40 or 45 unless they have other means of financing their retirement.

The ability to take pension rights earned on one job directly to another job is called "portability." Very few jobs and pension plans have portability. Some public employees, university teachers, and members of certain unions have portability to some extent. Even in these cases, some of the credit for a pension may not transfer.

Funding and Tax Considerations

Two other important considerations for a plan are the nature of its funding and tax provisions. *Funded plans* charge current income with pension liabilities in advance of the actual payment, and funds are set aside. To do this, an estimate of the ultimate liability must be made. Experts, called actuaries, evaluate data concerning the probable number of employees who will qualify for a pension, when they will take the pension, and how much it will be. The objective is to arrive at amounts that permit the plan to be reasonably funded to meet its obligations.

An *unfunded* plan is similar to our social security system in that payments to retirees are made out of current income. In an unfunded plan, the employees must hope that sufficient resources are available to cover retirement.

Even a funded plan may not assure that all necessary resources will be available. If the actuarial assumptions that have gone into the computations allow too small an actual contribution, inadequate funding may take place. ERISA attempts to regulate and control such practices.

Finally, the employer and employee must determine if the plan is *qualified* for federal tax purposes. A qualified pension plan, under the provisions of the Internal Revenue Service, allows the employer to deduct annual contributions to the pension plan as a tax-deductible item. From the employees' perspective, a qualified plan allows funds in the plan to earn income without taxation, and no tax is paid on the employer's contribution until benefits are received. A qualified pension plan must meet the appropriate requirements established under ERISA.

INDIVIDUAL PENSION PLANS

Our discussion of pension plans up until now has centered on employee-employer related pension plans. We now shift our attention to individual pension or retirement plans.

Many individuals are self-employed or are employed by firms without pension plans. Under the Economic Recovery Tax Act of 1981 and prior legislation, those who are not covered by employer-sponsored pension plans, and even those who are covered, can establish individual personal pension plans which allow some major tax advantages and thus conserve dollars for

retirement years. The two types of individual retirement plans receiving the greatest attention are Keogh plans and individual retirement accounts.

Keogh Plans

Keogh plans are pension plans for self-employed individuals. These plans originally stem from the Self-Employment Individuals Tax Retirement Act of 1962–HR10 (Keogh Act) and give participants the same tax advantages that qualified pension plans of corporations enjoy. The current rules permit 25 percent of allowable earned income up to a maximum of $30,000 to be deducted from taxable income and to earn returns on a nontaxable basis until paid out at retirement.[7] The money must be put in legally approved investments for retirement. The funds can be managed by a variety of financial institutions. The custodians can be changed once per year without penalty, and movement into different kinds of investments can be made as often as desired. Funds may not be withdrawn from the Keogh plan until the participant is at least 59½ years old, and withdrawal must begin by the end of the year in which age 70½ is reached. Most users of Keogh plans are self-employed doctors, dentists, lawyers, accountants, farmers, and businesspeople. Only those who become totally disabled or the dependents of those who die can withdraw funds early without penalty. The penalty for withdrawing without meeting the proper conditions is to nullify the plan and cause regular taxes and penalty taxes to become due. Also, another Keogh plan cannot be instituted for five years.[8]

Individual Retirement Accounts (IRAs)

Individual retirement accounts (IRAs) are similar to Keogh plans except that they were originally intended to be open to employees of firms who were not covered by an employer-sponsored plan. In the 1981 tax revisions, plans were opened to employees already covered by a sponsored plan. The maximum annual deduction is $2,000 for one person or $2,250 if there is also a nonworking spouse. If there are two working spouses, the maximum deduction is

---

[7] Effectively, the maximum allowable deduction is closer to 20 percent. The reason is that the contribution must be deducted from gross earned income to determine the base against which the 25 percent can be applied. Thus, if one has $50,000 in gross earned income and takes a $10,000 Keogh contribution deduction, this would lower allowable earned income to $40,000. While the $10,000 represents 25 percent of allowable earned income, it really is only 20 percent of gross earned income.

[8] There is also a plan, called a defined benefit Keogh plan, which allows even larger amounts to be tax deductible. Under this plan, the beneficiary of the plan is allowed to pay an amount into the plan depending on the amount of payout to be received upon retirement. The basic idea is to figure how much would have to be set aside each year until retirement year to receive a particular sum each year after retirement. Limitations do apply. The amount of the benefit cannot be larger than the amount earned when the plan was established regardless of the age of the person at that time.

$4,000. Deductions reduce taxable income and allow for the accumulation of funds that are not currently taxed. Taxation only begins when withdrawals are made.

It is permissible to deduct the appropriate dollar amount without any percentage limitation. In other words, if a person only earns $2,000 the *whole* $2,000 can be deducted and put into an IRA. The same rule would apply to larger permitted deductions up to $4,000. Prior to the Economic Recovery Tax Act of 1981, you could only put 15 percent of income into an IRA, with a maximum of $1,500. Thus, $10,000 of income was necessary to utilize the full $1,500 deduction. As with Keogh plans, the funds can not be withdrawn without penalty before the age of 59½ and withdrawals must begin by the end of the year in which age 70½ is reached.

Individual retirement accounts are formally established when contributions are turned over to a trustee. Often the trustee is a bank or savings and loan association. The trustee then invests the funds in such outlets as certificates of deposit, savings accounts, mutual fund shares, or other allowable investments. Similarly, an *individual retirement annuity* can be purchased from a life insurance company to serve the same purpose. The interested investor may wish to consult a banker, insurance agent, or stockbroker to determine what is the most appropriate avenue to follow.

In Table 21–3, we see the impact of different assumed rates of return on IRAs over 40 years. These are based on $2,000 contributions (maximum for individual), $2,250 contributions (maximum for worker with nonworking spouse), and $4,000 (maximum for two working spouses). It is assumed that the maximum contribution under each circumstance is made every year. In all likelihood, future tax legislation will allow for even larger annual contributions as the cost of living increases.

TABLE 21–3   40-Year Accumulation under IRAs

Annual contribution	Rate of return on funds		
	8 percent	10 percent	12 percent
$2,000	$ 518,120	$ 885,180	$1,534,180
2,250	582,885	995,828	1,725,953
4,000	1,036,240	1,770,360	3,068,360

We can see there are many different paths to becoming a millionaire. For example, a $2,000 annual contribution for 40 years at 12 percent will produce $1,534,180. Contributions are usually invested for three to five years and then rolled over into new investments. This process may take place many times over 40 years or any other time period. There are two major points that can be gleaned from Table 21–3. First of all, there is an extreme difference in final values between an 8 percent and a 12 percent rate of return. Although 12

percent is only one third higher than 8 percent, the returns after 40 years are three times as great. Secondly, there is a major impact of "no" taxation on income accumulation. For example, if a 50 percent tax were paid on the returns for each year, the 10 percent return would be reduced to 5 percent and the 40–year accumulation for the $2,000 annual contribution would be a mere $241,600 instead of $885,180.

A number of other tax-advantaged retirement plans are also available. These include simplified employee pension IRAs, profit sharing plans, tax-sheltered annuities under Section 403B of the Internal Revenue Code, and the use of professional corporations. These topics go beyond the intended scope of this chapter and may be found in texts specifically dealing with personal financial planning or life insurance.

ESTATE PLANNING

In developing a comprehensive financial plan, one must look beyond the requirements of retirement planning to consider estate planning as well. Many believe that estate planning is only for the wealthy. While the wealthy do have greater needs in terms of disposing of assets, those who are not wealthy may have equal needs in terms of carefully directing the application of their estate to take care of dependents or to effectively use limited resources. As an example, a young married couple with several children needs to make sure that funds are available for the childrens' education if the breadwinner dies; whereas a wealthy person in the same situation may know, within reason, that plenty is available for education and other purposes.

Another problem is that people lack awareness of the size of their estates. With the considerable inflation that has taken place over the years, estates are often much larger than assumed. If no estate planning takes place, unnecessary problems, unwarranted taxes, and misdirection of resources may occur. The conclusion is that almost everyone should at least review his or her potential estate and the needs and responsibilities of disposing of it. The subsequent discussion in this section centers around wills, trusts, and estate taxes.

Wills

One of the first steps of estate planning is to draft a will. This requires some preliminary homework to determine such items as a list of assets, approximate net worth, legal residence, and special family situations (divorces, children, remarriages, etc.). All of these items will be needed and helpful for other parts of estate planning as well.

A will is a legal document that directs the disposition of the owner's property upon death. If no will exists, a person who dies is said to have died intestate. In this case, the laws of each state provide for how the property is to be dispersed. Thus a primary reason for having a will is to ensure that your estate is divided in the amounts and order of preference that you wish instead of what state laws require.

Trusts

The legal device called a trust is a valuable tool for estate planners. The concept of a trust is that of a legal entity in which transfer of ownership of property takes place from an original owner (the creator of the trust) to another person (the trustee) for the benefit of someone else (the beneficiary).

Trusts may be testamentary or living, revocable or irrevocable. A testamentary trust is one created by a will. A living trust *(inter vivos)* is one that is established during the lifetime of the creator. If a trust is defined so that the creator may dissolve it and retake ownership of the property, it is a revocable trust. When the trust is irrevocable, the trust cannot be changed and the property it owns cannot be taken back by the creator.

Trusts are created for many reasons. Management of property is one. The property is taken care of by the trustee, and this may provide for expertise, continuity of management, and objectivity in management.

Decreasing or deferring taxes is also a major reason for using trusts. Property that produces income can be transferred to a trust so that the income

TABLE 21–4   Unified Rate Schedules for Federal Gift and Estate Taxes*

(1) Taxable estate more than	*(2)* Taxable estate less than or equal to	*(3)* Tax on amount in column (1)	*(4)* Rate of tax on excess over amount in column (1) (percent)
$ 0	$ 10,000	$ 0	18%
10,000	20,000	1,800	20
20,000	40,000	3,800	22
40,000	60,000	8,200	24
60,000	80,000	13,000	26
80,000	100,000	18,200	28
100,000	150,000	23,800	30
150,000	250,000	38,800	32
250,000	500,000	70,800	34
500,000	750,000	155,800	37
750,000	1,000,000	248,300	39
1,000,000	1,250,000	345,800	41
1,250,000	1,500,000	448,300	43
1,500,000	2,000,000	555,800	45
2,000,000	2,500,000	780,800	49
2,500,000	3,000,000	1,025,800	53
3,000,000	3,500,000	1,290,800	57
3,500,000	4,000,000	1,575,800	61
4,000,000	4,500,000	1,880,800	65
4,500,000	5,000,000	2,205,800	69
5,000,000	—	2,550,800	70

* Changes in upper-bracket rates of 50 percent or higher will take place through 1987. The maximum rate will eventually be 50 percent, starting at $2.5 million.

is paid to the trust or to the beneficiaries of the trust, such as minor children. The transfer of income from the creator's tax return lowers his taxes, and the tax bracket of a minor is often low enough so that little or no tax is required.

A problem relating to trusts is the fact that changes occurring long after the trust was established may make provisions of the trust inadequate. This is especially true with payments to beneficiaries when inflation exists. Income from the earnings of the trust may be inadequate to pay for a college education 20 years from now. This can be relieved by allowing use of part of the principal assets of the trust to supplement the funds earned. Use of the principal is termed "invasion" of the trust and can be written into the trust agreement. Other problems that develop over time can be partially or completely avoided by giving the trustee adequate flexibility to manage the trust's assets.

Estate and Gift Taxes

Estate taxes are imposed on the estate of a deceased person, and gift taxes are imposed on lifetime gifts that exceed the $10,000 per year gift allowance. For the purpose of computation of taxes payable, the two types of tax obligations are combined (estate and gift), and a unified tax rate is applied to both. Thus, the lifetime gifts subject to taxation and the value of an estate at time of death are added together to determine the total tax base against which the unified rate schedule is applied.

As implied above, anyone can give away $10,000 per year to any number of people without incurring a subsequent tax obligation. Actually, each spouse can give a child $10,000 per year ($20,000 total per year), This is known as gift-splitting. Thus, a husband and wife with three children could give away $60,000 per year without further tax obligation. Over 20 years, $1.2 million could be transferred in such a fashion.

Computation of Unified Federal Gift and Estate Tax

In Table 21–4 on p. 617, we see a unified tax rate schedule for federal gift and estate taxes. The tax obligation can be found by using column 3 (and column 4 where necessary). For example, on $40,000, the basic tax amount is $8,200 (column 3). On $50,000, we take the basic tax amount on $40,000 ($8,200) and multiply the additional $10,000 by 24 percent (the additional or marginal tax rate in column 4). This $2,400 is added to $8,200 to arrive at $10,600.

Prior to passage of the 1981 Economic Recovery Tax Act, a $47,000 unified tax credit was allowed. This $47,000 tax credit effectively freed the first $175,625 in an estate from taxation. Let's see how this works.

Tax on $150,000	$38,800
Tax on additional $25,625 (at 32 percent)	8,200
Total tax obligation	$47,000
Unified tax credit	−47,000
Tax obligation	$ 0

Only on amounts greater than $175,625 would a tax obligation occur. With the passage of the 1981 Economic Recovery Tax Act, the unified tax credit was changed each year from 1982 through 1987, allowing progressively larger estates to be exempt from taxation as indicated in Table 21–5.

TABLE 21–5   Unified Credits under the 1981 Economic Recovery Tax Act (ERTA)

Year	Unified credit	Equivalent exemption
1981	$ 47,000	$175,625
1982	62,800	225,000
1983	79,300	275,000
1984	96,300	325,000
1985	121,800	400,000
1986	155,800	500,000
1987 and forward	192,800	600,000

For example, in 1986, the unified tax credit is $155,800. This will exempt a $500,000 estate from taxation as indicated in Table 21–5.

In 1987 and thereafter, $600,000 of a taxable estate will be exempt from taxation. Thus on a $1 million estate, we would compute taxes as follows.

Taxes on $1,000,000 (Table 21–4)	$345,800
United tax credit (Table 21–5 for 1987)	192,800
Actual taxes owed	$153,000

On the $1 million estate, this only represents an average tax of 15.3 percent. Another way to look at this is to say that $153,000 represents the tax on estate values between $600,000 and $1 million. As indicated in Table 21–4, the marginal tax rate between $600,000 and $750,000 would be 37 percent, and between $750,000 and a $1 million, it would be 39%. The computed tax is:

$600,000 − $750,000 (representing $150,000) × 37%	=	$ 55,500
$750,000 − $1,000,000 (representing $250,000) × 39% =		97,500
Total tax	=	$153,000

Other Consequences of the 1981 Economic Recovery Tax Act Related to Estate Planning

The act also allowed all qualifying transfers between spouses to be free of gift or estate taxes (unlimited marital deduction). Thus, one spouse may completely transfer or leave an estate to his or her spouse without any immediate tax consequences. This is different from prior legislation in which the greater of $250,000 or one half of the adjusted estate could be passed onto a spouse.

Now the full amount is exempt from estate taxes. Of course, descendants of the surviving spouse may ultimately have to pay the estate taxes. The surviving spouse and the future heirs must be particularly aware of the ultimate tax consequences because the estate, which is free of taxes on the first pass due to the unlimited marital deduction, is likely to be larger than it would have been in the past.

The bill also provided an estate tax break for farmers, whose land is passed on to heirs categorized as "special use" land—that is, property valued as farmland rather than its "highest and best use." Previously, special use land could be transferred in an estate up to $500,000 below the highest and best use value. Under the 1981 Economic Recovery Tax Act, this was raised to $750,000.

Additional Comments on Estate Planning

A few additional comments about estate planning need to be made. We have made no specific points about state inheritance taxes, which naturally vary from state to state. Traditionally, they are smaller and of less consequence than federal estate taxes. Furthermore, state inheritance taxes may be used as credits against federal taxes. Nevertheless, it is possible that in the future with substantially reduced federal estate taxes (a $600,000 exemption in 1987), the only taxes that many families will pay will be relatively low state inheritance taxes.

In taking an overview of estate planning, some have suggested that the $600,000 exemption and other liberal provisions of the 1981 Economic Recovery Tax Act will make estate planning for tax purposes less important. However, with the presence of even modest inflation, estate values are likely to be substantially increased by the end of the century. While estate planning for tax purposes may have reduced importance for many, others must continue to contend with these issues. Financial advisers must remain aware of the various vehicles for passing along property and deferring taxes.[9]

SUMMARY

Retirement and estate planning considerations are important to comprehensive financial planning. First, objectives must be set based on a thorough evaluation of personal circumstances.

Even though the future is uncertain and returns from various investments may fluctuate greatly, future time is as much a benefit as it is a detriment to financial planning. Over time, unusual variations tend to smooth out and follow

---

[9] For example, the $600,000 exemption actually can become a $1.2 million exemption for a married couple. One spouse leaves $600,000 tax exempt to the heirs or descendants and the remaining $600,000 tax free to other spouse, who ultimately utilizes the $600,000 tax exemption to pass on the estate tax free to the heirs.

long-term trends that override short-term changes. Although common stock portfolios may go up or down 10 or 20 percent in a given year, over the long term, a normal anticipated return can be considered.

Many sources of retirement income are available to those who plan ahead. Common examples include social security, private pension plans, and individual retirement plans which include Keogh plans, individual retirement accounts (IRAs), and annuities. These can be combined with current investments in common stocks and real assets to provide a comprehensive investment package. Essentials of estate planning concern wills, trusts, and taxes. Wills permit transfer of property at death according to the wishes of the owner within legal limits. Trusts are legal entities that allow for control of property before and/or after death by transferring assets from an owner to a trustee. Numerous reasons for establishing trusts can be described, but tax advantages and management of assets are the most common.

Major taxes involved with estate planning are gift and estate taxes. The 1981 Economic Recovery Tax Act has increased the size of an exempt estate from $175,625 to $600,000 by 1987, increased the annual allowable gift from $3,000 to $10,000, provided for an unlimited marital deduction, and lowered maximum gift-estate tax rates. All of these factors are essential to estate planning and determining future tax exposure.

IMPORTANT WORDS AND CONCEPTS

Dollar-cost averaging
Private pension plans
Vesting
Individual retirement accounts (IRAs)
Individual retirement annuity
ERISA
Contributory pension plan
Noncontributory pension plan
Defined benefit plan
Defined contribution plan
Funded pension plan

Unfunded pension plan
Qualified pension plan
Keogh plan
Trust
Testamentory trust
Living trust (inter vivos)
Revocable trust
Irrevocable trust
Estate and gift taxes
Uniform tax rate schedule
Unified tax credit
Marital deduction

DISCUSSION QUESTIONS

1. Why does dollar-cost averaging force the investor to buy relatively more shares at lower stock prices?
2. What is meant by the fact that social security operates on a current-funding basis?
3. What is meant by the term *vesting* in a pension plan?

4. What is the difference between a contributory and noncontributory pension plan?
5. Explain why frequent job shifts may reduce retirement benefits.
6. What are the maximum contributions (deductions) that can be made to an individual retirement account (IRA) under the 1981 tax revisions?
7. What is the earliest age at which one can begin withdrawing funds from an IRA without penalty? By what age must withdrawals begin?
8. Explain how a trust set up for the benefit of minors may lower taxes.
9. What is the difference between a revocable and irrevocable trust?
10. Explain how gift taxes and estate taxes are combined.
11. Explain the general effect of the 1981 Economic Recovery Tax Act on the unified credit.
12. Why is estate planning also important to those who do not possess large wealth?
13. How might continued income from work affect one who receives social security benefits?
14. Can a very large earner expect to earn substantially more than an average earner under social security? Would the same principle apply to a private pension plan?
15. How does the 1981 Economic Recovery Tax Act affect the way that property can be transferred between spouses for estate purposes?

PROBLEMS

(For ease of calculations, make the assumption that cash flows come at the end of the period, as was done in the chapter.)

1. An individual will need $21,000 per year during retirement over a 14-year period. With an 8 percent discount rate, what is the present value of the annual needs?
2. Assume funds will be set aside each year for 12 years at 10 percent to meet the retirement need computed in Problem 1. How much will the annual contribution be?
3. Ms. Gray will need $15,000 the first year of her retirement. Her needs will go up 6 percent per year for the next 9 years (a total of 10 years of retirement). If Ms. Gray can earn 11 percent per year during the requirement period, what is the present value of her needs? (Round to the nearest dollar throughout your calculations.)
4. Assume in Problem 3 that Ms. Gray will begin putting away money to meet her retirement 20 years in advance of retirement. Compute the required amount(s) under the following assumptions.
   a. Equal annual contributions will be made for 20 years that earn 11 percent per year.
   b. Equal annual contributions will be made for 20 years that earn 15 percent per year.

    c. A single lump sum payment will be made 20 years in advance. The payment will earn 10 percent per year.

5. Under dollar-cost averaging, an investor will purchase $4,000 worth of stock each year for three years. The stock price is $25 in year 1, $16 in year 2, and $32 in year 3.

    a. Compute the average price.

    b. Compute the average cost.

    c. Explain why the average cost is less than the average price.

6. Mr. Means is a strong believer in dollar-cost averaging. He will purchase $4,800 worth of stock at the beginning of each year for the next 4 years. The stock is $32 in year 1, $24 in year 2, $16 in year 3, and $32 in year 4. It is now the beginning of year 5:

    a. At what stock quote in the market will he be at a break-even point in terms of his costs?

    b. Assume the stock paid $1 per share a year in dividends, and he gets the full dividend for each complete year he owned the stock. How does this change your answer in part a (what is the break-even stock price)?

7. Ms. Singleton lives alone. She has had a successful work history throughout her life and is now 67 years old. Normally her social security payments would be $8,500 per year. However, she is still earning $10,500 per year doing part-time work as an accountant.

    a. By how much will her social security benefits be reduced?

    b. At what age will all earnings restrictions be removed?

    c. How much would her total income have to be for her to have to pay taxes on social security benefits?

8. Mr. King has set up a Keogh plan. He has $100,000 in gross income. He intends to put $15,000 in the plan. What percent of allowable earned income will he be setting aside? What is the largest dollar deduction that is allowed to him under the law?

9. Assume you make annual contributions into an IRA plan for 40 years. Compute the ending value under the following assumption:

    a. You set aside $2,000 per year and earn a 9 percent annual return. (Use the appropriate table for 40 years.)

    b. You and your spouse set aside $4,000 per year and earn an 11 percent annual return.

10. Assume in Problem 9b that you and your spouse will take the accumulation after 40 years and allow it to grow for three more years at 11 percent before withdrawals begin. What is your total accumulation? (Disregard taxes.)

11. An estate has a value of $800,000.

    a. Compute the estate tax obligation before tax credits.

    b. In part a, in 1986, how much would the tax obligation after tax credits be?

12. An estate has a value of $1,200,000. If the year of settlement with the government is 1988, how much will the final tax obligation be?

SELECTED REFERENCES

"A Long Life Can Strain Your Finances." *Changing Times,* August 1980, pp. 61–62.

Ashley, Paul Prichard. *You and Your Will: The Planning and Management of Your Estate.* New York: McGraw-Hill, 1975.

Ball, Robert M. *Social Security Today and Tomorrow.* New York: Columbia University Press, 1978.

"Economic Recovery Tax Act of 1981." (An analysis.) Chicago: Arthur Andersen & Co., 1981.

Estimating Your Social Security Retirement Check—Using the Indexing Method. Washington, D.C.: U.S. Government Printing Office, 1984.

Hemphill, Charles F., Jr. *Wills and Trusts.* Englewood Cliffs, N.J.: Prentice-Hall, 1980.

Jacoby, Susan, "All about Pensions and Other Retirement Plans." *Working Woman,* April 1977, pp. 14–18.

Kahn, Arnold D. *Family Security through Estate Planning.* New York: McGraw-Hill, 1979.

Lippett, Peter E. *Estate Planning: What Anyone Who Owns Anything Must Know.* Reston, Va.: Reston Publishing, 1979.

Platt, Charles M. "Social Security, Will It Be There When You Need It?" *U.S. News & World Report,* April 1979, pp. 24–27.

Scharff, Edward E. "Planning Now for Retirement Later." *Money,* July 1979, pp. 33–37.

Unthank L. L., and Harry M. Behrendt. *What You Should Know about Individual Retirement Accounts.* Homewood, Ill.: Dow Jones-Irwin, 1978.

GLOSSARY

Abnormal return Gains beyond what the market would normally provide after adjustment for risk.

Adjustable rate mortgage A mortgage in which the interest rate is adjusted regularly to current market conditions. It is sometimes referred to as a variable rate mortgage.

Advances Increases in the prices of various stocks as measured between two points in time. Significant advances in a large number of stocks indicate a particular degree of market strength. Also see **Declines.**

After-acquired property clause The stipulation in a mortgage bond indenture requiring all real property subsequently obtained by the issuing firm to serve as additional bond security.

After-market performance The price experience of new issues in the market.

Alpha The value representing the difference between the return on a portfolio and a return on the market line that corresponds to a beta equal to the portfolio. If a portfolio manager performs at positive alpha levels, he would generate returns better than those available along the market line.

American depository receipts (ADRs) These securities represent the ownership interest in a foreign company's common stock. The process is as follows: the shares of the foreign company are purchased and put in trust in a foreign branch of a New York bank. The bank, in turn, receives and can issue depository receipts to the American shareholders of the foreign firm. These ADRs (i.e., depository receipts) allow foreign shares to be traded in the United States much like any other security. Through ADRs, one can purchase the stock of Sony Corporation, Honda Motor Co., Ltd., and hundreds of other foreign corporations.

American Exchange Market Value Index An index comprising all stocks on the American Stock Exchange. It is value-weighted.

Anticipated realized yield The return received on a bond held for a period other than that ending on the call date or the maturity date. In computing the anticipated realized yield, the investor considers both coupon payments and expected capital gains.

Arbitrage pricing theory A theory for explaining stock prices and stock returns. While the capital asset pricing model bases return solely on one form of systematic risk (market risk), arbitrage pricing theory can utilize several sources of systematic risk (GNP, unemployment, etc.). Under this theory, it is assumed that the investor will not be allowed to earn a return greater than that dictated by the various sources of systematic risk. To the extent that he does, arbitrageurs will eliminate the extra returns by selling the security and buying other comparable securities—thus the term *artibrage pricing theory.* Unlike the capital asset pricing model, there is no necessity to define K_M (the market rate of return).

Asset utilization ratios Ratios that indicate the number of times per year that assets are

turned over. They show the activity in the various asset accounts.

Average differential return The alpha value which indicates the difference between the return on a portfolio or fund and a return on the market line that corresponds to a beta equal to the portfolio or fund.

Balance sheet A financial statement that indicates, at a given point in time, what the firm owns and how these assets are financed in the form of liabilities and ownership interest.

Balanced fund A type of mutual fund that invests in common stock, bonds, and often preferred stock to try to provide income plus some capital gains.

Bankers' acceptance A short-term debt instrument usually issued in conjunction with a foreign trade transaction. The acceptance is a draft that is drawn on a bank for approval for future payment and is subsequently presented to the payer.

Barron's Confidence Index An indicator utilized by technical analysts who follow smart money rules. Movements in the index measure the expectations of bond investors, whom some technical analysts see as astute enough to foresee economic trends before the stock market has time to react.

Barron's Group Stock Averages Barron's publishes stock averages covering 32 industry groups. These averages are especially useful to the analyst who is following the performance of a specific industry relative to the general market.

Basis The difference between the futures price and the value of the underlying item. Thus on a stock index futures contract, basis represents the difference between the stock index futures price and the value of the underlying index. The basis may be either positive or negative, with the former indicating optimism and the latter signifying pessimism.

Basis point The unit of measure of change on interest-bearing instruments. One basis point is equal to .01 percent.

Best efforts The issuing firm, rather than the investment banker, assumes the risk for a distribution. The investment banker merely agrees to provide his best effort to sell the securities.

Beta A measurement of movement of a security with the market in general. It measures volatility. A high beta coefficient indicates high amounts of systematic risk.

Beta-related hedge A stock index futures hedge in which the relative volatility of the portfolio to the market is considered in determining the number of contracts necessary to offset a given dollar level of exposure. If a portfolio has a beta greater than one, then extra contracts may be necessary to compensate for high volatility.

Beta stability The amount of consistency in beta values over time. Instability means prior beta values may not be reflective of future beta values.

Black-Scholes Option Pricing Model A formal model used to determine the theoretical value of an option. Such factors as the riskless interest rate, the length of the option, and the volatility of the underlying security are considered. For a more complete discussion, see Appendix 13B.

Blind pool A form of limited partnership for real estate investments in which funds are provided to the general partner to select properties for investment.

Bond price sensitivity The sensitivity of a change in bond prices to a change in interest rates. Bond price sensitivity is influenced by the duration of the bond, in that the longer the duration of a bond, the greater the price sensitivity. A less sophisticated, but acceptable approach, is to tie price sensitivity to the maturity of the bond rather than the duration.

Bond swaps The term refers to selling out of a given bond position and immediately buying into another one with similar attributes in an attempt to improve overall portfolio return or performance.

Breadth of market indicators Overall market rules used by technical analysts in comparing broad market activity with trading activity in a few stocks. By comparing all advances and declines in NYSE-listed stocks, for example, with the Dow Jones Industrial Average, analysts attempt to judge when the market has changed directions.

Bull spread An option strategy utilized when the expectation is that the stock price will rise. The opposite is a bear spread.

Business cycle Short-term swings in economic activity encompassing expansionary and recessionary periods and generally occurring over two- to four-year periods.

Buying the spread A term indicating the cost from writing the call is more than the revenue of the short position. The opposite results in "selling the spread."

Call An option to buy 100 shares of common stock at a specified price for a given period of time.

Call provision A mechanism for repaying funds advanced through a bond issue. A provision of the bond indenture allows the issuer to retire bonds prior to maturity by paying holders a premium above principal.

Capital appreciation A growth in the value of a stock or other investments as opposed to income from dividends or interest.

Capital asset pricing model A model by which assets are valued based on their risk characteristics. The required return for an asset is related to its beta.

Capital market line The graphic representation of the relationship of risks and returns with various portfolios of assets. The line is part of the capital asset pricing model.

Cash settlement Closing out a futures or options contract for cash rather than calling for actual delivery of the underlying item specified in the contract—i.e., pork bellies, T-bills. The stock index futures markets and stock index options markets are *purely* cash settlement markets. There is never even the implied

potential for future delivery of the S&P 500 Stock Index or other indexes.

CBOE Chicago Board Options Exchange, the first exchange for call options.

Certificates of deposit Savings certificates which entitle the holder to the receipt of interest. These instruments are issued by commercial banks and savings and loans (or other thrift institutions) and have traditionally been in small amounts such as $1,000 to $10,000 or large amounts such as $100,000 (jumbo CDs).

Chartered Financial Analyst (CFA) A security analyst or portfolio manager who has been appropriately certified through experience requirements and testing.

Charting The use by technical analysts of charts and graphs to plot past stock price movements, which are used to predict future prices.

Closed-end fund An investment fund with a limited number of shares. Shares are available in the market only if present owners wish to sell their holdings. See **Open-end fund.**

Closing purchase transaction A transaction in which an investor who is a writer of an option intends to terminate his obligation.

Closing sale transaction A transaction in which an investor who is the holder of an outstanding security intends to liquidate his position as a holder.

Combined earnings and dividend model A model combining earnings per share and an earnings multiplier with a finite dividend model. Value is derived from both the present value of dividends and the present value of the future price of the stock based on the earnings multiplier (P/E).

Commercial paper A short-term credit instrument which is issued by large business corporations to the public. Commercial paper usually comes in minimum denominations of $25,000 and represents an unsecured promissory note.

Commission broker An individual who represents a stock brokerage firm at an exchange

and who executes sales and purchases stocks for the firm's clients across the nation.

Commodities Such tangible items as livestock, farm produce, and precious metals. Users and producers of comododities hedge against future price fluctuations by transferring risks to speculators through futures contracts.

Constant dollar method Adjusting for inflation in the financial statements by using the consumer price index.

Constant growth model A dividend valuation model that assumes a constant growth rate for dividends.

Construction and development trust A type of REIT that makes short-term loans to developers during their construction period.

Consumer price index An index used to measure the changes in the general price level.

Contrary opinion rules Guidelines, based on such factors as the odd-lot or the short sales position, used by technical analysts who predict stock market activity on the assumption that such groups as small traders or short sellers are often wrong. Also see **Smart money rules.**

Contributory pension plan An arrangement in which both the employer and employee contribute to the pension plan.

Conversion premium The amount, expressed as a dollar value or as a percentage, by which the price of the convertible security exceeds the current market value of the common stock into which it may be converted.

Conversion price The face value of a convertible security divided by the conversion ratio, giving the price of the underlying common stock at which the security is convertible. An investor would usually not convert the security into common stock unless the market price was greater than the conversion price.

Conversion ratio The number of shares of common stock an investor receives in exchanging convertible bonds or shares of convertible preferred stock for shares of common stock.

Conversion value The value of the underlying common stock represented by convertible bonds or convertible preferred stock. This dollar value is obtained by multiplying the conversion ratio by the per-share market price of the common stock.

Convertible security A corporate bond or a share of preferred stock which, at the option of the holder, can be converted into shares of common stock of the issuing corporation.

Correlation coefficient The measurement of joint movement between two variables.

Coupon rate The stated, fixed rate of interest paid on a bond.

Covered writer A writer of an option who owns the stock on which the option is written. If the stock is not owned, the writer is deemed naked.

Creditor claims Claims represented by debt instruments offered by financial institutions, industrial corporations, or the government.

Cross hedge A hedging position in which one form of security is used to hedge another form of security (often because differences in maturity dates or quality characteristics make a perfect hedge difficult to establish).

Currency fluctuations Changes in the relative value of one currency to another. For example, the French franc may advance or decline in relation to the dollar. To the extent a foreign currency appreciates relative to the dollar, returns on foreign investments will increase in terms of dollars. The opposite would be true for declining foreign currencies.

Currency futures Futures contracts for speculation or hedging in different nations' currencies.

Current cost method Adjusting for inflation in the financial statements by revaluing assets at their current cost.

Current ratio Current assets divided by current liabilities.

Current yield The annual dollar amount of interest paid on a bond divided by the price at

which the bond is currently trading in the market.

Cyclical Indicators Factors that economists can observe to measure the progress of economic cycles. Leading indicators move in a particular direction in advance of the movement of general business conditions, while lagging indicators change direction after general conditions, and coincident indicators move in unison with the economy.

Cyclical Industry An industry, such as automobiles, whose financial health is closely tied to the condition of the general economy. Such industries tend to make the type of products whose purchase can be postponed until the economy improves.

Data base A form of organized, stored data. It is usually fed into the computer for additional analysis.

Debenture An unsecured corporate bond.

Debt utilization ratios Ratios that indicate how the firm is financed between debt (lenders) and equity (owners), and the firm's ability for meeting cash payments due on fixed obligations, such as interest, lease payments, licensing fees, or sinking fund charges.

Declines Decreases in the prices of various stocks as measured between two points in time. Significant declines in a large number of stocks indicate a particular degree of market weakness. Also see **Advances.**

Deep discount bond A bond that has a coupon rate far below rates currently available on investments and which consequently can be traded only at a significant discount from par value. It may offer an opportunity for capital appreciation.

Defined benefit plan Under a defined benefit plan, the employee can calculate his or her pension based on a formula using such factors as years of service and average earnings.

Defined contribution plan Under a defined contribution plan, retirement benefits are a function of total contributions over the life of the plan and are not based on such factors as years of service or average earnings.

Diagonal spread A combination of a vertical and horizontal spread.

Dilution The reduction in earnings per share that occurs when earnings remain unchanged yet the number of shares outstanding increases, as in the conversion of convertible bonds or preferred stock into common stock.

Direct equity claim Representation of ownership interests through common stock or other instruments to purchase common stock, such as warrants and options.

Discount rate The interest rate at which future cash flows are discounted to a present value.

Dispersion The distribution of values or outcomes around an expected value.

Diversification Lack of concentration in any one item. A portfolio composed of many different securities is diversified.

Diversification benefits Risk reduction through a diversification of investments. Investments that are negatively correlated or that have low positive correlation provide the best diversification benefits. Such benefits may be particularly evident in an internationally diversified portfolio.

Dividend valuation model Any one of a number of stock valuation models based on the premise that the value of stock lies in the present value of its future dividend stream.

Dividend yield Annual dividends per share divided by market price.

Dollar-cost averaging Under this system, a fixed-dollar investment is placed in a given security (or portfolio) each period regardless of its price or the current market outlook. This reflects an attempt to buy more shares at a lower average price.

Dow Jones Industrial Average An index of stock market activity based on the price movements of 30 large corporations. The average is price-weighted, which means that each stock is effectively weighted by the magnitude of its price.

Dow theory The theory, developed by Charles Dow in the late 1890s and still in

use today, states that the analysis of long-term (primary) stock market trends can yield accurate predictions for future price movements.

Downside protection The protection that a convertible bond investor enjoys during a period of falling stock prices. While the underlying common stock and the convertible bond may both fall in value, the bond will fall only to a particular level because it has a fundamental, or pure, bond value based on its assured income stream.

Downside risk The possibility that an asset, such as a security, may fall in value as a result of fundamental factors or external market forces. The limit of the downside risk for a convertible bond can be computed as the difference between the bond's market price and its pure bond value divided by the market price.

Du Pont analysis A system of analyzing return on assets through examining the profit margin and asset turnover. Also, the value of return on equity is analyzed through evaluating return on assets and the debt/total assets ratio. Figure 7–2 summarizes the major components of the Du Pont system of analysis.

Duration The weighted average life of a bond. The weights are based on the present values of the individual cash flows relative to the present value of the total cash flows. Duration is a better measure than maturity when assessing the price sensitivity of bonds; that is, the impact of interest rate changes on bond prices can be more directly correlated to duration than to maturity.

Earnings per share The earnings available to holders of common stock divided by the number of common stock shares outstanding.

Earnings valuation model Any one of a number of stock valuation models based on the premise that a stock's value is some appropriate multiple of earnings per share.

Effective diversification The diversification of a portfolio to remove unsystematic risk.

Efficient frontier A set of portfolios of investments in which the investor receives maximum return for a given level of risk or a minimum risk for a given level of return.

Efficient hedge A hedge in which one side of the transaction effectively covers the exposed side in terms of movement.

Efficient market The capacity of the market to react to new information, to avoid rapid price fluctuations, and to engage in increased or reduced trading volume without realizing significant price changes. In an efficient market environment, securities are assumed to be correctly priced at any point in time.

Efficient market hypothesis The concept that there are many participants in the securities markets who are profit maximizing and alert to information so that there is almost instant adjustment to new information. The weak form of this hypothesis suggests that there is no relationship between past and future prices. The semi-strong form maintains that all forms of public information are already reflected in the price of a security so fundmental analysis cannot determine under- or overvaluation. The strong form suggests that all information, insider as well as public, is impounded in the value of a security.

Efficient portfolio A portfolio that combines assets so as to minimize the risk for a given level of return.

Equal-weighted index Each stock, regardless of total market value or price, is weighted equally. It is as if there were $100 invested in each and every stock in the index. The Value Line Index is a prime example of an equal-weighted index.

Equipment trust certificate A secured debt instrument used by firms in the transportation industry that provides for bond proceeds to purchase new equipment, which in turn is collateral for the bond issue.

Equity participation The lender also participates in an ownership interest in the property.

Equity trust A type of REIT that buys, operates, and sells real estate as an investment as opposed to construction and development trusts and mortgage trusts.

ERISA Employee Retirement Income Security Act of 1974 (commonly called the Pension Reform Act of 1974). The act requires that vesting after a certain period of time must take place. ERISA also prescribes minimum standards of eligibility for participation, disclosure to participant rules, and employer fiscal responsibility.

Estate and gift taxes Estate taxes are imposed on the estate of a deceased person, and gift taxes are imposed on lifetime gifts that exceed the $10,000-per-year gift allowance. For purposes of computation of taxes payable, the two types of tax obligations are combined (estate and gift), and a unified tax is applied to both.

Excess returns Returns in excess of the risk-free rate or in excess of a market measure such as the S&P 500 stock index.

Exchange listing A firm lists its shares on an exchange (such as the American or New York Stock Exchange).

Exercise price (warrant) The price at which the stock can be bought using the warrant.

Expectations hypothesis The hypothesis which explains the term structure of interest rates, stating that a long-term interest rate is the average of expected short-term interest rates over the applicable time period. If, for example, long-term rates are higher than short-term rates, then according to the expectations hypothesis, investors must expect that short-term rates will be increasing in coming periods.

Expected value The sum of possible outcomes times their probability of occurrence.

Extraordinary gains and losses Gains or losses from the sale of corporate fixed assets, lawsuits, or similar events that would not be expected to occur often, if ever again.

Fed The Federal Reserve serves as the central banking authority for the United States. The Fed enacts monetary policy, and it plays a major role in regulating commercial banking operations and controlling the money supply.

Federal deficit A situation in which the federal government spends more money than it receives through taxes and other revenue sources.

Federal surplus A situation in which taxes and other government revenues provide more money than is needed to cover government expenditures.

FIFO A method of inventory valuation in which it is assumed that inventory purchased first is sold first (first-in, first-out).

Financial asset A financial claim on an asset (rather than physical possession of a tangible asset) usually documented by a legal instrument, such as a stock certificate.

Financial service companies Firms that provide a broad range of financial services in order to diversify their consumer base. Services may include brokerage activities, insurance, banking, etc.

Fiscal policy Government spending and taxing practices designed to promote or inhibit various economic activities.

Floor broker An independent stockbroker who is a member of a stock exchange and who executes trades, for a fee, for commission brokers experiencing excessive volumes of trading.

Floor value A value which an income-producing security will not fall below because of the fundamental value attributable to its assured income stream.

Flow of funds analysis Analysis of the pattern of financial payments between business, government, and households.

Foreign currency effects To the extent a foreign currency appreciates relative to the dollar, returns on foreign investments will increase in terms of dollars. The opposite would be true for declining foreign currencies.

Foreign political risks The risks associated with investing in firms operating in foreign countries. There is the danger of nationalization of foreign firms or the blockage of capital flows to investors. There also may be the danger of violent overthrow of the political party in power, with all the associated implications. Punitive legislation against foreign firms or investors is another political risk.

Fourth market The direct trading between large institutional investors in blocks of listed stocks. The participants avoid paying brokerage commissions.

Fully diluted earnings per share The value of earnings per share that would be realized if all outstanding securities convertible into common stock were, in fact, converted.

Fundamental analysis The valuation of stocks based on fundamental factors, such as company earnings, growth prospects, etc.

Funded pension plan Current income is charged with pension liabilities in advance of the actual payment, and funds are set aside.

Futures contract An agreement that provides for sale or purchase of a specific amount of a commodity at a designated time in the future at a given price.

General obligation bonds A municipal bond backed by the full faith, credit, and "taxing power" of the issuing unit rather than the revenue from a given project.

Gift splitting Each spouse giving a child $10,000 per year for a total of $20,000, rather than the usual $10,000 available under the 1981 Economic Recovery Tax Act.

GNMA pass-through certificates These securities represent an undivided interest in a pool of federally insured mortgages. Actually, GNMA (the Government National Mortgage Association) buys a pool of mortgages from various lenders at a discount and then issues securities to the public against the mortgages. They are pass-through in that the holder of a GNMA certificate receives the interest and principal payment on the mortgages on a monthly basis.

Going public Selling formerly privately held shares to new investors on the over-the-counter market for the first time.

Government securities Bonds issued by federal, state, or local governmental units or government agencies. Whereas corporate securities' returns are paid through company earnings, government securities are repaid through taxes or the revenues from projects financed by the bonds.

Graduated payment mortgage A type of mortgage in which payments start out on a relatively low basis and increase over the life of the loan.

Greed index A contrary opinion index that measures how "greedy" investors are. Greed is thought to be synonymous with bullish sentiment, or optimism. Under the assumptions of the greed index, the more greedy or optimistic investors are, the more likely the market is to fall and vice versa.

Gross national product implicit price deflator A calculation made by the Department of Commerce which adjusts the prices of all goods and services in the GNP estimate for the effects of price change. It's a measure of inflation.

Growth company A company that exhibits rising returns on assets each year and sales that are growing at an increasing rate (growth phase of the life-cycle curve). Growth companies may not be as well known as growth stocks.

Growth stock The stock of a firm generally growing faster than the economy or market norm.

Hedging A process for lessening or eliminating risk by taking a position in the market opposite to your original position. For example, someone who owns wheat can sell a futures contract to protect against future price declines.

Horizontal spread Buying and writing two options with the same strike price but maturing in different months.

Ibbotson and Singuefield study A Univer-

sity of Chicago study examining comparative returns on stocks and fixed-income securities from the mid-1920s into the 1980s.

Immunization Immunizing or protecting a bond portfolio against the effects of changing interest rates on the ending value of the portfolio. The process is usually tied to a time horizon. In the process if interest rates go up, there will be a decline in the value of the portfolio, but a higher reinvestment rate opportunity for inflows. Conversely, if interest rates go down, there will be capital appreciation for the portfolio, but a lower reinvestment rate opportunity. By tying all the investment decisions to a specified duration period, the portfolio manager can take advantage of these counter forces to ensure a necessary outcome.

Income bond A corporate debt instrument on which interest is paid only if funds are available from current income.

Income statement A financial statement that shows the profitability of a firm over a given period of time.

Income statement method A method of forecasting earnings per share based on a projected income statement.

Indenture A lengthy, complicated legal document which spells out the borrowing firm's responsibilities to the individual lenders in a bond issue.

Index fund A fund investing in a portfolio of corporate stocks, the composition of which is determined by the Standard & Poor's 500 or some other index.

Indirect equity claim An indirect claim on common stock such as that achieved by placing funds in investment companies.

Individual retirement accounts (IRAs) Individual retirement plans. The maximum annual contribution is $2,000 for one person and $2,250 if there is a nonworking spouse. If there are two working spouses, the maximum contribution is $4,000. Contributions reduce taxable income and allow for the accumulation of funds that are not currently taxed.

Taxation only begins when withdrawals are made.

Individual retirement annuity A tax-deferred retirement annuity purchased from an insurance company. Benefits may be guaranteed in advance.

Industry factors The unique attributes that must be considered in analyzing a given industry or group of industries. Examples include industry structure, supply/demand of labor and materials, and government regulation.

Industry life cycle The movement of a firm or industry through stages of development, growth, expansion, and maturity.

Inflation A general increase in the prices of goods and services.

Inflation-adjusted accounting Restating financial statements to show the effect of inflation on the balance sheet and income statement. This is supplemental to the normal presentation based on historical data.

Inflationary expectations A value representing future expectations about the rate of inflation. This value, combined with the real rate of return, provides the risk-free required return for the investor.

Institutional investor A type of investor (as opposed to individual investors) representing organizations responsible for bringing together large pools of capital for investment. Institutional investors include investment companies, pension funds, life insurance companies, bank trust departments, and endowments and foundations.

In-the-money A term that indicates when the market price of a stock is above the striking price of the option. When the strike price is above the market price, the option is out-of-the-money.

Interest rate futures Futures contracts involving Treasury bills, Treasury bonds, Treasury notes, commercial paper, certificates of deposit, and GNMA certificates.

International tax problems Many foreign countries impose a 7.5 percent to 15 percent withholding tax against the dividends or inter-

est paid to nonresident holders of equity or debt securities. However, it is often possible for tax-exempt U.S. investors to secure an exemption or rebate on part or all of the withholding tax. Also, taxable U.S. investors can normally claim a U.S. tax credit for taxes paid in foreign countries. The problem is more likely to be one of inconvenience and paper shuffling rather than loss of funds.

Internationally oriented funds Mutual funds and closed-end investment companies that invest in worldwide securities. Some funds specialize in Asian holdings, others in South African, and so on. A listing of internationally oriented funds is presented in Table 18–12.

Intrinsic value Value of an option equal to market price minus the strike price.

Inverse pyramiding A process of leveraging to control commodities contracts in which the profits from one contract are used to purchase another contract on margin, and profits on this contract are applied to a third, and so on.

Investment The commitment of current funds in anticipation of the receipt of an increased return of funds at some point in the future.

Investment banker One who is primarily involved in the distribution of securities from the issuing corporation to the public. An investment banker also advises corporate clients on their financial strategy and may help to arrange mergers and acquisitions.

Investment banking The underwriting and distribution of a new securities issue in the primary market. The investment banker advises the issuing concern on price and other terms and normally guarantees sale, while overseeing distribution of the securities through the selling brokerage houses.

Investment companies A type of financial institution that takes proceeds of individual investors and reinvests them in securities according to their specific objectives. A popular type of investment company is the mutual fund.

Irrevocable trust The creator may not dissolve the trust and take back the property.

Jensen Measure of Portfolio Performance Jensen compares excess returns (total portfolio returns minus the risk-free rate) to what should be required in the market based on the portfolio beta. For example, if the portfolio beta is one, the portfolio has a systematic risk equal to the market, and the expected portfolio excess returns should be equal to market excess returns (the market rate of return minus the risk-free rate). The question then becomes, did the portfolio manager do better or worse than what is expected? The portfolio manager's excess returns can be compared to the market line of expected excess returns for any beta level.

Junk bonds High risk, low-grade bonds. They often perform like common stock and may provide interesting investment opportunities.

K_e The term representing anticipated rate of return equal to dividend yield plus expected growth in earnings and dividends. It is the discount rate applied to future dividends.

Keogh plan A retirement plan for self-employed individuals. The current rules permit 25 percent of annual earned income up to a maximum of $30,000 to be deducted from taxable income and to earn returns on a nontaxable basis until paid out at retirement. The funds may be invested in stocks, bonds, etc. Effectively, the maximum allowable deduction is closer to 20 percent because the contribution to the plan must be deducted from gross income to determine the base against which the 25 percent can be applied.

Key indicators Various market observations used by technical analysts to predict the directions of future market trends. Examples include the contrary opinion and smart money rules.

Least squares trendline A statistically developed linear trendline that minimizes the dis-

tance of the individual observations from the line.

Less developed countries Foreign countries that have not fully developed their economic system and productive capacity. Examples might include Chile, Jordan, Korea, Thailand, and Zimbabwe. A number of these less developed countries may represent good risk-reduction potential for U.S. investors because the factors that influence their economic welfare may be quite different from critical factors in the United States. Investments in these countries, at times, may also provide high returns.

LIFO A method of inventory valuation in which it is assumed that inventory purchased last is sold first (last-in, first-out).

Limit order A condition placed on a transaction executed through a stockbroker to assure that securities will be sold only if a specified minimum price is received, or purchased only if the price to be paid is no more than a given maximum.

Limited partnership A business arrangement in which there is the limited liability protection of a corporation with the tax provisions of a regular partnership. All profits or losses are directly assigned to the partners for tax purposes. The general partner has unlimited liability.

Lipper Mutual Fund Investment Performance Averages Lipper publishes indexes for growth funds, growth-with-income funds, and balanced funds. Lipper also shows year-to-date and weekly performance for many other categories of funds.

Liquidity The capacity of an investment to be retired for cash in a short period of time with a minimum capital loss.

Liquidity preference theory A theory related to the term structure of interest rates. The theory states that the term structure tends to be upward sloping more than any other pattern. This reflects a recognition of the fact that long maturity obligations are sub-ject to greater price change movements than short maturity obligations when interest rates change. Because of increased risk of holding longer-term maturities, investors demand a higher return to hold such securities. Thus they have a preference for short-term liquid obligations.

Liquidity ratios Ratios that demonstrate the firm's ability to pay off short-term obligations as they come due.

Living trust (Inter vivos) A trust that is established during the lifetime of the creator.

Long position A market transaction in which an investor purchases securities with the expectation of holding the securities for cash income or for resale at a higher price in the future. See also **Short position.**

Long-term gain and losses Gains and losses on securities held over six months. The capital gains tax rate applied to long-term transactions is 40 percent of that for short-term transactions.

Lorie and Fisher study A University of Chicago study indicating comparative returns on financial assets over half a decade. It is similar to the Ibbotson and Sinquefield study in many respects.

Margin account A trading account maintained with a brokerage firm on which the investor may borrow a percentage of the funds for the purchase of securities. The broker loans the fund at interest slightly above the prime rate.

Margin maintenance requirement The amount of money that must be "deposited" to hold a margin position if losses reduce the initial margin that was put up.

Margin requirements The amount of money that must be "deposited" to purchase a commodity contract or shares of stock on margin.

Marital deduction The avoidance of any immediate tax consequence in passing an estate from one spouse to another.

Market A mechanism for facilitating the exchange of assets through buyer-seller com-

munication. The communication, and not a central negotiating location, is the requisite condition for a market to exist, though some transactions (e.g., trades at the various stock exchanges) do involve a direct meeting of buyers and sellers or their agents.

Market capitalization The total market value of the firm. It is computed by multiplying shares outstanding times stock price.

Market line On a graph, excess returns are shown on the vertical axis and the portfolio beta is shown on the horizontal axis and the market line describes the relationship between the two.

Market rate of interest The coupon rate of interest paid on bonds currently issued. Of course, a previously issued bond which is currently traded may be sold at a discount or a premium so that the buyer in effect receives the market rate even if the coupon rate on this older bond is substantially higher or lower than market rates. The market rate is also known as the yield to maturity.

Market segmentation theory A theory related to the term structure of interest rates that focuses on the demand side of the market. There are several large institutional participants in the bond market, each with its own maturity preferences. Banks tend to prefer short-term liquid securities to match the nature of their deposits, whereas life insurance companies prefer long-term bonds to match their long-run obligations. The behavior of these two institutions and of savings and loans often creates pressure on short-term or long-term rates but very little on the intermediate market of five- to seven-year maturities. This theory helps to focus on the accumulation or liquidation of securities by institutions during the different phases of the business cycle and the resultant impact on the yield curve.

Maturity date The date at which outstanding principal must be repaid to bondholders.

Merger price premium The difference between the offering price per share and the market price per share of the merger candidate (before the impact of the offer).

Monetarist An economic analyst who feels that monetary policy tools, and not fiscal policy, can best provide a stable environment of sustained economic growth.

Monetary policy Direct control of interest rates or the money supply undertaken by the Federal Reserve to achieve economic objectives. Used in some cases to augment or offset the use of fiscal policy.

Money market account Accounts offered by financial institutions to compete with money market funds. The minimum deposit is $1,000, with a maximum of three checks drawn per month.

Money market fund A type of mutual fund which invests in short-term government securities, commercial paper, and repurchase agreements. Most offer check-writing privileges in minimums of $500.

Money supply The level of funds available at a given time for conducting transactions in our economy. The Federal Reserve can influence the money supply through its monetary policy tools. There are many different definitions of the money supply. For example, M1 is currency in circulation plus private checking deposits, including those in interest-bearing NOW accounts. M2 adds in savings accounts and money market mutual funds and so on.

Mortgage trust A form of REIT in which long-term loans are made to real estate investors.

Multinational corporations Firms that have operations in a number of foreign countries. Though precise definitions are difficult, a true multinational will probably operate in at least five different countries, with foreign sales equal to at least 40 to 50 percent of total sales. Multinationals are frequently found in such industries as oil, mainframe computers, and banking.

Municipal bonds Tax-exempt debt securities issued by state and local governments (including special political subdivisions).

Mutual fund A type of investment company that pools funds from investors and reinvests them. It is thought of as an open-end investment company because new shares can be sold to investors.

Mutual fund cash position An overall market rule which asserts that by examining the level of uncommitted funds held by large institutional investors, analysts can measure the potential demand for stocks and thereby anticipate market movements.

NASDAQ OTC Indexes Index measures for components of the over-the-counter market. The OTC Indexes are value-weighted.

National Association of Securities Dealers Automated Quotations System (NASDAQ) A computerized system that provides up-to-the-minute price quotations on over 4,000 of the more actively traded OTC stocks.

Net asset value A term often used in reference to the price of a share of a mutual fund. It is equal to the market value of the portfolio minus liabilities divided by the total number of shares outstanding in the fund.

Net debtor-creditor hypothesis Since inflation makes each dollar worth less, it is often argued that a person or firm that is a net debtor gains from inflation because payments of interest and return of principal are made with continually less valuable dollars. Conversely, a net creditor loses real capital because the loans are repaid in less valuable dollars.

Net working capital Current assets minus current liabilities.

New York Stock Exchange Index A market value-weighted measure of stock market changes for all stocks listed on the NYSE.

No-load mutual fund A mutual fund on which no sales commission must be paid. The funds' shares are sold, not through brokers but rather through the mail or other direct channels.

Nominal GNP Gross national product expressed in current, noninflation adjusted dollars.

Nominal return A return that has not been adjusted for inflation.

Nonconstant growth model A dividend valuation model that does not assume a constant growth rate for dividends.

Noncontributory pension plan An arrangement in which only the employer contributes to the pension plan. It is noncontributory for the employee.

Odd-lot dealer A member of a stock exchange who maintains an inventory of a particular firm's stock in order to sell odd lots (trades of less than 100 shares) to customers of the exchange.

Odd-lot theory The contrary opinion rule stating that small traders (who generally buy or sell odd lots) often misjudge market trends, selling just before upturns and buying before downturns. The theory has not been useful in predicting trends observed in recent years.

One hundred seventy-five percent declining-balance depreciation An accelerated depreciation method which represents the most rapid write-off of depreciation allowable on real estate (over 18 years) under the 1981 Economic Recovery Tax Act. In the IRS tables there is also an assumed shift to straight-line in the mid-life of the asset.

Open-end fund An investment company without a specified number of shares for trading; new shares can be created for new investors. It is called a mutual fund. See **Closed-end fund.**

Open-market operations The Federal Reserve's action of buying or selling government securities in order to expand or contract the amount of money in the economy.

Opening purchase transaction A transaction in which an investor intends to become the holder of an option.

Opening sale transaction A transaction in which an investor intends to be a writer of an option.

Operating margin Operating income divided by sales.

Option The right acquired for a consideration

to buy or sell something at a fixed price within a specified period of time.

Option premium The intrinsic value plus a speculative premium.

Option price The specified price at which the holder of a warrant may buy the shares to which the warrant entitles purchase.

Options Clearing Corporation Issues all options listed on the exchanges which trade in options.

Options on industry indexes An option index contract specifically tailored to a given industry. Thus, one who wishes to speculate on a given industry's performance or hedge against holdings in that industry can use industry index options (subindexes). Contracts apply to the S&P Computer and Business Equipment Index, the S&P Integrated International Oil Index, the S&P Transportation Index, and to many other industries.

Options on stock index futures An *option* to purchase a stock index *futures* contract at a specified price over a given time period. This security combines the options concept with the futures concept.

Organized exchanges Institutions, such as the New York Stock Exchange, the American Stock Exchange, or any of the smaller regional exchanges, that provide a central location for the buying and selling of securities.

OTC National Market System A segment of the OTC stock market made up of stocks that have a diversified geographical stockholder base and relatively large activity in their securities. Stocks in the National Market system receive enhanced market activity reporting through the NASDAQ system.

Overall market rules Guidelines, such as breadth of market indicators or mutual fund cash positions, used by technical analysts who predict stock market activity based on past activity.

Over-the-counter market Not a specific location but rather a communications network through which trades of bonds, nonlisted stocks, and other securities take place. Trad-

ing activity is overseen by the National Association of Securities Dealers (NASD).

Par bonds Bonds that are selling at their par or maturity values rather than at premium or discounted prices. Par value on a corporate bond is generally $1,000.

Par value (bond) The face value of a bond, generally $1,000 for corporate issues, higher denominations for government issues.

Partial hedge A hedge position in which only part of the risk is eliminated or lessened.

Payout ratio Annual dividends per share divided by annual earnings per share.

Peak The point in an economic cycle at which expansion ends and a recession begins.

Perpetual bond A bond with no maturity date.

Personal savings/personal disposable income The rate at which people are saving their disposable income. This has implications for the generation of funds to modernize plant and equipment and increase productivity.

Portfolio The term applied to a collection of securities or investments.

Portfolio effect The effect obtained when assets are combined into a portfolio. The interaction of the assets can provide risk reduction such that the portfolio standard deviation may be less than the standard deviation of any one asset in it.

Portfolio manager One who has responsibility for managing large pools of funds. Portfolio managers may be employed by insurance companies, mutual funds, bank trust departments, pension funds, and other institutional investors.

Preferred stock A hybrid security that generally provides fixed returns. Preferred stockholders are paid returns after bondholder claims are satisfied but before any returns are paid to common stockholders. Though preferred stock returns are fixed in amount, they are classified as dividends (not interest) and are not tax-deductible to the issuing firm.

Price/earnings ratio The multiplier applied to earnings per share to determine current

value. The P/E ratio is influenced by the earnings and sales growth of the firm, the risk or volatility of its performance, the debt-equity structure, and other factors.

Price ratios Ratios that relate the internal performance of the firm to the external judgment of the marketplace in terms of value.

Price-weighted average Each stock in the average is weighted by its price. The higher the price, the greater the relative weighting. The Dow Jones Industrials Average represents a price-weighted average.

Primary earnings per share A firm's adjusted earnings after taxes divided by the number of shares of common stock outstanding plus common stock equivalents. Common stock equivalents include warrants and other options along with convertible securities that are paying low returns at time of issue compared to other comparable securities.

Primary market A market in which an investor purchases an asset (via an investment banker) from the issuer of that asset. The purchase of newly issued shares of corporate stock is an example of primary market activity. Subsequent transfers of the particular asset take place in the secondary market. Also see the definition for **Secondary market.**

Private pension plans Nongovernment-sponsored pension plans. About 60 percent of nongovernmental employees are covered by a private pension plan.

Private placement The company sells its securities to private investors such as insurance companies, pension funds, etc. rather than through the public markets. Investment bankers may also aid in a private placement on a fee basis. Most private placements involve debt rather than common stock.

Profitability ratios Ratios that allow the analyst to measure the ability of the firm to earn an adequate return on sales, total assets, and invested capital.

Prospectus A document that must accompany a new issue of securities. It contains the same information appearing in the registration statement, such as a list of directors and officers, financial reports certified by a CPA, the underwriters, the purpose and use for the funds, and other reasonable information that investors need to know.

Public placement Public distribution of securities through the financial markets.

Pure bond value The fundamental value of a bond that represents a floor price below which the bond's value should not fall. The pure bond value is computed as the present value of all future interest payments added to the present value of the bond principal.

Pure pickup yield swap A bond swap where a bond owner thinks that he or she can increase the yield to maturity by selling a bond and buying a different bond of equal risk. This implies market disequilibrium.

Put An option to sell 100 shares of common stock at a specified price for a given period of time.

Qualified pension plan Under the provisions of the Internal Revenue Service, a qualified pension plan allows the employer to deduct annual contributions to the pension plan as a tax-deductible item. From the employees' perspective, a qualified plan allows funds in the plan to earn income without immediate taxation, and no tax is paid on the employer's contribution until benefits are received. A qualified pension plan must meet the appropriate requirements established under ERISA.

Quick ratio Current assets minus inventory (i.e., cash, marketable securities, and accounts receivables) divided by current liabilities.

R^2 The coefficient of determination. It measures the degree of association between the independent variable(s) and the dependent variable. It may take on a value anywhere between 0 and 1.

Real asset A tangible piece of property that may be seen, felt, held, or collected, such as real estate, gold, diamonds, etc.

Real estate investment trust (REIT) An organization similar to a mutual fund where investors pool funds that are invested in real

estate or used to make construction or mortgage loans.

Real GNP Gross national product expressed in dollars that have been adjusted for inflation.

Real rate of return The return that investors require for allowing others to use their money for a given time period. This is the value that investors demand for passing up immediate consumption and allowing others to use their savings until the funds are returned. Because the term *real* is employed, this means it is a value determined *before* inflation is added.

Recaptured depreciation When accelerated depreciation is taken and then the property is sold, part of the profit may be considered recaptured depreciation for tax purposes. It is taxed as ordinary income.

Registered trader A member of a stock exchange who trades for his or her own account rather than for the client of a brokerage firm.

Reinvestment assumption with bonds The assumed rate of reinvestment for inflows from a bond investment. It is normally assumed that inflows can be reinvested at the yield to maturity of the bond. This, however, may not be valid. Interest rates may go up or down as inflows from coupon payments come in and need to be reinvested. A more valid approach is to assign appropriate reinvestment rates to inflows and then determine how much the total investment will be worth at the end of a given time period. This process is known as terminal wealth analysis.

Reported income versus adjusted earnings Reported income is generally based on historical cost accounting, whereas adjusted earnings have been modified for the effect of inflation (on inventory and plant and equipment).

Reserve requirements Percentages of bank deposit balances stipulated by the Federal Reserve as unavailable for lending. By increasing or reducing reserve requirements, the Fed can contract or expand the money supply.

Resistance level The technical analyst's view that as long as a given long-term trend continues, prices of a particular stock or of the market as a whole will not rise above the upper end of the normal trading range (the resistance level) because at that point investors sell in an attempt to get even or take a profit.

Return on equity Net income divided by stockholders' equity.

Revenue bond A municipal bond supported by the revenue from a specific project, such as a toll road, bridge, or municipal colosseum.

Revocable trust The creator may eventually dissolve the trust and take back the property.

Risk Uncertainty concerning the outcome of an investment or other situation. It is often defined as variability of returns from an investment. The greater the range of possible outcomes, the greater the risk.

Risk-adjusted return The amount of return after adjustment for the level of risk incurred to achieve the return.

Risk-free rate The required rate of return before risk is explicitly considered. It is composed of the real rate of return plus a rate equivalent to inflationary expectations. It is referred to as R_F.

Risk premium A premium assumed to be paid to an investor for the risk inherent in an investment. It is added to the risk-free rate to get the overall required return on an investment.

Secondary market A market in which an investor purchases an asset from another investor rather than the issuing corporation. The activity of secondary markets sets prices and provides liquidity. Also see **Primary market.**

Secured bond A bond which is collateralized by the pledging of assets.

Securities Act of 1933 Enacted by Congress to curtail abuses by securities issuers, the law requires full disclosure of pertinent investment information and provides for penalties to officers of firms that do not comply.

Securities Acts Amendments of 1975 Enacted to increase competition in the securities markets, this legislation prohibits fixed commissions on public offerings of securities and

directs the Securities and Exchange Commission to develop a single, nationwide securities market.

Securities and Exchange Commission (SEC) The federal government agency created in 1934 to enforce securities laws. Issuers of securities must register detailed reports with the SEC, and the SEC polices such activities as insider trading, investor conspiracies, and the functionings of the securities exchanges.

Securities Exchange Act of 1934 Created the Securities and Exchange Commission to regulate the securities markets. The act further empowers the Board of Governors of the Federal Reserve System to control margin requirements.

Securities Investor Protection Corporation Created under the Securities Investor Protection Act of 1970, this agency oversees the liquidation of insolvent brokerage firms and provides insurance on investors' trading accounts.

Security analyst One who studies various industries and companies and provides research reports and valuation studies.

Security market line The graphic representation of risk (as measured by beta) and return for an individual security.

Selling short against the box A short sale of securities with the objective of deferring the payment of taxes. This requires a short sale against shares already owned so that shares owned are delivered to cover the short position as the transaction is completed.

Semi-strong form of efficient market hypothesis The hypothesis states that all public information is already impounded into the value of a security.

Serial bond A mechanism for repaying funds advanced through a bond issue. Regular payments systematically retire individual bonds with increasing maturities until, after many years, the entire series has been repaid.

Settle price The term for the closing price on futures contracts.

Shared appreciation mortgage A type of mortgage in which the lender participates in any increase in value associated with the property being mortgaged.

Sharpe Measure of Portfolio Performance Total portfolio return minus the risk-free rate divided by the portfolio standard deviation. It allows the portfolio manager to view his or her excess returns in relation to total risk. Comparisons between various portfolios can be made based on this relative risk measure.

Short position (short sale) A market transaction in which an investor sells borrowed securities in anticipation of a price decline. The investor's expectation is that the securities can be repurchased (to replace the borrowed shares) at a lower price in the future. Also see the definition for **Long position.**

Short sales position theory The contrary opinion rule stating that large volumes of short sales can signal an impending market upturn because short sales must be covered and thereby create their own demand. Also, the average short seller is often thought to be wrong.

Short-term gains and losses Gains and losses on securities held for six months or less. The stockholders' ordinary marginal tax rate applies.

Sinking fund A mechanism for repaying funds advanced through a bond issue. The issuer makes periodic payments to the trustee, who retires part of the issue by purchasing the bonds in the open market.

Small-firm effect A market theory that suggests that small firms produce superior returns compared to larger firms on both an absolute and risk-adjusted basis.

Smart money rules Guidelines, such as *Barron's* Confidence Index, used by technical analysts who predict stock market activity based on the assumption that sophisticated investors will correctly predict market trends and that their lead should be followed. Also see **Contrary opinion rules.**

Sources-and-uses-of-funds statement A

presentation of how changes in the balance sheet were financed over a period of time. Sources of funds include increases in stockholders' equity, decreases in assets, and increases in liabilities. Uses are represented by decreases in stockholders' equity, increases in assets, and decreases in liabilities.

Specialist or dealer hedge A specialist on an exchange or dealer in the over-the-counter market buys and sells stocks for his own inventory for temporary holding (as part of his market making function). At times, he may assume a larger temporary holding than desired with all the risks associated with that exposure. Stock index futures or options can reduce the market, or systematic, risk, although they cannot reduce the specific risk associated with a security.

Speculative premium The difference between an option or warrant's price and its intrinsic value. That an investor would pay something in excess of the intrinsic value indicates a speculative desire to hold the security in anticipation of future increases in the price of the underlying stock.

Spot market The term applied to the cash price for immediate transfer of a commodity as opposed to the futures market where no physical transfer takes place immediately.

Spreads A combination of options which consists of buying one option (going long) and writing an option (going short) on the same stock.

Standard & Poor's 500 Stock Index An index of 500 major U.S. Corporations. There are 400 industrial firms, 20 transportation firms, 40 utilities, and 40 financial firms. This index is value-weighted.

Standard & Poor's 400 Industrial Index An index which measures price movements in the stocks of 400 large industrial corporations listed on the New York Stock Exchange.

Standard & Poor's International Oil Index A value-weighted index of six oil firms. Options on the index have been traded on the Chicago Board Options Exchange.

Standard deviation A measure of dispersion that considers the spread of outcomes around the expected value.

Stock dividend A dividend paid by issuing more stock which results in retained earnings being capitalized.

Stock index futures A futures contract on a specific stock index, such as the Standard & Poor's 500 Stock Index or the NYSE Composite Index.

Stock index options An option contract to purchase (call) or sell (put) a stock index. Popular contracts include the S&P 100 Index, the American Exchange Major Market Index, and others. The purchaser of a stock index option pays an initial premium and then closes out the option at a given price in the future.

Stock repurchase A purchase by a firm of its own shares in the marketplace.

Stock split The result of a firm dividing its shares into more shares with a corresponding decrease in par value.

Stop order A mechanism for locking in gains or limiting losses on securities transactions. The investor is not assured of paying or receiving a particular price but rather agrees to accept the price prevailing when the broker is able to execute the order after prices have reached some predetermined figure.

Straddle A combination of a put and call on the same stock with the same strike price and expiration date.

Straight-line depreciation A method of depreciation in which the project cost is divided by the project life to calculate each year's depreciation amount.

Strong form of the efficient market hypothesis A hypothesis that says that all information, insider as well as public, is reflected in the price of a security.

Support level The technical analyst's view that as long as a given long-term trend continues, prices of a particular stock or of the market as a whole will not fall below the lower end of normal trading range (the sup-

port level) because at that point low prices stimulate demand.

Swaps The procedure of selling out of a given bond position and immediately buying into another one with similar attributes in an attempt to improve overall portfolio return or performance.

Syndicate A group of investment bankers which jointly shares the underwriting and distribution responsibilities in a large offering of new securities. Each participant is responsible for a predetermined sales volume. One or a few firms serve as the managing underwriters.

Synergy A more than proportionate increase in performance from the combination of two or more parts.

Systematic risk Risk inherent in an investment related to movements in the market that cannot be diversified away.

Tax hedge An investor may have accumulated a large return on a diversified portfolio in a given year. In order to maintain the profitable position, but defer the taxable gains until the next year, stock index future or options contracts may be employed. Of course, for individual securities, individual stock options may be used when available.

Tax swaps Selling out of one bond position and buying into a similar one in order to take advantage of a tax situation. For example, one might sell a bond that has a short-term capital loss in order to take the deduction, and replace it with a similar bond.

Technical analysis An analysis of price and volume data as well as other related market indicators to determine past trends that are believed to be predictable into the future. Charts and graphs are often utilized.

Term structure of interest rates This depicts the relationship between maturity and interest rates for a 20- to 25-year time horizon.

Terminal wealth table A table that indicates the ending or terminal wealth from a bond investment based on the reinvestment of the inflows at a specified rate (which may be different from the coupon rate). The initial investment can then be compared to the terminal wealth (compound interest plus principal) and an overall rate of return computed.

Testamentary trust A trust created by a will.

Third market The trading between dealers and institutional investors, through the over-the-counter market, of NYSE-listed stocks. The third market accounts for an extremely small share of total trading activity.

Trading range The spread of prices that a stock normally sells within.

Treasury bill A short-term U.S. government obligation. A Treasury bill is purchased at a discount and is negotiable.

Treasury bond A long-term (7 to 25 years) U.S. government bond.

Treasury note An intermediate-term (one to seven years) U.S. government bond.

Treasury stock Stock issued but not outstanding by virtue of being held (after it is repurchased) by the firm.

Trend analysis Comparative analysis of performance over time.

Treynor Measure of Portfolio Performance Total portfolio return minus the risk-free rate divided by the portfolio beta. Unlike the Sharpe Measure, which uses the portfolio standard deviation in the denominator, the risk measure here is the beta, or systematic risk. It enables the portfolio manager to view his or her excess returns in relation to non-diversifiable risk. The assumption is that all other types of risk have been diversified away. Once computed, the Treynor Measure allows for comparisons between different portfolios.

Trough The point in an economic cycle at which recession ends and expansion begins.

Trust A legal entity in which transfer of ownership of property from an original owner (the creator of the trust) to another person (the trustee) takes place for the benefit of someone else (the beneficiary).

Underpricing In selling formerly privately held shares to new investors in the over-the-counter market, the price might not fully reflect the value of the issue. Underpricing is

used to attempt to ensure the success of the initial distribution.

Underwriter hedge A hedge, based on stock index futures or options contracts, used to offset the risk exposure associated with the underwriting of new securities by an investment banker. If the market goes down, presumably the loss on the stock being underwritten will be compensated for by the gain on the stock index futures or option contract as a result of being able to repurchase it at a lower price. This, of course, is not a perfect hedge. It is possible that the stock could go down while the market is going up, and losses on both the stock and stock index contract would take place (writing options directly against the stock may be more efficient, but in many cases such options are not available).

Unfriendly takeover A merger or acquisition in which the firm acquired does not wish to be acquired.

Unfunded pension plan Payments to retirees are made out of current income and not out of prior funding.

Unified tax credit A credit against the estate and gift tax. Under the 1981 Economic Recovery Tax Act, the credit goes from $47,000 in 1981 to $192,800 in 1987. In 1987, this will provide an equivalent exemption of $600,000 for estate taxes.

Unified tax rate schedule The schedule applied to estate and gift taxes on a unified basis.

Unseasoned issue An issue that has not been formerly traded in the public markets.

Unsystematic risk Risk of an investment that is random in nature. It is not related to general market movements. It may represent the temporary influence of a competitor's new product, changes in raw material prices, or unusual economic or government influences on a firm. It may generally be diversified away.

Valuation The process of attributing a value to a security based on expectations of the future performance of the issuing concern, the relevant industry, and the economy as a whole.

Valuation model A representation of the components that provide the value of an investment, such as a dividend valuation model used to show the value of a common stock.

Value Line Index The index represents 1,700 companies from the New York and American Stock Exchanges and the over-the-counter market. Many individual investors use the Value Line Index because it more closely corresponds to the variety of stocks the average investor may have in his or her portfolio. It is an equal-weighted index, which means that each of the 1,700 stocks, regardless of market price, or total market value, is weighted equally.

Value-weighted index Each company in the index is weighted by its own total market value as a percentage of the total market value for all firms in the index. Most major indexes, such as the S&P 500, S&P 400, the NYSE Index, and the American Exchange Market Value Index, are value-weighted. With value-weighted indexes, large firms tend to be weighted more heavily than smaller firms.

Variability The possible different outcomes of an event. As an example, an investment with many possible different levels of return would have great variability.

Variable rate mortgage A mortgage in which the interest rate is adjusted regularly.

Vertical spread Buying and writing two contracts at different striking prices with the same month of expiration.

Vesting A legal term meaning that pension benefits or rights cannot be taken away.

Warrant A right or option to buy a stated number of shares of stock at a specified price over a given time period. It is usually of longer duration than a call option.

Warrant break-even The price movement in the underlying stock necessary for the warrant purchaser to break-even, that is, recover the initial purchase price of the warrant.

Weak form of efficient market hypothesis A hypothesis suggesting there is no relation-

ship between past and future prices of securities.

White knight A firm that "rescues" another firm from an unfriendly takeover by a third firm.

Wiesenberger Financial Services An advisory service that provides important information on mutual funds.

Wilshire 5,000 Equity Index A stock market measure comprising 5,000 equity securities. It includes all New York Stock Exchange and American Stock Exchange issues and the most active over-the-counter issues. The index represents the *total dollar value* of all 5,000 stocks. By measuring total dollar value, it is, in effect, a value-weighted measure.

World Index A value-weighted index of the performance in 19 major countries as compiled by Capital International, S.A., of Geneva, Switzerland. The United States alone makes up approximately 50 percent of the index because it is value-weighted by market size.

Yield curve A curve that shows interest rates at a specific point in time for all securities having equal risk but different maturity dates. Usually, government securities are used to construct such curves. The yield curve is also referred to as the term structure of interest rates.

Yield spread The difference between the yields received on two different types of bonds, or bonds with different ratings. It is important to investment strategy because during periods of economic uncertainty, spreads increase because investors demand larger premiums on risky issues to compensate for the greater chance of default.

Yield to call The interest yield that will be realized on a callable bond if it is held from a given purchase date until the date when it can be called by the issuer. The yield to call reflects the fact that lower overall returns may be realized if the issuer avoids some later payments by retiring the bonds early.

Yield to maturity The annualized rate of return that an investor will receive if a bond is held until its maturity date. It is the market rate of return. The yield-to-maturity formula includes any capital gains or losses that arise because the par value is greater or less than the current market price.

Ying, Lewellen, Schlarbaum, and Lease study A research study that indicates there may be an opportunity for abnormal returns on a risk-adjusted basis in the many weeks between announcement of listing and actual listing of a security.

Zero-coupon bonds Bonds that are designed to pay no interest, in which the return to the investor is in the form of capital appreciation over the life of the issue.

APPENDIXES

APPENDIX A

Compound sum of $1

Period	1%	2%	3%	4%	5%	6%	7%	8%	9%	10%	11%
1	1.010	1.020	1.030	1.040	1.050	1.060	1.070	1.080	1.090	1.100	1.110
2	1.020	1.040	1.061	1.082	1.103	1.124	1.145	1.166	1.188	1.210	1.232
3	1.030	1.061	1.093	1.125	1.158	1.191	1.225	1.260	1.295	1.331	1.368
4	1.041	1.082	1.126	1.170	1.216	1.262	1.311	1.360	1.412	1.464	1.518
5	1.051	1.104	1.159	1.217	1.276	1.338	1.403	1.469	1.539	1.611	1.685
6	1.062	1.126	1.194	1.265	1.340	1.419	1.501	1.587	1.677	1.772	1.870
7	1.072	1.149	1.230	1.316	1.407	1.504	1.606	1.714	1.828	1.949	2.076
8	1.083	1.172	1.267	1.369	1.477	1.594	1.718	1.851	1.993	2.144	2.305
9	1.094	1.195	1.305	1.423	1.551	1.689	1.838	1.999	2.172	2.358	2.558
10	1.105	1.219	1.344	1.480	1.629	1.791	1.967	2.159	2.367	2.594	2.839
11	1.116	1.243	1.384	1.539	1.710	1.898	2.105	2.332	2.580	2.853	3.152
12	1.127	1.268	1.426	1.601	1.796	2.012	2.252	2.518	2.813	3.138	3.498
13	1.138	1.294	1.469	1.665	1.886	2.133	2.410	2.720	3.066	3.452	3.883
14	1.149	1.319	1.513	1.732	1.980	2.261	2.579	2.937	3.342	3.797	4.310
15	1.161	1.346	1.558	1.801	2.079	2.397	2.759	3.172	3.642	4.177	4.785
16	1.173	1.373	1.605	1.873	2.183	2.540	2.952	3.426	3.970	4.595	5.311
17	1.184	1.400	1.653	1.948	2.292	2.693	3.159	3.700	4.328	5.054	5.895
18	1.196	1.428	1.702	2.026	2.407	2.854	3.380	3.996	4.717	5.560	6.544
19	1.208	1.457	1.754	2.107	2.527	3.026	3.617	4.316	5.142	6.116	7.263
20	1.220	1.486	1.806	2.191	2.653	3.207	3.870	4.661	5.604	6.727	8.062
25	1.282	1.641	2.094	2.666	3.386	4.292	5.427	6.848	8.623	10.835	13.585
30	1.348	1.811	2.427	3.243	4.322	5.743	7.612	10.063	13.268	17.449	22.892
40	1.489	2.208	3.262	4.801	7.040	10.286	14.974	21.725	31.409	45.259	65.001
50	1.645	2.692	4.384	7.107	11.467	18.420	29.457	46.902	74.358	117.39	184.57

APPENDIX A (concluded)

Compound sum of $1

Percent

Period	12%	13%	14%	15%	16%	17%	18%	19%	20%	25%	30%
1	1.120	1.130	1.140	1.150	1.160	1.170	1.180	1.190	1.200	1.250	1.300
2	1.254	1.277	1.300	1.323	1.346	1.369	1.392	1.416	1.440	1.563	1.690
3	1.405	1.443	1.482	1.521	1.561	1.602	1.643	1.685	1.728	1.953	2.197
4	1.574	1.630	1.689	1.749	1.811	1.874	1.939	2.005	2.074	2.441	2.856
5	1.762	1.842	1.925	2.011	2.100	2.192	2.288	2.386	2.488	3.052	3.713
6	1.974	2.082	2.195	2.313	2.436	2.565	2.700	2.840	2.986	3.815	4.827
7	2.211	2.353	2.502	2.660	2.826	3.001	3.185	3.379	3.583	4.768	6.276
8	2.476	2.658	2.853	3.059	3.278	3.511	3.759	4.021	4.300	5.960	8.157
9	2.773	3.004	3.252	3.518	3.803	4.108	4.435	4.785	5.160	7.451	10.604
10	3.106	3.395	3.707	4.046	4.411	4.807	5.234	5.696	6.192	9.313	13.786
11	3.479	3.836	4.226	4.652	5.117	5.624	6.176	6.777	7.430	11.642	17.922
12	3.896	4.335	4.818	5.350	5.936	6.580	7.288	8.064	8.916	14.552	23.298
13	4.363	4.898	5.492	6.153	6.886	7.699	8.599	9.596	10.699	18.190	30.288
14	4.887	5.535	6.261	7.076	7.988	9.007	10.147	11.420	12.839	22.737	39.374
15	5.474	6.254	7.138	8.137	9.266	10.539	11.974	13.590	15.407	28.422	51.186
16	6.130	7.067	8.137	9.358	10.748	12.330	14.129	16.172	18.488	35.527	66.542
17	6.866	7.986	9.276	10.761	12.468	14.426	16.672	19.244	22.186	44.409	86.504
18	7.690	9.024	10.575	12.375	14.463	16.879	19.673	22.091	26.623	55.511	112.46
19	8.613	10.197	12.056	14.232	16.777	19.748	23.214	27.252	31.948	69.389	146.19
20	9.646	11.523	13.743	16.367	19.461	23.106	27.393	32.429	38.338	86.736	190.05
25	17.000	21.231	26.462	32.919	40.874	50.658	62.669	77.388	95.396	264.70	705.64
30	29.960	39.116	50.950	66.212	85.850	111.07	143.37	184.68	237.38	807.79	2,620.0
40	93.051	132.78	188.88	267.86	378.72	533.87	750.38	1,051.7	1,469.8	7,523.2	36,119.
50	289.00	450.74	700.23	1,083.7	1,670.7	2,566.2	3,927.4	5,988.9	9,100.4	70,065.	497,929.

Source: Maurice Joy, *Introduction to Financial Management* (Homewood, Ill.: Richard D. Irwin, Inc. 1977).

APPENDIX B

Present value of $1

						Percent						
Period	1%	2%	3%	4%	5%	6%	7%	8%	9%	10%	11%	12%
1	0.990	0.980	0.971	0.962	0.952	0.943	0.935	0.926	0.917	0.909	0.901	0.893
2	0.980	0.961	0.943	0.925	0.907	0.890	0.873	0.857	0.842	0.826	0.812	0.797
3	0.971	0.942	0.915	0.889	0.864	0.840	0.816	0.794	0.772	0.751	0.731	0.712
4	0.961	0.924	0.885	0.855	0.823	0.792	0.763	0.735	0.708	0.683	0.659	0.636
5	0.951	0.906	0.863	0.822	0.784	0.747	0.713	0.681	0.650	0.621	0.593	0.567
6	0.942	0.888	0.837	0.790	0.746	0.705	0.666	0.630	0.596	0.564	0.535	0.507
7	0.933	0.871	0.813	0.760	0.711	0.665	0.623	0.583	0.547	0.513	0.482	0.452
8	0.923	0.853	0.789	0.731	0.677	0.627	0.582	0.540	0.502	0.467	0.434	0.404
9	0.914	0.837	0.766	0.703	0.645	0.592	0.544	0.500	0.460	0.424	0.391	0.361
10	0.905	0.820	0.744	0.676	0.614	0.558	0.508	0.463	0.422	0.386	0.352	0.322
11	0.896	0.804	0.722	0.650	0.585	0.527	0.475	0.429	0.388	0.350	0.317	0.287
12	0.887	0.788	0.701	0.625	0.557	0.497	0.444	0.397	0.356	0.319	0.286	0.257
13	0.879	0.773	0.681	0.601	0.530	0.469	0.415	0.368	0.326	0.290	0.258	0.229
14	0.870	0.758	0.661	0.577	0.505	0.442	0.388	0.340	0.299	0.263	0.232	0.205
15	0.861	0.743	0.642	0.555	0.481	0.417	0.362	0.315	0.275	0.239	0.209	0.183
16	0.853	0.728	0.623	0.534	0.458	0.394	0.339	0.292	0.252	0.218	0.188	0.163
17	0.844	0.714	0.605	0.513	0.436	0.371	0.317	0.270	0.231	0.198	0.170	0.146
18	0.836	0.700	0.587	0.494	0.416	0.350	0.296	0.250	0.212	0.180	0.153	0.130
19	0.828	0.686	0.570	0.475	0.396	0.331	0.277	0.232	0.194	0.164	0.138	0.116
20	0.820	0.673	0.554	0.456	0.377	0.312	0.258	0.215	0.178	0.149	0.124	0.104
25	0.780	0.610	0.478	0.375	0.295	0.233	0.184	0.146	0.116	0.092	0.074	0.059
30	0.742	0.552	0.412	0.308	0.231	0.174	0.131	0.099	0.075	0.057	0.044	0.033
40	0.672	0.453	0.307	0.208	0.142	0.097	0.067	0.046	0.032	0.022	0.015	0.011
50	0.608	0.372	0.228	0.141	0.087	0.054	0.034	0.021	0.013	0.009	0.005	0.003

APPENDIX B (concluded)

Present value of $1

Percent

Period	13%	14%	15%	16%	17%	18%	19%	20%	25%	30%	35%	40%	50%
1	0.885	0.877	0.870	0.862	0.855	0.847	0.840	0.833	0.800	0.769	0.741	0.714	0.667
2	0.783	0.769	0.756	0.743	0.731	0.718	0.706	0.694	0.640	0.592	0.549	0.510	0.444
3	0.693	0.675	0.658	0.641	0.624	0.609	0.593	0.579	0.512	0.455	0.406	0.364	0.296
4	0.613	0.592	0.572	0.552	0.534	0.515	0.499	0.482	0.410	0.350	0.301	0.260	0.198
5	0.543	0.519	0.497	0.476	0.456	0.437	0.419	0.402	0.320	0.269	0.223	0.186	0.132
6	0.480	0.456	0.432	0.410	0.390	0.370	0.352	0.335	0.262	0.207	0.165	0.133	0.088
7	0.425	0.400	0.376	0.354	0.333	0.314	0.296	0.279	0.210	0.159	0.122	0.095	0.059
8	0.376	0.351	0.327	0.305	0.285	0.266	0.249	0.233	0.168	0.123	0.091	0.068	0.039
9	0.333	0.300	0.284	0.263	0.243	0.225	0.209	0.194	0.134	0.094	0.067	0.048	0.026
10	0.295	0.270	0.247	0.227	0.208	0.191	0.176	0.162	0.107	0.073	0.050	0.035	0.017
11	0.261	0.237	0.215	0.195	0.178	0.162	0.148	0.135	0.086	0.056	0.037	0.025	0.012
12	0.231	0.208	0.187	0.168	0.152	0.137	0.124	0.112	0.069	0.043	0.027	0.018	0.008
13	0.204	0.182	0.163	0.145	0.130	0.116	0.104	0.093	0.055	0.033	0.020	0.013	0.005
14	0.181	0.160	0.141	0.125	0.111	0.099	0.088	0.078	0.044	0.025	0.015	0.009	0.003
15	0.160	0.140	0.123	0.108	0.095	0.084	0.074	0.065	0.035	0.020	0.011	0.006	0.002
16	0.141	0.123	0.107	0.093	0.081	0.071	0.062	0.054	0.028	0.015	0.008	0.005	0.002
17	0.125	0.108	0.093	0.080	0.069	0.060	0.052	0.045	0.023	0.012	0.006	0.003	0.001
18	0.111	0.095	0.081	0.069	0.059	0.051	0.044	0.038	0.018	0.009	0.005	0.002	0.001
19	0.098	0.083	0.070	0.060	0.051	0.043	0.037	0.031	0.014	0.007	0.003	0.002	0
20	0.087	0.073	0.061	0.051	0.043	0.037	0.031	0.026	0.012	0.005	0.002	0.001	0
25	0.047	0.038	0.030	0.024	0.020	0.016	0.013	0.010	0.004	0.001	0.001	0	0
30	0.026	0.020	0.015	0.012	0.009	0.007	0.005	0.004	0.001	0	0	0	0
40	0.008	0.005	0.004	0.003	0.002	0.001	0.001	0.001	0	0	0	0	0
50	0.002	0.001	0.001	0.001	0	0	0	0	0	0	0	0	0

Source: Maurice Joy, *Introduction to Financial Management* (Homewood, Ill.: Richard D. Irwin, Inc. 1977).

APPENDIX C

Compound sum of an annuity of $1

Percent

Period	1%	2%	3%	4%	5%	6%	7%	8%	9%	10%	11%
1	1.000	1.000	1.000	1.000	1.000	1.000	1.000	1.000	1.000	1.000	1.000
2	2.010	2.020	2.030	2.040	2.050	2.060	2.070	2.080	2.090	2.100	2.110
3	3.030	3.060	3.091	3.122	3.153	3.184	3.215	3.246	3.278	3.310	3.342
4	4.060	4.122	4.184	4.246	4.310	4.375	4.440	4.506	4.573	4.641	4.710
5	5.101	5.204	5.309	5.416	5.526	5.637	5.751	5.867	5.985	6.105	6.228
6	6.152	6.308	6.468	6.633	6.802	6.975	7.153	7.336	7.523	7.716	7.913
7	7.214	7.434	7.662	7.898	8.142	8.394	8.654	8.923	9.200	9.487	9.783
8	8.286	8.583	8.892	9.214	9.549	9.897	10.260	10.637	11.028	11.436	11.859
9	9.369	9.755	10.159	10.583	11.027	11.491	11.978	12.488	13.021	13.579	14.164
10	10.462	10.950	11.464	12.006	12.578	13.181	13.816	14.487	15.193	15.937	16.722
11	11.567	12.169	12.808	13.486	14.207	14.972	15.784	16.645	17.560	18.531	19.561
12	12.683	13.412	14.192	15.026	15.917	16.870	17.888	18.977	20.141	21.384	22.713
13	13.809	14.680	15.618	16.627	17.713	18.882	20.141	21.495	22.953	24.523	26.212
14	14.947	15.974	17.086	18.292	19.599	21.015	22.550	24.215	26.019	27.975	30.095
15	16.097	17.293	18.599	20.024	21.579	23.276	25.129	27.152	29.361	31.772	34.405
16	17.258	18.639	20.157	21.825	23.657	25.673	27.888	30.324	33.003	35.950	39.190
17	18.430	20.012	21.762	23.698	25.840	20.213	30.840	33.750	36.974	40.545	44.501
18	19.615	21.412	23.414	25.645	28.132	30.906	33.999	37.450	41.301	45.599	50.396
19	20.811	22.841	25.117	27.671	30.539	33.760	37.379	41.446	46.018	51.159	56.939
20	22.019	24.297	26.870	29.778	33.066	36.786	40.995	45.762	51.160	57.275	64.203
25	28.243	32.030	36.459	41.646	47.727	54.865	63.249	73.106	84.701	98.347	114.41
30	34.785	40.588	47.575	56.085	66.439	79.058	94.461	113.28	136.31	164.49	199.02
40	48.886	60.402	75.401	95.026	120.80	154.76	199.64	259.06	337.89	442.59	581.83
50	64.463	84.579	112.80	152.67	209.35	290.34	406.53	573.77	815.08	1,163.9	1,668.8

APPENDIX C (concluded)

Compound sum of an annuity of $1

Period	12%	13%	14%	15%	16%	17%	18%	19%	20%	25%	30%
Percent											
1	1.000	1.000	1.000	1.000	1.000	1.000	1.000	1.000	1.000	1.000	1.000
2	2.120	2.130	2.140	2.150	2.160	2.170	2.180	2.190	2.200	2.250	2.300
3	3.374	3.407	3.440	3.473	3.506	3.539	3.572	3.606	3.640	3.813	3.990
4	4.779	4.850	4.921	4.993	5.066	5.141	5.215	5.291	5.368	5.766	6.187
5	6.353	6.480	6.610	6.742	6.877	7.014	7.154	7.297	7.442	8.207	9.043
6	8.115	8.323	8.536	9.754	8.977	9.207	9.442	0.683	9.930	11.259	12.756
7	10.089	10.405	10.730	11.067	11.414	11.772	12.142	12.523	12.916	15.073	17.583
8	12.300	12.757	13.233	13.727	14.240	14.773	15.327	15.902	16.499	19.842	23.858
9	14.776	15.416	16.085	16.786	17.519	18.285	19.086	19.923	20.799	25.802	32.015
10	17.549	18.420	19.337	20.304	21.321	22.393	23.521	24.701	25.959	33.253	42.619
11	20.655	21.814	23.045	24.349	25.733	27.200	28.755	30.404	32.150	42.566	56.405
12	24.133	25.650	27.271	29.002	30.850	32.824	34.931	37.180	39.581	54.208	74.327
13	28.029	29.985	32.089	34.352	36.786	39.404	42.219	45.244	48.497	68.760	97.625
14	32.393	34.883	37.581	40.505	43.672	47.103	50.818	54.841	59.196	86.949	127.91
15	37.280	40.417	43.842	47.580	51.660	56.110	60.965	66.261	72.035	109.69	167.29
16	42.753	46.672	50.980	55.717	60.925	66.649	72.939	79.850	87.442	138.11	218.47
17	48.884	53.739	59.118	65.075	71.673	78.979	87.068	96.022	105.93	173.64	285.01
18	55.750	61.725	68.394	75.836	84.141	93.406	103.74	115.27	128.12	218.05	371.52
19	63.440	70.749	78.969	88.212	98.603	110.29	123.41	138.17	154.74	273.56	483.97
20	72.052	80.947	91.025	102.44	115.38	130.03	146.63	165.42	186.69	342.95	630.17
25	133.33	155.62	181.87	212.79	249.21	292.11	342.60	402.04	471.98	1,054.8	2,348.80
30	241.33	293.20	356.79	434.75	530.31	647.44	790.95	966.7	1,181.9	3,227.2	8,730.0
40	767.09	1,013.7	1,342.0	1,779.1	2,360.8	3,134.5	4,163.21	5,529.8	7,343.9	30,089.	120,393.
50	2,400.0	3,459.5	4,994.5	7,217.7	10,436.	15,090.	21,813.	31,515.	45,497.	280,256.	165,976.

Source: Maurice Joy, *Introduction to Financial Management* (Homewood, Ill.: Richard D. Irwin, Inc. 1977).

APPENDIX D

Present value of an annuity of $1

Percent

Period	1%	2%	3%	4%	5%	6%	7%	8%	9%	10%	11%	12%
1	0.990	0.980	0.971	0.962	0.952	0.943	0.935	0.926	0.917	0.909	0.901	0.893
2	1.970	1.942	1.913	1.886	1.859	1.833	1.808	1.783	1.759	1.736	1.713	1.690
3	2.941	2.884	2.829	2.775	2.723	2.673	2.624	2.577	2.531	2.487	2.444	2.402
4	3.902	3.808	3.717	3.630	3.546	3.465	3.387	3.312	3.240	3.170	3.102	3.037
5	4.853	4.713	4.580	4.452	4.329	4.212	4.100	3.993	3.890	3.791	3.696	3.605
6	5.795	5.601	5.417	5.242	5.076	4.917	4.767	4.623	4.486	4.355	4.231	4.111
7	6.728	6.472	6.230	6.002	5.786	5.582	5.389	5.206	5.033	4.868	4.712	4.564
8	7.652	7.325	7.020	6.733	6.463	6.210	5.971	5.747	5.535	5.335	5.146	4.968
9	8.566	8.162	7.786	7.435	7.108	6.802	6.515	6.247	5.995	5.759	5.537	5.328
10	9.471	8.983	8.530	8.111	7.722	7.360	7.024	6.710	6.418	6.145	5.889	5.650
11	10.368	9.787	9.253	8.760	8.306	7.887	7.499	7.139	6.805	6.495	6.207	5.938
12	11.255	10.575	9.954	9.385	8.863	8.384	7.943	7.536	7.161	6.814	6.492	6.194
13	12.134	11.348	10.635	9.986	9.394	8.853	8.358	7.904	7.487	7.103	6.750	6.424
14	13.004	12.106	11.296	10.563	9.899	9.295	8.745	8.244	7.786	7.367	6.982	6.628
15	13.865	12.849	11.939	11.118	10.380	9.712	9.108	8.559	8.061	7.606	7.191	6.811
16	14.718	13.578	12.561	11.652	10.838	10.106	9.447	8.851	8.313	7.824	7.379	6.974
17	15.562	14.292	13.166	12.166	11.274	10.477	9.763	9.122	8.544	8.022	7.549	7.102
18	16.398	14.992	13.754	12.659	11.690	10.828	10.059	9.372	8.756	8.201	7.702	7.250
19	17.226	15.678	14.324	13.134	12.085	11.158	10.336	9.604	8.950	8.365	7.839	7.366
20	18.046	16.351	14.877	13.590	12.462	11.470	10.594	9.818	9.129	8.514	7.963	7.469
25	22.023	19.523	17.413	15.622	14.094	12.783	11.654	10.675	9.823	9.077	8.422	7.843
30	25.808	22.396	19.600	17.292	15.372	13.765	12.409	11.258	10.274	9.427	8.694	8.055
40	32.835	27.355	23.115	19.793	17.159	15.046	13.332	11.925	10.757	9.779	8.951	8.244
50	39.196	31.424	25.730	21.482	18.256	15.762	13.801	12.233	10.962	9.915	9.042	8.304

APPENDIX D (concluded)

Present value of an annuity of $1

Percent

Period	13%	14%	15%	16%	17%	18%	19%	20%	25%	30%	35%	40%	50%
1	0.885	0.877	0.870	0.862	0.855	0.847	0.840	0.833	0.800	0.769	0.741	0.714	0.667
2	1.668	1.647	1.626	1.605	1.585	1.566	1.547	1.528	1.440	1.361	1.289	1.224	1.111
3	2.361	2.322	2.283	2.246	2.210	2.174	2.140	2.106	1.952	1.816	1.696	1.589	1.407
4	2.974	2.914	2.855	2.798	2.743	2.690	2.639	2.589	2.362	2.166	1.997	1.849	1.605
5	3.517	3.433	3.352	3.274	3.199	3.127	3.058	2.991	2.689	2.436	2.220	2.035	1.737
6	3.998	3.889	3.784	3.685	3.589	3.498	3.410	3.326	2.951	2.643	2.385	2.168	1.824
7	4.423	4.288	4.160	4.039	3.922	3.812	3.706	3.605	3.161	2.802	2.508	2.263	1.883
8	4.799	4.639	4.487	4.344	4.207	4.078	3.954	3.837	3.329	2.925	2.598	2.331	1.922
9	5.132	4.946	4.772	4.607	4.451	4.303	4.163	4.031	3.463	3.019	2.665	2.379	1.948
10	5.426	5.216	5.019	4.833	4.659	4.494	4.339	4.192	3.571	3.092	2.715	2.414	1.965
11	5.687	5.453	5.234	5.029	4.836	4.656	4.486	4.327	3.656	3.147	2.752	2.438	1.977
12	5.918	5.660	5.421	5.197	4.988	4.793	4.611	4.439	3.725	3.190	2.779	2.456	1.985
13	6.122	5.842	5.583	5.342	5.118	4.910	4.715	4.533	3.780	3.223	2.799	2.469	1.990
14	6.302	6.002	5.724	5.468	5.229	5.008	4.802	4.611	3.824	3.249	2.814	2.478	1.993
15	6.462	6.142	5.847	5.575	5.324	5.092	4.876	4.675	3.859	3.268	2.825	2.484	1.995
16	6.604	6.265	5.954	5.668	5.405	5.162	4.938	4.730	3.887	3.283	2.834	2.489	1.997
17	6.729	6.373	6.047	5.749	5.475	5.222	4.988	4.775	3.910	3.295	2.840	2.492	1.998
18	6.840	6.467	6.128	5.818	5.534	5.273	5.033	4.812	3.928	3.304	2.844	2.494	1.999
19	6.938	6.550	6.198	5.877	5.584	5.316	5.070	4.843	3.942	3.311	2.848	2.496	1.999
20	7.025	6.623	6.259	5.929	5.628	5.353	5.101	4.870	3.954	3.316	2.850	2.497	1.999
25	7.330	6.873	6.464	6.097	5.766	5.467	5.195	4.948	3.985	3.329	2.856	2.499	2.000
30	7.496	7.003	6.566	6.177	5.829	5.517	5.235	4.979	3.995	3.332	2.857	2.500	2.000
40	7.634	7.105	6.642	6.233	5.871	5.548	5.258	4.997	3.999	3.333	2.857	2.500	2.000
50	7.675	7.133	6.661	6.246	5.880	5.554	5.262	4.999	4.000	3.333	2.857	2.500	2.000

Source: Maurice Joy, Introduction to Financial Management (Homewood, Ill.: Richard D. Irwin, Inc. 1977).

Tables of squares and square roots

N	N²	√N	√10N	N	N²	√N	√10N
				50	2 500	7.071 068	22.36068
1	1	1.000 000	3.162 278	51	2 601	7.141 428	22.58318
2	4	1.414 214	4.472 136	52	2 704	7.211 103	22.80351
3	9	1.732 051	5.477 226	53	2 809	7.280 110	23.02173
4	16	2.000 000	6.324 555	54	2 916	7.348 469	23.23790
5	25	2.236 068	7.071 068	55	3 025	7.416 198	23.45208
6	36	2.449 490	7.745 967	56	3 136	7.483 315	23.66432
7	49	2.645 751	8.366 600	57	3 249	7.549 834	23.87467
8	64	2.828 427	8.944 272	58	3 364	7.615 773	24.08319
9	81	3.000 000	9.486 833	59	3 481	7.681 146	24.28992
10	100	3.162 278	10.00000	60	3 600	7.745 967	24.49490
11	121	3.316 625	10.48809	61	3 721	7.810 250	24.69818
12	144	3.464 102	10.95445	62	3 844	7.874 008	24.89980
13	169	3.605 551	11.40175	63	3 969	7.937 254	25.09980
14	196	3.741 657	11.83216	64	4 096	8.000 000	25.29822
15	225	3.872 983	12.24745	65	4 225	8.062 258	25.49510
16	256	4.000 000	12.64911	66	4 356	8.124 038	25.69047
17	289	4.123 106	13.03840	67	4 489	8.185 353	25.88436
18	324	4.242 641	13.41641	68	4 624	8.246 211	26.07681
19	361	4.358 899	13.78405	69	4 761	8.306 824	26.26785
20	400	4.472 136	14.14214	70	4 900	8.366 600	26.45751
21	441	4.582 576	14.49138	71	5 041	8.426 150	26.64583
22	484	4.690 416	14.83240	72	5 184	8.485 281	26.83282
23	529	4.795 832	15.16575	73	5 329	8.544 004	27.01851
24	576	4.898 979	15.49193	74	5 476	8.602 325	27.20294
25	625	5.000 000	15.81139	75	5 625	8.660 254	27.38613
26	676	5.099 020	16.12452	76	5 776	8.717 798	27.56810
27	729	5.196 152	16.43168	77	5 929	8.774 964	27.74887
28	784	5.291 503	16.73320	78	6 084	8.831 761	27.92848
29	841	5.385 165	17.02939	79	6 241	8.888 194	28.10694
30	900	5.477 226	17.32051	80	6 400	8.944 272	28.28427
31	961	5.567 764	17.60682	81	6 561	9.000 000	28.46050
32	1 024	5.656 854	17.88854	82	6 724	9.055 385	28.63564
33	1 089	5.744 563	18.16590	83	6 889	9.110 434	28.80972
34	1 156	5.830 952	18.43909	84	7 056	9.165 151	28.98275
35	1 225	5.916 080	18.70829	85	7 225	9.219 544	29.15476
36	1 296	6.000 000	18.97367	86	7 396	9.273 618	29.32576
37	1 369	6.082 763	19.23538	87	7 569	9.327 379	29.49576
38	1 444	6.164 414	19.49359	88	7 744	9.380 832	29.66479
39	1 521	6.244 998	19.74842	89	7 921	9.433 981	29.83287
40	1 600	6.324 555	20.00000	90	8 100	9.486 833	30.00000
41	1 681	6.403 124	20.24846	91	8 281	9.539 392	30.16621
42	1 764	6.480 741	20.49390	92	8 464	9.591 663	30.33150
43	1 849	6.557 439	20.73644	93	8 649	9.643 651	30.49590
44	1 936	6.633 250	20.97618	94	8 836	9.695 360	30.65942
45	2 025	6.708 204	21.21320	95	9 025	9.746 794	30.82207
46	2 116	6.782 330	21.44761	96	9 216	9.797 959	30.98387
47	2 209	6.855 655	21.67948	97	9 409	9.848 858	31.14482
48	2 304	6.928 203	21.90890	98	9 604	9.899 495	31.30495
49	2 401	7.000 000	22.13594	99	9 801	9.949 874	31.46427
50	2 500	7.071 068	22.36068	100	10 000	10.00000	31.62278

Tables of squares and square roots

N	N^2	$\sqrt{N}$	$\sqrt{10N}$	N	N^2	$\sqrt{N}$	$\sqrt{10N}$
100	10 000	10.00000	31.62278	150	22 500	12.24745	38.72983
101	10 201	10.04988	31.78050	151	22 801	12.28821	38.85872
102	10 404	10.09950	31.93744	152	23 104	12.32883	39.98718
103	10 609	10.14889	32.09361	153	23 409	12.36932	39.11521
104	10 816	10.19804	32.24903	154	23 716	12.40967	39.24283
105	11 025	10.24695	32.40370	155	24 025	12.44990	39.37004
106	11 236	10.29563	32.55764	156	24 336	12.45000	39.49684
107	11 449	10.34408	32.71085	157	24 649	12.52996	39.62323
108	11 664	10.39230	32.86335	158	24 964	12.56981	39.74921
109	11 881	10.44031	33.01515	159	25 281	12.60952	39.87480
110	12 100	10.48809	33.16625	160	25 600	12.64911	40.00000
111	12 321	10.53565	33.31666	161	25 921	12.68858	40.12481
112	12 544	10.58301	33.46640	162	26 244	12.72792	40.24922
113	12 769	10.63015	33.61547	163	26 569	12.76715	40.37326
114	12 996	10.67708	33.76389	164	26 896	12.80625	40.49691
115	13 225	10.72381	33.91165	165	27 225	12.84523	40.62019
116	13 456	10.77033	34.05877	166	27 556	12.88410	40.74310
117	13 689	10.81665	34.20526	167	27 889	12.92285	40.86563
118	13 924	10.86278	34.35113	168	28 224	12.96148	40.98780
119	14 161	10.90871	34.49638	169	28 561	13.00000	41.10961
120	14 400	10.95445	34.64102	170	28 900	13.03840	41.23106
121	14 641	11.00000	34.78505	171	29 241	13.07670	41.35215
122	14 884	11.04536	34.92850	172	29 584	13.11488	41.47288
123	15 129	11.09054	35.07136	173	29 929	13.15295	41.59327
124	15 376	11.13553	35.21363	174	30 276	13.19091	41.71331
125	15 625	11.18034	35.35534	175	30 625	13.22876	41.83300
126	15 876	11.22497	35.49648	176	30 976	13.26650	41.95235
127	16 129	11.26943	35.63706	177	31 329	13.30413	42.07137
128	16 384	11.31371	35.77709	178	31 684	13.34166	42.19005
129	16 641	11.35782	35.91657	179	32 041	13.37909	42.30839
130	16 900	11.40175	36.05551	180	32 400	13.41641	42.42641
131	17 161	11.44552	36.19392	181	32 761	13.45362	42.54409
132	17 424	11.48913	36.33180	182	33 124	13.49074	42.66146
133	17 689	11.53256	36.46917	183	33 489	13.52775	42.77850
134	17 956	11.57584	36.60601	184	33 856	13.56466	42.89522
135	18 225	11.61895	36.74235	185	34 225	13.60147	43.01163
136	18 496	11.66190	36.87818	186	34 596	13.63818	43.12772
137	18 769	11.70470	37.01351	187	34 969	13.67479	43.24350
138	19 044	11.74734	37.14835	188	35 344	13.71131	43.35897
139	19 321	11.78983	37.28270	189	35 721	13.74773	43.47413
140	19 600	11.83216	37.41657	190	36 100	13.78405	43.58899
141	19 881	11.87434	37.54997	191	36 481	13.82027	43.70355
142	20 164	11.91638	37.68289	192	36 864	13.85641	43.81780
143	20 449	11.95826	37.81534	193	37 249	13.89244	43.93177
144	20 736	12.00000	37.94733	194	37 636	13.92839	44.04543
145	21 025	12.04159	38.07887	195	38 025	13.96424	44.15880
146	21 316	12.08305	38.20995	196	38 416	14.00000	44.27189
147	21 609	12.12436	38.34058	197	38 809	14.03567	44.38468
148	21 904	12.16553	38.47077	198	39 204	14.07125	44.49719
149	22 201	12.20656	38.60052	199	39 601	14.10674	44.60942
150	22 500	12.24745	38.72983	200	40 000	14.14214	44.72136

Tables of squares and square roots

N	N²	√N	√10N	N	N²	√N	√10N
200	40 000	14.14214	44.72136	250	62 500	15.81139	50.00000
201	40 401	14.17745	44.83302	251	63 001	15.84298	50.09990
202	40 804	14.21267	44.94441	252	63 504	15.87451	50.19960
203	41 209	14.24781	45.05552	253	64 009	15.90597	50.29911
204	41 616	14.28296	45.16636	254	64 516	15.93738	50.39841
205	42 025	14.31782	45.27693	255	65 025	15.96872	50.49752
206	42 436	14.35270	45.38722	256	65 536	16.00000	50.59644
207	42 849	14.38749	45.49725	257	66 049	16.03122	50.69517
208	43 264	14.42221	45.60702	258	66 564	16.06238	50.79370
209	43 681	14.45683	45.71652	259	67 081	16.09348	50.89204
210	44 100	14.49138	45.82576	260	67 600	16.12452	50.99020
211	44 521	14.52584	45.93474	261	68 121	16.15549	51.08816
212	44 944	14.56022	46.04346	262	68 644	16.18641	51.18594
213	45 369	14.59452	46.15192	263	69 169	16.21727	51.28353
214	45 796	14.62874	46.26013	264	69 696	16.24808	51.38093
215	46 225	14.66288	46.36809	265	70 225	16.27882	51.47815
216	46 656	14.69694	46.47580	266	70 756	16.30951	51.57519
217	47 089	14.73092	46.58326	267	71 289	16.34013	51.67204
218	47 524	14.76482	46.69047	268	71 824	16.37071	51.76872
219	47 961	14.79865	46.79744	269	72 361	16.40122	51.86521
220	48 400	14.83240	46.90415	270	72 900	16.43168	51.96152
221	48 841	14.86607	47.01064	271	73 441	16.46208	52.05766
222	49 284	14.89966	47.11688	272	73 984	16.49242	52.15362
223	49 729	14.93318	47.22288	273	74 529	16.52271	52.24940
224	50 176	14.96663	47.32864	274	75 076	16.55295	52.34501
225	50 625	15.00000	47.43416	275	75 625	16.58312	52.44044
226	51 076	15.03330	47.53946	276	76 176	16.61325	52.53570
227	51 529	15.06652	47.64452	277	76 729	16.64332	52.63079
228	51 984	15.09967	47.74935	278	77 284	16.67333	52.72571
229	52 441	15.13275	47.85394	279	77 841	16.70329	52.82045
230	52 900	15.16575	47.95832	280	78 400	16.73320	52.91503
231	53 361	15.19868	48.06246	281	78 961	16.76305	53.00943
232	53 824	15.23155	48.16638	282	79 524	16.79286	53.10367
233	54 289	15.26434	48.27007	283	80 089	16.82260	53.19774
234	54 756	15.29706	48.37355	284	80 656	16.85230	53.29165
235	55 225	15.32971	48.47680	285	81 225	16.88194	53.38539
236	55 696	15.36229	48.57983	286	81 796	16.91153	53.47897
237	56 169	15.39480	48.68265	287	82 369	16.94107	53.57238
238	56 644	15.42725	48.78524	288	82 944	16.97056	53.66563
239	57 121	15.45962	48.88763	289	83 521	17.00000	53.75872
240	57 600	15.49193	48.98979	290	84 100	17.02939	53.85165
241	58 081	15.52417	49.09175	291	84 681	17.05872	53.94442
242	58 564	15.55635	49.19350	292	85 264	17.08801	54.03702
243	59 049	15.58846	49.29503	293	85 849	17.11724	54.12947
244	59 536	15.62050	49.39636	294	86 436	17.14643	54.22177
245	60 025	15.65248	49.49747	295	87 025	17.17556	54.31390
246	60 516	15.68439	49.59839	296	87 616	17.20465	54.40588
247	61 009	15.71623	49.69909	297	88 209	17.23369	54.49771
248	61 504	15.74802	49.79960	298	88 804	17.26268	54.58938
249	62 001	15.77973	49.89990	299	89 401	17.29162	54.68089
250	62 500	15.81139	50.00000	300	90 000	17.32051	54.77226

Tables of squares and square roots

N	N²	√N	√10N	N	N²	√N	√10N
300	90 000	17.32051	54.77226	350	122 500	18.70829	59.16080
301	90 601	17.34935	54.86347	351	123 201	18.73499	59.24525
302	91 204	17.37815	54.95453	352	123 904	18.76166	59.32959
303	91 809	17.40690	55.04544	353	124 609	18.78829	59.41380
304	92 416	17.43560	55.13620	354	125 316	18.81489	59.49790
305	93 025	17.46425	55.22681	355	126 025	18.84144	59.58188
306	93 636	17.49288	55.31727	356	126 736	18.86796	59.66574
307	94 249	17.52142	55.40758	357	127 449	18.89444	59.74948
308	94 864	17.54993	55.49775	358	128 164	18.92089	59.83310
309	95 481	17.57840	55.58777	359	128 881	18.94730	59.91661
310	96 100	17.60682	55.67764	360	129 600	18.97367	60.00000
311	96 721	17.63519	55.76737	361	130 321	19.00000	60.08328
312	97 344	17.66352	55.85696	362	131 044	19.02630	60.16644
313	97 969	17.69181	55.94640	363	131 769	19.05256	60.24948
314	98 596	17.72005	56.03670	364	132 496	19.07878	60.33241
315	99 225	17.74824	56.12486	365	133 225	19.10497	60.41523
316	99 856	17.77639	56.21388	366	133 956	19.13113	60.49793
317	100 489	17.80449	56.30275	367	134 689	19.15724	60.58052
318	101 124	17.83255	56.39149	368	135 424	19.18333	60.66300
319	101 761	17.86057	56.48008	369	136 161	19.20937	60.74537
320	102 400	17.88854	56.56854	370	136 900	19.23538	60.82763
321	103 041	17.91647	56.65686	371	137 641	19.26136	60.90977
322	103 684	17.94436	56.74504	372	138 384	19.28730	60.99180
323	104 329	17.97220	56.83309	373	139 129	19.31321	61.07373
324	104 976	18.00000	56.92100	374	139 876	19.33908	61.15554
325	105 625	18.02776	57.00877	375	140 625	19.36492	61.23724
326	106 276	18.05547	57.09641	376	141 376	19.39072	61.31884
327	106 929	18.08314	57.18391	377	142 129	19.41649	61.40033
328	107 584	18.11077	57.27128	378	142 884	19.44222	61.48170
329	108 241	18.13836	57.35852	379	143 641	19.46792	61.56298
330	108 900	18.16590	57.44563	380	144 000	19.49359	61.64414
331	109 561	18.19341	57.53260	381	145 161	19.51922	61.72520
332	110 224	18.22087	57.61944	382	145 924	19.54483	61.80615
333	110 889	18.24829	57.70615	383	146 689	19.57039	61.88699
334	111 556	18.27567	57.79273	384	147 456	19.59592	61.96773
335	112 225	18.30301	57. 87918	385	148 225	19.62142	62.04837
336	112 896	18.33030	57.96551	386	148 996	19.64688	62.12890
337	113 569	18.35756	58.05170	387	149 769	19.67232	62.20932
338	114 224	18.38478	57.13777	388	150 544	19.69772	62.28965
339	114 921	18.41195	58.22371	389	151 321	19.72308	62.36986
340	115 600	18.43909	58.30952	390	152 100	19.74842	62.44998
341	116 281	18.46619	58.39521	391	152 881	19.77372	62.52999
342	116 694	18.49324	58.48077	392	153 664	19.79899	62.60990
343	117 649	18.52026	58.56620	393	154 449	19.82423	62.68971
344	118 336	18.54724	58.65151	394	155 236	19.84943	62.76942
345	119 025	18.57418	58.73670	395	156 025	19.87461	62.84903
346	119 716	18.60108	58.82176	396	156 816	19.89975	62.92853
347	120 409	18.62794	58.90671	397	157 609	19.92486	63.00794
348	121 104	18.65476	58.99152	398	158 404	19.94994	63.08724
349	121 801	18.68154	59.07622	399	159 201	19.97498	63.16645
350	122 500	18.70829	59.16080	400	160 000	20.00000	63.24555

Tables of squares and square roots

N	N²	√N	√10N	N	N²	√N	√10N
400	160 000	20.00000	63.24555	450	202 500	21.21320	67.08204
401	160 801	20.02498	63.32456	451	203 401	21.23676	67.15653
402	161 604	20.04994	63.40347	452	204 304	21.26029	67.23095
403	162 409	20.07486	63.48228	453	205 209	21.28380	67.30527
404	163 216	20.09975	63.56099	454	206 116	21.30728	67.37952
405	164 025	20.12461	63.63961	455	207 025	21.33073	67.45369
406	164 836	20.14944	63.71813	456	207 936	21.35416	67.52777
407	165 649	20.17424	63.79655	457	208 849	21.37756	67.60178
408	166 464	20.19901	63.87488	458	209 764	21.40093	67.67570
409	167 281	20.22375	63.95311	459	210 681	21.42429	67.74954
410	168 100	20.24846	64.03124	460	211 600	21.44761	67.82330
411	168 921	20.27313	64.10928	461	212 521	21.47091	67.89698
412	169 744	20.29778	64.18723	462	213 444	21.49419	67.97058
413	170 569	20.32240	64.26508	463	214 369	21.51743	68.04410
414	171 396	20.34699	64.34283	464	215 296	21.54066	68.11755
415	172 225	20.37155	64.42049	465	216 225	21.56386	68.19091
416	173 056	20.39608	64.49806	466	217 156	21.58703	68.26419
417	173 889	20.42058	64.57554	467	218 089	21.61018	68.33740
418	174 724	20.44505	64.65292	468	219 024	21.63331	68.41053
419	175 561	20.46949	64.73021	469	219 961	21.65641	68.48357
420	176 400	20.49390	64.80741	470	220 900	21.67948	68.55655
421	177 241	20.51828	64.88451	471	221 841	21.70253	68.62944
422	178 084	20.54264	64.96153	472	222 784	21.72556	68.70226
423	178 929	20.56696	65.03845	473	223 729	21.74856	68.77500
424	179 776	20.59126	65.11528	474	224 676	21.77154	68.84706
425	180 625	20.61553	65.19202	475	225 625	21.79449	68.92024
426	181 476	20.63977	65.26808	476	226 576	21.81742	68.99275
427	182 329	20.66398	65.34524	477	227 529	21.84033	69.06519
428	183 184	20.68816	65.42171	478	228 484	21.86321	69.13754
429	184 041	20.71232	65.49809	479	229 441	21.88607	69.20983
430	184 900	20.73644	65.57439	480	230 400	21.90800	69.28203
431	185 761	20.76054	65.65059	481	231 361	21.93171	69.35416
432	186 624	20.78461	65.72671	482	232 324	21.95450	69.42622
433	187 489	20.80865	65.80274	483	233 280	21.97726	69.50820
434	188 356	20.83267	65.87868	484	234 256	22.00000	69.57011
435	189 225	20.85665	65.95453	485	235 225	22.02272	69.64194
436	190 096	20.88061	66.03030	486	236 196	22.04541	69.71370
437	190 969	20.90454	66.10598	487	237 169	22.06808	69.78530
438	191 844	20.92845	66.18157	488	238 144	22.09072	69.85700
439	192 721	20.95233	66.25708	489	239 121	22.11334	69.92853
440	193 600	20.97618	66.33250	490	240 100	22.13594	70.00000
441	194 481	21.00000	66.40783	491	241 081	22.15852	70.07139
442	195 364	21.02380	66.48308	492	242 064	22.18107	70.14271
443	196 249	21.04757	66.55825	493	243 049	22.20360	70.21396
444	197 136	21.07131	66.63332	494	244 036	22.22611	70.28513
445	198 025	21.09502	66.70832	495	245 025	22.24860	70.35624
446	198 916	21.11871	66.78323	496	246 016	22.27106	70.42727
447	199 809	21.14237	66.85806	497	247 009	22.29350	70.49823
448	200 704	21.16601	66.93280	498	248 004	22.31519	70.56912
449	201 601	21.18962	67.00746	499	249 001	22.33831	70.63993
450	202 500	21.21320	67.08204	500	250 000	22.36068	70.71068

Tables of squares and square roots

N	N²	√N	√10N	N	N²	√N	√10N
500	250 000	22.36068	70.71068	550	302 500	23.45208	74.16198
501	251 001	22.38303	70.78135	551	303 601	23.47339	74.22937
502	252 004	22.40536	70.85196	552	304 704	23.49468	74.29670
503	253 009	22.42766	70.92249	553	305 809	23.51595	74.36397
504	254 016	22.44994	70.99296	554	306 916	23.53720	74.43118
505	255 025	22.47221	71.06335	555	308 025	23.55844	74.49832
506	256 036	22.49444	71.13368	556	309 136	23.57965	74.56541
507	257 049	22.51666	71.20393	557	310 249	23.60085	74.63243
508	258 064	22.53886	71.27412	558	311 364	23.62202	74.69940
509	259 081	22.56103	71.34424	559	312 481	23.64318	74.76630
510	260 100	22.58318	71.41428	560	313 600	23.66432	74.83315
511	261 121	22.60531	71.48426	561	314 721	23.68544	74.89993
512	262 144	22.62742	71.55418	562	315 844	23.70654	74.96666
513	263 169	22.64950	71.62402	563	316 969	23.72762	75.03333
514	264 196	22.67157	71.69379	564	318 096	23.74686	75.09993
515	265 225	22.69361	71.76350	565	319 225	23.76973	75.16648
516	266 256	22.71563	71.83314	566	320 356	23.79075	75.23297
517	267 289	22.73763	71.90271	567	321 489	23.81176	75.29940
518	268 324	22.75961	71.97222	568	322 624	23.83275	75.36577
519	269 361	22.78157	72.04165	569	323 761	23.85372	75.43209
520	270 400	22.80351	72.11103	570	324 900	23.87467	75.49834
521	271 441	22.82542	72.18033	571	326 041	23.89561	75.56454
522	272 484	22.84732	72.24957	572	327 184	23.91652	75.63068
523	273 529	22.86919	72.31874	573	328 329	23.93742	75.69676
524	274 576	22.89105	72.38784	574	329 476	23.95830	75.76279
525	275 625	22.91288	72.45688	575	330 625	23.97916	75.82875
526	276 676	22.93469	72.52586	576	331 776	24.00000	75.89466
527	277 729	22.95648	72.59477	577	332 929	24.02082	75.96052
528	278 784	22.97825	72.66361	578	334 084	24.04163	76.02631
529	279 841	23.00000	72.73239	579	335 241	24.06242	76.09205
530	280 900	23.02173	72.80110	580	336 400	24.08319	76.15773
531	281 961	23.04344	72.86975	581	337 561	24.10394	76.22336
532	283 024	23.06513	72.93833	582	338 724	24.12468	76.28892
533	284 089	23.08679	73.00685	583	339 889	24.14539	76.35444
534	285 156	23.10844	73.07530	584	341 056	24.16609	76.41989
535	286 225	23.13007	73.14369	585	342 225	24.18677	76.48529
536	287 296	23.15167	73.21202	586	343 396	24.20744	76.55064
537	288 369	23.17326	73.28028	587	344 569	24.22808	76.61593
538	289 444	23.19483	73.34848	588	345 744	24.24871	76.68116
539	290 521	23.21637	73.41662	589	346 921	24.26932	76.74634
540	291 600	23.23790	73.48469	590	348 100	24.28992	76.81146
541	292 681	23.25941	73.55270	591	349 281	24.31049	76.87652
542	293 764	23.28089	73.62056	592	350 464	24.33105	76.94154
543	294 849	23.30236	73.68853	593	351 649	24.35159	77.00649
544	295 936	23.32381	73.75636	594	352 836	24.37212	77.07140
545	297 025	23.34524	73.82412	595	354 025	24.39262	77.13624
546	298 116	23.36664	73.89181	596	355 216	24.41311	77.20104
547	299 209	23.38803	73.95945	597	356 409	24.43358	77.26578
548	300 304	23.40940	74.02702	598	357 604	24.45404	77.33046
549	301 401	23.43075	74.09453	599	358 801	24.47448	77.39509
550	302 500	23.45208	74.16198	600	360 000	24.49490	77.45967

Tables of squares and square roots

N	N²	√N	√10N	N	N²	√N	√10N
600	360 000	24.49490	77.45967	650	422 500	25.49510	80.62258
601	361 201	24.51530	77.52419	651	423 801	25.51470	80.68457
602	362 404	24.53569	77.58868	652	425 409	25.53240	80.80130
603	363 609	24.55606	77.65307	653	426 409	25.55386	80.80842
604	364 816	24.57641	77.71744	654	427 716	25.57342	80.87027
605	366 025	24.59675	77.78175	655	429 025	25.59297	80.93207
606	367 736	24.61707	77.84600	656	430 336	25.61250	80.99383
607	368 449	24.63737	77.91020	657	431 649	25.63201	81.05554
608	369 664	24.65766	77.97435	658	432 964	25.65151	81.11720
609	370 881	24.67793	78.03845	659	434 281	25.67100	81.17881
610	372 100	24.69818	78.10250	660	435 600	25.69047	81.24038
611	373 321	24.71841	78.16649	661	436 921	25.70992	81.30191
612	374 544	24.73863	78.23043	662	438 244	25.72936	81.36338
613	375 769	24.75884	78.29432	663	439 569	25.74879	81.42481
614	376 996	24.77902	78.35815	664	440 896	25.76820	81.48620
615	378 225	24.79919	78.42194	665	442 225	25.78759	81.54753
616	379 456	24.81935	78.48567	666	443 556	25.80698	81.60882
617	380 689	24.83948	78.54935	667	444 889	25.82634	81.67007
618	381 924	24.85961	78.61298	668	446 224	25.84570	81.73127
619	383 161	24.87971	78.67655	669	447 561	25.86503	81.79242
620	384 400	24.89980	78.74008	670	448 900	25.88436	81.85353
621	385 641	24.91987	78.80355	671	450 241	25.90367	81.91459
622	386 884	24.93993	78.86698	672	451 584	25.92296	81.97561
623	388 129	24.95997	78.93035	673	452 929	25.94224	82.03658
624	389 376	24.97999	78.99367	674	454 276	25.96151	82.09750
625	390 625	25.00000	79.05694	675	455 625	25.98076	82.15838
626	391 876	25.01999	79.12016	676	456 976	26.00000	82.21922
627	393 129	25.03997	79.18333	677	458 329	26.01922	82.28001
628	394 384	25.05993	79.24645	678	459 684	26.03843	82.34076
629	395 641	25.07987	79.30952	679	461 041	26.05763	82.40146
630	396 900	25.09980	79.37254	680	462 400	26.07681	82.46211
631	398 161	25.11971	79.43551	681	463 761	26.09598	82.52272
632	399 424	25.13961	79.49843	682	465 124	26.11513	82.58329
633	400 689	25.15949	79.56130	683	466 489	26.13427	82.64381
634	401 956	25.17936	79.62412	684	467 856	26.15339	82.70429
635	403 225	25.19921	79.68689	685	469 225	26.17250	82.76473
636	404 496	25.21904	79.74961	686	470 596	26.19160	82.82512
637	405 769	25.23886	79.81228	687	471 969	26.21068	82.88546
638	407 044	25.25866	79.87490	688	473 344	26.22975	82.94577
639	408 321	25.27845	79.93748	689	474 721	26.24881	83.00602
640	409 600	25.29822	80.00000	690	476 100	26.26785	83.06624
641	410 881	25.31798	80.06248	691	477 481	26.28688	83.12641
642	412 164	25.33772	80.12490	692	478 864	26.30589	83.18654
643	413 449	25.35744	80.18728	693	480 249	26.32489	83.24662
644	414 736	25.37716	80.24961	694	481 636	26.34388	83.30666
645	416 025	25.39685	80.31189	695	483 025	26.36285	83.36666
646	417 316	25.41653	80.37413	696	484 416	26.38181	83.42661
647	418 609	25.43619	80.43631	697	485 809	26.40076	83.48653
648	419 904	25.45584	80.49845	698	487 204	26.41969	83.54639
649	421 201	25.47548	80.56054	699	488 601	26.43861	83.60622
650	422 500	25.49510	80.62258	700	490 000	26.45751	83.66600

Tables of squares and square roots

N	N²	√N	√10N	N	N²	√N	√10N
700	490 000	26.45751	83.66600	750	562 500	27.38613	86.60254
701	491 401	26.47640	83.72574	751	564 001	27.40438	86.66026
702	492 804	26.49528	83.78544	752	565 504	27.42262	86.71793
703	494 209	26.51415	83.84510	753	567 009	27.44085	86.77557
704	495 616	26.53300	83.90471	754	568 516	27.45906	86.83317
705	497 025	26.55184	83.96428	755	570 025	27.47726	86.89074
706	498 436	26.57066	84.02381	756	571 536	27.49545	86.94826
707	499 849	26.58947	84.08329	757	573 049	27.51363	87.00575
708	501 264	26.60827	84.14274	758	574 564	27.53180	87.06320
709	502 681	26.62705	84.20214	759	576 081	27.54995	87.12061
710	504 100	26.64583	84.26150	760	577 600	27.56810	87.17798
711	505 521	26.66458	84.32082	761	579 121	27.58623	87.23531
712	506 944	26.68333	84.38009	762	580 644	27.60435	87.29261
713	508 369	26.70206	84.43933	763	582 169	27.62245	87.34987
714	509 796	26.72078	84.49852	764	583 696	27.64055	87.40709
715	511 225	26.73948	84.55767	765	585 225	27.65863	87.46428
716	512 656	26.75818	84.61578	766	586 756	27.67671	87.52143
717	514 089	26.77686	84.67585	767	588 289	27.69476	87.57854
718	515 524	26.79552	84.73488	768	589 824	27.71281	87.63561
719	516 961	26.81418	84.79387	769	591 361	27.73085	87.69265
720	518 400	26.83282	84.85281	770	592 900	27.74887	87.74964
721	519 841	26.85144	84.91172	771	594 441	27.76689	87.80661
722	521 284	26.87006	84.97058	772	595 984	27.78489	87.86353
723	522 729	26.88866	85.02941	773	597 529	27.80288	87.92042
724	524 176	26.90725	85.08819	774	599 076	27.82086	87.97727
725	525 625	26.92582	85.14693	775	600 625	27.83882	88.03408
726	527 076	26.94439	85.20563	776	602 176	27.85678	88.09086
727	528 529	26.96294	85.26429	777	603 729	27.87472	88.14760
728	529 984	26.98148	85.32294	778	605 284	27.89265	88.20431
729	531 411	27.00000	85.38150	779	606 841	27.91057	88.26098
730	532 900	27.01851	85.44004	780	608 400	27.92848	88.31761
731	534 361	27.03701	85.49854	781	609 961	27.94638	88.37420
732	535 824	27.05550	85.55700	782	611 524	27.96426	88.43076
733	537 289	27.07397	85.61542	783	613 089	27.98214	88.48729
734	538 756	27.09243	85.67380	784	614 656	28.00000	88.54377
735	540 225	27.11088	85.73214	785	616 225	28.01785	88.60023
736	541 696	27.12932	85.79044	786	617 796	28.03569	88.65664
737	543 169	27.14774	85.84870	787	619 369	28.05352	88.71302
738	544 644	27.16616	85.90693	788	620 944	28.07134	88.76936
739	546 121	27.18455	85.96511	789	622 521	28.08914	88.82567
740	547 600	27.20294	86.02325	790	624 100	28.10694	88.88194
741	549 081	27.22132	86.08136	791	625 681	28.12472	88.93818
742	550 564	27.23968	86.13942	792	627 264	28.14249	88.99438
743	552 049	27.25803	86.20745	793	628 849	28.16026	89.05055
744	553 536	27.27636	86.25543	794	630 436	28.17801	89.10668
745	555 025	27.29469	86.31338	795	632 025	28.19574	89.16277
746	556 516	27.31300	86.37129	796	633 616	28.21347	89.21883
747	558 009	27.33130	86.42916	797	635 209	28.23119	89.27486
748	559 504	27.34959	86.48609	798	636 804	28.24889	89.33085
749	561 001	27.36786	86.54479	799	638 401	28.26659	89.38680
750	562 500	27.38613	86.60254	800	640 000	28.28427	89.44272

Tables of squares and square roots

N	N²	√N	√10N	N	N²	√N	√10N
800	640 000	28.28427	89.44272	850	722 500	29.15476	92.19544
801	641 601	28.30194	89.49860	851	724 201	29.17190	92.24966
802	643 204	28.31960	89.55445	852	725 904	29.18904	92.30385
803	644 809	28.33725	89.61027	853	727 609	29.20616	92.35800
804	646 416	28.35489	89.66605	854	729 316	29.22328	92.41212
805	648 025	28.37252	89.72179	855	731 025	29.24038	92.46621
806	649 636	28.39014	89.77750	856	732 736	29.25748	92.52027
807	651 249	28.40775	89.83318	857	734 449	29.27456	92.57429
808	652 864	28.42534	89.88882	858	736 164	29.29164	92.62829
809	654 481	28.44293	89.94443	859	737 881	29.30870	92.68225
810	656 100	28.46050	90.00000	860	739 600	29.32576	92.73618
811	657 721	28.47806	90.05554	861	741 321	29.34280	92.79009
812	659 344	28.49561	90.11104	862	743 044	29.35984	92.84396
813	660 969	28.51315	90.16651	863	744 769	29.37686	92.89779
814	662 596	28.53069	90.22195	864	746 496	29.39388	92.95160
815	664 225	28.54820	90.27735	865	748 225	29.41088	93.00538
816	665 856	28.56571	90.33272	866	749 956	29.42788	93.05912
817	667 489	28.58321	90.38805	867	751 689	29.44486	93.11283
818	669 124	28.60070	90.44335	868	753 424	29.46184	93.16652
819	670 761	28.61818	90.49862	869	755 161	29.47881	93.22017
820	672 400	28.63564	90.55385	870	756 900	29.49576	93.27379
821	674 041	28.65310	90.60905	871	758 641	29.51271	93.32738
822	675 684	28.67054	90.66422	872	760 384	29.52965	93.38094
823	677 329	28.68798	90.71935	873	762 129	29.54657	93.43447
824	678 976	28.70540	90.77445	874	763 876	29.56349	93.48797
825	680 625	28.72281	90.82951	875	765 625	29.58040	93.54143
826	682 276	28.74022	90.88454	876	767 376	29.59730	93.59487
827	683 929	28.75761	90.93954	877	769 129	29.61419	93.64828
828	685 584	28.77499	90.99451	878	770 884	29.63106	93.70165
829	687 241	28.79236	91.04944	879	772 641	29.64793	93.75500
830	688 900	28.80972	91.10434	880	774 400	29.66479	93.80832
831	690 561	28.82707	91.15920	881	776 161	29.68164	93.86160
832	692 224	28.84441	91.21403	882	777 924	29.69848	93.91486
833	693 889	28.86174	91.26883	883	779 689	29.71532	93.96808
834	695 556	28.87906	91.32360	884	781 456	29.73214	94.02027
835	697 225	28.89637	91.37833	885	783 225	29.74895	94.07444
836	698 896	28.91366	91.43304	886	784 996	29.76575	94.12757
837	700 569	28.93095	91.48770	887	786 769	29.78255	94.10868
838	702 244	28.94823	91.54234	888	788 544	29.79933	94.23375
839	703 921	28.96550	91.59694	889	790 321	29.81610	94.28680
840	705 600	28.98275	91.65151	890	792 100	29.83287	94.33981
841	707 281	29.00000	91.70605	891	793 881	29.84962	94.39280
842	708 964	29.01724	91.76056	892	795 664	29.86637	94.44575
843	710 649	29.03446	91.81503	893	797 449	29.88311	94.49868
844	712 336	29.05168	91.86947	894	799 236	29.89983	94.55157
845	714 025	29.06888	91.92388	895	801 025	29.91655	94.60444
846	715 716	29.08608	91.97826	896	802 816	29.93326	94.65728
847	717 409	29.10326	92.03260	897	804 609	29.94996	94.71008
848	719 104	29.12044	92.08692	898	806 404	29.96665	94.76286
849	720 801	29.13760	92.14120	899	808 201	29.98333	94.81561
850	722 500	29.15476	92.19544	900	810 000	30.00000	94.86833

Tables of squares and square roots

N	N²	√N	√10N	N	N²	√N	√10N
900	810 000	30.00000	94.86833	950	902 500	30.82207	97.46794
901	811 801	30.01666	94.92102	951	904 401	30.83829	97.51923
902	813 604	30.03331	94.97368	952	906 304	30.85450	97.57049
903	815 409	30.04996	95.02631	953	908 209	30.87070	97.62172
904	817 216	30.06659	95.07891	954	910.116	30.88689	97.67292
905	819 025	30.08322	95.13149	955	912 025	30.90307	97.72410
906	820 836	30.09938	95.18403	956	913 936	30.91925	97.77525
907	822 649	30.11644	95.23655	957	915 849	30.93542	97.82638
908	824 464	30.13304	95.28903	958	917 764	30.95158	97.87747
909	826 281	30.14963	95.34149	959	919 681	30.96773	97.92855
910	828 100	30.16621	95.39392	960	921 600	30.98387	97.97959
911	829 921	30.18278	95.44632	961	923 521	31.00000	98.03061
912	831 744	30.19934	95.49869	962	925 444	31.01612	98.08160
913	833 569	30.21589	95.55103	963	927 369	31.03224	98.13256
914	835 396	30.23243	95.60335	964	929 296	31.04835	98.18350
915	837 225	30.24897	95.65563	965	931 225	31.06445	98.23441
916	839 056	30.26549	95.70789	966	933 156	31.08054	98.28530
917	840 889	30.28201	95.76012	967	935 089	31.09662	98.33616
918	842 724	30.29851	95.81232	968	937 024	31.11270	98.38699
919	844 561	30.31501	95.86449	969	938 961	31.12876	98.43780
920	846 400	30.33150	95.91663	970	940 900	31.14482	98.48858
921	848 241	30.34798	95.96874	971	942 841	31.16087	98.53933
922	850 084	30.36445	96.02083	972	944 784	31.17691	98.59006
923	851 929	30.38092	96.07289	973	946 729	31.19295	98.64076
924	853 776	30.39735	96.12492	974	948 676	31.20897	98.69144
925	855 625	30.41381	96.17692	975	950 625	31.22499	98.74209
926	857 476	30.43025	96.22889	976	952 576	31.24100	98.79271
927	859 329	30.44667	96.28084	977	954 529	31.25700	98.84331
928	861 184	30.46309	96.33276	978	956 484	31.27299	98.89388
929	863 041	30.47950	96.38465	979	958 441	31.28898	98.94443
930	864 900	30.49590	96.43651	980	960 400	31.30495	98.99495
931	866 761	30.51229	96.48834	981	962 361	31.32092	99.04544
932	868 624	30.52868	96.54015	982	964 324	31.33688	99.09591
933	870 489	30.54505	96.59193	983	966 144	31.34021	99.10321
934	872 356	30.56141	96.64368	984	968 256	31.36877	99.19677
935	874 225	30.57777	96.69540	985	970 225	31.38471	99.24717
936	876 096	30.59412	96.74709	986	972 196	31.40064	99.29753
937	877 969	30.61046	96.79876	987	974 169	31.41656	99.34787
938	879 844	30.62679	96.85040	988	976 144	31.43247	99.39819
939	881 721	30.64311	96.90201	989	978 121	31.44837	99.44848
940	883 600	30.65942	96.95360	990	980 100	31.46427	99.49874
941	885 481	30.67572	97.00515	991	982 081	31.48015	99.54898
942	887 364	30.69202	97.05668	992	984 064	31.49603	99.54920
943	889 249	30.70831	97.10819	993	986 049	31.51190	99.64939
944	891 136	30.72458	97.15966	994	988 036	31.52777	99.69955
945	893 025	30.74085	97.21111	995	990 025	31.54362	99.74969
946	894 916	30.75711	97.26253	996	992 016	31.55947	99.79980
947	896 809	30.77337	97.31393	997	994 009	31.57531	99.84989
948	898 704	30.78961	97.36529	998	996 004	31.59114	99.89995
949	900 601	30.80584	97.41663	999	998 001	31.60696	99.94999
950	902 500	30.82207	97.46794	1000	1 000 000	31.62278	100.00000

Source: Donald H. Sanders, A. Franklin Murph, Robert J. Eng, *Statistics, A Fresh Approach* (New York: McGraw-Hill, Inc. 1976).

APPENDIX F: *Financial and Economic Data Bases*

PART I: STOCK MARKET DATA

DOW JONES INDUSTRIAL AVERAGES

STANDARD AND POOR'S INDEXES

Quarterly Dow Jones Industrial Stock Average

The table below lists the earnings (losses) of the Dow Jones Industrial Average based upon generally accepted accounting principles. The P/E ratio for the DJI correctly reflects deficit/negative earnings for the 1982 September and December quarters. The 1984 December 12-months dividend reflects $1.87½ GM dividend distribution value of one share of class E common for each 20 shares of common held. N.A.-Not available. d-Deficit.

Year	Quarter Ended	Clos. Avg.	Qtrly Chg.	% Chg.	Qtrly Earns	12-Mth Earns	P/E Ratio	12-Mth Divs	Divs Yield	Payout Ratio
1984	Dec. 31	1211.57	+ 4.86	+ 0.40	N.A.	N.A.	N.A.	60.63	5.00	N.A.
	Sept. 28	1206.71	+ 74.31	+ 6.56	29.08	108.11	11.2	58.41	4.84	.5402
	June 29	1132.40	− 32.49	− 2.79	35.02	102.07	11.1	57.67	5.09	.5650
	Mar. 30	1164.89	− 93.75	− 7.45	30.12	87.38	13.3	56.39	4.84	.6453
1983	Dec. 30	1258.64	+ 25.51	+ 2.07	13.89	72.45	17.4	56.33	4.47	.7775
	Sept. 30	1233.13	+ 11.17	+ 0.91	23.04	56.12	30.0	54.59	4.43	.9727
	June 30	1221.96	+ 91.93	+ 8.13	20.33	11.59	105.4	54.05	4.42	4.6635
	Mar. 31	1130.03	+ 83.49	+ 7.98	15.19	9.52	118.7	54.10	4.79	5.6828
1982	Dec. 31	1046.54	+ 150.29	+ 16.77	d2.44	9.15	114.4	54.14	5.17	5.9169
	Sept. 30	896.25	+ 84.32	+ 10.38	d21.49	35.15	25.5	55.55	6.20	1.5804
	June 30	811.93	− 10.84	− 1.32	18.26	79.90	10.2	55.84	6.88	.6989
	Mar. 31	822.77	− 52.23	− 5.97	14.82	97.13	8.5	56.28	6.84	.5794
1981	Dec. 31	875.00	+ 25.02	+ 2.94	23.56	113.71	7.7	56.22	6.42	.4944
	Sept. 30	849.98	− 126.90	− 12.99	23.26	123.32	6.9	56.18	6.61	.4539
	June 30	976.88	− 26.99	− 2.69	35.49	128.91	7.6	55.98	5.73	.4266
	Mar. 31	1003.87	+ 39.88	+ 4.14	31.40	123.60	8.1	54.99	5.48	.4449
1980	Dec. 31	963.99	+ 31.57	+ 3.39	33.17	121.86	7.9	54.36	5.64	.4461
	Sept. 30	932.42	+ 64.50	+ 7.43	28.85	111.58	8.4	53.83	5.77	.4824
	June 30	867.92	+ 82.17	+ 10.46	30.18	116.40	7.5	52.81	6.08	.4537
	Mar. 31	785.75	− 52.99	− 6.32	29.66	120.77	6.5	52.10	6.63	.4314
1979	Dec. 31	838.74	− 39.93	− 4.54	22.89	124.46	6.7	50.98	6.08	.4096
	Sept. 28	878.67	+ 36.69	+ 4.36	33.67	136.26	6.4	51.45	5.85	.3776
	June 29	841.98	− 20.20	− 2.34	34.55	128.99	6.5	50.35	5.98	.3903
	Mar. 30	862.18	+ 57.17	+ 7.10	33.35	124.10	6.9	49.48	5.74	.3987
1978	Dec. 29	805.01	− 60.81	− 7.02	34.69	112.79	7.1	48.52	6.03	.4302
	Sept. 29	865.82	+ 46.87	+ 5.72	26.40	101.59	8.5	47.42	5.48	.4668
	June 30	818.95	+ 61.59	+ 8.13	29.66	91.37	9.0	46.74	5.71	.5115
	Mar. 31	757.36	− 73.81	− 8.88	22.04	89.23	8.5	46.53	6.14	.5215
1977	Dec. 30	831.17	− 15.94	− 1.88	23.49	89.10	9.3	45.84	5.51	.5145
	Sept. 30	847.11	− 69.19	− 7.55	16.18	89.86	9.4	44.73	5.28	.4978
	June 30	916.30	− 2.83	− 0.31	27.52	97.18	9.4	43.85	4.79	.4512
	Mar. 31	919.13	− 85.52	− 8.51	21.91	95.51	9.6	42.63	4.64	.4463
1976	Dec. 31	1004.65	+ 14.46	+ 1.46	24.25	96.72	10.4	41.40	4.12	.4280
	Sept. 30	990.19	− 12.59	− 1.27	23.50	95.81	10.3	38.90	3.93	.4060
	June 30	1002.78	+ 3.33	+ 0.33	25.85	90.68	11.1	38.10	3.80	.4202
	Mar. 31	999.45	+ 147.04	+ 17.25	23.12	81.87	12.2	36.88	3.69	.4505
1975	Dec. 31	852.41	+ 58.53	+ 7.37	23.34	75.66	11.3	37.46	4.39	.4951
	Sept. 30	793.88	− 85.11	− 10.72	18.37	75.47	10.5	38.28	4.82	.5072
	June 30	878.99	+ 110.84	+ 12.61	17.04	83.83	10.5	38.66	4.40	.4612
	Mar. 31	768.15	+ 151.91	+ 24.65	16.91	93.47	8.2	38.56	5.02	.4125

Dow Jones Industrial Average
Earnings, Dividends and Price-Earnings Ratio

		Price	Earnings (by qtrs)	Preceding 12 mos. earnings	Price Earnings Ratio (col. 1 ÷ col. 3)	Dividends
1983	December 30	1258.94	. . . .	. . . .	. . . .	14.77
	September 30	1233.13	23.04	56.12	30.0	13.98
	June 30	1221.96	20.33	11.59	105.4	13.70
	March 31	1130.03	15.19	9.52	118.7	13.88
						56.33
1982	December 31	1046.54	d2.44	9.15	114.4	13.03
	September 30	896.25	d21.49	35.15	25.5	13.44
	June 30	811.93	18.26	79.90	10.2	13.75
	March 31	822.77	14.82	97.13	8.5	13.92
			9.15			54.14
1981	December 31	875.00	23.56	113.71	7.7	14.44
	September 30	849.98	23.26	123.32	6.9	13.73
	June 30	976.88	35.49	128.91	7.6	14.19
	March 31	1003.87	31.40	123.60	8.1	13.86
			113.71			56.22
1980	December 31	963.99	33.17	121.86	7.9	14.40
	September 30	932.42	28.85	111.58	8.4	13.53
	June 30	867.92	30.18	116.40	7.5	13.20
	March 31	785.75	29.66	120.77	6.5	13.23
			121.86			54.36
1979	December 31	838.74	22.89	124.46	6.7	13.87
	September 28	878.67	33.67	136.26	6.4	12.51
	June 29	841.98	34.55	128.99	6.5	12.49
	March 30	862.18	33.35	124.10	6.9	12.11
			124.46			50.98
1978	December 29	805.01	34.69	112.79	7.1	14.34
	September 29	865.82	26.40	101.59	8.5	11.41
	June 30	818.95	29.66	91.37	9.0	11.62
	March 31	757.36	22.04	89.23	8.5	11.15
			112.79			48.52

Earnings and Price-Earnings Ratio

Earnings on the Dow Jones industrial average are computed by adding the per share results of the latest quarter of each of the 30 components. This total is then divided by the then-current divisor. Having obtained the figure for the quarter, the four most recent quarterly figures are totaled to give the 12-month figure.

The industrial average stood at 1233.13 on September 30, 1983, for instance (see above). The 12-month earnings for that date were $56.12, being the sum of the four previous quarters ended September.

To obtain the price-earnings ratio on the industrials, the industrial average on a given date is divided by the 12-month earnings of the same date.

Source: *The Dow Jones Investor's Handbook* (Homewood, Ill.: Dow Jones-Irwin, 1984).

Dow Jones Industrial Average
Earnings, Dividends and Price-Earnings Ratio

		Price	Earnings (by qtrs)	Preceding 12 mos. earnings	Price Earnings Ratio (col. 1 ÷ col. 3)	Dividends
1977	December 30	831.17	23.49	89.10	9.3	13.24
	September 30	847.11	16.18	89.86	9.4	10.73
	June 30	916.30	27.52	97.18	9.4	11.41
	March 31	919.13	21.91	95.51	9.6	10.46
			89.10			45.84
1976	December 31	1004.65	24.25	96.72	10.4	12.13
	September 30	990.19	23.50	95.81	10.3	9.85
	June 30	1002.78	25.85	90.68	11.1	10.19
	March 31	999.45	23.12	81.87	12.2	9.23
			96.72			41.40
1975	December 31	852.41	23.34	75.66	11.3	9.63
	September 30	793.88	18.37	75.47	10.5	9.05
	June 30	878.99	17.04	83.83	10.5	8.97
	March 31	768.15	16.91	93.47	8.2	9.81
			75.66			37.46
1974	December 31	616.24	23.15	99.04	6.2	10.45
	September 30	607.87	26.73	99.73	6.1	9.43
	June 28	802.41	26.68	93.26	8.6	8.87
	March 29	846.68	22.48	89.46	9.5	8.97
			99.04			37.72
1973	December 31	850.86	23.84	86.17	9.9	10.62
	September 28	947.10	20.26	82.09	11.5	8.36
	June 29	891.71	22.88	77.56	11.5	8.27
	March 30	951.01	19.19	71.98	13.2	8.08
			86.17			35.33
1972	December 29	1020.02	19.76	67.11	15.2	8.99
	September 29	953.27	15.73	62.15	15.3	7.76
	June 30	929.03	17.30	58.87	15.8	7.87
	March 30	940.70	14.32	56.76	16.6	7.65
			67.11			32.27
1971	December 31	890.20	14.80	55.09	16.2	7.85
	September 30	887.19	12.45	53.43	16.6	7.51
	June 30	891.14	15.19	53.45	16.7	7.80
	March 31	904.37	12.65	52.36	17.3	7.70
			55.09			30.86
1970	December 31	838.92	13.14	51.02	16.4	8.25
	September 30	760.68	12.47	51.83	14.7	7.80
	June 30	683.53	14.10	53.18	12.8	7.80
	March 31	785.57	11.31	54.07	14.5	7.68
			51.02			31.53

Source: *The Dow Jones Investor's Handbook* (Homewood, Ill.: Dow Jones-Irwin, 1984).

Dow Jones Industrial Average
Earnings, Dividends and Price-Earnings Ratio

	Price	Earnings (by qtrs)	Preceding 12 mos. earnings	Price Earnings Ratio (col. 1 ÷ col. 3)	Dividends
1969 December 31	800.36	13.95	57.02	14.0	8.63
September 30	813.09	13.82	59.60	13.6	7.82
June 30	873.19	14.99	59.47	14.7	8.08
March 28	935.48	14.26	59.34	15.8	9.37
		57.02			33.90
1968 December 31	943.75	16.53	57.89	16.3	8.59
September 30	935.79	13.69	57.05	16.4	7.73
June 28	897.80	14.86	55.71	16.1	7.73
March 29	840.67	12.81	53.98	15.6	7.29
		57.89			31.34
1967 December 29	905.11	15.69	53.87	16.8	8.03
September 29	926.66	12.35	52.73	17.6	7.25
June 30	860.26	13.13	54.27	15.8	7.36
March 31	865.98	12.70	56.67	15.3	7.55
		53.87			30.19
1966 December 30	785.69	14.55	57.68	13.6	10.01
September 30	774.22	13.89	57.36	13.5	7.18
June 30	870.10	15.53	56.23	15.5	7.26
March 31	924.77	13.71	55.05	16.8	7.44
		57.68			31.89
1965 December 31	969.26	14.23	53.67	18.1	8.54
September 30	930.58	12.76	52.74	17.6	6.58
June 30	868.03	14.35	50.84	17.1	6.79
March 31	889.05	12.33	48.55	18.3	6.70
		53.67			28.61
1964 December 31	874.13	13.30	46.43	18.8	10.46
September 30	875.37	10.86	45.88	19.1	5.79
June 30	831.50	12.06	44.46	18.7	7.16
March 31	813.29	10.21	42.60	19.1	7.83
		46.43			31.24
1963 December 31	762.95	12.75	41.21	18.5	7.39
September 30	732.79	9.44	40.18	18.2	5.35
June 28	706.68	10.20	38.71	18.3	5.52
March 29	682.52	8.82	37.35	18.3	5.15
		41.21			23.41
1962 December 31	652.10	11.72	36.43	17.9	7.66
September 28	578.98	7.97	35.52	16.3	5.26
June 29	561.28	8.84	34.74	16.2	5.23
March 30	706.95	7.90	34.11	20.7	5.15
		36.43			23.30

Source: *The Dow Jones Investor's Handbook* (Homewood, Ill.: Dow Jones-Irwin, 1984).

Dow Jones Industrial Average
Earnings, Dividends and Price-Earnings Ratio

		Price	Earnings (by qtrs)	Preceding 12 mos. earnings	Price Earnings Ratio (col. 1 ÷ col. 3)	Dividends
1961	December 29	731.13	10.81	31.91	22.9	7.57
	September 29	701.21	7.19	29.03	24.2	5.09
	June 30	683.96	8.21	29.29	23.4	5.05
	March 30	676.63	5.70	29.53	22.9	5.00
			31.91			22.71
1960	December 31	615.89	7.93	32.21	19.1	6.55
	September 30	580.14	7.45	31.64	18.3	4.86
	June 30	640.62	8.45	31.26	20.5	4.83
	March 31	610.59	8.38	33.82	18.2	5.12
			32.21			21.36
1959	December 31	679.36	7.36	34.31	19.8	6.73
	September 30	631.68	7.07	35.70	17.7	4.53
	June 30	643.60	11.01	35.71	18.0	4.59
	March 31	601.71	8.87	31.04	19.4	4.89
			34.31			20.74
1958	December 31	583.65	8.75	27.95	20.9	5.83
	September 30	532.09	7.08	27.97	19.0	4.59
	June 30	478.18	6.34	29.41	16.3	4.62
	March 31	446.76	5.78	32.56	13.7	4.96
			27.95			20.00
1957	December 31	435.69	8.78	36.08	12.1	6.91
	September 30	456.30	8.51	36.70	12.4	4.91
	June 28	503.29	9.49	34.82	14.4	4.79
	March 29	474.81	9.30	34.30	13.8	5.00
			36.08			21.61
1956	December 31	499.47	9.40	33.34	15.0	8.17
	September 28	475.25	6.63	33.65	14.1	4.83
	June 29	492.78	8.97	35.51	13.9	4.98
	March 29	511.79	8.34	36.02	14.2	5.01
			33.34			22.99
1955	December 30	488.40	9.71	35.78	13.7	8.13
	September 30	466.62	8.49	34.41	13.6	4.25
	June 30	451.38	9.48	32.11	14.1	4.24
	March 31	409.70	8.10	29.65	13.8	4.96
			35.78			21.58
1954	December 31	404.39	8.34	28.18	14.4	5.76
	September 30	360.46	6.19	26.99	13.4	3.75
	June 30	333.53	7.02	27.52	12.1	3.92
	March 31	303.51	6.63	27.20	11.2	4.04
			28.18			17.47

Source: *The Dow Jones Investor's Handbook* (Homewood, Ill.: Dow Jones-Irwin, 1984).

Dow Jones Industrial Average
Earnings, Dividends and Price-Earnings Ratio

		Price	Earnings (by qtrs)	Preceding 12 mos. earnings	Price Earnings Ratio (col. 1 ÷ col. 3)	Dividends
1953	December 31	280.90	7.15	27.23	10.3	4.86
	September 30	264.04	6.72	27.63	9.6	3.53
	June 30	268.26	6.70	26.93	10.0	3.95
	March 31	279.87	6.66	25.78	10.9	3.77
			27.23			16.11
1952	December 31	291.90	7.55	24.78	11.8	4.62
	September 30	270.61	6.02	24.37	11.1	3.55
	June 30	274.35	5.55	24.06	11.4	3.55
	March 31	269.46	5.66	25.11	10.7	3.71
			24.78			15.43
1951	December 31	269.23	7.14	26.59	10.1	5.25
	September 28	271.16	5.71	29.02	9.3	3.72
	June 29	242.64	6.60	31.83	7.6	3.48
	March 31	247.94	7.14	32.40	7.7	3.89
			26.59			16.34
1950	December 30	235.41	9.57	30.70	7.7	6.26
	September 29	226.36	8.52	27.15	8.3	3.87
	June 30	209.11	7.17	24.99	8.4	2.98
	March 31	206.05	5.44	23.20	8.9	3.02
			30.70			16.13
1949	December 31	200.13	6.02	23.54	8.5	5.02
	September 30	182.51	6.36	24.66	7.4	2.32
	June 30	167.42	5.38	23.95	7.0	2.85
	March 31	177.10	5.78	23.79	7.4	2.60
			23.54			12.79
1948	December 31	177.30	7.14	23.07	7.7	4.32
	September 30	178.30	5.65	20.94	8.5	2.42
	June 30	189.46	5.22	19.60	9.7	2.59
	March 31	177.20	5.06	19.01	9.3	2.17
			23.07			11.50
1947	December 31	181.16	5.01	18.80	9.6	2.98
	September 30	177.49	4.31	18.66	9.5	2.09
	June 30	177.30	4.63	18.10	9.8	2.22
	March 31	177.20	4.85	16.62	10.7	1.92
			18.80			9.21
1946	December 31	177.20	4.87	13.63	13.0	2.45
	September 30	172.42	3.75	11.56	14.9	1.70
	June 28	205.62	3.15	10.24	20.1	1.78
	March 30	199.75	1.86	9.76	20.5	1.57
			13.63			7.50

Source: *The Dow Jones Investor's Handbook* (Homewood, Ill.: Dow Jones-Irwin, 1984).

YEARLY HIGHS AND LOWS OF DOW JONES AVERAGES

		—Industrials—		—Transportation—		—Utilities—	
		High	Low	High	Low	High	Low
1983	. . . .	1287.20	1027.04	612.57	434.24	140.70	119.51
1982	. . . .	1070.55	776.92	464.55	292.12	122.83	103.22
1981	. . . .	1024.05	824.01	447.38	335.48	117.81	101.28
1980	. . . .	1000.17	759.13	425.68	233.69	117.34	96.04
1979	. . . .	897.61	796.67	271.77	205.78	109.74	98.24
1978	. . . .	907.74	742.12	261.49	199.31	110.98	96.35
1977	. . . .	999.75	800.85	246.64	199.60	118.67	104.97
1976	. . . .	1014.79	858.71	237.03	175.69	108.38	84.52
1975	. . . .	881.81	632.04	174.57	146.47	87.07	72.02
1974	. . . .	891.66	577.60	202.45	125.93	95.09	57.93
1973	. . . .	1051.70	788.31	228.10	151.97	120.72	84.42
1972	. . . .	1036.27	889.15	275.71	212.24	124.14	105.06
1971	. . . .	950.82	797.97	248.33	169.70	128.39	108.03
1970	. . . .	842.00	631.16	183.31	116.69	121.84	95.86
1969	. . . .	968.85	769.93	279.88	169.03	139.95	106.31
1968	. . . .	985.21	825.13	279.48	214.58	141.30	119.79
1967	. . . .	943.08	786.41	274.49	205.16	140.43	120.97
1966	. . . .	995.15	744.32	271.72	184.34	152.39	118.96
1965	. . . .	969.26	840.59	249.55	187.29	163.32	149.84
1964	. . . .	891.71	766.08	224.91	178.81	155.71	137.30
1963	. . . .	767.21	646.69	179.46	142.03	144.37	129.19
1962	. . . .	726.01	535.76	149.83	114.86	130.85	103.11
1961	. . . .	734.91	610.25	152.92	131.06	135.90	99.75
1960	. . . .	685.47	566.05	160.43	123.37	100.07	85.02
1959	. . . .	679.36	574.46	173.56	146.65	94.70	85.05
1958	. . . .	583.65	436.89	157.91	99.89	91.00	68.94
1957	. . . .	520.77	419.79	157.67	95.67	74.61	62.10
1956	. . . .	521.05	462.35	181.23	150.44	71.77	63.03
1955	. . . .	488.40	388.20	167.83	137.84	66.68	61.39
1954	. . . .	404.39	279.87	146.23	94.84	62.47	52.22
1953	. . . .	293.79	255.49	112.21	90.56	53.88	47.87
1952	. . . .	292.00	256.35	112.53	82.03	52.64	47.53
1951	. . . .	276.37	238.99	90.08	72.39	47.22	41.47
1950	. . . .	235.47	196.81	77.89	51.24	44.26	37.40
1949	. . . .	200.52	161.60	54.29	41.03	41.31	33.36
1948	. . . .	193.16	165.39	64.95	48.13	36.04	31.65
1947	. . . .	186.85	163.21	53.42	41.16	37.55	32.28
1946	. . . .	212.50	163.12	63.31	44.69	43.74	33.20
1945	. . . .	195.82	151.35	64.89	47.03	39.15	26.15
1944	. . . .	152.53	134.22	48.40	33.45	26.37	21.74
1943	. . . .	145.82	119.26	38.30	27.59	22.30	14.69
1942	. . . .	119.71	92.92	29.28	23.31	14.94	10.58
1941	. . . .	133.59	106.34	30.88	24.25	20.65	13.51

Source: *The Dow Jones Investor's Handbook* (Homewood, Ill.: Dow Jones-Irwin, 1984).

YEARLY HIGHS AND LOWS OF DOW JONES AVERAGES

	—Industrials—		—Transportation—		—Utilities—	
	High	Low	High	Low	High	Low
1940	152.80	111.84	32.67	22.14	26.45	18.03
1939	155.92	121.44	35.90	24.14	27.10	20.71
1938	158.41	98.95	33.98	19.00	c25.19	c15.14
1937	194.40	113.64	64.46	28.91	37.54	19.65
1936	184.90	143.11	59.89	40.66	36.08	28.63
1935	148.44	96.71	41.84	27.31	29.78	14.46
1934	110.74	85.51	52.97	33.19	31.03	16.83
1933	108.67	50.16	56.53	23.42	37.73	19.33
1932	88.78	41.22	41.20	13.23	36.11	16.53
1931	194.36	73.79	111.58	31.42	73.40	30.55
1930	294.07	157.51	157.94	91.65	108.62	55.14
1929	381.17	198.69	189.11	128.07	144.61	64.72
1928	300.00	191.33	b152.70	b132.60	....	....
1927	202.40	152.73	144.82	119.92	....	....
1926	166.64	135.20	123.23	102.41	....	....
1925	159.39	115.00	112.93	92.82	....	....
1924	120.51	88.33	99.50	80.23	....	....
1923	105.38	85.76	90.63	76.78	....	....
1922	103.43	78.59	93.99	74.43	....	....
1921	81.50	63.90	77.56	65.52	....	....
1920	109.88	66.75	85.37	67.83	....	....
1919	119.62	79.15	91.13	73.63	....	....
1918	89.07	73.38	92.91	77.21	....	....
1917	99.18	65.95	105.76	70.75	....	....
1916	110.15	84.96	112.28	99.11	....	....
1915	99.21	54.22	108.28	87.85	....	....
1914	a83.43	a71.42	a109.43	a89.41	....	....
1913	88.57	72.11	118.10	100.50	....	....
1912	94.15	80.15	124.35	114.92	....	....
1911	87.06	72.94	123.86	109.80	....	....
1910	98.34	73.62	129.90	105.59	....	....
1909	100.53	79.91	134.46	113.90	....	....
1908	87.67	58.62	120.05	86.04	....	....

a—The high and low figures for the industrials and transportation are for the period ended July 31, 1914. The industrial average was composed of 12 stocks when the New York Stock Exchange closed in July 1914 because of World War I. In September 1916, a new list of 20 stocks was adopted and computed back to the opening of the Exchange on December 12, 1914. On October 1, 1928, the stocks comprising the industrial average was increased to 30. The high and low for the industrial average for December 1914 was 56.76 and 53.17, respectively. The high and low for transportation for December 1914 was 92.29 and 86.40.

b—On March 7, 1928, transportation components were increased to 20 from 12.

c—Since June 2, 1938, the utility average has been based on 15 stocks instead of 20.

Source: *The Dow Jones Investor's Handbook* (Homewood, Ill.: Dow Jones-Irwin, 1984).

Standard and Poor's 500 Composite Index

COMPOSITE—500 STOCKS

Per Share Data—Adjusted to stock price index level. Average of stock price indexes, 1941-1943=10

	Earnings Per Share	Dividends			Price 1941-1943=10		Price/Earn. Ratio		Div. Yields %	
		Per Share	% of Earn.		High	Low	High	Low	High	Low
1957	3.37	1.79	53.12		49.13	38.98	14.58	11.57	4.59	3.64
1958	2.89	1.75	60.55		55.21	40.33	19.10	13.96	4.33	3.17
1959	3.39	1.83	53.98		60.71	53.58	17.91	15.81	3.42	3.01
1960	3.27	1.95	59.63		60.39	52.30	18.47	15.99	3.73	3.23
1961	3.19	2.02	63.32		72.64	57.57	22.77	18.05	3.51	2.78
1962	3.67	2.13	58.04		71.13	52.53	19.38	14.26	4.07	2.99
1963	4.02	2.28	56.72		75.02	62.69	18.66	15.59	3.64	3.04
1964	4.55	2.50	54.95		86.28	75.43	18.96	16.58	3.31	2.90
1965	5.19	2.72	52.41		92.63	81.60	17.85	15.72	3.33	2.94
1966	5.55	2.87	51.71		94.06	73.20	16.95	13.19	3.92	3.05
1967	5.33	2.92	54.78		97.59	80.38	18.31	15.08	3.63	2.99
1968	5.76	3.07	53.30		108.37	87.72	18.81	15.23	3.50	2.83
1969	5.78	3.16	54.67		106.16	89.20	18.37	15.43	3.54	2.98
1970	5.13	3.14	61.21		93.46	69.29	18.22	13.51	4.53	3.36
1971	5.70	3.07	53.86		104.77	90.16	18.38	15.82	3.41	2.93
1972	6.42	3.15	49.07		119.12	101.67	18.55	15.84	3.10	2.64
1973	8.16	3.38	41.42		120.24	92.16	14.74	11.29	3.67	2.81
1974	8.89	3.60	40.49		99.80	62.28	11.23	7.01	5.78	3.61
1975	7.96	3.68	46.23		95.61	70.04	12.01	8.80	5.25	3.85
1976	9.91	4.05	40.87		107.83	90.90	10.88	9.17	4.46	3.76
1977	10.89	4.67	42.88		107.00	90.71	9.83	8.33	5.15	4.36
1978	12.33	5.07	41.12		106.99	86.90	8.68	7.05	5.83	4.74
1979	14.86	5.65	38.02		111.27	96.13	7.49	6.47	5.88	5.08
1980	14.82	6.16	41.57		140.52	98.22	9.48	6.63	6.27	4.38
1981	15.36	6.63	43.16		138.12	112.77	8.99	7.34	5.88	4.80
1982	12.64	6.87	54.35		143.02	102.42	11.31	8.10	6.71	4.80
1983	14.03	7.09	50.54		172.65	138.34	12.31	9.86	5.13	4.11

Source: *Standard & Poor's Analyst's Handbook* (New York: Standard & Poor's Corporation, 1984).

400 INDUSTRIALS*

Per Share Data — Adjusted to stock price index level. Average of stock price indexes, 1941-1943 = 10

	Sales	Oper. Profit	Profit Margin %	Depr.	Income Taxes	Earnings Per Share	Earnings % of Sales	Dividends Per Share	Dividends % of Earn.	Price 1941-1943=10 High	Price Low	Price/Earn. Ratio High	Price/Earn. Ratio Low	Div. Yields % High	Div. Yields % Low	Book Value Per Share	Book Value % Return	Working Capital	Capital Expenditures
1953	49.50	6.99	14.12	1.53	2.95	2.57	5.19	1.34	52.14	26.99	22.70	10.50	8.83	5.90	4.96	20.76	12.38	11.70	2.77
1954	46.19	6.50	14.07	1.66	2.29	2.69	5.82	1.45	53.90	37.24	24.84	13.84	9.23	5.84	3.89	22.09	12.18	12.19	2.77
1955	54.14	8.58	15.85	1.92	3.23	3.58	6.61	1.74	48.60	49.54	35.66	13.84	9.96	4.88	3.51	25.09	14.27	14.03	3.03
1956	54.73	8.36	15.27	2.04	2.96	3.50	6.40	1.84	52.57	53.28	45.71	15.22	13.06	4.03	3.45	26.35	13.28	13.91	4.14
1957	55.81	8.79	15.75	2.41	2.87	3.53	6.33	1.94	54.96	53.25	41.98	15.08	11.89	4.62	3.64	29.44	11.99	13.50	4.84
1958	53.48	7.70	14.40	2.38	2.40	2.95	5.52	1.86	63.05	58.97	43.20	19.99	14.64	4.31	3.15	30.66	9.62	14.27	3.58
1959	57.83	8.84	15.29	2.47	2.99	3.47	6.00	1.95	56.20	65.32	57.02	18.82	16.43	3.42	2.99	32.26	10.76	14.93	3.65
1960	59.47	8.73	14.68	2.56	2.87	3.40	5.72	2.00	58.82	65.02	55.34	19.12	16.28	3.61	3.08	33.74	10.08	15.29	4.23
1961	59.51	8.75	14.70	2.66	2.80	3.37	5.66	2.07	61.42	76.69	60.87	22.76	18.06	3.40	2.70	34.85	9.67	15.84	3.97
1962	64.63	9.81	15.18	2.89	3.16	3.83	5.93	2.20	57.44	75.22	54.80	19.64	14.31	4.01	2.92	36.37	10.53	16.85	4.41
1963	68.50	10.73	15.66	3.04	3.51	4.24	6.19	2.36	55.66	79.25	65.48	18.69	15.44	3.60	2.98	38.17	11.11	17.64	4.41
1964	73.19	11.67	15.94	3.24	3.70	4.85	6.63	2.58	53.20	91.29	79.74	18.82	16.44	3.24	2.83	40.23	12.06	18.07	5.71
1965	80.69	13.11	16.25	3.52	4.14	5.50	6.82	2.82	51.27	98.55	86.43	17.92	15.71	3.26	2.86	43.50	12.64	18.80	6.87
1966	88.46	14.48	16.37	3.87	4.35	5.87	6.64	2.95	50.26	100.60	77.89	17.14	13.27	3.79	2.93	45.59	12.88	19.48	8.26
1967	91.86	14.28	15.55	4.25	4.11	5.62	6.12	2.97	52.85	106.15	85.31	18.89	15.18	3.48	2.80	47.78	11.76	20.74	8.35
1968	101.49	16.08	15.84	4.56	5.14	6.16	6.07	3.16	51.30	118.03	95.05	19.16	15.43	3.32	2.68	50.21	12.27	21.08	8.65
1969	108.53	16.63	15.32	4.87	5.14	6.13	5.65	3.25	53.02	116.24	97.75	18.96	15.95	3.32	2.80	51.70	11.86	21.05	9.70
1970	109.85	15.54	14.15	5.17	4.23	5.41	4.92	3.20	59.15	102.87	75.58	19.01	13.97	4.23	3.11	52.65	10.28	20.70	10.25
1971	118.23	17.22	14.56	5.45	4.98	5.97	5.04	3.16	52.93	115.84	99.36	19.40	16.64	3.18	2.73	55.28	10.80	22.61	9.96
1972	128.79	19.39	15.06	5.76	5.90	6.83	5.30	3.22	47.14	132.95	112.19	19.47	16.43	2.87	2.42	58.34	11.71	24.41	10.08
1973	149.22	23.64	15.84	6.25	7.59	8.89	5.96	3.46	38.92	134.54	103.37	15.13	11.63	3.35	2.57	62.84	14.15	26.49	11.65
1974	182.10	27.97	15.36	6.86	10.22	9.61	5.28	3.71	38.61	111.65	69.53	11.62	7.24	5.34	3.32	67.81	14.17	28.47	14.65
1975	185.16	26.63	14.38	7.36	9.40	8.58	4.63	3.72	43.36	107.40	77.71	12.52	9.06	4.79	3.46	70.84	12.11	30.47	14.43
1976	202.66	29.23	14.42	7.58	10.21	10.69	5.27	4.22	39.48	120.89	101.64	11.31	9.51	4.15	3.49	76.26	14.02	31.89	14.92
1977	224.24	32.20	14.36	8.53	11.14	11.45	5.11	4.95	43.23	118.92	99.88	10.39	8.72	4.96	4.16	82.21	13.93	33.28	17.02
1978	251.32	36.19	14.40	9.64	12.14	13.04	5.19	5.37	41.18	118.71	95.52	9.10	7.33	5.63	4.53	89.34	14.60	34.88	19.70
1979	292.38	42.01	14.37	10.82	14.02	16.29	5.57	5.92	36.34	124.49	107.08	7.64	6.57	5.53	4.76	98.71	16.50	36.32	26.44
1980	327.36	43.08	13.16	12.37	13.67	16.12	4.92	6.49	40.26	160.96	111.09	9.99	6.89	5.84	4.03	108.33	14.88	36.52	29.86
1981	344.31	44.50	12.92	13.82	12.95	16.74	4.86	7.01	41.88	157.02	125.93	9.38	7.52	5.57	4.46	116.06	14.42	35.98	33.03
R1982	333.86	42.67	12.78	15.30	10.95	13.20	3.95	7.13	54.02	159.66	114.08	12.10	8.64	6.25	4.47	118.60	11.13	34.41	31.30
1983	334.58	45.81	13.69	16.16	12.13	14.78	4.42	7.32	49.53	194.84	154.95	13.18	10.48	4.72	3.76	121.66	12.15	36.74	24.86

NOTE: 1983 data incls. results of 'old' A.T.'; excls. $5.5 bil. charge
*Based on 68 individual groups.
Stock Price Indexes for this group extend back to 1918.

Source: Standard & Poor's *Analyst's Handbook* (New York: Standard & Poor's Corporation, 1984).

Standard and Poor's 400 Industrial Index
(Income Statement, Balance Sheet, Financial Ratios)

S & P 400
Per Share Data - Adjusted to Stock Price Index Level
Average of Stock Price Indexes, 1941 - 1943 = 10

Income Account —

	1983	1982	1981	1980	1979	1978
Sales	329.32	333.86	344.31	327.36	292.38	251.32
Costs & expenses	283.72	291.19	299.81	284.28	250.37	215.13
Operating income	45.61	42.67	44.50	43.08	42.01	36.19
Other income	5.10	5.42	6.93	5.55	4.14	2.84
Total income	50.70	48.09	51.42	48.63	46.15	39.02
Depreciation	16.09	15.30	13.82	12.37	10.82	9.64
Interest	7.56	8.23	7.49	5.95	4.58	3.84
Minority interest	0.21	0.19	0.22	0.33	0.29	0.23
Income taxes	11.98	10.95	12.95	13.67	14.02	12.14
Net income	14.87	13.41	16.94	16.31	16.45	13.17
Preferred dividends	0.34	0.26	0.24	0.22	0.19	0.16
Savings fr. com. stk. equiv.	0.03	0.04	0.04	0.04	0.03	0.03
Common earnings	14.56	13.20	16.74	16.12	16.29	13.04
Common dividends	7.25	7.13	7.01	6.49	5.92	5.37
Balance after dividends	7.31	6.06	9.73	9.63	10.38	7.67

Financial Ratios—

	1983	1982	1981	1980	1979	1978
Current ratio	1.5	1.5	1.5	1.6	1.6	1.7
Quick ratio	0.9	0.9	0.9	0.9	0.9	1.0
Debt to total assets (%)	23	24	23	22	22	22
Times interest earned	4.6	4.0	5.0	6.0	7.7	7.6
Inventory turnover	8.0	7.4	7.8	7.6	7.2	7.2
Total assets turnover	1.1	1.2	1.3	1.3	1.3	1.3
Profit margin (%)	13.85	12.78	12.92	13.16	14.37	14.40
Return on total assets (%)	5.08	4.64	6.22	6.47	7.24	6.58

Balance Sheet

Assets —

	1983	1982	1981	1980	1979	1978
Cash & equivalent	20.32	15.67	14.69	15.17	15.27	15.34
Receivables	44.90	41.90	40.68	39.93	38.80	33.39
Income tax refund	0.28	0.34	0.23	0.24	0.07	0.04
Inventories	41.30	44.99	44.02	42.83	40.42	35.09
Other current assets	4.88	5.21	4.71	4.12	3.19	2.68
Total current assets	107.04	104.68	103.29	101.51	97.65	86.44
Net property, plant, & equipment	141.15	144.06	134.37	120.03	106.89	94.15
Inv. & adv. to uncons. subs.	13.12	12.58	11.87	10.87	10.03	8.89
Intangibles	3.88	3.76	3.19	2.66	2.69	2.22
Other assets	16.79	15.72	15.58	13.23	7.65	6.43
Total assets	286.62	284.22	269.32	249.08	225.00	198.24

Liabilities —

	1983	1982	1981	1980	1979	1978
Notes payable	13.30	13.94	10.05	8.96	8.01	5.89
Current portion of long term debt	2.40	2.44	2.17	1.94	1.79	1.85
Accounts payable	27.03	25.16	26.07	25.71	23.75	19.88
Income tax payable	6.78	6.70	7.07	7.94	7.26	5.87
Accrued expenses	15.54	15.12	14.85	13.61	12.61	11.11
Other current liabilities	8.95	9.12	9.01	8.53	7.91	6.96
Total current liabilities	70.69	70.26	67.31	64.99	61.33	51.56
Long term debt	49.70	52.72	49.06	43.27	39.22	36.23
Deferred income tax	18.38	17.74	15.97	13.43	10.83	8.93
Minority interest	1.82	1.95	2.02	2.14	2.06	1.83
Other liabilities	17.20	15.04	12.31	10.97	6.90	5.45
Preferred stock	3.21	3.48	2.82	2.57	2.19	1.82
Common stock	9.40	11.33	11.17	10.64	10.37	10.34
Capital surplus	20.53	16.20	14.64	12.72	11.90	11.29
Retained earnings	95.71	95.50	94.03	88.35	80.20	70.78
Total liabilities	286.62	284.22	269.32	249.08	225.00	198.24

NA - Not Available
NM - Not Meaningful
Note: Data presented in the above format reflects results for only those companies which have reported; no estimates are used. This holds true for all industry groups. The tables in the front of the book do reflect estimated results for those companies which have not reported for fiscal 1983.

Source: *Standard & Poor's Analyst's Handbook* (New York: Standard & Poor's Corporation, 1984).

STOCK PRICE INDEXES—COMPOSITE†

(500 Stocks)

1941-1943 = 10

Monthly Averages of Daily Indexes

	Jan.	Feb.	Mar.	Apr.	May	June	July	Aug.	Sept.	Oct.	Nov.	Dec.	Avg.
1926	12.65	12.67	11.81	11.48	11.56	12.11	12.62	13.12	13.32	13.02	13.19	13.49	12.59
1927	13.40	13.66	13.87	14.21	14.70	14.89	15.22	16.03	16.94	16.68	17.06	17.46	15.34
1928	17.53	17.32	18.25	19.40	20.00	19.02	19.16	19.78	21.17	21.60	23.06	23.15	19.95
1929	24.86	24.99	25.43	25.28	25.66	26.15	28.48	30.10	31.30	27.99	20.58	21.40	26.02
1930	21.71	23.07	23.94	25.46	23.94	21.52	21.06	20.79	20.78	17.92	16.62	15.51	21.03
1931	15.98	17.20	17.53	15.86	14.33	13.87	14.33	13.90	11.83	10.25	10.39	8.44	13.66
1932	8.30	8.23	8.26	6.28	5.51	4.77	5.01	7.53	8.26	7.12	7.05	6.82	6.93
1933	7.09	6.25	6.23	6.89	8.87	10.39	11.23	10.67	10.58	9.55	9.78	9.97	8.96
1934	10.54	11.32	10.74	10.92	9.81	9.94	9.47	9.10	8.88	8.95	9.20	9.26	9.84
1935	9.26	8.98	8.41	9.04	9.75	10.12	10.65	11.37	11.61	11.92	13.04	13.04	10.60
1936	13.76	14.55	14.86	14.88	14.09	14.69	15.56	15.87	16.05	16.89	17.36	17.06	15.47
1937	17.59	18.11	18.09	17.01	16.25	15.64	16.57	16.74	14.37	12.28	11.20	11.02	15.41
1938	11.31	11.04	10.31	9.89	9.98	10.21	12.24	12.31	11.75	13.06	13.07	12.69	11.49
1939	12.50	12.40	12.39	10.83	11.23	11.43	11.71	11.54	12.77	12.90	12.67	12.37	12.06
1940	12.30	12.22	12.15	12.27	10.58	9.67	9.99	10.20	10.63	10.73	10.98	10.53	11.02
1941	10.55	9.89	9.95	9.64	9.43	9.76	10.26	10.21	10.24	9.83	9.37	8.76	9.82
1942	8.93	8.65	8.18	7.84	7.93	8.33	8.64	8.59	8.68	9.32	9.47	9.52	8.67
1943	10.09	10.69	11.07	11.44	11.89	12.10	12.35	11.74	11.99	11.88	11.33	11.48	11.50
1944	11.85	11.77	12.10	11.89	12.10	12.67	13.00	12.81	12.60	12.91	12.82	13.10	12.47
1945	13.49	13.94	13.93	14.28	14.82	15.09	14.78	14.83	15.84	16.50	17.04	17.33	15.16
1946	18.02	18.07	17.53	18.66	18.70	18.58	18.05	17.70	15.09	14.75	14.69	15.13	17.08
1947	15.21	15.80	15.16	14.60	14.34	14.84	15.77	15.46	15.06	15.45	15.27	15.03	15.17
1948	14.83	14.10	14.30	15.40	16.15	16.82	16.42	15.94	15.76	16.19	15.29	15.19	15.53
1949	15.36	14.77	14.91	14.89	14.78	13.97	14.76	15.29	15.49	15.89	16.11	16.54	15.23
1950	16.88	17.21	17.35	17.84	18.44	18.74	17.38	18.43	19.08	19.87	19.83	19.75	18.40
1951	21.21	22.00	21.63	21.92	21.93	21.55	21.93	22.89	23.48	23.36	22.71	23.41	22.34
1952	24.19	23.75	23.81	23.74	23.73	24.38	25.08	25.18	24.78	24.26	25.03	26.04	24.50
1953	26.18	25.86	25.99	24.71	24.84	23.95	24.29	24.39	23.27	23.97	24.50	24.83	24.73
1954	25.46	26.02	26.57	27.63	28.73	28.96	30.13	30.73	31.45	32.18	33.44	34.97	29.69
1955	35.60	36.79	36.50	37.76	37.60	39.78	42.69	42.43	44.34	42.11	44.95	45.37	40.49
1956	44.15	44.43	47.49	48.05	46.54	46.27	48.78	48.49	46.84	46.24	45.76	46.44	46.62
1957	45.43	43.47	44.03	45.05	46.78	47.55	48.51	45.84	43.98	41.24	40.35	40.33	44.38
1958	41.12	41.26	42.11	42.34	43.70	44.75	45.98	47.70	48.96	50.95	52.50	53.49	46.24
1959	55.62	54.77	56.15	57.10	57.96	57.46	59.74	59.40	57.05	57.00	57.23	59.06	57.38
1960	58.03	55.78	55.02	55.73	55.22	57.26	55.84	56.51	54.81	53.73	55.47	56.80	55.85
1961	59.72	62.17	64.12	65.83	66.50	65.62	65.44	67.79	67.26	68.00	71.08	71.74	68.27
1962	69.07	70.22	70.29	68.05	62.99	55.63	56.97	58.52	58.00	56.17	60.04	62.64	62.38
1963	65.06	65.92	65.67	68.76	70.14	70.11	69.07	70.98	72.85	73.03	72.62	74.17	69.87
1964	76.45	77.39	78.80	79.94	80.72	80.24	83.22	82.00	83.41	84.85	85.44	83.96	81.37
1965	86.12	86.75	86.83	87.97	89.28	85.04	84.91	86.49	89.38	91.39	92.15	91.73	88.17
1966	93.32	92.69	88.88	91.60	86.78	86.06	85.84	80.65	77.81	77.13	80.99	81.33	85.26
1967	84.45	87.36	89.42	90.96	92.59	91.43	93.01	94.49	95.81	95.66	92.66	95.30	91.93
1968	95.04	90.75	89.09	95.67	97.87	100.5	100.3	98.11	101.3	103.8	105.4	106.5	98.69
1969	102.0	101.5	99.30	101.3	104.6	99.14	94.71	94.18	94.51	95.52	96.21	91.11	97.84
1970	90.31	87.16	88.65	85.95	76.06	75.59	75.72	77.92	82.58	84.37	84.28	90.05	83.22
1971	93.49	97.11	99.60	103.0	101.6	99.72	99.00	97.24	99.40	97.29	92.78	99.17	98.29
1972	103.3	105.2	107.7	108.8	107.7	108.0	107.2	111.0	109.4	109.6	115.1	117.5	109.2
1973	118.4	114.2	112.4	110.3	107.2	104.8	105.8	103.8	105.6	109.8	102.0	94.78	107.4
1974	96.11	93.45	97.44	92.46	89.67	89.79	82.82	76.03	68.12	69.44	71.74	67.07	82.85
1975	72.56	80.10	83.78	84.72	90.10	92.40	92.49	85.71	84.67	88.57	90.07	88.70	86.16
1976	96.86	100.6	101.1	101.9	101.2	101.8	104.2	103.3	105.5	101.9	101.2	104.7	102.0
1977	103.8	101.0	100.6	99.05	98.76	99.29	100.2	97.75	96.23	93.74	94.28	93.82	98.20
1978	90.25	88.98	88.82	92.71	97.41	97.66	97.19	103.9	103.9	100.6	94.71	96.11	96.02
1979	99.71	98.23	100.1	102.1	99.73	101.7	102.7	107.4	108.6	104.5	103.7	107.8	103.0
1980	110.9	115.3	104.7	103.0	107.7	114.6	119.8	123.5	126.5	130.2	135.7	133.5	118.8
1981	133.0	128.4	133.2	134.4	131.7	132.3	129.1	129.6	118.3	119.8	122.9	123.8	128.1
1982	117.3	114.5	110.8	116.3	116.4	109.7	109.4	109.7	122.4	132.7	138.1	139.4	119.7
1983	144.3	146.8	151.9	157.7	164.1	166.4	167.0	162.4	167.2	167.7	165.2	164.4	160.4

Annual Range, and Close, of Daily Indexes

Year	High	Low	Close	Year	High	Low	Close	Year	High	Low	Close
1926	13.66	10.93	13.49	1946	19.25	14.12	15.30	1966	94.06	73.20	80.33
1927	17.71	13.18	17.66	1947	16.20	13.71	15.30	1967	97.59	80.38	96.47
1928	24.35	16.95	24.35	1948	17.06	13.84	15.20	1968	108.4	87.72	103.9
1929	31.92	17.66	21.45	1949	16.79	13.55	16.76	1969	106.2	89.20	92.06
1930	25.92	14.44	15.34	1950	20.43	16.65	20.41	1970	93.46	69.29	92.15
1931	18.17	7.72	8.12	1951	23.85	20.69	23.77	1971	104.8	90.16	102.1
1932	9.31	4.40	6.89	1952	26.59	23.09	26.57	1972	119.1	101.7	118.1
1933	12.20	5.53	10.10	1953	26.66	22.71	24.81	1973	120.2	92.16	97.55
1934	11.82	8.36	9.50	1954	35.98	24.80	35.98	1974	99.80	62.28	68.56
1935	13.46	8.06	13.43	1955	46.41	34.58	45.48	1975	95.61	70.04	90.19
1936	17.69	13.40	17.18	1956	49.74	43.11	46.67	1976	107.8	90.90	107.5
1937	18.68	10.17	10.55	1957	49.13	38.98	39.99	1977	107.0	90.71	95.10
1938	13.79	8.50	13.21	1958	55.21	40.33	55.21	1978	107.0	86.90	96.11
1939	13.23	10.18	12.49	1959	60.71	53.58	59.89	1979	111.3	96.13	107.9
1940	12.77	8.99	10.58	1960	60.39	52.30	58.11	1980	140.5	98.22	135.8
1941	10.86	8.37	8.69	1961	72.64	57.57	71.55	1981	138.1	112.8	122.6
1942	9.77	7.47	9.77	1962	71.13	52.32	63.10	1982	143.0	102.4	140.6
1943	12.64	9.84	11.67	1963	75.02	62.69	75.02	1983	172.7	138.3	164.9
1944	13.29	11.56	13.28	1964	86.28	75.43	84.75				
1945	17.68	13.21	17.36	1965	92.63	81.60	92.43				

INDUSTRIAL STOCKS†

(*400 Stocks)

Monthly Averages of Daily Indexes

1941–1943–10

	Jan.	Feb.	Mar.	Apr.	May	June	July	Aug.	Sept.	Oct.	Nov.	Dec.	Avg.
1926	10.04	10.10	9.38	9.06	9.12	9.59	10.06	10.52	10.67	10.46	10.58	10.84	10.04
1927	10.74	10.96	11.16	11.42	11.85	12.01	12.38	13.18	14.08	13.80	14.20	14.61	12.53
1928	14.68	14.43	15.34	16.35	16.74	15.96	16.18	16.80	18.11	18.70	19.94	19.75	16.92
1929	21.22	21.12	21.68	21.62	21.70	21.55	22.95	23.89	24.68	22.26	16.44	17.03	21.35
1930	17.13	18.06	18.73	19.93	18.60	16.68	16.41	16.33	16.21	13.84	12.97	12.17	16.42
1931	12.34	13.27	13.45	12.18	10.97	10.56	10.95	10.72	9.15	7.91	8.09	6.54	10.51
1932	6.39	6.33	6.35	4.83	4.27	3.80	4.00	5.94	6.39	5.49	5.45	5.18	5.37
1933	5.35	4.74	4.93	5.75	7.41	8.61	9.40	9.15	9.37	8.49	8.92	9.16	7.61
1934	9.56	10.11	9.63	9.86	8.88	8.96	8.60	8.41	8.22	8.31	8.70	8.81	9.00
1935	8.88	8.72	8.19	8.67	9.40	9.64	10.14	10.71	11.01	11.39	12.43	12.38	10.13
1936	12.96	13.71	14.12	14.20	13.44	13.93	14.66	14.96	15.17	16.04	16.69	16.41	14.69
1937	16.87	17.51	17.52	16.45	15.74	15.26	16.18	16.45	14.12	12.04	10.82	10.68	14.97
1938	11.10	10.89	10.22	[illegible]	9.78	10.07	12.12	12.29	11.81	12.98	12.96	12.63	11.39
1939	12.30	12.12	12.09	10.56	10.91	11.11	11.37	11.15	12.56	12.60	12.35	12.06	11.77
1940	11.95	11.87	11.84	11.94	10.28	9.34	9.55	9.79	10.26	10.39	10.73	10.34	10.69
1941	10.30	9.64	9.73	9.43	9.27	9.66	10.19	10.14	10.21	9.81	9.41	8.86	9.72
1942	8.95	8.67	8.24	7.93	8.01	8.47	8.82	8.76	8.84	9.45	9.56	9.68	8.78
1943	10.22	10.81	11.13	11.44	11.87	12.14	12.29	11.66	11.91	11.78	11.25	11.42	11.49
1944	11.78	11.63	11.95	11.75	11.98	12.58	12.90	12.67	12.47	12.76	12.67	12.90	12.34
1945	13.23	13.63	13.63	13.94	14.44	14.58	14.23	14.39	15.43	16.03	16.41	16.73	14.72
1946	17.34	17.38	16.85	18.02	18.04	17.85	17.42	17.12	14.65	14.35	14.20	14.58	16.48
1947	14.69	15.31	14.73	14.23	14.02	14.58	15.48	15.15	14.76	15.19	15.15	14.93	14.85
1948	14.60	13.88	14.07	15.19	15.92	16.65	16.21	15.74	15.53	16.02	15.16	15.11	15.34
1949	15.23	14.57	14.72	14.66	14.51	13.69	14.55	15.04	15.20	15.62	15.86	16.29	15.00
1950	16.56	16.90	17.03	17.58	18.27	18.68	17.31	18.47	19.18	20.06	20.05	19.92	18.33
1951	21.38	22.22	21.84	22.24	22.29	21.88	22.31	23.35	23.98	23.80	23.09	23.83	22.68
1952	24.61	24.05	24.04	23.96	23.94	24.66	25.49	25.53	25.06	24.48	25.24	26.29	24.78
1953	26.45	26.07	26.18	24.84	25.01	24.12	24.41	24.44	23.26	23.96	24.51	24.85	24.84
1954	25.55	26.12	26.72	27.97	29.21	29.43	30.64	31.26	32.20	33.17	34.56	36.14	30.25
1955	36.79	38.06	37.65	39.04	38.88	41.45	44.94	44.56	46.88	44.52	47.78	48.25	42.40
1956	46.88	47.13	50.59	51.38	49.64	49.38	52.27	51.89	50.15	49.52	48.92	49.79	49.80
1957	48.43	46.10	46.86	48.06	50.10	51.30	52.54	49.51	47.52	44.43	43.41	43.29	47.63
1958	43.98	44.01	44.97	45.09	46.51	47.62	48.96	51.00	52.40	54.55	56.11	57.09	49.36
1959	59.30	58.33	59.79	60.92	62.09	61.75	64.23	63.74	61.21	61.04	61.46	63.56	61.45
1960	62.27	59.60	58.71	59.46	58.84	61.06	59.25	59.96	57.96	56.90	58.89	60.22	59.43
1961	63.20	65.71	67.83	69.64	70.34	69.48	69.15	71.69	70.89	71.42	74.72	75.81	69.99
1962	72.99	74.22	74.22	71.64	66.32	58.32	59.61	61.29	60.67	58.66	62.90	65.59	65.54
1963	68.00	68.91	68.71	72.17	73.60	73.61	72.45	74.43	76.63	77.09	76.69	78.38	73.39
1964	80.85	81.96	83.64	84.92	85.79	85.13	88.19	86.70	88.27	89.75	90.36	88.71	86.19
1965	91.04	91.64	91.75	93.08	94.69	90.19	89.92	91.68	94.93	97.20	98.02	97.66	93.48
1966	99.56	99.11	95.04	98.17	92.85	92.14	91.95	86.40	83.11	82.01	86.10	86.50	91.08
1967	89.88	93.35	95.86	97.54	99.59	98.61	100.4	102.1	103.8	104.2	100.9	103.9	99.18
1968	103.1	98.33	96.77	104.4	107.0	109.7	109.2	106.8	110.5	113.3	114.8	116.0	107.5
1969	111.0	110.2	108.2	110.7	114.5	108.6	103.7	103.4	104.0	105.1	105.9	100.5	107.2
1970	99.40	95.73	96.95	94.01	83.16	82.96	83.00	85.40	90.66	92.85	92.58	98.72	91.29
1971	102.2	106.6	109.6	113.7	112.4	110.3	109.1	107.3	109.9	107.3	102.2	109.7	108.4
1972	114.1	116.9	119.7	121.3	120.2	120.8	120.0	124.4	122.3	122.4	128.3	131.1	121.8
1973	132.6	127.9	126.1	123.6	120.0	117.2	118.7	116.8	118.5	123.4	114.6	106.2	120.5
1974	107.2	104.1	109.0	103.7	101.2	101.6	93.54	85.51	76.54	77.57	80.17	74.80	92.91
1975	80.50	89.29	93.90	95.27	101.5	103.7	103.8	96.21	94.96	99.29	100.9	99.31	96.56
1976	108.5	113.0	113.7	114.7	113.8	114.5	117.0	115.6	118.2	114.0	113.0	116.3	114.3
1977	115.2	112.1	111.9	109.9	109.1	109.5	110.1	107.5	105.9	103.2	103.7	103.1	108.4
1978	99.34	97.95	97.65	102.1	107.7	108.0	107.4	115.0	115.1	111.6	105.2	106.9	106.2
1979	111.2	109.5	111.7	114.0	111.2	113.0	113.6	118.9	121.1	117.0	116.1	120.8	114.8
1980	124.7	130.9	118.7	115.6	120.8	128.8	135.2	140.2	143.7	148.4	155.1	152.2	134.5
1981	151.1	145.7	151.0	152.3	149.1	148.7	145.4	146.0	132.7	134.0	136.8	138.4	144.3
1982	131.1	127.6	122.9	129.2	129.7	122.6	122.5	122.3	137.1	148.1	153.9	156.0	133.6
1983	162.0	165.2	170.3	176.8	184.1	187.4	188.3	183.2	188.6	189.0	185.9	185.2	180.5

Annual Range, and Close, of Daily Indexes

Year	High	Low	Close	Year	High	Low	Close	Year	High	Low	Close
1926	11.01	8.63	10.83	1946	18.53	13.64	14.75	1966	100.6	77.89	85.24
1927	14.88	10.56	14.82	1947	15.83	13.40	15.18	1967	106.2	85.31	105.11
1928	20.85	14.05	20.85	1948	16.93	13.58	15.12	1968	118.0	95.05	113.0
1929	25.38	14.18	16.99	1949	16.52	13.23	16.49	1969	116.2	97.75	101.5
1930	20.32	11.33	11.90	1950	20.60	16.34	20.57	1970	102.9	75.58	100.9
1931	14.07	6.02	6.32	1951	24.33	20.85	24.24	1971	115.8	99.36	112.7
1932	7.26	3.52	5.18	1952	26.92	23.30	26.89	1972	133.0	112.2	131.9
1933	10.25	4.24	9.26	1953	26.99	22.70	24.87	1973	134.5	103.4	109.1
1934	10.54	7.63	9.12	1954	37.24	24.84	37.24	1974	111.7	69.53	76.47
1935	12.84	7.90	12.77	1955	49.54	35.66	48.44	1975	107.4	77.71	100.9
1936	17.02	12.67	16.50	1956	53.28	45.71	50.08	1976	120.9	101.6	119.5
1937	18.10	9.73	10.26	1957	53.25	41.98	42.86	1977	118.9	99.88	104.7
1938	13.66	8.39	13.07	1958	58.97	43.20	58.97	1978	118.7	95.52	107.2
1939	13.08	9.92	12.17	1959	65.32	57.02	64.50	1979	124.5	107.1	121.0
1940	12.42	8.70	10.37	1960	65.02	55.34	61.49	1980	161.0	111.1	154.5
1941	10.62	8.47	8.78	1961	76.69	60.87	75.72	1981	157.0	125.9	137.1
1942	9.94	7.54	9.93	1962	75.22	54.80	66.00	1982	159.7	114.1	157.6
1943	12.58	10.00	11.61	1963	79.25	65.48	79.25	1983	194.8	155.0	186.2
1944	13.18	11.43	13.05	1964	91.29	79.74	89.62				
1945	17.06	12.97	16.79	1965	98.55	86.43	98.47				

Source: *Standard & Poor's Statistics* (New York: Standard & Poor's Corporation, 1984).

PREFERRED STOCK PRICE INDEXES

Dollars per $100 par value

The indexes are based upon one price weekly (as of Wednesday's close), the monthly index being an average of the four or five weekly indexes of the month. These indexes have been based upon ten high grade non callable issues, the yield for each being determined and the average of the four median yields representing the group yield. The average yield has, in turn, been converted into an equivalent price basis (7%) for the composite price index.

Monthly Averages of Weekly Indexes

	Jan.	Feb.	Mar.	Apr.	May	June	July	Aug.	Sept.	Oct.	Nov.	Dec.	Avg.
1933	121.8	120.6	115.3	114.5	117.8	123.3	126.6	127.3	128.1	126.3	121.9	121.1	122.1
1934	123.6	128.2	129.7	131.4	132.6	133.6	135.6	135.2	132.7	131.6	135.7	140.5	132.5
1935	142.8	144.5	145.6	149.2	153.5	153.8	153.9	154.4	153.5	152.6	154.6	157.9	151.4
1936	159.2	160.8	162.6	162.7	161.4	161.7	162.4	163.1	162.1	161.4	160.9	164.5	161.9
1937	167.6	166.5	159.0	154.8	153.1	155.3	155.2	157.1	156.6	155.2	153.8	156.5	157.6
1938	157.2	158.2	156.0	154.3	157.2	158.8	160.9	163.6	165.5	166.9	169.7	168.9	161.4
1939	170.1	170.6	169.4	168.3	169.1	170.7	172.8	172.0	156.1	156.9	165.3	169.0	167.5
1940	172.2	171.0	169.6	170.5	166.5	159.9	166.1	167.0	168.6	170.8	171.6	176.2	169.2
1941	177.9	172.9	171.5	170.8	168.9	168.9	173.1	174.3	173.4	172.1	170.5	168.7	171.9
1942	166.3	165.1	159.8	154.8	156.3	159.2	162.0	164.0	164.0	165.5	165.4	166.9	162.4
1943	168.0	170.8	171.5	171.5	172.1	173.8	175.9	176.4	175.9	175.1	172.6	169.1	172.7
1944	171.2	172.7	173.4	174.1	173.2	175.8	177.6	176.9	177.4	177.4	178.5	180.9	175.8
1945	183.3	185.5	187.7	190.9	191.2	190.9	189.6	188.1	186.7	188.0	192.2	195.3	189.1
1946	197.9	200.5	203.1	204.9	201.9	202.4	204.1	203.4	196.2	191.6	189.3	186.2	198.5
1947	187.3	189.0	188.1	186.5	186.2	186.2	188.4	188.7	188.3	181.2	174.5	172.1	184.7
1948	169.5	167.5	170.1	169.8	171.6	172.8	169.5	166.9	166.5	163.8	166.2	168.7	168.6
1949	171.4	173.2	172.2	172.2	173.2	176.1	176.6	179.5	182.1	180.3	179.8	180.6	176.4
1950	182.8	182.4	183.8	183.5	183.1	182.0	178.5	181.9	181.7	180.5	180.7	179.9	181.7
1951	180.9	180.9	174.9	170.4	168.9	167.9	166.7	169.4	168.5	167.0	165.4	163.7	170.4
1952	164.2	165.9	168.2	172.2	173.4	173.3	171.1	169.9	170.2	168.3	169.8	170.3	169.7
1953	168.4	166.3	165.7	161.7	160.0	156.8	160.1	163.1	162.8	167.3	168.8	166.5	164.0
1954	168.7	171.8	173.3	174.3	173.8	172.9	173.3	174.7	175.8	178.1	178.9	178.3	174.5
1955	175.8	175.0	174.6	176.0	175.6	175.7	176.7	174.4	172.7	173.5	174.7	172.9	174.8
1956	173.9	175.7	174.5	168.7	166.0	167.8	168.2	165.1	159.6	158.5	153.7	151.4	165.3
1957	155.1	156.7	157.2	156.8	154.6	149.5	147.3	145.1	146.2	145.9	146.5	156.0	151.4
1958	160.7	159.9	158.3	160.4	162.4	163.5	160.5	157.5	153.0	150.8	150.7	151.1	157.4
1959	154.4	155.1	156.3	155.0	149.7	146.0	147.2	149.0	146.0	145.6	145.6	144.3	149.5
1960	143.8	145.3	147.1	148.6	147.3	147.7	148.9	151.9	149.2	147.5	146.3	144.8	147.4
1961	148.0	149.8	150.2	150.1	151.0	150.2	149.4	149.2	149.3	151.6	152.7	150.9	150.2
1962	152.6	155.0	156.2	157.2	157.3	155.0	152.7	154.0	155.7	155.8	157.4	158.3	155.6
1963	161.3	164.1	164.9	162.4	163.4	163.2	161.4	162.7	162.9	164.5	163.6	161.9	163.0
1964	162.4	162.6	161.2	160.1	158.8	158.9	160.3	163.5	164.8	164.8	164.7	165.6	162.3
1965	167.5	166.1	164.2	163.7	162.8	159.7	159.8	161.3	162.2	159.8	158.9	156.6	161.9
1966	155.2	151.1	144.8	146.5	145.0	142.1	139.9	135.3	133.8	132.7	134.5	133.5	141.2
1967	138.3	140.7	138.9	139.2	135.5	132.0	131.1	131.0	129.4	125.3	120.8	117.8	131.7
1968	122.9	123.9	130.8	119.5	118.0	118.7	121.9	125.2	124.4	121.6	120.3	118.1	121.3
1969	118.2	117.9	115.0	114.0	113.0	110.6	109.1	108.6	106.1	103.1	102.3	97.4	109.6
1970	99.8	99.3	100.6	100.3	96.5	92.4	92.0	94.6	95.8	95.6	95.9	101.7	97.0
1971	107.3	110.7	108.1	106.4	102.7	100.1	99.6	99.5	101.5	103.7	103.4	102.9	103.8
1972	106.7	105.0	103.6	101.3	101.4	101.0	100.1	101.5	100.0	99.5	101.2	101.2	101.9
1973	102.1	101.4	99.5	98.6	98.1	96.7	95.3	94.2	94.9	97.6	94.6	90.2	96.9
1974	92.2	93.7	92.7	89.5	86.3	84.9	83.3	81.4	78.4	79.8	81.4	79.7	85.3
1975	84.1	86.8	87.1	84.7	82.2	83.9	85.0	83.2	81.8	81.6	82.4	82.8	83.8
1976	85.8	87.5	86.8	87.1	86.9	86.4	86.7	87.7	88.6	89.9	89.8	90.9	87.8
1977	92.9	92.7	92.6	92.1	91.8	91.9	93.3	92.7	92.4	91.9	91.2	89.2	92.1
1978	88.35	87.66	86.80	86.88	86.37	84.23	83.26	84.76	85.02	84.50	83.02	79.27	85.01
1979	79.61	79.87	79.80	80.01	79.33	78.94	78.40	77.62	76.67	74.01	70.42	69.60	77.02
1980	68.84	66.40	61.57	62.83	68.63	71.59	71.40	69.76	69.02	65.84	61.72	58.63	66.35
1981	60.62	59.19	59.27	59.26	56.94	57.23	56.30	55.45	53.82	53.50	54.88	54.58	56.75
1982	53.06	53.02	53.98	54.30	55.67	54.03	52.86	54.80	56.41	59.83	62.60	62.55	56.09
1983	62.37	62.92	64.45	64.84	65.72	64.75	63.32	63.27	63.32	63.82	62.94	60.96	63.56

Annual Range, and Close, of Weekly Indexes

Year	High	Low	Close	Year	High	Low	Close	Year	High	Low	Close
1931	145.2	117.1	117.1	1949	183.3	169.1	181.4	1967	141.5	116.7	118.4
1932	121.5	99.3	119.9	1950	184.2	178.1	179.8	1968	125.8	116.3	116.5
1933	128.7	113.5	120.3	1951	181.7	161.9	161.9	1969	118.9	95.6	97.7
1934	141.4	121.3	140.9	1952	173.8	161.6	169.6	1970	103.0	89.3	101.2
1935	159.1	141.4	159.1	1953	169.6	156.2	166.7	1971	112.2	98.5	103.6
1936	165.5	158.7	165.5	1954	179.1	167.0	177.5	1972	107.9	99.2	101.0
1937	168.3	152.5	156.6	1955	177.4	172.0	172.6	1973	102.7	88.6	88.6
1938	170.7	153.5	167.5	1956	176.4	150.7	151.9	1974	94.7	77.6	78.7
1939	173.7	152.5	168.7	1957	158.2	144.2	157.7	1975	88.4	80.4	82.5
1940	178.1	159.1	178.1	1958	164.4	150.0	151.7	1976	91.5	83.1	91.5
1941	179.5	166.7	166.7	1959	157.3	142.7	142.8	1977	94.5	89.0	89.3
1942	167.1	152.5	166.7	1960	153.1	143.5	146.4	1978	89.42	78.32	78.52
1943	176.4	167.1	169.9	1961	153.0	146.4	150.7	1979	80.90	68.93	69.03
1944	181.9	170.7	181.9	1962	159.1	151.0	159.1	1980	73.16	57.96	57.88
1945	196.7	182.3	196.7	1963	165.2	159.1	161.2	1981	61.04	52.62	52.62
1946	205.3	185.7	185.7	1964	166.2	158.0	166.0	1982	65.35	52.43	61.47
1947	189.2	167.9	167.9	1965	168.7	155.2	155.2	1983	66.10	60.02	60.02
1948	173.7	163.6	169.5	1966	155.6	131.2	135.3				

PREFERRED STOCK YIELD INDEXES

Yield in percent.

The indexes are based upon one price weekly (as of Wednesday's close), the monthly index being an average of the four or five weekly indexes of the month. These indexes have been based upon ten high-grade non-callable issues, the yield for each being determined and the average of the four median yields representing the group yield. The average yield has, in turn, been converted into an equivalent price basis (7%) for the composite price index.

Monthly Averages of Weekly Indexes

	Jan.	Feb.	Mar.	Apr.	May	June	July	Aug.	Sept.	Oct.	Nov.	Dec.	Avg.
1933	5.75	5.81	6.07	6.12	5.95	5.68	5.53	5.50	5.47	5.55	5.74	5.78	5.75
1934	5.66	5.46	5.40	5.33	5.28	5.24	5.16	5.18	5.28	5.32	5.16	4.99	5.29
1935	4.90	4.85	4.81	4.69	4.56	4.55	4.55	4.54	4.56	4.59	4.53	4.43	4.63
1936	4.40	4.36	4.31	4.30	4.34	4.33	4.31	4.29	4.32	4.34	4.35	4.26	4.33
1937	4.18	4.21	4.40	4.52	4.57	4.51	4.51	4.46	4.47	4.51	4.55	4.47	4.45
1938	4.45	4.43	4.49	4.54	4.46	4.43	4.35	4.28	4.23	4.20	4.12	4.15	4.34
1939	4.12	4.11	4.13	4.16	4.14	4.10	4.05	4.07	4.49	4.47	4.24	4.14	4.19
1940	4.07	4.10	4.13	4.11	4.21	4.38	4.22	4.19	4.15	4.10	4.08	3.97	4.14
1941	3.94	4.05	4.08	4.10	4.15	4.15	4.05	4.02	4.04	4.07	4.01	4.15	4.08
1942	4.21	4.24	4.38	4.52	4.48	4.40	4.32	4.27	4.27	4.23	4.23	4.19	4.31
1943	4.17	4.10	4.08	4.08	4.07	4.03	3.98	3.97	3.98	4.00	4.06	4.14	4.06
1944	4.09	4.06	4.04	4.02	4.04	3.98	3.94	3.96	3.95	3.95	3.92	3.87	3.99
1945	3.82	3.78	3.73	3.67	3.66	3.67	3.69	3.72	3.75	3.72	3.64	3.59	3.70
1946	3.54	3.49	3.45	3.42	3.47	3.46	3.43	3.44	3.57	3.65	3.70	3.76	3.53
1947	3.74	3.71	3.72	3.75	3.76	3.76	3.72	3.71	3.72	3.86	4.01	4.07	3.79
1948	4.13	4.18	4.12	4.12	4.08	4.05	4.13	4.20	4.20	4.28	4.21	4.15	4.15
1949	4.09	4.04	4.07	4.07	4.04	3.98	3.97	3.90	3.85	3.88	3.89	3.88	3.97
1950	3.83	3.84	3.81	3.82	3.82	3.85	3.92	3.85	3.85	3.88	3.88	3.89	3.85
1951	3.87	3.87	4.00	4.11	4.15	4.17	4.20	4.13	4.16	4.19	4.23	4.28	4.11
1952	4.26	4.22	4.16	4.07	4.04	4.04	4.09	4.12	4.12	4.16	4.12	4.11	4.13
1953	4.16	4.21	4.23	4.33	4.38	4.47	4.37	4.30	4.30	4.19	4.15	4.20	4.27
1954	4.15	4.08	4.04	4.02	4.03	4.05	4.04	4.01	3.98	3.93	3.92	3.93	4.02
1955	3.98	4.00	4.01	3.98	3.99	3.98	3.96	4.01	4.06	4.04	4.01	4.05	4.01
1956	4.03	3.99	4.01	4.15	4.22	4.17	4.16	4.24	4.39	4.42	4.56	4.63	4.25
1957	4.51	4.47	4.46	4.47	4.53	4.69	4.75	4.83	4.79	4.80	4.78	4.49	4.63
1958	4.36	4.38	4.42	4.37	4.31	4.28	4.36	4.45	4.58	4.64	4.65	4.63	4.45
1959	4.54	4.52	4.48	4.51	4.68	4.79	4.75	4.70	4.80	4.81	4.81	4.85	4.69
1960	4.87	4.82	4.76	4.71	4.75	4.74	4.70	4.61	4.69	4.75	4.78	4.84	4.75
1961	4.73	4.68	4.66	4.67	4.63	4.66	4.69	4.69	4.69	4.62	4.59	4.64	4.66
1962	4.59	4.52	4.48	4.45	4.45	4.52	4.59	4.55	4.50	4.49	4.45	4.42	4.50
1963	4.34	4.27	4.24	4.31	4.29	4.29	4.34	4.30	4.30	4.26	4.28	4.32	4.30
1964	4.31	4.31	4.34	4.37	4.41	4.41	4.37	4.29	4.25	4.25	4.25	4.23	4.32
1965	4.18	4.22	4.26	4.28	4.30	4.38	4.38	4.34	4.32	4.38	4.41	4.47	4.33
1966	4.51	4.63	4.83	4.78	4.83	4.93	5.00	5.18	5.23	5.28	5.21	5.24	4.87
1967	5.07	4.98	5.04	5.03	5.17	5.30	5.34	5.35	5.41	5.59	5.79	5.95	5.34
1968	5.70	5.65	5.80	5.86	5.92	5.90	5.74	5.59	5.63	5.76	5.82	5.93	5.78
1969	5.93	5.94	6.09	6.14	6.20	6.33	6.42	6.45	6.61	6.79	6.84	7.19	6.41
1970	7.02	7.04	6.97	6.98	7.26	7.57	7.62	7.41	7.31	7.33	7.30	6.88	7.22
1971	6.53	6.32	6.48	6.59	6.82	6.99	7.03	7.04	6.90	6.75	6.78	6.81	6.75
1972	6.57	6.67	6.76	6.91	6.90	6.93	6.99	6.90	7.00	7.03	6.93	6.92	6.88
1973	6.85	6.91	7.03	7.11	7.13	7.25	7.35	7.43	7.38	7.18	7.40	7.76	7.23
1974	7.60	7.47	7.56	7.83	8.11	8.25	8.40	8.61	8.93	8.78	8.60	8.78	8.24
1975	8.33	8.07	8.04	8.27	8.51	8.34	8.24	8.41	8.56	8.58	8.50	8.46	8.36
1976	8.16	8.00	8.07	8.04	8.06	8.10	8.08	7.99	7.90	7.80	7.80	7.70	7.98
1977	7.54	7.55	7.56	7.60	7.63	7.62	7.51	7.55	7.58	7.62	7.67	7.85	7.61
1978	7.92	7.99	8.07	8.06	8.11	8.31	8.42	8.26	8.24	8.29	8.43	8.84	8.25
1979	8.79	8.77	8.77	8.75	8.82	8.87	8.93	9.02	9.13	9.46	9.95	10.06	9.11
1980	10.17	10.55	11.37	11.16	10.20	9.78	9.81	10.04	10.14	10.64	11.35	11.94	10.60
1981	11.55	11.83	11.81	11.81	12.30	12.23	12.43	12.63	13.01	13.09	12.76	12.83	12.36
1982	13.79	13.20	12.97	12.90	12.58	12.96	13.24	12.78	12.41	11.71	11.18	11.20	12.53
1983	11.23	11.13	10.86	10.80	10.65	10.81	11.06	11.07	11.06	10.97	11.12	11.49	11.02

Annual Range, and Close, of Weekly Indexes

Year	High	Low	Close	Year	High	Low	Close	Year	High	Low	Close
1933	6.17	5.44	5.82	1950	3.93	3.80	3.89	1967	6.00	4.95	5.91
1934	5.77	4.95	4.97	1951	4.32	3.85	4.32	1968	6.02	5.57	6.01
1935	4.95	4.40	4.40	1952	4.33	4.03	4.13	1969	7.33	5.88	7.16
1936	4.41	4.23	4.23	1953	4.48	4.13	4.20	1970	7.84	6.79	6.89
1937	4.59	4.16	4.47	1954	4.19	3.91	3.95	1971	7.10	6.24	6.76
1938	4.56	4.10	4.18	1955	4.07	3.96	4.06	1972	7.06	6.49	6.93
1939	4.59	4.03	4.15	1956	4.65	3.97	4.61	1973	7.90	6.82	7.90
1940	4.40	3.93	3.93	1957	4.86	4.42	4.44	1974	9.02	7.39	8.89
1941	4.20	3.90	4.20	1958	4.67	4.26	4.62	1975	8.70	7.92	8.48
1942	4.59	4.19	4.20	1959	4.90	4.45	4.90	1976	8.42	7.65	7.65
1943	4.19	3.97	4.12	1960	4.88	4.57	4.81	1977	7.87	7.41	7.84
1944	4.10	3.85	3.85	1961	4.78	4.58	4.65	1978	8.94	7.83	8.92
1945	3.84	3.56	3.56	1962	4.64	4.40	4.40	1979	10.16	8.71	10.14
1946	3.77	3.41	3.77	1963	4.40	4.24	4.34	1980	12.09	9.57	12.09
1947	4.17	3.70	4.17	1964	4.41	4.21	4.22	1981	13.30	11.47	13.30
1948	4.28	4.03	4.13	1965	4.51	4.15	4.51	1982	13.35	10.71	11.39
1949	4.14	3.82	3.86	1966	5.34	4.50	5.17	1983	11.66	10.59	11.66

Source: *Standard & Poor's Statistics* (New York: Standard & Poor's Corporation, 1984).

New York Stock Exchange

Composite Stock Index

Year	Open	High	Low	Close	Chg.
1983	79.79	*99.63	79.79	95.18	+14.15
1982	81.33	82.35	58.80	81.03	+ 9.92
1981	78.26	79.14	64.96	71.11	— 6.75
1980	60.69	81.02	55.30	77.86	+15.91
1979	53.93	63.39	53.88	61.95	+ 8.33
1978	51.82	60.38	48.37	53.62	+ 1.12
1977	57.69	57.69	49.78	52.50	— 5.38
1976	48.04	57.88	48.04	57.88	+10.24
1975	37.06	51.24	37.06	47.64	+11.51
1974	51.98	53.37	32.89	36.13	—15.69
1973	65.06	65.48	49.05	51.82	—12.66
1972	56.23	65.14	56.23	64.48	+ 8.05
1971	49.73	57.76	49.60	56.43	+ 6.20
1970	52.10	52.36	37.69	50.23	— 1.30
1969	58.94	59.32	49.31	51.53	— 7.37
1968	53.68	61.27	48.70	58.90	+ 5.07
1967	43.74	54.16	43.74	53.83	+10.11
1966	49.86	51.06	39.37	43.72	— 6.28
1965	45.37	50.00	43.64	50.00	+ 4.35
1964	40.47	46.49	40.47	45.65	+ 5.73
1963	34.41	39.92	34.41	39.92	+ 6.11
1962	37.34	38.02	28.20	33.81	— 4.58
1961	31.17	38.60	31.17	38.39	+ 7.45
1960	31.99	31.99	28.38	30.94	— 1.21
1959	29.54	32.39	28.94	32.15	+ 3.30
1958	21.71	28.85	21.45	28.85	+ 7.74
1957	24.43	26.30	20.92	21.11	— 3.24
1956	23.56	25.90	22.55	24.35	+ 0.64
1955	19.05	23.71	19.05	23.71	+ 4.31
1954	13.70	19.40	13.70	19.40	+ 5.80
1953	14.65	14.65	12.62	13.60	— 0.89
1952	13.70	14.49	13.31	14.49	+ 0.89
1951	12.28	13.89	12.28	13.60	+ 1.59
1950	10.06	12.01	9.85	12.01	+ 2.10

*Record high.

The New York Stock Exchange composite stock index has been computed on a daily basis since June 1, 1964. Prior to that date it was on a weekly basis. December 31, 1965, equals 50.

Source: *The Dow Jones Investor's Handbook* (Homewood, Ill.: Dow Jones-Irwin, 1984).

New York Stock Exchange
Cash Dividends and Yields on Common Stocks

Calendar Year	Number of Issues Listed at Year End	Number Paying Cash Dividends During Year	Estimated Aggregate Cash Payments (Millions)	a-Median Yield (%)	Calendar Year	Number of Issues Listed at Year End	Number Paying Cash Dividends During Year	Estimated Aggregate Cash Payments (Millions)	a-Median Yield (%)
1982	1,499	1,287	$62,224	4.1	1960	1,126	981	$9,872	4.2
1981	1,534	1,337	60,628	5.0	1959	1,092	953	9,337	3.8
1980	1,540	1,361	53,072	4.6	1958	1,086	961	8,711	4.1
1979	1,536	1,359	46,937	5.0	1957	1,098	991	8,807	6.1
1978	1,552	1,373	41,151	4.8	1956	1,077	975	8,341	5.2
1977	1,549	1,360	36,270	4.5	1955	1,076	982	7,488	4.6
1976	1,550	1,340	30,608	4.0	1954	1,076	968	6,439	4.7
1975	1,531	1,273	26,901	5.0	1953	1,069	964	5,874	6.3
1974	1,543	1,308	25,662	7.4	1952	1,067	975	5,595	6.0
1973	1,536	1,276	23,627	5.0	1951	1,054	961	5,467	6.5
1972	1,478	1,195	21,490	3.0	1950	1,039	930	5,404	6.7
1971	1,399	1,132	20,256	3.2	1949	1,017	887	4,235	7.0
1970	1,330	1,120	19,781	3.7	1948	986	883	3,806	7.8
1969	1,290	1,121	19,404	3.6	1947	964	851	3,255	6.3
1968	1,253	1,104	18,124	2.6	1946	933	798	2,669	4.8
1967	1,255	1,116	16,866	3.2	1945	881	746	2,275	3.6
1966	1,267	1,127	16,151	4.1	1944	864	717	2,223	5.0
1965	1,254	1,111	15,300	3.2	1943	845	687	2,063	6.1
1964	1,227	1,066	13,555	3.3	1942	834	648	1,997	7.8
1963	1,194	1,032	12,096	3.6	1941	834	627	2,281	9.3
1962	1,168	994	11,203	3.8	1940	829	577	2,099	6.1
1961	1,145	981	10,430	3.3	1939	825	504	1,833	..

a-Based on cash payments during the year and price at end of year for dividend-paying stocks only.

Source: *The Dow Jones Investor's Handbook* (Homewood, Ill.: Dow Jones-Irwin, 1984).

INTRODUCTION: THE VALUE LINE AVERAGES

Value Line computes four stock market averages; the Value Line Composite (based on the 1,700 stocks reviewed in the Value Line Investment Survey); the 1,500-stock Value Line Industrial Average (which eliminates railroad and utility stocks); the Value Line Railroad Average (14 stocks) and the Value Line Utility Average (177 stocks).

Value Line Averages are computed as follows: Every market day, the closing price of each stock is divided by the preceding day's close. Thus, for example, if a stock rises from 50 to 51½ (a 3 percent increase) the change would be expressed as 1.03; 51½ ÷ 50 = 1.03. Conversely, if a stock fell 3 percent from 50 to 48½, the change would be .97; 48½ ÷ 50 = .97. The changes for all stocks in the group would be geometrically averaged.[1] This final average change for the day is then multiplied by the prior day's closing Value Line Average. For example, if Monday's closing Value Line Composite is 140.10 and Tuesday's average change is 1.025, Tuesday's Value Line Composite is 143.60; 140.10 × 1.025 = 143.60. (The Value Line Averages use June 30, 1961, as a starting point; the averages for that day are set at 100.00.)

When stock dividends or splits occur, the preceding day's price is adjusted accordingly, and the index of change is computed using the above method. As stocks are added to the Value Line Investment Survey, the average is enlarged. Additions and deletions of stocks present no problem to the average because of its large base.

Like the Value Line Averages, the New York Stock Exchange Indices and the Standard & Poor's Averages use many stocks. But the NYSE and S&P measures focus on changes in *market value* rather than changes in stock price. (The market value of a company is its stock price multiplied by the number of shares outstanding.) Thus, a $50 stock with 10 million shares outstanding that moves by 3 percent has a greater impact on the "weighted" averages than another $50 stock that also moves by 3 percent but has only 2 million shares outstanding. Also, even if both companies have the same number of shares, a 3 percent price change in the stock that sells for $50 a share will have a greater impact on the average than a 3 percent change in the price of a stock that sells for $20. Although the Dow Jones Industrial Average is neither weighted by number of shares, nor broad—including as it does, only 30 stocks—the fluctu-

---

[1] A geometric average of n items is:

$$\sqrt[n]{\text{the product of all } n \text{ items.}}$$

Thus, the geometric average of 3, 4 and 5 (3 items) is:

$$\sqrt[3]{3 \times 4 \times 5} = \sqrt[3]{60} = 3.91$$

This is in contrast to an arithmetic average, which is:

$$\text{the sum of all } n \text{ items} \div n.$$

For 3, 4 and 5, the arithmetic average would be:

$$(3 + 4 + 5) \div 3 = 12 \div 3 = 4$$

ations of the Dow are similar to those of the S&P and NYSE averages. That's because the 30 Dow stocks are the shares of the largest companies in the country, and they account for about 25 percent of the total market value of all outstanding shares.

The NYSE and the S&P averages, because they are value weighted, are better measures of the *value of all shares outstanding* in the marketplace than of stock prices. Nor is the Dow an effective barometer of stock prices. Smaller companies are ignored. And those companies that are included don't have equal impacts on the index: The Dow is more responsive to trends in the price of a $20 stock than those of a $5 security.

Value Line's Averages give as much weight to a 3 percent fluctuation in the price of a stock with 2 million shares outstanding as to a 3 percent move in the price of a stock with 100 million shares. Also, the Value Line Averages give equal consideration to stocks that sell for $20 or $5 per share. Thus the Value Line Averages reflect changes in the *price of the typical stock.* The investor who wants to measure the performance of his individual stocks (as opposed to the performance of a diversified portfolio) or monitor trends in stock prices can better do so by referring to Value Line's broadly based, *equally weighted average* of stock prices than to weighted averages which are heavily dependent on large "blue chip" stocks.

Annual High-Low Ranges, 1961–1981

Value Line Composite Averages

Year	High	Date	Low	Date	Last
1961	106.78	12-1	99.62	7-21	105.33
1962	106.03	2-16	76.58	10-26	88.20
1963	102.64	9-13	91.23	1-4	100.21
1964	116.36	11-20	102.03	1-3	113.55
1965	135.47	12-21	111.09	6-28	135.11
1966	141.14	4-21	105.98	10-7	118.45
1967	156.27	10-9	119.25	1-3	152.89
1968	188.64	12-13	138.92	3-25	183.18
1969	183.63	1-2	127.40	12-17	130.56
1970	135.46	1-5	84.23	7-7	103.60
1971	125.76	4-28	97.36	11-23	112.94
1972	125.98	4-12	107.11	10-16	114.05
1973	116.20	1-3	70.50	12-13	73.61
1974	83.41	3-14	47.03	12-23	48.97
1975	80.88	7-15	51.12	1-2	70.69
1976	93.47	12-31	71.62	1-2	93.47
1977	96.34	7-22	86.53	10-25	93.92
1978	119.77	9-12	88.67	1-16	97.97
1979	125.25	10-5	98.88	1-2	121.91
1980	149.76	11-20	100.60	3-27	144.20
1981	159.03	6-15	125.66	9-25	137.81

Value Line Industrial Averages

Year	High	Date	Low	Date	Last
1961	105.72	12-8	99.61	7-21	104.71
1962	105.41	2-16	74.30	10-26	85.68
1963	99.77	10-25	88.65	1-4	97.52
1964	113.06	11-20	99.42	1-3	110.22
1965	135.10	12-17	108.22	6-28	134.34
1966	142.53	4-21	105.21	10-7	118.17
1967	163.09	10-9	119.03	1-3	160.00
1968	199.99	12-13	144.03	3-5	193.80
1969	194.38	1-3	133.80	12-17	137.00
1970	142.27	1-5	85.40	7-7	104.67
1971	129.92	4-28	98.89	11-23	115.84
1972	131.65	4-12	110.09	10-16	116.97
1973	119.33	1-3	70.45	12-13	73.53
1974	84.30	3-14	46.50	12-23	48.52
1975	82.22	7-15	50.61	1-2	70.93
1976	94.33	12-31	71.87	1-2	94.33
1977	96.67	7-22	86.48	10-25	94.52
1978	124.35	9-12	89.02	1-11	100.38
1979	130.33	10-5	101.33	1-2	127.01
1980	158.61	11-20	104.39	3-27	152.14
1981	169.62	6-15	132.01	9-25	145.06

Value Line Rail Averages

Year	High	Date	Low	Date	Last
1961	110.52	11-17	95.85	7-21	104.05
1962	110.65	2-9	79.93	6-22	96.68
1963	131.61	8-30	104.25	1-18	127.30
1964	177.80	10-21	129.90	1-8	160.87
1965	199.09	12-17	149.37	6-28	198.65
1966	224.12	2-15	144.06	10-7	157.18
1967	202.69	7-21	159.76	1-3	175.56
1968	213.69	12-13	160.74	3-25	210.01
1969	218.52	2-12	129.29	12-23	132.76
1970	140.71	3-3	81.66	7-7	112.64
1971	145.21	9-7	104.10	11-24	122.57
1972	127.86	1-28	101.98	10-31	104.05
1973	107.17	1-3	70.60	8-22	86.93
1974	94.22	1-3	56.98	9-16	60.66
1975	75.07	7-16	63.12	1-3	68.12
1976	100.25	12-29	69.27	1-2	99.94
1977	115.50	5-20	95.57	10-25	102.69
1978	122.26	9-8	97.32	10-31	103.02
1979	144.44	8-15	105.07	1-2	134.17
1980	207.16	11-28	122.27	3-27	198.12
1981	213.42	4-20	163.06	9-25	181.40

Value Line Utility Averages

Year	High	Date	Low	Date	Last
1961	116.94	11-24	100.00	6-30	111.70
1962	113.03	3-23	89.55	6-22	105.49
1963	118.45	9-6	107.66	1-4	114.09
1964	128.73	11-28	114.99	1-3	127.95
1965	134.10	3-4	123.50	6-29	127.90
1966	128.79	1-10	101.40	8-30	112.38
1967	118.79	4-20	105.89	11-20	109.59
1968	126.34	11-29	105.33	3-25	121.84
1969	123.14	2-7	91.88	12-17	94.65
1970	99.95	12-31	80.68	7-23	99.95
1971	105.40	1-19	89.69	11-24	96.93
1972	101.40	11-24	88.15	7-31	99.48
1973	100.21	1-8	75.11	12-5	79.13
1974	84.05	1-7	52.19	9-13	55.91
1975	76.98	6-25	58.79	1-2	75.63
1976	95.11	12-31	76.50	1-2	95.11
1977	101.63	7-22	92.45	3-28	96.57
1978	96.17	1-3	85.89	11-14	86.94
1979	98.63	8-31	87.53	1-2	93.86
1980	100.81	7-17	79.34	3-27	98.43
1981	101.71	1-6	89.72	9-25	96.26

Source: *Value Line Investment Survey,* Arnold Bernhardt & Company, Inc.

1973–83 Yearly Highs, Lows, Closes & Percent Changes for the Year

Index		1973	1974	1975	1976	1977
Composite	High	136.84 1/11	96.53 3/15	88.00 7/15	97.88 12/31	105.05 12/30
	Low	88.67 12/24	54.87 10/03	60.70 1/02	78.06 1/02	93.66 4/05
	Close	92.19	59.82	77.62	97.88	105.05
	% Change	−31.1	−35.1	+29.8	+26.1	+ 7.3
Industrial	High	136.97 1/11	89.78 3/15	93.79 7/15	100.12 12/31	109.43 12/30
	Low	80.15 12/24	54.21 10/03	57.22 1/02	81.44 1/02	96.29 4/26
	Close	83.57	56.46	80.95	100.12	109.43
	% Change	−36.9	−32.4	+43.4	+23.7	+ 9.3
Other Finance	High	151.93 1/11	111.60 1/23	88.47 6/24	101.57 12/31	105.65 7/25
	Low	102.93 12/24	57.16 10/03	64.70 1/02	79.36 1/02	97.04 4/06
	Close	107.50	63.43	79.02	101.57	105.53
	% Change	−27.8	−41.0	+24.6	+28.5	+ 3.9
Insurance	High	149.69 1/03	113.46 1/17	91.19 7/15	105.21 12/31	115.01 11/25
	Low	103.22 5/21	57.57 10/03	73.47 9/17	81.60 1/02	96.14 4/04
	Close	110.15	74.69	80.90	105.21	114.51
	% Change	−26.1	−32.2	+ 8.3	+30.0	+ 8.8
Bank	High	123.57 1/22	105.11 1/17	82.76 7/15	92.72 12/31	96.02 12/05
	Low	96.50 12/05	59.43 10/04	62.22 1/02	72.73 1/02	89.64 5/31,6/06
	Close	100.42	61.49	72.37	92.72	95.28
	% Change	−15.7	−38.8	+17.7	+28.1	+ 2.8
Utility	High	101.30 2/20	76.55 3/06	69.52 6/30	86.91 12/31	101.68 12/23
	Low	69.85 12/05	48.22 12/24	50.44 1/02	66.15 1/02	87.04 1/03
	Close	72.07	49.60	65.95	86.91	101.03
	% Change	−26.9	−31.2	+33.0	+31.8	+16.2
Transportation	High	124.95 1/12	96.66 3/15	90.92 7/14	105.78 4/20	104.40 7/22
	Low	77.65 12/21	61.24 12/23	66.67 1/06	85.97 1/02	91.60 4/25
	Close	81.04	65.79	85.52	101.28	97.68
	% Change	−31.0	−18.8	+30.0	+18.4	− 3.6

Index		1978	1979	1980	1981	1982	1983
Composite	High	139.25 9/13	152.29 10/05	208.15 11/28	223.47 5/29	240.70 12/08	328.91 06/24
	Low	99.09 1/11	117.84 1/02	124.09 3/27	175.03 9/28	159.14 8/13	230.59 01/03
	Close	117.98	151.14	202.34	195.84	232.41	278.60
	% Change	+12.3	+28.1	+33.9	− 3.2	+18.7	+19.9
Industrial	High	155.79 9/12	175.18 12/31	274.70 11/28	283.03 5/29	281.64 12/08	408.42 06/24
	Low	101.91 1/11	126.88 1/02	145.03 3/27	204.62 9/25	177.70 8/13	270.55 01/03
	Close	126.85	175.18	261.36	229.29	273.58	323.68
	% Change	+15.9	+38.1	+49.2	−12.3	+19.3	+18.3
Other Finance	High	129.85 9/13	139.50 8/24	154.07 12/31	182.10 6/25	216.40 12/08	284.39 09/26
	Low	101.11 1/16	114.18 1/02	106.35 3/27	154.61 1/02	152.45 8/13	206.86 01/04
	Close	114.43	130.92	154.07	176.20	207.50	227.53
	% Change	+ 8.4	+14.4	+17.7	+14.4	+17.8	+33.7
Insurance	High	144.14 9/11	166.31 10/05	184.71 9/23	204.77 6/15	236.76 12/06	287.34 05/10
	Low	106.71 1/16	126.58 1/02	128.74 3/27	166.10 2/13	163.78 8/13	217.33 01/24
	Close	127.24	162.03	166.81	194.31	226.40	257.63
	% Change	+11.1	+27.3	+ 3.0	+16.5	+16.5	+13.8

NASDAQ Index Comparisons, 1973–1983 (*continued*)

Index		1978	1979	1980	1981	1982	1983
Bank	High	111.56 10/13	115.81 8/31	118.58 12/24	144.06 12/01	160.73 11/12	203.75 12/30
	Low	93.96 1/11	102.09 1/03	91.99 3/27	118.59 1/02	127.84 8/13	155.68 01/12
	Close	102.33	108.24	118.39	143.13	156.37	203.75
	% Change	+ 7.4	+ 5.8	+ 9.4	+20.9	+ 9.3	+30.3
Utility	High	116.73 9/13	130.41 12/31	165.92 11/28	191.18 11/30	316.17 12/08	293.76 11/30
	Low	93.23 1/20	106.27 1/02	106.01 3/27	148.69 2/04	168.02 3/12	194.27 01/04
	Close	106.04	130.41	165.70	181.67	286.23	280.80
	% Change	+ 5.0	+23.0	+27.1	+ 9.6	+57.6	+43.6
Transportation	High	128.71 9/13	133.42 10/04	179.20 10/10	201.71 6/15	205.81 11/05	391.37 06/16
	Low	92.92 1/23	100.76 1/02	100.55 3/27	155.99 1/08	145.26 3/16	257.12 10/12
	Close	100.53	118.47	164.19	167.77	195.48	269.39
	% Change	+ 2.9	+17.8	+39.0	+ 2.2	+16.5	− 5.9

Source: *NASDAQ 1928 & 83 Fact Book*, National Association of Security Dealers, Inc.

PART II: INTEREST RATE DATA

MOODY'S U.S. GOVERNMENT BOND YIELD AVERAGES (Monthly Data)

MOODY'S CORPORATE and INDUSTRIAL BOND YIELDS (Monthly Data)

MOODY'S GOVERNMENT BOND YIELD AVERAGES

3-5 YEAR MATURITY, SELECTED ISSUES ①

	Annual	Jan.	Feb.	Mar.	Apr.	May	June	July	Aug.	Sept.	Oct.	Nov.	Dec.
1941	.73	.76	.81	.84	.81	.72	1.41	.67	.62	.62	.72	.98	1.10
1942	1.46	1.05	1.02	1.02	1.06	1.11	1.32	1.45	1.47	1.47	1.48	1.49	1.48
1943	1.34	1.43	1.41	1.40	1.39	1.36	.68	1.30	1.29	1.31	1.31	1.29	1.30
1944	1.33	1.30	1.32	1.36	1.36	1.35	1.34	1.31	1.30	1.31	1.35	1.34	1.35
1945	1.18	1.31	1.22	1.18	1.14	1.16	1.16	1.16	1.17	1.19	1.17	1.14	1.13
1946	1.16	1.06	.99	.96	1.10	1.16	1.15	1.15	1.19	1.27	1.29	1.28	1.30
1947	1.32	1.26	1.26	1.24	1.24	1.27	1.29	1.33	1.31	1.28	1.35	1.47	1.54
1948	1.62	1.63	1.63	1.60	1.58	1.51	1.49	1.56	1.65	1.69	1.71	1.69	1.64
1949	1.43	1.59	1.57	1.54	1.53	1.49	1.42	1.26	1.26	1.34	1.38	1.37	1.37
1950	1.50	1.39	1.44	1.45	1.45	1.45	1.47	1.45	1.45	1.55	1.65	1.62	1.64
1951	1.93	1.66	1.67	1.86	2.03	2.04	2.00	1.94	1.89	1.93	2.00	2.01	2.09
1952	2.13	2.08	2.07	2.02	1.93	1.95	2.04	2.14	2.29	2.28	2.26	2.25	2.30
1953	2.56	2.39	2.42	2.46	2.61	2.86	2.92	2.72	2.77	2.69	2.38	2.32	2.22
1954	1.82	2.04	1.84	1.80	1.71	1.78	1.79	1.69	1.74	1.80	1.85	1.90	1.94
1955	2.50	2.11	2.18	2.30	2.39	2.40	2.42	2.54	2.73	2.72	2.58	2.70	2.83
1956	3.12	2.74	2.65	2.83	3.11	3.04	2.87	2.97	3.36	3.43	3.29	3.49	3.65
1957	3.62	3.40	3.33	3.38	3.48	3.60	3.77	3.89	3.91	3.93	3.99	3.63	3.04
1958	2.90	2.77	2.67	2.50	2.33	2.25	2.25	2.54	3.11	3.57	3.63	3.60	3.65
1959	4.33	3.86	3.85	3.88	4.03	4.16	4.33	4.40	4.45	4.78	4.69	4.74	4.95
1960	3.99	4.87	4.66	4.24	4.23	4.42	4.06	3.71	3.50	3.50	3.61	3.68	3.51
1961	3.60	3.53	3.54	3.43	3.39	3.28	3.70	3.69	3.80	3.77	3.64	3.68	3.82
1962	3.57	3.84	3.77	3.55	3.48	3.53	3.51	3.71	3.57	3.56	3.46	3.46	3.44
1963	3.72	3.47	3.48	3.50	3.56	3.57	3.67	3.78	3.81	3.88	3.91	3.97	4.04
1964	4.06	4.06	4.02	4.15	4.18	4.07	4.03	3.99	3.99	4.03	4.04	4.04	4.07
1965	4.22	4.06	4.08	4.12	4.12	4.11	4.09	4.10	4.19	4.24	4.33	4.46	4.77
1966	5.16	4.89	5.02	4.94	4.86	4.94	5.01	5.22	5.58	5.62	5.38	5.43	5.43
1967	5.05	4.71	4.73	4.52	4.46	4.69	4.96	5.17	5.28	5.40	5.52	5.73	5.07
1968	5.60	5.52	5.58	5.77	5.69	5.95	5.71	5.44	5.32	5.31	5.42	5.47	5.99
1969	6.86	6.04	6.16	6.33	6.16	6.32	6.64	7.02	7.07	7.58	7.47	7.58	7.98
1970	7.34	8.14	7.80	7.20	7.49	7.97	7.86	7.58	7.56	7.24	7.06	6.36	5.87
1971	5.74	5.73	5.32	4.74	5.42	6.02	6.30	6.69	6.33	5.89	5.63	5.43	5.32
1972	5.77	5.28	5.43	5.64	5.92	5.58	5.65	5.74	5.84	6.09	6.07	5.96	5.98
1973	6.84	6.21	6.54	6.78	6.67	6.72	6.69	7.41	7.67	7.09	6.73	6.88	6.72
1974	7.73	6.87	6.70	7.26	7.92	8.16	8.06	8.32	8.57	8.31	7.91	7.58	7.15
1975	7.46	7.22	6.78	6.91	7.66	7.39	7.16	7.62	8.03	8.14	7.73	7.42	7.41
1976	6.83	7.08	7.09	7.14	6.87	7.23	7.30	7.13	6.90	6.75	6.40	6.23	5.85
1977	6.79	6.44	6.62	6.67	6.52	6.70	6.53	6.60	6.83	6.87	7.18	7.21	7.33
1978	8.23	7.64	7.69	7.71	7.84	8.02	8.24	8.46	8.24	8.32	8.53	8.91	9.13
1979	9.52	9.30	9.10	9.20	9.27	9.24	8.85	8.82	9.03	9.48	10.67	10.90	10.35
1980	11.29	10.67	12.48	13.31	11.50	9.44	8.97	9.34	10.63	11.44	11.77	12.83	13.12
1981	14.06	12.59	13.25	13.23	13.80	14.57	13.75	14.63	15.41	15.81	15.24	13.03	13.45
1982	12.83	14.39	14.38	13.77	13.77	13.45	14.12	13.81	12.64	12.17	10.81	10.32	10.27
1983	10.52	9.98	10.19	10.03	9.92	9.85	10.45	10.99	11.33	11.15	10.96	10.07	11.33

LONG-TERM BONDS ②

	Annual	Jan.	Feb.	Mar.	Apr.	May	June	July	Aug.	Sept.	Oct.	Nov.	Dec.
1941	2.05	2.12	2.22	2.12	2.07	2.04	2.01	1.98	2.01	2.02	1.98	2.34	2.47
1942	2.46	2.48	2.48	2.46	2.44	2.45	2.43	2.46	2.47	2.46	2.45	2.47	2.49
1943	2.47	2.46	2.46	2.48	2.48	2.46	2.45	2.45	2.46	2.48	2.48	2.48	2.49
1944	2.48	2.49	2.49	2.48	2.48	2.49	2.49	2.49	2.48	2.47	2.48	2.48	2.48
1945	2.37	2.44	2.38	2.40	2.39	2.39	2.35	2.34	2.36	2.37	2.35	2.33	2.33
1946	2.19	2.21	2.12	2.09	2.08	2.19	2.16	2.18	2.23	2.28	2.26	2.25	2.24
1947	2.25	2.21	2.21	2.19	2.19	2.19	2.22	2.25	2.24	2.24	2.27	2.36	2.39
1948	2.44	2.45	2.45	2.44	2.44	2.42	2.41	2.41	2.45	2.45	2.45	2.44	2.44
1949	2.31	2.42	2.39	2.38	2.38	2.38	2.38	2.27	2.24	2.22	2.22	2.20	2.19
1950	2.32	2.20	2.24	2.27	2.30	2.31	2.33	2.34	2.33	2.36	2.38	2.38	2.39
1951	2.57	2.39	2.40	2.47	2.56	2.63	2.65	2.63	2.57	2.56	2.61	2.66	2.70
1952	2.68	2.74	2.71	2.70	2.64	2.57	2.61	2.61	2.70	2.71	2.74	2.71	2.75
1953	2.94	2.80	2.83	2.89	2.97	3.12	3.13	3.04	3.05	3.01	2.87	2.86	2.79
1954	2.55	2.69	2.62	2.53	2.48	2.54	2.55	2.47	2.48	2.52	2.54	2.57	2.59
1955	2.84	2.68	2.77	2.78	2.82	2.81	2.82	2.91	2.95	2.92	2.87	2.89	2.91
1956	3.08	2.88	2.85	2.93	3.07	2.97	2.93	3.00	3.17	3.21	3.20	3.30	3.40
1957	3.47	3.34	3.22	3.26	3.32	3.40	3.58	3.60	3.63	3.66	3.73	3.57	3.30
1958	3.43	3.24	3.26	3.25	3.12	3.14	3.19	3.36	3.60	3.75	3.76	3.70	3.80
1959	4.07	3.90	3.92	3.92	4.01	4.08	4.09	4.11	4.10	4.26	4.11	4.12	4.27
1960	4.01	4.37	4.22	4.08	4.17	4.16	3.99	3.86	3.79	3.82	3.91	3.93	3.88
1961	3.90	3.89	3.81	3.78	3.80	3.73	3.88	3.90	4.00	4.02	3.98	3.98	4.06
1962	3.95	4.08	4.09	4.01	3.89	3.88	3.90	4.02	3.97	3.94	3.89	3.87	3.87
1963	4.00	3.88	3.92	3.93	3.97	3.97	4.00	4.01	3.99	4.04	4.07	4.10	4.14
1964	4.15	4.15	4.14	4.18	4.20	4.15	4.14	4.13	4.14	4.16	4.16	4.12	4.14
1965	4.21	4.14	4.16	4.15	4.15	4.14	4.14	4.14	4.19	4.25	4.28	4.34	4.43
1966	4.65	4.43	4.61	4.63	4.55	4.57	4.63	4.75	4.80	4.79	4.70	4.74	4.65
1967	4.85	4.40	4.47	4.45	4.51	4.76	4.86	4.86	4.95	4.98	5.18	5.43	5.36
1968	5.26	5.17	5.15	5.38	5.28	5.39	5.23	5.09	5.04	5.10	5.24	5.36	5.66
1969	6.12	5.74	5.86	6.05	5.86	5.85	6.06	6.07	6.02	6.32	6.27	6.51	6.81
1970	6.58	6.86	6.44	6.39	6.53	6.94	6.99	6.58	6.75	6.63	6.59	6.25	5.98
1971	5.70	5.93	5.85	5.73	5.77	6.00	5.88	5.80	5.68	5.47	5.36	5.40	5.53
1972	5.54	5.53	5.58	5.57	5.65	5.54	5.50	5.49	5.51	5.61	5.60	5.42	5.53
1973	6.21	5.80	5.99	6.11	6.02	6.16	6.24	6.45	6.76	6.32	6.16	6.24	6.25
1974	6.88	6.45	6.46	6.70	6.92	6.98	6.92	7.07	7.21	7.19	7.11	6.82	6.67
1975	6.96	6.58	6.51	6.65	6.99	6.94	6.85	6.93	7.13	7.29	7.28	7.20	7.16
1976	6.79	6.92	6.92	6.86	6.72	6.98	6.93	6.88	6.86	6.72	6.66	6.62	6.37
1977	7.53	7.35	7.53	7.57	7.50	7.57	7.43	7.45	7.50	7.45	7.60	7.67	7.77
1978	8.40	8.02	8.10	8.10	8.22	8.37	8.45	8.61	8.38	8.37	8.60	8.68	8.84
1979	9.26	8.93	8.94	8.99	9.03	9.11	8.84	8.85	8.89	9.14	9.93	10.38	10.08
1980	11.23	10.54	12.01	12.26	11.22	10.15	9.74	10.20	10.94	11.36	11.63	12.30	12.35
1981	13.31	12.05	12.68	12.59	13.08	13.44	12.82	13.49	14.05	14.05	14.59	13.08	13.28
1982	12.61	14.16	14.07	13.37	13.24	13.05	13.75	13.40	12.54	11.86	10.84	10.46	10.60
1983	11.17	10.64	10.89	10.65	10.49	10.52	11.44	11.78	11.62		11.55	11.68	11.81

① Selected notes and bonds maturing within 3 to 5 years. ② Long-term: due or callable after 15 years, Jan. 1941-March 1952; after 12 years, Apr. 1952-Mar. 1953; 10 years or more, beginning Apr. 1953.

Source: *Moody's Municipal & Government Manual,* vol. 2 (New York: Moody's Investor's Service Inc., 1984).

3-YEAR TREASURY*

	Jan.	Feb.	Mar.	Apr.	May	June	July	Aug.	Sept.	Oct.	Nov.	Dec.
1943	1.22	1.22	1.23	1.27	1.19	1.16	1.15	1.18	1.20	1.20	1.20	1.19
1944	1.22	1.24	1.27	1.23	1.21	1.24	1.20	1.19	1.17	1.23	1.25	1.30
1945	1.23	1.17	1.19	1.16	1.18	1.14	1.19	1.22	1.20	1.15	1.10	1.07
1946	0.96	0.92	1.00	1.10	1.12	1.09	1.11	1.13	1.23	1.22	1.23	1.20
1947	1.15	1.18	1.13	1.19	1.23	1.23	1.26	1.22	1.24	1.37	1.44	1.49
1948	1.48	1.49	1.47	1.47	1.39	1.46	1.49	1.56	1.61	1.63	1.60	1.54
1949	1.49	1.51	1.47	1.48	1.43	1.37	1.25	1.22	1.25	1.25	1.28	1.26
1950	1.33	1.33	1.36	1.41	1.39	1.43	1.39	1.45	1.59	1.64	1.62	1.68
1951	1.70	1.71	1.97	2.00	2.05	2.08	1.93	1.87	1.95	2.07	2.04	2.11
1952	2.06	2.10	2.04	1.94	1.96	2.07	2.20	2.34	2.30	2.24	2.25	2.34
1953	2.30	2.31	2.37	2.59	2.68	2.62	2.52	2.60	2.39	2.20	2.24	1.96
1954	1.88	1.57	1.52	1.43	1.60	1.43	1.44	1.49	1.66	1.75	1.73	1.79
1955	1.95	2.19	2.24	2.40	2.29	2.42	2.56	2.73	2.54	2.56	2.76	2.90
1956	2.62	2.68	2.88	3.14	2.93	2.94	3.20	3.42	3.43	3.39	3.66	3.66
1957	3.33	3.42	3.44	3.54	3.67	3.82	3.93	3.95	4.04	4.00	3.43	2.78
1958	2.65	2.41	2.32	2.12	1.97	2.15	2.43	3.33	3.65	3.57	3.56	3.70
1959	3.93	3.85	4.02	4.10	4.24	4.54	4.59	4.77	4.93	4.68	4.86	5.17
1960	4.86	4.83	4.14	4.32	4.37	3.98	3.47	3.42	3.41	3.52	3.71	3.34
1961	3.46	3.42	3.38	3.29	3.36	3.56	3.51	3.62	3.63	3.55	3.60	3.64
1962	3.75	3.57	3.40	3.35	3.34	3.48	3.66	3.41	3.34	3.26	3.35	3.38
1963	3.39	3.38	3.44	3.51	3.57	3.56	3.76	3.77	3.81	3.88	3.88	4.00
1964	3.99	4.00	4.16	4.10	4.02	3.96	3.93	3.95	3.99	4.01	4.07	4.09
1965	4.15	4.20	4.18	4.17	4.14	4.08	4.12	4.19	4.33	4.36	4.48	4.88
1966	4.89	5.04	4.92	4.91	5.05	5.04	5.21	6.11	5.72	5.38	5.42	4.93
1967	4.62	4.76	4.29	4.41	4.55	5.10	5.24	5.29	5.45	5.64	5.64	5.71
1968	5.53	5.69	5.81	5.95	6.05	5.87	5.52	5.53	5.46	5.61	5.73	6.51
1969	6.17	6.38	6.34	6.31	6.61	6.88	7.32	7.34	8.06	7.41	7.79	8.41
1970	8.20	7.62	7.20	7.73	8.14	7.72	7.57	7.43	7.01	6.90	5.71	5.75
1971	5.60	5.08	4.48	5.13	5.89	6.20	6.59	6.18	5.74	5.46	5.21	5.14
1972	5.00	5.19	5.45	5.78	5.38	5.54	5.65	5.69	5.95	5.89	5.82	5.89
1973	6.15	6.46	6.86	6.76	6.83	6.73	7.43	7.85	7.27	6.74	6.96	6.75
1974	6.87	6.66	7.20	7.97	8.16	8.09	8.33	8.64	8.40	7.91	7.62	7.20
1975	7.03	6.51	6.87	7.65	7.13	7.28	7.78	8.02	8.24	7.41	7.51	7.01
1976	6.91	6.93	6.95	6.84	7.37	7.10	7.05	6.74	6.62	6.36	5.80	5.61
1977	6.49	6.52	6.49	6.28	6.46	6.22	6.49	6.68	6.91	7.27	7.10	7.36
1978	7.52	7.66	7.67	7.82	8.12	8.37	8.39	8.34	8.50	8.76	9.04	9.55
1979	9.18	9.45	9.33	9.48	9.34	8.95	9.03	9.50	9.60	11.60	10.58	10.72
1980	11.06	13.79	13.76	10.32	8.92	9.27	9.44	11.64	12.44	12.49	13.19	12.43
1981	13.01	13.29	13.36	14.24	14.66	14.12	15.03	16.21	16.03	15.40	12.67	13.97
1982	14.74	13.87	14.39	13.67	13.67	14.90	13.82	12.45	12.04	10.81	10.31	10.03
1983	10.12	9.68	10.09	9.82	10.25	10.58	11.04	11.23	10.73	10.92	10.89	10.93

5-YEAR TREASURY*

	Jan.	Feb.	Mar.	Apr.	May	June	July	Aug.	Sept.	Oct.	Nov.	Dec.
1943	1.63	1.66	1.68	1.69	1.63	1.55	1.56	1.60	1.61	1.61	1.63	1.61
1944	1.62	1.61	1.62	1.62	1.62	1.64	1.64	1.62	1.62	1.64	1.64	1.66
1945	1.54	1.48	1.47	1.36	1.40	1.37	1.39	1.40	1.40	1.36	1.26	1.24
1946	1.14	1.11	1.15	1.29	1.31	1.27	1.29	1.33	1.43	1.43	1.46	1.44
1947	1.36	1.40	1.35	1.38	1.39	1.41	1.42	1.37	1.40	1.51	1.61	1.76
1948	1.76	1.77	1.74	1.73	1.62	1.68	1.73	1.83	1.84	1.86	1.81	1.74
1949	1.69	1.69	1.63	1.63	1.58	1.51	1.41	1.36	1.40	1.40	1.41	1.39
1950	1.45	1.45	1.48	1.54	1.50	1.57	1.49	1.55	1.68	1.72	1.71	1.76
1951	1.78	1.79	2.03	2.09	2.14	2.15	2.00	1.96	2.04	2.14	2.12	2.20
1952	2.14	2.19	2.12	2.04	2.13	2.22	2.33	2.42	2.44	2.34	2.34	2.39
1953	2.42	2.45	2.49	2.70	2.80	2.74	2.65	2.74	2.49	2.36	2.43	2.16
1954	2.09	1.98	1.85	1.75	1.95	1.80	1.85	1.87	1.95	2.05	2.07	2.13
1955	2.32	2.39	2.50	2.57	2.51	2.63	2.79	2.88	2.76	2.71	2.89	2.95
1956	2.74	2.75	3.00	3.17	2.95	3.03	3.24	3.48	3.40	3.46	3.65	3.58
1957	3.33	3.37	3.39	3.57	3.71	3.85	3.98	3.88	4.03	4.00	3.42	2.84
1958	2.76	2.66	2.54	2.38	2.38	2.54	2.88	3.48	3.77	3.78	3.60	3.87
1959	4.04	3.87	4.02	4.19	4.32	4.50	4.55	4.72	4.87	4.70	4.72	5.10
1960	4.85	4.78	4.24	4.38	4.43	4.07	3.65	3.64	3.64	3.72	3.96	3.60
1961	3.73	3.63	3.60	3.57	3.55	3.80	3.80	3.91	3.79	3.78	3.84	3.89
1962	4.00	3.83	3.64	3.62	3.61	3.72	3.87	3.65	3.64	3.55	3.62	3.56
1963	3.61	3.65	3.71	3.73	3.75	3.79	3.88	3.88	3.92	3.98	3.96	4.08
1964	4.07	4.08	4.21	4.16	4.11	4.04	4.06	4.06	4.06	4.09	4.12	4.14
1965	4.17	4.21	4.19	4.19	4.17	4.14	4.16	4.24	4.33	4.38	4.49	4.83
1966	4.87	5.04	4.90	4.91	5.03	5.04	5.21	5.98	5.38	5.21	5.37	4.88
1967	4.64	4.77	4.45	4.57	4.72	5.22	5.29	5.34	5.46	5.69	5.67	5.69
1968	5.55	5.70	5.83	5.92	6.04	5.86	5.55	5.58	5.52	5.67	5.77	6.45
1969	6.19	6.38	6.38	6.34	6.62	6.80	7.02	7.04	7.97	7.31	7.58	8.33
1970	8.14	7.56	7.24	7.82	8.10	7.79	7.61	7.50	7.18	7.15	6.18	6.05
1971	6.03	5.73	5.13	5.69	6.32	6.61	6.88	6.48	6.04	5.86	5.73	5.64
1972	5.48	5.63	5.88	6.14	5.80	5.88	5.94	6.00	6.25	6.15	6.06	6.12
1973	6.30	6.59	6.89	6.71	6.88	6.60	7.25	7.59	7.01	6.70	6.87	6.75
1974	6.83	6.75	7.22	7.87	7.99	7.88	8.15	8.50	8.25	7.88	7.63	7.32
1975	7.33	6.95	7.28	7.82	7.48	7.55	7.84	8.01	8.35	7.67	7.80	7.38
1976	7.35	7.32	7.27	7.24	7.60	7.46	7.46	7.19	7.08	6.82	6.25	6.19
1977	6.91	6.96	6.94	6.80	6.86	6.62	6.81	6.93	7.09	7.41	7.28	7.56
1978	7.70	7.83	7.85	8.00	8.23	8.43	8.47	8.26	8.42	8.65	8.81	9.24
1979	8.96	9.17	9.15	9.20	8.97	8.75	8.86	9.19	9.25	11.07	10.43	10.40
1980	10.85	13.43	12.90	10.22	9.58	9.79	9.79	11.84	12.28	12.21	12.71	12.09
1981	12.66	13.20	13.24	14.08	14.17	13.78	14.62	16.05	16.06	15.63	12.99	13.96
1982	14.50	13.54	14.17	13.34	13.32	14.55	13.50	12.20	12.22	11.31	10.99	10.51
1983	10.69	10.19	10.56	10.30	10.70	11.00	11.43	11.70	11.28	11.41	11.36	11.36

Source: *Moody's Municipal & Government Manual*, vol. 2 (New York: Moody's Investor's Service Inc., 1984).

91-DAY BILL RATE-AVG. FOR LAST OFFERING OF MONTH

	Jan.	Feb.	Mar.	Apr.	May	June	July	Aug.	Sept.	Oct.	Nov.	Dec.
1941	neg.	.086	.055	.097	.107	.087	.094	.090	.062	.151	.242	.310
1942	.220	.222	.221	.335	.365	.360	.372	.367	.373	.373	.368	.357
1943	.369	.369	.374	.373	.374	.375	.374	.375	.375	.375	.375	.373
1944	.374	.375	.375	.375	.374	.375	.375	.375	.375	.375	.375	.373
1945	.375	.375	.376	.375	.375	.375	.375	.375	.375	.375	.375	.373
1946	.375	.375	.375	.375	.376	.376	.376	.376	.375	.375	.376	.374
1947	.376	.376	.376	.376	.376	.376	.740	.766	.817	.895	.944	.952
1948	.990	.997	.996	.997	.997	.998	.997	1.072	1.109	1.120	1.147	1.157
1949	1.160	1.164	1.162	1.156	1.159	1.158	1.017	1.031	1.076	1.036	1.052	1.087
1950	1.103	1.132	1.145	1.166	1.167	1.172	1.174	1.285	1.324	1.316	1.383	1.382
1951	1.389	1.390	1.507	1.506	1.600	1.527	1.591	1.645	1.647	1.593	1.609	1.865
1952	1.589	1.563	1.592	1.616	1.728	1.682	1.877	1.899	1.635	1.757	1.931	2.228
1953	1.961	2.070	2.036	2.243	2.084	1.954	2.157	2.001	1.634	1.220	1.488	1.574
1954	0.998	0.986	1.030	0.886	0.718	0.635	0.800	0.983	0.984	1.007	0.897	1.175
1955	1.349	1.355	1.374	1.697	1.471	1.401	1.720	1.875	2.122	2.231	2.440	2.688
1956	2.245	2.429	2.422	2.788	2.573	2.535	2.303	2.832	2.986	2.907	3.174	3.217
1957	3.283	3.288	3.034	3.054	3.245	3.232	3.158	3.497	3.534	3.622	3.158	3.174
1958	2.202	1.202	1.189	1.055	0.635	1.006	0.984	2.162	2.511	2.647	2.723	2.739
1959	2.975	2.589	2.766	2.831	2.878	3.281	3.047	3.824	3.958	4.022	4.279	4.516
1960	4.116	4.168	2.792	3.317	3.497	2.399	2.404	2.518	2.286	2.129	2.396	2.120
1961	2.230	2.496	2.392	2.186	2.354	2.219	2.244	2.321	2.233	2.325	2.606	2.594
1962	2.688	2.664	2.719	2.740	2.656	2.792	2.892	2.806	2.749	2.742	2.853	2.894
1963	2.917	2.870	2.919	2.884	2.974	2.979	3.206	3.396	3.379	3.452	3.480	3.522
1964	3.501	3.547	3.550	3.446	3.475	3.478	3.475	3.513	3.542	3.567	3.758	3.867
1965	3.848	3.989	3.922	3.916	3.889	3.789	3.803	3.855	3.983	4.040	4.104	4.457
1966	4.596	4.696	4.555	4.630	4.641	4.435	4.818	5.087	5.503	5.246	5.202	4.747
1967	4.486	4.538	4.150	3.715	3.477	3.462	4.423	4.490	4.629	4.542	4.957	4.989
1968	4.846	5.063	5.186	5.499	5.696	5.238	5.190	5.194	5.182	5.471	5.488	6.199
1969	6.167	6.080	6.065	6.053	6.124	6.456	7.172	7.098	7.106	7.030	7.476	8.096
1970	7.888	6.812	6.330	6.876	7.133	6.421	6.345	6.342	5.807	5.831	5.084	4.803
1971	4.201	3.497	3.521	3.865	4.344	5.080	5.554	4.549	4.676	4.443	4.324	3.731
1972	3.367	3.446	3.849	3.513	3.762	4.023	3.794	4.332	4.644	4.767	4.886	5.111
1973	5.689	5.811	6.251	6.278	6.694	7.228	8.320	8.778	7.331	7.163	7.695	7.406
1974	7.778	7.188	8.300	8.909	7.983	7.841	7.698	9.908	7.002	7.892	7.328	7.113
1975	5.606	5.455	5.562	5.716	5.206	5.665	6.318	6.593	6.547	5.685	5.520	5.208
1976	4.763	4.870	4.929	4.909	5.495	5.368	5.194	5.091	5.072	4.929	4.466	4.296
1977	4.720	4.708	4.609	4.518	4.993	4.965	5.163	5.574	5.982	6.278	6.057	6.144
1978	6.440	6.429	6.310	6.294	6.658	6.967	6.895	7.323	8.106	8.454	9.166	9.388
1979	9.324	9.451	9.498	9.498	9.526	8.802	9.154	9.855	9.989	12.256	11.018	12.105
1980	12.038	13.700	15.037	10.788	7.675	8.149	8.221	10.124	11.524	12.331	14.384	13.908
1981	15.199	14.103	12.501	14.190	16.750	13.909	15.065	15.583	14.669	13.352	10.400	11.690
1982	13.364	12.430	13.399	12.469	11.520	13.269	10.550	8.604	7.801	8.031	8.280	7.975
1983	8.122	7.944	8.680	8.150	8.650	9.090	9.130	9.280	8.730	8.410	8.900	8.940

10-YEAR TREASURY*

	Jan.	Feb.	Mar.	Apr.	May	June	July	Aug.	Sept.	Oct.	Nov.	Dec.
1943	2.08	2.06	2.09	2.08	2.02	2.02	2.00	2.03	2.03	2.05	2.08	2.09
1944	2.09	2.06	2.05	2.06	2.06	2.07	2.07	2.05	2.05	2.07	2.06	2.06
1945	1.96	1.87	1.85	1.75	1.75	1.71	1.70	1.72	1.71	1.64	1.58	1.49
1946	1.38	1.43	1.45	1.58	1.61	1.59	1.64	1.71	1.74	1.75	1.79	1.70
1947	1.68	1.70	1.67	1.70	1.69	1.72	1.70	1.65	1.66	1.78	1.87	2.17
1948	2.17	2.17	2.12	2.08	1.96	2.08	2.07	2.16	2.15	2.19	2.11	2.05
1949	2.00	1.98	1.91	1.89	1.86	1.79	1.73	1.66	1.70	1.70	1.70	1.66
1950	1.74	1.73	1.74	1.79	1.76	1.82	1.75	1.80	1.91	1.95	1.93	1.96
1951	1.96	2.01	2.20	2.27	2.26	2.29	2.15	2.19	2.25	2.27	2.28	2.35
1952	2.31	2.35	2.29	2.20	2.35	2.37	2.37	2.42	2.64	2.52	2.50	2.52
1953	2.61	2.66	2.74	2.87	3.02	2.92	2.85	2.87	2.62	2.56	2.63	2.41
1954	2.37	2.37	2.41	2.33	2.37	2.39	2.36	2.43	2.45	2.44	2.49	2.51
1955	2.59	2.64	2.65	2.73	2.65	2.76	2.94	2.94	2.83	2.80	2.89	2.92
1956	2.80	2.83	2.99	3.13	2.90	2.99	3.14	3.37	3.26	3.39	3.53	3.51
1957	3.29	3.30	3.30	3.50	3.60	3.84	3.87	3.75	3.88	3.88	3.35	2.96
1958	2.92	2.88	2.79	2.67	2.69	2.92	3.23	3.52	3.79	3.78	3.62	4.01
1959	4.06	3.88	4.00	4.22	4.32	4.38	4.41	4.54	4.68	4.46	4.47	4.87
1960	4.78	4.57	4.31	4.37	4.29	4.09	3.80	3.79	3.76	3.92	4.10	3.81
1961	3.86	3.72	3.76	3.75	3.76	3.91	3.91	3.96	3.88	3.93	4.05	4.15
1962	4.19	4.09	3.91	3.86	3.91	3.97	4.03	3.92	3.94	3.89	3.95	3.85
1963	3.85	3.94	3.96	3.98	3.95	3.99	3.99	3.99	4.05	4.13	4.09	4.14
1964	4.16	4.14	4.22	4.22	4.20	4.15	4.21	4.21	4.18	4.19	4.18	4.18
1965	4.18	4.22	4.21	4.21	4.21	4.21	4.22	4.26	4.33	4.37	4.50	4.64
1966	4.70	4.96	4.84	4.85	4.89	4.89	5.05	5.53	5.12	4.94	5.13	4.72
1967	4.51	4.73	4.50	4.65	4.80	5.16	5.21	5.26	5.33	5.59	5.64	5.65
1968	5.51	5.63	5.78	5.70	5.93	5.70	5.37	5.45	5.40	5.56	5.72	6.18
1969	6.00	6.24	6.33	6.05	6.34	6.50	6.54	6.60	7.35	6.97	7.34	7.99
1970	7.64	7.10	7.00	7.77	8.20	7.66	7.28	7.35	7.16	7.30	6.29	6.46
1971	6.02	6.03	5.42	5.81	6.26	6.78	6.66	6.26	5.96	5.82	5.74	5.70
1972	5.88	5.66	6.01	6.11	5.96	5.96	5.82	6.21	6.37	6.31	6.29	6.40
1973	6.51	6.74	6.73	6.59	6.78	6.78	7.31	7.00	6.52	6.58	6.71	6.67
1974	6.91	6.85	7.16	7.61	7.72	7.53	7.75	8.19	7.89	7.59	7.35	7.12
1975	6.96	6.93	7.05	7.55	7.14	7.28	7.31	7.41	6.98	6.77	6.45	6.22
1976	7.24	7.26	7.12	7.18	7.34	7.26	7.23	7.05	7.21	7.30	7.58	7.77
1977	7.33	7.44	7.44	7.34	7.31	7.09	7.11	7.21	7.30	7.58	7.49	7.77
1978	7.93	8.00	8.04	8.15	8.33	8.49	8.52	8.29	8.45	8.67	8.72	9.02
1979	8.86	9.11	9.11	9.12	8.92	8.90	9.00	9.22	9.29	10.74	10.24	10.33
1980	11.10	13.07	12.50	10.53	9.88	9.97	10.31	11.48	11.97	12.06	12.34	11.82
1981	12.48	13.11	13.02	13.75	13.70	13.34	14.13	15.37	15.51	15.19	12.96	14.00
1982	14.57	13.83	14.11	13.25	13.21	14.30	13.54	12.45	11.80	10.78	10.53	10.32
1983	10.64	10.10	10.35	10.08	10.53	10.84	11.28	11.52	11.27	11.44	11.37	11.43

*Taken from a line, commonly called a yield curve, on last Tuesday of month.

Source: *Moody's Municipal & Government Manual,* vol. 2 (New York: Moody's Investor's Service Inc., 1984).

MOODY'S AVERAGE OF YIELDS ON Aaa CORPORATE BONDS (IN PERCENT)

Year	Aver.	Jan.	Feb.	Mar.	Apr.	May	June	July	Aug.	Sept.	Oct.	Nov.	Dec.
1984..	...	12.20	12.08	12.57	12.81	13.28	...	...	...	...	...	...	...
1983..	12.04	11.79	12.01	11.73	11.51	11.46	11.74	12.15	12.51	12.37	12.25	12.41	12.57
1982..	13.79	15.18	15.27	14.58	14.46	14.26	14.81	14.61	13.71	12.94	12.12	11.68	11.83
1981..	14.17	12.81	13.35	13.33	13.88	14.32	13.75	14.38	14.89	15.49	15.40	14.22	14.23
1980..	11.94	11.09	12.38	12.96	12.04	10.99	10.58	11.07	11.64	12.02	12.31	12.97	13.21
1979..	9.63	9.25	9.26	9.37	9.38	9.50	9.29	9.20	9.23	9.44	10.13	10.76	10.74
1978..	8.73	8.41	8.47	8.47	8.56	8.69	8.76	8.88	8.69	8.69	8.89	9.03	9.16
1977..	8.02	7.96	8.04	8.10	8.04	8.05	7.95	7.94	7.98	7.92	8.04	8.08	8.19
1976..	8.43	8.60	8.55	8.52	8.40	8.58	8.62	8.56	8.45	8.38	8.32	8.25	7.98
1975..	8.83	8.83	8.62	8.67	8.95	8.90	8.77	8.84	8.95	8.95	8.86	8.78	8.79
1974..	8.57	7.83	7.85	8.01	8.25	8.37	8.47	8.72	9.00	9.24	9.27	8.89	8.89
1973..	7.44	7.15	7.22	7.29	7.26	7.29	7.37	7.45	7.68	7.63	7.60	7.67	7.68
1972..	7.21	7.19	7.27	7.24	7.30	7.30	7.23	7.21	7.19	7.22	7.21	7.12	7.08
1971..	7.39	7.36	7.08	7.21	7.25	7.53	7.64	7.64	7.59	7.44	7.39	7.26	7.25
1970..	8.04	7.91	7.93	7.84	7.83	8.11	8.48	8.44	8.13	8.09	8.03	8.05	7.64
1969..	7.03	6.59	6.66	6.85	6.89	6.79	6.98	7.08	6.97	7.14	7.33	7.35	7.72
1968..	6.18	6.17	6.10	6.11	6.21	6.27	6.28	6.24	6.02	5.97	6.09	6.19	6.45
1967..	5.51	5.20	5.03	5.13	5.11	5.24	5.44	5.58	5.62	5.65	5.82	6.07	6.19
1966..	5.13	4.74	4.78	4.92	4.96	4.98	5.07	5.16	5.31	5.49	5.41	5.35	5.39
1965..	4.49	4.43	4.41	4.42	4.43	4.44	4.46	4.48	4.49	4.52	4.56	4.60	4.68
1964..	4.40	4.37	4.36	4.38	4.40	4.41	4.41	4.40	4.41	4.42	4.42	4.43	4.44
1963..	4.26	4.21	4.19	4.19	4.21	4.22	4.23	4.26	4.29	4.31	4.32	4.33	4.35
1962..	4.33	4.42	4.42	4.39	4.33	4.28	4.28	4.34	4.35	4.32	4.28	4.25	4.24
1961..	4.35	4.32	4.27	4.22	4.25	4.27	4.33	4.41	4.45	4.45	4.42	4.39	4.42
1960..	4.41	4.61	4.56	4.49	4.45	4.46	4.45	4.41	4.28	4.25	4.30	4.31	4.35
1959..	4.38	4.12	4.14	4.13	4.23	4.37	4.46	4.47	4.43	4.52	4.57	4.56	4.58
1958..	3.79	3.60	3.59	3.63	3.60	3.57	3.57	3.67	3.85	4.09	4.11	4.09	4.08
1957..	3.89	3.77	3.67	3.66	3.67	3.74	3.91	3.99	4.10	4.12	4.10	4.08	3.81
1956..	3.36	3.11	3.08	3.10	3.24	3.28	3.26	3.28	3.43	3.56	3.59	3.69	3.75
1955..	3.06	2.93	2.93	3.02	3.01	3.04	3.05	3.06	3.11	3.13	3.10	3.10	3.15
1954..	2.90	3.06	2.95	2.86	2.85	2.88	2.90	2.89	2.87	2.89	2.87	2.89	2.90
1953..	3.20	3.02	3.07	3.12	3.23	3.34	3.40	3.28	3.24	3.29	3.16	3.11	3.13
1952..	2.96	2.98	2.93	2.96	2.93	2.93	2.94	2.95	2.94	2.95	3.01	2.98	2.97
1951..	2.86	2.66	2.66	2.78	2.87	2.89	2.94	2.94	2.88	2.84	2.89	2.96	3.01
1950..	2.62	2.57	2.58	2.58	2.60	2.61	2.62	2.65	2.61	2.64	2.67	2.67	2.67
1949..	2.66	2.71	2.71	2.70	2.70	2.71	2.71	2.67	2.62	2.60	2.61	2.60	2.58
1948..	2.82	2.86	2.85	2.83	2.78	2.76	2.76	2.81	2.84	2.84	2.84	2.84	2.79
1947..	2.61	2.57	2.55	2.55	2.53	2.53	2.55	2.55	2.56	2.61	2.70	2.77	2.86
1946..	2.53	2.54	2.48	2.47	2.46	2.51	2.49	2.48	2.51	2.58	2.60	2.59	2.61
1945..	2.62	2.69	2.65	2.62	2.61	2.62	2.61	2.60	2.61	2.62	2.62	2.62	2.61
1944..	2.72	2.72	2.74	2.74	2.74	2.73	2.73	2.72	2.71	2.72	2.72	2.72	2.70
1943..	2.73	2.79	2.77	2.77	2.76	2.76	2.74	2.72	2.69	2.69	2.69	2.70	2.71	2.74
1942..	2.83	2.83	2.85	2.86	2.83	2.85	2.85	2.83	2.81	2.80	2.80	2.79	2.81
1941..	2.77	2.75	2.78	2.80	2.82	2.81	2.77	2.74	2.74	2.75	2.73	2.72	2.80
1940..	2.84	2.88	2.86	2.84	2.82	2.93	2.96	2.88	2.85	2.82	2.79	2.75	2.71
1939..	3.01	3.01	3.00	2.99	3.02	2.97	2.92	2.89	2.93	3.25	3.15	3.00	2.94
1938..	3.19	3.17	3.20	3.22	3.30	3.22	3.26	3.22	3.18	3.21	3.15	3.10	3.08
1937..	3.26	3.10	3.22	3.32	3.42	3.33	3.28	3.25	3.24	3.28	3.27	3.24	3.21
1936..	3.24	3.37	3.32	3.29	3.29	3.27	3.24	3.23	3.21	3.18	3.18	3.15	3.10
1935..	3.60	3.77	3.69	3.67	3.66	3.65	3.61	3.56	3.60	3.59	3.52	3.47	3.44
1934..	4.00	4.35	4.20	4.13	4.07	4.01	3.93	3.89	3.93	3.96	3.90	3.86	3.81
1933..	4.49	4.44	4.48	4.68	4.78	4.63	4.46	4.36	4.30	4.36	4.34	4.54	4.50
1932..	5.01	5.20	5.23	4.98	5.17	5.36	5.41	5.26	4.91	4.70	4.64	4.63	4.59
1931..	4.58	4.42	4.43	4.39	4.40	4.37	4.36	4.36	4.40	4.55	4.99	4.94	5.32
1930..	4.55	4.66	4.69	4.62	4.60	4.60	4.57	4.52	4.47	4.42	4.42	4.47	4.52
1929..	4.83	4.62	4.66	4.70	4.69	4.70	4.70	4.77	4.79	4.80	4.77	4.76	4.67
1928..	4.55	4.46	4.46	4.46	4.46	4.49	4.57	4.57	4.64	4.61	4.61	4.51	4.46
1927..	4.57	4.66	4.67	4.62	4.58	4.57	4.58	4.60	4.56	4.56	4.51	4.49	4.46
1926..	4.73	4.82	4.77	4.79	4.74	4.71	4.72	4.71	4.72	4.72	4.71	4.68	4.68
1925..	4.88	4.95	4.95	4.91	4.87	4.83	4.83	4.87	4.90	4.87	4.85	4.84	4.85
1924..	5.00	5.09	5.09	5.10	5.08	5.04	4.99	4.95	4.95	4.95	4.92	4.94	4.95
1923..	5.12	5.04	5.07	5.18	5.22	5.16	5.15	5.14	5.08	5.12	5.11	5.09	5.09
1922..	5.10	5.34	5.29	5.23	5.15	5.13	5.08	5.00	4.96	4.93	4.97	5.09	5.08
1921..	5.97	6.14	6.08	6.08	6.06	6.11	6.18	6.12	5.99	5.93	5.84	5.60	5.50
1920..	6.12	5.75	5.86	5.92	6.04	6.25	6.38	6.34	6.30	6.22	6.05	6.08	6.26
1919..	5.49	5.35	5.35	5.39	5.44	5.39	5.40	5.44	5.56	5.60	5.54	5.66	5.73

Source: *Moody's Industrial Manual* (New York: Moody's Investor's Service, 1984).

MOODY'S AVERAGE OF YIELDS ON Aa CORPORATE BONDS (IN PERCENT)

Year	Aver.	Jan.	Feb.	Mar.	Apr.	May	June	July	Aug.	Sept.	Oct.	Nov.	Dec.
1984..	...	12.71	12.70	13.22	13.48	14.10	...	...	...	...	...	...	...
1983..	12.42	12.35	12.58	12.32	12.06	11.95	12.15	12.39	12.72	12.62	12.49	12.61	12.76
1982..	14.41	15.75	15.72	15.21	14.90	14.77	15.26	15.21	14.48	13.72	12.97	12.51	12.44
1981..	14.75	13.52	13.89	13.90	14.39	14.88	14.41	14.79	15.42	15.95	15.82	14.97	15.00
1980..	12.50	11.56	12.73	13.51	13.06	11.91	11.39	11.43	12.09	12.52	12.68	13.34	13.78
1979..	9.94	9.48	9.50	9.61	9.65	9.86	9.66	9.49	9.53	9.70	10.46	11.22	11.15
1978..	8.92	8.59	8.65	8.66	8.73	8.84	8.95	9.07	8.96	8.92	9.07	9.24	9.33
1977..	8.24	8.16	8.26	8.28	8.28	8.28	8.19	8.12	8.17	8.15	8.26	8.34	8.40
1976	8.75	9.13	9.02	9.01	8.89	8.92	8.89	8.81	8.66	8.54	8.48	8.46	8.24
1975	9.17	9.13	8.91	8.92	9.19	9.24	9.13	9.13	9.23	9.35	9.32	9.23	9.25
1974	8.84	8.00	8.05	8.18	8.43	8.58	8.75	9.01	9.28	9.66	9.64	9.34	9.20
1973..	7.66	7.37	7.47	7.49	7.49	7.49	7.55	7.64	7.84	7.86	7.84	7.90	7.92
1972..	7.48	7.52	7.52	7.53	7.57	7.56	7.51	7.50	7.43	7.41	7.45	7.39	7.36
1971..	7.78	7.90	7.67	7.73	7.74	7.84	7.96	7.96	7.93	7.81	7.69	7.56	7.57
1970..	8.32	8.15	8.13	8.06	8.03	8.24	8.58	8.64	8.49	8.47	8.44	8.42	8.13
1969..	7.20	6.73	6.77	6.95	7.02	6.96	7.12	7.24	7.23	7.36	7.53	7.58	7.93
1968..	6.38	6.29	6.27	6.28	6.38	6.48	6.50	6.45	6.25	6.23	6.32	6.45	6.66
1967..	5.66	5.30	5.18	5.23	5.26	5.42	5.63	5.72	5.76	5.87	6.01	6.23	6.35
1966..	5.23	4.83	4.90	5.05	5.10	5.10	5.16	5.25	5.38	5.58	5.50	5.46	5.48
1965..	4.57	4.48	4.46	4.48	4.48	4.49	4.52	4.56	4.59	4.63	4.66	4.69	4.80
1964..	4.49	4.49	4.46	4.47	4.49	4.50	4.51	4.50	4.49	4.48	4.49	4.49	4.50
1963..	4.39	4.37	4.36	4.34	4.35	4.36	4.36	4.39	4.40	4.41	4.43	4.44	4.46
1962..	4.47	4.55	4.56	4.53	4.49	4.43	4.44	4.49	4.49	4.46	4.41	4.40	4.38
1961..	4.48	4.48	4.40	4.33	4.37	4.41	4.45	4.53	4.57	4.59	4.56	4.54	4.56
1960..	4.56	4.77	4.71	4.62	4.58	4.61	4.60	4.56	4.44	4.41	4.44	4.47	4.50
1959..	4.51	4.22	4.24	4.23	4.32	4.46	4.56	4.58	4.58	4.69	4.76	4.70	4.74
1958..	3.94	3.81	3.77	3.78	3.78	3.78	3.78	3.83	3.98	4.20	4.21	4.21	4.18
1957..	4.03	3.89	3.83	3.80	3.79	3.83	3.98	4.10	4.21	4.26	4.28	4.29	4.08
1956..	3.45	3.19	3.16	3.18	3.30	3.34	3.35	3.39	3.50	3.63	3.69	3.76	3.85
1955..	3.16	3.06	3.10	3.13	3.13	3.15	3.14	3.14	3.20	3.22	3.19	3.18	3.22
1954..	3.06	3.22	3.12	3.03	3.00	3.03	3.06	3.04	3.03	3.04	3.04	3.04	3.04
1953..	3.31	3.09	3.14	3.18	3.29	3.41	3.50	3.42	3.39	3.43	3.33	3.27	3.28
1952..	3.04	3.05	3.01	3.03	3.01	3.00	3.03	3.04	3.06	3.07	3.08	3.06	3.05
1951..	2.91	2.71	2.71	2.82	2.93	2.93	2.99	2.99	2.92	2.88	2.93	3.02	3.06
1950..	2.69	2.65	2.65	2.66	2.66	2.66	2.69	2.72	2.67	2.71	2.72	2.72	2.72
1949..	2.75	2.81	2.80	2.79	2.79	2.78	2.78	2.75	2.71	2.69	2.70	2.68	2.67
1948..	2.90	2.94	2.93	2.90	2.87	2.86	2.85	2.89	2.94	2.93	2.94	2.92	2.88
1947..	2.70	2.65	2.64	2.64	2.63	2.63	2.64	2.64	2.64	2.69	2.79	2.85	2.94
1946..	2.62	2.62	2.56	2.54	2.56	2.58	2.59	2.59	2.62	2.68	2.70	2.69	2.69
1945..	2.71	2.76	2.73	2.72	2.73	2.72	2.69	2.68	2.70	2.70	2.70	2.68	2.68
1944..	2.81	2.83	2.83	2.82	2.82	2.81	2.81	2.80	2.79	2.79	2.81	2.80	2.76
1943..	2.86	2.93	2.89	2.88	2.88	2.87	2.85	2.82	2.81	2.82	2.83	2.84	2.87
1942..	2.98	2.96	2.98	3.00	2.98	3.00	3.01	2.99	2.99	2.98	2.95	2.94	2.96
1941..	2.94	2.95	3.00	3.01	3.04	2.99	2.95	2.90	2.90	2.91	2.87	2.86	2.95
1940..	3.02	3.08	3.05	3.04	2.99	3.08	3.10	3.01	3.03	3.01	3.01	2.96	2.92
1939..	3.22	3.32	3.26	3.22	3.22	3.16	3.13	3.08	3.11	3.49	3.35	3.16	3.14
1938..	3.56	3.50	3.51	3.56	3.73	3.56	3.68	3.62	3.57	3.60	3.53	3.46	3.42
1937..	3.46	3.30	3.40	3.50	3.57	3.48	3.43	3.41	3.41	3.46	3.53	3.54	3.50
1936..	3.46	3.57	3.55	3.55	3.57	3.53	3.51	3.49	3.47	3.45	3.42	3.38	3.28
1935..	3.95	4.21	4.13	4.11	4.08	4.03	3.99	3.89	3.87	3.85	3.82	3.73	3.65
1934..	4.44	5.00	4.70	4.55	4.43	4.37	4.30	4.28	4.34	4.42	4.36	4.28	4.27
1933..	5.23	5.30	5.35	5.61	5.81	5.40	5.09	4.83	4.77	4.96	4.97	5.35	5.27
1932..	5.98	6.08	6.13	5.85	6.11	6.38	6.60	6.51	5.83	5.54	5.51	5.57	5.60
1931..	5.05	4.70	4.70	4.70	4.67	4.76	4.76	4.81	4.85	5.08	5.57	5.61	6.26
1930..	4.77	4.86	4.86	4.89	4.80	4.78	4.77	4.76	4.74	4.68	4.67	4.75	4.85
1929..	4.93	4.79	4.86	4.92	4.91	4.91	4.98	4.97	4.99	5.01	5.01	4.94	4.84
1928..	4.71	4.61	4.61	4.59	4.60	4.64	4.75	4.79	4.82	4.79	4.78	4.75	4.77
1927..	4.77	4.87	4.87	4.83	4.80	4.79	4.80	4.80	4.73	4.73	4.69	4.65	4.62
1926..	4.97	5.07	5.04	5.05	4.99	4.94	4.92	4.95	4.95	4.97	4.95	4.93	4.89
1925..	5.20	5.30	5.25	5.24	5.24	5.19	5.15	5.17	5.21	5.18	5.17	5.14	5.14
1924..	5.44	5.55	5.52	5.57	5.56	5.49	5.43	5.38	5.38	5.38	5.35	5.32	5.31
1923..	5.62	5.42	5.49	5.62	5.73	5.66	5.66	5.69	5.63	5.65	5.65	5.63	5.63
1922..	5.59	5.94	5.80	5.79	5.71	5.62	5.64	5.57	5.44	5.35	5.36	5.45	5.41
1921..	6.55	6.64	6.60	6.59	6.68	6.69	6.76	6.78	6.64	6.56	6.47	6.18	5.95
1920..	6.59	6.19	6.28	6.42	6.54	6.78	6.79	6.69	6.76	6.65	6.56	6.63	6.84
1919..	5.86	5.75	5.79	5.76	5.80	5.75	5.71	5.76	5.85	5.96	5.96	6.02	6.21

Source: *Moody's Industrial Manual* (New York: Moody's Investor's Service, 1984).

MOODY'S AVERAGE OF YIELDS ON A CORPORATE BONDS (IN PERCENT)

Year	Aver.	Jan.	Feb.	Mar.	Apr.	May	June	July	Aug.	Sept.	Oct.	Nov.	Dec.
1984..	...	13.13	13.11	13.54	13.77	14.37	...	...	...	...	...	...	...
1983..	13.10	13.53	13.52	13.15	12.86	12.68	12.88	12.99	13.17	13.11	12.97	13.09	13.21
1982..	15.43	16.19	16.35	16.12	15.95	15.70	16.07	16.20	15.70	15.07	14.34	13.81	13.66
1981..	15.29	13.83	14.27	14.47	14.82	15.43	15.08	15.36	15.76	16.36	16.47	15.82	15.75
1980..	12.89	11.88	12.99	13.97	13.55	12.35	11.89	11.95	12.44	12.97	13.05	13.59	14.03
1979..	10.20	9.72	9.68	9.81	9.88	10.00	9.89	9.75	9.85	10.03	10.83	11.50	11.46
1978..	9.12	8.76	8.79	8.83	8.93	9.05	9.18	9.33	9.18	9.11	9.26	9.48	9.53
1977..	8.49	8.45	8.49	8.55	8.55	8.55	8.46	8.40	8.40	8.37	8.48	8.56	8.57
[1]1976.	9.09	9.54	9.43	9.40	9.26	9.28	9.24	9.14	8.98	8.81	8.73	8.69	8.53
[1]1975$	9.65	9.81	9.51	9.37	9.62	9.79	9.67	9.61	9.68	9.74	9.72	9.64	9.67
[1]1974.	9.20	8.17	8.25	8.32	8.61	8.83	9.07	9.40	9.67	10.04	10.29	9.96	9.80
1973..	7.84	7.53	7.60	7.66	7.64	7.64	7.71	7.86	8.11	8.11	7.98	8.07	8.11
1972..	7.66	7.70	7.70	7.66	7.64	7.64	7.75	7.71	7.64	7.64	7.64	7.58	7.50
1971..	8.03	8.15	7.85	7.96	7.99	8.14	8.20	8.21	8.20	8.04	7.97	7.88	7.81
1970..	8.57	8.35	8.31	8.17	8.22	8.49	8.76	8.92	8.85	8.78	8.71	8.74	8.48
1969..	7.40	6.93	6.97	7.13	7.21	7.12	7.28	7.40	7.41	7.56	7.79	7.84	8.21
1968..	6.54	6.48	6.41	6.43	6.57	6.62	6.65	6.60	6.38	6.39	6.47	6.59	6.85
1967..	5.86	5.53	5.38	5.49	5.46	5.60	5.77	5.88	5.94	6.06	6.19	6.43	6.58
1966..	5.35	4.91	4.96	5.12	5.18	5.17	5.29	5.36	5.48	5.69	5.67	5.65	5.69
1965..	4.63	4.57	4.54	4.54	4.54	4.54	4.55	4.58	4.62	4.65	4.69	4.71	4.75
1964..	4.57	4.56	4.56	4.56	4.59	4.60	4.60	4.58	4.57	4.55	4.55	4.57	4.58
1963..	4.48	4.48	4.46	4.45	4.46	4.46	4.45	4.47	4.48	4.50	4.51	4.54	4.54
1962..	4.65	4.74	4.74	4.71	4.66	4.62	4.62	4.65	4.66	4.62	4.61	4.59	4.54
1961..	4.70	4.69	4.63	4.57	4.59	4.63	4.69	4.75	4.80	4.81	4.79	4.75	4.74
1960..	4.77	4.93	4.92	4.86	4.79	4.84	4.81	4.77	4.65	4.63	4.67	4.69	4.71
1959..	4.67	4.43	4.43	4.40	4.45	4.61	4.71	4.75	4.74	4.87	4.87	4.86	4.89
1958..	4.17	4.01	4.00	4.06	4.01	4.02	4.00	4.04	4.19	4.40	4.45	4.43	4.42
1957..	4.19	4.01	3.99	3.97	3.95	3.99	4.09	4.20	4.35	4.43	4.46	4.50	4.31
1956..	3.57	3.30	3.28	3.30	3.41	3.47	3.48	3.52	3.63	3.73	3.81	3.90	3.98
1955..	3.24	3.15	3.17	3.18	3.19	3.21	3.22	3.24	3.28	3.31	3.30	3.29	3.33
1954..	3.18	3.35	3.25	3.16	3.15	3.15	3.18	3.17	3.15	3.13	3.14	3.13	3.14
1953..	3.47	3.25	3.25	3.30	3.36	3.44	3.58	3.67	3.62	3.56	3.56	3.47	3.40
1952..	3.23	3.32	3.25	3.24	3.20	3.20	3.20	3.19	3.21	3.22	3.24	3.24	3.22
1951..	3.13	2.89	2.88	3.00	3.11	3.15	3.21	3.23	3.17	3.15	3.18	3.26	3.31
1950..	2.89	2.85	2.86	2.86	2.86	2.88	2.90	2.92	2.87	2.88	2.91	2.92	2.91
1949..	3.00	3.08	3.05	3.05	3.05	3.04	3.04	3.04	2.96	2.95	2.94	2.93	2.89
1948..	3.12	3.17	3.17	3.13	3.08	3.06	3.03	3.07	3.13	3.13	3.15	3.18	3.16
1947..	2.87	2.79	2.79	2.80	2.81	2.82	2.83	2.82	2.81	2.86	2.95	3.01	3.16
1946..	2.75	2.73	2.70	2.69	2.69	2.73	2.73	2.72	2.74	2.80	2.84	2.84	2.83
1945..	2.87	2.98	2.94	2.92	2.90	2.88	2.86	2.85	2.85	2.85	2.84	2.81	2.79
1944..	3.06	3.11	3.10	3.10	3.09	3.07	3.07	3.05	3.04	3.05	3.01	3.01	2.98
1943..	3.13	3.20	3.17	3.14	3.14	3.13	3.11	3.09	3.08	3.10	3.10	3.11	3.13
1942..	3.28	3.30	3.29	3.32	3.30	3.31	3.31	3.28	3.27	3.26	3.24	3.24	3.23
1941..	3.30	3.36	3.38	3.37	3.38	3.34	3.31	3.26	3.24	3.24	3.21	3.19	3.27
1940:.	3.57	3.69	3.68	3.65	3.59	3.65	3.70	3.57	3.55	3.52	3.48	3.40	3.36
1939..	3.89	3.97	3.94	3.87	3.97	3.92	3.86	3.83	3.80	4.05	3.94	3.78	3.74
1938..	4.22	4.20	4.24	4.34	4.49	4.28	4.41	4.21	4.13	4.20	4.08	4.02	4.02
1937..	4.01	3.77	3.85	3.97	4.04	3.98	3.96	3.94	3.94	4.02	4.16	4.24	4.20
1936..	4.02	4.21	4.12	4.10	4.12	4.11	4.09	4.05	3.99	3.94	3.90	3.85	3.78
1935..	4.55	4.74	4.63	4.67	4.69	4.59	4.52	4.46	4.49	4.48	4.49	4.45	4.35
1934..	5.08	5.72	5.24	5.12	4.97	4.96	4.96	4.93	5.09	5.17	5.00	4.93	4.86
1933..	6.09	6.16	6.30	6.64	6.85	6.29	5.88	5.58	5.51	5.70	5.76	6.22	6.21
1932..	7.20	7.06	7.06	6.80	7.48	8.40	8.50	8.19	6.84	6.45	6.44	6.53	6.61
1931..	6.01	5.26	5.29	5.30	5.52	5.65	5.75	5.64	5.88	6.29	6.88	6.90	7.70
1930..	5.13	5.23	5.25	5.25	5.12	5.07	5.08	5.06	5.00	4.94	5.06	5.21	5.43
1929..	5.28	5.10	5.14	5.24	5.23	5.24	5.31	5.32	5.39	5.43	5.38	5.33	5.21
1928..	5.01	4.91	4.92	4.92	4.91	4.96	5.07	5.07	5.10	5.07	5.04	4.99	5.08
1927..	5.04	5.11	5.13	5.12	5.06	5.05	5.06	5.04	5.01	5.01	4.97	4.94	4.92
1926..	5.24	5.38	5.33	5.34	5.27	5.18	5.18	5.21	5.23	5.23	5.23	5.51	5.46
1925..	5.55	5.70	5.61	5.66	5.63	5.46	5.44	5.51	5.56	5.53	5.54	5.17	5.46
1924..	5.93	6.16	6.18	6.10	6.09	6.00	5.90	5.79	5.84	5.83	5.78	5.72	5.72
1923..	6.17	6.04	6.07	6.24	6.25	6.17	6.19	6.21	6.06	6.15	6.23	6.22	6.20
1922..	6.03	6.41	6.33	6.22	6.05	5.93	5.97	5.88	5.85	5.79	5.91	5.99	6.04
1921..	7.28	7.52	7.50	7.53	7.53	7.50	7.58	7.53	7.43	7.23	7.03	6.62	6.39
1920..	7.41	6.88	7.15	7.11	7.34	7.60	7.58	7.62	7.69	7.48	7.34	7.45	7.71
1919..	6.48	6.42	6.45	6.48	6.40	6.35	6.26	6.26	6.44	6.56	6.52	6.70	6.91

Source: *Moody's Industrial Manual* (New York: Moody's Investor's Service, 1984).

MOODY'S AVERAGE OF YIELDS ON Baa CORPORATE BONDS (IN PERCENT)

Year	Aver.	Jan.	Feb.	Mar.	Apr.	May	June	July	Aug.	Sept.	Oct.	Nov.	Dec.
1984..	...	13.65	13.59	13.99	14.31	14.74	...	...	...	...	...	...	...
1983..	13.55	13.94	13.95	13.61	13.29	13.09	13.37	13.39	13.64	13.55	13.46	13.61	13.75
1982..	16.11	17.10	17.18	16.82	16.78	16.64	16.92	16.80	16.32	15.63	14.73	14.30	14.14
1981..	16.04	15.03	15.37	15.34	15.56	15.95	15.80	16.17	16.34	16.92	17.11	16.39	16.55
1980..	13.67	12.42	13.57	14.45	14.19	13.17	12.71	12.65	13.15	13.70	14.23	14.64	15.14
1979..	10.69	10.13	10.08	10.26	10.33	10.47	10.38	10.29	10.35	10.54	11.40	11.99	12.06
1978..	9.49	9.17	9.20	9.22	9.32	9.49	9.60	9.60	9.48	9.42	9.59	9.83	9.94
1977..	8.97	9.08	9.12	9.12	9.07	9.01	8.91	8.87	8.82	8.80	8.89	8.95	8.99
[1]1976..	9.75	10.41	10.24	10.12	9.94	9.86	9.89	9.82	9.64	9.40	9.29	9.23	9.12
[1]1975..	10.61	10.81	10.65	10.48	10.58	10.69	10.62	10.55	10.59	10.61	10.62	10.56	10.56
[1]1974..	9.50	8.48	8.53	8.62	8.87	9.05	9.27	9.48	9.77	10.18	10.48	10.60	10.63
1973..	8.24	7.90	7.97	8.03	8.09	8.06	8.13	8.24	8.53	8.63	8.41	8.42	8.48
1972..	8.16	8.23	8.23	8.24	8.24	8.23	8.20	8.23	8.19	8.09	8.06	7.99	7.93
1971..	8.56	8.74	8.39	8.46	8.45	8.62	8.75	8.76	8.76	8.59	8.48	8.38	8.38
1970..	9.11	8.86	8.78	8.63	8.70	8.98	9.25	9.40	9.44	9.39	9.33	9.38	9.12
1969..	7.81	7.32	7.30	7.51	7.54	7.52	7.70	7.84	7.86	8.05	8.22	8.25	8.65
1968..	6.94	6.84	6.80	6.85	6.97	7.03	7.07	6.98	6.82	6.79	6.84	7.01	7.23
1967..	6.23	5.97	5.82	5.85	5.83	5.96	6.15	6.26	6.33	6.40	6.52	6.72	6.93
1966..	5.67	5.06	5.12	5.32	5.41	5.48	5.58	5.68	5.83	6.09	6.10	6.13	6.18
1965..	4.87	4.80	4.78	4.78	4.80	4.81	4.85	4.88	4.88	4.91	4.93	4.95	5.02
1964..	4.83	4.83	4.83	4.83	4.85	4.85	4.85	4.83	4.82	4.82	4.81	4.81	4.81
1963..	4.86	4.91	4.89	4.88	4.87	4.85	4.84	4.84	4.83	4.84	4.83	4.84	4.85
1962..	5.02	5.08	5.07	5.04	5.02	5.00	5.02	5.05	5.06	5.03	4.99	4.96	4.92
1961..	5.08	5.10	5.07	5.02	5.01	5.01	5.03	5.09	5.11	5.12	5.13	5.11	5.10
1960..	5.19	5.34	5.34	5.25	5.20	5.28	5.26	5.22	5.08	5.01	5.11	5.08	5.10
1959..	5.05	4.87	4.89	4.85	4.86	4.96	5.04	5.08	5.09	5.18	5.28	5.26	5.28
1958..	4.73	4.83	4.66	4.68	4.67	4.62	4.55	4.53	4.67	4.87	4.92	4.87	4.85
1957..	4.71	4.49	4.47	4.43	4.44	4.52	4.63	4.73	4.82	4.93	4.99	5.09	5.03
1956..	3.88	3.60	3.58	3.60	3.68	3.73	3.76	3.80	3.93	4.07	4.17	4.24	4.37
1955..	3.53	3.45	3.47	3.48	3.49	3.50	3.51	3.52	3.56	3.59	3.59	3.58	3.62
1954..	3.51	3.71	3.61	3.51	3.47	3.47	3.49	3.50	3.49	3.47	3.46	3.45	3.45
1953..	3.74	3.51	3.53	3.57	3.65	3.78	3.86	3.86	3.85	3.88	3.82	3.75	3.74
1952..	3.52	3.59	3.53	3.51	3.50	3.49	3.50	3.53	3.51	3.52	3.54	3.53	3.51
1951..	3.41	3.17	3.16	3.23	3.35	3.40	3.49	3.53	3.50	3.46	3.50	3.56	3.61
1950..	3.24	3.24	3.24	3.24	3.23	3.25	3.28	3.32	3.23	3.21	3.22	3.22	3.20
1949..	3.42	3.46	3.45	3.47	3.45	3.45	3.47	3.46	3.40	3.37	3.36	3.35	3.31
1948..	3.47	3.52	3.53	3.53	3.47	3.38	3.34	3.37	3.44	3.45	3.50	3.53	3.53
1947..	3.24	3.13	3.12	3.15	3.16	3.17	3.21	3.18	3.17	3.23	3.35	3.44	3.52
1946..	3.05	3.01	2.95	2.94	2.96	3.02	3.03	3.03	3.03	3.10	3.15	3.17	3.17
1945..	3.29	3.46	3.41	3.38	3.36	3.32	3.29	3.26	3.26	3.24	3.20	3.15	3.10
1944..	3.61	3.76	3.72	3.70	3.68	3.63	3.59	3.57	3.55	3.56	3.55	3.53	3.49
1943..	3.91	4.16	4.08	4.01	3.96	3.91	3.88	3.81	3.81	3.83	3.82	3.83	3.82
1942..	4.28	4.29	4.29	4.30	4.26	4.27	4.33	4.30	4.28	4.26	4.24	4.25	4.28
1941..	4.33	4.38	4.42	4.38	4.33	4.32	4.31	4.28	4.27	4.30	4.28	4.28	4.38
1940..	4.75	4.86	4.83	4.80	4.74	4.94	5.11	4.80	4.76	4.66	4.56	4.48	4.45
1939..	4.96	5.12	5.05	4.89	5.15	5.07	4.91	4.84	4.85	5.00	4.88	4.85	4.92
1938..	5.80	5.89	5.97	6.30	6.47	6.06	6.25	5.63	5.49	5.65	5.36	5.23	5.27
1937..	5.03	4.49	4.53	4.68	4.84	4.84	4.93	4.91	4.92	5.16	5.52	5.82	5.73
1936..	4.77	5.00	4.80	4.86	4.91	4.94	4.90	4.84	4.74	4.62	4.54	4.52	4.53
1935..	5.75	5.98	5.95	6.26	6.13	5.94	5.77	5.67	5.58	5.53	5.54	5.43	5.30
1934..	6.32	7.01	6.27	6.26	6.01	6.05	6.06	6.13	6.49	6.57	6.40	6.37	6.23
1933..	7.76	8.01	8.37	8.91	9.12	7.74	7.07	6.62	6.77	7.27	7.49	7.98	7.75
1932..	9.30	9.13	8.87	8.83	10.46	11.63	11.52	10.79	8.22	7.61	7.87	8.24	8.42
1931..	7.62	6.41	6.38	6.44	6.72	7.15	7.36	7.08	7.47	8.07	9.04	8.93	10.42
1930..	5.90	5.92	5.89	5.73	5.70	5.72	5.78	5.77	5.73	5.65	5.94	6.25	6.71
1929..	5.90	5.63	5.66	5.79	5.80	5.80	5.94	5.95	6.04	6.12	6.11	6.03	5.95
1928..	5.48	5.35	5.33	5.32	5.33	5.42	5.55	5.58	5.61	5.59	5.58	5.55	5.60
1927..	5.48	5.61	5.59	5.54	5.48	5.50	5.50	5.55	5.48	5.42	5.38	5.35	5.32
1926..	5.87	6.09	6.02	6.05	5.98	5.86	5.80	5.79	5.81	5.79	5.81	5.77	5.68
1925..	6.27	6.44	6.36	6.36	6.41	6.30	6.18	6.20	6.24	6.20	6.17	6.17	6.15
1924..	6.83	7.24	7.14	7.08	7.03	6.97	6.82	6.67	6.69	6.73	6.62	6.54	6.46
1923..	7.24	6.98	6.97	7.09	7.17	7.17	7.21	7.34	7.38	7.38	7.46	7.40	7.38
1922..	7.08	7.70	7.55	7.45	7.14	6.89	6.97	6.89	6.85	6.75	6.78	6.98	7.02
1921..	8.35	8.50	8.42	8.55	8.53	8.52	8.56	8.48	8.51	8.34	8.34	7.88	7.61
1920..	8.20	7.78	7.94	7.97	8.17	8.39	8.39	8.52	8.39	8.14	7.99	8.21	8.56
1919..	7.25	7.12	7.20	7.15	7.23	7.09	7.04	7.06	7.13	7.27	7.34	7.54	7.77

[1] As of December 20, 1976, railroad bonds were removed from the combined Corporate Averages, retroactive to January 1974. This adjustment was necessary because of a lack of comparability to the Industrial and Public Utility averages, reflecting the limited availability of reasonably-current-coupon railroad bonds.

Source: *Moody's Industrial Manual* (New York: Moody's Investor's Service, 1984).

MOODY'S AVERAGE OF YIELDS ON Aaa INDUSTRIAL BONDS (IN PERCENT)

Year	Aver.	Jan.	Feb.	Mar.	Apr.	May	June	July	Aug.	Sept.	Oct.	Nov.	Dec.
1984..	...	12.01	12.08	12.57	12.81	13.28	...	...	...	...	...	...	...
1983..	11.56	11.28	11.54	11.27	11.03	10.91	11.25	11.61	11.99	11.87	11.83	12.00	12.14
1982..	13.35	14.57	14.66	14.09	14.07	13.83	14.30	14.24	13.43	12.64	11.81	11.24	11.34
1981..	13.70	12.31	12.75	12.81	13.33	13.81	13.35	13.87	14.36	14.92	14.97	13.99	13.93
1980..	11.57	10.85	12.01	12.59	11.81	10.74	10.27	10.65	11.17	11.58	11.83	12.53	12.79
1979..	9.39	9.01	9.01	9.11	9.15	9.30	9.08	8.98	8.99	9.18	9.87	10.52	10.51
1978..	8.58	8.31	8.37	8.36	8.43	8.54	8.60	8.73	8.52	8.54	8.72	8.87	8.98
1977..	7.86	7.77	7.86	7.92	7.86	7.87	7.77	7.78	7.82	7.76	7.88	7.93	8.04
1976..	8.23	8.33	8.29	8.30	8.20	8.43	8.40	8.33	8.26	8.18	8.14	8.12	7.81
1975..	8.61	8.65	8.44	8.52	8.78	8.75	8.61	8.62	8.69	8.68	8.57	8.52	8.51
1974..	8.42	7.65	7.70	7.87	8.13	8.26	8.34	8.60	8.89	9.12	9.03	8.69	8.74
1973..	7.28	6.96	7.04	7.12	7.08	7.13	7.23	7.28	7.56	7.48	7.43	7.50	7.50
1972..	6.97	6.90	7.00	6.93	7.01	7.00	6.93	6.98	6.96	7.03	7.01	6.94	6.90
1971..	7.05	7.01	6.68	6.80	6.91	7.21	7.28	7.32	7.28	7.14	7.08	6.97	6.95
1970..	7.77	7.76	7.73	7.61	7.58	7.76	8.16	8.19	7.83	7.79	7.75	7.75	7.31
1969..	6.93	6.47	6.53	6.73	6.81	6.69	6.88	7.03	6.95	7.04	7.21	7.21	7.58
1968..	6.12	6.09	6.05	6.08	6.16	6.22	6.24	6.20	5.97	5.91	6.04	6.12	6.38
1967..	5.49	5.13	5.04	5.14	5.13	5.21	5.41	5.58	5.62	5.66	5.77	6.06	6.14
1966..	5.12	4.72	4.81	4.95	4.97	4.98	5.05	5.11	5.29	5.49	5.37	5.32	5.36
1965..	4.45	4.36	4.35	4.35	4.36	4.39	4.44	4.46	4.47	4.50	4.52	4.58	4.67
1964..	4.32	4.28	4.24	4.27	4.31	4.32	4.31	4.32	4.35	4.36	4.38	4.37	4.37
1963..	4.14	4.06	4.04	4.04	4.07	4.08	4.09	4.15	4.19	4.21	4.22	4.23	4.26
1962..	4.18	4.30	4.31	4.28	4.19	4.11	4.14	4.22	4.22	4.16	4.09	4.07	4.08
1961..	4.21	4.16	4.09	4.04	4.09	4.11	4.20	4.28	4.29	4.32	4.29	4.27	4.33
1960..	4.28	4.49	4.44	4.37	4.33	4.34	4.34	4.29	4.13	4.12	4.15	4.16	4.21
1959..	4.27	4.00	4.03	4.01	4.15	4.28	4.38	4.35	4.30	4.43	4.44	4.43	4.45
1958..	3.61	3.42	3.43	3.46	3.39	3.33	3.32	3.46	3.68	4.03	3.98	3.93	3.93
1957..	3.76	3.68	3.53	3.54	3.52	3.63	3.89	3.91	4.01	3.97	3.93	3.94	3.58
1956..	3.30	3.05	3.01	3.08	3.22	3.22	3.17	3.21	3.36	3.50	3.51	3.59	3.70
1955..	3.00	2.86	2.93	2.97	2.95	2.99	3.00	2.98	3.06	3.07	3.05	3.03	3.10
1954..	2.82	3.00	2.85	2.78	2.78	2.81	2.84	2.81	2.79	2.80	2.77	2.80	2.84
1953..	3.12	2.97	3.01	3.05	3.16	3.29	3.37	3.19	3.12	3.17	3.06	3.03	3.05
1952..	2.88	2.87	2.82	2.87	2.85	2.86	2.87	2.87	2.86	2.87	2.95	2.91	2.88
1951..	2.78	2.59	2.60	2.74	2.82	2.81	2.87	2.87	2.80	2.74	2.81	2.86	2.88
1950..	2.55	2.50	2.51	2.52	2.53	2.53	2.54	2.58	2.54	2.57	2.60	2.60	2.60
1949..	2.58	2.60	2.61	2.61	2.61	2.63	2.64	2.59	2.53	2.52	2.53	2.53	2.51
1948..	2.71	2.76	2.74	2.71	2.67	2.65	2.65	2.70	2.74	2.73	2.73	2.73	2.67
1947..	2.53	2.49	2.47	2.46	2.45	2.46	2.47	2.46	2.47	2.53	2.60	2.68	2.76
1946..	2.44	2.42	2.38	2.39	2.43	2.47	2.42	2.40	2.42	2.51	2.50	2.48	2.51
1945..	2.49	2.54	2.50	2.47	2.50	2.52	2.51	2.49	2.47	2.48	2.46	2.48	2.48
1944..	2.57	2.49	2.53	2.57	2.59	2.58	2.59	2.59	2.58	2.58	2.58	2.59	2.56
1943..	2.49	2.54	2.52	2.51	2.51	2.49	2.48	2.46	2.46	2.47	2.48	2.50	2.50
1942..	2.57	2.59	2.59	2.61	2.56	2.60	2.60	2.57	2.56	2.56	2.54	2.54	2.56
1941..	2.50	2.36	2.44	2.51	2.57	2.57	2.57	2.52	2.49	2.51	2.48	2.48	2.56
1940..	2.44	2.47	2.44	2.41	2.38	2.60	2.57	2.57	2.52	2.45	2.40	2.34	2.28
1939..	2.67	2.62	2.61	2.63	2.69	2.65	2.65	2.57	2.51	3.03	2.90	2.68	2.59
1938..	2.85	2.87	2.93	2.92	2.96	2.85	2.86	2.86	2.82	2.87	2.82	2.74	2.72
1937..	3.06	2.90	3.05	3.10	3.27	3.12	3.04	3.04	3.02	3.12	3.06	2.99	2.97
1936..	3.03	3.13	3.08	3.05	3.07	3.08	3.07	3.06	3.01	2.95	2.99	2.94	2.91
1935..	3.53	3.82	3.72	3.69	3.65	3.62	3.57	3.50	3.53	3.48	3.31	3.24	3.25
1934..	4.02	4.37	4.23	4.19	4.13	4.04	3.93	3.87	3.91	3.93	3.89	3.85	3.84
1933..	4.53	4.50	4.56	4.74	4.88	4.74	4.50	4.42	4.35	4.39	4.36	4.46	4.46
1932..	5.09	5.45	5.37	5.18	5.26	5.35	5.47	5.30	4.96	4.75	4.67	4.68	4.64
1931..	4.71	4.59	4.51	4.51	4.54	4.54	4.49	4.47	4.47	4.65	5.12	5.07	5.50
1930..	4.69	4.80	4.84	4.76	4.71	4.72	4.69	4.64	4.60	4.57	4.57	4.64	4.68
1929..	4.86	4.77	4.81	4.83	4.82	4.85	4.90	4.91	4.90	4.92	4.91	4.91	4.80
1928..	4.73	4.66	4.66	4.68	4.66	4.69	4.73	4.79	4.82	4.79	4.77	4.76	4.77
1927..	4.76	4.85	4.84	4.81	4.80	4.77	4.76	4.78	4.77	4.75	4.68	4.68	4.64
1926..	4.93	5.03	5.01	5.04	5.00	4.95	4.93	4.89	4.88	4.88	4.83	4.85	4.86
1925..	5.11	5.19	5.19	5.18	5.10	5.10	5.11	5.09	5.12	5.10	5.03	5.04	5.05
1924..	5.28	5.33	5.34	5.35	5.34	5.33	5.29	5.26	5.24	5.25	5.23	5.21	5.21
1923..	5.37	5.33	5.33	5.38	5.42	5.42	5.41	5.40	5.38	5.36	5.33	5.31	5.31
1922..	5.35	5.60	5.52	5.45	5.38	5.38	5.37	5.27	5.23	5.19	5.21	5.26	5.37
1921..	6.15	6.34	6.25	6.23	6.21	6.22	6.28	6.26	6.16	6.16	6.15	5.87	5.65
1920..	6.19	5.74	5.83	5.91	6.01	6.21	6.47	6.44	6.41	6.42	6.26	6.26	6.35
1919..	5.55	5.53	5.51	5.53	5.58	5.53	5.44	5.45	5.50	5.57	5.60	5.65	5.69

Source: *Moody's Industrial Manual* (New York: Moody's Investor's Service, 1984).

MOODY'S AVERAGE OF YIELDS ON Baa INDUSTRIAL BONDS (IN PERCENT)

Year	Aver.	Jan.	Feb.	Mar.	Apr.	May	June	July	Aug.	Sept.	Oct.	Nov.	Dec.
1984..	. . .	13.24	13.13	13.42	13.78	14.21	. . .	. . .	. . .	. . .	. . .	. . .	. . .
1983..	12.90	13.33	13.27	12.89	12.52	12.12	12.57	12.76	13.07	12.99	12.95	13.10	13.27
1982..	15.77	16.36	16.51	16.47	16.55	16.60	16.63	16.50	16.28	15.57	14.35	13.79	13.58
1981..	15.48	14.76	14.87	14.84	14.98	15.24	15.29	15.35	15.48	16.08	16.50	16.28	16.07
1980..	13.39	11.92	12.73	13.64	14.03	13.41	12.78	12.54	12.79	13.33	14.03	14.48	14.98
1979..	10.42	9.96	9.89	9.98	10.11	10.24	10.19	10.11	10.20	10.29	10.91	11.50	11.61
1978..	9.35	9.07	9.11	9.07	9.10	9.27	9.40	9.45	9.43	9.36	9.49	9.66	9.79
1977..	8.87	8.99	9.04	9.04	8.97	8.88	8.80	8.75	8.72	8.74	8.77	8.84	8.90
1976..	9.67	10.26	10.17	10.07	9.92	9.81	9.76	9.75	9.61	9.33	9.17	9.12	9.03
1975..	10.26	10.02	9.98	10.01	10.30	10.42	10.39	10.30	10.31	10.35	10.34	10.33	10.33
1974..	9.14	8.38	8.37	8.42	8.69	8.85	9.03	9.23	9.39	9.78	9.92	9.81	9.85
1973..	8.07	7.80	7.85	7.94	8.00	7.89	7.99	8.10	8.34	8.35	8.12	8.17	8.29
1972..	7.99	8.01	8.02	8.07	8.07	8.10	8.01	8.01	8.00	7.95	7.96	7.86	7.80
1971..	8.37	8.46	8.04	8.18	8.19	8.51	8.71	8.74	8.60	8.43	8.34	8.16	8.13
1970..	9.00	8.84	8.76	8.57	8.65	8.82	9.05	9.22	9.32	9.29	9.22	9.28	8.92
1969..	7.76	7.29	7.26	7.44	7.41	7.47	7.65	7.76	7.87	8.02	8.17	8.15	8.58
1968..	6.90	6.79	6.79	6.81	6.86	6.95	7.05	6.98	6.75	6.76	6.82	7.01	7.25
1967..	6.21	6.02	5.90	5.90	5.81	5.87	6.06	6.24	6.31	6.43	6.53	6.67	6.82
1966..	5.68	5.09	5.14	5.29	5.32	5.44	5.61	5.74	5.92	6.18	6.14	6.13	6.18
1965..	4.92	4.85	4.84	4.83	4.88	4.88	4.91	4.93	4.95	4.96	4.98	5.00	5.05
1964..	4.87	4.90	4.88	4.88	4.89	4.91	4.91	4.88	4.85	4.84	4.84	4.84	4.85
1963..	4.90	4.90	4.89	4.90	4.91	4.91	4.89	4.90	4.90	4.90	4.89	4.89	4.90
1962..	4.98	5.07	5.05	4.96	4.93	4.93	4.93	5.00	5.06	4.96	4.91	4.91	4.90
1961..	5.10	5.13	5.08	5.02	5.05	5.05	5.06	5.12	5.13	5.14	5.16	5.13	5.10
1960..	5.11	5.17	5.17	5.08	5.06	5.20	5.20	5.17	5.05	4.99	5.05	5.05	5.11
1959..	4.91	4.77	4.80	4.76	4.77	4.80	4.87	4.92	4.96	5.02	5.07	5.09	5.12
1958..	4.59	4.75	4.63	4.60	4.56	4.50	4.44	4.39	4.44	4.64	4.71	4.72	4.74
1957..	4.79	4.62	4.64	4.57	4.55	4.60	4.73	4.81	4.90	5.00	5.03	5.04	4.97
1956..	3.84	3.55	3.52	3.55	3.65	3.69	3.71	3.75	3.89	4.02	4.13	4.22	4.42
1955..	3.47	3.38	3.40	3.41	3.42	3.44	3.45	3.47	3.53	3.54	3.53	3.53	3.56
1954..	3.40	3.59	3.46	3.35	3.31	3.34	3.39	3.43	3.40	3.38	3.37	3.36	3.36
1953..	3.55	3.27	3.29	3.34	3.44	3.54	3.65	3.69	3.70	3.72	3.68	3.63	3.64
1952..	3.20	3.18	3.15	3.16	3.17	3.16	3.16	3.17	3.18	3.21	3.25	3.29	3.28
1951..	3.04	2.84	2.84	2.91	2.98	3.02	3.10	3.13	3.11	3.09	3.12	3.15	3.18
1950..	2.86	2.86	2.85	2.83	2.85	2.85	2.86	2.88	2.86	2.85	2.86	2.86	2.85
1949..	3.02	3.10	3.09	3.07	3.06	3.05	3.06	3.03	2.99	2.96	2.96	2.93	2.90
1948..	3.13	3.18	3.18	3.19	3.16	3.10	3.04	3.04	3.11	3.12	3.16	3.16	3.15
1947..	2.92	2.87	2.85	2.86	2.85	2.83	2.86	2.88	2.90	2.92	3.01	3.08	3.16
1946..	2.84	2.83	2.80	2.80	2.81	2.84	2.83	2.83	2.80	2.83	2.86	2.88	2.91
1945..	2.96	3.02	2.99	2.99	2.98	2.96	2.97	2.97	2.98	2.95	2.93	2.89	2.88
1944..	3.15	3.30	3.25	3.24	3.24	3.17	3.09	3.10	3.11	3.10	3.10	3.08	3.05
1943..	3.38	3.49	3.47	3.48	3.44	3.42	3.38	3.30	3.29	3.31	3.31	3.33	3.33
1942..	3.55	3.62	3.63	3.62	3.54	3.50	3.49	3.47	3.49	3.54	3.56	3.54	3.56
1941..	3.65	3.78	3.78	3.76	3.74	3.70	3.67	3.61	3.58	3.54	3.48	3.50	3.60
1940..	4.08	4.13	4.11	4.07	4.02	4.22	4.38	4.20	4.15	4.06	3.96	3.88	3.82
1939..	4.25	4.27	4.27	4.25	4.39	4.33	4.22	4.20	4.19	4.37	4.27	4.14	4.15
1938..	4.49	4.48	4.53	4.67	4.73	4.54	4.60	4.44	4.39	4.49	4.37	4.32	4.36
1937..	4.25	3.94	3.99	4.13	4.21	4.16	4.16	4.16	4.12	4.22	4.49	4.69	4.70
1936..	4.07	4.16	4.13	4.13	4.15	4.13	4.12	4.11	4.06	4.02	3.99	3.93	3.96
1935..	4.51	4.74	4.70	4.67	4.68	4.57	4.54	4.43	4.45	4.44	4.36	4.30	4.28
1934..	5.15	5.54	5.31	5.28	5.09	5.06	5.03	4.98	5.13	5.22	5.17	5.05	4.88
1933..	6.36	7.04	7.54	7.99	7.71	6.64	6.03	5.59	5.44	5.49	5.52	5.68	5.70
1932..	8.76	9.78	9.16	8.53	9.35	10.30	10.64	10.29	7.93	7.21	7.25	7.39	7.32
1931..	8.03	6.59	6.55	6.72	7.17	7.93	8.08	7.65	7.88	8.61	9.46	9.22	10.50
1930..	6.09	6.21	6.11	5.91	5.82	5.84	5.99	5.95	5.88	5.81	6.21	6.43	6.90
1929..	6.02	5.82	5.79	5.88	5.84	5.89	6.05	5.98	6.01	6.13	6.19	6.35	6.25
1928..	5.71	5.54	5.49	5.51	5.55	5.68	5.80	5.86	5.84	5.80	5.79	5.84	5.85
1927..	5.61	5.80	5.75	5.63	5.54	5.60	5.63	5.63	5.64	5.56	5.49	5.50	5.52
1926..	6.11	6.29	6.23	6.22	6.21	6.12	6.06	6.09	6.04	6.05	6.06	6.06	5.89
1925..	6.37	6.54	6.46	6.45	6.47	6.48	6.34	6.35	6.32	6.29	6.21	6.25	6.23
1924..	6.87	7.16	7.11	7.08	7.02	6.96	6.87	6.80	6.84	6.75	6.71	6.60	6.55
1923..	7.06	7.02	6.99	6.97	6.93	6.84	6.90	7.10	7.17	7.15	7.21	7.24	7.21
1922..	7.12	7.50	7.51	7.45	7.15	6.92	6.97	6.92	6.91	6.81	6.86	7.16	7.22
1921..	8.10	8.50	8.23	8.42	8.33	8.16	8.14	8.07	8.11	8.14	8.07	7.68	7.36
1920..	7.94	7.48	7.63	7.82	7.81	8.04	8.12	8.23	8.12	7.83	7.64	8.06	8.54
1919..	6.99	6.96	7.04	7.00	7.07	6.97	6.78	6.78	6.83	6.90	6.90	6.97	7.35

The tables above give the monthly average yields of 40 long-term industrial bonds (10 **Aaa**, 10 **Aa**, 10 **A** and 10 **Baa**). Prior to 1928, 20 bonds were used. All yields are calculated to maturity dates and the list of bonds used is adjusted when required to reflect rating changes or other reasons so that each of the series is comparable throughout the entire period. Average yields for the periods presented are not intended to be indicative of yields which may prevail in the future.

Source: *Moody's Industrial Manual* (New York: Moody's Investor's Service, 1984).

PART III: ECONOMIC DATA

SUMMARY NATIONAL INCOME AND PRODUCT SERIES, ANNUALLY AND QUARTERLY: 1950—82

Table A.—Gross National Product

[Billions of dollars; quarterly data are seasonally adjusted at annual rates]

Year and quarter	GNP	Personal consumption expenditures				Gross private domestic investment				Net exports			Government purchases of goods and services			Final sales	Percent change from preceding period	
		Total	Durable goods	Nondurable goods	Services	Total	Nonresidential	Residential	CBI	Net	Exports	Imports	Total	Federal	State and local		GNP	Final sales
1950	286.5	192.0	30.8	98.2	63.0	53.8	27.3	19.8	6.8	2.2	14.4	12.2	38.5	18.7	19.8	279.7	10.9	7.0
1951	330.8	207.1	29.8	108.8	68.5	59.2	31.3	17.6	10.3	4.4	19.7	15.3	60.1	38.3	21.8	320.5	15.5	14.6
1952	348.0	217.1	29.1	113.9	74.0	52.1	31.3	17.7	3.1	3.2	19.1	15.9	75.6	52.4	23.2	344.8	5.2	7.6
1953	366.8	229.7	32.5	116.5	80.6	53.3	34.5	18.4	.4	1.3	18.0	16.7	82.5	57.5	25.0	366.3	5.4	6.2
1954	366.8	235.8	31.8	118.0	86.1	52.7	34.2	20.1	-1.5	2.5	18.7	16.2	75.8	47.9	27.8	368.4	0	.6
1955	400.0	253.7	38.6	122.9	92.1	68.4	38.5	23.9	6.0	3.0	21.0	18.0	75.0	44.5	30.6	394.1	9.0	7.0
1956	421.7	266.0	37.9	128.9	99.2	71.0	44.0	22.3	4.7	5.3	25.0	19.8	79.4	45.9	33.5	417.0	5.4	5.8
1957	444.0	280.4	39.3	135.2	105.9	69.2	47.0	20.9	1.3	7.3	28.1	20.8	87.1	50.0	37.1	442.6	5.3	6.1
1958	449.7	289.5	36.8	139.8	112.8	61.9	42.0	21.4	-1.5	3.3	24.2	21.0	95.0	53.9	41.1	451.2	1.3	1.9
1959	487.9	310.8	42.4	146.4	121.9	78.1	45.9	26.6	5.7	1.4	24.8	23.4	97.6	53.9	43.7	482.2	8.5	6.9
1960	506.5	324.9	43.1	151.1	130.7	75.9	48.5	24.5	3.0	5.5	28.9	23.4	100.3	53.7	46.5	503.6	3.8	4.4
1961	524.6	335.0	41.6	155.3	138.1	74.8	48.0	24.5	2.3	6.6	29.9	23.3	108.2	57.4	50.8	522.2	3.6	3.7
1962	565.0	355.2	46.7	161.6	147.0	85.4	52.2	27.0	6.3	6.4	31.8	25.4	118.0	63.7	54.3	558.8	7.7	7.0
1963	596.7	374.6	51.4	167.1	156.1	90.9	54.8	30.1	6.0	7.6	34.2	26.6	123.7	64.6	59.0	590.7	5.6	5.7
1964	637.7	400.5	56.4	176.9	167.1	97.4	61.0	30.7	5.6	10.1	38.8	28.8	129.8	65.2	64.6	632.1	6.9	7.0
1965	691.1	430.4	63.0	188.6	178.7	113.5	72.7	30.9	9.9	8.8	41.1	32.3	138.4	67.3	71.1	681.2	8.4	7.8
1966	756.0	465.1	68.0	204.7	192.4	125.7	83.1	28.5	14.1	6.5	44.6	38.1	158.7	78.8	79.8	741.9	9.4	8.9
1967	799.6	490.3	70.1	212.6	207.6	122.8	83.9	28.6	10.3	6.3	47.3	41.0	180.2	90.9	89.3	789.3	5.8	6.4
1968	873.4	536.9	80.5	230.6	225.8	133.3	90.7	34.8	7.9	4.3	52.4	48.1	199.0	98.0	101.0	865.5	9.2	9.7
1969	944.0	581.8	85.7	247.8	248.2	149.3	101.3	38.2	9.8	4.2	57.5	53.3	208.8	97.6	111.2	934.2	8.1	7.9
1970	992.7	621.7	85.2	265.7	270.8	144.2	103.9	37.1	3.2	6.7	65.7	59.0	220.1	95.7	124.4	989.5	5.2	5.9
1971	1,077.6	672.2	97.2	278.8	296.2	166.4	107.9	50.9	7.7	4.1	68.8	64.7	234.9	96.2	138.7	1,070.0	8.6	8.1
1972	1,185.9	737.1	111.1	300.6	325.3	195.0	121.0	63.8	10.2	.7	77.5	76.7	253.1	101.7	151.4	1,175.7	10.1	9.9
1973	1,326.4	812.0	123.3	333.4	355.2	229.8	143.3	68.0	18.5	14.2	109.6	95.4	270.4	102.0	168.5	1,307.9	11.8	11.2
1974	1,434.2	888.1	121.5	373.4	393.2	228.7	156.6	57.9	14.1	13.4	146.2	132.8	304.1	111.0	193.1	1,420.1	8.1	8.6
1975	1,549.2	976.4	132.2	407.3	437.0	206.1	157.7	55.3	-6.9	26.8	154.9	128.1	339.9	122.7	217.2	1,556.1	8.0	9.6
1976	1,718.0	1,084.3	156.8	441.7	485.7	257.9	174.1	72.0	11.8	13.8	170.9	157.1	362.1	129.2	232.9	1,706.2	10.9	9.6
1977	1,918.3	1,204.4	178.2	478.8	547.4	324.1	205.2	95.8	23.0	-4.0	182.7	186.7	393.8	143.4	250.4	1,895.3	11.7	11.1
1978	2,163.9	1,346.5	200.2	528.2	618.0	386.6	248.9	111.2	26.5	-1.1	218.7	219.8	431.9	153.6	278.3	2,137.4	12.8	12.8
1979	2,417.8	1,507.2	213.4	600.0	693.7	423.0	290.2	118.6	14.3	13.2	281.4	268.1	474.4	168.3	306.0	2,403.5	11.7	12.4
1980	2,631.7	1,668.1	214.7	668.8	784.5	401.9	308.8	102.9	-9.8	23.9	338.8	314.8	537.8	197.0	340.8	2,641.5	8.8	9.9
1981	2,954.1	1,857.2	236.1	733.9	887.1	474.9	352.2	104.3	18.5	26.3	368.8	342.5	595.7	229.2	366.5	2,935.6	12.2	11.1
1982	3,073.0	1,991.9	244.5	761.0	986.4	414.5	348.3	90.8	-24.5	17.4	347.6	330.2	649.2	258.7	390.5	3,097.5	4.0	5.5
1950: I	267.6	182.9	27.7	94.8	60.3	43.6	23.8	17.5	2.4	3.4	13.5	10.1	37.7	18.6	19.1	265.2	17.9	4.9
II	277.1	186.8	28.1	96.3	62.3	50.5	26.1	19.6	4.8	3.0	13.8	10.8	36.9	17.4	19.4	272.3	15.0	11.2
III	294.8	200.4	35.6	100.9	63.9	55.4	29.1	21.5	4.9	.9	14.5	13.6	38.0	18.0	20.0	289.9	28.0	28.4
IV	306.3	197.8	31.5	100.9	65.4	65.6	30.1	20.5	15.1	1.5	15.8	14.3	41.4	20.9	20.5	291.2	16.6	1.8
1951: I	320.4	208.3	33.8	107.6	66.9	60.7	30.3	19.9	10.5	1.7	17.3	15.6	49.6	28.7	20.9	309.9	19.7	28.2
II	328.3	203.8	28.9	107.1	67.9	63.9	31.3	17.4	15.2	3.8	19.7	15.9	56.7	35.1	21.6	313.1	10.2	4.1
III	335.0	206.2	28.3	109.0	69.0	58.7	31.9	16.4	10.4	5.8	20.7	15.0	64.4	42.3	22.1	324.7	8.5	15.7
IV	339.2	209.9	28.3	111.4	70.1	53.4	31.6	16.7	5.1	6.4	21.0	14.7	69.6	47.2	22.4	334.1	5.1	12.1
1952: I	341.9	211.1	28.9	110.8	71.5	54.1	31.8	17.1	5.2	5.7	21.3	15.6	70.9	48.3	22.6	336.7	3.2	3.2
II	342.1	215.1	29.0	113.0	73.1	47.5	32.3	17.6	-2.3	4.0	19.3	15.3	75.5	52.2	23.3	344.4	.3	9.5
III	347.8	217.2	27.3	115.0	74.9	51.1	29.2	17.6	4.3	2.0	17.9	15.9	77.5	54.3	23.1	343.5	6.8	-1.1
IV	360.0	225.0	31.4	116.9	76.7	55.7	31.9	18.4	5.4	1.0	18.0	17.0	78.3	54.6	23.8	354.6	14.8	13.5
1953: I	366.1	228.3	32.9	117.0	78.4	54.8	33.7	18.7	2.4	1.3	17.8	16.5	81.7	57.2	24.5	363.7	7.0	10.6
II	369.4	229.9	32.8	116.9	80.2	56.1	34.2	18.8	3.2	.8	18.0	17.1	82.6	58.1	24.4	366.3	3.7	2.9
III	368.4	230.5	32.5	116.2	81.8	54.2	35.2	18.2	.7	1.3	18.3	17.0	82.4	57.2	25.1	367.7	-1.1	1.6
IV	363.1	230.0	31.9	116.0	82.1	48.2	34.8	18.0	-4.5	1.6	17.8	16.3	83.4	57.6	25.8	367.6	-5.6	-.1
1954: I	362.5	231.9	31.2	117.1	83.6	49.5	33.9	18.1	-2.5	1.7	17.2	15.5	79.5	52.8	26.7	365.1	-.7	-2.8
II	362.3	234.3	31.8	117.1	85.3	50.4	33.8	19.4	-2.7	2.3	19.2	16.9	75.4	48.0	27.4	365.1	-.2	0
III	366.7	236.4	31.3	118.1	87.0	53.1	34.5	20.8	-2.2	2.6	18.7	16.0	74.6	46.2	28.4	368.9	5.0	4.3
IV	375.6	240.8	33.0	119.5	88.3	57.8	34.5	22.1	1.3	3.5	19.7	16.2	73.4	44.8	28.7	374.3	10.0	6.0
1955: I	388.2	246.8	36.2	120.5	90.1	63.5	35.0	23.9	4.6	3.6	20.5	16.9	74.3	44.5	29.8	383.5	14.1	10.2
II	396.2	251.9	38.6	122.2	91.1	67.9	37.4	24.5	6.1	2.3	20.2	17.9	74.1	43.7	30.3	390.1	8.5	7.0
III	404.8	256.0	40.3	123.3	92.4	70.1	39.9	24.1	6.0	3.3	21.5	18.3	75.4	44.7	30.7	398.7	9.0	9.2
IV	411.0	260.0	39.4	125.7	94.9	72.0	41.8	23.1	7.1	2.9	21.8	18.9	76.2	44.9	31.3	404.0	6.3	5.3
1956: I	412.8	261.4	37.6	127.2	96.5	70.8	42.3	22.5	6.0	3.4	23.2	19.8	77.2	44.9	32.3	406.8	1.7	2.8
II	418.4	263.9	37.6	128.1	98.1	70.4	43.4	22.7	4.3	4.9	24.6	19.8	79.3	46.2	33.1	414.1	5.5	7.4
III	423.5	266.8	37.3	129.4	100.1	71.3	44.9	22.3	4.1	5.6	25.7	20.1	79.7	45.8	33.9	419.4	4.9	5.2
IV	432.1	271.9	38.9	130.8	102.1	71.6	45.5	21.8	4.3	7.2	26.6	19.4	81.3	46.7	34.6	427.7	8.4	8.2
1957: I	440.2	276.1	40.0	132.5	103.6	69.8	46.5	21.3	2.1	8.0	29.0	21.0	86.2	50.3	35.9	438.1	7.7	10.1
II	442.3	278.3	39.5	133.9	104.9	69.8	46.6	20.8	2.3	7.6	28.7	21.1	86.6	49.9	36.7	440.0	1.9	1.7
III	449.4	282.8	39.1	137.2	106.5	71.8	47.9	20.7	3.2	7.4	28.0	20.6	87.5	50.1	37.5	446.3	6.6	5.8
IV	444.0	284.4	38.8	136.9	108.7	65.4	47.0	20.6	-2.2	6.1	26.6	20.5	88.1	49.6	38.5	446.2	-4.8	-.1
1958: I	436.8	284.0	36.8	137.6	109.6	57.8	43.2	20.0	-5.4	3.8	24.2	20.4	91.2	51.6	39.5	442.2	-6.3	-3.5
II	440.7	286.8	36.0	138.9	111.9	56.5	41.5	20.1	-5.1	3.2	24.2	21.0	94.2	53.6	40.6	445.8	3.7	3.3
III	453.9	291.7	36.7	140.8	114.2	62.5	40.9	21.6	.1	3.5	24.2	20.7	96.1	54.4	41.7	453.8	12.5	7.3
IV	467.0	295.4	38.0	141.9	115.5	70.4	42.4	23.9	4.1	2.4	24.2	21.8	98.7	55.9	42.7	462.8	12.1	8.3
1959: I	477.0	303.5	41.2	144.3	117.9	74.5	43.9	26.4	4.2	1.1	23.5	22.4	97.8	54.3	43.6	472.8	8.9	8.9
II	490.6	309.1	43.0	145.6	120.5	83.0	45.6	27.3	10.2	.4	24.0	23.6	98.0	54.3	43.7	480.4	11.9	6.6
III	489.0	314.2	43.9	147.1	123.2	75.2	47.1	26.7	1.4	2.1	26.0	24.0	97.5	53.7	43.8	487.6	-1.3	6.1
IV	495.0	316.2	41.6	148.7	125.9	79.7	47.1	25.9	6.8	2.1	25.7	23.6	97.0	53.3	43.7	488.2	5.0	.5
1960: I	506.9	319.8	43.0	148.8	128.0	86.0	49.0	26.6	10.5	3.8	27.7	23.9	97.3	52.3	44.9	496.4	10.0	6.9
II	506.3	325.9	43.9	151.8	130.2	76.4	49.2	24.3	2.8	4.7	28.7	24.0	99.3	53.1	46.2	503.4	-.5	5.8
III	508.0	326.0	43.4	151.4	131.2	74.2	48.0	23.5	2.6	6.1	29.5	23.4	101.8	54.6	47.2	505.4	1.4	1.5
IV	504.8	328.0	42.2	152.5	133.3	66.9	47.7	23.4	-4.2	7.3	29.5	22.3	102.7	54.8	47.9	509.0	-2.5	2.9
1961: I	508.2	328.5	39.7	153.9	135.0	66.9	46.7	23.4	-3.2	7.8	30.0	22.3	105.0	55.3	49.7	511.4	2.7	1.9
II	519.2	333.1	40.7	154.7	137.6	72.9	47.8	23.6	1.5	6.4	28.9	22.5	106.8	56.9	49.9	517.7	9.0	5.0
III	528.2	335.7	41.9	155.2	138.6	78.0	48.0	24.9	5.2	6.1	30.0	24.0	108.4	57.7	50.8	523.1	7.1	4.2
IV	542.6	342.7	44.0	157.4	141.4	81.3	49.6	25.9	5.8	6.3	30.8	24.5	112.3	59.6	52.7	536.7	11.3	10.9
1962: I	554.2	347.5	45.0	159.3	143.2	84.9	50.6	26.0	8.3	5.7	30.5	24.8	116.1	63.0	53.1	546.0	8.9	7.1
II	562.7	353.0	46.3	160.6	146.1	85.9	52.3	27.2	6.4	7.0	32.4	25.4	116.8	63.0	53.8	556.4	6.3	7.8
III	568.9	357.0	46.8	162.2	148.0	86.4	53.1	27.4	5.9	6.7	32.3	25.6	118.8	64.1	54.7	562.9	4.4	4.8
IV	574.3	363.4	48.8	164.1	150.5	84.5	52.7	27.3	4.5	6.0	32.0	26.0	120.4	64.8	55.6	569.8	3.9	5.0

Source: *Survey of Current Business* (Washington, D.C.: Department of Commerce, October 1983).

Table A.—Gross National Product—Continued

[Billions of dollars; quarterly data are seasonally adjusted at annual rates]

Year and quarter	GNP	Personal consumption expenditures				Gross private domestic investment				Net exports			Government purchases of goods and services			Final sales	Percent change from preceding period	
		Total	Durable goods	Nondurable goods	Services	Total	Nonresidential	Residential	CBI	Net	Exports	Imports	Total	Federal	State and local		GNP	Final sales
1963: I	582.0	367.2	49.8	165.2	152.1	86.4	52.5	28.3	5.7	6.3	31.9	25.6	122.1	64.9	57.2	576.3	5.4	4.6
II	590.7	371.2	51.1	165.9	154.1	90.4	54.0	30.3	6.1	7.9	34.3	26.4	121.3	63.3	58.0	584.6	6.1	5.9
III	601.8	377.8	51.9	168.3	157.7	92.3	55.6	30.3	6.5	7.3	34.6	27.2	124.3	64.5	59.8	595.3	7.7	7.5
IV	612.4	382.1	52.9	168.8	160.4	94.5	57.3	31.6	5.6	8.8	36.1	27.3	127.0	65.9	61.2	606.8	7.3	8.0
1964: I	625.3	390.6	55.0	172.7	162.9	95.6	58.3	31.9	5.4	10.7	38.3	27.6	128.3	65.9	62.4	619.9	8.7	8.9
II	634.0	397.9	56.4	175.7	165.7	96.7	60.2	30.7	5.9	9.4	37.8	28.4	130.0	65.8	64.2	628.2	5.7	5.5
III	642.8	405.9	58.2	179.1	168.5	96.8	62.1	30.3	4.5	10.1	39.2	29.1	130.0	64.7	65.3	638.3	5.7	6.6
IV	648.8	407.6	56.1	180.1	171.4	100.2	63.6	29.9	6.7	10.0	40.0	30.0	130.9	64.5	66.4	642.1	3.8	2.4
1965: I	668.8	417.9	61.6	182.6	173.7	111.5	68.2	31.0	12.3	7.9	36.9	29.1	131.6	63.9	67.7	656.5	13.0	9.3
II	681.7	424.3	61.5	186.0	176.9	111.8	71.1	31.2	9.5	10.0	42.6	32.7	135.6	65.8	69.8	672.2	7.9	9.9
III	696.4	432.9	63.3	189.5	180.1	114.2	74.0	31.0	9.2	9.2	42.3	33.0	140.1	67.6	72.6	687.2	8.9	9.3
IV	717.2	446.3	65.6	196.5	184.3	116.7	77.6	30.6	8.5	8.1	42.5	34.4	146.1	71.8	74.3	708.7	12.5	13.1
1966: I	738.5	456.2	68.7	200.5	187.0	124.8	80.8	30.9	13.1	7.5	43.4	36.0	150.0	73.6	76.4	725.4	12.4	9.8
II	750.0	460.6	66.0	203.9	190.6	127.4	82.9	29.9	14.5	6.7	43.8	37.0	155.3	76.8	78.5	735.4	6.4	5.6
III	760.6	469.4	68.5	206.8	194.1	123.5	84.0	28.1	11.3	5.7	45.0	39.4	162.0	81.5	80.5	749.3	5.8	7.8
IV	774.9	474.2	68.8	207.4	198.0	127.1	84.5	25.1	17.6	6.2	46.0	39.8	167.3	83.5	83.9	757.3	7.7	4.3
1967: I	780.7	478.7	67.3	209.6	201.9	120.2	83.0	24.8	12.4	7.0	47.5	40.6	174.9	88.6	86.3	768.4	3.1	6.0
II	788.6	487.5	70.6	211.2	205.7	117.1	83.5	27.6	6.0	6.7	46.8	40.1	177.3	89.4	88.0	782.7	4.1	7.6
III	805.7	494.0	70.8	213.4	209.8	123.5	83.6	29.7	10.2	6.3	46.9	40.6	182.0	92.1	89.9	795.6	9.0	6.8
IV	823.3	500.8	71.6	216.2	213.0	130.6	85.6	32.1	12.8	5.3	48.1	42.8	186.5	93.7	92.9	810.4	9.0	7.7
1968: I	841.2	517.6	76.8	223.1	217.8	127.1	89.5	33.0	4.6	4.1	49.8	45.7	192.4	96.0	96.4	836.6	9.0	13.6
II	867.2	530.2	78.7	228.2	223.2	133.6	88.5	34.5	10.7	4.9	51.8	46.9	198.6	98.8	99.7	856.5	13.0	9.9
III	884.9	545.7	83.0	234.2	228.4	133.8	90.3	35.0	8.5	4.4	54.3	49.9	201.0	98.6	102.3	876.3	8.4	9.6
IV	900.3	554.0	83.3	236.9	233.8	138.6	94.3	36.6	7.7	3.7	53.5	49.8	204.0	98.6	105.4	892.6	7.2	7.6
1969: I	921.2	565.8	85.3	241.3	239.2	147.1	97.8	38.9	10.4	3.9	49.7	45.9	204.5	97.0	107.5	910.8	9.6	8.4
II	937.4	576.9	85.7	245.9	245.3	149.4	100.0	39.1	10.4	3.7	59.0	55.3	207.4	97.2	110.3	927.1	7.2	7.3
III	955.3	586.7	85.9	249.9	250.9	154.1	103.4	38.4	12.3	3.9	59.5	55.6	210.7	98.3	112.4	943.1	7.9	7.1
IV	962.0	597.8	86.0	254.3	257.4	146.5	103.8	36.4	6.3	5.2	61.9	56.6	212.4	97.8	114.6	955.7	2.8	5.5
1970: I	972.0	607.8	84.9	260.2	262.8	141.3	103.3	36.4	1.6	6.5	63.6	57.1	216.4	98.0	118.4	970.5	4.2	6.3
II	986.3	616.9	86.3	263.5	267.1	143.6	104.3	34.9	4.4	8.1	66.7	58.6	217.7	95.8	122.0	981.9	6.0	4.8
III	1,003.6	628.1	87.3	267.3	273.6	147.8	105.2	36.5	6.0	6.6	66.1	59.6	221.1	94.2	126.9	997.6	7.2	6.5
IV	1,009.0	634.1	82.4	271.9	279.7	144.1	102.7	40.5	.9	5.5	66.2	60.7	225.3	95.0	130.3	1,008.1	2.2	4.3
1971: I	1,049.3	652.8	93.0	273.8	286.0	159.4	104.8	44.1	10.5	7.3	68.4	61.0	229.7	95.8	133.9	1,038.7	16.9	12.7
II	1,068.9	666.0	95.9	277.4	292.7	166.9	107.4	49.6	9.9	3.5	69.1	65.6	232.4	95.0	137.4	1,059.0	7.7	8.0
III	1,086.6	677.5	98.2	279.9	299.5	168.7	108.5	53.4	6.8	3.9	71.8	67.9	236.4	96.6	139.9	1,079.7	6.8	8.1
IV	1,105.8	692.6	102.0	284.0	306.6	170.6	110.9	56.4	3.3	1.7	66.0	64.3	240.9	97.4	143.4	1,102.4	7.3	8.7
1972: I	1,142.4	709.6	105.6	288.8	315.2	183.3	116.0	61.0	6.3	−.2	74.0	74.3	249.7	102.7	147.0	1,136.1	13.9	12.8
II	1,171.7	727.3	109.0	297.2	321.2	193.2	118.7	62.5	12.0	−.3	73.8	74.0	251.5	102.8	148.7	1,159.7	10.7	8.5
III	1,196.1	744.2	112.2	304.0	328.0	197.5	120.9	63.8	12.8	1.4	78.0	76.5	252.9	100.4	152.5	1,183.2	8.6	8.4
IV	1,233.5	767.0	117.6	312.6	336.8	206.1	128.4	68.0	9.8	2.1	84.1	82.1	258.3	100.8	157.5	1,223.7	13.1	14.4
1973: I	1,283.5	790.0	125.5	321.6	343.0	221.6	134.8	70.5	16.3	7.0	95.8	88.8	264.9	103.0	161.9	1,267.2	17.2	15.0
II	1,307.6	802.9	124.3	327.7	350.9	227.0	142.5	69.1	15.4	11.4	105.0	93.5	266.3	100.4	165.9	1,292.2	7.7	8.1
III	1,337.7	820.6	123.4	337.5	359.8	229.6	146.9	67.6	15.1	18.5	114.1	95.6	268.9	98.8	170.2	1,322.6	9.6	9.7
IV	1,376.7	834.3	120.2	346.8	367.3	240.9	149.0	64.8	27.1	19.8	123.5	103.6	281.6	105.8	175.9	1,349.6	12.2	8.4
1974: I	1,387.7	853.0	118.5	358.4	376.1	225.8	152.0	61.2	12.7	22.0	136.8	114.7	286.8	103.9	182.8	1,375.0	3.2	7.7
II	1,423.8	878.6	121.7	369.4	387.5	232.9	155.6	59.6	17.7	11.7	146.3	134.6	300.6	109.6	191.0	1,406.1	10.8	9.4
III	1,451.6	906.7	127.4	380.4	398.9	227.9	159.2	58.0	10.7	7.8	147.5	139.8	309.2	112.7	196.6	1,440.8	8.0	10.3
IV	1,473.8	914.1	118.5	385.1	410.4	228.0	159.5	53.1	15.4	12.1	154.2	142.1	319.7	117.8	201.9	1,458.4	6.3	5.0
1975: I	1,479.8	935.1	122.4	392.2	420.6	191.4	155.1	50.6	−14.3	25.6	156.0	130.3	327.7	119.2	208.5	1,494.1	1.6	10.2
II	1,516.7	961.6	127.1	402.5	432.0	193.0	155.2	52.5	−14.6	28.5	149.2	120.7	333.6	120.1	213.5	1,531.3	10.4	10.3
III	1,578.5	992.1	136.7	414.1	441.3	217.5	158.9	56.6	2.1	24.9	152.7	127.8	344.0	123.7	220.3	1,576.5	17.3	12.3
IV	1,621.8	1,016.9	142.6	420.4	453.9	222.4	161.8	61.4	−.8	28.1	161.9	133.8	354.3	127.9	226.4	1,622.5	11.4	12.2
1976: I	1,672.0	1,047.8	152.0	429.6	466.2	248.8	166.6	66.9	15.3	18.4	164.0	145.6	357.0	126.7	230.4	1,656.7	13.0	8.7
II	1,698.6	1,067.2	154.6	436.2	476.4	258.3	170.9	70.1	17.3	15.0	168.4	153.4	358.1	126.3	231.8	1,681.3	6.5	6.1
III	1,729.0	1,094.2	158.1	445.6	490.5	259.6	177.5	70.7	11.4	12.2	173.6	161.4	362.8	129.5	233.4	1,717.5	7.3	8.9
IV	1,772.5	1,127.9	162.6	455.5	509.8	264.7	181.3	80.2	3.3	9.4	177.5	168.1	370.4	134.3	236.2	1,769.2	10.5	12.6
1977: I	1,834.8	1,162.7	171.2	466.0	525.5	296.4	191.5	85.3	19.6	−2.1	177.9	180.0	377.9	135.8	242.1	1,815.2	14.8	10.8
II	1,895.1	1,186.8	175.5	474.5	536.8	319.4	200.8	95.4	23.3	−1.8	185.1	186.8	390.7	142.2	248.4	1,871.9	13.8	13.1
III	1,954.4	1,216.5	180.1	480.5	555.9	339.6	208.2	99.3	32.1	−.4	186.8	187.2	398.7	146.2	252.5	1,922.3	13.1	11.2
IV	1,988.9	1,251.8	186.0	494.3	571.5	340.7	220.5	103.2	17.1	−11.7	181.2	192.9	408.0	149.5	258.4	1,971.8	7.2	10.7
1978: I	2,031.7	1,276.4	184.9	502.7	588.8	354.2	226.8	102.1	25.3	−11.7	195.6	207.2	412.8	147.3	265.5	2,006.4	8.9	7.2
II	2,139.5	1,330.7	202.6	519.2	608.8	388.5	245.8	111.9	30.8	−4.1	213.1	217.2	424.4	149.2	275.3	2,108.7	23.0	22.0
III	2,202.5	1,367.5	203.7	534.9	628.8	394.6	256.4	114.8	23.5	1.2	224.0	222.9	439.3	156.1	283.2	2,179.1	12.3	14.0
IV	2,281.6	1,411.3	209.6	556.1	645.6	409.1	266.6	116.2	26.2	10.1	242.1	232.0	451.1	161.8	289.3	2,255.4	15.2	14.8
1979: I	2,335.5	1,446.3	211.1	569.3	666.0	415.1	277.1	116.4	21.5	17.2	256.1	238.9	456.9	164.4	292.5	2,314.0	9.8	10.8
II	2,377.9	1,476.0	208.7	586.0	681.3	428.3	283.7	118.2	26.4	9.1	268.2	259.1	464.5	163.2	301.2	2,351.5	7.5	6.6
III	2,454.8	1,528.3	217.3	609.3	701.7	431.9	298.4	121.8	11.8	16.1	290.6	274.5	478.5	168.0	310.5	2,443.1	13.6	16.5
IV	2,502.9	1,578.0	216.6	635.5	725.9	416.8	301.6	117.8	−2.6	10.5	310.5	300.0	497.6	177.8	319.8	2,505.5	8.1	10.6
1980: I	2,572.9	1,620.5	220.7	651.4	748.3	422.0	311.1	112.5	−1.6	12.8	335.3	322.5	517.6	188.1	329.6	2,574.5	11.7	11.5
II	2,578.8	1,626.4	200.8	658.2	767.5	394.3	299.3	92.0	3.0	22.5	336.8	314.2	535.5	199.0	336.5	2,575.7	.9	.2
III	2,639.1	1,683.4	213.8	671.9	797.6	379.5	307.5	97.5	−25.4	37.1	337.6	300.5	539.1	194.5	344.6	2,664.5	9.7	14.5
IV	2,736.0	1,741.9	223.6	693.7	824.6	411.7	317.3	109.5	−15.1	23.3	345.4	322.0	559.0	206.6	352.4	2,751.1	15.5	13.6
1981: I	2,866.6	1,802.8	236.9	716.3	849.6	455.5	333.1	111.6	10.9	31.9	367.3	335.4	576.3	215.7	360.5	2,855.7	20.5	16.1
II	2,912.5	1,835.8	233.4	730.6	871.8	472.1	347.6	109.5	15.0	21.1	369.2	348.1	583.5	220.4	363.2	2,897.5	6.6	6.0
III	3,004.9	1,886.1	243.5	741.1	901.5	495.8	360.6	101.7	33.6	22.8	367.5	344.7	600.3	232.4	367.9	2,971.4	13.3	10.6
IV	3,032.2	1,904.1	230.8	747.7	925.6	476.2	367.6	94.3	14.3	29.2	371.0	341.7	622.8	248.5	374.3	3,017.9	3.7	6.4
1982: I	3,021.4	1,938.9	239.4	749.7	949.7	422.9	361.3	87.3	−25.7	29.9	358.4	328.5	629.8	249.7	380.0	3,047.1	−1.4	3.9
II	3,070.2	1,972.8	242.9	754.7	975.2	432.5	352.7	91.0	−11.2	33.3	364.5	331.2	631.6	244.1	387.5	3,081.4	6.6	4.6
III	3,090.7	2,008.8	243.4	766.6	998.9	425.3	342.3	87.9	−4.9	.9	346.0	345.0	655.7	261.7	394.0	3,095.6	2.7	1.9
IV	3,109.6	2,046.9	252.1	773.0	1,021.8	377.4	337.0	96.8	−56.4	5.6	321.6	316.1	679.7	279.2	400.5	3,165.9	2.5	9.4

GNP Gross national product; CBI Change in business inventories.

Source: *Survey of Current Business* (Washington, D.C.: Department of Commerce, October 1983).

Table B.—Gross National Product in Constant Dollars

[Billions of 1972 dollars; quarterly data are seasonally adjusted at annual rates]

Year and quarter	GNP	Personal consumption expenditures				Gross private domestic investment				Net exports			Government purchases of goods and services			Final sales	Command GNP	Percent change from preceding period		
		Total	Durable goods	Non-durable goods	Serv-ices	Total	Nonresi-dential	Resi-dential	CBI	Net	Exports	Imports	Total	Federal	State and local			GNP	Final sales	Com-mand GNP
1950	534.8	337.3	42.6	161.8	132.9	93.5	50.0	33.0	10.6	5.9	23.6	17.7	98.1	47.3	50.8	524.2	532.1	8.7	5.6	8.2
1951	579.4	341.6	39.1	165.3	137.2	93.9	52.9	27.3	13.7	10.1	28.6	18.5	133.7	82.2	51.5	565.6	574.6	8.3	7.9	8.0
1952	600.8	350.1	38.0	171.2	140.9	83.0	52.1	26.6	4.3	7.9	27.9	20.0	159.8	107.2	52.7	596.5	596.8	3.7	5.5	3.9
1953	623.6	363.4	42.1	175.7	145.6	85.3	56.3	27.5	1.5	4.8	26.6	21.8	170.1	114.7	55.3	622.1	620.4	3.8	4.3	3.9
1954	616.1	370.0	42.5	177.0	150.5	83.1	55.4	29.9	−2.2	6.9	27.8	20.9	156.0	96.1	59.9	618.2	612.4	−1.2	−.6	−1.3
1955	657.5	394.1	51.1	185.4	157.6	103.8	61.3	34.8	7.7	7.3	30.7	23.4	152.3	88.2	64.1	649.8	654.1	6.7	5.1	6.8
1956	671.6	405.4	48.8	191.6	165.0	102.6	65.4	31.5	5.8	10.1	35.3	25.2	153.5	86.8	66.7	665.8	668.2	2.1	2.5	2.2
1957	683.8	413.8	48.6	194.9	170.3	97.0	66.2	29.2	1.5	11.8	38.0	26.1	161.2	90.6	70.6	682.2	681.1	1.8	2.5	1.9
1958	680.9	418.0	45.3	196.8	175.9	87.5	59.3	30.0	−1.8	5.6	33.2	27.6	169.8	93.4	76.4	682.7	679.6	−.4	.1	−.2
1959	721.7	440.4	50.7	205.0	184.8	108.0	63.6	37.4	7.0	2.7	33.8	31.1	170.6	91.4	79.2	714.7	720.9	6.0	4.7	6.1
1960	737.2	452.0	51.4	208.2	192.4	104.7	66.9	34.2	3.5	7.7	38.4	30.7	172.8	90.4	82.4	733.7	736.8	2.2	2.7	2.2
1961	756.6	461.4	49.3	211.9	200.2	103.9	66.7	34.3	3.0	8.5	39.3	30.9	182.9	95.3	87.5	753.7	757.0	2.6	2.7	2.7
1962	800.3	482.0	54.7	218.5	208.8	117.6	72.0	37.7	7.8	7.5	41.8	34.3	193.2	102.8	90.4	792.4	801.3	5.8	5.1	5.9
1963	832.5	500.5	59.7	223.0	217.8	125.1	75.1	42.5	7.5	9.4	44.8	35.4	197.6	101.8	95.8	825.0	833.2	4.0	4.1	4.0
1964	876.4	528.0	64.8	233.3	229.8	133.0	82.7	43.1	7.1	12.8	50.3	37.5	202.6	100.2	102.4	869.3	876.7	5.3	5.4	5.2
1965	929.3	557.5	72.6	244.0	240.9	151.9	97.4	42.7	11.8	10.1	51.7	41.6	209.8	100.3	109.5	917.5	930.5	6.0	5.5	6.1
1966	984.8	585.7	78.4	255.5	251.8	163.0	108.0	38.2	16.8	6.5	54.4	47.9	229.7	112.6	117.1	968.0	986.6	6.0	5.5	6.0
1967	1,011.4	602.7	79.5	259.5	263.7	154.9	105.6	37.1	12.2	5.4	56.7	51.3	248.5	125.1	123.4	999.2	1,013.9	2.7	3.2	2.8
1968	1,058.1	634.4	88.3	270.5	275.6	161.6	109.5	43.1	9.0	1.9	61.2	59.3	260.2	128.1	132.1	1,049.1	1,061.5	4.6	5.0	4.7
1969	1,087.6	657.9	91.8	277.3	288.8	171.4	116.8	43.6	11.1	.9	65.0	64.1	257.4	121.8	135.6	1,076.6	1,091.7	2.8	2.6	2.9
1970	1,085.6	672.1	89.1	283.7	299.3	158.5	113.8	41.0	3.8	3.9	70.5	66.6	251.1	110.6	140.5	1,081.8	1,089.2	−.2	.5	−.2
1971	1,122.4	696.8	98.2	288.7	309.9	173.9	112.2	53.7	8.1	1.6	71.0	69.3	250.1	103.7	146.4	1,114.3	1,125.2	3.4	3.0	3.3
1972	1,185.9	737.1	111.1	300.6	325.3	195.0	121.0	63.8	10.2	.7	77.5	76.7	253.1	101.7	151.4	1,175.7	1,185.9	5.7	5.5	5.4
1973	1,254.3	767.9	121.3	307.4	339.2	217.5	138.1	62.3	17.2	15.5	97.3	81.8	253.3	95.9	157.4	1,237.1	1,250.9	5.8	5.2	5.5
1974	1,246.3	762.8	112.3	302.5	348.0	195.5	135.7	48.2	11.6	27.8	108.5	80.7	260.3	96.6	163.6	1,234.7	1,226.7	−.6	−.2	−1.9
1975	1,231.6	779.4	112.7	307.5	359.3	154.8	119.3	42.2	−6.7	32.2	103.5	71.4	265.2	97.4	167.8	1,238.4	1,214.4	−1.2	.3	−1.0
1976	1,298.2	823.1	126.6	321.9	374.7	184.5	125.6	51.2	7.8	25.4	110.1	84.7	265.2	96.8	168.4	1,290.4	1,280.2	5.4	4.2	5.4
1977	1,369.7	864.3	138.0	333.4	393.0	214.2	140.3	60.7	13.3	22.0	112.9	90.9	269.2	100.4	168.8	1,356.4	1,345.8	5.5	5.1	5.1
1978	1,438.6	903.2	146.8	344.4	412.0	236.7	158.3	62.4	16.0	24.0	126.7	102.7	274.6	100.3	174.3	1,422.6	1,414.0	5.0	4.9	5.1
1979	1,479.4	927.6	147.2	353.1	427.3	236.3	169.9	59.1	7.3	37.2	146.2	109.0	278.3	102.1	176.2	1,472.2	1,447.6	2.8	3.5	2.4
1980	1,475.0	931.8	137.5	355.6	438.8	208.5	165.8	47.1	−4.4	50.3	159.1	108.8	284.3	106.4	177.9	1,479.4	1,433.0	−.3	.5	−1.0
1981	1,513.8	956.8	141.2	362.5	453.1	227.6	174.4	44.7	8.5	43.0	159.7	116.7	286.5	110.4	176.1	1,505.3	1,479.8	2.6	1.8	3.3
1982	1,485.4	970.2	139.8	364.2	466.2	194.5	166.1	37.8	−9.4	28.9	147.3	118.4	291.8	116.6	175.2	1,494.8	1,462.7	−1.9	−.7	−1.2
1950: I	512.6	327.7	38.9	160.1	128.6	79.6	44.8	30.3	4.4	6.8	22.6	15.9	98.6	48.1	50.4	508.2	511.3	19.1	8.1	18.6
II	526.4	333.6	39.2	161.7	132.7	89.8	48.9	33.2	7.7	6.8	23.3	16.5	96.2	45.4	50.8	518.7	524.1	11.2	8.5	10.5
III	543.8	348.0	49.0	164.4	134.6	96.0	53.0	35.0	8.0	4.3	23.8	19.5	95.5	44.5	50.9	535.8	540.7	13.9	13.8	13.3
IV	556.3	339.9	43.2	161.0	135.7	108.7	53.3	33.3	22.1	5.6	24.6	19.0	102.0	51.0	51.0	534.2	552.6	9.5	−1.2	9.1
1951: I	564.4	345.7	44.3	164.7	136.7	96.6	51.8	31.4	13.4	6.4	25.8	19.4	115.7	65.0	50.7	550.9	560.1	6.0	13.1	5.6
II	575.9	337.8	38.1	162.7	137.1	100.1	53.0	27.1	19.9	9.5	28.2	18.7	128.5	77.0	51.5	556.0	570.9	8.4	3.7	7.9
III	587.9	340.7	37.1	166.0	137.6	93.8	53.9	25.3	14.6	12.2	30.0	17.8	141.2	89.5	51.8	573.3	582.5	8.6	13.1	8.4
IV	589.1	342.1	36.9	167.7	137.5	85.3	52.8	25.5	7.0	12.5	30.5	18.0	149.2	97.4	51.8	582.1	584.4	.8	6.3	1.3
1952: I	593.7	342.7	37.5	166.5	138.7	86.4	53.1	26.0	7.3	11.7	30.8	19.1	152.9	100.7	52.2	586.4	589.1	3.2	3.0	3.2
II	594.3	348.6	38.3	170.3	140.0	77.4	53.6	26.5	−2.7	9.0	28.0	19.0	159.4	106.3	53.1	597.0	590.3	.4	7.4	.8
III	600.5	350.2	35.9	172.8	141.5	80.5	48.9	26.2	5.4	6.1	26.2	20.1	163.7	111.6	52.1	595.1	596.9	4.2	−1.3	4.6
IV	614.6	358.8	40.5	174.9	143.4	87.6	52.8	27.6	7.2	4.9	26.6	21.7	163.3	110.0	53.2	607.4	610.9	9.7	8.5	9.7
1953: I	623.2	362.8	42.3	176.1	144.4	87.6	55.6	28.0	3.9	5.0	26.3	21.3	167.7	113.5	54.3	619.2	619.8	5.7	8.0	6.0
II	628.3	364.6	41.9	176.6	146.0	89.1	55.9	28.2	5.1	4.4	26.8	22.4	170.2	115.9	54.3	623.2	625.0	3.3	2.6	3.4
III	624.4	363.6	41.8	175.2	146.6	86.0	57.0	27.1	1.9	4.8	27.0	22.2	170.0	114.4	55.6	622.5	621.3	−2.4	−.4	−2.3
IV	618.2	362.6	42.5	174.9	145.3	78.6	56.7	26.9	−5.0	5.0	26.3	21.3	172.0	115.1	56.9	623.2	615.2	−3.9	.4	−3.9
1954: I	610.5	363.5	40.9	175.8	146.8	79.1	55.3	27.3	−3.4	5.2	25.7	20.5	162.6	103.9	58.7	613.9	607.5	−4.9	−5.8	−4.9
II	608.1	366.2	41.4	175.0	149.7	79.7	54.8	29.0	−4.1	6.7	28.4	21.8	155.6	96.5	59.0	612.2	604.4	−1.6	−1.1	−2.1
III	616.9	371.8	42.4	177.2	152.1	84.0	56.0	30.8	−2.7	7.3	27.9	20.6	153.8	93.3	60.6	619.6	613.0	5.9	4.9	5.8
IV	628.4	378.6	45.1	180.0	153.4	89.7	55.6	32.7	1.5	8.4	29.3	20.9	151.7	90.8	60.9	627.0	624.6	7.7	4.8	7.8
1955: I	644.1	385.2	48.1	181.4	155.7	97.7	56.6	35.2	5.9	8.4	30.3	21.9	152.7	89.5	63.3	638.2	640.3	10.3	7.4	10.4
II	653.2	392.2	51.3	184.4	156.5	103.9	60.2	35.7	8.0	6.3	29.7	23.4	150.9	86.8	64.1	645.2	649.9	5.8	4.5	6.2
III	663.2	396.4	52.7	185.9	157.7	105.8	63.2	34.9	7.8	7.5	31.2	23.8	153.5	89.2	64.3	655.4	660.0	6.3	6.5	6.3
IV	669.5	402.6	52.2	189.8	160.6	107.8	65.2	33.3	9.2	7.1	31.4	24.4	152.0	87.2	64.8	660.2	666.1	3.8	3.0	3.7
1956: I	666.8	403.2	49.4	191.6	162.2	103.9	64.3	32.1	7.5	7.7	33.0	25.3	152.1	86.6	65.5	659.3	663.5	−1.6	−.6	−1.6
II	670.2	403.9	48.9	191.1	163.9	102.7	65.3	31.9	5.5	9.6	34.8	25.2	154.0	87.6	66.5	664.7	666.8	2.0	3.3	2.0
III	670.7	405.1	48.1	191.2	165.8	102.2	66.2	31.2	4.9	10.5	36.2	25.7	152.9	85.9	66.9	665.9	667.4	.3	.7	.4
IV	678.4	409.3	48.8	192.5	168.0	101.7	65.7	30.7	5.4	12.5	37.1	24.6	154.8	87.2	67.6	673.0	675.0	4.7	4.4	4.7
1957: I	683.5	411.7	49.9	193.1	168.7	98.4	66.1	29.9	2.5	13.2	39.4	26.2	160.1	91.0	69.2	681.0	680.3	3.0	4.8	3.2
II	684.1	412.4	48.8	193.9	169.7	98.0	65.9	29.2	2.9	12.6	39.1	26.4	161.1	91.3	69.8	681.2	681.0	.4	.1	.4
III	688.5	415.2	48.0	196.7	170.5	99.8	67.3	28.9	3.7	11.9	37.7	25.8	161.6	90.7	70.8	684.8	685.8	2.6	2.1	2.8
IV	679.1	416.0	47.9	195.7	172.3	91.7	65.7	29.0	−3.0	9.5	35.6	26.1	162.0	89.5	72.5	682.1	677.3	−5.3	−1.6	−4.9
1958: I	665.5	411.0	45.1	193.4	172.5	82.9	61.5	28.2	−6.8	6.5	33.0	26.5	165.0	90.9	74.2	672.3	664.0	−7.8	−5.7	−7.7
II	669.9	414.7	44.5	194.9	175.3	80.8	58.8	28.2	−6.2	5.6	33.2	27.6	168.7	93.2	75.6	676.1	668.5	2.7	2.3	2.8
III	685.9	420.9	45.1	198.3	177.5	88.1	57.6	30.2	.3	5.9	33.2	27.3	171.0	93.9	77.2	685.6	684.7	9.9	5.8	10.0
IV	702.5	425.4	46.6	200.6	178.2	98.0	59.3	33.5	5.3	4.3	33.2	28.9	174.7	96.0	78.7	697.2	701.4	10.0	7.0	10.2
1959: I	711.5	434.1	49.5	203.2	181.5	103.7	61.1	37.1	5.5	2.1	32.1	30.0	171.6	92.3	79.3	706.0	710.9	5.2	5.1	5.5
II	726.2	439.7	51.3	204.6	183.8	114.1	63.1	38.4	12.6	1.2	32.7	31.5	171.3	92.0	79.3	713.6	725.5	8.5	4.4	8.5
III	721.2	443.3	52.1	205.5	185.7	104.0	65.0	37.6	1.4	3.6	35.4	31.8	170.2	90.8	79.4	719.8	720.3	−2.8	3.5	−2.8
IV	727.9	444.6	49.7	206.8	188.1	110.2	65.1	36.4	8.7	3.8	34.9	31.1	169.3	90.3	79.0	719.2	726.9	3.8	−.3	3.7
1960: I	740.7	448.1	51.0	207.2	189.9	117.4	67.4	37.3	12.7	6.0	37.3	31.3	169.2	88.9	80.3	728.0	739.7	7.2	5.0	7.3
II	738.4	454.1	52.3	209.5	192.3	105.1	67.8	34.1	3.3	6.8	38.2	31.5	172.4	90.4	82.0	735.1	737.8	−1.2	4.0	−1.0
III	737.7	452.7	51.8	208.1	192.7	102.5	66.2	32.9	3.4	8.1	38.9	30.7	174.4	91.1	83.3	734.3	737.5	−.4	−.4	−.1
IV	732.1	453.2	50.5	208.1	194.6	93.8	66.3	32.7	−5.3	9.8	39.2	29.4	175.4	91.3	84.1	737.4	731.9	−3.0	1.7	−3.0
1961: I	737.7	454.0	47.7	209.6	196.7	94.0	65.2	32.9	−4.1	10.4	39.9	29.5	179.4	92.6	86.8	741.8	737.6	3.1	2.4	3.1
II	750.1	459.9	48.4	211.6	199.9	101.1	66.3	33.1	1.8	8.0	37.8	29.8	181.0	94.6	86.4	748.3	750.6	6.9	3.5	7.2
III	759.6	461.4	49.4	211.7	200.2	107.9	66.5	34.9	6.5	7.7	39.4	31.7	182.7	95.4	87.3	753.2	760.0	5.2	2.6	5.1
IV	779.0	470.3	51.8	214.8	203.7	112.6	68.6	36.3	7.7	7.8	40.3	32.5	188.4	98.7	89.7	771.3	779.6	10.6	10.0	10.7
1962: I	789.2	474.5	52.9	216.5	205.1	116.8	70.0	36.4	10.4	6.6	40.0	33.3	191.3	102.2	89.1	778.8	790.2	5.3	3.9	5.6
II	798.4	479.8	54.2	217.4	208.3	118.3	72.2	38.0	8.1	8.5	42.6	34.1	191.8	102.1	89.7	790.4	799.4	4.8	6.1	4.7
III	805.5	483.7	54.7	219.3	209.7	119.1	73.3	38.3	7.5	8.0	42.6	34.6	194.6	103.7	90.9	797.9	806.6	3.6	3.9	3.7
IV	808.0	490.0	57.0	220.8	212.1	116.0	72.5	38.2	5.3	7.0	42.2	35.2	195.0	103.2	91.8	802.6	809.1	1.2	2.4	1.3

Source: *Survey of Current Business* (Washington, D.C.: Department of Commerce, October 1983).

Table B.—Gross National Product in Constant Dollars—Continued

[Billions of 1972 dollars; quarterly data are seasonally adjusted at annual rates]

Year and quarter	GNP	Personal consumption expenditures				Gross private domestic investment				Net exports			Government purchases of goods and services			Final sales	Command GNP	Percent change from preceding period		
		Total	Durable goods	Nondurable goods	Services	Total	Nonresidential	Residential	CBI	Net	Exports	Imports	Total	Federal	State and local			GNP	Final sales	Command GNP
1963: I	815.0	493.1	58.2	221.5	213.4	118.7	71.8	39.5	7.4	7.4	41.9	34.5	195.8	102.2	93.6	807.6	816.0	3.5	2.5	3.5
II	826.7	497.4	59.4	222.4	215.7	124.6	74.1	42.6	7.9	9.6	44.8	35.2	195.1	100.6	94.4	818.8	827.6	5.8	5.7	5.8
III	839.8	503.9	60.1	224.1	219.7	127.3	76.1	43.1	8.0	9.2	45.2	36.0	199.3	102.3	96.9	831.7	840.2	6.5	6.5	6.2
IV	848.6	507.5	61.0	224.2	222.4	129.6	78.2	44.7	6.7	11.3	47.3	36.0	200.2	102.0	98.2	841.9	848.9	4.3	5.0	4.2
1964: I	864.2	516.6	63.2	228.2	225.2	131.8	79.3	45.6	6.9	14.0	50.0	36.0	201.7	101.8	99.9	857.3	864.1	7.5	7.5	7.4
II	873.7	525.6	64.8	232.2	228.7	132.4	81.6	43.4	7.4	12.3	49.2	36.9	203.4	101.3	102.1	866.3	873.7	4.5	4.3	4.5
III	880.9	534.3	66.8	236.1	231.4	131.5	83.9	42.1	5.5	12.8	50.6	37.9	202.3	99.1	103.3	875.4	881.3	3.3	4.3	3.5
IV	886.8	535.3	64.6	236.7	234.1	136.1	86.0	41.4	8.6	12.4	51.4	39.0	203.1	98.6	104.6	878.2	887.5	2.7	1.3	2.9
1965: I	906.7	546.0	70.5	239.2	236.2	149.4	91.7	42.9	14.8	9.0	46.7	37.7	202.3	96.8	105.5	891.9	907.9	9.3	6.4	9.5
II	919.7	550.7	70.6	240.9	239.2	150.5	95.6	43.6	11.3	11.2	53.6	42.4	207.2	99.0	108.2	908.3	921.4	5.8	7.6	6.1
III	934.1	559.2	73.1	244.1	242.1	152.4	98.9	42.5	11.0	10.6	53.1	42.5	211.8	100.5	111.3	923.1	935.3	6.4	6.6	6.2
IV	956.8	573.9	76.1	251.8	246.0	155.4	103.4	41.9	10.0	9.8	53.6	43.9	217.7	104.7	113.0	946.7	957.3	10.1	10.7	9.7
1966: I	975.4	581.2	79.7	253.5	248.0	164.8	106.7	42.4	15.6	8.2	54.1	45.8	221.2	106.5	114.7	959.8	976.7	8.0	5.6	8.4
II	979.3	582.3	76.3	255.4	250.6	165.0	108.1	39.8	17.1	7.1	53.8	46.7	224.8	108.8	116.0	962.2	980.7	1.6	1.0	1.6
III	987.9	588.6	78.8	257.2	252.6	160.3	109.0	37.7	13.6	5.1	54.6	49.5	234.0	116.8	117.2	974.3	989.9	3.6	5.1	3.8
IV	996.6	590.5	78.7	255.9	255.9	162.0	108.2	33.0	20.8	5.4	55.1	49.7	238.7	118.3	120.4	975.8	998.9	3.6	.6	3.7
1967: I	997.8	594.8	77.2	258.3	259.2	152.6	105.8	32.3	14.5	6.2	56.9	50.7	244.2	122.5	121.7	983.3	1,000.3	.5	3.1	.6
II	1,004.2	602.4	80.7	259.4	262.3	148.9	105.5	36.1	7.3	6.0	56.1	50.2	247.0	124.6	122.4	996.9	1,006.6	2.6	5.6	2.6
III	1,016.2	605.2	79.9	259.5	265.7	155.1	104.8	38.4	11.8	5.4	56.3	50.9	250.6	127.1	123.5	1,004.4	1,018.7	4.9	3.0	4.9
IV	1,027.3	608.2	80.1	260.8	267.4	163.0	106.3	41.5	15.2	3.9	57.4	53.5	252.2	126.3	125.9	1,012.2	1,030.1	4.4	3.1	4.5
1968: I	1,036.6	620.7	85.2	266.1	269.5	157.2	109.9	41.9	5.4	2.2	59.0	56.8	256.5	127.8	128.7	1,031.2	1,039.4	3.7	7.7	3.7
II	1,055.7	629.9	86.9	269.0	274.0	162.7	107.4	43.0	12.2	2.2	60.1	57.9	260.9	129.5	131.4	1,043.5	1,059.5	7.6	4.9	8.0
III	1,068.2	642.3	90.9	273.6	277.8	161.6	108.6	43.3	9.8	2.0	63.6	61.5	262.2	128.8	133.4	1,058.4	1,071.5	4.8	5.8	4.6
IV	1,071.8	644.7	90.4	273.3	281.0	164.9	112.3	44.0	8.6	1.2	62.3	61.1	261.1	126.5	134.6	1,063.2	1,075.2	1.4	1.9	1.4
1969: I	1,084.2	651.9	92.3	275.7	283.9	172.5	115.1	45.6	11.7	1.2	57.1	55.8	258.6	123.6	135.0	1,072.5	1,087.6	4.7	3.5	4.7
II	1,088.8	656.2	92.1	277.0	287.1	173.1	116.2	45.0	11.8	.4	67.4	67.0	259.2	123.5	135.7	1,077.0	1,092.9	1.7	1.7	2.0
III	1,092.0	659.6	91.7	277.7	290.2	175.4	118.5	43.2	13.7	.2	67.2	67.0	256.8	120.8	136.0	1,078.3	1,096.4	1.2	.5	1.3
IV	1,085.6	663.9	91.3	278.7	293.9	164.8	117.4	40.5	7.0	1.8	68.3	66.5	255.0	119.1	135.9	1,078.6	1,089.9	−2.3	.1	−2.4
1970: I	1,081.4	667.4	89.7	281.3	296.4	158.1	115.4	40.6	2.1	3.2	69.4	66.2	252.7	115.1	137.6	1,079.2	1,085.7	−1.5	.2	−1.5
II	1,083.0	670.5	90.7	282.4	297.4	158.3	115.0	38.4	5.0	4.5	71.5	67.0	249.6	110.9	138.7	1,077.9	1,087.7	.6	−.5	.7
III	1,093.3	676.5	91.1	284.5	300.8	161.6	114.7	40.4	6.5	4.3	70.6	66.3	250.9	108.8	142.1	1,086.8	1,096.3	3.9	3.3	3.2
IV	1,084.7	673.9	84.8	286.7	302.5	156.2	110.3	44.5	1.4	3.6	70.4	66.8	251.0	107.5	143.4	1,083.3	1,087.2	−3.1	−1.3	−3.3
1971: I	1,111.5	687.0	94.0	287.6	305.4	169.8	110.8	47.8	11.2	4.7	70.7	66.0	250.0	105.6	144.4	1,100.3	1,114.8	10.3	6.4	10.5
II	1,116.9	693.3	96.3	288.5	308.5	175.1	112.1	52.6	10.4	.3	71.2	70.9	248.3	102.6	145.7	1,106.5	1,120.5	2.0	2.3	2.1
III	1,125.7	698.2	99.0	288.4	310.8	175.3	112.2	56.0	7.0	1.7	74.2	72.5	250.6	104.1	146.5	1,118.7	1,128.2	3.2	4.5	2.8
IV	1,135.4	708.6	103.5	290.2	314.9	175.4	113.6	58.2	3.6	−.2	67.7	67.9	251.5	102.7	148.8	1,131.7	1,137.3	3.5	4.7	3.3
1972: I	1,157.2	718.6	106.2	292.4	320.0	186.0	117.3	62.4	6.3	−1.9	74.9	76.9	254.5	104.3	150.2	1,150.9	1,158.9	7.9	6.9	7.8
II	1,178.5	731.1	108.9	299.3	322.9	194.5	119.1	63.4	12.1	−.4	74.2	74.6	253.2	103.3	150.0	1,166.5	1,178.6	7.6	5.5	7.0
III	1,193.1	741.3	111.7	303.3	326.4	196.8	120.4	63.7	12.8	2.4	78.2	75.8	252.6	101.0	151.6	1,180.3	1,192.1	5.0	4.8	4.7
IV	1,214.8	757.1	117.6	307.6	331.9	202.7	127.2	65.7	9.7	2.9	82.5	79.6	252.1	98.1	154.0	1,205.1	1,213.9	7.5	8.7	7.5
1973: I	1,246.8	768.8	124.8	309.9	334.1	215.7	132.8	66.9	16.0	7.7	91.0	83.3	254.6	98.9	155.7	1,230.7	1,245.7	10.9	8.8	10.9
II	1,248.3	766.3	122.5	306.3	337.5	217.2	138.3	63.7	15.2	13.7	95.8	82.1	251.1	94.9	156.2	1,233.1	1,244.6	.5	.8	−.3
III	1,255.8	769.7	120.8	307.4	341.5	215.4	140.5	61.1	13.8	19.4	99.8	80.4	251.3	93.5	157.8	1,242.0	1,252.0	2.4	2.9	2.4
IV	1,266.1	766.7	117.2	306.0	343.5	221.8	140.7	57.4	23.7	21.2	102.4	81.2	256.4	96.3	160.1	1,242.4	1,260.4	3.3	.1	2.7
1974: I	1,253.3	761.2	114.4	302.6	344.2	206.3	140.3	52.8	13.2	28.2	108.0	79.8	257.5	95.3	162.2	1,240.1	1,240.4	−4.0	−.8	−6.2
II	1,254.7	764.1	114.7	302.6	346.8	200.9	138.2	50.1	12.6	28.9	111.4	82.5	260.8	96.9	163.9	1,242.1	1,232.9	.4	.7	−2.4
III	1,246.8	769.4	115.8	304.4	349.2	190.3	135.2	47.4	7.7	26.2	107.5	81.3	260.9	96.8	164.1	1,239.1	1,225.2	−2.5	−1.0	−2.5
IV	1,230.3	756.5	104.5	300.4	351.6	184.3	129.1	42.4	12.9	27.8	106.9	79.1	261.8	97.5	164.3	1,217.5	1,209.3	−5.2	−6.8	−5.1
1975: I	1,204.3	763.3	106.5	302.8	354.0	145.8	120.7	39.4	−14.3	32.1	104.0	71.9	263.0	96.8	166.2	1,218.6	1,186.3	−8.2	.4	−7.4
II	1,218.9	775.6	109.0	307.8	358.8	146.8	117.8	40.3	−11.3	33.5	100.3	66.8	263.0	96.5	166.5	1,230.2	1,201.1	4.9	3.9	5.1
III	1,246.1	785.4	115.9	309.0	360.5	163.3	119.2	43.1	1.0	30.8	102.5	71.7	266.6	98.1	168.4	1,245.1	1,229.3	9.2	4.9	9.7
IV	1,257.3	793.3	119.2	310.2	363.9	163.3	119.6	45.9	−2.3	32.3	107.4	75.1	268.3	98.2	170.2	1,259.5	1,240.7	3.6	4.7	3.8
1976: I	1,285.0	809.9	125.1	316.3	368.4	181.4	122.0	49.4	10.0	26.7	107.6	80.9	267.0	96.5	170.5	1,274.9	1,268.5	9.1	5.0	9.3
II	1,293.7	817.1	125.6	320.2	371.3	185.7	124.1	50.3	11.3	25.9	109.3	83.3	264.9	96.3	168.6	1,282.4	1,275.9	2.7	2.4	2.4
III	1,301.1	826.5	126.9	323.5	376.1	184.6	127.4	49.9	7.3	25.6	111.5	85.9	264.3	96.8	167.6	1,293.8	1,282.0	2.3	3.6	1.9
IV	1,313.1	838.9	128.5	327.5	382.8	186.3	128.9	55.0	2.4	23.4	111.9	88.5	264.5	97.4	167.1	1,310.6	1,294.6	3.7	5.3	4.0
1977: I	1,341.3	851.7	133.9	330.6	387.1	201.7	134.5	56.7	10.5	22.3	111.0	88.7	265.6	97.6	168.0	1,330.8	1,317.9	8.9	6.3	7.4
II	1,363.3	858.0	136.9	331.9	389.2	213.7	138.8	61.2	13.8	22.6	113.9	91.3	269.0	100.2	168.8	1,349.5	1,339.8	6.7	5.8	6.8
III	1,385.8	867.3	139.2	332.4	395.7	222.8	141.2	62.8	18.7	24.9	115.2	90.3	270.8	102.2	168.6	1,367.0	1,360.7	6.8	5.3	6.4
IV	1,388.4	880.4	142.0	338.7	399.7	218.5	146.5	61.9	10.1	18.1	111.4	93.2	271.4	101.8	169.6	1,378.3	1,364.7	.8	3.4	1.2
1978: I	1,400.0	883.8	139.4	339.1	405.3	226.7	148.5	60.9	17.3	19.1	118.1	99.0	270.4	98.8	171.6	1,382.8	1,375.4	3.4	1.3	3.2
II	1,437.0	901.1	149.8	341.0	410.3	239.9	157.9	63.7	18.4	22.4	124.3	101.9	273.6	99.0	174.7	1,418.6	1,412.7	11.0	10.8	11.3
III	1,448.8	908.6	147.9	345.3	415.4	238.0	161.6	63.1	13.3	25.3	128.8	103.5	276.8	101.1	175.7	1,435.5	1,424.0	3.3	4.9	3.2
IV	1,468.4	919.2	150.1	352.2	416.9	242.2	165.2	61.8	15.2	29.3	135.6	106.2	277.7	102.4	175.3	1,453.2	1,443.7	5.5	5.0	5.7
1979: I	1,472.6	921.2	148.6	349.9	422.8	241.5	168.0	60.7	12.9	33.4	138.8	105.4	276.4	102.2	174.2	1,459.7	1,446.8	1.1	1.8	.9
II	1,469.2	919.5	144.9	349.2	425.4	241.3	168.0	59.6	13.7	31.5	140.4	109.0	276.8	101.0	175.9	1,455.4	1,441.5	−.9	−1.2	−1.4
III	1,486.6	930.9	149.1	353.4	428.5	237.2	172.9	59.5	4.8	39.8	149.2	109.4	278.8	101.9	176.8	1,481.9	1,453.3	4.8	7.5	3.3
IV	1,489.3	938.6	146.3	359.8	432.6	225.3	170.9	56.7	−2.3	44.2	156.4	112.2	281.2	103.4	177.8	1,491.6	1,449.1	.7	2.7	−1.1
1980: I	1,496.4	938.3	145.2	358.5	434.5	224.3	171.8	53.0	−.5	49.8	164.4	114.5	284.0	105.8	178.1	1,496.9	1,451.1	1.9	1.4	.6
II	1,461.4	919.6	130.0	354.2	435.4	202.4	162.2	42.4	−2.1	52.6	161.0	108.4	286.8	109.3	177.5	1,463.6	1,416.6	−9.0	−8.6	−9.2
III	1,464.2	929.4	135.6	353.5	440.3	197.4	163.6	44.0	−10.1	53.4	156.4	102.9	284.0	106.2	177.8	1,474.4	1,423.5	.8	3.0	2.0
IV	1,477.9	940.0	139.0	356.2	444.7	210.0	165.7	49.0	−4.7	45.4	154.7	109.3	282.5	104.2	178.3	1,482.5	1,440.3	3.8	2.2	4.8
1981: I	1,510.1	953.6	145.4	359.8	448.3	222.7	170.9	48.8	3.0	48.3	160.6	112.4	285.6	107.3	178.3	1,507.0	1,472.5	9.0	6.8	9.2
II	1,512.5	954.7	140.5	362.7	451.5	229.5	173.4	47.3	8.9	44.1	160.7	116.6	284.1	107.9	176.2	1,503.6	1,475.5	.7	−.9	.8
III	1,525.8	962.9	143.9	363.6	455.5	236.3	177.0	43.1	16.1	39.8	159.0	119.1	286.8	111.8	175.0	1,509.7	1,493.9	3.6	1.6	5.1
IV	1,506.9	955.7	134.8	363.8	457.1	221.7	176.3	39.4	6.0	39.9	158.7	118.8	289.6	114.5	175.1	1,500.9	1,477.2	−4.9	−2.3	−4.4
1982: I	1,485.8	961.4	138.5	362.6	460.4	199.7	173.6	36.3	−10.2	35.2	151.8	116.6	289.4	114.5	174.9	1,495.9	1,461.2	−5.5	−1.3	−4.3
II	1,489.3	968.8	139.5	363.5	465.7	201.4	167.1	37.8	−3.4	33.4	154.5	121.1	285.8	110.3	175.4	1,492.7	1,468.1	1.0	−.8	1.9
III	1,485.7	971.0	138.2	364.7	468.2	198.4	163.3	36.5	−1.3	24.0	146.4	122.4	292.2	116.9	175.3	1,487.0	1,462.0	−1.0	−1.5	−1.6
IV	1,480.7	979.6	143.2	366.0	470.4	178.4	160.5	40.6	−22.7	23.0	136.5	113.5	299.7	124.4	175.2	1,503.4	1,459.7	−1.3	4.5	−.6

GNP Gross national product; CBI Change in business inventories.

Source: *Survey of Current Business* (Washington, D.C.: Department of Commerce, October 1983).

COMMODITY PRICES—CONSUMER PRICES

CONSUMER PRICE INDEX [1]

YEAR AND MONTH	All items, wage earners and clerical workers,revised (CPI-W) ★	All items, all urban consumers (CPI-U)	All items less shelter	All items less food	All items less medical care	Commodities Total [3]	Nondurables Total	Nondurables Nondurables less food	Durables [3]	Commodities less food [3]	Services Total [3]	Services less rent [3]	Food Total [4]	Food at home
														1967 = 100
1961	89.6		89.9	89.7	90.3	92.0	90.2	91.2	96.6	93.4	85.2	83.9	89.1	90.4
1962	90.6		90.9	90.8	91.2	92.8	90.9	91.8	97.6	94.1	86.8	85.5	89.9	91.0
1963	91.7		92.1	92.0	92.3	93.6	92.0	92.7	97.9	94.8	88.5	87.3	91.2	92.2
1964	92.9		93.2	93.2	93.5	94.6	93.0	93.5	98.8	95.6	90.2	89.2	92.4	93.2
1965	94.5		94.6	94.5	94.9	95.7	94.6	94.8	98.4	96.2	92.2	91.5	94.4	95.5
1966	97.2		97.4	96.7	97.7	98.2	98.1	97.0	98.5	97.5	95.8	95.3	99.1	100.3
1967	100.0		100.0	100.0	100.0	100.0	100.0	100.0	100.0	100.0	100.0	100.0	100.0	100.0
1968	104.2		104.1	104.4	104.1	103.7	103.9	104.1	103.1	103.7	105.2	105.7	103.6	103.2
1969	109.8		109.0	110.1	109.7	108.4	108.9	108.8	107.0	108.1	112.5	113.8	108.9	108.2
1970	116.3		114.4	116.7	116.1	113.5	114.0	113.1	111.8	112.5	121.6	123.7	114.9	113.7
1971	121.3		119.3	122.1	120.9	117.4	117.7	117.0	116.5	116.8	128.4	130.8	118.4	116.4
1972	125.3		122.9	125.8	124.9	120.9	121.7	119.8	118.9	119.4	133.3	135.9	123.5	121.6
1973	133.1		131.1	130.7	132.9	129.9	132.8	124.8	121.9	123.5	139.1	141.8	141.4	141.4
1974	147.7		146.1	143.7	147.7	145.5	151.0	140.9	130.6	136.6	152.1	156.0	161.7	162.4
1975	161.2		159.1	157.1	160.9	158.4	163.2	151.7	145.5	149.1	166.6	171.9	175.4	175.8
1976	170.5		168.3	167.5	169.7	165.2	169.2	158.3	154.3	156.6	180.4	186.8	180.8	179.5
1977	181.5	181.5	179.1	178.4	180.3	174.7	178.9	166.5	163.2	165.1	194.3	201.6	192.2	190.2
1978	195.3	195.4	191.3	191.2	194.0	187.1	192.0	174.3	173.9	174.7	210.9	219.4	211.4	210.2
1979	217.7	217.4	210.8	213.0	216.1	208.4	215.9	198.7	191.1	195.1	234.2	244.9	234.5	232.9
1980	247.0	246.8	235.5	244.0	245.5	233.9	245.0	235.2	210.4	222.0	270.3	285.1	254.6	251.5
1981	272.3	272.4	258.5	270.6	270.9	253.6	266.3	257.5	227.1	241.2	305.7	324.3	274.6	269.9
1982	288.6	289.1	273.3	288.4	286.8	263.8	273.6	261.6	241.1	250.9	333.3	354.2	285.7	279.2
1979:														
January	204.7	204.7	199.5	199.8	203.2	195.8	201.0	180.3	182.0	181.9	221.1	230.4	223.9	223.1
February	207.1	207.1	201.6	201.8	205.5	198.3	204.0	182.2	183.6	183.7	223.3	232.9	228.2	228.0
March	209.3	209.1	203.7	203.8	207.6	200.5	206.9	185.7	184.9	185.9	225.1	235.0	230.4	229.9
April	211.8	211.5	206.0	206.3	210.1	203.3	209.9	189.6	187.2	188.9	227.0	237.1	232.3	231.7
May	214.3	214.1	208.4	208.9	212.7	205.8	212.8	193.2	189.2	191.6	229.5	239.8	234.3	233.4
June	216.9	216.6	210.7	211.8	215.2	208.4	215.7	197.6	191.1	194.7	232.1	242.6	235.4	234.2
July	219.4	218.9	212.7	214.2	217.6	210.5	218.3	201.1	192.6	197.0	234.7	245.6	236.9	235.5
August	221.5	221.1	214.2	216.9	219.7	212.2	220.4	205.4	193.6	199.5	237.6	248.8	236.3	233.9
September	223.7	223.4	216.1	219.6	222.1	214.1	223.1	209.6	194.5	201.8	240.7	252.1	237.1	234.7
October	225.6	225.4	217.4	221.8	224.1	215.6	224.5	211.3	196.0	203.4	243.6	255.1	238.2	235.4
November	227.6	227.5	218.6	224.1	226.2	217.4	225.8	212.9	198.4	205.4	246.2	258.2	239.1	236.0
December	230.0	229.9	220.6	226.4	228.6	219.4	228.2	215.2	199.8	207.2	249.3	261.6	241.7	238.7
1980:														
January	233.3	233.2	223.4	229.9	231.9	222.4	232.0	220.5	201.3	210.4	253.1	266.1	243.8	240.6
February	236.5	236.4	226.6	233.5	235.0	225.2	236.3	227.3	202.1	213.8	256.8	270.2	244.9	241.3
March	239.9	239.8	229.6	237.1	238.4	228.0	240.3	232.6	203.0	216.7	261.3	275.4	247.3	243.6
April	242.6	242.5	231.7	239.9	241.1	229.9	242.2	234.6	204.9	218.6	265.3	280.0	249.1	245.3
May	245.1	244.9	233.4	242.6	243.6	231.4	243.2	235.5	207.1	220.2	269.2	284.4	250.4	246.5
June	247.8	247.6	234.9	245.5	246.4	232.8	244.5	236.3	208.6	221.4	274.2	290.0	252.0	248.0
July	248.0	247.8	236.4	245.1	246.5	234.1	245.9	236.6	209.8	222.2	272.4	287.6	254.8	251.5
August	249.6	249.4	238.5	246.3	248.1	236.7	248.3	237.8	212.4	224.2	272.5	287.4	258.7	256.3
September	251.9	251.7	241.0	248.6	250.4	239.0	250.2	239.3	215.3	226.6	274.8	289.8	261.1	258.9
October	254.1	253.9	242.1	250.9	252.6	240.7	251.0	239.6	218.1	228.3	277.9	293.2	262.4	260.0
November	256.4	256.2	243.6	253.2	254.9	242.5	252.4	240.5	220.6	230.0	280.9	296.4	264.5	262.1
December	258.7	258.4	245.2	255.5	257.1	243.8	254.1	242.0	221.1	231.0	284.7	300.7	266.4	263.9
1981:														
January	260.7	260.5	247.6	257.6	259.2	245.4	256.9	245.3	221.0	232.4	287.7	304.2	268.6	265.6
February	263.5	263.2	251.2	260.4	261.9	248.3	262.3	253.2	220.3	235.4	290.1	306.9	270.8	267.3
March	265.2	265.1	253.3	262.3	263.7	249.8	265.2	257.5	219.8	237.0	292.5	309.5	272.2	268.6
April	266.8	266.8	254.9	264.2	265.4	250.8	265.9	258.1	221.1	238.0	295.4	312.8	272.9	268.7
May	269.1	269.0	256.2	267.0	267.6	251.9	265.8	258.2	223.9	239.6	299.6	317.4	272.5	267.7
June	271.4	271.3	257.8	269.5	269.9	253.2	266.2	258.0	226.6	241.1	303.5	321.9	273.8	268.7
July	274.6	274.4	259.9	272.7	273.0	255.0	267.1	257.5	229.6	242.6	308.8	328.1	276.2	271.6
August	276.5	276.5	261.4	274.9	274.9	256.2	268.1	258.4	230.9	243.8	312.2	331.7	277.4	272.8
September	279.1	279.3	263.5	278.2	277.8	257.7	269.5	260.3	232.6	244.5	317.3	337.5	278.0	273.2
October	279.7	279.9	264.5	279.0	278.3	257.9	269.5	260.7	232.9	245.9	318.6	338.7	277.6	272.1
November	280.4	280.7	265.4	280.1	279.0	258.0	269.5	261.1	233.2	246.2	320.6	340.8	277.1	271.0
December	281.1	281.5	266.0	280.8	279.6	258.4	269.8	261.1	233.7	246.5	321.8	342.0	277.8	271.7
1982:														
January	282.1	282.5	267.4	281.4	280.6	258.8	270.8	260.2	233.4	245.9	323.9	344.2	281.0	275.3
February	282.9	283.4	268.3	282.1	281.5	259.5	271.7	260.1	233.7	246.0	325.3	345.7	283.3	278.0
March	282.5	283.1	268.5	281.7	280.9	258.8	270.7	258.4	233.5	245.2	325.5	345.7	283.0	277.1
April	283.7	284.3	268.7	282.9	282.1	258.9	269.3	255.0	235.8	245.0	328.4	349.1	283.9	277.9
May	286.5	287.1	270.6	286.0	284.9	261.5	270.7	256.2	239.8	247.8	331.8	352.8	285.5	279.8
June	290.1	290.6	273.8	289.7	288.4	265.1	274.4	261.2	243.2	251.9	334.9	356.5	287.8	282.6
July	291.8	292.2	275.3	291.5	289.9	266.5	275.7	263.0	244.7	253.5	337.0	358.5	288.5	282.8
August	292.4	292.8	275.7	292.5	290.5	266.4	275.5	263.6	244.6	253.8	338.9	360.5	287.4	280.8
September	292.8	293.3	276.9	292.9	290.8	266.6	276.2	264.6	244.1	253.9	339.7	361.3	287.6	280.6
October	293.6	294.1	277.9	294.0	291.5	267.5	276.5	265.7	246.0	255.4	340.3	361.6	287.0	279.4
November	293.2	293.6	278.1	293.6	290.8	267.8	276.4	266.1	246.6	256.0	338.6	359.3	286.4	278.3
December	292.0	292.4	278.2	292.1	289.5	267.7	275.8	264.7	247.3	255.8	335.6	355.5	286.5	277.8

Footnotes giving source of data and description of series appear in the section immediately following these tables.

★Monthly data prior to 1979 are shown on pp. 156 and 157.

Source: *Business Statistics,* a *Supplement to the Survey of Current Business* (Washington, D.C.: U.S. Department of Commerce, Bureau of Economic Analysis, 1982).

FINANCE—PROFITS AND DIVIDENDS

YEAR AND QUARTER	MANUFACTURING CORPORATIONS (FEDERAL TRADE COMMISSION) [1]																Dividends paid (cash), quarterly, all industries
	Net profits after taxes																
	All industries	Food and kindred products	Textile mill products	Paper and allied products	Chemicals and allied products	Petroleum and coal products	Stone, clay, and glass products	Primary nonferrous metal	Primary iron and steel	Fabricated metal products	Machinery (except electrical)	Electrical and electronic equipment	Transportation equipment (except motor vehicles and equipment)	Motor vehicles and equipment	All other manufacturing industries	
	Millions of dollars																
1961	15,311	1,325	280	583	2,045	3,090	543	488	803	445	1,061	1,024	298	1,488	1,722	8,551
1962	17,719	1,369	354	628	2,239	3,236	581	533	720	608	1,308	1,219	442	2,289	2,033	9,281
1963 [2]	19,483	1,449	354	634	2,427	3,831	593	563	938	668	1,432	1,299	444	2,562	2,041	9,868
1964	23,211	1,692	507	754	2,857	4,094	681	758	1,225	842	2,001	1,512	546	2,808	2,617	10,810
1965	27,521	1,896	694	[3] 753	3,188	4,442	761	970	1,401	1,151	2,499	1,926	721	3,496	[3] 3,285	11,979
1966	30,937	[4] 2,102	702	911	3,474	5,055	799	1,298	1,487	1,395	3,058	2,379	821	3,053	[4] 4,058	12,958
1967	29,008	2,130	540	[5] 796	3,261	5,497	672	1,061	1,165	1,316	2,893	2,297	809	2,356	3,884	13,262
1968	32,069	2,209	654	889	3,525	5,794	769	1,149	1,186	1,320	2,947	2,518	1,025	3,222	4,229	14,189
1969	33,248	2,382	621	987	3,591	5,884	822	1,414	1,221	1,326	3,138	2,594	945	2,845	4,835	15,058
1970	28,572	2,549	413	719	3,434	5,893	627	1,297	692	1,066	2,689	2,349	593	1,424	4,522	15,070
1971	31,038	2,754	558	501	3,780	5,829	853	621	748	1,070	2,489	2,563	585	3,097	4,990	15,252
1972	36,467	3,021	659	941	4,499	5,151	1,060	687	1,022	[6] 1,569	3,481	[6] 2,999	[6] 780	3,639	5,944	16,110
1973 [7]	48,259	3,723	831	1,427	5,670	[8] 7,759	1,266	1,343	1,695	2,207	4,936	3,883	933	4,122	7,079	17,734
1974	58,747	4,601	780	2,287	7,175	14,483	1,204	2,035	2,035	2,837	5,648	2,940	1,127	1,957	8,524	19,467
1975	49,135	5,154	409	1,801	6,703	9,307	968	663	2,280	2,523	6,311	2,564	1,039	1,737	7,481	19,968
1976	64,519	5,826	809	2,270	7,610	11,725	1,447	913	2,085	3,196	7,889	4,073	1,687	5,099	9,890	22,763
1977	70,366	5,575	828	2,367	8,060	12,179	1,686	873	864	3,458	9,131	5,383	1,989	6,133	11,840	26,585
1978	81,148	6,213	1,170	2,598	9,117	12,805	2,353	1,362	2,124	3,815	10,746	6,500	2,374	6,211	13,760	28,932
1979	98,698	7,340	1,340	3,723	10,896	21,936	2,373	2,691	2,185	4,431	11,530	7,386	3,189	4,382	15,314	32,491
1980	92,579	8,222	977	2,789	11,578	25,133	1,833	2,768	2,334	3,967	11,459	7,114	3,084	−3,424	14,745	36,495
1981	101,302	9,109	1,157	3,110	12,973	23,733	1,627	2,124	3,507	4,235	12,580	7,872	3,722	−209	15,762	40,317
1982	71,028	8,383	851	1,460	10,324	19,666	408	−333	−3,705	2,320	8,038	6,449	2,566	734	13,867	41,259
1979:																
January																
February																
March	22,666	1,456	246	867	2,746	3,976	287	607	617	1,017	2,682	1,808	666	2,164	3,527	7,126
April																
May																
June	26,795	1,919	355	917	2,938	5,256	749	749	966	1,272	3,006	1,926	884	1,917	3,941	8,170
July																
August																
September	24,746	2,171	381	1,162	2,632	5,732	770	609	743	1,091	2,763	1,735	815	−51	4,193	8,099
October																
November																
December	24,491	1,794	358	777	2,580	6,972	567	726	−141	1,051	3,079	1,917	824	352	3,635	9,096
1980:																
January																
February																
March	24,776	1,720	313	731	3,157	7,258	237	961	814	1,161	2,591	1,799	777	−210	3,467	8,788
April																
May																
June	22,423	1,844	230	740	2,774	6,675	480	769	529	928	2,890	1,694	804	−1,333	3,399	8,919
July																
August																
September	20,982	2,120	196	621	2,937	5,644	602	402	218	870	2,637	1,681	742	−1,626	3,938	8,920
October																
November																
December	24,398	2,538	238	697	2,710	5,556	514	636	773	1,008	3,341	1,940	761	−255	3,941	9,868
1981:																
January																
February																
March	24,372	2,106	243	769	3,525	5,395	238	835	921	1,022	2,745	2,164	1,111	−384	3,682	9,771
April																
May																
June	28,873	2,264	408	879	3,365	6,771	567	630	1,160	1,320	3,259	2,166	1,001	936	4,147	10,080
July																
August																
September	25,201	2,293	308	633	3,098	6,103	555	290	1,421	1,133	3,084	1,797	903	−622	4,205	9,703
October																
November																
December	22,856	2,446	198	829	2,985	5,464	267	369	5	760	3,492	1,745	707	−139	3,728	10,763
1982:																
January																
February																
March	19,042	1,895	110	418	2,963	5,164	−198	111	27	762	2,723	1,702	609	1	2,755	10,176
April																
May																
June	20,044	2,181	144	436	2,821	4,040	165	59	−276	833	2,377	1,717	653	1,072	3,822	10,437
July																
August																
September	17,828	1,845	258	408	2,478	5,225	280	−36	−906	433	1,786	1,602	706	−18	3,767	10,085
October																
November																
December	14,114	2,462	339	198	2,062	5,237	161	−467	−2,550	292	1,152	1,428	598	−321	3,523	10,561

Footnotes giving source of data and description of series appear in the section immediately following these tables.

Source: *Business Statistics,* a *Supplement to the Survey of Current Business* (Washington, D.C.: U.S. Department of Commerce, Bureau of Economic Analysis, 1982).

INDEX

This book has been set Quadex 202, in 10 and 9 point Garamond Book, leaded 2 points. Part numbers are 24 point Garamond Book Italic and part titles are 24 point Garamond Book. Chapter numbers are 18 point Garamond Book Italic and chapter titles are 18 point Garamond Book. The size of the type page is 28 by 48½ picas.